THE INTERNATIONAL INTELLECTUAL PROPERTY SYSTEM
COMMENTARY AND MATERIALS
PART ONE

The International Intellectual Property System

Commentary and Materials

Part One

by
Frederick Abbott,
Thomas Cottier
&
Francis Gurry

KLUWER LAW
INTERNATIONAL

The Hague • London • Boston

Published by Kluwer Law International,
P.O. Box 85889, 2508 CN The Hague, The Netherlands.

Sold and distributed in the U.S.A. and Canada
by Kluwer Law International,
675 Massachusetts Avenue, Cambridge, MA 02139, U.S.A.
tel: (617) 354-0140; fax: (617) 354-8595

In all other countries, sold and distributed
by Kluwer Law International,
P.O. Box 85889, 2508 CN The Hague, The Netherlands
tel: 31 70 308 1562; fax: 31 70 308 1555

ISBN 9041194126 (Part One)
ISBN 9041193227 (set)

To our children

Annie

Céline

Devin

Emma

Maurice

Ryan

Samuel

and

Thomas

Contents

PART ONE

CHAPTER I
INTRODUCTION TO INTELLECTUAL PROPERTY:
FORMS AND POLICIES

A. Intellectual Property in the Global Economy: An Introduction   1
    Frederick M. Abbott, *Protecting First World Assets in the Third
    World: Intellectual Property Negotiations in the GATT
    Multilateral Framework* (1989)   5
    Thomas Cottier, *Intellectual Property in International Trade
    Law and Policy: The GATT Connection* (1992)   10
    Francis Gurry, *The Evolution of Technology and Markets and
    the Management of Intellectual Property Rights* (1997)   12
    Lester Thurow, HEAD TO HEAD (1992)   16
       Notes and Questions   18
B. The Various Rights   21
   1. Introduction to the Forms of Intellectual Property   21
   2. Patent   25
     a. The Nature and Subject Matter of the Patent   25
     b. Scope of Patentable Subject Matter   28
       Diamond v. Chakrabarty, 447 U.S. 303 (1980)   29
       Notes and Questions   41

    c.   Novelty, Inventive Step and Enabling Disclosure   42
        Biogen v. Medeva, [1997] RPC (1996)   45
            Notes and Questions   63
3. Plant Variety Protection   65
    a.   The Nature and Subject Matter of Plant Variety
        Protection   65
    b.   Farmer's Privilege   68
        Asgrow Seed Company v. Winterboer, 513 U.S. 179 (1995)   68
            Notes and Questions   80
4. Copyright   81
    a.   The Nature and Subject Matter of the Copyright   81
    b.   Idea Versus Expression   83
        Frau X v. Frau Y & Z Publishing House, BGE 113 II 306
        ([1989] ECC 232) (1987)   85
            Notes and Questions   92
    c.   Computer Software   93
        Lotus v. Borland, 49 F.3d 807 (1995)   95
            Notes and Questions   109
5. Industrial Designs   110
    a.   The Nature and Subject Matter of Industrial Designs   110
    b.   Design Patent   115
        Best Lock v. Ilco Unican, 94 F.3d 1563 (1996)   115
            Notes and Questions   123
    c.   Industrial Design   124
        Volvo v. FH SA, SMI 1991, 153 ff (1990)   124
            Notes and Questions   128
6. Trademark   128
    a.   The Nature and Function of the Trademark   128
    b.   Color as Trademark   131
        Qualitex v. Jacobson, 514 U.S. 159 (1995)   132
            Notes and Questions   144
    c.   Function of Trademark in Intra-Community Trade   146
        IHT Internationale Heiztechnik v. Ideal Standard, [1994]
        3CMLR 857, (1994)   147
            Notes and Questions   160
7. Integrated Circuit Layout-Design Protection   162
    a.   The Origin and Nature of the *Sui Generis* IC Layout-
        Design Right   162

      b.   Substantial Similarity and Reverse Engineering   164
          Brooktree v. Advanced Micro Devices, 977 F.2d
          1555 (1992)   166
              Notes and Questions   182

   8.   Geographical Indication of Origin   185
      a.   The Nature and Function of the Geographical
          Indication   185
      b.   The Goodwill Function of the Geographical Indication   187
          Winzersekt v. Rheinland-Pfalz, Case C-306/93, [1995] 2
          CMLR 718 (1994)   188
              Notes and Questions   195

   9.   Undisclosed Information   196
      a.   The Nature and Subject Matter of Undisclosed
          Information   196
      b.   Relationship Between Patent and Trade Secret
          Protection   198
          Kewanee Oil v. Bicron, 416 U.S. 470 (1974)   199
              Notes and Questions   217
      c.   Confidential Business Information and Governmental
          Institutions   218
          Akzo Chemie v. Commission, Case 53/85 (1986)   219
              Notes and Questions   222

C. Policies Underlying the Grant of IPRs   222
   1.   Historical Skepticism   224
      Fritz Machlup, *An Economic Review of the Patent System*
      (1958)   224
          Notes and Questions   246
   2.   Modern Acceptance in the Courts   250
      Hilton-Davis v. Warner-Jenkinson, 62 F.3d. 1512 (1995)   251
   3.   Skepticism on the International Plane   254
      Edith Tilton Penrose, *Summary and Conclusions*, in THE
      ECONOMICS OF THE INTERNATIONAL PATENT SYSTEM (1951)   255
          Notes and Questions   264
   4.   Modern Trend of Acceptance on the International Plane   265
      Carlos Primo Braga and Carsten Fink, *The Economic
      Justification for the Grant of Intellectual Property Rights:
      Patterns of Convergence and Conflict* (1997)   226
          Notes and Questions   281

5. IPRs in the Post-Industrial Age 284
J. H. Reichman, *Charting the Collapse of the Patent-Copyright Dichotomy: Premises for a Restructured International Intellectual Property System* (1995) 285
  Notes and Questions 299

CHAPTER II
ORGANIZATIONS AND INTERNATIONAL COOPERATION

A. Multilateral Organizations 301
 1. The World Intellectual Property Organization (WIPO) 303
  International Bureau of WIPO, *World Intellectual Property Organization and The International Bureau of WIPO* 303
  a. WIPO as an Institution for Securing Rights 308
   Francis Gurry, *The Evolution of Technology and Markets and the Management of Intellectual Property Rights* (1997) 309
    Notes and Questions 312
 2. The World Trade Organization 314
  a. WTO Secretariat, *What is the World Trade Organization?* 314
  b. The World Trade Organization Framework 320
   First Report of the International Trade Law Committee of the International Law Association 320
    Notes and Questions 326
  c. The WTO TRIPS Agreement 326
   i. Pre-TRIPS Agreement Protection of IPRs 326
    Frederick M. Abbott, *Protecting First World Assets in the Third World: Intellectual Property Negotiations in the GATT Multilateral Framework* (1989) 327
    Notes and Questions 339
   ii. The TRIPS Agreement as Described by the Advocates General to the European Court of Justice 340
    Re The Uruguay Round Treaties, Court of Justice of the European Communities, [1995] 1 CMLR 205, (1994) 340

		Notes and Questions	352
	d.	The WTO Dispute Settlement System	353
		Frederick M. Abbott, *Incomplete Rule Systems, System Incompatibilities and Suboptimal Solutions: Changing the Dynamic of Dispute Settlement and Avoidance in Trade Relations between Japan and the United States* (1999)	353
		Notes and Questions	357
	3.	The Relationship between WIPO and the WTO	358
		Frederick M. Abbott, *The Future of the Multilateral Trading System in the Context of TRIPS* (1997)	358
		Notes and Questions	374
	4.	Development and Environmental Organizations	374
		a. Multilateral Institutions of the United Nations System	374
		b. Limited Membership Institutions	376
		Organisation for Economic Cooperation and Development (OECD), *What is the OECD?*	377
		Notes and Questions	382
B.	Regional Institutions		383
	1.	Introduction	383
		Proceedings of the American Society of International Law (1996), *International Institutions and Economic Integration; Remarks by Frederick M. Abbott (overview), Charlene Barshefsky (APEC, NAFTA and the FTAA), Marcos Castrioto de Azambuja (Mercosur)*	385
		Notes and Questions	398
	2.	The European Union, the WTO and TRIPS	399
		a. The Political and Legal Structure and Process of the European Union	400
		J.H.H. Weiler, *The Transformation of Europe* (1991)	400
		Notes and Questions	421
		b. The External IPRs Relations of the EU and the TRIPS Agreement	422
		i. Competence to Conclude the TRIPS Agreement	422
		Re The Uruguay Round Treaties, [1995] 1 CMLR 205 (1994)	424
		Notes and Questions	434
		ii. EU External Relations and Mixed Agreements	435

Thomas Cottier, *Dispute Settlement in the World Trade Organization: Characteristics and Structural Implications for the European Union* (1998)   435

Notes and Questions   437

3. The North American Free Trade Agreement IPRs Regime   438
Frederick M. Abbott, LAW AND POLICY OF REGIONAL INTEGRATION: THE NAFTA AND WESTERN HEMISPHERIC INTEGRATION IN THE WORLD TRADE ORGANIZATION SYSTEM (1995)   439

Notes and Questions   442

4. The Mercosur IPRs Regime   443
Wilfrido Fernández, *Mercosur and its Implications for Industrial Property* (1995)   443

Notes and Questions   454

5. The APEC IPRs Regime   455
APEC Secretariat, *Asia-Pacific Economic Cooperation, Intellectual Property Rights*   456

Notes and Questions   458

C. Regional Institutions Securing Rights   461

1. The European Union and European Patent Office   461
Friedrich-Karl Beier, *The European Patent System* (1981)   462

Notes and Questions   468

2. The EU Office for Harmonisation in the Internal Market (Trade Marks and Industrial Designs)   469
Office for Harmonisation in the Internal Market (Trade Marks and Designs)   469

Notes and Questions   474

3. The EU System for the Registration of Plant Varieties   474
Community Plant Variety Rights Office (CPVO)   475

4. Other Regional Arrangements for Securing IPRs   475
International Bureau of WIPO, *Regional Cooperation in the Field of Industrial Property*   476

Notes and Questions   480

D. Bilateral Arrangements   481

Notes and Questions   482

E. Non-Governmental Organizations   483

CHAPTER III
SOURCES AND BASIC PRINCIPLES

A. Sources of International Law   485
    1. Treaty Law   487
    2. Customary International law   488
    3. Precedents and Doctrine   491
    4. General Principles of Law   494
       Ralph A. Newman, *The Precepts of Equity* (1973)   496
          Notes and Questions   501
B. The Potential Impact of Human Rights   501
    Human Rights Instruments   504
          Notes and Questions   506
C. Justice and the Potential Impact of Sustainable Development   507
          Notes and Questions   508
D. The Impact of International Law   508
    1. The Interpretation of International Agreements and the
       Doctrine of Legitimate Expectations   508
       India   Patent Protection for Pharmaceutical and Agricultural
       Chemical Products, Report of the Panel, World Trade
       Organization (1997)   511
          Notes and Questions   532
       India — Patent Protection for Pharmaceutical and Agricultural
       Chemical Products, Report of the Appellate Body (1997)   533
          Notes and Questions   556
    2. The Doctrine of Consistent Interpretation   558
       Thomas Cottier and Krista Nadakavukaren Schefer, *The*
       Relationship of World Trade Organization Law, National and
       Regional Law (1998)   558
       Hermès International v. FHT Marketing Choice BV, Case
       C-53/96 (1998)   561
          Notes and Questions   572
    3. The Doctrine of Direct Effect   572
       Thomas Cottier and Krista Nadakavukaren Schefer, *The*
       Relationship of World Trade Organization Law, National and
       Regional Law (1998)   574
          Notes and Questions   586
E. Basic Principles and Features   587

1. National Treatment and Reciprocity — 587
   Paul Katzenberger, *TRIPs and Copyright Law* (1996) — 591
      Notes and Questions — 593
2. Most Favored Nation Treatment — 596
   Paul Katzenberger, *TRIPs and Copyright Law* (1996) — 598
      Notes and Questions — 601
3. Territoriality — 602
      Notes and Questions — 603
4. Ubiquity and Exhaustion of Rights — 604
   Thomas Cottier and Marc Stucki, *Parallel Imports in Patent, Copyright and Industrial Design Law — The Scope of European and International Public Law* (1996) — 605
      Note — 608
5. Right of Priority — 608
      Notes and Questions — 610
6. Duration of Intellectual Property Rights — 610
   TRIPS Agreement Norms on Duration — 611
      Notes and Questions — 613
7. Intellectual Step — 613
   Norms on Intellectual Step — 615
      Notes and Questions — 617
8. Dissemination of Protected Information — 618
   International Bureau of WIPO, *Patent Documents as a Source of Technological Information* — 621
      Notes and Questions — 624
9. Transparency of Rules — 625
   Norms on Transparency — 626
      Notes and Questions — 627
10. Enforceability of IPRs — 627
    Thomas Dreier, *TRIPs and the Enforcement of Intellectual Property Rights* (1996) — 628
      Notes and Questions — 631

CHAPTER IV
NORMS AND NORM-MAKING IN THE
INTERNATIONAL IPRS SYSTEM

A. Introduction — 633
B. The Paris Convention — 634

1. Historical Context   634
   Edith Tilton Penrose, *The Development of the International
   Convention for the Protection of Industrial Property*, in
   THE ECONOMICS OF THE INTERNATIONAL PATENT SYSTEM
   (1951)   635
       Notes and Questions   645
2. The Treaty Text Explored   647
   WIPO, *Paris Convention for the Protection of Industrial
   Property (1883)*   647
   Paris Convention for the Protection of Industrial
   Property   652
       Notes and Questions   661
3. The Independence of Patents   662
   a. Independence in the Courts   662
      Cuno v. Pall, 729 F. Supp. 234 (1989)   663
       Notes and Questions   671
   b. Independence of Patents and the Free Movement of
      Goods   672
      BBS Kraftfahrzeugtechnik v. Rasimex Japan, Supreme
      Court of Japan (1997)   674
       Notes and Questions   676
4. The Right of Priority   676
   Gehard Schricker, *Problems of Convention Priority for
   Patent Applications* (1967)   678
       Notes and Questions   685
C. The Patent Norms of the WTO TRIPS Agreement   685
1. Negotiation of the TRIPS Agreement Norms   686
   Thomas Cottier, *The Prospects for Intellectual Property in
   GATT* (1991)   686
2. The Resulting Agreement   697
   Adrian Otten and Hannu Wager, *Compliance with TRIPS:
   The Emerging World* View (1996)   697
   WTO Agreement on Trade-Related Aspects of Intellectual
   Property Rights   702
       Notes and Questions   708
3. Compulsory Licensing and the Balance of Rights   710
   Elizabeth Henderson, *TRIPs and the Third World:
   The Example of Pharmaceutical Patents in India* (1997)   712
       Notes and Questions   717

4. Interpreting the Patent Norms of the TRIPS Agreement   718
Frederick M. Abbott, *WTO Dispute Settlement and the
Agreement on Trade-Related Aspects of Intellectual Property
Rights* (1997)   719
Notes and Questions   732
D. The European Patent Convention (EPC) Norms   733
1. The Establishment of EPC Norms   733
Friedrich-Karl Beier, *The European Patent System* (1981)   734
Notes and Questions   739
EPC Convention on the Grant of European Patents   740
Notes and Questions   748
2. Case Law of the European Patent Office   749
Procter & Gamble, Decision of Technical Board of Appeal
3.3.1, dated 3 May 1996   751
Notes and Questions   760
Mycogen, Decision of Technical Board of Appeal 3.3.4, dated
8 May 1996   761
Notes and Questions   775
3. The EPC, the European Communities and the Community
Patent Convention   776
Commission of the European Communities, *Promoting
innovation through patents, Green Paper on the Community
patent and the patent system in Europe* (1997)   777
Notes and Questions   806
E. The NAFTA Patent Norms   808
NAFTA Patent Provisions   809
Notes and Questions   817
F. The Andean Pact Patent and Technology Transfer Provisions   818
1. The Andean Experiment   818
Frederick M. Abbott, *Bargaining Power and Strategy in the
Foreign Investment Process: A Current Andean Code Analysis*
(1975)   819
Notes and Questions   824
2. Adapting to a New Reality   825
Andean Pact: Decision 344 Regarding Common Provisions
on Industrial Property   825
Notes and Questions   836
G. National Patent Norms   837

1.	Comparison of U.S. PTO, EPO and Japan Patent Office Rules	837
	Trilateral Project 24.1 — Biotechnology Comparative Study on Biotechnology Patent Practices, Comparative Study Report	838
	Notes and Questions	843
2.	The Patent System of China	844
	Dr. Gao Lulin, *China's Intellectual Property Protection System in Progress* (1998)	845
	Notes and Questions	854
3.	The Japanese Patent Experience	854
	Guntram Rahn, *Japanese Experience of the Relation Between Industrial Property and Development* (1988)	855
	Notes and Questions	859
H.	International Copyright Norms	860
	Sam Ricketson, *The Birth of the Berne Union* (1986)	861
	Notes and Questions	869
I.	The Berne Convention	870
1.	Terms of the Berne Convention	870
	WIPO International Bureau, *International Protection of Copyright and Neighboring Rights, Berne Convention for the Protection of Literary and Artistic Works (1886)*	870
	Berne Convention for the Protection of Literary and Artistic Works	874
	Notes and Questions	894
2.	The Berne Convention in National Law	896
	SUISA (Swiss Society of Authors and Publishers) v. Rediffusion [1982] ECC 481 (1981)	897
	Notes and Questions	906
J.	The WIPO Copyright Treaty	906
	Pamela Samuelson, *The U.S. Digital Agenda at WIPO* (1997)	908
	Notes and Questions	939
	International Bureau of WIPO, *WIPO Copyright Treaty (WCT)* (1996)	941
	WIPO Copyright Treaty	943
	Notes and Questions	949
K.	The WIPO Performances and Phonograms Treaty (WPPT)	950
1.	Introduction	950

Schweizerische Interpreten-Gesellschaft and Others v. X and Z,
    [1986] ECC 384, (1984)   950
        Notes and Questions   960
  2. The WPPT and the Rome Convention   960
    International Bureau of WIPO, *WIPO Performances and*
      Phonograms Treaty (WPPT) (1996)   961
    WIPO Performances and Phonograms Treaty   965
    Rome Convention, 1961 — International Convention for the
    Protection of Performers, Producers of Phonograms and
    Broadcasting Organisations   974
        Notes and Questions   983
L. TRIPS Agreement Copyright Provisions   984
  Thomas Cottier, *The Prospects For Intellectual Property in*
    GATT (1991)   985
  Adrian Otten and Hannu Wager, *Compliance with TRIPS: The*
    Emerging World View (1996)   986
  Agreement on Trade-Related Aspects of Intellectual
    Property Rights   988
        Notes and Questions   991
M. Copyright in the European Union and the United States   992
  1. The Path of Approximation   992
    Warner Brothers Inc. and Metronome Video ApS v. Erik Viuff
    Christiansen, 1988 ECJ CELEX LEXIS 2016, Judgment
    of the Court of 17 May 1988   992
        Notes and Questions   997
    a. The Rental Rights Directive   998
      Council Directive 92/100/EEC of 19 November 1992
      on rental right and lending right and on certain rights
      related to copyright in the field of intellectual property   998
        Notes and Questions   1006
    b. The Copyright Directive   1006
      Council Directive 93/98/EEC of 29 October 1993
      harmonizing the term of protection of copyright and
      certain related rights   1007
        Notes and Questions   1012
    c. Database Protection and the Database Directive   1012
      i. Databases in U.S. Law   1013
        Feist Publications v. Rural Telephone Service, 499
        U.S. 340 (1991)   1013

		Notes and Questions	1029
	ii.	The EU Database Directive	1030
		Common Position (EC) No 20/95 adopted by the	
		Council on 10 July 1995 with a view to adopting	
		Directive 95//EC of the European Parliament and of	
		the Council . . . on the legal protection of databases	1031
		Notes and Questions	1039
	2.	Free Movement and Copyrighted Works	1040
	a.	Films and Broadcasts Within the EU	1040
		Coditel v. Cine Vog Films, [1980] ECR 881, [1981]	
		2 CMLR 362 (1980)	1041
		Notes and Questions	1046
	b.	Copyright and International Trade	1046
		Quality King Distributors v. L'anza Research	
		International, 1998 U.S. LEXIS 1606 (1998)	1047
		Notes and Questions	1060

N. The NAFTA and Copyright — 1062
NAFTA Copyright Provisions — 1063
Notes and Questions — 1066

O. Copyright Law of China — 1066
Adolph Dietz, *The New Copyright Law of the People's Republic of China — An Introduction* (1991) — 1067
Notes and Questions — 1082

P. Moral Rights — 1083
1. Moral Rights in Continental Europe — 1085
Angelica Huston v. Turner Entertainment Co, French Cour de Cassation, [1992] ECC 334 (1991) — 1085
Notes and Questions — 1086
2. Moral Rights in the United States — 1087
a. The Copyright Act and the Lanham Act — 1087
Terry Gilliam, Graham Chapman, Terry Jones, Michael Palin, John Cleese and Eric Idle, individually and collectively performing as the professional group known as "Monty Python" v. American Broadcasting Companies, Inc., 538 F.(1976) — 1087
Notes and Questions — 1102
b. The Visual Artists Rights Act of 1990 — 1102
John Carter, et al. v. Helmsley-Spear, (2d Cir. 1995), 71 F.3d 77 (1995) — 1103

		Notes and Questions	1118
Q.	Computer Software		1119
	1.	The European Union	1121
		a. The Inventive Step in Germany	1121
		Re The Protection of Computer Programs,	
		Bundesgerichtshof, [1986] ECC 498, (1985)	1122
		Notes and Questions	1134
		b. Rejection of the Inventive Step by the Union: The	
		Software Directive	1135
		Council Directive of 14 May 1991 on the legal	
		protection of computer programs, (91/250/EEC)	1135
		Notes and Questions	1140
		c. The New European Software Environment	1141
		Michael Lehmann, *The New Software Contract Under*	
		European and German Copyright Law (1994)	1142
		Notes and Questions	1151
	2.	The United States	1152
		a. The State of the Art in U.S. Software Doctrine	1152
		Computer Associates International v. Altai, 982 F.2d 693	
		(1992)	1153
		Notes and Questions	1194
		b. Copyright Versus Patent Revisited	1195
		Pamela Samuelson, Randall Davis, Mitchell D. Kapor, &	
		J.H. Reichman, *A Manifesto Concerning the Legal*	
		Protection of Computer Programs (1994)	1196
		Notes and Questions	1201
R.	Satellite Signals and Cable Transmission		1202
	1.	The Brussels Convention of 1974	1202
		Convention Relating to the Distribution of Programme-	
		Carrying Signals Transmitted by Satellite, Done at Brussels	
		on May 21, 1974	1203
		Notes	1207
	2.	Satellite Signals in the European Union	1207
		Re Satellite Television Broadcasting (Case 4 Ob 44/92), [1994]	
		ECC 526	1207
		Council Directive 93/83/EEC of 27 September 1993 on the	
		coordination of certain rules concerning copyright and	

rights related to copyright applicable to satellite broadcasting
and cable retransmission 1211
Notes and Questions 1218

PART TWO

S. Trademarks at the Multilateral Level 1219
1. Introduction 1219
2. The Paris Convention and Trademarks 1219
WIPO, Introduction to Intellectual Property — Theory
and Practice (1997) 1220
Paris Convention for the Protection of Industrial Property 1233
Notes and Questions 1246
3. The TRIPS Agreement and Trademarks 1247
Annette Kur, *Trademark Provisions of the TRIPs Agreement*
(1996) 1247
WTO TRIPS Agreement Text, Section 2: Trademarks 1261
Notes and Questions 1264
T. Trademarks at the Regional Level 1265
1. EU Trademarks Approximation 1265
Opinion of Advocate General Jacobs, 29 Jan. 1998, *Silhouette*
International Schmied GmbH & Co. KG v.
Hartlauer Handelsgesellschaft mbH (Case C-355/96) 1267
Annette Kur, *Harmonization of the Trademark Laws in*
Europe — An Overview (1997) 1269
First Council Directive of 21 December 1988 to
approximate the laws of the Member States relating to
trade marks (89/104/EEC) 1273
Notes and Questions 1285
Deutsche Renault AG v. Audi AG (Case C-317/91),
[1995] 1 CMLR 461 1287
Notes and Questions 1297
2. EU Trademarks Unification 1297
Office for Harmonisation in the Internal Market, *The*
OHIM and the Community Trade Mark 1299
Council Regulation, *The Community Trade Mark Regulation*
(1993) 1307

Notes and Questions 1336
3. NAFTA Trademark Provisions 1337
NAFTA Text 1337
Notes and Questions 1340
U. The Function of the Trademark in International Trade 1341
1. European Doctrine 1341
a. Intra-Union Exhaustion 1341
b. International Exhaustion 1342
i. Member State Doctrine Prior to the Trade Marks
Directive and the *Silhouette* Case 1342
Revlon v. Cripps & Lee, [1980] FSR 85 (1979) 1343
Notes and Questions 1353
ii. EU Doctrine After the Trade Marks Directive and the
Silhouette Case 1354
Silhouette v. Hartlauer, [1998] 2 CMLR 953 (1998) 1355
Notes and Questions 1363
iii. European Free Trade Association (EFTA) Doctrine 1364
Mag Intrument v. California Trading, (Case E-2/97)
[1998] 1 CMLR 331 (1997) 1364
Notes and Questions 1372
iv. Switzerland and the TRIPS Agreement 1372
Silhouette v. Hartlauer 1373
Chanel Geneva and Chanel Glarus v. EPA, BGE
122 II 469 (1996) 1374
Notes and Questions 1385
2. United States Doctrine 1386
K mart v. Cartier, 486 U.S. 281 (1988) 1387
Notes and Questions 1424

CHAPTER V
OBTAINING PROTECTION

A. Variations Relating to Form of IPR 1427
B. Patents at the Multilateral Level 1430
1. The Patent Cooperation Treaty System 1430
International Bureau of WIPO, *Basic Facts about the Patent
Cooperation Treaty* 1433
Patent Cooperation Treaty 1441

	PCT Timeline A	1465
	Notes	1467
C.	Patents at the Regional Level	1468
	European Patent Office, *How to obtain a European patent*	1468
	EPC Convention on the Grant of European Patents (European Patent Convention)	1470
	Notes and Questions	1490
D.	Trademarks at the Multilateral Level	1491
	International Bureau of WIPO, *Trademark Law Treaty ("TLT") (1994)*	1494
	Trade Mark Law Treaty	1496
	International Bureau of WIPO, *Nice Agreement Concerning the International Classification of Goods and Services for the Purposes of the Registration of Marks (1957)*	1499
	Nice Agreement Concerning the International Classification of Goods and Services for the Purposes of the Registration of Marks (1957)	1500
	Notes	1502
	WIPO, *Guide to the International Registration of Marks under the Madrid Agreement and the Madrid Protocol* (1997)	1502
	Madrid Agreement Concerning the International Registration of Marks	1513
	Protocol Relating to the Madrid Agreement Concerning the International Registration of Marks	1522
	Notes and Questions	1534
E.	Trademarks at the Regional Level	1535
	Office for Harmonisation in the Internal Market, *The Community Trade Mark in Practice*	1536
	Council Regulation (EC) No 40/94 of 20 December 1993 on the Community trade mark	1544
	Notes and Questions	1566

CHAPTER VI
DISPUTE SETTLEMENT AND ENFORCEMENT
OF RIGHTS

| A. | Government to Government Action on the International Plane | 1569 |
| | 1. TRIPS Agreement Enforcement Obligations | 1569 |

Frederick M. Abbott, *WTO Dispute Settlement and the Agreement on Trade-Related Aspects of Intellectual Property Rights* (1997)   1570

      Notes and Questions   1575

  2. The Process of Government to Government Action   1575

     a. Authority of the U.S. Trade Representative Under Section 301 and Special 301   1576

       Frederick M. Abbott, *Protecting First World Assets in the Third World: Intellectual Property Negotiations in the GATT Multilateral Framework* (1989)   1578

       Section 301 and Special 301   1580

       Notes and Questions   1591

     b. China-U.S. Agreements on IPRs Protection   1592

       1992 Memorandum of Understanding Between the Government of the People's Republic of China and the Government of the United States of America on the Protection of Intellectual Property   1593

       China-United States: Agreement Regarding Intellectual Property Rights (1995)   1600

       Notes and Questions   1607

     c. The European Union Analogue to Section 301: The Trade Barriers Regulation   1608

       Council Regulation (EC) No 3286/94 of 22 December 1994 laying down Community procedures in the field of the common commercial policy in order to ensure the exercise of the Community's rights under international trade rules, in particular those established under the auspices of the World Trade Organization   1609

       European Commission decision regarding AKZO complaint with respect to Section 337 of U.S. Tariff Act of 1930   1622

       GATT Panel Report on United States – Section 337 of the Tariff Act of 1930   1629

       Notes and Questions   1648

B. Enforcement of IPRs Within the Stream of Commerce   1649

  1. The EC Regulation on Counterfeit Goods   1650

     Council Regulation (EC) No 3295/94 of 22 December 1994 laying down measures to prohibit the release for free

circulation, export, re-export or entry for a suspensive
procedure of counterfeit and pirated goods 1650
  Notes and Questions 1661
 2. U.S. Legislation Concerning Infringing Imports 1662
  a. Relief Under Section 337 of the Tariff Act of 1930 1662
   Duracell v. U.S. International Trade Commission, (CAFC
   1985) 778 F.2d 1578 1664
   Section 337 of the Tariff Act of 1930 1667
   Notes and Questions 1672
  b. Other U.S. Legislation Regulating Infringing Imports 1673
   i. Section 602 of the Copyright Act of 1976 1673
    Title 17. Copyrights Chapter 6. Manufacturing
    Requirements and Importation 1674
   ii. Section 42 of the Lanham Act and Section 526 of
    the Tariff Act of 1930 1675
    Lever Brothers v. United States (CAFC 1993), 981
    F.2d 1330 1676
    Section 42 of the Lanham Act 1689
    Section 526 of the Tariff Act of 1930 1691
    Notes and Questions 1692
 3. Private Action Against Infringing Imports 1694
  Babbit Electronics v. Dynascan, (11th Cir. 1994), 38 F.3d 1161 1695
  Notes and Questions 1727
 4. Criminal Penalties for Trade in IPRs Protected Goods and
  Services 1728
  Title 18. Crimes and Criminal Procedure — 18 USCS
  §§ 2318 & 2320 (1998) 1728
  Notes and Questions 1732
C. Arbitration of IPRs-Related Disputes 1732
 WIPO, *About the Arbitration and Mediation Center* 1733
  Notes and Questions 1738

CHAPTER VII
TENSION WITH OTHER AREAS
OF PUBLIC POLICY

A. IPRs and Competition 1741

Contents

1. Competition and the Global Marketplace — 1743
Frederick M. Abbott, *Public Policy and Global Technological Integration: An Introduction* (1997) — 1743
Thomas Cottier and Ingo Meitinger, *The TRIPs Agreement without a Competition Agreement?* (1998) — 1750
Notes and Questions — 1761
2. European Union Competition Law and IPRs — 1762
Frederick M. Abbott, *First Report (Final) to the Committee on International Trade Law of the International Law Association on the Subject of Parallel Importation* (1997) — 1762
Notes and Questions — 1766
Radio Telefís Eireann (RTE) and Independent Television Publications Ltd (ITP) v. Commission, ECJ, 1995 ECJ Celex Lexis 1716 (1995) — 1767
Notes and Questions — 1779
3. Exhaustion of IPRs, Trade and Competition — 1779
Frederick M. Abbott, *Discussion Paper for Conference on Exhaustion of Intellectual Property Rights and Parallel Importation in World Trade* (1998) — 1780
Thomas Cottier, *The WTO System and Exhaustion of Rights* (1998) — 1796
Marco C.E.J. Bronckers, *The Exhaustion of Patent Rights Under WTO Law* (1998) — 1804
Notes and Questions — 1817
B. Biotechnology, Genetic Resources and Traditional Intellectual Property Rights (TIPRs) — 1819
Thomas Cottier, *The Protection of Genetic Resources and Traditional Knowledge: Towards More Specific Rights and Obligations in World Trade Law* (1998) — 1820
Notes and Questions — 1848
C. Diffusion of Knowledge and Other Areas of Tension — 1851
Carlos A. Primo Braga, Carsten Fink and Claudia Paz Sepulveda, *Intellectual Property Rights and Economic Development* (1998) — 1851
Notes and Questions — 1860
D. Freedom of Information and Protection of IPRs — 1861
Online Copyright Infringement Liability Limitation Act — 1863
Notes and Questions — 1875

CHAPTER VIII
DEALING WITH THE FUTURE:
THE EVOLUTION OF TECHNOLOGY
AND MARKETS

A. The Impact of New Technologies on the Forms of IPR   1877
    1. The WIPO Internet Domain Name Process   1878
        Final Report of the WIPO Internet Domain Name
        Process, *The Management of Internet Names and Addresses:*
        Intellectual Property Issues (1999)   1879
            Notes and Questions   1965
    2. The Internet Corporation for Assigned Names and Numbers
        (ICANN)   1967
        U.S. Department of Commerce, *Management of Internet*
        Names and Addresses (1998)   1968
            Notes and Questions   1985
B. Global Electronic Commerce and IPRs   1986
    WTO Declaration on Global Electronic Commerce
        (20 May1998)   1987
    OECD Ministerial Conference, *A Borderless World: Realising the*
        Potential of Global Electronic Commerce, OECD Action Plan for
        Electronic Commerce (1998)   1988
            Notes and Questions   1989
C. Challenges to International Institutions   1990
    Adrian Otten, *Implementation of the TRIPS Agreement and*
        Prospects for Its Further Development (1998)   1991
            Notes and Questions   2006
    Carlos A. Primo Braga, Carsten Fink and Claudia Paz
        Sepulveda, *Intellectual Property Rights and Economic*
        Development (1998)   2008
            Notes and Questions   2017
    Francis Gurry, *The Evolution of Technology and Markets and*
        the Management of Intellectual Property Rights (1997) 2018
            Notes and Questions   2026

Preface

The world economy is increasingly driven by intellectual capital: knowledge, inventions, expressions of creativity and the accumulated education, training and skills embodied in the scientific, engineering and professional workforce. At the advent of the 21st Century, intellectual capital is surpassing in importance the components of physical capital — land, natural resources and manual labor — as the main source of wealth creation. Unlike physical capital, intellectual capital is highly mobile and circulates the globe with even greater ease since the arrival of digital networks and, in particular, the Internet. The physical border — the old container of national policy, the national economy and national cultural homogeneity — is increasingly less apt to serve as an organizing concept for regulating the rights and obligations that attach to the flow of intellectual capital on the borderless and multifunctional medium of digital networks.

This book responds to a new and complex era — an era in which rapid technological change has become the norm, in which markets are transnational and legal systems are required continuously to adapt in order to promote and protect the interests of industry, art and the consumer. Intellectual property has become a controlling factor of wealth as the use of emerging key technologies is essentially framed by intellectual property regulation. Based upon national traditions, government regulators, encouraged by business and cultural interests, have labored to create an adequate framework to protect it around the world. The elaboration of an adequate and effective global framework for the protection of intellectual property rights (IPRs) has been at the forefront of the business agenda of developed countries since the mid-1980s, yet its contours have only slowly entered the mainstream of the legal profession and the law school classroom. Many quarters of the globe find the protection of intellectual property is in its initial stages and are faced with the challenge of adjusting and absorbing a new global regime with all its various economic and cultural implications.

We seek in this book to provide a resource for law students, practicing lawyers, judges, government officials, non-governmental organizations and members of the legal academy interested in learning about the benefits and difficulties of an emerging international system for the regulation of intellectual property. We have endeavored to synthesize a complex and elaborate regulatory framework within a single accessible resource. The changing nature of the international IPRs environment suggests the need to develop common or shared regulatory approaches to IPRs across the many national and regional legal systems. We hope that this book will contribute towards building these shared understandings.

We try to present a comprehensive picture of the international intellectual property system, giving attention to the multiple forms of IPR, the policies underlying them, the rules which govern their grant and the mechanisms by which they are enforced. Legislative materials, judicial decisions and commentary are integrated in this single resource, allowing for comparative studies and the search for common ground among different regulatory and cultural traditions in law and policy. Unlike other books, we focus on international law aspects of intellectual property protection and seek to prepare common ground for further developments. Relevant portions of referenced international agreements are included directly in this text, rather than in a separate documentary supplement. The international IPRs system relies heavily on such international agreements as a source of norms, and without direct reference to these norms it is difficult to appreciate the system. Judicial decisions are edited to reduce length, yet longer portions of these decisions appear than is sometimes the case with educational resources. During the editorial process we were struck by how difficult it would be for readers to analyze complex IPRs decisions without their context intact.

This book is intended both as a teaching and as a reference resource. For the typical law school teaching period of a single semester, the instructor will certainly need to select among various paths through the international IPRs system. In presenting an integrated perspective on the international IPRs system — including its history, economics and social implications — we have tried to convey its functioning as part of a larger worldwide framework of laws and institutions. We hope that this justifies the length of the text.

Permission to reproduce

The authors extend their thanks to all of those whose work appears in this book for their permission to reproduce these materials. Permission to reproduce has been generously granted by the American Society of International Law, Johns Hopkins University Press, Kluwer Law International, Lexis-Nexis Publishers, William Morrow & Co., the Vanderbilt Journal of Transnational Law, the World Intellectual Property Organization, Carlos Primo Braga, Marco Bronckers, Adolph Dietz, Thomas Dreier, Wilfrido Fernández, Carsten Fink, Elizabeth Henderson, Tadayoshi Homma, Paul Katzenberger, Annette Kur, Michael Lehmann, Ralph Newman, Adrian Otten, Jerome Reichman, Sam Ricketson, Pamela Samuelson, Claudia Paz Sepulveda and Joseph Weiler.

Authors' statement

The views expressed by the authors in this book are personal and, in respect of Francis Gurry, do not necessarily reflect the views of the World Intellectual Property Organization (WIPO).

Form and Format

A few words about form and formatting:

Footnotes. We have eliminated most of the footnotes from the excerpted texts which are reproduced in this book. Where footnotes have been retained, they are referenced with their original published numbering. Therefore footnotes appear out of sequence when they appear in conjunction with excerpted texts and judicial decisions.

Spelling and abbreviation conventions. The customary English-language spelling and appearance of certain terms relating to IPRs differ as between the continents. For example, in the United States *trademark* is spelled as a single word, while in Europe *trade mark* is spelled as two words. Throughout this book, U.S.-English language spelling conventions are adopted when they appear in the authors' commentary. However, when excerpts are included, the spelling convention of the author of the excerpt is generally retained. Also, the original spelling is generally maintained in formal legislative texts, such as European Union directives and regulations.

In this book, *Trade-Related Aspects of Intellectual Property Rights* is generally abbreviated as *TRIPS* in authors' commentary, while also appearing as *TRIPs* when originally presented as such in excerpts and legal texts. Customary practice regarding this abbreviation varies. For example, *TRIPS* is used by the World Trade Organization while *TRIPs* is used by the European Union.

Acknowledgments

In preparing this text the authors have had the benefit of research assistance from various quarters. Of special note is the diligent work of two doctoral students and research fellows at the Institute of European and International Economic Law at the University of Berne: Benoit Merkt and Ingo Meitinger. They were instrumental in searching and selecting appropriate materials and preparing draft comments and questions. Barabara Rutz, a former law student, assisted in scanning and formatting documents. Without the help of these young colleagues, the contribution from the Berne side would not have come about. Participation of the Institute was facilitated by the Weickert Foundation.

At the World Intellectual Property Organization, Gary Smith and Isabel Boutillon are owed thanks for their insights into the operation of the Patent Cooperation Treaty system. Thanks are also due to Adrian Otten at the World Trade Organization and Carlos Primo Braga at the World Bank for their generosity in sharing thoughts on the evolution of the international IPRs system.

On the editorial side, Cathy Abbott acted as editor of first instance, assuring that the authors' ideas were rendered in a way that would make sense to a reader. Marianne White acted as editor of second instance, assuring that the various pieces of the book fit together properly, and preparing a draft index. Monique Roy acted as editor of third instance, assisting with the proofreading of typeset text.

Particular thanks are due to John Berger, the publisher of this book at Kluwer Law International. John has been involved in the production of this book since its inception. He has supported the authors throughout the production process, and has provided all possible aid at each stage. The more or less timely completion of this book is in no small measure due to John's exceptional efforts.

We hope that you will find this book stimulating and useful. We encourage you to contact us with suggestions for improvement to future editions.

Frederick Abbott   Thomas Cottier   Francis Gurry
Chicago   Berne   Geneva

June 1999

CHAPTER I

Introduction to Intellectual Property: Forms and Policies

A. Intellectual Property in the Global Economy: An Introduction

The growing integration of global society in many parts of the world is a fact. The business manager increasingly thinks in terms of the international market for goods and services. Capital moves around the world in the greatest haste, seeking its highest return. Information flows with rather limited regard for national boundaries. Cultural exchange is facilitated by transnational mass media, and this exchange increasingly affects our lives and traditions. Digital and networking technology enable all forms of information, whether text, sound or image, to be reduced to binary code and to be transmitted on the Internet to any point on the globe almost instantaneously.

International rules and institutions that seek to regulate this integrated globe are rapidly evolving to cope with change. Nowhere is this evolution occurring more rapidly than in the field of the regulation of intellectual property rights. This rapid evolution is the result of a number of contemporaneous phenomena.

The pace of technological development that initially accelerated during the Second World War is now breath-taking. The evolution of computing technology has vastly expanded the capacity of the scientist and engineer to solve technical problems. Space-based telescopes aid astronomers and astro-physicists to unravel the mysteries of the universe; microbiologists and genetic engineers manipulate life forms as children have long manipulated building blocks.

Advances in technology rapidly enter the stream of commerce, affecting the techniques of industrial production, promotion and distribution. Industrial engineers perfect techniques of mass production employing sophisticated and untiring robotic machinery. In the services industries, new technologies facilitate rapid transportation and business transactions. Businesses demand the expansion of markets for selling and consuming. Cultural activities transcend the national theatre. The national border becomes a hindrance to all these endeavors, save where that national border can be exploited to profitable advantage.

As goods and services move more freely and quickly throughout an increasingly integrated global economy, producers and distributors need to assure that the creative or innovative elements of these goods and services, and the elements that give these goods and services their unique character and, thus, their competitive advantage, are protected against misappropriation. The absence of effective protection of intellectual property in many parts of the world in essence amounts to new types of trade barriers. Indeed, the reduction of tariffs and quantitative restrictions remains of limited effect if, at the same time, imported products may be freely copied and reproduced at considerably lower costs. The more that products and services contain intellectual property rights (IPRs) components, the more such barriers have effects in international trade.

For such reasons, demands for increased levels of IPRs protection emerged with intensity in the early 1980s. These demands led to the negotiation of a major new international IPRs protection agreement in the GATT — now the World Trade Organization (WTO). The Agreement on Trade-Related Aspects of Intellectual Property Rights (TRIPS Agreement) that entered into force on January 1, 1995 adds important texture to the international IPRs landscape. This includes the prescription of minimum levels of substantive IPRs protection for all WTO Member countries, a requirement of providing adequate enforcement mechanisms (including judicial processes), and the potential for authorization of trade sanctions against a Member that fails to implement the requirements.

However, the TRIPS Agreement is but the latest step in a trend toward an integrated global system for the protection of IPRs that began to take concrete shape in the late 1800s with the conclusion of the Paris Convention for the Protection of Industrial Property (1883) and the Berne Convention for the Protection of Literary and Artistic Works (1886). In fact, these conventions rank first in the effort to build a multilateral framework in support of international trade and cultural exchange. Many of the same concerns that led to the conclusion of the TRIPS Agreement were voiced by producers and artists more than a century ago. The Paris and Berne Conventions did not go as far as the TRIPS Agreement in addressing the interests of producers and artists in the protection of IPRs, both because the relatively underdeveloped nature of international commercial and cultural exchanges created less opportunity for abuse of intellectual property rights across borders and because the system of international institutions and the international legal system as a consequence needed to be far less mature in the late 1800s.

The establishment of institutions such as the United Nations and the International Monetary Fund at the end of the Second World War, the subsequent development of the GATT, the founding of the European Economic Community in 1957/58 and the establishment of the World Intellectual Property Organization in the late 1960s, opened new frontiers in international legal regulation. Yet for a long time, international standard setting in IPRs was met with scepticism on the part of newly independent nations, and progress was difficult to achieve under the umbrella of the Paris and Berne Conventions. Until the TRIPS Agreement, the international IPRs system mainly focused on facilitating and coordinating national and international registration of rights.

The development of a more comprehensive framework of international institutions paved the way for a more highly integrated system for the protection of IPRs than was possible in the late 1800s. Even so, it is interesting to observe that efforts to protect IPRs on a transnational basis are at the cutting edge of international legal development, both a century ago and today.

This book seeks to provide a new perspective for transnational learning. The materials do not exclusively focus on a particular jurisdiction. Instead, they draw from different sources, primarily U.S. and European and, of course, international law, with a view of intellectual property rights as building blocks of what is increasingly developing into a body of globally relevant rules based on shared perceptions of law. At the same time, the cases and materials selected also associate intellectual property rights with characteristics of different legal systems, and assist the reader in better understanding existing divergences which have been, and increasingly will be, addressed in future international negotiations — bringing about a positive global integration of intellectual property regimes.

By referring to the international intellectual property rights *system* we do not intend to suggest that there is a single integrated global mechanism for the protection of IPRs. This is far from the case. International IPRs protection remains grounded in the national legal systems of each country, and to a certain extent in the legal systems of integrated regions, such as the European Union. Nevertheless, important strides have been made in effectively achieving a truly global framework. Various conventions administered by the World Intellectual Property Organization (WIPO) and the WTO provide a broad multilateral framework of IPRs rules for the international community, and new agreements are continually in negotiation. There are a variety of mechanisms for securing IPRs protection on a multilateral basis — most notably the Patent Cooperation Treaty (PCT) mechanism and the Madrid Agreement concerning the International Registration of Marks administered by WIPO — and there is a proliferation of such mechanisms at the regional level. In particular, the European Union and the European Patent Organization increasingly provide the IPRs protection framework for Europe. Other regional arrangements, such as NAFTA and Mercosur, have set out to define minimum standards of IPR protection.

After a brief overview of global IPRs protection issues, this text begins by introducing the various intellectual property rights through an examination of court decisions in different national/regional jurisdictions. Though many students or practitioners who use this book will be familiar with the basic forms of IPRs, they may nevertheless find it useful to see how these forms are defined and approached in different national/regional legal systems. Of course, the introductory cases make reference to procedures and institutions that will be covered in more detail in subsequent chapters of the book, but we trust that these references will not be an obstacle to an appreciation of the introductory cases.

Following this introduction, we turn in Chapter II to the institutions that regulate the international protection of IPRs at the broad multilateral and regional levels. Chapter III examines general principles of international law and intellectual property, such as the national treatment and most favored nation principles, and the doctrine of legitimate expectations as to conditions of competition in WTO law. Chapter IV deals, in detail, with the content and scope of protection of the various rights in international law and regional law. Chapter V sets out rules and procedures for international registration of IPRs. Chapter VI deals with the field of enforcement and dispute settlement, a field of increasing importance in the context of assuring effective protection and of assuring good governance around the world. Chapter VII discusses issues of interfacing intellectual property with other fields of international and regional law. The complex relationship of competition law and IPRs, issues in biotechnology, and issues involving the flow of knowledge and information in cyberspace, will be introduced and discussed at this stage. We further explore the future in Chapter VIII, including how new technologies will affect the form and governance of IPRs (with emphasis on the Internet), what impact the growth of global electronic commerce will have on IPRs regulation, and how the developing countries may best adapt to the new global technological environment.

Excerpts from texts by the authors of this book and by Lester Thurow follow. The first excerpt discusses factors that over the past several decades gave rise to an increased interest in international aspects of IPRs, and considers why and how this interest was reflected in the field of international trade regulation. The next depicts three different generations of discriminatory trade barriers and locates the field of intellectual property within the most recent one. The third highlights the role of technology and the concomitant emphasis on research and development in post-industrial economies. The fourth excerpt identifies technology as an instrument of international economic competition, and suggests that there is a new type of comparative advantage at work in the international economy.

Protecting First World Assets in the Third World: Intellectual Property Negotiations in the GATT Multilateral Framework

Frederick M. Abbott*

*****

II. The Intellectual Property Problem

A. Treatment in the GATT

The expanding significance of intellectual property as an element of national wealth might, in retrospect, have been apparent in the immediate post-World War II environment. Certainly, the emergence of radar, radio field communications, rockets, and atomic weapons as pivotal components

---

*22 Vand.J.Transnat'l L. 689 (1989).

of military strategy pointed to an increasingly important role for science and technology in the postwar era. Nevertheless, if a glimmer of events to come was available to the 1940s statesman, the General Agreement did not reflect it.... The General Agreement does not address the extraterritorial protection of intellectual property rights in any explicit manner.

Two developments subsequent to the drafting of the General Agreement lent scope and intensity to what will be referred to as the "intellectual property problem." The first was the tremendous growth in the significance of technology to the industrialized countries. Constant innovation has become the hallmark of the economies of the OECD countries, and the technology/innovation component of exports — both tangible and intangible — has become a major factor in international economic competition. The second development was the dramatic increase in the relative significance of international trade to world gross economic product and the concomitant intensification of international economic interdependence (no doubt reflecting to some extent the success of the GATT). These two factors — technology as a major component of national wealth, and heightened economic interdependence — create a situation that demands attention.

B. Defining the Intellectual Property Problem

The intellectual property problem involves the unintended transfer of wealth from the industrialized country economies to the developing and newly industrialized country (NIC) economies. In this case, wealth takes the form of technology protected in the industrialized countries by patent and trade secret, goodwill protected by trademark and other indication of origin, expression protected by copyright, and design protected by design patent and semiconductor layout protection legislation. Intellectual property is intangible wealth, often easily appropriated and reproduced. Unlike tangible wealth, which must be mined, grown, or manufactured and is therefore subject to finite limitations of ownership or use, intellectual property wealth can be reproduced and used without depriving its creator/owner of possession or use and almost without practical limit. Once created, the marginal cost of reproduction is often near zero. The intellectual property problem therefore concerns devising a mechanism for protecting industrialized country intangible wealth, distinctly requiring the cooperation of developing countries and NICs, which by providing such protection forego a potential economic windfall.

Demands for protection of intellectual property are often based (implicitly or explicitly) on a theory of natural law or moral right — the idea that intellectual property is naturally owned by the person who creates it and that appropriation from that person without compensation is wrongful (whether such appropriation is purely domestic or international). However, national policies on the scope of legitimized intellectual property rights vary widely depending on the results of a cost/benefit analysis balancing the immediate public welfare against long-term interests in private capital formation. National policy, as opposed to natural law, has shaped the grant of the intellectual property right. While a combination of self-interest and equity have given rise to a system in which states grant to foreign nationals intellectual property rights protection equivalent to that accorded to local entities, the scope of local protection has not been intuitively derived from natural law.

C. What the Intellectual Property Problem Is Not

An influential segment of the United States intellectual property community is promoting developing country protection of intellectual property based on claimed benefits to those countries.[16] However, the

---

[16]*See, e.g.,* INTELLECTUAL PROPERTY RIGHTS: GLOBAL CONSENSUS, GLOBAL CONFLICT 20-21 (R.M. GADBAW & T. RICHARDS EDS. 1988). . . .

While not empirically substantiated, industrialized country economists argue that increased levels of intellectual property protection will produce a variety of short- and long-term benefits for developing countries. They suggest that increased levels of developing country patent protection will: (1) encourage technology transfers and investment from the industrialized economies to the developing economies by providing an hospitable environment; (2) stimulate local innovation and technology infrastructures (by providing an environment in which local innovators are encouraged both to create and share their creations); (3) encourage domestic investment in local technology-based industries; and (4) promote exports by opening markets otherwise closed to those manufacturing without authorization. In the trademark area they suggest that developing country protection will increase the local introduction of new foreign discoveries and the diffusion of information necessary to make consumer markets function efficiently by permitting consumers to make educated choices about goods of varying quality. In the copyright area they suggest that enhanced intellectual property protection stimulates local innovation and the flow of ideas from abroad. Industrialized country economists recognize that there is a short-term loss from enhanced protection that will be absorbed by developing countries, in the form of lost pirate revenues and the reallocation of resources, but contend that these losses will be compensated for by the long-term benefits enumerated above. *See, e.g.,* MacLaughlin, Richards & Kenny, *The Economic Sig-*

intellectual property problem is not a failure by the developing countries to recognize the social or economic utility of granting and protecting rights in intellectual property. In the industrialized countries themselves, the most well-reasoned studies of patent systems have been inconclusive with respect to the social or economic utility of those systems. Machlup, Hamilton, and Jewkes each concluded by different routes that continuation of the industrialized country patent systems is justified because they exist and do not appear to do any great harm. No significant empirical study as yet has demonstrated the beneficial impact of the patent grant on economic growth or social development. A study yielding such results might indeed be possible, but it is in the realm of the future. Attempting to persuade developing countries that the industrialized countries are promoting enhanced intellectual property protection to accelerate the former's economic growth is neither necessary nor appropriate at this point. The intellectual property debate stands on firmer ground if premised on recognition that the industrialized countries are attempting to protect an increasingly important component of their national wealth.

D. Quantifying the Intellectual Property Problem

Quantifying the intellectual property problem in terms of financial losses to industrialized country business enterprises due to unintended (or unauthorized) appropriation of intellectual property by developing country enterprises is difficult because it involves several highly uncertain factors. First, losses to industrialized country enterprises take the form of lost revenue opportunities, and calculation of such losses requires the hypothesis of unaffected revenues. Second, because intellectual property is often easy to reproduce and difficult to trace, the extent of unauthorized appropriation and use involves speculation. Data collected from industrialized country enterprises by government agencies or trade organizations are not

---

nificance of Piracy, in Gadbaw & Richards, *id.*, at 89-91, 97-108; Sherwood, *The Benefits Developing Countries Gain from Safeguarding Intellectual Property* (June 1988) (unpublished, in author's files). A more evenhanded, if more limited, view of the potential ways in which national patent systems might stimulate growth in developing countries — primarily based on the capacity of such systems to disseminate technical information — is found in Lecture by Klaus Pfanner, WIPO Deputy Director General, *The Usefulness of National and International Protection of Inventions*, reprinted in WORLD INTELLECTUAL PROPERTY ORGANIZATION [WIPO], THE USE OF THE PATENT SYSTEM BY INDUSTRIAL ENTERPRISES IN DEVELOPING COUNTRIES 43, 51-54 (1982).

likely to be subject to the kind of rigorous examination required for a least-biased estimate of losses. Cautionary observations aside, several attempts to quantify intellectual property losses have been made, the most recent and influential of which is a report produced by the United States International Trade Commission (ITC) in 1988 at the request of the United States Trade Representative (USTR) (ITC Report).The USTR asked the ITC to prepare a comprehensive study of "distortions in U.S. worldwide trade associated with deficiencies in the protection provided by foreign countries to U.S. intellectual property rights." The ITC was requested to consider distortions caused by trademark counterfeiting, as well as infringement and misappropriation of copyrights, patents, semiconductor chip design, trade secrets, and other types of intellectual property. The ITC compiled its data from a questionnaire sent to 736 United States companies, including all Fortune 500 companies, for the year 1986. The ITC estimated 1986 aggregate worldwide losses to United States companies responding to its questionnaire at $23.8 billion. Based on "reasonable" (but not statistically valid) assumptions, the ITC Report extrapolated this data to estimate that worldwide losses to United States industries in 1986 ranged from $43 billion to $61 billion. The ITC Report attributed a significant concentration of estimated losses to certain developing countries and NICs: Brazil, China, Hong Kong, India, Mexico, Nigeria, the Republic of Korea, and Taiwan. Reporting firms accounting for eighty-four percent of aggregate losses in 1986 indicated that in the last fifteen years losses from inadequate intellectual property rights protection had grown moderately or greatly; the ITC Report attributed this phenomenon to two factors:

> First, the situation has undoubtedly deteriorated in the past 15 years; international trade has increased markedly; production capabilities in countries with less than adequate protection have increased; and U.S. firms have made increasing efforts to exploit foreign markets and use foreign production sites. All these factors increase the exposure of U.S. firms to intellectual-property violations. Concurrent with these developments, the overall awareness of the importance of intellectual property to profitability has increased substantially in U.S. business; thus the respondents are far more aware of losses stemming from inadequate intellectual property protection than they were 15 years ago.

Quantifications of intellectual property losses, although subject to question over amount (and whether quasi-empirical or anecdotal), identify a relatively consistent list of countries whose lack of legislation or enforcement results in a significant level of unauthorized appropriation of industrialized country intellectual property. As a broad characterization, and with very limited exception, these states are either newly-industrialized or developing. The industries that appear most affected are chemicals and pharmaceuticals, computer software, and entertainment (audio and video).

Intellectual Property in International Trade Law and Policy: The GATT Connection

Thomas Cottier*

1. From Tariffs to Intellectual Property

Trade policy in the early post World War II era focused on gradual reduction of tariffs and the elimination of preferential systems. Rates were high, stemming from protectionist policies of the great recession of the 1930s. Moreover, preferential imperial, and therefore discriminatory, tariffs were elaborate in colonial systems. The 1947 General Agreement on Tariffs and Trade (GATT) provided, in essence, a framework for a gradual and, as it turned out, successful process of reduction of tariffs. In seven rounds of multilateral negotiations, a general level of some 40 percent in 1947 sank to an average of 4.7 percent among the main industrialized nations after the 1974–1979 Tokyo Round. Actual average levels are even lower, and further cuts of about 30 percent are expected in the present Uruguay Round. Principles and provisions of the General Agreement were modeled, in the beginning, to accompany this process and to avoid frustration and circumvention by other means, in particular quantitative import restrictions, subsidies or discriminatory taxes on imports. Indeed, the gradual reduction, and even elimination of tariffs within customs unions and free trade arrangements, increasingly shifted the emphasis on non-tariff measures, which began to replace tariffs as main instruments of governmental trade and economic policies. Quantitative restrictions, export subsidies, anti-dumping measures, technical norms and standards, balance of pay-

---

*1 Aussenwirtschaft, Issue 1, at 79-105 (1992).

ment measures, labeling requirements, import licensing, rules on government procurement, "voluntary" import obligation or export restriction agreements (VER) and other imaginative tools became additional and widely used instruments for political ends, both in developing (beside higher and often still non-bound tariffs) as well as in industrialized countries. With beginnings in the Kennedy Round, such non-tariff barriers became, beside the classical process of tariff-reductions, the main objects of trade negotiations in the Tokyo Round. The results have remained under review and further elaboration also in the present Uruguay Round. Beside partial and important reforms of the 1947 General Agreement, changes are also expected in the fields covered by the Tokyo Round agreements such as anti-dumping, technical barriers to trade, import licensing procedures, subsidies and countervailing duties and government procurement.

It is due to substantial tariff reductions and — to use GATT terminology — increasing legal disciplines in the field of non-tariff measures, but foremost to an ever-increasing importance of high technology and service industries, that a third generation of non-tariff barriers was brought to attention during the 1980s. This generation encompasses a number of issues, ranging from domestic farm support to restrictive regulation of service industries, of investments and, finally, the protection of intellectual property. What do these subjects share in common? They stem from different fields of law, public and private, but the common trait, perhaps, is that they all are mainly part of the general internal legal system. They are not directly geared to classical international trade relations, but they have been affecting such relations more and more in terms of limiting market access while other barriers were gradually dismantled or at least legally disciplined. The great political difficulties in reaching final agreement in key issues of the Round, such as reduction of agricultural support systems, but also failure to achieve substantial stream-lining of conditions for investment, or to bring about presently considerable liberalization of trade in services beyond bindings and a first and important step to establish a framework for liberalization, all stem from this very fact. The main difficulties to be settled in the area of intellectual property or trade-related aspects of intellectual property rights (TRIPs) have similar roots. The issue of patentability of pharmaceuticals, foodstuffs or living matter, i.e. the problem how far exceptions to patentability should be allowed to go, or, in copyright, how the relationships of authors, producers, performers and users should be arranged, are perhaps the most prominent examples in showing how far international negotiations and regulations have penetrated contemporary, controversial, socially, ethical or culturally sensitive issues of the domestic political process. The example of patenting life forms and genetic engineering also indicates why such problems are difficult to settle on the international level, and that successful resolution requires a domestic political and democratic process which is carried out in a parallel timespan, if not before.

International trade law has come a long way. It has definitively left the stage of mere transboundary action. More than ever before, international trade regulation today amounts to the ambition of assuring fair competition in a globalizing market economy. The subject dealt with in the Structural Impediment Initiative (U.S.-Japan), ranging from saving and investment patterns, land policy, distribution systems, exclusionary business practices, "keiretsu" relationship (closely related corporate relationship through mutual stock-holding, interlocking directorates and other means) to pricing mechanisms may demonstrate, as a forerunner, future directions of multilateral trade and economic relations, and how far they are penetrating domestic law and policy. Foreign and domestic economic affairs can no longer be separated; and the increasing importance and attention paid to foreign policy in general, formerly of true interest often merely to a few, is a natural effect of such developments.

The Evolution of Technology and Markets and the Management of Intellectual Property Rights

Francis Gurry*

The transition that intellectual property has undergone from backroom specialty to boardroom and ministerial concern is perhaps most dramatically reflected on the international level in the Agreement on Trade Related Aspects of Intellectual Property (TRIPS), concluded as part of the Uruguay Round accords that led to the establishment of the World Trade Organization (WTO). While TRIPS may be the most dramatic example of

---

*In PUBLIC POLICY AND GLOBAL TECHNOLOGICAL INTEGRATION 25 (F. M. ABBOTT AND D. J. GERBER EDS., 1997).

heightened international attention to intellectual property, it should nevertheless be understood as but a single response to economic and industrial change that is much more broadly based than trade, and whose effects will require policy management of a far more widespread, complex and sophisticated nature than that which a single multilateral trade accord can provide.

The economic and industrial change that was the root cause of the inclusion of intellectual property in the Uruguay Round accords can be described in a variety of ways. Various phrases have been coined to describe it, such as the post-industrial society, the information revolution or the information age. Stated at its broadest, the change signals the transition from an economy in which the central source of wealth generation was physical capital to one in which that central source is increasingly becoming intellectual capital.

There are many signs of this transition. Investment in the generation of intellectual capital through research and development (R&D) has steadily increased across the industrialized countries. Over the twenty years from 1972 to 1991, the amount of resources invested in R&D by the G7 countries increased from an average of 1.80% of GDP to an average of 2.25% of GDP. For individual corporations, the amounts invested in R&D expenditure are often prodigious. In 1992, for example, three corporations, General Motors, Siemens, and IBM, each spent over 5 billion dollars on R&D. It is difficult to imagine many investments in physical capital of this magnitude by a corporation, let alone on a recurrent, annual basis, as is the case for R&D.

Not surprisingly, the composition of the work force reflects a corresponding evolution. The number of scientific and engineering workers engaged in R&D in France, Germany, Italy, Japan, the United Kingdom, and the United States of America rose from 788,500 in 1965 to 1,887,100 in 1989, or from around 162 per 10,000 persons in the labor force to 326 per 10,000.

Investment in the generation of intellectual capital may be seen as both the cause and effect of the increasingly prominent position of the high-tech industries, which are identified by the Organisation for Economic Co-operation and Development (OECD) as those industries with the highest R&D intensities. The production of high-tech manufactures by the major industrialized countries, in constant dollar terms, doubled from

1981 to 1992, while production of other manufactured goods grew by twenty-nine percent. In consequence, the output of the high-tech industries represented twenty-two percent of global production of all manufactured goods in 1992, whereas, in 1981, it represented only fourteen percent.

In an age where intellectual capital is increasingly the source of wealth generation, intellectual property assumes critical significance as the means of control of the newest, and potentially most commercially attractive, elements of intellectual capital. The evolution of the demand for the protection of intellectual property reflects the new significance of intellectual property. Patents provide a ready example. At the end of the 1993, a total of 3.9 million patents were in force throughout the world. The demand for new patent rights is increasing at an extraordinary rate, the total number of patent applications worldwide having arisen from 1,371,806 in 1989 to 1,965,487 in 1993, an increase of 43.3%. In Japan, to take but one, admittedly leading, example, the two millionth patent was granted in December 1995. It took ninety-five years (from 1885 to 1980) to grant the first million patents in Japan, whereas it took only fifteen years (from 1980 to 1995) to grant the next million patents.

The new significance of intellectual capital and the increased demand for intellectual property are both occurring within the context of the globalization of markets. In this process of globalization, intellectual capital has been a vector of internationalization and intellectual property has been an instrument of competitive positioning in global markets.

As a vector, intellectual capital has provided the key elements of the infrastructure that has permitted markets to become globalized. Transportation, communications, and telecommunications are the heart of the high-tech industries and have provided the means by which physical barriers to global markets have been overcome. Of the six industries identified by the OECD as high-tech, three — aerospace, office and computing equipment, and communications equipment — have been primary agents of globalization.

Intellectual property is peculiarly adapted to exploitation within global markets. Being the intangible expression of an invention, design, sign or other expression of an idea, or, more simply, information, it may, unlike physical property, be used simultaneously in different physical markets. Patents for inventions or industrial designs may be exploited wherever the physical conditions exist to permit the embodiment of the invention or the design in a product. Trademarks are potent means for enabling the market presence of corporations to be signaled in the same manner and with the same identity wherever the corporation's goods or services are available. Information technologies and, in particular, digitization, have permitted what is, at base, a single expression to be distributed in a variety of different media. The book has become also the film at the cinema, the video at home, the CD-ROM, and the video game.

There is much evidence of the use of intellectual property as a central instrument in competitive positioning in the context of globalized markets. The increased demand for patents, referred to above, is largely a reflection of increased geographical coverage sought for the protection of inventions. Protection is sought not in a single market, but across each of the markets where it is considered that the invention can be viably exploited. Whereas, as mentioned above, the number of patent applications filed worldwide rose from 1989 to 1993 by 593,681 applications, or by 43.3%, the number of first filings, that is, applications filed for the first time around the world, as opposed to applications claiming the priority of an application already filed elsewhere in the world, rose by only 88,414 applications, or by sixteen percent. Thus, the bulk of the new applications filed worldwide represents the endeavor to obtain protection for the same invention filed across a broader range of countries.

The increased opportunities for international cooperation brought about by globalized markets, together with the high cost and high risk of investment in R&D, have led to a significant increase in inter-firm collaboration and alliances in the generation of intellectual capital. A database maintained in the Netherlands on strategic technology partnerships indicates that, whereas the number of international multi-firm R&D alliances recorded between 1973 and 1976 was eighty-six, the number of such alliances recorded between 1985 and 1988 was 988.

It is clear also that internationalization in the area of intellectual capital is occurring not only through strategic multi-firm alliances, but also through internationalization on all levels of the activities and management of a single enterprise. A single firm can spread its R&D, procurement, production and marketing throughout the world, as the example of Canon indicates. In 1992, Canon had, outside Japan, 9 research centers, 54 manufacturing facilities, 185 marketing subsidiaries and 40 global procurement subsidiaries. More generally, the number of overseas manufacturing operations of Japanese electronic corporations rose from 654 in 1988 to 1015 in 1993.

What are the challenges for policy management presented by the new significance of intellectual property in internationalized markets fueled by intellectual capital, and how are they being met? The challenges are manifold and many of them are such that appropriate precedents for their treatment are not readily available.

Head to Head

Lester Thurow*

Technology

In the past comparative advantage was a function of natural-resources endowments and factor proportions (capital-labor ratios). Cotton was grown in the American South because the climate and soil were right. Slavery provided abundant labor. Cotton was spun in New England because it had the capital to harness available waterpower. Each industry had its natural location.

Consider what are commonly believed to be the seven key industries of the next few decades — microelectronics, biotechnology, the new materials industries, civilian aviation, telecommunications, robots plus machine tools, and computers plus software. All are brainpower industries. Each could be located anywhere on the face of the globe. Where they will be located depends upon who can organize the brainpower to capture them. In the century ahead comparative advantage will be man-made.

Since technology lies behind man-made comparative advantage, research and development becomes critical. In the past the economic winners were those who invented new products. The British in the nineteenth century and the Americans in the twentieth century got rich doing so. But in the twenty-first century sustainable competitive advantage will come much more out of new process technologies and much less out of new product technologies. Reverse engineering has become an art form. New products can easily be reproduced. What used to be primary (inventing new prod-

---

*HEAD TO HEAD at 45-47 (1992).

16

ucts) becomes secondary, and what used to be secondary (inventing and perfecting new processes) becomes primary.

If R&D spending by private firms is examined, American firms spend two thirds of their money on new products and one third on new processes. The Japanese do exactly the opposite — one third on new products, two thirds on new processes. Not surprisingly, both sets of firms do well where they concentrate their talent. While the Americans earn higher rates of return on new product technologies, Japanese firms earn higher rates of return on new processes.

Someone, however, is making a mistake. Both strategies cannot be correct. In this case the someone is the United States. Its spending patterns are wrong, but they are wrong because they used to be right. In the early 1960s it was conventional wisdom, and also true, that the rate of return on investment in new product R&D was almost always higher than that on new process R&D. A new product gave the inventor a monopoly power to set higher prices and earn higher profits. With a new product, there were no competitors.

In contrast, a new process left the inventor in a competitive business. Competitors knew how to make the product, and they would always lower their prices to match the inventor's prices as long as they were covering marginal costs in their old facilities. To make monopoly rents on process technologies, it was necessary to drive one's competitors out of business. To do this, new process technologies had to have average costs below the marginal costs of old process technologies. Since marginal costs are typically far below average costs, an enormous (and very unlikely) process breakthrough was necessary if one were to establish a monopoly position with better process technologies. Driving one's competitor out of business was also likely to get one into trouble with the antitrust laws. It was simply rational to spend most of a firm's R&D money on new product development.

While Americans focused on product technologies, Japan and West Germany focused on process technologies. They did so not because they were smarter than Americans but because the United States had such a technical lead in the 1950s and 1960s that it was virtually impossible for either Japan or West Germany to become leaders in the development of new products. They could only hope to compete in existing markets that Americans were exiting. As a result, Japan and West Germany invested less of their GNP in R&D, and what they did invest was invested more heavily in process R&D. They had no choice.

But what was a good American strategy thirty years ago, a focus on new product technologies, is today a poor strategy. Levels of technical sophistication in Germany, Japan, and the United States are now very different, and reverse engineering has become a highly developed art form. The nature of the change can be seen in the economic history of three leading new products introduced into the mass consumer market in the past two decades: the video camera and recorder, the fax, and the CD player. Americans invented the video camera and recorder and the fax; Europeans (the Dutch) invented the CD player. But measured in terms of sales, employment, and profits, all three have become Japanese products.

The moral of the story is clear. Those who can make a product cheaper can take it away from the inventor. In today's world it does very little good to invent a new product if the inventor is not the cheapest producer of that product. What necessity forced upon West Germany and Japan thirty years ago happens to be the right long-run R&D strategy today.

Notes and Questions

1. The preceding excerpts seek to depict the evolution and importance of intellectual property on the agenda of international trade regulation. When the Abbott article was published in 1989, there was still considerably uncertainty and controversy whether a substantial agreement on intellectual property should and could be reached within the realm of GATT and the Uruguay Round of multilateral trade negotiations. At the time of the 1989 Montreal Mid-Term Review, little beyond a somewhat more detailed agenda for trade negotiation on issues in addition to the combating of piracy and counterfeiting was agreed. The article focuses on and recalls the basic claims of industrialized countries, led by the United States. During early negotiations, developing countries still largely adhered to perspectives developed during the 1970s which conceived of IPRs protection as detrimental to their interests. This perspective had made progress on addressing industrialized country concerns within the specialized U.N. organization, WIPO, virtually impossible. It is important to stress that the TRIPS negotiations contributed significantly to a mutual learning process. In addition to geopolitical factors such as the end of the Cold War, these negotiations helped to bridge fundamental differences in perception between the developed and developing worlds.

With the advent of the TRIPS Agreement, and the competitive quest for attracting investment in the process of globalization, the question whether developing countries should provide higher levels of IPRs protection appears to be largely settled. Nevertheless, there persists among some government officials and scholars, particularly in the developing world, a substantial degree of doubt about the wisdom and equity of the TRIPS Agreement. This may presage continuing conflict within the international political and economic systems.

In a recently published article, Abbott stresses the importance of closing the gap between rich and poor nations, offering this perspective on the international IPRs system: "the most critical policy issue to be addressed at the international level with respect to the international intellectual property system of laws and institutions is how it can best be constructed and implemented to facilitate economic growth and social welfare in the developing and newly-industrializing countries."[1]

The Gurry article, written after the conclusion of the Uruguay Round, set outs the main factors which currently put — and will keep — intellectual property protection high on the legal agenda in international negotiations and cooperation.

2. The preceding excerpts lay out a number of factors accounting for increased worldwide attention to IPRs protection: (1) high research and development costs; (2) changing structure of the global workforce; (3) demands of businesses to control the latest products; (4) the integration of markets; (5) the potential for IPRs to aid in market penetration, especially with respect to product or service positioning; and (6) increased firm collaborations and alliances. What additional factors might be at work?

3. Cottier describes the TRIPS negotiations as part of a third generation of efforts to bring about the dismantling of trade barriers. How is the third generation of trade barriers distinguished from previous ones? In BEING DIGITAL, Nicolas Negroponte said "GATT is about atoms."[2] If the GATT is about atoms, what might the new WTO be about?

4. The excerpt from the book by Lester Thurow reflects one economist's view on technological competition between major industrialized countries,

---

[1]Frederick M. Abbott, *The Enduring Enigma of TRIPS: A Challenge to the World Economic System*, 1 JIEL 497 (1998).
[2]NICHOLAS NEGROPONTE, BEING DIGITAL (1995), at 11.

arguing in favor of investing in R&D relating to processes, rather than new products. What is Thurow's reasoning? During the late 1990s, the economy of the United States was substantially more dynamic than those of Japan and Germany. Does this imply that Thurow was mistaken, or might it imply some change in U.S. industrial behavior?

5. Does the text by Thurow suggest why the 1980s and 1990s witnessed a dramatic drive towards enhanced protection of IPRs as compared to more traditional property rights? What is Thurow's perspective on the evolution of comparative advantage?

6. In discussing demands for increased international IPRs protection, references are often made by IPRs specialists, economists and others to *high technology products* or *industries* that are said to have assumed special significance for achieving higher rates of economic growth. Laura Tyson has described the concept of the high technology industry this way:

> Conceptually, a high technology industry is one in which knowledge is a prime source of competitive advantage for producers, who in turn make large investments in knowledge creation. Reflecting this definition, high-technology industries are usually identified as those with above-average spending on research and development, above-average employment of scientists and engineers, or both.[3]

Determining what constitutes a *high technology product* may involve an element of subjective judgment.[4] Not all products made by high technology industries are high technology products, since the result of a large-scale R&D effort may be an elegant yet technically unsophisticated end-product. Similarly, the fact that a product is protected by patent or other IPR does not alone make it a high technology product, since a high level of technological sophistication is not a prerequisite of patent protection. A high technology product is generally the result not only of above-average R&D spending and/or higher than average input by scientists and engineers, but also may require the employment of scientifically sophisticated manufac-

---

[3]Laura D'Andrea Tyson, Who's Bashing Whom: Trade Conflict in High Technology Industries 18 (1992)(citation omitted).

[4]Tyson notes that the classification of products as "high technology" is approached by trade economists using a number of different systems, some of which incorporate the subjective judgment of experts and analysts. *Id.* at Table 2.1 (notes).

turing techniques, and/or be capable of operation only by technically skilled individuals. Is the concept of high technology useful as a policy instrument and, if so, how? Do you think that the concept is likely to be enduring, that is, do you think that it will still be used in the year 2050?

B. The Various Rights

1. Introduction to the Forms of Intellectual Property

From an economic perspective, intellectual property rights grant a more or less extensive monopoly right over the economic exploitation of ideas, the expression of ideas and distinctive words or symbols. It is a matter of protecting investment, creating incentive for future investment and facilitating identification in distributed markets. The possibility of hindering others from free-riding on the investment of capital and labor amounts to the most important economic function of these rights.

From a legal perspective, however, we need to examine intellectual property in its different constituent components and forms. The distinctions among the forms are important because the various forms imply different legal effects.

Intellectual Property and Intellectual Property Rights

The term *intellectual property* refers to a defined set of the intangible products of human activity. It refers to an idea, the expression of an idea or the expression of an identity that is capable of being ascribed to a person. The term *intellectual property right* refers to a bundle of legally enforceable interests that a person may hold with respect to intellectual property. Sometimes intellectual property is defined as the negative of real property and personal (or movable) property. While perhaps formally possible, this definition is overbroad.

The *set* (that is, the group belonging together) of intangible products of human activity is legally *defined* because not all such products are *intellectual property*. For example, an electronic wire transfer of funds is the product of human activity and it is intangible, but it is not intellectual property.

Intellectual property is *intangible* even though its manifestation or visible form may be set or fixed in something tangible. For example, an artist may express him or her self with a brush and paints on a canvas. The resulting painting is a tangible product that embodies the creative activity of the artist. The painting itself is not intellectual property. Only the creativity of the artist that is visible in the painting is intellectual property.

Intellectual property is the product of *human* activity. Intervening steps performed by machine potentially deprive intangible products of their character as intellectual property. For example, a human may write a computer program that embodies intellectual property (that is, the creative expression of its author embodied in the program). This computer program may itself be capable of writing a new computer program. Whether the subsequent computer program itself embodies creative human expression and should benefit from IPRs protection is not yet fully settled.

The *holder* of an intellectual property *right* has the legally recognized capacity to authorize or prevent others from acting in certain ways with respect to that intellectual property.

Intellectual property rights are of limited or unlimited *duration*. Some of the various rights are of limited duration, such as patents, design, and copyright. Others may provide an entitlement for unlimited duration. For example, an artist's *moral right* to prevent the mutilation of his or her artistic work might be of indefinite duration. Similarly, trademark rights are renewable without limitation. Trade secrets may exist as long as relevant conditions are met. When the right expires, intellectual property may either be said to lose its character as *property* since it may no longer be owned or possessed, or it may be said to become the common property of the public (*i.e.* to enter the public domain). The two perspectives may entail, in particular cases, different legal consequences.

The intellectual property *right* is *ubiquitous*. This means that the entitlement — unlike real or movable property — is not limited to a particular physical body incorporating the rights. It is present and incorporated in all actual and virtual realizations of the intellectual property which it protects. This feature makes intellectual property significantly different from physical property (movable and real property) and the rights attached to it. This distinction will explain a number of particular features of IPRs in international trade regulation which do not exist for physical property.

Defining *what* rights with respect to intellectual property are legally enforceable is the subject of intellectual property *law*. The distribution of legal competence among nations, regional organizations and international organizations to define, grant and enforce intellectual property rights forms the *international* component of intellectual property law, and is the focus of this book.

The Forms of Intellectual Property Rights

There are different *forms* of intellectual property. These forms are generally referred to by the *right* that attaches to them. For example, a patent is a right with respect to an invention. The patent is not the invention itself, but defines the types of rights enjoyed with respect to the invention. Not all inventions are patented, and thus one refers to a *patented product* or a *patented invention*. Various legal criteria must be met before the intangible product of human activity is characterized as a form of intellectual property subject to a *right*. This relationship can be similarly defined for all forms of IPRs.

The major forms of intellectual property right are:

1. Patent (and related industrial design right);
2. Copyright (and related neighboring rights);
3. Trademark (and related service mark);
4. Integrated Circuit Layout Right;
5. Geographical Indication of Origin;
6. Plant Variety Right; and
7. Undisclosed Information (Trade Secret).

As indicated above, within the various broad forms of intellectual property right there are subforms. The relationship between these forms and subforms is not always clear and may vary over time. For example, as indicated above, in addition to the utility patent there is the design patent. In many legal traditions, however, design rights are considered to be a subset of copyright, rather than patent, reflecting the hybrid character of design rights as part industrial and part artistic. Copyright has its *neighboring rights* such as broadcast rights. However, it is arguable that neighboring rights doctrine is becoming obsolete as performance, broadcast and related rights are incorporated in the TRIPS Agreement and new WIPO treaties as components of copyright.

The relationship among different forms of intellectual property rights is not always easy to define. An idea or expression of an idea may be protectable under various forms. For example, a computer program may be protected under copyright or under patent law. For the creator, it is generally a matter of choosing the most efficient form of protection in terms of cost and duration. Sometimes, protection is assured by sequentially using different forms. For example, a pharmaceutical product may first be protected by patent, but may ultimately rely on trademark protection for many more years. In each case the legal effect of the protection is different. Where patent rights are relied on, the inventive element of the pharmaceutical product is given legal protection. Where trademark rights are relied on, the identity of the maker of the product in the marketplace is given legal protection. In economic terms, the effect is to enable the creator to secure a return on investment in the creation and differentiation of its product.

Finally, it should be noted that one of the goals of IPRs — consumer protection and fair competition — may be pursued in parallel by different means, in particular by way of laws and rules on unfair competition. For example, passing off may be remedied both under unfair competition laws and trademark laws. Generally speaking, it may be said that the various forms of IPRs prevail, as specific entitlements, over broader doctrines and rules of unfair competition.

Historically, national governments were largely free to define intellectual property, the scope of intellectual property rights, and the ways and means to enforce such rights, as a matter of domestic law, within certain broad constraints that were imposed by international agreements to which such governments may have assented. Over the past two decades, the range of discretion permitted to national governments in defining intellectual property has increasingly become a subject of concern among industry and artist groups, and efforts have been made to harmonize these definitions in a number of fora, including the World Intellectual Property Organization (WIPO), the World Trade Organization (WTO) and the European Union (EU). We will examine these efforts in detail later in this book. The important point for present purposes is that today we can describe the different forms of intellectual property for most nations (and regions) of the world in a fairly consistent manner. We will illustrate issues surrounding the various forms of intellectual property with judicial decisions from different national courts. It is important to bear in mind that there will be variations in the national rules relating to what qualifies for intellectual property rights protection among nations and regions. Nonetheless, the economic functions and descriptions of IPRs are largely common among developed legal systems. The following section seeks to define and introduce the functions of the various rights and their common features around the world.

2. Patent

a. The Nature and Subject Matter of the Patent

A *patent* is a right granted to the inventor of a technological product or process that is new (or novel), useful (or is capable of industrial application), and involves an inventive step (or is non-obvious). In return for making the invention, more precisely the technical rule, publicly known, a patent entitles the inventor to exclude others from making, using, selling or importing the invention for a period of time, generally twenty years from the date the patent application is filed. While patents share these common general features in most countries, it is important to note that legal definitions as to scope, entitlements, fields of technology and exceptions still vary considerably and have not been fully harmonized in international law.

Virtually any kind of invention in the different fields of technology may be patented, though there are certain limitations. For example, inventions that would be harmful to public order or the environment may be excluded from patentability, as may inventions with respect to surgical procedures.

The most important inherent limitation on patentable subject matter revolves around the sometimes blurred distinction between an *invention* and a *discovery*. Laws of nature or scientific principles that a researcher may "find" are not patentable. For example, imagine that a scientist discovers that a certain previously unknown form of magnetic wave strikes the earth's atmosphere from deep space, and that this kind of wave has an adverse effect on the transmission of data between the earth and communications satellites. Such a discovery may have enormous commercial implications, perhaps leading to the invention of a device that filters out the harmful effect of the waves. The inventor of the filtering device may be entitled to a patent. The discoverer of the magnetic wave cannot patent his or her discovery. Today, the distinction between discovery and invention is of increasing importance in the fields of genetic engineering and biotechnology.

Patent laws generally rely upon four essential criteria for the grant of exclusive rights:

- The first criterion and major qualification for a patent is that an invention be *new* or *novel*. This means that the invention (product or process) has not been anticipated by (is not present in) prior art. In other words, the invention has not been disclosed or described before the date of the patent application filing. A patent application will, generally, be defeated by an anticipating disclosure anywhere in the world. A so-called "prior art search" by a patent examiner should take into account information about prior art from throughout the world. Naturally, there may be controversy between an inventor and the patent examiner about whether a particular prior art disclosure in fact anticipates an invention. A prior inventor may have described a device similar, but not identical, to the subsequent inventor's device. The patent examiner must determine whether the second device is sufficiently different from the first device (sufficiently new) to qualify for a patent.

- The second criterion for patenting is that an invention be *useful* or *capable of industrial application*. Until fairly recently, it seemed that the requirement of utility was not terribly important to the patenting process since very few otherwise patentable inventions failed to meet this criterion. Some commercial use, it seemed, could be found for most anything. However, recent developments in the fields of biotechnology and chemistry have made it possible for researchers to develop new molecules and compounds with relative ease, yet without, at least initially, any immediate application for such molecules or compounds in mind. The question then arises to what extent patents should be granted on these "speculative" inventions, since a proliferation of patent grants might impede research by other persons. The criterion of *utility* has thus reemerged as a critical one in the evaluation of claims for inventions.

- The third criterion of *involving an inventive step* or *non-obviousness* is very important. An invention is *obvious* if it would be an apparent improvement to prior art to a person reasonably skilled in the art practiced by the invention. For example, imagine that someone has been granted a patent on the clip that is used to keep ballpoint pens fastened to shirt pockets. Suppose that the patent application described a clip with a pointed tip, and that such clips as described in the application were soon found to tear holes in shirt pockets. A second person submits a patent application describing the same clip, but with a rounded end. The rounded end prevents shirt pockets from tearing. Such an invention may be *new* and *useful*, but it is probably too *obvious* to qualify for a patent (it lacks an *inventive step*).

* The fourth criterion with respect to the grant of the patent is that an inventor shall have disclosed in the patent application either a means for *enabling* the practice of the invention (generally for Europe), or the best known means for practicing the invention (for the United States). One reaon for this criterion lies in the contract theory of the award of a patent: the patent applicant is awarded exclusive rights in return for the disclosure to society of a new, useful and non-obvious invention. This contract between society and the inventor can only be executed if persons other than the inventor are able to benefit from the inventor's disclosure. Another objective of this requirement is to distinguish true inventions from speculative concepts of would-be inventors about future possibilities. A claimed invention should function as described. Of course, many inventors would prefer to secure their patents without telling others just exactly how to go about making or using the invention. There is a constant tension between patent examiners and inventors as to whether the inventors are complying with this disclosure obligation, a tension which some applicants seek to exploit by endeavoring to obtain the exclusive rights deriving from the grant of a patent without, however, disclosing too much to their competitors.

There are other factors, varying in different jurisdictions, that go into determining whether or not a patent will be granted to an inventor. These factors include whether the inventor is the first to file a patent application on the product or process (or, in the United States, whether the person submitting the patent application is the first-in-time inventor of the product or process) (both requirements are other ways of viewing the novelty criterion). Inventors in different countries may be working on the same (or similar) projects at the same time, and may file patent applications on the same invention in different countries based upon independent work. Treaties regulating the international intellectual property system provide rules as to which inventor is entitled to a patent under these circumstances. This treaty system is examined later in the book.

It should be apparent that application of the tests of patentability by patent examiners and courts involves a large number of subjectivities, or human judgments, both great and small. These subjective judgments provide the basis for uncertainty concerning the validity (or strength) of patents. This uncertainty may affect the willingness of investors to commit capital to the production of patented inventions or the decision whether to patent or to retain an invention as a trade secret. These subjective judgments are the food for litigation between patent holders and those whom they sue for infringement. It is most unlikely that any set of legal rules, however seemingly comprehensive, will eliminate disputes over the validity of patents. On the other hand, considerable economic efficiency benefits may arise if patent examiners around the world apply similar criteria to judge whether inventions are new, useful and non-obvious.

---

b. Scope of Patentable Subject Matter

Diamond v. Chakrabarty is a decision by the U.S. Supreme Court that addresses the scope of patentable subject matter. In the United States there is a federal court system, and there are court systems for the separate states. Patents are the subject of federal legislative power, and patent cases are exclusively subject to the jurisdiction of the federal courts. Patent cases may arise either in the form of appeals from determinations by the Patent and Trademark Office (PTO), or in the form of private civil litigation, such as private suits for patent infringement. Civil claims are brought in one of the many federal district courts located throughout the United States, depending upon the amenability of a defendant to suit in a particular location. While most decisions of federal district courts are appealed to one of twelve Circuit Courts of Appeal located in different regions of the country, appeals from district court patent decisions may be heard only by the Court of Appeals for the Federal Circuit (CAFC), located in Washington, D.C. Likewise, decisions of the PTO (a federal agency) are directly and indirectly appealed to the CAFC. The federal court system as it applies to patent cases is therefore more centralized than it is in respect to most other kinds of cases in which the Courts of Appeal may divide on common questions. As a matter of history, the Supreme Court has only infrequently granted the right of appeal in patent cases (although in the past few years it has done so with some frequency). A good portion of the Supreme Court's time is generally occupied with resolving splits among the Courts of Appeal, but since there is only one Circuit Court that decides patent appeals (the CAFC), the Supreme Court need not occupy itself with resolving splits on patent questions.

In *Chakrabarty* the Supreme Court addresses the question whether an artificially created life form — in this case a new form of bacterium obtained by genetic alteration — is patentable subject matter. The Court observes a boundary line between the discovery of a naturally occurring life form which is not patentable, and the creation of a new life form. The Court looks at the U.S. Constitution and at the history of the patent statutes dating back to 1793. It perceives an intention on the part of the U.S. Congress to open a broad field to inventors. In a much-quoted passage, the Court refers to the intent of Congress to extend the scope of patentable subject matter to "'anything under the sun that is made by man.'" The Court dismisses arguments grounded in the fear that the genetic alteration of life forms may lead to social harm, saying that it is up to the legislature to address such concerns. The Court also dismisses the argument that the legislature must act to bring new technologies within the scope of patent protection. It observes that the very nature of invention precludes Congress from knowing in advance what kinds of subject matter might be covered in the future.

Diamond, Commissioner of Patents and Trademarks v. Chakrabarty

Supreme Court of The United States
447 U.S. 303; 1980 U.S. LEXIS 112 (1980)

Prior History:
Certiorari To The United States Court Of Customs And Patent Appeals.
Disposition: 596 F.2d 952, affirmed.

Syllabus: Title 35 U. S. C. § 101 provides for the issuance of a patent to a person who invents or discovers "any" new and useful "manufacture" or "composition of matter." Respondent filed a patent application relating to his invention of a human-made, genetically engineered bacterium capable of

breaking down crude oil, a property which is possessed by no naturally occurring bacteria. A patent examiner's rejection of the patent application's
claims for the new bacteria was affirmed by the Patent Office Board of Appeals on the ground that living things are not patentable subject matter
under § 101. The Court of Customs and Patent Appeals reversed, concluding that the fact that micro-organisms are alive is without legal significance
for purposes of the patent law.

*****

Judges: Burger, C. J., Delivered the Opinion of the Court, in Which Stewart,
Blackmun, Rehnquist, and Stevens, JJ., Joined. Brennan, J., Filed a Dissenting Opinion, in Which White, Marshall, and Powell, JJ.

Opinion: Mr. Chief Justice Burger delivered the opinion of the Court.

We granted certiorari to determine whether a live, human-made micro-
organism is patentable subject matter under 35 U. S. C. § 101.

I

In 1972, respondent Chakrabarty, a microbiologist, filed a patent application, assigned to the General Electric Co. The application asserted 36
claims related to Chakrabarty's invention of "a bacterium from the genus
Pseudomonas containing therein at least two stable energy-generating plasmids, each of said plasmids providing a separate hydrocarbon degradative
pathway."[1] This human-made, genetically engineered bacterium is capable
of breaking down multiple components of crude oil. Because of this prop-

---

[1]Plasmids are hereditary units physically separate from the chromosomes of the cell. In
prior research, Chakrabarty and an associate discovered that plasmids control the oil
degradation abilities of certain bacteria. In particular, the two researchers discovered
plasmids capable of degrading camphor and octane, two components of crude oil. In
the work represented by the patent application at issue here, Chakrabarty discovered a
process by which four different plasmids, capable of degrading four different oil components, could be transferred to and maintained stably in a single Pseudomonas bacterium, which itself has no capacity for degrading oil.

erty, which is possessed by no naturally occurring bacteria, Chakrabarty's invention is believed to have significant value for the treatment of oil spills.[2]

Chakrabarty's patent claims were of three types: first, process claims for the method of producing the bacteria; second, claims for an inoculum comprised of a carrier material floating on water, such as straw, and the new bacteria; and third, claims to the bacteria themselves. The patent examiner allowed the claims falling into the first two categories, but rejected claims for the bacteria. His decision rested on two grounds: (1) that micro-organisms are "products of nature," and (2) that as living things they are not patentable subject matter under 35 U. S. C. § 101.

Chakrabarty appealed the rejection of these claims to the Patent Office Board of Appeals, and the Board affirmed the examiner on the second ground.[3] Relying on the legislative history of the 1930 Plant Patent Act, in which Congress extended patent protection to certain asexually reproduced plants, the Board concluded that § 101 was not intended to cover living things such as these laboratory created micro-organisms.

The Court of Customs and Patent Appeals, by a divided vote, reversed on the authority of its prior decision in In re Bergy, 563 F.2d 1031, 1038 (1977), which held that "the fact that microorganisms . . . are alive . . . [is] without legal significance" for purposes of the patent law.[4] . . .

*****

II

The Constitution grants Congress broad power to legislate to "promote the Progress of Science and useful Arts, by securing for limited Times

---

[2]At present, biological control of oil spills requires the use of a mixture of naturally occurring bacteria, each capable of degrading one component of the oil complex. In this way, oil is decomposed into simpler substances which can serve as food for aquatic life. However, for various reasons, only a portion of any such mixed culture survives to attack the oil spill. By breaking down multiple components of oil, Chakrabarty's micro-organism promises more efficient and rapid oil-spill control.

[3]The Board concluded that the new bacteria were not "products of nature," because Pseudomonas bacteria containing two or more different energy-generating plasmids are not naturally occurring.

[4]Bergy involved a patent application for a pure culture of the micro-organism Streptomyces vellosus found to be useful in the production of lincomycin, an antibiotic.

to Authors and Inventors the exclusive Right to their respective Writings and Discoveries." Art. I, § 8, cl. 8. The patent laws promote this progress by offering inventors exclusive rights for a limited period as an incentive for their inventiveness and research efforts. Kewanee Oil Co. v. Bicron Corp., 416 U.S. 470, 480-481 (1974); Universal Oil Co. v. Globe Co., 322 U.S. 471, 484 (1944). The authority of Congress is exercised in the hope that "[the] productive effort thereby fostered will have a positive effect on society through the introduction of new products and processes of manufacture into the economy, and the emanations by way of increased employment and better lives for our citizens." Kewanee, supra, at 480.

The question before us in this case is a narrow one of statutory interpretation requiring us to construe 35 U. S. C. § 101, which provides:

> Whoever invents or discovers any new and useful process, machine, manufacture, or composition of matter, or any new and useful improvement thereof, may obtain a patent therefor, subject to the conditions and requirements of this title.

Specifically, we must determine whether respondent's micro-organism constitutes a "manufacture" or "composition of matter" within the meaning of the statute.[5]

III

In cases of statutory construction we begin, of course, with the language of the statute. Southeastern Community College v. Davis, 442 U.S. 397, 405 (1979). And "unless otherwise defined, words will be interpreted as taking their ordinary, contemporary, common meaning." Perrin v. United States, 444 U.S. 37, 42 (1979). We have also cautioned that courts "should not read into the patent laws limitations and conditions which the legislature has not expressed." United States v. Dubilier Condenser Corp., 289 U.S. 178, 199 (1933).

Guided by these canons of construction, this Court has read the term "manufacture" in § 101 in accordance with its dictionary definition to mean "the production of articles for use from raw or prepared materials by giving to these materials new forms, qualities, properties, or combinations,

---

[5]This case does not involve the other "conditions and requirements" of the patent laws, such as novelty and nonobviousness. 35 U. S. C. §§ 102, 103.

whether by hand-labor or by machinery." American Fruit Growers, Inc. v. Brogdex Co., 283 U.S. 1, 11 (1931). Similarly, "composition of matter" has been construed consistent with its common usage to include "all compositions of two or more substances and . . . all composite articles, whether they be the results of chemical union, or of mechanical mixture, or whether they be gases, fluids, powders or solids." Shell Development Co. v. Watson, 149 F.Supp. 279, 280 (DC 1957) (citing 1 A. Deller, Walker on Patents § 14, p. 55 (1st ed. 1937)). In choosing such expansive terms as "manufacture" and "composition of matter," modified by the comprehensive "any," Congress plainly contemplated that the patent laws would be given wide scope.

The relevant legislative history also supports a broad construction. The Patent Act of 1793, authored by Thomas Jefferson, defined statutory subject matter as "any new and useful art, machine, manufacture, or composition of matter, or any new or useful improvement [thereof]." Act of Feb. 21, 1793, § 1, 1 Stat. 319. The Act embodied Jefferson's philosophy that "ingenuity should receive a liberal encouragement." 5 Writings of Thomas Jefferson 75-76 (Washington ed. 1871). See Graham v. John Deere Co., 383 U.S. 1, 7-10 (1966). Subsequent patent statutes in 1836, 1870, and 1874 employed this same broad language. In 1952, when the patent laws were recodified, Congress replaced the word "art" with "process," but otherwise left Jefferson's language intact. The Committee Reports accompanying the 1952 Act inform us that Congress intended statutory subject matter to "include anything under the sun that is made by man." S. Rep. No. 1979, 82d Cong., 2d Sess., 5 (1952); H. R. Rep. No. 1923, 82d Cong., 2d Sess., 6 (1952).[6]

This is not to suggest that § 101 has no limits or that it embraces every discovery. The laws of nature, physical phenomena, and abstract ideas have been held not patentable. See Parker v. Flook, 437 U.S. 584 (1978); Gottschalk v. Benson, 409 U.S. 63, 67 (1972); Funk Brothers Seed Co. v. Kalo Inoculant Co., 333 U.S. 127, 130 (1948); O'Reilly v. Morse, 15 How. 62, 112-121 (1854); Le Roy v. Tatham, 14 How. 156, 175 (1853). Thus, a new mineral discovered in the earth or a new plant found in the wild is not patentable subject matter. Likewise, Einstein could not patent his celebrated

---

[6]This same language was employed by P. J. Federico, a principal draftsman of the 1952 recodification, in his testimony regarding that legislation: "[Under] section 101 a person may have invented a machine or a manufacture, which may include anything under the sun that is made by man. . . ." Hearings on H. R. 3760 before Subcommittee No. 3 of the House Committee on the Judiciary, 82d Cong., 1st Sess., 37 (1951).

law that $E=mc^2$; nor could Newton have patented the law of gravity. Such discoveries are "manifestations of . . . nature, free to all men and reserved exclusively to none." Funk, supra, at 130.

Judged in this light, respondent's micro-organism plainly qualifies as patentable subject matter. His claim is not to a hitherto unknown natural phenomenon, but to a nonnaturally occurring manufacture or composition of matter — a product of human ingenuity "having a distinctive name, character [and] use." Hartranft v. Wiegmann, 121 U.S. 609, 615 (1887). The point is underscored dramatically by comparison of the invention here with that in Funk. There, the patentee had discovered that there existed in nature certain species of root-nodule bacteria which did not exert a mutually inhibitive effect on each other. He used that discovery to produce a mixed culture capable of inoculating the seeds of leguminous plants. Concluding that the patentee had discovered "only some of the handiwork of nature," the Court ruled the product nonpatentable:

> Each of the species of root-nodule bacteria contained in the package infects the same group of leguminous plants which it always infected. No species acquires a different use. The combination of species produces no new bacteria, no change in the six species of bacteria, and no enlargement of the range of their utility. Each species has the same effect it always had. The bacteria perform in their natural way. Their use in combination does not improve in any way their natural functioning. They serve the ends nature originally provided and act quite independently of any effort of the patentee. (333 U.S., at 131)

Here, by contrast, the patentee has produced a new bacterium with markedly different characteristics from any found in nature and one having the potential for significant utility. His discovery is not nature's handiwork, but his own; accordingly it is patentable subject matter under § 101.

IV

Two contrary arguments are advanced, neither of which we find persuasive.

(A)

The petitioner's first argument rests on the enactment of the 1930 Plant Patent Act, which afforded patent protection to certain asexually reproduced plants, and the 1970 Plant Variety Protection Act, which authorized protection for certain sexually reproduced plants but excluded bacteria from its protection.[7] In the petitioner's view, the passage of these Acts evidences congressional understanding that the terms "manufacture" or "composition of matter" do not include living things; if they did, the petitioner argues, neither Act would have been necessary.

We reject this argument. Prior to 1930, two factors were thought to remove plants from patent protection. The first was the belief that plants, even those artificially bred, were products of nature for purposes of the patent law. This position appears to have derived from the decision of the Patent Office in Ex parte Latimer, 1889 Dec. Com. Pat. 123, in which a patent claim for fiber found in the needle of the Pinus australis was rejected. The Commissioner reasoned that a contrary result would permit "patents [to] be obtained upon the trees of the forest and the plants of the earth, which of course would be unreasonable and impossible." Id., at 126. The Latimer case, it seems, came to "[set] forth the general stand taken in these matters" that plants were natural products not subject to patent protection. Thorne, Relation of Patent Law to Natural Products, 6 J. Pat. Off. Soc. 23, 24 (1923).[8] The second obstacle to patent protection for plants was the fact that plants were thought not amenable to the "written description" requirement of the patent law. See 35 U. S. C. § 112. Because new plants may differ from old only in color or perfume, differentiation by written description was often impossible. See Hearings on H. R. 11372 before the House

---

[7]The Plant Patent Act of 1930, 35 U. S. C. § 161, provides in relevant part:

Whoever invents or discovers and asexually reproduces any distinct and new variety of plant, including cultivated sports, mutants, hybrids, and newly found seedlings, other than a tuber propogated plant or a plant found in an uncultivated state, may obtain a patent therefor. . . .

The Plant Variety Protection Act of 1970, provides in relevant part:

The breeder of any novel variety of sexually reproduced plant (other than fungi, bacteria, or first generation hybrids) who has so reproduced the variety, or his successor in interest, shall be entitled to plant variety protection therefor. . . . 84 Stat. 1547, 7 U. S. C. § 2402 (a).

See generally, 3 A. Deller, Walker on Patents, ch. IX (2d ed. 1964); R. Allyn, The First Plant Patents (1934).

[8]Writing three years after the passage of the 1930 Act, R. Cook, Editor of the Journal of Heredity, commented: "It is a little hard for plant men to understand why [Art. I, § 8] of the Constitution should not have been earlier construed to include the promotion of the art of plant breeding. The reason for this is probably to be found in the principle that natural products are not patentable." Florists Exchange and Horticultural Tade World, July 15, 1933, p. 9.

Committee on Patents, 71st Cong., 2d Sess., 7 (1930) (memorandum of Patent Commissioner Robertson).

In enacting the Plant Patent Act, Congress addressed both of these concerns. It explained at length its belief that the work of the plant breeder "in aid of nature" was patentable invention. S. Rep. No. 315, 71st Cong., 2d Sess., 6-8 (1930); H. R. Rep. No. 1129, 71st Cong., 2d Sess., 7-9 (1930). And it relaxed the written description requirement in favor of "a description . . . as complete as is reasonably possible." 35 U. S. C. § 162. No Committee or Member of Congress, however, expressed the broader view, now urged by the petitioner, that the terms "manufacture" or "composition of matter" exclude living things. The sole support for that position in the legislative history of the 1930 Act is found in the conclusory statement of Secretary of Agriculture Hyde, in a letter to the Chairmen of the House and Senate Committees considering the 1930 Act, that "the patent laws . . . at the present time are understood to cover only inventions or discoveries in the field of inanimate nature." See S. Rep. No. 315, supra, at Appendix A; H. R. Rep. No. 1129, supra, at Appendix A. Secretary Hyde's opinion, however, is not entitled to controlling weight. His views were solicited on the administration of the new law and not on the scope of patentable subject matter — an area beyond his competence. Moreover, there is language in the House and Senate Committee Reports suggesting that to the extent Congress considered the matter it found the Secretary's dichotomy unpersuasive. The Reports observe:

> There is a clear and logical distinction *between the discovery of a new variety of plant and of certain inanimate things,* such, for example, as a new and useful natural mineral. The mineral is created wholly by nature unassisted by man. . . . On the other hand, a plant discovery resulting from cultivation is unique, isolated, and is not repeated by nature, nor can it be reproduced by nature unaided by man. . . . (S. Rep. No. 315, supra, at 6; H. R. Rep. No. 1129, supra, at 7) (emphasis added).

Congress thus recognized that the relevant distinction was not between living and inanimate things, but between products of nature, whether living or not, and human-made inventions. Here, respondent's micro-organism is the result of human ingenuity and research. Hence, the passage of the Plant Patent Act affords the Government no support.

Nor does the passage of the 1970 Plant Variety Protection Act support the Government's position. As the Government acknowledges, sexually re-produced plants were not included under the 1930 Act because new vari-eties could not be reproduced true-to-type through seedlings. Brief for Petitioner 27, n. 31. By 1970, however, it was generally recognized that true-to-type reproduction was possible and that plant patent protection was therefore appropriate. The 1970 Act extended that protection. There is nothing in its language or history to suggest that it was enacted because § 101 did not include living things.

In particular, we find nothing in the exclusion of bacteria from plant variety protection to support the petitioner's position. See n. 7, supra. The legislative history gives no reason for this exclusion. As the Court of Cus-toms and Patent Appeals suggested, it may simply reflect congressional agreement with the result reached by that court in deciding In re Arzberger, 27 C. C. P. A. (Pat.) 1315, 112 F.2d 834 (1940), which held that bacteria were not plants for the purposes of the 1930 Act. Or it may reflect the fact that prior to 1970 the Patent Office had issued patents for bacteria under § 101.[9] In any event, absent some clear indication that Congress "focused on [the] issues . . . directly related to the one presently before the Court," SEC v. Sloan, 436 U.S. 103, 120-121 (1978), there is no basis for reading into its ac-tions an intent to modify the plain meaning of the words found in § 101. See TVA v. Hill, 437 U.S. 153, 189-193 (1978); United States v. Price, 361 U.S. 304, 313 (1960).

(B)

The petitioner's second argument is that micro-organisms cannot qualify as patentable subject matter until Congress expressly authorizes such protection. His position rests on the fact that genetic technology was un-foreseen when Congress enacted § 101. From this it is argued that resolution of the patentability of inventions such as respondent's should be left to Con-

---

[9]In 1873, the Patent Office granted Louis Pasteur a patent on "yeast, free from organic germs of disease, as an article of manufacture." And in 1967 and 1968, immediately prior to the passage of the Plant Variety Protection Act, that Office granted two patents which, as the petitioner concedes, state claims for living micro-organisms. See Reply Brief for Petitioner 3, and n. 2.

gress. The legislative process, the petitioner argues, is best equipped to weigh the competing economic, social, and scientific considerations involved, and to determine whether living organisms produced by genetic engineering should receive patent protection. In support of this position, the petitioner relies on our recent holding in Parker v. Flook, 437 U.S. 584 (1978), and the statement that the judiciary "must proceed cautiously when . . . asked to extend patent rights into areas wholly unforeseen by Congress." Id., at 596.

It is, of course, correct that Congress, not the courts, must define the limits of patentability; but it is equally true that once Congress has spoken it is "the province and duty of the judicial department to say what the law is." Marbury v. Madison, 1 Cranch 137, 177 (1803). Congress has performed its constitutional role in defining patentable subject matter in § 101; we perform ours in construing the language Congress has employed. In so doing, our obligation is to take statutes as we find them, guided, if ambiguity appears, by the legislative history and statutory purpose. Here, we perceive no ambiguity. The subject-matter provisions of the patent law have been cast in broad terms to fulfill the constitutional and statutory goal of promoting "the Progress of Science and the useful Arts" with all that means for the social and economic benefits envisioned by Jefferson. Broad general language is not necessarily ambiguous when congressional objectives require broad terms.

Nothing in Flook is to the contrary. That case applied our prior precedents to determine that a "claim for an improved method of calculation, even when tied to a specific end use, is unpatentable subject matter under § 101." 437 U.S., at 595, n. 18. The Court carefully scrutinized the claim at issue to determine whether it was precluded from patent protection under "the principles underlying the prohibition against patents for 'ideas' or phenomena of nature." Id., at 593. We have done that here. Flook did not announce a new principle that inventions in areas not contemplated by Congress when the patent laws were enacted are unpatentable per se.

To read that concept into Flook would frustrate the purposes of the patent law. This Court frequently has observed that a statute is not to be confined to the "particular [applications] . . . contemplated by the legislators." Barr v. United States, 324 U.S. 83, 90 (1945). Accord, Browder v. United States, 312 U.S. 335, 339 (1941); Puerto Rico v. Shell Co., 302 U.S. 253, 257 (1937). This is especially true in the field of patent law. A rule that unanticipated inventions are without protection would conflict with the core concept of the patent law that anticipation undermines patentability. See Graham v. John Deere Co., 383 U.S., at 12-17. Mr. Justice Douglas reminded that the inventions most benefiting mankind are those that "push back the frontiers of chemistry, physics, and the like." Great A. & P. Tea Co. v. Supermarket Corp., 340 U.S. 147, 154 (1950) (concurring opinion). Congress employed broad general language in drafting § 101 precisely because such inventions are often unforeseeable.[10]

To buttress his argument, the petitioner, with the support of amicus, points to grave risks that may be generated by research endeavors such as respondent's. The briefs present a gruesome parade of horribles. Scientists, among them Nobel laureates, are quoted suggesting that genetic research may pose a serious threat to the human race, or, at the very least, that the dangers are far too substantial to permit such research to proceed apace at this time. We are told that genetic research and related technological developments may spread pollution and disease, that it may result in a loss of genetic diversity, and that its practice may tend to depreciate the value of human life. These arguments are forcefully, even passionately, presented; they remind us that, at times, human ingenuity seems unable to control fully the forces it creates — that, with Hamlet, it is sometimes better "to bear those ills we have than fly to others that we know not of."

It is argued that this Court should weigh these potential hazards in considering whether respondent's invention is patentable subject matter under § 101. We disagree. The grant or denial of patents on micro-organisms is not likely to put an end to genetic research or to its attendant risks. The large amount of research that has already occurred when no researcher had sure knowledge that patent protection would be available suggests that legislative or judicial fiat as to patentability will not deter the scientific mind from probing into the unknown any more than Canute could command the tides. Whether respondent's claims are patentable may determine whether research efforts are accelerated by the hope of reward or slowed by want of incentives, but that is all.

What is more important is that we are without competence to entertain these arguments — either to brush them aside as fantasies generated

---

[10]Even an abbreviated list of patented inventions underscores the point: telegraph (Morse, No. 1,647); telephone (Bell, No. 174,465); electric lamp (Edison, No. 223,898); airplane (the Wrights, No. 821,393); transistor (Bardeen & Brattain, No. 2,524,035); neutronic reactor (Fermi & Szilard, No. 2,708,656); laser (Schawlow & Townes, No. 2,929,922). See generally Revolutionary Ideas, Patents & Progress in America, United States Patent and Trademark Office (1976).

by fear of the unknown, or to act on them. The choice we are urged to make is a matter of high policy for resolution within the legislative process after the kind of investigation, examination, and study that legislative bodies can provide and courts cannot. That process involves the balancing of competing values and interests, which in our democratic system is the business of elected representatives. Whatever their validity, the contentions now pressed on us should be addressed to the political branches of the Government, the Congress and the Executive, and not to the courts.[11]

We have emphasized in the recent past that "[our] individual appraisal of the wisdom or unwisdom of a particular [legislative] course . . . is to be put aside in the process of interpreting a statute." TVA v. Hill, 437 U.S., at 194. Our task, rather, is the narrow one of determining what Congress meant by the words it used in the statute; once that is done our powers are exhausted. Congress is free to amend § 101 so as to exclude from patent protection organisms produced by genetic engineering. Cf. 42 U. S. C. § 2181 (a), exempting from patent protection inventions "useful solely in the utilization of special nuclear material or atomic energy in an atomic weapon." Or it may choose to craft a statute specifically designed for such living things. But, until Congress takes such action, this Court must construe the language of § 101 as it is. The language of that section fairly embraces respondent's invention.

Accordingly, the judgment of the Court of Customs and Patent Appeals is

Affirmed.

---

[11]We are not to be understood as suggesting that the political branches have been laggard in the consideration of the problems related to genetic research and technology. They have already taken action. In 1976, for example, the National Institutes of Health released guidelines for NIH-sponsored genetic research which established conditions under which such research could be performed. 41 Fed. Reg. 27902. In 1978 those guidelines were revised and relaxed. 43 Fed. Reg. 60080, 60108, 60134. And Committees of the Congress have held extensive hearings on these matters. See, e. g., Hearings on Genetic Engineering before the Subcommittee on Health of the Senate Committee on Labor and Public Welfare, 94th Cong., 1st Sess. (1975); Hearings before the Subcommittee on Science, Technology, and Space of the Senate Committee on Commerce, Science, and Transportation, 95th Cong., 1st Sess. (1977); Hearings on H. R. 4759 et al. before the Subcommittee on Health and the Environment of the House Committee on Interstate and Foreign Commerce, 95th Cong., 1st Sess. (1977).

Notes and Questions

1. The U.S. Supreme Court concludes that the legislature (in this case the U.S. Congress) has spoken clearly in adopting statutory language that includes the possibility of patenting life forms, and that to change this would require further legislative action. Generally speaking, a legislature or parliament is the branch of government considered to most directly reflect the "voice of the people". Legislative representatives are elected by voters living within particular districts or regions and are more likely than other national officials to be responsive to the specific views of people living in defined areas. A President, Chancellor, Prime Minister or other executive leader of government is usually elected by the population at large or by a majority of members of parliament, and is expected to reflect the broader perspectives of the voting public. Judges are often appointed by the executive (and perhaps confirmed by the legislature).

IPRs rules are made for most countries at the level of a "democratic" legislature or parliament, in which pressure is brought to bear on members of the legislature by constituents and by the process of seeking re-election by such constituents. As we proceed through this book, consider the process by which rules regarding IPRs are made and implemented at the international level. As a general proposition such rules are made by the treaty-making process. We will examine the treaty-making process later in the book. Who are the constituents in the forum (international organizations) in which treaties are made? You might now begin to reflect on whether there may be a "democracy deficit" at the international level of IPRs rule-making. This is a question relevant to all aspects of international economic law rule-making.

2. In 1936, Julian Huxley said: "Biology is as important as the sciences of lifeless matter, and biotechnology will in the long run be more important than mechanical and chemical engineering."[1] How important do you think that the decision in *Diamond v. Chakrabarty* will be in the realization of Huxley's prophecy?

---

[1]*Chairman's Introductory Address* in L. HOGBEN, THE RETREAT FROM REASON (1936).

3. No country or region in fact grants patent protection for any invention under the sun that is made by a person. Patents are granted to promote general social welfare interests. Yet there are cases in which governments foresee potential harms to society from granting patents that would outweigh this general social interest in granting them. The WTO TRIPS Agreement identifies and limits the subject matter areas which governments may declare off limits to patent protection. Might this lead to conflicts between WTO Member governments in the future?

---

c. Novelty, Inventive Step and Enabling Disclosure

In the United Kingdom, the House of Lords refers both to the upper chamber of the Parliament and to the highest judicial body of the land. They are effectively separate bodies. Judges of the House of Lords are referred to as Law Lords. The following decision by the House of Lords, *Biogen v. Medeva*, introduces the concepts involved in the patent, including *new*-ness (or *novelty*), *involving an inventive step* (or *non-obviousness*), and the requirement of *sufficient* or *enabling* disclosure. Lord Hoffman's opinion asks whether there may be some requirement for a patentable *invention* in U.K. law beyond the statutory requirements that a product or process be new, involve an inventive step, and be capable of industrial application. He concludes that, for present purposes at least, there is no such requirement. This case illustrates the general acceptance of the patentability of biotechnology inventions in the United Kingdom, and the relationship between the European Patent Convention system and European national patent systems. The decision by the House of Lords in this case touches upon some of the most interesting questions in the field of patent law.

Professor Murray of the United Kingdom invented a process for synthesizing an antigen (the precursor of a vaccine) for the Hepatitis B virus. Murray's research involved the use of recombinant DNA techniques in a trial and error process that produced the antigen, but in an inefficient way. Murray developed his process in the face of a number of technical obstacles that might have dissuaded other scientists from attempting it. Murray's invention was owned by Biogen, a company which he helped to found. Biogen filed a patent application that claimed essentially all recombinant DNA processes by which the antigen Murray synthesized could be produced.

At the time of Prof. Murray's initial research and success, it was widely accepted that if an entire DNA strand of the Hepatitis B virus could be sequenced (or mapped), then it would be a relatively simple matter to produce the antigen that Murray succeeded in synthesizing with his trial and error method. However, at the time Murray undertook his research, it was very costly and time consuming to sequence a gene, and the use of this method was effectively precluded. Shortly after Murray's initial success with the trial and error method, it became much cheaper and easier to sequence genes. This development, for all intents and purposes, rendered Murray's first method of producing the antigen of little value, since any producer would now use a sequencing technique.

Murray and Biogen contended that the claims of their first patent application (Biogen 1) entitled Biogen to a monopoly on all recombinant methods of producing the antigen — not only the early trial and error method, but the later more efficient sequencing method as well.

One question which the House of Lords had to answer was whether Murray's work included the *inventive step* required of a patentable invention. The U.K. Appeals Court had doubted the presence of an inventive step, since researchers in Murray's field generally knew that if enough time and money were spent on his problem, a solution would be found. The only thing that distinguished Murray from other scientists was his willingness to undertake research in the face of long odds. This was, in view of the Appeals Court, not an inventive process that Murray undertook, but a commercial decision.

The House of Lords, on the other hand, observes that many (if not most) inventions today are the result of a calculated commercial decision. If such decision-making precludes patenting, there might be few patents issued. The House of Lords, while suggesting it considered Murray's process to involve a sufficient inventive step, does not expressly decide this issue because it decides the case on other grounds.

The House of Lords invokes the concept of the *enabling disclosure*, and asks whether Biogen in its patent application in fact disclosed the more efficient sequencing method of producing the antigen. Its conclusion is that Biogen did not, and thus that its claim for all recombinant methods of producing the antigen are overbroad. It is as if, the Law Lords say, the Wright Brothers upon inventing the fixed wing propeller aircraft claimed all methods of heavier than air flight. In the Court's view, allowing the Biogen claim would be giving it a far wider scope than was justified. Allowing claims of this scope, without requiring sufficient enabling disclosure, would be an impediment to scientific development.

Another problem that confronted the House of Lords was that the Technical Board of the European Patent Office (EPO) had ruled that Biogen's patent was valid. The EPO is established under the terms of the European Patent Convention (EPC) and issues patents with respect to more than fifteen countries in Europe (not limited to European Community countries).[1] An EPO patent is granted following a traditional patent examination by the EPO, and it is granted with respect to all EPO members which have been designated by an applicant. Once the patent is granted, however, it is governed by the law of the country in which it is practiced, in the *Biogen* case the United Kingdom. Moreover, there is in the EPO system a *post-grant opposition* procedure that permits parties believing a patent should not have been granted to challenge the grant within a set time period. Biogen's patent was subject to such a challenge by Medeva before the EPO Technical Board. We will examine the EPC/EPO arrangement in detail later on.

At more or less the same time that Medeva challenged the Biogen patent at the EPO, Biogen sued Medeva in the U.K. courts to block Medeva's alleged patent infringement. Medeva counter-sued for invalidity of the patent under the UK Patent Act. During the same time period, both the EPO and the U.K. courts were considering the validity of the Biogen patent — and they ultimately reached different results! This is not a common occurrence, given the subjective judgments involved in determining whether the conditions of patentability are fulfilled that are referred to above. Since U.K. law governs the substance of the Biogen patent in the United Kingdom, Biogen has lost its protection there — but not in the rest of the EPO countries where it has designated patent protection.

---

[1] At the time of this writing there are 19 EPO member states — Austria, Belgium, Switzerland, Cyprus, Germany, Denmark, Spain, Finland, France, United Kingdom, Hellenic Republic (Greece), Ireland, Italy, Liechtenstein, Luxembourg, Monaco, Netherlands, Portugal and Sweden. Membership is likely to increase in the near future.

Biogen Inc v. Medeva PLC

House of Lords
[1997] RPC 1
31 October 1996

Lord Hoffmann: My Lords,

1. Genetic Engineering.

In this appeal your Lordships' House has for the first time to consider the validity of a patent for products of genetic engineering. This is a technology which has developed only during the last 25 years, in consequence of the great advances which have been made in our knowledge of the genetic code contained in every living cell. The code is embodied in a molecule of deoxyribonucleic acid ("DNA") which directs the cell to make the proteins which the organism requires. Genetic engineering or "recombinant DNA technology" consists of altering the DNA of a suitable cell so that it produces a protein which in nature occurs in another organism. In this way it has been possible to manufacture products of great medical importance which could not have been made by orthodox chemical synthesis.

2. The patent in suit.

The principal claim of the patent in suit is for an artificially constructed molecule of DNA carrying a genetic code which, when introduced into a suitable host cell, will cause that cell to make antigens of the virus hepatitis B ("HBV"). I shall have to describe in much greater detail what antigens are and how the invention enables them to be made. Suffice if for the moment to say that HBV is a widespread human virus, often causing fatal diseases of the liver, and that its antigens can be used both to test for whether someone has the virus and to make a vaccine which can give immunity against infection.

3. Biogen and Professor Murray.

The patent is based upon experimental work done in 1978 by Professor Sir Kenneth Murray of Edinburgh University. Recombinant DNA technology was then in its promising infancy. In February 1978 Professor Murray and a number of other molecular biologists of international repute, together with financial backers, met in Geneva and decided to found Biogen Inc, the patentee company ("Biogen"), for the purpose of exploiting the technology for commercial purposes. One of the first projects upon which they agreed was to try to make the antigens of HBV. Professor Murray began work in the spring of that year and in November reported that he had produced two of the known HBV antigens in colonies of cultured bacteria.

4. History of the proceedings and legal issues.

On 22 December 1978 Biogen filed a United Kingdom patent application describing what Professor Murray had done. This application, known in the proceedings as "Biogen 1" forms the basis of a claim to priority in respect of a later application filed with the European Patent Office ("EPO") in Munich on 21 December 1979. The European Patent was granted on 11 July 1990 and opposition proceedings were dismissed on appeal by the EPO on 28 July 1994.

Meanwhile, in 1992 Biogen began infringement proceedings against the respondent, Medeva plc, which was proposing to market what it described as a third-generation hepatitis B vaccine made by recombinant DNA technology in colonies of mammalian cells. Medeva counterclaimed for revocation. It alleged that the patent was invalid on a number of grounds. I shall briefly mention those which are still relied upon without at this stage making any comment or doing more than to refer to the sections of the Patents Act 1977 on which the objections are based. They are, first, that the claimed invention was obvious (sections 1(1)(b) and 3), both at the date of application for the patent in suit and at the date of Biogen 1. Secondly, that Biogen was not entitled to the priority date of Biogen 1 because it did not "support" the invention claimed in the patent (section 5(2)(a)). Thirdly, that the claimed invention was not an invention (section 1(1)), and fourthly, that the description in the specification was insufficient (section 72(1)(c)). Biogen concedes that the claimed invention was obvious at the date when the application for the European patent was filed but not that it was on the date of Biogen 1.

Aldous J held that the claims in the patent were supported by the matter disclosed in Biogen 1 and that it was accordingly entitled to the earlier priority date. He dismissed all the objections and held the patent valid and infringed. The Court of Appeal (Nourse, Peter Gibson and Hobhouse LJJ) allowed an appeal. Hobhouse LJ gave the judgment of the court. He held that Biogen 1 did not support the claimed invention and that in any case it was obvious at the earlier date. He would have been inclined, but for Medeva's counsel's lack of enthusiasm for the point, to hold that it was not an invention at all. He also held the description in the specification to be insufficient. From this comprehensive reverse Biogen appeals to your Lordships' House.

5. The state of the art in 1978.

In this appeal much turns upon identifying the inventive step, if any, in what Professor Murray did. There is no doubt that he was the first person to make HBV antigens by recombinant DNA technology. It does not however follow that he was inventive. The technology was developing very fast and recent developments might have made its use for that purpose obvious. Even if it was not, it does not follow that "making HBV antigens by recombinant DNA technology" would be the right way to describe his inventive step. Whenever anything inventive is done for the first time it is the result of the addition of a new idea to the existing stock of knowledge. Sometimes, it is the idea of using established techniques to do something which no one had previously thought of doing. In that case, the inventive idea will be doing the new thing. Sometimes, it is finding a way of doing something which people had wanted to do but could not think how. The inventive idea would be the way of achieving the goal. In yet other cases, many people may have a general idea of how they might achieve a goal but [do] not know how to solve a particular problem which stands in their way. If someone devises a way of solving the problem, his inventive step will be that solution, but not the goal itself or the general method of achieving it. To discover precisely what constituted the inventive step, one must therefore examine the state of the art of molecular biology in 1978. Would it have been a new idea to think of making HBV antigens at all? Or would that have been a goal which people had thought about but did not know how to achieve? If the latter, would it have been inventive to think in general terms of using recombinant DNA technology? Or would that also have been something which many molecular biologists would have wanted to do if only they could think of how to overcome particular difficulties which stood in their way? . . .

*****

8. Patentable Inventions

Section 1(1) of the 1977 Act defines "patentable inventions". It says:

1(1) A patent may be granted only for an invention in respect of which the following conditions are satisfied, that is to say —

(a) the invention is new;
(b) it involves an inventive step;
(c) it is capable of industrial application;
(d) the grant of a patent for it is not excluded by subsections (2) and (3) below; and references in this Act to a patentable invention shall be construed accordingly.

9. What is an invention?

The Act thus lays down various conditions, both positive (in paragraphs (a) to (c)) and negative (in paragraph (d)) which an invention must satisfy in order to be a "patentable invention". This scheme might suggest that logically one should first decide whether the claimed invention can properly be described as an invention at all. Only if this question receives an affirmative answer would it be necessary to go on to consider whether the invention satisfies the prescribed conditions for being "patentable". In practice, however, I have no doubt that in most cases this would be a mistake and cause unnecessary difficulty.

The Act does not define the concept of an invention. Section 1(1) was intended to reflect, "as nearly as practicable", article 52 of the European Patent Convention ("EPC"): see section 130(7) of the 1977 Act. Article 52 also has no definition of an invention. It seems that the parties to the EPC were unable to agree upon one: see Singer and Singer, The European Patent Convention (English edn 1995 by Ralph Lunzer), paragraph 52.04). But the reason why the parties were content to do without a definition was that they recognised that the question would almost invariably be academic. The four conditions in section 1(1) do a great deal more than restrict the class of "inventions" which may be patented. They probably also contain every element of the concept of an invention in ordinary speech. I say probably, because in the absence of a definition one cannot say with certainty that one might not come across something which satisfied all the conditions but could not be described as an invention. But the draftsmen of the Convention and the Act, as well as counsel at the bar, were unable to think of any examples. Just in case one should appear, section 1(5) gives the Secretary of

State power to vary the list of matters excluded by paragraph (d) "for the purpose of maintaining them in conformity with developments in science and technology".

As the four conditions are relatively familiar ground, elucidated by definitions in the Act and the jurisprudence of the courts and the EPO, it will normally be more convenient to start by deciding whether they are satisfied. In virtually every case this will be the end of the inquiry. There may one day be a case in which it is necessary to decide whether something which satisfies the conditions can be called an invention, but that question can wait until it arises.

One can of course imagine cases in which the alleged subject-matter is so obviously not an invention that it is tempting to take an axe to the problem by dismissing the claim without inquiring too closely into which of the conditions has not been satisfied. So in Genentech Inc's Patent [1989] RPC 147, 264 Mustill LJ said, by reference to the ordinary speech meaning of "invention":

> You cannot invent water, although you certainly can invent ways in which it may be distilled or synthesised.

This is obviously right and in such a case it may seem pedantic to say that water fails the condition in paragraph (a) of section 1(1) because it is not new. Unfortunately, most cases which come before the courts are more difficult. Judges would therefore be well advised to put on one side their intuitive sense of what constitutes an invention until they have considered the questions of novelty, inventiveness and so forth. In the present case, I think that Medeva's counsel was right to resist the invitation of the Court of Appeal to make submissions on whether the claims constituted an invention.

10. Inventive Step

I will therefore first consider the question of whether what Professor Murray did in 1978 involved, as at the date of Biogen 1, an inventive step. Section 3 says:

> An invention shall be taken to involve an inventive step if it is not obvious to a person skilled in the art, having regard to any matter which forms part of the state of the art by virtue only of section 2(2) above ...
> Section 2(2) defines the state of the art:

The state of the art in the case of an invention shall be taken to comprise all matter (whether a product, a process, information about either or anything else) which has at any time before the priority date of that invention been made available to the public (whether in the United Kingdom or elsewhere) by written or oral description, by use or in any other way.

The question is therefore whether what Professor Murray did was obvious having regard to all matter which had been made available to the public before 22 December 1978. Aldous J, after hearing expert evidence about what people skilled in the art of recombinant DNA technology would have thought and done at the time, held that it was not. I will summarise his reasoning. He followed the procedure suggested by Oliver LJ in Windsurfing International Inc v Tabur Marine (Great Britain) Ltd [1985] RPC 59, 73-74 by dividing the inquiry into four steps:

The first is to identify the inventive concept embodied in the patent in suit. Thereafter, the court has to assume the mantle of the normally skilled but unimaginative addressee in the art at the priority date and impute to him what was, at that date, common general knowledge in the art in question. The third step is to identify what, if any, differences exist between the matter cited as being "known or used" and the alleged invention. Finally, the court has to ask itself whether, viewed without any knowledge of the alleged invention, those differences constitute steps which would have been obvious to the skilled man or whether they require any degree of invention.

Aldous J identified the inventive concept as "the idea or decision to express a polypeptide displaying HBV antigen specificity in a suitable host". The identification of the inventive concept is, as I have said, critical to this case and I shall have more to say about it later. At this stage I only observe that as formulated by Aldous J, the inventive concept means, in effect, having the idea of making HBV antigens by recombinant DNA technology. But that seems to me to be putting the matter far too wide. The idea of making HBV antigens by recombinant DNA technology was shared by everyone at the Geneva meeting of Biogen in February 1978 and no doubt by others working in the field, just as the idea of flying in an heavier-than-air machine had existed for centuries before the Wright brothers. The problem which required invention was to find a way of doing it.

Aldous J then considered what would have been known to the man skilled in the art. I have already summarised what relevant information would have been available to the public in 1978. In particular, Aldous J considered the importance of the Villa-Komaroff paper and said:

> It is accepted that once a decision [had] been made to try expression of the HBV genome, the technique set out in Villa-Komaroff would have been sufficient to enable it to be carried out. Thus the difference between the prior art and the inventive concept is the idea or decision to express a polypeptide displaying HBV antigen specificity in a suitable host. ([1995] RPC 25, 58.)

Again, I think that this is not a sufficiently specific way of stating the inventive concept. The general idea of expressing the gene for a polypeptide displaying HBV antigen specificity in a suitable host was, as I have said, fairly widely entertained. The inventive concept was the notion that Professor Murray's method of achieving the goal — creating large fragments of genomic DNA, ligating them to pBR322 and introducing the hybrid molecule into E coli — would work.

Aldous J then considered what strategies would have been available in 1978 to a skilled man who wanted to achieve the goal of making HBV antigens by recombinant DNA technology. One (strategy A) was to try to find out more about HBV and its DNA. In particular, one would sequence the genome. This would provide the information upon which a decision could be made as to whether and if so how to express the relevant genes. The alternative (strategy B) was, as Professor Murray had done, to take the genomic DNA and try to express it in E coli. Biogen's case, as recorded by the judge, was that — "it was not until the sequence had been obtained, with the knowledge that introns would not be a problem, that the skilled man would seriously consider expression of HBV antigens." ([1995] RPC 25, 64.)

The judge accepted this submission and held that strategy B would not have been obvious in 1978. He said:

> In the present case, there is no evidence to suggest that anyone, other than Biogen, contemplated expression of the HBV antigen in December 1978, despite the fact that the skilled man must have read the Villa-Komaroff paper and there was an incentive to do so. The reason may

well be that stated in the patent, namely the skilled man was put off by introns. ([1995] RPC 25, 65.)

He also rejected the argument that strategy A was an obvious way of making the antigens. The evidence showed only that sequencing might show that there were no introns and that the gene could be expressed in bacteria but there was no ground for assuming that it would.

In the Court of Appeal, Hobhouse LJ held that strategy B was obvious. The decision to adopt it was a "matter of business judgment", a "mere commercial decision". Biogen had made a decision "to pursue an identified goal by known means". I think, with all respect to the closely-reasoned judgment of Hobhouse LJ, that the reference to a commercial decision is an irrelevancy. The fact that a given experimental strategy was adopted for commercial reasons, because the anticipated rewards seemed to justify the necessary expenditure, is no reason why that strategy should not involve an inventive step. An inventor need not pursue his experiment untouched by thoughts of gain. Most patents are the result of research programmes undertaken on the basis of hard-headed cost-benefit analysis. Nor do I think that the analogy of a bet is particularly helpful. In Genentech Inc's Patent [1989] RPC 147, 281, Mustill LJ said, in my opinion rightly, that "it cannot . . . be assumed that inventiveness must have been involved somewhere, just because a wager on success could have been placed at long odds". The question is not what the odds were but whether there was an inventive step.

Having said this, I do think that Hobhouse LJ was substantially correct in saying that Professor Murray had chosen to pursue an identified goal by known means. The goal of obtaining HBV antigens by recombinant DNA technology was obvious and the Villa-Komaroff method was by then part of the state of the art. If, therefore, the inventive concept was simply, as Aldous J said, "the idea or decision to express a polypeptide displaying HBV antigen specificity in a suitable host", I would agree with Hobhouse LJ that, so stated, the concept was obvious. It is however clear from the reasoning of Aldous J that in order to explain why he regarded the decision as involving an inventive step it is necessary to describe it with rather more particularity. A proper statement of the inventive concept needs to include some express or implied reference to the problem which it required invention to overcome. The reasons why the expert witnesses thought it was not obvious to try the expression of genomic HBV DNA in E coli were for the most part concerned with the uncertainties, in the absence of sequence information, about the presence of the HBV antigen genes in the Dane particle DNA, the perceived difficulties of expressing genomic eukaryotic DNA in a prokaryotic host, and, specifically, the problem of introns. It seems to me, therefore, that a more accurate way of stating the inventive concept as it appeared to Aldous J is to say that it was the idea of trying to express unsequenced eukaryotic DNA in a prokaryotic host.

The question of whether an invention was obvious had been called "a kind of jury question" (see Jenkins LJ in Allmanna Svenska Elektriska A/B v The Burntisland Shipbuilding Co Ltd (1952) 69 RPC 63, 70) and should be treated with appropriate respect by an appellate court. It is true that in Benmax v Austin Motor Co Ltd [1955] AC 370 ((1955) 72 RPC 39, 42) this House decided that, while the judge's findings of primary fact, particularly if founded upon an assessment of the credibility of witnesses, were virtually unassailable, an appellate court would be more ready to differ from the judge's evaluation of those facts by reference to some legal standard such as negligence or obviousness. In drawing this distinction, however, Viscount Simonds went on to observe, at page 374, that it was "subject only to the weight which should, as a matter of course, be given to the opinion of the learned judge". The need for appellate caution in reversing the judge's evaluation of the facts is based upon much more solid grounds than professional courtesy. It is because specific findings of fact, even by the most meticulous judge, are inherently an incomplete statement of the impression which was made upon him by the primary evidence. His expressed findings are always surrounded by a penumbra of imprecision as to emphasis, relative weight, minor qualification and nuance (as Renan said, la verite est dans une nuance), of which time and language do not permit exact expression, but which may play an important part in the judge's overall evaluation. It would in my view be wrong to treat Benmax as authorising or requiring an appellate court to undertake a de novo evaluation of the facts in all cases in which no question of the credibility of witnesses is involved. Where the application of a legal standard such as negligence or obviousness involves no question of principle but is simply a matter of degree, an appellate court should be very cautious in differing from the judge's evaluation.

In the present case I think that the reason why Hobhouse LJ differed from the judge on the question of obviousness was not because of any failure to give sufficient weight to the judge's evaluation of the evidence but because he took at face value the judge's statement of the inventive concept. On the other hand, if the concept is reformulated in accordance with the judge's reasoning as I have suggested, the argument for the existence of an inventive step is much stronger. If no question of principle were involved, I think it would be wrong to interfere with the judge's assessment. But the inventiveness alleged in this case is of a very unusual kind. It is said to consist in attempting something which a man less skilled in the art might have regarded as obvious, but which the expert would have thought so beset by obstacles as not to be worth trying. In Raleigh Cycle Co Ltd v H Miller & Co Ltd (1946) 63 RPC 113 the Court of Appeal was prepared to assume that it could be inventive to realise that a bicycle hub dynamo of conventional design could function satisfactorily even though it rotated at a lower speed than was previously thought essential. There may be a question of principle here but, like the Court of Appeal in that case, I shall not pursue the question of whether this amounts to an inventive step for the purposes of patent law because I am content to assume, without deciding, that what Professor Murray did was not obvious.

11. Priority date

The next question is whether, given that Biogen 1 disclosed what would at the time have been a patentable invention, it "supports" the invention actually claimed in the patent in suit. This question must be answered in the affirmative if Biogen is to be able to rely on the date of Biogen 1 as its priority date in accordance with section 5(2)(a). The relevant provisions are as follows:

> 5(1) For the purposes of this Act the priority date of an invention to which an application for a patent relates and also of any matter (whether or not the same as the invention) contained in any such application is, except as provided by the following provisions of this Act, the date of filing the application.
> (2) If in or in connection with an application for a patent (the application in suit) a declaration is made, whether by the applicant or any predecessor in title of his, complying with the relevant requirements of rules and specifying one or more earlier relevant applications for the purposes of this section made by the applicant or a predecessor in title of his and each having a date of filing during the period of twelve months immediately preceding the date of filing the application in suit, then —
> (a) if an invention to which the application in suit relates is supported by matter disclosed in the earlier relevant application or applications, the priority date of that invention shall instead of being the date of filing

the application in suit be the date of filing the relevant application in which that matter was disclosed or, if it was disclosed in more than one relevant application, the earliest of them;

In Asahi Kasei Kogyo KK's Application [1991] RPC 485 this House decided that for matter to be capable of supporting an invention within the meaning of section 5(2)(a) it must contain an "enabling disclosure", that is to say, it must disclose the invention in a way which will enable it to be performed by a person skilled in the art. This construction has not been challenged by the appellants before your Lordships' House. It is however important to notice the relationship between the requirement of "support" in section 5(2)(a) and certain other provisions of the Act which share the concept of an enabling disclosure.

The concept of an enabling disclosure is central to the law of patents. For present purposes, it touches the matters in issue at three different points. First, as we have seen, it forms part of the requirement of "support" in section 5(2)(a). Secondly, it is one of the requirements of a valid application in section 14. And thirdly, it is essential to one of the grounds for the revocation of a patent in section 72. I shall start with section 14. Subsection (3) says:

> The specification of an application shall disclose the invention in a manner which is clear enough and complete enough for the invention to be performed by a person skilled in the art.

This is plainly a requirement of an "enabling disclosure". In addition, subsection (5)(c) says that the claim or claims shall be "supported by the description". It was by reference to subsection (3) that Lord Oliver of Aylmerton, who gave the leading speech in Asahi, reasoned at page 536 that a description would not "support" the claims for the purpose of subsection (5)(c) unless it contained sufficient material to enable the specification to constitute the enabling disclosure which subsection (3) required: "the Act can hardly have contemplated a complete application for a patent lacking some of the material necessary to sustain the claims made". By parity of reasoning, he said that "support" must have the same meaning in section 5(2)(a).

The absence of an enabling disclosure is likewise one of the grounds for the revocation of a patent specified in section 72(1). Paragraph (c) says that one such ground is that —

the specification of the patent does not disclose the invention clearly enough and completely enough for it to be performed by a person skilled in the art.

This is entirely in accordance with what one would expect. The requirement of an enabling disclosure in a patent application is a matter of substance and not form. Its absence should therefore be a ground not only for refusal of the application but also for revocation of the patent after grant. Similarly, the same concept is involved in the question of whether the patent is entitled to priority from an earlier application. This is not to say that the question in each case is the same. The purposes for which the question is being asked are different. But the underlying concept is the same.

*****

The need for an enabling disclosure to satisfy the requirements of support under section 5(2)(a), valid application under section 14 and sufficiency under section 72(1)(c) has, I think, been plain and undisputed since the decision in Asahi. What has been less clear is what the concept of an enabling disclosure means. Part of the difficulty has been caused by a misinterpretation of what the Technical Board of Appeal of the EPO said in Genentech I/Polypeptide expression (T 292/85) [1989] OJ EPO 275. This was a patent for a plasmid suitable for transforming a bacterial host which included an expression control sequence or "regulon" which could enable the expression of foreign DNA as a recoverable polypeptide. The Examining Division was willing to grant a patent only in respect of the plasmids, bacteria and polypeptides known at the date of application. The Technical Board of Appeal allowed the appeal, saying that the Examining Division had taken too narrow a view of the requirement of enabling disclosure:

> What is also important in the present case is the irrelevancy of the particular choice of a variant within the functional terms "bacteria", "regulon" or "plasmid". It is not just that some result within the range of polypeptides is obtained in each case but it is the same polypeptide which is expressed, independent of the choice of these means . . . Unless variants of components are also embraced in the claims, which are, now or later on, equally suitable to achieve the same effect in a manner which could not have been envisaged without the invention, the protection provided by the patent would be ineffectual . . . The character of the invention this time is one of general methodology which is fully applica-

ble with any starting material, and is, as it was already stated, also independent from the known, trivial, or inventive character of the end-products. (paras 3.1.3, 3.1.5, 3.3.2.)

In other words, the applicants had invented a general principle for enabling plasmids to control the expression of polypeptides in bacteria and there was no reason to believe that it would not work equally well with any plasmid, bacterium or polypeptide. The patent was therefore granted in general terms.

In Molnlycke AB v Procter & Gamble Ltd [1992] FSR 549, however, Morritt J interpreted this decision to mean that it was a general rule of European patent law that an invention was sufficiently disclosed if the skilled man could make a single embodiment. This interpretation was followed by Aldous J in Chiron Corporation v Organon Teknika Ltd [1994] FSR 202, although I think I detect in his judgment some surprise that the EPO should have adopted such a mechanistic and impoverished approach to the concept of enabling disclosure. As we shall see, he applied the same rule in the present case.

In fact the Board in Genentech I/Polypeptide expression was doing no more than apply a principle of patent law which has long been established in the United Kingdom, namely, that the specification must enable the invention to be performed to the full extent of the monopoly claimed. If the invention discloses a principle capable of general application, the claims may be in correspondingly general terms. The patentee need not show that he has proved its application in every individual instance. On the other hand, if the claims include a number of discrete methods or products, the patentee must enable the invention to be performed in respect of each of them.

Thus if the patentee has hit upon a new product which has a beneficial effect but cannot demonstrate that there is a common principle by which that effect will be shared by other products of the same class, he will be entitled to a patent for that product but not for the class, even though some may subsequently turn out to have the same beneficial effect: see May & Baker Ltd v Boots Pure Drug Co Ltd (1950) 67 RPC 23, 50. On the other hand, if he has disclosed a beneficial property which is common to the class, he will be entitled to a patent for all products of that class (assuming them to be new) even though he has not himself made more than one or two of them.

Since Genentech I/Polypeptide expression the EPO has several times reasserted the well established principles for what amounts to sufficiency of disclosure. In particular, in Exxon/Fuel Oils (T 409/91) [1994] OJ EPO 653, paragraph 3.3, the Technical Board of Appeal said of the provision in the European Patent Convention equivalent to section 14(5)(c) of the Act:

> Furthermore, Article 84 EPC also requires that the claims must be supported by the description, in other words, it is the definition of the invention in the claims that needs support. In the Board's judgment, this requirement reflects the general legal principle that the extent of the patent monopoly, as defined by the claims, should correspond to the technical contribution to the art in order for it to be supported, or justified.

12. Support for the claims

I come therefore to the question of whether Biogen 1 contained an enabling disclosure which supported the claims in the patent in suit. The argument before Aldous J seems to have concentrated on the questions of whether it had been shown that Professor Murray's method was capable of making both HBcAg and HBsAg and whether it would work in eukaryotic as well as bacterial hosts. The judge, following his earlier decision in Chiron Corporation v Organon Teknika Ltd [1994] FSR 202, said that it would be enough if the specification enabled one embodiment to be made. As there was no doubt that Professor Murray had made HBcAg in cultures of E coli, that was an end of the matter. In case it was considered that the claims really amounted to two inventions, one for making HBcAg and another for HBsAg, he found that the skilled man would also have been able to make HBsAg. Having heard the evidence of Professor Murray and others, he said:

> Upon the evidence, I conclude that Biogen did express and demonstrate expression of the surface antigen using the techniques described in the specification. ([1995] RPC 25, 50)

The disclosure was therefore sufficient in respect of both inventions.

In the opposition proceedings in the EPO, the argument proceeded upon similar lines. The only issue on sufficiency seems to have been whether the invention could produce HBsAg as well as HBcAg. The Technical Board, like Aldous J, found as a fact that it could. The question of whether the method could be used in other hosts was not argued, the opponents thinking (probably rightly) that this point was concluded against them by the EPO decision in Genentech I/Polypeptide expression. In fact, if Professor Murray's method worked in a prokaryotic host, despite the possibility that such a host might not be able to cope with introns, it was even more likely to work in a eukaryotic host, which was better equipped for dealing with them. For my part, therefore, I would not differ from the findings of either Aldous J or the Technical Board in rejecting both these grounds of opposition.

In the Court of Appeal, Hobhouse LJ began his judgment by saying that he did not believe that the court was differing from Aldous J "on any question of the acceptance of the evidence of witnesses or primary scientific fact". He nevertheless made a thorough re-examination of the evidence on whether the method disclosed in Biogen 1 had enabled the making of HBsAg and came to the conclusion that it had not. He said:

> The outcome of this evidence is that whatever results the plaintiff obtained in 1978 did not amount to evidence justifying a claim to have produced a recombinant DNA molecule which enabled the expression of HBsAg in E coli (or any other host). ([1995] RPC 25, 112)

I am bound to say that I regret the decision of the Court of Appeal to revisit the evidence upon which the judge made his finding of fact. For the reasons given earlier in relation to the issue of obviousness, I think that this was a question on which greater respect should have been paid to the judge's findings. The Court of Appeal's reversal of the judge on this issue greatly lengthened the hearing before your Lordships' House, as no doubt it had done in the Court of Appeal. The House was invited to undertake a minute examination of the facts with a view to restoring the findings of the judge. It was even offered inspection of the autoradiographs claimed to show the positive results upon which Professor Murray had based his claim to success — an offer which your Lordships felt able to decline. But I think that your Lordships learned enough of the detailed facts to form the view that the judge's decision was one which was open to him upon the evidence and should not have been disturbed.

But the fact that the skilled man following the teaching of Biogen 1 would have been able to make HBcAg and HBsAg in bacterial cells, or indeed in any cells, does not conclude the matter. I think that in concentrating upon the question of whether Professor Murray's invention could, so to speak, deliver the goods across the full width of the patent or priority document, the courts and the EPO allowed their attention to be diverted from what seems to me in this particular case the critical issue. It is not whether the claimed invention could deliver the goods, but whether the claims cover other ways in which they might be delivered: ways which owe nothing to the teaching of the patent or any principle which it disclosed.

It will be remembered that in Genentech I/Polypeptide expression the Technical Board spoke of the need for the patent to give protection against other ways of achieving the same effect "in a manner which could not have been envisaged without the invention". This shows that there is more than one way in which the breadth of a claim may exceed the technical contribution to the art embodied in the invention. The patent may claim results which it does not enable, such as making a wide class of products when it enables only one of those products and discloses no principle which would enable others to be made. Or it may claim every way of achieving a result when it enables only one way and it is possible to envisage other ways of achieving that result which make no use of the invention.

One example of an excessive claim of the latter kind is the famous case of O'Reilly v Morse (1854) 56 US (15 How) 62 in the Supreme Court of the United States. Samuel Morse was the first person to discover a practical method of electric telegraphy and took out a patent in which he claimed any use of electricity for "making or printing intelligible characters, signs, or letter, at any distances". The Supreme Court rejected the claim as too broad. Professor Chisum, in his book on Patents (vol 1, § 1.03 [2] summarises the decision as follows:

> Before Morse's invention, the scientific community saw the possibility of achieving communication by the 'galvanic' current but did not know any means of achieving that result. Morse discovered one means and attempted to claim all others.

A similar English case is British United Shoe Machinery Co Ltd v Simon Collier Ltd (1908) 26 RPC 21. The patentee invented a piece of machinery for automatically trimming the soles of boots and shoes by means of a cam. One of the claims was in general terms for automatic means of trimming soles. Parker J said, at pages 49-50:

> (The) problem was simply how to do automatically what could already be done by the skill of the workman. On the other hand, the principle which the inventor applies for the solution of the problem is the capacity of a cam to vary the relative positions of two parts of a machine while the machine is running. Assuming this principle to be new, it might be

possible for the inventor, having shown one method of applying it to the solution of the problem, to protect himself during the life of his patent from any other method of applying it for the same purpose, but I do not think that the novelty of the principle applied would enable him to make a valid claim for all means of solving the problem whether the same or a different principle were applied to its solution.

I return therefore to consider the technical contribution to the art which Professor Murray made in 1978 and disclosed in Biogen 1. As it seems to me, it consisted in showing that despite the uncertainties which then existed over the DNA of the Dane particle — in particular whether it included the antigen genes and whether it had introns — known recombinant techniques could nevertheless be used to make the antigens in a prokaryotic host cell. As I have said, I accept the judge's findings that the method was shown to be capable of making both antigens and I am willing to accept that it would work in any otherwise suitable host cell. Does this contribution justify a claim to a monopoly of any recombinant method of making the antigens? In my view it does not. The claimed invention is too broad. Its excessive breadth is due, not to the inability of the teaching to produce all the promised results, but to the fact that the same results could be produced by different means. Professor Murray had won a brilliant Napoleonic victory in cutting through the uncertainties which existed in his day to achieve the desired result. But his success did not in my view establish any new principle which his successors had to follow if they were to achieve the same results. The inventive step, as I have said, was the idea of trying to express unsequenced eukaryotic DNA in a prokaryotic host. Biogen 1 discloses that the way to do it is to choose the restriction enzymes likely to cleave the Dane particle DNA into the largest fragments. This, if anything, was the original element in what Professor Murray did. But once the DNA had been sequenced, no one would choose restriction enzymes on this basis. They would choose those which digested the sites closest to the relevant gene or the part of the gene which expressed an antigenic fragment of the polypeptide. The metaphor used by one of the witnesses was that before the genome had been sequenced everyone was working in the dark. Professor Murray invented a way of working with the genome in the dark. But he did not switch on the light and once the light was on his method was no longer needed. Nor, once they could use vectors for mammalian cells, would they be concerned with the same problem of introns which had so exercised those skilled in the art in 1978. Of course there might be other problems, but Biogen 1 did not teach how to solve them. The respondents Medeva, who use restriction enzymes based on knowledge of the HBV genome and mammalian host cells, owe nothing to Professor Murray's invention.

It is said that what Professor Murray showed by his invention was that it could be done. HBV antigens could be produced by expressing Dane particle DNA in a host cell. Those who followed, even by different routes, could have greater confidence by reason of his success. I do not think that this is enough to justify a monopoly of the whole field. I suppose it could be said that Samuel Morse had shown that electric telegraphy could be done. The Wright Brothers showed that heavier-than-air flight was possible, but that did not entitle them to a monopoly of heavier-than-air flying machines. It is inevitable in a young science, like electricity in the early nineteenth century or flying at the turn of the last century or recombinant DNA technology in the 1970s, that dramatically new things will be done for the first time. The technical contribution made in such cases deserves to be recognised. But care is needed not to stifle further research and healthy competition by allowing the first person who has found a way of achieving an obviously desirable goal to monopolise every other way of doing so. (See Merges and Nelson, On the Complex Economics of Patent Scope (1990) 90 Columbia Law Review 839.)

I would therefore hold that Biogen 1 did not support the invention as claimed in the European Patent and that it is therefore not entitled to the priority date of Biogen 1. As it is conceded that the invention was obvious when the patent application was filed, it is invalid.

13. The EPO decision.

I must at this point say something about the decision of the Technical Board of the EPO, which dismissed opposition proceedings and held the patent valid. Decisions of the EPO on questions of law are, as this House said in Merrell Dow Pharmaceuticals Inc v HN Norton & Co Ltd [1996] RPC 76, 82, of considerable persuasive authority. But the decision of the EPO in this case did not, as it seems to me, proceed on any principle different from those I have endeavoured to apply. The Board held, as I have been willing to assume, that the invention described in Biogen 1 was not obvious at the priority date. On the other hand it held that the disclosure in Biogen 1 was in respect of the same invention as that claimed in the patent and, contrary to my view hereafter expressed, that such disclosure was sufficient to enable the invention to be performed to the full extent of the claims. But in arriving at this conclusion, the Board directed its attention solely to the question of whether the teaching in Biogen 1 would enable the man skilled in the art to achieve expression of HBsAg as well as HBcAg. Nothing was said about whether the claims were too broad because expression could also be achieved without the use of the teaching which it contained, by a method of which it could not be said, in the words of the Technical Board in Genentech I, that it was "in a manner which could not have been envisaged without the invention". But the principle upon which I have come to the conclusion that on this ground the patent is invalid is also, as I have said, clearly stated in decisions of the EPO such as Genentech I and Exxon. I would not therefore regard the outcome of this appeal as suggesting any divergence between the jurisprudence of this court and that of the EPO.

14. Sufficiency

If your Lordships are agreed that, lacking the support of an earlier priority date, the patent is invalid for obviousness, it is unnecessary to consider whether it was also invalid for insufficiency and therefore liable to be revoked under section 72(1)(c). But the reasoning by which I have come to the conclusion that the patent was not entitled to the earlier priority also, in my view, leads to the conclusion that it was insufficient. . . .

*****

I would dismiss the appeal.

Disposition:

Appeal dismissed.

Notes and Questions

1. Lord Hoffmann expresses doubt whether there are criteria for an invention other than that a product or process be new, capable of industrial application and involve an inventive step. Can you suggest an added element? The patent system is often justified as a stimulus to inventive activity

through enhanced financial reward (or potential reward). If an invention is achieved by a commercial decision to invest capital in pursuit of a widely identified goal, can the patent grant be said to have stimulated inventive activity? Has it instead stimulated the investment of capital? Is there a difference?

2. In the well-known Star Trek science fiction series, people (including alien people) are moved about from one point in space to another by means of the "transporter." The transporter has become so much a part of global culture that most of us likely assume it is only a matter of time (even if a very long time) before people are "beaming" from one place to another. Should the producers of the Star Trek series have filed a patent application on the transporter before they first publicly introduced it?

When it was introduced, was the concept of the transporter new?[1]

When it was introduced, was the concept of the transporter capable of industrial application?

When it was introduced, did the concept of the transporter involve an inventive step?

If the Star Trek transporter was new, capable of industrial application and involved an inventive step, why should not a patent examiner have recommended the grant of a patent? Could the producers of the Star Trek series have provided an enabling disclosure?

3. In 1997 a group of scientists in Scotland announced the successful "cloning" of a sheep named Dolly. A patent application has been filed on this invention. What do you think has been claimed in the patent application? How might the holding in *Biogen* limit the scope of the claims?

4. Lord Hoffmann says that the EPO Technical Board dismissed Medeva's opposition to the Biogen patent without considering the grounds on which the House of Lords invalidates the patent for the United Kingdom. According to Lord Hoffmann, what was the substance of the challenge considered by the Technical Board, and what is the additional ground considered by the House of Lords?

---

[1] Staying within the science fiction genre, consider, for example, the teleportation device that played a prominent role in an early science fiction film, The Fly, with Vincent Price.

3. Plant Variety Protection

a. The Nature and Subject Matter of Plant Variety Protection

Innovation in the field of agriculture has been important to human civilization since farmers first began to cultivate crops. Increasing crop yields has long been a goal of agricultural research and development. Two phenomena at work today in the international community have led to a heightened interest in the means for protecting new varieties of plants. These phenomena are, first, a rapidly growing world population which will almost certainly place strains on global food production capacity over the next several decades; and second, advances in biotechnology which have facilitated the creation of new plant varieties with improved agricultural characteristics (such as resistance to disease).

Up until the 1930s, there was strong sentiment against granting patent protection for new varieties of plants. The U.S. Supreme Court discussed some of the reasons for this sentiment in *Diamond v. Chakrabarty*.[1] On a technological level, it was not apparent that particular varieties of plants could be reproduced in a manner that maintained their characteristics over time. On an administrative level, it was considered difficult or impracticable to describe in words the unique characteristics of plant varieties, and this made the formulation of patent claims and descriptions impracticable. The United States adopted a statutory framework for granting "plant patents" in 1930. As noted in *Chakrabarty*, the Plant Patent Act addressed the technological problem of maintaining "true to type" characteristics by limiting protection to new varieties of "asexually" reproduced plants. If the act of propagation depended on using material of the plant being reproduced, the characteristics of the next generation could be assured. On the administrative level, the Plant Patent Act also relaxed the written description requirement of the general patent law to allow for reasonably complete description. Other countries followed the United States with various forms of plant patent protection, and with more limited forms of plant variety protection directed, for example, to the marketing of certified seed varieties. In the United States, the Plant Variety Protection Act of 1970 extended

---

[1] *See supra*, § B, 2, b.

patent-like protection to new varieties of "sexually" reproduced plants. By 1970, authorities in the United States had concluded that it was possible to maintain the characteristics of certain plant varieties across generations, even when new generations were produced from seeds. A detailed discussion of the different protections afforded under the Plant Patent Act and the Plant Variety Protection Act (PVPA) in the United States can be found in *Imazio Nursery v. Dania Greenhouses*, 69 F.3d 1560 (CAFC 1995).

The protection of plant varieties has long been controversial at the international level. A major part of agricultural research and development historically has been financed and/or undertaken by public authorities, and the results of this research have often been made freely available. There has been reluctance to apply IPRs-related limitations to the fruits of public research, and there has been some worry that private sector dominance of the agricultural research area would have adverse consequences, particularly in developing countries. Plants are living things and, as was discussed in *Chakrabarty*, there has been concern about the propriety of subjecting (a) products of nature and (b) living things, to IPRs protection. Moreover, it is difficult to balance the interests of farmers in the use and resale of seeds and other plant propagating material (under so-called "farmer's privileges"), on one hand, and the interests of the creators/producers of such material in earning reasonable returns on investment, on the other.

Multilateral efforts toward plant variety protection began with the 1961 Act of the International Convention for the Protection of New Varieties of Plants (UPOV). This was followed by revisions, notably a 1978 Act, and most recently a 1991 Act of the UPOV. The 1991 Act is entered into force in April 1998. It provides the most commonly used set of rules for the international protection of plant varieties. The WTO TRIPS Agreement requires that its members provide for the protection of plant varieties either by patent "or by *sui generis* system of protection or by any combination thereof" (Article 27(3)). This requirement is subject to review in 1999.

Using the rules of the 1991 Act of the UPOV as a reference point, a system of plant variety protection should grant a plant "breeder's right" with respect to a "variety" which is "new," "distinct," "uniform" and "stable." These criteria differ from the criteria for the grant of a utility patent.

"Novelty" refers more to commercial or market novelty than technological novelty and requires that a variety has not been sold or marketed in the country where the application is filed earlier than one year before the filing date. The variety may not have been sold or marketed in the territory of any other UPOV country earlier than four years before that same filing date (and earlier than six years for trees or vines).

"Distinctness" requires that a variety be clearly distinguishable from other commonly known varieties.

"Uniformity" of a variety requires that, subject to variation that may be expected from its propagation, the variety must be sufficiently uniform in its relevant characteristics.

"Stability" requires that the relevant characteristics of the variety remain unchanged after repeated propagation.

In addition, the variety must be given a "denomination," that is, a name that will not be misleading or confusing as to the value of the variety or the identity of the breeder.

The plant breeder's right extends to seven acts in respect to propagating material of a variety that require the breeder's authorization: (1) production or reproduction (multiplication); (2) conditioning for the purpose of propagation; (3) offering for sale; (4) selling or other marketing; (5) exporting; (6) importing; and (7) stocking for any of the purposes mentioned in (1) to (6).

The breeder's right is subject to certain limited exceptions (e.g., acts done for experimental purposes). In addition, each party to the UPOV *may* allow farmers certain privileges with respect to use of protected varieties for reproduction on their farm holdings.

The duration of the breeder's right must be a minimum of twenty years from the date of grant, and for trees and vines a minimum of twenty-five years.

The UPOV Convention provides for a one-year priority period from the date of filing the first application in a UPOV member. It also requires each country party to extend national treatment to persons of other UPOV members.

The WTO TRIPS Agreement does not require that members adhere to the UPOV Convention, nor does it incorporate provisions of the UPOV (as it does, for example, with respect to the Berne Convention). While the UPOV Convention may to a certain extent reflect an evolving worldwide standard of plant variety protection, the Convention maintains a limited membership and does not yet represent a uniform system of globally applicable rules (as of March 31, 1999, there were 39 states party to the various Acts of the UPOV Convention).

The European Patent Convention (EPC) generally excludes the patenting of plant varieties. However, there is a European Union system for the registration of plant varieties. This system is outlined in Chapter II, section C.3.

b. Farmer's Privilege

One of the principal differences between the U.S. Plant Patent Act and the PVPA lies in the scope of protection afforded to breeders. The PVPA provides an exception that permits farmers to make specific use of seeds generated from protected stock, while the Plant Patent Act does not provide farmers with a corresponding privilege to reproduce from protected stock. This difference has significant financial implications both for breeders and farmers. As the following decision by the U.S. Supreme Court indicates, the scope of farmer's privileges under the PVPA has not been easy to determine from the language of the statute. We include the following decision not to focus on the problematic syntax of the PVPA, but rather to illustrate the very important concept of farmer's privileges — which promises to be the source of controversy in future international negotiations on plant breeders' rights.

Asgrow Seed Company, Petitioner v. Denny Winterboer and Becky Winterboer, dba Deebees

Supreme Court of the United States
513 U.S. 179; 1995 U.S. LEXIS 693 (1995)

Prior History: on Writ of Certiorari to the United States Court of Appeals for the Federal Circuit. Disposition: 982 F. 2d 486, reversed.

Syllabus: Petitioner Asgrow Seed Company has protected two varieties of soybean seed under the Plant Variety Protection Act of 1970 (PVPA), which extends patent-like protection to novel varieties of sexually reproduced plants (plants grown from seed). After respondent farmers planted 265 acres of Asgrow's seed and sold the entire salable crop — enough to plant 10,000 acres — to other farmers for use as seed, Asgrow filed suit, alleging infringement under, inter alia, 7 U.S.C. § 2541(1), for selling or offering to sell the seed, and § 2541(3), for "sexually multiplying the novel varieties as a step in marketing [them] (for growing purposes)." Respondents contended that they were entitled to a statutory exemption from liability under § 2543, which provides in relevant part that "except to the extent that such action may constitute an infringement under [§ 2541(3)]," a farmer may "save seed . . . and use such saved seed in the production of a crop for use on his farm, or for sale as provided in this section: Provided, That" such saved seed can be sold for reproductive purposes where both buyer and seller are farmers "whose primary farming occupation is the growing of crops for sale for other than reproductive purposes." In granting Asgrow summary judgment, the District Court found that the exemption allows a farmer to save and resell to other farmers only the amount of seed the seller would need to replant his own fields. The Court of Appeals reversed, holding that § 2543 permits a farmer to sell up to half of every crop he produces from PVPA-protected seed, so long as he sells the other half for food or feed.

Held: A farmer who meets the requirements set forth in § 2543's proviso may sell for reproductive purposes only such seed as he has saved for the purpose of replanting his own acreage. . . .

(a) Respondents were not eligible for the § 2543 exemption if their planting and harvesting were conducted "as a step in marketing" under § 2541(3), for the parties do not dispute that these actions constituted "sexual multiplication" of novel varieties. Since the PVPA does not define "marketing," the term should be given its ordinary meaning. Marketing ordinarily refers to the act of holding forth property for sale, together with the activities preparatory thereto, but does not require that there be extensive promotional or merchandising activities connected with the selling. . . .

(b) By reason of the proviso, the first sentence of § 2543 allows seed that has been preserved for reproductive purposes (saved seed) to be sold for such purposes. However, the structure of the sentence is such that this authorization does not extend to saved seed that was grown for the purpose of sale (marketing) for replanting, because that would violate § 2541(3). As a practical matter, this means that only seed that has been saved by the farmer to replant his own acreage can be sold. Thus, a farmer who saves seeds to replant his acreage, but changes his plans, may sell the seeds for replanting under the proviso's terms. The statute's language stands in the way of the limitation the Court of Appeals found in the amount of seed that can be sold. . . .

Judges: Scalia, J., delivered the opinion of the Court, in which Rehnquist, C. J., and O'connor, Kennedy, Souter, Thomas, Ginsburg, and Breyer, JJ., Joined. Stevens, J., filed a dissenting opinion. . . .

Opinion: Justice Scalia delivered the opinion of the Court.

The Plant Variety Protection Act of 1970, 7 U.S.C. § 2321 et seq., protects owners of novel seed varieties against unauthorized sales of their seed for replanting purposes. An exemption, however, allows farmers to make some sales of protected variety seed to other farmers. This case raises the question whether there is a limit to the quantity of protected seed that a farmer can sell under this exemption.

I

In 1970, Congress passed the Plant Variety Protection Act (PVPA), 84 Stat. 1542, 7 U.S.C. § 2321 et seq., in order to provide developers of novel plant varieties with "adequate encouragement for research, and for marketing when appropriate, to yield for the public the benefits of new varieties," § 2581. The PVPA extends patent-like protection to novel varieties of sexually reproduced plants (that is, plants grown from seed) which parallels the protection afforded asexually reproduced plant varieties (that is, varieties reproduced by propagation or grafting) under Chapter 15 of the Patent Act. See 35 U.S.C. §§ 161-164.

The developer of a novel variety obtains PVPA coverage by acquiring a certificate of protection from the Plant Variety Protection Office. See 7 U.S.C. §§ 2421, 2422, 2481-2483. This confers on the owner the exclusive right for 18 years to "exclude others from selling the variety, or offering it for sale, or reproducing it, or importing it, or exporting it, or using it in producing (as distinguished from developing) a hybrid or different variety therefrom." § 2483.

Petitioner, Asgrow Seed Company, is the holder of PVPA certificates protecting two novel varieties of soybean seed, which it calls A1937 and A2234. Respondents, Dennis and Becky Winterboer, are Iowa farmers whose farm spans 800 acres of Clay County, in the northwest corner of the State. The Winterboers have incorporated under the name "D-Double-U Corporation" and do business under the name "DeeBee's Feed and Seed." In addition to growing crops for sale as food and livestock feed, since 1987 the Winterboers have derived a sizable portion of their income from "brown-bag" sales of their crops to other farmers to use as seed. A brown-bag sale occurs when a farmer purchases seed from a seed company, such as Asgrow, plants the seed in his own fields, harvests the crop, cleans it, and then sells the reproduced seed to other farmers (usually in nondescript brown bags) for them to plant as crop seed on their own farms. During 1990, the Winterboers planted 265 acres of A1937 and A2234, and sold the entire salable crop, 10,529 bushels, to others for use as seed — enough to plant 10,000 acres. The average sale price was $8.70 per bushel, compared with a then-current price of $16.20 to $16.80 per bushel to obtain varieties A1937 and A2234 directly from Asgrow.

Concerned that the Winterboers were making a business out of selling its protected seed, Asgrow sent a local farmer, Robert Ness, to the Winterboer farm to make a purchase. Mr. Winterboer informed Ness that he could sell him soybean seed that was "just like" Asgrow varieties A1937 and A2234. Ness purchased 20 bags of each; a plant biologist for Asgrow tested the seeds and determined that they were indeed A1937 and A2234.

Asgrow brought suit against the Winterboers in the Federal District Court for the Northern District of Iowa, seeking damages and a permanent injunction against sale of seed harvested from crops grown from A1937 and A2234. The complaint alleged infringement under 7 U.S.C. § 2541(1), for selling or offering to sell Asgrow's protected soybean varieties; under § 2541(3), for sexually multiplying Asgrow's novel varieties as a step in marketing those varieties for growing purposes; and under § 2541(6), for dispensing the novel varieties to others in a form that could be propagated without providing notice that the seeds were of a protected variety.[1]

---

[1]At the time the infringement action was filed, § 2541 provided in full:

> Except as otherwise provided in this subchapter, it shall be an infringement of the rights of the owner of a novel variety to perform without authority, any of the following acts in the United States, or in commerce which can be regulated by Congress or affecting such commerce, prior to expiration of the right to plant variety protection but after either the issue of the certificate or the distribution of a novel plant variety with the notice under section 2567 of this title:
>
> (1) sell the novel variety, or offer it or expose it for sale, deliver it, ship it, consign it, exchange it, or solicit an offer to buy it, or any other transfer of title or possession of it;
>
> (2) import the novel variety into, or export it from, the United States;
>
> (3) sexually multiply the novel variety as a step in marketing (for growing purposes) the variety; or
>
> (4) use the novel variety in producing (as distinguished from developing) a hybrid or different variety therefrom; or
>
> (5) use seed which had been marked "Unauthorized Propagation Prohibited" or "Unautho-

The Winterboers did not deny that Asgrow held valid certificates of protection covering A1937 and A2234, and that they had sold seed produced from those varieties for others to use as seed. Their defense, at least to the §§ 2541(1) and (3) charges, rested upon the contention that their sales fell within the statutory exemption from infringement liability found in 7 U.S.C. § 2543. That section, entitled "Right to save seed; crop exemption," reads in relevant part as follows:

> Except to the extent that such action may constitute an infringement under subsections (3) and (4) of section 2541 of this title, it shall not infringe any right hereunder for a person to save seed produced by him from seed obtained, or descended from seed obtained, by authority of the owner of the variety for seeding purposes and use such saved seed in the production of a crop for use on his farm, or for sale as provided in this section: Provided, That without regard to the provisions of section 2541(3) of this title it shall not infringe any right hereunder for a person, whose primary farming occupation is the growing of crops for sale for other than reproductive purposes, to sell such saved seed to other persons so engaged, for reproductive purposes, provided such sale is in compliance with such State laws governing the sale of seed as may be applicable. A bona fide sale for other than reproductive purposes, made in channels usual for such other purposes, of seed produced on a farm either from seed obtained by authority of the owner for seeding purposes or from seed produced by descent on such farm from seed obtained by authority of the owner for seeding purposes shall not constitute an infringement. . . .[2]

---

rized Seed Multiplication Prohibited" or progeny thereof to propagate the novel variety; or

    (6) dispense the novel variety to another, in a form which can be propagated, without notice as to being a protected variety under which it was received; or

    (7) perform any of the foregoing acts even in instances in which the novel variety is multiplied other than sexually, except in pursuance of a valid United States plant patent; or

    (8) instigate or actively induce performance of any of the foregoing acts.

In October 1992, Congress amended § 2541, designating the prior text as subsection (a) and adding a subsection (b), the provisions of which are not relevant here. Curiously, however, the references in § 2543 to the infringement provisions of § 2541 were not amended to reflect this change. For clarity's sake, therefore, we will continue to refer to the infringement provisions under their prior designations, e.g., §§ 2541(1)-(8), rather than their current designations, e.g., §§ 2541(a)(1)-(8).

[2]Congress has recently amended this section by striking from the first sentence the words "'section: Provided, That' and all that follows through the period and inserting 'section.'" Plant Variety Protection Act Amendments of 1994, Pub. L. 103-349, 108 Stat.

The Winterboers argued that this language gave them the right to sell an unlimited amount of seed produced from a protected variety, subject only to the conditions that both buyer and seller be farmers "whose primary farming occupation is the growing of crops for sale for other than reproductive purposes," and that all sales comply with state law. Asgrow maintained that the exemption allows a farmer to save and resell to other farmers only the amount of seed the seller would need to replant his own fields — a limitation that the Winterboers' sales greatly exceeded. The District Court agreed with Asgrow and granted summary judgment in its favor. 795 F. Supp. 915 (1991).

The United States Court of Appeals for the Federal Circuit reversed. 982 F.2d 486 (1992). Although "recognizing that, without meaningful limitations, the crop exemption [of § 2543] could undercut much of the PVPA's incentives," id., at 491, the Court of Appeals saw nothing in § 2543 that would limit the sale of protected seed (for reproductive purposes) to the amount necessary to plant the seller's own acreage. Rather, as the Court of Appeals read the statute, § 2543 permits a farmer to sell up to half of every crop he produces from PVPA-protected seed to another farmer for use as seed, so long as he sells the other 50 percent of the crop grown from that specific variety for nonreproductive purposes, e.g., for food or feed. The Federal Circuit denied Asgrow's petition for rehearing and suggestion for rehearing en banc by a vote of six judges to five. 989 F.2d 478 (1993). We granted certiorari. 511 U.S. 1029 (1994).

II

It may be well to acknowledge at the outset that it is quite impossible to make complete sense of the provision at issue here. One need go no further than the very first words of its title to establish that. Section 2543 does not, as that title claims and the ensuing text says, reserve any "right to save seed" — since nothing elsewhere in the Act remotely prohibits the saving of seed. Nor, under any possible analysis, is the proviso in the first sentence of § 2543 ("Provided, That") really a proviso.

3136, 3142. That amendment has the effect of eliminating the exemption from infringement liability for farmers who sell PVPA-protected seed to other farmers for reproductive purposes. That action, however, has no bearing on the resolution of the present case, since the amendments affect only those certificates issued after April 4, 1995, that were not pending on or before that date. See id., §§ 14(a), 15, 108 Stat. 3144, 3145.

With this advance warning that not all mysteries will be solved, we enter the verbal maze of § 2543. The entrance, we discover, is actually an exit, since the provision begins by excepting certain activities from its operation: "*Except to the extent that such action may constitute an infringement under subsections (3) and (4) of section 2541 of this title,* it shall not infringe any right hereunder for a person to save seed produced by him . . . and use such saved seed in the production of a crop for use on his farm, or for sale as provided in this section . . . ." (Emphasis added.) Thus, a farmer does not qualify for the exemption from infringement liability if he has

(3) sexually multiplied the novel variety as a step in marketing (for growing purposes) the variety; or

(4) used the novel variety in producing (as distinguished from developing) a hybrid or different variety therefrom. (7 U.S.C. §§ 2541(3)-(4))

In 1990, the Winterboers planted 265 acres of Asgrow protected variety seed and collected a harvest of 12,037 bushels of soybeans. The parties do not dispute that this act of planting and harvesting constituted "sexual multiplication" of the novel varieties. See 7 U.S.C. § 2401(f) (defining "sexually reproduced" seed to include "any production of a variety by seed"). The Winterboers sold almost all of these beans for use as seed (i.e., "for growing purposes"), without Asgrow's consent. The central question in this case, then, is whether the Winterboers' planting and harvesting were conducted "as a step in marketing" Asgrow's protected seed varieties for growing purposes. If they were, the Winterboers were not eligible for the § 2543 exemption, and the District Court was right to grant summary judgment to Asgrow.

The PVPA does not define "marketing." When terms used in a statute are undefined, we give them their ordinary meaning. FDIC v. Meyer, 510 U.S. 471, 476, 127 L. Ed. 2d 308, 114 S. Ct. 996 (1994). The Federal Circuit believed that the word "marketing" requires "extensive or coordinated selling activities, such as advertising, using an intervening sales representative, or similar extended merchandising or retail activities." 982 F.2d at 492. We disagree. Marketing ordinarily refers to the act of holding forth property for sale, together with the activities preparatory thereto (in the present case, cleaning, drying, bagging, and pricing the seeds). The word does not require that the promotional or merchandising activities connected with the selling be extensive. One can market apples by simply displaying them on a cart with a price tag; or market a stock by simply listing it on a stock exchange; or market a house (we would normally say "place it on the market") by simply setting a "for sale" sign on the front lawn. Indeed, some dictionaries give as one meaning "market" simply "to sell." See, e.g., Oxford Universal Dictionary 1208 (3d ed. 1955); Webster's New International Dictionary 1504 (2d ed. 1950). Of course, effective selling often involves extensive promotional activities, and when they occur they are all part of the "marketing." But even when the holding forth for sale relies upon no more than word-of-mouth advertising, a marketing of goods is in process. Moreover, even if the word "marketing" could, in one of its meanings, demand extensive promotion, we see no reason why the law at issue here would intend that meaning. That would have the effect of preserving PVPA protection for less valuable plant varieties, but eliminating it for varieties so desirable that they can be marketed by word of mouth; as well as the effect of requiring courts to ponder the difficult question of how much promotion is necessary to constitute marketing. We think that when the statute refers to sexually multiplying a variety "as a step in marketing," it means growing seed of the variety for the purpose of putting the crop up for sale.[3] Under the exception set out in the first clause of § 2543, then, a farmer is not eligible for the § 2543 exemption if he plants and saves seeds for the purpose of selling the seeds that they produce for replanting.

Section 2543 next provides that, so long as a person is not violating either §§ 2541(3) or (4),

> it shall not infringe any right hereunder for a person to *save seed* produced by him from seed obtained, or descended from seed obtained, by

---

[3]The dissent asserts that the Federal Circuit's more demanding interpretation of "marketing" is supported by the ancient doctrine disfavoring restraints on alienation of property, see post, ... The wellspring of that doctrine, of course, is concern for property rights, and in the context of the PVPA it is the dissent's interpretation, rather than ours, which belittles that concern. The whole purpose of the statute is to create a valuable property in the product of botanical research by giving the developer the right to "exclude others from selling the variety, or offering it for sale, or reproducing it, or importing it, or exporting it," etc. 7 U.S.C. § 2483. Applying the rule disfavoring restraints on alienation to interpretation of the PVPA is rather like applying the rule disfavoring restraints upon freedom of contract to interpretation of the Sherman Act.

authority of the owner of the variety for seeding purposes and use *such saved seed* in the production of a crop for use on his farm, or for sale as provided in this section . . . . (Emphasis added.)

Farmers generally grow crops to sell. A harvested soybean crop is typically removed from the farmer's premises in short order and taken to a grain elevator or processor. Sometimes, however, in the case of a plant such as the soybean, in which the crop is the seed, the farmer will have a portion of his crop cleaned and stored as seed for replanting his fields next season. We think it clear that this seed saved for replanting is what the provision under discussion means by "saved seed" — not merely regular uncleaned crop that is stored for later market sale or use as fodder.

*****

To summarize: By reason of its proviso the first sentence of § 2543 allows seed that has been preserved for reproductive purposes ("saved seed") to be sold for such purposes. The structure of the sentence is such, however, that this authorization does *not* extend to saved seed that was grown *for the very purpose* of sale ("marketing") for replanting — because in that case, § 2541(3) would be violated, and the above-discussed exception to the exemption would apply. As a practical matter, since § 2541(1) prohibits all unauthorized transfer of title to, or possession of, the protected variety, this means that the only seed that can be sold under the proviso is seed that has been saved by the farmer to replant his own acreage.[5] (We think that limitation is also apparent from the text of the crop exemption, which per-

---

[5]For crops such as soybeans, in which the seed and the harvest are one and the same, this will mean enough seeds for one year's crop on that acreage. Since the germination rate of a batch of seed declines over time, the soybean farmer will get the year-after-next's seeds from next year's harvest. That is not so for some vegetable crops, in which the seed is not the harvest, and a portion of the crop must be permitted to overripen ("go to seed") in order to obtain seeds. One of the amici in the Court of Appeals asserted (and the parties before us did not dispute) that it is the practice of vegetable farmers to "grow" seeds only every four or five years, and to "brown bag" enough seed for four or five future crops. A vegetable farmer who sets aside protected seed with subsequent replantings in mind, but who later abandons his plan (because he has sold his farm, for example), would under our analysis be able to sell all his saved seed, even though it would plant (in a single year) four or five times his current acreage.

mits a farm crop from saved seeds to be sold — for nonreproductive purposes — only if those saved seeds were "produced by descent *on such farm*."
(Emphasis added.) It is in our view the proviso in § 2543, and not the crop
exemption, that authorizes the permitted buyers of saved seeds to sell the
crops they produce.) Thus, if a farmer saves seeds to replant his acreage, but
for some reason changes his plans, he may instead sell those seeds for replanting under the terms set forth in the proviso (or of course sell them for
nonreproductive purposes under the crop exemption).

It remains to discuss one final feature of the proviso authorizing limited sales for reproductive purposes. The proviso allows sales of saved seed
for replanting purposes only between persons "whose primary farming occupation is the growing of crops for sale for other than reproductive purposes." The Federal Circuit, which rejected the proposition that the only
seed sellable under the exemption is seed saved for the farmer's own replanting, sought to achieve some limitation upon the quantity of seed that
can be sold for reproductive purposes by adopting a "crop-by-crop" approach to the "primary farming occupation" requirement of the proviso.
"Buyers or sellers of brown bag seed qualify for the crop exemption," it concluded, "only if they produce a larger crop from a protected seed for consumption (or other nonreproductive purposes) than for sale as seed." 982
F.2d at 490. That is to say, the brown-bag seller can sell no more than half of
his protected crop for seed. The words of the statute, however, stand in the
way of this creative (if somewhat insubstantial) limitation. To ask what is a
farmer's "primary farming occupation" is to ask what constitutes the bulk
of his total farming business. Selling crops for other than reproductive purposes must constitute the preponderance of the farmer's business, not just
the preponderance of his business in the protected seed. There is simply no
way to derive from this text the narrower focus that the Federal Circuit applied. Thus, if the quantity of seed that can be sold is not limited as we have
described — by reference to the original purpose for which the seed is
saved — then it is barely limited at all (i.e., limited only by the volume or
worth of the selling farmer's total crop sales for other than reproductive
purposes). This seems to us a most unlikely result.

* * *

We hold that a farmer who meets the requirements set forth in the
proviso to § 2543 may sell for reproductive purposes only such seed as he

has saved for the purpose of replanting his own acreage. While the meaning of the text is by no means clear, this is in our view the only reading that comports with the statutory purpose of affording "adequate encouragement for research, and for marketing when appropriate, to yield for the public the benefits of new varieties." 7 U.S.C. § 2581. Because we find the sales here were unlawful, we do not reach the second question on which we granted certiorari — whether sales authorized under § 2543 remain subject to the notice requirement of § 2541(6).

The judgment of the Court of Appeals for the Federal Circuit is Reversed.

Dissent: Justice Stevens, dissenting.

The key to this statutory puzzle is the meaning of the phrase, "as a step in marketing," as used in 7 U.S.C. § 2541(a)(3) (1988 ed., Supp. V). If it is synonymous with "for the purpose of selling," as the Court holds, . . . then the majority's comprehensive exposition of the statute is correct. I record my dissent only because that phrase conveys a different message to me.

There must be a reason why Congress used the word "marketing" rather than the more common term "selling." Indeed, in § 2541(a)(1), contained in the same subsection of the statute as the crucial language, Congress made it an act of infringement to "sell the novel variety." Yet, in § 2541(a)(3), a mere two clauses later, Congress eschewed the word "sell" in favor of "marketing." Because Congress obviously could have prohibited sexual multiplication "as a step in selling," I presume that when it elected to prohibit sexual multiplication only "as a step in marketing (for growing purposes) the variety," Congress meant something different.

Moreover, as used in this statute, "marketing" must be narrower, not broader, than selling. The majority is correct that one meaning of "marketing" is the act of selling and all acts preparatory thereto. See ante, . . . But Congress has prohibited only one preparatory act — that of sexual multiplication — and only when it is a step in marketing. Under the majority's broad definition of "marketing," prohibiting sexual multiplication "as a step in marketing" can be no broader than prohibiting sexual multiplication "as a step in selling," because all steps in marketing are, ultimately, steps in selling. If "marketing" can be no broader than "selling," and if Congress did not intend the two terms to be coextensive, then "marketing" must encompass something less than all "selling."

The statute as a whole — and as interpreted by the Court of Appeals — indicates that Congress intended to preserve the farmer's right to engage in so-called "brown-bag sales" of seed to neighboring farmers. Congress limited that right by the express requirement that such sales may not constitute the "primary farming occupation" of either the buyer or the seller. Moreover, § 2541(a)(3) makes it abundantly clear that the unauthorized participation in "marketing" of protected varieties is taboo. If one interprets "marketing" to refer to a subcategory of selling activities, namely merchandising through farm cooperatives, wholesalers, retailers, or other commercial distributors, the entire statute seems to make sense. I think Congress wanted to allow any ordinary brown-bag sale from one farmer to another; but, as the Court of Appeals concluded, it did not want to permit farmers to compete with seed manufacturers on their own ground, through "extensive or coordinated selling activities, such as advertising, using an intervening sales representative, or similar extended merchandising or retail activities." 982 F.2d 486, 492 (CA Fed. 1992).

This reading of the statute is consistent with our time-honored practice of viewing restraints on the alienation of property with disfavor. See, e.g., Sexton v. Wheaton, 21 U.S. 229, 8 Wheat. 229, 242, 5 L. Ed. 603 (1823) (opinion of Marshall, C. J.)*. The seed at issue is part of a crop planted and harvested by a farmer on his own property. Generally the owner of personal property — even a patented or copyrighted article — is free to dispose of that property as he sees fit. See, e. g., United States v. Univis Lens Co., 316 U.S. 241, 250-252, 86 L. Ed. 1408, 62 S. Ct. 1088 (1942); Bobbs-Merrill Co. v. Straus, 210 U.S. 339, 350-351, 52 L. Ed. 1086, 28 S. Ct. 722 (1908). A statutory restraint on this basic freedom should be expressed clearly and unambiguously. Cf. Deepsouth Packing Co. v. Laitram Corp., 406 U.S. 518, 530-531, 32 L. Ed. 2d 273, 92 S. Ct. 1700 (1972). As the majority recognizes, the meaning of this statute is "by no means clear." . . . Accordingly, both because I am persuaded that the Court of Appeals correctly interpreted the intent of Congress, and because doubts should be resolved against purported restraints on freedom, I would affirm the judgment below.

---

*"It would seem to be a consequence of that absolute power which a man possesses over his own property, that he may make any disposition of it which does not interfere with the existing rights of others, and such disposition, if it be fair and real, will be valid. The limitations on this power are those only which are prescribed by law." Sexton v. Wheaton, 8 Wheat. at 242.

Notes and Questions

1. With the advent of modern biotechnology, the borderline between the patent and plant variety protection becomes increasingly difficult to draw. The problem of granting a farmer's privilege arises, and it is noteworthy that a final compromise in the EC Directive of 6 July 1998 on the legal protection of biotechnological inventions was only achieved in Europe upon introducing, *inter alia*, a farmer's privilege.

2. How would you address the competing interests of the farmer and the seed developer/producer in the light of the statutory language and the main purposes of the PVPA? Would it be sufficient to bar commercial exploitation of seeds by farming cooperatives and large scale commercial operators?

3. In *Diamond v. Chakrabarty*,[1] the U.S. Supreme Court addressed the Plant Patent Act and the PVPA. It identified some of the reasons why plant varieties were considered outside the boundaries of traditional patent protection. What were those reasons? The subject of plant variety protection has become an increasingly important one because of large scale investments in research and development looking toward the creation of new agricultural products, and because of the interests of developing countries and indigenous peoples in protecting plant varieties that may have been developed over long periods of time. Should traditional patent protection be available for a plant variety that has been cultivated somewhere for several hundred years?

4. In the new age of biotechnology, is there any need for a specific regime to protect plant varieties, or might this better be addressed within a comprehensive regime to protect biotechnology inventions?

5. The farmer's privilege is a generally accepted exemption from plant variety protection. What do you think justifies it? Is it in accordance with the traditional theories underlying protection of inventions? Do you think, for example, that hospitals should be exempted from the patent protection accorded to pharmaceutical producers? Is a system that excludes one of its

---

[1] *See supra*, § B, 2, b.

major market sectors consistent with the general principles underlying IPRs protection?

6. Protection of plant varieties has historically been criticized, and this criticism will probably last as long as this IPR exist? Do you consider it unethical to grant IPRs on animals and plants?

4. Copyright

a. The Nature and Subject Matter of the Copyright

The copyright is granted to authors and artists to protect their creative expression against unauthorized copying or reproduction. Unlike the patent, the copyright does not establish a monopoly relating to the contents of the creation; ideas and thoughts remain in the public domain and can be freely used in different forms of expression. Theoretically, a person who independently creates a work identical or similar to that of the first author is entitled to produce and distribute his or her independent creation.

The copyright covers virtually all forms of creative expression — such as books, paintings, films, recordings and performances. Most recently, by default, copyright became the most commonly used IPR for the protection of computer software, and this use of the copyright has led to a significant blurring of lines between the traditional domains of *industrial property* and *authors' and artists' rights*.

The protection afforded by copyright is of substantially longer duration than that afforded by patent. The typical duration of copyright is the author's life plus fifty years.[1] This long duration is partially justified by the fact that copyright is *weaker* than the patent right, since it does not preclude independent creation.

The protection afforded by copyright is subject to important exceptions, the most notable of which are rights of *fair use* accorded to certain

---

[1]Later in the book we will examine recent European Union and U.S. legislation that harmonizes the term of copyright for the life of the author plus 70 years.

copying and distribution. Fair use doctrines permit portions of otherwise copyrighted works to be used, for example, for news reference and instructional purposes.

The Berne Convention for the Protection of Literary and Artistic works establishes certain so-called *moral rights* in favor of authors. These include the right of attribution and the right to prevent a mutilation or other abuse of the work that would disparage the reputation of the author. An author's moral rights are considered inalienable — they cannot be waived or released — and they are not subject to sale or transfer in connection with the author's *economic rights* in a work. It is conventional wisdom that major distinctions exist between the common law copyright systems (e.g., the American and British) and the continental European copyright systems (e.g., the French) on the subject of moral rights, with the common law systems being less protective of authors. Most likely, conventional wisdom exaggerates these differences.

Copyright is granted only in respect to *creative* expression. Determining what constitutes *creativity* for this purpose presents some difficulties that may result in a lack of uniform treatment of the same work in different countries or regions. The typical example of a work that may lack the requisite creative element is a *database* that represents the compilation of publicly available data. So, for example, a telecommunications company that publishes a listing of telephone numbers may invest a great deal of time and effort in assembling data into a useful form (i.e., a telephone directory). However, there may be nothing about the arrangement of a telephone directory that is unique or that might involve an author's distinctive contribution.[2] The listing in the telephone directory may not be protected by copyright as a *database,* and for this reason efforts are being pressed by major compilers of such databases for the negotiation of a new international agreement on this subject, to provide a *sui generis* form of *database protection.* Although some legal systems initially attempted to impose a minimum requirement of creative spark or innovation on the authors of computer programs as a condition of granting copyright protection, this approach was eventually abandoned.[3]

---

[2]*See, e.g.,* U.S. Supreme Court decision in *Feist,* discussed *infra* Ch. IV, § L, 1, c.

[3]*See* discussion of German Federal Supreme Court decision in Re The Protection of Computer Programs, and the EC Software Directive, *infra* Ch. IV, § Q, 1. Note also that courts in the United States have imposed constraints on the copyrighting of software

In addition to protecting the author's initial expression, copyright also protects against the unauthorized distribution of derivative works, such as *translations* and *adaptations*.

The unauthorized reproduction of an author's work may take the form of direct or literal copying, in which case infringement of the author's rights may be relatively easy to determine (bearing in mind that there are defenses to literal copying, for example, under fair use doctrine). Unauthorized reproduction may also take the form of indirect or nonliteral copying, in which case the copying party is modifying the protected work in order to avoid the appearance of reproducing it. In the case of nonliteral copying, courts apply various tests to determine whether an allegedly infringing work is sufficiently similar to a protected work to violate the author's copyright. In the United States, for example, the traditional legal test is whether an allegedly infringing work is "substantially similar" to the protected work. Application of this test generally requires the use of subjective judgment.

Computer technology has made possible the transformation of expressive works into digital electronic format. This has greatly facilitated the reproduction, transmission and retransmission of expressive works. The capacity for use of digital technology to reproduce and distribute expressive works is of great benefit to global society as knowledge, information and culture can be shared widely. The same capacity is also perceived as a threat to the traditional interests of copyright holders who fear loss of control over the right to reproduce (and therefore to derive income from) their expressive works. The flow of digital data across national borders is less constrained than the flow of physical goods (using "trade routes" such as the Internet), and copyright issues arising from the digitization of information have a substantial international dimension.

b. Idea Versus Expression

Copyright protection extends to authors' and artists' creative expression. Legislatures and courts have consistently interpreted the term "expression" to exclude the protection of ideas or methods that might be embodied in an expressive work. In the following case, the Swiss Supreme Court considers the distinction between expression and idea in the copyright context.

---

based on functionality and method of operation considerations (*see* Lotus v. Borland, *infra* § B, 4, c, and Computer Associates v. Altai, *infra*, Ch. IV, § Q, 2, a).

Frau X filed suit against Frau Y and Z Publishing House for infringement of copyright, alleging that Frau Y used written results of Frau X's research in a public presentation before that research was published.[4] In addition to claiming infringement of protected expression, Frau X claimed that Frau Y infringed her moral rights because she gave the impression to her audience that she was the author of the work by Frau X. The court provides a good summary of the Swiss approach to the moral rights question (moral rights will be treated in detail in Chapter IV).

The judicial system in Switzerland, typical for continental Europe, generally consists of three levels: first the Bezirksgericht (Circuit Court), which has first instance jurisdiction within a small geographic region. The Obergericht or Kantonsgericht (Court of Appeals) is the second level, which decides all appeals in one state (a "Canton") of Switzerland. The highest Swiss Court is the Federal Court, located in Lausanne. In addition to performing the usual tasks of judicial review, this court, in the area of private law, acts as a court of second appeal with a view to bringing about the uniform interpretation of federal law in the Swiss federalist structure. Unlike the U.S. Supreme Court, the Swiss Federal Court does not have discretion to decide whether or not an appeal should be considered.

---

[4]The case relies upon the Swiss Copyright Act of 1922, but the basic rules remain valid under the new Act of 1992, which has been largely modeled to conform with the respective directives of the European Community.

Frau X v. Frau Y & Z Publishing House[*]

Bundesgericht (Swiss Federal Court)
BGE 113 II 306 ([1989] ECC 232) (translation, as adjusted)
17 June 1987

*****

Facts:

Frau X was a student of psychology at Zurich University. Both her work for a licentiate and her dissertation were concerned with the life and work of the first child psychoanalyst, Hermine von Hug-Hellmuth. At the end of 1983, intending to have the results of her work published, she approached the Z publishing house. The publisher's reader informed her by telephone in March 1984 that publication of the two works in the form in which they then were was not possible but the publisher would be interested in the manuscripts if they were to be reworked. The reader added that she had passed the manuscripts on for an opinion to Frau Y, who, as Frau X knew, had announced a forthcoming lecture at the Zurich Psychoanalytic Seminar on 'H Hug-Hellmuth and W Schmidt'. Frau Y subsequently also got in touch with Frau X.

The lecture took place on 10 May 1984; it was recorded on a tape which is stored in the library of the Psychoanalytic Seminar. It is not clear whether the lecture has been published in an appropriate form.

In May 1985 Frau X started legal proceedings against Frau Y and the Z publishing house seeking in particular an injunction under threat of penalty on the first defendant against using any quotations or results of scientific research from either of her two unpublished manuscripts unless they were acknowledged as being such. She also asked that the first defendant be ordered to pay her 2,000 Sfr plus interest by way of moral redress

---

[*]Editors' Note: In Swiss legal practice, names are deleted from published opinions with a view to protect the plaintiff's and defendant's privacy and integrity.

and that both defendants be jointly held liable to pay 500 Sfr plus interest by way of damages.

The Zurich Obergericht (court of appeal) dismissed the action on 20 November 1986 on the grounds that the first defendant had not infringed any copyright or droit moral of the plaintiff and had not been guilty of unfair competition, that the second defendant was not responsible for the action of its reader, and that the plaintiff had suffered no harm as a result of the passing on of the manuscript.

The plaintiff has appealed against that judgment in which she maintains her claims.

Decision:

*****

3. The plaintiff objects that the Obergericht was wrong in finding that there was no infringement by the first defendant of her copyright under section 1(2) of the Copyright Act. She argues in particular that a comparison of her work with the lecture in issue shows that various passages in her manuscripts are quoted and their substantive content is adopted in part. She says that the Court below did not go into the matter at all. Her theses were of an independent character, were the result of a personal intellectual performance and therefore should not have been quoted before publication even in extracts. The content of scientific works was not generally free for copyright purposes, so that, contrary to the view of the court below, it was not admissible to consider individual empirical facts in isolation or to refuse protection in advance in the case of scientific data and theses. Since the individual content of such works had to be sought in the selection and scientific processing of material which they undertook, the aspects relevant for copyright purposes had to be considered as a connected whole before it was possible to make a judgment on whether protection was available to the work.

(a) Literary works fall within the concept of a protected work within the meaning of section 1 of the Copyright Act if the specific presentation does not merely contain what is common property but, when taken as a whole, is to be regarded as a result of intellectual creative activity of an individual character or as the expression of a new original idea; for originality and individuality also count as essential characteristics of a protected work. (See 110 IV BGE 105 E 2; 106 II BGE 73-74; 100 II BGE 172, with further references in each case.) A scientific work is also covered by the statutory definition if it shows a minimum standard of creative performance. But for these purposes a scientific idea as such does not come into consideration. What a scientist states about external circumstances, operations or other matters of fact becomes free once it is published so far as the content is concerned, and is not in itself protected for copyright purposes even if it conveys new discoveries or has been worked out with effort (88 IV BGE 127). The content of a scientific idea is not the intellectual work involved therein but consists in the fact that it reveals previously unknown or little known facts. The result of the work, therefore, is freely usable as regards content, as befits the purpose of scientific investigation, which is oriented towards free access. Reservations remain only in the case of scientific discoveries in the technical field, which in appropriate cases can be subject to patent rights or protection by reference to secrecy or confidentiality. (Troller, Immaterialguterrecht I (3rd ed), p 355; Kummer, Das urheberrechtlich schutzbare Werk, pp 106 et seq.)

On the other hand, the specific presentation of a scientific work can be entitled to protection. This includes in the first instance the external form in which the work is communicated if it is clearly distinct from other persons' written work with the same content. For these purposes it evidently cannot be overlooked that for the author of such a work narrow boundaries tend to be set as regards its written formulation because he must adhere to specific sets of facts and in particular to technical language if he wishes to be taken seriously and to be understood (88 IV BGE 129). Where the form of communication is so tightly constricted by the scientific content that there is no longer any room for an individual or original formulation copyright protection disappears for that reason. (Kummer, op cit p 108.) In addition to the form given to it, a scientific work can also exhibit individual characteristics in the way in which it plans, selects and treats, and arranges and articulates the material, and it can thus establish copyright protection (88 IV BGE 127; Troller, op cit I p 356, n 26; Ulmer, Urheber- und Verlsagsrecht (3rd ed), p 123.) Section 70 of the German Copyright Act is interpreted in the same way. (Judgments of the Federal Supreme Court at [1975] GRUR 667 et seq and [1982] UFITA 143 et seq.) Contrary to the plaintiff's view, however, it is not admissible to extend the copyright protection still further to the content of scientific works, as is advocated by some writers on the basis of the German conception. (Haberstumpf zur Individualitat wissenschaftlicher Sprachwerke, p 77 et seq, and at [1983] UFITA 41 et seq.)

Where, as in the present case, scientific works are concerned, an infringement of copyright may accordingly arise as a result of a third person adopting the specific form in which the work is presented or imitating it in its essential aspects. It is necessary to bear in mind in this connection that not only the work's scientific propositions as such but also forms of expression predetermined by them are freely available to the public, and furthermore that the selection, recording and articulation of the subject-matter only qualify for protection as a whole or in relation to connected parts of the work, but not so far as it simply concerns details of the work, such as data, evidence, examples or similar statements. The taking over of such details, even if they are many, is not an infringement of copyright because scientific statements which are common property do not become protected parts of a work as a result of the treatment or presentation of the subject-matter, which can confer copyright protection. Nor is this position altered by the principle that not only the work as a whole but also its individual parts can be entitled to protection if they satisfy the necessary conditions for protection (85 II BGE 123 E 3).

(b) When those criteria are applied there can be no objections under Federal law to the view of the court below that the first defendant did not infringe any copyright owned by the plaintiff. At any rate, in so far as the first defendant adopted quotations and biographic details, one is dealing with pre-existing statements which are therefore in the public domain, nor do they enjoy copyright protection in respect of their content or of the predetermined form in which they are communicated. Accordingly the scientific thesis that the role of Hermine von Hug-Hellmuth must be seen in the light of the dispute between Freud and Jung about the origin of neuroses is not protected as a scientific proposition by reason of its content but at the most by reason of the characteristic written form in which it is expressed. The judgment in question found that in the proceedings at cantonal level the plaintiff did not argue that this thesis was adopted by the first defendant in the external form in which it was communicated in the plaintiff's two works. Accordingly the first defendant was able to consider the scientific propositions of the thesis in her lecture without infringing the plaintiff's copyright.

The position is not altered by the fact the plaintiff's two works were not published at the date when it is alleged that they were taken over. The publication of a protected work is decisive for the ability to quote passages from it or make it known publicly. (Ss 12(1)4 and 42 1(d) of The Copyright Act; Troller op cit II p 704; Ulmer op cit p 313; Lutz Die Schranken des Urheberrechts nach Schweizerischem Recht, Diss Zurich 1964, p 47; E Sciaroni, Das Zitatrecht, Diss Freiburg 1970 p 28.) But publication does not affect the distinction between the free and the restricted use of a work. There is therefore no need to decide whether the plaintiff's two works already counted as published for the purposes of the Act when approved by the faculty. It must still be borne in mind that the prohibition on quoting from unpublished works does not protect the author's publishing right, but his or her claim to prevent a distorting representation of the work and to reserve to himself or herself the right to determine the final version; and that condition is sufficiently satisfied if the work is fixed as regard its essential parts, which is generally the case where the competent body of an institute of further education has passed the work. (Cf Lutz, op cit p 47.)

4. The plaintiff further accuses the first defendant of infringing her droit moral. According to the judgment under appeal that allegation had to be rejected because the quotations, data and propositions which were undoubtedly adopted were nevertheless not of such moment that one could talk of usurpation of the work, and because there was no other prejudice to the plaintiff's scientific reputation.

(a) Under Swiss legal theory and legislation an author is protected not only in his or her power to dispose of the work as the object of property rights, but also as regards his personal relationship to the work, that is as regards his droit moral as author, which are conceived as being a part or special aspect of general droit moral. The protection of that special droit moral arises in part from the provisions of the Copyright Act, such as section 42(1) and (2) but above all from section 28 of the Civil Code and section 49 of the Code of Obligations which expressly remain unaffected in section 44, second sentence, of the Copyright Act. The protection arises further from Article 6 bis of the Berne Union Convention, and it first occurs in the revision made in Rome in 1928 (96 II BGE 420 E 6, with references).

Under section 28 of the Civil Code it is a condition precedent for claims arising out of droit moral that there is unlawful interference in personal relationships, which are understood as being the sphere of private life and the home, as well as a person's professional and private reputation. That is not to say that any relationship of the author to the work is sufficient to turn an alleged interference into an infringement of a personal right; for the general principle does not grant any claim to an exclusive right of disposal if the author's reputation is not affected; such an approach to the matter would have the end-result of creating a monopoly under section 28 of the Civil Code in something which is designated as freely available to the public under the statutory provisions on the specific subject-matter. The special statutory provision has precedence over the general provisions of the Civil Code and governs the area to which it applies to the exclusion of other rules. It is therefore not admissible to attempt to fill alleged gaps in copyright law by an indirect route through the general principle (110 II BGE 417 E 3a, with references). In the matter of copyright this principle only covers claims which are not subject to the rules of the legislation on the specific subject-matter, such as the author's claim to have his scientific achievement acknowledged, to have his work protected against distortion, or to have access to research documentation. (Engel in [1982] GRUR 709 et seq.) This corresponds to Article 6bis(1) of the Berne Union Convention, under which, independently of the author's copyright and even after transfer of such copyright, the author still has the right in particular to object to any distortion, mutilation or other alteration of the work which could be prejudicial to his honour or reputation; under the 1948 Revision the concept also includes anything else which would be prejudicial. For these purposes it is sufficient that the alteration or other prejudicial action is apt to injure his reputation or honour (96 II BGE 421).

(b) The plaintiff attacks the first defendant's manner of proceeding inasmuch as the latter took quotations, data and propositions from her works without stating the source. She supports her claim in this respect with section 26(2) of the Copyright Act, but overlooks the fact that, as shown by heading III, that provision belongs to 'Exceptions from Copyright Protection', and therefore presupposes a protected work or a protected part of a work. (Troller, op cit II, p 704; Sciaroni, op cit, pp 28 et seq.) What is available for public use, however, enjoys no copyright protection, and therefore also establishes no duty to attach a statement of source to quotations. The plaintiff, therefore, is likewise unable to derive anything from the general right of personality which will protect her scientific statements, regardless of whether or not her works have to be treated as published.

The Obergericht must also be agreed with in its finding that there was no infringement of the plaintiff's right to acknowledgment of her scientific achievement. It is true that rights of personality give the author a claim in particular to the protection of any reputation and honour which the work may establish for him (84 II BGE 573); he can also oppose the usurpation of authorship by third parties. As the court below correctly held, however, that presupposes that the work is claimed as an individual achievement as regards its essential parts or characteristic features. That cannot be seriously maintained in the present case, especially as according to the findings on the factual aspects the quotations, data and propositions taken over word-for-word or merely in substance cannot qualify for copyright protection.

5. In the same way the accusation that the first defendant's actions are to be regarded as a breach of good faith for the purposes of section 1 of the Unfair Competition Act fails in the first instance by reason of the fact that conduct which is not to be objected to under the specific legislative provisions on intangible property rights also does not in principle contravene the provisions of the Unfair Competition Act (110 IV BGE 107 E 4 and 108 II BGE 331 E 5a, with citation). No doubt on the basis of the general stipulation contained in section 1(1) of the Act an exception would be made for the case of conduct which amounts to a systematic approximation or a deliberate covert approach to another person's work (108 II BGE 74-75 and 332; 104 II BGE 334 E 5b). But this is clearly not such a case. The passages listed by the defendant, consisting of three quotations, five items biographical data and a scientific proposition (thesis), which are allegedly extracted from her two works, make it impossible to conclude that the first defendant, in the exercise of an economic activity, usurped rights in specific parts of the work or even the authorship of the whole presentation, as the plaintiff seeks to argue.

Finally, the plaintiff claims damages for breach of contract and on the grounds of vicarious liability because the reader of the second defendant acting without authority and therefore unlawfully passed her manuscripts on to the first defendant. It is not necessary for present purposes to decide how the facts stand with regard to those claims, for the plaintiff acknowledges in the appeal that she authorised the first defendant to refer to both works under certain 'restrictive' conditions. In so doing she herself removes the basis of her objection that the publishing company passed the manuscripts on without authority and thereby made it possible for the first defendant to adopt the passages in question.

Appeal dismissed. Judgment of the lower court reaffirmed.

Notes and Questions

1. How did the court define the boundary between protectable expression and unprotectable content or idea?

2. The Court suggests that the means for expressing scientific ideas may be sufficiently constrained such that this expression cannot be an independently creative act for copyright purposes. In what cases are scientific propositions so clearly "true" in an objective sense that the personality of the researcher is not part of the scientific proposition? If a scientific proposition turns out to be false, does this falsity turn the proposition into creative expression within the scope of copyright protection?

3. Does the author in this case have "personal rights" in her work that copyright has not adequately protected? Do you agree with the Court's view that if material used in the lecture is not protected as creative expression, then its author cannot have a moral right in the work?

4. Compilations of factual material are protected by copyright if their arrangement embodies a creative act by the compiler. Why is Frau X's work not protected as a compilation?

5. Traditionally, U.S. and British copyright law required registration to obtain a copyright. With adherence to the Berne Convention, both countries abandoned this condition, since the Berne Convention states that the enjoyment and exercise of authors' rights shall not be subject to any formality. But, whereas Great Britain fully eliminated the registration requirement, the U.S. still permits registration and encourages right holders to register by giving them an initial advantage in litigation. Are there reasonable grounds not to require registration of copyrights? Conversely, what justifies registration requirements with respect to patents, plant varieties, industrial designs, integrated circuit layout designs and trademarks?

5. Toward the end of its opinion, the Swiss Federal Court considers the plaintiff's unfair competition claim. While accepting that the usurpation of another person's work might constitute unfair competition, the Court says

that the offending conduct must be systematic or involve a deliberate approach to the other person. In this regard, the Court says that appropriation, *inter alia*, of plaintiff's thesis makes it impossible to conclude that a sufficiently great usurpation occurred. Perhaps the Court was not terribly impressed by the plaintiff's thesis. But as a general proposition, might not a single scientific proposition or thesis be of enormous economic and social value such that its usurpation would constitute a great harm to its creator? What if a physicist had broken into Albert Einstein's apartment in Berne and shortly thereafter published Einsteins's theory of relativity under a different name?

6. Law professors and other academics make their reputations — and thus help determine their living conditions — on the basis of their creative scholarship. Law professors routinely circulate their work to colleagues prior to publication for criticism, editorial suggestion, and so forth, with the aim of improving the final product. Though it is certainly not unheard of, it is in fact rather rare to hear a complaint that one professor has "misappropriated" another's unpublished thesis. What do you think might motivate law professors, or research scientists, to respect the interests of their colleagues in such work? Is it protection by copyright or unfair competition law? Is it high moral standards? Is some other potential "collegial sanctioning mechanism" at work? Does such a sanctioning mechanism operate in the business sector?

---

c. Computer Software

Lotus v. Borland is one in a long line of cases decided by U.S. courts regarding the scope of copyright protection for computer software. As computer software became an important tool of business and its commercial value became apparent in the early 1970s, individuals and businesses that invested in software development searched for the legal means to protect their investments. None of the existing forms of IPRs protection appeared to suit computer software particularly well. The computer program, consisting of a series of instructions that operate a computer, did not appear to fall within the traditional domain of patent protection because of its similarity to a method of calculation. The computer program seemed an unlikely candidate for copyright protection since copyright has traditionally been the domain of authors and artists who composed works of literature and art, and software did not seem to share the characteristics of a work of literature or art.

As government officials and business managers searched contentiously for a *sui generis* form of IPRs protection for software, lawyers used the tools at hand, and convinced the courts that the expression of a computer software programmer was just as well entitled to copyright protection as the expression of a painter. Nonetheless, the basic idea that software might be protectable by copyright left open a myriad of questions. Was this protection limited to human-readable language (i.e., source code), or might expression that could only be read by a computer (i.e., object code) also be protectable? Was only the written software code protectable, or was the output of the program in the form of a visual display also protectable? If a specific set of instructions was required to cause the computer equipment to perform a function, did this functional element deprive that set of instructions of a copyrightable character? How would the courts go about deciding whether a similar, but not identical, program infringed a copyrighted program?

U.S. courts have answered all of these questions, though some with far more certainty and clarity than others. We will consider the international aspects of software protection in more detail later on in the book. For present purposes, the *Lotus v. Borland* case illustrates one of the limits on the use of the copyright to protect computer software. Copyright protects authors' expression. It does not protect ideas as such, or methods of operation. When a set of expressive elements is embodied in a computer program to serve a purely functional purpose, in this case permitting users to input and manipulate data, it loses its character as creative expression. It is instead a *method of operation* that is analogous to an unprotectable *idea* or *concept*. The symbols through which the user of the Lotus spreadsheet program is able to enter data for manipulation by the program are compared by the court to the buttons on a video cassette recorder (VCR) that allow a user to Play, Stop and Rewind a cassette. The symbols on VCR buttons are not copyrightable subject matter. They are methods of operating the VCR. To permit them to be copyrighted would create a substantial impediment to the commercial development of products.

Lotus Development Corporation, Plaintiff, Appellee, v. Borland International, Inc., Defendant, Appellant.

United States Court of Appeals for the First Circuit
49 F.3d 807; 1995 U.S. App. LEXIS 4618

March 9, 1995, Decided

Subsequent History: As Corrected March 23, 1995.
Prior History: Appeal from the United States District Court for the District of Massachusetts.

***

Judges: Before Torruella, Chief Judge, Boudin and Stahl, Circuit Judges.

Opinion: Stahl, Circuit Judge. This appeal requires us to decide whether a computer menu command hierarchy is copyrightable subject matter. In particular, we must decide whether, as the district court held, plaintiff-appellee Lotus Development Corporation's copyright in Lotus 1-2-3, a computer spreadsheet program, was infringed by defendant-appellant Borland International, Inc., when Borland copied the Lotus 1-2-3 menu command hierarchy into its Quattro and Quattro Pro computer spreadsheet programs. . . .

I.

Background

Lotus 1-2-3 is a spreadsheet program that enables users to perform accounting functions electronically on a computer. Users manipulate and control the program via a series of menu commands, such as "Copy," "Print," and "Quit." Users choose commands either by highlighting them on the screen or by typing their first letter. In all, Lotus 1-2-3 has 469 commands arranged into more than 50 menus and submenus.

Lotus 1-2-3, like many computer programs, allows users to write what are called "macros." By writing a macro, a user can designate a series of command choices with a single macro keystroke. Then, to execute that series of commands in multiple parts of the spreadsheet, rather than typing the whole series each time, the user only needs to type the single pre-programmed macro keystroke, causing the program to recall and perform the designated series of commands automatically. Thus, Lotus 1-2-3 macros shorten the time needed to set up and operate the program.

Borland released its first Quattro program to the public in 1987, after Borland's engineers had labored over its development for nearly three years. Borland's objective was to develop a spreadsheet program far superior to existing programs, including Lotus 1-2-3. In Borland's words, "from the time of its initial release . . . Quattro included enormous innovations over competing spreadsheet products."

The district court found, and Borland does not now contest, that Borland included in its Quattro and Quattro Pro version 1.0 programs "a virtually identical copy of the entire 1-2-3 menu tree." *Borland III*, 831 F. Supp. at 212 (emphasis in original). In so doing, Borland did not copy any of Lotus's underlying computer code; it copied only the words and structure of Lotus's menu command hierarchy. Borland included the Lotus menu command hierarchy in its programs to make them compatible with Lotus 1-2-3 so that spreadsheet users who were already familiar with Lotus 1-2-3 would be able to switch to the Borland programs without having to learn new commands or rewrite their Lotus macros.

In its Quattro and Quattro Pro version 1.0 programs, Borland achieved compatibility with Lotus 1-2-3 by offering its users an alternate user interface, the "Lotus Emulation Interface." By activating the Emulation Interface, Borland users would see the Lotus menu commands on their screens and could interact with Quattro or Quattro Pro as if using Lotus 1-2-3, albeit with a slightly different looking screen and with many Borland options not available on Lotus 1-2-3. In effect, Borland allowed users to choose how they wanted to communicate with Borland's spreadsheet programs: either by using menu commands designed by Borland, or by using the commands and command structure used in Lotus 1-2-3 augmented by Borland-added commands.

*****

The district court ruled that the Lotus menu command hierarchy was copyrightable expression because

[a] very satisfactory spreadsheet menu tree can be constructed using different commands and a different command structure from those of Lotus 1-2-3. In fact, Borland has constructed just such an alternate tree for use in Quattro Pro's native mode. Even if one holds the arrangement of menu commands constant, it is possible to generate literally millions of satisfactory menu trees by varying the menu commands employed.

Borland II, 799 F. Supp. at 217. The district court demonstrated this by offering alternate command words for the ten commands that appear in Lotus's main menu. Id. For example, the district court stated that "the 'Quit' command could be named 'Exit' without any other modifications," and that "the 'Copy' command could be called 'Clone,' 'Ditto,' 'Duplicate,' 'Imitate,' 'Mimic,' 'Replicate,' and 'Reproduce,' among others." Id. Because so many variations were possible, the district court concluded that the Lotus developers' choice and arrangement of command terms, reflected in the Lotus menu command hierarchy, constituted copyrightable expression.

In granting partial summary judgment to Lotus, the district court held that Borland had infringed Lotus's copyright in Lotus 1-2-3:

> As a matter of law, Borland's Quattro products infringe the Lotus 1-2-3 copyright because of (1) the extent of copying of the "menu commands" and "menu structure" that is not genuinely disputed in this case, (2) the extent to which the copied elements of the "menu commands" and "menu structure" contain expressive aspects separable from the functions of the "menu commands" and "menu structure," and (3) the scope of those copied expressive aspects as an integral part of Lotus 1-2-3.

*****

This appeal concerns only Borland's copying of the Lotus menu command hierarchy into its Quattro programs and Borland's affirmative defenses to such copying. . . .

II.

Discussion

On appeal, Borland does not dispute that it factually copied the words and arrangement of the Lotus menu command hierarchy. Rather, Borland argues that it "lawfully copied the unprotectable menus of Lotus 1-2-3." Borland contends that the Lotus menu command hierarchy is not copyrightable because it is a system, method of operation, process, or procedure foreclosed from protection by 17 U.S.C. § 102(b). Borland also raises a number of affirmative defenses.

A. Copyright Infringement Generally

To establish copyright infringement, a plaintiff must prove "(1) ownership of a valid copyright, and (2) copying of constituent elements of the work that are original." Feist Publications, Inc. v. Rural Tel. Serv. Co., 499 U.S. 340, 361, 113 L. Ed. 2d 358, 111 S. Ct. 1282 (1991); see also Data Gen. Corp. v. Grumman Sys. Support Corp., 36 F.3d 1147, 1160 n.19 (1st Cir. 1994); Concrete Mach. Co. v. Classic Lawn Ornaments, Inc., 843 F.2d 600, 605 (1st Cir. 1988). To show ownership of a valid copyright and therefore satisfy Feist's first prong, a plaintiff must prove that the work as a whole is original and that the plaintiff complied with applicable statutory formalities. See Engineering Dynamics, Inc. v. Structural Software, Inc., 26 F.3d 1335, 1340 (5th Cir. 1994). "In judicial proceedings, a certificate of copyright registration constitutes prima facie evidence of copyrightability and shifts the burden to the defendant to demonstrate why the copyright is not valid." Bibbero Sys., Inc. v. Colwell Sys., Inc., 893 F.2d 1104, 1106 (9th Cir. 1990); see also 17 U.S.C. § 410(c); Folio Impressions, Inc. v. Byer California, 937 F.2d 759, 763 (2d Cir. 1991) (presumption of validity may be rebutted).

To show actionable copying and therefore satisfy Feist's second prong, a plaintiff must first prove that the alleged infringer copied plaintiff's copyrighted work as a factual matter; to do this, he or she may either present direct evidence of factual copying or, if that is unavailable, evidence that the alleged infringer had access to the copyrighted work and that the offending and copyrighted works are so similar that the court may infer that there was factual copying (i.e., probative similarity). Engineering Dynamics, 26 F.3d at 1340; see also Concrete Mach., 843 F.2d at 606. The plaintiff must then prove that the copying of copyrighted material was so extensive that it rendered the offending and copyrighted works substantially similar. See Engineering Dynamics, 26 F.3d at 1341.

In this appeal, we are faced only with whether the Lotus menu command hierarchy is copyrightable subject matter in the first instance, for Borland concedes that Lotus has a valid copyright in Lotus 1-2-3 as a whole[5] and admits to factually copying the Lotus menu command hierarchy. As a result, this appeal is in a very different posture from most copyright-infringement cases, for copyright infringement generally turns on whether the defendant has copied protected expression as a factual matter. Because of this different posture, most copyright-infringement cases provide only limited help to us in deciding this appeal. This is true even with respect to those copyright-infringement cases that deal with computers and computer software.

B. Matter of First Impression

Whether a computer menu command hierarchy constitutes copyrightable subject matter is a matter of first impression in this court. While some other courts appear to have touched on it briefly in dicta, see, e.g., Autoskill, Inc. v. National Educ. Support Sys., Inc., 994 F.2d 1476, 1495 n.23 (10th Cir.), cert. denied, 126 L. Ed. 2d 254, 114 S. Ct. 307 (1993), we know of no cases that deal with the copyrightability of a menu command hierarchy standing on its own (i.e., without other elements of the user interface, such as screen displays, in issue). Thus we are navigating in uncharted waters.

Borland vigorously argues, however, that the Supreme Court charted our course more than 100 years ago when it decided Baker v. Selden, 101 U.S. 99, 25 L. Ed. 841 (1879). In Baker v. Selden, the Court held that Selden's copyright over the textbook in which he explained his new way to do accounting did not grant him a monopoly on the use of his accounting system.[6] Borland argues:

---

[5]Computer programs receive copyright protection as "literary works." See 17 U.S.C. § 102(a)(1) (granting protection to "literary works") and 17 U.S.C. § 101 (defining "literary works" as "works . . . expressed in words, numbers, or other verbal or numerical symbols or indicia, regardless of the nature of the material objects, such as books, periodicals, phonorecords, film, tapes, disks, or cards, in which they are embodied" (emphasis added)); see also H.R. Rep. No. 1476, 94th Cong., 2d Sess. 54 (1976), reprinted in 1976 U.S.C.C.A.N. 5659, 5667 ("The term 'literary works' . . . includes computer data bases, and computer programs to the extent that they incorporate authorship in the programmer's expression of original ideas, as distinguished from the ideas themselves.").

[6]Selden's system of double-entry bookkeeping is the now almost-universal T-accounts system

The facts of Baker v. Selden, and even the arguments advanced by the parties in that case, are identical to those in this case. The only difference is that the "user interface" of Selden's system was implemented by pen and paper rather than by computer.

To demonstrate that Baker v. Selden and this appeal both involve accounting systems, Borland even supplied this court with a video that, with special effects, shows Selden's paper forms "melting" into a computer screen and transforming into Lotus 1-2-3.

We do not think that Baker v. Selden is nearly as analogous to this appeal as Borland claims. Of course, Lotus 1-2-3 is a computer spreadsheet, and as such its grid of horizontal rows and vertical columns certainly resembles an accounting ledger or any other paper spreadsheet. Those grids, however, are not at issue in this appeal for, unlike Selden, Lotus does not claim to have a monopoly over its accounting system. Rather, this appeal involves Lotus's monopoly over the commands it uses to operate the computer. Accordingly, this appeal is not, as Borland contends, "identical" to Baker v. Selden.

C. Altai

Before we analyze whether the Lotus menu command hierarchy is a system, method of operation, process, or procedure, we first consider the applicability of the test the Second Circuit set forth in Computer Assoc. Int'l, Inc. v. Altai, Inc., 982 F.2d 693 (2d Cir. 1992).[7] The Second Circuit designed its Altai test to deal with the fact that computer programs, copyrighted as "literary works," can be infringed by what is known as "nonliteral" copying, which is copying that is paraphrased or loosely paraphrased rather than word for word. See id. at 701 (citing nonliteral-copying cases); see also 3 Melville B. Nimmer & David Nimmer, Nimmer on Copyright § 13.03[A][1] (1993). When faced with nonliteral-copying cases, courts must determine whether similarities are due merely to the fact that the two works share the same underlying idea or whether they instead indi-

---

[7]We consider the Altai test because both parties and many of the amici focus on it so heavily. Borland, in particular, is highly critical of the district court for not employing the Altai test. Borland does not, however, indicate how using that test would have been dispositive in Borland's favor. Interestingly, Borland appears to contradict its own reasoning at times by criticizing the applicability of the Altai test.

cate that the second author copied the first author's expression. The Second Circuit designed its Altai test to deal with this situation in the computer context, specifically with whether one computer program copied nonliteral expression from another program's code.

The Altai test involves three steps: abstraction, filtration, and comparison. The abstraction step requires courts to "dissect the allegedly copied program's structure and isolate each level of abstraction contained within it." Altai, 982 F.2d at 707. This step enables courts to identify the appropriate framework within which to separate protectable expression from unprotected ideas. Second, courts apply a "filtration" step in which they examine "the structural components at each level of abstraction to determine whether their particular inclusion at that level was 'idea' or was dictated by considerations of efficiency, so as to be necessarily incidental to that idea; required by factors external to the program itself; or taken from the public domain." Id. Finally, courts compare the protected elements of the infringed work (i.e., those that survived the filtration screening) to the corresponding elements of the allegedly infringing work to determine whether there was sufficient copying of protected material to constitute infringement. Id. at 710.

In the instant appeal, we are not confronted with alleged nonliteral copying of computer code. Rather, we are faced with Borland's deliberate, literal copying of the Lotus menu command hierarchy. Thus, we must determine not whether nonliteral copying occurred in some amorphous sense, but rather whether the literal copying of the Lotus menu command hierarchy constitutes copyright infringement.

While the Altai test may provide a useful framework for assessing the alleged nonliteral copying of computer code, we find it to be of little help in assessing whether the literal copying of a menu command hierarchy constitutes copyright infringement. In fact, we think that the Altai test in this context may actually be misleading because, in instructing courts to abstract the various levels, it seems to encourage them to find a base level that includes copyrightable subject matter that, if literally copied, would make the copier liable for copyright infringement.[8] While that base (or literal) level

---

[8]We recognize that Altai never states that every work contains a copyrightable "nugget" of protectable expression. Nonetheless, the implication is that for literal copying, "it is not necessary to determine the level of abstraction at which similarity ceases to consist of an 'expression of ideas,' because literal similarity by definition is always a similarity as

would not be at issue in a nonliteral-copying case like Altai, it is precisely what is at issue in this appeal. We think that abstracting menu command hierarchies down to their individual word and menu levels and then filtering idea from expression at that stage, as both the Altai and the district court tests require, obscures the more fundamental question of whether a menu command hierarchy can be copyrighted at all. The initial inquiry should not be whether individual components of a menu command hierarchy are expressive, but rather whether the menu command hierarchy as a whole can be copyrighted. But see Gates Rubber Co. v. Bando Chem. Indus., Ltd., 9 F.3d 823 (10th Cir. 1993) (endorsing Altai's abstraction-filtration-comparison test as a way of determining whether "menus and sorting criteria" are copyrightable).

D. The Lotus Menu Command Hierarchy: A "Method of Operation"

Borland argues that the Lotus menu command hierarchy is uncopyrightable because it is a system, method of operation, process, or procedure foreclosed from copyright protection by 17 U.S.C. § 102(b). Section 102(b) states: "In no case does copyright protection for an original work of authorship extend to any idea, procedure, process, system, method of operation, concept, principle, or discovery, regardless of the form in which it is described, explained, illustrated, or embodied in such work." Because we conclude that the Lotus menu command hierarchy is a method of operation, we do not consider whether it could also be a system, process, or procedure.

We think that "method of operation," as that term is used in §102(b), refers to the means by which a person operates something, whether it be a car, a food processor, or a computer. Thus a text describing how to operate something would not extend copyright protection to the method of operation itself; other people would be free to employ that method and to describe it in their own words. Similarly, if a new method of operation is used rather than described, other people would still be free to employ or describe that method.

---

to the expression of ideas." 3 Melville B. Nimmer & David Nimmer, Nimmer on Copyright § 13.03[A](2) (1993).

We hold that the Lotus menu command hierarchy is an uncopy-rightable "method of operation." The Lotus menu command hierarchy provides the means by which users control and operate Lotus 1-2-3. If users wish to copy material, for example, they use the "Copy" command. If users wish to print material, they use the "Print" command. Users must use the command terms to tell the computer what to do. Without the menu command hierarchy, users would not be able to access and control, or indeed make use of, Lotus 1-2-3's functional capabilities.

The Lotus menu command hierarchy does not merely explain and present Lotus 1-2-3's functional capabilities to the user; it also serves as the method by which the program is operated and controlled. The Lotus menu command hierarchy is different from the Lotus long prompts, for the long prompts are not necessary to the operation of the program; users could operate Lotus 1-2-3 even if there were no long prompts.[9] The Lotus menu command hierarchy is also different from the Lotus screen displays, for users need not "use" any expressive aspects of the screen displays in order to operate Lotus 1-2-3; because the way the screens look has little bearing on how users control the program, the screen displays are not part of Lotus 1-2-3's "method of operation."[10] The Lotus menu command hierarchy is also different from the underlying computer code, because while code is necessary for the program to work, its precise formulation is not. In other words, to offer the same capabilities as Lotus 1-2-3, Borland did not have to copy Lotus's underlying code (and indeed it did not); to allow users to operate its programs in substantially the same way, however, Borland had to copy the Lotus menu command hierarchy. Thus the Lotus 1-2-3 code is not a uncopyrightable "method of operation."[11]

---

[9]As the Lotus long prompts are not before us on appeal, we take no position on their copyrightability, although we do note that a strong argument could be made that the brief explanations they provide "merge" with the underlying idea of explaining such functions. See Morrissey v. Procter & Gamble Co., 379 F.2d 675, 678-79 (1st Cir. 1967) (when the possible ways to express an idea are limited, the expression "merges" with the idea and is therefore uncopyrightable; when merger occurs, identical copying is permitted).

[10]As they are not before us on appeal, we take no position on whether the Lotus 1-2-3 screen displays constitute original expression capable of being copyrighted.

[11]Because the Lotus 1-2-3 code is not before us on appeal, we take no position on whether it is copyrightable. We note, however, that original computer codes generally

The district court held that the Lotus menu command hierarchy, with its specific choice and arrangement of command terms, constituted an "expression" of the "idea" of operating a computer program with commands arranged hierarchically into menus and submenus. Borland II, 799 F. Supp. at 216. Under the district court's reasoning, Lotus's decision to employ hierarchically arranged command terms to operate its program could not foreclose its competitors from also employing hierarchically arranged command terms to operate their programs, but it did foreclose them from employing the specific command terms and arrangement that Lotus had used. In effect, the district court limited Lotus 1-2-3's "method of operation" to an abstraction.

Accepting the district court's finding that the Lotus developers made some expressive choices in choosing and arranging the Lotus command terms, we nonetheless hold that that expression is not copyrightable because it is part of Lotus 1-2-3's "method of operation." We do not think that "methods of operation" are limited to abstractions; rather, they are the means by which a user operates something. If specific words are essential to operating something, then they are part of a "method of operation" and, as such, are unprotectable. This is so whether they must be highlighted, typed in, or even spoken, as computer programs no doubt will soon be controlled by spoken words.

The fact that Lotus developers could have designed the Lotus menu command hierarchy differently is immaterial to the question of whether it is a "method of operation." In other words, our initial inquiry is not whether the Lotus menu command hierarchy incorporates any expression.[12] Rather, our initial inquiry is whether the Lotus menu command hierarchy is a "method of operation." Concluding, as we do, that users operate Lotus 1-2-3 by using the Lotus menu command hierarchy, and that the entire Lotus menu command hierarchy is essential to operating Lotus 1-2-3, we do not inquire further whether that method of operation could have been designed differently. The "expressive" choices of what to name the command terms and how to arrange them do not magically change the uncopyrightable menu command hierarchy into copyrightable subject matter.

---

are protected by copyright. See, e.g., Altai, 982 F.2d at 702 ("It is now well settled that the literal elements of computer programs, i.e., their source and object codes, are the subject of copyright protection.") (citing cases).

[12] We think that the Altai test would contemplate this being the initial inquiry.

Our holding that "methods of operation" are not limited to mere abstractions is bolstered by Baker v. Selden. In Baker, the Supreme Court explained that

> the teachings of science and the rules and methods of useful art have their final end in application and use; and this application and use are what the public derive from the publication of a book which teaches them. . . . The description of the art in a book, though entitled to the benefit of copyright, lays no foundation for an exclusive claim to the art itself. The object of the one is explanation; the object of the other is use. The former may be secured by copyright. The latter can only be secured, if it can be secured at all, by letters-patent.

Baker v. Selden, 101 U.S. at 104-05. Lotus wrote its menu command hierarchy so that people could learn it and use it. Accordingly, it falls squarely within the prohibition on copyright protection established in Baker v. Selden and codified by Congress in § 102(b).

In many ways, the Lotus menu command hierarchy is like the buttons used to control, say, a video cassette recorder ("VCR"). A VCR is a machine that enables one to watch and record video tapes. Users operate VCRs by pressing a series of buttons that are typically labelled "Record, Play, Reverse, Fast Forward, Pause, Stop/Eject." That the buttons are arranged and labeled does not make them a "literary work," nor does it make them an "expression" of the abstract "method of operating" a VCR via a set of labeled buttons. Instead, the buttons are themselves the "method of operating" the VCR.

When a Lotus 1-2-3 user chooses a command, either by highlighting it on the screen or by typing its first letter, he or she effectively pushes a button. Highlighting the "Print" command on the screen, or typing the letter "P," is analogous to pressing a VCR button labeled "Play."

Just as one could not operate a buttonless VCR, it would be impossible to operate Lotus 1-2-3 without employing its menu command hierarchy. Thus the Lotus command terms are not equivalent to the labels on the VCR's buttons, but are instead equivalent to the buttons themselves. Unlike the labels on a VCR's buttons, which merely make operating a VCR easier by indicating the buttons' functions, the Lotus menu commands are essential to operating Lotus 1-2-3. Without the menu commands, there would be no way to "push" the Lotus buttons, as one could push unlabeled VCR buttons. While Lotus could probably have designed a user interface for which the command terms were mere labels, it did not do so here. Lotus 1-2-3 depends for its operation on use of the precise command terms that make up the Lotus menu command hierarchy.

One might argue that the buttons for operating a VCR are not analogous to the commands for operating a computer program because VCRs are not copyrightable, whereas computer programs are. VCRs may not be copyrighted because they do not fit within any of the § 102(a) categories of copyrightable works; the closest they come is "sculptural work." Sculptural works, however, are subject to a "useful-article" exception whereby "the design of a useful article . . . shall be considered a pictorial, graphic, or sculptural work only if, and only to the extent that, such design incorporates pictorial, graphic, or sculptural features that can be identified separately from, and are capable of existing independently of, the utilitarian aspects of the article." 17 U.S.C. § 101. A "useful article" is "an article having an intrinsic utilitarian function that is not merely to portray the appearance of the article or to convey information." Id. Whatever expression there may be in the arrangement of the parts of a VCR is not capable of existing separately from the VCR itself, so an ordinary VCR would not be copyrightable.

Computer programs, unlike VCRs, are copyrightable as "literary works." 17 U.S.C. § 102(a). Accordingly, one might argue, the "buttons" used to operate a computer program are not like the buttons used to operate a VCR, for they are not subject to a useful-article exception. The response, of course, is that the arrangement of buttons on a VCR would not be copyrightable even without a useful-article exception, because the buttons are an uncopyrightable "method of operation." Similarly, the "buttons" of a computer program are also an uncopyrightable "method of operation."

That the Lotus menu command hierarchy is a "method of operation" becomes clearer when one considers program compatibility. Under Lotus's theory, if a user uses several different programs, he or she must learn how to perform the same operation in a different way for each program used. For example, if the user wanted the computer to print material, then the user would have to learn not just one method of operating the computer such that it prints, but many different methods. We find this absurd. The fact that there may be many different ways to operate a computer program, or even many different ways to operate a computer program using a set of hierarchically arranged command terms, does not make the actual method of operation chosen copyrightable; it still functions as a method for operating the computer and as such is uncopyrightable.

Consider also that users employ the Lotus menu command hierarchy in writing macros. Under the district court's holding, if the user wrote a macro to shorten the time needed to perform a certain operation in Lotus 1-2-3, the user would be unable to use that macro to shorten the time needed to perform that same operation in another program. Rather, the user would have to rewrite his or her macro using that other program's menu command hierarchy. This is despite the fact that the macro is clearly the user's own work product. We think that forcing the user to cause the computer to perform the same operation in a different way ignores Congress's direction in § 102(b) that "methods of operation" are not copyrightable. That programs can offer users the ability to write macros in many different ways does not change the fact that, once written, the macro allows the user to perform an operation automatically. As the Lotus menu command hierarchy serves as the basis for Lotus 1-2-3 macros, the Lotus menu command hierarchy is a "method of operation."

In holding that expression that is part of a "method of operation" cannot be copyrighted, we do not understand ourselves to go against the Supreme Court's holding in Feist. In Feist, the Court explained:

> The primary objective of copyright is not to reward the labor of authors, but to promote the Progress of Science and useful Arts. To this end, copyright assures authors the right to their original expression, but encourages others to build freely upon the ideas and information conveyed by a work.

Feist, 499 U.S. at 349-50 (quotations and citations omitted). We do not think that the Court's statement that "copyright assures authors the right to their original expression" indicates that all expression is necessarily copyrightable; while original expression is necessary for copyright protection, we do not think that it is alone sufficient. Courts must still inquire whether original expression falls within one of the categories foreclosed from copyright protection by § 102(b), such as being a "method of operation."

We also note that in most contexts, there is no need to "build" upon other people's expression, for the ideas conveyed by that expression can be conveyed by someone else without copying the first author's expression.[13] In the context of methods of operation, however, "building" requires the

---

[13]When there are a limited number of ways to express an idea, however, the expression "merges" with the idea and becomes uncopyrightable. Morrissey, 379 F.2d at 678-79.

use of the precise method of operation already employed; otherwise, "building" would require dismantling, too. Original developers are not the only people entitled to build on the methods of operation they create; anyone can. Thus, Borland may build on the method of operation that Lotus designed and may use the Lotus menu command hierarchy in doing so.

Our holding that methods of operation are not limited to abstractions goes against Autoskill, 994 F.2d at 1495 n.23, in which the Tenth Circuit rejected the defendant's argument that the keying procedure used in a computer program was an uncopyrightable "procedure" or "method of operation" under § 102(b). The program at issue, which was designed to test and train students with reading deficiencies, id. at 1481, required students to select responses to the program's queries "by pressing the 1, 2, or 3 keys." Id. at 1495 n.23. The Tenth Circuit held that, "for purposes of the preliminary injunction, . . . the record showed that [this] keying procedure reflected at least a minimal degree of creativity," as required by Feist for copyright protection. Id. As an initial matter, we question whether a programmer's decision to have users select a response by pressing the 1, 2, or 3 keys is original. More importantly, however, we fail to see how "a student selecting a response by pressing the 1, 2, or 3 keys," id., can be anything but an unprotectable method of operation.[14]

III.

Conclusion

Because we hold that the Lotus menu command hierarchy is uncopyrightable subject matter, we further hold that Borland did not infringe Lotus's copyright by copying it. Accordingly, we need not consider any of Borland's affirmative defenses. The judgment of the district court is

Reversed.

---

[14]The Ninth Circuit has also indicated in dicta that "menus, and keystrokes" may be copyrightable. Brown Bag Software v. Symantec Corp., 960 F.2d 1465, 1477 (9th Cir.), cert. denied, BB Asset Management, Inc. v. Symantec Corp., 121 L. Ed. 2d 141, 113 S. Ct. 198 (1992). In that case, however, the plaintiff did not show that the defendant had copied the plaintiff's menus or keystrokes, so the court was not directly faced with whether the menus or keystrokes constituted an unprotectable method of operation. Id.

Notes and Questions

1. In a concurring opinion, Judge Boudin considers and rejects an alternative approach to that followed in the majority opinion. Judge Boudin wonders whether Lotus might be found to maintain a copyright in the menu command hierarchy, while the court might devise a new doctrine that Borland's use of the Lotus menu command hierarchy is "privileged." This new "privileged use" doctrine would be analogous to fair use doctrine. Borland's use would be permitted because it made a distinctive contribution in its own menu command system, and it incorporated the Lotus menu only to facilitate use of its program by former Lotus users. Judge Boudin rejects this alternative because it would be difficult to administer, and outcomes would be unpredictable. He ultimately concludes that the majority result is the best alternative under imperfect circumstances. Might you prefer Judge Boudin's privileged use suggestion?

2. The *Lotus* court concludes that the menu command hierarchy is unprotectable subject matter because it constitutes a "method of operation." Yet is not a computer program itself a method of operating a computer? The program instructs the central processor regarding computations that should be undertaken, it instructs the computer where the resulting information should be transmitted, stored, displayed, and so forth. How is the menu command hierarchy distinguishable from the underlying program? Is it distinguishable only because earlier courts have held that computer software is copyrightable subject matter?

3. We are mainly concerned with how various IPRs rules are created and applied internationally. Rules relating to protection of computer software raise intriguing questions as we consider their application in diverse legal systems. Consider, for example, the complexity of the *Altai* court's three-step analysis as outlined by the *Lotus* court (i.e., abstraction, filtration and comparison). The *Altai* procedure for evaluating claims of non-literal infringement requires the evaluation of computer programs by experts who are able to follow the steps of programs written in source code. These experts must extract the essential elements of an allegedly infringed program so that the court may determine which elements were dictated by functional considerations, and it must ultimately compare the remaining expressive elements with the allegedly infringing program for substantial

similarity. This process is exceedingly difficult when all of the essential ingredients are present in the courtroom — sophisticated trial counsel, expert witnesses, and a well developed set of legal rules. Such litigation is time-consuming and expensive. How realistic is it to expect courts in countries with less sophisticated legal systems to conduct litigation based on the kind of procedure followed by the *Altai* court? Might we need some less complex and subjective rules?

One answer to the foregoing question may be that most copyright infringement complaints in countries with less sophisticated legal systems are likely to involve "literal infringement" or simple counterfeiting, such as illegal copying and distribution of program CDs with no attempt to disguise the program being copied rather than infringements between competitors, each of which is developing new programs. In such cases, complex tests such as that used by the *Altai* court will not be required. Yet consider the great and growing sophistication of the computer software industries in many developing economies and economies in transition. Is it a valid assumption that Chinese, Indian and Russian programmers are unable to modify sophisticated programs to create the impression that copying has not taken place?

4. Patents are granted for twenty years from the date of filing of the application. Copyright has a minimum term of the author's life plus fifty years (Berne Convention and TRIPS Agreement), and now for the author's life plus seventy years in the European Union and United States. Why should protection for computer software have such long duration? How many computer programs written today will be commercially relevant in fifty (or seventy) years, or even in fifteen years?

---

5. Industrial Designs

a. The Nature and Subject Matter of Industrial Designs

Producers may invest heavily in creating an outward appearance of their products which they believe will appeal to consumers. An attractively designed product may command a significantly higher price in the market than an ordinary product. To take but one example, a plain cotton T-shirt and an Italian designer blouse may serve precisely the same function in protecting a person's skin from the elements. The basic materials comprising these two products may be more or less equivalent. Yet the consumer is often willing to travel a long distance and pay a far higher price for the Italian designer blouse than the T-shirt because the designer blouse appeals to the consumer's taste or subjective preference, and because the Italian producer may have invested in advertising which the consumer associates with the attractively designed product.

Design is a particularly important means of differentiating products with similar technical performance. Thus, design is of special significance in industries where the possibilities of technological innovation have been exhausted, such as footware, clothing, furniture and crockery.

Design has an intense relationship with function. On the one hand, design possibilities are limited by function. At a certain stage, extravagance or fantasy in design can impede function. There may be endless ways in which to conceive of the appearance of a shoe or an airplane, but not all of them will result in a functional piece of footware or a vehicle that flies. On the other hand, design can facilitate function. Certain designs of motor vehicles take advantage of aerodynamics and decrease air resistance to increase speed or reduce fuel consumption.

The protection of industrial designs has long been problematic. The traditional forms of IPRs protection — copyright, patent and trademark — can be applicable in many cases, but nevertheless their application poses technical problems. Copyright, for example, protects the creative expression of artists and authors. There are few significant restrictions on the type of media in which expressions may be embodied for copyright purposes, so that many industrially applicable designs (i.e. creative expressions) will be protected by copyright. However, there are substantial drawbacks to relying on copyright for design protection. Copyright, as we have already observed, does not protect idea or function, so that copyright will not protect a design to the extent that it is functional. Distinguishing between expression and function presents legislators and courts with a formidable task. From a pragmatic enforceability standpoint, it is significant that copyright protects only against "reproduction" or copying. Independent creation is not precluded. In order to successfully pursue a copyright infringement action, the party claiming infringement must either affirmatively demonstrate that the alleged infringer copied the work, or must present circumstantial evidence (e.g., the alleged infringer had access to the work and the two works are alike) sufficient to persuade a trier of fact that copying took place.

A utility patent may protect a functional design. However, a functional design must meet the ordinary criteria for patentability: novelty, utility and non-obviousness. If a design is created to appeal to the consumer's subjective preference, that design may not be "useful" in the utility patent sense. Furthermore, a design may be new, but it may not represent a high degree of technical sophistication compared to the prior art. Its newness may reside more in an original artistic expression than in technologically improved performance characteristics. Moreover, the expense and effort that is required to obtain a utility patent, even when this is possible, may outweigh the economic gains that the producer would expect from securing one.

The design of a product is often closely associated with the trademark or brand of the producer, and trademark protection should preclude a potential competitor from marketing an identical product using the same trademark. But trademark protection is addressed to the word or symbol that constitutes the mark, rather than the whole outward appearance of the product.

The drawbacks associated with traditional forms of IPRs protection have led many countries and regions to adopt forms of protection specifically directed at industrial designs.

In general, there are two main systems for obtaining protection for industrial designs. The first, which is the most widely used throughout the world, assimilates designs more to copyright than to patents. Under this system, which is prevalent in Europe, a design is deposited or registered in the pertinent industrial property office and protection is granted without any substantive examination by the office of the novelty of the design. Countries practicing this system of protection consider that it is impossible to examine a design against the prior art, since there is no comprehensive collection of all designs made by humankind. Rather, they leave the task of ensuring that protection is not given inappropriately to the market: competitors will challenge inappropriate grants of protection when their interests are affected by protection being granted to a design that is not new.

The second system assimilates designs more to patents than to copyright. Under this system, applications for the protection of designs are subjected to a substantive examination by the concerned industrial property office. This is the system that is practiced in the United States, where it is possible to obtain a "design patent." This system, described in the *Best Lock* case below, subjects industrial designs to the usual criteria of patentability of the utility patent law, with the significant exception that a design must be "ornamental" rather than functional. In U.S. law, a design patent is granted for a period of fourteen years. As with an application for a utility patent, an application for a design patent is subject to examination by the Patent and Trademark Office. The design patent protects its holder against infringement by an independent creator; that is, the holder does not need to demonstrate that the design was copied.

Other countries that practice the substantive examination of industrial designs included Australia, Japan, Hungary, Norway, Sweden and the United Kingdom. Of these countries Australia, Sweden and the United Kingdom have abandoned the substantive examination of industrial design applications and moved to a system of simple registration.

The EU has debated the adoption of a directive on the legal protection of designs for a number of years, and in late September 1998 the organs of the Union appeared ready to conclude and adopt this directive. The directive would approximate the laws of the member states with respect to design protection, requiring each member state to adopt of system of protection meeting certain criteria. The directive would establish criteria for design protection, including that a design be "new" and "have individual character". Designs would be subject to registration, and to examination as to whether the relevant criteria for protection are met.

According to the EU directive, "design means the appearance of the whole or a part of a product resulting from the features of, in particular, the lines, contours, colours, shape, texture and/or materials of the product itself and/or its ornamentation." (Art. 1(a)). As to "individual character," a "design shall be considered to have individual character if the overall impression it produces on the informed user differs from the overall impression produced on such a user by any design which has been made available to the public before the date of filing of the application for registration or, if priority is claimed, the date of priority." (Art. 5(1)). Also, "[i]n assessing individual character, the degree of freedom of the designer in developing the design will be taken into consideration." (Art. 5(2)).

Under the EU directive, the term of the design right would be a total of twenty-five years, but the EU member states may elect to grant this right in five year increments, renewable at the request of the right holder. (Art. 10). The holder of a design right would have "the exclusive right to use [the design] and to prevent any third party not having his consent from using it," including through making, offering, putting on the market, importing, exporting, using or stocking (Art. 12(1)). These rights would be expressly subject to the rule of intra-Union exhaustion (Art. 15).

The major stumbling block to adoption of the EU directive on the legal protection of designs related to controversy over the treatment of automobile spare parts. The EC Commission had proposed a system of equitable remuneration which would have permitted makers of visible spare parts (e.g., bumpers) to use designs of the automobile producers. Ultimately, a compromise on this issue left it in the hands of the member states for the time being.

The *Volvo* decision of the Swiss Federal Court, which follows the *Best Lock* case, illustrates the application of design protection legislation to automobile spare parts. This decision reflects one continental European approach to industrial design protection, although it should be recalled that Switzerland is not an EU member state.

While there is a multilateral agreement administered by WIPO which provides a system for the deposit of industrial designs (The Hague Agreement Concerning the International Deposit of Industrial Designs, initially concluded in 1925), this agreement has a rather limited membership (29 Contracting States) and is at present not widely used. Negotiations are ongoing in WIPO for a revision of the Hague Agreement that would accommodate the interests of a wider number of countries. A diplomatic conference will be held in June 1999 to conclude the new Act of the Hague Agreement. The aims of the diplomatic conference are twofold. First, it is desired to change the fee and registration system to accommodate the interests of the fashion and textile industries, which typically produce a large number of designs, only a few of which prove to be commercially successful. Rather than having to pay full registration fees for all designs produced and registered, it is planned to enable a fraction of the fees to be paid on application, with the remainder payable only in respect of those designs for which the creators wish to continue to seek protection. Secondly, the Hague Agreement was designed for countries having a simple registration system of protection and it is planned to revise it so as to permit countries practicing substantive examination of industrial design applications to participate also in the Agreement.

The WTO TRIPS Agreement (Art. 25) obligates Members to protect industrial designs that are new or original for a period of ten years. Members may exclude functional designs from such protection. Members are to assure that textile designs are subject to protection through a system which does not impose unreasonable cost, examination or publication hurdles. Copyright protection may be used for this protection of textile designs. The holder of a design right shall be able to prevent others from making, selling or importing articles embodying the design.

---

b. Design Patent

Best Lock Corporation, Plaintiff-Appellant, v. Ilco Unican Corporation, Defendant-Appellee.

United States Court of Appeals for the Federal Circuit
94 F.3d 1563; 1996 U.S. App. LEXIS 22415 (1996)

Prior History: Appealed from: U.S. District Court for the Southern District of Indiana (Indianapolis). Judge McKinney.

Disposition: Affirmed
Judges: Before Archer, Chief Judge, Newman and Lourie, Circuit Judges. Opinion for the Court Filed by Circuit Judge Lourie. Dissenting Opinion Filed by Circuit Judge Newman.
Opinion: Lourie, Circuit Judge.

Best Lock Corporation appeals from the final decision of the United States District Court for the Southern District of Indiana in which the court held that Best Lock's U.S. Design Patent 327,636 was invalid. Best Lock Corp. v. Ilco Unican Corp., 896 F. Supp. 836, 36 U.S.P.Q.2D (BNA) 1527 (S.D. Ind. 1995). Because the court did not clearly err in finding that the claimed design was functional and hence not ornamental, we affirm.

Background

This case involves a design patent for a key "blade." A typical key consists of a bow, which allows the user to turn the key in a corresponding lock, and a blade, which is the portion of the key inserted into the lock's keyway. When a key is manufactured, the key blade is "blank," i.e., the blade has not been cut or "bitted" with the combination required to operate the corresponding lock. Although a blank key blade will not operate the lock, the profile of the key blade is manufactured to fit into the corresponding lock's keyway. Subsequently, the blank key blade is cut to match the corresponding lock's combination.

In the replacement key market, a locksmith or a retail store with a key duplicating facility stocks blank key blades with various key profiles. The locksmith or retailer makes a replacement key by first selecting the appropriate blank key blade. This is done by matching the key blade profile with the corresponding lock keyway. Then, the locksmith or retailer cuts the blade of the key blank with the combination required to operate the lock.

Best Lock manufactures and sells locks and keys used to maintain security at industrial, commercial, and institutional facilities. At these facilities, it is often feared that the keys used in their locks may readily be duplicated. Consequently, key and lock manufacturers, including Best Lock, have attempted to restrict unauthorized access to duplicate key blanks by obtaining utility or design patent protection on the keys. By obtaining patent protection, a company hopes to control the market for duplicate key blanks during the life of the patent.[1]

Best Lock is the assignee of the two patents that were at issue before the district court, U.S. Patent 5,136,869 and U.S. Design Patent 327,636. The '869 patent, entitled "High Security Key and Cylinder Lock Assembly," claims an improved key blade and cylinder lock assembly that provides a wider key profile than standard keys and includes other features to deter lock picking. The '636 patent, entitled "Portion of a Key Blade Blank," claims the ornamental design for the operative portion of a key blade blank. In addition to the '636 design patent, Best Lock is the assignee of 33 other design patents on key blade designs. It also is the assignee of 34 design patents directed to keyways designed to mate with the key blades claimed in Best Lock's 34 key blade design patents. The '636 patent is the only design patent at issue on appeal. . . .

Ilco manufactures duplicate and replacement key blanks for existing locks. It sells its replacement key blanks to locksmiths and replacement key retailers. In 1993, Ilco copied the design of a Best Lock key, which had a key

---

[1] Key and lock manufacturers also use other methods to restrict access to duplicate key blanks. For example, some manufacturers limit the sale of a particular type of lock and key to a single customer or particular geographic region, thereby making consumer demand for replacement keys for that particular lock design so small that replacement key manufacturers have no incentive to manufacture duplicate key blanks.

blade shaped like the design shown in the '636 patent. It subsequently distributed key blanks with that key blade shape at the annual convention of the Associated Locksmiths of America. In response, Best sued Ilco, alleging, inter alia, infringement of the '636 design patent and the '869 utility patent. Ilco counterclaimed, seeking a declaratory judgment of invalidity and noninfringement of both patents.

After a ten-day bench trial, the district court held that the '869 patent claims were invalid under 35 U.S.C. § 102 because the claims were anticipated by the prior art. Best Lock Corp. v. Ilco Unican Corp., 896 F. Supp. 836, 837, 36 U.S.P.Q.2D (BNA) 1527, 1528 (S.D. Ind. 1995). Best Lock has not appealed that holding. The court also held that the '636 design patent was invalid. In particular, the court found that Best Lock's key blades were not "a matter of ornamental concern to the purchaser or the user." Id. at 843, 36 U.S.P.Q.2D (BNA) at 1534. The court further found that the design patent was invalid because the shape of the blank key blade was dictated by its function. Id. Best Lock appeals, challenging the district court's decision regarding the '636 patent.

Discussion

Under 35 U.S.C. § 171, a design patent may be granted for a "new, original and ornamental design for an article of manufacture." However, if the design claimed in a design patent is dictated solely by the function of the article of manufacture, the patent is invalid because the design is not ornamental. See Bonito Boats, Inc. v. Thunder Craft Boats, Inc., 489 U.S. 141, 148, 9 U.S.P.Q.2D (BNA) 1847, 1851, 103 L. Ed. 2d 118, 109 S. Ct. 971 (1989) ("To qualify for protection, a design must present an aesthetically pleasing appearance that is not dictated by function alone, and must satisfy the other criteria of patentability."); see also In re Carletti, 51 C.C.P.A. 1094, 328 F.2d 1020, 1022, 140 U.S.P.Q. (BNA) 653, 654 (CCPA 1964) ("It has long been settled that when a configuration is the result of functional considerations only, the resulting design is not patentable as an ornamental design for the simple reason that it is not 'ornamental' — was not created for the purpose of ornamenting."). A design is not dictated solely by its function when alternative designs for the article of manufacture are available. See L.A. Gear, Inc. v. Thom McAn Shoe Co., 988 F.2d 1117, 1123, 25 U.S.P.Q.2D (BNA) 1913, 1917 (Fed. Cir.), cert. denied, 510 U.S. 908, 114 S. Ct. 291, 126 L. Ed. 2d 240 (1993). We review for clear error the district court's determination that the design claimed in the '636 patent is functional. See id. at 1124, 25 U.S.P.Q.2D (BNA) at 1917.

On appeal, Best Lock argues that the court erred in holding the '636 design patent invalid as being directed solely to a functional design. As support, it asserts that although a particular key and its corresponding lock must mate to operate the lock, an unlimited number of key blade and corresponding keyway designs are available. Choice of any particular design is arbitrary. Thus, Best Lock maintains that the key blade blank may have any number of different shapes and is therefore not dictated solely by functional concerns.

We disagree. The design shown in the claim of the '636 patent is limited to a blank key blade as shown in Figures 1-5 of the patent. Best Lock did not claim a design for the entire key.[2] See 37 C.F.R. § 1.153 (1995) (The claim of a design patent "shall be in formal terms to the ornamental design for the article . . . as shown, or as shown and described.") (emphasis added). The parties do not dispute that the key blade must be designed as shown in order to perform its intended function — to fit into its corresponding lock's keyway. An attempt to create a key blade with a different design would necessarily fail because no alternative blank key blade would fit the corresponding lock. In fact, Best Lock admitted that no other shaped key blade would fit into the corresponding keyway, and it presented no evidence to the contrary. Therefore, we find no clear error in the court's finding that the claimed key blade design was dictated solely by the key blade's function. Any aesthetic appeal of the key blade design shown in the '636 patent is the inevitable result of having a shape that is dictated solely by functional concerns.

Further, Best Lock's assertion that a variety of possible shapes of interfaces between keys and locks exists does not compel a different result. Clearly, different interfaces between key blades and corresponding lock keyways can be designed to permit the combination to function as a lock and key set. However, Best Lock's patent does not claim the combination of a lock and corresponding key. Instead, the claim in the '636 design patent is limited to a key blade, which must be designed as shown in the '636 patent in order to perform its intended function.

---

[2] As our predecessor court previously held, a design for an article of manufacture may be embodied in less than all of an article of manufacture. . . . at In re Zahn, 617 F.2d 261, 267, 204 U.S.P.Q. (BNA) 988, 994 (CCPA 1980).

Moreover, the fact that Best Lock also has a design patent on the keyway that mates with the key blade shown in the '636 patent does not alter our analysis. The existence of a separate patent on the keyway is irrelevant to the construction of the '636 patent claim and to the ultimate determination that the claimed design is dictated solely by function. See Elmer v. ICC Fabricating, Inc., 67 F.3d 1571, 1577, 36 U.S.P.Q.2D (BNA) 1417, 1421 (Fed. Cir. 1995) (construing design patent as limited to the article of manufacture "as shown and described" in the patent). The validity of a patent must be evaluated based on what it claims rather than on the totality of the claims of multiple patents.

For the foregoing reasons, the district court's finding that the claimed design is solely governed by functional concerns is not clearly erroneous. Consequently, we affirm its resulting conclusion that the '636 patent is invalid under 35 U.S.C. § 171 for failure to satisfy the statute's ornamentality requirement.

Affirmed

Dissent: Newman, Circuit Judge, dissenting.

I respectfully dissent. The design of this key blade profile meets the statutory criteria of design patent subject matter. The design statute defines this subject matter as follows:

> 35 U.S.C. §171 Patents for designs
> Whoever invents any new, original and ornamental design for an article of manufacture may obtain a patent therefor, subject to the conditions and requirements of this title.
> The provisions of this title relating to patents for inventions shall apply to patents for designs, except as otherwise provided.

Whether the design of the D'636 patent is otherwise patentable, for example on the criteria of originality or non-obviousness, was not reached by the district court and is not before us. However, the panel majority has misapplied 35 U.S.C. '171 in holding that the arbitrary design of the key profile is "functional" because it mates with its matching keyway.

The design of the key profile is not removed from access to the design statute because the key fits a matching keyway. That two articles are designed in harmony does not deprive the design of access to the design patent law. The design of the key profile is not determined by the function of the key to fit the lock. In the case at bar there are said to be "thousands" of alternative key blade profiles.

The district court concluded that the design of the D'636 patent was not "a matter of ornamental concern to the purchaser or the user," and thus held that the design was functional. The statute requires that the subject of a design patent be an ornamental design of a useful object. However, "ornamental" does not always mean artistic or pleasing to the eye. The Court of Customs and Patent Appeals early recognized that "the beauty and ornamentation requisite in design patents is not confined to such as may be found in the 'aesthetic or fine arts.'" In re Koehring, 17 C.C.P.A. 774, 37 F.2d 421, 422 (CCPA 1930).

Recognizing that ornamentation is in the eye of the beholder, the courts have sought a more objective standard in the general rule that a design is "ornamental" for purposes of 35 U.S.C. §171 when it is not primarily functional. See In re Carletti, 51 C.C.P.A. 1094, 328 F.2d 1020, 140 U.S.P.Q. (BNA) 653 (CCPA 1964) ("To qualify for protection, a design must present an aesthetically pleasing appearance that is not dictated by function alone."). However, the article itself must have a utility in order for its design features to be patentable under 35 U.S.C. §171. See L.A. Gear, Inc. v. Thom McAn Shoe Co., 988 F.2d 1117, 1123, 25 U.S.P.Q.2D (BNA) 1913, 1917 (Fed. Cir.) ("A design patent is directed to the appearance of an article of manufacture. An article of manufacture necessarily serves a utilitarian purpose, and the design of a useful article is deemed to be functional when the appearance of the claimed design is 'dictated by' the use or purpose of the article."), cert. denied, 510 U.S. 908, 126 L. Ed. 2d 240, 114 S. Ct. 291 (1993).

If the design is dictated by the function performed by the article of manufacture, the design is not patentable. Power Controls Corp. v. Hybrinetics, Inc., 806 F.2d 234, 238, 231 U.S.P.Q. (BNA) 774, 777 (Fed. Cir. 1986). See Bonito Boats, Inc. v. Thunder Craft Boats, Inc., 489 U.S. 141, 148, 9 U.S.P.Q.2D (BNA) 1847, 1851, 103 L. Ed. 2d 118, 109 S. Ct. 971 (1989) ("To qualify for protection, a design must present an aesthetically pleasing appearance that is not dictated by function alone, and must satisfy the other criteria of patentability."). A design is "not dictated by function alone" when there are alternative designs or configurations available for the article of manufacture, as in the case before us.

The legal principles governing design patents have their foundation in the important decision of Gorham Co. v. White, 81 U.S. (14 Wall.) 511, 20 L. Ed. 731 (1871), wherein the Supreme Court explained:

The appearance may be the result of peculiarity of configuration, or of ornament alone, or of both conjointly, but, in whatever way produced, it is the new thing, or product, which the patent law regards.

81 U.S. at 525. Courts have measured the term "ornamental" by the non-functionality that distinguishes the subject of a design patent from a utility patent, while recognizing that the design of a useful article is not insulated from the utility of the article. A review of patentable designs in general illustrates the mixture of functional and non-functional features embraced in the patented design. See, e.g., Winner Int'l Corp. v. Wolo Mfg. Corp., 905 F.2d 375, 15 U.S.P.Q.2D (BNA) 1076 (Fed. Cir. 1990) (design of steering wheel lock); Lee v. Dayton-Hudson Corp., 838 F.2d 1186, 5 U.S.P.Q.2D (BNA) 1625 (Fed. Cir. 1988) (design patent for massage device); FMC Corp. v. Hennessy Indus., Inc., 836 F.2d 521, 5 U.S.P.Q.2D (BNA) 1272 (Fed. Cir. 1987) (design patent for changer for tubeless tires); Unette Corp. v. Unit Pack Co., 785 F.2d 1026, 228 U.S.P.Q. (BNA) 933 (Fed. Cir. 1986) (container for dispensing liquids); In re Igarashi, 228 U.S.P.Q. (BNA) 463 (Bd. Pat. App. & Interf. 1985) (tire tread design); Trans-World Mfg. Corp. v. Al Nyman & Sons, Inc., 750 F.2d 1552, 224 U.S.P.Q. (BNA) 259 (Fed. Cir. 1984) (design for eyeglass display rack).

An effective design patent law must recognize the distinction between functionality of the article and of the particular design of the article or features thereof. See L.A. Gear, supra, (the sneaker tongue, moustache, delta wing, and side mesh, were useful parts of the sneaker, but the overall design of these features and the shoe was not dictated by function alone). This interaction of form and function does not remove the design from the statutory scope of the design patent law, or defeat the statutory patentability of a primarily non-functional design, although it is not always easy to draw a bright line between the functionality of an article and its design, as discussed by J.H. Reichman, Design Protection and the New Technologies: The United States Experience in a Transnational Perspective, 19 Balt. L. Rev. 6 (1989), for design patents often appear on quite mundane articles of manufacture. See, e.g., Tone Bros., Inc. v. Sysco Corp., 28 F.3d 1192, 31 U.S.P.Q.2D (BNA) 1321 (Fed. Cir. 1994) (bottle for spices); In re Klein, 987 F.2d 1569, 26 U.S.P.Q.2D (BNA) 1133 (Fed. Cir. 1993) (roof or siding shingle); KeyStone Retaining Wall Sys., Inc. v. Westrock, Inc., 997 F.2d 1444, 27 U.S.P.Q.2D (BNA) 1297 (Fed. Cir. 1993) (concrete block for retaining wall); In re Webb, 916 F.2d 1553, 16 U.S.P.Q.2D (BNA) 1433 (Fed. Cir. 1990) (femoral hip stem prosthesis); In re Cho, 813 F.2d 378, 1 U.S.P.Q.2D (BNA)

1662 (Fed. Cir. 1987) (bottle cap); Pacific Furniture Mfg. Co. v. Preview Furniture Corp., 800 F.2d 1111, 231 U.S.P.Q. (BNA) 67 (Fed. Cir. 1986) (upholstered armchair); Litton Sys., Inc. v. Whirlpool Corp., 728 F.2d 1423, 221 U.S.P.Q. (BNA) 97 (Fed. Cir. 1984) (microwave oven); In re Koehring, 17 C.C.P.A. 774, 37 F.2d 421 (CCPA 1930) (concrete mixing truck).

The design of the key blade profile is primarily non-functional, as the Patent and Trademark Office recognized in granting the patent in suit. The Manual of Patent Examining Procedure defines "design" as follows for purposes of §171:

> The design of an object consists of the visual characteristics or aspects displayed by the object. It is the appearance presented by the object which creates a visual impact upon the mind of the observer.

Since a design is manifested in appearance, the subject matter of a design patent application may relate to the configuration or shape of an object, to the surface ornamentation on an object, or both.

Design is inseparable from the object to which it is applied and cannot exist alone merely as a scheme of surface ornamentation. It must be a definite, preconceived thing, capable of reproduction and not merely the chance result of a method. MPEP §1502 (6th ed. 1995). See also 1 D. Chisum, Patents §1.04[2][a] (1996) ("[A] design rests on appearance created by the configuration of the article, surface ornamentation, or a combination of configuration and ornamentation.") (footnote omitted).

The parties to this litigation agree that there are myriad possible designs of key profiles. All keys require, of course, mating keyways. In holding that because the key must fit a keyway, the abstract design of the key profile is converted to one solely of function, the court creates an exception to design patent subject matter. An arbitrary design of a useful article is not statutorily excluded from §171 simply because in use it interacts with an article of complementary design. Although precedent is sparse, it is contrary to this holding. In Motorola Inc. v. Alexander Mfg. Co., 786 F. Supp. 808, 21 U.S.P.Q.2D (BNA) 1573 (N.D. Iowa 1991), the only United States case on this point of which we are aware, the court considered a design patent for a battery housing intended for use in a portable phone. Since the battery housing had to fit into the phone and a battery charger, the accused infringer argued that this function dictated the design. The court disagreed:

> The design of the battery housing was not dictated by the design of the battery charger because the charger did not exist when the housing was

designed. The design of the phone was done concurrently with the battery housing. Therefore, the design of the battery housing cannot fairly be said to have been "dictated" by the design of the phone.

Id. at 812, 21 U.S.P.Q.2D at 1557. This reasoning is equally apt in this case. The design of the key profile was not dictated by the design of the keyway, and indeed the two share the same arbitrary design.

In sum, the fact that the key blade is the mate of a keyway does not convert the arbitrary key profile into a primarily functional design. It is not the design of the key profile that is functional, but the key itself. Thus I must, respectfully, dissent from the ruling of the panel majority that the design of the key blade profile is not patentable because the key blade requires a mating keyway.

Notes and Questions

1. Do you think the decision might have been different if Best Lock Corp. had registered the key blades and the lock as one design?

2. Why must a design be ornamental to be protected? Some countries provide protection for utility models, which incorporate functionally useful features. Might it make sense to combine the concepts of the design patent and the utility model?

3. It is sometimes said that design protection lies between the copyright and patent right — that is, somewhere between the protection of expression and idea. The design right fills a gap lying between these two forms of protection. What other forms of intellectual creation fall into gaps between different forms of protection?

4. During the Uruguay Round TRIPS Agreement negotiations, some industries actively sought improvements in design protection while other industries opposed them. The automotive industry favored lower standards for protection of designs, while the insurance industry sought to increase the required level of originality. The clothing fashion design industry complained about the inefficiency of industrial design protection and called for more a efficient and rapid registration system (or improved protection

through copyright). Why did these industries take the positions that they did?

---

c. Industrial Design

AB Volvo v. FH SA

Bundesgericht (Swiss Federal Court)
SMI 1991, 153 ff.*
15 October 1990

*****

Plaintiff is the owner of the registered industrial design no. 107 439 for a left-side fender that was installed in Volvo automobiles of the 200 series from 1975 onwards. Since 1986 at the latest, defendant — dealing in automobile accessories and spare parts — has been on the market offering fenders which emanate from his own production and which correspond to the registered industrial design. On March 16th 1988, plaintiff sued defendant at the Canton of Zurich's Court of Commerce (Handelsgericht des Kantons Zürich) for ascertainment of an infringement of industrial design and of a violation of competition, for abstaining from such activities in the future, for production of privileged documents, for damages, and for publication of the decision; defendant is counterclaiming for cancellation of industrial design no. 107 439.

On February 27th 1990, the Court of Commerce rejected the suit and did not enter judgment for the counterclaim because the duration of protection for plaintiff's industrial design had expired in December 1989. Plaintiff is appealing against the Court of Commerce's decision and is pursuing his original claims.

The Federal Supreme Court takes into consideration:

(2) The Court of Commerce has denied the registered fender its protectability as an industrial design on the grounds that the shape is to a large

---

*Translation by B. Austin.

extent conditioned by technical necessity and is lacking in the required novelty. Plaintiff maintains that the court of first instance applied the terms of federal law of "industrial design" in the sense of Industrial Design Act, art. 2 as well as "novelty" in the sense of Industrial Design Act, art. 12 (1) incorrectly and had therefore erred in not imposing the sanctions pursuant to articles 24 (2 to 4), 25, and 30 against defendant.

a)

aa) Industrial Design Act, art. 2 defines an industrial design which is amenable to legal protection as an external design, also in conjunction with colors, which is meant to serve as the prototype for the commercial manufacturing of an object. Moreover, from Industrial Design Act, art. 3 it follows that the shape has to be given to the object in order to appeal to one's taste or one's sense of beauty (Federal Supreme Court Reporter (hereafter "FSCR") 95 II 472): protection for industrial design cannot be claimed for a shape that is conditioned by the manner of its production, by requirements of usefulness or by the technical effect of an object.

bb) Registration of an industrial design is invalid if it is not novel at the time of registration, i.e. if it is already known to the general public or to concerned business circles (Industrial Design Act, art. 12 (1); FSCR 105 II 299 Cons. 2; 104 II 326 Cons. 3). The novelty of an industrial design is to be negated, too, if the owner himself has made use of it before registration (FSCR 104 II 326 Cons. 3a with reference).

cc) According to jurisdiction, a shape does not have to be the result of a creative activity in order to qualify for protection as an industrial design; yet neither may it be obvious but instead must lend itself to a certain originality and therefore be seen to have commanded a minimal amount of mental effort (FSCR 104 II 329 Cons. 3; 95 II 429, 92 II 204 Cons. 4). On the one hand, this originality and material novelty is given to shapes whose characteristic features cannot be detected in the previously known, on the other hand, also in industrial designs that build upon previously known shapes yet simultaneously rearrange them in a fashion that a significantly different and uniform effect comes into being; such an effect is lacking when a previously known shape is solely altered in its details or when previously known shapes are assembled as a mosaic and are not brought to a clearly recognizable uniform effect (Troller, Immaterialgüterrecht, 3rd edition, p. 406).

The degree of originality that is required in order to establish the protectability of an industrial design corresponds to the limits that the law states for the imitation of protected shapes (FSCR 84 II 661 Cons. 2e). Accordingly, the distinctness from the previously known must be evident and not merely perceptible upon careful comparison Industrial Design Act, art. 24 11)). In this case, it is not the abilities of observation or evaluation of an expert but those of an interested layman, especially one entertaining intentions to purchase, that must be taken into consideration; although the layman must demonstrate a certain attentiveness in his observation of the objects to be compared, his judgment will be influenced more by his overall impression and by common features than by minor deviations (FSCR 83 II 484; see also FSCR 104 II 330; 84 II 661 Cons. 2e; Furler, Kommentar zum deutschen Geschmacksmustergesetz, N. 18 f of § 5).

dd) A peculiarity exists in this case under consideration insofar as fenders form a component of the automobile's body as a whole, therefore their aesthetic effect is not intended to unfold for themselves alone but rather for a greater whole. Therefore, it appears appropriate to view the registered fender in its aesthetic function within the automobile's body as a whole — as demanded by plaintiff — and not in isolation from it (see Nirk/Kurze, Kommentar zum deutschen Geschmacksmustergesetz, N. 55 ff. of § 1; BGH in GRUR 89/1987, p. 518 ff., with remarks by Gerstenberg). However, it remains to be stressed that in order to be able to judge the protectability only the aesthetic effect of the object registered as an industrial design can be taken into account; plaintiff, too, recognizes this explicitly. The outcome of this case, therefore, does not depend upon the novelty or originality of the automobile's body as a whole; rather, it is only decisive whether a novel and sufficiently original aesthetic effect is emanating from the fenders within this scope.

b)

aa) With his industrial design no. 107 439, plaintiff has only registered the left-side fender of the Volvo automobile of the 200 series. Defendant subscribes to the point of view that, therefore, as regards the right-side fender an infringement of industrial design cannot come into question in the first place. Whether this is, in fact, the case can be left undecided, since the registered industrial design is invalid anyway, as the following will demonstrate.

bb) Undisputedly, the Volvo automobile of the 200 series is identical to the older 100 series from the windscreen onwards to the rear. In the front section the following differences to the predecessor series strike the eye: the grill of the radiator is designed differently, the headlights and blinkers are arranged differently and the bumper has become more massive. The drawing of lines at the front end of the fender had to be adapted to these changes. For the protection of industrial design' however, this adaptation must be disregarded because it is conditioned by technical necessity, as correctly pointed out by the Court of Commerce, since it guarantees as seamless as possible a connection to the adjacent parts of the automobile's body — which is in itself already required for reasons of aerodynamics. As for the rest, the differences between the fender of the 200 series and those of the 100 series are negligible: the omission for the wheel is marginally larger, the upper edge slopes off slightly less precipitously, at the lower edge the line from the omission for the wheel to the bumper is drawn somewhat differently, and, finally, the new fender is a little longer than its predecessor. In contrast to this, the elements decisive for one's overall impression — the wide, smooth side-surface and the progression of the decorative ledge — have remained unaltered. Especially when the fenders are not viewed in isolation but rather in the context of the entire automobile's body, it becomes apparent that new aesthetical accentuations that may claim a certain originality for themselves are not set by the fenders but by the grill of the radiator, the headlights, the blinkers and the bumper. When the Court of Commerce reaches the conclusion that, in contrast to the 100 series, the fender of the 200 series is wanting in originality prerequisite for its protection as an industrial design, this would appear to be thoroughly appropriate; by no means can it be claimed that the court of first instance violated federal laws.

cc) For the protectability of plaintiff's registered industrial design to be denied it suffices that the required originality is lacking when compared with the fender of the previous series which itself was not protected as an industrial design. Furthermore, whether the design of the registered fender coincided with numerous other shapes of fenders, as assumed by the Court of Commerce, may be left undecided. Plaintiff's complaints of a violation of Civil Law Code, art. 8 and of an "obvious oversight" in the sense of Court Organization Act, art. 63 (2) in this context are void as far as there need not be a judgment entered in any event due to a lack of substantiation (Court Organization Act, art. 55 (1) let. c) (Cons. lb ex ante).

Notes and Questions

1. The Swiss Federal Court discusses the degree of novelty or originality necessary to qualify for industrial design protection. What criteria do utility patent laws use to determine whether inventions are sufficiently creative in light of prior art? Does the criterion of non-obviousness (or inventive step) play this role?

2. Why does Volvo's claim for industrial design protection fail? If Volvo had registered its earlier fender design, would this have made a difference?

3. Most automobile manufacturers would assert that their cars are "aerodynamically" shaped so as to avoid wind resistance, and to enhance traction. If the shape of an automobile body is intended to improve a car's aerodynamic characteristics, does this preclude industrial design protection for its replacement body parts? Does this functional aspect preclude copyright protection?

6. Trademark

a. The Nature and Function of the Trademark

A trademark[1] is a sign used on a good or in connection with the marketing of a product, including goods and services. Saying that the sign is used "on" a good or "in connection with the marketing" of a product means that it may appear not only on the goods themselves, but also on the container or wrapper of the goods when they are sold. Saying that the sign is used "in connection with the marketing" of a product refers mainly to the appearance of the sign in advertisements (newspaper, television, etc.) or in the windows of the stores in which the product is sold. Where a trademark is used in connection with services, it is sometimes specifically called a "ser-

---

[1] In the United States, "trademark" is generally spelled as a single word. In Europe, "trade mark" is generally spelled as two words. In this book, the U.S. spelling convention is used, except in reference to EU legislation in which the European convention is formally used.

128

vice mark." Service marks are used, for example, in connection with the operation of hotels, airlines, banks, insurance companies and travel agencies. With the growth of service industries such marks and their protection have become as important as traditional trademarks relating to goods. Generally speaking, it can be said that the trademark is for the consumer the most visible and most tangible form of intellectual property.

Trademark laws confer on the proprietor the exclusive right to prevent all third parties not having the consent of the owner from using in the course of trade any sign which is identical with the trademark or any sign whose similarity to the trademark is such that there exists a likelihood of confusion on the part of the public between the sign and the trademark. From the consumer point of view, a trademark is a symbol needed to distinguish between competing products and services in a market economy that is increasingly complex. Many distribution channels and distance lie between the producer and the consumer. The trademark is the recognizable sign that the consumer can use in distributed markets to associate the product with its origin. The protection of trademarks is without limitation in time. Initial registration and each renewal of a trademark has to be for a term of at least seven years under the terms of the TRIPS Agreement.

In general, it may be said that trademarks traditionally perform four main functions. These functions relate to the distinguishing of marked goods and services, their origin, their quality and their promotion in the marketplace. While the first two functions mentioned concern the legal quality of the mark, the latter ones are essentially economic and commercial.

- The first and primary function of a trademark is to distinguish the products of an enterprise from products of other enterprises and to distinguish products of an enterprise from other products or services of the same enterprise. The trademark helps the consumer to identify a product which was already known to him or which was advertised.
- The second function of trademarks is to refer to a particular quality of products for which the trademark is used and stands for. Here the trademark essentially protects investment in labor and capital and the goodwill achieved through these efforts in the marketplace. The legal quality of this function, however, is controversial and not generally recognized.

- The third traditional function of a trademark is to relate a particular product to the producer. It indicates the origin of the product for which the mark is used. With the possibility, however, to detach the trademark from a particular producer and product and to license the trademark (franchising), this function no longer seems to be an essential legal component of a trademark.
- The fourth and last function of trademarks is to promote the marketing and sale of products and the marketing and rendering of services.

The sign constituting the trademark may consist of one or more distinctive words (including personal names), letters, numbers, pictures, color and drawings and the distinctive form of a product (for example, the shape of a Coke bottle). Advanced legislation even offers the possibility of including sound (sound marks and scents). In all cases, the signs must not be "descriptive" or "generic," which means they must not be commonly used in society. The purpose of excluding descriptive or generic terms is to prevent one producer from arrogating to itself the word used in the language to describe the product itself. That word should be available to all producers of the product to describe the item.

Trademarks are traditionally conferred nationally either by virtue of formal registration, or because of a reputation generated by actual trading.

The protection that law gives to a trademark consists essentially of making it illegal for any entity other than the owner of the trademark to use the trademark or a sign similar to it, at least in connection with goods for which the trademark was registered or with goods similar to such goods.

The advantage of having a trademark registered is that if a rival trader uses the same or a similar mark, it will be difficult for that rival to resist a claim that he or she is not entitled to do so. The main disadvantage of trademark registration is that it costs money. This disadvantage is accentuated if one undertaking applies for registration in many countries, which happens more and more often due to the globalization of business activities and the consequent need for a global protection. We will see how international registration systems accommodate this need.

From an international point of view, the concept of national trademark protection, as with the exclusivity of other intellectual property rights, leads to the partitioning of international markets. It will be seen that the main problems relating to trademarks in international and European law relate to this aspect.

---

b. Color as Trademark

Qualitex v. Jacobson is a landmark decision of the U.S. Supreme Court addressing the question whether or not, and under which circumstances, the Lanham Trademark Act of 1946 permits registration of color alone as a trademark. According to the Court, a mere color, purely and simply, may meet the basic legal requirements for use as a trademark, based upon the broad and encompassing wording of the statute, as well as underlying principles of trademark law.

The Court notes that a color is capable of satisfying the more important part of the definition of a trademark, which requires that a person "use" or "intend to use" the mark in order to "identify and distinguish his or her goods, including a unique product, from those manufactured or sold by others and to indicate the source of the goods, even if that source is unknown." This is the first function of trademark law referred to above.

The Court further notes that trademark law, by preventing others from copying, reduces the consumers's costs of shopping and the cost of making purchasing decisions. It quickly and easily assures a potential customer that the item with the mark is made by the same producer as other similarly marked items that he or she liked or disliked in the past. This correlates to the second function of trademarks listed in the introductory note.

Further, the Court notes that trademark law helps to assure a producer that it will reap the financial, reputation-related rewards associated with a desirable product. This is the fourth and last function related to the marketing and sale of products and the marketing and rendering of services.

There is no reference in this case to the third traditional function of trademark which is to relate a particular product to the producer by way of indicating the origin of the product for which the mark is used. Indeed, the consumer is not interested in the genealogy of trademarks. As we noted above, this function is controversial. The *Ideal Standard*[1] case decided by

---

[1] *See infra*, § B, 8, c.

the European Court of Justice nevertheless illustrates that the function of trademarks as indication of the origin of a product still is of importance in the context of consumer confusion.

Qualitex Company, Petitioner v. Jacobson Products Company, Inc.

Supreme Court of the United States
514 U.S. 159; 115 S. Ct. 1300; 1995 U.S. LEXIS 2408
March 28, 1995, Decided

Prior History: On Writ of Certiorari to the United States Court of Appeals for the Ninth Circuit.

Disposition: 13 F.3d 1297, reversed.

Syllabus:

Petitioner Qualitex Company has for years colored the dry cleaning press pads it manufactures with a special shade of green-gold. After respondent Jacobson Products (a Qualitex rival) began to use a similar shade on its own press pads, Qualitex registered its color as a trademark and added a trademark infringement count to the suit it had previously filed challenging Jacobson's use of the green-gold color. Qualitex won in the District Court, but the Ninth Circuit set aside the judgment on the infringement claim because, in its view, the Lanham Trademark Act of 1946 does not permit registration of color alone as a trademark.

Held: The Lanham Act permits the registration of a trademark that consists, purely and simply, of a color.

(a) That color alone can meet the basic legal requirements for use as a trademark is demonstrated both by the language of the Act, which describes the universe of things that can qualify as a trademark in the broadest of terms, 15 U.S.C. § 1127, and by the underlying principles of trademark law, including the requirements that the mark "identify and distinguish [the seller's] goods . . . from those manufactured or sold by others and to indicate [their] source," ibid., and that it not be "functional," see, e.g., Inwood Laboratories, Inc. v. Ives Laboratories, Inc., 456 U.S. 844, 850, n. 10, 72 L. Ed. 2d 606, 102 S. Ct. 2182. The District Court's findings (accepted by the Ninth Circuit and here undisputed) show Qualitex's green-gold color has met these requirements. It acts as a symbol. Because customers identify the color as Qualitex's, it has developed secondary meaning, see, e.g., id., at 851, n. 11, and thereby identifies the press pads' source. And, the color serves no other function. (Although it is important to use some color on press pads to avoid noticeable stains, the court found no competitive need in the industry for the green-gold color, since other colors are equally usable.) Accordingly, unless there is some special reason that convincingly militates against the use of color alone as a trademark, trademark law protects Qualitex's use of its green-gold color.

(b) Jacobson's various special reasons why the law should forbid the use of color alone as a trademark — that a contrary holding (1) will produce uncertainty and unresolvable court disputes about what shades of a color a competitor may lawfully use; (2) is unworkable in light of the limited supply of colors that will soon be depleted by competitors; (3) is contradicted by many older cases, including decisions of this Court interpreting pre-Lanham Act trademark law; and (4) is unnecessary because firms already may use color as part of a trademark and may rely on "trade dress" protection — are unpersuasive.

13 F.3d 1297, reversed.

Judges: Breyer, J., delivered the opinion for a unanimous Court.

Opinion: Justice Breyer delivered the opinion of the Court.

The question in this case is whether the Lanham Trademark Act of 1946 (Lanham Act), 15 U.S.C. §§ 1051-1127 (1988 ed. and Supp. V), permits the registration of a trademark that consists, purely and simply, of a color. We conclude that, sometimes, a color will meet ordinary legal trademark requirements. And, when it does so, no special legal rule prevents color alone from serving as a trademark.

I

The case before us grows out of petitioner Qualitex Company's use (since the 1950's) of a special shade of green-gold color on the pads that it makes and sells to dry cleaning firms for use on dry cleaning presses. In 1989 respondent Jacobson Products (a Qualitex rival) began to sell its own press pads to dry cleaning firms; and it colored those pads a similar green-gold. In 1991 Qualitex registered the special green-gold color on press pads with the Patent and Trademark Office as a trademark. Registration No. 1,633,711 (Feb. 5, 1991). Qualitex subsequently added a trademark infringement count, 15 U.S.C. § 1114(1), to an unfair competition claim, § 1125(a), in a lawsuit it had already filed challenging Jacobson's use of the green-gold color.

Qualitex won the lawsuit in the District Court. 21 U.S.P.Q.2D (BNA) 1457 (CD Cal. 1991). But, the Court of Appeals for the Ninth Circuit set aside the judgment in Qualitex's favor on the trademark infringement claim because, in that Circuit's view, the Lanham Act does not permit Qualitex, or anyone else, to register "color alone" as a trademark. 13 F.3d 1297, 1300, 1302 (1994).

The courts of appeals have differed as to whether or not the law recognizes the use of color alone as a trademark. Compare NutraSweet Co. v. Stadt Corp., 917 F.2d 1024, 1028 (CA7 1990) (absolute prohibition against protection of color alone), with In re Owens-Corning Fiberglas Corp., 774 F.2d 1116, 1128 (CA Fed. 1985) (allowing registration of color pink for fiberglass insulation), and Master Distributors, Inc. v. Pako Corp., 986 F.2d 219, 224 (CA8 1993) (declining to establish per se prohibition against protecting color alone as a trademark). Therefore, this Court granted certiorari. 512 U.S. 1287 (1994). We now hold that there is no rule absolutely barring the use of color alone, and we reverse the judgment of the Ninth Circuit.

II

The Lanham Act gives a seller or producer the exclusive right to "register" a trademark, 15 U.S.C. § 1052 (1988 ed. and Supp. V), and to prevent his or her competitors from using that trademark, § 1114(1). Both the language of the Act and the basic underlying principles of trademark law would seem to include color within the universe of things that can qualify as a trademark. The language of the Lanham Act describes that universe in the broadest of terms. It says that trademarks "include any word, name, symbol, or device, or any combination thereof." § 1127. Since human beings might use as a "symbol" or "device" almost anything at all that is capable of carrying meaning, this language, read literally, is not restrictive. The courts and the Patent and Trademark Office have authorized for use as a mark a particular shape (of a Coca-Cola bottle), a particular sound (of NBC's three chimes), and even a particular scent (of plumeria blossoms on sewing thread). . . . If a shape, a sound, and a fragrance can act as symbols why, one might ask, can a color not do the same?

A color is also capable of satisfying the more important part of the statutory definition of a trademark, which requires that a person "use" or "intend to use" the mark

> to identify and distinguish his or her goods, including a unique product,
> from those manufactured or sold by others and to indicate the source of
> the goods, even if that source is unknown. (15 U.S.C. § 1127)

True, a product's color is unlike "fanciful," "arbitrary," or "suggestive" words or designs, which almost automatically tell a customer that they refer to a brand. Abercrombie & Fitch Co. v. Hunting World, Inc., 537 F.2d 4, 9-10 (CA2 1976) (Friendly, J.); see Two Pesos, Inc. v. Taco Cabana, Inc., 505 U.S., (1992) (slip op., at 6-7). The imaginary word "Suntost," or the words "Suntost Marmalade," on a jar of orange jam immediately would signal a brand or a product "source"; the jam's orange color does not do so. But, over time, customers may come to treat a particular color on a product or its packaging (say, a color that in context seems unusual, such as pink on a firm's insulating material or red on the head of a large industrial bolt) as signifying a brand. And, if so, that color would have come to identify and distinguish the goods — i.e. to "indicate" their "source" — much in the way that descriptive words on a product (say, "Trim" on nail clippers or "Car-Freshner" on deodorizer) can come to indicate a product's origin. See, e.g., J. Wiss & Sons Co. v. W. E. Bassett Co., 462 F.2d 567, 59 C.C.P.A. 1269, 1271 (Pat.), 462 F.2d 567, 569 (1972); Car-Freshner Corp. v. Turtle Wax, Inc., 268 F. Supp. 162, 164 (SDNY 1967). In this circumstance, trademark law says that the word (e.g., "Trim"), although not inherently distinctive, has developed "secondary meaning." See Inwood Laboratories, Inc. v. Ives Laboratories, Inc., 456 U.S. 844, 851, n. 11, 72 L. Ed. 2d 606, 102 S. Ct. 2182 (1982) ("secondary meaning" is acquired when "in the minds of the public, the primary significance of a product feature . . . is to identify the source of the product rather than the product itself"). Again, one might ask, if trademark law permits a descriptive word with secondary meaning to act as a mark, why would it not permit a color, under similar circumstances, to do the same?

We cannot find in the basic objectives of trademark law any obvious theoretical objection to the use of color alone as a trademark, where that color has attained "secondary meaning" and therefore identifies and distinguishes a particular brand (and thus indicates its "source"). In principle, trademark law, by preventing others from copying a source-identifying mark, "reduces the customer's costs of shopping and making purchasing decisions," 1 J. McCarthy, McCarthy on Trademarks and Unfair Competition § 2.01[2], p. 2-3 (3d ed. 1994) (hereinafter McCarthy), for it quickly and easily assures a potential customer that this item — the item with this mark — is made by the same producer as other similarly marked items that he or she liked (or disliked) in the past. At the same time, the law helps assure a producer that it (and not an imitating competitor) will reap the financial, reputation-related rewards associated with a desirable product. The law thereby "encourages the production of quality products," ibid., and simultaneously discourages those who hope to sell inferior products by capitalizing on a consumer's inability quickly to evaluate the quality of an item offered for sale. See, e.g., 3 L. Altman, Callmann on Unfair Competition, Trademarks and Monopolies § 17.03 (4th ed. 1983); Landes & Posner, The Economics of Trademark Law, 78 T. M. Rep. 267, 271-272 (1988); Park 'N Fly, Inc. v. Dollar Park and Fly, Inc., 469 U.S. 189, 198, 83 L. Ed. 2d 582, 105 S. Ct. 658 (1985); S. Rep. No. 100-515, p. 4 (1988). It is the source-distinguishing ability of a mark — not its ontological status as color, shape, fragrance, word, or sign — that permits it to serve these basic purposes. See Landes & Posner, Trademark Law: An Economic Perspective, 30 J. Law & Econ. 265, 290 (1987). And, for that reason, it is difficult to find, in basic trademark objectives, a reason to disqualify absolutely the use of a color as a mark.

Neither can we find a principled objection to the use of color as a mark in the important "functionality" doctrine of trademark law. The functionality doctrine prevents trademark law, which seeks to promote competition by protecting a firm's reputation, from instead inhibiting legitimate competition by allowing a producer to control a useful product feature. It is the province of patent law, not trademark law, to encourage invention by granting inventors a monopoly over new product designs or functions for a limited time, 35 U.S.C. §§ 154, 173, after which competitors are free to use the innovation. If a product's functional features could be used as trademarks, however, a monopoly over such features could be obtained without regard to whether they qualify as patents and could be extended forever (because trademarks may be renewed in perpetuity). See Kellogg Co. v. National Biscuit Co., 305 U.S. 111, 119-120, 83 L. Ed. 73, 59 S. Ct. 109 (1938) (Brandeis, J.); Inwood Laboratories, Inc., supra, at 863 (White, J., concurring in result) ("A functional characteristic is 'an important ingredient in the commercial success of the product,' and, after expiration of a patent, it is no more the property of the originator than the product itself") (citation omitted). Functionality doctrine therefore would require, to take an imaginary example, that even if customers have come to identify the special illumination-enhancing shape of a new patented light bulb with a particular manufacturer, the manufacturer may not use that shape as a trademark, for doing so, after the patent had expired, would impede competition — not by protecting the reputation of the original bulb maker, but by frustrating competitors' legitimate efforts to produce an equivalent illumination-enhancing bulb. See, e.g., Kellogg Co., supra, at 119-120 (trademark law cannot be used to extend monopoly over "pillow" shape of shredded wheat biscuit after the patent for that shape had expired). This Court consequently has explained that, "in general terms, a product feature is functional," and cannot serve as a trademark, "if it is essential to the use or purpose of the article or if it affects the cost or quality of the article," that is, if exclusive use of the feature would put competitors at a significant non-reputation-related disadvantage. Inwood Laboratories, Inc., 456 U.S. at 850, n. 10. Although sometimes color plays an important role (unrelated to source identification) in making a product more desirable, sometimes it does not. And, this latter fact — the fact that sometimes color is not essential to a product's use or purpose and does not affect cost or quality — indicates that the doctrine of "functionality" does not create an absolute bar to the use of color alone as a mark. See Owens-Corning, 774 F.2d at 1123 (pink color of insulation in wall "performs no non-trademark function").

It would seem, then, that color alone, at least sometimes, can meet the basic legal requirements for use as a trademark. It can act as a symbol that distinguishes a firm's goods and identifies their source, without serving any other significant function. See U.S. Dept. of Commerce, Patent and Trademark Office, Trademark Manual of Examining Procedure § 1202.04(e), p. 1202-13 (2d ed. May, 1993) (hereinafter PTO Manual) (approving trademark registration of color alone where it "has become distinctive of the applicant's goods in commerce," provided that "there is [no] competitive need for colors to remain available in the industry" and the color is not "functional"); see also 1 McCarthy §§ 3.01[1], 7.26 ("requirements for qualification of a word or symbol as a trademark" are that it be (1) a "symbol," (2) "used . . . as a mark," (3) "to identify and distinguish the seller's goods from goods made or sold by others," but that it not be "functional"). Indeed, the District Court, in this case, entered findings (accepted by the Ninth Circuit) that show Qualitex's green-gold press pad color has met these requirements. The green-gold color acts as a symbol. Having developed secondary meaning (for customers identified the green-gold color as Qualitex's), it identifies the press pads' source. And, the green-gold color serves no other function. (Although it is important to use some color on press pads to avoid noticeable stains, the court found "no competitive need in the press pad industry for the green-gold color, since other colors are equally usable." 21 U.S.P.Q.2D (BNA) at 1460.) Accordingly, unless there is some special reason that convincingly militates against the use of color alone as a trademark, trademark law would protect Qualitex's use of the green-gold color on its press pads.

III

Respondent Jacobson Products says that there are four special reasons why the law should forbid the use of color alone as a trademark. We shall explain, in turn, why we, ultimately, find them unpersuasive.

First, Jacobson says that, if the law permits the use of color as a trademark, it will produce uncertainty and unresolvable court disputes about what shades of a color a competitor may lawfully use. Because lighting (morning sun, twilight mist) will affect perceptions of protected color, competitors and courts will suffer from "shade confusion" as they try to decide whether use of a similar color on a similar product does, or does not, confuse customers and thereby infringe a trademark. Jacobson adds that the "shade confusion" problem is "more difficult" and "far different from" the "determination of the similarity of words or symbols." Brief for Respondent 22.

We do not believe, however, that color, in this respect, is special. Courts traditionally decide quite difficult questions about whether two words or phrases or symbols are sufficiently similar, in context, to confuse buyers. They have had to compare, for example, such words as "Bonamine" and "Dramamine" (motion-sickness remedies); "Huggies" and "Dougies" (diapers); "Cheracol" and "Syrocol" (cough syrup); "Cyclone" and "Tornado" (wire fences); and "Mattres" and "1-800-Mattres" (mattress franchisor telephone numbers). . . . Legal standards exist to guide courts in making such comparisons. See, e.g., 2 McCarthy § 15.08; 1 McCarthy §§ 11.24-11.25 ("Strong" marks, with greater secondary meaning, receive broader protection than "weak" marks). We do not see why courts could not apply those standards to a color, replicating, if necessary, lighting conditions under which a colored product is normally sold. See Ebert, Trademark Protection in Color: Do It By the Numbers!, 84 T. M. Rep. 379, 405 (1994). Indeed, courts already have done so in cases where a trademark consists of a color plus a design, i.e., a colored symbol such as a gold stripe (around a sewer pipe), a yellow strand of wire rope, or a "brilliant yellow" band (on ampules). . . .

Second, Jacobson argues, as have others, that colors are in limited supply. See, e.g., NutraSweet Co., 917 F.2d at 1028; Campbell Soup Co. v. Armour & Co., 175 F.2d 795, 798 (CA3 1949). Jacobson claims that, if one of many competitors can appropriate a particular color for use as a trademark, and each competitor then tries to do the same, the supply of colors will soon be depleted. Put in its strongest form, this argument would concede that "hundreds of color pigments are manufactured and thousands of colors can be obtained by mixing." L. Cheskin, Colors: What They Can Do For You 47 (1947). But, it would add that, in the context of a particular product, only some colors are usable. By the time one discards colors that, say, for reasons of customer appeal, are not usable, and adds the shades that competitors cannot use lest they risk infringing a similar, registered shade, then one is left with only a handful of possible colors. And, under these circumstances, to permit one, or a few, producers to use colors as trademarks will "deplete" the supply of usable colors to the point where a competitor's inability to find a suitable color will put that competitor at a significant disadvantage.

This argument is unpersuasive, however, largely because it relies on an occasional problem to justify a blanket prohibition. When a color serves as a mark, normally alternative colors will likely be available for similar use by others. See, e.g., Owens-Corning, 774 F.2d at 1121 (pink insulation). More-over, if that is not so — if a "color depletion" or "color scarcity" problem does arise — the trademark doctrine of "functionality" normally would seem available to prevent the anticompetitive consequences that Jacobson's argument posits, thereby minimizing that argument's practical force.

The functionality doctrine, as we have said, forbids the use of a product's feature as a trademark where doing so will put a competitor at a significant disadvantage because the feature is "essential to the use or purpose of the article" or "affects [its] cost or quality." Inwood Laboratories, Inc., 456 U.S. at 850, n. 10. The functionality doctrine thus protects competitors against a disadvantage (unrelated to recognition or reputation) that trademark protection might otherwise impose, namely their inability reasonably to replicate important non-reputation-related product features. For example, this Court has written that competitors might be free to copy the color of a medical pill where that color serves to identify the kind of medication (e.g., a type of blood medicine) in addition to its source. See id., at 853, 858, n. 20 ("Some patients commingle medications in a container and rely on color to differentiate one from another"); see also J. Ginsburg, D. Goldberg, & A. Greenbaum, Trademark and Unfair Competition Law 194-195 (1991) (noting that drug color cases "have more to do with public health policy" regarding generic drug substitution "than with trademark law"). And, the federal courts have demonstrated that they can apply this doctrine in a careful and reasoned manner, with sensitivity to the effect on competition. Although we need not comment on the merits of specific cases, we note that lower courts have permitted competitors to copy the green color of farm machinery (because customers wanted their farm equipment to match) and have barred the use of black as a trademark on outboard boat motors (because black has the special functional attributes of decreasing the apparent size of the motor and ensuring compatibility with many different boat colors). See Deere & Co. v. Farmhand, Inc., 560 F. Supp. 85, 98 (SD Iowa 1982), aff'd, 721 F.2d 253 (CA8 1983); Brunswick Corp. v. British Seagull Ltd., 35 F.3d 1527, 1532 (CA Fed. 1994), cert. pending, No. 94-1075; see also Nor-Am Chemical v. O. M. Scott & Sons Co., 4 U.S.P.Q.2D (BNA) 1316, 1320 (ED Pa. 1987) (blue color of fertilizer held functional because it indicated the presence of nitrogen). The Restatement (Third) of Unfair Competition adds that, if a design's "aesthetic value" lies in its ability to "confer a significant benefit that cannot practically be duplicated by the use of alternative designs," then the design is "functional." Restatement (Third) of Unfair Competition § 17, Comment c, pp. 175-176 (1995). The "ultimate test of aesthetic functionality," it explains, "is whether the recognition of trademark rights would significantly hinder competition." Id., at 176.

The upshot is that, where a color serves a significant nontrademark function — whether to distinguish a heart pill from a digestive medicine or to satisfy the "noble instinct for giving the right touch of beauty to common and necessary things," G. K. Chesterton, Simplicity and Tolstoy 61 (1912) — courts will examine whether its use as a mark would permit one competitor (or a group) to interfere with legitimate (nontrademark-related) competition through actual or potential exclusive use of an important product ingredient. That examination should not discourage firms from creating aesthetically pleasing mark designs, for it is open to their competitors to do the same. See, e.g., W. T. Rogers Co. v. Keene, 778 F.2d 334, 343 (CA7 1985) (Posner, J.). But, ordinarily, it should prevent the anticompetitive consequences of Jacobson's hypothetical "color depletion" argument, when, and if, the circumstances of a particular case threaten "color depletion."

Third, Jacobson points to many older cases — including Supreme Court cases — in support of its position. In 1878, this Court described the common-law definition of trademark rather broadly to "consist of a name, symbol, figure, letter, form, or device, if adopted and used by a manufacturer or merchant in order to designate the goods he manufactures or sells to distinguish the same from those manufactured or sold by another." McLean v. Fleming, 96 U.S. 245, 254, 24 L. Ed. 828. Yet, in interpreting the Trademark Acts of 1881 and 1905, 21 Stat. 502, 33 Stat. 724, which retained that common-law definition, the Court questioned "whether mere color can constitute a valid trade-mark," A. Leschen & Sons Rope Co. v. Broderick & Bascom Rope Co., 201 U.S. 166, 171, 50 L. Ed. 710, 26 S. Ct. 425 (1906), and suggested that the "product including the coloring matter is free to all who make it." Coca-Cola Co. v. Koke Co. of America, 254 U.S. 143, 147, 65 L. Ed. 189, 41 S. Ct. 113 (1920). Even though these statements amounted to dicta, lower courts interpreted them as forbidding protection for color alone. See, e.g., Campbell Soup Co., 175 F.2d at 798, and n. 9; Life Savers Corp. v. Curtiss Candy Co., 182 F.2d 4, 9 (CA7 1950) (quoting Campbell Soup).

These Supreme Court cases, however, interpreted trademark law as it existed before 1946, when Congress enacted the Lanham Act. The Lanham Act significantly changed and liberalized the common law to "dispense with mere technical prohibitions," S. Rep. No. 1333, 79th Cong., 2d Sess., 3 (1946), most notably, by permitting trademark registration of descriptive words (say, "U-Build-It" model airplanes) where they had acquired "secondary meaning." See Abercrombie & Fitch Co., 537 F.2d at 9 (Friendly, J.). The Lanham Act extended protection to descriptive marks by making clear that (with certain explicit exceptions not relevant here),

> nothing . . . shall prevent the registration of a mark used by the applicant which has become distinctive of the applicant's goods in commerce. 15 U.S.C. § 1052(f) (1988 ed., Supp. V)

This language permits an ordinary word, normally used for a nontrademark purpose (e.g., description), to act as a trademark where it has gained "secondary meaning." Its logic would appear to apply to color as well. Indeed, in 1985, the Federal Circuit considered the significance of the Lanham Act's changes as they related to color and held that trademark protection for color was consistent with the

> jurisprudence under the Lanham Act developed in accordance with the statutory principle that if a mark is capable of being or becoming distinctive of [the] applicant's goods in commerce, then it is capable of serving as a trademark. (Owens-Corning, 774 F.2d at 1120)

In 1988 Congress amended the Lanham Act, revising portions of the definitional language, but left unchanged the language here relevant. § 134, 102 Stat. 3946, 15 U.S.C. § 1127. It enacted these amendments against the following background: (1) the Federal Circuit had decided Owens-Corning; (2) the Patent and Trademark Office had adopted a clear policy (which it still maintains) permitting registration of color as a trademark, see PTO Manual § 1202.04(e) (at p. 1200-12 of the January 1986 edition and p. 1202-13 of the May 1993 edition); and (3) the Trademark Commission had written a report, which recommended that "the terms 'symbol, or device' . . . not be deleted or narrowed to preclude registration of such things as a color, shape, smell, sound, or configuration which functions as a mark," The United States Trademark Association Trademark Review Commission Report and Recommendations to USTA President and Board of Directors, 77 T. M. Rep. 375, 421 (1987) (hereinafter Trademark Commission); see also 133 Cong. Rec. 32812c (1987) (statement of Sen. DeConcini) ("The bill I am introducing today is based on the Commission's report and recommendations"). This background strongly suggests that the language "any word, name, symbol, or device," 15 U.S.C. § 1127, had come to include color. And, when it amended the statute, Congress retained these terms. Indeed, the Senate Report accompanying the Lanham Act revision explicitly referred to this background understanding, in saying that the "revised definition intentionally retains . . . the words 'symbol or device' so as not to preclude the registration of colors, shapes, sounds or configurations where they function as trademarks." S. Rep. No. 100-515, at 44. (In addition, the statute retained language providing that "no trademark by which the goods of the applicant may be distinguished from the goods of others shall be refused registration . . . on account of its nature" (except for certain specified reasons not relevant here). 15 U.S.C. § 1052 (1988 ed., Supp V)).

This history undercuts the authority of the precedent on which Jacobson relies. Much of the pre-1985 case law rested on statements in Supreme Court opinions that interpreted pre-Lanham Act trademark law and were not directly related to the holdings in those cases. Moreover, we believe the Federal Circuit was right in 1985 when it found that the 1946 Lanham Act embodied crucial legal changes that liberalized the law to permit the use of color alone as a trademark (under appropriate circumstances). At a minimum, the Lanham Act's changes left the courts free to reevaluate the pre-existing legal precedent which had absolutely forbidden the use of color alone as a trademark. Finally, when Congress re-enacted the terms "word, name, symbol, or device" in 1988, it did so against a legal background in which those terms had come to include color, and its statutory revision embraced that understanding.

Fourth, Jacobson argues that there is no need to permit color alone to function as a trademark because a firm already may use color as part of a trademark, say, as a colored circle or colored letter or colored word, and may rely upon "trade dress" protection, under § 43(a) of the Lanham Act, if a competitor copies its color and thereby causes consumer confusion regarding the overall appearance of the competing products or their packaging, see 15 U.S.C. § 1125(a) (1988 ed., Supp. V). The first part of this argument begs the question. One can understand why a firm might find it difficult to place a usable symbol or word on a product (say, a large industrial bolt that customers normally see from a distance); and, in such instances, a firm might want to use color, pure and simple, instead of color as part of a design. Neither is the second portion of the argument convincing. Trademark law helps the holder of a mark in many ways that "trade dress" protection does not. See 15 U.S.C. § 1124 (ability to prevent importation of confusingly similar goods); § 1072 (constructive notice of ownership); § 1065 (incontestible status); § 1057(b) (prima facie evidence of validity and ownership). Thus, one can easily find reasons why the law might provide trademark protection in addition to trade dress protection.

IV

Having determined that a color may sometimes meet the basic legal requirements for use as a trademark and that respondent Jacobson's arguments do not justify a special legal rule preventing color alone from serving as a trademark (and, in light of the District Court's here undisputed findings that Qualitex's use of the green-gold color on its press pads meets the basic trademark requirements), we conclude that the Ninth Circuit erred in barring Qualitex's use of color as a trademark. For these reasons, the judgment of the Ninth Circuit is

Reversed.

Notes and Questions

1. Note that the ruling of the United States Supreme Court, based upon statutory language and functions of trademark, does not imply that colors, purely and solely, may equally establish protectable trademarks in other jurisdictions. Some jurisdictions have considered colors to have a generic nature and have reasoned that they need to be combined with other elements in order to achieve the necessary distinctiveness. The notion and scope of trademark still may vary, in detail, from country to country. An illustrative example from another country is the Swiss "Milka" case. The food products firm Kraft Jacobs Suchard wanted to register the color mauve as a trademark for its chocolate, also known as "Milka". The registration was initially denied by the Swiss Federal Institute of Intellectual Property as well as the Rekurskommission (Commission of Appeals) (FBDM 1995 I 73). Only after Kraft Jacobs Suchard filed the color as a well-known trademark, was the registration granted. It remains an open question whether the Federal

Institute will make the same decision on future applications, or if it will go back to its former more restrictive practice.

2. Do you suppose that *Qualitex vs. Jacobson* may have influenced the new approach to colors in Swiss trademark law? What is the economic, commercial and marketing impact if colors as such are being protected in the U.S., but not in other major markets of the globe? Might there be any impact on the creation of uniform global trademarks?

3. A common form of media advertising involves combining the visual and aural image of an exciting or interesting event with a trademark — without conveying any direct information about a product. The objective is to associate a particular trademark with a positive (or even a negative) feeling such as success, endurance or courage, so that when the consumer is faced with a choice among products, he or she will be drawn to the one displaying the trademark that was advertised. In these circumstances, what function is the trademark performing?

4. In Case No. 95491 of December 17, 1998, the Swedish Court of Patent Appeals (Patentbesvärfättens) approved the first trademark registration in Sweden of a melody, a popular tune used by Swedish ice-cream carts (trademark application No. 9211287, submitted originally in 1992). The Court noted that melodies may be graphically represented by notes. Do you consider that melodies are the proper subject of trademark protection and, if so, in what circumstances should their registration as trademarks be envisaged?

5. For many years it was a requirement of trademark law in some countries that for a trademark to be registered it must have appeared on a good in the stream of commerce. Pursuant to the TRIPS Agreement, countries must allow the possibility of registering trademarks before goods are introduced. This is but one element of a distinct trend in international trademark law to disassociate trademarks from products. Further evidence of this trend is the right to assign and transfer trademarks in the absence of the sale of the underlying business. Are new theories of the function of the trademark needed?

6. Internet domain names are addresses of computers on the Internet. Some of the questions they have raised in connection with traditional IPRs, such as trademarks, are considered in Chapter VIII, below. Do you think

that you should be able to register a domain name, such as *amazon.com* as a trademark? Does the ".com" form part of the mark? What is associated by the consumer with such a domain name?

---

c. Function of the Trademark in Intra-Community Trade

The basic facts of the case are as follows: Until 1984, the American Standard group owned the trademark "Ideal Standard" both in France and in Germany for the marketing of sanitary fittings and heating equipment. The trademark was owned through two different subsidiaries: Ideal-Standard SA in France and Ideal-Standard GmbH in Germany. In 1984, following financial difficulties, Ideal Standard France assigned its trademark to an independent French company. Ownership of the trademark then passed to another company (Compagnie internationale du chauffage "CICh") which also had no economic link with the American Standard group. CICh then tried to market its heating products in Germany under the trademark "Ideal Standard." Ideal Standard Germany objected to the imports and obtained a ruling in the German court of first instance upholding its right to block the importation. On appeal, the Oberlandsgericht Dusseldorf referred to the European Court of Justice (ECJ) for a preliminary ruling under article 177 EC Treaty a question concerning the compatibility with EU law of restrictions of the use of the mark Ideal Standard in Germany.

Ideal Standard is a typical trademark case arising in the context of the EU and regional integration. It illustrates the territorial nature and the independence of national trademarks conflicting with the principle of free movement of goods in EU law. While trademark rights are essential conditions of competition, they create (as other exclusive rights) tensions with free trade and amount to trade barriers. In this case, the ECJ concluded that the prohibition on the use of the name Ideal Standard in Germany amounted to a measure having equivalent effect to a quantitative restriction under the terms of Article 30 EC. However, it went on to find that the measure was acceptable under Article 36 EC, which includes a reference to the protection of intellectual property rights, and allows for trade restrictions necessary to protect the legitimate exercise of such rights. We will consider in detail the relationship between IPRs and trade in Chapters IV and VII.

Consider here in particular the Court's assessment of the essential functions of a trademark. According to the ECJ, the purpose of a trademark is to protect owners against third parties who might take advantage of the trademark and its reputation. It also suggests that another essential function consists in assuring that all the goods bearing the mark have been produced under the control of a single undertaking which is accountable for their quality.

IHT Internationale Heiztechnik GmbH and Another v Ideal-Standard GmbH and Another

(Case C-9/93)
The Court of Justice of the European Communities
[1994] 3 CMLR 857

22 JUNE 1994

Panel: Presiding, Due CJ; Mancini, Moitino de Almeida, Diez de Velasco PPC; Kakouris, Joliet (Rapporteur), Schockweiler, Rodriguez Iglesias, Zuleeg, Kapteyn, Murray JJ

Headnote:

Reference from Germany by the Oberlandesgericht (Regional Court of Appeal), Dusseldorf, under Article 177 EC.

Decision:

By order of 15 December 1992, received at the Court on 12 January 1993, the Oberlandesgericht (Higher Regional Court) Dusseldorf referred to the Court for a preliminary ruling under Article 177 EEC a question on the interpretation of Articles 30 and 36 EEC in order to assess the compatibility with Community law of restrictions on the use of a name where a group of companies held, through subsidiaries, a trade mark consisting of that name in several Member States of the Community and where that trade mark was assigned, for one Member State only and for some of the products for which it had been registered, to an undertaking outside the group.

That question arose in a dispute between Ideal-Standard GmbH and IHT, both German companies, regarding the use in Germany of the trade mark "Ideal Standard" for heating equipment manufactured in France by IHT's parent, Compagnie Internationale de Chauffage ("CICh").

Until 1984 the American Standard group held, through its German and French subsidiaries — Ideal-Standard GmbH and Ideal-Standard SA — the trade mark "Ideal Standard" in Germany and in France for sanitary fittings and heating equipment.

In July 1984 the French subsidiary of that group, Ideal-Standard SA, sold the trade mark for the heating equipment sector, with its heating business, to Societe Generale de Fonderie ("SGF"), a French company with which it had no links. That trade mark assignment related to France (including the overseas departments and territories), Tunisia and Algeria.

The background to that assignment was the following. From 1976 Ideal-Standard SA had been in financial difficulties. Insolvency proceedings were opened. A management agreement was concluded between the trustees and another French company set up by, inter alios, SGF. That company carried on Ideal-Standard SA's production and sales activities. The management agreement came to an end in 1980. The business of Ideal-Standard SA's heating equipment division remained unsatisfactory. In view of SGF's interest in maintaining the heating equipment division and its marketing in France under the device "Ideal Standard", Ideal-Standard SA assigned the trade mark and transferred the production plants for the heating division referred to [above] to SGF. SGF later assigned the trade mark to another French company, CICh, which, like SGF, is part of the French Nord-Est group and has no links with the American Standard group.

Ideal-Standard GmbH brought proceedings against IHT for infringement of its trade mark and its commercial name by marketing in Germany heating equipment bearing the trade mark "Ideal Standard" manufactured in France by CICh. Ideal-Standard GmbH was still the owner of the trade mark "Ideal Standard" in Germany both for sanitary fittings and for heating equipment although it had stopped manufacturing and marketing heating equipment in 1976.

The action seeks an injunction against IHT from marketing in Germany heating equipment bearing the trade mark "Ideal Standard" and from using that trade mark on various commercial documents.

At first instance the proceedings were heard by the Landgericht (Regional Court) Dusseldorf which, by judgment of 25 February 1992, upheld the claim.

The Landgericht held first that there was risk of confusion. The device used — the name "Ideal Standard" — was identical. Moreover, the products were sufficiently close for the relevant users, seeing the same device on the products, to be led to believe that they came from the same undertaking.

The Landgericht further held that there was no reason for it to avail itself of its power to refer a question to the Court of Justice under Article 177 of the Treaty on the interpretation of Articles 30 and 36 of the Treaty. It reviewed the judgments in Case 192/73, VAN ZUYLEN v HAG (HAG I) ([1974] ECR 731, [1974] 2 CMLR 127) and Case C-10/89, CNL-SUCAL v HAG (HAG II) ([1990] I ECR 3711, [1990] 3 CMLR 571) and held that the reasoning of the Court in HAG II "suffices to show that there is no longer any foundation for the doctrine of common origin, not only in the context of the facts underlying that decision, that is cases of expropriation in a Member State, but also in cases of voluntary division of ownership of a trade mark originally in single ownership, which is the position in this case".

IHT appealed against that judgment to the Oberlandesgericht Dusseldorf which, referring to HAG II, considered whether this case should, as the Landgericht had held, be decided in the same way pursuant to Community law.

Accordingly, the Oberlandesgericht referred the following question to the Court of Justice for a preliminary ruling:

> Does it constitute an unlawful restriction of intra-Community trade, within the meaning of Articles 30 and 36 EEC, for an undertaking carrying on business in Member State A which is a subsidiary of a manufacturer of heating systems based in Member State B to be prohibited from using as a trade mark the name 'Ideal Standard' on the grounds of risk of confusion with a mark having the same origin, where the name 'Ideal Standard' is lawfully used by the manufacturer in its home country by virtue of a trade mark registered there which it has acquired by means of a legal transaction and which was originally the property of a company affiliated to the undertaking which is opposing, in Member State A, the importation of goods marked 'Ideal Standard'?

It is common ground that a prohibition on the use in Germany by IHT of the name "Ideal Standard" for heating equipment would constitute a measure having equivalent effect to a quantitative restriction under Article

149

30. The question is, therefore, whether that prohibition may be justified under Article 36 of the Treaty.

It is appropriate first of all to review certain key features of trade mark law and the case law of the Court on Articles 30 and 36 of the Treaty in order to identify the precise legal context of the national court's question.

The similarity of the products and the risk of confusion

The HAG II case, whose bearing on the main proceedings is the point of the question put by the national court, related to a situation where it was not just the name that was identical but also the products marketed by the parties to the dispute. This dispute, by contrast, relates to the use of an identical device for different products since Ideal-Standard GmbH is relying on its registration of the trade mark "Ideal Standard" for sanitary fittings in order to oppose the use of that device for heating equipment.

It is common ground that the right of prohibition stemming from a protected trade mark, whether protected by registration or on some other basis, extends beyond the products for which the trade mark has been acquired. The object of trade mark law is to protect owners against contrivances of third parties who might seek, by creating a risk of confusion amongst consumers, to take advantage of the reputation accruing to the trade mark: see Case 102/77, HOFFMANN-LA ROCHE v CENTRAFARM. That risk may arise from the use of an identical device for products different from those for which a trade mark has been acquired (by registration or otherwise) where the products in question are sufficiently close to induce users seeing the same device on those products to conclude that the products come from the same undertaking. Similarity of the products is thus part of the concept of risk of confusion and must be assessed in relation to the purpose of trade mark law.

In its observations the Commission warned against taking the broad view of the risk of confusion and similarity of products taken by the German courts, since it is liable to have restrictive effects, not covered by Article 36 EEC, on the free movement of goods.

As regards the period before the entry into force of the First Council Directive (89/104) to approximate the laws of the Member States relating to trade marks, which was postponed to 31 December 1992 by Article 1 of Council Decision 92/10, that being the material period for the main dispute, the Court held in Case C-317/91, DEUTSCHE RENAULT v AUDI that "the determination of the criteria allowing the conclusion to be drawn that there is a risk of confusion is part of the detailed rules for protection of trade marks, which . . . are a matter for national law" and "Community law does not lay down any criterion requiring a strict interpretation of the risk of confusion."

However, as was held in DEUTSCHE RENAULT, application of national law continues to be subject to the limits set out in the second sentence of Article 36 of the Treaty: there must be no arbitrary discrimination or disguised restriction on trade between Member States. There would, in particular, be a disguised restriction if the national court were to conduct an arbitrary assessment of the similarity of products. As soon as application of national law as to similarity of the products led to arbitrary discrimination or a disguised restriction, the obstacle to imports could not anyway be justified under Article 36. Moreover, if the competent national court were finally to hold that the products in question were not similar, there would be no obstacle to imports susceptible of justification under Article 36.

Subject to those reservations, it is for the court hearing the main proceedings to assess the similarity of the products in question. Since that is a question involving determination of the facts of which only the national court can have direct knowledge and so, to that extent, is outside the Court's jurisdiction under Article 177, the Court must proceed on the assumption that there is a risk of confusion. The problem therefore arises on the same basis as if the products for which the trade mark was assigned and those covered by the registration relied on in Germany were identical.

The territorial nature and independence of national trade mark rights

Since this case concerns a situation where the trade mark has been assigned for one State only and the question whether the solution in HAG II regarding the splitting of a mark as a result of sequestration also applies in the event of splitting by voluntary act, it should be noted first, as the United Kingdom pointed out, that national trade mark rights are not only territorial but also independent of each other.

National trade mark rights are first of all territorial. This principle of territoriality, which is recognised under international treaty law, means that it is the law of the country where protection of a trade mark is sought which determines the conditions of that protection. Moreover, national law can only provide relief in respect of acts performed on the national territory in question.

Article 36 EEC itself, by allowing certain restrictions on imports on grounds of protection of intellectual property, presupposes that in principle the legislation of the importing State applies to acts performed in that State in relation to the imported product. A restriction on importation permitted by that legislation will of course escape Article 30 only if it is covered by Article 36.

National trade mark rights are also independent of each other

The principle of the independence of trade marks is expressed in Article 6(3) of the Paris Union Convention for the Protection of Industrial Property of 20 March 1883, as last revised at Stockholm on 14 July 1967 which provides: "A mark duly registered in a country of the Union shall be regarded as independent of marks registered in other countries of the Union . . ."

That principle has led to recognition that a trade mark right may be assigned for one country without at the same time being assigned by its owner in other countries.

The possibility of independent assignments is first of all implicit in Article 6quater of the Paris Union Convention.

Some national laws permit the transfer of the trade mark without a concomitant transfer of the undertaking whilst others continue to require that the undertaking should be transferred with the trade mark. In some countries the requirement of the concomitant transfer of the undertaking was even interpreted as necessitating the transfer of the whole undertaking even if certain parts of it were situated in countries other than that for which the transfer was proposed. The transfer of a trade mark for one country therefore almost necessarily entailed the transfer of the trade mark for other countries.

That is why Article 6quater of the Paris Union Convention provided:

> When, in accordance with the law of a country of the Union, the assignment of mark is valid only if it takes place at the same time as the transfer of the business or goodwill to which the mark belongs, it shall suffice for the recognition of such validity that the portion of the business or

goodwill located in that country be transferred to the assignee, together with the exclusive right to manufacture in the said country, or to sell therein the goods bearing the mark assigned.

By thus making possible the assignment of a trade mark for one country without the concomitant transfer of the trade mark in another country, Article 6quater of the Paris Union Convention presupposes that such independent assignments may be made.

The principle of the independence of trade marks is, moreover, expressly enshrined in Article 9ter(2) of the Madrid Agreement concerning the International Registration of Marks of 14 April 1891, as last revised at Stockholm in 1967, which provides: "The International Bureau shall likewise record the assignment of an international mark in respect of one or several of the contracting countries only."

Unified laws, which bring the territory of several States into a single territory for purposes of trade mark law, such as the Uniform Benelux Act on Trade Marks for Goods (annexed to the Convention Benelux en Matière de Marques de Produits, or Council Regulation 40/94 on the Community trade mark render void transfers of trade marks for only one part of the territory to which they apply. However, those unified laws do not, any more than national laws, make the validity of a trade mark assignment for the territory to which they apply conditional on the concomitant assignment of the trade mark for the territory of third States.

The case law on Articles 30 and 36 trade mark law and parallel imports

On the basis of the second sentence of Article 36 of the Treaty the Court has consistently held:

> Inasmuch as it provides an exception to one of the fundamental principles of the Common Market, Article 36 in fact only admits of derogations from the free movement of goods where such derogations are justified for the purpose of safeguarding rights which constitute the specific subject-matter of this property.

In relation to trade marks, the specific subject-matter of the industrial property is the guarantee that the owner of the trade mark has the exclusive right to use that trade mark, for the purpose of putting products protected by the trade mark into circulation for the first time, and is therefore intended to protect him against competitors wishing to take advantage of the status and reputation of the trade mark by selling products illegally bearing that trade mark.

An obstacle to the free movement of goods may arise out of the existence, within a national legislation concerning industrial and commercial properly, of provisions laying down that a trade mark owner's right is not exhausted when the product protected by the trade mark is marketed in another Member State, with the result that the trade mark owner can [oppose] importation of the product into his own Member State when it has been marketed in another Member State.

Such an obstacle is not justified when the product has been put onto the market in a legal manner in the Member State from which it has been imported, by the trade mark owner himself or with his consent, so that there can be no question of abuse or infringement of the trade mark.

In fact, if a trade mark owner could prevent the import of protected products marketed by him or with his consent in another Member State, he would be able to partition off national markets and thereby restrict trade between Member States, in a situation where no such restriction was necessary to guarantee the essence of the exclusive right flowing from the trade mark (see Case 16/74, CENTRAFARM v WINTHROP).

So, application of a national law which would give the trade mark owner in the importing State the right to oppose the marketing of products which have been put into circulation in the exporting State by him or with his consent is precluded as contrary to Articles 30 and 36. This principle, known as the exhaustion of rights, applies where the owner of the trade mark in the importing State and the owner of the trade mark in the exporting State are the same or where, even if they are separate persons, they are economically linked. A number of situations are covered: products put into circulation by the same undertaking, by a licensee, by a parent company, by a subsidiary of the same group, or by an exclusive distributor.

There are numerous instances in national case law and Community case law where the trade mark had been assigned to a subsidiary or to an exclusive distributor in order to enable those undertakings to protect their national markets against parallel imports by taking advantage of restrictive approaches to the exhaustion of rights in the national laws of some States.

Articles 30 and 36 defeat such manipulation of trade marks rights since they preclude national laws which enable the holder of the right to oppose imports.

In the situations described above . . . the function of the trade mark is in no way called in question by freedom to import. As was held in HAG II: "For the trade mark to be able to fulfil [its] role, it must offer a guarantee that all goods bearing it have been produced under the control of a single undertaking which is accountable for their quality." In all the cases mentioned, control was in the hands of a single body: the group of companies in the case of products put into circulation by a subsidiary; the manufacturer in the case of products marketed by the distributor; the licensor in the case of products marketed by a licensee. In the case of a licence, the licensor can control the quality of the licensee's products by including in the contract clauses requiring the licensee to comply with his instructions and giving him the possibility of verifying such compliance. The origin which the trade mark is intended to guarantee is the same: it is not defined by reference to the manufacturer but by reference to the point of control of manufacture (see the statement of grounds for the Benelux Convention and the Uniform Act).

It must further be stressed that the decisive factor is the possibility of control over the quality of goods, not the actual exercise of that control. Accordingly, a national law allowing the licensor to oppose importation of the licensee's products on grounds of poor quality would be precluded as contrary to Articles 30 and 36: if the licensor tolerates the manufacture of poor quality products, despite having contractual means of preventing it, he must bear the responsibility. Similarly if the manufacture of products is decentralised within a group of companies and the subsidiaries in each of the Member States manufacture products whose quality is geared to the particularities of each national market, a national law which enabled one subsidiary of the group to oppose the marketing in the territory of that State of products manufactured by an affiliated company on grounds of those quality differences would also be precluded. Articles 30 and 36 require the group to bear the consequences of its choice.

Articles 30 and 36 thus debar the application of national laws which allow recourse to trade mark rights in order to prevent the free movement of a product bearing a trade mark whose use is under unitary control.

The situation where unitary control of the trade mark has been severed following assignment for one or several Member States only

The problem posed by the Oberlandesgericht's question is whether the same principles apply where the trade mark has been assigned, for one or several Member States only, to an undertaking which has no economic link with the assignor and the assignor opposes the marketing, in the State in which he has retained the trade mark, of products to which the trade mark has been affixed by the assignee.

That situation must be clearly distinguished from the case where the imported products come from a licensee or a subsidiary to which ownership of the trade mark right has been assigned in the exporting State: a contract of assignment by itself, that is in the absence of any economic link, does not give the assignor any means of controlling the quality of products which are marketed by the assignee and to which the latter has affixed the trade mark.

The Commission has submitted that by assigning in France the trade mark "Ideal Standard" for heating equipment to a third company, the American Standard group gave implied consent to that third company putting heating equipment into circulation in France bearing that trade mark. Because of that implied consent, it should not be possible to prohibit the marketing in Germany of heating equipment bearing the assigned trade mark.

That view must be rejected. The consent implicit in any assignment is not the consent required for application of the doctrine of exhaustion of rights. For that, the owner of the right in the importing State must, directly or indirectly, be able to determine the products to which the trade mark may be affixed in the exporting State and to control their quality. That power is lost if, by assignment, control over the trade mark is surrendered to a third party having no economic link with the assignor.

The insulation of markets where, for two Member States of the Community, there are separate trade mark owners having no economic links is a result that has already been accepted by the Court in HAG II. However, since that was a case where unitary ownership was divided following sequestration, it has been submitted that the same result does not have to be adopted in the case of voluntary division.

That view cannot be accepted because it is contrary to the reasoning of the Court in HAG II. The Court began by noting that trade mark rights are an essential element in the system of undistorted competition which the Treaty seeks to establish. It went on to recall the identifying function of trade marks, and in a passage cited above, the conditions for trade marks to be able to fulfil that role. The Court further noted that the scope of the exclusive right which is the specific subject-matter of the trade mark must be determined having regard to its function. It stressed that in that case the determinant factor was absence of consent of the proprietor of the trade mark in the importing State to the putting into circulation in the exporting State of products marketed by the proprietor of the right in the latter State. It concluded that free movement of the goods would undermine the essential function of the trade mark: consumers would no longer be able to identify for certain the origin of the marked goods and the proprietor of the trade mark could be held responsible for the poor quality of goods for which he was in no way accountable.

Those considerations apply, as was rightly stressed by the United Kingdom and Germany and was held by the Landgericht Dusseldorf at first instance, whether the splitting of the trade mark originally held by the same owner is due to an act of public authority or a contractual assignment.

IHT in particular has submitted that the owner of a trade mark who assigns the trade mark in one Member State, while retaining it in others, must accept the consequences of the weakening of the identifying function of the trade mark flowing from that assignment. By a territorially limited assignment, the owner voluntarily renounces his position as the only person marketing goods bearing the trade mark in question in the Community.

That argument must be rejected. It fails to take account of the fact that, since trade mark rights are territorial, the function of the trade mark is to be assessed by reference to a particular territory (HAG II).

IHT has further argued that the French subsidiary, Ideal-Standard SA, has adjusted itself in France to a situation where products (such as heating equipment and sanitary fittings) from different sources may be marketed under the same trade mark on the same national territory. The conduct of the German subsidiary of the same group which opposes the marketing of the heating equipment in Germany under the trade mark "Ideal Standard" is therefore abusive.

That argument cannot be upheld either.

First of all, the assignment was made only for France. The effect of that argument, if it were accepted, would, as the German Government points out, be that assignment of the right for France would entail permission to use the device in Germany, whereas assignments and licences always relate, having regard to the territorial nature of national trade mark rights, to a specified territory.

Moreover, and most importantly, French law, which governs the assignment in question here, permits assignments of trade marks confined to certain products, with the result that similar products from different sources may be in circulation on French territory under the same trade mark, whereas German law, by prohibiting assignments of trade marks confined to certain products, seeks to prevent such co-existence. The effect of IHT's argument, if it were accepted, would be to extend to the importing State whose law opposes such co-existence the solution prevailing in the exporting State despite the territorial nature of the rights in question.

Starting from the position that assignment to an assignee having no links with the assignor would lead to the existence of separate sources within a single territory and that, in order to safeguard the function of the trade mark, it would then be necessary to allow prohibition of export of the assignee's products to the assignor's territory and vice versa, unified laws, to avoid creating such obstacles to the free movement of goods, render void assignments made for only part of the territory covered by the rights they create. By limiting the right to dispose of the trade mark in this way, such unified laws ensure single ownership throughout the territory to which they apply and guarantee free movement of the product.

Thus, the Uniform Benelux Act on Trade Marks for Goods, whose objective was to unify the territory of the three States for trade mark purposes (statement of grounds), provided that, from the date of its entry into force, a trade mark could be granted only for the whole of Benelux (statement of grounds). To that end it further provided that trade mark assignments not effected for the whole of Benelux were void.

The regulation on the Community trade mark referred to above also creates a right with a unitary character. Subject to certain exceptions (see in this respect Article 106 on the prohibition of use of Community trade marks and Article 107 on prior rights applicable to particular localities), the Community trade mark "shall have equal effect throughout the Community: it shall not be registered, transferred or surrendered or be the subject of a decision revoking the rights of the proprietor or declaring it invalid, nor shall its use be prohibited, save in respect of the whole Community" (Article 1(2)).

However, unlike the Benelux Act, "the Community law relating to trade marks . . . does not replace the laws of the Member States on trade marks" (fifth recital in the preamble to the regulation on the Community trade mark). The Community trade mark is merely superimposed on the national rights. Undertakings are in no way obliged to take out Community trade marks (fifth recital). Moreover, the existence of earlier national rights may be an obstacle to the registration of a Community trade mark since, under Article 8 of the regulation, the owner of a trade mark in a single Member State may oppose the registration of a Community trade mark by the proprietor of national rights for identical or similar products in all the other Member States. That provision cannot be interpreted as precluding the assignment of national trade marks for one or more States of the Community only. It is therefore apparent that the regulation on the Community trade mark does not render void assignments of national marks which are confined to certain States of the Community.

That sanction cannot be introduced through case law. To hold that the national laws are measures having equivalent effect which fall under Article 30 and are not justified by Article 36, in that, given the independence of national rights (see . . . above), they do not, at present, make the validity of assignments for the territories to which they apply conditional on the concomitant assignment of the trade mark for the other States of the Community, would have the effect of imposing on the States a positive obligation, namely to embody in their laws a rule rendering void assignments of national trade marks made for part only of the Community.

It is for the Community legislature to impose such an obligation on the Member States by a directive adopted under Article 100a EEC, elimination of the obstacles arising from the territoriality of national trade marks being necessary for the establishment and functioning of the internal market, or itself to enact that rule directly by a regulation adopted under the same provision.

It should be added that, where undertakings independent of each other make trade mark assignments following a market-sharing agreement, the prohibition of anti-competitive agreements under Article 85 applies and assignments which give effect to that agreement are consequently void. However, as the United Kingdom rightly pointed out, that rule and the accompanying sanction cannot be applied mechanically to every assignment. Before a trade mark assignment can be treated as giving effect to an agreement prohibited under Article 85, it is necessary to analyse the context, the commitments underlying the assignment, the intention of the parties and the consideration for the assignment.

In view of the foregoing, the answer to the Oberlandesgericht Dusseldorf's question must be that there is no unlawful restriction on trade between Member States within the meaning of Articles 30 and 36 where a subsidiary operating in Member State A of a manufacturer established in Member State B is to be enjoined from using as a trade mark the name "Ideal Standard" because of the risk of confusion with a device having the same origin, even if the manufacturer is lawfully using that name in his country of origin under a trade mark protected there, he acquired that trade mark by assignment and the trade mark originally belonged to a company affiliated to the undertaking which, in Member State A, opposes the importation of goods bearing the trade mark "Ideal Standard".

*****

On those grounds, THE COURT, in answer to the question referred to it by the Oberlandesgericht Dusseldorf, by order of 15 December 1992,

Hereby Rules:

There is no unlawful restriction on trade between Member States within the meaning of Articles 30 and 36 where a subsidiary operating in Member State A of a manufacturer established in Member State B is to be enjoined from using as a trade mark the name "Ideal Standard" because of the risk of confusion with a device having the same origin, even if the manufacturer is lawfully using that name in his country of origin under a trade mark protected there, he acquired that trade mark by assignment and the trade mark originally belonged to a company affiliated to the undertaking which, in Member State A, opposes the importation of goods bearing the trade mark "Ideal Standard".

Notes and Questions

1. Article 30[1] of the EC Treaty provides:

    Quantitative restrictions on imports and all measures having equivalent effect shall, without prejudice to the following provisions, be prohibited between Member States.

    Article 36 of the EC Treaty provides:

    The provisions of Articles 30 to 34 shall not preclude prohibitions or restrictions on imports, exports or goods in transit justified on grounds of public morality, public policy or public security; the protection of health and life of humans, animals or plants; the protection of national treasures possessing artistic, historic or archaeological value; or the protection of industrial and commercial property. Such prohibitions

---

[1] The numbering of the articles of the EC Treaty will be modified as a consequence of the Amsterdam Treaty. Articles 30 and 36 will become articles 28 and 30 respectively.

or restrictions shall not, however, constitute a means of arbitrary discrimination or a disguised restriction on trade between Member States.

One of the principal objectives of the European Economic Community (established in 1958) was to eliminate tariffs and quotas that inhibited trade between its member states. Shortly after the Community came into being, the ECJ perceived that the free movement of goods and services might be substantially impaired by forms of regulation more subtle than tariffs and quotas, such as through the adoption of national regulatory schemes that directly or indirectly discriminated against outsiders. The EC Treaty did not specifically address each more subtle form of discrimination, so the Court began to fashion a jurisprudence based on Article 30 which characterized these other forms of discriminatory regulation as measures with the "equivalent effect" of quotas. There is today an extensive body of ECJ case law interpreting and applying Article 30, and considering its relationship to Article 36. We will study more of this jurisprudence as it relates to IPRs later in the book.

2. The ECJ's decision in *Ideal Standard* identifies an important paradox in international law as it relates to trademarks. The ECJ notes that a main function of the trademark is to indicate the source of goods so as to permit consumers to identify their quality. This same function of the mark was stressed by the U.S. Supreme Court in *Qualitex*. Yet the ECJ accepts that a trademark holder may sell and transfer its mark for a particular country (based on the principle of independence) to a party over which it will have absolutely no control — except, according to the ECJ, that the seller of the trademark may block the importation of goods bearing the transferee's identical mark into other countries where the seller of the mark continues to hold equivalent trademark rights (based on the principle of territoriality).[2] The paradox is that consumers are expected to associate the mark with goods of a particular enterprise, thereby identifying quality characteristics, while goods bearing identical trademarks may be placed on different markets by different enterprises without a common quality control standard.

---

[2]This is an exception to the ECJ's own "intra-Union exhaustion" jurisprudence, which holds that when goods are placed on the market in any member state of the Union with the consent of the trademark holder, a parallel trademark in another member state may not be used to block importation.

Does the ECJ's decision in *Ideal Standard* adequately account for the realities of the global (or European) marketplace? If a German construction contractor or real estate developer does business in France, will that person know that "Ideal Standard" heating equipment sold in France is made by a different company than the one that makes "Ideal Standard" sanitary fixtures in Germany? The economic function of the trademark is to make markets more efficient by allowing consumers to determine quality characteristics quickly — without extensive investigation. How will the German construction contractor determine the "lineage" of its equipment? Will the contractor investigate corporate records and trademark registrations in France?

---

7. Integrated Circuit Layout-Design Protection

a. The Origin and Nature of the *Sui Generis* IC Layout-Design Right

The protection of intellectual property in integrated circuit (or semiconductor device) layout-design is a *sui generis* form of IPR that developed largely in the 1980s. The initial impetus came from the U.S. semiconductor industry, which pursued and obtained domestic legislation on the subject. Similar legislation soon followed in Japan and the EU.[1] In 1989, the Treaty on Intellectual Property in respect of Integrated Circuits (IC Treaty) was concluded. This Treaty has not entered into force because of industry concerns over certain terms. The TRIPS Agreement, however, incorporates the substantive provisions of the IC Treaty, with amendments designed to address those concerns.

An integrated circuit (IC) or semiconductor device is produced by depositing and etching a pattern of electricity-conducting materials, e.g., aluminum, and insulating material on to a semiconducting base, usually silicon. The pattern forms a series of transistors designed to perform computational functions. By designing smaller transistors and placing them closer together, engineers can produce ICs that run faster.

The pattern that is deposited and etched on to a semiconducting base

---

[1]For these legislative references, see Frederick M. Abbott, *Introductory Note to WIPO: Treaty on Intellectual Property in Respect of Integrated Circuits*, 28 I.L.M. 1477 (1989), at note 3.

is embodied in a three-dimensional map, referred to as a *mask work, layout-design* or *topography*, that is used to guide the complex equipment that creates the physical end-product IC. Once such a mask work is created, it can be used by any semiconductor foundry with the requisite technical expertise to produce the subject IC. The objective of the IC producer is to assure that its competitors are not able to use a mask work it has developed to create an identical or substantially similar product.

Engineers are able to reverse engineer a mask work starting with a finished IC product. This is a complex and costly process. Nevertheless, a reverse-engineered IC may be significantly less expensive to produce than a newly-developed product.

Integrated circuit layout-design protection generally entitles the right holder to prohibit the unauthorized *reproduction* of its mask work in an IC. The use of the term *reproduction* in IC protection legislation, and in the IC Treaty, signifies that it is the *copying* of a protected design which is prohibited by the IC Treaty, since Article 9 of the Berne Convention uses the term *reproduction* to define the act which a copyright holder is entitled to authorize. In this regard, IC protection is more similar to copyright than patent protection. However, the term of IC layout-design protection generally is ten years, which is a considerably shorter term than copyright protection, and about half that of patent protection.

IC layout-design protection is generally secured by registration of the mask work with an appropriate national or regional authority, although certain countries, such as Sweden, provide for protection without registration. Examination of the application by such an authority to determine whether the mask work meets the substantive requirement of originality is not a precondition of registration demanded by the terms of the IC Treaty, and a substantive examination is not ordinarily undertaken by registering authorities. However, such a substantive examination does not appear to be precluded by the terms of the IC Treaty. Whether a registered mask work or layout-design meets the relevant standards for protection is generally a matter that is left for the market to resolve through civil litigation following registration.[2]

In its decision in the following case, *Brooktree v. Advanced Micro Devices*, the U.S. Court of Appeals for the Federal Circuit explains why the IC

---

[2]Note, for example, that pursuant to the U.S. Semiconductor Chip Protection Act (1984), registration with the Copyright Office establishes a presumption that a mask work is protected, thereby placing the burden of proof on a party challenging the entitlement to protection. 17 U.S.C. §908(f).

industry concluded that a *sui generis* form of IPR was needed to protect its commercial interests.

b. Substantial Similarity and Reverse Engineering

In our earlier discussion of the patent, we noted that in the United States all appeals of lower court patent decisions are heard by the Court of Appeals for the Federal Circuit (CAFC) located in Washington D.C. The *Brooktree* case involved claims of both patent infringement and infringement of a protected semiconductor mask work. While an appeal solely regarding semiconductor mask work infringement would ordinarily have been heard by the Court of Appeals for the Ninth Circuit, the appeal on patent issues required that the case be decided by the CAFC. The CAFC indicates, however, that it will apply the "discernable law of the Ninth Circuit" regarding mask work infringement issues, reflecting the fact that it is not granted the same kind of power to consolidate U.S. mask work law as it is to consolidate U.S. patent law.

The CAFC offers an explanation of how semiconductor mask works came to be the subject of a *sui generis* or product-specific form of IPR. Regarding copyright, the concern of the semiconductor industry was that courts would find the layout-design of semiconductor devices to be dictated by utilitarian concerns. In other words, the arrangement of electronic features would be found to take a specific form because that was necessary to make the semiconductor device perform its functions. Copyright does not protect ideas as such, or methods of operation. Recall, for example, that in *Lotus v. Borland*, reviewed earlier, the court found that Lotus's spreadsheet command structure constituted a method of operation not protected by copyright. Though U.S. courts did not definitively rule on the copyrightable character of semiconductor mask works before the industry began its efforts to obtain a new form of protection, the industry perceived a substantial risk that such works would not be protected.

Patent presented other problems. As a matter of principle, a semiconductor device produced by a mask work, or a mask work itself, may qualify for patent protection. A semiconductor device is certainly capable of being a novel, useful and non-obvious product. A mask work in its own right might constitute a process for producing that product. However, most advances in semiconductor technology are incremental — they build on a great deal of prior research and published literature. This means that in many cases it will be difficult to separate the novel element from the prior art, and this may create difficulties in obtaining protection and in prosecuting patent infringement cases. Second, the process of securing a patent may be lengthy, and patent protection generally does not apply before a patent is granted.[3] Since many semiconductor advances have a short *useful life*, patent protection may come too late to help the innovator. Finally, the question whether the solution to a semiconductor development problem would be obvious to a person skilled in the art may be difficult to answer, and again may constitute an obstacle to obtaining protection and to successful prosecution of an infringement action. In sum, while patent protection may be available for a semiconductor and mask work, and while in some cases a patent may provide the ideal form of protection, in many cases the patent will present difficulties.

Note the CAFC's analogy to copyright and the doctrine of "substantial similarity" for determining whether a mask work is infringed. The reproduction of a relatively small portion of a mask work may constitute infringement, if that portion is of particular importance to the performance of the product. Likewise, cosmetic differences may not save an alternative layout-design from constituting infringement. In the United States, whether there is infringement is a question of fact decided by a jury.

AMD's primary defense to the infringement claim is that its new design is the result of reverse engineering permitted by the Semiconductor Chip Protection Act (and also, though not relevant in this case, by the IC Treaty). A design arrived at by reverse engineering must in any event be original. Reverse engineering may provide some additional leeway for similarity in design. In this case, AMD's defense was rejected by the jury, and this decision was affirmed by the Court of Appeals because, in the final analysis, AMD simply copied Brooktree's layout-design.

---

[3]There are some exceptions based on publication of applications, which we will study later.

Brooktree Corporation, Plaintiff/Cross-Appellant, v. Advanced Micro Devices, Inc., Defendant/Appellant

United States Court of Appeals for the Federal Circuit
977 F.2d 1555; 1992 U.S. App. LEXIS 25567

October 9, 1992, Decided

Subsequent History: Petition for Rehearing Denied January 4, 1993, Reported at 1993 U.S. App. LEXIS 415.

Prior History: Appealed from: U.S. District Court for the Southern District of California. Judge Enright

Disposition: Affirmed.

Judges: Before Newman, Michel, and Rader, Circuit Judges.

Opinion:

Newman, Circuit Judge.

Brooktree Corporation brought suit against Advanced Micro Devices, Inc. (herein AMD) for patent infringement, 35 U.S.C. § 271, and infringement of mask work registrations, 17 U.S.C. § 910, in connection with certain semiconductor chips used in color video displays. The United States District Court for the Southern District of California entered judgment that the patents were valid and infringed and that the registered mask works were infringed, assessing damages.[1]

The principal issues on appeal arise under the Patent Act, of which the Federal Circuit has exclusive appellate jurisdiction, 28 U.S.C. § 1295(a)(1), and the Semiconductor Chip Protection Act, of which this court's appellate jurisdiction is pendent. Thus for issues of fact and law under the Semicon-

---

[1]Brooktree Corp. v. Advanced Micro Devices, Inc., 757 F. Supp. 1088, 18 USPQ2d 1692 (S.D. Cal. 1990).

ductor Chip Protection Act we apply the discernable law of the Ninth Circuit, in accordance with the principles set forth in Atari, Inc. v. JS&A Group, Inc., 747 F.2d 1422, 1438-40, 223 USPQ 1074, 108687 (Fed. Cir. 1984) (en banc) (applying copyright law of the circuit in which the case was tried, thus avoiding creating new opportunities for forum shopping). Judicial consideration of the Semiconductor Chip Protection Act has thus far been sparse, and we have given particular attention to the statute and its history, for the parties dispute significant aspects of statutory interpretation.

This case occasioned a lengthy trial over the course of seven weeks before the jury, in consecutive determinations of liability and damages. The jury verdicts were the subject of duly filed motions for judgment notwithstanding the verdict and for a new trial, which motions were denied by the district court. AMD charges error on issues of mask work infringement and damages, and also on issues of patent validity, infringement, and willfulness. Brooktree cross-appeals certain damages rulings, and the denial of attorney fees under both the Patent Act and the Semiconductor Chip Protection Act.

I

Mask Works

The Semiconductor Chip Protection Act

The Semiconductor Chip Protection Act of 1984, Pub. L. 98-620, Title III, 98 Stat. 3347, codified at 17 U.S.C. §§ 901-914, arose from concerns that existing intellectual property laws did not provide adequate protection of proprietary rights in semiconductor chips that had been designed to perform a particular function. The Act, enacted after extensive congressional consideration and hearings over several years, adopted relevant aspects of existing intellectual property law, but for the most part created a new law, specifically adapted to the protection of design layouts of semiconductor chips.

Chip design layouts embody the selection and configuration of electrical components and connections in order to achieve the desired electronic functions. The electrical elements are configured in three dimensions, and are built up in layers by means of a series of "masks" whereby, using photographic depositing and etching techniques, layers of metallic, insulating, and semiconductor material are deposited in the desired pattern on a wafer of silicon. This set of masks is called a "mask work", and is part of the semiconductor chip product. The statute defines a mask work as:

a series of related images, however fixed or encoded

(A) having or representing the predetermined, three dimensional pattern of metallic, insulating, or semiconductor material present or removed from the layers of a semiconductor chip product; and

(B) in which series the relation of the images to one another is that each image has the pattern of the surface of one form of a semiconductor chip product.

17 U.S.C. § 901(a)(2). The semiconductor chip product in turn is defined as:

the final or intermediate form of any product —

(A) having two or more layers of metallic, insulating, or semiconductor material, deposited or otherwise placed on, or etched away or otherwise removed from, a piece of semiconductor material in accordance with a predetermined pattern; and

(B) intended to perform electronic circuitry functions.

17 U.S.C. § 901(a)(1).

The design of a satisfactory chip layout may require extensive effort and be extremely time consuming, particularly as new and improved electronic capabilities are sought to be created. A new semiconductor chip may incur large research and development costs, yet after the layout is imprinted in the mask work and the chip is available in commerce, it can be copied at a fraction of the cost to the originator. Thus there was concern that widespread copying of new chip layouts would have adverse effects on innovative advances in semiconductor technology, as stated in the Senate Report:

In the semiconductor industry, innovation is indispensable; research breakthroughs are essential to the life and health of the industry. But research and innovation in the design of semiconductor chips are threatened by the inadequacies of existing legal protection against piracy and unauthorized copying. This problem, which is so critical to this essential sector of the American economy, is addressed by the Semiconductor Chip Protection Act of 1984.

* * *

The Semiconductor Chip Protection Act of 1984, . . . would prohibit "chip piracy" — the unauthorized copying and distribution of semiconductor chip products copied from the original creators of such works.

S. Rep. No. 425, 98th Cong., 2d Sess., 1 (1984) (hereinafter Senate Report).

In the evolution of the Semiconductor Chip Protection Act it was first proposed simply to amend the Copyright Act, 17 U.S.C. § 101 et seq., to include semiconductor chip products and mask works as subject of copyright. See H.R. 1028, 98th Cong., 1st Sess. (1983). However, although some courts had interpreted copyright law as applicable to computer software imbedded in a semiconductor chip, see Apple Computer, Inc. v. Franklin Commuter Corp., 714 F.2d 1240, 1249, 219 USPQ 113, 121 (3d Cir. 1983), cert. dismissed, 464 U.S. 1033 (1984), it was uncertain whether the copyright law could protect against copying of the pattern on the chip itself, if the pattern was deemed inseparable from the utilitarian function of the chip. Indeed, the Copyright Office had refused to register patterns on printed circuit boards and semiconductor chips because no separate artistic aspects had been demonstrated. Copyright Protection for Semiconductor Chips: Hearings on H.R. 1028 Before the Subcomm. on Courts, Civil Liberties, and the Administration of Justice of the House Comm. on the Judiciary, 98th Cong., 1st Sess., 77 (1983) (hereinafter 1983 House Hearings) (statement of Dorothy Schrader, Associate Register of Copyrights for Legal Affairs). Concern was also expressed that extension of the copyright law to accommodate the problems of mask works would distort certain settled copyright doctrines, such as fair use. 1983 House Hearings at 16-17 (statement of Jon A. Baumgarten, Copyright Counsel, Association of American Publishers, Inc.)

The patent system alone was deemed not to provide the desired scope of protection of mask works. Although electronic circuitry and electronic components are within the statutory subject matter of patentable invention, see 35 U.S.C. § 101, and some original circuitry may be patentable if it also meets the requirements of the Patent Act, as is illustrated in this case, Congress sought more expeditious protection against copying of original circuit layouts, whether or not they met the criteria of patentable invention. Senate Report at 8.

The Semiconductor Chip Protection Act of 1984 was an innovative solution to this new problem of technology-based industry. While some copyright principles underlie the law, as do some attributes of patent law, the Act was uniquely adapted to semiconductor mask works, in order to achieve appropriate protection for original designs while meeting the competitive needs of the industry and serving the public interest.

The Semiconductor Chip Protection Act provides for the grant of certain exclusive rights to owners of registered mask works, including the exclusive right "to reproduce the mask work by optical, electronic, or any other means", and the exclusive right "to import or distribute a semiconductor chip product in which the mask work is embodied". 17 U.S.C. § 905. Mask works that are not "original", or that consist of "designs that are staple, commonplace, or familiar in the semiconductor industry, or variations of such designs, combined in a way that, considered as a whole, is not original", are excluded from protection. 17 U.S.C. § 902(b). Protection is also not extended to any "idea, procedure, process, system, method of operation, concept, principle, or discovery, regardless of the form in which it is described, explained, illustrated or embodied" in the mask work. 17 U.S.C. § 902(c).

The sponsors and supporters of this legislation foresaw that there would be areas of uncertainty in application of this new law to particular situations, and referred to "gray areas" wherein factual situations could arise that would not have easy answers. Those areas are emphasized by both parties in the assignments of error on this appeal.

Brooktree's Mask Work Registrations

Brooktree was granted mask work registration MW 2873 on August 6, 1987, and registration MW 3838 on July 6, 1988, for its chips identified as Bt451 and Bt458. These Brooktree chips embody a circuit design that combines the functions of a static random access memory (SRAM) and a digital to analog converter (DAC). This circuitry, sometimes referred to as

RAMDAC, acts as a "color palette", producing the colors in color video displays having high speed and enhanced picture resolution. A Brooktree witness described these chips as a technological breakthrough, exceeding limits in speed and performance that had been believed impossible to exceed. Brooktree stated that a single Bt458 chip replaced a previously used set of 36 chips (an AMD product) and offered many advantages. A Brooktree witness testified that these chips were extremely successful commercially, and were soon incorporated into new designs for video display systems made by several large manufacturers.

A critical component of the Brooktree chips is the core cell, a ten-transistor SRAM cell which is repeated over six thousand times in an array covering about eighty percent of the chip area. Each core cell consists of ten transistors and metal conductors electrically connecting the transistors throughout the three dimensions of the multilayered cell. Brooktree charged that this core cell was copied by AMD, thus infringing Brooktree's mask work registrations.

AMD does not challenge the validity of these mask work registrations, or dispute Brooktree's position that its chips are protected under the Semiconductor Chip Protection Act. AMD does, however, assert that its accused chips are not infringements, for reasons we shall discuss.

Infringement

The Semiconductor Chip Protection Act defines an "infringing semiconductor chip product" as one which is "made, imported, or distributed in violation of the exclusive rights" of the mask work owner. 17 U.S.C. § 901(a)(9). The text of the Semiconductor Chip Protection Act sets forth the subject matter of protection in terms of certain exclusive rights, including, inter alia, the exclusive right to "reproduce the mask work", 17 U.S.C. § 905. This usage mirrors the words of the Copyright Act, which states the exclusive rights of copyright owners "to reproduce the copyrighted work". 17 U.S.C. § 106. Although the Semiconductor Chip Protection Act does not uses the word "copy" to describe infringement, the parallel language reflects the incorporation of the well-explicated copyright principle of substantial similarity into the Semiconductor Chip Protection Act, as discussed infra.

The jury instruction on the criteria for establishing infringement included the instruction that infringement requires substantial similarity to a material portion of the registered mask work:

To establish infringement, Brooktree must show that A.M.D.'s mask works are substantially similar to a material portion of the mask works in Brooktree's chips covered by Brooktree's mask work registration. No hard and fast rule or percentage governs what constitutes a, quote, "substantial similarity." Substantial similarity may exist where an important part of the mask work is copied, even though the percentage of the entire chip which is copied may be relatively small. It is not required that A.M.D. make a copy of the entire mask work embodied in the Brooktree chip.

AMD states that it does not on appeal challenge this jury instruction. Instead, AMD argues that because the non-SRAM portion of its accused chip was not copied, the chips are not "substantially similar", whatever the materiality of the SRAM cell to the total mask work. It was undisputed that there was not duplication of the entire chip. AMD states that the Semiconductor Chip Protection Act requires copying of the entire chip, and therefore that it was entitled to judgment in its favor as a matter of law, or at least to a new trial on the issue.

The principle of substantial similarity recognizes that the existence of differences between an accused and copyrighted work may not negate infringement if a material portion of the copyrighted work is appropriated. Shaw v. Lindheim, 919 F.2d 1353, 1362, 15 USPQ2d 1516, 1523 (9th Cir. 1990). If the copied portion is qualitatively important, the finder of fact may properly find substantial similarity under copyright law, Baxter v. MCA, Inc., 812 F.2d 421, 425, 2 USPQ2d 1059, 1063 (9th Cir.), cert. denied, 484 U.S. 954, 98 L. Ed. 2d 372, 108 S. Ct. 346 (1987), and under the Semiconductor Chip Protection Act.

Brooktree agrees that the SRAM portion of the accused chips covers only eighty percent of the chip area, and that the remaining circuitry was not copied by AMD. Infringement under the statute does not require that all parts of the accused chip be copied. The district court's explanation to the jury was in full accord with the statutory grant of exclusive rights to reproduce the mask work. The statutory interpretation now pressed by AMD, viz., that the entire chip must have been copied, is unsupported. Indeed, the House Report states that it was contemplated that the cell layout alone could be misappropriated:

Mask works sometimes contain substantial areas of (so-called "cells") whose layouts involve creativity and are commercially valuable. In appropriate fact settings, the misappropriation of such a cell — assuming it meets the original standards of this chapter — could be the basis for an infringement action under this chapter.

H.R. Rep. No. 781, 98th Cong., 2d Sess., 26-27 (1984), reprinted in 1984 U.S. Code Cong. & Admin. News 5750 (hereinafter House Report) (footnote omitted). As explained in the Explanatory Memorandum — Mathias-Leahy Amendment to S. 1201, 130 Cong. Rec. S12,916 (daily ed. Oct. 3, 1984) (hereinafter Mathias-Leahy Memorandum), written to explain the House and Senate bills as they were enacted, id. at S12,923, the Congressional intention was to protect against "piecemeal copying" and "copying of a material portion" of a chip:

> ... the amendment, like both bills, incorporates the familiar copyright principle of substantial similarity. Although as a practical matter, copying of an insubstantial portion of a chip and independent design of the remainder is not likely, copying of a material portion nevertheless constitutes infringement. This concept is particularly important in the semiconductor industry, where it may be economical, for example, to copy 75% of a mask work from one chip and combine that with 25% of another mask work, if the copies are transferable modules, such as units from a cell library.
>
> As the Senate report notes, no hard and fast percentages govern what constitutes a "substantial" copying because substantial similarity may exist where an important part of a mask work is copied even though the percentage copied may be relatively small. Nonetheless, mask work owners are protected not only from wholesale copying but also against piecemeal copying of substantial or material portions of one or more mask works.

Mathias-Leahy Memorandum at S12,917.

Whether an appropriation of a cell layout constitutes infringement in a particular case is for the trier of fact, and can not be decided as a matter of law. See Sid & Marty Krofft Television Productions, Inc. v. McDonald's Corp., 562 F.2d 1157, 1164, 196 USPQ 97, 102-03 (9th Cir. 1977) (question of substantial similarity under copyright law is for the trier of fact). We shall discuss this question post, for it was litigated in the context of AMD's defense of reverse engineering.

The Reverse Engineering Defense

AMD's position at trial, and on appeal, was that its core cell was the product of reverse engineering of the Brooktree chip, and therefore does not constitute infringement under the Semiconductor Chip Protection Act. Reverse engineering is a statutory defense, included in the Act upon extensive congressional attention to the workings of the semiconductor chip industry.

The statute provides that it is not an infringement of a registered mask work for

(1) a person to reproduce the mask work solely for the purpose of teaching, analyzing, or evaluating the concepts or techniques embodied in the mask work or the circuitry, logic flow, or organization of components used in the mask work; or

(2) a person who performs the analysis or evaluation described in paragraph (1) to incorporate the results of such conduct in an original mask work which is made to be distributed.

17 U.S.C. § 906(a). The statute thus provides that one engaged in reverse engineering shall not be liable for infringement when the end product is itself original. In performing reverse engineering a person may disassemble, study, and analyze an existing chip in order to understand it. This knowledge may be used to create an original chip having a different design layout, but which performs the same or equivalent function as the existing chip, without penalty or prohibition. Congress was told by industry representatives that reverse engineering was an accepted and fair practice, and leads to improved chips having "form, fit, and function" compatibility with the existing chip, thereby serving competition while advancing the state of technology. Senate Report at 21.

Much attention was given by Congress and by witnesses to the question of how to determine whether a chip layout was born of legitimate reverse engineering or of copying. It was foreseen that there would be a "gray area" wherein the rights of the parties, on the facts of a particular chip design, would require resolution on a fact-dependent, case-by-case basis. The following colloquy illustrates concerns raised at the hearings:

Rep. EDWARDS: . . . Is the chief reservation here the idea that reverse engineering, which all the witnesses agree is appropriate, might be confused with pirating and that any kind of reverse engineering might be interpreted under this law as pirating?

Mr. MacPHERSON (of Fairchild Camera & Instrument Corp.): I think that's one of the very strong concerns that we have, yes. There is a very gray area here in the very nature of reverse engineering, which would leave an individual engaged in that practice uncertain what his ultimate rights would be should he use that particular result in another product.

Copyright Protection for Imprinted Design Patterns on Semiconductor Chips: Hearings Before the Subcomm. on Courts, Civil Liberties, and the Administration of Justice of the House Comm. on the Judiciary, 96th Cong., 1st Sess., 66 (1979).

This aspect was explored over the several years of legislative gestation. The reverse engineering procedure was described by witnesses, and distinguished in purpose and mechanism from the copying against which the Semiconductor Chip Protection Act was intended to guard. It was explained that a person engaged in reverse engineering seeks to understand the design of the original chip with the object of improving the circuitry, the chip layout, or both. The presence of innovation and improvement was stressed as the hallmark of an original layout. A witness explained the difference as determining "was anything innovative done in the process or was it simply a reproduction of what was already there?" The Semiconductor Chip Protection Act of 1983: Hearings on S. 1201 Before the Subcomm. on Patents, Copyrights, and Trademarks of the Senate Comm. on the Judiciary, 98th Cong., 1st Sess., 84 (1983) (testimony of Stanley C. Corwin). Another witness explained that reverse engineering generally produces a "paper trail" recording the engineer's efforts to understand the original chip and to design a different version after reverse engineering:

Whenever there is a true case of reverse engineering, the second firm will have prepared a great deal of paper — logic and circuit diagrams, trial layouts, computer simulations of the chip, and the like; it will also have invested thousands of hours of work. All of these can be documented by reference to the firm's ordinary business records. A pirate has no such papers, for the pirate does none of this work. Therefore,

175

whether there has been a true reverse engineering job or just a job of copying can be shown by looking at the defendant's records. The paper trail of a chip tells a discerning observer whether the chip is a copy or embodies the effort of reverse engineering.

Senate Report at 22 (quoting statement of Leslie L. Valdasz, Senior Vice President, Intel Corporation). The Committee reports and the statements of the Semiconductor Chip Protection Act's supporters show the belief that evidence of the presence or absence of such a paper trail would significantly reduce the gray area between legitimate and illegitimate behavior. See Mathias-Leahy Memorandum at S12,917; House Report at 21.

Senators Mathias and Leahy explained that § 906(a) includes a provision

> to clarify the intent of both chambers that competitors are permitted not only to study the protected mask works, but also to use the results of that study to design, distribute and import semiconductor chip products embodying their own original mask works.

> * * *

> The end product of the reverse engineering process is not an infringement, and itself qualifies for protection under the Act, if it is an original mask work as contrasted with a substantial copy. If the resulting semiconductor chip product is not substantially identical to the original, and its design involved significant toil and investment, so that it is not mere plagiarism, it does not infringe the original chip, even if the layout of the two chips is, in substantial part, similar.

Mathias-Leahy Memorandum at S12,917.

In illuminating the meaning of "original" in the context of reverse engineering, Senators Mathias and Leahy distinguished between a substantial copy, on one hand, and the product of reverse engineering which might be similar to the original, but if not a substantial copy would not be an infringement. For the latter, the "paper trail" was expected to document efforts in "analyzing, or evaluating the concepts or techniques embodied in the mask work or the circuitry, logic flow, or organization of components used in the mask work", as the effort required would be reflected in the documents. Id.

AMD's defense was that its chips were independently designed after the Brooktree chips were subjected to reverse engineering to learn the Brooktree design. The question of whether AMD's activities were acceptable reverse engineering, or unacceptable copying, was explained to the jury as follows:

> Reverse engineering is permitted and is authorized by the Chip Protection Act. It is not infringement of an owner's exclusive right and protected mask work for another person, through reverse-engineering, to photograph and to study the mask work for the purpose of analyzing its circuitry — correction — the circuitry, logic flow and organization of the components used in the mask work and to incorporate such analysis into an original mask work.
>
> The end product of the reverse-engineering process may be an original mask work, and therefore not an infringing mask work, if the resulting semiconductor chip product is not substantially identical to the protected mask work and its design involved significant toil and investment so that it is not mere plagiarism.
>
> You should place great weight on the existence of reverse paperwork trail in determining whether the defendant's mask work is an original mask work from reverse-engineering.
>
> A.M.D. mask work constitutes an original mask work if A.M.D.'s mask work incorporates its own new design elements which offered improvements over or an alternative to Brooktree's mask work.

These instructions focus the jury on whether AMD produced an original mask work, as the statute requires. The instructions were not challenged by AMD on its motion for new trial or on appeal, and were adapted from AMD's proposed instructions. Brooktree calls the instructions "too lenient". Whether or not too lenient, they were not objected to by AMD at trial, and are not now criticized by AMD as incorrect. They are the law applied in this case. See Fed. R. Civ. P. 51; Herrington v. County of Sonoma, 834 F.2d 1488, 1500 n.12 (9th Cir. 1987), cert. denied, 489 U.S. 1090, 103 L. Ed. 2d 860, 109 S. Ct. 1557 (1989) (failure to object to a jury instruction precludes appellate review).

The Trial

The factual premises of the issues of infringement and AMD's reverse engineering defense were extensively explored at trial, through examination and cross-examination of witnesses, exhibits, displays, and attorney argument. To summarize, AMD argued at trial, and repeats on this appeal, that it did not intend to copy Brooktree's layout, and did not do so. AMD pointed to its "paper trail" of its two and a half years of effort at a cost in excess of three million dollars. AMD stated that if its intent had been to copy the Brooktree layout, it would simply have directed duplication of the circuit layouts, requiring a matter of months, not years. AMD stressed differences between its chips and those of Brooktree, and pointed out its aversion to piracy. According to AMD, this case is not in the gray area where reasonable minds could differ over whether there was reverse engineering or copying. AMD argues that Congress could not have intended that mask work infringement be found in the circumstances of this case, and that this court should hold, as a matter of law, that AMD did not infringe Brooktree's mask work registrations.

Brooktree, on its part, argued that AMD's cell layout is not original, but was directly copied from Brooktree's SRAM core cell, and repeated 6,000 times. Brooktree stressed AMD's lengthy and expensive failures at designing a layout. Brooktree observed that AMD had incorrectly analyzed Brooktree's chip during its attempts at reverse engineering, and that throughout this entire period of attempted duplication of function, AMD was unable to come close to Brooktree's results. Brooktree pointed to the rapidity with which AMD changed to Brooktree's layout when the error in analysis was discovered, AMD immediately producing, without further experimentation, a substantially identical SRAM cell.

At trial there was extensive evidence of AMD's design efforts, including its full paper trail. Evidence included the following: William Plants, AMD's assigned designer of the SRAM core cell, testified that AMD initiated a project to design a color palette chip in January, 1986, based on Brooktree's announcement of such a chip the previous November and introduction of its Bt451 chip in February 1986. In April AMD obtained several Brooktree Bt451 chips. Plants opened up one of the chips and had it photographed, including blow-ups of the SRAM portion, which he said was of particular interest to him. After studying the chip he prepared a "reverse engineering report" in June, 1986. Plants incorrectly concluded that the Brooktree chip had eight transistors in each SRAM cell rather than ten. Plants then abandoned his efforts to design an SRAM cell based on six transistors, and attempted, over the next six months, to create an SRAM core cell design based on eight transistors. These attempts were not successful.

There was evidence of increasing pressure to complete the design, including suggestions by AMD supervisors that Plants reexamine the Brooktree chip because the project had gotten "bogged down". Plants did so some time in late January or early February. Plants testified that it was toward the end of January 1987 when he changed to a ten-transistor design in the same arrangement as Brooktree's design. Plants admitted that he did "solve the problem in a week" by adopting the ten-transistor design. Plants denied, however, that he learned of the ten-transistor design from his reexamination of the Brooktree chip, but explained that the design had been suggested to him by a job candidate he interviewed during that period. That candidate did not testify, and an AMD witness said he was dead.

There was extensive exploration at trial of the events during this period, of Plants' design processes, and of the timing and other details of the successful AMD ten-transistor design. For instance, Plants testified that his reexamination of the Brooktree chip was prompted not by pressure from his supervisors, but by a memory flash, like a "bolt from the blue", of something he had seen previously in the Brooktree chip.

In addition, there was extensive testimony and demonstrative and documentary evidence that the similarities in the circuit designs led to the substantial identity between the layouts of the Brooktree and AMD core cells. For example, Plants testified that in laying out the ten-transistor SRAM cell for fabrication in silicon, he never changed the locations of the ten transistors in his design, and never considered alternatives to Brooktree's transistor arrangement. Michael Brunolli, the engineer responsible for the layout of the Brooktree SRAM cell, testified that, in contrast, he had gone through about six changes of transistor layout before he achieved the final design.

Brooktree's expert witness Richard Crisp testified that the layout of the Brooktree SRAM cell was unique and original, and was not a commonplace or staple design. Crisp stated that the most important factor in layout of the SRAM cell is the location of the transistors. Crisp showed the jury exhibits picturing alternative layouts of electrically identical ten-transistor SRAM core cells in other chips, illustrating different layouts of the same circuitry. Plants had agreed that "you could conceivably come up with an infinite number of layouts" for the ten-transistor cell.

Plants admitted that the metal lines connecting the transistors in one layer of his layout were in the same sequence or order as the corresponding lines in the Brooktree chip, although his design had an extra metal line in it.

Crisp testified that the extra metal line in AMD's layout did not relate to any function of the SRAM core cell itself. Plants also admitted that he originally included 45-degree angled portions in the polysilicon layer of his initial layout, a feature found in the Brooktree layout. Plants said he later removed the angles at the request of AMD's production engineers because it was incompatible with AMD's process methodology. Brunolli testified that the 45-degree angled portions arose in his design as a result of design rules used at Brooktree, and that he chose the angles to make his cell layout more compact.

Crisp testified that the transistors, which "form the substance of the cell" were "grouped together in the same way" in the AMD and Brooktree layouts. Crisp showed a videotape of the Brooktree and AMD SRAM cells side-by-side and then overlaid. (This tape was shown four times, including once in the jury room.) He stopped the tape at various points to illustrate the similarities in the layout of the two chips, and explained that the differences were primarily the esult of AMD's smaller technology and removal of the 45-degree angles. Crisp testified that the differences between the cells were "very minor, trivial, insignificant", and "insignificant electrically", and that "the substance of the cells is the same." Plants had testified that minor differences in design layout would arise because the differing technologies of AMD and Brooktree resulted in each firm having different standard design rules for layout of semiconductor chips.

The standard of review is whether there was legally sufficient evidence (often called "substantial evidence") whereby a reasonable jury could have reached the verdict reached by this jury. Transgo, Inc. v. Ajac Transmission Parts Corp., 768 F.2d 1001, 1014, 227 USPQ 598, 602 (9th Cir. 1985), cert. denied, 474 U.S. 1059, 88 L. Ed. 2d 778, 106 S. Ct. 802 (1986). Rule 50 as amended states that judgment as a matter of law shall be granted when "a party has been fully heard with respect to an issue and there is no legally sufficient evidentiary basis for a reasonable jury to have found for that party with respect to that issue". Fed. R. Civ. P. 50(a)(1) (1992). This standard posits that a reasonable jury would have assessed the credibility of witnesses, considered and weighed the evidence presented by both sides, and applied the law in accordance with the court's instructions.

A reasonable jury could have placed weight on the evidence that AMD did not use an alternative transistor configuration but used Brooktree's configuration. A reasonable jury could have inferred that AMD's paper trail, insofar as it related to the SRAM cell, related entirely to AMD's failures, and that as soon as the Brooktree chip was correctly deciphered by reverse engineering, AMD did not create its own design but copied the Brooktree design. A reasonable jury could have resolved credibility questions in favor of Brooktree. Issues of credibility of witnesses are for the jury, and are not amenable to appellate review. Nicholson v. Rushen, 767 F.2d 1426, 1427 (9th Cir. 1985).

AMD argues on appeal that the sheer volume of paper established the reverse engineering defense "as a matter of law". AMD appears to misperceive the process, whereby the jury is instructed on the law, and applies the law to the facts and inferences reasonably drawn therefrom, based on the evidence adduced at trial. When there was sufficient evidence to support the verdict in light of the entire record, and upon correct or unobjected instructions of law, the jury's verdict must stand. . . . Reversal is proper only if the evidence permits only one reasonable conclusion. . . .

The jury was instructed on the law of the reverse engineering defense, and was told to place "great weight" on the paper trail. The correctness of a jury instruction is a question of law and, if objection to the instruction was timely made at trial, is reviewed on appeal to determine whether, on the whole, the jury instructions were adequate to ensure that the jury fully understood the legal issues for each element of the case. . . .

AMD's proposed interpretation of the reverse engineering defense is not supported in the statute. 17 U.S.C. § 906(a) requires, as an element of the defense of reverse engineering, that the product be original. The Senate Report described reverse engineering as activity that "spurs innovation and technological progress, as competitors seek to develop ever faster or more efficient chips, to perform similar or related functions". Senate Report at 21. The statute does not reflect an intent to excuse copying, as a matter of law, if the copier had first tried and failed to do the job without copying. The paper trail is evidence of independent effort, but it is not conclusive or incontrovertible proof of either originality or the absence of copying.

The questions of originality and copying are heavily fact-dependent, not absolutes of law. Where the evidence is such that reasonable minds could draw different conclusions, such questions are the province of the jury, as illustrated in analogous copyright cases, e.g., Twentieth Century-Fox Film Corp. v. MCA, Inc., 715 F.2d 1327, 1329, 217 USPQ 611, 612 (9th Cir. 1983) (question of whether there was copying was a "close enough question" to require trial); Dezendorf v. Twentieth Century-Fox Film Corp., 99 F.2d 850, 851 (9th Cir. 1938) (issue of originality is for the jury, not for the court).

AMD points out that there was conflicting evidence as to whether the AMD chips were improved. For example, AMD points to evidence that its accused chips were smaller, and as a result faster, than those of Brooktree, while Brooktree points to evidence that this was because AMD used 1.6 micron technology as opposed to Brooktree's older 2 micron technology. (The micron size refers to the length across a transistor gate.)

There was also extensive evidence of differences in the circuit layouts, and their significance. For example, AMD's expert, Dominick Richiuso, testified to specific differences between the AMD and Brooktree chips in the layouts of the interconnections between the SRAM cells and other portions of the chips, and in the SRAM cells themselves. These differences were acknowledged by Brooktree's expert Crisp, who testified that the similarities in the chip layouts, including the locations and interconnections of the transistors, were of far greater significance than the differences.

These fact-dependent areas were thoroughly aired at trial. The grant of judgment as a matter of law, by the trial judge or by the appellate court, is appropriate only when the evidence, with inferences drawn favorably to the party with the verdict, could not reasonably support the verdict. Dean v. Trans World Airlines, Inc., 924 F.2d 805, 810 (9th Cir. 1991).

We conclude that there was a legally sufficient evidentiary basis whereby a reasonable jury could have found infringement of the mask work registrations. The judgment is affirmed.

******

Notes and Questions

1. The practice of reverse engineering is common to many industries. Generally speaking, a company that introduces a new product will not turn over its designs to its competitors. These competitors, seeking to maintain their share of the market, will buy the new product and examine it. There is nothing inherently wrongful in examining a product that one lawfully purchases — and it is in the nature of competitive markets that business enter-

prises will seek to acquire the best information about the activities of their competitors. Moreover, the progress of science and industry is promoted if businesses are continually seeking to enhance their understanding of new developments, and to add their own improvements.

When may reverse engineering be wrongful?

This may depend on the form of IPR that protects a product. Patent applicants are required to disclose their inventions as a condition of being granted a patent, so it is most unlikely that examining a patented invention would be wrongful. One is precluded from making a product that is the same as a patented product even as a result of reverse engineering. Making a product that innovates over a reverse-engineered product does not violate the patentee's rights. What separates a patented product from a new product may of course be the subject of dispute.

Reverse engineering raises more difficult questions in the copyright area, particularly as it relates to computer software. Sellers/licensors of software generally do not provide copies of the "source code" (or human readable program instructions) to purchasers/licensees. In order to analyze a program, a competitor must "reverse compile" or "decompile" the "object code" (or machine readable instructions) of the program — that is, converting from the object code to the source code. In performing this reverse compilation, the competitor may be making an unauthorized copy (reproduction) or adaptation of the program. If the terms of a software sale or license do not permit this, the copyright holder may be able to prevent it.

But this does not end the inquiry. For example, the purchaser of a new program may have other programs which must be adapted to operate with it, so that the purchaser has a need to examine the way in which the new program functions. Manufacturers of computer hardware may need to understand the way in which software operates in order to design their systems to work properly with it. Is reverse engineering to perform these functions a "fair use" of copyrighted programs? The EU seeks to address these questions in its computer software directive which we will examine in Chapter IV.

Finally, if purchasers/licensees of computer software are prevented from analyzing it by the traditional rules of copyright law, have computer software programmers obtained a stronger form of IPRs protection under copyright law than they would have under patent law? Once again, is copyright well-suited to the protection of producer and consumer interests in computer software?

2. One implication of the U.S. Semiconductor Chip Protection Act is that by furnishing evidence of a reverse engineering paper trail, the producer of an IC is given more leeway than it would otherwise have to approximate the registered layout-design of another IC producer. The paper trail reflects investment in research which is said to distinguish the legitimate reverse engineering firm from the mere "counterfeiter." But "original" IC designs do not in any case infringe the rights of registered mask work holders, so why is more leeway needed by the reverse engineering firm? Are there two standards of originality — one for reverse engineering firms and one for others? What distinguishes them?

3. Attempts to establish integrated circuit layout-design protection on the multilateral level followed very soon upon the first introduction of such protection on the national level. The first national law, the U.S. Semiconductor Chip Protection Act, was enacted in 1984. The first multilateral agreement, the Treaty on Intellectual Property in Respect of Integrated Circuits, was concluded just five years later, in 1989. As noted above, the IC Treaty has never entered into force because of perceived deficiencies in the standards of protection which it provides. At the diplomatic conference in Washington D.C. at which the IC Treaty was concluded, developing countries expressed the fear that multilateral protection would favor only the countries that produced integrated circuits which, at the time, were mainly countries in the European Union, Japan and the United States. They also expressed the fear that multilateral protection might inhibit the development of production capacity in their own countries. The industrialized countries, on the other hand, drew attention to the considerable investment involved in creating an IC layout-design and the relative ease of copying. How are these competing interests of suspicion of developments that are occurring only in the industrialized world, on the one hand, and the desire to protect investment in innovations that enhance the quality of life, on the other hand, accommodated at the multilateral level? Is the tension between these interests constant and will it be, for example, reflected in the adjustment of the intellectual property system to the digital economy?

8. Geographical Indication of Origin

a. The Nature and Function of the Geographical Indication

A geographical indication is a sign or denomination by which the link of a product to a particular locality, region or country is legally protected. It provides exclusive rights for the use of geographical names in relation to a particular product, and prevents deceptive use of such names. The right essentially protects the goodwill associated with the name or the advantages or characteristics of a locality that lead to the reputation for quality of the particular products of that locality. Legal notions vary from one legal system to another, and we do not find well-defined common features in place throughout the world. Generally speaking, indications of source and appellations of origin may be distinguished.

An *indication of source* is constituted by any denomination, expression or sign indicating that a product or service originates in a country, a region or specific place (for instance, "made in . . , "). Here, no particular quality of the product is legally required. As a general rule, the use of false or deceptive indications of source is unlawful. An *appellation of origin* is constituted by the denomination of a country, a region or a specific place which serves to designate a product originating there, the qualities of which are due *exclusively or essentially to the geographical environment*, in other words to natural and/or human factors. Here, a link to the quality of the product and the locality is legally required. Generally, the use of an appellation of origin is lawful only for a certain circle of persons or enterprises located in the geographical area concerned and only in connection with the specific products originating therein (for instance, "Chianti", "Bordeaux"). Indications of source and appellations of origin provide exclusive rights which allow the prevention and remedy of the deceptive use of local names and the use of geographical names in connection with a product unrelated to that region.

Geographical indications traditionally fulfill two main functions.

- The promotion of products having certain characteristics is of considerable benefit to the region or area where the products are manufactured and to the area where they are marketed. Geographical indications protect producers of these regions or areas against unauthorized exploitation of the goodwill created by the quality of the products and the advertising appeal of the respective locality or region by competitors and their products. Entire sectors, such as wine growing, depend upon effective protection of geographical indications.

• Geographical indications are important sources of information for the consumer in an increasingly diverse market as to the origin, quality and reputation of a product. Moreover, the quest for specialized products generates a growing demand for products having an identifiable geographical origin.

The concept of geographical indication essentially originated in Europe where it has mainly been related to agricultural products and foodstuffs, eventually expanding to certain industrial products (e.g., Swiss watch). In other parts of the world, recognition of rights relating to geographical indications is far more restricted. This field of law is not uniform, but varies from one country to another. Many products in the New World and Third World bear traditional European names.

While some nations specifically recognize such title, others, such as the United States, protect the functions of geographical indications under general trade mark law, prohibiting deceptive use of geographical names. In addition, these functions can partly be assumed by collective marks and so-called guaranty marks which assure a certain quality of the products bearing such names by the imposition of regulatory controls. Moreover, the field of geographical indications increasingly overlaps with labeling requirements which, imposed or voluntarily, may indicate geographical origin (e.g., tropical wood) or the quality or methods of production (e.g., organic food). Finally, the legal relationship between geographical indications and rules of origin, used to define the origin of a product for purposes of tariffs and other trade policies, raises difficult and unsettled issues.

The field of geographical indications is subject to increasing international harmonization, in particular within the EU. The EC Council has issued a regulation on the protection of geographical indications and designations of origin for agricultural products and foodstuffs, to which the following case relates (Council Regulation 2081/92 of 14 July 1992 on the protection of geographical indications and designations of origin for agricultural products and foodstuffs, O.J. No. L 208, of 24.7.1992). The regulation lays down a procedure for the registration of a designation of origin or a geographical indication. First steps toward establishing common international legal rules regarding geographical indications were also taken in the TRIPS Agreement within the WTO.

Geographical indications are regularly conferred nationally or internationally following a formal procedure of registration. In some countries (e.g., Switzerland) such rights exist without registration. In international law and relations, protected geographical names usually are the object of bilaterally agreed lists of protected names. This is how legal security is achieved in distinguishing them from generic names in the countries concerned.

In addition, there is one multilateral agreement for the international registration of *appellations of origin,* which is administered by WIPO, the Lisbon Agreement for the Protection of Appellations of Origin and their International Registration. Only 18 countries, however, were party to the Lisbon Agreement as of April 1, 1999. Under the Agreement, the contracting states undertake to protect appellations that are registered pursuant to the Agreement. There were 835 registrations of appellations as of April 1, 1999.

b. The Goodwill Function of the Geographical Indication

In *Winzersekt,* a German wine growers' association challenges the validity of a Council Regulation governing geographical indications of origin. The Regulation prescribes that after a transition period, persons who are not entitled to designate their sparkling wine as "champagne" will not be able to indicate that their wine is produced using the "methode champenoise." The German producers have not used, and do not wish to use, the designation "champagne" for their sparkling wine, which is produced using the same method as champagne produced in France. They have, however, for many years indicated on the labels of their sparkling wine (known as "sekt" in German) that it is produced using the *champagne method,* and they contend that the Council's act depriving them of the right to do this unfairly prejudices their economic interests and property rights. The alternative descriptions of production method permitted by the Council Regulation, such as use of the *traditional method,* do not in their view adequately protect their economic interests, since these alternative descriptions do not convey sufficient information to the consumer. The ECJ affirmed the lawfulness of the Regulation. The case is of interest primarily for two reasons:

187

First, the ECJ opinion indicates that the geographical indication has a purpose beyond that of protecting the consumer against confusion about the origin of goods. It also protects the *goodwill investment* of a region which produces genuine goods against misappropriation by others who have not made the same investment in goodwill. In other words, *champagne method* has a value because of the investment of French sparkling wine producers in producing their specific product, and German wine producers may not *free ride* on this investment. Note that under the Regulation protection is a matter of public law and does not depend on the infringement of consumer interests.

Second, the case expounds the relationship between geographical indications, property rights and the right to pursue a trade or business. Winzersekt argues that without permission to capitalize on the French method of bottle fermentation — unusual in Germany — it may go out of business. The Court conceives the protection of geographical indications of regions to be a legitimate limitation on property rights and free trade due to broad legislative discretion in agriculture and the fact that alternative indications may be use. We can learn from this case that the scope of content of intellectual property rights has to be balanced with acquired property rights and interests in free and uninhibited trade.

SMW Winzersekt GmbH v Land Rheinland-Pfalz (C-306/93)

The Court of Justice of the European Communities
[1995] 2 CMLR 718

13 December 1994

Panel: Presiding, Rodriguez Iglesias CJ; Schockweiler, Kapteyn PPC; Mancini, Kakouris, Moitinho de Almeida, Murray JJ

Headnote:

Reference from Germany by the Verwaltungsgericht (Administrative Court) Mainz, under Article 177 EEC.

*****

Decision:

By order of 25 March 1993, received at the Court on 4 June 1993, the Verwaltungsgericht (Administrative Court) Mainz referred for a preliminary ruling under Article 177 EEC a question on the validity of the second and third subparagraphs of Article 6(5) of Council Regulation 2333/92 laying down general rules for the description and presentation of sparkling wines and aerated sparkling wines ("Regulation 2333/92").

That question arose in a dispute between SMW Winzersekt GmbH ("Winzersekt") and the Land Rheinland-Pfalz concerning the use after 31 August 1994 of the term "Flaschengarung im Champagnerverfahren" ("bottle-fermented by the champagne method") to describe certain quality sparkling wines produced in a specified region ("quality sparkling wines psr").

Regulation 2333/92 was adopted following numerous amendments to Council Regulation 3309/85 laying down general rules for the description and presentation of sparkling wines and aerated sparkling wines ("Regulation 3309/85").

According to the second recital in the preamble to Regulation 2333/92, the purpose of the description of sparkling wines and aerated sparkling wines is to provide potential final customers and public bodies responsible for organising and supervising the marketing of the products concerned with sufficiently clear and accurate information to enable them to form an opinion of the products.

The tenth recital in the preamble to Regulation 2333/92 states that the special provisions relating to the quality wines produced in specified regions ("quality wines psr") were laid down by Council Regulation 823/87 laying down special provisions relating to quality wines produced in specified regions and that those provisions establish precise rules for the use of names of specified regions in the description of quality wines psr, including quality sparkling wines psr. In accordance with those rules, only the geographical name of a wine-growing area which produces wine possessing special quality characteristics may be used to designate a quality sparkling wine psr.

Finally, the twenty-second recital in the preamble to Regulation 2333/92 states that provision should be made for the adoption of transitional arrangements, in particular so that products which comply with the national rules on description and presentation applying before the entry into force of Regulation 2333/92, but not with the new Community rules, may be marketed.

Those objectives were implemented by, in particular, Article 6 of Regulation 2333/92, which corresponds in all essential respects to Article 6 of Regulation 3309/85. Article 6 of Regulation 2333/92 provides inter alia as follows:

1. The name of a geographical unit other than a specified region, and smaller than a Member State or a third country, may be used only to supplement the description of:
   — a quality sparkling wine psr,
   . . .
Use of such a name shall be allowed only if:
(a) it conforms to the rules of the Member State or third country in which the sparkling wine was produced;
(b) the geographical unit in question is defined exactly;
(c) all the grapes from which the product was obtained came from that geographical unit, with the exception of the products contained in tirage liqueur or expedition liqueur;
(d) in the case of a quality sparkling wine psr, the geographical unit is situated within the specified region whose name the wine bears;

   . . .

4. The expressions "bottle-fermented by the traditional method" or "traditional method" or "classical method" or "classical traditional method" and any expressions resulting from a translation of them may be used only to describe:
   — a quality sparkling wine psr,
   . . .
Use of one of the expressions referred to in the first subparagraph shall be allowed only if the product:
(a) was made sparkling by a second alcoholic fermentation in the bottle
(b) stayed without interruption in contact with the lees for at least nine months in the same undertaking from the time when the cuvee was constituted;
(c) was separated from the lees by disgorging.

5. An expression relating to a method of production which includes the name of a specified region or of another geographical unit, or a term derived from either of these, may be used only to describe:

— a quality sparkling wine psr,

...

Such expressions may be used only to describe a product entitled to one of the geographical ascriptions referred to in the first subparagraph.

However, reference to the method of production known as "methode champenoise" may, if such a usage were traditional, be used together with an equivalent expression relating to that method of production for five wine-growing years from 1 September 1989 for wines not entitled to the registered designation "Champagne".

Furthermore, use of an expression referred to in the third subparagraph shall not be permitted unless the conditions referred to in the second subparagraph of paragraph 4 are complied with.

Winzersekt is an association of wine-growers who produce sparkling wine from wines of the Mosel-Saar-Ruwer region using a process referred to as "methode champenoise", which means in particular that fermentation takes place in the bottle and the cuvee is separated from the lees by disgorging. The quality sparkling wines psr thus produced are marketed under the description "Flaschengarung im Champagnerverfahren" ("bottle-fermented by the champagne method") or "klassische Flaschengarung methode champenoise" ("classical bottle fermentation — methode champenoise").

By a binding judgment of 2 February 1989, the Verwaltungsgericht Mainz held that Winzersekt was entitled until 31 August 1994 to use the designation "methode champenoise" in the above descriptions for its products which satisfied the requirements of traditional bottle fermentation.

On 7 January 1992 Winzersekt applied to the Ministry of Agriculture, Viticulture and Forests of the Land Rheinland-Pfalz for a "binding statement" as to whether it would be lawfully entitled to continue to use the description "Flaschengarung im Champagnerverfahren" after 31 August 1994. By decision of 15 January 1992 the Ministry, referring to the judgment of the Verwaltungsgericht Mainz of 2 February 1989, stated that pursuant to Article 6(5) of Regulation 3309/85 the use of that designation could not be permitted after 31 August 1994.

On 4 February 1992 Winzersekt brought proceedings in the Verwaltungsgericht Mainz for a declaration that it would still be entitled to use that designation after 31 August 1994. As it took the view that the outcome of the proceedings depended on the validity of the second and third sub-paragraphs of Article 6(5) of Regulation 2333/92, the First Chamber of the Verwaltungsgericht Mainz decided to stay proceedings and refer the following question to the Court for a preliminary ruling:

> Are the provisions of Article 6(5), second and third subpara-graphs, of Council Regulation 2333/92 invalid in so far as they provide that from September 1994, for quality sparkling wines produced in specified regions from wines not entitled to the registered designation of origin "Champagne", reference to the method of production known as "methode champenoise" together with an equivalent expression relating to that method of production is not to be permitted?

*****

Substance

It follows from the documents on the case-file and the arguments before the Court that the validity of the second and third subparagraphs of Article 6(5) of Regulation 2333/92 has been challenged in the light of two principles or groups of principles: on the one hand, the right to property and the freedom to pursue a trade or profession and, on the other, the general principle of equal treatment.

The right to property and the freedom to pursue a trade or profession

Winzersekt takes the view that the contested provision adversely affects both its right to property and its right freely to pursue a trade or profession, which form part of the general principles of Community law. It submits in that connection that the designation "methode champenoise" is of fundamental importance for its commercial activity in so far as that designation enables it to make the public aware of its method of production. That method distinguishes it from the vast majority of German producers of sparkling wine, whose production method is either that of closed-tank fermentation or that of racking, two methods that are less onerous than the "methode champenoise" and which enable those producers to offer their products to consumers at much more attractive prices than Winzersekt. Winzersekt also submits that the designation forms part of its assets and should benefit from the protection granted to property rights. If Winzersekt were unable to continue to use the designation "methode champ-

192

enoise", it would be placed at a competitive disadvantage and its very existence might be jeopardised.

It should be pointed out in this respect that in matters concerning the common agricultural policy the Community legislature has a broad discretion which corresponds to the political responsibilities given to it by Articles 40 and 43 of the Treaty and that the Court has, on several occasions, held that the lawfulness of a measure adopted in that sphere can be affected only if the measure is manifestly inappropriate, having regard to the objective which the competent institution is seeking to pursue.

Account must also be taken of the Court's case law to the effect that the right to property and the freedom to pursue a trade or business are not absolute but must be viewed in relation to their social function. Consequently, the exercise of the right to property and the freedom to pursue a trade or profession may be restricted, particularly in the context of the common organisation of a market, provided that those restrictions in fact correspond to objectives of general interest pursued by the Community and do not constitute a disproportionate and intolerable interference, impairing the very substance of the rights guaranteed.

With regard to the infringement of the right to property alleged by Winzersekt, the designation "methode champenoise" is a term which, prior to the adoption of the regulation, all producers of sparkling wines were entitled to use. The prohibition of the use of that designation cannot be regarded as an infringement of an alleged property right vested in Winzersekt.

So far as concerns the impairment of the freedom to pursue a trade or profession, the second and third subparagraphs of Article 6(5) of Regulation 2333/92 do not impair the very substance of the right freely to exercise a trade or profession relied on by Winzersekt since those provisions affect only the arrangements governing the exercise of that right and do not jeopardise its very existence. It is for that reason necessary to determine whether those provisions pursue objectives of general interest, do not affect the position of producers such as Winzersekt in a disproportionate manner and, consequently, whether the Council exceeded the limits of its discretion in this case.

It should be noted in this regard that among the objectives pursued by Regulation 2333/92, that of the protection of registered designations or indications of the geographical origin of wines is an objective of general interest. In order to achieve that objective, the Council was entitled to regard it as essential, on the one hand, that the final consumer should receive sufficiently accurate information to enable him to form an opinion of the products in question and, on the other hand, that the producer should not derive advantage, for his own product, from a reputation established for a similar product by producers from a different region. This implies that a wine producer cannot be authorised to use, in descriptions relating to the method of production of his products, geographical indications which do not correspond to the actual provenance of the wine.

That objective is implemented in particular by Article 6 of Regulation 2333/92, which provides that the use of terms relating to a production method may refer to the name of a geographical unit only where the wine in question is entitled to use that geographical indication.

It follows that the prohibition laid down in that provision is not manifestly inappropriate in relation to the objective of the regulation at issue.

Furthermore, by adopting transitional arrangements such as those set out in the third subparagraph of Article 6(5) of the regulation and by allowing producers who, like Winzersekt, used the designation "methode champenoise" to have recourse to the alternative expressions contained in Article 6(4) of Regulation 2333/92, such as "bottle-fermented by the traditional method", "traditional method", "classical method" or "classical traditional method" and any expressions resulting from a translation of those terms, the Council took account of the position of those producers. In those circumstances, the contested provision cannot be regarded as disproportionate.

It follows that the second and third subparagraphs of Article 6(5) of Regulation 2333/92 pursue objectives of general interest and cannot be regarded as constituting a disproportionate interference with the position of producers such as Winzersekt. In those circumstances, it must be held that the Council did not exceed the limits of its discretion in adopting those provisions.

The general principle of equal treatment

In this regard, the Court has consistently held that the principle of equal treatment requires that similar situations should not be treated differently and that different situations should not be treated identically unless such differentiation is objectively justified."

In the present case, the second and third subparagraphs of Article 6(5) of Regulation 2333/92 apply to all producers of sparkling wines in the Community with the exception of those who are entitled to use the registered designation "Champagne". The fact of entitlement to use that registered designation is an objective matter which can justify a difference in treatment. In those circumstances, a difference in the treatment of each of those two groups of producers is justified.

The reply to the national court must accordingly be that examination of the question submitted has not revealed any factor of such a kind as to affect the validity of the second and third subparagraphs of Article 6(5) of Council Regulation 2333/92.

*****

On those grounds, THE COURT, in answer to the question referred to it by the Verwaltungsgericht Mainz, by order of 25 March 1993,

Hereby Rules:

Examination of the question submitted has not revealed any factor of such a kind as to affect the validity of the second and third subparagraphs of Article 6(5) of Council Regulation 2333/92 laying down general rules for the description and presentation of sparkling wines and aerated sparkling wines.

Notes and Questions

1. One of the difficulties affecting the field of geographical indications is the challenge of drawing distinctions *in fact* between the quality of goods produced in different regions. Is there really a difference between sparkling wines produced by the champagne method in France as compared with sparkling wines produced by the traditional method in Germany? How should government officials go about measuring this difference? Is it the difficulty in objectively differentiating between the quality of products that has led to a growing emphasis on the goodwill protection function of the geographical indication of origin?

2. For many years American cheese producers have used the designation "Swiss cheese" for a type of cheese that is produced and marketed in Switzerland under the name "Emmenthal." Should the cheese producers of Switzerland be able to prevent further use of the "Swiss cheese" designation on cheese produced in the United States? Are American consumers confused about the origin of the cheese they are buying? Are the interests of producers of cheese in Switzerland being adversely affected?

3. The authorities of Tuscany became concerned in recent years at the use of photographs and film footage of the Tuscan countryside to convey a sense of beauty and tranquility in the advertising of many different products and services that had nothing to do with Tuscany. They considered this to be misleading and an unfair appropriation of the special image and features of a particular geographical area. Do you think that intellectual property protection and, in particular, the protection of geographical indications can or should concern itself with this sort of problem?

---

9. Undisclosed Information

a. The Nature and Subject Matter of Undisclosed Information

Undisclosed information refers to information of a confidential or secret nature that has commercial value and which its holder takes reasonable steps to protect from disclosure. The term undisclosed information is used in the TRIPS Agreement to refer to the same kind of information that is embodied in the common law concept of trade secret. Prior to the conclusion of the TRIPS Agreement there was no multilateral convention or treaty specifically requiring the protection of undisclosed information, although the general provisions of the Paris Convention for the Protection of Industrial Property regarding unfair competition (Art. 10*bis*) may be understood to require some form of trade secret protection.

Trade secret or undisclosed information is not subject to a specific test of novelty or non-obviousness as is the technical information that may be protected by patent. Since a trade secret may incorporate data that is in the public domain, one of the main difficulties in characterizing this data as the subject of protection is how to distinguish it from information that is openly accessible for public use. The TRIPS Agreement approaches this difficulty by defining *secret* information as that which "is not, as a body or in the precise configuration and assembly of its components, generally known or readily accessible to persons within the circles that normally deal with the kind of information in question" (Art. 39(2)(a)).

Trade secret or undisclosed information may take many forms. These forms include secret manufacturing processes and formulas, customer and supplier lists of a trade or business, food preparation recipes, and business strategies.

The second criterion of trade secret (after its confidential character) is that the data has *commercial value* which, in the terms of the TRIPS Agreement, must be "because [the data] is secret." In other words, according to the TRIPS Agreement, the fact of the secrecy of the data must provide an advantage to its holder over potential competitors. If the data were made generally available in its specific form, the holder would lose its commercial advantage.

The third criterion is that the person in control of the data has taken "reasonable steps under the circumstances" to keep it secret (TRIPS, Art. 39(2)(c)). This standard by definition imposes different requirements depending on the circumstances of the holder of the data. Steps such as requiring employees to execute confidentiality agreements and limiting access to sensitive information are some of those that would customarily be used by a business to keep its data secret.

Trade secret or undisclosed information may be protected as long as the data remains secret and has commercial value. This characteristic clearly distinguishes trade secret protection from patent protection. Businesses may prefer to rely on trade secret when they are able to do so in order to take advantage of this potentially long duration. Securing a patent requires that the applicant disclose the invention and, at the expiry of the patent term, the invention may be imitated by others. The limited term of the patent is a drawback for business.

Why do not inventors routinely rely on trade secret in light of the advantage of its potentially long duration? The drawback of the trade secret is that it only protects information which the holder controls (in secret). It does not preclude competitors of a business from copying a product once it is on the market, or from reverse engineering a process. This significantly limits the utility of the trade secret where the secret becomes apparent upon the marketing of the product. If the trade secret relates to a process, however, which can be practiced within the confines of the holder's factory or plant, the secret may be able to be maintained even after any product produced as a result of the process is marketed.

One of the most frequently cited commercially successful uses of trade secret is the protection of the secret recipe or formula for Coca-Cola. Though the Coca-Cola Company might have obtained a patent on its formula 100 years ago, that patent would have long ago expired, and its competitors would have been free to imitate its formula. By using trade secret protection, the company has maintained a highly profitable advantage over competitors for a very long time.

The TRIPS Agreement does not require that laws for the protection of undisclosed information or trade secret take a particular form. National approaches to such protection have tended to vary widely, and such variation may well continue.

Business enterprises face the risk of disclosure of trade secret information not only in their dealings with other businesses, but also in their dealings with governments. There are a number of situations in which businesses are legally required to provide data to regulatory and enforcement authorities which, if disclosed, might harm their competitive situation. This includes data submitted in the process of obtaining regulatory approval of new products (as in the pharmaceuticals industry), data submitted in the investigation of anti-competitive activities, and so forth. The TRIPS Agreement includes a specific requirement that governments take steps to protect information submitted for the approval of pharmaceutical and agricultural chemical products.

---

b. Relationship Between Patent and Trade Secret Protection

In the following case, the Supreme Court of the United States clarifies the relationship between patent and trade secret law. Patent law in the United States is federal law, whereas trade secret law is in the domain of the states, and has traditionally been governed by state common law (i.e., case law). Many of the states have by now implemented statutory trade secret protection, some of which is based on the Uniform Trade Secret Act.

Kewanee Oil Co. v. Bicron Corp. et al.

Supreme Court of the United States

416 U.S. 470; 94 S. Ct. 1879; 1974 U.S. LEXIS 134 (1974)

Prior history: Certiorari to the United States Court of Appeals for the Sixth Circuit.

Disposition: 478 F.2d 1074, reversed and remanded for reinstatement of District Court Judgment.

Judges: Burger, C. J., delivered the opinion of the Court, in which Stewart, White, Blackmun, and Rehnquist, JJ., joined. Marshall, J., filed an opinion concurring in the result, post, p. 493. Douglas, J., filed a dissenting opinion, in which Brennan, J., joined . . . Powell, J., took no part in the decision of the case.

Opinion: Mr. Chief Justice Burger delivered the opinion of the Court.

We granted certiorari to resolve a question on which there is a conflict in the courts of appeals: whether state trade secret protection is pre-empted by operation of the federal patent law. In the instant case the Court of Appeals for the Sixth Circuit held that there was preemption. The Courts of Appeals for the Second, Fourth, Fifth, and Ninth Circuits have reached the opposite conclusion.

I.

Harshaw Chemical Co., an unincorporated division of petitioner, is a leading manufacturer of a type of synthetic crystal which is useful in the detection of ionizing radiation. In 1949 Harshaw commenced research into the growth of this type crystal and was able to produce one less than two inches in diameter. By 1966, as the result of expenditures in excess of $1 million, Harshaw was able to grow a 17-inch crystal, something no one else had done previously. Harshaw had developed many processes, procedures, and manufacturing techniques in the purification of raw materials and the growth and encapsulation of the crystals which enabled it to accomplish this feat. Some of these processes Harshaw considers to be trade secrets.

The individual respondents are former employees of Harshaw who formed or later joined respondent Bicron. While at Harshaw the individual respondents executed, as a condition of employment, at least one agreement each, requiring them not to disclose confidential information or trade secrets obtained as employees of Harshaw. Bicron was formed in August 1969 to compete with Harshaw in the production of the crystals, and by April 1970, had grown a 17-inch crystal.

Petitioner brought this diversity action in United States District Court for the Northern District of Ohio seeking injunctive relief and damages for the misappropriation of trade secrets. The District Court, applying Ohio trade secret law, granted a permanent injunction against the disclosure or use by respondents of 20 of the 40 claimed trade secrets until such time as the trade secrets had been released to the public, had otherwise generally become available to the public, or had been obtained by respondents from sources having the legal right to convey the information.

The Court of Appeals for the Sixth Circuit held that the findings of fact by the District Court were not clearly erroneous, and that it was evident from the record that the individual respondents appropriated to the benefit of Bicron secret information on processes obtained while they were employees at Harshaw. Further, the Court of Appeals held that the District Court properly applied Ohio law relating to trade secrets. Nevertheless, the Court of Appeals reversed the District Court, finding Ohio's trade secret law to be in conflict with the patent laws of the United States. The Court of Appeals reasoned that Ohio could not grant monopoly protection to processes and manufacturing techniques that were appropriate subjects for consideration under 35 U. S. C. § 101 for a federal patent but which had been in commercial use for over one year and so were no longer eligible for patent protection under 35 U. S. C. § 102 (b). We hold that Ohio's law of trade secrets is not preempted by the patent laws of the United States, and, accordingly, we reverse.

II.

Ohio has adopted the widely relied-upon definition of a trade secret found at Restatement of Torts § 757, comment b (1939). B. F. Goodrich Co. v. Wohlgemuth, 117 Ohio App. 493, 498, 192 N. E. 2d 99, 104 (1963); W. R.

Grace & Co. v. Hargadine, 392 F.2d 9, 14 (CA6 1968). According to the Restatement,

> [a] trade secret may consist of any formula, pattern, device or compilation of information which is used in one's business, and which gives him an opportunity to obtain an advantage over competitors who do not know or use it. It may be a formula for a chemical compound, a process of manufacturing, treating or preserving materials, a pattern for a machine or other device, or a list of customers.

The subject of a trade secret must be secret, and must not be of public knowledge or of a general knowledge in the trade or business. B. F. Goodrich Co. v. Wohlgemuth, supra, at 499, 192 N. E. 2d, at 104; National Tube Co. v. Eastern Tube Co., 3 Ohio C. C. R. (n. s.) 459, 462 (1902), aff'd, 69 Ohio St. 560, 70 N. E. 1127 (1903). This necessary element of secrecy is not lost, however, if the holder of the trade secret reveals the trade secret to another "in confidence, and under an implied obligation not to use or disclose it." Cincinnati Bell Foundry Co. v. Dodds, 10 Ohio Dec. Reprint 154, 156, 19 Weekly L. Bull. 84 (Super. Ct. 1887). These others may include those of the holder's "employees to whom it is necessary to confide it, in order to apply it to the uses for which it is intended." National Tube Co. v. Eastern Tube Co., supra, at 462. Often the recipient of confidential knowledge of the subject of a trade secret is a licensee of its holder. See Lear, Inc. v. Adkins, 395 U.S. 653 (1969). The protection accorded the trade secret holder is against the disclosure or unauthorized use of the trade secret by those to whom the secret has been confided under the express or implied restriction of nondisclosure or nonuse.[4] The law also protects the holder of a trade secret against disclosure or use when the knowledge is gained, not by the owner's volition, but by some "improper means," Restatement of Torts §

---

[4]Ohio Rev. Code Ann. § 1333.51 (C) (Supp. 1973) provides:

No person, having obtained possession of an article representing a trade secret or access thereto with the owner's consent, shall convert such article to his own use or that of another person, or thereafter without the owner's consent make or cause to be made a copy of such article, or exhibit such article to another.

Ohio Rev. Code Ann. § 1333.99 (E) (Supp. 1973) provides:

Whoever violates section 1333.51 of the Revised Code shall be fined not more than five thousand dollars, imprisoned not less than one nor more than ten years, or both.

757 (a), which may include theft, wiretapping, or even aerial reconnaissance. A trade secret law, however, does not offer protection against discovery by fair and honest means, such as by independent invention, accidental disclosure, or by so-called reverse engineering, that is by starting with the known product and working backward to divine the process which aided in its development or manufacture.

Novelty, in the patent law sense, is not required for a trade secret, W. R. Grace & Co. v. Hargadine, 392 F.2d, at 14. "Quite clearly discovery is something less than invention." A. O. Smith Corp. v. Petroleum Iron Works Co., 73 F.2d 531, 538 (CA6 1934), modified to increase scope of injunction, 74 F.2d 934 (1935). However, some novelty will be required if merely because that which does not possess novelty is usually known; secrecy, in the context of trade secrets, thus implies at least minimal novelty.

The subject matter of a patent is limited to a "process, machine, manufacture, or composition of matter, or . . . improvement thereof," 35 U. S. C. § 101, which fulfills the three conditions of novelty and utility as articulated and defined in 35 U. S. C. §§ 101 and 102, and nonobviousness, as set out in 35 U. S. C. § 103. If an invention meets the rigorous statutory tests for the issuance of a patent, the patent is granted, for a period of 17 years, giving what has been described as the "right of exclusion," R. Ellis, Patent Assignments and Licenses § 4, p. 7 (2d ed. 1943). This protection goes not only to copying the subject matter, which is forbidden under the Copyright Act, 17 U. S. C. § 1 et seq., but also to independent creation.

III.

The first issue we deal with is whether the States are forbidden to act at all in the area of protection of the kinds of intellectual property which may make up the subject matter of trade secrets.

Article I, § 8, cl. 8, of the Constitution grants to the Congress the power

> to promote the Progress of Science and useful Arts, by securing for limited Times to Authors and Inventors the exclusive Right to their respective Writings and Discoveries . . . .

In the 1972 Term, in Goldstein v. California, 412 U.S. 546 (1973), we held that the cl. 8 grant of power to Congress was not exclusive and that, at least in the case of writings, the States were not prohibited from encouraging and protecting the efforts of those within their borders by appropriate legislation. The States could, therefore, protect against the unauthorized rerecording for sale of performances fixed on records or tapes, even though those performances qualified as "writings" in the constitutional sense and Congress was empowered to legislate regarding such performances and could pre-empt the area if it chose to do so. This determination was premised on the great diversity of interests in our Nation — the essentially nonuniform character of the appreciation of intellectual achievements in the various States. Evidence for this came from patents granted by the States in the 18th century. 412 U.S., at 557. Just as the States may exercise regulatory power over writings so may the States regulate with respect to discoveries. States may hold diverse viewpoints in protecting intellectual property relating to invention as they do in protecting the intellectual property relating to the subject matter of copyright. The only limitation on the States is that in regulating the area of patents and copyrights they do not conflict with the operation of the laws in this area passed by Congress, and it is to that more difficult question we now turn.

IV.

The question of whether the trade secret law of Ohio is void under the Supremacy Clause involves a consideration of whether that law "stands as an obstacle to the accomplishment and execution of the full purposes and objectives of Congress." Hines v. Davidowitz, 312 U.S. 52, 67 (1941). See Florida Avocado Growers v. Paul, 373 U.S. 132, 141 (1963). We stated in Sears, Roebuck & Co. v. Stiffel Co., 376 U.S. 225, 229 (1964), that when state law touches upon the area of federal statutes enacted pursuant to constitutional authority, "it is 'familiar doctrine' that the federal policy 'may not be set at naught, or its benefits denied' by the state law. Sola Elec. Co. v. Jefferson Elec. Co., 317 U.S. 173, 176 (1942). This is true, of course, even if the state law is enacted in the exercise of otherwise undoubted state power."

The laws which the Court of Appeals in this case held to be in conflict with the Ohio law of trade secrets were the patent laws passed by the Congress in the unchallenged exercise of its clear power under Art. I, § 8, cl. 8, of the Constitution. The patent law does not explicitly endorse or forbid the operation of trade secret law. However, as we have noted, if the scheme of protection developed by Ohio respecting trade secrets "clashes with the objectives of the federal patent laws," Sears, Roebuck & Co. v. Stiffel Co., supra, at 231, then the state law must fall. To determine whether the Ohio law "clashes" with the federal law it is helpful to examine the objectives of both the patent and trade secret laws. The stated objective of the Constitution in granting the power to Congress to legislate in the area of intellectual property is to "promote the Progress of Science and useful Arts." The patent laws promote this progress by offering a right of exclusion for a limited period as an incentive to inventors to risk the often enormous costs in terms of time, research, and development. The productive effort thereby fostered will have a positive effect on society through the introduction of new products and processes of manufacture into the economy, and the emanations by way of increased employment and better lives for our citizens. In return for the right of exclusion — this "reward for inventions," Universal Oil Co. v. Globe Co., 322 U.S. 471, 484 (1944) — the patent laws impose upon the inventor a requirement of disclosure. To insure adequate and full disclosure so that upon the expiration of the 17-year period "the knowledge of the invention enures to the people, who are thus enabled without restriction to practice it and profit by its use," United States v. Dubilier Condenser Corp., 289 U.S. 178, 187 (1933), the patent laws require[10] that the patent application shall include a full and clear description of the invention and "of the manner and process of making and using it" so that any person skilled in the art may make and use the invention. 35 U. S. C. § 112. When a patent is granted and the information contained in it is circulated to the general public and those especially skilled in the trade, such additions to the general store of knowledge are of such importance to the public weal that the Federal Government is willing to pay the high price of 17 years of exclusive use for its disclosure, which disclosure, it is assumed, will stimulate ideas and the eventual development of further significant advances in the art. The Court has also articulated another policy of the patent law: that which is in the public domain cannot be removed therefrom by action of the States.

> Federal law requires that all ideas in general circulation be dedicated to the common good unless they are protected by a valid patent. (Lear, Inc. v. Adkins, 395 U.S., at 668)

See also Goldstein v. California, 412 U.S., at 570-571; Sears, Roebuck & Co. v. Stiffel Co., supra; Compco Corp. v. Day-Brite Lighting, Inc., 376 U.S. 234,

---

[10]35 U. S. C. § 111.

237-238 (1964); International News Service v. Associated Press, 248 U.S. 215, 250 (1918) (Brandeis, J., dissenting)

The maintenance of standards of commercial ethics and the encouragement of invention are the broadly stated policies behind trade secret law. "The necessity of good faith and honest, fair dealing, is the very life and spirit of the commercial world." National Tube Co. v. Eastern Tube Co., 3 Ohio C. C. R. (n. s.), at 462. In A. O. Smith Corp. v. Petroleum Iron Works Co., 73 F.2d, at 539, the Court emphasized that even though a discovery may not be patentable, that does not

> destroy the value of the discovery to one who makes it, or advantage the
> competitor who by unfair means, or as the beneficiary of a broken faith,
> obtains the desired knowledge without himself paying the price in labor,
> money, or machines expended by the discoverer.

In Wexler v. Greenberg, 399 Pa. 569, 578-579, 160 A. 2d 430, 434-435 (1960), the Pennsylvania Supreme Court noted the importance of trade secret protection to the subsidization of research and development and to increased economic efficiency within large companies through the dispersion of responsibilities for creative developments.

Having now in mind the objectives of both the patent and trade secret law, we turn to an examination of the interaction of these systems of protection of intellectual property — one established by the Congress and the other by a State — to determine whether and under what circumstances the latter might constitute "too great an encroachment on the federal patent system to be tolerated." Sears, Roebuck & Co. v. Stiffel Co., 376 U.S., at 232. As we noted earlier, trade secret law protects items which would not be proper subjects for consideration for patent protection under 35 U. S. C. § 101. As in the case of the recordings in Goldstein v. California, Congress, with respect to nonpatentable subject matter, "has drawn no balance; rather, it has left the area unattended, and no reason exists why the State should not be free to act." Goldstein v. California, supra, at 570 (footnote omitted). Since no patent is available for a discovery, however useful, novel, and nonobvious, unless it falls within one of the express categories of patentable subject matter of 35 U. S. C. § 101, the holder of such a discovery would have no reason to apply for a patent whether trade secret protection existed or not. Abolition of trade secret protection would, therefore, not result in increased disclosure to the public of discoveries in the area of nonpatentable subject matter. Also, it is hard to see how the public would be benefitted by disclosure of customer lists or advertising campaigns; in fact, keeping such items secret encourages businesses to initiate new and individualized plans of operation, and constructive competition results. This, in turn, leads to a greater variety of business methods than would otherwise be the case if privately developed marketing and other data were passed illicitly among firms involved in the same enterprise.

Congress has spoken in the area of those discoveries which fall within one of the categories of patentable subject matter of 35 U. S. C. § 101 and which are, therefore, of a nature that would be subject to consideration for a patent. Processes, machines, manufactures, compositions of matter, and improvements thereof, which meet the tests of utility, novelty, and nonobviousness are entitled to be patented, but those which do not, are not. The question remains whether those items which are proper subjects for consideration for a patent may also have available the alternative protection accorded by trade secret law.

Certainly the patent policy of encouraging invention is not disturbed by the existence of another form of incentive to invention. In this respect the two systems are not and never would be in conflict. Similarly, the policy that matter once in the public domain must remain in the public domain is not incompatible with the existence of trade secret protection. By definition a trade secret has not been placed in the public domain.[13]

The more difficult objective of the patent law to reconcile with trade secret law is that of disclosure, the quid pro quo of the right to exclude. Universal Oil Co. v. Globe Co., 322 U.S., at 484. We are helped in this stage of the analysis by Judge Henry Friendly's opinion in Painton & Co. v. Bourns, Inc., 442 F.2d 216 (CA2 1971). There the Court of Appeals thought it useful, in determining whether inventors will refrain because of the existence of trade secret law from applying for patents, thereby depriving the public from learning of the invention, to distinguish between three categories of trade secrets:

> (1) the trade secret believed by its owner to constitute a validly patentable invention; (2) the trade secret known to its owner not to be

---

[13]An invention may be placed "in public use or on sale" within the meaning of 35 U. S. C. § 102 (b) without losing its secret character. Painton & Co. v. Bourns, Inc., 442 F.2d, at 224 n. 6; Metallizing Engineering Co. v. Kenyon Bearing & Auto Parts Co., 153 F.2d 516, 520 (CA2), cert. denied, 328 U.S. 840 (1946).

so patentable; and (3) the trade secret whose valid patentability is considered dubious. Id., at 224.

Trade secret protection in each of these categories would run against breaches of confidence — the employee and licensee situations — and theft and other forms of industrial espionage.

As to the trade secret known not to meet the standards of patentability, very little in the way of disclosure would be accomplished by abolishing trade secret protection. With trade secrets of nonpatentable subject matter, the patent alternative would not reasonably be available to the inventor. "There can be no public interest in stimulating developers of such [unpatentable] knowhow to flood an overburdened Patent Office with applications [for] what they do not consider patentable." Ibid. The mere filing of applications doomed to be turned down by the Patent Office will bring forth no new public knowledge or enlightenment, since under federal statute and regulation patent applications and abandoned patent applications are held by the Patent Office in confidence and are not open to public inspection. 35 U. S. C. § 122; 37 CFR § 1.14 (b).

Even as the extension of trade secret protection to patentable subject matter that the owner knows will not meet the standards of patentability will not conflict with the patent policy of disclosure, it will have a decidedly beneficial effect on society. Trade secret law will encourage invention in areas where patent law does not reach, and will prompt the independent innovator to proceed with the discovery and exploitation of his invention. Competition is fostered and the public is not deprived of the use of valuable, if not quite patentable, invention.

Even if trade secret protection against the faithless employee were abolished, inventive and exploitive effort in the area of patentable subject matter that did not meet the standards of patentability would continue, although at a reduced level. Alternatively with the effort that remained, however, would come an increase in the amount of self-help that innovative companies would employ. Knowledge would be widely dispersed among the employees of those still active in research. Security precautions necessarily would be increased, and salaries and fringe benefits of those few officers or employees who had to know the whole of the secret invention would be fixed in an amount thought sufficient to assure their loyalty. Smaller companies would be placed at a distinct economic disadvantage, since the costs of this kind of self-help could be great, and the cost to the public of the use of this invention would be increased. The innovative entrepreneur with limited resources would tend to confine his research efforts to himself and those few he felt he could trust without the ultimate assurance of legal protection against breaches of confidence. As a result, organized scientific and technological research could become fragmented, and society, as a whole, would suffer.

Another problem that would arise if state trade secret protection were precluded is in the area of licensing others to exploit secret processes. The holder of a trade secret would not likely share his secret with a manufacturer who cannot be placed under binding legal obligation to pay a license fee or to protect the secret. The result would be to hoard rather than disseminate knowledge. Painton & Co. v. Bourns, Inc., 442 F.2d, at 223. Instead, then, of licensing others to use his invention and making the most efficient use of existing manufacturing and marketing structures within the industry, the trade secret holder would tend either to limit his utilization of the invention, thereby depriving the public of the maximum benefit of its use, or engage in the time-consuming and economically wasteful enterprise of constructing duplicative manufacturing and marketing mechanisms for the exploitation of the invention. The detrimental misallocation of resources and economic waste that would thus take place if trade secret protection were abolished with respect to employees or licensees cannot be justified by reference to any policy that the federal patent law seeks to advance. Nothing in the patent law requires that States refrain from action to prevent industrial espionage. In addition to the increased costs for protection from burglary, wiretapping, bribery, and the other means used to misappropriate trade secrets, there is the inevitable cost to the basic decency of society when one firm steals from another. A most fundamental human right, that of privacy, is threatened when industrial espionage is condoned or is made profitable; the state interest in denying profit to such illegal ventures is unchallengeable.

The next category of patentable subject matter to deal with is the invention whose holder has a legitimate doubt as to its patentability. The risk of eventual patent invalidity by the courts and the costs associated with that risk may well impel some with a good-faith doubt as to patentability not to take the trouble to seek to obtain and defend patent protection for their discoveries, regardless of the existence of trade secret protection. Trade secret protection would assist those inventors in the more efficient exploitation of their discoveries and not conflict with the patent law. In most cases of genuine doubt as to patent validity the potential rewards of patent protection are so far superior to those accruing to holders of trade secrets, that the holders of such inventions will seek patent protection, ignoring the trade secret route. For those inventors "on the line" as to whether to seek patent protection, the abolition of trade secret protection might encourage some to apply for a patent who otherwise would not have done so. For some of those so encouraged, no patent will be granted and the result

> will have been an unnecessary postponement in the divulging of the trade secret to persons willing to pay for it. If [the patent does issue], it may well be invalid, yet many will prefer to pay a modest royalty than to contest it, even though Lear allows them to accept a license and pursue the contest without paying royalties while the fight goes on. The result in such a case would be unjustified royalty payments from many who would prefer not to pay them rather than agreed fees from one or a few who are entirely willing to do so. (Painton & Co. v. Bourns, Inc., 442 F.2d, at 225)

The point is that those who might be encouraged to file for patents by the absence of trade secret law will include inventors possessing the chaff as well as the wheat. Some of the chaff — the nonpatentable discoveries — will be thrown out by the Patent Office, but in the meantime society will have been deprived of use of those discoveries through trade secret-protected licensing. Some of the chaff may not be thrown out. This Court has noted the difference between the standards used by the Patent Office and the courts to determine patentability. Graham v. John Deere Co., 383 U.S. 1, 18 (1966). In Lear, Inc. v. Adkins, 395 U.S. 653 (1969), the Court thought that an invalid patent was so serious a threat to the free use of ideas already in the public domain that the Court permitted licensees of the patent holder to challenge the validity of the patent. Better had the invalid patent never been issued. More of those patents would likely issue if trade secret law were abolished. Eliminating trade secret law for the doubtfully patentable invention is thus likely to have deleterious effects on society and patent policy which we cannot say are balanced out by the speculative gain which might result from the encouragement of some inventors with doubt-fully patentable inventions which deserve patent protection to come forward and apply for patents. There is no conflict, then, between trade secret law and the patent law policy of disclosure, at least insofar as the first two categories of patentable subject matter are concerned.

The final category of patentable subject matter to deal with is the clearly patentable invention, i. e., that invention which the owner believes to meet the standards of patentability. It is here that the federal interest in disclosure is at its peak; these inventions, novel, useful and nonobvious, are "'the things which are worth to the public the embarrassment of an exclusive patent.'" Graham v. John Deere Co., supra, at 9 (quoting Thomas Jefferson). The interest of the public is that the bargain of 17 years of exclusive use in return for disclosure be accepted. If a State, through a system of protection, were to cause a substantial risk that holders of patentable inventions would not seek patents, but rather would rely on the state protection, we would be compelled to hold that such a system could not constitutionally continue to exist. In the case of trade secret law no reasonable risk of deterrence from patent application by those who can reasonably expect to be granted patents exists. Trade secret law provides far weaker protection in many respects than the patent law. While trade secret law does not forbid the discovery of the trade secret by fair and honest means, e. g., independent creation or reverse engineering, patent law operates "against the world," forbidding any use of the invention for whatever purpose for a significant length of time. The holder of a trade secret also takes a substantial risk that the secret will be passed on to his competitors, by theft or by breach of a confidential relationship, in a manner not easily susceptible of discovery or proof. Painton & Co. v. Bourns, Inc., 442 F.2d, at 224. Where patent law acts as a barrier, trade secret law functions relatively as a sieve. The possibility that an inventor who believes his invention meets the standards of patentability will sit back, rely on trade secret law, and after one year of use forfeit any right to patent protection, 35 U. S. C. § 102 (b), is remote indeed.

Nor does society face much risk that scientific or technological progress will be impeded by the rare inventor with a patentable invention who chooses trade secret protection over patent protection. The ripeness-of-time concept of invention, developed from the study of the many independent multiple discoveries in history, predicts that if a particular individual had not made a particular discovery others would have, and in probably a relatively short period of time. If something is to be discovered at all very likely it will be discovered by more than one person. Singletons and Multiples in Science (1961), in R. Merton, The Sociology of Science 343 (1973); J. Cole & S. Cole, Social Stratification in Science 12-13, 229-230

(1973); Ogburn & Thomas, Are Inventions Inevitable?, 37 Pol. Sci. Q. 83 (1922).[19] Even were an inventor to keep his discovery completely to himself, something that neither the patent nor trade secret laws forbid, there is a high probability that it will be soon independently developed. If the invention, though still a trade secret, is put into public use, the competition is alerted to the existence of the inventor's solution to the problem and may be encouraged to make an extra effort to independently find the solution thus known to be possible. The inventor faces pressures not only from private industry, but from the skilled scientists who work in our universities and our other great publicly supported centers of learning and research.

We conclude that the extension of trade secret protection to clearly patentable inventions does not conflict with the patent policy of disclosure. Perhaps because trade secret law does not produce any positive effects in the area of clearly patentable inventions, as opposed to the beneficial effects resulting from trade secret protection in the areas of the doubtfully patentable and the clearly unpatentable inventions, it has been suggested that partial pre-emption may be appropriate, and that courts should refuse to apply trade secret protection to inventions which the holder should have patented, and which would have been, thereby, disclosed.[20] However, since there is no real possibility that trade secret law will conflict with the federal policy favoring disclosure of clearly patentable inventions partial pre-emption is inappropriate. Partial pre-emption, furthermore, could well create serious problems for state courts in the administration of trade secret law. As a preliminary matter in trade secret actions, state courts would be obliged to distinguish between what a reasonable inventor would and would not correctly consider to be clearly patentable, with the holder of the trade secret arguing that the invention was not patentable and the misappropriator of the trade secret arguing its undoubted novelty, utility, and

---

[19]See J. Watson, The Double Helix (1968). If Watson and Crick had not discovered the structure of DNA it is likely that Linus Pauling would have made the discovery soon. Other examples of multiple discovery are listed at length in the Ogburn and Thomas article.

[20]See Note, Patent Preemption of Trade Secret Protection of Inventions Meeting Judicial Standards of Patentability, 87 Harv. L. Rev. 807 (1974); Brief for the United States as Amicus Curiae, presenting the view within the Government favoring limited pre-emption (which view is not that of the United States, which believes that patent law does not preempt state trade secret law).

nonobviousness. Federal courts have a difficult enough time trying to determine whether an invention, narrowed by the patent application procedure and fixed in the specifications which describe the invention for which the patent has been granted, is patentable. Although state courts in some circumstances must join federal courts in judging whether an issued patent is valid, Lear, Inc. v. Adkins, supra, it would be undesirable to impose the almost impossible burden on state courts to determine the patentability — in fact and in the mind of a reasonable inventor — of a discovery which has not been patented and remains entirely uncircumscribed by expert analysis in the administrative process. Neither complete nor partial pre-emption of state trade secret law is justified.

Our conclusion that patent law does not pre-empt trade secret law is in accord with prior cases of this Court. Universal Oil Co. v. Globe Co., 322 U.S., at 484; United States v. Dubilier Condenser Corp., 289 U.S., at 186-187; Becher v. Contoure Laboratories, 279 U.S. 388, 391 (1929); Du Pont Powder Co. v. Masland, 244 U.S. 100, 102 (1917); Dr. Miles Medical Co. v. Park & Sons Co., 220 U.S. 373, 402-403 (1911); Board of Trade v. Christie Grain & Stock Co., 198 U.S. 236, 250-251 (1905).[23] Trade secret law and patent law have co-existed in this country for over one hundred years. Each has its particular role to play, and the operation of one does not take away from the need for the other. Trade secret law encourages the development and exploitation of those items of lesser or different invention than might be accorded protection under the patent laws, but which items still have an important part to play in the technological and scientific advancement of the Nation. Trade secret law promotes the sharing of knowledge, and the efficient operation of industry; it permits the individual inventor to reap the rewards of his labor by contracting with a company large enough to develop and exploit it. Congress, by its silence over these many years, has seen the wisdom of allowing the States to enforce trade secret protection. Until Congress takes affirmative action to the contrary, States should be free to grant protection to trade secrets.

Since we hold that Ohio trade secret law is not preempted by the federal patent law, the judgment of the Court of Appeals for the Sixth Circuit

---

[23]The Court of Appeals below relied, in part, on Kendall v. Winsor, 21 How. 322 (1859), a case decided nine years before trade secret law was imported into this country from England by means of the landmark case of Peabody v. Norfolk, 98 Mass. 452 (1868).

is reversed, and the case is remanded to the Court of Appeals with directions to reinstate the judgment of the District Court.

It is so ordered.

Concur: Mr. Justice Marshall, concurring in the result.

Unlike the Court, I do not believe that the possibility that an inventor with a patentable invention will rely on state trade secret law rather than apply for a patent is "remote indeed." Ante, . . . State trade secret law provides substantial protection to the inventor who intends to use or sell the invention himself rather than license it to others, protection which in its unlimited duration is clearly superior to the 17-year monopoly afforded by the patent laws. I have no doubt that the existence of trade secret protection provides in some instances a substantial disincentive to entrance into the patent system, and thus deprives society of the benefits of public disclosure of the invention which it is the policy of the patent laws to encourage. This case may well be such an instance.

But my view of sound policy in this area does not dispose of this case. Rather, the question presented in this case is whether Congress, in enacting the patent laws, intended merely to offer inventors a limited monopoly in exchange for disclosure of their invention, or instead to exert pressure on inventors to enter into this exchange by withdrawing any alternative possibility of legal protection for their inventions. I am persuaded that the former is the case. State trade secret laws and the federal patent laws have co-existed for many, many years. During this time, Congress has repeatedly demonstrated its full awareness of the existence of the trade secret system, without any indication of disapproval. Indeed, Congress has in a number of instances given explicit federal protection to trade secret information provided to federal agencies. See, e. g., 5 U. S. C. § 552 (b)(4); 18 U. S. C. § 1905; see generally Appendix to Brief for Petitioner. Because of this, I conclude that there is "neither such actual conflict between the two schemes of regulation that both cannot stand in the same area, nor evidence of a congressional design to preempt the field." Florida Avocado Growers v. Paul, 373 U.S. 132, 141 (1963). I therefore concur in the result reached by the majority of the Court.

Dissent: Mr. Justice Douglas, with Whom Mr. Justice Brennan concurs, dissenting.

Today's decision is at war with the philosophy of Sears, Roebuck & Co. v. Stiffel Co., 376 U.S. 225, and Compco Corp. v. Day-Brite Lighting, Inc., 376 U.S. 234. Those cases involved patents — one of a pole lamp and one of fluorescent lighting fixtures each of which was declared invalid. The lower courts held, however, that though the patents were invalid the sale of identical or confusingly similar products to the products of the patentees violated state unfair competition laws. We held that when an article is unprotected by a patent, state law may not forbid others to copy it, because every article not covered by a valid patent is in the public domain. Congress in the patent laws decided that where no patent existed, free competition should prevail; that where a patent is rightfully issued, the right to exclude others should obtain for no longer than 17 years, and that the States may not "under some other law, such as that forbidding unfair competition, give protection of a kind that clashes with the objectives of the federal patent laws,"[1] 376 U.S., at 231.

The product involved in this suit, sodium iodide synthetic crystals, was a product that could be patented but was not. Harshaw the inventor apparently contributed greatly to the technology in that field by developing processes, procedures, and techniques that produced much larger crystals than any competitor. These processes, procedures, and techniques were also patentable; but no patent was sought. Rather Harshaw sought to protect its trade secrets by contracts with its employees. And the District Court found that, as a result of those secrecy precautions, "not sufficient disclosure occurred so as to place the claimed trade secrets in the public domain"; and those findings were sustained by the Court of Appeals.

The District Court issued a permanent injunction against respondents, ex-employees, restraining them from using the processes used by Harshaw. By a patent which would require full disclosure Harshaw could have obtained a 17-year monopoly against the world. By the District Court's injunction, which the Court approves and reinstates, Harshaw gets a permanent injunction running into perpetuity against respondents. In Sears, as in the present case, an injunction against the unfair competitor is-

---

[1]Here as in Lear, Inc. v. Adkins, 395 U.S. 653, 674, which held that a licensee of a patent is not precluded by a contract from challenging the patent, for if he were, that would defeat the policy of the patent laws: "enforcing this contractual provision would undermine the strong federal policy favoring the full and free use of ideas in the public domain."

sued. We said: "To allow a State by use of its law of unfair competition to prevent the copying of an article which represents too slight an advance to be patented would be to permit the State to block off from the public something which federal law has said belongs to the public. The result would be that while federal law grants only 14 or 17 years' protection to genuine inventions, see 35 U. S. C. §§ 154, 173, States could allow perpetual protection to articles too lacking in novelty to merit any patent at all under federal constitutional standards. This would be too great an encroachment on the federal patent system to be tolerated." 376 U.S., at 231-232. The conflict with the patent laws is obvious. The decision of Congress to adopt a patent system was based on the idea that there will be much more innovation if discoveries are disclosed and patented than there will be when everyone works in secret. Society thus fosters a free exchange of technological information at the cost of a limited 17-year monopoly.[2]

A trade secret[3], unlike a patent, has no property dimension. That was the view of the Court of Appeals, 478 F.2d 1074, 1081; and its decision is

---

[2]"The holding [of the Court of Appeals] in Kewanee seems correct. If it is permissible for an inventor to use the law of unfair competition as a substitute for patenting, certain categories of inventions would receive privileged protection under that law. Thus a new laser, television set, or airplane could not be protected because inventions which by their nature cannot be put into commercial use without disclosure, are not eligible for trade secret protection after they are put on the market. Those that can be maintained are eligible. But as the basic economic function of the patent system is to encourage the making and commercialization of inventions, there seems to be no justification for providing incentives beyond those provided by the patent law to discriminate between different categories of inventions, i. e., those that may inherently be kept secret and those that may not. Moreover, state rules which would grant such incentives seem to conflict with the economic quid pro quo underlying patent protection; i. e., a monopoly limited in time, in return for full disclosure of the invention. Thus federal law has struck a balance between incentives for inventors and the public's right to a competitive economy. In this sense, the patent law is an integral part of federal competitive policy." Adelman, Secrecy and Patenting: Some Proposals for Resolving the Conflict, 1 APLA Quarterly Journal 296, 298-299 (1973).

[3]Trade secrets often are unpatentable. In that event there is no federal policy which is contravened when an injunction to bar disclosure of a trade secret is issued. Moreover, insofar as foreign patents are involved our federal patent policy is obviously irrelevant. S. Oppenheim, Unfair Trade Practices 264-265 (2d ed. 1965). As respects further contrasts between patents and trade secrets see Milgrim, Trade Secret Protection and Licensing, 4 Pat. L. Rev. 375 (1972).

supported by what Mr. Justice Holmes said in Du Pont Powder Co. v. Masland, 244 U.S. 100, 102:

> The word property as applied to trade-marks and trade secrets is an un-analyzed expression of certain secondary consequences of the primary fact that the law makes some rudimentary requirements of good faith. Whether the plaintiffs have any valuable secret or not the defendant knows the facts, whatever they are, through a special confidence that he accepted. The property may be denied but the confidence cannot be. Therefore the starting point for the present matter is not property or due process of law, but that the defendant stood in confidential relations with the plaintiffs, or one of them. These have given place to hostility, and the first thing to be made sure of is that the defendant shall not fraudulently abuse the trust reposed in him. It is the usual incident of confidential relations. If there is any disadvantage in the fact that he knew the plaintiffs' secrets he must take the burden with the good.[4]

A suit to redress theft of a trade secret is grounded in tort damages for breach of a contract — a historic remedy, Cataphote Corp. v. Hudson, 422 F.2d 1290. Damages for breach of a confidential relation are not pre-empted by this patent law, but an injunction against use is pre-empted because the patent law states the only monopoly over trade secrets that is enforceable by specific performance; and that monopoly exacts as a price full disclosure. A trade secret can be protected only by being kept secret. Damages for breach of a contract are one thing; an injunction barring disclosure does service for the protection accorded valid patents and is therefore pre-empted.

---

[4]As to Goldstein v. California, 412 U.S. 546, the ruling of Mr. Justice Bradley concerning the distinction between patents and copyright is relevant:

The difference between the two things, letters-patent and copyright, may be illustrated by reference to the subjects just enumerated. Take the case of medicines. Certain mixtures are found to be of great value in the healing art. If the discoverer writes and publishes a book on the subject (as regular physicians generally do), he gains no exclusive right to the manufacture and sale of the medicine; he gives that to the public. If he desires to acquire such exclusive right, he must obtain a patent for the mixture as a new art, manufacture, or composition of matter. He may copyright his book, if he pleases; but that only secures to him the exclusive right of printing and publishing his book. So of all other inventions or discoveries. Baker v. Selden, 101 U.S. 99, 102-103.

From the findings of fact of the lower courts, the process involved in this litigation was unique, such a great discovery as to make its patentability a virtual certainty. Yet the Court's opinion reflects a vigorous activist antipatent philosophy. My objection is not because it is activist. This is a problem that involves no neutral principle. The Constitution in Art. I, § 8, cl. 8, expresses the activist policy which Congress has enforced by statutes. It is that constitutional policy which we should enforce, not our individual notions of the public good.

I would affirm the judgment below.

Notes and Questions

1. An enterprise often has to chose between patent and trade secret protection. Both systems have their advantages and disadvantages. Trade secret protection can last forever, whereas patents are limited to twenty years. Trade secrets always bear the risk of being disclosed to the public and therefore losing their protection, while to obtain a patent it is a condition to disclose the invention. Moreover, trade secret protection provides no rights against an independent discoverer, whereas patent protection does.

2. One of the most interesting issues in the trade secret field involves the relationship between knowledge gained by an employee in the ordinary course of practicing a trade or profession, and the proprietary information of an employer. In the archetypal Silicon Valley case, an employee has worked for several years at a semiconductor producing company, and leaves to work for another company in the same business. During his or her work for the first employer, the employee may have learned a great deal about producing semiconductors, and this knowledge will almost certainly make that employee more valuable to the second employer. The employee will have signed a confidentiality agreement with the first employer, but it is impracticable for the employee to surrender the useful knowledge he or she has gained. Some of that knowledge would be considered a trade secret by the first employer. Can this employer prevent the former employee from working for another semiconductor producer? In Silicon Valley, at least, the courts have been reluctant to impose restraints on the free movement of

workers, and have generally required the showing of a specific act of misappropriation of an industrial secret — such as the taking of important documents — before imposing liability on an employee, or his or her new employer. It is often noted that the free movement of highly skilled workers in Silicon Valley is one of the engines of the success of that region.

3. It can be observed that the choice between trade secret protection and patent protection for enterprises is like choosing a political party for individuals. There are enterprises which never file for a patent and consider trade secret protection advantageous compared to patent law. In the chemical industry patent protection is usually preferred, whereas the machine industry tends to choose trade secret protection. What do you think might account for this?

4. Especially in the countries of the European continent, trade secret protection is not as important as the other intellectual property rights. This does not mean that European inventors do not have trade secrets. Do you think that the classical IPRs (patent, copyright, trademark, industrial design) are sufficient to protect the intellectual creations of mankind, or might there be some holes in the system if we do not grant trade secret protection?

---

c. Confidential Business Information and Governmental Institutions

The risk of disclosure exists not only between private parties, but also with respect to public sector institutions (e.g., IP registration offices or competition surveillance authorities). There are many procedures that oblige enterprises or individuals to disclose confidential information, and the risk of the information becoming public is evident. The *AKZO* case is the landmark decision in EU law concerning the obligation of the European Commission to treat business secrets as confidential. In this case, the Commission asked for several sensitive documents in a competition law investigation. AKZO was obliged to produce these documents to the Commission by Article 213 of the EC Treaty as well as the corresponding provisions of Regulation No. 17 dealing with competition procedure. Later, the Commission transmitted some of the documents to the intervener, and it informed

AKZO only afterwards. In considering whether the Commission's action was proper, the ECJ interpreted the secrecy obligation of the Commission in relation to the access rights of third parties, and it found a high-level duty to protect business secrets.

AKZO Chemie BV and AKZO Chemie UK Ltd. v. Commission of the European Communities.

Judgment of the Court (Fifth Chamber) of 24 June 1986.
Case 53/85.
Court of Justice of the European Communities

Prior history: application requesting the Court to declare void the decision of the Commission of the European Communities of 14 December 1984 concerning the communication to a third party of documents stated to be confidential, disposition: on those grounds, the Court (fifth chamber) hereby:

(1) Declares void the decision which the Commission notified to the applicant by letter of 18 December 1984;
(2) Dismisses the remainder of the application;
(3) Orders the Commission to pay the costs.

Introduction: In case 53/85 AKZO Chemie BV . . .

vs.

Commission of the European Communities . . .

*****

Application requesting the Court to declare void the decision of the Commission of the European Communities of 14 December 1984 concerning the communication to a third party of documents stated to be confidential,

*****

Judgment by: Joliet

Judgment:

*****

Substance of the case

The applicant puts forward three submissions in support of its application. In the first place, it alleges that by communicating to ECS certain documents which were all in some way confidential, the Commission acted in breach of its obligation not to disclose information which is covered by the obligation of professional secrecy or which is subject to protection as a business secret. In the second place, by communicating to ECS certain documents which the latter could use in the legal proceedings pending in the United Kingdom, the Commission infringed Article 20(1) of Regulation No. 17/62 which provides that information acquired by the Commission in the exercise of its powers of investigation may be used only for the purpose for which it was obtained. Finally, the Commission has infringed Article 185 of the Treaty inasmuch as, by implementing its decision before notifying it to the applicant, it deprived the latter of the possibility of applying for an order suspending the operation of that decision at the same time as it instituted proceedings for annulment.

The Commission, with whose arguments the intervener essentially agrees, considers first of all that documents constituting evidence of an infringement of Article 86 of the Treaty, such as those communicated to ECS, are not of a confidential nature. It goes on to emphasize that ECS was given access to the documents only on the express condition that it would not use them for any purpose other than the proceedings before the Commission. Finally, it denies that there was any infringement of Article 185 of the Treaty because it did not adopt any decision which could be the subject of an application for annulment.

In the first place, it must be borne in mind that Article 214 of the Treaty requires the officials and other servants of the institutions of the Community not to disclose information in their possession of the kind covered by the obligation of professional secrecy. Article 20 of Regulation No. 17/62, which implements that provision in regard to the rules applicable to undertakings, contains in paragraph (2) a special provision worded as follows: "without prejudice to the provisions of Articles 19 and 21, the Commission and the competent authorities of the member states, their officials and other servants shall not disclose information acquired by them as a result of the application of this Regulation and of the kind covered by the obligation of professional secrecy."

The provisions of Articles 19 and 21, the application of which is thus reserved, deal with the Commission's obligations in regard to hearings and the publication of decisions. It follows that the obligation of professional secrecy laid down in Article 20(2) is mitigated in regard to third parties on whom Article 19(2) confers the right to be heard, that is to say in regard, in particular, to a third party who has made a complaint. The Commission may communicate to such a party certain information covered by the obligation of professional secrecy in so far as it is necessary to do so for the proper conduct of the investigation.

However, that power does not apply to all documents of the kind covered by the obligation of professional secrecy. Article 19(3) which provides for the publication of notices prior to the granting of negative clearance or exemptions, and Article 21 which provides for the publication of certain decisions, both require the Commission to have regard to the legitimate interest of undertakings in the protection of their business secrets. Business secrets are thus afforded very special protection. Although they deal with particular situations, those provisions must be regarded as the expression of a general principle which applies during the course of the administrative procedure. It follows that a third party who has submitted a complaint may not in any circumstances be given access to documents containing business secrets. Any other solution would lead to the unacceptable consequence that an undertaking might be inspired to lodge a complaint with the Commission solely in order to gain access to its competitors' business secrets.

It is undoubtedly for the Commission to assess whether or not a particular document contains business secrets. After giving an undertaking an opportunity to state its views, the Commission is required to adopt a decision in that connection which contains an adequate statement of the reasons on which it is based and which must be notified to the undertaking concerned. Having regard to the extremely serious damage which could result from improper communication of documents to a competitor, the Commission must, before implementing its decision, give the undertaking an opportunity to bring an action before the Court with a view to having the assessments made reviewed by it and to preventing disclosure of the documents in question.

In this case, the Commission gave the undertaking concerned an opportunity to make its position known and adopted a decision containing an adequate statement of the reasons on which it was based and concerning both the confidential nature of the documents at issue and the possibility of communicating them. At the same time, however, by an act which cannot be severed from that decision, the Commission decided to hand over the documents to the third party who had made the complaint even before it notified its findings to that undertaking. It thus made it impossible for the undertaking to avail itself of the means of redress provided by Article 173 in conjunction with Article 185 of the Treaty with a view to preventing the implementation of a contested decision.

That being the case, the decision which the Commission notified to the applicant by letter of 18 December 1984 must be declared void without there being any need to determine whether the documents communicated to the intervener did in fact contain business secrets.

Notes and Questions

1. Two important examples in which government offices must protect business secrets have been mentioned above. In what other areas of law do enterprises have to submit information that should not be disclosed?

2. Does it make sense to have different approaches to protection of undisclosed information depending on the recipient of information? If yes, why does the enterprise-to-governmental institution relationship require different treatment than the enterprise-to-enterprise relationship?

C. Policies Underlying the Grant of IPRs

As government decision makers consider the scope of protection that should be granted to IPRs holders, they must consider the objectives they expect to achieve with these grants. Perspectives on the role of IPRs may vary across time and culture. The views of policy makers in the industrial-ized countries — where large scale investment in research and develop-ment takes place and whose industries enjoy advantages in the creation of IPRs-related productive assets — may be quite different from the views of policy makers in the developing and newly-industrializing countries where there is heavy reliance on technologies generated elsewhere. Some policy experts argue that strong IPRs protection systems inherently play a positive role at all stages of economic development. Others suggest that different levels of IPRs protection may be more appropriate at different stages of eco-nomic development.

Economists have had difficulty determining the effects of IPRs protec-tion systems even in the highly industrialized countries where there appears to be general acknowledgment that such systems have a positive effect on economic growth and social welfare. A major reason for this difficulty in-volves the problem of "disaggregation." There are many reasons why partic-ular businesses, industries and national economies are successful or unsuccessful. Factors include local resource endowment, education of the labor force, availability of capital, and size and dynamism of the local mar-ket. In examining the success or failure of a particular business, an industry segment, or a national economy, it is difficult to isolate and evaluate a sin-gle factor or variable contributing to that success or failure. This is all the more difficult when these factors involve intangibles such as IPRs, and when the effects of IPRs may depend in significant measure on private sec-tor expectations concerning future conditions of competition.

When attention is turned to the role of IPRs in economic develop-ment, the problems of disaggregation multiply. Do IPRs have the same ef-fects in the least developed and more advanced developing economies? In agrarian and manufacturing economies? In free market, social market and totalitarian economies? In countries which are parties to a regional integra-tion arrangement and those which are not?

Determining the effect in fact of IPRs on economic development would require the collection and analysis of empirical data that might demonstrate cause and effect. Though there are efforts underway to assem-ble such data, study in this area continues to be hampered by its absence.

All intellectual property laws — national, regional and interna-tional — reflect a balancing of interests among various individuals and groups; for example, with respect to patent laws: inventors, investors of cap-ital and consumers. Debate concerning developments in the international intellectual property system takes place within the framework of these various interests.

1. Historical Skepticism

The first reading contains portions of a seminal economic work by Fritz Machlup, *An Economic Review of the Patent System*, which was in the form of a report prepared for the Subcommittee on Patents, Trademarks and Copyrights of the U.S. Senate Judiciary Committee as part of a study of the U.S. patent system. The report was published in 1958. The policy issues Machlup identifies with respect to patents pertain in differing measure to other forms of IPRs, though each form of IP protection presents certain unique issues.

Though economists studying the international intellectual property system today work with highly sophisticated economic models to attempt to determine the impact of different levels of IPRs protection on the international economic system, these models can function no better than their theoretical foundation permits.

An Economic Review of the Patent System

By Fritz Machlup*

I. Introduction

Patent, the adjective means "open," and patent, the noun, is the customary abbreviation of "open letter." The official name is "letters patent," a literal translation of the Latin "litterae patentes." Letters patent are official documents by which certain rights, privileges, ranks, or titles are conferred. Among the better known of such "open letters" are patents of appointment (of officers, military, judicial, colonial), patents of nobility, patents of precedence, patents of land conveyance, patents of monopoly, patents of inven-

---

*Subcomm. On Patents, Trademarks and Copyrights, of the Committee on the Judiciary, 85th Congress, 2d Sess.

tion. Patents of invention confer the right to exclude others from using a particular invention. When the term "patent" is used without qualification, it nowadays refers usually to inventors' rights. Similarly, the French "brevet," derived from the Latin "litterae breves" (brief letters), is a document granting a right or privilege, and usually stands for "brevet d'invention."

Defined more accurately, a patent confers the right to secure the enforcement power of the state in excluding unauthorized persons, for a specified number of years, from making commercial use of a clearly identified invention. Patents of invention are commonly classed with other laws or measures for the protection of so-called "intellectual property" or "industrial property." This class includes the protection of exclusivity for copyrights, trademarks, trade names, artistic designs, and industrial designs, besides technical inventions; other types of "products of intellectual labor" have at various times been proposed as worthy of public protection. It has seemed "unjust" to many, for example, that the inventor or a new gadget should be protected, and, perhaps, become rich, while the savant who discovered the principle on which the invention is based should be without protection and without material reward for his services to society. Yet, proposals to extend government protection of "intellectual property" to scientific discoveries have everywhere been rejected as impractical and undesirable.

II. Historical Survey

A. Early History (Before 1624)

The oldest examples of grants of exclusive rights by kings and rulers to private inventors and innovators to practice their new arts or skills go back to the 14th century. Probably the first "patent law," in the sense of a general promise of exclusive rights to inventors, was enacted in 1474 by the Republic of Venice. In the 16th century, patents were widely used by German princes, some of whom had a well-reasoned policy of granting privileges on the basis of a careful consideration of the utility and novelty of the inventions and, also, of the burden which would be imposed on the country by excluding others from the use of these inventions and by enabling the patentees to charge higher prices.

Some of the exclusive privileges were on new inventions; others on skilled crafts imported from abroad. Some of the privileges were for limited periods; others forever. (For example, the canton Bern in Switzerland granted in 1577 to inventor Zobell a "permanent exclusive privilege.") Some of the privileges granted protection against imitation and therefore, competition, and thus created monopoly rights. Others, however, granted protection from the restrictive regulations of guilds, and thus were designed to reduce existing monopoly positions and to increase competition. In view of the latter type of privilege, patents have occasionally been credited with liberating industry from restrictive regulations by guilds and local authorities and with aiding the industrial revolution in England. In France, the persecution of innovators by guilds of craftsmen continued far into the 18th century. (For example, in 1726, the weavers'guild threatened design printers with sever punishment, including death.) Royal patent privileges were sometimes conferred, not to grant exclusive rights, but to grant permission to do what was prohibited under existing rules.

Many of the privileges, however, served neither to reward inventors and protect innovators, nor to exempt innovators from restrictive regulations, nor to promote the development of industry in general, but just to grant profitable monopoly rights to favorites of the court or to supporters of the royal coffers. Patents of monopoly of this sort became very numerous in England after 1560, and the abuses led to increasing public discontent. In 1603, in the "Case of Monopolies," a court declared a monopoly in playing cards void under common law, and in 1623-24 Parliament passed the Statute of Monopolies (21 Jac. I., cap. 3) forbidding the granting by the Crown of exclusive rights to trade, with the exception of patent monopolies to the "first and true inventor" of a new manufacture. It is this emphasis of the law, that only the first and true inventor could be granted a monopoly patent, which justified designation of the Statute of Monopolies as the "Magna Carta of the rights of inventors."

B. The Spread of the Patent System (1624-1850)

The Statute of Monopolies is the basis of the present British patent law, and became the model for the laws elsewhere. Some of the Colonies were the first to follow: Massachusetts, for example, in 1641. To South Carolina goes the credit for enacting, in 1691, the first "general" patent law, as distinguished from authorization to the Crown to make patent grants. The larger countries of Europe were much slower. An edict of King Louis XV of France, in 1762, did little more than prohibit permanent privileges and provide for inventors' patents limited to 15 years. In 1791, the Constitutional Assembly passed a comprehensive patent law, in which the inventor's right in his creation was declared a "property right" based on the "rights of man."

In the United States of America, the Constitution of 1787 had given Congress the power:

> to promote the Progress of Science and useful Arts, by securing for limited Times to Authors and Inventors the exclusive Right to their respective Writings and Discoveries.

Under this power, the Congress passed the first patent law in 1790 and amended it in 1793.

The next country to adopt patent legislation was Austria. In 1794, a Hofdekret (royal decree) announced the establishment of a patent system, and in 1810 such a law was enacted. Opposed to the doctrine of the inventor's "natural rights," it provided, and the amended act of 1820 repeated, that inventors had neither any property rights in their inventions nor any rights to patents; the Government reserved its prerogative to grant privileges to restrict what was called their subjects' "natural rights to imitate" an inventor's idea.

Four different legal philosophies about the nature of the inventor's legal right were thus expressed in the patent laws of the various countries: the French, recognizing a property right of the inventor in his invention and deriving from it his right to obtain a patent; the American, silent on the property question, but stressing the inventor's legal right to a patent; the English, recognizing the monopoly character of the patent, and regarding it in theory as a grant of royal favor, but in practice regularly allowing the inventor's claim to receive a patent on his invention; the Austrian, insisting that the inventor has no right to protection, but may, as a matter of policy, be granted a privilege if in the public interest.

Regardless of these differences concerning the inventor's rights, in one form or another, the patent system, in the sense of a system of inventor's protection regulated by statutory law, spread to other countries. Patent laws were enacted in Russia in 1812; Prussia, 1815; Belgium and the Netherlands, 1817; Spain, 1820; Bavaria, 1825; Sardinia, 1826; the Vatican State, 1833; Sweden, 1834; Wurttemberg, 1836; Portugal, 1837; Saxonia, 1843.

C. The Rise of an Antipatent Movement (1850-1873)

During the second quarter of the 19th century various groups pressed for the strengthening of the patent system and for its expansion. In Britain, they wanted patents made more easily obtainable and more effectively enforceable. In Germany a unified patent system was sought after an agreement of the Zollverein in 1842 had reduced the value of patents by permitting patented articles to be imported from member states. Petitions in Switzerland, partly inspired by German interests, asked for patent legislation. Provoked by such pressures and in line with the free-trade movement of the period, an antipatent movement started in most countries of Europe.

Parliamentary committees and royal commissions in Britain investigated the operation of the patent system in 1851-52, in 1862-65, and again in 1869-72. Some of the testimony was so damaging to the repute of the patent system that leading statesmen urged its abolition. A patent-reform bill, providing for stricter examination of applications, a reduction of the term of protection to 7 years, and compulsory licensing of all patents, was passed by the House of Lords.

In Germany several trade associations and chambers of commerce recommended abolition of the patent laws, the Kongress deutscher Volkswirte in 1863 condemned "patents of invention as injurious to common welfare;" the Government of Prussia decided to oppose the adoption of a patent law by the North German Federation; and Chancellor Bismarck in 1868 announced his objections to the principle of patent protection.

In Switzerland, the only industrial country of Europe that had remained without patent legislation, the legislature rejected proposals in 1849, 1851, 1854, and twice in 1863, the last time with a reference to the fact that "economists of greatest competence" had declared the principle of patent protection to be "pernicious and indefensible."

In the Netherlands the majority of the Parliament was convinced that "a good law of patents is an impossibility." The abolitionists won and, in 1869, the patent law was repealed.

D. The Victory of the Patent Advocates (1873-1910)

The tide turned in 1873, when the antipatent movement collapsed rather suddenly, after a most impressive propaganda campaign by the groups interested in patent protection. The following reasons have been given for the sudden change: the great depression, the rise of protectionism that came with it, the rise of nationalism, and the willingness of the patent advocates to accept a compromise.

The free-trade idea had been the chief ideological support of the antipatent movement: patent protection had been attacked along with tariff protection. Now, "thanks to the bad crisis," public opinion had turned away from "the pernicious theory . . . of free competition and free trade" (Reichstagsabgeordneter Ackermann, opening the debate on the German patent bill in 1877).

The strategic compromise was the acceptance of the principle of compulsory licensing — of compelling all patentees to license others to use the invention at reasonable compensation. This idea had been proposed in 1790 in the United States Senate, in 1851 in the House of Lords in Britain, in 1853 by a German official, in 1858, 1861, and 1863 at various conferences of British scientific organizations, and now in 1873 at the Patent Congress held at the Vienna World's Fair. The patent advocates and the free traders compromised on this general limitation on the patentees' monopoly power. (Despite the resolution of the Patent Congress, the actual adoption of compulsory licensing has been rather slow in some countries, and is still resisted in the United States of America.)

The defeat or disappearance of the opposition was reflected in the actions of the legislatures of several countries. In Britain the drastic reform bill that had passed the House of Lords was withdrawn in the House of Commons in 1874. In Germany a uniform patent law for the entire Reich was adopted in 1877. Japan, which had adopted her first patent law in 1872 only to abolish it again in 1873, enacted another law in 1885. Switzerland, more conservative than other nations, held out longer; a referendum in 1882 still rejected patent legislation, but a new referendum in 1887 enabled the legislature to pass a law. Patentability of inventions in the chemical and textile industries was limited by a requirement of mechanical models for all patented inventions. But this limitation was deleted from the law by an amendment in 1907, after Germany had threatened higher tariffs on certain

Swiss products. The Netherlands, the last bastion of "free trade in inventions," reintroduced a patent system in 1910, to become effective in 1912.

* * *

IV. Economic Theory

A. Early Economic Opinion: 1750-1850

The English classical economists accepted the traditional view that, in the words of Adam Smith (1776), monopoly was "necessarily hurtful to society," but a temporary monopoly granted to an inventor was a good way of rewarding his risk and expense. Jeremy Bentham (1785), comparing rewards by bonus payments with rewards by "exclusive privileges," held that the latter method was "best proportioned, most natural, and least burdensome"; "it produces an infinite effect and costs nothing." The "protection against imitators" is necessary because "he who has no hope that he shall reap will not take the trouble to sow." John Stuart Mill (1848) urged that "the condemnation of monopolies ought not to extend to patents." The inventor "ought to be both compensated and rewarded"; not to reward him would be "a gross immorality." The temporary "exclusive privilege" was preferable to a governmental bonus because it avoided "discretion" and secured a reward proportional to the "usefulness" of the invention, a reward paid by the consumer who benefits from it.

The German cameralists had reservations. Johann Heinrich G. von Justi (1758) was in favor of rewards and encouragements to inventors, but not "by privileges leading to monopoly positions." Ludwig Heinrich Jakob (1809) approved of patents only for inventions that had been particularly expensive and "could not just as easily have been made by others"; patents for "accidental inventions" and "insignificant artifices" could easily paralyze the industry of others and, therefore, would be iniquitous. Johann Friedrich Lotz (1822) conceded that it might be "fair and economically advantageous for a nation to compensate the inventor" for efforts and expenses, but that it was "very questionable whether monopolization of his invention is the right kind of compensation." Karl Heinrich Rau (1844), on the other hand, found that, though "some important inventions are made by accident," many require great effort and one "would not make such sacrifices if he could not hope for a period of protection from encroachment by competitors in the use of his invention."

*****

B. The Chief Arguments for Patent Protection

While the early opinions on the patent system were expressed merely in occasional comments and remarks contained in general treatises on political economy, economists during the great patent controversy of the second half of the 19th century wrote articles, pamphlets, and books on the economics of exclusive rights. The arguments for and against the patent system have not changed much since that time.

Patent protection for inventors is advocated on ethical grounds in the name of "justice" or "natural right" — or on pragmatic grounds — in the name of "promotion of the public interest." In some views, ethical and pragmatic considerations are combined, largely because conduct is regarded as ethical if and because it benefits society. Others recognize the possibility of conflict between requirements of justice and material usefulness to society, and they may seek justice even at the expense of material benefits, or material benefits at the expense of justice.

The four best-known positions on which advocates of patent protection for inventors have rested their case may be characterized as the "natural-law" thesis, the "reward-by-monopoly" thesis, the "monopoly-profit-incentive" thesis, and the "exchange-for-secrets" thesis.

The "natural-law" thesis assumes that man has a natural property right in his own ideas. Appropriation of his ideas by others, that is, their unauthorized use, must be condemned as stealing. Society is morally obligated to recognize and protect this property right. Property is, in essence, exclusive. Hence, enforcement of exclusivity in the use of a patented invention is the only appropriate way for society to recognize this property right.

The "reward-by-monopoly" thesis assumes that justice requires that a man receive reward for his services in proportion to their usefulness to society, and that, where needed, society must intervene to secure him such reward. Inventors render useful services, and the most appropriate way to secure them commensurate rewards is by means of temporary monopolies in the form of exclusive patent rights in their inventions.

The "monopoly-profit-incentive" thesis assumes that industrial progress is desirable, that inventions and their industrial exploitation are necessary for such progress, but that inventions and/or their exploitation will not be obtained in sufficient measure if inventors and capitalists can hope only for such profits as the competitive exploitation of all technical knowledge will permit. To make it worthwhile for inventors and their capitalist backers to make their efforts and risk their money, society must intervene to increase their profit expectations. The simplest, cheapest, and most effective way for society to hold out these incentives is to grant temporary monopolies in the form of exclusive patent right in inventions.

The "exchange-for-secrets" thesis presumes a bargain between inventor and society, the former surrendering the possession of secret knowledge in exchange for the protection of a temporary exclusivity in its industrial use. The presupposition again is that industrial progress at a sustained rate is desirable but cannot be obtained if inventors and innovating entrepreneurs keep inventions secret; in this case the new technology may only much later become available for general use; indeed, technological secrets may die with their inventors and forever be lost to society. Hence, it is in the interest of society to bargain with the inventor and make him disclose his secret for the use of future generations. This can best be done by offering him exclusive patent rights in return for public disclosure of the invention.

* * *

Since the relevant period of profitable exploitation of an innovation is a conjecture about the future — no matter whether the anticipation rests on the natural headstart or on the term of a patent grant or on the interval before the emergence of a substitute invention — what counts most in this respect is whether entrepreneurs, by and large, are optimistic or pessimistic. Fritz Machlup — the author of the present study — has written in an earlier book:

> For the pessimistic monopolist we can plausibly generalize that open avenues of technological advance will remain untried. Investment in industrial research, development and innovation will not appear promising in view of the supposedly imminent advent of competition. Inventions will be suppressed if the time for the amortization of the required new investments seems too short.

... [W]e may point to the possibility of the opposite error, the over optimistic entrepreneur who underestimates the actual degree of pliopoly [i.e., newcomers' competition] and overestimates the safe period. He need not be an actual monopolist, nor even imagine that he is one; it suffices that he believes it will take his competitors-imitators or makers of substitutes-longer than it actually does to start competing with him. This optimism is the best promoter of technical progress. Progress calls for both innovation and imitation. If firms anticipate rapid imitation, they will not risk expensive innovation. But if imitation is rapid while the firms expect it to be slow, society will get the benefit of innovation as well as of rapid imitation.

To buy innovation by paying with unnecessarily long delays of imitation is a poor bargain for society to make. Imitation always and necessarily lags behind innovation. It will be the best deal from the point of view of society if innovators optimistically overestimate this lag. If they expect the lag to be longer than it actually is, innovation will be enhanced and imitation will not be delayed. That it may create this socially wholesome illusion on the part of innovators is the strongest justification for a well-designed patent system.

A.C. Pigou included "the perfecting of inventions and improvements in industrial processes" in the —

class of divergences between marginal private net product and the marginal social net product . . . [because] the whole of the extra reward, which they at first bring to their inventor, is very quickly transferred from him to the general public in the form of reduced prices. The patent laws aim, in effect, at bringing marginal private net product and marginal social net product more closely together.

This formulation of the aim of the patent system commands widest agreement among economic theorists, though not all economists would agree that government interventions should be resorted to whenever divergences between social and private "marginal net products" are found; nor would all agree that the patent system was the best kind of government intervention for the particular purpose. Frank H. Knight has serious doubts in this respect and proposes that-

it would seem to be a matter of political development to provide a better way of rewarding these [inventive] services than even a temporary monopoly of their use . . .

F.A. Hayek expresses the same misgivings:

> In the field of industrial patents in particular we shall have seriously to examine whether the award of a monopoly privilege is really the most appropriate and effective form of reward for the kind of risk bearing which investment in scientific research involves.

An interesting statement is offered by Joan Robinson of what she calls "the paradox of patents":

> A patent is a device to prevent the diffusion of new methods before the original investor has recovered profit adequate to induce the requisite investment. The justification of the patent system is that by slowing down the diffusion of technical progress it insures that there will be more progress to diffuse. The patent system introduces some of the greatest of the complexities in the capitalist rules of the game and leads to many anomalies. Since it is rooted in a contradiction, there can be no such thing as an ideally beneficial patent system, and it is bound to produce negative results in particular instances, impeding progress unnecessarily, even if its general effect is favorable on balance.

* * * * *

The most outspoken critic of the patent system in modern times has been Sir Arnold Plant. At one point in his argument he refers to "exceptional cases" in which "special inducements" would be necessary to secure funds for "prolonged research and experiment" on specified, socially desirable invention. He continues:

> A patent system applicable to inventions in general clearly cannot be justified, however, by exceptional circumstances of this kind. Economics, in short, has not yet evolved any apparatus of analysis which would enable us to pronounce upon the relative productivity of this particular infant industry — the production of inventions; nor does it provide any criteria for the approval of this method of special encouragement.

After examining the case for general compulsory licensing as a reform designed to facilitate "the operation of competitive forces" within the patent system, Plant concludes:

Expedients such as licenses of right, nevertheless, cannot repair the lack of theoretical principle behind the whole patent system. They can only serve to confine the evils of monopoly within the limits contemplated by the legislators; and, as I have endeavoured to show, the science of economics, as it stands today, furnishes no basis of justification for this enormous experiment in the encouragement of a particular activity by enabling monopolistic price control.

John Jewkes, in a book published in 1958, pays his respect to Plant's "classic" study, which he recommends as "the departure point for any modern study of the patent system." Jewkes, who presents much evidence indicating the continued importance of the individual inventor, holds that —

So long as the survival of the individual inventor is not utterly despaired of . . . and so long as nothing better can be suggested for the purpose, there is a very strong case for the retention of the patent system.

But Jewkes is far from eulogizing the system. This is what he has to say about it:

It is easy enough to perceive the weaknesses, even the absurdities, of the patent system and the reasons why conflicting opinions as to its value are to be found. Its very principles are paradoxical. It is meant to encourage over the long period the widest possible use of knowledge, but it starts out by conferring upon the inventor the power to restrict to himself the use of that knowledge. It grants statutory monopolies but it arose out of an act to curb monopoly. It flourished most vigorously in the 19th century, the great period of economic competition, and even now it is more robustly defended and embodies the most extensive monopoly rights in those countries which most tenaciously adhere to the competitive system of private enterprise. It is a crude and inconsistent system. It is based upon the assumption that the right and proper reward for the innovator is the monopoly profit he can extract in an arbitrarily fixed period. It offers the same reward to all inventors, irrespective of the intellectual merits of their inventions. It provides rewards for certain kinds of discoveries but usually confers no such rewards for other kinds of discover, . . . The standards of patentability, the patent period, the conditions attached to the patent have varied greatly from time to time in the same country and vary as between different countries.

235

The patent system lacks logic. It postulates something called "invention" but in fact no satisfactory definition of "invention" has ever appeared, and the courts, in their search for guiding rules, have produced an almost incredible tangle of conflicting doctrines. This confusion has led to extensive and costly litigation. Its critics have described the patent right as merely "something which has to be defended in the courts" and, because it may put the individual inventor at a disadvantage against the larger corporations, as "a lottery in which it is hardly worthwhile taking out a ticket."

The system, too, is wasteful. It gives protection for 16 years (or thereabouts) whilst in fact over nine-tenths of the patents do not remain active for the whole of this period. It is dangerous in that the monopoly it confers can often be widened by its owner into fields and forms which it was never intended he should possess.

It is almost impossible to conceive of any existing social institution so faulty in so many ways. It survives only because there seems to be nothing better.

* * * * *

G. Some Confusions, Inconsistencies, and Fallacies

The discussions in the last section or two have been somewhat apart from the main stream of the debate on the traditional issues concerning the patent system. Some of these issues cannot be finally resolved inasmuch as they rest on unprovable articles of faith or morals. Others, however, involve confusions which can be clarified, inconsistencies which can be shown up, or fallacies which can be exposed. The arguments — the confuted or the confuting ones — will for the most part be recognizable as those advanced by a number of writers mentioned in the previous survey of economic opinion.

A slight inconsistency can be discovered with regard to the bargain theory — that patent protection is exchanged for the disclosure of secrets. The theory asserts that great benefits are obtained for society by securing the general availability, after 17 years or so, of now secret information; actual patenting practice, however, implies that others may be ready any minute to put the same information to work. Is the conviction that valuable technical information might remain secret for years, if not forever, fully consistent with the attorney's advice to his clients that they rush to the

Patent Office lest someone else with the same idea beat them to it? If several inventors actually come up with the same idea, is it likely to be one that anybody could have kept secret? And is not society likely to lose, then, by restricting the use of such an idea for several years?

The contention that the first inventor has by "natural law" a "property right" in his invention does not go well with the provision (also enunciated in the French law of 1791) that whoever introduces a foreign invention should have the same rights as if he were the inventor. Nor does the notion of the inventor's "natural property right" in the invention — not to be confused with the property right in the patent — go well with the accepted principles that certain kinds of invention are not patentable, that all patents should expire within 14 or 17 years, and that they may be revoked earlier or licensed to others in case of an "abuse of the monopoly," for instance, through nonworking or insufficient use of the invention. A "natural property right" is just the opposite of a "limited conditional, and revocable monopoly grant."

The problem of what are "natural rights," or rights under natural law, is one of legal and political philosophy, and controversies about it are usually moot. But the assertion that the recognition of anybody's exclusive rights in an invention, or in its commercial use, "takes nothing away from the public" is a fallacy which can be rebutted, and has been for centuries. The various "freedoms" or "rights" which individuals would enjoy if no exclusive rights were granted to patentees have often been listed. In particular, those who independently develop the technological ideas already patented by someone else are barred from using the fruits of their own labor, and those who would have freely imitated these inventions are deprived of the right to imitate — which some regard as a "right" not less "natural" than any other. The suppression or restriction of these and other rights may be in the public interest, and one might perhaps say that patents take "little" from the public compared with the benefits that accrue to it. But to contend that they take "nothing" is simply wrong.

The meaning and object of "property" and "property rights" are shrouded by confusions, which, however, are more troublesome to lawyers than to economists. But it is almost embarrassing how often the controversial idea of a property right in an *invention* is confused with the noncontroversial idea of a property right in a *patent*.

A confusion which might encumber economic analysis if it were widespread is that between "property" and "monopoly." There is the idea that "property" and "monopoly" are one and the same thing from the economic point of view, and that the "owner" of an invention has a monopoly of its use just as the owner of a house has a "monopoly" of the use of the house. This idea runs counter to the fact that anyone who builds a house exactly like one built earlier by someone else will be permitted to use it or sell it — even if he has copied it — whereas anyone who develops a technology exactly like one developed earlier by someone else will be prohibited, by the patent rights granted to the "first inventor" from using it or selling it — even if his work was entirely independent.

An old fallacy relates to the "adequacy" of the "reward" to the inventor. The assertion has been made, and is still being repeated, that the "rewards" which inventors or their assignees earn through profits from exclusive use of the patented inventions are in proportions to the "social usefulness" of these inventions. There is no reason why this should be so, and in fact no such proportionality, or approximate proportionality, can possibly be shown. It is well known that several inventions which have later proved to be of immense usefulness to society were somewhat "ahead of their time" when they were made and patented, and have earned nothing for their creators. It is firmly established that patents on some trivial gadgets have earned millions for their owners while patents on technically highly significant processes have been financially unrewarding. In general, the profits made from the commercial exploitation of a patent depend in part on the degree of restriction on the output produced under the patent. It is more than probable that the socially most important inventions, say, of drugs or vaccines for the cure or prevention of cancer, would not be allowed to be exploited with the same monopolistic restrictions that are freely tolerated in the exploitation of patents on hair curlers, bottle caps, or television screens.

The most perplexing and disturbing confusions occur in discussions about the "value of patents." This is no wonder, what with the large number of possible meanings in the minds of the writers on the subject: they may be talking about (a) the value of patents to their owners, (b) the value of patents to society, (c) the value of the patent system to society, (d) the value of patented inventions to their users, (e) the value of patented inventions to society, (f) the value of patent-induced inventions to society. But even this in not all, because the social value of inventions may depend on the degree to which they are used, and the value of patents to their owners on the way they are exploited.

Singling out, from this long list, (b) the value of patents to society — and making quite sure that this refers neither to the social benefits of the patent system nor to the social value of the inventions, which are altogether different matters — it is worth pointing out that existing domestic patents held by domestic owners cannot be reasonably regarded as parts of the national wealth or as sources of real national income. To regard them so is as fallacious as it would be to include in national wealth such things as the right of a businessman to exclude others from using his trade name, or the right of a (domestic) creditor to collect from his (domestic) debtors, or to include such things as (domestic) money, securities, damage claims, and lottery tickets. The right of a person to keep others from doing something is no social asset and, again, somebody's right to keep others from using his invention should not be confused with the invention itself. To confuse an important invention with the patent that excludes people from using it is like confusing an important bridge with the tollgates that close it to many who might want to use it. No statistics of national wealth would ever include (domestic) "patent property." And the "destruction of patent property" — though it may affect the future performance of the economy — would leave the Nations's wealth, as it is now understood in social accounting, unimpaired. (An exception must be noted concerning foreign patent rights. One may regard domestic holdings of foreign patents as claims to future royalties and profits earned abroad and, hence, as assets; of course, foreign holdings of domestic patents, establishing foreign rights to future royalties and profits earned here, should then have to be counted among the liabilities and, therefore, as deductions from national wealth.)

The idea that social benefits may be derived from the operation of the patent system misleads many into assuming, without further argument, that social benefits can be derived from existing patents. If one accepts the theory that patent protection has the social function of serving as an incentive for inventive activity, one accepts, by implication, that the beneficial effects of this incentive system must flow, not from existing patents, but from the hope for future profits from future patents; this hope may induce people to undertake certain risky investments and useful activities — to wit, financing and arranging industrial research — which they might not undertake otherwise. Existing patents, on the other hand, restrict the use of inventions already known, and thus they reduce temporarily the full contribution these inventions could make to national output. These restrictions are neither "odious" nor unlawful, nor contrary to public policy; they are "necessary" if any profit is to be derived from the patents. But they are still restrictions, keeping output smaller than it might be otherwise. Consequently, existing patents impose a burden on society, a burden which it has decided to carry in order to hold out to people the chance of obtaining future profits from future patents on future inventions. That existing patents are a social cost, not a social benefit, is most readily appreciated when the patented invention is of such extraordinary importance that society would not tolerate even a temporary restriction in its use. The great inventor of the polio vaccine, Dr. Salk, generously contributed his idea to society without applying for a patent. If he had taken a patent on his process and sold it to a company which exploited it restrictively enough to make high profits, would the American public have stood for it?

The preceding considerations concerning the social benefits derived from patents concerned the theory that the patent system is designed to stimulate invention. Other theories — not often clearly expounded — stress other incentives as the essential functions of the system: to stimulate innovation and to stimulate investment. Inventing, innovating, and investing are different activities, though usually not properly separated in analysis. They may, of course, be interrelated; a big investment may be required to finance inventive activity; innovation also usually involves investment of capital; innovation, moreover, may be based on a patented invention, constituting, in effect, its commercial exploitation. But there need not be such relationship: innovation may be based on nonpatentable inventions or even on nontechnological ideas, and investment may be for new though not novel plant and equipment. Now, under the theory that the patent system is designed to stimulate innovation, existing patents (and pending patents) will play a direct role in the realization of this objective. The point is that *inventive* activity must precede the patent, whereas *innovating* activity may follow it. But the justification of the patent system as an incentive for innovating enterprise and for entrepreneurial investment would call for different supporting arguments than the justification as an incentive for invention. These arguments might have to include a demonstration that innovations based on patentable inventions are socially more desirable than other innovations, and that the free-enterprise system would not, without monopoly incentives, generate investment opportunities to an adequate extent — propositions which the supporters of the theories in question might not be willing to entertain. Moreover, there would be the additional question whether the promotion of innovating enterprise and of entrepreneurial investment can be held to be subsumed in the promotion of "science and the useful arts" which the Constitution of the United States stipulated as the sole objective of patent legislation.

* * * * *

N. Evaluation of the Patent System as a Whole

A comparison, even though speculative, of the incremental benefits and costs associated with a little more or a little less patent protection, is more feasible than is an attempt to assess the "total effects" of the system. An economic evaluation of the patent system as a whole implies an analysis of the differences between its existence and non-existence — perhaps a hopeless task. Nevertheless several different effects, some beneficial some harmful, have been attributed to the operation of the patent system, and must be reviewed in an attempt at evaluation.

That the patent system succeeds in eliciting the disclosure of technological secrets is a claim widely asserted though often denied. The chief question is whether, by and large, the period over which inventions could be kept secret, or in which the first invention would not be duplicated by other inventors, is longer than the period for which patents are granted. A negative answer is strongly suggested by the simple reflection that inventions probably are patented only when the inventor or user fears that others would soon find out his secret or independently come upon the same idea. It would follow that the patent system can elicit only those technological secrets which without a patent system would be likely to be dispersed even sooner than they become free for public use under patent protection.

This conclusion disregards the possibility that all the competitors who eventually find out about the novel technology or find it independently will try to keep it secret. However, this would be a "secret" shared by all whose knowledge really matters. For if there is enough competition among those who are "in the know," the interests of the community are safeguarded. But there is another advantage in prompt and full disclosure under the patent system, which is not secured through the process of individual detection or multiple invention. Disclosure of an invention through the patent grant may give "ideas" to technicians in other industries who would not, as a rule, go out of their ways to "find" the technical information in question but may be glad to take a hint when it is "thrown" at them through publication in the official gazette. In other words, dissemination of technical ideas to outsiders should be considered separately from the availability of the invention to those who would like to use it in competition with the first inventor.

The claim that the patent system serves to disseminate technological information, and that this accelerates the growth of productivity in the economy, is not questioned. In some countries, though not in all, the patent offices have collected and made publicly available the vast amount of technical information contained in the hundreds of thousands of patents, current and past. But, while this store of knowledge in public print is a very desirable byproduct of the patent system, it is not necessarily dependent on it; conceivably, similar collections of technical knowledge could be compiled, perhaps no less efficiently, by special agencies in the absence of patents.*

Apart from any effects upon the size of the national income, the patent system affects the distribution of income. Indeed this is its purpose from the point of view of the "just reward" theory: to transfer some of the income increase produced by newly invented technology to the people responsible for it. The recipients of this income transfer are often pictured to be those ingenious, independent fellows called "garret inventors" or "basement inventors"; it was said that they would be helped by the patent system in their endeavors to go into business for themselves or to sell their rights to one of the several businessmen competing to acquire these rights for practical application of the inventions. Yet this is not how things work today. The majority of "inventors" are employees of corporations, many working on the staff of research departments of very big firms. The income transferred from the consumers is received by the corporations to cover their research and development cost (if written off immediately), or as part of their profit either to be reinvested (perhaps in research equipment and innovations) or to be distributed to stockholders. Is what the consumers pay on this score (as part of the price of the goods and services they buy) more, or

---

*It is difficult to compare two methods of dissemination if one of them has not been tried. Would the "compilers" be able to get the cooperation of industry? Would the prestige of public recognition be an inducement for making information available to the compilers? It must be borne in mind that the present method of disclosure is not designed to inform and to instruct; on the contrary, patent applicants often try to disclose as little as possible, and only in terms of the claims of the patents. "Dissemination" might be more effectively achieved by different methods.

is it less, than the increase in real income which results — has resulted? Will result? — from the corporate research and development work? If it is true that the total outlay for such work is increased under the patent incentive, this increase means more demand for research personnel and thus will raise the salaries of the entire staff, old and new, although it is only the additions to the staff that will increase the rate at which new technology is created. If the supply of research workers should be completely inelastic, there will be only increased salaries but not more inventing; and if the corporations should know this, or for any other reasons fail to increase their outlays for inventive and innovating activities, there will be only increased corporate profits resulting from the patent system. But one never can tell, perhaps the income redistribution accomplished by the system is only a modest portion of the increase in national product which the system induces and which would not occur without it.

The incentive effects of the patent system, which are supposed to yield the new inventions and innovations which in turn produce an increase in national output, are the result of profit expectation based on restrictions of the output produced with the aid of the patented inventions. These output restrictions are the very essence of the patent system because only by restricting output below the competitive level can the patent secure an income to its owner. There need not be any contradiction between the output restrictions and output expansions effected by the patent system. While each existing patent may restrict the utilization of a recently developed piece of technology and thus reduce the output of particular products in particular industries, the system as a whole may promote the development and application of ever new technologies and thus permit an accelerated increase in national product. One is reminded of the famous analogy of the automobile brakes which permit motorists to drive with greater speed. The patents are here likened to the brakes which the "drivers" (entrepreneurs) in the economy can apply and which are to give them the courage to accelerate its progress. The "braking" is the direct and absolutely certain effect, the encouragement is only an indirect effect and not quite so certain, though rather plausible. The output restrictions based on patents are primary effects and testable; the incentive effects are secondary and more conjectural.

These incentives are supposed to generate technological inventions plus innovations — innovations being the first commercial application of a new idea. Invention without application is useless; practical application may depend on patent protection even where invention does not. Thus, even if the patent system were proved to be unnecessary for the promotion of invention — that is, if an adequate flow of inventions were forthcoming without patent incentive — patents might still be needed as encouragement for investment and enterprise to introduce untried techniques and products.

To be eager to do something is not enough if the necessary funds are lacking. Some observers have placed less emphasis on the need for patents as an *incentive* for investment in industrial research, development, and practical innovation than on the need for them as sources of *finance* for such investment. They have argued that only the monopoly profits derived from existing market positions based on past patents can provide the funds for new incentive work and innovating ventures. This argument was perhaps suggested by the observation that the largest research laboratories are in fact maintained by corporations with the strongest patent positions and with high and stable earnings. This, however, does not mean that other firms, not drawing on patent-monopoly profits, could not afford to invest in research. What it probably does mean is that the patent system, because of certain scientific and technological developments of the time, favors certain types of industry, such as chemical and electronic, and that this occasions both the accumulation of masses of patents and the intensive search for new patentable inventions in these industries. But even this explanation probably exaggerates the role of patent monopolies in industrial research. It seems very likely that even without any patents, past, present, or future, firms in these industries would carry on research, development, and innovation because the opportunities for the search for new processes and new products are so excellent in these fields that no firm could hope to maintain its position in the industry if it did not constantly strive to keep ahead of its competitors by developing and using new technologies.

We find ourselves confronted with conflicting theories. On the basis of the theory of the "competitive compulsion to keep ahead" one might think that firms would invent and innovate even without patent protection. But on the basis of the theory of the "competitive elimination of profits" one might think that without patent protection it would not pay to invent and to innovate, and that firms could not afford to invest in research and development. On the strength of the theory of the "sufficiency of the innovator's headstart" one might think that many innovators would have enough time to recover their costs of innovation. But on the strength of the theory of the "nearly perfect competition from imitators" one might think that few innovators would get away without losses.

No conclusive empirical evidence is available to decide this conflict of theories. That the automobile industry developed partly despite patents (when it still had to overcome the barrier of the basic Selden patent) and partly independently of patents (since it refrained from enforcing the exclusive rights obtained) is some presumptive evidence against the theory of the need for patent protection. That in Switzerland and the Netherlands industrial development proceeded rapidly when these countries had no patent laws is not conclusive because, one might say, they shared the fruits of the patent systems elsewhere and profited from the free imitation of technologies developed abroad — an instance of sharing the benefits without sharing the cost. That experts in the chemical, electronic, and other industries testify that their firms could not maintain their research laboratories without patent protection may persuade some, but probably should be discounted as self-serving testimony. That countries with patent laws have made rapid technical progress does not compel the inference that their progress would have been slower without patent laws. None of the empirical evidence at our disposal and none of the theoretical arguments presented either confirms or confutes the belief that the patent system has promoted the progress of the technical arts and the productivity of the economy.

O. Concluding Remarks

The statements winding up the discussion in the preceding section look like a disappointingly inconclusive conclusion of a rather lengthy economic review of the patent system. Some explanatory remarks, therefore, seem to be in order.

It should be said, first of all, that scholars must not lack the courage to admit freely that there are many questions to which definite answers are not possible, or not yet possible. They need not be ashamed of coming forth with a frank declaration of ignorance. And they may make a contribution to knowledge if they state the reasons why they do not know the answers, and what kind of objective information they would have to have for an approach toward the answers.

The "inconclusive conclusions," it will be remembered, referred to an attempted "Evaluation of the Patent System as a Whole." The literature abounds with discussions of the "economic consequences" of the patent system, purporting to present definitive judgments, without even stating the assumptions on which the arguments are based, let alone submitting supporting evidence for the actual realization of these assumptions. No economist, on the basis of present knowledge, could possibly state with certainty that the patent system, as it now operates, confers a net benefit or a net loss upon society. The best he can do is to state assumptions and make guesses about the extent to which reality corresponds to these assumptions.

If one does not know whether a system "as a whole" (in contrast to certain features of it) is good or bad, the safest "policy conclusion" is to "muddle through" — either with it, if one has long lived with it, or without it, if one has lived without it. If we did not have a patent system, it would be irresponsible, on the basis of our present knowledge of its economic consequences, to recommend instituting one. But since we have had a patent system for a long time, it would be irresponsible, on the basis of our present knowledge, to recommend abolishing it. This last statement refers to a country such as the United States of America — not to a small country and not a predominantly nonindustrial country, where a different weight of argument might well suggest another conclusion.

While the student of the economics of the patent system must, provisionally, disqualify himself on the question of the effects of the system *as a whole* on a large industrial economy, he need not disqualify himself as a judge of proposed *changes* in the existing system. While economic analysis does not yet provide a basis for choosing between "all or nothing," it does provide a sufficiently firm basis for decisions about "a little more or a little less" of various ingredients of the patent system. Factual data of various kinds may be needed even before some of these decisions can be made with confidence. But a team of well-trained economic researchers and analysts should be able to obtain enough information to reach competent conclusions on questions of patent reform. The kind of analysis that could form the framework for such research has been indicated in the present study.

Notes and Questions

The questions raised by Fritz Machlup regarding the policies underlying the grant of patents remain at least as important today as they were in the late 1950s. While tools of economic analysis have grown much more sophisticated, there nevertheless remain large gaps in our collective understanding of what the grant of patents accomplishes, how and why.[1] We will see an example of state of the art modeling of the economic impact of patents on trade by Primo Braga and Fink later in this section, noting here that these economists acknowledge the significant obstacles to our understanding of the role of patents in the international arena.

Machlup's observations are not limited to a particular patent system. He employs an historical and a comparative perspective. Today's predominant world view of patents may not be tomorrow's. The American and German view of patents may not be the Brazilian or Chinese view.

1. The Natural Rights Approach

Machlup discusses in some depth the idea that the patent right is a *natural right* that derives from the humanity of the inventor — because the inventor creates, the inventor owns. Machlup rejects natural rights as a justification for the patent system. If we assume that human creation justifies ownership of an invention (i.e., a right to control its exploitation), how much does that tell us? It might tell us that creators should not be arbitrarily deprived of an interest in their creation. But as we begin to focus on specific issues, the gaps in guidance become apparent. Should the term of patent protection be five, ten or twenty years? Should an invention made in Tokyo provide a right to prevent exploitation by others in Toronto? If *natural rights* justify the grant of a patent in an invention, why should they not justify the grant of a patent in a discovery?

If the right to own an invention is a *natural right*, why did nature make it so easy for others to reproduce an invention? Perhaps nature intended that humans imitate each other's creative activities so as to promote the wide distribution of new technologies. If nature had intended humans to control the exploitation of their own ideas, should nature have provided each of us with natural anti-counterfeiting protection?

2. Stimulating Invention by Reward

Another argument in support of the patent grant is that the availability of the patent monopoly promotes invention. There has yet to be a significant empirical study that confirms this hypothesis. The most persuasive

---

[1]One of the best such studies is WILLIAM D. NORDHAUS, INVENTION, GROWTH AND WELFARE (1969). Even at this level of sophistication, it is apparent that economic models do not fully capture the complexity of the patent system and its impact.

studies to date suggest that inventors create for a variety of reasons, often for the personal satisfaction they derive from making a contribution to society or from solving a vexing technical problem.[2]

If we assume that in the emerging 21st century economy many inventions are the result of the application of large scale expenditure to discrete or defined problems — recall the *Biogen*[3] case — is it possible that the correlation between the availability of the patent grant and the promotion of invention may have shifted since the time when Machlup wrote? The invention of a new pharmaceutical product, for example, may not have so much to do with a creative spark of genius on the part of an inventor, but instead be dependent on methodical trial and error testing of different molecular combinations. Is it possible that without the availability of the patent grant pharmaceutical companies would not invest as heavily in research and development (R&D), and therefore new inventions would not emerge? Have perhaps the criteria for patentability undergone a subtle change since the 1950s?

Economists have labeled the problem confronting firms undertaking R&D expenditure as that of the "incomplete appropriability of knowledge."[4] Firms that invest in the production of knowledge must confront the fact that it is difficult, if not impossible, to completely protect the result of their investment – some of the new knowledge will diffuse to other firms and into the public domain. The patent is a partial solution to this problem. It allows the investing firm to appropriate a return on its investment by protecting an invention against duplication. Even so, a patent does not completely protect the investor in R&D. The patentee must disclose its new knowledge, and this disclosure will at some level benefit competing firms (either immediately or in the future when the patent expires). Competing firms may study the patented invention as a tool for creating other new products (that are not the equivalent of the patented product), and there will almost always be difficulties in policing the market against the misappropriation of patented technology.

---

[2]The best study of the impact of the patent system on inventors is that of J. JEWKES, D. SAWERS AND S. STILLERMAN, THE SOURCES OF INVENTION (1958), referred to by Machlup.
[3]*See supra*, § B, 2, c.
[4]*See* Kenneth J. Arrow, *Economic Welfare and the Allocation of Resources for Invention, in* THE RATE AND DIRECTION OF INVENTIVE ACTIVITY: ECONOMIC AND SOCIAL FACTORS 609 (1962).

Patents may encourage invention particularly when the inventive process involves the application of existing technology to a defined problem in a situation in which there is a relatively high likelihood of success. Is it wise to provide a high level of protection (i.e., a patent) to the results of such undertakings?

Certain patents cover basic or seminal inventions, such as the jet engine, television, the semiconductor integrated circuit or the technique of genetic manipulation. Others are granted for inventions that are incremental advances in a field that is already quite well described. Some patented inventions are enormously successful in the market. Others are never commercially exploited. Yet the conditions accompanying the patent grant are the same for all inventions that qualify for protection, whether they are basic or incremental, commercially successful or market failures. Should the patent system differentiate more between inventions and, in order to stimulate the right kind of invention, grant greater rights to basic inventions? If so, how could this be achieved?

3. Encouragement of Investment

A hypothesis that Machlup finds plausible is that the patent grant encourages investment in the production and distribution of the invention. Given that inventors will invent for reasons of their own, investors nevertheless will be more inclined to undertake the expenditure of capital necessary to exploit an invention if they have the benefit of the patent monopoly to assist in penetration and defense of the market.

While Machlup suggests that this justification for the patent may be reasonable, he also suggests that investors who operate on this basis may be deluding themselves. In fact, patents may create a false sense of security because, *inter alia*, competitors that observe the patent holder achieving a high rate of return are likely to enter the market with other products that serve a comparable purpose, and the capacity to earn monopoly returns may be short-lived. If this is correct, says Machlup, then this is a beneficial illusion for the economy as a whole. That is, patents may be less destructive to competitive markets than is commonly assumed.

4. Society's Bargain for Disclosure

Does the data published from the patent application benefit the public sufficiently to justify the patent grant? This is a difficult question to answer. Even if inventors are under a legal requirement to provide sufficient

249

(or best known means) disclosure, inventors have an economic interest in making things difficult for potential competitors.

At the international level, do disclosures by advanced industries in the Organisation for Economic Cooperation and Development (OECD) countries benefit industries in developing countries if the latter lack the infrastructure to make use of the disclosed knowledge? At present, there are over 30 million patent documents that have been published around the world. The most comprehensive access to such documents is by way of a commerical search service. If developing country industries cannot make use of the information disclosed in patent applications, should consumers in developing countries pay monopoly prices for patented products? Should they pay these prices to assure the future availability of useful products even if they are not made locally?

Machlup scoffs at the idea that a pharmaceutical company with an invention critical to public health — such as the polio vaccine — would be allowed to exploit it at a high monopoly price. Is this a reflection of Machlup's naivete, or have attitudes toward the virtues of the market shifted since the late 1950s?

Machlup's conclusion for the United States is among the foundational perspectives on the value of patents: based on what is known, if there were no patent system he could not recommend creating one; yet, because the United States has a patent system and the economy appears to be functioning relatively well, based on what is known, he could not recommend getting rid of it.

Machlup limits his conclusion to a large industrial country such as the United States — it may *not*, he says, apply to "a small country and not [apply to] a predominantly nonindustrial country, where a different weight of argument might well suggest another conclusion." What other conclusion(s) do you think Machlup may have had in mind?

---

2. Modern Acceptance in the Courts

The following excerpt from the concurring opinion of Judge Newman in the *Hilton Davis* case[1] suggests that Machlup's skeptical approach to the

---

[1]The decision of the Court of Appeals for the Federal Circuit in this case was subsequently affirmed by the Supreme Court in Warner-Jenkinson v. Hilton Davis, 117 S. Ct.

value of the patent system is outside the mainstream of opinion today. In her opinion supporting the *doctrine of equivalents* in U.S. patent law,[2] Judge Newman accepts the premise that patents promote research and development, thereby increasing the stock of knowledge, and that patents promote the commercialization of new technologies, thereby enhancing net social welfare.

Hilton Davis Chemical Co., Plaintiff-Appellee, v. Warner-Jenkinson Company, Inc., Defendant-Appellant

United States Court of Appeals for the Federal Circuit
62 F.3d 1512; 1995 U.S. App. LEXIS 21069
August 8, 1995, Decided

Subsequent History:

As Amended August 21, 1995.

Prior History: Appealed from: U.S. District Court for the Southern District of Ohio, Western Division. Judge Weber.

Disposition: Affirmed

*****

Newman, Circuit Judge, concurring.

*****

Technologic Innovation and the National Interest

Technologic innovation has driven the American economy, over the past century, to the exclusion of virtually all other growth factors. Many

---

1040 (1997).
[2]The doctrine of equivalents prescribes the extent to which products and processes similar, but not identical, to those described in patent claims infringe on the rights of the patent holder.

students of technologic change have explained that innovative activity is fundamental to industrial vigor, developing new markets while enhancing productivity and competitiveness, thereby strengthening and enriching the nation. *E.g.*, F.M. Scherer, Innovation and Growth (1984); Robert Solow, Technical Change and the Aggregate Production Function, 39 Rev. Econ. & Stat. 312 (1957). The role of patents in this activity is of increasing scholarly interest. *E.g.*, David Silverstein, Patents, Science and Innovation: Historical Linkages and Implications for Global Technological Competitiveness, 17 Rutgers Computer & Tech. L.J. 261 (1991); Zvi Griliches, Patents: Recent Trends and Puzzles, in Brookings Papers on Economic Activity: Microeconomics 291 (Martin N. Baily & Clifford Winston eds., 1989). The technology-user community has always had a practical comprehension of the value of various innovation incentives in particular commercial contexts. *See* Domestic Policy Review of Industrial Innovation, Department of Commerce (1979).[1]

*****

I need not belabor that the economic risk in developing new technology is high, that the potential return must warrant the risk, and that the return must pay for the failures as well as the successes. *See* Paul A. Samuelson & William D. Nordhaus, Economics 658 (12th ed. 1985) (in general, a higher return is required for higher risk than for lower risk investment). The goal on which we must concentrate is the public welfare, as summarized in Mazer v. Stein, 347 U.S. 201, 219, 100 U.S.P.Q. (BNA) 325, 333, 98 L. Ed. 630, 74 S. Ct. 460 (1954):

The economic philosophy behind the clause empowering Congress to grant patents and copyrights is the conviction that encouragement of individual effort by personal gain is the best way to advance public welfare through the talents of authors and inventors in "Science and useful Art."

The principle is today of international force, as the United States seeks to enhance its national strength and international trade with the aid of intellectual property. Indeed, recent economic history illustrates the stagna-

---

[1] I use the term "innovation" in Schumpeter's meaning of the combination of invention and investment. Joseph A. Schumpeter, Capitalism, Socialism, and Democracy (3d ed. 1950). Schumpeter was one of the first economists formally to recognize that invention of itself produces no economic effect, while patent-based innovation has a positive impact on the economic system as new industries and new goods displace the old.

tion of the economy coinciding with periods of diminished industrial investment in technologic advance. Professor Griliches, supra, at 291, wrote "Among the many explanations for the worldwide productivity slowdown in the 1970s, the exhaustion of inventive and technological opportunities remains a major suspect."

*****

Most (but perhaps not all) students of technologic innovation today accept the proposition that there is a larger welfare benefit when the inventor is protected against appropriability by a competitor who did not bear the commercial risk. The cost of substantially imitating an established product, with or without improvements, is usually lower, and always less risky, than the originator's cost of creating, developing, and marketing the new product. Such a competitor can act in a shorter time than was needed by the patentee, and undercut the return to the patentee. *See* Edwin Mansfield, Mark Schwartz & Samuel Wagner, Imitation Costs and Patents: An Empirical Study, 91 Econ. J. 907 (1981). Because of the diminished risk-weighted incentive to the originator, it has generally been concluded that "total welfare, but not the welfare of consumers, would be increased by making it more difficult to produce close substitutes for existing products." Stanley M. Besen & Leo J. Raskind, An Introduction to the Law and Economics of Intellectual Property, 5 J. Econ. Persp. 3, 5 n.2 (1991).

*****

Competition in research and development is important to the nation. There are important distinctions between competition in the research (inventing) stage and in commercial activity. Competition in research, however inefficient its economics, serves the advancement of knowledge in myriad ways. It is often observed that investment in commercialization tends to be more risk-sensitive than investment in research, apparently since the costs of product development and capital plant often dwarf the cost of making the invention. Yet industrial innovation is served by the patent system when the commercial investment is made. To the extent that the doctrine of equivalents enlarges the value of the patent to the innovator it also increases the net social value, as well as serving as a risk-reducing factor in commercial investment. The relevant economic theories on these points are varied, and the analyses are interesting. *See, e.g.,* Janusz A. Ordover, Economic Foundations and Considerations in Protecting Industrial and Intellectual Property, 53 Antitrust L.J. 503, 506-07 (1985) (discussing the effects on innovative efforts of competition in research and development).

The complexities of these relationships far exceed the highlights I have touched. On the present state of the law I have concluded that the doctrine of equivalents, on balance, serves the interest of justice and the public interest in the advancement of technology, by supporting the creativity of originators while requiring appropriators to adopt more than insubstantial technologic change.

---

3. Skepticism on the International Plane

Fritz Machlup's study of the patent system and Judge Newman's concurring opinion are both principally directed at the patent system of a single country – in this case the United States – though both writings suggest that the economic effects of the patent system of the United States must be considered in an international context.

Edith Tilton Penrose was a long time colleague of and collaborator with Fritz Machlup. He observes in his forward to her book, THE ECONOMICS OF THE INTERNATIONAL PATENT SYSTEM (1951):

> The discussion of the economics of the international patent system, and in particular of the international patent [Paris] Convention, has been almost devoid of contributions by *bona fide* economists. The international patent Convention is now 67 years old and the literature on it is by no means small. But scrutinize it and you will find only a handful of economists writing on this subject, even as they address themselves more to peripheral issues than to the fundamental economic issue — the balance of costs and gains.
>
> The book by Dr. Edith Penrose is the first of its kind . . . the economic analysis of the international patent system is both novel and controversial. The parts of the study that deal with the economic evaluation of various provisions will undoubtedly draw fire, because several dogmas which legal experts have held in great respect are exposed to the bright searchlight of a skilled economic analyst and are shown to be untenable. One may safely predict that many members of the American patent bar, and especially international patent lawyers, will intensely dislike some of the views expressed and perhaps all of the suggestions contained in this book.

But the views and suggestions of Mrs. Penrose are not out of line with the current thinking of the more enlightened patent experts.

Following are the Summary and Conclusions of the pioneering work by Edith Tilton Penrose. Her observations and questions, rather than becoming antiquated over time, are of the most compelling import today.

The Economics of the International Patent System

By Edith Tilton Penrose*

Chapter XI

Summary and Conclusions

In this chapter I shall briefly recapitulate the argument of this study, the propositions I have tried to establish and the implications of the prevailing assumptions about the international extension of the patent system.

I.

The patent of invention is a monopoly privilege of ancient origin granted for the purpose of encouraging innovation. It was first systematically used in Venice in the 14th and 15th centuries and has today been adopted by nearly all countries. The only serious attack on the principle of the patent system took place in the 19th century under the influence of the free trade movement. It was defeated but it served to emphasize the economic effects of the restrictions on industry that are inherent in the patent system and that most countries try to reduce by placing specific limitations on the monopoly granted.

II.

The origin of the patent system is clearly economic. In the 19th century attempts were made to justify it by appealing to a "natural" property

---

*Johns Hopkins Press 1951.

right in ideas and to an inventor's moral right to receive a reward for his services. Although vestiges of the latter still crop up in patent discussions, today the primary arguments for the patent system are economic. Patents are held to be necessary to persuade inventors to disclose their secrets and to encourage the making and introduction of inventions.[1]

III.

Theories of natural property rights, idealistic visions of a world drawn together in international unity, and pressures from manufacturers in industrial countries combined to advance the cause of the international protection of patentees. After a series of conferences the International Convention for the Protection of Industrial Property was signed in 1883 creating the International Union for the Protection of Industrial Property. Today forty countries are members of the Union.

The Convention is founded on two basic principles: 1) that foreigners should receive in each country the same treatment as the nationals of that country; and 2) that the first applicant for a patent on an invention in one country should have a right of priority over all other applicants to obtain patents on the same invention in other countries. Most countries have always felt, however, that the grant of unconditional patents to foreigners would retard their economic development and the most controversial issues in the international conferences have centered around the question of what restrictions a country should be permitted to place on its patents.

IV.

Before the International Convention was created a patentee in one country could generally obtain patents on his invention in other countries, but he faced many special difficulties in those countries and was frequently discriminated against. The purpose of the Convention is to reduce the difficulties and eliminate the discrimination. It thus formally sanctions the

---

[1] I have not in this study attempted to appraise the influence of national patent systems on the rate of invention. Most countries have adopted some form of patent law under which patents are also granted on inventions already patented and worked in other countries and I am only concerned with the economics of this arrangement.

principle that a patentee in one country ought to be able to obtain patents on his invention in all other countries with a minimum of difficulty. In other words, the Convention rests on the assumption that it is insufficient for a patentee to obtain a monopoly on his invention in one country only and that he ought to obtain a worldwide monopoly.

The deliberate adoption of this economic policy can be justified on economic grounds only if the gains that accrue to society from it exceed the costs incurred because of it. It is indeed awkward that the costs cannot be measured nor the gains counted. As a result the optimum limits of the patent system, whether with respect to time, space, patentability or restrictions on the use of the grant, must always remain a subject of controversy. There is no doubt, however, that the costs have been underestimated.

It is generally assumed that the economic justification for the international extension of the patent system lies in its effects upon the advance of technology and the development of industry. Upon analysis, however, it appears that if one were to rely on this justification one would have to conclude that on balance the social cost of extending the patent system internationally exceeds the gain to be derived from it for the world as a whole. Nearly all foreign patenting is done by already industrialized countries, and the question of the effect of the prospect of patents in foreign markets on the rate of invention is a question of the extent to which the expected increment of profit arising from the geographical extension of the limits of patent protection will stimulate additional invention. There are many factors to be taken into consideration: the size of the national market, the nature of national industry, the types of invention, the motivation of inventors and the methods of financing invention. I have concluded that on balance the effect on invention of a system in which patents in many countries can be obtained is probably negligible for the world as a whole although it may be important for some firms and for some inventions. With respect to the introduction of inventions, there is little evidence that business men in industrial countries require patent protection to encourage them to adopt inventions which have already been developed to a commercial stage elsewhere.

But whatever may be the effect of the international extension of the patent system on the rate of invention or innovation, a heavy social cost is incurred. The patent method of encouraging invention operates by restricting the use of new inventions in order that a monopoly rent may be earned by the patentees to recompense them for the expenses and risks of making or introducing new inventions. The social costs to which this restriction gives rise appear in the first instance as increased prices and royalty payments. The more fundamental and important cost, however, is the production lost through the less efficient use of resources when new techniques cannot be freely used and when monopoly power is extended by means of patent agreements.[5]

V.

A few individual countries may gain from the system in which foreign patents are permitted. Industrial exporting countries obtain monopoly profits resulting from the increased price of exports; in some instances patent protection may enable exporting countries to retain a market against competitors or to surmount tariff barriers. The majority of countries, however, probably lose, since the higher price of patented imports, royalty payments to foreign patentees and in particular the restriction on their own use of new techniques constitute a cost much greater than is generally realized and the benefit derived from patent protection in foreign countries is much less than is usually assumed.

Under these circumstances if individual countries weigh the costs and gains of granting patents on inventions already patented and primarily used in other countries, most of them could easily conclude that the costs exceed the gains and that it is not to their benefit to grant them. The reasons why any particular country has adopted a policy of granting such patents can, of course, be explained only in terms of its history and of the pressures that have influenced its government. These pressures include those of exporting firms who wish to obtain protection abroad, of patent lawyers, of spokesmen for "internationalism," and — of particular importance for many of the smaller countries — the pressure exerted by the larger industrial countries to persuade the smaller ones to adopt "suitable" patent laws. On the other hand, most countries have realized that the social costs of granting unrestricted patents on inventions primarily worked abroad

---

[5]See discussion of the sources of costs and gains in an international extension of the patent system. . . . The costs with which we are concerned are not the costs of making the inventions but the social cost of the patent method of encouraging them.

would exceed any benefit to be obtained and have accordingly placed special restrictions on such patents.[9]

VI.

From the point of view of the world economy and of the economies of individual countries, the usual justification for the establishment of an international patent system — that it promotes technological progress — is not convincing. But the mere existence of national laws creates an economic problem which can only be met by an international extension of patent protection. In order to show this clearly I have examined what would be the economic consequences of a prohibition of international patenting, that is, of a system in which a patentee could obtain a patent in one national market only. Such a system would have the effect of enabling producers of patented products to obtain as a result of their patents higher profits in one country than in other countries. The prospect of such profits, which are unrelated to the underlying economic factors, would, therefore, exert an uneconomic influence on the international location of industry.[10]

Let us assume for the moment that a patentee is permitted to obtain a patent on his invention only in the country in which he produces. There is nothing, however, to prevent him from deciding to produce only in the country in which he wants a patent; the choice of plant location in many industries is not independent of market considerations. If the location of a plant in one area would permit monopoly profits to be obtained which would be foregone if the plant were located in another area, an intelligent producer would include the possibility of obtaining these profits in his calculations regarding the most profitable location of his plant. Thus a strong incentive would be created for patentees to locate their plants in larger industrial countries merely because they could there obtain a monopoly profit greater than elsewhere. If the expected monopoly profits were very great, a producer might well find it desirable to incur considerably higher

---

[9]This is particularly brought out in the Swiss controversy over the inauguration of patent protection. . . .

[10]Because a short summary statement of the argument in this section would be misleading, I am giving a large part of the argument just as it appears in Chapter VI. . . .

costs of production in order to obtain the protected market. In addition, industrial research and technical innovations would tend to concentrate in these countries.

This tendency for patentees who wish to sell in the larger markets to take out their patents in those markets would have still other consequences. A patent has a double effect within the territory in which it is valid: it prevents others from producing or selling in that territory. But outside that territory the products or processes are free from the patent restrictions. Hence if an invention could only be patented in one country, there would be an incentive for firms who wished to use the invention, to establish plants outside the territory covered by the patent and there produce for the rest of the world. Thus the exporting industries of the countries in which the larger number of patents were taken out would suffer, since when one firm holds a patent on an important new process, all other firms producing competitive products in that industry are at a disadvantage. In industries where all firms produce largely for foreign markets and are in competition with foreign firms in foreign markets, the firms without access to new developments would not only be at a disadvantage compared with the firm holding the patent in the domestic market but also with respect to the rest of the world: firms in the rest of the world could freely use any of the new techniques. Not only is the monopolistic position of the patentee firm increased within the domestic industry, but for no sound economic reason the domestic industry, other than the patentee firm is handicapped in relation to foreign industry.[11]

If the patentee were not required to produce in the country in which he takes out his patent, the fear of losing and the hope of safeguarding his patent monopoly in this or that market would not enter into the calculations of the producer in determining the location of his plant. Yet the position of the countries containing the larger markets would be even more adversely affected. The tendency for patents to be concentrated in these markets would be strengthened and the restrictions on industry in these countries would consequently be increased. It is part of the purpose of the patent system to retard the development of competitors of the patentee in order to enable him to earn a reward for his innovating enterprise, but it is

---

[11]Foreign branch plants of domestic firms are of course here considered as part of "foreign industry."

difficult to justify a discrimination between these competitors by which one group is retarded — the group unfortunate enough to be in the country selected for the patent — while all others are left free. The patentee firm may gain very little by this secondary effect since it may be selling in markets which would not be served by the restricted group of firms and the latter may suffer very much. If the patentee is not allowed to extend his monopoly over the greater part of his market, the patent, in securing protection to him against competitors, automatically discriminates between these competitors. This alone is sufficient to justify some international arrangement regarding foreign patents.

Because of the social costs of the international extension of patenting, however, any international arrangement regarding foreign patenting should meet three conditions: 1) It should prevent the exploitation of the weaker industrial countries by the stronger. 2) It should reduce the influence of patents on the location of industrial activity. 3) It should reduce the social cost to each country of granting patents on inventions developed and primarily worked abroad. The present International Convention has made considerable advances in all three directions but with respect to the third, much more needs to be done.

VII.

Two methods of reducing the social costs to a country of granting patents on inventions developed and primarily worked abroad have been widely used. The oldest is compulsory working.[12] Most countries have at some time adopted compulsory working laws in order to ensure that all patents granted are worked in the country granting them. This method is not only ineffective and frequently nothing but a clumsy way of obtaining access to foreign inventions for domestic firms, but it also conflicts with the second of the functions of an international patent arrangement since it establishes an uneconomic influence on the location of industry of the sort

---

[12] Compulsory working means that the law requires a patentee or his licensee to produce under the patent in the country granting the patent, although a patentee is usually exempt from this requirement if he can produce "acceptable excuses" instead. Until recently revocation of the patent was the chief penalty for failure to work. Now compulsory licensing is becoming more commonly adopted.

discussed in the previous section. The efforts of the International Union for the Protection of Industrial Property to eliminate such requirements are therefore in the right direction.

VIII.

The second method of reducing the cost of the patent monopoly is that of compulsory licensing.[14] This is by far the most effective and flexible method and enables the state to prevent most of the more serious restrictions on industry. It could be used very effectively to undermine the monopoly power of several of the more powerful international cartels whose position is largely based on their control of the patent rights to industrial processes in the larger industrial countries; and it could be used to ensure that patented new techniques developed abroad are available to domestic industries wishing to use them.

The International Convention places restrictions on the right of countries to subject patents to compulsory licensing. These restrictions should be eliminated and countries should be encouraged to use this device to break up some of the more serious of the monopolistic restrictions on the use of new techniques.

IX.

The Convention has been attacked by those who are concerned about the rise of international monopolistic practices, especially of international cartels. Although it is true that the Convention is one-sided, being more concerned with the rights of patentees than with the public interest in these rights, and that undue restrictions are placed on the use of compulsory licensing, the Convention itself cannot be held responsible for the existing evils of international patent practices merely because it has not outlawed them, for, conversely, it certainly has not sanctioned them. The difficulty lies with the national patent laws and national policies existing independently of the Convention. So long as national patent laws exist, an interna-

---

[14] Under compulsory licensing a patentee is required by law to license his patent to another producer who wishes to use it upon payment of a reasonable royalty. . . .

tional convention on patents is desirable, but the patent policies of national governments and their trade and monopoly policies have not been very well coordinated and this lack of coordination is reflected in the one-sided nature of the Convention.

The Convention has also been criticised by the friends of international patent protection because it does not establish uniformity of patent practice in administrative matters. The laws and practices of different countries are very different and it has not yet proved possible to obtain substantial agreement on any uniform provisions. This is indeed a real weakness of the Convention, for if international patenting is to be permitted, a reduction of legal and administrative difficulties is desirable not only from the point of view of patentees but also in the general interest. The more difficult and expensive international patenting is, the more the large, well financed, and legally equipped firms have an advantage over smaller firms. Indeed a single international patent valid in all Union countries, long the ideal of ardent supporters of international patenting, is a desirable, though far-distant goal, providing that the patented technique is made easily available at a reasonable royalty to all who wish to use it.

X.

Although an international patent Convention between the industrial countries of the world is desirable, the non-industrial countries, few of whose nationals want patents in foreign countries, have nothing to gain from granting patents to foreign firms. In view of the desirability of encouraging the development of these countries and of the fact that foreign patents tend more to restrict than to advance their industrial techniques, such countries should be exempt from any international patent arrangements.

XI.

Up to the present, the regime for the international protection of patent rights has been developed primarily in the interest of patentees. The gains to be derived from an extension of the patent system have been stressed, but the concomitant increase in social costs has been seriously neglected. So far as it goes, the International Convention has not been to any important extent incompatible with the best interests of the world economy. Nonetheless, the Convention in no way helps to alleviate the restrictions on trade and industrial activity which unregulated international patenting permits. A reconsideration of its provisions from this point of view is in order.

Notes and Questions

1. Edith Tilton Penrose supports the early international patent system established by the Paris Convention mainly because it should prevent a distortion in the international allocation of productive resources. If inventors could effectively patent their inventions in only one country, they would be likely to locate their production facilities in densely populated industrialized countries where they could maximize their monopoly returns. Penrose explains that this would have a number of undesirable effects. It might well lead to a concentration of R&D activities in already well-off countries. It would also place domestic competitors of the patent holder in these countries at a disadvantage *vis-à-vis* foreign producers of the same product, unencumbered by patent restrictions.

2. Penrose sees little reason why developing countries should find it desirable to provide patent protection to foreign inventors, and proposes to exempt developing countries from any international patent arrangements.

3. Penrose introduces us to the concept of the compulsory patent license. A compulsory patent license is granted by a government without the consent of the patent holder, and it permits the exploitation of rights otherwise controlled by the patent holder. The license may be granted in favor of a private enterprise or in favor of the government itself. Compulsory licensing will be considered further in Chapter IV.

4. Penrose alerts us to the question whether international patent protection may foster higher levels of industrial concentration. Again, this question is probably more trenchant today than it was when Penrose raised it in 1951.

5. Penrose's perspective on the value of an international patenting system for developing countries is out of synch with current OECD industry views, and perhaps with the predominant current trend in opinion among international economists (*see* the Primo Braga and Fink contribution which follows).

Nevertheless, Penrose returns us again to the question whether the same level of IPRs protection is appropriate for all countries.

---

4. Modern Trend of Acceptance on the International Plane

In 1997, one of the authors of this book wrote:

> Recent studies of the role of intellectual property in the international economic system have largely been generated by industry sources to support the GATT Uruguay Round TRIPS Agreement. There are a few significant recent scholarly studies of the role of intellectual property rights in the international trading system. These studies clearly acknowledge the existence of critical information gaps, and the lack of empirical foundation for claims frequently made by industry concerning the benefits of high levels of IPRs protection.[1]

Following is an excerpt from one of the significant recent scholarly studies to which the author referred.

Carlos Primo Braga and Carsten Fink introduce an important new element into the international IPRs economic equation: the digital revolution. Advances in computer technology have greatly facilitated the reproduction and worldwide transmission of information. Holders of IPRs fear that the digital revolution will undermine their efforts at protection. Are classical forms of IPRs protection — such as the patent — becoming less relevant in the post-industrial economy?

---

[1]Frederick M. Abbott, *Public Policy and Global Technological Integration: An Introduction, in* PUBLIC POLICY AND GLOBAL TECHNOLOGICAL INTEGRATION 3, 6-7 (F. M. Abbott & D. J. Gerber eds., 1997).

The Economic Justification for the Grant of Intellectual Property Rights: Patterns of Convergence and Conflict

Carlos A. Primo Braga and Carsten Fink*

Introduction

The debate concerning the economic implications of intellectual property rights ("IPRs") is an old one. The globalization of economic activities and the dawning of the digital era have added new dimensions to this debate. As international transactions involving knowledge-intensive products expand, frictions concerning IPRs protection have also increased, fostering demands for international convergence toward higher standards of protection at a worldwide level. The digital "revolution," in turn, by promoting the convergence of telecommunications, computers, and media has created new challenges for existing legal instruments of protection.

This paper reviews some aspects of the contemporary debate on the economics of intellectual property rights by discussing the above mentioned patterns of convergence (i.e., with respect to geographical coverage and with respect to technology). The process of convergence at international level is an ongoing development that will be strengthened by the recently negotiated "Agreement on Trade-Related Aspects of Intellectual Property Rights" ("TRIPS"). In a parallel development, the technological convergence generated by the "digital" revolution challenges traditional forms of protection and the "consensus" in favor of higher standards of IPRs protection. In the future, the "battlefield" for those engaged in strengthening IPRs protection will be determined not so much by geography, but mainly by the economics of production of knowledge-intensive products in a "digital" environment.

I. The Economics of IPRs

The conventional economic rationale for the protection of IPRs is often framed in terms of Arrow's seminal work concerning the incomplete

---

*In Public Policy and Global Technological Integration 99 (F. M. Abbott and D. J. Gerber eds., 1997)

appropriability of knowledge.[3] IPRs can be understood as second-best solutions to the problems created by the "public good" nature of knowledge. To the extent that they enhance "appropriability," IPRs are expected to foster investment in research and development ("R&D") and knowledge creation. They create, however, a static distortion as they constrain the current consumption of knowledge, by enhancing the market power of title holders. In short, IPRs involve a "bargain" between the producers of knowledge and society, which is mediated by the government.

The above rationale is typically used to explain the economics of patent and copyright laws. With respect to trademarks and industrial designs, the basis for protection is more often framed in terms of incentives for investments in reputation (quality) rather than innovation *per se*. Trade secrets, in turn, are rationalized as a necessary supplement to the patent system. Their main positive role is to foster innovations that do not comply with the strict requirements for patentability of products and processes. In this paper, we focus our analysis on IPRs as instruments to promote the creation of knowledge.

The long-term trend with respect to IPRs protection in developed economies has been clearly in the direction of the strengthening of these rights. As pointed out by Winter, however, there is no clear theoretical presumption that a movement towards stronger standards of protection will be always welfare enhancing. Patent races may lead to over-investment in R&D. Private returns may exceed social returns as protection increases and inventors can appropriate additional gains in assets that are complementary to the innovation. And the increase in static distortions in the consumption of knowledge (because of monopolistic practices) may overcome the dynamic benefits of additional R&D.

In spite of these considerations, there is broad recognition that IPRs systems play an important role in the promotion of technological progress. It is true that other institutional arrangements can be used to foster the generation of knowledge without necessarily relying on property rights. The direct production of knowledge by the government, as well as the reliance on subsidies and/or government procurement to foster R&D activities by the private sector illustrate some of the available alternatives. But

---

[3] *See* Kenneth J. Arrow, *Economic Welfare and the Allocation of Resources for Invention, in* THE RATE AND DIRECTION OF INVENTIVE ACTIVITY: ECONOMIC AND SOCIAL FACTORS 609 (1962).

historical hindsight suggests that market-driven incentives (as exemplified by the proprietary approach) provide the most effective way to organize economic activities, including the creation of knowledge through R&D.

Many questions with respect to the normative implications of IPRs regimes remain unanswered, however. Is the international harmonization of IPRs regimes toward higher standards of protection welfare improving? Are IPRs in a digital environment an effective instrument to promote knowledge creation or just a nuisance? In what follows, we review some of the theoretical aspects of the debate concerning these issues.

II. The International Dimension

IPRs are territorial in nature. Nations must reach accommodation as their residents seek protection for their works abroad. The TRIPS negotiations in the context of the Uruguay Round of multilateral trade negotiations can be characterized as the most recent chapter in the long history of attempts to deal with the issue of extra-territoriality of IPRs. What was new in this context was the acceptance of minimum standards of protection (not only in terms of coverage of subject matter and scope of protection, but also with respect to enforcement) and the "universal" coverage of the agreement (special and differential treatment for developing countries is limited to the concession of generous transition periods). As discussed in Primo Braga, TRIPS will promote a much greater level of "harmonization" of IPRs protection than was believed feasible a few years ago.

The caveats that apply to the desirability of ever stronger protection for IPRs at the national level gain an additional dimension when the analysis moves to the international level. If the existing (or potential) title-holders are predominantly foreigners, the strengthening of protection raises the possibility of an international rent transfer.[4] The net welfare impact of the reform for the country will depend on how local consumers and producers are affected, as well as on its implications for world levels (and composition) of R&D.

---

[4]Available statistics suggests that this is a valid description of the situation of developing countries. By 1982, of the 200,000 patents awarded by developing countries, for example, 175,000 (87.5 percent) were awarded to foreign patentees. For the major developing countries, the share was around 79 percent. *See* WORLD INTELLECTUAL PROPERTY ORGANIZATION, 100 YEARS OF INDUSTRIAL PROPERTY STATSITICS (1983); Arvind Subramanian, *Putting Some Numbers on the TRIPS Pharmaceutical Debate*, INT'L J. TECH. MGMT. 1, 1-17 (1994).

Many different scenarios can be modeled to capture these effects. If a country is small (i.e., its IPRs regime does not affect world R&D) and it has limited production and innovation capabilities, higher standards of protection are likely to be welfare improving as long as they permit access to products that would not be available otherwise. If, however, the country has some production capabilities (a proxy for its capacity to imitate), but limited innovative capacity (as measured by its R&D basis, for example), higher standards of protection are likely to have a negative welfare impact, as local producers are displaced, prices rise and a rent transfer from local consumers and producers to foreign title-holders ensues. Finally, if the small country has both well developed production and innovative capabilities (as in the case of the East Asian newly industrialized economies), the result will be indeterminate, depending on the elasticity of supply of domestic innovations with respect to IPRs protection.

On the other hand, if the developing country is large enough to affect innovation in the North, then one has also to take into account the possibility of an increase (or reorganization) of R&D investments on a global scale. In such a scenario, higher levels of protection in the South may be a better solution for the world as a whole in a dynamic sense, even if the immediate losses for the South are bigger than the benefits for innovators in the North.

This brief review underscores the limitations of normative recommendations concerning changes in the rules for IPRs at world level. The strengthening of IPRs protection will have different welfare implications depending on the characteristics of each country. Generalizations can only be made if strong assumptions are adopted. For example, if one assumes that the supply of innovations in the South (i.e., in the developing world) is rather inelastic and that IPRs regimes are of limited relevance in influencing trade, foreign direct investment and technology transfer then it follows that the Agreement is in essence an exercise in rent transfer. A much more optimistic view of its welfare implications for developing countries, however, can be put together if the opposite assumptions are held.

III. The Technological Dimension

The dawning of the digital era poses another set of problems for IPRs regimes. The merger of computer and telecommunication technologies has allowed the explosive growth of computer-mediated networks and the gradual emergence of a global information infrastructure (i.e., a network of

269

networks with global reach and multi-media capabilities). The Internet environment provides an exciting "window" into this future.

Some of the problems for IPRs raised by the emergence of the global information infrastructure ("GII") are not exactly new. It is true that the GII, by promoting the "end of geography," gives a new relevance to the issue of extra-territoriality and increases the demand for convergence among national IPRs regimes. This, however, can be characterized as the next stage in the process of economic globalization. The GII also expands the possibilities for dissemination of information (through copying) and, eventually, for activities that infringe on someone's IPRs. Here, again it can be argued that this is simply another chapter in the history of technological progress and that as in the case of xerox, audio and video-tape capabilities the law will adapt — as time goes by — to face these new challenges. The expansion of legitimate video-tape rental facilities around the world illustrates how the legal system can cope with decreasing costs of copying, while enforcing the protection of IPRs.

There are, however, some issues that are new and for which no definitive answers are available. The frontiers between carriers and content providers become fuzzy in the GII. With a few computer strokes one can download copyrighted material in numerous bulletin board systems ("BBS") around the world in an anonymous fashion. By prosecuting infringing BBS operators (carriers . . .), one can discourage infringement, but this may inhibit the expansion of the very value-added services that make the GII meaningful. In the same vein, the possibilities for digital manipulation (and dissemination) of copyrighted material are expanding (e.g., colorization of black-and-white movies, multi-media experiments, databases in networks . . .), and friction among right-holders and users is also bound to increase. For those who are optmistic about the capacity of conventional IPRs laws to deal with these new issues, history is a strong ally to the extent that it highlights the capacity of the system to adapt and address the needs of new technologies (e.g., the protection of software).

Another type of concern reenergized by the proliferation of electronic networks is the question of IPRs and market power. It has been pointed out, for example, that the optimal level of protection for software that benefits from significant network externalities (i.e., software that becomes more valuable as the number of users increase) should be lower than is the case for non-network software. It can be argued, however, that this does not require changes in the IPRs regime. It only highlights the importance of having effective competition laws in parallel to IPRs protection.

A more fundamental question, however, is posed by these technological developments. It can be stated as follows: is there anything intrinsic to the economics of the digital era that makes the rationale for IPRs protection obsolete?

There are some analysts who believe that to be the case. Barlow argues that encryption (i.e., technology), rather than laws, provides the only effective way to protect intellectual property in "cyberspace." The gist of his arguments can be captured by the following propositions: (i) "all information wants to be free"; (ii) the economics of information in a networked economy will increasingly be associated with relationships (*e.g.*, ancillary services) rather than property; (iii) the transaction costs to enforce IPRs in a networked environment are too high.

Some aspects of propositions (i) and (iii) can be addressed by the supporters of IPRs orthodoxy without major problems. After all, IPRs do not protect information in the abstract. In the case of copyright, for example, the requirement of creativity allows one to argue that the protection of intellectual property promotes the production of knowledge and works of art without hampering the possibilities of dissemination of information *stricto sensu*. In the same vein, the issue of transaction costs is not a new phenomenon and IPRs laws have been flexible enough to cope with this problem as illustrated by the special treatment given to private use of copyrighted works in most countries. From this perspective, laws will adapt gradually as experience with the economics of a digital environments accumulates. In sum, no revolutionary change is required.

Proposition (ii), however, poses a more fundamental challenge to IPRs orthodoxy. This line of reasoning is further developed in Dyson. If the economics of networks evolves in such a way that the competitiveness of content providers in the GII is enhanced by distributing their intellectual property for free, while charging for ancillary services and products, then the enforcement of IPRs in this environment will lose its relevance over time. Empirical analyses of this type of phenomenon, however, are still in their infancy. In this context, support for immediate radical changes in the legal system remains limited to the fringes of the relevant industries.

IV. Empirical Analyses About the Effects of Convergence

The economic implications of international and technological convergence are in essence empirical questions. As already noted, empirical analyses of the impact of IPRs in digital environments remain limited and most assertions at this stage rely on theoretical models. In this section, we review some of the empirical literature available about the effects of international convergence.

The point of departure for this analysis is the proposition that the TRIPS Agreement will typically foster higher standards of IPRs protection in the South (i.e., the developing countries) than the ones prevailing in 1994. Accordingly, it will promote greater convergence among IPRs regimes around the world. There are costs and benefits for countries engaged in the strengthening of their IPRs regimes. Costs associated with the required changes include additional administrative and enforcement costs, increase in payments for foreigners' proprietary knowledge, price increases associated with greater market power for knowledge producers, the costs of displacement of "pirate" activities, and the opportunity cost of additional R&D. Potential benefits include new inventions fostered by higher levels of R&D at domestic and international level, and greater technology and foreign direct investment ("FDI") flows. Moreover, convergence is expected to affect trade flows in products that rely on IPRs protection.

In what follows, the discussion focuses on the main potential implications of the TRIPs agreement. First, the potential impact of strengthening IPRs on trade, FDI and the transfer of technology is discussed. The basic premise is that these effects may generate allocative and dynamic benefits for the countries in question. After that, attention is given to the rent transfer aspects of the Agreement, its impact on local producers and on R&D investments in the North and in the South.

V. IPRs and Trade Flows

IPRs regimes may influence trade flows. Stern, for example, points out that discrepancies among national IPRs regimes generate effects analogous to non-tariff barriers. Exporters in the North have additional costs when exporting to the South (as compared to North-North trade) as they have to engage in activities designed to inhibit local imitation. It can also be argued that the international harmonization of IPRs regimes diminishes the transaction costs of operating in different regulatory environments.

The net impact on trade flows of strengthening protection of IPRs in the South is, however, ambiguous. As pointed out by Maskus and Penubarti, the higher level of protection fosters two conflicting effects. First, it will enhance the market power of the title holder, reducing the elasticity of demand for his/her products. Second, it will expand the net demand for the protected products as imitators are displaced. The net trade effect will depend on which effect dominates. If the market-power effect is bigger than the market-expansion effect then trade flows may decrease in the aftermath of the reform. If the opposite holds, then strengthening IPRs protection will lead to trade expansion. In other words, the net trade effect of the TRIPS Agreement is in essence an empirical question.

Ferrantino, using data from the early 1980s, investigates the role of IPRs regimes in influencing U.S. arm's-length trade, intra-firm trade and "establishment-trade" (i.e., sales of U.S. overseas affiliates in the local market). . . .

Ferrantino's overall results suggest at best a weak association between IPRs and arm's-length U.S. exports (only the length of patent protection shows a significant positive impact), no influence of IPRs on establishment trade, but significant effects with respect to intra-firm trade. His main conclusion is that intra-firm exports tend to be higher in the case of countries with weaker IPRs protection. This is interpreted as an indication that U.S. transnational corporations prefer to maintain production within U.S. borders and engage in intra-firm trade rather than risk the loss of proprietary information by adopting a more integrated system of production in partner countries that have weaker IPRs regime.

Using bilateral data for the U.S. from 1989 covering thirty-five partner countries, we estimated a gravity model for the same dependent variables analyzed in Ferrantino (1993): arm's length trade, intra-firm trade, and "establishment trade" for U.S. companies. . . . The performance of the model is quite good; . . . . Positive coefficients for the IPRs index are found in all equations, but the coefficient is statistically significant only with respect to arm's length trade in contrast to Ferrantino's result. Taking this result at its face value, it seems that market expansion dominates market-power effects — that is, stronger IPRs protection promotes more trade.

This result is confirmed by Maskus and Penubarti, who use an augmented version of the Helpman-Krugman model of monopolistic competition in examining bilateral trade flows. . . .

The results obtained suggest that firms are influenced by the strength of importing countries' patent regimes when engaging in export activities. Countries with stronger patent regimes import more than what is predicted by the Helpman-Krugman model. Moreover, the impact of patent protection on trade flows is found to be bigger in the larger developing countries.

Following Maskus and Penubarti's methodology, we estimated a similar model with bilateral trade flows as a share of aggregate expenditure as dependent variable. . . . The results [are] . . . [i]n accordance with Maskus and Penubarti, they show a positive impact of patent protection on trade flows within the Helpman-Krugman model. However, when turning to the interacted variables, our result suggests the impact of IPRs on trade flows to be weaker in large developing countries and stronger in small developing countries.

Maskus and Penubarti also analyze sectoral exports by clustering industries in three different categories of expected sensitivity to patent laws: high sensitivity (R&D-intensive industries and those industries that have reported significant damages from "piracy"), low sensitivity, and other industries. They find that on average the coefficients for the patent index in the least patent-sensitive industries seem to be more significant and bigger than for the most sensitive industries. They interpret this result as related either to larger market-power effects or to the interplay between trade and FDI decisions in highly sensitive industries (with FDI replacing trade as a mode of delivery in countries with weaker patent regimes). They also argue that the patent index may be capturing other dimensions of the IPRs regime (*e.g.*, copyright and trademark protection) that are relevant for the low-patent-sensitivity group.

In sum, there is mounting evidence that IPRs are indeed "trade-related." These results are, of course, model specific and should be interpreted with care. They suggest, however, that the implementation of TRIPS will have a net trade creating impact. Although no precise welfare predictions can be derived from them, they suggest that TRIPS may have a positive allocative impact at global level and that market-expansion will dominate the market-power effect in developing countries.

VI. IPRs and FDI

It is often argued that foreign firms avoid investing in countries with weak IPRs regimes. The magnitude of the impact of weak protection on Foreign Direct Investment ("FDI") decisions, however, is debatable. First, evidence based on surveys of foreign investors that identify IPRs as a relevant variable for FDI decisions tend also to point out that other considerations — in essence the overall investment climate of the country — are more important. Second, as already pointed out, FDI may replace trade flows as firms try to maintain control of proprietary information in countries with weak IPRs protection. In this case, the impact of TRIPS would be to diminish the incentives for FDI at the margin for R&D-intensive industries.

Mansfield provides some new insights on the IPRs-FDI link. His analysis, based on survey data collected from patent attorneys and executives of major U.S. manufacturing firms, makes clear that IPRs regimes are relevant for some, but not all types of FDI decisions. Not surprisingly, IPRs protection was found to be much more relevant for decisions on investment in R&D facilities than for FDI in sales and distribution outlets. Sharp differences were also found concerning the perceptions of different industries on the importance of IPRs regimes in influencing their decisions on FDI. While the chemical (and pharmaceutical) industry reported that IPRs played a major role in their decisions with respect to investment in joint ventures abroad, the metals and food industries considered IPRs protection to have marginal significance.

Mansfield also reports ongoing econometric work that tries to explain U.S. foreign direct investment flows to the sixteen countries encompassed by his survey, using the host-country GDP and his own index of protection as independent variables (a dummy for Mexico is also included in the model). The overall results are not particularly robust, but when Japan and Spain are excluded from the sample, he does find that both aggregate manufacturing FDI flows as well as FDI flows to certain industries (particularly machinery and food) are sensitive to weaknesses in IPRs regimes — that is, U.S. FDI flows increase with the perceived strength of the IPRs regime.

A similar exercise was implemented by the authors, relying on a larger set of countries and the Rapp and Rozek index. . . . The results are most powerful with respect to manufacturing as a whole. . . . The coefficient on the Rapp and Rozek index shows IPRs to have a positive impact on the level of U.S. investment abroad. The sectoral results are less robust, although the coefficient on the Rapp and Rozek index always shows a positive sign and is statistically significant for "primary and fabricated metals" and "electric and electronic equipment."

These results are tentative and additional work needs to be done in this area. In particular, a formal model of equilibrium of the international distribution of FDI is needed for one to derive more precise inferences about the IPRs-FDI link. It can be argued, however, that in a world characterized by growing competition for FDI flows, future compliance with the minimum standards of the TRIPS Agreement will be perceived as a threshold indicator. It will influence perceptions of foreign investors about the relative attractiveness of competing investment locations, even though its direct impact on FDI flows at country level remains an open question.

VII. IPRs and Transfer of Technology

Probably the most traditional argument for intellectual property rights protection in developing countries is that technology owners are less willing to transfer proprietary knowledge to countries with weak protection because of the risk of "piracy." Support for this proposition typically comes from surveys of firms in the North. Mansfield, for example, finds that U.S. firms "tend to regard intellectual property protection as being more important in decisions regarding the transfer of advanced technology than in investment decisions."

Some analysts, however, remain skeptical about the relevance of this effect. Subramanian points out that North-South conflict occurs mainly in those fields (e.g., pharmaceutical and chemical products, software) where imitation is possible independently of technology transfer. Accordingly, the potential benefits of higher IPRs protection are disputed to the extent that imitation is argued to be a sound alternative for formal transfer of technology. Nogues in turn argues "that the decision to license and transfer technology depends much more on the legal strength of the licensing agreement and the adaptable capacity of the buyer to absorb technology" than on the strength of the IPRs regime.

It is important to acknowledge, however, that firms in the North react to copying by investing in "masking" technologies (e.g., encryption of software codes) that raise the costs of imitation. Moreover, lack of protection in sectors that are imitation-prone influences the overall perception of the IPRs regime in the developing country. If the country is perceived not to be playing by the "rules of the game," it will find it increasingly difficult to obtain the transfer of technology in fields in which the cooperation of the inventor is fundamental. Finally, it can be argued that imitation as a "mode" of technology transfer will be of limited efficacy to the extent that knowledge about a particular technology is "tacit" and "circumstantial." On balance, one should expect more North-South transference of technology in response to the TRIPS Agreement.

VIII. IPRs and Rent Transfer

One of the main concerns of developing countries with respect to the TRIPS Agreement is related to the potential impact of higher standards of protection on domestic prices and with respect to rent transfer abroad. The potential for rent transfer is significant to the extent that, as already noted, non-residents account for most of the patents granted in developing countries.

The introduction of patents for pharmaceutical inventions, for example, has attracted considerable attention. This is an area in which many developing countries do not offer IPRs protection and where price levels are closely monitored in the context of health policies and other social objectives. Estimates of price increases, domestic welfare losses (encompassing consumer surplus and domestic producer surplus losses) and potential rent transfers (as measured by the rise in foreign profits) are available in the literature. As expected, the static effects of the introduction of patent for pharmaceutical inventions in developing countries imply domestic welfare losses for the South which are larger than the benefits accrued to innovators in the North. The estimates, however, are quite sensitive to assumptions concerning market structure and firm behavior.

A worst case scenario in terms of welfare losses and rent transfer can be developed if one assumes that a domestic competitive industry becomes a foreign-owned monopoly as a consequence of the introduction of patents. The domestic welfare loss is determined by the significant price increase that occurs in such a scenario. If the original market structure is characterized by a duopoly with a domestic and a foreign firm that evolves into a foreign controlled monopoly, then the scope for a price increase is limited, but a significant welfare loss still ensues mainly as a consequence of the loss in domestic producer surplus.

As Maskus and Konan point out, however, these scenarios do not capture in a realistic fashion the market for pharmaceutical products in most developing countries. Once one assumes that in the pre-reform situation the dominant foreign firm faces a competitive fringe of imitators and, eventually, of producers of generic drugs that are close substitutes for the patented drugs, the results change. First, the price impact and consumer surplus losses are significantly reduced. They will be larger in countries in which the competitive fringe of imitators is relatively bigger (e.g., India, Argentina) than in others where imitators have a more limited market share to start with (e.g., Brazil). Second, the potential for rent transfers also decreases dramatically.

The basic message of these exercises is that although the TRIPS Agreement will generate rent transfers from the South to the North, the magnitude of these transfers is unlikely to be as large as in the worst case scenarios discussed above. Moreover, as discussed in Subramanian, the transitional provisions of the Agreement further dilute these static losses. It takes on average ten years after a patent is filed for a drug to receive marketing approval. Accordingly, the direct impact of the Agreement will only begin to be felt in developing countries by 2005. And the full impact — that is, complete displacement of imitators — will only materialize by 2015, assuming a linear rate of introduction of new drugs in the world pharmaceutical market.

IX. IPRs and the Displacement of Pirates

Estimates of revenues foregone by innovators in the North due to weak IPRs protection in the South vary widely, but there is no doubt that the values involved are significant. In the same vein, the economic interests of "pirates" (that is those free riding on intellectual property of others, independently of the legality of their actions) in the South are substantial, particularly in those industries in which imitation is relatively easy (e.g., trademarked goods, software).

The displacement of "pirates" *per se* does not necessarily entail a social welfare loss, as these producers may be replaced by others operating under licenses from foreign title-holders. There is some evidence, from countries that have reformed their IPRs regimes (e.g., Singapore), that "pirates" often are well positioned to switch to legitimate activities once the legal environment changes, particularly in industries characterized by low barriers to entry (e.g., production of video and audio cassettes).

For trademarked goods the issue is in essence one of enforcement. As mentioned before, institutional weaknesses and lack of resources are expected to continue to constrain developing countries despite their TRIPS obligations. This is an area in which technical and financial assistance from the North can play an important role, assuming that the political will to curb "piracy" is mustered.

X. IPRs and Investments in R&D

The analysis so far has concentrated mainly on the allocative implications of the TRIPS Agreement. This is a partial approach to the extent that it does not take into account potential dynamic benefits associated with the strengthening of IPRs regimes. The impact of TRIPS on R&D investments in both developed and developing countries is the main issue in this context.

Evidence on the response of investments in R&D in developing countries to changes in IPRs protection remains scarce. Still, there is growing appreciation for the role played by innovation in economic development. Gould and Gruben, for example, have found evidence that IPRs protection has a marginally significant positive effect on economic growth. They attribute this to the role of IPRs in fostering R&D investments. They also find that the contribution of IPRs to economic growth increases with the openness of the economy. Based on these results, an argument can be made that the trade liberalization fostered by the Uruguay Round will enhance the potential dynamic benefits of the TRIPS Agreement. More research, however, is needed to confirm this proposition.

Another aspect of the TRIPS-R&D link concerns the potential impact of higher protection of IPRs in the South on R&D investments in the North. The small-country assumption adopted in the analysis of the pharmaceutical industry, for example, may not be appropriate on aggregate terms or with respect to products of special relevance to developing countries (e.g., drugs to fight tropical diseases). The relevance of such a proposition remains an empirical question, but in theory it opens the door for "Pareto-efficient" bargains between developed and developing countries.

The Agreement may also affect the composition of R&D investments in the South. Agricultural research in developing countries, for example, has traditionally been implemented by the public sector. The introduction of protection for plant varieties is expected to foster the privatization of agricultural research. The reaction of national or international governmental research centers to this trend is likely to have important economic implications. As innovators claim IPRs over plant varieties, the policy of free exchange of germplasm among research centers will have to be adapted. A danger in this context, is the adoption of cumbersome bureaucratic procedures for germplasm exchanges in response to the introduction of property rights.

Summing up, from a static perspective, the Agreement is an exercise in rent transfer from the South to the North. Its negative welfare implications for developing countries are, however, significantly diluted by the long transitional periods adopted. Moreover, there are positive-sum games that can be explored by developing and developed countries in the areas of trade, foreign direct investment, and transfer of technology as protection of IPRs is strengthened.

XI. Concluding Remarks

The patterns of convergence discussed in this paper have different implications for the economic debate about IPRs. As countries introduce the minimum standards of protection required by the TRIPS Agreement, a gradual strengthening of IPRs on a global scale will ensue. In this context, international convergence is happening at a faster pace than most analysts believed possible ten years ago.

It is true that this process of international convergence should not be interpreted as announcing the end of international frictions concerning IPRs protection. The question of enforcement and differences in the scope of protection across countries will continue to generate debate. Moreover, the achievements of the TRIPS Agreement fall short of the expectations of knowledge-intensive industries in developed countries. Unilateral action as a lever to promote change will continue to be supported by these industries. It is fair to say, however, that the prospects for international convergence remain favorable and this is consistent with a gradual strengthening of IPRs around the globe.

The technological convergence promoted by the digital revolution, in turn, raises new challenges for IPRs regimes. Our understanding of the implications of global networks and the digital environment for IPRs is still limited. In the near future, however, technological convergence is more likely to weaken than to reinforce the trend toward stronger IPRs protection identified above.

Notes and Questions

1. The excerpt from the article by Primo Braga and Fink points to many of the important conceptual issues underlying the grant and protection of IPRs at the international level. As Francis Gurry and Laura Tyson have already pointed out to us, the great preponderance of patents are held worldwide by OECD country industrial enterprises, and it is largely these concerns that will be exploiting patents in the developing countries, at least for the time being. This raises the prospect of a rent transfer from the developing to the industrialized countries. The critical question is whether this rent transfer will be more than offset by dynamic economic gains in the developing countries that result from introducing more comprehensive IPRs protection systems.

2. Patents held by industrialized country-based enterprises in developing countries can be exploited by the establishment of local production facilities, by exporting products protected by patent to the developing country, and/or by licensing patented technology to locally-owned enterprises. Might the extent to which knowledge is diffused into the local economy depend at least to some extent on the way in which patented foreign technology is exploited in a developing country? Which form of exploitation might be the most likely to result in technology diffusion? Why might foreign patent holders favor or disfavor that form of exploitation? Consider in this regard the deliberations of the International Conference for the Protection of Industrial Property held in Paris in November 1880, which was to give rise ultimately to the Paris Convention.[1] Article 4 of the draft convention

---

[1] See ACTS OF THE INTERNATIONAL CONFERENCE FOR THE PROTECTION OF INDUSTRIAL PROPERTY 44-45, Berne, International Bureau of the Paris Union (2nd ed. 1902); authors' translations.

considered by the Conference read: "The owner of a patent shall have the right to import into the country where the patent has been granted to him objects manufactured in one or other of the contracting countries without the importation being a reason for forfeiture of the patent." The Belgian delegate to the Conference, in the discussions on this draft article, observed "that it was only in France that legislation prohibited absolutely the importation by the patentee of objects manufactured abroad. In Belgium, while a similar provision did not exist, the principles current in relation to exploitation nevertheless prohibited the patentee from importing into the Kingdom [of Belgium] objects manufactured abroad. In order to exploit, within the meaning of Belgian law, it was necessary to manufacture the patented object in Belgium; it was intended, by that requirement, to benefit the national industrial workforce. Consequently, the patentee who limited himself to importing objects manufactured abroad to put them on sale in Belgium was not exploiting his invention in the legal sense, and faced, by that fact, the forfeiture of his rights. The principle should not, however, be applied in too absolute a manner: for example, if a patentee only imported a small quantity of objects, and manufactured in Belgium on a relatively large scale, he would only have contributed in a very restrained way to removing the benefit to national industry, and it would be invidious to provide for the forfeiture of his patent."

The President of the Conference, Senator Bozérian of France, stated "that he did not hesitate to declare that he considered the pertinent provision of the French law to be barbarous and, in addition, to be absolutely useless. It had been inserted in the law to protect national industry; but it did not respond to this objective, and it was of a nature to carry serious prejudice to trade, without any corresponding interest for industry."

3. Advocates of high levels of IPRs protection argue that providing such protection encourages foreign direct investment (FDI). A recent United Nations study concluded that there was little evidence of such a correlation.[2] In fact, over the past decade there is a strong correlation between the

---

[2]U.N. TRANSNAT'L CORP. & MGMT. DIV., U.N. DEP'T OF ECONOMICS AND SOCIAL DEVELOPMENT, INTELLECTUAL PROPERTY RIGHTS AND FOREIGN DIRECT INVESTMENT, U.N. Doc. ST/CTC/SER.A/24, U.N. Sales No. E.93.II.A.10 (1993).

United States Trade Representative's list of worst IPRs violators and the highest levels of U.S. FDI.[3] Whether FDI flows to a particular country is certain to be determined by a variety of factors, among which the expected rate of GDP growth is likely to be most significant. It is quite difficult to separate out a country's level of IPRs protection as a factor influencing FDI flow. A country with a weak IPRs protection system may attract large-scale FDI. However, it might attract more FDI with a higher level of protection, and/or it might attract more advanced technologies with a higher level of protection. China offers a potential market of over 1 billion consumers. A weak IPRs protection system may pose risks to foreign investors, but these risks may be worth taking.

4. Does the technology of a wholly-owned subsidiary of a U.S., Europe- or Japan-based enterprise diffuse into a developing country economy sufficiently to justify the payment by consumers there of monopoly rents on patented technology and products? As Primo Braga and Fink observe, this is a question to which there is at present no conclusive answer.

5. Primo Braga and Fink suggest that there is mounting evidence that high levels of IPRs protection may increase aggregate world trade, yet they note the absence of evidence regarding how the benefits from gains in trade may be allocated. What countries do you think may be most likely to capture the gains from increased world trade in IPRs protected goods and services?

6. Some politicians and commentators speak of world trade as if it were a "zero-sum game"; that is, that gains achieved by one country/player imply losses to another country/player. If this were true, then it might be convincingly argued that the industrialized countries should not seek to promote technological advancement and economic growth in developing countries, since the industrialized countries will suffer loses in welfare as the developing countries become more economically competitive. Is international trade a zero-sum game, or are gains from trade shared as each country is

---

[3]The countries that received the highest levels of FDI in the period covered by the U.N. study included China, Brazil, Argentina and Thailand.

able to exchange its goods and services for those produced more efficiently by others?

7. Should individuals living in the OECD countries care about whether developing country economies succeed? The humanitarian may answer that we all have a stake in the well-being of people wherever they may live. Even the pragmatist in an industrialized country may see the value of assuring that the schism between industrialized and developing economies is not too wide. Public order disturbances in the developing countries have a way of impacting on industrialized country economies, and on global security interests as well.

8. If it turned out the developing countries were adversely affected by the grant of high levels of patent and other IPRs protection, how might they go about rebalancing the international IPRs system? Might they employ tax policies?

---

5. IPRs in the Post-Industrial Age

In the following excerpt, Jerome Reichman asks us to reconsider the IPRs paradigm that is characterized by a distinction between *industrial property* (the "hard" IPR of the patent) and *authors' and artists' rights* (the "soft" IPR of the copyright). Reichman points to a proliferation of IPRs that have emerged to cover new technologies, or that have been adapted to cover old technologies now deemed worthy of protection. He suggests that the present international IPRs protection system has lost its focus — that there is no cohesive policy foundation on which government decision-makers are basing their actions.

Fitting new technologies into an old paradigm may not be the best way to carry out international public policy. There are risks that overprotection may stymie research and development and the introduction of new products, and may impede the creation of new artistic works. There are likewise risks that underprotection may discourage investment in new and useful technologies. Reichman suggests that there must be a way to provide IPRs protection in the post-industrial world economy that will more appropriately balance public and private interests — a new IPRs paradigm.

Charting the Collapse of the Patent-Copyright Dichotomy: Premises for a Restructured International Intellectual Property System

J.H. Reichman*

Introduction

Governments adopt intellectual property laws in the belief that a privileged, monopolistic domain operating on the margins of the free-market economy promotes long-term cultural and technological progress better than a regime of unbridled competition. Ordinary tangible goods that acquire value by satisfying known human needs in more or less standardized ways cannot escape the price-setting function of the competitive market. In contrast, intellectual goods acquire value by deviating from standard solutions to known human needs in ways that yield more efficient outcomes or that capture the public's fancy. Because intellectual goods define relevant market segments in terms of the novelty or the originality they purvey, their creators invent their own markets by stimulating demand for goods that did not previously exist.

By the end of the twentieth century, the role of intellectual property rights in stimulating post-industrial economic development had become so vital that it figured on the agenda for the Uruguay Round of multilateral trade negotiations. The Final Act embodying the results of that Round incorporates an Agreement on Trade-Related Aspects of Intellectual Property Rights ("TRIPS" Agreement) into the Marrakesh Agreement Establishing the World Trade Organization ("WTO"). The universal minimum standards of protection set out in the TRIPS Agreement tend to detach intellectual property rights from their historical roots in territorial law and to align them more closely with general norms of public and private international law applicable to older, more tangible forms of property.

In so doing, however, the drafters of the TRIPS Agreement undertook no new economic or legal analysis to justify or validate the elevation of pre-existing intellectual property rights to the status of universal norms. On the

---

*13 CARDOZO ARTS & ENT. L.J. 475 (1995).

contrary, they deliberately built upon the Paris Convention for the Protection of Industrial Property (1883) and the Berne Convention for the Protection of Literary and Artistic Works (1886), as progressively developed and supplemented by other international agreements. These "Great Conventions," as they are known, established a worldwide constitutional framework that directly or indirectly configures the various domestic systems on which it rests. Their nineteenth-century conceptual underpinnings remain central to the operations of the international intellectual property system as further broadened and strengthened by the TRIPS Agreement.

This Article is one in a series of studies that questions the capability of this inherited institutional framework to meet the needs of creators, innovators and investors operating under the changed conditions of an Information Age. It re-examines certain negative economic premises underlying the patent and copyright paradigms and explains how these premises are tacitly implemented in a compartmentalized, bipolar framework that supports the international intellectual property system as historically conceived. The Article then suggests that a proliferation of hybrid legal regimes falling outside this classical framework routinely violates its cardinal economic premises and disrupts the historical balance between free competition and legal incentives to create. Once these hybrid or deviant regimes are taken into account, the real structure of the international intellectual property system as it empirically operates at the end of the twentieth century differs radically from the bipolar structure embodied in the Great Conventions at the end of the nineteenth century.

The Article concludes with the thought that efforts to balance the public and private interests at stake in devising legal incentives for twenty-first-century innovation are likely to produce cycles of under- and overprotection until the economic implications of existing hybrid legal regimes are better understood. Another study, entitled Legal Hybrids Between the Patent and Copyright Paradigms, has recently begun this task. Meanwhile, the discrepancies between the nineteenth-century historical construct and the twentieth-century empirical realities charted in this Article suggest that the TRIPS Agreement could yield fewer beneficial results than anticipated and, in some areas, could even compound the social disutilities stemming from an obsolete and increasingly dysfunctional institutional framework. The Article ends by reaffirming the need for a new intellectual property paradigm specifically devised for the conditions that induce legislators everywhere to enact hybrid regimes that deviate from the legal and economic logic of the international intellectual property system as historically conceived.

I. Bipolar Structure of the International Intellectual Property System

The term "intellectual property" was not coined until the late nineteenth century. Only when Josef Kohler and Edmond Picard perceived that copyright, patent, and trademark laws had more in common with each other than with the older forms of property known to Roman law was it recognized that a new class of rights in intangible creations had arisen. Their use of the term "intellectual property" thus coincided with the drive for international regulation of both artistic and industrial property, a movement destined to produce a fully articulated and universally recognized legal discourse in little more than a century.

A. Nature and Limits of the Dominant Intellectual Property Paradigms

Taken together, the Paris and Berne Conventions purport to subdivide the international intellectual property system into two hermetically sealed compartments separated by a common line of demarcation. Literary and artistic property rights occupy one of these compartments; so-called industrial property rights occupy the other.

1. The Patent and Copyright Subsystems

The origins of the bipolar structure can be traced to cornerstone provisions of the Great Conventions extant since their inception and to corresponding state practices recognized by most developed intellectual property systems. On the one hand, Article 1 of the Berne Convention established "a Union for the protection of the rights of authors in their literary and artistic works." Such works, categorized at length in Article 2(1), should receive automatic and mandatory protection in the domestic copyright laws of the member states. To avoid censorship and to liberate authors from overt and covert forms of patronage, these laws entitle almost all independently created works falling within the designated subject matter categories to a generous but relatively soft form of protection against copying only that lasts a long period of time.

On the other hand, Articles 1(1) and 1(2) of the Paris Convention established "a Union for the protection of industrial property" and identified certain legal institutions as the "object" of industrial property protection, namely, "patents, utility models, industrial designs, trademarks, service marks, trade names, indications of source . . . and the repression of unfair competition." While some international minimum standards and the rule of national treatment apply to all these institutions, the Paris Convention entrusted the protection of industrial creations primarily to "the various kinds of industrial patents recognized by the laws of the countries of the Union." The patent paradigm and variants thereof classically confer a tougher form of protection on strict formal and substantive conditions for a relatively short period of time.

2. The Historical Line of Demarcation

Because the domestic patent and copyright regimes afford fundamentally different types of protection, the line of demarcation between the Paris and Berne Conventions becomes of paramount importance. A line that appears unclear or poorly defended will tempt entrepreneurs to circumvent the strict prerequisites of patent law, with its basic requirements of novelty, utility, and nonobviousness, in order to shelter industrial creations within the more receptive and generous embrace of copyright law, which applies without regard to artistic merit. An unclear line of demarcation also leads to the risk that the same subject matter will attract different proprietary regimes. This, in turn, renders classical intellectual property theory incoherent and breeds endless contradictions.

A body of historical evidence pertaining to industrial design makes it logical to characterize this line of demarcation in terms of a discredited dichotomy between "art" and "utility." However, the international conventions did not expressly sanction this interpretation or others, equally intractable, that appeal to philosophical or even political biases. Rather, the Great Conventions took a more empirical approach, adopted for mundane economic purposes, that turned on the definition of "industrial property" in Article 1(3) of the Paris Convention.

This definition deliberately left nothing to the discretion of the member states. It dictated that "industrial property shall be understood in the broadest sense and shall apply not only to industry and commerce proper, but likewise to agricultural and extractive industries and to all manufactured or natural products, for example, wines, grain, tobacco leaf, fruit, cattle, minerals, mineral waters, beer, flowers, and flour." In effect, this provision casts "industrial property" in terms of every conceivable product available for sale on the general products market in order "to avoid excluding . . . activities or products which would otherwise run the risk of not being assimilated to those of industry proper." Its sole major exclusion is for those literary and artistic works subject to domestic copyright laws that were later covered by Article 2(1) of the Berne Convention and by Article I of the Universal Copyright Convention (U.C.C.).

Apart from the rule of national treatment, states members of the Paris Union are seldom required to take any particular action with regard to any of the product categories listed in this broad definition of industrial property. The industrial property defined in Article 1(3) thus constitutes the true subject matter of protection under the Paris Convention, as distinct from the legal regimes, such as the domestic patent and trademark laws, through which its protection may or may not be perfected. At the same time, the definition of industrial property functionally determines the jurisdictional reach of the Paris Convention in relation to the international copyright conventions. In effect, this line of demarcation appears to turn not strictly on the "art versus utility" criterion, but rather on the distinction between "products" of industrial and commercial activity "in the broadest sense" that are sold on the general products market, and literary and artistic "productions" that are not.

In principle, the patent and copyright subsystems thus meet each other face to face across this common frontier. The clarity of this juncture is enhanced by noting that domestic and international industrial property laws normally exclude technical writings as such from eligibility as patentable subject matter. Conversely, technical and utilitarian writings normally fall within the jurisdiction of national and international copyright laws, at least to the extent of their expression and not their ideas.

That this line of demarcation has become less air tight and unequivocal over time than the nineteenth-century draftsmen had intended cannot be denied. The old puzzle of industrial art (i.e., commercial designs) and the new puzzle of industrial literature (i.e., computer programs), for example, conjure up endless ambiguities. For present purposes, nonetheless, it suffices to establish, first, that "industrial property" and "literary and artistic works" entirely occupied the classical intellectual property universe at the international level; and second, that the predominant legal subsystems operating within that universe of discourse were historically separated by a line of demarcation cast in terms of the general products market. As will be seen from the next section, this bipolar structure rested upon a shrewd economic calculus.

*****

To understand why the classical intellectual property system has begun to break down, one must first grasp the nature and role of the[ir] negative premises. One must then test the accuracy of the behavioral assumptions on which they rest against the realities of legislative and judicial action in the second half of the twentieth century. . . .

*****

For example, the positive modalities of patent law are known to provide inventors in developed countries with an absolute right of exclusion for a relatively short period of time if they satisfy the strict substantive prerequisites of novelty, utility, and above all, nonobviousness. Yet, one also finds at least four negative economic premises implicit in the structural arrangements given these modalities:

1) Unpatented innovations remain subject to price competition and may be imitated if disclosed;
2) Undisclosed, unpatented innovations may be reverse-engineered but not stolen;
3) Patented inventions are not infringed by nonequivalent innovation;
4) Unfair competition law should not repress imitation of unpatented products in the absence of confusion or deception.

*****

Similarly, the positive modalities of copyright law (or of "authors' rights" laws as they are known in most non-English-speaking countries) provide virtually all authors and artists who independently create their own works with relatively soft protection against copying only that lasts a very long period of time. By the same token, one also finds at least four negative economic premises implicit in the structural arrangements given these modalities:

1) Noncopyrightable productions or components thereof remain subject to price competition and may be imitated if disclosed.

2) Nonprotectable ideas underlying clusters of independent creation may be used but may not be stolen [built-in reverse-engineering].

3) Cultural policies are not applicable to the general products market.

4) Unfair competition laws should not limit users' rights in the absence of confusion or deception.

*****

1. Patents for Inventions

Taken together, these negative premises serve to remind both partisans and critics of the patent system that its strict substantive prerequisites — when faithfully applied — implicitly ensure that the great bulk of non-patentable innovation remains subject to price competition on the general products market. The competitors' rights freely to imitate any unpatented products once distributed to the public thus constitute a normative premise of the free-market economy, one that presumably benefits consumers by gearing prices to production efficiencies and to incremental technical progress.

*****

2. Literary and Artistic Works

Taken together, the negative economic premises identified above further remind both partisans and critics of intellectual property law that the mature copyright paradigm is predicated on the very absence of the natural lead time that trade secret law attempts to defend. Because authors normally embody their intangible creations in tangible mediums of expression, the distribution of these material supports to the public at large negates any further possibility of concealing the product of creative know-how in the manner of trade secrets. Because every artistic work thus bears its author's intellectual creation on its face, would-be competitors need only obtain some tangible embodiment of that expression to duplicate it without incurring the investment of time, money, or skill inherent in the process of reverse-engineering unpatented industrial innovation. Third parties who rapidly duplicate a successful literary or artistic work may reduce the author's natural lead time to zero, or even minus zero if they possess sufficient market power, simply by selling the same artistic production at a price below the average cost to publish or disseminate the original work. The copyright system thus deals with intellectual goods not protectable as trade secrets that require no reverse-engineering to appropriate.

*****

2. The Deviant Regimes

*****

. . . [I]n Marginal Zone A (on the industrial property side of the dividing line), one finds such deviant protective regimes as utility model laws, registered design laws, plant variety protection laws, and unregistered design protection laws (like that the United Kingdom enacted in 1988). Also included in this zone are recent unfair competition laws that, to varying degrees, restrain third parties from copying unpatented, noncopyrightable innovation without any corresponding investment of their own. Logically included in this zone . . . are several other hybrid regimes, both existing and proposed, such as sui generis regimes protecting typeface designs; regimes that issue inventors' certificates or that reward individual rationalization proposals (largely a heritage of the centrally planned economies); and, arguably, proposed amendments to the United States patent law that would lower the standards of eligibility for certain discoveries in biogenetic engineering.

*****

Similarly, in Marginal Zone B (on the artistic property side of the dividing line), one finds such deviant regimes as sui generis laws protecting computer programs (now largely superseded); laws protecting integrated circuit designs on copyright-like principles; and miscellaneous sui generis laws protecting such items as data bases and catalogues, applied art, and engineering projects. Also included in this zone is the European Union's experimental adaptation of copyright law to computer programs, as well as certain aberrational experiments in the domestic copyright laws, such as full copyright protection of functional designs in the United Kingdom (now superseded); full copyright protection of mostly non-functional appearance designs in France; and modified forms of copyright protection for certain borderline functional works, such as measures concerning technical drawings and engineering projects in Germany and the United States. Logically included in Marginal Zone B . . . are the more traditional rights, related to or "neighboring" on copyright law, which protect performers, broadcasting organizations, and the producers of sound recordings, and which turn out to be less deviant than appears on the surface.

*****

Some of these misfits or mutants are truly new and readily identifiable with today's important new technologies. Others, however, are almost as old as the world's intellectual property system itself. . . .

*****

II. Empirical Limits of the Classical Bipolar Structure

The survey of deviant regimes . . . confirms that the classical "vision that subdivided world intellectual property law into discrete and mutually exclusive compartments for industrial and artistic property has irretrievably broken down."[131] To the extent that the patent and copyright models underlying the Great Conventions represent a coherent theory about the way intellectual creations behave in the world at large, that theory has been discredited by its inability to account for, or adequately deal with, the behavior of so many commercially valuable intellectual creations that actually inhabit that universe.

The real objects of protection that increasingly elude the classical scheme often constitute the cutting edge of technological innovation at the end of the twentieth century; they account for an ever growing share of the gross domestic products in both developed and developing countries. Yet,

---

[131]J.H. Reichman, Legal Hybrids Between the Patent and Copyright Paradigms, 94 Colum. L. Rev. 2432 (1994), at 2500 [hereinafter Legal Hybrids]; see generally id. at 2453-2504.

one cannot reconcile the hybrid legal regimes summoned to protect these creations with the economic justifications of the classical intellectual property system. On the contrary, the proponents of these regimes invariably make a virtue out of a vice by justifying the need for new intellectual property rights in terms of the shortcomings or limits of the dominant legal paradigms.

In these and other respects, the hybrid legal regimes proliferating within today's international intellectual property system resemble the Ptolemaic epicycles with which the earth-centered theory of the universe was continually adjusted in a bygone day. These adjustments enable observers only to account for past deviations from existing norms without being able to predict the behavior of the relevant legal constellations in the future.

*****

To escape these after-the-fact rationalizations, a helpful first step is to reconsider the theoretical foundations of the classical framework in order to obtain a more precise understanding of how — and where — it empirically accommodates the deviant regimes. . . .

*****

That the objects of the deviant regimes actually resemble each other more than they resemble works of art or industrial inventions is of capital importance in arriving at a systematic clarification of the marginal cases in general. It should be remembered that Kohler and Picard coined the term "intellectual property" because they thought patents, copyrights, and trade marks had more in common with each other than with the categories of tangible property inherited from antiquity. That the creations governed by hybrid legal regimes resemble each other more than they resemble the true objects of classical copyright and patent systems likewise suggests that one is witnessing the formation of a new intellectual property paradigm that has much to reveal about the economics of competition in a post-industrial marketplace.

*****

The survey of legal hybrids revealed, in short, that the worldwide intellectual property system now routinely dispenses its legal monopolies to less than nonobvious innovation that competes on the general products market. Regardless of whether the hybrid legal regimes that increasingly occupy the forefront of attention protect cutting-edge technologies or more traditional forms of innovation, they defy the economic and social justifications for the classical intellectual property systems that were put forward at the end of the nineteenth century.

2. Cumulative Restraints on Trade

The anti-competitive effects likely to ensue from this creeping generalization of the "two-market conundrum" are potentially more far-reaching than those that the older marginal cases might have engendered fifty to a hundred years ago. In the nineteenth century, for example, industrial design was truly marginal in the economic sense, because industrial objects reproduced in series still competed on the basis of technical yields, not style; moreover, electronic information processing had yet to be invented. Today, instead, industrial design drives the products market and computer programs constitute a primary engine of economic development. Yet, because virtually every product bears a functionally integrated configuration that could fall within, say, an unregistered design law or increasingly, within a utility model law, and because every computer program is potentially copyrightable, the cumulative effect of the marginal cases is to suspend the operation of the normal rules of competition at the very core of the postindustrial economy.

Taken one by one, the protection provided by each of the hybrid legal regimes seeks to overcome the free-rider problem that threatens to inhibit investment in a particular type of innovation. Taken together, these regimes introduce a strong protectionist bias into domestic economies driven by constant innovation that contradicts even the liberalizing thrust of multilateral trade negotiations seeking greater competition in an integrated world market. The risk is that liberalization . . . will largely affect traditional products of the industrial revolution, while producers of nontraditional, high-tech products and processes increasingly take ad hoc protectionist barriers for granted on both the domestic and international markets.

The protectionist tide rising with respect to nontraditional objects of legal protection could thus offset competitive gains expected to flow from the harmonization of laws pertaining to more traditional objects of protection whose relative share of total investment in research and development seems likely to decline over time.

These transnational legislative trends have virtually eclipsed the cautious and skeptical view of intellectual property rights that prevailed in the nineteenth and early twentieth centuries. In that period, compelling economic and social justifications were required for any legal monopoly that derogated from the basic norm of free competition. Even the paradigmatic intellectual property regimes recognized in the Paris and Berne Conventions accordingly evolved with strict limitations and exceptions that balance the public interest in competition against specific incentives to create. "In contrast, the hybrid legal regimes appear to have been crafted without comparable inhibitions."[175] They represent an improvised set of responses to sectoral protectionist demands that lack any coherent theoretical foundations and that rest upon altogether different economic premises.

The competitive mandate of nineteenth-century economic law is thus giving way to an assortment of hybrid legal regimes under which virtually every product of important new technologies will come freighted with some improvised grant of exclusive property rights. As the protectionist momentum building up in the sphere of nontraditional innovation continues unabated, moreover, the paradigmatic foundations of the international intellectual property system are further destabilized by the tendency of patent, copyright and trademark laws to mutate under the pressure of events. Both tendencies lack any unifying principle or standards to guide courts and administrators, and history shows that both are likely to breed recurring cyclical states of chronic under- and over-protection.

It may be doubted that nineteenth-century notions of unrestricted competition adequately meet the needs of a post-industrial economy in which the most valuable commercial products often consist of costly, intangible bundles of information that third parties can duplicate without defraying the costs of their own research and development. . . . [W]hat the empirical survey of legal hybrids showed, if nothing else, was that application of the nineteenth-century competitive model, as adjusted by its classical patent and copyright systems, had become increasingly chimerical in

---

[175]Id. at at 2503.

practice. That model has been overwhelmed by the rise and rapid expansion of a countervailing group of deviant models that apply different and seldom explored economic principles.

The bigger picture that emerges from the empirical survey of legal hybrids does not, therefore, concern just the evolution of intellectual property rights. It concerns the changing nature of competition in the so-called information society, changes that all the attention bestowed on the classical patent and copyright systems in recent years may paradoxically have obscured. In effect, the hybrid legal regimes "turn the nineteenth-century outlook upside down by presupposing a universe of commercial intercourse in which legal protection becomes a necessary and constant component of economic life." If, as the old cliche declares, the classical patent and copyright systems were once islands of protection in a sea of competition, the legal hybrids — taken together — conjure up the vision of a sea of protection in which intrepid entrepreneurs encounter remote islands of free competition.

3. Need for a New Intellectual Property Paradigm

Governments seeking to maintain high levels of investment in technological innovation face an increasingly difficult task as the twentieth century draws to a close. They must preserve or restore the bases for healthy competition at a time when information is increasingly becoming the medium from which the most socially valuable artifacts are likely to be constructed. This task will require the elaboration of a new intellectual property paradigm that looks "beyond art and inventions."[182] Such a paradigm must deal directly with the pervasive threat of market failure facing investors in unpatentable, noncopyrightable innovation under present-day conditions, without multiplying ill-conceived, socially harmful regimes of exclusive property rights.

*****

Taken together, these studies demonstrate that the failure of the patent and copyright models to deal adequately with the most important new technologies, including computer programs, biogenetic engineering, and

---

[182] . . . see generally, id. at 2504-06.

industrial designs, does not stem from inherent conceptual defects in those models. Rather, the real problems arise from a breakdown of classical trade secret law under modern conditions. In effect, the nineteenth-century view of competition takes it for granted that some measure of natural lead time will result from the duty of second comers to reverse-engineer unpatented, noncopyrightable innovation by proper means. In other words, competition with respect to the products of incremental innovation — as distinct from patentable inventions and copyrightable literary or artistic works — presupposes that trade secret laws (or equivalent laws of confidential information) typically supply enough lead time to overcome the problem of appropriability inherent in public goods.

On analysis, trade secret law can most usefully be conceived as a set of default liability rules regulating relations between members of any given technical community. These rules provide innovators with natural lead time and they require second comers to contribute, directly or indirectly, to the technical community's overall costs of research and development. Although trade secret laws always suffered from the risk of irrational and capricious results at the margins, where secrecy either did not exist at all or proved impervious to reverse-engineering, the total competitive picture entails an "historical dependence of intellectual property systems on a substratum of liability rules."

These ancillary liability rules break down under modern conditions, however, because information becomes a primary medium of construction for the most innovative products and also because the design components of new technologies — which transcend the old product-process distinction of patent law — are routinely embodied in the end products that are distributed in the open market. As a result, "incremental innovation bearing know-how on its face" tends to obtain zero lead time from classical trade secret law in most design-rich or design-dependent applications of advanced technical know-how to industry. The resulting threat of market failure leads to the proliferation of hybrid legal regimes, usually built on modified patent and copyright principles, that have cropped up here and abroad. Collectively evaluated, their cumulative restraints on competition appear worse, in the sense of overprotection, than the chronic state of underprotection they seek to redress.

The solution to the real problems facing twenty-first century innovation is not mindlessly to multiply exclusive property rights for each new technology that heaves into sight. Rather, the task is to develop a substitute liability regime that rationalizes the economic functions of classical trade secret law under the very different conditions of an Information Age: it requires, so to speak, the formulation of a "portable trade secret" regime whose economic benefits do not depend on the often socially irrelevant condition of actual secrecy. To this end, [this writer has suggested that a] "default liability regime for applied know-how" [might be] devised specifically for unpatentable, noncopyrightable innovations that fall into the penumbra between the international patent and copyright systems. It [would provide] innovators with short periods of artificial lead time in which to recoup their investment, and it also endows competitors with a menu of standardized, automatic licenses that encourage them to make incremental improvements while contributing to the originator's costs of research and development. This minimalist, pro-competitive approach overcomes market failure and the attendant free-rider problem without multiplying exclusive property rights or creating other barriers to entry.

These and other studies thus confirm that today's most commercially valuable applications of scientific and technical know-how to industry often fall through the cracks of the classical bipolar structure enshrined in existing international conventions, including the TRIPS Agreement. Policymakers charged with the task of restructuring the world's intellectual property system have yet to grasp the true nature of the problems that limit the flow of investment to incremental innovation under present-day conditions. As a result, the bases for healthy competition in an integrated world market risk being constantly undermined by a chronic shortage of natural lead time and by a welter of anticompetitive trade restraints that Ptolemaic tinkering with an obsolete historical construct tends to engender. Sooner or later, unless legislators combat these twin evils in the interests of a more rational and constructive approach that seeks to place both innovators and borrowers in a win-win position over time, an increasingly discredited intellectual property system risks collapsing of its own protectionist weight.

Notes and Questions

1. What concerns does Jerome Reichman express with respect to the proliferation of new forms of IPRs protection? Is he concerned that legislators are not sufficiently skeptical of demands for new forms of protection? How

can legislators adopt new forms of IPRs protection without a theoretical foundation that predicts the consequences of their actions? Yet, if the technologies they address are indeed new, how could this theoretical foundation have developed? Do all IPRs share a common theoretical foundation?

2. As we proceed through the remainder of the book, you will study a variety of IPRs instruments developed to address advances in technology. Try to identify unifying or coherent policy bases for these measures. Do the legislative measures of governments generally reflect coherent policy foundations? How else do government measures come about? Is there anything unique about government measures in respect to IPRs (as compared, for example, to government measures in respect to the agricultural sector)? Does the growing "internationalization" of IPRs law require that more coherent underlying policy foundations be formulated?

CHAPTER II

Organizations and International Cooperation

A. Multilateral Organizations

The international system for the protection of intellectual property is governed by institutions that are organized and that operate on a range of levels. The main organizations at the international or multilateral level are the World Intellectual Property Organization (WIPO) and World Trade Organization (WTO). Beyond these organizations which deal with IPRs in a specialized and comprehensive manner, the subject matter has become of increasing and growing importance to several organizations of the United Nations system in addition to WIPO. The World Bank plays an important role in the international IPRs system through its financing programs to facilitate technology transfer and capacity-building, and through its training programs. The United Nations Conference on Trade and Development (UNCTAD), the United Nations Environment Program (UNEP), and the United Nations Development Program (UNDP) are each involved with IPRs issues, especially from the development point of view. The activities of the Food and Agriculture Organization (FAO), the International Telecommunications Union (ITU) and the World Health Organization (WHO) are directly and indirectly affected by developments in the international IPRs field. Limited membership organizations such as the Organisation for Economic Cooperation and Development (OECD) are also major actors in the international IPRs dialogue.

Many regional institutions situated throughout the world are involved in regulating IPRs. The Andean Group, APEC, European Union (EU), Mercosur and NAFTA, among other such institutions, play broad roles in governing trade and social welfare matters. Other regional institutions, such as the European Patent Office and African Regional Industrial Property Organization (ARIPO), are exclusively concerned with IPRs matters. National governments continue to play a central role in IPRs governance. As IPRs are important components of economic regulation, national regulation of

IPRs takes place mainly at the central (e.g., federal) government level. In some countries, subfederal units of government (such as the states of the United States) continue to exercise substantial authority in a few areas (such as trade secret regulation). In Germany and Switzerland, the Länder and Cantons no longer play a significant role in IPRs policy-making and administration, with limited exceptions such as the regulation of geographical indications.

Until the GATT Uruguay Round of trade negotiations that commenced in 1986, WIPO played the preeminent role in the international regulation of IPRs. For a variety of reasons, industry groups throughout the industrialized world grew dissatisfied with the development of the treaty system administered by WIPO. One of the main objectives of U.S., EU, Japanese and other industrialized country trade negotiators in the Uruguay Round was to establish a new and comprehensive international framework for the protection of IPRs that would address the shortcomings identified by industry. The overall objective was to shift the IPRs regulatory focus away from WIPO and to the GATT — now the WTO. Among other purposes, this would permit the use of trade-based remedies to enforce international IPRs standards.

The Uruguay Round negotiations on trade-related aspects of intellectual property rights (TRIPS) were long, complex and contentious. When the Uruguay Round was brought to an end in late 1993, industrialized countries had achieved what they sought — if not more — in the new Agreement on Trade-Related Aspects of Intellectual Property Rights (TRIPS Agreement). In the following sections, we first examine the basic structure and role of WIPO. We then turn to the issues confronting trade negotiators as they sought to bring IPRs into the GATT, and finally we examine the bipolar structure of international IPRs regulation that emerged when the Agreement Establishing the World Trade Organization entered into force on January 1, 1995. As you will see, while the international IPRs regulation center of gravity has to some extent shifted, the results of the Uruguay Round at the institutional level are not so clear-cut as might have been foreseen.

1. The World Intellectual Property Organization (WIPO)
International Bureau of WIPO*

History

The World Intellectual Property Organization (WIPO), which is located in Geneva, Switzerland, was established by a convention (the Convention Establishing the World Intellectual Property Organization), which was concluded at Stockholm in 1967 and which entered into force in 1970.

The origins of the Organization, however, go back to the nineteenth century when the Paris Convention for the Protection of Industrial Property was concluded in 1883 and the Berne Convention for the Protection of Literary and Artistic Works was concluded in 1886. Both Conventions provided for the establishment of an "International Bureau" or secretariat, which were united in 1893 and functioned under various names until 1970, when they were replaced by the International Bureau of Intellectual Property by virtue of the WIPO Convention.

WIPO became a specialized agency of the United Nations system of organizations in 1974. Under the Agreement between WIPO and the United Nations pursuant to which it became a specialized agency, WIPO is responsible for taking action for promoting creative intellectual activity and for facilitating the transfer of technology to the developing countries in order to accelerate their economic, social and cultural development.

Constitutional Structure

WIPO is a constitutionally complex organization. The WIPO Convention acts as an umbrella convention establishing the Organization, its constituent organs and its secretariat. It is an administrative treaty only, which imposes no substantive obligations in the field of intellectual property. Those substantive obligations are established in separate treaties, each of

---

*http://www.wipo.int.

which has its own set of contracting parties and, usually, its own constituent organ through which those contracting parties act. Cohesion between the various treaties is achieved by a common secretariat and, since recent years, a common budgetary and financial system. In addition, the organs of each treaty administered by WIPO meet simultaneously, in practice once every year, and address a common program of work and activities carried out by the Organization.

The Treaties Falling Under the WIPO Umbrella

The treaties administered by WIPO and, as of April 1, 1999, their respective numbers of contracting States, are as follows:

1. Convention Establishing the World Intellectual Property Organization (171 States);

2. Paris Convention for the Protection of Industrial Property (153 States);

3. Berne Convention for the Protection of Literary and Artistic Works (136 States);

4. Madrid Agreement for the Repression of False or Deceptive Indications of Source on Goods (31 States);

5. Madrid Agreement Concerning the International Registration of Marks (51 States) and Protocol Relating to the Madrid Agreement Concerning the International Registration of Marks (37 States);

6. Hague Agreement Concerning the International Deposit of Industrial Designs (29 States);

7. Nice Agreement Concerning the International Classification of Goods and Services for the Purposes of the Registration of Marks (58 States);

8. Lisbon Agreement for the Protection of Appellations of Origin and their International Registration (19 States);

9. International Convention for the Protection of Performers, Producers of Phonograms and Broadcasting Organisations (Rome Convention, administered jointly with the ILO and Unesco) (58 States);

10. Locarno Agreement Establishing an International Classification for Industrial Designs (35 States);

11. Patent Cooperation Treaty (100 States);

12. Strasbourg Agreement Concerning the International Patent Classification (43 States);

13. Convention for the Protection of Producers of Phonograms Against Unauthorized Duplication of Their Phonograms (Geneva (Phonograms) Convention) (57 States);

14. Vienna Agreement Establishing an International Classification of the Figurative Elements of Marks (13 States);

15. Convention Relating to the Distribution of Programme-Carrying Signals Transmitted by Satellite (23 States);

16. Budapest Treaty on the International Recognition of the Deposit of Microorganisms for the Purposes of Patent Procedure (45 States);

17. Nairobi Treaty on the Protection of the Olympic Symbol (39 States);

18. Treaty on the International Registration of Audiovisual Works (13 States);

19. Trademark Law Treaty (22 States).

In addition, the WIPO Copyright Treaty and the WIPO Performances and Phonograms Treaty were concluded under the auspices of WIPO in 1996. Each requires 30 accessions or ratifications to enter into force. As at April 1, 1999, seven States had acceded to or ratified the former, while five States had acceded to or ratified the latter.

As can be seen from the differing numbers of contracting States to each of the abovementioned treaties, there is no obligation on the part of a State member of WIPO to accede to any of the other treaties administered by WIPO. It is for each State to choose which, if any, treaties it will accede to and, thus, to what degree of intensity it wishes to participate in the international system constituted by the treaties.

Program and Activities of WIPO

The program and activities of WIPO may be divided into five main areas:

Global Protection Systems

WIPO administers four systems which enable users to apply for or obtain protection in multiple countries through a single international procedure:

(i) The Patent Cooperation Treaty (PCT), under which an applicant can, through one international application, apply for patent protection in any or all of 100 contracting States. In 1998, 67,007 international applications were filed under the PCT. Taking into account the number of countries designated in those applications, they were equivalent to 4.8 million national patent applications.

(ii) The Madrid System for the international registration of marks, under which an applicant can apply for and obtain a trademark registration in any or all of 51 contracting States. In 1998, there were 20,020 international registrations of marks under the Madrid system, equivalent to some 240,000 national registrations.

(iii) The Hague Agreement Concerning the International Deposit of Industrial Designs, under which an applicant can, through a single international deposit (application) obtain industrial design protection in up to 29 contracting States. In 1998, there were 3,970 international deposits (registrations or renewals of registrations) under the Hague Agreement.

(iv) The Lisbon Agreement for the Protection of Appellations of Origin and their International Registration, under which protection may be obtained, through a single international registration, for an appellation of origin in 18 contracting States. A registration has continuing validity. To date, there have been 835 registrations.

Progressive Development of International Intellectual Property Law

The treaties administered by WIPO which establish substantive obligations in the field of intellectual property represent the result of the past efforts of WIPO to develop international intellectual property law. Those efforts continue especially with respect to the approximation of national procedural and substantive patent and trademark laws, the adjustment of the intellectual property system to the digital economy and electronic commerce, and the exploration of appropriate means of protecting folklore, cultural heritage and indigenous knowledge. The latest results of the WIPO program in this area were the WIPO Copyright Treaty and the WIPO Performances and Phonograms Treaty, which were concluded in 1996 and which establish important adjustments of the international copyright system to the digital age, and the final report of the WIPO Internet Domain Name Process, which contains recommendations to the Internet Corporation for Assigned Names and Numbers (ICANN) on a variety of matters relating to the intersection of domain names and trademarks, including dispute-resolution procedures.

Cooperation for Development

An important part of WIPO's program is directed at providing legislative and administrative advice and infrastructure development for developing countries to enable them to modernize their intellectual property systems, exploit intellectual property to the benefit of their economies and comply with the provisions of the WTO Agreement on Trade Related Aspects of Intellectual Property Rights.

Inter-Office Technical Cooperation

A specialized, but nonetheless important, activity of WIPO is related to the standardization of practices and working systems amongst industrial property offices. WIPO administers international classification systems for patents (under the Strasbourg Agreement Concerning the International

Patent Classification), trademarks (under the Nice Agreement Concerning the International Classification of Goods and Services for the Purposes of the Registration of Marks and the Vienna Agreement Establishing an International Classification of the Figurative Elements of Marks) and industrial designs (under the Locarno Agreement Establishing an International Classification for Industrial Designs). While of a technical and administrative nature, these classification systems are important components of the international intellectual property system. They ensure that patent applications and patent grants are classified in a consistent and systematic manner which permits the search and retrieval of the technical information contained in patents. Likewise, they facilitate the search of trademark and industrial design registrations by applicants wishing to avoid collisions with prior registrations.

Dispute Resolution Between Private Parties

The WIPO Arbitration and Mediation Center administers arbitration and mediation procedures for resolving international commercial disputes involving intellectual property. A single procedure of arbitration or mediation can offer a cost-effective means of resolving a multijurisdictional dispute over intellectual property rights.

Finance and Staff

WIPO has an annual budget of around 200 million Swiss francs (approximately 130 USD). It is unusual in the United Nations system in being largely self-financed. 90% of its income comes from fees for services rendered under the global protection systems and other activities, while around 10% comes from Member State contributions.

As at April 1, 1999, WIPO had around 850 staff, including short-term employees or consultants.

---

a. WIPO as an Institution for Securing Rights

Creating an effective and efficient international IPRs protection system requires the establishment of mechanisms by which rights may be secured. Francis Gurry reflects on the role which WIPO plays in providing such mechanisms, and on some of the gaps in the present system. We will study the registration mechanisms in detail later on in the book.

The Evolution of Technology and Markets and the Management of Intellectual Property Rights

Francis Gurry*

*****

Servicing Globalized Demand

Intellectual property titles are national in nature. Users seeking protection across different markets are obliged to file separate national applications, often requiring different administrative formalities and legal conditions to be satisfied, in each country in which they seek protection. Some relief from this administrative burden is provided by regional systems, which provide either for the processing and grant on the regional level of separate national titles in the participating member states of the regional system, such as the regional patent and industrial design system administered by the African Regional Industrial Property Office (ARIPO), or the regional patent system administered by the European Patent Organization (EPO), or for the processing and grant of regional titles, such as the regional system for patents, trademarks, and industrial designs administered by the African Intellectual Property Organization (OAPI), the regional patent system administered by the Eurasian Patent Organization or the regional trademarks system administered by the Office of Harmonization for the Internal Market (OHIM) of the European Union. From the point of view of users, however, there is an obvious need for international systems to facilitate the task of obtaining protection for intellectual property on a

---

*In Public Policy and Global Technological Integration 25 (F. M. Abbott and D. J. Gerber eds., 1997).

global basis. These systems exist and are administered by the World Intellectual Property Organization (WIPO).

In the area of patents, the Patent Cooperation Treaty (PCT) provides a system under which applicants may file one international application which is valid in all contracting states designated by the applicants. Certain of the ensuing stages of the processing of the application take place on the international level, while the final stages are reserved for the national phase administered by the national (or regional) patent office. The stages that take place at the international level are the publication of the application, an international search of the application and, at the option of the applicant, an international preliminary examination of the application.

The PCT has met with extraordinary success, which has provided eloquent testimony to the need for an international system. The PCT commenced only in 1978. In 1995, 38,906 international applications were filed which, after taking into account the number of designations in such applications, amounted to 1,807,216 national applications. There are now eighty-nine states party to the PCT, covering all of the industrialized world and major areas of the developing world and states with economies in transition from centrally planned economies.

In the area of trademarks, the Madrid Agreement Concerning the International Registration of Marks provides an international system under which a single application can result in a single international registration with the effect of a national registration in all of the designated contracting states. Forty-six countries are party to the Madrid Agreement. At present, there are some 328,000 international registrations in force under the Madrid Agreement, with 18,852 new international applications having been filed in 1995.

The Madrid Agreement has suffered from a geographical coverage that is less than fully international in the states that are party to the Agreement. In 1989, a Protocol to the Madrid Agreement Concerning the International Registration of Marks was concluded, which entered into force in 1996. The Madrid Protocol offers the possibility of greatly enlarging the geographical coverage of the Madrid system. Of the thirteen states that have so far become party to the Madrid Protocol, five were not previously party to the Madrid Agreement, providing an encouraging sign for the prospect of a more global trademark registration system. The participation of the United States of America in the new system is, however, subject to a difficulty. While legislation has been passed by Congress for the ratification of the

Madrid Protocol, the legislation will not take effect for as long as the European Union has the possibility of a vote additional to those of its member states in the administrative machinery established under the Madrid Protocol.

In the area of industrial designs, an international system is administered by WIPO under the Hague Agreement Concerning the International Deposit of Industrial Designs. The Hague Agreement regrettably enjoys a limited geographical participation, only twenty-six states being party to the Agreement, with some 3549 new international deposits being received in 1995. Efforts are underway at WIPO for a revision of the Hague system with a view to enlarging its geographical coverage. Those efforts require the development of a new system that will, on the one hand, preserve the simplicity and ease of use of the existing system, while allowing that system to be expanded in such a way as to accommodate the needs of those countries whose law requires an examination of the novelty of applications for design protection and, thus, a more complex administrative processing machinery.

A further aspect of servicing globalized demand is the provision of an even playing field for users of intellectual property, which gives assurance to intellectual property owners that their intellectual property will enjoy an adequate level of protection and not be subject to unnecessary restrictions or unusual conditions in different countries. This need is met by international norms, which are contained, in the first place, in various treaties administered by WIPO, such as the Paris Convention for the Protection of Industrial Property and the Berne Convention for the Protection of Literary and Artistic Works, and, secondly, by the TRIPS Agreement, which adopts most of the norms established in the WIPO-administered treaties and supplements and extends them so as to provide a comprehensive international code on the protection of intellectual property.

Intellectual property is, however, by definition concerned with the latest and most sophisticated technological advances. It is hardly to be expected, therefore, that even the comprehensive nature of the TRIPS Agreement will be adequate to deal with needs for international norms in the field of intellectual property that may be produced by the future evolution of the technological basis of the economy. International norm-making in an age in which intellectual capital assumes increasing importance in the generation of wealth promises to be, however, a far more complex exercise than it has been in the past. There are a number of currents that cross, and may increasingly be expected to cross, the trajectory of the demand for new international norms. These include tension with competing areas of public policy; the need for swift response posed by new technological developments and the ability of the multilateral process to accommodate such swift response; the definition of the extent to which protection can go and the balancing of that extent with the need for the diffusion of the benefits of intellectual capital; the definition of the needs, and of the means of satisfying the needs of developing economies; machinery for the resolution of disputes; and the coordination of increasingly complex institutional architecture.

Notes and Questions

1. We will observe in the following article dealing with the background of the GATT Uruguay Round negotiations that IPRs regulation was brought within the WTO framework largely because of perceived weaknesses in the WIPO administered international IPRs system. One of the fascinating results of the TRIPS negotiations is the emergence and strengthening of WIPO as a major international institution — a development that may seem almost paradoxical. The attention that has been focused on WIPO might be grounded in a variety of factors:

a. WIPO is a specialized agency with expertise in IPRs, which the WTO is not, and there is a compelling need for an expert institution in which to develop new IPRs rules.

b. The WTO is a relatively slow moving organization in which major developments are usually accommodated in the process known as "rounds," and WIPO is capable of moving more quickly. This is particularly important in view of the dynamic pace at which the need for improvements to IPRs occur.

c. The role of WIPO in providing mechanisms for securing protection on a worldwide basis, in particular through the Patent Cooperation Treaty system, has become increasingly important and promises to become even more-so.

d. WIPO can provide technical assistance to developing and developed countries. This function is necessary to create infrastructures that should facilitate transfers of technology, to aid in achieving compliance with the TRIPS Agreement, and to assist in transforming the IPRs legal frameworks of former command economy countries.

2. WIPO is a specialized agency of the United Nations. Its relationship with the UN is defined by agreement. The United Nations Charter establishes goals for the UN that are considerably more far reaching than the goals of the WTO. The WTO is mainly concerned with promoting worldwide economic growth and employment in accordance with the principle of sustainable development. The broader goals of the UN include maintaining peace and security, and promoting human rights and social progress for all peoples. Should this difference in the overarching goals of the UN and WTO be reflected in different policy approaches to international IPRs regulation in WIPO and the WTO?

3. It is essential to note that both WIPO and the WTO are governed by decisions of their member countries, and that the secretariats of each organization act under the direction of these members. Popular press reporting may sometimes convey the impression that there is a substantial independent policy formulation function within WIPO and the WTO. These reports may not adequately convey the extent to which the member countries exercise and guard their authority. Within the governments of WIPO member countries, different ministries and departments may be responsible for policy formulation regarding WIPO and the WTO, and indeed for other international organizations such as UNEP and UNDP. Is this division of policy-making authority likely to cause domestic tensions? How is IPRs policy coordination arranged within your government? How would you suggest that it be arranged?

4. Upon the proposal of the United States, WIPO members decided to commit substantial additional resources to the creation of a dedicated worldwide intellectual property network that will link the industrial property offices of the world and ultimately, provide a means for the online registration of IPRs in countries around the world. The creation of such a

system might appear as the logical outgrowth of the TRIPS Agreement negotiations which sought to establish greater worldwide legal security for OECD country companies investing in research and development (R & D) and undertaking other creative activity. If such a system were effective in significantly strengthening IPRs protection in the developing countries, this might also have important implications for the diffusion of technology, rent transfer and other matters we explored in Chapter I.

5. Francis Gurry points to the increasingly complex institutional architecture for the regulation of IPRs, and to the necessity for coordinating this system. How might you recommend going about this coordination? This question is addressed later in this Chapter in an article by Abbott that suggests the idea of a joint WIPO/WTO IPRs Council.

6. As you read through the next section on the WTO, try to formulate and clarify the reasons why the central forum for IPRs policy making in certain core areas has moved from WIPO to the WTO. Consider further whether and why you believe this move is a positive one.

2. The World Trade Organization

a. What is the World Trade Organization?
WTO Secretariat*

The World Trade Organization (WTO) is the only international body dealing with the rules of trade between nations. At its heart are the WTO agreements, negotiated and signed by the bulk of the world's trading nations. These documents provide the legal ground-rules for international commerce. They are essentially contracts, binding governments to keep their trade policies within agreed limits. Although negotiated and signed by governments, the goal is to help producers of goods and services, exporters, and importers conduct their business.

---

*http://www.wto.org.

Three main purposes

The system's overriding purpose is to help trade flow as freely as possible — so long as there are no undesirable side-effects. That partly means removing obstacles. It also means ensuring that individuals, companies and governments know what the trade rules are around the world, and giving them the confidence that there will be no sudden changes of policy. In other words, the rules have to be "transparent" and predictable.

Because the agreements are drafted and signed by the community of trading nations, often after considerable debate and controversy, one of the WTO's most important functions is to serve as a forum for trade negotiations.

A third important side to the WTO's work is dispute settlement. Trade relations often involve conflicting interests. Contracts and agreements, including those painstakingly negotiated in the WTO system, often need interpreting. The most harmonious way to settle these differences is through some neutral procedure based on an agreed legal foundation. That is the purpose behind the dispute settlement process written into the WTO agreements.

Two years old, but not so young

The WTO began life on 1 January 1995, but its trading system is half a century older. Since 1948, the General Agreement on Tariffs and Trade (GATT) had provided the rules for the system. Before long it gave birth to an unofficial, de facto international organization, also known informally as GATT, and over the years GATT evolved through several rounds of negotiations.

The latest and largest round, was the Uruguay Round which lasted from 1986 to 1994 and led to the WTO's creation. Whereas GATT had mainly dealt with trade in goods, the WTO and its agreements now cover trade in services, and in traded inventions, creations and designs (intellectual property).

Principles of the trading system

The WTO agreements are lengthy and complex because they are legal texts covering a wide range of activities. They deal with: agriculture, textiles and clothing, banking, telecommunications, government purchases, industrial standards, food sanitation regulations, intellectual property, and much more. But a number of simple, fundamental principles run throughout all of these documents. These principles are the foundation of the multilateral trading system.

The principles

The trading system should be . . .

without discrimination — a country should not discriminate between its trading partners (they are all, equally, granted "most-favoured-nation" or MFN status); and it should not discriminate between its own and foreign products, services or nationals (they are given "national treatment").

freer — with barriers coming down through negotiation

predictable — foreign companies, investors and governments should be confident that trade barriers (including tariffs, non-tariff barriers and other measures) should not be raised arbitrarily; more and more tariff rates and market-opening commitments are "bound" in the WTO.

more competitive — by discouraging "unfair" practices such as export subsidies and dumping products at below cost to gain market share.

more beneficial for less developed countries — by giving them more time to adjust, greater flexibility, and special privileges.

A closer look at these principles: Trade without discrimination

1. Most-favoured-nation (MFN): treating other people equally

Under the WTO Agreements, countries cannot normally discriminate between their trading partners. Grant someone a special favour (such as a lower customs duty rate for one of their products) and you have to do the same for all other WTO members.

This principle is known as most-favoured-nation (MFN) treatment. It is so important that it is the first article of the General Agreement on Tariffs and Trade (GATT), which governs trade in goods. MFN is also a priority in the General Agreement on Trade in Services (GATS) Article 2) and the Agreement on Trade-Related Aspects of Intellectual Property Rights

(TRIPS) (Article 4), although in each agreement the principle is handled slightly differently. Together, those three agreements cover all three main areas of trade handled by the WTO.

Some exceptions are allowed. For example, countries within a region can set up a free trade agreement that does not apply to goods from outside the group. Or a country can raise barriers against products from specific countries that are considered to be traded unfairly. And in services, countries are allowed, in limited circumstances, to discriminate. But the agreements only permit these exceptions under strict conditions. In general, MFN means that every time a country lowers a trade barrier or opens up a market, it has to do so for the same goods or services from all its trading partners — whether rich or poor, weak or strong.

2. National treatment: treating foreigners and locals equally

Imported and locally-produced goods should be treated equally — at least after the foreign goods have entered the market. The same should apply to foreign and domestic services, and to foreign and local trademarks, copyrights and patents. This principle of "national treatment" (giving others the same treatment as one's own nationals) is also found in all the three main WTO agreements (Article 3 of GATT, Article 17 of GATS and Article 3 of TRIPS), although once again the principle is handled slightly differently in each of these.

National treatment only applies once a product, service or item of intellectual property has entered the market. Therefore, charging customs duty on an import is not a violation of national treatment even if locally-produced products are not charged an equivalent tax.

Freer trade: gradually, through negotiation

Lowering trade barriers is one of the most obvious means of encouraging trade. The barriers concerned include customs duties (or tariffs) and measures such as import bans or quotas that restrict quantities selectively. From time to time other issues such as red tape and exchange rate policies have also been discussed.

Since GATT's creation in 1947-48 there have been eight rounds of trade negotiations. At first these focused on lowering tariffs (customs duties) on imported goods. As a result of the negotiations, by the late 1980s industrial countries' tariff rates on industrial goods had fallen steadily to about 6.3%.

317

But by the 1980s, the negotiations had expanded to cover non-tariff barriers on goods, and to the new areas such as services and intellectual property.

Opening markets can be beneficial, but it also requires adjustment. The WTO agreements allow countries to introduce changes gradually, through "progressive liberalization". Developing countries are usually given longer to fulfil their obligations.

Predictability: through binding

Sometimes, promising not to raise a trade barrier can be as important as lowering one, because the promise gives businesses a clearer view of their future opportunities. With stability and predictability, investment is encouraged, jobs are created and consumers can fully enjoy the benefits of competition — choice and lower prices. The multilateral trading system is an attempt by governments to make the business environment stable and predictable.

In the WTO, when countries agree to open their markets for goods or services, they "bind" their commitments. For goods, these bindings amount to ceilings on customs tariff rates. Sometimes countries tax imports at rates that are lower than the bound rates. Frequently this is the case in developing countries. In developed countries the rates actually charged and the bound rates tend to be the same.

A country can change its bindings, but only after negotiating with its trading partners, which could mean compensating them for loss of trade. One of the achievements of the Uruguay Round of multilateral trade talks was to increase the amount of trade under binding commitments. In agriculture, 100% of products now have bound tariffs. The result of all this: a substantially higher degree of market security for traders and investors.

The system tries to improve predictability and stability in other ways as well. One way is to discourage the use of quotas and other measures used to set limits on quantities of imports — administering quotas can lead to more red-tape and accusations of unfair play. Another is to make countries' trade rules as clear and public ("transparent") as possible. Many WTO agreements require governments to disclose their policies and practices publicly within the country or by notifying the WTO. The regular surveillance of national trade policies through the Trade Policy Review Mechanism provides a further means of encouraging transparency both domestically and at the multilateral level.

318

Promoting fair competition

The WTO is sometimes described as a "free trade" institution, but that is not entirely accurate. The system does allow tariffs and, in limited circumstances, other forms of protection. More accurately, it is a system of rules dedicated to open, fair and undistorted competition.

The rules on non-discrimination — MFN and national treatment — are designed to secure fair conditions of trade. So too are those on dumping (exporting at below cost to gain market share) and subsidies. The issues are complex, and the rules try to establish what is fair or unfair, and how governments can respond, in particular by charging additional import duties calculated to compensate for damage caused by unfair trade.

Many of the other WTO agreements aim to support fair competition: in agriculture, intellectual property, services, for example. The agreement on government procurement (a "plurilateral" agreement because it is signed by only a few WTO members) extends competition rules to purchases by thousands of "government" entities in many countries. And so on.

Encouraging development and economic reform

It is widely recognized by economists and trade experts that the WTO system contributes to development. It is also recognized that the least-developed countries need flexibility in the time they take to implement the agreements. And the agreements themselves inherit the earlier provisions of GATT that allow for special assistance and trade concessions for developing countries.

Over three-quarters of WTO members are developing countries and countries in transition to market economies. During the seven and a half years of the Uruguay Round, over 60 of these countries implemented trade liberalization programmes autonomously. At the same time, developing countries and transition economies were much more active and influential in the Uruguay Round negotiations than in any previous round.

This trend effectively killed the notion that the trading system existed only for industrialized countries. It also changed the previous emphasis on exempting developing countries from certain GATT provisions and agreements.

At the end of the Uruguay Round, developing countries were prepared to take on most of the obligations that are required of developed countries. But the agreements did give them transition periods to adjust to the more unfamiliar and, perhaps, difficult WTO provisions — particularly so for the poorest, "least-developed" countries. A ministerial decision adopted at the end of the round gives least developed countries extra flexibility in implementing WTO agreements. It says better-off countries should accelerate implementing market access commitments on goods exported by the least-developed countries, and it seeks increased technical assistance for them.

b. The World Trade Organization Framework

The International Trade Law Committee (ITLC) of the International Law Association (ILA) is composed of trade law experts from around the world. The ITLC was founded in 1992, and in 1994 it issued its First Report in connection with the ILA Biennial Conference in Buenos Aires. In the following excerpt from the First Report, the ITLC summarizes the accomplishments of the GATT Uruguay Round, looking forward to the entry into force of the WTO Agreement on January 1, 1995. As the First Report stresses, one of the most significant accomplishments of the Uruguay Round was to create a "single undertaking" international organization the general rules of which would be applicable to all Members.

Committee on International Trade Law
First Report of the Committee*
Prof. Thomas Oppermann, Chair
Profs. E.-U. Petersmann and F. M. Abbott, Rapporteurs

*****

II. *The 1994 Agreement Establishing the World Trade Organization (WTO)*

2. The successful conclusion of the Uruguay Round negotiations on 15 April 1994, and the entry into force — on 1 January 1994 — of the world's two largest free trade area agreements: the European Economic Area (EEA)

---

*International Law Association, Buenos Aires Conference, 14-20 August 1994.

between the EC and 5 EFTA countries and the North American Free Trade Area (NAFTA) between Canada, Mexico and the USA, reflect a new generation of international economic law. Fifty years after the Bretton Woods Conference, the signing of the WTO Agreement on 15 April 1994 at the Ministerial Conference at Marrakesh completes the legal structure of the Bretton Woods system based on the IMF, the World Bank and the new WTO, and lays the legal foundation for a new world trading system for the 21st century. Like the GATT, the IMF and other international organizations, the WTO will serve essentially three different functions:

A. *The WTO Agreement as a new legal Code of Conduct for World Trade*

3. As a framework agreement and code of conduct, the WTO Agreement sets out the basic rights and duties for the policies of its member countries and lays down a new legal basis for international movements of goods, services, persons, trade-related investments and intellectual property rights. The most radical innovation of the WTO Agreement is its "single agreement approach" which aims "to develop an integrated, more viable and durable multilateral trading system encompassing the General Agreement on Tariffs and Trade, the results of past trade liberalization efforts, and all the results of the Uruguay Round of multilateral trade negotiations" (Preamble) including the General Agreement on Trade in Services and the Agreement on Trade-Related Intellectual Property Rights. The WTO Agreement integrates the about 30 Uruguay Round Agreements and 200 previous GATT Agreements into one single legal framework. The new "GATT 1994" in Annex 1A of the WTO Agreement is "legally distinct" from the old "GATT 1947", as subsequently amended (Article II:4). The requirement that acceptance of the WTO Agreement "shall apply to this Agreement and the Multilateral Trade Agreements annexed thereto" (Article XIV: 1), and the additional requirement that all WTO members must accept a "GATT Schedule of Concessions" as well as a "GATS Schedule of Specific Services Commitments" (cf. Article XI:1), were designed to remedy four major deficiencies of the current world trading system based on GATT law:

a) The *fragmented nature of the current "GATT a la carte"*, where only a minority of the 122 GATT member countries have also accepted the rights and obligations under the various Tokyo Round Agreements, will be replaced by a "single agreement approach" requiring full membership of all WTO member countries in all "multilateral trade agreements" listed in Annexes 1-3 of the WTO Agreement. The uniformity of the new "WTO legal system" will be strengthened by the "integrated dispute settlement system" (Annex 2) and "trade policy review mechanism" (Annex 3) which are applicable to all "multilateral trade agreements". Only the four "plurilateral trade agreements" (on trade in civil aircraft, government procurement, dairy products and bovine meat) listed in Annex 4 have a limited membership, even though they are "part of this (WTO) Agreement for those Members that have accepted them" (Article XI:3 WTO Agreement).

b) The *frequent GATT practice of "free-riding"*, under which many less-developed GATT contracting parties had never undertaken substantial tariff liberalization commitments, will be limited by the requirement that all WTO member countries must undertake both a "GATT Schedule of Concessions" as well as a "GATS Schedule of Specific Services Commitments". During the Uruguay Round of multilateral trade negotiations in GATT (1986-1994), many developing countries played a very active role and engaged in far-reaching programmes of trade liberalization and deregulation. The "single undertaking approach", requiring acceptance of essentially all Uruguay Round results by all WTO member countries (cf. Articles XI, XII and XIV of the WTO Agreement), is expected to promote more liberty, more rule of law and more welfare through more trade, investments and a larger international division of labour and income growth in all countries.

c) The *still limited GATT membership* is, at least in the long run, likely to become more universal once WTO member countries withdraw from the old "GATT 1947" and thereby set strong incentives for WTO membership as the only means to secure legal access to the important world markets. The fact that 25 countries have joined the GATT since the beginning of the Uruguay Round, and that an additional 19 countries were negotiating their accession to GATT in early 1994, illustrates that most countries correctly perceive their national interest in increasing their national welfare through trade and through membership in GATT and in the WTO.

d) Unlike the *flimsy legal basis of the "GATT 1947"* which never entered into force and was applied on the basis of a "Protocol of Provisional Application" subject to a "grandfather clause" that exempted GATT-inconsistent mandatory "existing legislation", the WTO Agreement is expected to enter into force in 1995 on a definitive basis without any "provisional application clause" and general "grandfather clause" similar to the GATT Protocol of Provisional Application.

4. Apart from the above-mentioned "systemic changes", the basic principles and "code of conduct" of the "GATT 1994" remain essentially the same as those of the "GATT 1947", as amended. According to Article II of the WTO Agreement, the "Multilateral Trade Agreements" listed in Annexes 1, 2 and 3 are "integral parts of this Agreement, binding on all Members". They include:

a) The *"Agreements on Trade in Goods"* listed in Annex 1A. They include the "GATT 1994" and 6 Uruguay Round Understandings on the interpretation of various GATT Articles (II, XII, XVII, XVIII, XXIV, XXV, XXVIII); the Uruguay Round Protocol of Concessions to the GATT 1994; and 12 additional multilateral Agreements on Agriculture, Sanitary and Phytosanitary Measures, Textiles and Clothing, Technical Barriers to Trade, Trade-Related Investment Measures (TRIMS), Customs Valuation, Antidumping Measures, Preshipment Inspection, Rules of Origin, Import Licensing Procedures, Subsidies and Countervailing Measures, and on Safeguards. The gist of these Understandings and Agreements is to give further precision to and strengthen the existing general GATT rules, especially with regard to agricultural, textiles and "grey area" trade restrictions which have escaped effective GATT legal disciplines for a long time.

b) The *General Agreement on Trade in Services* (GATS) which provides for a new set of multilateral rules for the fastest-growing sector of world trade and creates a framework for a continuous process of liberalization of services trade. The GATS rests on three pillars:

— *First*, a framework agreement applicable to all WTO Member countries and to any service in any sector, except services supplied in the exercise of governmental authority neither on a commercial basis nor in competition with other service suppliers. Some of the basic provisions — for instance on most-favoured-nation treatment, transparency, admissibility of preferential integration agreements, domestic regulation, judicial review, monopolies, restrictions to safeguard the balance of payments, general exceptions and security exceptions, dispute settlement and enforcement — are modelled on the corresponding principles of GATT law.

— *Second*, the national Schedules of "market access commitments", "national treatment commitments" and other "additional commitments", as well as the national lists of temporary most-favoured-nation exemptions. Unlike international trade in goods. international services trade is often regulated primarily by domestic regulations rather than by border measures. This is due to the fact that many international services are traded not through the supply of services from one country to the territory of another, but within the territory of one country to the consumers of another country (e.g. tourism) or through the presence of foreign natural service suppliers (e.g. foreign construction workers, consultants) or foreign service providing entities abroad (e.g. supply of banking services through foreign banks or subsidiaries). This frequent interrelationship between international movements of services, persons and capital makes the international regulation and liberalization of services trade much more complex compared to trade in goods. The GATS therefore provides not only for "market access commitments" (e.g. to eliminate limitations on the number of service providers and service operations) and "national treatment commitments" but also for other "additional commitments, including "those regarding qualifications, standards or licensing matters" (Article XVIII). Article XIX GATS provides for "successive rounds of negotiations" on the progressive liberalization of international trade in services.

— *Third*, a number of Annexes addressing the special situations of individual services sectors such as financial services, telecommunications, air transport services. maritime transport services and movement of natural persons supplying services. For instance, the "Annex on Financial Services" (such as banking and insurance) lays down the right of parties to take prudential measures, including for the protection of investors, deposit holders and policy holders, and to ensure the integrity and stability of the financial system. The Annex on Telecommunications requires, *inter alia*, that access to and use of public telecommunications services and networks be accorded to another party, on reasonable and nondiscriminatory terms, to permit the supply of a service included in its Schedule. The Annex on Air Transport Services excludes from the agreement's coverage "traffic rights, however granted" (largely bilateral air service agreements conferring landing rights) and "services directly related to the exercise of traffic rights", except for aircraft repair and maintenance services, the selling and marketing of air transport services, and computer reservation system services.

Even though the GATS presents only a first step on the long way towards liberalization of trade in services and leaves many questions open (such as the need for competition rules and the controversies about a "cultural exception"), its worldwide legal political and economic significance may turn out to be similar to that of the GATT itself.

c) *The Agreement on Trade-Related Aspects of Intellectual Property Rights (TRIPS)* in Annex 1C of the WTO Agreement provides for "adequate standards and principles concerning the availability, scope and use of trade-related intellectual property rights," "effective and appropriate means for the enforcement of trade-related intellectual property rights, and "effective and expeditious procedures for the multilateral prevention and settlement of disputes between governments" (Preamble). The legal principles underlying the TRIPS Agreement are in part based on those of GATT law (e.g. the national treatment and most-favoured-nation treatment requirements in Articles 3 and 4). But the explicit recognition "that intellectual property rights are private rights" (Preamble), the legal requirement of compliance with existing intellectual property conventions (Article 2), the various competition rules on prevention of abuses of intellectual property rights by right-holders (e.g. Articles 8, 40), and the relatively high minimum standards for the protection and enforcement of copyrights and related rights, trademarks, geographical indications, industrial designs, patents, layout-designs and undisclosed information also illustrate that the TRIPS Agreement introduces many new legal principles into the multilateral trading system based on GATT. The formal linkage between multilateral trade rules and relevant intellectual property agreements may serve as a model for similar future agreements, for instance on "trade-related environmental measures" and "trade-related anticompetitive practices".

d) The integrated *Understanding on Rules and Procedures Governing the Settlement of Disputes* (Annex 2) as well as the *Trade Policy Review Mechanism* (Annex 3), which are applicable to all multilateral trade agreements . . .

Notes and Questions

1. The WTO is an "organic" institution. It has evolved from a bare bones agreement applicable to trade in goods and largely designed to reduce tariff barriers, to a detailed and complex legal and institutional arrangement also covering services and IPRs. There are critics of the WTO who claim that it deprives national and local governments of their "sovereign" right to regulate as they see fit. Why do governments adhere to international agreements that limit their flexibility to act? Is it out of a charitable impulse, or is there a self-interest in this behavior? The United States, which many countries perceive as the dominant force in the WTO, may also be home to the most vocal critics of the WTO on "sovereignty" grounds. What might account for the seeming paradox that the country which most often sees its demands met, also may be the most sensitive to being deprived of its freedom to act?

c. The WTO TRIPS Agreement

i. Pre-TRIPS Agreement Protection of IPRs

Excerpts from articles by Frederick Abbott and Thomas Cottier in Chapter I considered the underlying forces that gave rise to negotiation of the TRIPS Agreement in the GATT Uruguay Round. In the following excerpt from the Abbott article, we examine the structure for the protection of IPRs that existed prior to conclusion of the Uruguay Round, why that structure was considered inadequate, and what obstacles stood in the way of incorporating IPRs protection within the GATT framework.

We do this not only to provide historical background, but because the GATT — now the WTO — is an organic institution. Its Members are entitled to assert rights based on what their legitimate or reasonable expectations were upon entering into the WTO Agreement (an important aspect of the Agreement that we will explore in Chapter III). A Member's reasonable expectations may in part be reflected in what went on at the negotiating table.

As we explore various substantive rules of the TRIPS Agreement in later chapters, we will return to the article by Thomas Cottier for insights into the negotiation of specific substantive rules of the Agreement.

Protecting First World Assets in the Third World: Intellectual Property Negotiations in the GATT Multilateral Framework

Frederick M. Abbott*

*****

III. The Current System for the International Protection of Intellectual Property and its Shortcomings

A. The Treaty System

The current international system for the protection of intellectual property consists of a variety of treaties administered by international organizations (primarily the World Intellectual Property Organization, or WIPO), which essentially coordinate nation-state legal regimes that are relied upon to provide both substantive norms and enforcement procedures. The principal international treaty for the protection of patents, trademarks, and industrial designs is the Paris Convention for the Protection of Industrial Property (Paris Convention), which was concluded in 1883, was last revised in 1967, and has ninety-eight Member States.** WIPO administers the Paris Convention. The principal features of the Paris Convention are the obligation of states to extend national treatment to residents of other states and a right of priority to applicants of foreign Member States for their patent, trademark, and design filings. The Paris Convention permits

---

*22 VAND. J. TRANSNAT'L L. 689 (1989).
**Authors' note: there has been a substantial increase in the number of countries adhering to the Paris and Berne Conventions since this article was published in 1989.

Member States to take legislative measures providing for the grant of compulsory licenses for patents in, for example, cases of non-work.

Proponents of enhanced intellectual property protection criticize the Paris Convention with respect to patents because: (1) it does not adequately address the subject matter of technologies; (2) it does not set a minimum patent term; (3) it does not expressly provide for payment of full compensation for compulsory licenses; (4) it is too permissive with respect to the granting of compulsory licenses; and (5) though providing for recourse to the International Court of Justice in disputes between Member States, the Convention does not establish standards for national enforcement and cannot, in any event, be considered to provide a meaningful dispute settlement mechanism. Critics express similar concerns over the lack of substantive standards and enforcement mechanisms for trademarks.

The most important international treaty for protecting copyright is the Berne Convention for the Protection of Literary and Artistic Works (Berne Convention). The Berne Convention is administered by WIPO. Major features of the Berne Convention, to which over seventy-five states are parties, are the extension of national treatment to foreign authors; the recognition of a minimum copyright term (generally the life of the author plus fifty years); the establishment of "moral rights" of authors (e.g., granting the right to authors to protect the integrity of artistic works after transfer of their economic interests); and the requirement of a lack of formalities for obtaining copyright protection. Like the Paris Convention, the Berne Convention provides for the submission of disputes over its interpretation or application to the International Court of Justice. On October 20, 1988, the United States Senate approved accession to the Berne Convention, partly in an effort to allay international doubt as to the United States commitment to protect intellectual property.

The Berne Convention is primarily criticized for its lack of an effective dispute settlement mechanism. The attitude of the United States copyright industries toward this treaty has been summarized as follows:

> The protection offered by these rules, however, cannot cure many of the intellectual property problems faced today by America's creative industries. First, national treatment becomes meaningless when the national laws of developing countries are inadequate, or not enforced. Second, the limited number of signatories and the Conventions' [referring also

to the Universal Copyright Convention] lack of application to non-member countries also diminish their effectiveness. Finally, the lack of mechanisms for consultations, for dispute settlement or for remedying violations limits their usefulness.

In addition to its failure to provide adequate substantive norms and dispute settlement procedures, the current treaty system is criticized for its lack of attention to certain important subject matter areas. No international treaty exists regarding the protection of trade secrets (although most countries would appear to grant some form of local protection). There is sufficient doubt as to the protection afforded to semiconductor layout under existing copyright law that a significant number of countries, including the United States and Japan, have adopted sui generis legislation covering the protection of such designs. The Council of the European Communities adopted a 1986 directive obliging all European Communities Member States to adopt such laws.

On May 26, 1989, a diplomatic conference in Washington, D.C., adopted a Treaty on Intellectual Property in Respect of Integrated Circuits, to be administered by WIPO. The United States and Japan, however, opposed the treaty. Included in the provisions apparently objectionable to the United States are: (1) a minimum duration of protection of eight years; (2) liberal rules with respect to compulsory licensing; (3) a dispute settlement procedure that is too "politicized" (in the words of a United States official) and that, unlike the GATT dispute settlement procedure, would not permit the imposition of meaningful sanctions; and (4) the absence of compensation for innocent infringement following notice.

B. National Systems

The international treaty system, while providing minimum substantive standards in a few intellectual property rights areas, does not presently operate as an effective substantive rule-making system, nor does it meaningfully address domestic enforcement procedures. These matters are presently reserved to the internal legal systems of individual states, and as such substantial disparities prevail in substantive rules, enforcement procedures, and enforcement practices. The scope of the basic substantive differences is apparent from a review of the WIPO Report to the GATT working group on trade-related aspects of intellectual property (TRIPS), which provides a comprehensive, although general, current survey of the intellectual property laws in force throughout the world (both in GATT and non-GATT countries).

In a 1989 Foreign Trade Barriers Report (FTB Report), the USTR's [United States Trade Representative's] office identified the most serious existing defects (from the standpoint of United States Government) in important foreign intellectual property legal regimes. The findings in the FTB Report were consistent with those in the earlier ITC Report, but were set out in terms of substantive law and enforcement deficiencies rather than as quantifications of losses. . . . Taken together, the ITC [International Trade Commission] and FTB Reports highlight in a significant number of developing countries and NICs [newly-industrialized countries] a lack of patent subject matter coverage for chemicals and pharmaceuticals, short patent terms and overly permissive compulsory patent licensing, and inadequate copyright legislation and enforcement with respect to the audio, video, and software sectors.

C. The United States Bilateral Approach

While pronouncing GATT-based multilateral negotiations its preferred strategy for resolving trade problems, the United States Government has undertaken an intense program of direct bilateral negotiations, coupled with the threat and use of unilateral economic sanctions, to attempt to improve foreign protection for United States intellectual property rights owners. Although existing unfair foreign trading practices legislation already addressed inadequate protection of intellectual property rights and was used in several intellectual property disputes, Congress heightened the priority of the intellectual property issue in the enactment of the Omnibus Trade and Competitiveness Act of 1988 (1988 Trade Act) by outlining an explicit program of executive action. Congressional action took the form of amendments to foreign unfair trading practices legislation (originally enacted as section 301 of the Trade Act of 1974). These amendments, which generally give the appearance of limiting executive discretion with respect to trade barriers investigations and remedies, require the USTR to (1) identify countries that deny adequate and effective protection of intellectual property rights; (2) identify "priority" countries that are the most egregious intellectual property rights transgressors and that do not undertake or make progress in negotiations with the USTR; and (3) initiate accelerated section 301 investigations with regard to the practices of the identified priority countries (which may lead to the taking of remedial action). On May 25, 1989, the Office of the USTR, using these newly-christened "Special 301" provisions of the 1988 Trade Act, placed seventeen countries on an intellectual property "Watch List" and eight countries on a "Priority Watch List." The USTR did not identify any "priority" countries, because, while the eight Priority Watch List countries met some or all of the statutory criteria for Priority country identification, they had made progress in recent bilateral or multilateral negotiations and therefore fell (at least temporarily) within a statutory exemptions. The USTR indicated her intention to review the Priority Watch List no later than November 1, 1989, to consider progress under an accelerated action plan for pursuing negotiations with each country named. The USTR press release accompanying the Watch List and Priority Watch List identifications stated:

— As a result of this extensive review, the USTR concluded that no foreign country currently meets every standard for adequate and effective intellectual property protection as set forth in the U.S. proposal on intellectual property tabled in the Uruguay Round.
— Thus the USTR has determined that all countries are eligible for potential priority designation based on the standards of the U.S. Uruguay Round proposal, because all countries "deny adequate and effective protection of intellectual property rights" within the meaning of the statute.

D. The Brazilian Pharmaceutical Patent Dispute

At the end of 1988, the USTR, acting on a complaint from the Pharmaceutical Manufacturers Association (PMA), imposed approximately $40 million in ad valorem tariffs on a variety of Brazilian imports as a consequence of Brazil's continuing refusal to extend product and process patent coverage to pharmaceuticals. Brazil has contended that its patent policies are fully consistent with its international legal obligations, both under the international intellectual property treaty system and the GATT. The intellectual property treaty system does not mandate specific subject matter (e.g., pharmaceutical product or process) coverage, and Brazil's patent laws do not discriminate against foreign imports. Brazil lodged a complaint with the GATT, charging that the retaliatory and discriminatory United States tariffs violate the latter's obligations under the General Agreement (including respect for the Most Favored Nation principle). After initial objection by the United States, a GATT panel formed to decide the dispute. According to a senior GATT official, Brazil's position has received the "most massive support we have ever seen in a panel dispute," accompanied by a complete absence of support for the United States position.

United States actions under section 301 are evidence of a government and industry resolve to halt an unintended transfer of wealth from the United States. No doubt exists, however, that this program meets a high degree of foreign resistance, risks significant damage to United States foreign policy interests, and is terribly inefficient. Moreover, gains achieved by United States negotiators are passed on at no cost to its major trade competitors in the European Communities and Japan, thus strengthening the argument for a multilateral approach.

IV. The GATT as an Intellectual Property Forum

A. The Intellectual Property Mandate

As observed at the outset of this Article, the General Agreement is virtually silent on intellectual property matters. The first effort by the United States to heighten GATT sensitivity to intellectual property protection was a proposal for an anti-counterfeiting code made during the GATT Tokyo Round negotiations in the late 1970s. The developing countries did not actively participate in these code negotiations, a final text was not agreed upon, and formal GATT action on the proposed code did not take place. As plans for the next round of GATT negotiations were laid, United States (and European Communities) objectives for GATT involvement in intellectual property matters expanded. The United States Congress, in the Trade and Tariff Act of 1984, emphasized the importance it attached to negotiations on intellectual property protection. Following highly contentious negotiations during much of 1985 and 1986, the United States, with support from the European Communities and other OECD countries, persuaded the full GATT membership to include in the September 20, 1986, Uruguay Round Ministerial Declaration a mandate for negotiations on trade-related aspects of intellectual property rights. The mandate provided:

> In order to reduce the distortions and impediments to international trade, and taking into account the need to promote effective and ade-

quate protection of intellectual property rights, and to ensure that measures and procedures to enforce intellectual property rights do not themselves become barriers to legitimate trade, the negotiations shall aim to clarify GATT provisions and elaborate as appropriate new rules and disciplines.

This new mandate was controversial because both before and after its adoption, a significant number of developing countries insisted that the GATT should not and does not contemplate the negotiation of substantive intellectual property standards. According to developing countries such as Brazil and India, WIPO is the appropriate forum for the negotiation of intellectual property standards. As a result of the Uruguay Round mandate, a GATT working group on TRIPS was established. Not until April 1989 did the developing countries agree to let negotiations on substantive standards proceed, reserving the issue of the GATT's competence to promulgate new rules.

*****

V. Intellectual Property within the GATT Framework

As discussed at the outset of this Article, two major issues must be addressed in the process of incorporating intellectual property rights protection into the GATT framework. The first issue, which was expressly reserved in the Uruguay Round Ministerial Declaration and in the Framework Agreement, concerns the choice of an institutional arrangement or mechanism for incorporating intellectual property protection within the GATT. The second issue concerns the extent of the industrialized countries' duty to adhere to the GATT principle of reciprocity in the intellectual property negotiations.

A. The Institutional Arrangement

1. Matching Solutions to Problems

The institutional mechanism chosen to resolve the intellectual property problem must match the particular problem posed. Although attempting to characterize broadly the trade problems facing the GATT may be somewhat imprecise, the problems might usefully be separated into those of more and less inclusive dimension. Thus, for example, the excessive tariff structures in place at the end of the Second World War were of global dimension and required an inclusive solution if a liberal worldwide trading order — based on extensive most favored nation treatment — was to be established. On the other hand, the present existence of barriers to trade in services may significantly impair aggregate trade with respect to the more highly industrialized countries as a group, such that a non-inclusive (i.e., exclusive) remedy among a limited number of countries would have a high degree of present economic utility, so as to justify only limited participation, at least in the short term.

The intellectual property problem, while, in fact, distinct from most problems previously addressed by the GATT in that its cause lies within the developing countries and NICs, with adverse consequences affecting primarily the industrialized countries, must be categorized as an inclusive or global problem in that the remedy must apply outside those countries that have historically been parties to the exclusive GATT agreements referred to as codes. New intellectual property norms must be effective in and regulate the conduct of the developing countries. The parties must therefore negotiate an inclusive remedy in some form of a generalized GATT amendment . . . .

*****

2. The Exclusive Approach and its Unsuitability for Intellectual Property

One of the two GATT amendment mechanisms that came into use at the conclusion of the Tokyo Round in 1979 was the adoption by a limited group of countries of separate GATT agreements or codes. The need for the code mechanism became apparent as the Tokyo Round progressed and it was clear that many of the projects undertaken in the round were of interest only to a limited number of the GATT Contracting Parties, primarily the OECD countries. Codes are simply agreements between GATT Contracting Parties that choose to adopt them and are not applicable to countries that do not adopt them. Thus, the Anti-dumping, Subsidies, Government Procurement, and Technical Standards Codes are each adopted by about thirty-five of the more than ninety GATT Contracting Parties, establishing norms among an exclusive group — primarily the OECD.

In its intellectual property proposal, the United States expressed a preference for a code and noted that it would apply only among signatories. The United States relied on a vague generalization — the creation of a "discipline" — and more concretely on the establishment of a mechanism for multilateral dispute settlement to demonstrate the potential utility of a code. Neither of these claims of utility is strong enough to support a code approach to the intellectual property problem. Although at some level a less than fully consensual intellectual property agreement may have a persuasive effect on non-participants, a code whose participants largely represent the OECD countries would have very little persuasive effect because: (1) the goal of the code is not to harmonize intellectual property laws; and (2) the rules in the OECD countries already are largely the same. A "discipline" therefore already exists. Similarly, establishment of a multilateral dispute settlement mechanism among the OECD countries is not a satisfactory objective of the Uruguay Round. While something arguably can be gained by bringing intellectual property disputes between the United States, Canada, and Japan, for example, into the GATT, this objective can hardly be worth six years of intensive and potentially counterproductive negotiations. A GATT solution that includes the developing countries and NICs is essential.

The hidden agenda of the United States may be to make its current policy of pressuring developing countries and NICs into reforming their intellectual property regimes at least quasi-"GATT-legal." At present, no convincing justification exists within the GATT or the international treaty system for unilaterally imposed United States trade-related intellectual property sanctions (e.g., against Brazil in the pharmaceutical patent dispute), and the United States is under considerable pressure to halt the imposition of such sanctions. An exclusive intellectual property code could, in theory, establish a strong minority position that trade sanctions are an appropriate response to intellectual property disputes.

If this is United States policy, the question arises whether it will not merely intensify the schism between North and South by more clearly defining the opposing camps — with the position of the developing countries arguably enhanced because of the perceived need of the United States and other industrialized countries to negotiate a new code arrangement (perhaps conceding the present inapplicability of the GATT). The United States may be better served by foregoing a code and standing firm with its position that the GATT is inherently defective and or that failure to provide intellectual property protection nullifies or impairs existing GATT benefits — and by acting on the basis of this position despite threatened counter-measures. Because of the prospects for intensifying the North/South schism without achieving any demonstrable end, the code is a poor, if not counterproductive, choice for resolving the inclusive intellectual property problem.

The primary advantage of the code mechanism is, of course, that a limited or exclusive amendment may be achieved when a quasi-consensual or consensual amendment could not be. When there is a significant amount of affected trade among code signatories there may be a significant economic utility in the code's adoption. Once established, the code may provide an important framework for dispute settlement. The absence of the potential utility of an intellectual property code may be usefully contrasted with the potential utility of a code to eliminate barriers to trade in services. A myriad of barriers stand against the establishment of service businesses throughout the OECD countries, and a great deal of potential trade may be created by an agreement solely among the OECD countries. It is in this context that an exclusive code has a high present utility and in which a lack of participation by the developing countries may have only a marginal adverse effect.

*****

5. Transitional Arrangements

Whichever institutional mechanism implements the intellectual property amendment, it should incorporate transitional arrangements that will minimize economic dislocations for the developing countries. Transitional procedures are a common feature of changed trading arrangements, and transitional procedures that give special relief to less economically developed countries are not uncommon. As evidenced by the intellectual property Framework Agreement, the concept of a transitional arrangement has become a formal part of the TRIPs agenda.

In concrete terms, an intellectual property amendment could consist of three sets of norms of substance and enforcement procedure. The "final" set would apply to the industrialized countries and select NICs. A second set would apply to most NICs and developing countries. A third set would apply to the least developed countries. A maximum period of ten years might, for example, be established for movement upward through each set of standards. Transitional standards might well differentiate between areas in which more compelling developing country and NIC public interests are involved (pharmaceuticals and foodstuffs), justifying longer compliance deadlines, and areas in which less compelling interests are involved (unauthorized appropriation of video copyright), where rapid adherence would be expected. Standards governing the granting of and compensation for compulsory licenses could be tightened during the transitional periods. Transitional sets of norms would provide a limited incentive to the developing countries by limiting immediate economic and social dislocations. The interests of the industrialized countries would be served by an effective, if perhaps longer-term, solution to the intellectual property problem.

B. Reciprocity Concessions

1. Reciprocity Within the GATT

The concept of "reciprocity" is firmly imbedded in the GATT. Long observes that "although reciprocity as a legal concept has not been defined by the Contracting Parties, it is a fundamental principle occupying a central position in the General Agreement.". . . Reciprocity, as accepted in GATT practice, means that a country need not make a trade concession unless it receives something in return — a quid pro quo. Likewise, a country deprived of benefits previously negotiated in the GATT is entitled to withdraw concessions previously granted by it. There is no accepted formula for calculating the value of a trade concession, and no reciprocity formula exists. The vast array of intangibles involved in the multilateral trade negotiating process (e.g., the calculation of anticipated changes in demand based on the removal of a trade barrier) do not lend much support to the development of a formula. Nevertheless, all other things being equal, GATT Contracting Parties that make a trade concession are as a matter of GATT law and practice entitled to receive a concession in return. As a corollary, the use of "brute" economic bargaining power (e.g., in the form of a threatened denial of access to an already opened market) is not condoned. With respect to the intellectual property problem, the question arises whether agreement by the developing countries to provide enhanced intellectual property rights protection would constitute a trade concession within the bounds of the reciprocity principle on the one hand, or would constitute the remedy of a defect inherent in the GATT arrangement or explicit agreement to preexisting (though implicit) GATT obligations on the other.

*****

4. Renegotiation of a Long-Term Agreement

*****

In the case of intellectual property, both North and South have a good faith, albeit differing, perspective concerning the spirit (if not the letter) of the General Agreement. Absolute acceptance of each perspective yields a significantly different result both with respect to the norms to be observed and the obligation to compensate for changes. In such circumstances, a compromise is appropriate. Intellectual property should be protected because it is now an essential component of industrialized country national wealth and because the need for such protection resulted from evolutionary forces. However, immediate and strict compliance with new intellectual property standards would result in painful dislocations that should be ameliorated through a transitional approach. Compensation or reciprocal trade concessions should be paid because an existing bargain is being altered, but strict reciprocity is not appropriate because the bargain must have contemplated the incorporation of economic progress. As a compromise, compensation might take the form of concessions adequate to ameliorate short-term economic dislocations in the developing countries . . . — as opposed to concessions that would compensate for the long-term costs of payment for foreign intellectual property . . . . Over the long term, intellectual property should be treated on the same basis as other traded commodities, and appropriations or transfers of intellectual property at less than full value should be subject to the same considerations as any other below-value appropriations or transfers, whether prohibited, compensated for, or treated as other forms of economic aid. As discussed in . . . this Article, such long-term protection is necessary to satisfy industrialized country interests in the protection of an increasingly important component of national wealth and to preserve the liberal trading system.

5. The Available Package of Concessions

There are variety of concessions that the industrialized countries might grant to the developing countries in exchange for a GATT agreement on the protection of intellectual property. These range from concessions with respect to compensation due for intellectual property itself, to concessions in other trade areas, to concessions not technically within the international trade regime. As a practical matter, a package of concessions may be most suitable.

*****

Notes and Questions

1. One of the primary interests of an important group of developing countries in the Uruguay Round negotiations was to obtain agreement by the EU to reduce its high level of agricultural subsidies. These subsidies allow farmers in the EU to sell at low prices in world markets, and reduce the profitability of developing country agricultural production and exports. The United States offered to press the EU to reduce agricultural subsidies in exchange for developing country acceptance of the TRIPS Agreement.

Toward the end of the Uruguay Round negotiations, the EU (under particularly intense pressure from the French government) refused to agree to a level of subsidies reductions that met U.S. demands. Only after the Round threatened to unravel did the EU and United States agree on an agriculture compromise which was significantly less successful in reducing EU subsidies than the developing countries had hoped. Nevertheless, the TRIPS Agreement was concluded as part of a Uruguay Round bargain which included the granting of concessions to developing countries in the fields of agriculture and textiles, and the incorporation of transition periods in favor of developing countries in the TRIPS Agreement and other parts of the WTO Agreement text. The United States seemed to agree that it would cease its practice of threatening and imposing trade sanctions on developing countries for their IPRs-related practices so long as they complied with the terms of the TRIPS Agreement. Oddly enough, in approving the Uruguay Round Agreements, the U.S. Congress amended U.S. Section 301 legislation to permit the USTR to impose trade sanctions on countries for their IPRs-related practices, even if they are in compliance with the TRIPS Agreement. On what basis do you suppose that the U.S. Congress might have undertaken this action?

2. It is an interesting question whether developing countries finally assented to the TRIPS Agreement because their views as to the potential benefits of introducing IPRs protection systems changed during the course of the Uruguay Round, or whether they did so to preserve other benefits of participation in the GATT system (and to avoid U.S. and EU trade sanctions). With a sound answer to this question, we might be better able to predict the course of developing country compliance with the TRIPS

Agreement. Even among seasoned trade negotiators, there remains a substantial divergence of views as to what ultimately caused the developing countries to accept the Agreement. One might suggest that if the developing countries had come to see the benefits of IPRs protection, they could have acted to adopt protection systems without the obligations imposed by the TRIPS Agreement. Yet, might it be a political advantage to governments, when seeking to promote legislation that is unpopular among a large group of their citizens, to adopt it under "compulsion"?

ii. The TRIPS Agreement as Described by the
Advocates General to the European Court of Justice

Shortly before the signing of the WTO Agreement in Marrakesh in April 1994, the European Commission requested an advisory opinion from the European Court of Justice (ECJ) on the question whether the European Community (EC) possessed sole competence to accede to the WTO Agreement, or whether the EC shared that competence with its member states. In other words, which entity or entities should be party to the WTO Agreement? We will examine the structure of the European Union/Community and study the ECJ's opinion on this question in the next section.

Following is an extract from the factual background prepared by the Advocates General to the Court which describes the TRIPS Agreement. While we will examine particular provisions in more detail later, it should be useful at this point to have an overview of the agreement.

Re The Uruguay Round Treaties (Opinion 1/94)

The Court of Justice of the European Communities
[1995] 1 CMLR 205
15 November 1994

PANEL: Presiding, Rodriguez Iglesias CJ; Joliet (Rapporteur), Schockweiler, Kapteyn, Gulmann, Mancini, Kakouris, Moitinho de Almeida, Murray, Edward, La Pergola JJ

Headnote:

Opinion under Article 228(6) EC.

Provisions considered:

EC 43, 100a, 113, 235

*****

Facts:

I. Agreements resulting from the Uruguay Round

The "most complex negotiations in world history" (in the words of the Council) ended with the signature in Marrakesh on 15 April 1994 of the Final Act embodying the results of the Uruguay Round of Multilateral Trade Negotiations. Those negotiations took seven years, starting with the Punta del Este Ministerial Declaration of 20 September 1986. The representatives of the governments and of the European Communities who drew up the Final Act agreed on the desirability of its coming into force on 1 January 1995 or as early as possible thereafter.

The Final Act contains an agreement establishing the World Trade Organisation (hereinafter "the WTO Agreement") to provide a common institutional framework for the conduct of trade relations among the members. The agreement does not comprise any provisions of a substantive nature. Such provisions are contained in the annexes, which contain various "multilateral trade agreements" forming an integral part of the WTO Agreement.

They include:

— the Multilateral Agreements on Trade in Goods, including GATT 1994 (Annex 1A);
— the General Agreement on Trade in Services (Annex 1B);
— the Agreement on Trade-Related Aspects of Intellectual Property Rights (Annex 1C);

— an understanding on rules and procedures governing the settlement of disputes ("the Dispute Settlement Understanding") (Annex 2);
— a trade policy review mechanism (Annex 3).

The WTO Agreement and its annexes form a single "package". States wishing to become members of the WTO are obliged to accept all the multilateral agreements negotiated in the Uruguay Round. The procedure for the settlement of disputes applies to all those multilateral agreements. Under the procedure, recourse may be had, in the last resort, to what is known as "cross-retaliation". The breach of any one element of the agreements as a whole (whether in the sector of goods, services or intellectual property rights) can be redressed by retaliation in a different sector (Article 22(3)(b) of the Dispute Settlement Understanding) or under another agreement (Article 22(3)(c) of the Understanding). Moreover, as the Commission states, "compensation similarly can be offered in another sector or under a different agreement than the one where the breach took place".

This single "package" system brings to an end what has been termed "GATT a la carte". The individual agreements resulting from the Tokyo Round involved variable levels of participation. Furthermore, each agreement had its own procedure for the settlement of disputes.

Also annexed to the WTO Agreement are four plurilateral agreements (relating respectively to government procurement, trade in civil aircraft, the dairy sector and bovine meat). In those fields, an exception is allowed to the principle of a single "package"; the agreements are to be binding only on those members of the WTO who accept them. However, the dispute settlement procedure is to apply in the relations between parties who accept them.

*****

X. Analysis of the GATS and the TRIPs Agreement

*****

B. TRIPs

1. Objectives and raison d'etre

The primary objective of the TRIPs Agreement, as the French Government points out, is to strengthen and harmonise, on a global scale, the protection of intellectual property.

The French Government states that, in the light of the failure of the efforts made to achieve that aim in other contexts and, in particular, the work carried out between 1980 and 1984 in revising the Paris Convention for the Protection of Industrial Property, the developed countries insisted that intellectual property rights should be included in the Uruguay Round in such a way as to take advantage of the dynamics of GATT as a whole (together with its provisions regarding negotiation) and its machinery for the settlement of disputes.

As the Commission points out, trade in counterfeit products in certain non-member countries (counterfeit trade marks, imitation products, infringement of patent rights in products or processes, pirated books, records and videocassettes) causes considerable harm to Community industry. The lack of effective protection of intellectual property rights in certain non-member countries is regarded as having the same effect on "goods subject to intellectual property rights" as any other restriction on imports.

The Commission notes that retaliatory trade measures have been applied both by the United States and by the Community against countries which either provided inadequate protection for intellectual property or discriminated between their trading partners. Those measures have prompted developing countries to accept the idea of stronger protection of intellectual property, even though they hitherto tended to regard that branch of the law as an instrument of exploitation on the part of the industrialised economies. Furthermore, the Commission states that the developing countries are becoming more and more aware of the possible benefits of stronger protection of intellectual property, including greater incentives for local innovation.

2. The scope of the TRIPs Agreement and the methods adopted for the achievement of its objectives

The TRIPs Agreement is extremely wide in scope, since it covers both literary and artistic property (copyright and related rights) and industrial property (trade marks, geographical indications of provenance and origin, patents, designs and models, know-how), excluding, however, new varieties of plants (Article 1(2) of TRIPs).

Part I (Articles 1 to 8) contains general provisions and basic principles. Part II (Articles 9 to 40) lays down standards concerning the availability, scope and use of intellectual property rights. Part III (Articles 41 to 61) lays down rules on the enforcement of intellectual property rights. Part IV (Article 62) covers procedures for the acquisition and maintenance of intellectual property rights. Part V (Articles 63 and 64) concerns the settlement of disputes. Part VI (Articles 65 to 67) contains transitional provisions and Part VII (Articles 68 to 73) lays down institutional and final provisions.

The TRIPs Agreement seeks to establish a minimum level of protection of intellectual property. The members countries are free under that Agreement both to implement more extensive protection and to determine the most appropriate method of giving effect to its provisions (Article 1(1) of the TRIPs Agreement).

The applicability of the agreement is determined according to a personal criterion (rights attaching to certain natural and legal persons who are nationals of other countries; Article 1(3) of the TRIPs Agreement).

The TRIPs Agreement lays down the principles of national treatment (Article 3) and most-favoured-nation treatment (Article 4). There are certain exceptions to those two principles. The principle of national treatment is subject to the exceptions already provided in the Paris Convention for the Protection of Industrial Property, the Berne Convention for the Protection of Literary and Artistic Works, the Rome Convention for the Protection of Performers, Producers of Phonograms and Broadcasting Organisations and the Washington Treaty on Intellectual Property in Respect of Integrated Circuits. Furthermore, the national treatment obligation is restricted, as regards performers, producers of phonograms and broadcasting organisations, to the rights provided by the TRIPs Agreement itself (Article 3(1) of the TRIPs Agreement).

As the Council observes, the objectives of the TRIPs Agreement are pursued in two different ways: first, by reference to international conventions which, in the words of the Commission, enjoyed "a relatively wide degree of acceptance", that is to say, the Paris Convention on industrial property and the Berne Convention on literary and artistic works, which also seek to achieve the harmonisation of rights and national treatment in non-harmonised fields, and, second, as the Commission observes, by means of certain substantive provisions ("plus-elements") "in areas of intellectual property where the participating countries felt the immediate need to extend the areas of protection".

The reference to the Paris Convention encompasses all the substantive provisions of that convention, excluding only the institutional, final and transitional provisions (Article 2(1) of the TRIPs Agreement). The reference to the Berne Convention also covers all the substantive provisions of that convention apart from those relating to authors' moral rights (Article 9(1) of the TRIPs Agreement).

The specific substantive provisions are set out in Parts II, III and IV of the TRIPs Agreement.

There is one important issue which is not addressed by those specific substantive provisions: the exhaustion of rights. One of the general provisions of the TRIPs Agreement states as follows:

> For the purposes of dispute settlement under this Agreement, subject to the provisions of Articles 3 [national treatment] and 4 [most-favoured-nation treatment], nothing in this Agreement shall he used to address the issue of the exhaustion of intellectual property rights.

It will be recalled that the principle of exhaustion precludes the holders of intellectual property rights from being able to rely on those rights in order to control the movement of products which they have themselves placed on the market or which have been placed on the market with their consent. According to the Commission, it follows from Article 6 of the TRIPs Agreement that if a TRIPs Member applies the principle of 'national' exhaustion (or 'regional' exhaustion for customs unions or free trade areas), the dispute settlement provisions of TRIPs (including both violation and non-violation complaints) cannot be invoked.

The Member States of the Community, which are obliged to apply the principle of exhaustion in intra-Community trade, are free not to apply it if the product which is imported originates from a non-member country; the same applies in relation to the Community itself.

However, if a Member State does apply the principle of exhaustion to its nationals, without restricting it to goods put into circulation in a Member State of the Community, it must also apply it in that way to nationals of non-member countries, pursuant to the principle of national treatment. Similarly, the principle of most-favoured-nation treatment precludes any TRIPs Member from applying different rules depending on whether persons are nationals of one non-member country or of another.

According to the Commission, Article 6 of the TRIPs Agreement will enable a member country "to continue opposing parallel imports of goods . . . marketed abroad [ie in a non-member country] by the intellectual property owner or with his consent". The Commission considers that the restriction of the principle of exhaustion to intra-Community trade is necessary in order to respect the provisions of EC law and to allow Community rightholders to conquer foreign markets [ie those in non-member countries] whilst maintaining some control on (re)importation of technology-based goods in the Community.

3. The specific substantive provisions

(a) Copyright and related rights

Copyright protection extends to expressions and not to ideas, procedures, methods of operation or mathematical concepts as such (Article 9(2) of the TRIPs Agreement). The minimum term of protection is prescribed (Article 12).

Computer programs are protected as literary works under the Berne Convention (Article 10(1) of the TRIPs Agreement).

The related rights of performers, producers of phonograms and broadcasting organisations are recognised and defined (Article 14 of the TRIPs Agreement).

Rental rights are to be granted to authors of computer programs. Such rights are to be granted to the authors of cinematographic works only where such rental has "led to widespread copying of such works which is materially impairing the exclusive right of reproduction conferred in [the member country in question] on authors and their successors in title".

(b) Industrial property

(i) Trade marks

The protection to be given to trade marks applies both to those relating to goods and to those relating to services.

Signs capable of constituting a trade mark are specified and the rights conferred by a trade mark are defined (Articles 15(1) and 16(1) of the TRIPs Agreement).

The registrability of a mark may be made dependent on its use, but such use may not be a condition for filing an application for registration (Article 15(3)). The minimum term of registration and of any renewal thereof is presented (Article 18). Where use is required to maintain a registration, the TRIPs Agreement lays down a minimum period of non-use after which the registration of the trade mark may be cancelled (Article 19).

The protection of well-known marks within the meaning of Article 6bis of the Paris Convention is extended to marks relating to services (Article 16(2)) and beyond the ambit of similar products (Article 16(3)).

TRIPs Members may determine conditions for the licensing and assignment of trade marks. However, the compulsory licensing of trade marks is not permitted and a trade mark may be assigned without the transfer of the business to which the mark belongs.

(ii) Geographical indications

Section 3 of Part II of TRIPs lays down very detailed provisions regarding the protection to be given to geographical indications, which are defined as "indications which identify a good as originating in the territory of a Member, or a region or locality in that territory, where a given quality, reputation or other characteristic of the good is essentially attributable to its geographical origin" (Article 22(1) of the TRIPs Agreement).

Generally, the aim is to prevent:

(a) the use of any means in the designation or presentation of a good that indicates or suggests that the good in question originates in a geographical area other than the true place of origin in a manner which misleads the public as to the geographical origin of the good;

(b) any use which constitutes an act of unfair competition within the meaning of Article 10b is of the Paris Convention (1967) [Article 22(2) of the TRIPs Agreement].

Additional protection is to be provided for geographical indications for wines and spirits: the means of preventing the use of a geographical indication identifying wines or spirits not originating in the place indicated must also be available "where the true origin of the goods is indicated or the geographical indication is used in translation or accompanied by expressions such as 'kind', 'type', 'style', 'imitation' or the like" (Article 23(1) of the TRIPs Agreement).

However, those rules are to apply only for the future, since it is provided that:

> Nothing in this section shall require a Member to prevent continued and similar use of a particular geographical indication of another Member identifying wines or spirits in connection with goods or services by any of its nationals or domiciliaries who have used that geographical indication in a continuous manner with regard to the same or related goods or services in the territory of that Member either (a) for at least 10 years preceding 15 April 1994 or (b) in good faith preceding that date [Article 24(4) of the TRIPs Agreement].

(iii) Industrial designs

Industrial designs are also covered by the TRIPs Agreement. Protection is to be afforded to industrial designs which are new or original (Article 25(1)). The scope of such protection is laid down and its minimum duration is prescribed (Article 26).

As regards textiles in particular, the requirements for securing protection must not be such that they unreasonably impair the opportunity to obtain such protection (Article 25(2) of the TRIPs Agreement).

(iv) Patents

Section 5 of Part II on patents first sets out provisions concerning patentability (Article 27). Patents are to be available without discrimination for any inventions, whether products or processes, in all fields of technology (ibid). However, developing countries are permitted for a certain period to defer the obligation to extend product patent protection to areas of technology not so protectable under their national laws on the general date of application of the Agreement (Article 65(4)). The rights conferred by a patent are defined (Article 28) and must be for a term of at least 20 years (Article 33). Lastly, Article 31 lays down provisions limiting the circumstances in which compulsory licences may be granted.

(v) Layout designs (topographies) of integrated circuits

The provisions relating to topographies of integrated circuits are intended to remedy the deficiencies in the Washington Treaty on Intellectual Property in Respect of Integrated Circuits. They define both the scope of the protection to be conferred (Article 36) and the term of protection (Article 38).

(vi) Protection of undisclosed technical information

TRIPs Members are obliged to protect undisclosed information against unfair competition (Article 39(1)). The lawful holders of such information are to have the possibility of preventing it from being "disclosed to, acquired by, or used by others without their consent in a manner contrary to honest commercial practices". That protection is conditional on the information being secret, having commercial value because it is secret and having been subject to steps by the person lawfully in control of it to keep it secret (Article 39(2)).

(vii) Control of anti-competitive practices in contractual licences

The Members agree that some licensing practices or conditions pertaining to intellectual property rights which restrain competition may have adverse effects on trade and may impede the transfer and dissemination of technology (Article 40). Consequently, the TRIPs Agreement confers on them the right to specify practices or conditions which may constitute an abuse of intellectual property rights and to adopt appropriate measures to prevent or control such practices.

4. Specific procedural provisions (enforcement of intellectual property rights)

It is not enough, in order to achieve a minimum level of uniform protection for intellectual property, to define the content of the various rights to be recognised. It is necessary in addition to provide "effective and appropriate means" for their enforcement (see the preamble to the TRIPs Agreement). This is the reason for Part III of the TRIPs Agreement, relating to the procedures to be established by the Members to permit effective action against any act of infringement of intellectual property rights covered by the TRIPs Agreement (Article 41(1)). Part III sets out, first, the measures which the holders of intellectual property rights may require the judicial, administrative and customs authorities to take against infringements and threatened infringements of their rights (see (a) below) and, second, provides that the procedures by which such measures may be obtained must fulfil certain requirements (see (b) below).

(a) Corrective measures

The TRIPs Agreement lays down measures for the termination and restraint of infringements of intellectual property rights (injunctions, damages, the confiscation or destruction of counterfeit objects, criminal sanctions) and also measures for the prevention of infringements of intellectual property rights (provisional measures, suspension of release by customs authorities).

The judicial authorities are to have the authority to order a party to desist from an infringement of the intellectual property rights of a person bringing proceedings (Article 44(1)).

The judicial authorities are to have the power to order the infringer to pay the holder of the right infringed adequate damages where that infringer knew, or had reasonable grounds for knowing, that his action infringed an intellectual property right (Article 45(1)).

The judicial authorities are further to have authority to order that goods which infringe an intellectual property right be disposed of without compensation outside the channels of commerce or, unless this would be contrary to existing constitutional requirements, destroyed (Article 46).

Criminal sanctions, extending to imprisonment, are to be applicable in cases of wilful trade mark counterfeiting or copyright piracy on a commercial scale (Article 61).

Preventive measures fall into two categories.

On the one hand, the judicial authorities are to have the authority to order prompt and effective provisional measures to prevent an infringement of any intellectual property right from occurring (Article 50(1)). Where appropriate, those measures may be adopted inaudita altera parte (Article 50(2)), although the defendant may subsequently apply for a review (Article 50(4)).

On the other, the Members are to adopt procedures to enable a right holder who has valid grounds for suspecting that the importation of counterfeit trade mark or pirated copyright goods may take place to lodge an application in writing with the competent administrative or judicial authorities for the suspension by the customs authorities of the release into free circulation of such goods. Members may envisage similar measures in respect of other infringements of intellectual property rights (Article 51).

Such measures for the suspension of the release of goods into free circulation are also of a provisional nature. Their continuation is conditional on the initiation of proceedings to determine the merits of the case (see Article 55).

(b) Procedural safeguards

Procedures concerning the enforcement of intellectual property rights must be fair and equitable (Article 41(2)). The requirement of fair and equitable procedures is expressed in a number of different ways.

The holders of rights are to have access to civil judicial procedures concerning the enforcement of intellectual property rights and defendants are to have the right to written notice which is timely and contains sufficient detail, including the basis of the claims (Article 42). The parties must be allowed to be represented by independent legal counsel and overly burdensome requirements must not be imposed concerning mandatory personal appearances (Article 42). All parties to such procedures are to be entitled to substantiate their claims and to present all relevant evidence (Article 42), and to require the production by the opposing party of evidence which is in its possession (Article 43). Decisions on the merits must be based solely on evidence in respect of which the parties were offered the opportunity to be heard and should preferably be in writing and reasoned (Article 41(3)).

The parties are to have an opportunity for review by a judicial authority of final administrative decisions and of initial judicial decisions (Article 41(4)).

There must exist authority to award damages against holders of intellectual property rights who abuse or have unjustified recourse to the procedures available to them (Article 48(1)).

Notes and Questions

1. There are three main components of the TRIPS Agreement: (a) minimum substantive standards of IPRs protection to be adopted by all WTO Members; (b) obligations imposed on all Members to establish effective systems of IPRs enforcement, and; (c) incorporation of intergovernmental dispute settlement procedures applicable to all Members, including the possibility of trade sanctions in the event of non-compliance with a ruling by the Dispute Settlement Body.

2. Each country, such as China, that is seeking to join the WTO must negotiate a Protocol of Accession with WTO Members. The Protocol spells out specific trade-liberalizing obligations the new Member accepts, in addition to the general obligations of WTO membership. One question facing an applicant for membership such as China is whether it will be considered a "developing country" Member, and, therefore, whether it will be entitled to take advantage of certain privileges — such as the right to implement the TRIPS Agreement over an extended transition period. The Chinese government, while generally claiming the right to be considered a developing country Member if and when it accedes to the WTO, has nevertheless indicated that it intends to forego the TRIPS Agreement transition periods. It is willing to fully implement the TRIPS Agreement upon its entry into the WTO.

3. The TRIPS Agreement transition arrangements are set forth in terms of a period of years from the entry into force of the Agreement. There is no explicit provision for extending these periods to countries later acceding to the WTO. Do you think that special accommodations should be made for developing countries (and countries in transition to market economy) that are late joiners of the TRIPS Agreement, so that they may undertake to comply over a period of years?

4. There are a number of areas of international concern as to which the adoption of a TRIPS-type legal system might be useful. Would such a system be useful for environmental protection or the regulation of competition? Some environmental groups criticize the WTO for paying attention to the interests of IPRs holders while ignoring the environment. Why might

WTO Members be more sympathetic to addressing the concerns of IPRs holders than addressing environmental (or labor union) concerns?

d. The WTO Dispute Settlement System

As noted previously, the Uruguay Round negotiations resulted in a substantial change to the way in which disputes were settled in the former GATT system. The new WTO dispute settlement system is briefly described in the following excerpt. This description concludes with reference to so-called "non-violation" complaints. In Chapter 3 we will study the first WTO panel and Appellate Body decisions regarding implementation of the TRIPS Agreement which, *inter alia,* addresses the non-violation form of action.

Incomplete Rule Systems, System Incompatibilities and Suboptimal Solutions: Changing the Dynamic of Dispute Settlement and Avoidance in Trade Relations Between Japan and the United States

Frederick M. Abbott*

*****

D. From Consensus to Quasi-Judicial Dispute Settlement

1. The General Practice

The WTO Agreement has transformed the GATT dispute settlement system from a consensus-based system to a quasi-judicial system. Both the old and new systems derive from Article XXIII of the GATT which generally provided for a system of consultation, to be followed by recommendations from the Members as appropriate, to authorization of the withdrawal

---

*16 Ariz. J. Int'l & Comp. L (forthcoming 1999). Prepared in connection with Joint Workshop on Japan-U.S. Economic Relations.

353

of trade concessions as required. The basic Article XXIII provisions evolved over time into a panel dispute settlement system which was codified in a 1979 Understanding on Dispute Settlement. In this system, the GATT Council received complaints from Members, and could agree by consensus to establish a panel of experts, generally consisting of three individuals, who were charged with drafting a report with respect to a dispute. The report might make recommendations concerning measures to be taken by a complained-against Member in order to conform its rules to the GATT. In order for the report of the panel to be binding on a complained-against Member, the GATT Council was required to adopt the report by a consensus of its Members, including the complained-against Member. Although this system of dispute settlement appears to have functioned effectively for much of recent GATT history, there was a perception that the consensus-based system resulted in the failure to establish panels and avoidance of panel rulings, and that the system was therefore insufficiently law-based.

The Dispute Settlement Understanding [DSU] adopted in connection with the conclusion of the Uruguay Round substantially alters the prior GATT dispute settlement practice. The DSU applies to the settlement of disputes under all of the multilateral trade agreements (MTAs). Following a mandatory consultation period, a panel of experts will be appointed by the WTO Secretariat (or Director-General if necessary), unless the Dispute Settlement Body (DSB) votes by consensus against the establishment of a panel. The report of the panel will be adopted by the DSB unless there is a consensus vote against adoption, or unless a disputing party appeals the decision to the newly created Appellate Body. If an appeal is undertaken, the ruling of the Appellate Body is adopted by the DSB, unless there is a consensus against adoption. Since there is little prospect that a consensus will exist against the adoption of a report, for all intents and purposes the adoption of panel reports is now automatic.

The automatic adoption of panel reports is coupled with other important features of the new DSU. The DSU provides that Members are expected to resolve disputes involving interpretation and application of WTO rules, or "impediment[s] to the attainment of any objective of the covered agreements," under the rules and procedures of the DSU. Moreover, a Member is not to impose trade sanctions on another Member for an alleged violation of WTO rules without the authorization of the DSB. The DSU thus generally prohibits the unilateral imposition of trade sanctions with respect to matters within the scope of the WTO regulatory system.

Another important innovation of the DSU is the prescription of more rigorous timetables for the settlement of disputes. In addition to rules limiting the time within which panels and the Appellate Body must issue their reports, the DSU provides guidelines as to the time frame in which Members are expected to implement recommendations and rulings of the DSB.

The dispute settlement procedure of the GATT 1947 involved a political negotiation directed at achieving a consensus among the disputing Members. Although this procedure may have been largely successful in resolving disputes, it lacked the legal character of a judicial procedure. A judicial procedure requires that the decision-making function be performed by a neutral decision-maker, *i.e.* one without a direct interest in the outcome of the dispute. The assumption underlying the judicial procedure is that the law applicable to the parties will govern the outcome of the dispute, and not the self-interest of the parties. Under the GATT 1947 system, the interests of the Members and the willingness of the Members to make concessions with respect to those interests were central to the outcome of a dispute.

The WTO DSU removes WTO Members from the center of the decision-making function by making the establishment of panels and the adoption of panel reports automatic. The panels and Appellate Body assume the role of primary decision-makers. Since panels are appointed on a case by case basis, the panelists act in the capacity of arbitrators rather than judges. Members of the Appellate Body serve for extended terms and have the independent character of appellate judges. On the whole, it seems fitting to refer to the new DSU procedure as "quasi-judicial." The underlying assumption of the new WTO system is that the law is the master of the Members. The outcome of a dispute settlement procedure should not, at least nominally, be based on a political negotiation.

E. What is within the Scope of WTO Dispute Settlement?

... Members of the WTO ... have [as such] agreed to settle certain disputes by recourse to the DSU. There is nothing in the WTO Agreement or DSU that prevents Members of the WTO from agreeing between themselves to settle a specific dispute or class of disputes through alternative dispute settlement mechanisms. However, it is important to consider the scope of the class of disputes that [Members] have already agreed to settle by recourse to the DSU. The critical text in this regard is Article 23 DSU, which states:

Article 23
Strengthening of the Multilateral System

1. When Members seek the redress of *a violation of obligations or other nullification or impairment of benefits under the covered agreements or an impediment to the attainment of any objective of the covered agreements*, they shall have recourse to, and abide by, the rules and procedures of this Understanding.

2. In such cases, Members shall: (a) not make a determination to the effect that a violation has occurred, that benefits have been nullified or impaired or that the attainment of any objective of the covered agreements has been impeded, except through recourse to dispute settlement in accordance with the rules and procedures of this Understanding, and shall make any such determination consistent with the findings contained in the panel or Appellate Body report adopted by the DSB or an arbitration award rendered under this Understanding; . . .[68]

Article 23 of the DSU must be read in conjunction with Article XXIII of the GATT 1994, Article XXIII of the GATS, and Article 64 of the TRIPS Agreement. Article 23 DSU and Article XXIII GATT 1994, in conjunction, contemplate several different kinds of disputes. Specifically:

---

[68] Article 23 continues:

(b) follow the procedures set forth in Article 21 to determine the reasonable period of time for the Member concerned to implement the recommendations and rulings; and (c) follow the procedures set forth in Article 22 to determine the level of suspension of concessions or other obligations and obtain DSB authorization in accordance with those procedures before suspending concessions or other obligations under the covered agreements in response to the failure of the Member concerned to implement the recommendations and rulings within that reasonable period of time.

Article 2:2 of the DSU is also relevant to the scope of the Member's obligations, providing:

2. The dispute settlement system of the WTO is a central element in providing security and predictability to the multilateral trading system. The Members recognize that it serves to preserve the rights and obligations of Members under the covered agreements, and to clarify the existing provisions of those agreements in accordance with customary rules of interpretation of public international law. Recommendations and rulings of the DSB cannot add to or diminish the rights and obligations provided in the covered agreements.

1. Disputes involving a violation of the terms of the GATT 1994 ("violation complaints");

2. Disputes not involving a violation of the GATT 1994, but involving conduct by a Member that nullifies or impairs the benefits of another Member under the agreement, or that interferes with the attainment of an objective of the agreement ("non-violation complaints"), and;

3. Disputes involving "any other situation" ("situation complaints").

Article 23 of GATS (with Article 23 DSU) contemplates violation and non-violation complaints, but does not refer to situation complaints. Article 64 of the TRIPS Agreement (with Article 23 DSU) contemplates only violation complaints for the first five years after its entry into force, with the issue of non-violation complaints and situation complaints to be considered by the Ministerial Conference during that period. If no consensus is reached by the Ministerial Conference by the end of the five year period, then non-violation complaints and situation complaints might be brought under the TRIPS Agreement.

Article 23 DSU adds a mandatory character to the dispute settlement provisions of the GATT/WTO. Article XXIII GATT 1947 was permissive in its terms. Article 23 DSU says that *if* a complaint is covered by the terms of the DSU, then a Member with a complaint *must* resolve the dispute under the DSU (unless the disputing Members agree among themselves to do otherwise).

Notes and Questions

1. It was often suggested that the former GATT dispute system worked well precisely because it allowed governments to veto decisions against them. Before an adverse decision was accepted by a government, it could test the waters at home to make sure that political reaction would not be unduly harsh. The new WTO system removes this safety valve. It is a system that is more "law-based" in the traditional sense of that concept, but it also seems

to carry with it a higher degree of political risk. Do you think that governments made the right decision in moving towards a more judicially-oriented rule system in the WTO?

---

3. The Relationship Between WIPO and the WTO

There are two international organizations with wide government membership that are principally responsible for regulating the international intellectual property system — WIPO and the WTO. The following excerpt discusses the complex relationship between the two organizations and various issues raised by their potentially overlapping competences. Which organization should be responsible for overseeing the negotiation of new rules? What if members of the two organizations adopt different rules? How should dispute settlement competences be allocated?

The Future of the Multilateral Trading System in the Context of TRIPS

Frederick M. Abbott*

*****

II. The Basic Institutional Arrangement

A. The WTO

The TRIPS Agreement entered into force on January 1, 1995. Application of the rules of the Agreement is obligatory for Members in accordance with transitional arrangements. On January 1, 1996 the rules of the TRIPS Agreement became obligatory for developed country Members. At the same time, provisions with respect to national and most favored nation treatment became obligatory for all WTO Members. Developing country Members, Members in transformation from centrally-planned to market

---

*20 HASTINGS INT'L & COMP. L. REV. 661 (1997).

economies, and least developed Members, may elect to take advantage of transition periods ranging from 5 to 10 years, depending on the IPRs subject matter involved and their level of economic development. Most TRIPS Agreement rules will become obligatory for developing and transforming Members on January 1, 2000.

Pursuant to the terms of the WTO Agreement, the Council for Trade-Related Aspects of Intellectual Property Rights (TRIPS Council) has been established as a component of the WTO governing structure. Each Member of the WTO is entitled to membership on the TRIPS Council. The TRIPS Council is responsible, *inter alia*, for monitoring operation of the TRIPS Agreement, including implementation of its obligations by Members. The TRIPS Council is assisted by the WTO Secretariat, particularly by the Director for Intellectual Property and Investment, who is assisted by a small staff.

An important factor in the genesis of the TRIPS Agreement was a perception among certain interested groups in the OECD countries that the international IPRs system administered by WIPO was insufficiently strong in terms of the establishment of substantive rules and the maintenance of mechanisms for the enforcement of those rules. Although certain WIPO-administered conventions permit the referral of disputes to the International Court of Justice for resolution, no such referral has ever been made, and this procedure was perceived by OECD governments to be inadequate. A central purpose of the TRIPS Agreement negotiations was to move the center of gravity in the international IPRs arena from WIPO to the new WTO. The WTO would become the central arena for the negotiation of primary international IPRs standards. Most importantly, WTO institutional mechanisms would be used to police the new international IPRs order. Disputes arising under the TRIPS Agreement are now subject to resolution by the WTO Dispute Settlement Body (DSB) in accordance with the terms of the Dispute Settlement Understanding (DSU). Trade sanctions may be collectively authorized to assure compliance by WTO Members with TRIPS obligations.

B. WIPO

WIPO is a Specialized Agency of the United Nations. As a matter of institutional history, the central objectives of WIPO have been to provide a forum for international cooperation in the development of rules to define

IPRs, to administer the rules agreed upon, and to provide technical assistance to Contracting States which desire it. The objectives of WIPO have been carried out by the negotiation of multilateral IPRs conventions, including periodic revisions to such conventions (*e.g.*, with respect to the Paris and Berne Conventions), the establishment of a Secretariat capable of administration at the international level (*e.g.*, to administer the Patent Cooperation Treaty), and the creation of a staff of IPRs specialists capable of rendering technical assistance (*e.g.*, through the presentation of training programs). WIPO is largely funded through revenues from its IPRs administration operations, with Contracting States contributing only about 20 per cent of its operating budget.

C. Cooperative Mechanisms

Ex post facto cooperation between the WTO and WIPO was foreseen. The TRIPS Agreement specifically directs the TRIPS Council to establish mechanisms for cooperation with WIPO, and suggests that the two organizations might work together in the establishment of a common register of Member IPRs laws and regulations. The TRIPS Agreement and related WTO agreements are permissive in the sense of enhanced cooperation between the WTO and WIPO. The TRIPS Council, for example, at the request of its Members might seek guidance from WIPO in the context of dispute settlement. During periodic reviews of TRIPS Agreement implementation, the TRIPS Council might consult with WIPO concerning the evolution of multilateral IPRs rules.

Formal actions have been taken to facilitate cooperation between the two international organizations. In December 1995 the Director General of WIPO and the Director General of the WTO signed an agreement that facilitates exchange of the texts of laws and regulations of WTO and WIPO members. The WIPO-WTO Agreement also establishes a basic framework for cooperation in providing technical assistance relating to the TRIPS Agreement to developing country members of each organization. The WTO TRIPS Council and the WIPO Governing Bodies have taken additional steps that facilitate cooperation. The WIPO Coordination Committee (composed of representatives of the WIPO Contracting States), to be assisted by the Secretariat, has been designated by the WIPO Governing Bodies as the channel of communication between the two organizations. The TRIPS Council has decided that the WTO and WIPO should use a uniform system for notification by Members of IPRs laws, and has agreed that this uniform system will be administered by WIPO. The TRIPS Council has requested that WIPO provide assistance to Members in drafting and implementing TRIPS-compliant IPRs legislation. WIPO Contracting States have voted a substantial increase in resources for assisting countries in modernizing their IP legislation and administrative infrastructures. Each of these decisions and actions constitutes a significant step toward defining and establishing a cooperative and mutually supportive relationship between the WTO and WIPO.

II. Potential Sources of Inter-Institutional Tension

A. Rule-Making and Enforcement

1. Rule-Making Conflicts

There is a clear basis for conflict involving the rule-making activities of the WTO in the TRIPS context, and WIPO. The potential dispute settlement activities of the WTO and WIPO also represent a potential source of tension. The TRIPS Agreement does not suspend the independent operation of WIPO-administered multilateral IPRs conventions. There is not a complete correspondence between the Members of the WTO and the Contracting States of the WIPO conventions. New IPRs conventions are under negotiation in WIPO, as are amendments and supplements to existing IPRs conventions, including those incorporated by reference in the TRIPS Agreement. The TRIPS Council will review the implementation of the TRIPS Agreement, and propose changes to this agreement as necessary or desirable.

The Agreement Establishing the WTO (WTO Agreement) and the TRIPS Agreement provide two basic alternatives for amendment of the TRIPS Agreement. First, the TRIPS Council may submit a proposal for amendment of the TRIPS Agreement to the WTO Ministerial Conference, following which the proposal will be subject to the ordinary amendment procedure of the WTO. Under that procedure, the approval of a two-thirds majority of the Ministerial Conference is required to submit an amending proposal to the Members for acceptance. An amendment becomes effective for Members that have accepted it following their two-thirds acceptance. Members may require the approval of their national parliaments prior to accepting an amendment to the TRIPS Agreement, so that this first amendment procedure may rather be time-consuming.

The WTO and TRIPS Agreements establish an expedited amendment procedure for cases in which the purpose of the amendment is to "adjust . . . to higher levels of protection of intellectual property rights achieved, and in force, in other multilateral agreements and accepted under those agreements by all Members of the WTO." A proposal for such amendment requires a consensus vote of the TRIPS Council, and such amendment may thereafter be adopted by the WTO Ministerial Conference "without further formal acceptance process." Decisions of the Ministerial Conference are ordinarily taken by consensus, but in the absence of consensus by a majority of the votes cast. Since any proposal under this expedited procedure will have been subject to consensus voting in the TRIPS Council, a lower voting threshold at the Ministerial Conference should not create difficulties. The most difficult threshold question with respect to use of this expedited procedure is whether all Members of the WTO will accept a multilateral agreement negotiated under WIPO auspices. Although the Paris and Berne Conventions are the subject to wide adherence, based upon the historical record it would be unusual for all 120 or so WTO Members to be parties to a WIPO agreement.

Rule-making activities in the field of the multilateral regulation of IPRs have assumed great importance and are the focus of intense interest. Questions relating to the protection of information transmitted across the Internet system, the protection of satellite broadcasts against misappropriation, and the time and place at which the exhaustion of IPRs occurs, all loom large at the moment. There is obvious need for additional rule-making in a number of other areas, and the present rate of technological change makes it difficult to predict where and when new issues will surface. Governments and interest groups may have strong preferences with regard to the forum where rules are negotiated for reasons relating, *inter alia*, to perceptions as to where they hold the greatest negotiating strength, and perceptions as to where they most likely will be able to enforce new rules.

The recently completed negotiations under WIPO auspices of two treaties on copyright and neighboring rights, and the postponement of consideration of a related third treaty (on database protection), illustrate the process by which substantive rules will continue to be adopted by the WIPO Contracting States. Provisions of the WIPO draft Treaty on Certain Questions Concerning the Protection of Literary and Artistic Works, and the Treaty for the Protection of the Rights of Performers and Producers of Phonograms, are intended to clarify the scope of protection for authors and artists as the media for the creation and dissemination of artistic works has been reshaped over the past several decades. Proposals for these draft treaties produced an intense debate among disparate groups whose interests would be affected by their adoption. If the treaties are ratified and enter into force, substantive rules governing the international protection of copyrighted material will change as among state parties to the agreements. In order for these changes to be adopted by WTO Members as part of their TRIPS Agreement obligations, action must be taken in accordance with the WTO procedures outlined above.

There is no guarantee that governments participating in negotiations in both the WTO and WIPO will maintain the same perspective on desirable rules in each forum. Some governments may conclude that non-compliance with rules agreed to at WIPO should not be subject to the potential application of trade sanctions in the WTO. Some governments may send trade specialists to negotiate in the WTO, and IPRs specialists to negotiate in WIPO, and these negotiators may not speak with the same voice.

State practice under both the TRIPS Agreement and the WIPO-administered conventions will continue, and will involve state parties that are contemporaneously parties to all of the relevant international instruments, and state parties that are not. Additional protocols and regulatory provisions may be adopted in WIPO that are not contemporaneously approved or adopted in the TRIPS forum. These developments may lead to situations in which states may be in compliance with the rules of the TRIPS Agreement and in derogation of rules of WIPO-administered conventions, and *vice versa*.

2. WTO Dispute Settlement

Analysis of the WTO Dispute Settlement Understanding (DSU) and its application with respect to disputes arising under the TRIPS Agreement suggests that WTO dispute settlement panels will be required in some circumstances to refer to practice under multilateral IPRs conventions administered by WIPO in order to effectively interpret the TRIPS Agreement. The TRIPS Agreement establishes minimum international IPRs substantive rules of three types. The first type is established by the incorporation of provisions of existing multilateral IPRs conventions administered by

WIPO, such as copyright standards that incorporate Berne Convention provisions. The second type consists of rules that are unique to the TRIPS Agreement, such as the rules that establish the subject matter of patent protection. The third type consists of hybrid rules which clarify or amend rules of existing multilateral IPRs conventions, such as a rule clarifying that computer software is copyrightable subject matter. Interpretative practices may vary depending upon which of the three types of TRIPS Agreement rules are being applied. Practice under the WIPO conventions precedes and post-dates entry into force of the TRIPS Agreement. WTO dispute settlement panels will need to sort out the relationship between state practice under WIPO conventions pre- and post-dating the TRIPS Agreement, and the interpretative impact of state practice among parties that are not parties to the WTO Agreement. This is a task well within the competence of WTO panels, but illustrates the jurisprudential issues that are created by the concurrent operation of rule-making bodies acting upon the same subject matter.

The WIPO Secretariat is not authorized by its charter documents to render interpretations of WIPO-administered conventions on behalf of its Contracting States. Yet the WIPO Secretariat may play a role in WTO dispute settlement in a number of ways. A WTO dispute settlement panel may request that the Secretariat provide advice on a technical issue (such as by providing the negotiating history of a particular provision) that does not constitute an interpretative act. A member of the WIPO Secretariat might be asked to serve as a member of a WTO dispute settlement panel. This is certainly permissible under the terms of the TRIPS Agreement and the DSU. Moreover, the Director-General of WIPO has already furnished an informal memorandum to a Contracting State official regarding interpretation of a provision of a WIPO-administered convention that is the subject of an ongoing dispute between two WTO Members.

3. WIPO Dispute Settlement

A Committee of Experts has been convened under WIPO auspices to examine the preparation of a Draft Treaty on the Settlement of Disputes Between States in the Field of Intellectual Property. This Committee first met in 1990, and active discussions concerning the Draft Treaty are continuing as of early 1997. A most striking aspect of these negotiations within WIPO is that they are being pursued with considerable vigor by many of the same OECD governments that moved the international IPRs center of gravity from WIPO into the WTO.

There are sound reasons in favor of the establishment of an IPRs dispute settlement forum outside of the WTO DSU. First, not all potential IPRs disputes are subject to WTO dispute settlement. Second, not all parties to multilateral IPRs conventions are Members of the WTO, and so are not subject to WTO dispute settlement. Third, and perhaps most importantly, the creation of a dispute settlement forum outside the WTO may permit states to resolve IPRs-related disputes in an environment less politically-charged than the WTO. In the WTO the stakes of dispute settlement are often amplified by intense media scrutiny and domestic political pressure on the state participants. States may find it useful to be able to submit IPRs-related disputes to neutral dispute settlement without the threat of trade sanctions looming against losing parties.

4. The Relationship between WTO and WIPO Dispute Settlement

The potential establishment of a WIPO dispute settlement mechanism raises several significant issues with respect to the WTO and TRIPS Agreement. The initial WIPO Draft Treaty set forth a number of alternative spheres of application for the WIPO dispute settlement mechanism. These initial proposals proved controversial, primarily because they did not define the consequences of the initiation of dispute settlement in either the WIPO or WTO forum. Work has continued on refining the formula for the sphere of application of the Draft Treaty. The Committee of Experts remains divided over the proper approach, with several delegations seeking to assure that WTO dispute settlement is given priority within its sphere of application.

It remains to be clarified whether, and to what extent, the WTO DSU and TRIPS Agreement may foreclose the WTO Member parties to IPRs disputes from invoking the jurisdiction of dispute settlement fora outside the WTO. As a matter of principle, it would appear desirable to suspend initiation of proceedings in a forum that is not first selected for the duration because the existence of parallel proceedings is likely to exacerbate inter-institutional tensions. However, there is a corresponding need to minimize the risk that states will choose to initiate proceedings in one forum in order to delay proceedings in another.

There is no unique problem in the trade/IPRs field created by the potential existence of alternative decisions on the same subject matter. WTO Members would retain the power to authorize trade sanctions in the event a Member did not comply with a DSB recommendation or ruling. From a WTO perspective there should not therefore be great concern that the force of its rulings would be undermined by WIPO rulings, since a Member would not be able to avoid abiding by a WTO ruling by invoking an alternative WIPO ruling, so long as the latter are not deemed binding for the WTO.

B. Developing Country Institutional Perspective

It was evident prior to the outset of the Uruguay Round and throughout the Round that the developing countries perceive WIPO as a forum more favorable to their interests than the WTO. There are several possible explanations for this preference, and the explanation probably involves a combination of factors. First, insofar as the developing countries could have maintained the supremacy of WIPO in the field of IPRs, they might have avoided the threat of trade sanctions as a potential consequence of failing to protect OECD-based IPRs. It would logically be in the interests of developing countries to maintain the supremacy of a forum which did not threaten them. Second, WIPO has a history of assisting developing countries in preparing laws, in training IPRs office personnel and in assisting in the creation of patent protection system infrastructure (e.g., by providing prior art files on CD-ROM). The WIPO Secretariat therefore may be perceived as friendly to developing country interests. Third, WIPO has always operated on the system of one country, one vote, and the treaty negotiation system of WIPO lacks the intensity of pressure for reaching strict consensus that is in some circumstances present in the WTO. The developing countries appear to perceive that the political balance of power in WIPO is somewhat more favorable to them than the balance in the WTO.

It would therefore not be surprising to find the developing countries advocating a substantial continuing role for WIPO in the international IPRs field, though it is apparent that at least for the time being they have lost the battle concerning the potential for trade sanctions emanating from the WTO. If the OECD countries continue to perceive their IPRs-related interests as they did throughout the Uruguay Round, they might be expected to continue to support a stronger role for the WTO. Yet as has been seen with respect to the Draft Treaty on the Settlement of Disputes Between States in the Field of Intellectual Property, there may not be the consensus of opinion within the OECD that trade specialists expected.

C. Trade and IPRs Cultures

There may also be a difference in cultures among the international trade community and the international IPRs community that manifests itself in different governmental perspectives at the WTO and WIPO. Officials in IPRs offices in the OECD and developing countries may have been frustrated by the transfer of principal authority in the IPRs sphere to the trade specialists during the Uruguay Round negotiations, and there may be a certain pressure among the IPRs officials to reassert the centrality of WIPO in the international IPRs field. IPRs officials are more accustomed to a skeptical public policy analysis of IPRs protection issues than are trade specialists. The field of IPRs protection has historically included a strong undercurrent of skepticism in its scholarly literature.

The potential of a cultural difference between the IPRs and trade specialists is at least worthy of bringing to the surface for discussion since the theme of cultural differences has permeated the debate concerning the place of environmental rules in the international trading system. It is also worth noting that the WTO has made considerable progress in adapting its culture to environmental interests over the past several years.

The foregoing suggests the potential for conflict in the creation and implementation of separate IPRs rules within the WTO and WIPO, the potential for conflict in dispute settlement, a potential struggle for supremacy involving developing and developed country interests, and a potential clash of institutional cultures.

D. The Status Quo

Some of the potential inter-institutional conflicts involving the WTO and WIPO, such as those that may arise in connection with the parallel track negotiation of new substantive rules, may be substantially ameliorated through action at the national (and regional) level. If each national government takes steps to assure the consistency of its positions in the WTO and WIPO forums, this would reduce the possibility of conflicting results and the creation of inter-institutional tensions. The importance to the national government of assuring that the trade and IPRs communities speak with one voice should not be minimized in this context.

Moreover, a certain level of inter-institutional rivalry and tension may be healthy. This is one of the values, for example, of regional integration mechanisms within the WTO system; that is, regional systems may generate innovative solutions that thereafter may be incorporated within the broader WTO framework. The same may apply as between the WTO and WIPO, as parallel track developments generate alternative solutions to IPRs-related problems.

The WTO and WIPO will co-exist, and will eventually settle their differences, without any major institutional adjustments. Nevertheless, some useful suggestions might be made.

III. Inter-Institutional Proposals

A. Institutional Objectives

As a matter of institutional history, the roles of the GATT/WTO and WIPO have been largely complementary. A review of the historical objectives of the GATT/WTO and WIPO, and their existing institutional strengths, suggests that their roles should remain largely complementary, and that the goal of public planners over the next two decades should be to refine the distribution of roles between the two institutions.

The TRIPS Agreement negotiations were based on the recognition of a close relationship between IPRs and international economic activity, and the acknowledgment of a certain gap between the GATT and WIPO systems. The WIPO system facilitated the creation of IPRs at the international level, but it did not assure their enforcement. The GATT system assured the enforcement of liberal trade rules, but did not recognize the principle of IPRs protection.

1. The GATT/WTO System

As a matter of institutional history, the central objective of the GATT/WTO has been to provide the operating framework for the progressive liberalization of the global trading system. This objective has been carried out by the establishment of certain general principles to govern the international trading system (*e.g.*, MFN and national treatment), the negotiation of reductions in markets access barriers (*e.g.*, tariffs and quotas), the reduction of general principles to specific norms (*e.g.*, the Tokyo Round agreements on technical barriers and antidumping), and the consensus resolution of disputes (*i.e.* the Article XXIII-based dispute settlement system). The institutional objectives of the new WTO are largely identical to that of the former GATT, adding a broader scope of subject matter coverage (*i.e.* the new area agreements, including TRIPS), and attention to the principle of sustainable development (*e.g.*, the preamble to the WTO Agreement), while at the same time appearing to move away from consensus-based dispute resolution.

In the field of IPRs, the WTO should maintain its principal objective of facilitating the liberalization of the international trading system so as to promote worldwide economic growth. In the field of IPRs, trade liberalization is understood as providing assurance against the misappropriation of an agreed-upon basket of IPRs assets. Just as an effective international trading system does not tolerate the misappropriation of imported goods as they pass through customs, so the system should not tolerate the misappropriation of the agreed-upon basket of IPRs assets as they cross territorial boundaries. Such misappropriation would upset the competitive balance foreseen by the WTO Agreement, and the goal of the WTO and its Dispute Settlement Understanding is to maintain, and restore when necessary, that competitive balance. Consensus within the WTO as to the proper basket of IPRs assets deserving of protection may fluctuate over time, and changes in such consensus can be reflected in the primary instrument expressing that consensus, the TRIPS Agreement.

2. The WIPO System

The WIPO system evolved over a long period of time in response to technological changes, and in response to recognition that the coordination of international rules to protect IPRs was necessary to the effective promotion of the transborder flow of expression and ideas. The historical objective of WIPO was to provide a framework for international cooperation in the field of IPRs, and not to act as an international IPRs enforcement body. In light of this goal, WIPO evolved relatively efficient systems for the development of new international IPRs rules, for the administration of agreed-upon systems, and for the provision of technical training to facilitate the development and maintenance of the international IPRs system.

B. The On-Going Allocation of Responsibilities

In light of institutional objectives in the field of IPRs, the primary role of the WTO should be to maintain the competitive balance in trade among WTO Members as foreseen by the TRIPS Agreement. The primary role of WIPO should be to promote technological development, particularly in the developing countries, to provide a forum for the negotiation of new multilateral IPRs rules (in coordination with the TRIPS Council), and to administer multilateral IPRs conventions as at present.

1. Rule-Making

The negotiation of new multilateral IPRs conventions and the refinements of existing conventions may be continued in the WIPO forum. The Contracting States of WIPO have successfully collaborated in the formulation and adoption of substantive IPRs rules. Customary practices that have evolved in WIPO for the elaboration of new rules should continue to serve in the new dual-institutional framework. The role of the WTO in respect to such new rules should be to identify changes in the global IPRs environment that may result in a shift in the competitive balance among Members, to bring these changes to the attention of WIPO Contracting States to initiate the negotiation of new rules where appropriate, and to adopt changes as necessary to the TRIPS Agreement to establish a new consensus on the competitive balance. Changes to the TRIPS Agreement may be based on new rules agreed to in WIPO. Such changes may also be achieved directly through negotiations within the WTO, for instance regarding media and cultural issues that are closely related to services, or if negotiations on sensitive issues would require room for cross-concessions in other fields which the WIPO forum cannot provide (for example, progress in other areas important to developing countries, such as the elimination of agricultural subsidies). WIPO Committees of Experts, through the WIPO Coordination Committee, could notify the TRIPS Council of proposed changes to multilateral IPRs rules, and provide an analysis of the potential impact of those changes. The TRIPS Council may furnish a response to WIPO, pointing out where a different approach may be desirable from a trade standpoint. The use of WIPO as an initial venue for the negotiation of new rules would not foreclose negotiations in the WTO regarding the same or different subject matter.

2. Dispute Settlement

The proper allocation of dispute settlement responsibilities is very important. The completion of the WIPO Dispute Settlement Treaty would provide an appropriate complementary dispute settlement forum to that of the WTO DSB. The WIPO forum might be allocated primary responsibility for the settlement of disputes concerning the interpretation of substantive IPRs rules, with the WTO forum being allocated principal responsibility for the maintenance and restoration of competitive balance in the field of trade. A dispute involving interpretation of an IPRs standards might first be adjudicated at WIPO. A complaint based on a finding of a violation of substantive standards could thereafter be brought to the WTO, adding an allegation of harm to the competitive balance (*i.e.* nullification or impairment). The WTO could serve as dispute settlement forum of first instance when the issue of enforcement of agreed-upon standards within a national legal system is present. The IPRs Council (see proposal *infra*) could be charged with proposing the proper dispute settlement forum of first instance if a conflict between the parties arises; though a consensus voting structure in the IPRs Council will require a default procedure.

3. Developmental Assistance

The strength of WIPO as an institution is its technical expertise and skill in administration. Perhaps the major issue confronting the international economic system in connection with IPRs and technology is how to deal with existing disparities in levels of technological capacity among states. WIPO is well suited to playing the major role in formulating and executing programs to aid in global technological development, with the active cooperation of the TRIPS Council and other WTO bodies. This is a primary objective for the international economic system and for its institutions.

4. Administration

There is no reason to suggest that WIPO should not continue in its role as international IPRs administrator, for example with respect to the Patent Cooperation Treaty, since this is a task to which it is institutionally suited.

One may not ignore the issue of financial resources, which may be at the heart of government decision-making with respect to the allocation of competences between the WTO and WIPO. WIPO generates much of its own resources and should not require major budgetary enhancements in order to continue to fulfill its role as principal international IPRs-system regulator. Its staff is largely in place. The WTO would require a major infusion of resources to take over in many of the areas that WIPO presently operates. In the absence of a compelling reason for a change, it is doubtful that governments will choose to undertake a major change in the scale of the WTO Secretariat's operations.

C. New Institutional Arrangements

1. Cooperation

Cooperation between the WTO and WIPO might well be formalized at the institutional level, and the creation of a charter document that defines primary areas of institutional responsibility may be useful. An Inter-Institutional IPRs and Trade Governing Council (IPRs Council) might be created. The WTO TRIPS Council and the WIPO Governing Bodies (or Coordination Committee) could be equally represented on this body. At its initiation, the IPRs Council might make decisions only by consensus, thus rendering the precise allocation of seats as between WTO and WIPO Members less than critical. The Chair of the IPRs Council might be rotated annually or biennially between the Chair of the TRIPS Council and the Chair of the WIPO Governing Bodies.

The IPRs Council would serve to coordinate the activities of the WTO and WIPO across the range of IPRs-related activities, including dispute settlement. The IPRs Council would seek to facilitate cooperation between the WTO Committee on Trade and Development and WIPO so as to enhance progress in the field of technological development.

One of the objectives of the IPRs Council would be to explore mechanisms for creating a greater complementarity between WTO and WIPO membership. This would include the pursuit of a more universal adherence to the WIPO-administered IPRs conventions so as to reduce the possibility of conflict between WTO and WIPO on the basis of membership disparities.

2. Potential Consolidation

A cooperative institutional approach involving the WTO and WIPO would be the most desirable for at least the medium term (10 to 15 years). Whether a consolidation of the WTO and WIPO over the longer term may be desirable is an intriguing question. One might imagine that over the course of several decades the WTO would evolve into a international economic institution at which constitutional-level decisions would be made across a broader spectrum of subject matter areas. One might imagine that a decision-making structure would evolve which would adequately reflect both the effective international economic power of states and a wide range of individual and group interests. Outside the area of core decision-making which would be undertaken at the WTO, international economic decision-making and administration would be distributed to its appropriate level, whether international, regional, national or local.

In such a broad framework, international economic organizations other than the WTO might function in the manner of executive Ministries operating under the policy direction of the center. The Ministries might be responsible for executing the details of policy. WIPO might become an executive operating arm of the WTO. The principal policy decisions with respect to the international IPRs system would be made within the WTO constitutional power structure, and policy would be executed within WIPO. A vertical chain of command would exist. As with all such chains, uncertainties in the execution of policy may arise. Procedures for dealing with such uncertainties would need to be worked out.

At the present time one should hesitate to consolidate the role of WIPO under the direction of the WTO. There is some reason to question whether the WTO is sufficiently developed as an institution to recommend a significant enhancement of its role as a public policy planning and execution agency in situations involving developmental and consumer interests. Reference may be made here to a certain "democracy deficit." This deficit evidences itself in a lack of transparency, and is reflected in an environment for the negotiation of rules that is heavily weighted in favor of the existing distribution of market-based power. There is no better place than the WTO for carrying out the present purposes of the WTO. However, if the role of the WTO in formulating public policy is to be significantly enhanced, the global constitutional implications of such an enhancement must thought through with care.

Notes and Questions

1. The WTO and WIPO are not by any means the only multilateral international institutions concerned with IPRs. The World Bank is playing an increasingly important role in this area as it attempts to identify and fund projects that will contribute to the diffusion and use of technology in developing and newly-industrializing countries. The International Telecommunications Union (ITU) is involved in Internet governance issues that are closely tied to IPRs (this is discussed further in Chapter VIII). The Food and Agriculture Organization (FAO) and related organizations are concerned with the rights of farmers in regard to genetic resources. In fact, virtually all international institutions are affected by IPRs governance issues.

2. Abbott observes that IPRs policy specialists are more attuned to a skeptical approach to IPRs protection than are trade specialists, bearing in mind the works of Fritz Machlup, Walton Hamilton and others who pioneered research into the role of IPRs in economic development. Are IPRs policy specialists still skeptical about claims to the economic and social welfare benefits of IPRs protection, or has this tradition of skepticism perhaps fallen away in the past decade? Is it perhaps now the trade specialists who are the skeptics?

4. Development and Environmental Organizations

a. Multilateral Institutions of the United Nations System

WIPO and the WTO are international institutions whose charters are specifically directed towards the governance of IPRs. However, as we have previously noted, there are many international institutions whose activities are directly and indirectly affected by IPRs rules. Some of these other institutions will play a significant role in the future evolution of the international IPRs system. Examples of such institutions include the World Bank, the Food and Agriculture Organization, the International Telecommunications Union, the United Nations Conference on Trade and Development, the United Nations Environment Program, the United Nations Development Program and the World Health Organization. All of these institutions are part of the UN system of organizations.

While the basic mission of the World Bank is to promote economic development by providing loans to developing countries, the Bank in fact plays a much broader role in the economic development process through a vast array of advisory, technical assistance, development, education and training programs. In recent years, the Bank has begun to focus attention on the process of technological capacity building in the developing countries. To this end, the Bank is active in studying the role of IPRs in the economic development process in order to determine, *inter alia,* the extent to which its resources should be committed to assisting in the process of building IPRs-related infrastructure (such as patent and trademark offices). In advising its developing country clients, the Bank becomes involved in questions such as whether a proposed project includes useful mechanisms for technology transfer, and how these mechanisms might be improved.

The Food and Agriculture Organization (FAO) promotes the alleviation of hunger. One of its main missions is to increase the world food supply. The agricultural sectors in developed and developing countries are increasingly dependent on advances in biotechnology (including plant genetics) to increase crop yields. As private enterprises play an increasingly important role in agriculture related R&D, the scope of IPRs protection for biotechnological inventions and new varieties of plants takes on added interest. In addition, producers in developed and developing countries are interested in matters such as the protection of geographical indications of origin with respect to agricultural products.

The International Telecommunications Union (ITU) seeks to assure the smooth functioning of the global telecommunications infrastructure. As the focus of the telecommunications world has shifted from voice telephone to data transmission, and as the Internet and other international data networks have become of increasing importance, the ITU has become deeply involved in issues arising out of the complex relationships between telecommunications carriers and content providers. The interests of the content providers are often framed in terms of their interests in IPRs protection.

The United Nations Conference on Trade and Development (UNCTAD) is concerned with the role of trade and investment in enhancing economic development in the developing countries. UNCTAD has produced a number of important studies on the role of IPRs in the economic development process.

The United Nations Environment Program (UNEP) and the United Nations Development Program (UNDP) are concerned both with achieving sustainable development in the international economy and in promoting the interests of developing countries. High on the sustainable development agenda is the protection of genetic resources (biodiversity). The protection of biodiverse resources may depend upon the extent to which such resources may be commercially exploited, and the capacity for commercial exploitation may depend upon the level of IPRs protection such resources are afforded. UNEP and UNPD are concerned with how the wealth that accrues from the commercial exploitation of biodiverse resources will be shared among the developing countries which house most of such resources, and the private enterprises of industrialized countries which may be most capable of commercially exploiting them.

The World Health Organization (WHO) seeks to promote improvements in health care around the world. The extent of patent protection on pharmaceutical products (and related IPRs issues) are of great interest to the WHO, as patents may affect both the pricing and availability of drugs. The delegations of member states of WHO are usually composed of officials from Ministries of Health, whose focus is on the most efficient means of delivery of health care and the reduction of disease. The executive Board of WHO is in the process of recommending to the World Health Assembly a Revised Drug Strategy. The preamble to the draft resolution on the Revised Drug Strategy under consideration in early 1999 notes "that there are trade issues which require a public health perspective," recognizes "that the TRIPS Agreement provides scope for the protection of public health" and takes note "of concerns of many Member States about the impact of relevant international agreements, including trade agreements, on local manufacturing capacity and on access to and prices of pharmaceuticals in developing and least developed countries."

b. Limited Membership Institutions

In addition to multilateral institutions with wide membership (such as those that are part of the UN system), and regional institutions that reflect the interests of countries that are in geographic proximity, there are many international institutions with a relatively limited membership based on certain common interests. Among these institutions is the Organisation for Economic Cooperation and Development (OECD), the membership of which is more or less synonymous with the "industrialized" countries. The OECD often acts as an incubator for ideas that move from the limited circle of industrialized countries to the wider arena of the WTO. The interests of the industrialized countries in achieving higher levels of IPRs protection at the multilateral level was intensively discussed at the OECD both before and during the TRIPS negotiations. The OECD is well known for its excellent research staff. Following is a more detailed description of this organization.

Organisation for Economic Cooperation and Development (OECD)
OECD Secretariat*

What is the OECD?

The Organisation for Economic Co-operation and Development is a Paris-based intergovernmental organisation whose purpose is to provide its 29 Member countries** with a forum in which governments can compare their experiences, discuss the problems they share and seek solutions which can then be applied within their own national contexts. The Organisation is thus entirely at the service of its Member countries. It forms a homogeneous entity in that each Member country is committed to the principles of the market economy and pluralistic democracy.

The fundamental task of the OECD is straightforward: namely to enable its members to consult and co-operate with each other in order to

---

*http://www.oecd.org (visited 08-21-98).

**OECD Member Countries (and date of joining): Australia (1971), Austria (1961), Belgium (1961),Canada (1961), Czech Republic (1995), Denmark (1961), Finland (1969), France (1961), Germany (1961), Greece (1961), Hungary (1996), Iceland (1961), Ireland (1961), Italy (1961), Japan (1964), Korea (1996), Luxembourg (1961), Mexico (1994), The Netherlands (1961), New Zealand (1973), Norway (1961), Poland (1996), Portugal (1961), Spain (1961), Sweden (1961), Switzerland (1961), Turkey (1961),United Kingdom (1961),United States (1961).

achieve the highest sustainable economic growth in their countries and improve the economic and social well-being of their populations.

The OECD offers advice and makes recommendations to its members to help them to define their policies. On occasion its also arbitrates negotiations of multilateral agreements and establishes legal codes in certain areas of activity.

The Organisation is a forum for objective, skilled and independent dialogue which permits a thorough understanding and true assessment of the problems posed in today's increasingly complex world. The great comparative advantages of the OECD are its multidisciplinary approach — a capacity to cover all areas of government activity in a consistent way — and its system of consensus building through peer pressure. Within the different committees the peer pressure system encourages countries to be transparent, to provide explanations and justifications, and to be self-critical where necessary, the practice of self-assessment being the most original characteristic of the OECD.

How the OECD Works

The purpose of the OECD is to boost prosperity by helping to knit a web of compatible policies and practices across countries that are part of an ever more globalised world.

It accomplishes this purpose through a systematic review and analysis of nearly every element that can affect economic and social policy — from agriculture to environment, education to trade and foreign investment.

The OECD collects and analyses a unique body of data that allows comparisons of statistics across countries and provides macro-economic and micro-economic research and policy advice in fields that mirror policy-making ministries in governments.

This work, which is often made public in publications, underpins discussions by Member countries, who send experts and policy makers to meet in specialised committees and groups for each of about 200 subject areas.

Committee discussions can lead to formal agreements or rules to foster international fairness in particular parts of the economy, such as international investment, capital movements or export credits, environmental protection and combating bribery.

More often, however, discussion at the OECD is designed to contribute to better domestic policy making and more co-ordinated interna-

378

tional practice — both of which build healthier economies, create more employment, and foster trade for the benefit of OECD and non-OECD countries alike. This role is at least as important today as it was when the OECD was formed more than three decades ago.

How the OECD Is Organised

[T]he OECD comprises two main structures:
   the Council and the Committees
   the Secretariat

linked by the Secretary-General, who is chairman of the Council.

The Council

The Council is the supreme authority of the OECD and holds the decision-making power. It is composed of a representative from each Member country as well as a representative from the European Commission. The OECD ambassadors meet regularly to develop general directives on the work to be undertaken. Once each year, the Council meets at the level of Ministers. On this occasion, the Ministers of Foreign Affairs, Economics, Finance and Trade address the major problems of the moment and set the priorities for the work of the OECD for the following year. The Secretary-General of the OECD presides over the Council.

The Committees

Committees for particular subject areas, such as education, environment, trade, and investment, are comprised of specialist representatives from Member countries. Committee meetings as well as meetings of sub-groups are held regularly, and provide a forum where experts and senior policy advisors from government administrations request, review and contribute to work that will improve policy making. Meetings at ministerial level of these specialised committees are also held occasionally. Several thousand national officials get together in around 200 committees and many working groups existing within the OECD. They provide the raw data. They also develop the concrete recommendations that emerge from results of ad hoc studies and often put them into practice. It is in the heart of these committees that the future actions of Member countries take shape.

Committees usually reach decisions by consensus, and each country's position is given equal weight.

The Secretariat

The exchange of views between OECD Member countries relies on information and analysis provided by a Secretariat based in Paris. This group of eminent specialists undertakes research, gathers the facts, compares, analyses and forecasts changes in spheres extending from the macroeconomy to the environment, and from new technology to education. The Secretariat is directed by the Secretary-General, assisted by four Deputy Secretaries-General.

*****

. . . All countries have an equal voice in the OECD, irrespective of the size of their budget contribution.

Trade

Although the OECD forum has not been used to conduct formal international negotiations on trade — this role resides in the World Trade Organisation (WTO) — the promotion of trade liberalisation has always been central to the OECD mandate. As early as 1960, its Convention set the goal of contributing to the expansion of world trade on a multilateral basis in accordance with international obligations. The Trade Committee and its general Working Party were created at the birth of the OECD to fulfill that mandate.

Within this context, the OECD has striven to respond with flexibility to the needs of its Member countries, as these needs have changed considerably over the Organisation's history. During the 1960s and 1970s, the main concern of OECD Member countries in the area of trade was to reduce the very restrictive customs tariffs and import restrictions which had been inherited from the Depression of the1930s and the economic disruptions owing to World War II. Today, the Organisation has come to play a vital role in complementing the work of the WTO to promote the multilateral trading system by focusing more on the extension of this liberalisation to OECD non-Member countries and, within the OECD grouping, on dismantling secondary or tertiary trade barriers.

*****

Throughout the process, the Trade Committee has built up complementary working relationships with other international institutions, such as the United Nations Conference on Trade and Development (UNCTAD), the International Labour Organization (ILO), and more importantly, the WTO. Leaving effective trade negotiations to the latter, the OECD develops a longer-term vision of the development of international trade relations. It provides a unique forum to set out the analytical basis required to understand the issues and to discuss among its Member countries a range of "blueprints" for improving the architecture of international economic relations. In the past, the Trade Directorate has conducted pioneering work in areas such as government purchasing, trade in services, the role of intellectual property for trade, and restrictions on foreign investment, which was subsequently used in the Tokyo and Uruguay Rounds of multilateral trade negotiations. It is now launching an ambitious programme on the new dimensions of market access at the dawn of the 21st century.

*****

The Directorate for Science, Technology and Industry

The Directorate for Science, Technology and Industry (DSTI) deals with issues relating to science and technology, information and communications technologies and industry.

Science and technology (S&T) are the major source of economic growth and human progress, and they will take on greater importance as we move into the 21st century. The period ahead will be dynamic but unpredictable, as ways of making productive use of human knowledge change over time and vary across countries. The DSTI deals with such frontier issues, and its task is to identify means of advancing S&T. Today, information and communications technologies are dramatically changing how we produce things and send information. Messages, images and sounds can be transmitted instantaneously to anywhere on the planet. However, the ability of countries, companies and individuals to make use of these technologies differs, with the result that the impact on industrial competitiveness and social well-being is sweeping but uneven. Other new technologies, such as biotechnology, presents similar challenges. OECD countries are trying to understand how to meet these challenges in order to identify the most effective ways of maximising the benefits of new technologies while minimising their adverse effects.

An internationally competitive industrial base is crucial to economic and social well-being. It is through industry that the public obtains the tangible benefits of science and technology. As industry is generally located in regions with a favourable business climate, creating appropriate framework conditions and infrastructure under increasingly tight resource constraints presents an important challenge.

*****

Notes and Questions

1. The WTO TRIPS Agreement is of paramount importance in the field of IPRs protection because its rules are broadly applicable to over 130 Member countries of the WTO, because the Agreement requires that its rules be enforced within these WTO Members, and because WTO Members face the loss of trade privileges if they fail to comply TRIPS Agreement rules. Yet other important international organizations have interests that are affected by the IPRs rules adopted in the WTO. The WTO Agreement encourages cooperation between the WTO and other institutions — including those within the UN system. The TRIPS Agreement specifically envisions cooperation with WIPO. How would you propose that the interests of other international organizations be taken into account in the work of the WTO TRIPS Council? Is it enough that the same governments are represented on the TRIPS Council and in other international institutions?

2. The interests of the industrialized countries are considered within the framework of the OECD. Work at the OECD often leads to more or less common positions that are thereafter taken up at the WTO and other multilateral institutions. The developing countries have also worked to achieve common positions. Throughout the 1970s and much of the 1980s, some of this cooperation was undertaken among the so-called "Group of 77." Yet the developing countries have had a difficult time in making their positions stick in multilateral negotiations — such as in the negotiation of the TRIPS

Agreement. Part of the reason for this is that the interests of the developing countries are in fact rather diverse, depending on natural resource endowment, location, population, level of development and so forth. What other reasons might account for the relative difficulty of the developing countries in achieving their diplomatic aims?

B. Regional Institutions

1. Introduction

We have observed that regional institutions play a significant role in the international IPRs system. In this section, we explore these institutions. We first look at regional institutions in their broad context, that is, beyond their role in the governance of IPRs. In order to understand how these regional institutions approach IPRs governance, we should be aware of their political, economic and social dynamics.

The European Union (EU) as a regional institution has undertaken to harmonize or approximate IPRs laws of its member states. The EC Treaty does not expressly grant the Union organs power to regulate in the field of IPRs. Instead, the Union organs have acted on the basis of their general power to approximate member state laws in order to facilitate the broad goals of the Union — to create a single market in which goods, services, persons and capital move freely. In the view of the Council and Commission, variations in member state laws with respect to IPRs may act to distort trade and investment patterns. The extent to which the Union might act to preempt member state laws in the IPRs field through the power to approximate is not fully settled.

Article 36 of the EC Treaty authorizes the member states to adopt laws restricting the free movement of goods to protect IPRs, reflecting a territorially-based view of IPRs protection. However, the ECJ has interpreted this authority restrictively, having early on in Community history developed the intra-Union exhaustion doctrine that we first studied in the *Ideal Standard* case in Chapter I.

The EU strives to create an economically efficient single market, and its governing organs also seek to assure that the single market economy is competitive with economies of other countries and regions. In recent years, as the Union governing organs have addressed IPRs subject matter, the goal of promoting technological competitiveness within the global market has been articulated. The EC Treaty specifically contemplates the development and implementation of regional R & D programs. EU IPRs policies are related to EU R & D programs since the scope of IPRs protection may affect the manner in which newly-developed technologies are commercialized.

It should be noted that EU rules on IPRs also apply to Norway, Iceland and the Principality of Liechtenstein, based upon the Agreement Establishing the European Economic Area (Article 13, Protocol 28 and Annex XVII)(EEA Agreement). While the EEA Agreement fully harmonizes IPRs in regard to internal relations among the EU and these three European Free Trade Area (EFTA) countries, the Agreement does not necessarily bring about a coherent legal regime in regard to third country relations. This is particularly true with regard to parallel imports, discussed in Chapter IV, VII and elsewhere. Differences in EU and EFTA external relations arise from the fact that the EEA Agreement does not create a customs union. Customs unions to a certain extent require that members follow coordinated external commercial policy. The EEA is an association agreement which leaves third country relations within the domain of the EFTA Member States.

Technology transfer and IPRs policies played a major role in the Andean Pact's innovative development strategy of the early 1970s. These policies, adopted among a regional arrangement initially comprised of six Andean nations, reflected a then-prevalent hostility to industrialized country economic power in the developing world. The Andean Pact members essentially attempted to alter the balance of economic bargaining power *vis-à-vis* industrialized countries by joining together in adopting measures which placed significant limitations on IPRs grants, licensing and royalty arrangements. Perspectives have changed; the Andean Pact has now largely re-entered the market economy fold, and it has substantially revised its IPRs policies and laws to reflect TRIPS Agreement obligations.

The first excerpt in this section is taken from the 1996 proceedings of the American Society of International Law. After introductory remarks by Frederick Abbott that note broad trends in regional integration and divergences in integration goals, U.S. Trade Representative Charlene Barshefsky discusses the structure of the Asia-Pacific Economic Cooperation (APEC) forum and the various regional integration arrangements in the Americas, including the Free Trade Area of the Americas (FTAA) that is under negotiation. The FTAA is expected to have a substantial IPRs component. Following this presentation, Marcos de Azambuja, Brazil's Ambassador to Argentina, elaborates on the structure and operation of the Mercosur.

Following the American Society proceedings is an excerpt from an article by Joseph Weiler which looks in depth at the political and legal evolution of the EU. Then comes the Advisory Opinion of the European Court of Justice regarding the EC's accession to the WTO, as it specifically addresses the TRIPS Agreement. This opinion will introduce us to the role of the EU in governing IPRs, and the external relations powers of the EU with respect to IPRs.

We then turn to study of the regional institutional structures that are specifically directed at IPRs governance. Some regional institutions, such as the European Union, have elaborated a body of substantive rules, and in later chapters we will be closely examining these rules. However, in this section we limit the focus to basic institutional arrangements.

International Institutions and Economic Integration*

*****

Remarks by Frederick M. Abbott

The question put to this meeting is, "Are International Institutions Doing Their Job?" This panel will examine the institutions that are part of the process of regional economic integration. Regional economic integration may be understood in a narrow or in a broad sense. In a narrow sense, it may be understood to refer to the formation of customs unions, free trade areas and services liberalization arrangements under the rules of the General Agreement on Tariffs and Trade (GATT), Article XXIV, and the General

---

*The American Society of International Law, Proceedings of the 90th Annual Meeting, "Are International Institutions Doing Their Job?", March 27-30, 1996, Washington, D.C., 90 ASIL Proc. 508 (1996).

Agreement on Trade in Services (GATS), Article 5. The rules of the World Trade Organization (WTO) are silent regarding the kinds of institutional structures that might be used to govern or regulate these arrangements, requiring only that certain criteria with respect to the elimination of barriers to the flow of goods and services are met, and that the members of the arrangement (and the European Communities/Union as a member itself) otherwise comply with WTO rules.

In a broader sense, regional economic integration refers to the process by which a group of states gradually integrate their economic, social and political processes. In this broader sense, regional economic integration refers to removing impediments to the flow of goods, services, persons, capital and ideas. It may include the goal of progressive harmonization of national laws to facilitate this process. It may include social goals such as the protection and promotion of a healthy environment, protection against abusive exploitation of labor, and the promotion of technological development. In Europe, for example, the regional integration process has proceeded from the European Coal and Steel Community (ECSC), to the European Economic Community (EEC), to the European Communities (EC), and now to the European Union (EU), at each phase of the process enhancing the scope and goals of the regional integration undertaking well beyond the goal of creating economic efficiencies in the production and distribution of goods.

To address the question of whether institutions for regional economic integration are doing their job, we must naturally begin by asking, What is the job they have to do? The goals of the major regional integration arrangements at the moment are decidedly different. The goals of the North American Free Trade Agreement (NAFTA) and nascent Free Trade Area of the Americas (FTAA) are in the more narrow range of the classical free trade area which focuses on the elimination of barriers to the flow of goods and services. Limitations on the agenda of the NAFTA should not be overstated, as the North American Commission for Environmental Cooperation (NACEC), for example, has made a very promising start in the pursuit of progressive social goals. The Mercosur is in a middle ground, with the establishment of a common external commercial policy, macroeconomic coordination and consultation on social matters.

The goals of the European Union are ambitious, and extend not only to the free movement of persons, but to the recognition of the citizen of the

Union who enjoys voting rights in the state of residence. There is new provision for the creation of common foreign and security policies, and cooperation in justice and home affairs. There is a plan for the creation of a common currency. The EU has long maintained the goals of environmental protection and the protection of the rights of workers, and these goals have recently been expanded. The EU envisions cooperation in the development of technological infrastructure, and technological and other assistance to the less developed member states. The EU, of course, maintains a common external commercial policy that guides all member state external commercial relations, with the occasional member state tug on the reins.

Many of us might readily be prepared to offer our own value judgment as to which set of goals is optimal for a regional integration arrangement. We might side with Jean Monnet and Helmut Kohl, or with Charles de Gaulle and Margaret Thatcher. Perhaps it is best to leave this subjective judgment aside for present purposes. The relevant point for today's proceeding is that the institutions of regional economic integration are doing jobs that are the same in some respects, and substantially (if not radically) different in others. The job performance of each institutional structure may be properly evaluated only in light of its goal context or agenda.

Every person in this room is familiar at least at a high level of generality with the institutional structures of the NAFTA and EU, and perhaps to a somewhat lesser extent with the Mercosur. These are three rather distinct models. In the past five years, with the creation of the Canada-U.S. Free Trade Area, followed by the NAFTA, and with the creation of the Mercosur, we have been presented with a genuine opportunity for comparing regional integration experiences among large industrial economies. I say this not unmindful of the early Latin American integration experiences, such as the Latin American Free Trade Association (LAFTA), but in recognition of a broad consensus among Latin American governments and scholars that LAFTA did not quite get it right.

The NAFTA institutions are limited, and operate largely as a forum for consultation and consensus-based cooperation. The charter of the NAFTA Free Trade Commission (FTC) does not include general powers to issue legislative rules binding on the NAFTA parties, and there is no provision for a common external policy. Dispute settlement is largely an intergovernmental process, and with narrow exception the actual implementation of panel recommendations is a matter to be agreed upon by political decision makers.[7] Self-executing effect for the NAFTA has been denied in the United States by an act of Congress.

The EU structure is complex, and this is not an appropriate place to lay out any details. Suffice it to say that the EU Council and Commission have legislative powers that may be exercised with direct or indirect effect; that legislation may in some circumstances be adopted by qualified majority voting; that the EC Treaty is authoritatively interpreted by the European Court of Justice (ECJ), whose decisions are binding on the member states and individuals; that individuals may directly rely on the Treaty as a source of rights; and that there is an increasingly active and effective Parliament. The European Commission is responsible for negotiating and pursuing the common commercial policy on behalf of the Union and its member states.

No one would suggest that the EU integration process is without its serious difficulties. Real or imagined concerns with domination by Brussels-based Eurocrats crystallized in the member states during the Maastricht Treaty ratification process and led to a strengthening of decision-making rules based on the "subsidiarity" principle. The move to a common currency is frustrated by persistently high levels of unemployment in some member states. Economic pressures arising from low-wage sources of production outside the Union are creating an internal political force that favors restrictions on market access, mirroring the U.S. political process. "Mad cow disease" is at the moment infecting the Union governing processes. The establishment of an ambitious agenda is not itself a guarantee of success.

The creation of the Mercosur institutional structure through the adoption of the Common Market Treaty of Asunción of 1991, the Brasilia Protocol on Dispute Settlement, also of 1991, and the Protocol of Ouro Preto on the Institutional Structure of the Mercosur of December 1994, may be the most interesting development in the field of regional integration in the past decade. The Mercosur institutional structure contains a

---

[7] *See* NAFTA, Art. 2018:

    1. On receipt of the final report of a panel, the disputing Parties shall agree on the resolution of the dispute, which normally shall conform with the determinations and recommendations of the panel, and shall notify their Sections of the Secretariat of any agreed resolution of any dispute.

    2. Wherever possible, the resolution shall be non-implementation or removal of a measure not conforming with this Agreement or causing nullification or impairment in the sense of Annex 2004 or, failing such a resolution, compensation.

number of innovative features that deserve close attention both from NAFTA planners and from the architects of the FTAA. These include a consensus-based decisional structure that incorporates the power to adopt rules binding on states parties, a dispute resolution system that mandates compliance, and a novel interparliamentary consultation arrangement designed to facilitate the implementation of decisions and enhance parliamentary input into the integration process. We look forward to hearing about these features in greater detail from Ambassador de Azambuja.

Though each of our panelists will take his or her own approach to today's subject matter, I believe that it may be useful to briefly raise a few questions concerning institutions for regional economic integration that our panelists may wish to address in their presentations, or that we might return to during the discussion period.

First, are the institutional structures of the EU, Mercosur and NAFTA dictated by the specific goals of these arrangements, or does some other factor or factors give rise to the unique characteristics of each arrangement? For example, does the comparatively limited agenda of the NAFTA dictate the absence of centralized decision-making power, or is this rather the result of preoccupations within the U.S. body politic with so-called sovereignty concerns? Is there prospect for a more comprehensive set of institutions in the FTAA?

Second, and I think perhaps most important, do regional institutions play a major or decisive role in promoting the momentum of integration? Ernst Haas first suggested, in *The Uniting of Europe*, that strong regional institutions would create a spill-over effect that would accelerate and deepen the integration process. If the forward momentum of integration is stalled — if Chile does not accede to the NAFTA or if the common European currency is aborted — will the regional integration process disintegrate, and what might be the consequences? Was the postwar creation of a comparatively strong EU institutional structure, with a potentially powerful spill-over effect, a historically unique event, or could a similar arrangement realistically be contemplated elsewhere? How have the Mercosur governments managed to create their middle ground arrangement? Is the vehicle of the interparliamentary institution viewed as critical to the success of the Mercosur? Are there variations in domestic political structure that facilitate integration momentum? To what extent does the fact that European Executive authorities (such as prime ministers) generally enjoy the support of the Parliament or National Assembly facilitate European cooperation? How could such cooperation/support be facilitated in the United States? Might the creation of an interparliamentary structure within the NAFTA and FTAA along the lines of the Mercosur encourage the Western hemispheric integration movement?

Third and finally, a hypothetical postulate for reflection: that regional integration is the inevitable outgrowth of technological development in the fields of transport, telecommunications and mass-scale production, and that we as human beings are exercising very limited control over the phenomenon.[12] To some extent, the actions of national and regional institutions may temporarily speed or stall integration process, but in the final analysis we are simply observers of what science has set in motion. In this context, the role of integration planners is to assure that the fruits of the technological revolution are to improve, rather than corrupt, the human living environment.

Remarks by Charlene Barshefsky*

I would actually like to talk about the FTAA and about the Asian Pacific Economic Cooperation forum (APEC) and suggest that in the context of those arrangements institution building will clearly be evolutionary and not a matter of *a priori* thought.

There are very interesting dichotomies between the FTAA integration process and the APEC process. Let me take the architecture and institutional point first. In Asia there is very little trade architecture of any sort on a regional or on a subregional basis. There are two subregional arrangements, the arrangement among the ASEAN countries called the ASEAN Free Trade Arrangement (AFTA) and the Australia-New Zealand Closer Economic Relations Trade Agreement (CER).

There are relatively few bilateral arrangements for free and open trade in the region. One reason that the United States has taken such a lead role in the APEC is that we view the notion of regional architecture as critical over time, not only to U.S. commercial interests but also to U.S. diplomatic and security interests. Institution building is something that for the Asia-

---

[12]Foreshadowed in KARL W. DEUTSCH, POLITICAL COMMUNITY AT THE INTERNATIONAL LEVEL (1954).

*U.S. Trade Representative.

Pacific region, particularly in the economic sphere, is relatively new and untested and rather controversial.

The Western hemisphere abounds in architecture. There are five major subregional arrangements, of which NAFTA is only one. There is Mercosur, the Centro-American Common Market (CACM), the Andean Group or Development Corporation (ADC), and the Caribbean Community (CARICOM). There are, conservatively speaking, about a zillion bilateral arrangements, a multitude of multilateral arrangements and a couple of quadrilateral arrangements.

Of course, all the countries in the region, the United States included, are very fond of their own particular brand of arrangement, with the result that we abound in architecture but there is at this point no overriding harmonizing structure. The FTAA is intended, in large measure to rationalize the varying rules and regulations, to expand upon these existing arrangements, and ultimately to arrive at a genuine free trade area that would be hemisphere-wide, where either a country is in for the whole arrangement or it is not in at all, very much like the single undertaking of the Uruguay Round. But even in the FTAA process and maybe because of the existing architecture, the notion of institution building is equally controversial. There really is no consensus about what this overarching framework ought to look like and what sub-institutions should form a part of it.

Going back to APEC (but this is also true for the Western hemisphere), there are two kinds of consensuses that need to be formed before we can actually talk about institutional structures. The first is the political-level consensus; that is, to ask among a group of countries what is it that we want to accomplish? Do we have a common goal? Do we have a common vision? In the APEC context this political consensus was achieved in the course of two meetings.

A first meeting initiated by President Clinton took place in November 1993 in Seattle. There it was agreed that APEC — which had been a rather loose consultative forum — ought to be a forum in which trade liberalizations would occur and as to which we could agree to common policy and substantive goals. A year later, in November of 1994, President Suharto of Indonesia chaired APEC — it is a rotating chairmanship — and said to the leaders: "We all agree that we want to use APEC as a trade liberalizing forum. Why don't we agree on free and open trade by a specific date." And he extracted from the APEC countries, some reluctantly, commitments for free and open trade by the year 2010 for developed countries, and 2020 for developing countries. Political consensus was achieved not through any institutional structure but on a very direct basis, among the leaders themselves, meeting alone with no bureaucrats around, with no recording device in the room.

By contrast the FTAA abounds in architecture — in regional and subregional institutions. How was the political consensus achieved? Exactly the same way as in the APEC context. President Clinton called together the other thirty-three democratically elected leaders of the hemisphere and said: "Why don't we have a free trade area of the Americas: basically, at some point get rid of all these disparate agreements and have a genuine WTO-compatible free trade area." The leaders agreed. In our hemisphere there is a tremendous movement toward market economics and the view that an open economy is likely to be a more wealthy economy. Again political consensus was achieved with no institutions, no bureaucrats, and only one note-taker in the room. It is the leaders' getting together and talking among themselves and arriving at a common vision.

Then we have the question of substantive work. Political declarations are great. But at some point, these declarations must be translated into substantive work. Take the APEC example. Very little exists in the way of institutions economically. APEC has gone about the substantive work of translating this vision into some sort of reality by setting up a series of working groups — now there are ten of them of varying types — and by having a series of essentially plenary meetings called the SOM (Senior Officials Meetings), which take place roughly quarterly, sometimes more frequently. Here in plenary sessions major policy decisions are made, and the working groups often either carry out those policy decisions or do work that is an adjunct to the policy decision.

So in Seattle there were a number of working groups that gave reports in various areas. By the time of the meeting in Indonesia it was decided that if the goal is free and open trade, there needed to be some more structured environment apart from just the working groups, and so the SOM members had cut out for them the task of translating this 2010/2020 vision into a reality. This past year in November, Japan chaired APEC and at the Osaka meeting these plenary sessions in conjunction with the working groups came up with an action plan that covered fifteen areas, including everything from government procurement to tariffs and nontariff barriers. An additional directive was put forward that each country should elaborate a plan in order to move toward open and free trade in all of the areas or sectors listed. Here there is not any formal institutional structure either, but there is a lot of very concrete work coming out of APEC, using a working group format with plenary sessions.

FTAA follows the same model. It abounds in architecture, but the form it uses is exactly the same as in the case of APEC. Here again there is a series of working groups. At the Denver trade ministerial meeting following the Miami meeting, seven working groups were set up in order to do some baseline data collection and information gathering, and in Cartagena last week four more groups were set up which cover the NAFTA chapters in terms of subject matter.

Last, there are vice-ministerial plenary sessions in which more basic policy decisions are made, including discussions on the questions of paths to the FTAA and what the ultimate architecture might look like. Here again, although the hemisphere is awash in agreements, basically the movement toward the goal of increasingly liberalized trade is done in very much the same way as in the APEC process. This has occurred, however, for different reasons: While in Asia institutional structures are not particularly sought after in areas of economics, in Latin America everybody is so wedded to their particular structures that countries — in many instances — almost have to start from scratch.

I think both these processes are absolutely critical from the point of view of U.S. interests. Asia is the fastest growing region in the world, but we are continually outstripped by competitors from Japan, Europe and elsewhere. Our relationship with Asia has been dominated by security relationships and by the notion that the U.S. presence in Asia is critical for stability in the region. That is still true, but certainly the United States has broader interests as well, including definite commercial interests in seeing a stable and prosperous Asia and in seeing the United States being an economic anchor within this constellation.

In Latin America we are well anchored, but trade barriers remain relatively high. Nonetheless, forty-five cents of every Latin American dollar used to buy imports buys U.S. goods. In many countries in the region, the United States supplies well over 70 percent of everything that they import. We can certainly do better, and a free trade area of the Americas would enhance our prospects, as well as other countries' prospects, with respect to our market.

All of that is to say, that the economic interests at stake are ultimately what led to the political-level consensus, and the political-level consensus ultimately is what will lead to substantive-level consensus . . . The set of institutions arising from the substantive consensus will grow gradually and only with respect to a perceived need for additional institutions in both parts of the world.

Professor ABBOTT: It seemed to me from your presentation that politics — that is, creating consensus among the parties involved — must lead the institutions. Do you think that in the Western hemisphere this implies that the United States should take the initiative? Could perhaps the Mercosur or the Latin American governments lead for a year or two?

Ambassador BARSHEFSKY: This is a very difficult question to answer. Certainly, the Mercosur is a very important trade group and Brazil's leadership in that group seems to me critical and unquestioned. There is a tendency, however, among the Mercosur countries to move more slowly than the United States would, and this comes in part from the belief among the Mercosur countries that there needs to be a perfection of the Mercosur arrangement itself before they can move to the FTAA integration process.

On the other hand, I think business interests in both regions are such that integration will proceed relatively quickly. From my own experience having chaired several meetings in our hemisphere, countries, including the Mercosur, still look to the United States in search of leadership, and the United States views itself as the hemispheric leader. I do not see any particular change in that. I assume your question arises because of the lack of fast track authority in the United States, but I did not detect with respect to the Cartagena meeting that the lack of fast track authority altered the general view that the United States remains the hemispheric leader.

Mercosur: a Pragmatic Regional Building Block

By Ambassador Marcos Castrioto de Azambuja*

Mercosur is an interesting exercise in open-handed regionalism that is seen by its members as a necessary building block for future associative endeavors, be they with the European Union or NAFTA. It is remarkable that Argentina, Brazil, Paraguay and Uruguay — with Chile and Bolivia in an associate capacity — have been able, from 1991 to 1996, to put together a

---

*Ambassador of Brazil to Argentina. The opinions of this paper express only the views of the author and do not necessarily represent any official position.

free trade zone that is also an imperfect customs union and that this project has advanced farther and more smoothly than could realistically have been anticipated.

After a long decade that for them was largely lost in terms of economic achievements, the four original members decided to set in motion an association taking advantage of four fundamental preconditions that were achieved more or less at the same time by them all:

(1) the establishment of profound and stable democratic regimes;
(2) the awareness that the import substitution cycle had run its course;
(3) the adoption of rational and broadly orthodox macroeconomic policies; and
(4) the awareness that in a global environment their economies had to adapt and become more open and competitive.

Once this awareness and the indispensable political will converged, the process went ahead at considerable speed, taking advantage of extraordinary cultural, institutional and linguistic affinities that had always existed among the countries. It helped that for over a century there had been no major conflict, armed or otherwise.

Another important factor that helped to speed up the pace of negotiations was the acceptance that the customs union to be established would be at the beginning an incomplete one, with each member being allowed to set up, for a limited period of time, a substantial list of exceptions, ample enough to safeguard its fundamental concerns but not so wide to make the concept of a customs union empty of real meaning and validity. Other factors that contributed to the fast pace of negotiations were that the national negotiating teams remained essentially stable through the years and that decisions were taken always seeking to avoid the setting up of permanent international or supranational arrangements that could generate bureaucratic inertia.

In fact, negotiations within Mercosur have been carried out basically by a decentralized structure of ten working subgroups, each one of them charged with specific issues: communications; mining; technical guidelines; financial matters; transport and infrastructure; environment; industry; agriculture; energy; and labor, employment and social security matters.

It is helpful to indicate the instruments that have been created by the Asunción Treaty of 1991 and by the Ouro Preto Protocol of December 1994 to allow Mercosur business to be conducted in an orderly fashion:

- The *Common Market Council* (CMC), formed by the Foreign Affairs Ministers and Economic Ministers of the four partners, is the highest level agency of Mercosur, with authority to conduct its policy according to the objectives and time frames set forth in the Asunción Treaty. The meetings take place whenever necessary, but at least once a year. The Presidents of the member states usually take part in the annual CMC meeting.
- The *Common Market Group* (GMC), coordinated by the Ministries of Foreign Affairs of the member states, is the chief executive body of Mercosur, to which the above mentioned working subgroups are subordinated.
- The *Mercosur Trade Commission* (CCM), also coordinated by the Ministries of Foreign Affairs, assists the Common Market Group, striving to apply the instruments of common business policy agreed on by the member nations with regard to operations of the customs union.
- The *Joint Parliamentary Committee* (CPC) represents the legislative branches of the member nations, having an advisory and decision-making nature, with powers to submit proposals as well.
- The *Administrative Office* (SAM) is responsible for the documentation of Mercosur.
- Finally, the *Economic and Social Advisory Forum* (FCES) represents nongovernmental sectors of the member nations.

As we can see, Mercosur has an intergovernmental structure without a permanent staff. It has neither a parliament nor court of justice. The mechanism for settlement of disputes consists of a flexible system based on direct negotiations, on the fostering of consensus by the Mercosur Trade Commission or by the Common Market Group and, as a last resort, on arbitration procedures handled by an ad hoc tribunal.

It is important to note that the coordination for Mercosur matters rotates every six months among its four founding members and rules have been developed so as to make it possible to have a certain uniformity of procedures as well as an organized memory of what has been decided. We are proud of the path Mercosur has followed, having avoided so far the creation of a vast administrative machinery that had been a burdensome hindrance of previous Latin American efforts of association and integration.

In due course, more elaborate structures will have to be created and Mercosur will have to acquire a more precise legal and political identity, if for no other reason than in order to negotiate on an equal footing with the European Union and other international groupings. I am personally reluctant, however, to acknowledge the necessity to speed up this administrative structuring of Mercosur, for I think that so far the current arrangements have met the challenge of overcoming problems that have cropped up along their way.

It was a wise decision for Mercosur authorities to establish a list of agreements that could be reached and to postpone issues that are not ripe enough for constructive negotiations. Although my assessments of what Mercosur has achieved so far is extremely positive, I should not hide the fact that there are many challenges ahead and I would like to list seven that have to be faced in the next months or years.

First, given the pace of international negotiations, Mercosur will not be given the time to settle down at its own leisure and will have to respond positively to the overtures made by other international groupings and associations. It will have to develop its own style and specific procedures and institutions so as to better interact with other international arrangements.

Second, the joining of new members in Mercosur will probably require a more formal arrangement, in order to ensure an egalitarian participation by such newcomers in the decision-making process.

Third, Mercosur has suffered from a rather acute lack of theoretical and conceptional thinking and will have to engage universities and academic centers in a far more active way, so as to receive the necessary inputs to make it a coherent and purposeful entity.

Fourth, Mercosur needs more vital participation by the national communities of the four founding members, including their societal groups and trade unions, so as to fulfill the requirements of contemporary democratic legitimacy.

Fifth, physical integration problems remain a stranglehold and the interplay of four national bureaucracies firmly entrenched in their habits remains a significant obstacle.

Sixth, there are major problems concerning manpower movements and validation of university and technical degrees and certificates among the four founders. Failure to work out effective compromises in these areas could lead to considerable difficulties.

Seventh, another objective is to involve more directly local governments in the integration process and to act in a manner so as to provide a level playing field for small enterprises that so far have been left out.

For a system that is only five years old, Mercosur is, I believe, an outstanding example of what open-handed regionalism can do. The experience acquired in its functioning by its members will enable them to approach larger and more complex scenarios. This will require mature consideration and extensive and delicate negotiations with other groups that have longer trajectories and much more time to organize themselves in an effective manner.

*****

Notes and Questions

1. The importance of the trend toward regional integration for the international IPRs system should not be minimized. The EU was initially thought not to have competence to harmonize the IPRs laws of its member states since the EC Treaty did not expressly confer this competence on the Community. As the Union has evolved over a period of forty years, it has gradually assumed the major role in IPRs regulation in Europe. A similar process of IPRs convergence and integration might well take place (or has already taken place) in other regional arrangements.

As a general matter, trade specialists worry that the move toward more powerful regional institutions may end up diminishing the effectiveness of the WTO and undercut a broad multilateral approach to trade liberalization. We have already seen in the EU some efforts to adopt regional IPRs policies that may discriminate against parties who create content outside the Union (see, e.g., the provisions of the Database Directive discussed in Chapter IV). Though it is conceivable that regional arrangements might evolve into IPRs "fortresses," in which only locally-based innovators would be protected, this does not at the moment seem to be a realistic threat to the WIPO-WTO TRIPS Agreement multilateral IPRs system. It is, however, a prospect worthy of some attention.

Consider, for example, that in a recent decision involving EU rules on the international exhaustion of trademarks, *Silhouette v. Hartlauer,*[1] the Court emphasizes that the First Trade Marks Directive preempts member state autonomy and precludes the member states from adopting their own external IPRs-related policies.

2. Intellectual property harmonization in Europe has not been exclusively an EU matter. The Council of Europe, founded in 1949, which oversees implementation of the European Convention on Human Rights, has a tradition of dealing with certain aspects of copyright in the context of cultural and media policy coordination. The Council has concluded a number of conventions mainly relating to transboundary radio and television broadcasts. The most recent is the European Convention relating to Questions on Copyright Law and Neighbouring Rights in the Framework of Transfrontier Broadcasting by Satellite, which was done at Strasbourg in 1994, but has not yet entered into force. Though the Council of Europe played an important role in addressing certain European IPRs issues for a number of years, most of this function has been taken over by the EU.

3. Developing countries may find it useful to pursue regional public and private R & D strategies because this allows for the pooling of limited resources toward common goals. Do such strategies require coordination of IPRs policies? Might variations in the terms and scope of national IPRs protection distort the results of collective R&D strategies in favor of particular countries or enterprises?

---

2. The European Union, the WTO and TRIPS

The European Union plays an increasingly important role in the formulation of IPRs policies and rules both on a regional basis, and in the context of its external or foreign relations. Just as the United States has long had a major impact on the way in which international rules on IPRs have developed, arising out of the importance of the U.S. economy to the global economy, so the EU today has a similar impact. It is very difficult to understand

---

[1]*See infra*, Chapter IV, § U,1,b,ii.

EU IPRs policy divorced from an understanding of the political and legal structure and processes of the EU as a whole. In the following excerpt, Joseph Weiler portrays the historical evolution of the EU as a political and legal entity.

---

a. The Political and Legal Structure and Process of the European Union

The Transformation of Europe

J.H.H. Weiler*

Introduction

In 1951, France, Germany, Italy, and the Benelux countries concluded the Treaty of Paris establishing the European Coal and Steel Community. Lofty in its aspirations, and innovative in some of its institutional arrangements, this polity was perceived, by the actors themselves — as well as by the developers of an impressive academic theoretical apparatus, who were quick to perceive events — as an avant garde international organization ushering forth a new model for transnational discourse. Very quickly, however, reality dissipated the dream, and again quickly following events, the academic apparatus was abandoned.

Forty years later, the European Community is a transformed polity. It now comprises twelve Member States, has a population of 340 million citizens, and constitutes the largest trading bloc in the world. But the notion of "transformation" surely comes from changes deeper than its geography and demography. That Europe has been transformed in a more radical fashion is difficult to doubt. Indeed, in the face of that remarkable (and often lucrative) growth industry, 1992 commentary, doubt may be construed as subversion.

The surface manifestations of this alleged transformation are legion, ranging (in the eyes of the beholder, of course) from the trivial and ridiculous to the important and sublime. Consider the changes in the following:

---

*100 YALE L.J. 2403 (1991).

(1) the scope of Community action. Notice how naturally the Member States and their Western allies have turned to the Community to take the lead role in assisting the development and reconstruction of Eastern Europe. A mere decade or two ago, such an overt foreign policy posture for the Community would have been bitterly contested by its very own Member States.

(2) the mode of Community action. The European Commission now plays a central role in dictating the Community agenda and in shaping the content of its policy and norms. As recently as the late 1960's, the survival of supranationalism was a speculative matter, while in the 1970's, the Commission, self-critical and demoralized, was perceived as an overblown and overpaid secretariat of the Community.

(3) the image and perception of the European Community. Changes in these are usually more telling signs than the reality they represent. In public discourse, "Europe" increasingly means the European Community in much the same way that "America" means the United States.

But these surface manifestations are just that — the seismographer's tell-tale line reflecting deeper, below-the-surface movement in need of interpretation. Arguably, the most significant change in Europe, justifying appellations such as "transformation" and "metamorphosis," concerns the evolving relationship between the Community and its Member States.

How can this transformation in the relationship between the Member States and the Community be conceptualized?

In a recent case, the European Court of Justice spoke matter-of-factly of the EEC Treaty as "the basic constitutional charter" of the Community. On this reading, the Treaties have been "constitutionalized" and the Community has become an entity whose closest structural model is no longer an international organization but a denser, yet nonunitary polity, principally the federal state. Put differently, the Community's "operating system" is no longer governed by general principles of public international law, but by a specified interstate governmental structure defined by a constitutional charter and constitutional principles.

This judicial characterization, endlessly repeated in the literature, underscores the fact that not simply the content of Community-Member State discourse has changed. The very architecture of the relationship, the group of structural rules that define the mode of discourse, has mutated. Also, the characterization gives us, as analytical tools, the main concepts developed in evaluating nonunitary (principally federal) polities. We can compare the Community to known entities within meaningful paradigms.

This characterization might, however, lead to flawed analysis. It might be read (and has been read) as suggesting that the cardinal material locus of change has been the realm of law and that the principal actor has been the European Court. But this would be deceptive. Legal and constitutional structural change have been crucial, but only in their interaction with the Community political process.

The characterization might also suggest a principal temporal locus of change, a kind of "Big Bang" theory. It would almost be natural, and in any event very tempting, to locate such a temporal point in that well-known series of events that have shaken the Community since the mid-1980's and that are encapsulated in that larger-than-life date, 1992. There is, after all, a plethora of literature which hails 1992 as the key seismic event in the Community geology. But, one should resist that temptation too. This is not to deny the importance of 1992 and the changes introduced in the late 1980's to the structure and process of Community life and to the relationship between Community and Member States. But even if 1992 is a seismic mutation, explosive and visible, it is nonetheless in the nature of an eruption.

My claim is that the 1992 eruption was preceded by two deeper, and hence for less visible, profound mutations of the very foundational strata of the Community, each taking place in a rather distinct period in the Community's evolution. The importance of these earlier subterranean mutations is both empirical and cognitive. Empirically, the 1992 capsule was both shaped by, and is significant because of, the earlier Community mutations. Cognitively, we cannot understand the 1992 eruption and the potential of its shockwaves without a prior understanding of the deeper mutations that conditioned it.

Thus, although I accept that the Community has been transformed profoundly, I believe this transformation occurred in three distinct phases. In each of the phases a fundamental feature in the relationship of the Community to its Member States mutated; only the combination of all three can be said to have transformed the Community's "operating system" as a nonunitary polity.

*****

402

I. 1958 to the Mid-1970's: the Foundational Period — Toward a Theory of Equilibrium

The importance of developments in this early period cannot be overstated. They transcend anything that has happened since. It is in this period that the Community assumed, in stark change from the original conception of the Treaty, its basic legal and political characteristics. But understanding the dynamics of the Foundational Period is of more than historical interest; the patterns of Community-Member State interaction that crystalized in this period conditioned all subsequent developments in Europe.

*****

1. The Foundational Period: The "Constitutionalization" of the Community Legal Structure

Starting in 1963 and continuing into the early 1970's and beyond, the European Court of Justice in a series of landmark decisions established four doctrines that fixed the relationship between Community law and Member State law and rendered that relationship indistinguishable from analogous legal relationships in constitutional federal states.

a. The Doctrine of Direct Effect

The judicial doctrine of direct effect, introduced in 1963 and developed subsequently, provides the following presumption: Community legal norms that are clear, precise, and self-sufficient (not requiring further legislative measures by the authorities of the Community or the Member States) must be regarded as the law of the land in the sphere of application of Community law. Direct effect (a rule of construction in result) applies to all actions producing legal effects in the Community: the Treaty itself and secondary legislation. Moreover, with the exception of one type of Community legislation, direct effect operates not only in creating enforceable legal obligations between the Member States and individuals, but also among individuals inter se. Critically, being part of the law of the land means that Community norms may be invoked by individuals before their state courts, which must provide adequate legal remedies for the E.C. norms just as if they were enacted by the state legislature.

The implications of this doctrine were and are far reaching. The European Court reversed the normal presumption of public international law whereby international legal obligations are result-oriented and addressed to states. Public international law typically allows the internal constitutional order of a state to determine the method and extent to which international obligations may, if at all, produce effects for individuals within the legal order of the state. Under the normal canons of international law, even when the international obligation itself, such as a trade agreement or a human rights convention, is intended to bestow rights (or duties) on individuals within a state, if the state fails to bestow the rights, the individual cannot invoke the international obligation before national courts, unless internal constitutional or statutory law, to which public international law is indifferent, provides for such a remedy. The typical remedy under public international law in such a case would be an inter-state claim. The main import of the Community doctrine of direct effect was not simply the conceptual change it ushered forth. In practice direct effect meant that Member States violating their Community obligations could not shift the locus of dispute to the interstate or Community plane. They would be faced with legal actions before their own courts at the suit of individuals within their own legal order.

Individuals (and their lawyers) noticed this practical implication, and the number of cases brought on the basis of this doctrine grew exponentially. Effectively, individuals in real cases and controversies (usually against state public authorities) became the principal "guardians" of the legal integrity of Community law within Europe similar to the way that individuals in the United States have been the principal actors in ensuring the vindication of the Bill of Rights and other federal law.

b. The Doctrine of Supremacy

The doctrine of direct effect might not strike all observers as that revolutionary, especially those observers coming from a monist constitutional order in which international treaties upon ratification are transposed automatically into the municipal legal order and in which some provisions of international treaties may be recognized as "self-executing." The full impact of direct effect is realized in combination with the second "constitutionalizing" doctrine, supremacy. Unlike some federal constitutions, the Treaty does not include a specific "supremacy clause." However, in a series of cases starting in 1964 the Court has pronounced an uncompromising version of supremacy: in the sphere of application of Community law, any Community norm, be it an article of the Treaty (the Constitutional Charter) or a minuscule administrative regulation enacted by the Commission, "trumps" conflicting national law whether enacted before or after the Community norm. Additionally, although this has never been stated explicitly, the Court has the "Kompetenz-Kompetenz" in the Community legal order, i.e. it is the body that determines which norms come within the sphere of application of Community law.

In light of supremacy the full significance of direct effect becomes transparent. Typically, in monist or quasi-monist states like the United States, although treaty provisions, including self-executing ones, may be received automatically into the municipal legal order, their normative status is equivalent to national legislation. Thus the normal rule of "later in time" (lex posteriori derogat lex anteriori) governs the relationship between the treaty provision and conflicting national legislation. A national legislature unhappy with an internalized treaty norm simply enacts a conflicting national measure and the transposition will have vanished for all internal practical effects. By contrast, in the Community, because of the doctrine of supremacy, the E.C. norm, which by virtue of the doctrine of direct effect must be regarded as part of the Law of the Land, will prevail even in these circumstances. The combination of the two doctrines means that Community norms that produce direct effects are not merely the Law of the Land but the "Higher Law" of the Land. Parallels to this kind of constitutional architecture may, with very few exceptions, be found only in the internal constitutional order of federal states.

c. The Doctrine of Implied Powers

One possible rationale underlying the Court's jurisprudence in both direct effect and supremacy has been its attempt to maximize the efficiency by which the Community performs the tasks entrusted to it by the Treaty. As part of this rationale, one must consider the question of specific powers granted the Community to perform these tasks. Direct effect and supremacy will not serve their functions if the Community does not have the necessary instruments at its disposal. The issue in which this consideration came to the fore, in 1970, was the treaty-making power of the Community. The full realization of many E.C. internal policies clearly depended on the ability of the Community to negotiate and conclude international treaties with third parties. As is the case with Member States, the problems facing the Community do not respect its internal territorial and jurisdictional boundaries. The Treaty itself was rather sparing in granting the Community treaty-making power, limiting it to a few specified cases.

In its landmark decision of that period (the period circa 1971) the European Court held that the grant of internal competence must be read as implying an external treaty-making power. The European Court added that Community international agreements would be binding not only on the Community as such, but also, as appropriate, on and within the Member States.The significance of this ruling goes beyond the issue of treaty-making power. With this decision, subsequently replicated in different contexts, the European Court added another rung in its constitutional ladder: powers would be implied in favor of the Community where they were necessary to serve legitimate ends pursued by it. Beyond its enormous practical ramifications, the critical point was the willingness of the Court to sidestep the presumptive rule of interpretation typical in international law, that treaties must be interpreted in a manner that minimizes encroachment on state sovereignty. The Court favored a teleological, purposive rule drawn from the book of constitutional interpretation.

In a parallel, although much less noticed, development, the European Court began to develop its jurisprudence on the relationship between areas of Community and Member State competence. The Treaty itself is silent on this issue. It may have been presumed that all authority granted to the Community was to be shared concurrently with the Member States, subject only to the emerging principle of supremacy. Member States could adopt national policies and laws, provided these did not contradict Community law in the same sphere.

In a bifurcated line of jurisprudence laid in place in the early 1970's and continued thereafter, the European Court developed two complementary doctrines: exclusivity and preemption. In a number of fields, most importantly in common commercial policy, the European Court held that the powers of the Community were exclusive. Member States were precluded from taking any action per se, whether or not their action conflicted with a positive measure of Community law. In other fields the exclusivity was not an a priori notion. Instead, only positive Community legislation in these fields triggered a preemptive effect, barring Member States from any action, whether or not in actual conflict with Community law, according to specific criteria developed by the Court.

Exclusivity and preemption not only constitute an additional constitutional layer on those already mentioned but also have had a profound effect on Community decisionmaking. Where a field has been preempted or is exclusive and action is needed, the Member States are pushed to act jointly.

d. The Doctrine of Human Rights

The last major constitutional tremor was in the field of human rights. The Treaty contains no Bill of Rights and there is no explicit provision for judicial review of an alleged violation of human rights. In a much discussed line of cases starting in 1969, the Court asserted that it would, nonetheless, review Community measures for any violation of fundamental human rights, adopting for its criteria the constitutional traditions common to the Member States and the international human rights conventions to which the Member States subscribed. This enormously complex jurisprudence will be discussed later in this Article, but its symbolic significance in a "constitution-building" exercise deserves mention here. The principal message was that the arrogation of power to the Community implicit in the other three doctrines would not be left unchecked. Community norms, at times derived only from an implied grant of power, often directly effective, and always supreme, would be subjected to a human rights scrutiny by the Court. This scrutiny is important given the "Democracy Deficit" in Community decisionmaking.

If nothing else, this jurisprudence was as clear an indication as any of the audacious self-perception of the European Court. The measure of creative interpretation of the Treaty was so great as to be consonant with a self-image of a constitutional court in a "constitutional" polity. It should be noted further that the human rights jurisprudence had, paradoxically, the hallmarks of the deepest jurists' prudence. The success of the European Court's bold moves with regard to the doctrines of direct effect, supremacy, implied powers, and human rights ultimately would depend on their reception by the highest constitutional courts in the different Member States.

The most delicate issue in this context was that of supremacy. National courts were likely to accept direct effect and implied-powers, but found it difficult to swallow the notion that Community law must prevail even in the face of an explicit later-in-time provision of a national legislature to whom, psychologically, if not in fact constitutionally, Member State courts owed allegiance. Accepting supremacy of Community law without some guarantee that this supreme law would not violate rights fundamental to the legal patrimony of an individual Member State would be virtually impossible. This especially would be true in Member States like Italy and Germany where human rights enjoy constitutional protection. Thus, even if protection of human rights per se need not be indispensable to fashioning a federal-type constitution, it was critical to the acceptance by courts in the Member States of the other elements of constitution-building. One by one, the highest jurisdictions in the Member States accepted the new judicial architecture of Europe.

The skeptic may, however, be justified in challenging the "new legal order" I have described incorporating these doctrines, especially the sharp lines it tries to draw in differentiating the "new" Community order from the "old" public international law order. After all, a cardinal principle of international law is its supremacy over national law. The notion of direct effect, or at least self-execution, is also known to international law, and implied powers jurisprudence has operated in the jurisprudence of the International Court of Justice as well. If international law shares these notions of supremacy, direct effect, and implied powers, the skeptic may be correct in challenging the characterization of Community development in the Foundational Period as something out of the ordinary.

One reply is that the Community phenomenon represents a quantitative change of such a magnitude that it is qualitative in nature. Direct effect may exist in international law but it is operationalized in so few instances that it must be regarded as the exception which proves the general rule of its virtual nonexistence. In the Community order direct effect is presumptive. The question of supremacy, however, brings the key difference between the two systems into sharp relief. International law is as uncompromising as Community law in asserting that its norms are supreme over conflicting national norms. But, international law's horizontal system of enforcement, which is typically actuated through the principles of state responsibility, reciprocity, and counter measures, gives the notion of supremacy an exceptionally rarified quality, making it difficult to grasp and radically different from that found in the constitutional orders of states with centralized enforcement monopolies.

The constitutionalization claim regarding the Treaties establishing the European Community can only be sustained by adding one more layer of analysis: the system of judicial remedies and enforcement. It is this system, as interpreted and operationalized by the European judicial branch, that truly differentiates the Community legal order from the horizontality of classical public international law.

2. The Community System of Judicial Review

As mentioned above, the hierarchy of norms within the European Community is typical of a nonunitary system. The Higher Law of the Community is, of course, the Treaty itself. Neither Community organs nor the Member States may violate the Treaty in their legislative and administrative actions. In addition, Member States may not violate Community regulations, directives, and decisions. Not surprisingly, then, the Community features a double-limbed system of judicial review, operating on two levels. Two sets of legislative acts and administrative measures are subject to judicial review: (1) the measures of the Community itself (principally acts of the Council of Ministers, Commission, and European Parliament), which are reviewable for conformity with the Treaties; and (2) the acts of the Member States, which are reviewable for their conformity with Community law and policy, including the above-mentioned secondary legislation.

*****

a. Judicial Review at the Community Level

Either the Commission or an individual Member State may, in accordance with Articles 169-72 of the EEC Treaty, bring an action against a Member State for failure to fulfill its obligations under the Treaty. Generally, this failure takes the form either of inaction in implementing a Community obligation or enactment of a national measure contrary to Community obligations. The existence of a mandatory and exclusive forum for adjudication of these types of disputes sets the Community apart from many international organizations.

The role of the Commission is even more special. As one commentator noted, "[u]nder traditional international law the enforcement of treaty obligations is a matter to be settled amongst the Contracting Parties themselves. Article 169, in contrast, enables an independent Community body, the Commission, to invoke the compulsory jurisdiction of the European Court against a defaulting Member State."[38]

At the same time, the "intergovernmental" character of this procedure and the consequent limitations on its efficacy are clear. Four weaknesses are particularly glaring:

(1) the procedure is political in nature; the Commission (appropriately) may have nonlegal reasons not to initiate a prosecution;

(2) a centralized agency with limited human resources is unable adequately to identify, process, and monitor all possible Member State violations and infringements;

(3) Article 169 may be inappropriate to apply to small violations; even if small violations are properly identified, dedicating Commission resources to infringements that do not raise an important principle or create a major economic impact is wasteful; and finally, and most importantly,

(4) no real enforcement exists; proceedings conclude with a "declaratory" judgment of the European Court without enforcement sanctions.

b. Judicial Review at the Member State Level

The weaknesses of Articles 169-172 are remedied to an extent by judicial review within the judicial systems of the Member States in collaboration with the European Court of Justice. Article 177 provides, inter alia, that when a question concerning the interpretation of the Treaty is raised before a national court, the court may suspend the national proceedings and request a preliminary ruling from the European Court of Justice in Luxembourg on the correct interpretation of the Treaty. If the national court is the court of last resort, then it must request a European Court ruling. Once this ruling is made, it is remitted back to the national court which gives, on the basis of the ruling, the opinion in the case before it. The national courts and

---

[38] Evans, *The Enforcement Procedure of Article 169 EEC: Commission Discretion*, 4 EUR. L. REV. 442, 443 (1979).

the European Court are thus integrated into a unitary system of judicial review.

The European Court and national courts have made good use of this procedure. On its face the purpose of Article 177 is simply to ensure uniform interpretation of Community law throughout the Member States. That, apparently, is how the framers of the Treaty understood it. However, very often the factual situation in which Article 177 comes into play involves an individual litigant pleading in national court that a rule, measure, or national practice should not be applied because it violates the Community obligations of the Member State. In this manner the attempts of Member States to practice selective Community membership by disregarding their obligations have become regularly adjudicated before their own national courts. On submission of the case, the European Court has rendered its interpretation of Community law within the factual context of the case before it. Theoretically, the European Court may not itself rule on the application of Community law. But, as one scholar notes:

> [I]t is no secret . . . that in practice, when making preliminary rulings the Court has often transgressed the theoretical border line . . . . [I]t provides the national judge with an answer in which questions of law and of fact are sufficiently interwoven as to leave the national judge with only little discretion and flexibility in making his final decision.[40]

The fact that the national court renders the final judgment is crucial to the procedure. The binding effect and enforcement value of such a decision, coming from a Member State's own court, may be contrasted with a similar decision handed down in declaratory fashion by the European Court under the previously discussed Article 169 procedure. A national court opinion takes care of the most dramatic weakness of the Article 169 procedure: the ability of a Member State, in extremis, to disregard the strictures of the European Court. Under the 177 procedure this disregard is impossible. A state, in our Western democracies, cannot disobey its own courts.

The other weaknesses of the 169 procedure are also remedied to some extent: individual litigants are usually not politically motivated in bringing their actions; small as well as big violations are adjudicated; and, in terms of

---

[40]Rasmussen, *Why is Article 173 Interpreted Against Private Plaintiffs?*, 5 EUR. L. REV. 112, 125 (1980).

monitoring, the Community citizen becomes, willy-nilly, a decentralized agent for monitoring compliance by Member States with their Treaty obligations.

The Article 177 system is not complete, however. Not all violations come before national courts; the success of the system depends on the collaboration between national courts and the European Court of Justice; and Member States may, and often have, utilized the delays of the system to defer ruling.

On the other hand, the overall effect of the judicial remedies cannot be denied. The combination of the "constitutionalization" and the system of judicial remedies to a large extent nationalized Community obligations and introduced on the Community level the habit of obedience and the respect for the rule of law which traditionally is less associated with international obligations than national ones.

It is at this juncture that one may speculate about the most profound difference between the Community legal order and international law generally. The combined effect of constitutionalization and the evolution of the system of remedies results, in my view, in the removal from the Community legal order of the most central legal artifact of international law: the notion (and doctrinal apparatus) of exclusive state responsibility with its concomitant principles of reciprocity and countermeasures. The Community legal order, on this view, is a truly self-contained legal regime with no recourse to the mechanism of state responsibility, at least as traditionally understood, and therefore to reciprocity and countermeasures, even in the face of actual or potential failure. Without these features, so central to the classic international legal order, the Community truly becomes something "new."

At the end of the day the debate about the theoretical difference between international law and Community law may have the relevance of some long-lasting theological disputes — i.e. none at all. Whatever the differences in theory, there can be no argument that the Community legal order as it emerged from the Foundational Period appeared in its operation much closer to a working constitutional order, a fact which, as will shortly emerge, had a fundamental impact on the way in which it was treated by its Member States.

*****

412

II. 1973 to the Mid-1980's: Mutation of Jurisdiction and Competences

A. Introduction

The period of the mid-1970's to the mid-1980's is traditionally considered a stagnant epoch in European integration. The momentum created by the accession of Great Britain, Ireland, and Denmark did not last long. The Oil Crisis of late 1973 displayed a Community unable to develop a common external posture. Internally the three new Member States, two of which, the U.K. and Denmark, were often recalcitrant partners, burdened the decisionmaking process, forcing it to a grinding pace. It is not surprising that much attention was given in that period to proposals to address a seriously deteriorating institutional framework and to relaunch the Community.

And yet it is in this politically stagnant period that another large scale mutation in the constitutional architecture of the Community took place, a mutation that has received far less attention than the constitutional revolution in the Foundational Period. It concerned the principle of division of competences between Community and Member States.

In most federal polities the demarcation of competences between the general polity and its constituent units is the most explosive of "federal" battlegrounds. Traditionally, the relationship in nonunitary systems is conceptualized by the principle of enumerated powers. The principle has no fixed content and its interpretation varies from system to system; in some it has a stricter and in others a more relaxed construction. Typically, the strength by which this principle is upheld (or, at least, the shrillness of the rhetoric surrounding it) reflects the strength of the belief in the importance of preserving the original distribution of legislative powers as a defining feature of the polity. Thus, there can be little doubt about the very different ethos that underscored the evolution of, for example, the Canadian and U.S. federalisms, in their formative periods and beyond, regarding enumeration. Nowhere is this different ethos clearer than in the judicial rhetoric of enumeration. The dicta of Lord Atkin and Chief Justice Marshall concerning powers are the theater pieces of this rhetoric. Likewise, the recurring laments over the "death of federalism" in this or that federation are typically associated with a critique of a relaxed attitude towards enumeration and an inevitable shift of power to the center at the expense of the states.

413

The different views about the strictness or flexibility of enumeration reflects a basic understanding of federalism and integration. Returning to the Canadian/U.S. comparison, we find the Atkin and Marshall dicta reconceptualized as follows: Wade, in the context of the Canadian experience, suggests that:

> The essential elements of a federal constitution are that powers are divided between the central and provincial governments and that neither has legal power to encroach upon the domain of the other, except through the proper process of constitutional amendment . . . . [T]he spirit . . . which is inherent in the whole federal situation [is] that neither side, so to speak, should have it in its power to invade the sphere of the other.[69]

In contrast, Sandalow, reflecting on the U.S. experience, suggests that:

> The disintegrative potential of [questions concerning the legality of governmental action] is especially great when they [challenge] the distribution of authority in a divided or federal system. . . . [Where] Congress determines that a national solution is appropriate for one or another economic issue, its power to fashion one is not likely to be limited by constitutional divisions of power between it and the state legislatures.[70]

These differences in approach could be explained by formal differences in the structure of the British North American Act (which predated the current Canadian Constitution) as compared to the U.S. Constitution. But they also disclose a principled difference in the way the two systems value enumerated powers within the federal architecture, a difference between ends and means, functions and values. In the Wade conception of the Canadian system the division of powers was considered a per se value, an end in itself. The form of divided governance was considered to be on par with the other fundamental purposes of a government, such as obtaining security, order, and welfare, and was viewed as part of its democratic architecture. In the

---

[69]Wade, *Amendment of the Constitution of Canada: The Role of the United Kingdom Parliament* in BRITISH NORTH AMERICA ACTS: THE ROLE OF PARLIAMENT, 2 HC 42, at 102, 108 (1981) (memorandum and evidence submitted to the Foreign Affairs Committee of the House of Commons).

[70]Sandalow, *The Expansion of Federal Legislative Authority*, in COURTS AND FREE MARKETS 49, 49-50 (1982) (I have reversed the order of quoted sentences).

United States, the federal distribution retained its constitutional importance as the system evolved. In practice, however, it would seem that the principle of division was subjected to higher values and invoked as a useful means for achieving other objectives of the U.S. union. To the extent that the division became an obstacle for the achievement of such aims it was sacrificed. We may refer to this approach as a functional one. The dichotomy is, of course, not total; we find strands of both the functional and per se approaches in each of the systems. Nevertheless, clear differences exist in the weight given to each of the strands and in the evolution of the two federations. In addition, the legal debate about division of powers was (and remains) frequently the code for battles over raw power between different loci of governance, an aspect ultimately of crucial importance.

In Europe, the Treaty itself does not precisely define the material limits of Community jurisdiction. But it is clear that, in a system that rejected a "melting pot" ethos and explicitly in the preamble to its constituent instrument affirms the importance of "an ever closer union among the peoples of Europe," that saw power being bestowed by the Member State on the Community (with residual power thus retained by the Member States) and consecrated in an international Treaty containing a clause that effectively conditions revision of the treaty on ratification by parliaments of all Member States, the "original" understanding was that the principle of enumeration would be strict and that jurisdictional enlargement (rationae materia) could not be lightly undertaken. This understanding was shared not only by scholars, but also by the Member States and the political organs of the Community, as evidenced by their practices, as well as by the Court of Justice itself. In its most famous decision, *Van Gend & Loos*, the Court affirmed that the Community constitutes "a new legal order of international law for the benefit of which the states have limited their sovereign rights, albeit in limited fields."[76] And earlier, in even more striking language, albeit related to the Coal and Steel Community, the Court explained that,

> [t]he Treaty rests on a derogation of sovereignty consented by the Member States to supranational jurisdiction for an object strictly determined. The legal principle at the basis of the Treaty is a principle of limited competence. The Community is a legal person of public law and

---

[76]Case 26/62, N.V. Algemene transport — en Expeditie Oderneming Van Gend & Loos v. Nederlandse administratie der belastingen, 1963 E.C.R.

to this effect it has the necessary legal capacity to exercise its functions but only those.[77]

In light of the Member States' vigorous reaction to the constitutional mutation of the Community during the Foundational Period, seizing effective control of Community governance, and the fact that a lax attitude to enumeration would indeed seem to result in a strengthening of the center at the expense of the states, we would expect that this "original" understanding of strict enumeration would be tenaciously preserved.

I characterize the period of the 1970's to the early 1980's as a second and fundamental phase in the transformation of Europe. In this period the Community order mutated almost as significantly as it did in the Foundational Period. In the 1970's and early 1980's, the principle of enumerated powers as a constraint on Community material jurisdiction (absent Treaty revision) substantially eroded and in practice virtually disappeared. Constitutionally, no core of sovereign state powers was left beyond the reach of the Community. Put differently, if the constitutional revolution was celebrated in the 1960's albeit "in limited fields," the 1970's saw the erosion of these limits. As an eminent authority assesses the Community today: "There simply is no nucleus of sovereignty that the Member States can invoke, as such, against the Community."[80]

*****

III. 1992 AND BEYOND

A. Introduction

The 1992 program and the Single European Act (SEA) determine both the current agenda of the Community and its modus operandi. Neither instrument is on its face functionally radical; the White Paper goal of achieving a single market merely restates, with some nuances, the classical (Treaty

---

[77] Joined Cases 7/56, 3-7/57, Dinecke Algera v. Common Assembly of the European Coal and Steel Community, 1957-58 E.C.R. 39. . . .

[80]Lenaerts, *Constitutionalism and the Many Faces of Federalism*, 38 Am. J. Comp. L. 205, 220 (1990). Note that Lenaerts refers in this statement to what I have termed in this article "absorption."

of Rome) objective of establishing a common market. The bulk of the 1992 program is little more than a legislative timetable for achieving in seven years what the Community should have accomplished in the preceding thirty. The SEA is even less powerful. Its forays into environmental policy and the like fail to break new jurisdictional ground, and its majority voting provisions, designed to harmonize non-tariff barriers to trade, seem to utilize such restrictive language, and open such glaring new loopholes, that even some of the most authoritative commentators believed the innovations caused more harm than good in the Community. Clearly, the European Parliament and the Commission were far from thrilled with the new act.

And yet, with the hindsight of just three years, it has become clear that 1992 and the SEA do constitute an eruption of significant proportions. Some of the evidence is very transparent. First, for the first time since the very early years of the Community, if ever, the Commission plays the political role clearly intended for it by the Treaty of Rome. In stark contrast to its nature during the Foundational Period and the 1970's and early 1980's, the Commission in large measure both sets the Community agenda and acts as a power broker in the legislative process.

Second, the decisionmaking process takes much less time. Dossiers that would have languished and in some cases did languish in impotence for years in the Brussels corridors now emerge as legislation often in a matter of months.

For the first time, the interdependence of the policy areas at the new-found focal point of power in Brussels creates a dynamic resembling the almost forgotten predictions of neo-functionalist spillover. The ever-widening scope of the legislative and policy agenda of the Community manifests this dynamic. The agreement to convene two new intergovernmental conferences to deal with economic and monetary union just three years after the adoption of the SEA symbolizes the ever-widening scope of the agenda, as does the increased perception of the Community and its institutions as a necessary, legitimate, and at times effective locus for direct constituency appeal.

But if the instruments themselves (especially the SEA) are so meager, how can one explain the changes they have wrought?

*****

B. Structural Background to 1992 and the Single European Act —
The Tension and its Resolution

*****

The key to the success of the 1992 strategy occurred when the Member States themselves agreed to majority voting. They took this step clearly not as a dramatic political step toward a higher level of European integration in the abstract, but rather as a low-key technical necessity in realizing the "non-controversial" objectives of the White Paper. This movement found expression in the single most important provision of the SEA, Article 100a.

As indicated above, this provision at face value seems minimalist and even destructive. First, the move to majority voting in Article 100a is couched as a residual measure and derogation from the principal measure, which requires unanimity, namely old Article 100. Second, the exception to Article 100a, Article 100a(4), was drafted in an even more restrictive form by the heads of state and government themselves. The exception states that for enactments by majority voting a Member State may, despite the existence of a Community norm, adopt national safeguard measures. Indeed, this exception may be seen as an ingenious attempt by the Member States to retain the equilibrium of the Foundational Period in the new context of majority voting.

If, after the adoption of a harmonization measure by the Council acting by a qualified majority, a Member State deems it necessary to apply national provisions on grounds of major needs referred to in Article 36 . . . it shall notify the Commission of these provisions. The Commission shall confirm the provisions involved after having verified that they are not a means of arbitrary discrimination or a disguised restriction on trade between Member States. By way of derogation from the procedure laid down in Articles 169 and 170, the Commission or any Member State may bring the matter directly before the Court of Justice if it considers that another Member State is making improper use of the powers provided for in this Article.

The essence of the original equilibrium rested on the acceptance by the Member States of a comprehensive Community discipline on the condition that each would have a determinative Voice, the veto, in the establishment of new norms. In Article 100a, the Member States, by accepting a passage to majority voting, seemed to be destroying one of the two pillars of the foundational equilibrium. But, by allowing a Member State to derogate from a measure even in the face of a Community norm (adopted by a majority!) the other pillar of comprehensive Community jurisdiction seems to be equally eroded, thereby restoring the equilibrium. The exception breaks, of course, the rule of preemption established by the Court in cases where harmonization measures were adopted.

*****

Although the language of the provision suggests the new system was intended as a derogation, the prevailing view is that Article 100a has become the "default" procedure for most internal market legislation, and that the procedure of other articles is an exception. Significantly, the connection between Article 100a and Article 8a means that majority voting should take place, except where specifically excluded, for all measures needed to achieve the objective of an internal market. The internal market is defined as "an area without internal frontiers in which the free movement of goods, persons, services and capital is ensured." This requirement of majority voting extends the scope of Article 100a procedure beyond the harmonization of technical standards affecting the free movement of goods. The net result is that few cases exist that would compel resort to the old legal basis and its unanimity requirement. The Commission proposes the legal basis of decisions; any change of such basis would be subject itself to a unanimous Council vote, which would be difficult to achieve. In any event, even if Council could change the legal basis, the Court, if a challenge were brought, would tend to side with the Commission on issues of legal basis.

Likewise, and contrary to some of the doomsday predictions, the derogation to the principle of preemption in Article 100a(4), so carefully crafted by prime ministers and presidents, has had and must have very little impact. It allows a Member State to adopt, under strict conditions and subject to judicial review, unilateral derogation of Community harmonizing measures when the Member State seeks to uphold a higher level of protection. But that does not seem to be the real battlefield of majority voting. The real battlefield is regulation by the Community in areas in which Member States may feel that they do not want any regulation at all, let alone a higher Community standard.

419

The sharpest impact, however, of majority voting under the SEA does not turn on these rather fine points. Earlier I explained that, although the language of the Luxembourg Accord* suggested its invocation only when asserting a vital national interest, its significance rested in the fact that practically all decisionmaking was conducted under the shadow of the veto and resulted in general consensus politics.

Likewise, the significance of Article 100a was its impact on all Community decisionmaking. Probably the most significant text is not the SEA, but the consequently changed rules of procedure of the Council of Ministers, which explain the rather simple mechanism for going to a majority vote. Thus, Article 100a's impact is that practically all Community decisionmaking is conducted under the shadow of the vote (where the Treaty provides for such vote). The Luxembourg Accord, if not eliminated completely, has been rather restricted. For example, it could not be used in the areas in which Article 100a provides the legal basis for measures. In addition, to judge from the assiduousness with which the Member States argue about legal bases, which determine whether a measure is adopted by majority or unanimity, it is rather clear that they do not feel free to invoke the Luxembourg Accord at whim. If the Accord persists at all, it depends on the assertion of a truly vital national interest, accepted as such by the other Member States, and the possibility of any Member State forcing a vote on the issue under the new rules of procedure. In other words, in accordance with the new rules, to invoke the Luxembourg Accord a Member State must persuade at least half the Member States of the "vitality" of the national interest claimed.

---

*Authors' note: earlier in this article, Joseph Weiler explained:

During the Foundational Period, in every phase of decisionmaking, the Member States, often at the expense of the Commission, assumed a dominant say. The cataclysmic event was the 1965 crisis brought about by France, which objected to the entry into force of the Treaty provisions that would actually introduce majority voting at the end of the Transitional Period. The crisis was "resolved" by the legally dubious Luxembourg Accord whereby, de facto, each and every Member State could veto Community proposed legislation. [The text may be found in B:2 ENCYCLOPEDIA OF EUROPEAN COMMUNITY LAW PB10-336. Although the Accord does not as such sanction the veto power, "a convention giving each Member State, in effect, a right of veto in respect of its 'very important interests' was established by the practice of the Council after 1965." Id. at PB10-337.] This signaled the rapid collapse of all other supranational features of Community decisionmaking. (At pages 2422-23)

Notes and Questions

1. Legal doctrines such as those of "direct effect" and "supremacy" may seem far removed from the everyday world of the practicing IPRs lawyer, but their importance to the practitioner should not be underestimated. Consider, for example, that many EU legislative enactments concerning IPRs take the form of "directives" (described below) which require that member states adopt laws, but do not prescribe their precise form. If a copyright lawyer in Germany believes that his or her client should benefit from rules of an EU directive that are not adequately reflected in German law, may the German lawyer invoke the terms of the directive to prevail over German law in the German courts? This is a question of direct effect. The doctrine of direct effect is further explored in Chapter III. How might the doctrine of supremacy affect the practical interests of IPRs lawyers and their clients?

2. On a similar note, the procedures for the adoption of Union legislation determine the way in which IPRs legislation is adopted. The move to qualified majority voting has certainly made it easier for the Union to adopt IPRs rules. It is important to observe here that the voting procedures described by Joseph Weiler in 1991 underwent another substantial transformation as a consequence of the Maastricht Treaty on European Union of 1993. The Maastricht Treaty substantially enhanced the role of the European Parliament in the legislative process. While the Parliament still does not have the power to initiate legislation, its powers to influence the ultimate form of legislation are now rather considerable. The European Parliament has played a significant role in the recent adoption of EU legislation on matters such as the protection of biotechnological inventions and the protection of designs.

b. The External IPRs Relations of the EU and the TRIPS Agreement

i. Competence to Conclude the TRIPS Agreement

The following extract from the opinion of the ECJ makes reference to the four principal institutions of the European Union/Communities — the Council, the Commission, the Parliament and, of course, the Court of Justice itself.

The Council is the main legislative organ of the EU. It is composed of a ministerial level representative from each member state. The minister who represents a member may vary from meeting to meeting. The Council acts by adopting "directives," "regulations" and "decisions".

A *directive* is an instruction to the member states that obligates them to bring their legislation into conformity with its requirements, but leaves to the discretion of each member state the precise means of achieving this goal. The directive will establish a date as of which conformity must be achieved. Directives generally may not be directly relied upon as a source of rights by EU persons, though they may sometimes be directly relied upon if a member state fails to implement its obligations within the time period established by the directive.

A *regulation* is in essence an ordinary piece of legislation that applies directly in the law of the member states, and without the requirement of implementing legislation. In appropriate cases, regulations may be relied upon by EU persons as a direct source of rights.

A *decision* is an order directed at a particular person.

As discussed by Joseph Weiler above, the Council adopts directives, regulations and decisions either by unanimous or by "qualified majority" voting. The voting procedure that is required in a particular situation is prescribed by the EC Treaty. Member states are accorded different numbers of votes for use in the qualified majority voting procedure, taking into account the varying populations of the member states and other factors.

The Commission is the executive institution of the EU. It is composed of seventeen Commissioners who head twenty "directorates" (which are more or less analogous to U.S. federal agencies). The Commissioners are independent of the member states, yet positions as Commissioner are allocated among nationals of the member states. The Commissioners act according to the principal of "collegiality," which in essence is a consensus decision-making procedure.

The Commission is responsible for assuring that the law of the Union is implemented, and for proposing legislative initiatives to the Council. The Commission has limited powers to issue regulations on its own authority (mainly in the competition law area), but often issues regulations based on Council-delegated authority.

The European Parliament is a popularly elected body of representatives. Each member state is allocated a number of seats in the Parliament. A national of the EU may vote for the representative of the member state in which he or she is residing.

The Parliament reviews legislation proposed by the Council, and it may act on that legislation in a number of ways depending on the subject matter. In some instances, the Parliament has the power to force the Council to move from qualified majority to unanimous voting. In other cases, the Parliament may defeat Council proposals. The Parliament does not have the power to adopt EU legislation on its own accord.

The European Court of Justice is the guardian of the EC Treaty. It hears complaints brought by the EU organs, by the member states and by individuals. Complaints by individuals usually reach the Court by referral from member state courts. Decisions of the ECJ are binding on the Union organs, member states and individuals.

In the following opinion, the ECJ considers whether the EC has exclusive competence to conclude the WTO TRIPS Agreement, or whether that agreement should be concluded as a "mixed" agreement with adherence by the EC and the member states.

Re The Uruguay Round Treaties (Opinion 1/94)
The Court of Justice of the European Communities
[1995] 1 CMLR 205

15 November 1994

Panel: Presiding, Rodriguez Iglesias CJ; Joliet (Rapporteur), Schockweiler, Kapteyn, Gulmann, Mancini, Kakouris, Moitinho de Almeida, Murray, Edward, La Pergola JJ

Headnote:

Opinion under Article 228(6) EC.

Provisions considered:

EC 43, 100a, 113, 235

*****

Opinion [of the Court]:

I. Introduction

The questions put to the Court by the Commission in its request for an Opinion, submitted pursuant to Article 228(6) of the Treaty establishing the European Community, seek to ascertain, first, whether or not the Community has exclusive competence to conclude the Multilateral Agreements on Trade in Goods, in so far as those Agreements concern ECSC products and Euratom products. Those questions further relate to the exclusive competence the Community may enjoy by virtue of either Article 113 EC, or the parallelism of internal and external competence, or Articles 100a or 235 EC, to conclude the General Agreement on Trade in Services (hereinafter "GATS") and the Agreement on Trade-Related Aspects of Intellectual Property Rights, including trade in counterfeit goods (hereinafter "TRIPs").

Those agreements are annexed to the Agreement establishing the World Trade Organisation (hereinafter "the WTO Agreement"). The WTO Agreement establishes a common institutional framework for the conduct of trade relations among its members in matters related to the agreements and legal instruments annexed to it (Article II(1) of the WTO Agreement). Those agreements embody the results of the Uruguay Round multilateral trade negotiations launched by the Punta del Este Ministerial Declaration of 20 September 1986.

Having approved that declaration, the Council and the Member States decided, "in order to ensure the maximum consistency in the conduct of the negotiations", that "the Commission would act as the sole negotiator on behalf of the Community and the Member States". However, it was stated in the minutes of the meeting that that "decision [did] not prejudge the question of the competence of the Community or the Member States on particular issues".

On 15 December 1993, the Trade Negotiations Committee, a body specially set up by the Punta del Este Conference to conclude the Uruguay Round negotiations, meeting at the level of senior officials, approved the Final Act embodying the results of the Uruguay Round multilateral trade negotiations.

At its meeting on 7 and 8 March 1994, the Council decided to proceed to the signature of the Final Act and the WTO Agreement. It authorised the President of the Council and Commissioner Sir Leon Brittan to sign the Final Act and the WTO Agreement at Marrakesh on 15 April 1994 on behalf of the Council of the European Union. The representatives of the Member States, who took the view that those acts "also (covered) matters of national competence", agreed on the same date that they would proceed to sign the Final Act and the WTO Agreement. The Commission, for its part, had recorded in the minutes its view that "the Final Act (. . . .) and the agreements annexed there to fall exclusively within the competence of the European Community".

The Commission submitted its request for an Opinion on 6 April 1994. It asked the following questions:

As regards the results of the Uruguay Round GATT trade talks contained in the Final Act of 15 December 1993:

(1) Does the European Community have the competence to conclude all parts of the Agreement establishing the WTO concerning trade in Services

(GATS) and trade-related aspects of intellectual property rights including trade in counterfeit goods (TRIPs) on the basis of the EC Treaty, more particularly on the basis of Article 113 EC alone, or in combination with Article 100a EC and/or Article 235 EC?

*****

(3) If the answer to the above . . . . question[s] is in the affirmative, does this affect the ability of Member States to conclude the WTO Agreement, in the light of the agreement already reached that they will be original Members of the WTO?

The agreements resulting from the Uruguay Round were indeed signed at Marrakesh on 15 April 1994. On behalf on the Community and its Member States, they were signed in accordance with the decisions referred to above. . . .

The request for an Opinion submitted by the Commission was served on the Council and the Member States on 24 May 1994.

*****

VII. Article 113 EC Treaty, GATS and TRIPs

The Commission's main contention is that the conclusion of both GATS and TRIPs falls within the exclusive competence conferred on the Community in commercial policy matters by Article 113 EC. That point of view has been vigorously disputed, as to its essentials, by the Council, by the Member States which have submitted observations and by the European Parliament, which has been permitted, at its request, to submit observations. It is therefore appropriate to begin by examining the Commission's main contention, with reference to GATS and TRIPs respectively.

*****

B. TRIPs

The Commission's argument in support of its contention that the Community has exclusive competence under Article 113 is essentially that the rules concerning intellectual property rights are closely linked to trade in the products and services to which they apply.

It should be noted, first, that Section 4 of Part III of TRIPs, which concerns the means of enforcement of intellectual property rights, contains specific rules as to measures to be applied at border crossing points. As the United Kingdom has pointed out, that section has its counterpart in the provisions of Council Regulation 3842/86 laying down measures to prohibit the release for free circulation of counterfeit goods. Inasmuch as that regulation concerns the prohibition of the release into free circulation of counterfeit goods, it was rightly based on Article 113 of the Treaty: it relates to measures to be taken by the customs authorities at the external frontiers of the Community. Since measures of that type can be adopted autonomously by the Community institutions on the basis of Article 113 EC, it is for the Community alone to conclude international agreements on such matters.

However, as regards matters other than the provisions of TRIPs on the release into free circulation of counterfeit goods, the Commission's arguments cannot be accepted.

Admittedly, there is a connection between intellectual property and trade in goods. Intellectual property rights enable those holding them to prevent third parties from carrying out certain acts. The power to prohibit the use of a trade mark, the manufacture of a product, the copying of a design or the reproduction of a book, a disc or a videocassette inevitably has effects on trade. Intellectual property rights are moreover specifically designed to produce such effects. That is not enough to bring them within the scope of Article 113. Intellectual property rights do not relate specifically to international trade; they affect internal trade just as much as, if not more than, international trade.

As the French Government has rightly observed, the primary objective of TRIPs is to strengthen and harmonise the protection of intellectual property on a worldwide scale. The Commission has itself conceded that, since TRIPs lays down rules in fields in which there are no Community harmonisation measures, its conclusion would make it possible at the same time to achieve harmonisation within the Community and thereby to contribute to the establishment and functioning of the Common Market.

It should be noted here that, at the level of internal legislation, the Community is competent, in the field of intellectual property, to harmonise national laws pursuant to Articles 100 and 100a and may use Article 235 as the basis for creating new rights superimposed on national rights, as it did in Council Regulation 40/94 on the Community trade mark. Those measures are subject to voting rules (unanimity in the case of Articles 100 and 235) or rules of procedure (consultation of the Parliament in the case of Articles 100 and 235, the joint decision-making procedure in the case of Article 100a) which are different from those applicable under Article 113.

If the Community were to be recognised as having exclusive competence to enter into agreements with non-member countries to harmonise the protection of intellectual property and, at the same time, to achieve harmonisation at Community level, the Community institutions would be able to escape the internal constraints to which they are subject in relation to procedures and to rules as to voting.

Institutional practice in relation to autonomous measures or external agreements adopted on the basis of Article 113 cannot alter this conclusion.

The Commission cites three cases in which, by virtue of the "new commercial policy instrument" (Council Regulation 2641/84 on the strengthening of the common commercial policy with regard in particular to protection against illicit commercial practices, which was itself based on Article 113 of the Treaty), procedures were opened to defend the Community's intellectual property interests: Commission Decision 87/251 of 12 March 1987 on the initiation of an international consultation and disputes settlement procedure concerning a United States measure excluding imports of certain aramid fibres into the United States of America; notice of initiation of an "illicit commercial practice" procedure concerning the unauthorised reproduction of sound recordings in Indonesia; notice of initiation of an examination procedure concerning an illicit commercial practice, within the meaning of Council Regulation 2641/84, consisting of piracy of Community sound recordings in Thailand.

The measures which may be taken pursuant to that regulation in response to a lack of protection in a non-member country of intellectual property rights held by Community undertakings (or to discrimination against them in that field) are unrelated to the harmonisation of intellectual property protection which is the primary objective of TRIPs. According to Article 10(3) of Regulation 2641/84, cited above, those measures are: the suspension or withdrawal of any concession resulting from commercial policy negotiations; the raising of existing customs duties or the introduction of any other charge on imports; and the introduction of quantitative restrictions or any other measures modifying import or export conditions in trade with the non-member country concerned. All those measures fall, by their very nature, within the ambit of commercial policy.

The Commission also relies on measures adopted by the Community in relation to Korea within the framework of Council Regulation 4257/88 applying generalised tariff preferences for 1989 in respect of certain industrial products originating in developing countries. Since Korea had discriminated between its trading partners as regards protection of intellectual property (see the nineteenth recital in the preamble to the regulation), the Community suspended the generalised tariff preferences in respect of its products (Article 1(3) of the regulation).

That argument is no more convincing than the preceding one. Since the grant of generalised preferences is a commercial policy measure, as the Court has held (see the "Generalised tariff preferences" judgment in Case 45/86, EC COMMISSION v EC COUNCIL), so too is their suspension. That does not in any way show that the Community has exclusive competence pursuant to Article 113 to conclude an agreement with non-member countries to harmonise the protection of intellectual property worldwide.

In support of its argument, the Commission has also cited provisions relating to the protection of intellectual property in certain agreements with non-member countries concluded on the basis of Article 113 of the Treaty.

It should be noted that those provisions are extremely limited in scope. The agreement between the European Economic Community and the People's Republic of China on trade in textile products, initialled on 9 December 1988, and the agreement between the European Economic Community and the Union of Soviet Socialist Republics on trade in textile products, initialled on 11 December 1989, merely provides for a consultation procedure in relation to the protection of trade marks or designs in respect of textile products. Moreover, the three interim agreements concluded between the Community and certain east European countries (Agreement with Hungary of 16 December 1991; Agreement with the Czech and Slovak Federal Republic of 16 December 1991; Agreement with the Republic of Bulgaria of 8 March 1993) all contain identically worded clauses (Articles 35, 36 and 37 respectively) calling upon those countries to improve the protection of intellectual property in order to provide, within a given time, "a level of protection similar to that provided in the Community" by Community acts. As the French Government has rightly observed, clauses of that type are binding only on the non-member country which is party to the agreement.

The fact that the Community and its institutions are entitled to incorporate within external agreements otherwise falling within the ambit of Article 113 ancillary provisions for the organisation of purely consultative procedures or clauses calling on the other party to raise the level of protection of intellectual property does not mean that the Community has exclusive competence to conclude an international agreement of the type and scope of TRIPs.

Lastly, it is indeed true, as the Commission states, that the Agreement with the Republic of Austria of 23 December 1988 on the control and reciprocal protection of quality wines and "retsina" wine and the Agreement with Australia of 26 and 31 January 1994 on trade in wine contain provisions relating to the reciprocal protection of descriptions of wines. The names of Austrian wine-growing regions are reserved exclusively, within the territory of the Community, to the Austrian wines to which they apply and may be used only in accordance with the conditions laid down in the Austrian rules (Article 3(3) of the agreement). A similar provision is contained in the agreement with Australia (Article 7(3)).

However, as is plain from the preamble to Council Decision 94/184 of 24 January 1994 concerning the conclusion of an Agreement between the European Community and Australia on trade in wine, that agreement was reached at Community level, because its provisions are directly linked to measures covered by the common agricultural policy, and specifically by the Community rules on wine and winegrowing. Moreover, that precedent does not provide support for any argument in relation to patents and designs, the protection of undisclosed technical information, trade marks or copyright, which are also covered by TRIPs.

In the light of the foregoing, it must be held that, apart from those of its provisions which concern the prohibition of the release into free circulation of counterfeit goods, TRIPs does not fall within the scope of the common commercial policy.

VIII. The Community's implied external powers, GATS and TRIPs

In the event of the Court rejecting its main contention that the Community has exclusive competence pursuant to Article 113, the Commission maintains in the alternative that the Community's exclusive competence to conclude GATS and TRIPs flows implicitly from the provisions of the Treaty establishing its internal competence, or from the existence of legislative acts of the institutions giving effect to that internal competence, or else from the need to enter into international commitments with a view to achieving an internal Community objective. The Commission also argues that, even if the Community does not have adequate powers on the basis of specific provisions of the Treaty or legislative acts of the institutions, it has exclusive competence by virtue of Articles 100a and 235 of the Treaty. The Council and the Member States which have submitted observations acknowledge that the Community has certain powers, but deny that they are exclusive.

A. GATS

*****

The Commission puts forward here both internal and external reasons to justify participation by the Community, and by the Community alone, in the conclusion of GATS and TRIPs. At internal level, the Commission maintains that, without such participation, the coherence of the internal market would be impaired. At external level, the European Community cannot allow itself to remain inactive on the international stage: the need for the conclusion of the WTO Agreement and its annexes, reflecting a global approach to international trade (embracing goods, services and intellectual property), is not in dispute.

*****

B. TRIPs

In support of its claim that the Community has exclusive competence to conclude TRIPs, the Commission relies on the existence of legislative acts of the institutions which could be affected within the meaning of the AETR judgment if the Member States were jointly to participate in its conclusion, and, as with GATS, on the need for the Community to participate in the agreement in order to achieve one of the objectives set out in the Treaty (the "Opinion 1/76 doctrine"), as well as on Articles 100a and 235.

The relevance of the reference to Opinion 1/76 is just as disputable in the case of TRIPs as in the case of GATS: unification or harmonisation of intellectual property rights in the Community context does not necessarily have to be accompanied by agreements with non-member countries in order to be effective.

Moreover, Articles 100a and 235 of the Treaty cannot in themselves confer exclusive competence on the Community, as stated above.

It only remains, therefore, to consider whether the subordinate legislative acts adopted in the Community context could be affected within the meaning of the AETR judgment if the Member States were to participate in the conclusion of TRIPs, as the Commission maintains.

Suffice it to say on that point that the harmonisation achieved within the Community in certain areas covered by TRIPs is only partial and that, in other areas, no harmonisation has been envisaged. There has been only partial harmonisation as regards trade marks, for example: it is apparent from the third recital in the preamble to the First Council Directive 89/104 to approximate the laws of the Member States relating to trade marks ([1989] OJ L40/1) that it is confined to the approximation of national laws "which most directly affect the functioning of the internal market". In other areas covered by TRIPs, no Community harmonisation measures have been adopted. That is the position as regards the protection of undisclosed technical information, as regards industrial designs, in respect of which proposals have merely been submitted, and as regards patents. With regard to patents, the only acts referred to by the Commission are conventions which are intergovernmental in origin, and not Community acts: the Munich Convention of 5 October 1973 on the Grant of European Patents and the Luxembourg Agreement of 15 December 1989 relating to Community Patents, which has not yet, however, entered into force.

Some of the Governments which have submitted observations have argued that the provisions of TRIPs relating to the measures to be adopted to secure the effective protection of intellectual property rights, such as those ensuring a fair and just procedure, the rules regarding the submission of evidence, the right to be heard, the giving of reasons for decisions, the right of appeal, interim measures and the award of damages, fall within the competence of the Member States. If that argument is to be understood as meaning that all those matters are within some sort of domain reserved to the Member States, it cannot be accepted. The Community is certainly competent to harmonise national rules on those matters, in so far as, in the words of Article 100 of the Treaty, they "directly affect the establishment or functioning of the common market". But the fact remains that the Community institutions have not hitherto exercised their powers in the field of the "enforcement of intellectual property rights", except in Regulation 3842/86 (cited above) laying down measures to prohibit the release for free circulation of counterfeit goods.

432

It follows that the Community and its Member States are jointly competent to conclude TRIPs.

IX. The duty of co-operation between the Member States and the Community institutions

At the hearing, the Commission drew the Court's attention to the problems which would arise, as regards the administration of the agreements, if the Community and the Member States were recognised as sharing competence to participate in the conclusion of the GATS and TRIPs agreements. While it is true that, in the negotiation of the agreements, the procedure under Article 113 of the Treaty prevailed subject to certain very minor adjustments, the Member States will, in the context of the WTO, undoubtedly seek to express their views individually on matters falling within their competence whenever no consensus has been found. Furthermore, interminable discussions will ensue to determine whether a given matter falls within the competence of the Community, so that the Community mechanisms laid down by the relevant provisions of the Treaty will apply, or whether it is within the competence of the Member States, in which case the consensus rule will operate. The Community's unity of action vis-à-vis the rest of the world will thus be undermined and its negotiating power greatly weakened.

In response to that concern, which is quite legitimate, it must be stressed, first, that any problems which may arise in implementation of the WTO Agreement and its annexes as regards the co-ordination necessary to ensure unity of action where the Community and the Member States participate jointly cannot modify the answer to the question of competence, that being a prior use. As the Council has pointed out, resolution of the issue of the allocation of competence cannot depend on problems which may possibly arise in administration of the agreements.

Next, where it is apparent that the subject-matter of an agreement or convention falls in part within the competence of the Community and in part within that of the Member States, it is essential to ensure close co-operation between the Member States and the Community institutions, both in the process of negotiation and conclusion and in the fulfilment of the commitments entered into. That obligation to co-operate flows from the requirement of unity in the international representation of the Community ...

The duty to co-operate is all the more imperative in the case of agreements such as those annexed to the WTO Agreement, which are inextricably interlinked, and in view of the cross-retaliation measures established by the Dispute Settlement Understanding. Thus, in the absence of close co-operation, where a Member State, duly authorised within its sphere of competence to take cross-retaliation measures, considered that they would be ineffective if taken in the fields covered by GATS or TRIPs, it would not, under Community law, be empowered to retaliate in the area of trade in goods, since that is an area which on any view falls within the exclusive competence of the Community under Article 113 of the Treaty. Conversely, if the Community were given the right to retaliate in the sector of goods but found itself incapable of exercising that right, it would, in the absence of close co-operation, find itself unable, in law, to retaliate in the areas covered by GATS or TRIPs, those being within the competence of the Member States.

The Commission's third question having been put only on the assumption that the Court recognised that the Community had exclusive competence, it does not call for reply.

In Conclusion, The Court gives the following opinion:

1. The Community has sole competence, pursuant to Article 113 EC, to conclude the Multilateral Agreements on Trade in Goods.

2. The Community and its Member States are jointly competent to conclude GATS.

3. The Community and its Member States are jointly competent to conclude TRIPs.

Notes and Questions

1. The ECJ refuses to acknowledge exclusive competence of the Union governing organs in the field of IPRs on the basis of its *ERTA* (or *AETR*) decision.[1] In that case the Court held that if the EU had adopted harmonizing

---

[1] Case 22/70, Commission of the European Communities v. Council of the European Communities, 1971 E.C.R. 263.

measures in a particular area, then even in the absence of an express grant of exclusive competence in the EC Treaty, the EU organs would assume exclusive competence for the conduct of external relations in that area to avoid conflict with the internal harmonizing measures. In this case concerning the TRIPS Agreement, the Court says that the EU has not yet achieved a sufficient level of harmonization in the IPRs area for the *ERTA* rationale to be applicable. As we proceed to review the various EU directives, regulations and other EU harmonizing measures throughout this book, consider whether the Court would make the same decision today.

2. The Court uses the First Trade Marks Directive as an example of an EU measure that is not a complete harmonizing (or approximation) measure, and which therefore should be discounted in the context of its *ERTA* rationale. In a subsequent decision involving the international exhaustion of trademarks, *Silhouette v. Hartlauer*,[2] the Court holds that the same Trade Marks Directive has effectively eliminated Member State discretion in the substantive trademark law field, and particularly with respect to external relations involving trademarks. Does this later decision reflect changed circumstances within the EU, or are the decisions inconsistent?

---

ii. EU External Relations and Mixed Agreements

Dispute Settlement in the World Trade Organization: Characteristics and Structural Implications for the European Union

Thomas Cottier*

*****

4.1.2. The Problem of Mixed Agreements

WTO dispute settlement is not without practical and legal implications for the concept of shared competences between the EC and Member

---

[2]*See infra*, Ch. IV, § V,1,b,ii.
*COMMON MKT L. REV. 1998 (forthcoming).

states (mixed agreements) in the new WTO areas of trade in services and intellectual property, both under existing rules in accordance with advisory opinion I/94 and the revisions of Art. 113 TEC by the Amsterdam Treaty. External relations' competence in these fields partly remains with the Member States unless the matter is explicitly and unanimously transferred to the Communities, presumably in the course of internal harmonization. At the same time, the EC is responsible under international law for compliance with these agreements due to full membership of the Communities in the World Trade Organization. Members of the WTO may therefore bring complaints in such matters against the EC, one or more Member States, or both, due to individual membership in the World Trade Organization. As a practical matter, Members, in particular the United States, have demonstrated a preference to bring complaints directly against the EC Member State, the law of which is claimed to be inconsistent with WTO obligations. This strategy may serve to solve disputes of a particular and unique nature with the Member State concerned. It also may be used to single out and target specific Member States to bring about a test case and to take advantage from the fact that national governments do not dispose of extensive experience in WTO dispute settlement similar to the expertise acquired by the Commission over many years in GATT. In all cases alike, however, the effects of dispute settlement are difficult to confine to a particular national jurisdiction within the single European market. In the case of sanctions, in particular cross-sanctions, measures may well be targeted on that particular economy. Yet, they are likely to spill over to other Member States and may affect them and the Union at large. For some authors, separate action by Member States no longer possibly exists.

It would therefore seem desirable for Member States to seek cooperation and support of the Commission in all cases concerned. In all cases brought against individual Members States, such cooperation was indeed established on an ad hoc basis. These experiences may facilitate new attempts to establish a Code of Conduct and to put such cooperation and interaction on a regular footing. The dilemma, of course, remains that the Commission often might not share the interests of a Member State but would rather prefer to see commitments under WTO law honored, rather sooner than later. From an outside view, this would leave the EC in an odd situation. Members States are being picked upon while Community lawyers stand by idly or act *contre coeur* in defense before a panel, and let in fact others do the job to bring about compliance of the Member State with WTO rules. This calculus may be without harm as long as such complaints are of a contained and isolated nature and do not affect broader issues of Community interests and European legal traditions. In test cases against Member States involving broader issues, cooperation, coordination among all the Member States and the Commission will be indispensable. If, for example, claims to improve enforcement in copy right law in the field of software should amount to call for punitive damages — a concept not known in civil law and an area not yet harmonized in the Community — either by extensive interpretation or, after the year 2000, by non-violation complaints, it will be necessary to develop shared European positions and strategies. WTO dispute settlement, in other words, may in fact stimulate legal harmonization among Member States and involvement of the Union. As before, external pressures to adjust the law in order to respond to modern needs may call for adjustment and continue to bring about internal reallocations of powers, formally or informally.

All of this, of course, is a matter of speculation at present times. There is no extensive experience to that effect. The concept of shared competences and mixed agreements in the field of WTO law may have advantages from a point of view of subsidiarity and internal power relations of Member States and the Union. From an external perspective, however, the concept hardly reinforces the position of Europe in relations with other Members of the WTO, in particular the United States. Dispute settlement may be engaged to divide and rule.

Notes and Questions

1. The "mixed" agreement has been a feature of the EU relationship with the GATT since the conclusion of the Tokyo Round in 1979. As Thomas Cottier observes, in addition to reflecting some uncertainty as to the allocation of legislative and enforcement competences within the EU, the mixed agreement presents certain difficulties to countries which are outside the Union. For example, if a third country has a complaint concerning implementation of the TRIPS Agreement, does it present that complaint to the European Commission or to an individual EU member state where the problem may be occurring? Against what entity is a WTO dispute settlement claim brought? If the complaining country eventually imposes trade

sanctions, does it impose them against the EU or against the member state? When negotiating with the Commission, is it certain that the Commission is speaking on behalf of the member states?

---

3. The North American Free Trade Agreement IPRs Regime

The North American Free Trade Agreement (NAFTA) was created with a different set of goals than the EU. Whereas the founders of the EU envisioned the gradual political and social integration of Europe — in addition to economic integration — through the operation of common governmental institutions, the founders of the NAFTA were pursuing a more limited economic agenda. The NAFTA is aimed at removing barriers to the free movement of goods, services and capital, and to removing obstacles to the movement of persons for the purpose of performing business-related activities.

The NAFTA's institutional structure is considerably different than that of the EU. The NAFTA institutional structure is headed by a Free Trade Commission (FTC) composed of one Minister or Cabinet level official of each country Party. The FTC supervises implementation of the agreement, and it oversees operation of the dispute settlement mechanism. The NAFTA creates a substantial number of working groups that assist in the implementation of specific parts of the agreement — such as the technical standards provisions — and these working groups are subordinate to the FTC. The NAFTA arrangement also includes "side agreements" with respect to labor and environmental matters, and these side agreements create their own institutional arrangements. The NAFTA establishes a Secretariat with limited responsibilities. These largely involve keeping track of the activities of the FTC and working groups.

Unlike the EU Council, the NAFTA FTC is not a legislative organ. While the FTC ministers have the power to make decisions defined by the terms of the NAFTA — which decisions are largely inherent in their powers as executive ministers of their respective governments — the FTC ministers do not adopt legislation for the NAFTA Parties. There is no NAFTA parliamentary body. Disputes between NAFTA Parties are resolved by panels of arbitrators chosen from rosters established by the Parties, and the decisions of these panels are referred to the Parties for implementation at the political level (except in the limited case of antidumping and countervailing duty decisions which are binding without additional political implementation). Individuals do not have recourse to general NAFTA dispute settlement (though individuals have certain rights to require the initiation of antidumping and countervailing duty dispute settlement proceedings, and there is limited individual access to certain complaint procedures under the environmental and, to a lesser extent, the labor, side agreements).

The NAFTA contains a separate chapter devoted to IPRs protection, which is described in the following excerpt. The NAFTA was completed before the WTO TRIPS Agreement, and the IPRs provisions of the NAFTA were modeled on a largely finalized draft of the TRIPS Agreement. Though there are, as noted in the excerpt, some differences between the two agreements, they are not major ones.

What may be of some interest is that a NAFTA Party may in most cases elect to bring a complaint regarding an IPRs matter either to the WTO Dispute Settlement Body or under the NAFTA dispute settlement mechanism. In theory, one could see different bodies of jurisprudence arising in the separate fora — though it seems unlikely that dispute panels in either forum would go out of their way to achieve such an end.

Law and Policy of Regional Integration:
The NAFTA and Western Hemispheric Integration in the World Trade Organization System (1995)

Frederick M. Abbott*

Chapter Five

*****

II. The NAFTA Intellectual Property Regime

The NAFTA chapter on Intellectual Property [Chapter Seventeen] is part of a broad global undertaking to incorporate intellectual property rights protection into regimes governing international trade. This under-

---

*Kluwer Law International (1995).

taking effectively commenced with the 1986 GATT Uruguay Round mandate which authorized the initiation of negotiations concerning trade-related aspects of intellectual property rights (TRIPS). It culminated on a broad multilateral level with the approval in December 1993 of the WTO Agreement on Trade-Related Aspects of Intellectual Property Rights [hereinafter WTO TRIPS Agreement]. The NAFTA text was negotiated principally on the basis of the Dunkel Draft text of the TRIPS Agreement, and it is comparable in almost all essential respects to the final WTO TRIPS Agreement text. Both the NAFTA and WTO TRIPS texts establish substantive standards for the protection of patents, trademarks, copyrights and neighboring rights, industrial designs, integrated circuit layouts, trade secrets, and geographical indications of origin. Both texts also require that parties adopt and maintain effective civil and criminal enforcement mechanisms with respect to the substantive IPRs rules. The NAFTA and WTO TRIPS texts will for the most part result in the multilateral application of IPRs standards comparable to those presently in place in the OECD countries.

Mexico began several years ago to overhaul its intellectual property rights (IPRs) regime to begin to approximate it with industrialized country standards. The impact of the NAFTA and TRIPS texts on Mexico will not therefore be terribly dramatic. The principal effects appear to be that Mexico will broaden the scope of "pipeline" protection granted to pharmaceutical and agricultural products that may have not have been available prior to conclusion of the NAFTA, provide IPRs protection for integrated circuit layouts, and expressly protect encrypted programming satellite signals with civil and criminal measures. Mexico has entered fairly broad reservations in the NAFTA with respect to its broadcast and film industries, requiring that a majority of time of each day's live broadcast programs feature Mexican nationals, limiting non-national ownership in cable service providers to minority interests, and requiring that thirty percent of per theater movie screen time be reserved for Mexican persons.

It may be that the NAFTA IPRs negotiations were more significant from a U.S. standpoint with respect to Canada because during the course of the NAFTA negotiations Canada agreed to eliminate an exceptionally permissive compulsory licensing regime applicable to pharmaceuticals. The NAFTA, on the other hand, carries forward Canada's protection of its cultural industries from the CUSFTA (making it applicable to all third countries). The cultural exemption permits Canada to discriminate in terms of services, investment and copyright protection in favor of its nationals, though Canada apparently has no intention of invoking the exemption in practice. The United States has reserved its right to withdraw comparable benefits if Canada invokes the exemption.

The principal change to U.S. IPRs law mandated by the NAFTA relates to the date of invention for Canadian and Mexican patents. Under current U.S. patent law, the earliest date of invention for inventions made outside the United States is the date of initial filing of a patent application. For inventions made in the United States the actual date of invention is used. Thus U.S. law discriminates on the basis of the place where an invention is made. The NAFTA prohibits discrimination with respect to patents on the basis of the place of invention in the Parties. It resulted in an amendment to U.S. patent law with respect to inventions made in Canada and Mexico.

The WTO TRIPS Agreement contains a broad national treatment provision. Therefore, the TRIPS Agreement requires the NAFTA parties to extend all of the IPRs benefits they have accorded to each other under the NAFTA to third countries. Bear in mind that the exemption in GATS Article V for services liberalizing agreements does not apply to IPRs agreements. In fact the European Union at one point in the Uruguay Round negotiations tabled a TRIPS proposal which would have permitted regional groups to adopt discriminatory IPRs regimes, though it subsequently explained that its proposal had been too broadly drafted and did not reflect its intention. It must be noted that the WTO TRIPS Agreement contains a general most favored nation provision. However, this MFN provision exempts from the MFN obligation rights granted under preexisting international IPRs agreements (which include the NAFTA). Nevertheless, because the WTO TRIPS Agreement contains both national and MFN treatment provisions, non-Parties to the NAFTA should still be entitled to receive treatment from each Party at least as favorable as that which each Party accords to its own nationals.

The NAFTA does in some cases provide for higher levels of protection than the WTO TRIPS Agreement. Because the TRIPS Agreement requires the extension of national treatment, and does not contain an exemption for RIAs, these benefits should be passed on to third countries. By failing to recognize this requirement, the NAFTA Parties could come into conflict with their WTO obligations, but there is no reason to believe that they will choose to do so.

The Canadian and Mexican reservations protecting their cultural industries are troubling from the standpoint of IPRs rights holders who at least potentially face market access restrictions. The United States and the

European Union fought an intense battle in the Uruguay Round negotiations regarding the permissibility of market access restrictions on audio-visual and related services and products. This battle was inconclusive. The WTO Agreement does not directly address the subject, and both sides reserved their positions. In view of this situation, the NAFTA reservations with respect to audio-visual services and products are unlikely to be considered inconsistent with the WTO Agreement.

Notes and Questions

1. Since the NAFTA entered into force, there has been a steady stream of complaints from the U.S. audio-visual sector about the enforcement of copyright laws in Mexico. The government of Mexico has substantially increased the funding of its copyright enforcement agency, but action against copyright violators is hampered by more general problems affecting Mexico's law enforcement system. The United States Trade Representative's Office is under pressure from the U.S. copyright industries to take some action against Mexico in order to compel the government to step up its enforcement efforts. In the context of the broad relationship between the United States and Mexico, how should USTR prioritize this situation? Options would include extended negotiations and cooperation which might not yield "on the ground" results for a number of years, and a hard line approach in which the U.S. demands immediate compliance with NAFTA/TRIPS enforcement obligations (coupled with a threat of trade sanctions).

2. Both Canada and Mexico express concerns with potential U.S. domination of their "cultural industries." Both are concerned that economies of scale in the U.S. audio-visual sector allow American companies to market and sell products such as movies, television programs, books and magazines at prices well below those of local Canadian and Mexican producers. Do provisions of the NAFTA (and TRIPS Agreement) which require Canada and Mexico to protect U.S. IPRs holders (in the same way as they protect Canadian and Mexican IPRs holders) prohibit these countries from restricting access to the Canadian and Mexican audio-visual markets? (Note that NAFTA rules regarding the free movement of goods, services

and investment also play a significant role in answering this market access question.)

4. The Mercosur IPRs Regime

We were introduced to the institutional structure of the Mercosur by the remarks of Ambassador de Azembuja. We turn now to the Mercosur provisions and activities specifically directed to IPRs. The following excerpt by Wilfrido Fernández lays out the basic approach of the Mercosur in respect to IPRs matters.

Mercosur and its Implications for Industrial Property

Wilfrido Fernández*

Introduction

6.1 Latin America has not escaped the worldwide trend towards an ever-increasing formation of a global market. The developments that have been taking place in this part of the world are living examples of this, namely Mercosur (Brazil, Argentina, Uruguay and Paraguay), the Andean Pact (Venezuela, Colombia, Ecuador, Peru and Bolivia) and the North American Free Trade Agreement (NAFTA) (Canada, USA and Mexico), which appears to be affecting not only Mexico, but also other Latin American countries. Consequently, the area of industrial property will be affected by such a trend. This chapter will give a current overview of the most recent developments within the Mercosur structure in relation to industrial property. Mercosur identifies the so-called Common Market of the South (*Mercado Común del Sur*) established in 1991 by Brazil, Argentina, Uruguay and Paraguay.

---

*In INTERNATIONAL INTELLECTUAL PROPERTY LAW (D. CAMPBELL AND S. COTTER EDS., 1995), at 131 et seq.

Implications of a supranational common market

6.2 ***** The common market form of integration chosen by Brazil, Argentina, Uruguay and Paraguay (the Mercosur countries) requires the establishment of identical market conditions in all of the Member Countries. The reduction, harmonization and, subsequently, the abolition of all the customs barriers, seeking to obtain a complete free flow of goods, must necessarily be the first step with regard to the development of a common market. Restrictions upon exportation and importation, as well as any kind of discrimination established by a national market, or by private agreements, are simply incompatible with the principle of the free flow of goods that essentially defines a common market.

Common market and industrial property rights

6.3 Traditionally industrial property rights have been applied territorially. For example, a patent right is only valid in the country where it was issued. Within a specific period of time, the production affected by the patent is monopolised only in that country, not automatically in the other countries which are members of the common market. As a consequence of the patent right, the importation of products protected by the right into the country which has granted the patent is forbidden, even if the goods are legally produced outside that country. The issuing of a licence under a national patent regime does not authorise the licensee to exploit an invention outside the country, since third parties, beneficiaries of other national patents or licensees abroad can oppose such exploitation with justifiable grounds. It can be seen, therefore, that as a result of different patent rights, a division of the territory of the common market can take place. The same situation arises with other categories of industrial property, such as trademarks, industrial designs and utility models. It can be shown that conflict between the concepts upon which the common market is based and the territorial enforcement of industrial property rights is inevitable.

Common market and trademark rights

6.4 By analysing the field of trademarks in a common market scenario. Two types of conflict can be recognized:

1. The conflict between the structure of the common market which defends the principle of free competition within its territory, on the one hand, and on the other, the right of exclusivity, that arises from a trademark granted in a Member Country; and

2. The conflict caused by the same structure of the common market which tends towards the removal of any hurdle to the free flow of goods within its territory *vis-à-vis* the trademark rights themselves which allow the owner of a national trademark to oppose the importation into the country where the trademark is registered, of goods bearing an identical or confusingly similar trademark.

Mercosur and the principles of industrial property

6.5 The treaty establishing the Common Market of the South (*Mercado Común del Sur*) is comprised of 24 articles and four annexes. This treaty, which is known as the Treaty of Asunción or the Treaty of Mercosur, was signed in Asunción, Paraguay in March of 1991, and has been ratified by all the Member Country congresses. The Treaty establishes a common market which was due to be fully implemented by 31 December 1994. The text of the Treaty states that this common market will naturally sustain the free flow of goods among the Member Countries. In order to accomplish this, it is specifically mentioned that all the tariff and non-tariff measures of any kind must be eliminated. According to the Treaty, the member countries must coordinate their policies in order to secure uniform conditions of competition in the Member Countries and, of course, they are obliged to establish common rules of commercial competition. In annex I, entitled Programme of Free Trade (*Programa de Liberacion Comercial*), it is established that restriction in the above-cited sense can be administrative, financial or of any other type, whereby a Member Country can impede or make difficult, by unilateral decision, commerce between the Member Countries. This creates the first conflict between the Mercosur structure and the principles of industrial property, since the goal of Mercosur is the free flow of goods among the Member Countries and industrial property rights can constitute, in principle, a restriction to such free flow of goods.

The Treaty of Asunción does not contain rules relating to industrial property like the Treaty of Rome, establishing the European Community which has a higher degree of integration than a common market. The implementing of its rules has been delegated to the competent institutional structure. Unlike the Treaty of Asunción, the Treaty of Rome expressly stated that any prohibition or restriction which could impede the free flow of goods arising from an industrial property right could only be exercised if it did not constitute a means of arbitrary discrimination or restriction upon the trade between the Member Countries. The European Court of Justice has gradually elaborated upon its doctrine regarding the interpretation of this rule. At this stage, it should be clarified that the Treaty of Asunción, establishing the Mercosur, does not impede the enforcement of the respective national industrial property rights granted by any Member Country.

Legal structure of a common market

6.6 The legal structure related to any supranational common market can involve the following three stages:

1. Harmonisation in interpreting the national laws of the Member Countries and the insertion in the jurisprudence of the principles of the common market, at which stage, the exercise of the national rights must be harmonised, taking into account those supranational principles established by the creation of a common market;

2. Harmonisation of the respective national laws, which stage means that the Member Countries maintain their national legislation, but the key rules of the respective national laws have a common normative reference and must provide a standard of minimum uniform protection or a fixed standard leading to national rights which are substantially uniform; and

3. The creation of a uniform supranational common market law which can either replace completely each different national legislation, or can co-exist as a parallel system with that legislation.

6.7 Within Mercosur, efforts are now being made to reach the second stage. The possibility of reaching the third stage has not yet been discussed.

Parallel imports

6.8 Parallel imports will, of course, be one of the crucial topics to be discussed. At present, the Treaty of Mercosur does not contain any criteria regarding this subject. Sufficient provision for community exhaustion of rights should be established, whereby parallel imports (always considering those performed within the same territory of the common market) cannot be prevented as long as the products are genuine. It should be added that the products, even the genuine ones which have been traded outside the territory of the common market with the consent of the legitimate industrial property right owner, be subject to a ban on importation to the Member Countries of Mercosur. This is a view based upon an evaluation of the European experience. Officially, the subject has already been discussed by the Industrial Property Committee of Mercosur and it has also been included in the agenda of the Interparliamentary Committee of Mercosur. However, no final decision has yet been taken regarding this subject.

Forum for dispute resolution within Mercosur

6.9 Considering the absence of any rule relating to industrial property within the Treaty of Mercosur, it is obviously a priority to provide for a systematic normative structure, without essentially affecting the national legislations, establishing a clear criteria regarding the resolution of disputes within the Mercosur regime. As soon as possible, a competent forum for the interpretation of the Mercosur rules must be established, taking as models the European Court of Justice and, under the Andean Pact, the Court of Justice of the Cartagena agreement which is seated in Quito, Ecuador.*****
[Authors' note: Since the publication of this article, a dispute settlement protocol has been adopted by the Mercosur.**]

Present institutional structure

6.10 An Interparliamentary Committee has been established within the Mercosur structure. In an initial meeting which took place in Asunción in

---

**Mercosur (Argentina, Brazil, Paraguay And Uruguay): Protocol of Brasilia for the Settlement of Disputes [Done at Brasilia, December 17, 1991], 36 I.L.M. 691 (May 1997).

June 1992, it was agreed that the topic of industrial property should be discussed by such a committee. A specific agenda of the following 14 items was compiled:

(1) Patent exploitation;
(2) Compulsory licences;
(3) Duration of patents;
(4) Grace period;
(5) Exclusion of patentability;
(6) Retroactivity;
(7) Parallel imports;
(8) Shifting of the burden of proof;
(9) Patentability in the field of biotechnology;
(10) Supranational structure for resolution of controversies;
(11) Consumer defence;
(12) Well-known trademarks;
(13) Unfair competition; and
(14) Protection of industries established in the Member Countries.

6.11 Notwithstanding this good start in the parliamentary area, little improvement has been made up to now. It appears that none of the four member congresses have considered this agenda and none of them have submitted conclusions to the Interparliamentary Committee of Mercosur. On the other hand, some improvement has been seen with regard to the activities within the structure of Mercosur identified as "Subgroup 7", dealing with technological and industrial policy. This subgroup initially organised a first seminar on industrial property for the Mercosur countries in June of 1992. Even the Interamerican Association of Industrial Property was officially represented at this event. Later in the same month, a meeting of government officers working in the area of industrial property took place in Brasilia, Brazil. One of the main recommendations which emerged from the meeting was the establishing of a specific Committee of Industrial Property with an official agenda, which was initially structured in the following way:

1. To evaluate the national rights of industrial property of the Member Countries, considering the juridical, technical and administrative aspects;

448

2. To examine the participation of the Mercosur countries in the different conventions and treaties regarding industrial property;

3. To analyse the possibilities of implementing co-operation and mutual assistance among the different Industrial Property Offices; and

4. To evaluate and suggest the actions necessary to obtain the effective co-operation and assistance of the international institutions in the area of industrial property to the Mercosur countries. It should be noted that the Interamerican Association of Industrial Property Office was again officially represented in this second event. Later, in November of 1992 in Montevideo, Uruguay, the first official meeting of the committee took place.

6.12 The resolution that officially created that committee expressly stated that the topic of industrial property has great relevance for any work leading to the harmonization of the industrial and technological policies within Mercosur. This first official meeting was not attended by a representative from Paraguay. It was agreed at the meeting that the first area of industrial property to be addressed was going to be the subject of trademarks. In that sense, it was also agreed by the representatives of the Member Countries present to immediately proceed with the evaluation of the symmetries and asymmetries of the Member Countries. Its was also agreed that the committee was entitled to proceed with comparative studies regarding the industrial property protection systems in other areas of integration of the world.

In March 1993, the second official meeting of the Committee of Industrial Property took place in Montevideo, Uruguay. Unfortunately again, this time no representative of Argentina attended the event. It was agreed as a consequence of the meeting to exchange ideas regarding any prospective co-operation from the World Intellectual Property Organisation (WIPO). The Brazilian delegation suggested the speeding up of item (b) of the initial agenda approved by the committee, that is, the evaluation of the participation of the different countries of Mercosur in the different conventions and treaties regarding industrial property. It was also decided that in order to give more efficiency to the committee work, an administrative co-ordinator's post would need to be created based upon a rotational term of six months of the different national delegations. The Brazilian delegation was elected as the first co-ordinator. In June of 1993, the third official meeting of the Committee of Industrial Property took place in Asunción, Paraguay. For the first time, all Member Countries were represented. A comparative evaluation of the different trademark systems of the four Member Countries was performed, covering the following 16 relevant aspects:

(1) Applicable legal rules;
(2) System of laws;
(3) Requirements to be a trademark owner;
(4) Duration of the trademark registration;
(5) Protection of well-known trademarks;
(6) Requirements of use;
(7) Registration procedure;
(8) Scope of the trademark protection;
(9) Signs not registrable as trademarks;
(10) Rights of the trademark owner;
(11) Assignment and transfer of rights;
(12) License for use;
(13) Administrative censure;
(14) Judicial censure;
(15) Infringements and remedies; and
(16) Geographical indications.

6.13 The Brazilian delegation expressed its concern in this third meeting that the beginning of the studies related to the area of patents should not be delayed. At the same time, it was agreed in this meeting that there be a joint seminar of the Committee of Industrial Property, created within the "Subgroup 7", and the Interparliamentary Committee of Mercosur. The possibility of harmonization regarding the concept of use was discussed and the subject of protection of well-known trademarks was also analysed in order to detect the present asymmetries in this field in the legislation of the four Member Countries. The whole agenda covered again the above 16 items regarding trademarks. Co-operation from WIPO was also discussed in relation to the legislative harmonisation process which will be taking place in the four Member Countries.

In September of 1993 the fourth meeting of the Committee of Industrial Property organised within the Mercosur institutional structure took place in Montevideo, Uruguay. In relation to trademarks the discussion continued regarding the 16 topics included in the official agenda, and always with the goal of the harmonization process which is to take place among the four Member Countries. In October of 1993, representatives of the four Member States of Mercosur met in Geneva with the Director General of WIPO to discuss collaborative efforts. It was agreed that WIPO would conduct studies and present recommendations on the treatment of intellectual property in the Mercosur countries at a meeting in one of the Member States in 1994. Hereby detailed for a better illustration is the official chronogram established as far as this field within the institutional Framework of Mercosur:

(1) December 1992 — evaluation of the national laws of intellectual property;
(2) June 1993 — evaluation of the international and regional conventions and treaties regarding industrial property;
(3) June 1993 — analysis of the possibilities of international co-operation;
(4) June 1993 — analysis of the possibilities of co-operation among the Industrial Property Offices of the four Member Countries;
(5) December 1993 — analysis of the symmetries and asymmetries of the national legislations;
(6) March 1994 — elaboration of the proposals for the regional treatment of intellectual property;
(7) May 1994 — discussions of the proposals for the regional treatment of intellectual property;
(8) Drafting of the final document; and
(9) July 1994 — submission of the final document to the GMC (*Grupo Mercado Común*, the executive body of Mercosur) for its evaluation and final implementation.

6.14 The committee had an initial deadline to prepare the final proposal document regarding the regional treatment of industrial property in the Mercosur countries of July 1994. However, it seems that such deadline will have to be extended given the present stage of the committee work which has suffered some delays. Up to December 1994, the Industrial Property Committee held nine official meetings. By such date, the Committee drafted an Agreement of Harmonisation of Industrial Property Legislation within the Mercosur countries regarding trademarks and indications of source and denominations of origin. The draft follows the guidelines of the

Paris Conventions and the Agreement on Trade-Related Aspects of Intellectual Property Rights (TRIPS), and deals, among other things, with waiver of translations and legalisations of documents, equal treatment of foreign and national parties, definition of trademarks, priority in such area, extension of article 6 bis of the Paris Convention to the field of services, protection of trademarks of exceptional reputation, duration and renewal of trademark registrations, exhaustion of rights, use of trademarks, cancellation of trademarks due to lack of use and definition of indications of source and denominations of origin with a prohibition on their registrability as trademarks. This draft Agreement has been submitted to the higher authority of the Mercosur structure which has so far not evaluated the draft. On the other hand, nothing has been drafted yet regarding patents, utility models, industrial designs and copyrights.

Present stage of industrial property legislation in Member Countries

6.15 The varying protection given to industrial property that nowadays exists in the different Member Countries of Mercosur can easily provoke, in the absence of a common normative structure and in the absence of an effective legislative harmonisation, a situation in which a Member Country that still does not recognise such rights could require the others to also not recognise these rights. This would mean that products originating in the first Member Country may freely circulate in the territories of the other Member Countries. As an illustrative example, Argentina and Paraguav do not have a utility model legislation, whereas Uruguay and Brazil do have that type of legislation. In this regard, a Member Country cannot be required to withdraw protection from an invention in order to make possible the importation of copies originating in another Member Country where the protection does not exist. With regard to patents, for example, all the Member Countries of Mercosur protect the patent of invention. Nevertheless, nowadays. there is no uniform criteria as to the patentability of some types of invention. For instance, in all of the Member Countries of Mercosur, pharmaceutical products are not patentable, but in Brazil not even the pharmaceutical processes are patentable, nor are the chemical products and processes which are patentable in the other Member Countries.

In this case, Brazil could not require the other Member Countries to restrict their protection, so that the goods it freely circulates within the

Brazilian territory due to non-patentability may also be circulated in the same way in the other Member Countries. It should be noted that the new Brazilian Code of Industrial Property, already approved by the House of Representatives and pending before the Senate, allows patentability in the areas mentioned. Also, with regard to patents, a similar problem could arise with revalidation patents, which up to now have been allowed in Argentina, Paraguay and Uruguay, but not in Brazil. As far as trademarks are concerned, the present asymmetries among the Member Countries regarding the concept of use should be a matter of serious consideration. In Paraguay, use is basically irrelevant within the trademark system, whereas, in the other Member Countries, the concept of use has gradually gained relevance.

Finally, the four members of Mercosur now protect industrial models. In Argentina and Paraguay the term of protection is five years, renewable for two more periods; in Uruguay the term of protection is five years, but is only renewable for one more period, and in Brazil the term of protection is 10 years. It is obvious that the possibility of a longer protection for industrial models in Argentina and Paraguay, in practice, could mean a restriction upon the circulation in those countries, for a longer period of time, of an industrial model that could very well be already in the public domain in the other Member Countries. As has already been stressed by the Brazilian delegation within the Industrial Property Committee, attention should be given to the fact that not all of the Member Countries of Mercosur are members of some regional conventions and treaties; for instance, Brazil, Paraguay and Uruguay are presently members of the Interamerican Convention regarding Patents of Invention and Industrial Drawings and Models, but Brazil is not. Also, Paraguay is presently a member of the Interamerican Convention regarding Trademark and Commercial Protection, but not Argentina, Brazil or Uruguay.

Conclusion

6.16 This has been a brief overview of some of the different problems that will be faced with regard to the Mercosur regime. It is obvious that the nature of these problems is complex and it will take time to reach a harmonised criteria within the Member Countries to deal with them. It is precisely because of this that the job of structuring the common normative reference, that is, the structuring of a competent Mercosur forum for resolution of disputes, and at least the task of harmonising the interpretative criteria of the present national rules, as well as subsequently the harmonisation of the legislation, should now have maximum priority. As far as industrial property is concerned, it may be concluded that any harmonization work should always be conducted under the premise of maximising the protection of industrial property rights, and to avoid a situation whereby a country that today gives protection, may not grant protection in the future. This means that the process of harmonization should be performed gradually, always taking into consideration that protection should be stressed and never diminished. It is also estimated that, considering the European experience, every dispute must be resolved by taking as a premise the respect of industrial property rights, which are known to be essential for the technological and economical development of the Member Countries. Such is precisely the present criteria of the European Court of Justice which, in recent years, has stressed, and given more relevance to, the concept of pragmatism. In addition, it has been successfully trying to reach a fair equilibrium when facing the classic concept that arises in any common market (which has been discussed above), leaving aside its initial criteria of giving preference to the free flow of goods to such a degree that once endangered not only the exercise, but also the existence, of industrial property rights.

Finally, it should be noted that the establishing of Mercosur has already been beneficial for the protection of industrial property in that Paraguay, who, at the time of the signing of the Treaty of Mercosur, was the only Member Country who was not a party to the Paris Convention, in January of 1994, largely due to Mercosur, adhered to that Convention. This is, of course, a very favourable step not only for the harmonization process, but also with regard to the expansion of the protection of industrial property rights.

Notes and Questions

1. The article by Wilfrido Fernández indicates that the Mercosur had not yet adopted measures to harmonize the national IPRs laws of its members. This remains the situation as of mid-1998. Changes to Mercosur country IPRs laws will affect both Mercosur and non-Mercosur persons (as a consequence of the TRIPS Agreement national treatment obligation). Compli-

cated IPRs-related political relations between the Mercosur countries and the United States may be causing the Mercosur IPRs harmonization process to move along rather slowly. The Mercosur is a dynamic regional arrangement, and it is not to be doubted that progress will be made in the adoption of common IPRs rules and procedures.

2. USTR Barshefsky described the process of negotiating a Free Trade Area of the Americas (FTAA). It is contemplated that the FTAA will contain regional IPRs rules, and an FTAA working group on TRIPS has been established. Discussion among U.S. IPRs industry groups has focused on creating a TRIPS-plus IPRs regime in the FTAA. The FTAA will somehow need to accommodate the different IPRs regimes of the Western Hemisphere — not only those of approximately thirty-five nations, but also of the various existing regional arrangements such as the Andean Pact, NAFTA, Mercosur, CARICOM and so forth. Some of the regional IPRs arrangements are rather complex, and each reflects a different approach to IPRs governance. Do you think it will be feasible in the FTAA to pursue a harmonized approach to the governance of IPRs such as we have seen evolve in the EU? Could such an approach take shape in the absence of common institutions such as an FTAA Court of Justice?

---

5. The APEC IPRs Regime

USTR Barshefsky introduced us to the general institutional framework of the Asia-Pacific Economic Cooperation (APEC) forum. The loose consultative structure of APEC might suggest that its IPRs-related activities will revolve largely around coordination among governments and the sharing of information, and for the moment at least that is the case. The importance of these activities for IPRs specialists should not be underestimated, since the absence of *transparency* can be a major impediment to the successful protection of rights. It is very difficult to obtain protection when the laws and regulations cannot be found.

The following are excerpts from the APEC Secretariat Internet Web-Site which briefly describe APEC's IPRs-related activities. One example of the on-line listing of an APEC member's IPRs laws and regulations (for the People's Republic of China) is reproduced.

Asia-Pacific Economic Cooperation
(APEC) — Intellectual Property Rights *

Background

In 1995, the 18 APEC economic leaders adopted the Osaka Action Agenda, which includes the Intellectual Property Rights (IPR) area as one of the 15 areas where all members will seek the liberalization and facilitation of trade and investment. Japan convened the three "IPR Get-Together" meetings, aiming at developing detailed action programs for each item of Osaka Action Agenda Collective Actions. A copy of the relevant excerpt from the Osaka Action Agenda is attached.

Progress

A Matrix Report Format has been finalized. The Work Plan describing concrete collective actions for 1996-7 and Initial Thoughts (explanatory note for the format) were approved at the Cebu CTI meeting in May 1996. As each economy reflects this Work Plan in its own Matrix Report, actions which will be taken by each member economy will be almost consistent with each other.

Progress has already been made on some of the seven items of the Collective Action Plan, i.e. item (b): the Survey and item (c): the Contact Points List. Under these two items, the Contact Points List was finalized in August and a consolidated version of Part I (domestic IPR legislation) of the Survey will be finalized soon. The Contact Points List will be put on the E-mail in 1997. At the third IPR Get-Together in August, members agreed that implementation of each Collective Action would be pursued at the initiative of respective lead economies.

In addition, as approved at SOM II in Cebu in May 1996, APEC Industrial Property Rights Symposium was held in Tokyo in August 1996, to provide an opportunity to deepen dialogue on industrial property policy among APEC member economies.

---

*http://www.apecsec.org.sg (visited July 23, 1997).

*****

Excerpt From The Osaka Action Agenda: Intellectual Property Rights

Objective

APEC economies will ensure adequate and effective protection, including legislation, administration and enforcement, of intellectual property rights in the Asia-Pacific region based on the principles of MFN treatment, national treatment and transparency as set out in the TRIPS Agreement and other related agreements.

Guidelines

Each APEC economy will:
1. ensure that intellectual property rights are granted expeditiously;
2. ensure that adequate and effective civil and administrative procedures and remedies are available against infringement of intellectual property rights; and
3. provide and expand bilateral technical cooperation in relation to areas such as patent search and examination, computerization and human resources development for the implementation of the TRIPS Agreement and acceleration thereof.

Collective Actions

APEC economies will:
1. deepen the dialogue on intellectual property policy among APEC economies;
2. survey the current status of intellectual property rights protection in each APEC economy including the related statutes and corresponding jurisprudence, administrative guidelines and activities of related organizations;
3. develop a contact point list of public and business/private sector experts on intellectual property rights and a list of law enforcement officers, the latter list for the purpose of establishing a network to prevent cross-border flow of counterfeits;
4. exchange information on well-known trademarks as a first step in examining the possibility of establishing an APEC-wide trademark system;

5. exchange information on current intellectual property rights administrative systems with a view to simplifying and standardizing administrative systems throughout the region;

6. study measures, including development of principles, for the effective enforcement of intellectual property rights; and

7. implement fully the TRIPS Agreement no later than 1 January 2000, and examine ways to facilitate technical cooperation to this end.

Notes and Questions

1. As noted at the outset of this section, there is a wide range of regional institutions that participate in the international intellectual property system. Over the past decade, regional arrangements have proliferated, and this trend appears to be continuing. Whether or not the proliferation of regional arrangements is a positive development for the international economic system as a whole, or specifically for the international intellectual property system, are much debated questions. Though many economists venture that regional arrangements may usefully serve as "building blocs" for a more integrated global economy, there are also dangers inherent in regionalization. Most importantly, regionalization may increase the risk that the international system will break down among competing groups which no longer see major advantages to broad multilateral cooperation. This would almost undoubtedly lead to economic contraction for the world economy as a whole. In relation to IPRs, some degree of regionalization appears to present advantages in consolidating and simplifying the procedures used to secure IPRs protection, and it may also accelerate the harmonization of substantive laws. However, at least two risks inhere in this process. First, there is a risk that by focusing on regional IPRs arrangements, governments will pay less attention to the establishment of an effective global IPRs protection framework. Second, in some parts of the world the proliferation of regional arrangements has been so extensive that new layers of law are continually being laid upon existing ones, creating confusion rather than simplification.

2. There are a number of other important regional arrangements whose activities extend to the regulation of IPRs. These include the Andean Pact

APEC IPR Activities

Intellectual Property Survey

Part I: List of relevant legislation and regulations as well as agencies responsible for developing and administering the laws and regulations.

APEC Member: People's Republic of China

Specific Intellectual Property Rights	Relevant Legislation	Relevant Agency (i) Development of Law	Relevant Agency (ii) Administration of Law
Copyright and Related Rights	Copyright Law of the PRC Implementing Regulations of the Copyright Law International Copyright Treaties Implementing Rules Criminal Law of the PRC (Art 217 & 218; to be effective from 1 Oct 1997 Regulations on the Protection of Computer Software	National Copyright Administration	National Copyright Administration and Local Copyright Administrations
Trademarks	Trademark Law of the PRC Implementing Regulations under the Trademark Law Criminal Law of the PRC (Art 213, 214 & 215)	Trademark Office of the State Administration for Industry and Commerce (SAIC)	Trademark Office of the SAIC & its local offices
Patents	Patent Law of PRC Implementing Regulations under the Patent Law Criminal Law of the PRC (Art 216)	Patent Office of China (CPO)	CPO and its local Administrative Authorities

Plant Variety Rights	Regulations on protection of Plant Varieties (to be effective from 1 Oct 97)	Administrations of Agriculture and Forestry under the State Council	
Designs	Patent Law of China	CPO	CPO and its local administrative authorities
Geographical Indications			
Layout Designs of Integrated Circuits	(being drafted)		
Protection of Undisclosed Information	Law on combating Unfair Competition in the PRC / Criminal Law of the PRC	People's Court ; SAIC	SAIC & its local offices
Control of Anti Competitive Practices	Law of the PRC on Combating Unfair Competition	People's Court; SAIC	SAIC & its local offices
IPRs	The General Principles of the Civil Law of the PRC		
Civil and Administrative Enforcement Remedies			
Border Measures	Regulations of Customs Protection of IPRs / Implementing Rules of Customs Protection of IPRs	Customs General Administration (CGA)	CGA & its major customs houses and port customs houses
Criminal Offenses	Criminal Law of PRC (Art 213 — 220)	People's Court	

whose structure and activities are discussed later in this book,[1] as well the arrangement established by the Central American Agreement for the Protection of Industrial Property (which establishes uniform legislation for certain forms of IPR, but not a central registration office). African regional systems for the grant and registration of IPRs are discussed in the next section.[2]

C. Regional Institutions Securing Rights

We have seen that regional institutions approach the subject of IPRs governance in a variety of ways. Some regions create centralized institutions that perform specific IPRs-related functions, such as processing applications for the grant or registration of IPRs. Such institutions vary depending on the IPRs subject matter with which they are concerned, e.g., patent or trademark, and depending on the specific scope of their charters. The most important regional IPRs institution to date is the European Patent Office. In this section of the book we provide an overview of some of the regional arrangements for securing IPRs. Later in the book we will examine the operation of several of these regional institutions more closely.[1]

1. The European Union and European Patent Office

One of the most important European institutions governing IPRs is not an EU institution. The European Patent Office (EPO), established by the Convention on the Grant of the European Patent (EPC), headquartered in Munich, plays an extremely important role in the regulation of IPRs in Europe. This institution is described in the following article by Friedrich-Karl Beier. At the time this article was written, Beier was Managing Director of the Max Planck Institute for Foreign and International Patent, Copyright, and Competition Law in Munich.

---

[1]See infra, Ch. IV, § F.
[2]See infra, Ch. II, § C, 4.
[1]See infra Chs. IV-VI.

The European Patent System

Friedrich — Karl Beier*

I. Introduction

One of the classic objectives of comparative law research is to reduce or overcome existing dissimilarities in national laws through harmonization or unification. Every comparative lawyer is aware of the great difficulties in departing from long-established, deeply-rooted national solutions and will be pleased if small progress can be noted at the end of all harmonization endeavors. In this context, it may be of interest, even for non-specialized lawyers, to take notice of the unification process in the area of European patent law, which recently has led to the creation of a new patent law system in Europe.

II. The History of Patent Law Unification in Europe

The idea of developing a harmonized or unified patent system in Europe originated as early as 1949 with the Council of Europe. The underlying rationale was the general wish to contribute to harmonizing national law, to better understanding and improve relations between the peoples of Europe, as well as the specific understanding that the fragmented national approach to protect technical inventions was contrary to good sense and rational economic behavior. It seemed unreasonable that the inventor, in order to get protection for the same invention in several countries, had to file separate applications in each country and that these patent applications had to be examined by different patent offices under different standards using different procedures.

The first plans discussed by the Council of Europe sought to end or at least reduce this multiple workload for inventors and patent offices, but were ahead of their time. These plans set in motion the European idea in patent law and created a healthy climate of understanding between patent specialists, but led to only modest results. Two conventions were adopted, one harmonizing certain patent application formalities and the other creating an international classification system. More far-reaching proposals for

*14 VAND. J. TRANSNAT'L L. 1 (1981).

cooperation did not come forward. The experts realized that any proposal for a harmonized or uniform granting procedure would have no chance without a common understanding of certain basic concepts of substantive patent law, in particular, the conditions for patentability. The difficult task of developing such a common understanding was undertaken by the Expert Committee for Patents of the Council of Europe in the late 1950s. On the basis of comparative law studies, the experts attempted to reconcile the various national concepts of patentable subject matter, novelty, obviousness, technical progress, industrial applicability, and the widely dissimilar concepts on interpretation of patents. After more than eight years, these endeavours were finished successfully with the adoption of the Strasbourg Convention of 1963 on the Unification of Certain Points of Substantive Law on Patent for Invention.

This important step forward would not have been taken so quickly, however, if the patent unification process had not received an important push in the meantime. The previously missing impetus was provided by the creation of the European Economic Community (EEC) in 1957. Soon after the Treaty of Rome took effect, it became clear that the existence of six national patent systems was inconsistent with the main objective of the treaty, the establishment of a common market. The territorial nature of national industrial property rights was an obstacle to the free flow of goods within the Common Market, and a solution had to be found to overcome these undesired consequences. Since harmonization or complete unification of the national patent laws of the member states would not affect the territorial nature of national industrial property rights and their potential divisive effects in the market, the idea of creating a uniform European patent system was reborn and determined all further considerations.

Work was resumed in 1969 by a small EEC working group under the chairmanship of Dr. Haertel, who was President of the German Patent Office at that time. Supported by fresh European *élan*, the working group produced a Preliminary Draft of an Agreement on a European Patent Law in November 1962. This draft contained complete provisions for a new supranational patent system for the six EEC countries. It was designed to be an additional system of protection coexisting with the national patent systems of the member states. The main purpose of the new system was the grant of European patents having effect in all member states through a common granting authority, the European Patent Office, under European rules and standards of patentability.

Although the experts agreed on nearly all of the patent law solutions in the 1962 draft, the governments of the EEC countries were unable to agree on certain political issues. The Common Market patent was a victim of the general crisis in the Common Market in the mid 1960s. The work came to a complete standstill in 1965 and was not resumed until 1970. Surprisingly, the initiative for resumption came from the French Government, which urged the speedy establishment of a European patent system not restricted to Common Market boundaries. Under these new auspices, the deliberations started again and were successfully brought to an end within a very short period.

III. The New European Patent System

The new European system of patent protection consists of three main elements or subsystems:

(1) The *European* patent system created by the European Patent Convention, adopted at Munich in 1973;

(2) the *Common Market patent system* created by the Community Patent Convention, adopted at Luxembourg in 1975; and

(3) the *harmonization of national patent systems* in Europe.

The first and most important element is the Convention on the Grant of European Patents, which provides for a uniform patent granting procedure. This procedure begins with the filing of a European patent application and ends, after novelty research and examination, with the granting of a European patent through a common administrative authority, the European Patent Office in Munich. This European patent does not, however, provide uniform legal protection in all contracting states. It leads, rather, to a bundle of a national patens with effects and rights having their substantive legal basis in the national laws of the individual contracting states.

The Munich Convention embraces not only the nine European Community countries, but also tends to include all other European countries which are interested in the introduction of a modern search and examination system for their territories. Over twenty European countries took part in the Munich Diplomatic Conference, including a socialist country, Yugoslavia. The Munich Convention was signed by sixteen countries, the nine EEC states and seven other West European countries.

After completion of the ratification procedure and the necessary preparations for the opening of the European Patent Office the Munich Patent Convention entered into force on October 7, 1977. It presently includes the following eleven contracting states: seven of the nine EEC countries, Belgium, the Federal Republic of Germany, France, the United Kingdom, Italy, Luxembourg, and the Netherlands and four non-EEC countries, Austria, Sweden, Switzerland, and Liechtenstein. The European Patent Office started its work on November 1, 1977, with its main office in Munich and a branch office, which conducts formal examination and search, in the Hague. On June 1, 1978, the first European patent applications were filed and during the first eighteen months of its activity, a total of 16,500 applications were received. The system now provides for substantial examination in all fields of technology, and the first European patents were granted in January 1980.

The basis for the second element of the overall European patent protection system is the Convention on the European Patent for the Common Market, also referred to as the Community Patent Convention or the Luxembourg Convention, which was adopted at Luxembourg on December 15, 1975. That instrument is a supplemental convention for the nine EEC countries, and its territorial effect is limited to the Common Market. The rules of the Luxembourg Convention take over where the rules of the Munich Convention leave off, after the grant of the European patent. Its objective is to prevent the dismemberment of the European bundle patent granted in Munich for the Common Market. Accordingly, it transforms a part of that bundle into a unitary, so-called Community patent for the EEC countries. This patent enjoys uniform protection in all EEC countries and cannot be used to split up the Common Market. It can only be filed, granted, transferred, and cancelled for the whole territory of all the member states of the Common Market. Unfortunately, the coming-into effect of the Luxembourg Convention has been delayed due to constitutional difficulties in Denmark and Ireland. As a consequence, the second element of the overall European patent system, the Common Market patent, which may be called the hard-core of the European patent, is still missing.

The final element of the European patent system consists of a far-reaching harmonization of national patent laws. The original concept was that the establishment of the new European patent system should leave the national patent systems of the contracting states totally unaffected. In adopting the new system, no member state was obliged to abandon its own system of protection, to close its national patent office, or to change its national patent law. This realistic approach, coexistence between the unchanged national patent systems and a new, modern system for European patents, greatly facilitated agreement between experts coming from different countries. Trying to find modern legal solutions for the European patent, they were ready to adopt notions that departed from their own traditional legal concept. But, after having agreed to these new solutions for the European patent system, each contracting state realized that it would be unwise to leave the national patent laws unchanged. This understanding caused a complete departure from the original idea and has led to a far-reaching harmonization of the national patent laws in Europe during the last five years. In adhering to the Munich Patent Convention, each contracting state has simultaneously adapted its national patent legislation to the main rules of the Munich Patent Convention and, also, to a large extent, to the rules of the Luxembourg Patent Convention, which are not yet in effect. In many instances, the provisions of these international conventions have been adopted word-for-word in the implementing laws enacted during the last five years in the Federal Republic of Germany, France, the Netherlands, the United Kingdom, Switzerland, Sweden, and others, and this has been done without any legal obligation to harmonize national legislation.

The persuasive power of the European patent system has therefore, brought forward a degree of unification of patent law in Western Europe which no one envisioned ten years ago. Even the conservative English have, without much hesitation, discarded many sacred principles of their national patent law dating back to the famous Statute of Monopolies of 1623. They have adopted a new patent law, which, in its form and content, is no longer a true British statute since it incorporates many continental-European concepts and solutions. This quasi-automatic harmonizing effect, emanating from a convincing international text not originally intended to harmonize national laws, is an astonishing phenomenon. It should also find attention in other fields of law in which the unification process is hindered by widely differing national concepts. It is almost a miracle that such far-reaching harmonization of law could have been attained in the field of patent protection, an area which was always and is still regarded as an instrument of national economic policy.

IV. The Munich Patent Convention

Let me now give some further comments on the first and most important element of the overall European patent system, the European Patent Convention of 1973.

A. General Remarks—The European Patent Organization

The Munich Patent Convention is an impressive document with 178 carefully drafted and systematically arranged articles. Complemented by several protocols and implementing regulations, which consist of 106 explanatory rules, it contains a complete set of rules dealing with the establishment and working of the European patent organization and the granting procedure of the European Patent Office without reference to national law.

The Convention establishes a European patent organization which has its seat in Munich and consists of the European Patent Office (EPO) and the Administrative Council. The EPO is an international administrative agency with a staff whose members come from all of the contracting states. It is led by a president and several vice-presidents. It is competent to examine and grant European patents, and its activities are supervised by the Administrative Council. The Council consists of representatives of the contracting states and, in addition to its budgetary and control functions, it has legislative competence to amend some of the provisions of the Convention and the Implementing Regulations.

*****

VI. Conclusion

The formation of the European patent system, which I have presented here only in part and which is still missing one essential element, the Common Market patent, constitutes a milestone in the development of international patent law. No event since the Paris Convention for the Protection of Industrial Property in 1883 has so drastically changed the system of protection of inventions as the European patent system will. I do not except the Patent Cooperation Treaty (PCT) signed in Washington in 1970 and entered into force over two years ago. It certainly overcomes the territorial approach of the Paris Convention in that it provides for an international patent application and a single novelty search for several countries. But it leaves the substantive law, as well as the patent granting and examination procedure and the final act of granting the monopoly, to the competence of the individual state for which protection is sought. Notwithstanding the progress attained in international cooperation by the Paris Convention and the PCT, the legal basis of international patent protection still remains, as 100 years before, the grant of national patents, through national patent authorities, according to national laws. This territorial or national phase of patent law will be overcome by the European patent system.

We are at the beginning of a new, supranational phase of patent law development. Even though limited in direct effect to Western Europe, the European patent system will certainly provide a model for the establishment of other regional patent systems and will also influence the further development of national patent systems outside of Europe. This seems to me an encouraging perspective which is so urgently needed in our divided world.

Notes and Questions

1. Membership in the EPC has increased since the publication of Beier's article in 1981. There are now 19 member countries, and six countries which have Extension Agreements under which they agree to extend to their territories the protection conferred by the grant of European patents. (Membership in the EU has increased to 15 member states.) The Community Patent Convention referred to by Beier never entered into force so that, for the moment at least, the EPC patents granted by the EPO remain subject to the substantive national patent laws of each EPC member. This, however, is only the beginning of the story which we will examine in detail in Chapters IV and V. The European Commission is proposing that the European Union essentially take over the functions of the EPO for EU members, so that there would in the end be an EU patent system administered by Union organs.

2. If the EU strives to create a "single market", what would the rationale be for maintaining separate member state patent laws? If you do not think that there is a persuasive rationale, how would your analysis change if we asked

the same question about the international patent system? Why might it be useful for each country to maintain its own substantive patent law?

3. Our discussion of the EPC system is limited here to the basic institutional arrangement. We will examine the EPC patent system, including conditions of patentability and granting (and opposition) proceedings in subsequent Chapters.

---

2. The EU Office for Harmonisation in the Internal Market (Trade Marks and Industrial Designs)

The European Union maintains a rather complex legal and institutional structure with respect to the registration and enforcement of trademark rights. The Trade Marks Directive seeks to establish a more or less uniform approach to trademarks throughout the member states, but nevertheless leaves each member state to grant and enforce trademark rights within its territory. The EU has also adopted the Community Trade Mark Regulation which provides for the registration of unitary (and indivisible) trademarks with effects throughout the Union. This EU-wide registration system is administered by the newly-established Office for Harmonisation in the Internal Market (OHIM) in Alicante, Spain. A number of EU member states are also party to the Madrid Agreement on Trademarks administered by WIPO, which provides yet another system for registration. In Chapter V, we will study the relationship among these various arrangements. Following is a brief description of the OHIM.

Office for Harmonisation in the Internal Market (Trade Marks and Designs) OHIM*

The Trade Mark and Internationalization of Markets

1.1. Enhancing the value of one's trade mark: a strategy for businesses

---

*http://europa/agencies/ohim.

The trade mark is a key element of company policy: enhancing its value means holding on to or acquiring market shares. The businessman's tasks are not confined to organization and production. A company's goods and services, as well as its image, must be visible on the market. The trade mark is an indispensable instrument for communicating with the public. It enriches and enhances the consumer's relationship with the goods and services by associating distinctive values with them. The trade mark does not just identify the origin of goods: it establishes a relationship with the consumer based on trust by staking the company's reputation and offering a guarantee of consistent quality. A trade mark is a capital good. It can be commercially exploited by licensing, franchising, merchandising and sponsorship. As a marketing tool it may even constitute the company's main asset.

1.2. The trade mark and the internal European market

The completion of the 'common market' or 'internal market' is forcing companies to change their trade mark policy. Since 1 January 1993, the free movement of goods, persons, services and capital within the Community has given a European dimension to the trade mark policies of an increasing number of companies. Those which still base this policy on their main market — their national market — will, in ever increasing numbers, become aware of the requirements of the European market.

1.3. Instruments available before the creation of the Community trade mark

Prior to the introduction of the Community trade mark, companies could protect their trade marks throughout the European Union in two ways: nationally and internationally. Registration at national level involves registering identical trade marks in each Member State of the European Union. Registration at international level makes it possible to obtain a number of trade marks, the validity of which is limited to the countries party to the Madrid Agreement. This involves applying to the World Intellectual Property Organization in Geneva on the basis of a trade mark already registered in a country party to the Agreement. This route is available only to companies having their headquarters or a real and effective establishment in those

470

countries. The Madrid Agreement covers only about 40 countries: nine countries of the European Union (Belgium, Germany, Spain, France, Italy, Luxembourg, the Netherlands, Austria, and Portugal), Switzerland, and the majority of the countries of Central and Eastern Europe. The other Member States of the European Union and its main trading partners, notably the USA and Japan, are not members of the Madrid Agreement.

1.4. The role of the Community trade mark

The Community trade mark offers the advantage of uniform protection in all countries of the European Union on the strength of a single registration procedure with the Office for Harmonization. It is both an alternative to, and complementary to, the two previous procedures: each of the three types of trade mark offers a level of protection adapted to specific business needs. The national trade mark offers protection limited to the market of a single country. The Community trade mark offers protection for the entire market within the European Union. The international trade mark meets the particular needs to obtain protection also in the countries outside the European Community. These three types of trade mark are not mutually exclusive: various links between them allow companies to develop their protection system according to their needs. A link is soon to be established with the Madrid Agreement by means of a Protocol which may soon enter into force.

The Community Trade Mark and the Office for Harmonisation in the Internal Market (OHIM)

2.1. OHIM

2.1.1. The Office for Harmonisation's task

The Office's task is to promote and manage trade marks and designs within the European Union. It carries out registration procedures for titles to Community industrial property. It keeps public registers of these titles. It shares with the courts in Member States of the European Union the task of pronouncing judgment on requests for invalidation of registered titles.

2.1.2. An independent European public establishment

The Office is a public establishment which enjoys legal, administrative and financial independence. The Office was created under European Community law and is a European Community body with its own legal personality. Its activities are subject to Community law. The Community courts — the Court of First Instance and the Court of Justice of the European Communities — are responsible for overseeing the legality of the Office's decisions. The Office is responsible for balancing its budget from its own revenue, which is derived mainly from registration fees and fees for the renewal of trade mark protection.

2.1.3. Location of the Office

The Office's headquarters are in Alicante, which is situated on the Spanish Mediterranean coast . . . The Office is housed temporarily in an avenue in the centre of Alicante . . . in a modern building where it will be possible to deal with the public's requirements for the first few years. The permanent headquarters will be built almost on the sea-shore, on the edge of the town, half-way between Alicante and the airport.

The Advantages of the Community Trade Mark

2.2.1. What are the advantages of the Community trade mark?

The Community trade mark gives its proprietor a uniform right applicable in all Member States of the European Union on the strength of a single procedure which simplifies trade mark policies at European level. It fulfils the three essential functions of a trade mark at European level: it identifies the origin of goods and services, guarantees consistent quality through evidence of the company's commitment vis-à-vis the consumer, and is a form of communication, a basis for publicity and advertising. The Community trade mark may be used as a manufacturer's mark, a mark for goods of a trading company, or service mark. It may also take the form of a collective trade mark: properly applied, the regulation governing the use of the collective trade mark guarantees the origin, the nature and the quality of goods and services by making them distinguishable, which is beneficial to members of the association or body owning the trade mark. The Community trade mark covers a market of more than 350 million consumers who enjoy some of the highest living standards in the world. It is the ideal instrument to meet the challenges of this market. The Community trade mark is obtained by registration in the Register kept by the Harmonization Office. When registered, transferred or allowed to lapse, the effect of such action is Community-wide. It is valid for a period of 10 years and may be renewed indefinitely. The rules of law applicable to it are similar to those applied to national trade marks by the Member States. Companies will therefore find themselves in a familiar environment, just on a larger scale.

2.2.2. The Community trade mark and national trade marks

The Community trade mark may be obtained for a sign which is either applied for directly at the Harmonization Office or which has been applied for previously through a national office. It does not imply revocation of previous national or international protection, but merely makes such protection more effective and more manageable. A newly-created sign adapted to the various languages, cultures and customs within the European market may be protected directly by applying for first registration as a Community trade mark at the Harmonization Office. A Community trade mark may protect a sign which has already been filed at a national office of a country party to the Paris Convention or to the Agreement on trade-related aspects of intellectual property rights concluded under GATT (TRIPs Agreement). In this case, a right of priority may be claimed for a period of six months. A national trade mark or series of national trade marks may be registered as a Community trade mark irrespective of their age. The company will thus have the perfect instrument to meet the challenges of the internal market. Opting for the Community trade mark does not imply the abandonment of national trade marks. The company may retain these as long as it wishes. The seniority of a national mark may be claimed at the Harmonization Office, even if the national trade mark is subsequently cancelled or surrendered in favour of a Community trade mark. The company enjoys the same

rights as if the national trade mark were still registered. In the event of refusal to register an application, or the revocation or annulment of a Community trade mark, applications for national trade marks may be made in
all countries of the European Union in which there are no such grounds for
refusal, revocation or annulment. The advantage of priority or seniority is
therefore maintained, as are any investment and advertising campaigns
previously carried out in these countries.

Notes and Questions

1. Efforts to bring about a EC wide system of protection of industrial designs have been under way for many years since initial proposals submitted
by the Max-Planck Institute for Foreign and International Patent, Copyright and Competition Law in 1991 (Towards a European Design Law, Munich 1991, 22 IIC 523), further elaborated by a 1991 Green Paper on the
Legal Protection of Industrial Designs (111/f/5131/91-EN), resulting in a
successive round of draft proposals for a unitary, community-wide design
right (COM(93)342, [1994] O.J. C37/20 final). The approach broadly follows the Community Trade Mark Regulation. Filing and registration is
likely to be with the OHIM (which may also explain why it was not simply
termed the European Trade Mark Office). The approach in design law has
been the same as in trademark law: It has been planned to harmonize
national laws by a directive (see Ch. I,B,5 *supra*), and thereafter to make
available a community-wide design right through a regulation. The substantial controversy surrounding adoption of the Design Directive leaves
some uncertainty regarding the timetable for a Union-wide design registration system.

3. The EU System for the Registration of Plant Varieties

In Chapter I we discussed the ongoing evolution of the legal protection of plant varieties. Following is a brief description of the EU plant variety registration office.

Community Plant Variety Rights Office (CPVO)*

The EC Commission began its work on community plant variety protection at about the same time as with trademarks and design protection. An initial proposal of a Community plant variety right (CPVR) was submitted in 1990. The Council Regulation EC No 2100/94 of 27 July 1994 on Community Plant Variety Rights was adopted on July 27, 1994, and has been operational since April 27, 1995. A special registration office was established in 1995. The Community Plant Variety Rights Office (CPVO) was temporarily located in Brussels, but, after the decision of the Council of the European Community of December 6, 1996, moved to its own premises in Angers, France. The CPVO is an independent body of the EC. It is exclusively responsible for the implementation of the new regime of Community plant variety rights. At the CPVO, individuals may obtain a Community-wide right. The CPVR exists in addtition to national plant variety rights.

Unlike the situation with trademarks, the implementation of the Community-wide plant variety right was not accompanied or preceded by a directive on the harmonization of national plant variety legislation (due to the fact that such national legislation is largely based upon the 1991 UPOV Convention). Importantly, national and European registration at the CPVO in Angers are mutually exclusive. Thus, it is not possible to register the same variety both at national offices and at the CPVO. In substance, the requirements of the Regulation for filing and registration are similar to those provided for by the 1991 UPOV Convention of 1991. The official languages of the CPVO comprise all official languages of the EC. By June 1998, more than 7000 applications had been filed and 3100 varieties registered by the Angers Office.

---

4. Other Regional Arrangements for Securing IPRs

The following paper from the International Bureau of WIPO describes two African regional IPRs systems for the granting and registration of IPRs.

---

*Adapted from an information sheet prepared by the CVPO.

Regional Cooperation in the Field of Industrial Property

International Bureau of WIPO*

*****

African Regional Industrial Property Organization (ARIPO)**

9. Since 1973, WIPO and the United Nations Economic Commission for Africa (ECA) have been collaborating to assist the governments of English-speaking African countries in their efforts to harmonize and develop their industrial property systems to create the appropriate intergovernmental structures to this effect.

10. Those efforts resulted in the adoption, by a Diplomatic Conference held at Lusaka, Zambia, in December 1976, and at which 13 governments of English-speaking African countries were represented, of an Agreement on the Creation of an Industrial Property Organization for English-speaking Africa (ESARIPO). The Agreement entered into force on February 15, 1978. In December 1985 the Organization changed its name to African Regional Industrial Property Organization (ARIPO), by decision of its Council. At present the following 14 countries are members of ARIPO: Botswana, Gambia, Ghana, Kenya, Lesotho, Malawi, Sierra Leone, Somalia, Sudan, Swaziland, Tanzania, Uganda, Zambia and Zimbabwe. Membership in ARIPO is open to Ethiopia, Liberia, Mauritius, Nigeria and Seychelles, all of which participate in the Organization's activities. ARIPO has its headquarters in Harare, Zimbabwe.

11. The objectives of ARIPO are, *inter alia*:

— to promote the harmonization and development of the industrial property laws, and matters related thereto, appropriate to the needs of its members and of the region as a whole;

---

*WIPO/CEIPI/PI/SB/98/5, Sept. 1998.
**Formerly known as the Industrial Property Organization for English-speaking Africa (ESARIPO).

— to establish such common services or organs as may be necessary or desirable for the coordination, harmonization and development of the industrial property activities affecting its members;

— to assist its members in the development and acquisition of suitable technology; and

— to evolve a common view in industrial property matters.

12. Upon the request of (ES)ARIPO, WIPO, in association with the ECA, assisted the Organization in the establishment of a Patent Documentation and Information Centre, at its headquarters in Harare. The purpose of the center is to promote the objectives of ARIPO by providing member States with technological information available for patent and patent-related documentation in order to assist those States in the achievement of their development objectives.

13. The establishment of the center, after an initial preparatory assistance phase, commenced in 1981 within the framework of a UNDP financed project with WIPO, in association with the ECA, as Executing Agency.

14. Within the framework of its Committees for Patent Matters and for Trade Mark and Industrial Design Matters, the Organization has developed Model Laws on Patents and on Trade Marks to assist its member States in the strengthening of their legislation in those respective fields.

15. A Protocol on Patents and Industrial Designs Within the Framework of (ES)ARIPO, adopted at a Special Meeting held in Harare in December 1982, entered into force on April 25, 1984, initially among Ghana, Malawi, Sudan, Uganda and Zimbabwe. Since then, Botswana, Gambia, Kenya, Lesotho, Swaziland and Zambia have joined the Protocol, bringing the total to 11 member countries party thereto.

16. The Protocol establishes a system under which patent and industrial design applications are processed and granted or registered, as the case may be, on behalf of Contracting States designated in the applications, by the Office of ARIPO. The scheme established by the Protocol enables the technical processing of patent and industrial design applications, and the administration of granted patents and industrial designs, to be undertaken by

477

a central authority. Any designated State has the right, however, where an application does not conform to the provisions of the Protocol or to those of its national industrial property legislation, to declare, *prior to the grant of the patent or registration of the industrial design*, that, if granted or registered, such grant or registration will have no effect within the territory of that State. Where no declaration is made, the grant of the patent or registration of the industrial design by ARIPO has the same effect as any grant or registration carried out under the national law of the States designated in the relevant application.

17. Part of the income generated from application and maintenance fees under the Protocol is used for the Office of ARIPO while the remainder is distributed among the Contracting States concerned.

18. On the occasion of its annual session held in Banjul (The Gambia) in 1993, the Administrative Council of ARIPO agreed on a Protocol on Trademarks, under which it will be possible to file applications with the ARIPO office. Under the said Protocol, once in force, the ARIPO Office will have the competence to process applications and to register trademarks and service marks on behalf of Contracting States designated in the applications. At the 1994 session of the Council held in Kasane (Botswana), the said Protocol was signed by six member countries. It will enter into force after three member states have deposited their instruments of ratification or accession.

19. Also in 1993, the Administrative Council had, in principle, agreed that PCT applicants should be able to designate, for an ARIPO patent, States which are party to both the PCT and the Harare Protocol. In 1994, the Administrative Council of ARIPO adopted the necessary amendments to the Harare Protocol, and its Implementing Regulations, with effect from July 1, 1994. As a result, it has been possible, from that date, for PCT applicants to designate, for an ARIPO patent, the States of Ghana, Kenya, Lesotho, Sierra Leone, Swaziland, Uganda, Zimbabwe, Malawi and Sudan, the nine Contracting States of the Harare Protocol which, as of now, are Members of the PCT.

African Intellectual Property Organization (OAPI)***

***The acronym corresponds to the French name (Organization africaine de la propriété intellectuelle).

20. A system of intergovernmental cooperation in the field of industrial property among 12 French-speaking African countries was established by the Libreville Agreement of 1962 for the creation of an African and Malagasy Office of Industrial Property (OAMPI). The Libreville Agreement was subsequently revised by the Bangui Agreement Relating to the Creation of an African Intellectual Property Organization (OAPI), which entered into force on February 8, 1982. The Libreville Agreement established, among the member States, a common system for the grant and maintenance of industrial property titles (patents, trademark registrations, industrial design registrations) in accordance with uniform legislation contained in Annexes to the Agreement, which are applicable in each member State. At present, 14 countries (Benin, Burkina Faso, Cameroon, Central African Republic, Chad, Congo, Côte d'Ivoire, Gabon, Guinea, Mali, Mauritania, Niger, Senegal, Togo) are members of OAPI. The system provides for common formalities for the grant of industrial property titles by a central industrial property office, the African Intellectual Property Organization (OAPI), situated in Yaoundé (Cameroon), which acts as the industrial property office for each of the member States.

21. Under the system, titles granted by the central office have effect in all member States; there is no possibility of limiting the effect to only one or some of the member States. Applications are normally filed with the central office in Yaoundé; however, nationals of member States may file applications with national administrations, which then have to transmit the applications to the central office; national administrations cannot grant titles themselves.

22. The industrial property rights granted have the effect of national industrial property rights in each of the Contracting States, i.e., not of supranational titles of protection.

23. Apart from certain modifications in the uniform substantive law (e.g., the gradual introduction of examination of patent applications for compliance with the substantive requirements of patentability), the main features of the revision introduced by the Bangui Agreement include the extension of OAPI's field of competence to copyright and the protection of the cultural heritage, and the inclusion, in addition to patents, marks and industrial designs, of the following objects of industrial property: trade names,

utility models, appellations of origin, indications of source and unfair competition. The uniform substantive law with respect to each object of intellectual property is set forth in separate annexes to the Agreement.

24. Upon the request of OAPI, WIPO has assisted it in the establishment, within the headquarters in Yaoundé, of a Patent Documentation and Information Department (Departement de la documentation et de l'information en matière de brevets (DEDIB)). The aim of DEDIB is to contribute to the technological and industrial development of the member States by putting at the disposal of governments, research institutions, industry and other users of such information technological information based on a collection of patent documentation and to establish a network of national industrial property structures in the OAPI member States for liaison with the Organization. The establishment of DEDIB and of the network of national structures was accomplished with the assistance of the United Nations Development Programme (UNDP) under a project, covering the period 1979 to 1982, of which WIPO was the Executing Agency.

25. OAPI is financed entirely from the income it receives from fees it collects for the grant and administration of industrial property rights.

Notes and Questions

1. The establishment of regional offices and rules for the granting and maintenance of IPRs would certainly appear to be advantageous in terms of promoting economic efficiencies. As efforts underway at WIPO to develop worldwide infrastructures for the electronic granting of IPRs in various fields proceed, there will be a need to integrate this multilateral process of integration with the regional process of integration in the IPRs field.

2. Governments have limited resources. As resources are invested in creating regional IPRs infrastructures, less attention is devoted to the broader multilateral framework established by WIPO and the WTO. Would governments be better off bypassing a regional IPRs system integration phase and

concentrating on multilateral endeavors? What advantages do governments see in the regional approach?

D. Bilateral Arrangements

In addition to multilateral institutions such as the WTO and regional institutions such as the EU, there are many bilateral — or state to state (and region to state) — arrangements with respect to IPRs. Bilateral agreements relating to IPRs were a traditional way to bring about selective harmonization (or preferences) before bilateral IPRs strategies gave way to multilateral strategies in WIPO and the WTO. Certain categories of agreements even today are often of a bilateral nature because of the subject matter which they cover: This applies to agreements on the protection of geographical indications, such as wines. Switzerland, for example, has concluded agreements on geographical indications with Germany, Argentina, Bulgaria, Spain, France, Hungary, Portugal, the Czech Republic and the Slovak Republic. These agreements essentially consist of listings of particular geographical names from a given country which are made subject to mutual recognition.

A further group of bilateral agreements form part of trade policy in the absence of multilateral disciplines. After the fall of the Berlin Wall, and while the TRIPS Agreement was not yet adopted (pending completion of negotiations, particularly in the field of agriculture), the United States, the EU and governments of other industrialized countries increasingly included IPRs standards in bilateral trade agreements. So, for example, the agreement between the EU and the People's Republic of China and the association and cooperation agreements between the EU and various Central and Eastern European countries (that envision an eventual enlargement of the EU) include obligations to protect IPRs. Some of these agreements are referred to in a passage from the opinion of the ECJ on Accession to the WTO which we studied earlier.

The EFTA States have jointly concluded agreements with some of the Eastern and Central European countries (Bulgaria, Czech Republic, Hungary, Poland, Romania, Slovakia). The provisions in these agreements primarily show the intention of the parties to provide an appropriate level of IPRs protection. These treaties entered into force in 1994.

Like the EU, the United States routinely concludes bilateral agreements, particularly with developing countries, that include provisions obligating the parties to protect IPRs. Some of these agreements are based on a model Bilateral Investment Treaty (BIT) which has been developed by the United States and is used to establish commercial legal relations with the developing world. These BITs includes obligations to protect IPRs. In recent years the United States has concluded several bilateral agreements in respect to IPRs protection in the context of settling U.S. complaints that arise under its "Section 301" and "Special 301" legislation. The two most comprehensive and interesting of these agreements were entered into with the People's Republic of China. We will examine U.S. Section 301, Special 301 and the IPRs agreements with China in Chapter VI.

Notes and Questions

1. One of the oldest bilateral treaties on IPRs in Europe is the Swiss-Liechtenstein Treaty on patents which entered into force in 1923 (SR 0.232.149.514). The agreement established a joint patent regime for both jurisdictions exclusively administered by the Swiss authorities. A recent revision clarified that Switzerland and the Principality of Liechtenstein operate as a single entity with respect to applications at the EPO and under the Patent Cooperation Treaty (PCT), although both are independent members of these respective international systems. Another example of an early bilateral agreement is the German-Swiss agreement on the mutual protection of patents, trademarks and designs (SR 0.232.149.136), which is still in force.

2. Are bilateral trade agreement IPRs provisions modeled after TRIPS Agreement provisions of any practical importance? What about provisions in agreements with non-member States of the WTO, such as China or Russia? Should the provisions of these agreements be construed in accordance with the provisions of the TRIPS Agreement?

3. In a recent U.S. Supreme Court case involving the importation of copyrighted goods,[1] the U.S. government took the position that certain imports

---

[1]See *Quality King Distributors v. L'anza Research International*, U.S. Supreme Court, 1998 U.S. LEXIS 1606, March 9, 1998, *infra* Ch. IV, § M,2,b.

should be restricted because a few recently concluded U.S. trade agreements with developing countries required the restriction of such imports. The U.S. government argued to the Supreme Court that the U.S. would breach its treaty obligations if the Court interpreted the federal Copyright Act to allow the subject imports. This form of advocacy troubled some U.S. IPRs experts because it suggested that the executive branch might seek to impose important domestic IPRs policies through non-transparent action in the foreign relations field. The Supreme Court sharply rejected the U.S. government's argument based on the trade agreements.

2. In approaching the conclusion of this Chapter, we observe that the international IPRs system incorporates institutions and rules at the multilateral level, the regional level, the national level and the subnational level. These institutions and rules interact with each other to create a highly complex system.

E. Non-Governmental Organizations

As with many other areas of international governance, non-governmental organizations (NGOs) play an increasingly active role in the formulation and implementation of IPRs policies. NGOs take many forms and represent a wide range of interests. In the IPRs area, the most active of these groups represent industry interests. These include NGOs formed by particular industry sectors, such as the pharmaceuticals sector (for example, the International Federation of Pharmaceuticals Manufacturers Associations (IFPMA)), and NGOs with interests in a particular form of IPRs protection, such as copyright (for example, the International Intellectual Property Alliance (IIPA)) and trademark (for example, the International Trademark Association (INTA)). NGOs are also often formed by lawyers with interests in IPRs subject matter (such as the American Intellectual Property Law Association (AIPLA)), and these lawyers' associations take public positions on international IPRs policy and legislation. A recent phenomenon is the formation of coalitions of interest groups with stakes in the outcome of negotiations on particular IPRs treaties. This phenomenon is discussed in an article by Pamela Samuelson on the negotiation of the WIPO Copyright Treaty that appears in Chapter IV. In this negotiation, an unlikely coalition of telecommunications service providers, scientific research groups and library interest groups was formed and worked together successfully.

As traditional non-profit organizations concerned with the protection of consumer interests, the environment, health care, and so forth, have come to appreciate the ways in which the scope of IPRs protection may affect their interests, these groups have also become increasingly active in public debate on IPRs protection issues.

International organizations have different policies towards the participation of NGOs in their work programs. NGOs are not permitted to participate in the negotiations that take place within the WTO and its organs. In contrast, WIPO has a developed system for the accreditation of NGOs as observers, with the right to speak at meetings, subject to the control of the presiding officer. NGOs participate as observers in WIPO diplomatic conferences and in member-state committees in which the preparatory work for diplomatic conferences is undertaken. In addition, the Director General of WIPO established in 1999 an Industry Advisory Commission to provide advice on program activities of WIPO. Do you consider that the international legislative and negotiation process is enriched or impeded by the participation of NGOs?

CHAPTER III

Sources and Basic Principles

In the first two chapters we observed that intellectual property protection essentially relies on a combination of national, regional and international law. While specific rights and obligations are mainly — and variably — defined and put into operation by national law (and increasingly also by regional law), international law provides the overarching framework for interfacing national and regional regulatory systems. It governs the transnational aspects of IPRs. It establishes basic principles for the international IPRs system, and it increasingly plays a role in harmonizing substantive and procedural rules in the process of globalization.

This chapter discusses the main sources of international law and how they conceptually relate to national and regional law, with particular focus on the processes of interpretation and application of IPRs standards. It sets out the principal substantive and procedural principles of international intellectual property protection before these matters are addressed in detail later in the book. We provide this synthesizing perspective on basic principals because it may aid students and policy-makers in viewing the international IPRs system as being based on a coherent body of underlying concepts. Some basic IPRs principles also serve as general principles operating in the international trading system. Some are specific to IPRs.

A. Sources of International Law

The legal sources of international law applicable to the international IPRs system, as for any other field of international law, are generally considered to be set forth and reflected in Article 38 of the Statute of the International Court of Justice.

Article 38

1. The Court, whose function is to decide in accordance with international law such disputes as are submitted to it, shall apply:

a. international conventions, whether general or particular, establishing rules expressly recognized by the contesting states;

b. international custom, as evidence of a general practice accepted as law;

c. the general principles of law recognized by civilized nations;

d. subject to the provisions of Article 59 [which *inter alia* allows the Court to call witnesses and experts] judicial decisions and the teachings of the most highly qualified publicists of the various nations, as subsidiary means for the determination of rules of law.

2. This provision shall not prejudice the power of the Court to decide a case ex aequo et bono, if the parties agree thereto.

Article 38 was initially drafted in 1920 by a ten-person Advisory Committee of Jurists to the Council of the League of Nations.[1] It became part of the Statute of the Permanent Court of International Justice of the League of Nations, and was incorporated almost verbatim into the 1945 Statute of the International Court of Justice (ICJ), today often referred to as the World Court. This list of sources still reflects the main contemporary sources of international law. At the same time, it may not adequately capture certain of the more recent evolutions in recognized principles of law. It is difficult, for example, to classify basic constitutional principles of international law such as the right to self-determination as purely matters of treaty or customary law. The same holds true for the concept of basic human rights. Moreover, Article 38 does not address the legal nature of recommendations and decisions of international organizations. Finally, this list does not establish any formal hierarchy of sources. It leaves the relationship between treaty law and customary law open.

In the context of the international IPRs system, the uncertain relationship among different sources of international law has not so far raised seri-

---

[1]For a detailed discussion of the history and the interpretation of Article 38 of the Statute, see Richard D. Kearney, *Sources of Law and the International Court of Justice, in* II THE FUTURE OF THE INTERNATIONAL COURT OF JUSTICE 610 (L. GROSS ED., 1976).

ous difficulties. The international IPRs system has been predominantly grounded in treaty norms. Questions of interpretation and application of these norms have been addressed by reference to the law of treaties. In the future, other sources of international law — in particular "general principles of law" — may play a more important role in the international IPRs system, especially as this system is now effectively open to quasi-judicial dispute settlement under the umbrella of the WTO.

1. Treaty Law

In the first two chapters, we referred to the 1883 multilateral Paris Convention for the Protection of Industrial Property and the 1886 Berne Convention for the Protection of Literary and Artistic Works. The negotiation of these treaties was among the very first attempts to bring about international harmonization of basic concepts of law. This was long before comparable efforts were undertaken after the Second World War in the field of trade and investment. In Chapter IV, we will briefly examine the negotiating history of each of the major IPRs treaties.

In Chapter II, we studied the structure of various international organizations, such as WIPO and the WTO, and of various regional institutions, such as the European Union, NAFTA and Mercosur. Each of these organizations or institutions is established by a treaty or treaties. Treaties among larger groups of countries and regions are generally referred to as "multilateral" treaties or agreements. Treaties among smaller groups of countries are sometimes (particularly by economists) referred to as "minilateral" agreements.[2] There is no single generally accepted broad term for agreements by which regional organizations or institutions are constituted.[3] This situation is partly explained by the fact that regional organizations and institutions differ fairly widely in their scope and structure, and the terminology used to describe their charter treaty is often fairly specific to the particular regional

---

[2] The WTO Agreement incorporates certain agreements to which some, but not all, WTO Members are party. These are referred to as "plurilateral" agreements, though the term "plurilateral" has not otherwise been a term of general usage in treaty law.

[3] Terms including "regional agreement," "regional arrangement," "regional integration mechanism," "regional trading arrangement," "customs union agreement," "free trade area agreement," "common market agreement" and others may be used to describe agreements establishing regional institutions or organizations, depending on the context.

arrangement. An agreement between two countries is generally referred to as a "bilateral" treaty.

Rules of international law governing the interpretation and application of treaties are generally set forth in the Vienna Convention on the Law of Treaties of 1969 (VCLT or Vienna Convention).[4] Most countries are parties to the Vienna Convention. The United States, as a notable exception, has not adhered to the Vienna Convention, but has indicated that it accepts the terms of the Convention as reflecting customary international law applicable to treaties. The Vienna Convention prescribes rules regarding the formation, amendment, interpretation and performance of treaties. It also prescribes rules regarding some aspects of relationships between different sets of treaty norms. In the interpretation and application of the norms of the various WIPO and WTO multilateral agreements, as well as in interpreting and applying bilateral agreements, the rules of the Vienna Convention will generally be applied.

As noted in the excerpt by Joseph Weiler regarding the EU,[5] regional organizations may or may not be governed by the rules of the Vienna Convention. The ECJ views the EC Treaty in the nature of a constitutional charter among member states, and so considers that a jurisprudence specific to the EU applies in the interpretation and application of the EC Treaty. Whether other regional organizations and institutions will consider their charters to be governed by the Vienna Convention, or by their own special internal jurisprudence, will depend upon the circumstances of each case.

Later in this section, we will examine decisions of a WTO panel and the WTO Appellate Body in a case involving a U.S. complaint against India for failing to implement TRIPS Agreement "mailbox" obligations. In their decisions, the panel and Appellate Body make extensive reference to the law of the Vienna Convention.

2. Customary International Law

To date, the sources of international law other than treaty law, as expressed in Article 38 of the ICJ Statute, have been of much less importance

---

[4]Vienna Convention on the Law of Treaties, May 23, 1969, 1155 UNTS 331 (entered into force Jan. 27, 1980), U.N. Doc. A/Conf. 39 (1969).
[5]See supra, Ch. II, § B, 2, a.

to the international IPRs system than to the classical domains of international law. Indeed, it would appear that the link between international IPRs law and the full body of international law has not been fully established. This is due not only to the fact that IPRs law has, for a long time, been highly specialized. It is also due to the fact that international lawyers, as a general proposition, have not exhibited interest in IPRs subject matter comparable to interest exhibited in other areas (for example, regarding international security law and the law of the sea), and interdisciplinary links between international lawyers and IPRs lawyers remain to be further developed in doctrine and practice.

Customary international law is defined both by evidence of state practice and by shared perceptions of law (*opinio iuris sive necessitatis*). Traditionally, rules of customary international law evolve over substantial periods of time as nations engage in more or less consistent patterns of conduct which reflect their shared perception of the required behavior in particular situations.[6]

Nationally and internationally, regulation of IPRs has been a domain of legislation (including treaty). This "positivist" tradition of the IPRs field is likely to change. Regulation of IPRs is subject to the effects of rapid technological change. New problems often cannot be solved by recourse to positive rules relating to past technologies.

In addition, in the area of electronic commerce and, more generally, the "regulation" of the Internet, there is a strong tendency emerging to prefer private-sector based self-regulation in many areas, including IPRs, to legislative solutions. The U.S.-Japan Joint Statement on Electronic Commerce of May 15, 1998, contained, as two of its general principles, the statements that "The private sector should lead in the development of electronic commerce and in establishing business practices," and that "Governments should encourage self-regulation through codes of conduct, model contracts, guidelines, and enforcement mechanisms developed by the private sector." In connection with domain names, the Joint Statement noted that "In order to reach its full potential, the system for registering, allocating and governing domain names should be global, fair and market-based and reflect the geo-

---

[6]The question whether "instant custom" may arise based on an immediate and widespread acceptance of new rules is debated, and we do not intend to address this issue by reference to the traditional conception of customary international law.

graphically and functionally diverse nature of the Internet. The said system should also give business the confidence that trademark rights are to be protected by establishing a self-regulatory regime on a global basis."

Will such self-regulatory schemes form the basis of customary law that can be applied as a source of international IPRs regulation? The speed with which they will need to be developed and applied poses a difficulty. Similarly, it is difficult to see how customary law will emerge in the field of copyright law relating to computer technology, which has doubled its potential every second year during the last five decades. These circumstances are at odds with customary law, which, by tradition has required long-standing practice, and an essentially stable societal and economic environment, to evolve.

Nevertheless, it is remarkable that the link to customary international law has not been made in the interest of protecting the intellectual property of foreigners against unlawful taking or excessively restrictive use. Limitations on takings of alien-owned property including, in particular, the principles of full and prompt, or equitable, compensation have not been applied to intellectual property.[7]

This fact may be partly explained by history. In the context of nationalization (which includes the context of decolonization), the objects of takings and expropriations were tangible property — either real or movable — such as oil or gas. Case law, doctrine and successive legal instruments, such as the 1974 Charter of Economic Rights and Duties of States, emerged against this background.[8] The problem of formal or informal taking of intellectual property was not addressed in this historical milieu. Despite the fact that the actions and issues are comparable — at least from an economic point of view — problems of piracy, copying and compulsory licensing of IPRs have not been approached on the basis of principles of customary law.

A number of factors may explain this situation. First, as we have noted, the international IPRs field has mainly been regulated by treaty, including bilateral investment protection agreements. Second, customary law has

---

[7]See generally, Burns H. Weston, *The New International Economic Order and the Deprivation of Foreign Proprietary Wealth: Reflections upon the Contemporary International Law Debate, in* RICHARD B. LILLICH, INTERNATIONAL LAW OF STATE RESPONSIBILITY FOR INJURIES TO ALIENS (1983).

[8]14 I.L.M. 251 (1975).

largely addressed formal government takings, and has been less concerned with the problem of informal, *de facto* and/or "creeping" takings. This situation may be gradually changing in light of the experience of the U.S. — Iran Claims Tribunal, which was explicitly authorized to look into informal takings.[9] Third, takings of IPRs often occur at the hands of the private sector, albeit with the tolerance of governments.

The foregoing illustration relating to the evolution of customary international law with respect to nationalization and expropriation suggests that the relationship between customary international law and the international IPRs system should be further explored. One question to consider is the extent to which the principles of customary law applying to the protection of real and movable property should apply to IPRs. Moreover, it would be interesting to examine to what extent other principles of customary law, such as *pacta sunt servanda*,[10] non-intervention,[11] territorial integrity,[12] self-defense,[13] prohibition of force and coercion,[14] and legal equality of states[15] are important to the IPRs field.

3. Precedents and Doctrine

Judicial precedent is an important source of law in the international IPRs system. As we see throughout this book, judicial decisions provide a backbone for the system. Yet, almost all of the decisions we examine emanate either from national or regional judges. This is largely due to the absence, prior to establishment of the WTO, of an efficient international dispute settlement mechanism. Until the inception of the WTO, the international IPRs system produced virtually no international legal precedents

---

[9] *See* George H. Aldrich, *What Constitutes a Compensable Taking of Property? The Decision of the Iran-United States Claims Tribunal*, 88 AJIL 585 (1994).

[10] The rule that international agreements should be performed in good faith.

[11] The rule that states should not, save in prescribed circumstances, interfere in the internal affairs of other states.

[12] The rule that the territorial boundaries of each state are secure against changes brought about by threat or use of force, and that each state is sovereign within its own territory.

[13] The rule that states possess an inherent right of self-defense against threat or use of force by other states.

[14] The rule that no state should use force or threat of force to impair the territorial integrity or political independence of another state.

[15] The rule that each state is juridically equal as a subject of international law.

in the sense of decisions by international adjudicatory authorities. While the ICJ has jurisdiction to adjudicate matters relating to international IPR conventions (Article 28, Paris Convention and Article 33, Berne Convention), no cases were brought before the Permanent Court of International Justice, and no cases have been brought so far before the ICJ. The same holds true, to date, for international arbitration. There is almost nothing to draw from case law in terms of precedents in international law. This situation has left many uncertainties in respect to the principal IPRs treaties.

The situation has changed with the advent of the WTO TRIPS Agreement, and a first case will be discussed shortly. Decisions of the Dispute Settlement Body (DSB) based upon recommendations by a panel or the Appellate Body (AB) will emerge as important precedents for the future of the international IPRs system. While the decisions are binding, the reasoning of the panel or AB does not amount to *stare decisis*, as this concept is generally unknown in international law.[16] Future panels are obliged to consider the arguments and reasoning of past GATT panels and WTO panels and AB recommendations,[17] but they may deviate, for good cause, from prior decisions.

Although there may be debate as to whether such action is required by the WTO Agreement, it would promote the rule of law in the international economic system if national and regional courts would give effect to decisions of WTO panels and the AB when such decisions specifically affect matters under their jurisdiction.[18] National and regional courts should also

---

[16]*Stare decisis* doctrine, as it is known in national legal systems, generally requires that legal rules be applied by one nation's courts in a consistent manner in equivalent sets of circumstances. Once a determination has been made as to the proper interpretation of a rule of law, that determination should be applied in comparable cases involving different parties. However, in international law each state is sovereign and, in recognition of this sovereignty, it is accepted that the method of application of a legal rule in one set of circumstances involving a sovereign entity(ies) does not require an identical application of the same legal rule to an equivalent set of circumstances involving another sovereign entity. That is, judicial interpretations in respect of one sovereign entity do not automatically bind another sovereign entity.

[17]*See infra*, India-Patent Protection, Report of the Appellate Body at para. 13 with a quotation of the Report of the Appellate Body in the case *Japan — Taxes on Alcoholic Beverages*.

[18]*See* Thomas Cottier, *Dispute Settlement in the World Trade Organization: Characteristics and Structural Implications for the European Union*, 35 CMLRev 325 (1998).

take into account the reasoning and interpretations of panels and the AB, though they are not bound by them. It is recommended to follow such reasoning and interpretations unless there are compelling reasons to do otherwise since it is important to build a coherent system, and this will not be the case if the rules of international agreements are construed at variance in different national or regional jurisdictions. Overall, the precedents set by the bodies of the WTO will be of more than a merely subsidiary character, as might appear contemplated by Article 38(1)(d) of the Statute of the ICJ.

Today, most precedents of general importance in the IPRs field stem from national or regional courts. These rulings are not primary sources of international law under Article 38 of the Statute of the ICJ, though they are important in constituting the body of general principles of law (which is a primary source, see below), and they may be used as subsidiary sources. As a practical matter, these cases are of utmost importance, and should be considered in deciding similar or comparable issues. Core concepts, such as the doctrine of exhaustion,[19] are primarily shaped and framed by national and regional courts, and it is important that courts take their decisions while fully informed about trends and developments in other jurisdictions. A wide variety of learned societies, journals and electronic resources provide ample information regarding these precedents. National and regional court precedents are, as this book tries to explain, of key importance to bringing about judicial coherence of the overall system. The international IPRs field could not have evolved without a strong comparativist approach, and such an approach will likely serve well in the future.

Article 38 of the ICJ Statute refers to the writings of highly qualified jurists as a subsidiary or secondary source of international law. It is too early to tell what influence prominent authors will have in international IPRs adjudication. The WTO AB occasionally refers to leading authors. Common law courts (for example, British and U.S. courts) refer to scholarly works, though this occurs much more frequently in the civil law tradition. The Swiss Federal Court, as example, frequently refers to scholars in order to explore different views, and to substantiate its own decisions. Recourse to the international academic community should be an important element in bringing about an overall coherence of the IPRs system, and should be further encouraged on the international, regional and national levels of law.

---

[19]See, e.g., Ideal Standard, supra Ch. I, § B, 6, c; and infra this chapter.

493

4. General Principles of Law

For the international IPRs system, general principles of law are perhaps the most important source of law outside treaty law. General principles apply extensively to national, regional and to international law, and they have the potential of substantially contributing to the coherence of the overall system. Moreover, general principles are applicable to the conduct of private parties. As IPRs are in the main held and used by private operators, general principles of law are well suited to be applied to the IPRs field.

General principles have not figured prominently in IPRs adjudication, but some recent decisions have employed them extensively. For example, in Chapter IV we will study the decision of an EPO Technical Board of Appeal (*Procter & Gamble*) in which general principles of law in relation to the doctrine of *res judicata* are used as a central source of law in interpreting the EPC. The advent of efficient dispute settlement under the umbrella of the WTO should also enhance the role of general principles.

The term "general principles of law," as found in Article 38(1)(c) Statute of the ICJ, does not refer to principles of international law which are formally part of customary or treaty law (such as the principle that treaties should be performed in good faith), but refers instead to principles of law common to the different legal systems of the world. These general principles operate in all areas of the law, including IPRs regulation. They contain the most valuable general body of law — a record of human nature, experience and wisdom, often essential to resolving difficult conflicts. It is not intended that national laws be adopted "lock, stock and barrel," but the principles underlying such laws can be important in filling gaps and lacunae, and they may guide courts in the process of interpreting international and regional law.[20]

General principles of law, recognized in international law, comprise a considerable body of rules which are important to the interpretation and administration of IPRs. There are, to begin with, principles relating to good

---

[20]*See generally* OSCAR SCHACHTER, INTERNATIONAL LAW IN THEORY AND PRACTICE 49-58 (1991); for a comprehenive classical analysis see WILFRIED JENKS, THE PROSPECTS OF INTERNATIONAL ADJUDICATION 316-427 (1964); B. CHENG, GENERAL PRINCIPLES OF LAW APPLIED BY INTERNATIONAL COURTS AND TRIBUNALS (1953); CHARLES DE VISSCHER, DE L'ÉQUITÉ DANS LE RÈGLEMENT ARBITRAL OU JUDICIAIRE DES LITIGES DE DROIT INTERNATIONAL PUBLIC (1972).

faith and equity.[21] These include, for example, the principle that reasonable expectations based upon the conduct of another person will be protected.[22] They arguably contain common law maxims, including: "He who seeks equity must do equity"; "Equity looks to the intent, rather than to the form" or, in other words, "In absolute equity things should be judged by what they are and not by what they are called"; "Equity aids the vigilant and not the indolent," and; "Equity regards the balance of convenience."[23] Most importantly, the doctrines of abuse of rights (*abus de droit*, important in the relationship between IPRs and competition law[24]), and estoppel and acquiescence, flow from the principle of good faith.[25]

General principles of equity also include: "No one may transfer more than he has"[26] (arguably important in trademarks and parallel importation[27]); the principle of *lex specialis*,[28] the latter in time rule,[29] the prohibition against retroactive laws,[30] and the principle of proportionality.[31]

---

[21]For a comprehensive review and analysis see Ralph A. Newman, *The General Principles of Equity* in: EQUITY IN THE WORLD'S LEGAL SYSTEMS: A COMPARATIVE STUDY 599-604 (R.A. NEWMAN ED.,1973).

[22]*Id.* at 603.

[23]*See* Jenks, *supra* note 20, at 413 with references to international awards referring to these maxims. Newman, *supra* note 21, at 599 concluded, based upon comparative studies, that equity not only entails the principles of good faith, but also consideration of honesty and generosity (see *infra* this subsection).

[24]Doctrines regarding abuse of rights flow from the idea that legal entitlements do not confer untettered discretion regarding the uses that may be made of such entitlements See infra, Chapter VII.

[25]Closely related doctrines of estoppel and acquiescence refer to circumstances in which parties may as a consequence of their own conduct be precluded from asserting rights that might otherwise have been available to them. *See* JOERG PAUL MUELLER, VERTRAUENSSCHUTZ IM VÖLKERRECHT (1971); Joerg Paul Mueller & Thomas Cottier, *in* 7 ENCYCLOPEDIA OF PUBLIC INTERNATIONAL LAW (1982)(at "estoppel and acquiescence").

[26]Nemo plus iuris transferre potest quam ipse habet.

[27]*See infra*, Chapters IV and VII.

[28]Specific rules take precedence over general rules. *Lex specialis derogat generalis.*

[29]Absent an intervening rule, a law adopted later in time is presumed to take precedence over a law earlier in time to the extent of a conflict. *Lex posterior derogat priori.*

[30]Laws should not impose new obligations or displace rights with respect to acts which have already occurred.

[31]The rule that laws should not impose obligations in excess of those reasonable necessary to address circumstances which give rise to them. The doctrine of proportionality is a centerpiece of European Court of Justice jurisprudence.

There are recent evolutions in the field of equity, addressing in particular the goals of "sustainable development." However, concepts such as intergenerational equity are not part of general principles of law common to different legal systems. They are addressed in the next section, which considers the impact of human rights jurisprudence.[32]

The following excerpt contains a concise summary of principles of equity which are found in major legal systems around the world. Some of these principles may, at least initially, appear somewhat dated — or naive — in the present global business environment, in which the sharp operator is often applauded for taking advantage of opportunity. Yet consider these principles from the standpoint of the arbitrator called upon to resolve a dispute between enterprises with an interest in maintaining long term relations. Might the application of some of these principles of fairness help to fashion decisions that accommodate longer term interests?

The Precepts of Equity

Ralph A. Newman*

Out of the slow but continuous process, through the ages, of the moralization of the law, there can be detected a small number of fundamental principles, more fully articulated in the Anglo-American experience but present in nearly all legal systems, the distillation of experience in the resolution of human confrontations. The existence of these principles is established by the Anglo-American history of the administration of equity for hundreds of years in a separate court. . . . When we reduce these principles of equity to their basic elements, we find that the principles, and nearly all the rules of private law in which they have been applied, rest on the moral precepts of good faith, honesty and generosity. The principles of equity which are based on these precepts are the legal profile of moral precepts which express the ethical and moral experience of mankind; which are

---

[32]We also recall principles of natural justice — including fairness, reciprocity, consideration of the particular circumstances of a case — which principles in recent time often have been superseded by human rights guarantees and have lost something of their operational importance. Schachter, *supra* note 20, at 55.

The General Principles of Equity in EQUITY IN THE WORLD'S LEGAL SYSTEMS: A COMPARATIVE STUDY 599-604 (R.A. NEWMAN ED.,1973).

found in all systems of ethics, morals and religion, and which rest on the eternal postulate of human brotherhood. Equity may be defined as the expression of standards of decent and honorable conduct which are the mark of a morally mature society.

The equitable precept of good faith originated in contractual and fiduciary obligations, but it applies to all violations of confidence. The equitable standard of good faith requires putting one's cards on the table. It forbids overreaching by any form of cunning, and includes the duty to disclose. In equity cheating is as reprehensible as it is in morals, without regard to the way the cheating is done. Good faith forbids exacting a hard bargain. The bargaining process is looked upon as a transaction between persons who are aware of all material facts and neither of whom need bargain under the pressure of controlling economic compulsion exerted by his adversary, even though such compulsion does not amount to the concepts of duress or undue influence of strict law. Good faith extends to obligations to strangers. It applies not only to the formation and interpretation of contracts but also to their performance. The course of dealing which has just been described is in accordance with the code of fair play of everyday ethics, is written into the civil codes in almost all civil law systems and is thoroughly established in Anglo-American equity. In some civil law countries, especially Switzerland and Germany, contractual relationships entail the continuing obligation, after the conclusion of the contract, to assist a party to the contract to achieve the realization of his contractual expectations by providing him with protection, information, supply and cooperation.

The equitable precept of honesty is relevant whenever benefits have been obtained gratuitously, in bad faith, or by accident or mistake under circumstances in which the acquirer would be unjustly enriched at another person's expense if the acquirer were permitted to retain the benefits. It should be noted that the precept of honesty does not explain all cases of unjust enrichment, most of which fall within the precept of generosity, as will be explained presently. The distinction is clear; nobody except perhaps a lawyer would say that a person who insists on retaining property obtained through accident or mistake — for example through payments made to a person whom he had wrongly supposed to be a creditor —, or through gift from a defrauder or through purchase from a known defrauder, was an honest man, nor would the term generosity be appropriate to describe the nature of the obligation. The return of property obtained under such circumstances would not be characterized in morals as generous conduct, nor should it be regarded in law as anything other than simple honesty. An agent or other fiduciary who gains a personal profit out of his relationship would be acting in bad faith as well as dishonestly. In all these situations relief is administered as part of the law of unjust enrichment.

Of the moral precepts of good faith, honesty and generosity, the precept of generosity, based essentially on a degree of sacrifice, is the most important and pervasive. The equitable conception of generosity requires the relinquishment of, or compensation for, benefits acquired or positions of unfair advantage arising out of services rendered by mistake, or out of consensual agreements or from ownership of real property. Obligations falling within the precept of generosity fall into four broad classifications which cut across the conventional divisions of law into contracts, quasi contract, property and tort. One of these categories consists of cases in which the assertion of a right would be of no material benefit, or of only relatively slight benefit. Another category comprises cases in which only a comparatively trifling effort or expenditure would be required to avert serious hardship to another person. A third category consists of cases which require payment for benefits obtained by services rendered, or improvements of property made without valid prior authorization. In the three foregoing categories there are no contractual relationships which according to strict interpretation of the rights involved would justify the retention of the benefits without making restitution. The fourth category is made up in part of cases in which benefits have been received in the course of consensual relationships, for example part performance of legally unenforceable contracts, and in which, therefore, the retention of benefits would be justified according to strict law. The other part of this category is made up of cases arising out of delictual encounters, where strict liability may apply. This fourth category requires not merely the relinquishment of rights or payment for benefits received, but requires assuming or sharing the burden resulting from accident or mistake. Generosity includes forebearance and consideration for rights of others. It will be seen that the concepts of honesty and generosity cover two classes of unjust enrichment. The concept of honesty applies in cases of unjust enrichment where there has been no prior agreement between the persons concerned for the adjustment of their interests. The concept of generosity applies in cases where the possibility of such eventual enrichment was inherent, even if not expressly envisaged, in a prior consensual agreement, a situation in which the enrichment would according to strict law be justified.

Out of the basic precepts of good faith, honesty and generosity there have evolved in the decisions of the courts of equity in England and the

United States, reproducing corresponding results of the positive law and jurisprudence in the civil law, twelve fundamental principles which are the distillation of the ethical experience of the various streams which constitute the sources of modern western law. These principles are sometimes expressed but must usually be found by a study of judicial decisions and of legislation. The principles sometimes overlap, as in the area of unjust enrichment, producing legal institutions which are the expression of more than one principle. The principles of equity, unlike the rules of strict law, are, because of their nature, drawn broadly so as to be capable of flexible application. For this reason the relationship between the principles and the rules of application is less visible than in strict law, and it is therefore even more necessary than in strict law to study the pragmatic operation of the principles in order to find out what they really mean.

The Fundamental Principles of Equity

Principles based on the precept of honesty:

I. Rights should be based on substance instead of form.

II. Agreements made with full awareness of their consequences must be carried out specifically if this is practicable and does not conflict with public or private interests of controlling importance.

Principles based on the precept of good faith:

III. The law will not allow the unscrupulous to carry out their plans.

IV. Reasonable expectations based on the conduct of another person will be protected.

V. Men must act in good faith with regard to those with whom they are dealing and those who may be affected by their action. Good faith requires fair dealing, affirmative disclosure of material facts and assistance to others in achieving the full benefit of contractual relationships.

Principles based on the precept of generosity:

VI. Relinquishment of rights, or affirmative conduct, may be required to the extent that is reasonably necessary to mitigate damage.

VII. Agreements made by mistake will not be enforced unless reliance on the agreement has led to a serious change of position.

VIII. The exercise of rights must not interfere with the reasonable exercise of rights of other persons or with the reasonable use of their property or emergency use of one's own property by another person.

IX. The burdens of misfortune arising out of human relationships or encounters should be fairly shared among the persons immediately concerned or among the members of the community.

X. The law will not permit the exercise of rights for the sole purpose of injuring other persons.

Principles based on both honesty and generosity:

XI. Performance of agreements will be excused, or the obligation will be modified, by reason of accident, unanticipated difficulty or failure to perform essential reciprocal obligations.

XII. Benefits obtained through accident or mistake must be relinquished, or restitution made, to those better entitled to the benefits.

     Although principles VIII and IX are both embraced within a broader principle that the law will establish a fair balance between conflicting interests, i.e., balance the hardship, a principle identified in the essays on equity in canon law and in Italian law, it seems that splitting up this broader principle clarifies the problem more specifically. An additional principle, adjustment of hardship in proportion to the wealth of the parties, originally in force in the USSR and Hungary but currently in force only in Dutch, Islamic, Argentine and Swedish law, seems never to have been in force in any other system. The principle of equality before the law, emphasized by Hobbes and regarded in Roman law, in the law of the Netherlands and in French law as a principle of equity, applies to all law and is not peculiar to equity. Consideration of the particular circumstances of the individual case, emphasized in canon law and in many civil law systems and emphasized by Pound as one of the most essential features of equity, is not an exclusively equitable principle because it is a requirement of all law and moreover provides no help in resolving the criteria for decision. Although additional principles will undoubtedly appear in the course of time, it is believed that the principles stated embrace all of the fundamental principles of equity which are to be found in different systems.

Notes and Questions

1. For many years, the field of international law was dominated by concern with issues of war and peace, and with the conduct of diplomatic relations between nations. The emergence after the Second World War of wide interest at the international level in the field of human rights represented one major evolution of concern in this field. Most recently, the development of the Internet — with its capacity for moving information and business opportunity around the globe virtually instantaneously — has led to a surge in interest in the international legal principles which govern the allocation of jurisdiction to prescribe and enforce law. This interest is reflected in the WIPO Final Report on Domain Names, which we study in Chapter VIII.

2. General principles of law may be relevant both to resolving substantive disputes between parties, and to determining the procedural rules which adjudicatory bodies will follow. For example, the *Proctor and Gamble* decision of the EPO Technical Board, mentioned above, concerns a procedural rule. Which of the general principles of law discussed above appear relevant to legal procedure?

B. The Potential Impact of Human Rights

In Chapter I, we reviewed the policy foundations of international IPRs protection. We noted that determinations as to the nature and scope of IPRs protection involve a balancing of social and economic welfare interests. Debates about the foundation of IPRs — whether they are, for example, rooted in natural law or industrial policy — tend not to be very revealing in terms of policy formulation because, regardless of the foundation of IPRs, social and economic welfare interests remain to be balanced.

However, worldwide attention to international human rights standards includes interest in whether — and the extent to which — the right to IPRs protection is part of the panoply of human rights that individuals enjoy. The protection of human creativity and the fruits of one's labor seem closely related to human rights concerns, and the question arises how the two fields are related. References to IPRs in human rights instruments are not extensive and, until recently, IPRs issues were rarely discussed by the human rights community. Efforts to bring about a better understanding of the relationship between human rights and intellectual property rights are currently under way.

In analyzing this relationship, two basic issues should be distinguished: (1) what is the foundation and legitimizing source of IPRs and (2) what is the impact of human rights norms in shaping and applying existing IPRs?

Based upon broad statements contained in the Universal Declaration of Human Rights and the International Covenant on Economic, Social and Cultural Rights, it would seem possible to argue that the international IPRs system is at least partially based in human rights. From this point of view, it would follow that protection of moral and material interests resulting from scientific, literary and artistic activities would exist independently of legislation, and be protected even in its absence. From a practical point of view, the key question would amount to whether IPRs protection could be claimed solely on the basis of human rights standards, and in the absence of a corresponding national or regional IPRs legislative regime. The answer would depend on whether the rights are self-executing.[1] With respect to rights subject to a registration and filing system, it would seem unlikely that they would be considered self-executing. On the other hand, this would seem possible in relation to copyright. In any case, a human rights standard might imply an obligation on the state to provide an appropriate IPRs system, and to enact necessary legislation and establish administrative machinery.

---

[1] In Chapter II, Joseph Weiler introduced the doctrine of "direct effect" in EU law, and later in this chapter we examine the same doctrine in international and national law. The doctrine of direct effect is also referred to as the doctrine of "self-executing" effect, particularly in U.S. jurisprudence. Arguably there are several meanings to the doctrine of self-executing effect. For present purposes, suffice it to say that an individual may directly rely on a norm of international law as a source of rights (*i.e.* it is "self-executing") if the norm is intended to serve as a direct source of rights and if the norm is sufficiently precise that it may be applied by a court. Whether an international norm is self-executing depends both on the character of the norm, and on the constitutional regime of the state in which it is invoked.

It remains unclear how far IPRs protection would expand as a matter of human rights. Would it envelope the rights of corporations, and thus juridical persons? Or, more likely, is the right limited to the human individual seeking protection of his or her own work and efforts? It would seem evident that such protection would only encompass a fraction of the entire IPRs system, and could hardly provide its entire foundation. Consider also the limited duration of most IPRs, discussed *infra*. How can limited duration be reconciled with a concept of inalienable fundamental rights?

Indeed, both from an historical and a functional angle, it is difficult to argue that national IPRs systems or the international IPRs system are based upon the concept of human rights. Human rights have been answers to specific and fundamental threats to individuals in human history. They establish specific zones of protection and cannot entail the design of an overall economic concept. Moreover, the international IPRs system may conversely be argued to amount to a system of limitations on fundamental rights. It is a part of economic law and market regulation which in effect limits economic liberties to the extent these are recognized in constitutional law (e.g., Wirtschaftsfreiheit or liberté économique in Germany and Switzerland). From this perspective, the granting of intellectual IPRs amounts to a monopoly, for which a sound legal basis is required in statutory law.

IPRs protection emerged on a functional basis, expanding in accordance with the economic needs of different industries and countries. A utilitarian approach can now be observed in the ongoing development of the system, as new technologies and markets arise. The fundamental debates on private versus public ownership of knowledge are informed by perceived economic advantage and disadvantage. These debates are likely to persist, and little ground can be gained by recourse to human rights standards.

Since the international IPRs system exists at a fairly high level of refinement, debate concerning its foundation may seem rather esoteric. However, issues of premise or foundation may appear more relevant as we consider the justification for entirely new types of rights, in particular the right of protection for traditional knowledge (so-called Traditional Intellectual Property Rights (TIPRs)(considered in detail in Chapter VIII). These are claims based on broad concepts of equity and justice. Moreover, they often address communities, moreso than individuals, and human rights pertaining to individuals may not provide an adequate philosophical foundation for these aspirational norms.

While human rights norms may not provide an adequate foundation for IPRs, these standards may influence the shaping and interpretation of

IPRs to a larger extent than they currently do. As with any other rules, those regarding IPRs should be construed so as to be consistent with fundamental rights. In specific contexts — in particular when addressing the status of individuals and their personalities — the invocation of human rights may well make a difference. For example, trademark protection may be grounded in the protection of a person's reputation, and not only in the avoidance of consumer confusion. An inventor may retain his or her rights to some degree, even if the economic potential of the invention in question has been transferred to an employer. Such effects may flow not just from human rights standards which explicitly refer to IPRs, but from a host of rights, including freedom of the press or freedom of expression. In particular cases, it may be necessary to explore how such rights influence the international IPRs system with a view to preserving basic human rights within a utilitarian concept of IPRs protection. In Chapter VIII, as illustration, we will further explore the tension between IPRs and freedom of information and expression.

Explicit references to IPRs can be found in the Universal Declaration of Human Rights and the International Convenant on Social, Economic and Cultural Rights, excerpts from which follow. The protection of property rights is addressed in regional human rights instruments, while a new generation of IPRs is proclaimed by way of the natural resources rights of indigenous peoples.

Human Rights Instruments

Article 27(2), Universal Declaration of Human Rights (1948)

Everyone has the right to protection of the moral and material interests resulting from any scientific, literary or artistic production of which he is the author.

Article 15, International Covenant on Economic, Social and Cultural Rights (1966)

1. The States parties to the present Covenant recognize the right of everyone:

*****

c. To benefit from the protection of the moral and material interests resulting from any scientific, literary or artistic production of which he is the author.

2. The steps to be taken by the States Parties to the present Covenant to achieve the full realization of this right shall include those necessary for the conservation, the development and the diffusion of science and culture.

*****

Regional instruments contain provisions relating to the protection of property rights in general:

Article 1, Protocol to the European Convention on Human Rights — Protection of property

Every natural or legal person is entitled to the peaceful enjoyment of his possessions. No one shall be deprived of his possessions except in the public interest and subject to the conditions provided for by law and by the general principles of international law.

The preceding provisions shall not, however, in any way impair the right of a State to enforce such laws as it deems necessary to control the use of property in accordance with the general interest or to secure the payment of taxes or other contributions or penalties.

Article 21, American Convention on Human Rights (1969)

1. Everyone has the right to the use and enjoyment of his property. The law may subordinate such use and enjoyment to the interest of society.

*****

Article 14, African Charter on Human Rights and Peoples' Rights (1981)

The right to property shall be guaranteed. It may only be encroached upon in the interest of public need or in the general interest of the community and in accordance with the provisions of appropriate laws.

The more recent instrument, which follows, addresses the issue of intellectual property rights in the context of traditional resource rights of indigenous peoples. These rights, broadly defined to encompass cultural rights and protection of traditional identities, introduced a new dimension to both the concept of human rights and intellectual property rights.

Article 29, Draft Declaration on Rights of Indigenous Peoples[2]

Indigenous peoples are entitled to the recognition of the full ownership, control and protection of their cultural and intellectual property.

They have the right to special measures to control, develop and protect their sciences, technologies and cultural manifestations, including human and other genetic resources, seeds, medicines, knowledge of the properties of fauna and flora, oral traditions, literatures, designs and visual and performing arts.

Notes and Questions

1. The more recent treaties on human rights generally mention neither IPRs in general nor copyright in specific. They contain provisions on property in general. Do you think this shows a tendency to exclude IPRs from the human rights area?

2. Does the guarantee of right to property include intellectual property? If yes, what does the vanishing of explicit IPRs protection mean for the pro-

---

[2]United Nations Commission on Human Rights Sub-Commission on Prevention of Discrimination and Protection of Minorities: Draft United Nations Declaration on The Rights of Indigenous Peoples, 34 I.L.M. 541 (1995).

tection of property rights in general? Will the inclusion of IPRs protection make it more difficult to secure protection for real and movable property?

3. Do you think the development of specific human rights standards of IPRs protection should be encouraged?

4. The Universal Declaration of Human Rights recognizes the right not to be subjected to arbitrary interference with one's privacy, family, home or correspondence (Article 12). The Internet is a multifunctional medium that is used for commercial, research, educational and social purposes. It is also a medium that raises concerns over the ease with which copyright infringing material can be posted and disseminated globally. Copyright owners are seeking to have access to databases containing the names and contact details of all persons who operate a website, so that they can trace infringers. How do you think the right of privacy and the right to benefit from the protection of interests resulting from literary and artistic productions can be reconciled on the Internet?

C. Justice and the Potential Impact of Sustainable Development

While human rights may not provide an appropriate foundation for IPRs (but may nevertheless influence their contents and administration), broad and somewhat elusive ideas of justice are important in shaping the international IPRs system. All laws and regulations, whatever the field, are grounded in (often unspoken) concepts and precepts of justice. IPRs regimes evolved on the basis of utilitarian concepts, and justice was seen in furthering the common good by honoring investment and creativity.

Technological advances throughout the last century were facilitated by the emerging international IPRs system. Yet to what extent did the system also contribute to the depletion of natural resources and to endangering the global environment and commons? Since adoption of the Stockholm principles in 1972, and the principles of the Rio Declaration in 1992, attention has been directed to the goals of sustainable development, and what the idea of intergenerational equity means to the international IPRs system. How should these concepts and principles affect the evolution of the IPRs system? How do they affect the field of biotechnology? We will turn to these issues in Chapter VIII, particularly in dealing with the the treatment of genetic resources and traditional IPRs. Yet it is important to observe in connection with sources of international law, that the international IPRs system cannot be considered in isolation. It has to be responsive to prevailing concepts of justice. It has to adapt to the emerging aspirational norms of international law.

Notes and Questions

1. The preamble to the WTO Agreement provides that WTO Members should attend to the requirements of sustainable development. What implications might this reference have for interpretation of the TRIPS Agreement? What is the potential impact of the emerging principle of sustainable development more generally for the international IPRs system? What areas are likely to be most affected?

D. The Impact of International Law

This section deals with the impact of international law on the international IPRs system. We first look at the principles of treaty interpretation, and consider how national IPRs legislation should be evaluated in light of treaty terms. In this context, we deal with the doctrine of legitimate expectations. We then consider the extent to which international law can and should be taken into account before national or regional courts of law. We examine the doctrine of consistent interpretation, and the more controversial doctrine of direct effect.

1. The Interpretation of International Agreements and the Doctrine of Legitimate Expectations

Articles 31 and 32 of the Vienna Convention on the Law of Treaties sets forth the main principles of treaty interpretation in international law:

Article 31, Vienna Convention — General Rule of Interpretation

(1) A treaty shall be interpreted in good faith in accordance with the ordinary meaning to be given to the terms of the treaty in their context and in the light of its object and purpose.

(2) The context for the purpose of the interpretation of a treaty shall comprise, in addition to the text, including its preamble and annexes:

(a) any agreement relating to the treaty which was made between all the parties in connection with the conclusion of the treaty;

(b) any instrument which was made by one or more parties in connection with the conclusion of the treaty and accepted by the other parties as an instrument related to the treaty.

(3) There shall be taken into account, together with the context:

(a) any subsequent agreement between the parties regarding the interpretation of the treaty or the application of its provisions;

(b) any subsequent practice in the application of the treaty which establishes the agreement of the parties regarding its interpretation;

(c) any relevant rules of international law applicable in the relations between the parties.

(4) A special meaning shall be given to a term if it is established that the parties so intended.

Article 32, Vienna Convention — Supplementary Means of Interpretation

Recourse may be had to supplementary means of interpretation, including the preparatory work of the treaty and the circumstances of its conclusion, in order to confirm the meaning resulting from the application of article 31, or to determine the meaning when the interpretation according to article 31:

(a) leaves the meaning ambiguous or obscure; or

(b) leads to a result which is manifestly absurd or unreasonable.

As mentioned earlier, these principles are equally applicable to the interpretation of bilateral or multilateral agreements pertaining to the protection of intellectual property. Article 31(1), VCLT, contains four keys to interpretation: the ordinary meaning of the terms, the context, the object and the purpose of the agreement, and the requirement to construe the norm in good faith. How do these key elements of interpretation relate to the field of IPRs? The first decision to address this question was the 1997 WTO panel report on *India — Patent Protection for Pharmaceuticals*. The panel developed the doctrine of legitimate expectations, which was eventually overruled and rejected by the AB.

The complaint by the United States alleged India's failure to implement its obligation with respect to establishing a "mailbox" for the receipt of patent applications pursuant to Article 70:8, TRIPS Agreement, and to establishing a mechanism for the granting of exclusive marketing rights pursuant to Article 70:9. Despite receiving a draft bill from the Executive, India's Parliament failed to adopt legislation to amend the national Patent Act to explicitly authorize the filing of mailbox applications. Instead, an accommodation for such filing was made by way of administrative practice. India argued that this practice would satisfy its obligations under international law.

The mailbox provision of Article 70:8, TRIPs Agreement, resulted from the fact that developing countries are allowed to postpone the introduction of product patents for new subject matter areas for a transition period of up to ten years (Article 65:4). An obligation to accept applications for pharmaceutical and agricultural chemical patents under examination in developed countries (so-called "pipeline" products) during the transition period was introduced for the developing countries, with a view that effective patent protection would immediately go into effect for the remainder of the patent term extending from the initial filing or priority date. Moreover, it was agreed that as of the initial date of filing (and for a maximum of five years), and with patent protection still absent, an "exclusive marketing right" for the product would be granted by the developing country, provided that government regulatory approval for the product had been granted in that country — thus resulting in a *de facto* monopoly on the market. This rather complicated constellation resulted as a compromise between industrialized countries, which insisted on immediate protection in all markets, and developing countries, which insisted on long transitional arrangements.

India — Patent Protection: Report of the Panel
India — Patent Protection for Pharmaceutical and Agricultural Chemical Products*

Report of the Panel

*****

I. Introduction

1.1 On 2 July 1996, the United States requested India to hold consultations pursuant to Article 4 of the Understanding on Rules and Procedures Governing the Settlement of Disputes (DSU) and Article 64 of the Agreement on Trade-Related Aspects of Intellectual Property Rights (TRIPS) regarding the absence in India of either patent protection for pharmaceutical and agricultural chemical products or formal systems that permit the filing of patent applications for pharmaceutical and agricultural chemical products and that provide exclusive marketing rights in such products (WT/DS50/1). No mutually satisfactory solution was reached in these consultations, held on 27 July 1996. The United States requested the Dispute Settlement Body (DSB), in a communication dated 7 November 1996, to establish a panel to examine the matter (WT/DS50/4). At its meeting of 20 November 1996, the DSB agreed to establish a panel with standard terms of reference in accordance with Article 6 of the DSU.

1.2 In document WT/DS50/5 of 5 February 1997, the DSB was informed that the terms of reference and the composition of the Panel were as follows:

---

*World Trade Organization, Report of the Panel, WT/DS50/R, 5 Sept. 1997.

Terms of reference

"To examine, in the light of the relevant provisions of the covered agreements cited by the United States in document WT/DS50/4, the matter referred to the DSB by the United States in that document and to make such findings as will assist the DSB in making the recommendations or in giving the rulings provided for in those agreements."

Composition

Chairman: Mr. Thomas Cottier
Panelists: Mr. Douglas Chester
                    Mr. Yanyong Phuangrach

1.3   The Panel heard the parties to the dispute on 15 April and 13 May 1997. The Panel decided to give the parties the chance to comment, after the second session, in writing on each other's arguments related to the United States' claim based on Article 63, which claim had been made for the first time at the first session. The interim report was issued to the parties on 27 June 1997. Only India requested the Panel to review parts of the interim report and no request was received to hold an additional meeting.

II.   Factual Aspects

2.1   The questions before this Panel concern the obligations India has as a WTO Member by virtue of certain transitional provisions of the TRIPS Agreement and are to be divided into questions related to the provisions of Article 70.8 of the TRIPS Agreement and questions related to the provisions of Article 70.9 of that Agreement. In respect of these questions, issues were also raised relating to the publication and notification provisions of Article 63.

2.2   Obligations arising under international agreements or treaties are not, by their own force, binding in Indian domestic law. Appropriate legislative or executive action has to be taken for bringing them into force.

2.3   On 31 December 1994, the President of India promulgated the Patents (Amendment) Ordinance 1994, to amend the Patents Act 1970 to provide a means in the Act for the filing and handling of patent applications for pharmaceutical or agricultural chemical products (as required by subparagraph (a) of Article 70.8 of the TRIPS Agreement) and for the grant of exclusive marketing rights with respect to the products that are the subject of such patent applications (as required by Article 70.9 of the Agreement).[1] This Ordinance was issued in exercise of the powers conferred upon the President by clause (1) of Article 123 of the Indian Constitution, which enables the President to legislate when Parliament (either House or both Houses) is not in session and the President "is satisfied that circumstances exist which render it necessary for him to take immediate action". The Ordinance became effective on 1 January 1995 and lapsed on 26 March 1995, since legislation of this kind ceases to apply at the expiration of six weeks from the re-assembly of Parliament.

2.4 At the time of the promulgation of the Patents (Amendment) Ordinance 1994, a Press Note was issued providing an explanation of its background and purposes. According to paragraph 4 of this Press Note, the Indian Government had set up an Expert Group which had been entrusted with the task of suggesting specific amendments necessary in Indian laws to comply with India's obligations under the provisions of Articles 70.8 and 70.9 of the TRIPS Agreement and also to safeguard India's interests in this regard; this Expert Group had recommended a set of measures on which decisions had been taken by the Government. The Ordinance was also notified by India to the Council for TRIPS under Article 63.2 of the TRIPS Agreement (which notification had been distributed as document IP/N/1/IND/1). During this period, 125 applications had been received and filed.

2.5 A Patents (Amendment) Bill 1995, which was intended to give permanent legislative effect to the provisions of the Ordinance, was introduced in the Lok Sabha (Lower House) of the Indian Parliament in March 1995. This Bill was passed by the Lok Sabha and was then introduced in the Rajya Sabha (Upper House). In the Rajya Sabha, the Bill was referred to a Select

---

[1] The Patents (Amendment) Ordinance 1994 stipulated, in essence, that applications claiming patent protection for pharmaceutical and agricultural chemical product inventions could be made, although such inventions were not patentable, and that their handling would be postponed until 1 January 2005 or until an application for the grant of an exclusive marketing right for the product in question was made, if such would occur earlier; the Ordinance also laid down the procedures for applications for the grant of exclusive marketing rights, the scope of these rights and their enforcement.

Committee of the House for examination and report. The Select Committee started its work but could not present its report before the dissolution of the Lok Sabha on 10 May 1996. The Patents (Amendment) Bill 1995 lapsed with the dissolution of the 10th Lok Sabha on that date.

(a) Article 70.8

2.6   At the time that the period of validity of the Ordinance expired, the Patents (Amendment) Bill 1995 was still being debated. India informed the Panel that, in the light of this situation, the Indian executive authorities decided, in April 1995, to instruct the patent offices in India to continue to receive patent applications for pharmaceutical and agricultural chemical products and to store them separately for processing as and when the change in the Indian patent law to make such subject matter patentable would take effect. No record of this decision or of any administrative guidelines issued to or within the patent offices of India to this effect was made available to the Panel.

2.7   No public notice was given at that time of this administrative decision and no notification concerning it was made to the Council for TRIPS. However, on 2 August 1996, the Indian Minister of Industry responded to a question asked by a member of the Lok Sabha concerning whether applications for product patents in the pharmaceutical, food and agricultural chemical areas had been received in anticipation of changes in the Indian Patents Act 1970 in accordance with the requirements of the World Trade Organization; as reflected at Annex 2 of this report, the Minister responded by stating that the patent offices had received 893 patent applications in the field of drug or medicine from Indian as well as foreign companies/institutions up to 15 July 1996 and that applications for patents would be taken up for examination after 1 January 2005 as per the WTO Agreement.

2.8   Under Indian patent law, patent applications for pharmaceutical or agricultural chemical products made by any person entitled to apply under Section 6 of the Patents Act 1970 are subject to the same fee as any other patent application being received and allotted a filing date and advertised in the Official Gazette with serial number, filing date, name of applicant and title of invention. Under the administrative arrangements of the Indian patent offices pursuant to the decision taken in April 1995, such applications are, however, unlike other patent applications, being stored separately and not referred by the Controller to an examiner as specified in Section 12 of the Act.

2.9 The legal authority for these administrative arrangements that has been cited by India is Article 73(1)(a) of the Indian Constitution in conjunction with the Indian Patents Act 1970. Article 73(1) reads as follows:

> *Extent of executive power of the Union.* (1) Subject to the provisions of this Constitution, the executive power of the Union shall extend
>
> > (a) to the matters with respect to which Parliament has power to make laws; and
>
> > (b) to the exercise of such rights, authority and jurisdiction as are exercisable by the Government of India by virtue of any treaty or agreement:
>
> Provided that the executive power referred to in sub-clause (a) shall not, save as expressly provided in this Constitution or in any law made by Parliament, extend in any State to matters with respect to which the Legislature of the State has also power to make laws.

2.10 The full text of the provisions of the Patents Act of relevance to the case in hand can be found at Annex 1 of this report. For the purposes of the case in hand, the main aspects of these provisions that are of relevance are as follows:

— Chapter III (Sections 6 through 11) deals with applications for patents. These provisions do not require that applications for patents must be limited to patentable subject matter. In respect of the subject matter of the claims, they only require that such applications should be for inventions.

— Inventions are defined in Section 2(1)(j) as, *inter alia*, any new and useful substance produced by manufacture, including any new and useful improvement of such a substance.

— Section 5 makes it clear that inventions claiming substances intended for use, or capable of being used, as a food, medicine or drug or relating to substances prepared or produced by chemical processes are not in themselves patentable, but methods or processes for their manufacture are. Under Section 2(1)(l)(iv) the term 'medicine or drug' includes insecticides, germicides, fungicides, weedicides and all other substances intended to be used for the protection or preservation of plants.

— Chapter IV of the Patents Act concerns the examination of applications. Section 12 requires that, when the complete specification has been filed[2] in respect of an application for a patent the application shall be referred by the Controller General of Patents, Designs and Trademarks to an examiner. The examiner shall ordinarily report to the Controller within a period of 18 months on, *inter alia*, whether the application and the specification are in accordance with the requirements of the Act and whether there is any lawful ground for objecting to the grant of the patent under the Act.

— Paragraph 2 of Section 15 states that, if it appears to the Controller that the invention claimed in the specification is not patentable under the Act, he shall refuse the application.

2.11   India informed the Panel that, between 1 January 1995 and 15 February 1997, a total of 1,339 applications for pharmaceutical and agricultural chemical products had been received and registered. Of these applications, United States' companies had filed 318 applications for pharmaceutical product patents and 45 applications for agricultural chemical product patents. On the day the Patents (Amendment) Ordinance 1994 had lapsed, 125 applications had been received and filed (41 made by US companies); prior to 15 February 1997, out of the other 1,214 applications (322 by US companies), 605 had been received and filed prior to the day the Patents (Amendment) Bill 1995 had lapsed.

(b)   Article 70.9

---

[2]Pursuant to Section 9, the complete specification must normally be filed within 12 months of the date of the filing of the application, which can be extended to 15 months, failing which the application is deemed abandoned.

2.12   The Indian executive authorities do not have the legal powers under present Indian law to accord exclusive marketing rights in accordance with the provisions of Article 70.9. No request for the grant of exclusive marketing rights has so far been submitted to the Indian authorities.

*****

VII.   Findings

*****

C.   Interpretation of the TRIPS Agreement

7.18   Before examining specific measures in dispute, we first deal with a general interpretative issue, namely standards applicable to interpretation of the TRIPS Agreement. In the first instance, Article 3.2 of the DSU directs panels to clarify the provisions of the covered agreements, including the TRIPS Agreement, "in accordance with customary rules of interpretation of public international law". As a number of recent panel reports and Appellate Body reports have pointed out, customary rules of interpretation of public international law are embodied in the text of the 1969 Vienna Convention on the Law of Treaties ("Vienna Convention"). Article 31(1) of the Vienna Convention provides:

> A treaty shall be interpreted in good faith in accordance with the ordinary meaning to be given to the terms of the treaty in their context and in the light of its object and purpose.

Accordingly, the TRIPS Agreement must be interpreted in good faith in light of (i) the ordinary meaning of its terms, (ii) the context and (iii) its object and purpose. In our view, good faith interpretation requires the protection of legitimate expectations derived from the protection of intellectual property rights provided for in the Agreement. A similar view has also been taken in the *Underwear* panel report:

> [T]he relevant provisions [of the Agreement on Textiles and Clothing] have to be interpreted in good faith. Based upon the wording, the context and the overall purpose of the Agreement, exporting Members can . . . legitimately expect that market access and investments made

would not be frustrated by importing Members taking improper recourse to such action. [79]

7.19   Second, we must bear in mind that the TRIPS Agreement, the entire text of which was newly negotiated in the Uruguay Round and occupies a relatively self-contained, *sui generis* status in the WTO Agreement, nevertheless is an integral part of the WTO system, which itself builds upon the experience over nearly half a century under the General Agreement on Tariffs and Trade 1947 ("GATT 1947"). Indeed, Article XVI:1 of the WTO Agreement provides:

> Except as otherwise provided under this Agreement or the Multilateral Trade Agreements, the WTO shall be guided by the decisions, procedures and customary practices followed by the CONTRACTING PARTIES to GATT 1947 and the bodies established in the framework of GATT 1947.

Since the TRIPS Agreement is one of the Multilateral Trade Agreements, we must be guided by the jurisprudence established under GATT 1947 in interpreting the provisions of the TRIPS Agreement unless there is a contrary provision. As the Appellate Body indicated in the *Japan — Alcoholic Beverages* case, adopted panel reports "create legitimate expectations among WTO Members, and, therefore, should be taken into account where they are relevant to any dispute".[80] Indeed, in light of the fact that the TRIPS Agreement was negotiated as a part of the overall balance of concessions in the Uruguay Round, it would be inappropriate not to apply the same principles in interpreting the TRIPS Agreement as those applicable to the interpretation of other parts of the WTO Agreement.

7.20   The protection of legitimate expectations of Members regarding the conditions of competition is a well-established GATT principle, which derives in part from Article XXIII, the basic dispute settlement provisions of GATT (and the WTO).[81] Regarding Article III of GATT, the panel on *Italian*

---

[79]Panel Report on "United States — Restrictions on Imports of Cotton and Man-made Fibre Underwear", adopted on 25 February 1997, WT/DS24/R, para. 7.20

[80]Appellate Body Report on "Japan — Taxes on Alcoholic Beverages", adopted on 1 November 1996, WT/DS8/AB/R, WT/DS10/AB/R, WT/DS13/AB/R, page 14.

[81]We note in this regard that Article 64 of the TRIPS Agreement (on dispute settlement) provides for the application of Article XXIII of GATT 1994, as elaborated by the DSU, to the settlement of disputes under the TRIPS Agreement.

Agricultural Machinery stated that "the intent of the drafters was to provide equal conditions of competition once goods had been cleared through customs".[82] This principle was later elaborated by the *Superfund* panel, which stated that "[t]he general prohibition of quantitative restrictions under Article XI . . . and the national treatment obligation of Article III . . . have the same rationale, namely to protect expectations of the contracting parties as to the competitive relationship between their products and those of the other contracting parties".[83] The panel on *Section 337*, which dealt with issues involving protection of intellectual property at the border, also reached similar conclusions.[84]

7.21   The protection of legitimate expectations is central to creating security and predictability in the multilateral trading system. In this connection, we note that disciplines formed under GATT 1947 (so-called GATT *acquis*) were primarily directed at the treatment of the goods of other countries, while rules under the TRIPS Agreement mainly deal with the treatment of nationals of other WTO Members. While this calls for the concept of the protection of legitimate expectations to apply in the TRIPS areas to the competitive relationship between a Member's own nationals and those of other Members (rather than between domestically produced goods and the goods of other Members, as in the goods area), it does not in our view make inapplicable the underlying principle. The Preamble to the TRIPS Agreement, which recognizes the need for new rules and disciplines concerning "the applicability of the basic principles of GATT 1994 . . .", provides a useful context in this regard.

7.22   In conclusion, we find that, when interpreting the text of the TRIPS Agreement, the legitimate expectations of WTO Members concerning the TRIPS Agreement must be taken into account, as well as standards of interpretation developed in past panel reports in the GATT framework, in particular those laying down the principle of the protection of conditions of competition flowing from multilateral trade agreements.

---

[82]Panel Report on "Italian Discrimination against Imported Agricultural Machinery", adopted on 23 October 1958, BISD 7S/60, para. 12-13.
[83]Panel Report on "United States — Taxes on Petroleum and Certain Imported Substances", adopted on 17 June 1987, BISD 34S/136, para. 5.2.2
[84]Panel Report on "United States — Section 337 of the Tariff Act of 1930", adopted on 7 November 1989, BISD 36S/345, para. 5.13

D.   Article 70.8

7.23   We now turn to the examination of the United States' claim on Article 70.8 of the TRIPS Agreement. Article 70.8 provides as follows:

> Where a Member does not make available as of the date of entry into force of the WTO Agreement patent protection for pharmaceutical and agricultural chemical products commensurate with its obligations under Article 27, that Member shall:

>> (a) notwithstanding the provisions of Part VI, provide as from the date of entry into force of the WTO Agreement a means by which applications for patents for such inventions can be filed;

>> (b) apply to these applications, as of the date of application of this Agreement, the criteria for patentability as laid down in this Agreement as if those criteria were being applied on the date of filing in that Member or, where priority is available and claimed, the priority date of the application; and

>> (c) provide patent protection in accordance with this Agreement as from the grant of the patent and for the remainder of the patent term, counted from the filing date in accordance with Article 33 of this Agreement, for those of these applications that meet the criteria for protection referred to in subparagraph (b).

The United States claims that India has failed to fulfil its obligations under this paragraph by not establishing a valid system for receiving "mailbox" applications. In this regard, we note that the only obligation India currently assumes under this paragraph is that of subparagraph (a), the effective date of which is "the date of entry into force of the WTO Agreement", i.e., 1 January 1995. Obligations under subparagraphs (b) and (c) will become binding on India only "as of the date of application of this Agreement", which in this particular instance means no later than 1 January 2005 by virtue of the provisions of paragraphs 2 and 4 of Article 65 of the TRIPS Agreement. Thus, the question before this Panel is whether India has taken the action necessary to implement its obligations under subparagraph (a) of Article 70.8.

Nature of the Obligations

7.24   Subparagraph (a) of Article 70.8, like all other provisions of the covered agreements, must be interpreted in good faith in light of (i) the ordinary meaning of its terms; (ii) the context; and (iii) its object and purpose, following the rules set out in Article 31(1) of the Vienna Convention.[85]

7.25   Subparagraph (a) starts with the phrase "notwithstanding the provisions of Part VI". This indicates that this provision is an exception to the transitional arrangements contained in Part VI of the TRIPS Agreement. Thus, if a Member does not make available as of 1 January 1995 patent protection for pharmaceutical and agricultural chemical products commensurate with its obligations under Article 27, that Member cannot avail itself of a transitional period under Article 65 regarding the operation of this subparagraph. This is clear from the textual analysis, and in any event is not in dispute between the parties. The substantive obligation to be assumed by such a Member as from 1 January 1995 is to provide "a means" by which applications for patents for inventions in respect of pharmaceutical and agricultural chemical products "can be filed". The analysis of the ordinary meaning of these terms alone does not lead to a definitive interpretation as to what sort of "means" is required by this subparagraph.

7.26   We thus need to analyze the context of this subparagraph. The means for filing is necessary because, under subparagraphs (b) and (c), a Member which does not make patents available as of 1 January 1995 for pharmaceutical and agricultural chemical products must examine, after the expiry of the transitional period, the applications so filed and must accord patent protection for those products that meet certain criteria. In addition, the Member is obligated to grant exclusive marketing rights to those products that meet the conditions set out in Article 70.9 even during the transitional period. The terms of subparagraph (a) must be understood in this context.

7.27   Furthermore, the object and purpose of Article 70.8 must be taken into account in our analysis. There seems to be a common understanding between the parties to the dispute regarding the object and purpose of subparagraph (a). India concedes that the purpose of subparagraph (a) is to

---

[85]See paragraph 7.18 above.

"*ensure* that each patent applicant obtains a date of filing on the basis of which patent protection [can] be granted as from the date on which Article 27 applies and that exclusive marketing rights [can] be granted to products at the point at which they are eligible for such rights" (*emphasis added*).[86] We affirm this view. The object and purpose of Article 70.8(a) can be derived from the structure of the TRIPS Agreement. Article 27 requires that patents be made available in all fields of technology, subject to certain narrow exceptions. Article 65 provides for transitional periods for developing countries: in general five years from the entry into force of the WTO Agreement, i.e. 1 January 2000, and an additional five years to provide for product patents in areas of technology not so patentable as of 1 January 2000. Thus, in such areas of technology, developing countries are not required to provide product patent protection until 1 January 2005. However, these transitional provisions are not applicable to Article 70.8, which ensures that, if product patent protection is not already available for pharmaceutical and agricultural chemical product inventions, a means must be in place as of 1 January 1995 which allows for the entitlement to file patent applications for such inventions and the allocation of filing and priority dates to them so that the novelty of the inventions in question and the priority of the applications claiming their protection can be preserved for the purposes of determining their eligibility for protection by a patent at the time that product patent protection will be available for these inventions, i.e. at the latest after the expiry of the transitional period.

7.28 In order to achieve the object and purpose of Article 70.8, there must be a mechanism to preserve the novelty of pharmaceutical and agricultural chemical inventions which are currently outside the scope of product patent protection and the priority of applications claiming their protection, for the purposes of determining their eligibility for protection by patents. Once these inventions can be protected by product patents, Article 27 requires them to be available for, at least, those inventions that are (i) new, (ii) involve an inventive step and (iii) are capable of industrial application. In accordance with the normal meaning of these conditions, an invention is new and involves an inventive step if, at the filing date or, if applicable, the priority date of the application in which patent protection is claimed, the invention did not form part of the prior art and required an inventive step

---

[86]Paragraph 4.9 above.

to be deduced from that prior art by a person skilled in the art. Thus, in order to prevent the loss of the novelty of an invention in this sense, filing and priority dates need to have a sound legal basis if the provisions of Article 70.8 are to fulfil their purpose. Moreover, if available, a filing must entitle the applicant to claim priority on the basis of an earlier filing in respect of the claimed invention over applications with subsequent filing or priority dates. Without legally sound filing and priority dates, the mechanism to be established on the basis of Article 70.8 will be rendered inoperational. In our view, preservation of novelty and priority in respect of applications for product patents in respect of pharmaceutical and agricultural chemical inventions so as to provide for effective future patent protection after examination of the applications as of, at the latest, 1 January 2005 is the central object and purpose of Article 70.8(a). This is a special obligation imposed on those Members benefitting from the transitional arrangements.

7.29   The findings above can be confirmed by the negotiating history of the TRIPS Agreement.[87] We note that in the negotiation of the TRIPS Agreement the question of patent protection for pharmaceutical and agricultural chemical products was a key issue, which was negotiated as part of a complex of related issues concerning the scope of the protection to be accorded to patents and some related rights and the timing of the economic impact of such protection. A critical part of the deal struck was that developing countries that did not provide product patent protection for pharmaceuticals and agricultural chemicals were permitted to delay the introduction thereof for a period of ten years from the entry into force of the WTO Agreement. However, if they chose to do so, they were required to put in place a means by which patent applications for such inventions could be filed so as to allow the preservation of their novelty and priority for the purposes of determining their eligibility for protection by a patent after the expiry of the transitional period. In addition, they were required to provide also for exclusive marketing rights in respect of the products in question if those products obtained marketing approval during the transitional period, subject to a number of conditions. It is our view that this means that

---

[87]We note that Article 32 of the Vienna Convention gives the negotiating history a status of "supplementary means of interpretation" only. Here we use it only to confirm the meaning resulting from the application of the rules set out in Article 31 of the Vienna Convention.

Article 70.8(a) requires the developing countries in question to establish a means that not only appropriately allows for the entitlement to file mailbox applications and the allocation of filing and priority dates to them, but also takes away any reasonable doubts as to whether mailbox applications and eventual patents based on them could be rejected or invalidated because, at the filing or priority date, the matter for which protection was sought was unpatentable in the country in question.

7.30   Finally, we recall that one of the precepts developed under GATT 1947 is that rules and disciplines governing the multilateral trading system serve to protect legitimate expectations of Members as to the competitive relationship between their products and those of the other Members.[88] As the *Superfund* panel pointed out, such rules and disciplines "are not only to protect current trade but also to create the predictability needed to plan future trade".[89] Predictability in the intellectual property regime is indeed essential for the nationals of WTO Members when they make trade and investment decisions in the course of their businesses.

7.31   To sum up, in determining whether India has taken the action necessary to implement its obligations under subparagraph (a) of Article 70.8, we need to examine whether the current Indian system for the receipt of mailbox applications can sufficiently protect the legitimate expectations of other WTO Members as to the competitive relationship between their nationals and those of other Members, by ensuring the preservation of novelty and priority in respect of products which were the subject of mailbox applications. Our findings are not based on the notion that, to implement Article 70.8(a) fully, a Member must already, as of 1 January 1995, have created the rights that will be granted after 2005: i.e., the Member must already have amended its patent law to provide that mailbox applications *will* lead to the grant of patents after 2005 if the conditions foreseen in paragraphs (b) and (c) of Article 70.8 are met. Rather, as indicated in paragraphs 7.28 and 7.29 above, our view is that Article 70.8(a) requires the Members in question to establish a means that not only appropriately allows for the entitlement to file mailbox applications and the allocation of filing and prior-

---

[88]See paragraphs 7.20 and 7.21 above.
[89]Panel Report on "United States — Taxes on Petroleum and Certain Imported Substances", *op. cit.*, para. 5.2.2.

ity dates to them, but also provides a sound legal basis to preserve novelty and priority as of those dates, so as to eliminate any reasonable doubts regarding whether mailbox applications and eventual patents based on them could be rejected or invalidated because, at the filing or priority date, the matter for which protection was sought was unpatentable in the country in question. Since we are not concluding that immediate action should be taken to give effect to the conditions of competition that must prevail after 1 January 2005 through the mechanism of Article 70.8 (b) and (c), we do not consider our findings would have the implications for the transitional periods under other WTO agreements to which India has alluded.[90] We are, however, of the view that India does have an obligation to take legislative measures as from 1 January 1995 to the extent that such measures are necessary in India to implement Article 70.8(a) in the way indicated above. In other words, we do not agree with India that the transitional arrangements of the TRIPS Agreement necessarily relieve India of the obligation to make legislative changes in its patent regime during the first five years of operation of the Agreement. As indicated in paragraph 7.28 above, Article 70.8(a) is a special obligation linked with the possibility of some developing country Members to avail themselves of an extended transitional period until 1 January 2005. Not to require this provision to be implemented with a sound legal basis would upset the delicate balance of the transitional arrangements of Articles 65, 70.8 and 70.9 that was negotiated during the Uruguay Round.

Mechanism for Implementing the Obligations

7.32 The United States claims that Indian law must be modified to implement India's obligations under Article 70.8 and that the current administrative practice of receiving mailbox applications is not a valid "means" for implementation. The United States claims that the Indian administration itself had admitted the necessity of legislative changes when it promulgated the Patents (Amendment) Ordinance 1994, the issuance of which was permissible only if the President "is satisfied that the circumstances exist which render it necessary for him to take immediate action" under Article 123 of the Indian Constitution.[91] To this argument, India essentially points out

---

[90]See paragraph 4.9 above.
[91]See paragraphs 4.3 and 7.3 above.

that Article 70.8 does not prescribe the choice of a particular method of implementation. India further points out that the purpose of Article 123 of the Indian Constitution is to enable legislation even when Parliament is not in session, and the United States' reading of the term "necessary" is an incorrect one.[92]

7.33   In respect of this particular issue, we note that Article 1.1 of the TRIPS Agreement provides in part as follows:

> Members shall be free to determine the appropriate method of implementing the provisions of this Agreement within their own legal system and practice.

Thus, it is up to India to decide how to implement its obligations under Article 70.8. We therefore find that the mere fact that India relies on an administrative practice to receive mailbox applications without legislative changes does not in itself constitute a violation of India's obligations under subparagraph (a) of Article 70.8. The lapse of the Patents (Amendment) Ordinance 1994, which was promulgated for the purpose of specifically addressing these obligations, does not automatically mean the lack of a "means" for filing patent applications for pharmaceutical and agricultural chemical products in India.

7.34   However, in order to make an objective assessment regarding the consistency of the current Indian mechanism with the TRIPS Agreement, as required under Article 11 of the DSU, we must ask ourselves the following question: can that mechanism achieve the object and purpose of Article 70.8 and thereby protect the legitimate expectations of other WTO Members, by ensuring the preservation of novelty and priority in respect of products which were the subject of mailbox applications? To answer this, we need to analyze the current Indian system from the viewpoint of whether it ensures the degree of legal security and predictability for patent applicants of other WTO Members that they are entitled to legitimately expect under the provisions of Article 70.8(a). There appear to be a few serious problems.

---

[92]See paragraph 4.6 above.

7.35   First, under Section 12(1) of the Patents Act 1970, when the complete specification has been filed in respect of a patent application, the Controller must refer the matter to an examiner. Section 12(2) clearly obliges the examiner ordinarily to complete examination within 18 months from the date of reference from the Controller.[93] Under Section 15(2) of the Patents Act, any application for the grant of a patent on a pharmaceutical or agricultural chemical product must be refused by the Controller for lack of patentability.[94] In light of these provisions, the current administrative practice creates a certain degree of legal insecurity in that it requires Indian officials to ignore certain mandatory provisions of the Patents Act. We recall that the *Malt Beverages* panel dealt with a similar issue. There, the respondent offered as a defence that certain GATT-inconsistent legislation was not currently enforced. The panel rejected this defence by stating as follows:

> Even if Massachusetts may not currently be using its police powers to enforce this mandatory legislation, the measure continues to be mandatory legislation which may influence the decisions of economic operators. Hence, a non-enforcement of a mandatory law in respect of imported products does not ensure that imported beer and wine are not treated less favourably than like domestic products to which the law does not apply.[95]

We find great force in this line of reasoning. There is no denying that economic operators -in this case potential patent applicants — are influenced by the legal insecurity created by the continued existence of mandatory legislation that requires the rejection of product patent applications in respect of pharmaceutical and agricultural chemical products. We note that the present situation is slightly different from the *Malt Beverages* case in that India is entitled to retain this mandatory legislation until 1 January 2005 by

---

[93]See paragraph 2.10 above.
[94]*Id.* Furthermore, under Section 9 of the Patents Act, a complete specification must be filed within 12 months of the filing of a provisional application, failing which the application is deemed abandoned ...
[95]Panel Report on "United States — Measures Affecting Alcoholic and Malt Beverages", adopted on 19 June 1992, BISD 39S/206, para. 5.60.

virtue of Article 65.4 of the TRIPS Agreement. The existence of the legislation *per se* is not a problem under the TRIPS Agreement. However, in the absence of clear assurance that applications for pharmaceutical and agricultural chemical product patents will not be rejected and that novelty and priority will be preserved despite the wording of the Patents Act, the legal insecurity remains.

7.36   This legal insecurity is further compounded by the lapse of the Patents (Amendment) Ordinance 1994, which formally and publicly established legal procedures for the receipt of mailbox applications. This is a particular problem according to the United States because a group of Indian patent law experts advised the Indian Government that a formal legal basis for mailbox applications was required to give them legitimacy under Indian law. Although India counters that the group issued no specific report on this issue and that the group contained patent law and not constitutional law experts, a press note issued at the time of the promulgation of the Ordinance indicates that the Ordinance was based in part on the group's recommendations.[96]

7.37   Second, even if Patent Office officials do not examine and reject mailbox applications, a competitor might seek a judicial order to force them to do so in order to obtain rejection of a patent claim.[97] If the competitor successfully establishes the illegality of the separate storage and non- examination of mailbox applications before a court, the filing of those applications could be rendered meaningless. The evidence submitted by India — two Supreme Court rulings on administrative practices — does

---

[96]See paragraph 2.4 above. We also note that the Preamble to the Patents Ordinance contained the following passage: ". . . whereas with a view to meeting India's obligations, it has become necessary to amend the Patents Act 1970 in conformity with the obligations under the [WTO] agreement . . . " (see document IP/N/1/IND/1). While India is, as discussed above, free to choose the legal form of implementing its obligations under the WTO Agreement, we note that India has not officially and publicly changed or corrected the view expressed in this Preamble.

[97]Because, under the current Indian system, patent applications for pharmaceutical and agricultural chemical products are not examined and such applications are not published, competitors might not be in a position to raise objections. However, since data such as the title of the invention, the filing date of the application and the name of the applicant are publicized in the Official Gazette, competitors will often be able to find out with which patent applications filed in other countries the applications correspond.

not sufficiently demonstrate that a court will uphold the validity of administrative actions which apparently contradict mandatory legislation. One case cited by India involved a situation where the administrative practice was not contrary to the statutory provisions. In the other case, the Supreme Court reached a conclusion that administrative guidelines had no statutory force and conferred no right on any citizen to complain that they were not being met.[98] These cases may confirm the Indian position that its reliance on an administrative practice regarding the handling of pharmaceutical and agricultural chemical product patent applications is not unconstitutional, but they do not specifically answer the question we are facing, i.e., whether a court will uphold the validity of administrative actions which apparently contradict mandatory legislation.

7.38 Third, despite India's commitment to seek legislative changes before the expiry of the transitional period available to it, without a sufficient legal basis now for preserving novelty and priority, there would remain doubt during the transitional period regarding the eligibility of these products for future patent protection. As a result, the legal status of patent applications in respect of these products would remain insecure and unpredictable for a possibly long period, which could last until 1 January 2005.

7.39 The fact that patent applications have been filed in respect of pharmaceutical and agricultural chemical products does not alter the situation. It is unknowable how many applications would have been filed if an appropriate system had been in place. As it appears that a number of United States' pharmaceutical companies do not believe that India has established a mailbox application system, and consequently have not filed applications for patent protection of pharmaceutical products,[99] it is reasonable to assume that potential applicants both in India and outside the country have lost opportunities for patent protection for their products in a belief that there is no mechanism to secure their rights. In this regard, we note that the interests of those persons who would have filed patent applications had there been an appropriate mechanism in place after the expiry of the Patents (Amendment) Ordinance 1994 should be protected, since the lack of an adequate mailbox application system has effectively deprived them of

---

[98]See paragraphs 4.10 and 4.12 above.
[99]See Annex 3 of this report.

benefits which they would have enjoyed in the future under the TRIPS Agreement.

7.40   The United States has raised these questions in a persuasive manner. As the Appellate Body report on *Shirts and Blouses* points out, "a party claiming a violation of a provision of the WTO Agreement by another Member must assert and prove its claim".[100] In this case, it is the United States that claims a violation by India of Article 70.8 of the TRIPS Agreement. Therefore, it is up to the United States to put forward evidence and legal arguments sufficient to demonstrate that action by India is inconsistent with the obligations assumed by India under Article 70.8. In our view, the United States has successfully put forward such evidence and arguments. Then, again to paraphrase the Appellate Body, the onus shifts to India to bring forward evidence and arguments to disprove the claim. We are not convinced that India has been able to do so.

7.41   In consideration of the above, we find that the lack of legal security in the operation of the mailbox system in India is such that the system cannot adequately achieve the object and purpose of Article 70.8 and protect legitimate expectations contained therein for inventors of pharmaceutical and agricultural chemical products. It would be extremely difficult to make informed trade and investment decisions based upon the current legal situation in India. To quote again from the *Superfund* panel, "the predictability needed to plan future trade" cannot be created under the system.[101] Thus, security and predictability in the multilateral trading system, which is one of the central goals of the dispute settlement mechanism, cannot be achieved. Consequently, the answer to the question we posed ourselves in paragraph 7.34 above clearly cannot be answered in the affirmative.

7.42   Furthermore, independently of India's transparency obligations under Article 63, we believe that there is a serious issue in the current Indian system of mailbox applications in that it is not made public. Within

---

[100]Appellate Body Report on "United States — Measure Affecting Imports of Woven Wool Shirts and Blouses from India", adopted on 23 May 1997, WT/DS33/AB/R, page 16.
[101]See paragraph 7.30 above.

the context of Article 70.8, it may be questioned whether unpublicized administrative practices can be regarded as "a means by which applications for patents for such inventions *can* be filed". If the means is not publicized, how can an inventor file a claim? India argues that "it [is] sufficient that individual companies that [wish] to submit an application [can] obtain the necessary information from the relevant authorities".[102] In our view, the mere existence of such possibility is hardly sufficient, even if we take into account the fact that economic operators in this area are usually well informed about systems for the protection of their rights. There must be a guarantee that the public — including interested nationals of other WTO Members — is adequately informed. For potential applicants from other WTO Members to be adequately informed, it is arguable that they must not only have information about the existence of a system for the filing of patent applications for pharmaceutical and agricultural chemical products, but also be informed of the purpose of such a system, i.e., to protect the novelty of the inventions in question and the priority of the applications claiming their protection so that the applications concerned are capable of leading to the grant of a patent under the conditions of subparagraphs (b) and (c) of Article 70.8, and to lead to the grant of exclusive marketing rights under the conditions set out in Article 70.9 even during the transitional period. Otherwise, the security and predictability necessary for the operation of the TRIPS Agreement would be lost, and legitimate expectations of interested nationals of other WTO Members would not be protected. However, we make no specific finding on the points discussed in this paragraph, since we deal in more detail with the transparency claim in the following section.

7.43   In conclusion, we find that India has failed to take the action necessary to implement its obligations under subparagraph (a) of Article 70.8 because of the lack of legal security regarding the status of product patent applications in respect of pharmaceutical and agricultural chemical products under the system it presently operates.

*****

---

[102]See paragraph 4.7 above.

Notes and Questions

1. The panel refers to the VCLT, which provides that the terms of a treaty should be interpreted in its context and in light of the object and purpose of the treaty. The panel develops criteria to assess the measures taken to implement the mailbox provision, and concludes that the legitimate expectations of Members as to the implementation of the provisions of the TRIPS Agreement deserve protection. In the view of the panel, the way for India to fulfill the legitimate expectations of the United States and patent applicants is to provide a sound legal mechanism to receive and protect patent applications — so as to remove reasonable doubts as to whether patent applications will be protected.

What is the foundation of the doctrine of legitimate expectations in the panel report? Consider different sources in GATT and WTO jurisprudence and the Vienna Convention on which the panel relies (paras. 7.18 - 7.22; paras. 7.24 - 7.31).

2. How does the panel assess the mechanism put in place by India to respond to the mailbox provision of the TRIPS Agreement? Is the matter dealt with as a question of law, of fact, or both? (paras. 7.32 - 7.33).

3. There is discussion in the panel report concerning the status of the Indian administrative measures from the perspective of whether such measures are permitted by the Indian Constitution (para. 7.37). Does the panel resolve the issue of the constitutionality of the measures which India alleges fulfill its TRIPS obligations?

4. The panel did not prescribe any particular manner in which the mailbox provision and the requirement of exclusive marketing rights should be implemented (para. 7.33). What criteria did it prescribe?

5. The panel indicates that conditions of legal security are important to private enterprise decision-making (cf. para. 7.41). From the standpoint of the broader purposes of the WTO — to promote enhanced global productivity and economic growth — what interests are served by allowing private

operators to make decisions in a more secure environment? Is consumer welfare potentially enhanced? Why?

India — Patent Protection: Report of the Appellate Body

Following is the Report of the AB in this same dispute settlement proceding. Because this is the first TRIPS Agreement dispute to reach the AB, the Report is included almost in its entirety. Take note of the AB's response to the doctrine of legitimate expectations as developed by the panel.

India — Patent Protection for Pharmaceutical and Agricultural Chemical Products
Report of the Appellate Body

India, *Appellant*
United States, *Appellee*
European Communities, *Third Participant*
Present:
    Lacarte-Muró, Presiding Member
    Bacchus, Member
    Beeby, Member

I. Introduction

1. India appeals from certain issues of law and legal interpretations in the Panel Report, *India — Patent Protection for Pharmaceutical and Agricultural Chemical Products* (the "Panel Report"). The Panel was established to consider a complaint by the United States against India concerning the absence in India of either patent protection for pharmaceutical and agricultural chemical products under Article 27 of the *Agreement on Trade-Related Aspects of Intellectual Property* (the "*TRIPS Agreement*"), or of a means for the filing of patent applications for pharmaceutical and agricultural chemical products pursuant to Article 70.8 of the *TRIPS Agreement* and of legal

authority for the granting of exclusive marketing rights for such products pursuant to Article 70.9 of the *TRIPS Agreement*. The relevant factual aspects of India's "legal regime" for patent protection for pharmaceutical and agricultural chemical products are described at paragraphs 2.1 to 2.12 of the Panel Report.

2. The Panel Report was circulated to the Members of the World Trade Organization (the "WTO") on 5 September 1997. The Panel reached the following conclusions:

> On the basis of the findings set out above, the Panel concludes that India has not complied with its obligations under Article 70.8(a) and, in the alternative, paragraphs 1 and 2 of Article 63 of the TRIPS Agreement, because it has failed to establish a mechanism that adequately preserves novelty and priority in respect of applications for product patents in respect of pharmaceutical and agricultural chemical inventions during the transitional period to which it is entitled under Article 65 of the Agreement, and to publish and notify adequately information about such a mechanism; and that India has not complied with its obligations under Article 70.9 of the TRIPS Agreement, because it has failed to establish a system for the grant of exclusive marketing rights.

The Panel made the following recommendation:

> The Panel recommends that the Dispute Settlement Body request India to bring its transitional regime for patent protection of pharmaceutical and agricultural chemical products into conformity with its obligations under the TRIPS Agreement . . .

3. On 15 October 1997, India notified the Dispute Settlement Body (the "DSB") of its intention to appeal certain issues of law covered in the Panel Report and legal interpretations developed by the Panel, pursuant to paragraph 4 of Article 16 of the *Understanding on Rules and Procedures Governing the Settlement of Disputes* (the "DSU"), and filed a Notice of Appeal with the Appellate Body, pursuant to Rule 20 of the *Working Procedures for Appellate Review* (the "*Working Procedures*"). On 27 October 1997, India filed an appellant's submission. On 10 November 1997, the United States filed an appellee's submission pursuant to Rule 22 of the *Working Procedures*. That

same day, the European Communities filed a third participant's submission pursuant to Rule 24 of the *Working Procedures*. The oral hearing provided for in Rule 27 of the *Working Procedures* was held on 14 November 1997. At the oral hearing, the participants and third participant presented their arguments and answered questions from the Division of the Appellate Body hearing the appeal.

****

III. Issues Raised In This Appeal

28. The appellant, India, raises the following issues in this appeal:

(a) What is the proper interpretation to be given to the requirement in Article 70.8(a) of the *TRIPS Agreement* that a Member shall provide "a means" by which applications for patents for inventions relating to pharmaceutical or agricultural chemical products can be filed?

(b) Did the panel err in its treatment of Indian municipal law, or in its application of the burden of proof, in examining whether India had complied with its obligations under Article 70.8(a) of the *TRIPS Agreement*?

(c) Does Article 70.9 of the *TRIPS Agreement* require that there must be a "mechanism" in place to provide for the grant of exclusive marketing rights effective as from the date of entry into force of the *WTO Agreement*?

*****

IV. The *TRIPS Agreement*

29. The *TRIPS Agreement* is one of the new agreements negotiated and concluded in the Uruguay Round of multilateral trade negotiations. The *TRIPS Agreement* brings intellectual property within the world trading system for the first time by imposing certain obligations on Members in the area of trade-related intellectual property rights. As one of the covered agreements under the DSU, the *TRIPS Agreement* is subject to the dispute

settlement rules and procedures of that Understanding. The dispute that gives rise to this case represents the first time the *TRIPS Agreement* has been submitted to the scrutiny of the WTO dispute settlement system.

30. Among the many provisions of the *TRIPS Agreement* are certain specific obligations relating to patent protection for pharmaceutical and agricultural chemical products. With respect to patentable subject matter, Article 27.1 of the *TRIPS Agreement* provides generally:

> Subject to the provisions of paragraphs 2 and 3, patents shall be available for any inventions, whether products or processes, in all fields of technology, provided that they are new, involve an inventive step and are capable of industrial application. Subject to paragraph 4 of Article 65, paragraph 8 of Article 70 and paragraph 3 of this Article, patents shall be available and patent rights enjoyable without discrimination as to the place of invention, the field of technology and whether products are imported or locally produced. (footnote deleted)

31. However, Article 65 of the *TRIPS Agreement* provides, in pertinent part:

> 1. Subject to the provisions of paragraphs 2, 3 and 4, no Member shall be obliged to apply the provisions of this Agreement before the expiry of a general period of one year following the date of entry into force of the WTO Agreement.

> 2. A developing country Member is entitled to delay for a further period of four years the date of application, as defined in paragraph 1, of the provisions of this Agreement other than Articles 3, 4 and 5.

> . . .

> 4. To the extent that a developing country Member is obliged by this Agreement to extend product patent protection to areas of technology not so protectable in its territory on the general date of application of this Agreement for that Member, as defined in paragraph 2, it may delay the application of the provisions on product patents of Section 5 of Part II to such areas of technology for an additional period of five years.

5. A Member availing itself of a transitional period under paragraphs 1, 2, 3 or 4 shall ensure that any changes in its laws, regulations and practice made during that period do not result in a lesser degree of consistency with the provisions of this Agreement.

32. With respect to patent protection for pharmaceutical and agricultural chemical products, certain specific obligations are found in Articles 70.8 and 70.9 of the *TRIPS Agreement*. The interpretation of these specific obligations is the subject of this dispute. Our task is to address the legal issues arising from this dispute that are raised in this appeal.

V. Interpretation of the *TRIPS Agreement*

33. As one of the fundamental issues in this appeal, India has questioned the Panel's enunciation and application of a general interpretative principle which, the Panel stated, "must be taken into account" in interpreting the provisions of the *TRIPS Agreement*. The Panel found that:

> ... when interpreting the text of the TRIPS Agreement, the legitimate expectations of WTO Members concerning the TRIPS Agreement must be taken into account, as well as standards of interpretation developed in past panel reports in the GATT framework, in particular those laying down the principle of the protection of conditions of competition flowing from multilateral trade agreements.

India argues that the Panel's invocation of this principle caused the Panel to misinterpret both Article 70.8 and Article 70.9 and led the Panel to err in determining whether India had complied with those obligations.

34. The Panel stated that:

> The protection of legitimate expectations of Members regarding the conditions of competition is a well-established GATT principle, which derives in part from Article XXIII, the basic dispute settlement provisions of GATT (and the WTO).

The Panel also referred to certain GATT 1947 panel reports[20] as authority for this principle. The Panel noted that whereas the "disciplines formed

---

[20]In particular: Panel Report, *Italian Discrimination Against Imported Agricultural Machinery*, adopted 23 October 1958, BISD 7S/60, paras. 12-13; Panel Report, *United*

under GATT 1947 (so-called GATT *acquis*) were primarily directed at the treatment of the goods of other countries", "the concept of the protection of legitimate expectations" in relation to the *TRIPS Agreement* applies to "the competitive relationship between a Member's own nationals and those of other Members (rather than between domestically produced goods and the goods of other Members, as in the goods area)".

35. In *Japan — Taxes on Alcoholic Beverages*, on the status of adopted panel reports, we acknowledged:

> Article XVI:1 of the *WTO Agreement* and paragraph 1(b)(iv) of the language of Annex 1A incorporating the GATT 1994 into the *WTO Agreement* bring the legal history and experience under the GATT 1947 into the new realm of the WTO in a way that ensures continuity and consistency in a smooth transition from the GATT 1947 system. This affirms the importance to the Members of the WTO of the experience acquired by the CONTRACTING PARTIES to the GATT 1947 — and acknowledges the continuing relevance of that experience to the new trading system served by the WTO. Adopted panel reports are an important part of the GATT *acquis*.[22]

36. Although the Panel states that it is merely applying a "well-established GATT principle", the Panel's reasoning does not accurately reflect GATT/WTO practice. In developing its interpretative principle, the Panel merges, and thereby confuses, two different concepts from previous GATT practice. One is the concept of protecting the expectations of contracting parties as to the competitive relationship between their products and the products of other contracting parties. This is a concept that was developed in the context of *violation* complaints involving Articles III and XI, brought under Article XXIII:1(a), of the GATT 1947. The other is the concept of the protection of the reasonable expectations of contracting parties relating to market access concessions. This is a concept that was developed in the context of *non-violation* complaints brought under Article XXIII:1(b) of the GATT.

States — *Taxes on Petroleum and Certain Imported Substances*, adopted 17 June 1987, BISD 34S/136, para. 5.22; and Panel Report, *United States — Section 337 of the Tariff Act of 1930*, adopted 7 November 1989, BISD 36S/345, para. 5.13.

[22]Adopted 1 November 1996, WT/DS8/AB/R, WT/DS10/AB/R, WT/DS11/AB/R, p. 14.

37. Article 64.1 of the *TRIPS Agreement* incorporates by reference Article XXIII of the GATT 1994 as the general dispute settlement provision governing the *TRIPS Agreement*.[23]The provisions of Articles XXII and XXIII of GATT 1994 as elaborated and applied by the Dispute Settlement Understanding shall apply to consultations and the settlement of disputes under this Agreement except as otherwise specifically provided herein. Thus, we have no quarrel in principle with the notion that past GATT practice with respect to Article XXIII is pertinent to interpretation of the *TRIPS Agreement*. However, such interpretation must show proper appreciation of the different bases for action under Article XXIII.

38. Article XXIII:1 of the GATT 1994 sets out the various causes of action on which a Member may base a complaint. A Member may have recourse to dispute settlement under Article XXIII when it considers that:

> . . . any benefit accruing to it directly or indirectly under this Agreement is being nullified or impaired or that the attainment of any objective of the Agreement is being impeded as the result of
>
> (*a*) the failure of another contracting party to carry out its obligations under this Agreement, or
>
> (*b*) the application by another contracting party of any measure, whether or not it conflicts with the provisions of this Agreement, or
>
> (*c*) the existence of any other situation.[24]

39. Article XXIII:1(a) involves so-called "violation" complaints. These are disputes that arise from an alleged failure by a Member to carry out its obligations. During nearly fifty years of experience, Article XXIII:1(a) has formed the basis of almost all disputes under the GATT 1947 and the *WTO Agreement*. In contrast, Article XXIII:1(b) involves so-called "non-violation" complaints. These are disputes that do not require an allegation of a violation of an obligation. The basis of a cause of action under Article XXIII:1(b) is not necessarily a violation of the rules, but rather the nullification or impairment of a benefit accruing to a Member under a covered agreement. In

---

[23]Article 64.1 of the *TRIPS Agreement* reads: . . .
[24]Article XXIII:1 of the GATT 1994.

the history of the GATT/WTO, there have been only a handful of "non-violation" cases arising under Article XXIII:1(b).[25] Article XXIII:1(c), covering what are commonly called "situation" complaints, has never been the foundation for a recommendation or ruling of the GATT CONTRACTING PARTIES or the Dispute Settlement Body, although it has formed the basis for parties' arguments before panels in a small number of cases.[26]

40. In the context of violation complaints made under Article XXIII:1(a), it is true that panels examining claims under Articles III and XI of the GATT have frequently stated that the purpose of these articles is to protect the expectations of Members concerning the competitive relationship between imported and domestic products, as opposed to expectations concerning trade volumes. However, this statement is often made *after* a panel has found a violation of, for example, Article III or Article XI that establishes a *prima facie* case of nullification or impairment.[27] At that point in its reasoning, the panel is examining whether the defending party has been able to rebut the charge of nullification or impairment. It is in this context

---

[25]Previous panels have found "non-violation" nullification or impairment in only four of 14 cases where it was alleged: Working Party Report, *Australia — Subsidy on Ammonium Sulphate*, adopted 3 April 1950, BISD II/188; Panel Report, *Germany — Imports of Sardines*, adopted 31 October 1952, BISD IS/53; Panel Report, *Germany — Import Duties on Starch and Potato Flour*, noted 16 February 1955, BISD 3S/77; and Panel Report, *European Communities — Payments and Subsidies Paid to Processors and Producers of Oilseeds and Related Animal-Feed Proteins*, adopted 25 January 1990, BISD 37S/86.

[26]See, generally, F. Roessler, "The Concept of Nullification and Impairment in the Legal System of the World Trade Organization" in E.-U. Petersmann (ed.), *International Trade Law and the GATT/WTO Dispute Settlement System* (Kluwer, 1997), pp. 123-142; and E.-U. Petersmann, *The GATT/WTO Dispute Settlement System: International Law, International Organizations and Dispute Settlement* (Kluwer, 1997), pp. 170-176.

[27]See, for example: Working Party Report, *Brazilian Internal Taxes*, adopted 30 June 1949, BISD II/181, para. 16; Panel Report, *United States — Taxes on Petroleum and Certain Imported Substances*, adopted 17 June 1987, BISD 34S/136, para. 5.1.9; Panel Report, *Canada — Administration of the Foreign Investment Review Act*, adopted 7 February 1984, BISD 30S/140, para. 6.6; Panel Report, *Japanese Measures on Imports of Leather*, adopted 15/16 May 1984, BISD 31S/94, para. 55; Panel Report, *Japan — Customs Duties, Taxes and Labelling Practices on Imported Wines and Alcoholic Beverages*, adopted 10 November 1987, BISD 34S/83, para. 5.11; Panel Report, *European Economic Community — Restrictions on Imports of Apples*, adopted 22 June 1989, BISD 36S/135, para. 5.25; and Panel Report, *United States — Measures Affecting the Importation, Internal Sale and Use of Tobacco*, adopted 4 October 1994, DS44/R, para. 99.

that panels have referred to the expectations of Members concerning the conditions of competition.

41. The doctrine of protecting the "reasonable expectations" of contracting parties developed in the context of "non-violation" complaints brought under Article XXIII:1(b) of the GATT 1947. Some of the rules and procedures concerning "non-violation" cases have been codified in Article 26.1 of the DSU. "Non-violation" complaints are rooted in the GATT's origins as an agreement intended to protect the reciprocal tariff concessions negotiated among the contracting parties under Article II.[28] In the absence of substantive legal rules in many areas relating to international trade, the "non-violation" provision of Article XXIII:1(b) was aimed at preventing contracting parties from using non-tariff barriers or other policy measures to negate the benefits of negotiated tariff concessions. Under Article XXIII:1(b) of the GATT 1994, a Member can bring a "non-violation" complaint when the negotiated balance of concessions between Members is upset by the application of a measure, whether or not this measure is inconsistent with the provisions of the covered agreement. The ultimate goal is not the withdrawal of the measure concerned, but rather achieving a mutually satisfactory adjustment, usually by means of compensation.[29]

42. Article 64.2 of the *TRIPS Agreement* states:

> Subparagraphs 1(b) and 1(c) of Article XXIII of GATT 1994 shall not apply to the settlement of disputes under this Agreement for a period of five years from the date of entry into force of the WTO Agreement.

The meaning of this provision is clear: the *only* cause of action permitted under the *TRIPS Agreement* during the first five years after the entry into force of the *WTO Agreement* is a "violation" complaint under Article XXIII:1(a) of the GATT 1994. This case involves allegations of violation of obligations under the *TRIPS Agreement*. However, the Panel's invocation of the "legitimate expectations" of Members relating to conditions of competition melds the legally-distinct bases for "violation" and "non-violation"

---

[28]See, in general, E.-U. Petersmann, "Violation Complaints and Non-violation Complaints in International Law" (1991) *German Yearbook of International Law* 175.
[29]This is codified in Article 26.1(b) of the DSU.

complaints under Article XXIII of the GATT 1994 into one uniform cause of action. This is not consistent with either Article XXIII of the GATT 1994 or Article 64 of the *TRIPS Agreement*. Whether or not "non-violation" complaints should be available for disputes under the *TRIPS Agreement* is a matter that remains to be determined by the Council for Trade- Related Aspects of Intellectual Property (the "Council for TRIPS") pursuant to Article 64.3 of the *TRIPS Agreement*. It is *not* a matter to be resolved through interpretation by panels or by the Appellate Body.

43. In addition to relying on the GATT *acquis*, the Panel relies also on the customary rules of interpretation of public international law as a basis for the interpretative principle it offers for the *TRIPS Agreement*. Specifically, the Panel relies on Article 31 of the *Vienna Convention*, which provides in part:

> 1. A treaty shall be interpreted in good faith in accordance with the ordinary meaning to be given to the terms of the treaty in their context and in the light of its object and purpose.

44. With this customary rule of interpretation in mind, the Panel stated that:

> In our view, good faith interpretation requires the protection of legitimate expectations derived from the protection of intellectual property rights provided for in the Agreement.

45. The Panel misapplies Article 31 of the *Vienna Convention*. The Panel misunderstands the concept of legitimate expectations in the context of the customary rules of interpretation of public international law. The legitimate expectations of the parties to a treaty are reflected in the language of the treaty itself. The duty of a treaty interpreter is to examine the words of the treaty to determine the intentions of the parties. This should be done in accordance with the principles of treaty interpretation set out in Article 31 of the *Vienna Convention*. But these principles of interpretation neither require nor condone the imputation into a treaty of words that are not there or the importation into a treaty of concepts that were not intended.

24. In *United States — Standards for Reformulated and Conventional Gaso-line*[31], we set out the proper approach to be applied in interpreting the *WTO Agreement* in accordance with the rules in Article 31 of the *Vienna Convention*. These rules must be respected and applied in interpreting the *TRIPS Agreement* or any other covered agreement. The Panel in this case has created its own interpretative principle, which is consistent with neither the customary rules of interpretation of public international law nor established GATT/WTO practice. Both panels and the Appellate Body must be guided by the rules of treaty interpretation set out in the *Vienna Convention*, and must not add to or diminish rights and obligations provided in the *WTO Agreement*.

47. This conclusion is dictated by two separate and very specific provisions of the DSU. Article 3.2 of the DSU provides that the dispute settlement system of the WTO:

> . . . serves to preserve the rights and obligations of the Members under the covered agreements, and to clarify the existing provisions of those agreements in accordance with customary rules of interpretation of public international law. Recommendations and rulings of the DSB cannot add to or diminish the rights and obligations provided in the covered agreements.

Furthermore, Article 19.2 of the DSU provides:

> In accordance with paragraph 2 of Article 3, in their findings and recommendations, the panel and Appellate Body cannot add to or diminish the rights and obligations provided in the covered agreements.

These provisions speak for themselves. Unquestionably, both panels and the Appellate Body are bound by them.

48. For these reasons, we do not agree with the Panel that the legitimate expectations of Members *and* private rights holders concerning conditions of competition must always be taken into account in interpreting the *TRIPS Agreement*.

---

[31]Adopted 20 May 1996, WT/DS2/AB/R, pp. 16-17.

VI. Article 70.8

49. Article 70.8 states:

> Where a Member does not make available as of the date of entry into force of the WTO Agreement patent protection for pharmaceutical and agricultural chemical products commensurate with its obligations under Article 27, that Member shall:
>
> (a) notwithstanding the provisions of Part VI, provide as from the date of entry into force of the WTO Agreement a means by which applications for patents for such inventions can be filed;
>
> (b) apply to these applications, as of the date of application of this Agreement, the criteria for patentability as laid down in this Agreement as if those criteria were being applied on the date of filing in that Member or, where priority is available and claimed, the priority date of the application; and
>
> (c) provide patent protection in accordance with this Agreement as from the grant of the patent and for the remainder of the patent term, counted from the filing date in accordance with Article 33 of this Agreement, for those of these applications that meet the criteria for protection referred to in subparagraph (b).

50. With respect to Article 70.8(a), the Panel found that:

> ... Article 70.8(a) requires the Members in question to establish a means that not only appropriately allows for the entitlement to file mailbox applications and the allocation of filing and priority dates to them, but also provides a sound legal basis to preserve novelty and priority as of those dates, so as to eliminate any reasonable doubts regarding whether mailbox applications and eventual patents based on them could be rejected or invalidated because, at the filing or priority date, the matter for which protection was sought was unpatentable in the country in question.

51. In India's view, the obligations in Article 70.8(a) are met by a developing country Member where it establishes a mailbox for receiving, dating and storing patent applications for pharmaceutical and agricultural chem-

ical products in a manner that properly allots filing and priority dates to those applications in accordance with paragraphs (b) and (c) of Article 70.8. India asserts that the Panel established an additional obligation "to create legal certainty that the patent applications and the eventual patents based on them will not be rejected or invalidated in the future". This, India argues, is a legal error by the Panel.

52. The introductory clause to Article 70.8 provides that it applies "[w]here a Member does not make available as of the date of entry into force of the WTO Agreement patent protection for pharmaceutical and agricultural chemical products commensurate with its obligations under Article 27 . . ." of the *TRIPS Agreement*. Article 27 requires that patents be made available "for any inventions, whether products or processes, in all fields of technology", subject to certain exceptions. However, pursuant to paragraphs 1, 2 and 4 of Article 65, a developing country Member may delay providing product patent protection in areas of technology not protectable in its territory on the general date of application of the *TRIPS Agreement* for that Member until 1 January 2005. Article 70.8 relates specifically and exclusively to situations where a Member does not provide, as of 1 January 1995, patent protection for pharmaceutical and agricultural chemical products.

53. By its terms, Article 70.8(a) applies "notwithstanding the provisions of Part VI" of the *TRIPS Agreement*. Part VI of the *TRIPS Agreement*, consisting of Articles 65, 66 and 67, allows for certain "transitional arrangements" in the application of certain provisions of the *TRIPS Agreement*. These "transitional arrangements", which allow a Member to delay the application of some of the obligations in the *TRIPS Agreement* for certain specified periods[35], do not apply to Article 70.8. Thus, although there are "transitional

---

[35]Pursuant to Article 65.1, all Members were entitled to delay the application of most of the provisions of the *TRIPS Agreement* for one year after the date of entry into force of the *WTO Agreement*. Pursuant to Article 65.2, developing country Members are generally entitled to a delay of a further four years. Where a developing country Member is obliged to extend patent protection to areas of technology to which it did not extend such protection on the general date of application of the *TRIPS Agreement* for that Member, Article 65.4 states that that developing country Member may delay the application of the provisions on product patents to such areas of technology for an additional period of five years.

arrangements" which allow developing country Members, in particular, more time to implement certain of their obligations under the *TRIPS Agreement*, no such "transitional arrangements" exist for the obligations in Article 70.8.

54. Article 70.8(a) imposes an obligation on Members to provide "a means" by which mailbox applications can be filed "from the date of entry into force of the WTO Agreement". Thus, this obligation has been in force since 1 January 1995. The issue before us in this appeal is not whether this obligation exists or whether this obligation is now in force. Clearly, it exists, and, equally clearly, it is in force now. The issue before us in this appeal is: what precisely is the "means" for filing mailbox applications that is contemplated and required by Article 70.8(a)? To answer this question, we must interpret the terms of Article 70.8(a).

55. We agree with the Panel that "[t]he analysis of the ordinary meaning of these terms alone does not lead to a definitive interpretation as to what sort of 'means' is required by this subparagraph". Therefore, in accordance with the general rules of treaty interpretation set out in Article 31 of the *Vienna Convention*, to discern the meaning of the terms in Article 70.8(a), we must also read this provision in its context, and in light of the object and purpose of the *TRIPS Agreement*.

56. Paragraphs (b) and (c) of Article 70.8 constitute part of the context for interpreting Article 70.8(a). Paragraphs (b) and (c) of Article 70.8 require that the "means" provided by a Member under Article 70.8(a) must allow the filing of applications for patents for pharmaceutical and agricultural chemical products from 1 January 1995 and preserve the dates of filing and priority of those applications, so that the criteria for patentability may be applied as of those dates, and so that the patent protection eventually granted is dated back to the filing date. In this respect, we agree with the Panel that,

> ... in order to prevent the loss of the novelty of an invention ... filing and priority dates need to have a sound legal basis if the provisions of Article 70.8 are to fulfil their purpose. Moreover, if available, a filing must entitle the applicant to claim priority on the basis of an earlier fil-

ing in respect of the claimed invention over applications with subsequent filing or priority dates. Without legally sound filing and priority dates, the mechanism to be established on the basis of Article 70.8 will be rendered inoperational.

57. On this, the Panel is clearly correct. The Panel's interpretation here is consistent also with the object and purpose of the *TRIPS Agreement*. The Agreement takes into account, *inter alia*, "the need to promote effective and adequate protection of intellectual property rights".[38] We believe the Panel was correct in finding that the "means" that the Member concerned is obliged to provide under Article 70.8(a) must allow for "the entitlement to file mailbox applications and the allocation of filing and priority dates to them". Furthermore, the Panel was correct in finding that the "means" established under Article 70.8(a) must also provide "a sound legal basis to preserve novelty and priority as of those dates". These findings flow inescapably from the necessary operation of paragraphs (b) and (c) of Article 70.8.

58. However, we do *not* agree with the Panel that Article 70.8(a) requires a Member to establish a means "so as to eliminate any reasonable doubts regarding whether mailbox applications and eventual patents based on them could be rejected or invalidated because, at the filing or priority date, the matter for which protection was sought was unpatentable in the country in question". India is *entitled*, by the "transitional arrangements" in paragraphs 1, 2 and 4 of Article 65, to delay application of Article 27 for patents for pharmaceutical and agricultural chemical products until 1 January 2005. In our view, India is obliged, by Article 70.8(a), to provide a legal mechanism for the filing of mailbox applications that provides a sound legal basis to preserve both the novelty of the inventions and the priority of the applications as of the relevant filing and priority dates. No more.

59. But what constitutes such a sound legal basis in Indian law? To answer this question, we must recall first an important general rule in the *TRIPS Agreement*. Article 1.1 of the *TRIPS Agreement* states, in pertinent part:

---

[38]Preamble to the *TRIPS Agreement*.

> ... Members shall be free to determine the appropriate method of implementing the provisions of this Agreement within their own legal system and practice.

Members, therefore, are free to determine how best to meet their obligations under the *TRIPS Agreement* within the context of their own legal systems. And, as a Member, India is "free to determine the appropriate method of implementing" its obligations under the *TRIPS Agreement* within the context of its own legal system.

60. India insists that it has done that. India contends that it has established, through "administrative instructions", a "means" consistent with Article 70.8(a) of the *TRIPS Agreement*. According to India, these "administrative instructions" establish a mechanism that provides a sound legal basis to preserve the novelty of the inventions and the priority of the applications as of the relevant filing and priority dates consistent with Article 70.8(a) of the *TRIPS Agreement*. According to India, pursuant to these "administrative instructions", the Patent Office has been directed to store applications for patents for pharmaceutical and agricultural chemical products separately for future action pursuant to Article 70.8, and the Controller General of Patents Designs and Trademarks ("the Controller") has been instructed not to refer them to an examiner until 1 January 2005. According to India, these "administrative instructions" are legally valid in Indian law, as they are reflected in the Minister's Statement to Parliament of 2 August 1996. And, according to India:

> There is ... *absolute certainty* that India can, when patents are due in accordance with subparagraphs (b) and (c) of Article 70.8, decide to grant such patents on the basis of the applications currently submitted and determine the novelty and priority of the inventions in accordance with the date of these applications. (emphasis added)

61. India has not provided any text of these "administrative instructions" either to the Panel or to us.

62. Whatever their substance or their import, these "administrative instructions" were not the initial "means" chosen by the Government of India

to meet India's obligations under Article 70.8(a) of the *TRIPS Agreement*. The Government of India's initial preference for establishing a "means" for filing mailbox applications under Article 70.8(a) was the Patents (Amendment) Ordinance (the "Ordinance"), promulgated by the President of India on 31 December 1994 pursuant to Article 123 of India's Constitution. Article 123 enables the President to promulgate an ordinance when Parliament is not in session, and when the President is satisfied "that circumstances exist which render it necessary for him to take immediate action". India notified the Ordinance to the Council for TRIPS, pursuant to Article 63.2 of the *TRIPS Agreement*, on 6 March 1995. In accordance with the terms of Article 123 of India's Constitution, the Ordinance expired on 26 March 1995, six weeks after the reassembly of Parliament. This was followed by an unsuccessful effort to enact the Patents (Amendment) Bill 1995 to implement the contents of the Ordinance on a permanent basis.[47] This Bill was introduced in the Lok Sabha (Lower House) in March 1995. After being passed by the Lok Sabha, it was referred to a Select Committee of the Rajya Sabha (Upper House) for examination and report. However, the Bill was subsequently not enacted due to the dissolution of Parliament on 10 May 1996. From these actions, it is apparent that the Government of India initially considered the enactment of amending legislation to be necessary in order to implement its obligations under Article 70.8(a). However, India maintains that the "administrative instructions" issued in April 1995 effectively continued the mailbox system established by the Ordinance, thus obviating the need for a formal amendment to the Patents Act or for a new notification to the Council for TRIPS.

63. With respect to India's "administrative instructions", the Panel found that "the current administrative practice creates a certain degree of legal insecurity in that it requires Indian officials to ignore certain mandatory provisions of the Patents Act"; and that "even if Patent Office officials do not examine and reject mailbox applications, a competitor might seek a judicial order to do so in order to obtain rejection of a patent claim".

---

[47] We note that an Expert Group advised the Indian Government that a formal legal basis was required to make the mailbox system valid under Indian law. See Panel Report, para. 7.36.

64. India asserts that the Panel erred in its treatment of India's municipal law because municipal law is a fact that must be established before an international tribunal by the party relying on it. In India's view, the Panel did not assess the Indian law as a fact to be established by the United States, but rather as a law to be interpreted by the Panel. India argues that the Panel should have given India the benefit of the doubt as to the status of its mailbox system under Indian domestic law. India claims, furthermore, that the Panel should have sought guidance from India on matters relating to the interpretation of Indian law.

65. In public international law, an international tribunal may treat municipal law in several ways.[52] Municipal law may serve as evidence of facts and may provide evidence of state practice. However, municipal law may also constitute evidence of compliance or non-compliance with international obligations. For example, in *Certain German Interests in Polish Upper Silesia*, the Permanent Court of International Justice observed:

> It might be asked whether a difficulty does not arise from the fact that the Court would have to deal with the Polish law of July 14th, 1920. This, however, does not appear to be the case. From the standpoint of International Law and of the Court which is its organ, municipal laws are merely facts which express the will and constitute the activities of States, in the same manner as do legal decisions and administrative measures. *The Court is certainly not called upon to interpret the Polish law as such; but there is nothing to prevent the Court's giving judgment on the question whether or not, in applying that law, Poland is acting in conformity with its obligations towards Germany under the Geneva Convention.*[53] (emphasis added)

66. In this case, the Panel was simply performing its task in determining whether India's "administrative instructions" for receiving mailbox applications were in conformity with India's obligations under Article 70.8(a) of the *TRIPS Agreement*. It is clear that an examination of the relevant aspects of Indian municipal law and, in particular, the relevant provisions of the Patents Act as they relate to the "administrative instructions", is essential to

---

[52]See, for example, I. Brownlie, *Principles of Public International Law*, 4th ed. (Clarendon Press, 1990), pp. 40-42.
[53][1926], PCIJ Rep., Series A, No. 7, p. 19.

determining whether India has complied with its obligations under Article 70.8(a). There was simply no way for the Panel to make this determination without engaging in an examination of Indian law. But, as in the case cited above before the Permanent Court of International Justice, in this case, the Panel was not interpreting Indian law "as such"; rather, the Panel was examining Indian law solely for the purpose of determining whether India had met its obligations under the *TRIPS Agreement*. To say that the Panel should have done otherwise would be to say that only India can assess whether Indian law is consistent with India's obligations under the *WTO Agreement*. This, clearly, cannot be so.

67. Previous GATT/WTO panels also have conducted a detailed examination of the domestic law of a Member in assessing the conformity of that domestic law with the relevant GATT/WTO obligations. For example, in *United States — Section 337 of the Tariff Act of 1930*,[54] the panel conducted a detailed examination of the relevant United States' legislation and practice, including the remedies available under Section 337 as well as the differences between patent-based Section 337 proceedings and federal district court proceedings, in order to determine whether Section 337 was inconsistent with Article III:4 of the GATT 1947. This seems to us to be a comparable case.

68. And, just as it was necessary for the Panel in this case to seek a detailed understanding of the operation of the Patents Act as it relates to the "administrative instructions" in order to assess whether India had complied with Article 70.8(a), so, too, is it necessary for us in this appeal to review the Panel's examination of the same Indian domestic law.

69. To do so, we must look at the specific provisions of the Patents Act. Section 5(a) of the Patents Act provides that substances "intended for use, or capable of being used, as food or as medicine or drug" are not patentable. "When the complete specification has been led in respect of an application for a patent", section 12(1) *requires* the Controller to refer that application and that specification to an examiner. Moreover, section 15(2) of the Patents Act states that the Controller "shall refuse" an application in respect

---

[54]Adopted 7 November 1989, BISD 36S/345.

of a substance that is not patentable. We agree with the Panel that these provisions of the Patents Act are mandatory. And, like the Panel, we are not persuaded that India's "administrative instructions" would prevail over the contradictory mandatory provisions of the Patents Act. We note also that, in issuing these "administrative instructions", the Government of India did not avail itself of the provisions of section 159 of the Patents Act, which allows the Central Government "to make rules for carrying out the provisions of [the] Act" or section 160 of the Patents Act, which requires that such rules be laid before each House of the Indian Parliament. We are told by India that such rulemaking was not required for the "administrative instructions" at issue here. But this, too, seems to be inconsistent with the mandatory provisions of the Patents Act.

70. We are not persuaded by India's explanation of these seeming contradictions. Accordingly, we are not persuaded that India's "administrative instructions" would survive a legal challenge under the Patents Act. And, consequently, we are not persuaded that India's "administrative instructions" provide a sound legal basis to preserve novelty of inventions and priority of applications as of the relevant filing and priority dates.

71. For these reasons, we agree with the Panel's conclusion that India's "administrative instructions" for receiving mailbox applications are inconsistent with Article 70.8(a) of the *TRIPS Agreement*.

72. India raises the additional argument that the Panel erred in its application of the burden of proof in assessing Indian municipal law. In particular, India alleges that the Panel, after having required the United States merely to raise "reasonable doubts" suggesting a violation of Article 70.8, placed the burden on India to dispel such doubts.

73. The Panel states:

> As the Appellate Body report on *Shirts and Blouses* points out, "a party claiming a violation of a provision of the WTO Agreement by another Member must assert and prove its claim". In this case, it is the United States that claims a violation by India of Article 70.8 of the TRIPS Agreement. Therefore, it is up to the United States to put forward evidence and legal arguments sufficient to demonstrate that action by India is inconsistent with the obligations assumed by India under Article 70.8. In our view, the United States has successfully put forward such evidence

and arguments. Then, . . . the onus shifts to India to bring forward evidence and arguments to disprove the claim. We are not convinced that India has been able to do so (footnotes deleted).[58]

74. This statement of the Panel is a legally correct characterization of the approach to burden of proof that we set out in *United States — Shirts and Blouses*.[59] However, it is not sufficient for a panel to enunciate the correct approach to burden of proof; a panel must also apply the burden of proof correctly. A careful reading of paragraphs 7.35 and 7.37 of the Panel Report reveals that the Panel has done so in this case. These paragraphs show that the United States put forward evidence and arguments that India's "administrative instructions" pertaining to mailbox applications were legally insufficient to prevail over the application of certain mandatory provisions of the Patents Act. India put forward rebuttal evidence and arguments. India misinterprets what the Panel said about "reasonable doubts". The Panel did not require the United States merely to raise "reasonable doubts" before the burden shifted to India. Rather, after properly requiring the United States to establish a *prima facie* case and after hearing India's rebuttal evidence and arguments, the Panel concluded that *it* had "reasonable doubts" that the "administrative instructions" would prevail over the mandatory provisions of the Patents Act if a challenge were brought in an Indian court.

75. For these reasons, we conclude that the Panel applied the burden of proof correctly in assessing the compliance of India's domestic law with Article 70.8(a) of the *TRIPS Agreement*.

VII. Article 70.9

76. Article 70.9 of the *TRIPS Agreement* reads:

> Where a product is the subject of a patent application in a Member in accordance with paragraph 8(a), exclusive marketing rights shall be granted, notwithstanding the provisions of Part VI, for a period of five years after obtaining marketing approval in that Member or until a product patent is granted or rejected in that Member, whichever period is shorter, provided that, subsequent to the entry into force of the WTO

---

[58]Panel Report, para. 7.40.
[59]Adopted 23 May 1997, WT/DS33/AB/R, p. 16.

Agreement, a patent application has been filed and a patent granted for that product in another Member and marketing approval obtained in such other Member.

77. With respect to Article 70.9, the Panel found:

> Based on customary rules of treaty interpretation, we have reached the conclusion that under Article 70.9 there must be a mechanism ready for the grant of exclusive marketing rights at any time subsequent to the date of entry into force of the WTO Agreement.

78. India argues that Article 70.9 establishes an obligation to grant exclusive marketing rights for a product that is the subject of a patent application under Article 70.8(a) after all the other conditions specified in Article 70.9 have been fulfilled. India asserts that there are many provisions in the *TRIPS Agreement* that, unlike Article 70.9, explicitly oblige Members to change their domestic laws to authorize their domestic authorities to take certain action before the need to take such action actually arises.[62] India maintains that the Panel's interpretation of Article 70.9 has the consequence that the transitional arrangements in Article 65 allow developing country Members to postpone legislative changes in all fields of technology except the most "sensitive" ones, pharmaceutical and agricultural chemical products. India claims that the Panel turned an obligation to take action in the future into an obligation to take action immediately.

79. India's arguments must be examined in the light of Article XVI:4 of the *WTO Agreement*, which requires that:

---

[62] ***; for example, India asserts that according to Articles 42-48 of the *TRIPS Agreement*, the judicial authorities of Members "shall have the authority" to grant certain rights. Article 51 obliges Members to "adopt procedures" to enable right holders to prevent the release of counterfeited or pirated products from customs. Article 39.2 requires Members to give natural and legal persons "the possibility of preventing" the disclosure of information. According to Article 25.1 "Members shall provide for the protection" of certain industrial designs and Article 22.2 obliges Members to "provide the legal means for interested parties to prevent" certain misuses of geographical indications. India further asserts that a comparison of the terms of Article 70.9 with those of Article 27 according to which "patents shall be available" for inventions is revealing.

Each Member shall ensure the conformity of its laws, regulations and administrative procedures with its obligations as provided in the annexed Agreements.

80. Moreover, India acknowledged before the Panel and in this appeal that, under Indian law, it is necessary to enact legislation in order to grant exclusive marketing rights in compliance with the provisions of Article 70.9. This was already implied in the Ordinance, which contained detailed provisions for the grant of exclusive marketing rights in India effective 1 January 1995. However, with the expiry of the Ordinance on 26 March 1995, no legal basis remained, and with the failure to enact the Patents (Amendment) Bill 1995 due to the dissolution of Parliament on 10 May 1996, no legal basis currently exists, for the grant of exclusive marketing rights in India. India notified the Council for TRIPS of the promulgation of the Ordinance pursuant to Article 63.2 of the *TRIPS Agreement*, but has failed as yet to notify the Council for TRIPS that the Ordinance has expired.

81. Given India's admissions that legislation is necessary in order to grant exclusive marketing rights in compliance with Article 70.9 and that it does not currently have such legislation, the issue for us to consider in this appeal is whether a failure to have in place a mechanism ready for the grant of exclusive marketing rights, effective *as from the date of entry into force* of the *WTO Agreement*, constitutes a violation of India's obligations under Article 70.9 of the *TRIPS Agreement*.

82. By its terms, Article 70.9 applies only in situations where a product patent application is filed under Article 70.8(a). Like Article 70.8(a), Article 70.9 applies "notwithstanding the provisions of Part VI". Article 70.9 specifically refers to Article 70.8(a), and they operate in tandem to provide a package of rights and obligations that apply *during* the transitional periods contemplated in Article 65. It is obvious, therefore, that both Article 70.8(a) *and* Article 70.9 are intended to apply as from the date of entry into force of the *WTO Agreement*.

83. India has an obligation to implement the provisions of Article 70.9 of the *TRIPS Agreement* effective as from the date of entry into force of the *WTO Agreement*, that is, 1 January 1995. India concedes that legislation is needed to implement this obligation. India has not enacted such legislation.

To give meaning and effect to the rights and obligations under Article 70.9 of the *TRIPS Agreement*, such legislation should have been in effect since 1 January 1995.

84. For these reasons, we agree with the Panel that India should have had a mechanism in place to provide for the grant of exclusive marketing rights effective as from the date of entry into force of the *WTO Agreement*, and, therefore, we agree with the Panel that India is in violation of Article 70.9 of the *TRIPS Agreement*.

*****

IX. Findings and Conclusions

97. For the reasons set out in this Report, the Appellate Body:

(a) upholds the Panel's conclusion that India has not complied with its obligations under Article 70.8(a) to establish "a means" that adequately preserves novelty and priority in respect of applications for product patents in respect of pharmaceutical and agricultural chemical inventions during the transitional periods provided for in Article 65 of the *TRIPS Agreement*;

(b) upholds the Panel's conclusion that India has not complied with its obligations under Article 70.9 of the *TRIPS Agreement*; and

*****

98. The Appellate Body *recommends* that the Dispute Settlement Body request India to bring its legal regime for patent protection of pharmaceutical and agricultural chemical products into conformity with India's obligations under Articles 70.8 and 70.9 of the *TRIPS Agreement*.

Notes and Questions

1. At the outset of the Appellate Body (AB) Report, the AB said the panel is correct in referring to and applying the accumulated body of "legal history

and experience" of the GATT 1947 in the present case (*e.g.*, at para. 35). This body of accumulated experience is generally referred to as the "GATT *acquis*", and the WTO Agreement expressly contemplates this bringing forward of GATT 1947 history.

2. The AB agrees with the panel as to result on the Article 70 questions, but differs as to legal reasoning. What is the main point of departure between the AB and the panel? The AB says that the panel's approach is incompatible with a proper analysis under the Vienna Convention (para. 45-48). The AB decides that interpreting the TRIPS Agreement to give effect to "legitimate expectations" — in the panel's terms, to remove "reasonable doubts" — goes beyond textual analysis and into the realm of the non-violation complaint under Article XXIII:1:b of the GATT Agreement (para. 19).

Do you agree with this assessment? What are the foundations and the purposes of so called non-violation complaints under Article XXIII:1:b which, for the time being, are excluded from the realm of the TRIPS Agreement (see Article 26 DSU; Article 64:3, TRIPS Agreement)?

3. How would you describe the difference between the doctrine of legitimate expectations and the concept of the non violation complaint?

4. As the AB observes, the TRIPS Agreement rule against the bringing of non-violation complaints will expire on January 1, 2000, unless it is extended by action of the WTO Ministerial Conference. Recall that IPRs generally grant "negative rights" to holders: patents accord rights to prevent others from making, using, selling and importing; copyrights accord rights to prevent others from reproducing. Are IPRs intended to provide the kind of "market access" rights which the AB says underlies the concept of non-violation nullification or impairment? Why might governments be concerned about extending the non-violation form of action into the TRIPS arena? Can you imagine formally lawful arrangements which may result in nullification and impairment of TRIPS rights?

5. India objects to the panel's analysis of its domestic law. India suggests that the panel should have deferred to the Indian government's analysis of its legal system. India is in essence arguing against outside interference in its domestic affairs — a classical "sovereignty" concern. How did the AB deal

with this argument? Did the AB treat the matter as a question of fact or law? How was the burden of proof allocated (paras. 64-77)?

2. The Doctrine of Consistent Interpretation

We turn now to another aspect of the relationship between international, regional and national law, examining to what extent national or regional courts should respect and take into account rights and obligations enshrined in international agreements. A state party to a treaty is bound by that agreement on the basis of the principle of *pacta sunt servanda*, enshrined in Article 26 of the Vienna Convention. Generally speaking, this obligation only affects its relation with third states,[1] and does not resolve the question to what extent the agreement must be honored domestically. These are essentially questions of national (and regional) constitutional law, which may vary from country to country. The first doctrine of paramount importance is the doctrine of consistent interpretation. This doctrine is addressed in an article by Thomas Cottier and Krista Schefer, which is then followed by the *Hermès* decision of the ECJ.

The Relationship between World Trade Organization Law, National and Regional Law

Thomas Cottier and Krista Nadakavukaren Schefer*

*****

2. The Relationship Between World Trade Organization Rules and National or Regional Law Before National or Regional Authorities and Courts of Law

---

[1]A state party to a treaty may also be obligated with respect to individuals in the human rights context. This was not the classical conception of treaty law at the time the VCLT was negotiated, and so is not expressly addressed by its terms.
*1 JIEL 83 (1998).

Interpretation and application of national or regional rules in accordance with World Trade Organization rules: the doctrine of consistent interpretation

Before turning to the difficult issue of direct effect, attention should be drawn to the important rule of consistent interpretation. According to this doctrine, where a national rule allows for different interpretations, national or regional law has to be construed in accordance with international obligations. In many instances, conformity in interpretation allows bridging alleged divergences between international, national or regional law, making adherence to both a treaty and national law possible. Jurisprudence from both the USA, the European Communities, and Switzerland adhere to this principle.

In the USA, the doctrine of consistent interpretation was introduced early in the history of the Supreme Court. In the case *Charming Betsy* [2 Cranch 64 (1804)], Chief Justice Marshall held, "an act of Congress ought never to be construed to violate the law of nations if any other construction is possible".

The European Court of Justice (ECJ) used a similar reasoning in *Werner and Leifer* [Case C-70/94 [1995] ECR I-3189 and Case C-83/94, [1995] ECR I-3231], referring to Article XI of GATT to confirm and support its findings. In *Commission v Federal Republic of Germany Case* [C-61/94, [1996] ECR I 3989], the Court, inspired by *Marleasing* [Case C-106/89, [1990] ECR I -4135] and successive case law, explicitly stated the rule of consistent interpretation to apply to external relations based on international agreements. The Court referred first to the general rules of treaty interpretation "requiring the parties to any agreement to do so in good faith in its performance" and that "the Community must interpret [the International Dairy Arrangement's] terms in such a way as to encourage the attainment of the objectives pursued" [*Marleasing*, at paras. 30-31]. It then held that Community legislation ought to be construed in a manner consistent with the international agreement concerned:

> When the wording of secondary Community legislation is open to more than one interpretation, preference should be given as far as possible to the interpretation which renders the provision consistent with the [EC] Treaty. Likewise, an implementing regulation must, if possible, be given the interpretation consistent with the basic regulation (see C-90/92 *Dr Tretter v Hauptzollamt Stuttgart-Ost* [1993] ECR I-3569 paragraph 11).

> Similarly, the primacy of international agreements concluded by the Community over provisions of secondary Community legislation means that such provision must, so far as possible, be interpreted in a manner that is consistent with those agreements. [*Marleasing*, at para. 52]

Given the reasoning of the Court on the primacy of international law, the rule of consistent interpretation should also apply to rules of the EC Treaty and not be limited to secondary legislation. The doctrine, on the other hand, finds its limitation in constellations where the wording and purpose of EC law cannot be found compatible with international obligations. It is here that the issue of direct effect will come into play.

In its 1968 decision *Frigero v EVED*, [94 I 669 (1968)] the Swiss Supreme Court established that national law has to be applied and construed in accordance with international obligations whenever there are doubts as to the proper meaning of the domestic statutory language. This also applies to WTO law. In *Chanel S.A.*, [122 III 469 (1996)] the Swiss Supreme Court, in deciding a fundamental issue on parallel importation in trademarks, took recourse, inter alia, to Article 16 of the TRIPS Agreement in order to construe Swiss trademark law which had been textually modelled after the 1988 First Trade Mark directive of the European Communities.

As Ernst-Ulrich Petersmann urged national and Community courts to interpret laws to be GATT-conforming, we assert now that this doctrine of conformity in interpretation remains of paramount importance in the context of the WTO. Courts are able to take international obligations into account when national law is broadly framed and where there is no fundamental conflict between national and international rules. The WTO trade rules are often more detailed than those in national legislation (particularly the legislation of the civil law tradition). More detailed language can be found in the agreements and it should be used to define the content of rights and obligations. In our view, interpreting domestic laws in conformity with the WTO avoids the traditional or statutory prohibitions on courts to base decisions on international law. The concept therefore can assist all members of the WTO alike in honoring the principle of *pacta sunt servanda*. Moreover, the principle of consistent interpretation not only applies to WTO members operating under a monist tradition. It is an equally useful and necessary concept for courts with a dualist approach to international law. Judges should not apply and construe national rules without giving regard to pertinent international obligations within the bounds of national law. They share in the responsibility of all state bodies under the principle of *pacta sunt servanda* to avoid, to the utmost extent possible, conflicts and clashes with international law and therefore the risks of international disputes and retaliation.

The WTO rules, so far, have not been frequently involved before courts of law. This is partly because worldwide the subject is not widely taught at law schools and neither attorneys nor judges are sufficiently familiar with the matter in order to argue their cases consistently with detailed WTO obligations, as construed by WTO panels and the Appellate Body. In dualist countries, the gap is even larger and WTO rules are sometimes treated with benign neglect or even amused disrespect. The doctrine of consistent interpretation clearly needs to be further spread as the prime inroad of WTO rules in daily operations of national or regional authorities and courts of law. Much depends on the successful education and training of lawyers in WTO law; the doctrine of consistent interpretation is bound to remain largely irrelevant, despite *Charming Betsy*, *Commission v Germany*, *Frigerio* or *Chanel*, until basic knowledge of and sensitization to WTO rules has taken place in the legal community at large. All this can be done without treading on the more sensitive grounds of direct effect. This problem, to which we now turn, should no longer impair the potential of the principle of consistent interpretation in international law.

*****

Hermès International v. FHT Marketing Choice BV

(Case C-53/96)
The Court of Justice of the European Communities
16 June 1998

The Court: G.C. Rodríguez Iglesias, President, C. Gulmann, H. Ragnemalm and M. Wathelet (Presidents of Chambers), G.F. Mancini, J.C. Moitinho de Almeida, P.J.G. Kapteyn, J.L. Murray, D.A.O. Edward (Rapporteur), J.-P.

Puissochet, G. Hirsch, P. Jann and L. Sevón, Judges, Advocate General: G. Tesauro, Registrar: L. Hewlett, Administrator . . .

Judgment:

1. By order of 1 February 1996, received at the Court on 22 February 1996, the Arrondissementsrechtbank (District Court) Amsterdam referred to the Court for a preliminary ruling under Article 177 of the EC Treaty a question on the interpretation of Article 50(6) of the Agreement on Trade-Related Aspects of Intellectual Property Rights (hereinafter "the TRIPS Agreement"), as set out in Annex 1 C to the Agreement establishing the World Trade Organisation (hereinafter "the WTO Agreement"), approved on behalf of the Community, as regards matters within its competence, in Council Decision 94/800/EC of 22 December 1994 (OJ 1994 L 336, p. 1).

2. That question was raised in proceedings between Hermès International (hereinafter "Hermès"), a partnership limited by shares governed by French law, and FHT Marketing Choice BV (hereinafter "FHT"), a company incorporated under Netherlands law, concerning trade-mark rights owned by Hermès.

Legal background

3. Article 99(1) of Council Regulation (EC) No 40/94 of 20 December 1993 on the Community trade mark (OJ 1994 L 11, p. 1) states, under the heading "Provisional and protective measures", as follows: "Application may be made to the courts of a Member State, including Community trade mark courts, for such provisional, including protective, measures in respect of a Community trade mark or Community trade mark application as may be available under the law of that State in respect of a national trade mark, even if, under this Regulation, a Community trade mark court of another Member State has jurisdiction as to the substance of the matter."

4. Under Article 143(1) that regulation was to enter into force on the sixtieth day following the day of its publication in the Official Journal of the European Communities. The regulation was published on 14 January 1994 and therefore entered into force on 15 March 1994.

5. Article 1 of Decision 94/800 provides as follows: "The following multi-lateral agreements and acts are hereby approved on behalf of the European Community with regard to that portion of them which falls within the competence of the European Community: — the Agreement establishing the World Trade Organization, and also the Agreements in Annexes 1, 2 and 3 to that Agreement. . . ."

6. Article 50 of the TRIPS Agreement provides:

1. The judicial authorities shall have the authority to order prompt and effective provisional measures: (a) to prevent an infringement of any intellectual property right from occurring, and in particular to prevent the entry into the channels of commerce in their jurisdiction of goods, including imported goods immediately after customs clearance; (b) to preserve relevant evidence in regard to the alleged infringement.

2. The judicial authorities shall have the authority to adopt provisional measures *inaudita altera parte* where appropriate, in particular where any delay is likely to cause irreparable harm to the right holder, or where there is a demonstrable risk of evidence being destroyed.

3. The judicial authorities shall have the authority to require the applicant to provide any reasonably available evidence in order to satisfy themselves with a sufficient degree of certainty that the applicant is the right holder and that the applicant's right is being infringed or that such infringement is imminent, and to order the applicant to provide a security or equivalent assurance sufficient to protect the defendant and to prevent abuse.

4. Where provisional measures have been adopted *inaudita altera parte*, the parties affected shall be given notice, without delay after the execution of the measures at the latest. A review, including a right to be heard, shall take place upon request of the defendant with a view to deciding, within a reasonable period after the notification of the measures, whether these measures shall be modified, revoked or confirmed.

. . .

6. Without prejudice to paragraph 4, provisional measures taken on the basis of paragraphs 1 and 2 shall, upon request by the defendant, be revoked or otherwise cease to have effect, if proceedings leading to a decision on the merits of the case are not initiated within a reasonable period, to be determined by the judicial authority ordering the measures where a Member's law so permits or, in the absence of such a determination, not to exceed 20 working days or 31 calendar days, whichever is the longer. . . .

7. The Final Act embodying the results of the Uruguay Round of multilateral trade negotiations (hereinafter "the Final Act") and, subject to conclusion, the WTO Agreement were signed in Marrakech on 15 April 1994 by the representatives of the Community and of the Member States.

8. Article 289(1) of the Netherlands Code of Civil Procedure (hereinafter "the Code") provides as follows:

In all cases in which, having regard to the interests of the parties, an immediate provisional measure is necessary on grounds of urgency, the application may be made at a hearing which the President shall hold for that purpose on working days which he shall fix.

9. In such a case, Article 290(2) of the Code provides that the parties may appear before the President under his "voluntary jurisdiction" to grant interim measures, in which case the applicant must be represented at the hearing by counsel, whereas the defendant may appear in person or be represented by counsel.

10. According to Article 292 of the Code, an interim measure adopted by the President does not prejudge the examination of the merits of the main proceedings.

11. Lastly, under Article 295 of the Code, an appeal against the provisional order may be lodged before the Gerechtshof (Court of Appeal) within two weeks of the delivery of that decision.

The facts in the main proceedings

12. By virtue of international registrations R 196 756 and R 199 735 designating the Benelux, Hermès is proprietor of the name "Hermès" and the name and device "Hermès" as trade marks.

13. Hermès applies those trade marks to inter alia neckties which it markets through a selective distribution system. In the Netherlands, "Hermès" neckties are sold by Galerie & Faïence BV and by the boutique Le Duc in Scheveningen and Zeist respectively.

14. On 21 December 1995, Hermès, believing that FHT was marketing copies of its ties, seized, with leave of the President of the Arrondissementsrechtbank Amsterdam, 10 ties in the possession of FHT itself and attached 453 ties held by PTT Post BV to the order of FHT.

15. On 2 January 1996, Hermès then applied to the President of the same court for an interim order requiring FHT to cease infringement of its copyright and trade mark. Hermès also requested the adoption of all measures necessary to bring the infringement definitively to an end.

16. In the order for reference, the President of the Arrondissementsrechtbank found that Hermès' claim that the ties seized at its request were counterfeit was plausible and that FHT could not reasonably argue that it had acted in good faith. He therefore granted Hermès' application and ordered FHT to cease any present or future infringement of Hermès' exclusive copyright and trade-mark rights.

17. In the same proceedings Hermès also requested the President of the Arrondissementsrechtbank to fix a period of three months from the date of service of the interim decision as the period within which FHT could, under Article 50(6), request revocation of those provisional measures and a period of 14 days as the period within which Hermès could initiate proceedings on the merits of the case, that period to run from the date on which FHT requested revocation.

18. The President of the Arrondissementsrechtbank considers that this last request of Hermès' cannot be granted, because Article 50(6) of the TRIPS

Agreement does not place any time-limit on the defendant's right to request revocation of provisional measures. He considers that the intention of that provision is, on the contrary, to allow the defendant to request revocation of a provisional measure at any time prior to delivery of judgment in the main proceedings. The period envisaged in that provision for initiation of proceedings on the merits cannot therefore be determined by reference to a period within which the defendant must request revocation of the provisional measures.

19. Nevertheless, the President of the Arrondissementsrechtbank is uncertain whether a period should be fixed within which Hermès must initiate proceedings on the merits. Such an obligation would be required if the measure ordered in the interim proceedings in question constituted a "provisional measure" within the meaning of Article 50 of the TRIPS Agreement.

20. The President of the Arrondissementsrechtbank observes that in interim proceedings under Netherlands law the defendant is summoned to appear, the parties have the right to be heard, and the judge hearing the application for interim measures makes an assessment of the substance of the case, which he also sets out in a reasoned written decision, against which an appeal may be lodged. Moreover, although the parties then have the right to initiate proceedings on the merits, in matters falling within the scope of the TRIPS Agreement they normally abide by the interim decision.

21. In those circumstances, the national court decided to stay proceedings and to refer the following question to the Court for a preliminary ruling: "Does an interim measure, as, for example, provided for in Article 289 et seq. of the Code of Civil Procedure, whereby an immediate, enforceable measure may be sought, fall within the scope of the expression 'provisional measures' within the meaning of Article 50 of the Agreement on Trade-Related Aspects of Intellectual Property Rights?"

Jurisdiction of the Court of Justice

22. The Netherlands, French and United Kingdom Governments have submitted that the Court of Justice has no jurisdiction to answer the question.

23. They refer in that regard to paragraph 104 of Opinion 1/94 of 15 November 1994 ([1994] ECR I-5267), in which the Court held that the provisions of the TRIPS Agreement relating to "measures ... to secure the effective protection of intellectual property rights", such as Article 50, essentially fall within the competence of the Member States and not that of the Community, on the ground that at the date when that Opinion was delivered, the Community had not exercised its internal competence in this area apart from in Council Regulation (EEC) No 3842/86 of 1 December 1986 laying down measures to prohibit the release for free circulation of counterfeit goods (OJ 1986 L 357, p. 1). According to the Netherlands, French and United Kingdom Governments, since the Community has still not adopted any further harmonising measures in the area in question, Article 50 of the TRIPS Agreement does not fall within the scope of application of Community law and the Court of Justice therefore has no jurisdiction to interpret that provision.

24. It should be pointed out, however, that the WTO Agreement was concluded by the Community and ratified by its Member States without any allocation between them of their respective obligations towards the other contracting parties.

25. Equally, without there being any need to determine the extent of the obligations assumed by the Community in concluding the agreement, it should be noted that when the Final Act and the WTO Agreement were signed by the Community and its Member States on 15 April 1994, Regulation No 40/94 had been in force for one month.

26. Article 50(1) of the TRIPS Agreement requires that judicial authorities of the contracting parties be authorised to order "provisional measures" to protect the interests of proprietors of trade-mark rights conferred under the laws of those parties. To that end, Article 50 lays down various procedural rules applicable to applications for the adoption of such measures.

27. Under Article 99 of Regulation No 40/94, rights arising from a Community trade mark may be safeguarded by the adoption of "provisional, including protective, measures".

567

28. It is true that the measures envisaged by Article 99 and the relevant procedural rules are those provided for by the domestic law of the Member State concerned for the purposes of the national trade mark. However, since the Community is a party to the TRIPS Agreement and since that agreement applies to the Community trade mark, the courts referred to in Article 99 of Regulation No 40/94, when called upon to apply national rules with a view to ordering provisional measures for the protection of rights arising under a Community trade mark, are required to do so, as far as possible, in the light of the wording and purpose of Article 50 of the TRIPS Agreement (see, by analogy, Case C-286/90 Poulsen and Diva Navigation [1992] ECR I-6019, paragraph 9, and Case C-61/94 Commission v Germany [1996] ECR I-3989, paragraph 52).

29. It follows that the Court has, in any event, jurisdiction to interpret Article 50 of the TRIPS Agreement.

30. It is immaterial that the dispute in the main proceedings concerns trade marks whose international registrations designate the Benelux.

31. First, it is solely for the national court hearing the dispute, which must assume responsibility for the order to be made, to assess the need for a preliminary ruling so as to enable it to give its judgment. Consequently, where the question referred to it concerns a provision which it has jurisdiction to interpret, the Court of Justice is, in principle, bound to give a ruling (see, to that effect, Joined Cases C-297/88 and C-197/89 Dzodzi [1990] ECR I-3763, paragraphs 34 and 35, and Case C-231/89 Gmurzynska-Bscher [1990] ECR I-4003, paragraphs 19 and 20).

32. Second, where a provision can apply both to situations falling within the scope of national law and to situations falling within the scope of Community law, it is clearly in the Community interest that, in order to forestall future differences of interpretation, that provision should be interpreted uniformly, whatever the circumstances in which it is to apply (see, to that effect, Case C-130/95 Giloy v Hauptzollamt Frankfurt am Main-Ost [1997] ECR I-4291, paragraph 28, and Case C-28/95 Leur-Bloem v Inspecteur der Belastingdienst/Ondernemingen [1997] ECR I-4161, paragraph 34). In the present case, as has been pointed out in paragraph 28 above, Article 50 of

the TRIPS Agreement applies to Community trade marks as well as to national trade marks.

33. The Court therefore has jurisdiction to rule on the question submitted by the national court.

The question referred for a preliminary ruling

34. The national court asks whether a measure whose purpose is to put an end to alleged infringements of a trade-mark right and which is adopted in the course of a procedure distinguished by the following features: — the measure is characterised under national law as an "immediate provisional measure" and its adoption must be made "on grounds of urgency", — the opposing party is summoned and is heard if he appears before the court, — the decision adopting the measure is reasoned and given in writing following an assessment of the substance of the case by the judge hearing the interim application, — an appeal may be lodged against the decision, and — although the parties remain free to initiate proceedings on the merits of the case, the decision is usually accepted by the parties as a "final" resolution of their dispute, is to be regarded as a "provisional measure" within the meaning of Article 50 of the TRIPS Agreement.

35. It should be stressed at the outset that, although the issue of the direct effect of Article 50 of the TRIPS Agreement has been argued, the Court is not required to give a ruling on that question, but only to answer the question of interpretation submitted to it by the national court so as to enable that court to interpret Netherlands procedural rules in the light of that article.

36. According to Article 50(1) of the TRIPS Agreement, that article applies to "prompt and effective" measures, whose purpose is to "prevent an infringement of any intellectual property right from occurring".

37. A measure such as the order made by the national court in the main proceedings meets that definition. Its purpose is to put an end to an infringement of trade mark rights; it is expressly characterised in national law as an "immediate provisional measure"; and it is adopted "on grounds of urgency".

38. Furthermore, it is common ground that the parties have the right, whether or not they make use of it, to initiate, following the adoption of the

measure in question, proceedings on the merits of the case. Thus, in law, the measure is not regarded as definitive.

39. The conclusion that a measure such as the order made by the national court is a "provisional measure" within the meaning of Article 50 of the TRIPS Agreement is not affected by the other characteristics of that order.

40. First, as to the fact that the other party is summoned and is entitled to be heard, it should be observed that Article 50(2) of the TRIPS Agreement provides that "where appropriate" provisional measures may be ordered "*inaudita altera parte*" and that Article 50(4) lays down specific procedures in that regard. Although those provisions allow for the adoption, where appropriate, of provisional measures *inaudita altera parte* that cannot mean that only measures adopted in that way are to be characterised as provisional for the purposes of Article 50 of the TRIPS Agreement. It is, on the contrary, clear from those provisions that in all other cases provisional measures are to be adopted in accordance with the principle *audi alteram partem*.

41. Second, the fact that the judge hearing the application for interim measures gives a reasoned decision in writing does not preclude that decision being characterised as a "provisional measure" within the meaning of Article 50 of the TRIPS Agreement, since that provision lays down no rule as to the form of the decision ordering such a measure.

42. Third, there is nothing in the wording of Article 50 of the TRIPS Agreement to indicate that the measures to which that article refers must be adopted without an assessment by the judge of the substantive aspects of the case. On the contrary, Article 50(3), in terms of which the judicial authorities are to have authority to require the applicant to provide any reasonably available evidence in order to satisfy themselves with a sufficient degree of certainty that his right is being infringed or that such infringement is imminent, implies that the "provisional measures" are based, at least to a certain extent, upon such an assessment.

43. Fourth, as regards the fact that an appeal may be brought against a measure such as that in question in the main proceedings in this case, it should be observed that, although Article 50(4) of the TRIPS Agreement expressly provides for the possibility of requesting a "review" where the

provisional measure has been adopted *inaudita altera parte*, no provision of that article precludes that "provisional measures" should in general be open to appeal.

44. Lastly, any possible willingness of the parties to accept the interim judgment as a "final" resolution of their dispute cannot alter the legal nature of a measure characterised as "provisional" for the purposes of Article 50 of the TRIPS Agreement.

45. The answer to the question submitted must therefore be that a measure whose purpose is to put an end to alleged infringements of a trade-mark right and which is adopted in the course of a procedure distinguished by the following features: — the measure is characterised under national law as an "immediate provisional measure" and its adoption must be required "on grounds of urgency", — the opposing party is summoned and is heard if he appears before the court, — the decision adopting the measure is reasoned and given in writing following an assessment of the substance of the case by the judge hearing the interim application, — an appeal may be lodged against the decision, and — although the parties remain free to initiate proceedings on the merits of the case, the decision is usually accepted by the parties as a "final" resolution of their dispute, is to be regarded as a "provisional measure" within the meaning of Article 50 of the TRIPS Agreement

*****

On those grounds, The Court, in answer to the question referred to it by the Arrondissementsrechtbank Amsterdam by order of 1 February 1996,

Hereby Rules:

A measure whose purpose is to put an end to alleged infringements of a trade-mark right and which is adopted in the course of a procedure distinguished by the following features: — the measure is characterised under national law as an "immediate provisional measure" and its adoption must be required "on grounds of urgency", — the opposing party is summoned and is heard if he appears before the court, — the decision adopting the measure is reasoned and given in writing following an assessment of the substance of the case by the judge hearing the interim application, — an appeal may lodged against the decision, and — although the parties remain free to initiate proceedings on the merits of the case, the decision is usually accepted by the parties as a "final" resolution of their dispute, is to be regarded as a "provisional measure" within the meaning of Article 50 of the Agreement on Trade-Related Aspects of Intellectual Property Rights, as set out in Annex 1 C to the Agreement establishing the World Trade Organisation, approved on behalf of the Community, as regards matters within its competence, in Council Decision 94/800/EC of 22 December 1994.

Notes and Questions

1. The *Hermès International* case is the first judgment of the European Court of Justice construing and applying the TRIPS Agreement. It is perhaps not an accident that the first case arose in the context of procedural rules. Indeed, the rules of "Part III — Section 2: Civil and Administrative Procedures and Remedies" are particularly detailed and offer ample opportunities for consistent interpretation. Procedural rules, in particular in civil law countries, are often less detailed than substantive rules. The particular nature and character of these TRIPS provisions stem from the effort to combine Anglo-American common law and civil law rules.

2. The Court construed a Dutch provision on civil procedure not in light of EU law, but in accordance with Article 50 of the TRIPS Agreement. How did the Court proceed? Did it invoke the doctrine of consistent interpretation? What is its underlying rationale for examining whether Dutch law must prescribe a fixed period within which to initiate proceedings on the merits of the alleged trademark infringement?

3. While the issue of the direct effect of the TRIPS Agreement was argued, the Court did not address this issue in substance (para. 35). How was it possible to dispose the case without granting direct effect?

---

3. The Doctrine of Direct Effect

We now turn to the second and more controversial doctrine of direct effect of international agreements. In Chapter II, we studied an article by

Joseph Weiler which considered the doctrine of direct effect in EU law. The principal issue examined in that context was the extent to which the EC Treaty and secondary EU legislation are directly applicable in the law of the member states. Here we examine the doctrine of direct (or self-executing) effect in relation to international law more generally — bearing in mind that the EC Treaty is viewed by the ECJ as a constitutional charter which has juridical characteristics different than general international law.

It is apparent that giving direct effect or granting self-execution to international norms considerably reinforces their impact — as such norms provide direct entitlements for private parties. Directly effective (or self-executing) norms can be relied upon by individuals in courts, and may render national or regional law inapplicable to the extent that the latter rules cannot be construed in accordance with international law under the doctrine of consistent interpretation. It is not surprising that this doctrine is controversial. As for any other field of law, application of the doctrine of direct effect with regard to IPRs norms depends on national or regional constitutional law.

It should be noted at the outset that the doctrine of direct effect can only be deployed in legal systems which follow the concept of monism of national and international law. It cannot apply in countries operating under the concept of dualism, with its strict separation of international and national or regional law. In so-called "dualist" countries, the legal effect of international agreements is limited to international relations in accord with the principle of *pacta sunt servanda*. International law does not have status in domestic law, and private parties can only rely on such law to the extent that domestic statutes so prescribe.

Notwithstanding that direct or self-executing effect within monist systems is a matter of national law, commonalities among monist systems can be observed. As relevant international rules are to be applied by courts of law, they must be justiciable rules (i.e., courts must be able to apply them). Normally, it is said that rules have to be sufficiently precise in order to grant rights and obligations to private parties. The test essentially seeks to separate out norms which prescribe further implementation of a program, which norms inherently need implementation by the legislature in order to become operational. Such norms are not justiciable. However, we learn from the field of human rights that openly textured rules and principles may also be justiciable — that density (i.e. level of detail) and precision are not necessarily critical. The central issue may rather be whether courts consider the subject matter within their field of competence. This will often be

573

the case in the field of IPRs, as they pertain — by their very nature — to private rights in national and regional law. Indeed, IPRs agreements in a number of European countries have a long tradition of direct effect. The discussion of this topic was newly invigorated with the advent of the WTO. The following excerpt provides a succinct survey of the doctrine in the European Union, the United States and Switzerland. It focuses on trade regulation — as to which IPRs have become a mainstay with the conclusion of the TRIPS Agreement.

The Relationship between World Trade Organization Law, National and Regional Law

Thomas Cottier and Krista Nadakavukaren Schefer*

*****

The relationship of World Trade Organization rules and inconsistent national or regional rules: the problem of direct effect

1. The concept of direct effect

In cases of explicit conflict between WTO rules and national or regional rules (situations which cannot be remedied by consistent interpretation), a situation of conflict exists in a domestic context and with domestic law. While international law clearly prevails as a matter of international relations under state responsibility discussed above, the matter is controversial and unresolved as a matter of domestic or EC law. It is generally addressed under the doctrine of direct effect or self-executing effect of international law rules, these terms being used interchangeably in the present context.

In this study, "direct effect" is used to mean that a private person in a state (or Union, respectively) may base a claim in, and be granted relief from, the domestic courts of that state against another private person or the state on the basis of the state's obligations under an international treaty.

---

*1 JIEL 83 (1998).

Such claims can be made without a transformation of the obligation by national or regional rule-makers. They may equally be made against implementing legislation on grounds that such legislation is not compatible with international law.

Direct effect brings about the empowerment of three actors: the administration, private actors, and the courts. The administration is empowered to act without specific internal legislation, directly relying upon treaty provisions, provided that the legislator or the government decides to act this way. Private actors directly derive rights and assume obligations under a self-executing treaty. Importantly, they may use such rights and obligations to challenge domestic law. But foremost, the position of courts is reinforced *vis-à-vis* government and national or regional legislators to the extent that the courts may overrule national or regional rules inconsistent with treaty obligations based upon supremacy of international law. Direct effect, in other words, has a fundamental impact on constitutional power relations among domestic actors, private and public.

Whether or not a rule is apt for such an application has been a matter of national or regional law and doctrine. The issue only exists under constitutions that follow the monist doctrine. It does not come up in dualist systems, absent explicit treaty or statutory provisions which empower authorities to rely directly upon international law. Nevertheless, state practice in monist countries has developed comparable criteria which rely upon intention, context and purpose of the treaty. The criteria centre, explicitly or implicitly, around the precision ("Bestimmtheit") of the rule concerned. Moreover, the matter of direct effect is not one of the entire treaty, but rather focuses on individual provisions. Behind the criteria of sufficient precision we find the concept, often unexpressed, of justiciability of the rule. The rights and obligations of a rule, in other words, need to be of a quality which can be understood and applied by courts within their competences. Thus, obligations of a clearly programmatic nature (e.g., a negotiating programme) which need further work on the international level or by national or regional legislation cannot be self-executing.

Justiciability cannot be determined merely on the basis of the wording of a norm. In many instances, courts have applied and construed broad principles, such as general human rights guarantees. They have done so because the application of such broad rules and principles has been considered to be within the competence of courts of law in determining individual rights and obligations. Such determination may be made by looking at the

575

wording and context of the provision, but it can also be found in the intent of negotiators and national legislators. Looking at WTO rules, there can be little doubt that most of them are sufficiently precise to be construed by courts. This is equally true for exceptions which do not show structural differences to comparable norms in national or regional law. Moreover, to the extent that principles, rules and exceptions are being applied and legally construed by panels and the Appellate Body — and indeed made more precise by this very process of creating precedents — they can be increasingly applied, and relied upon, by national courts in many instances. The basic problem lies in determining whether these rules are in a national court's competence as set out within the national structures of government and the separation of powers. It can be readily seen, therefore, that the underlying issue (except for clearly programmatic norms) again is a problem of national or regional constitutional law. Answers cannot be found on the level of international law and the WTO.

*****

The present status of World Trade Organization Agreements in national and regional law systems

The judicial history of direct effect of GATT rules in court practice is well documented. Such effect was formerly accorded in a limited number of cases only, in particular in Italy and exceptionally in the USA prior to the Tokyo Round. The doctrine of direct effect, however, did not succeed in shaping general relations between GATT and national or regional law since such effect was denied in *International Fruit* [Joined Cases 21 to 24/72 [1972], ECR 1219] by the European Court of Justice in 1972. We briefly look at three typical jurisdictions: The EC as a constitution-in-the-making, the USA as a superpower, and Switzerland as an example of a medium-sized trading nation.

1. European Union

Perhaps no other court of law is more aware of the liberalizing and powerful results of direct effect than the European Court of Justice (ECJ or the Court). Ever since *van Gend en Loos*, the Court has construed textually programmatic EC norms as constituting individual rights having direct effect. This, together with the doctrine of primauté (*Costa v. Enel*), gave EU law predominance over national law. In parallel the Court developed a doctrine of direct effect and effet utile for regional trade agreements, in particular the EFTA Agreements and Association Agreements. This reinforced the market access rights of foreign exporters into the Community to a considerable degree. Foreigners are now in a position to invoke the provisions of these Agreements before the ECJ notwithstanding the fact that there exists international dispute settlement machinery.

The Court's case law with respect to the GATT presents a stark contrast to its doctrine of effet utile within the European context. There are two main arguments the Court has consistently used for denying the direct effect of the GATT: (i) the GATT has been considered to be an instrument of negotiations, rather than adjudication; and (ii) the GATT's provisions are not considered to be sufficiently precise for the purpose of direct effect. This assessment is not merely applied in order to determine direct effect in terms of the rights of individuals before the courts of law, but also in the context of disputes brought by a Member State against the Community, where criteria of denying direct effect strictly speaking are not in place.

On the other hand, it is important to note that the Court's attitudes to GATT (and presumably to the WTO) rules are nuanced. Besides applying the important doctrine of consistent interpretation, the Court has taken recourse to GATT law where an EC instrument directly refers to GATT rules on anti-dumping. Moreover, the Court did not find any difficulty in construing GATT rules in the context of assessing the trade practices of trading partners within the 1984 "New Instrument" (now the Trade Barriers Regulation). Finally, in a dispute involving national measures of a member state, the Court found no difficulty construing in great detail the GATT International Dairy Arrangement.

With the advent of the WTO, the Court may re-evaluate the arguments set out in prior case law. First, the traditional argument of vagueness loses credibility in light of (a) additional concretization of GATT and (b) an increasing number of panel reports elaborated under judicial proceedings and providing specific guidance for interpretation. Second, the major changes in dispute settlement, in particular the introduction of the Appellate Body, cannot remain without an impact. Third, the qualification of GATS and TRIPs as being mixed agreements, to be ratified both by the EU and the member states, raises the issue of independent interpretation and qualification of these agreements by the national courts of law in their own right.

It is not entirely clear whether the judicial policy of the Court and the Council is binding upon the member states of the EU. It should be emphasized that TRIPs and GATS are mixed agreements. They were ratified by the European Communities as well as the Member States in accordance with Advisory Opinion I/94 of the European Court of Justice [*supra* this book, Chapter II]. Courts of the Member States, in particular those in Germany and Austria (as well as Swiss courts), have taken recourse to the provisions of the Berne and Paris Conventions — provisions which are now being incorporated into the TRIPs Agreement. It is difficult to see why such rules should alter their quality (the more so since obligations have been clarified by the "plus Berne and Paris approach" of the TRIPs Agreement). Clearly, most of them are not merely apt for the purpose of consistent interpretation of national laws, but also for direct effect. Interestingly, the German government partly acknowledged direct effect of substantive standards of the TRIPs Agreement. The matter, however, is far from uniformly settled in the EU. Courts in the UK have denied direct effect not only on grounds of UK law, but also on grounds of EU law. In his judgment, the High Court Judge particularly emphasized arguments and consideration of reciprocity in rejecting the proposition of direct effect of the TRIPs Agreement by way of EU law.

The dual membership of the EU and the Member States to the WTO is perhaps the most important policy argument in favour of reassessing judicial policies in the EU. The effects of protecting instruments inconsistent with WTO obligations are interesting to observe. While the issue of direct effect of GATT rules (and the relationship of GATT and EU law under Article 234 para. 1 EC Treaty) has been controversial among lower German administrative courts, defence strategies against GATT inconsistent instruments have shifted towards constitutional arguments. The cost of denying direct effect to GATT rules is potential turmoil within the EU's legal order. Following the German Bundesverfassungsgericht in its decision on the Maastricht treaty, the Verwaltungsgericht Frankfurt am Main has held EU regulation 404/93 partly inapplicable on grounds of German constitutional law [*Atlanta Fruchthandelsgesellschaft*, Case 1 E 798/95 (v), 1 E 2929/93]. This correlation is of great importance. The policy of the ECJ of ignoring the GATT for the sake of securing secondary EU law may undermine EU law from a different angle and lead to an erosion of the primacy of EU law over national law and to Rechtszersplitterung: serious fragmentation, disruption and weakening of the emerging internal federal structure of EU law.

Politically, the courts have been discouraged from reassessing the situation under the WTO Agreements by the Council Decision Implementing the Uruguay Round. Preambular language qualifies the Uruguay Round agreements as unfit for direct effect; and it is unclear to what extent the recital is binding on either the ECJ or the national courts. In *Lenzing AG* [1996] RPC 245], the statement was given considerable weight in refuting direct effect of the TRIPs Agreement by way of EU law in the UK. On the other hand, it should be noted that the Dublin II proposals for a new Article 113a EC Treaty, plainly banning the direct effect of multilateral trade agreements in the new areas (TRIPs, investment and services) as a matter of primary, and thus constitutional, EU law was not retained at the Amsterdam ministerial conference of 1997. The situation thus is controversial and far from settled.

2. United States of America

Prevailing attitudes within the EU are a clear reflection of the legal situation in the USA. In the field of trade regulation, the USA adopted a "non-policy" of applying some treaty provisions directly and refusing to apply others in national courts, with no very clear method of analysis.

The Comments to the Restatement (Third) of Foreign Relations Law of the United States suggests that in the case of no express request by the Executive or Congress for implementing legislation, a treaty signed by the USA is presumed to be self-executing. Those studying the courts' applications of direct effect nevertheless are often faced with examining the judges' analyses of the negotiators' intent. A decision from the Ninth Circuit explaining the judicial interpretation of self-execution in the USA has become the standard reference for US lawyers. The opinion states:

> The extent to which an international agreement establishes affirmative and judicially enforceable obligations without implementing legislation must be determined in each case by reference to many contextual factors: the purposes of the treaty and the objectives of its creators, the implementation, the availability and feasibility of alternative enforcement methods, and the immediate and long-range social consequences of self-execution or non-self-execution. [*People of Saipan v. United States Department of Interior*, 502 F. 2d 90 (9ᵗʰ Cir. 1974)]

Trade treaties have historically been granted self-executing status in US courts. Individuals victim to unlawful expropriations, for instance, have successfully invoked the USA's Friendship, Commerce and Navigation treaties with the offending foreign state to protest such actions. Recently, however, ratification of the USA's three most important free trade agreements was made contingent upon the inclusion of an explicit denial of each agreement's self-execution. Such is also the case with the WTO Agreements. In the field of trade regulation, we observe a significant departure from established traditions of direct effect under the US constitution. While denial of such effect by the President or the Senate through means of a mere "declaration" or "condition" is controversial, the exclusion was introduced by way of implementing congressional legislation in the case of the WTO.

The language of the US WTO implementing legislation explicitly prohibits the direct reliance on the Agreement by the courts in cases brought by or against individuals or states. While the federal government may, looking to the implementing legislation, sue a federal agency or state based upon an alleged violation of WTO obligations, an individual's case based on GATT, GATS, or TRIPs will be dismissed for lack of standing. It would be interesting to study whether courts would even be allowed to hear arguments based on WTO rules, under the *Betsy* doctrine of consistent interpretation, if brought forth in a private suit.

The foreseeable future does not seem to hold much promise for a change in the USA's views on direct effect of the WTO Agreements. Attorney Gary Horlick, a close observer of US trade policy, notes that political leaders in the USA have cast doubt on whether the WTO should have any effect in US law, most notably the Clinton Administration, which claims that it would ignore any inconvenient panel rulings and prefer to pay compensation. More internationally minded members of the Bar would probably be supportive, others (either because of protectionist clients or out of genuine conviction) would oppose direct effect loudly enough for the public to believe that there is no consensus in the legal community.

3. Switzerland

While direct effect is strongly discouraged by the major trading partners and dominant powers within the WTO system, it is interesting to observe that these attitudes are not necessarily shared by governments of medium-sized trading nations. Switzerland is a monistic nation in terms of international legal obligations. Indeed, Swiss courts have perhaps been generally more willing than other nations' judiciaries to recognize treaty provisions as self-executing, and international law prevails over domestic legislation.

However, in actuality, the Swiss' application of internationally negotiated rules is not without important exception in case law. The Supreme

Court has met demands of direct effect of international trade rules with utmost caution. While it was affirmed with regard to the EFTA Convention [*Banque de Crédit*, BGE 98 Ia 385 (1972)] it had been denied to private operators for the Swiss EC Free Trade Agreement of 1972 on several accounts. In 1986, the Swiss Federal Court held (in line with the ECJ) the GATT to be not available to an individual in Swiss courts of law [*Adams*, BGE 104 IV 175 (1978)]. The Court's reasoning was that the language of the provisions in question was too vague to be applied by the courts. Such grounds, say many commentators, were not well-founded at the time of the decision, and would be even less valid for the much more detailed WTO Agreements. Beyond wording, it is evident that direct effect of trade agreements was, at the time, at odds with weak legislation on competition law and a high density of cartels as a main trait of the Swiss economy. This has changed in the mean-time. In this context, the language of the Executive found in the explanatory notes of the Uruguay Round implementing legislation is telling. Policies of affirming the possibility of direct effect, strongly argued for by the government in the context of the Swiss EC Free Trade Agreement and of primacy of international law were upheld, albeit more moderately, in the case of global WTO law. With respect to private claims based upon the TRIPs Agreement provisions, the Executive, supported by scholars, has stated that direct effect is to be afforded the Agreement. For the other Agreements, the Executive implies that it would want the Court to recognize at least some of the provisions of the specific agreements as self-executing. The Executive first reaffirms its commitment to the general principles used to determine whether a treaty provision has direct effect — referring as well to the Swiss Court's earlier GATT decision analysis — and then declares that each WTO Agreement's treaty provision must be examined separately to make such a determination. Without further indicating its position on particular obligations, the Executive states that "for certain provisions in the various Agreements, the possibility [that they will be given direct effect] cannot be excluded".

While leaving the matter to the courts, the Swiss Executive, and unlike the EC Council, has not, at any rate, discouraged the judiciary from developing a doctrine of direct effect. Moreover, unlike the US Congress, direct effect of the WTO Agreement has not been an issue before Parliament and no attempt to exclude it by statutory language was ever undertaken.

In July of 1997, the Swiss Federal Court once again addressed a claim arguing in part that a national regime for auctioning import licenses was a violation of Switzerland's GATT obligations [Decision 2A.496/1996].

While the Court explicitly refrained from deciding *obiter dictum* whether the WTO Agreements are to be considered directly effective in Switzerland, the current Court — unlike the High Court in the UK — did acknowledge the changed circumstances under the new WTO Agreement as significant. However, the Court also commented that several of the new WTO Agreements still have unclear or flexible provisions, leaving open sufficient doubt of what direction the future decisions will take as to prevent the making of reliable predictions. The Court did rely to a large extent on academic writings on the various WTO provisions, and with Swiss jurists favouring direct effect combined with changing general attitudes in legislation towards competition policy and the abolition of internal trade barriers since the 1992 rejection of the European Economic Area (EEA) Agreement, it is not unlikely that many provisions of the WTO Agreements will be recognized as self-executing in Swiss courts of law.

The political economy of denying direct effect

The recent and predominant attitudes towards direct effect in the EU and the USA, as well as by the Swiss Supreme Court, can be explained in terms of political economy which explains the frequently hidden agenda of actors and authors. Much of the following has already been set forth by the authors referred to above. It is apparent that in the USA and the European Communities, as well as in many other countries, the effect of WTO rules is intended to be limited to international responsibility without threatening the predominance of national (or Community) rules in a domestic context. It is a strategy of combining the utmost effect of WTO law abroad with a view to foster market access rights while leaving traditional constitutional allocations of power at home as unimpaired as possible. Also, it is apparent that none of even the major players is in a position to impose its domestic consensus or majority rule on any of the other members. Divergence with national law therefore cannot be excluded, and WTO may impair national regulations. Denial of direct effect therefore offers an exit route to escape such divergencies. To a large extent the political economy of denying direct effect reflects predominant producers' interests in major trading nations, and the unilateral granting of procedural rights and domestic enforcement of WTO obligations is bound to be seen as the equivalent of a trade concession. From an economic or individual rights' point of view, it is difficult to sustain the denial of direct effect of suitable rules. The matter, however, is more than an expression of protectionism. Constitutional structural issues are involved. This is what John Jackson categorizes as a "hierarchy of norms" problem, and is in our opinion of tremendous practical importance for coming to a consensus on what to do about the direct effect of the WTO Agreements.

The maintenance of the domestic constitution's primacy within a national system can be justified by a number of arguments and structural concerns of 'constitutional economy' which need to be carefully examined and balanced against apparent economic advantages of direct effect. First, as the WTO Agreements reach more deeply into national legal systems and more directly affect the life of the individual, distribution of powers within national or regional governance will be altered. Direct effect not only enhances the powers of private actors in foreign policy, but it also enhances the powers of courts vis-a-vis rule-making authorities and the executive branch. Giving direct effect to WTO rules in agriculture, for example, fundamentally shifts powers from the EC Council and Parliament not only to the Commission, but also the European Courts. In the USA, direct effect would be to the detriment of Congress and its constitutional power to regulate foreign commerce, arguably the most important foreign policy prerogative of the 21st century. Direct effect might give courts a role for which neither the judges nor the constitutional framework are sufficiently prepared.

Second, foreign policy and economic policy are increasingly indistinguishable. Constitutional shifts induced by direct effect not only affect foreign relations but have equally profound impacts on traditional allocations of domestic constitutional powers.

Third, limitations imposed by courts on the basis of the direct effect of WTO provisions may either hinder foreign policy goals which no longer can be pursued by other (military) means or spur a formal or, more likely, informal retreat from WTO membership. The USA and the European Union have a great deal of global responsibility. Both depend on effective instruments of foreign policy to negotiate and to fulfill these responsibilities. They have potentially extensive retaliatory powers. In this context, considerations of a level playing field in external relations, particularly among the major powers, is paramount. Considerations of reciprocity in terms of enforcement of rights and obligations essentially drive executive and judicial foreign policies in order to keep a balance of power. Few are prepared to accept that WTO rules have more bite at home than abroad.

The implications of direct effect on the constitutional economy need to be carefully examined for all countries. The shift of essential regulatory activities to the international level of WTO law does not leave any member unimpaired. Yet, concerns of global responsibility and foreign policy are less important for most countries. Importantly, they do not dispose of significant retaliatory powers. The market is too small, and dependence on foreign markets paramount. These qualities and strong reliance on the law to secure market access abroad successfully make direct effect easier to offer. Switzerland, like many of the smaller trading nations, therefore, is in a better position to employ the doctrine of direct effect by virtue of having less individual weight in influencing global affairs. Direct effect should help remedy the inherently protectionist interests that often dominate domestic politics. Smaller countries may set an example to others by emphasizing the benefits of judicially securing market access. They are in a better position to add yet another element to the constitutional doctrine of checks and balances: vertical separation of powers. To the same degree as interstate commerce is protected by means of individual constitutional rights in a domestic context, international commerce can be secured by granting effective checking rights to the international systems as applied by international bodies and by national courts.

Legal problems of direct effect in World Trade Organization law

The legal doctrine of direct effect and the political economy depending on overall foreign policy responsibilities reaffirm that we are dealing with a problem currently addressed primarily at the national or regional level. Yet there are unsolved problems on the level of WTO law as well. These problems are not mainly found on the level of substantive rules. Most norms of WTO Law can be construed as readily by national courts as they can be by panels and the Appellate Body. And nothing prevents a court from denying direct effect where norms are considered to be of a programmatic and non-judicial nature because it is thought that they need further elaboration in the process of negotiations or implementation by the legislative or executive branch. The problem lies in the system of enforcing WTO rights.

Under the DSU and Article XXIII of the GATT, the Members of the WTO have a primary obligation to remedy laws and practices held to be inconsistent with their obligations under the treaties. Nevertheless, a Member may offer adequate compensation in diplomatic negotiations until a solution to the problem can be found domestically. While no obligation exists to accept such an offer, there is no right to seek immediate removal of the measure. The Member whose benefits were nullified and impaired may merely withdraw concessions, if necessary by means of cross-sanctions.

A court giving direct effect to WTO rules cannot offer the intermediate stage of granting temporary compensation. Upon ruling that a national or regional rule or practice is inconsistent with WTO obligations, the court will have to remedy the inconsistency immediately by refusing to apply national law. Given the legal effect of precedent in common law, such rulings will have far-reaching consequences. To a lesser extent, this is true in civil law traditions as well. In both traditions, legislators will be practically obliged to change the law to take the court's ruling into account, or will have to pass a new law overriding the WTO provision in the national context. The options of temporary compensation and of accepting sanctions instead are no longer available.

Whether such effects are compatible with rights and obligations of Members under the WTO is questionable. On one hand, it may be argued that the existence of international remedies under a treaty does not rule out direct effect. If this is generally denied, direct effect could not take place at all: all treaties are subject to state responsibility and therefore are subject to international remedies. The ECJ (unlike the Swiss Supreme Court) correctly held in Kupferberg that the existence of international dispute settlement machinery does not exclude direct effect of Free Trade Agreements. On the other hand, direct effect curtails options for state conduct on the international level from the point of view of assuring level playing fields in trade policy. The ECJ concluded in International Fruit for reasons of reciprocity that direct effect of GATT rules cannot be granted.

By granting direct effect, a member may generally waive effective recourse to temporary compensation and be subjected to sanctions instead of remedying inconsistencies of its law. In many instances, this can be done without harm, in particular if the dispute does not bear upon touchy political issues. While this considerably reinforces the WTO system, such a further move to a strict concept of *pacta sunt servanda* would possibly require further changes to the DSU in coming negotiations or the designing of new responses open to courts of law. Unilateral waiver of rights to compensation and options to prefer sanctions are unlikely in the light of level playing field arguments and political needs for reciprocity in the case of major trading partners. Moreover, non-violation complaints and the present lack of obligations to perform pose particular problems in regard to direct effect.

All this demonstrates that the issue implies the elaboration of appropriate rules coordinating political actions and judicial avenues, in the WTO and/or unilaterally within the Members of the Organization.

It was seen that similar issues arise in the context of implementing adjudicated dispute settlement decisions of the WTO. However, the problem here is limited to a specific case and the interaction between compensation and domestic judicial enforcement of the decision can be developed and solved more readily.

*****

Notes and Questions

1. The doctrines of consistent interpretation and of direct effect are often confused. How would you distinguish their respective functions and differences?

2. Imagine that direct effect is granted in your country to the protection of undisclosed information under Article 39, TRIPS Agreement. What are the likely implications? What are the main changes that will occur in the field of trade secret protection?

3. What are the main arguments for and against direct effect of IPRs rules (both substantive norms and enforcement standards)? How would direct effect impact the overall international IPRs system? While the advantages are apparent for the strengthening of IPRs, is the relative lack of democratic legitimacy of global rules a serious impediment to direct effect? What might be done about this?

4. How would you recommend bringing about coherent doctrine and practice of direct effect among the major trading countries? If one country is prepared to recognize a doctrine of direct effect, and allow individuals to invoke international IPRs rules in its courts without additional legislation, while other countries do not recognize direct effect, should this lack of reciprocity discourage the first country from unilaterally allowing the doctrine to operate?

E. Basic Principles and Features

We observed in Chapter I that different forms of intellectual property, while serving comparable economic functions, exhibit significant legal differences. Rules pertaining to different forms are often specific and cannot be readily applied to other features of the international IPRs system. Moreover, rules vary among different jurisdictions and legal cultures. There are limits to generalization about the basic concepts underlying IPRs. Likewise, there are limits to generalization about the international IPRs system. Nevertheless, IPRs embody certain shared concepts which are generally common to different forms, and certain shared general principles are at the heart of the overarching and organizing structure of the international IPRs system. These principles operate in tandem.

Unlike customary international law or general principles of law, discussed above, the basic principles and features of the international IPRs system are grounded in treaty law. They are part of "positive" law. They apply to IPRs holders to the extent that these persons enjoy the benefits of international agreements concluded by their respective states. While basic principles may emerge at some stage to form part of general customary international law, this stage is far from being realized. Furthermore, it is doubtful whether this stage will be reached so long as traditional — and currently prevailing — policies of overall reciprocity of rights and obligations are prevalent throughout the international community. Nonetheless, particularly with the advent of the WTO and the entry into force of the TRIPS Agreement, an ever-increasing number of states follow certain principles that may be called *(quasi-)universal* principles of the international IPRs system.

1. National Treatment and Reciprocity

It is appropriate to start with the principle of "national treatment," which is one of the oldest organizing principles found in international trade and investment agreements. This was a core feature of Nineteenth Century bilateral agreements, establishing the fundamental tenet of non-discrimination: foreign nationals or entitled subject matter (such as goods, services or investment) shall not be treated less favorably than domestic nationals or subject matter. This principle, eventually enshrined in the GATT

1947 and the 1995 WTO agreements, including Article 3 of the TRIPS Agreement, is of paramount importance in bringing about level playing fields and fair conditions of competition for foreign products. It is equally a fundamental principle of political economy: As political systems tend to favor domestic constituencies and voters, it is the task of international agreements to bring about a proper rebalancing of these shortcomings. Mutual interest in furthering fair conditions of competition on foreign markets provides ample incentive for this rebalancing.

National treatment also effectively functions as a substitute for international harmonization. To the extent that states concentrate on national law, and progress in international law is slow (as it was after decolonization and before the Uruguay Round), the principle of national treatment allows the international community to automatically benefit from improved standards in municipal law or regional law introduced mainly for the welfare (and at request of) domestic right holders.

In the field of IPRs, national treatment has been part of the international system from the very beginning. Articles 2 and 3 of the 1883 Paris Convention enshrined the principle, and ever since it has been part of all multilateral IPRs agreements:

Article 2, Paris Convention

(1) Nationals of any country of the Union shall, as regards the protection of industrial property, enjoy in all the other countries of the Union the advantages that their respective laws now grant, or may hereafter grant, to nationals; all without prejudice to the rights specially provided for by this Convention. Consequently, they shall have the same protection as the latter, and the same legal remedy against any infringement of their rights, provided that the conditions and formalities imposed upon nationals are complied with.

(2) However, no requirement as to domicile or establishment in the country where protection is claimed may be imposed upon nationals of countries of the Union for the enjoyment of any industrial property rights.

(3) The provisions of the laws of each of the countries of the Union relating to judicial and administrative procedure and to jurisdiction,

and to the designation of an address for service or the appointment of an agent, which may be required by the laws on industrial property are expressly reserved.

Article 3, Paris Convention

Nationals of countries outside the Union who are domiciled or who have real and effective industrial or commercial establishments in the territory of one of the countries of the Union shall be treated in the same manner as nationals of the countries of the Union.

Article 3 of the TRIPS Agreement contains the most comprehensive statement of the principle and its exceptions under existing and partially incorporated international agreements.

Article 3, TRIPS Agreement

1. Each Member shall accord to the nationals of other Members treatment no less favourable than that it accords to its own nationals with regard to the protection[3] of intellectual property, subject to the exceptions already provided in, respectively, the Paris Convention (1967), the Berne Convention (1971), the Rome Convention or the Treaty on Intellectual Property in Respect of Integrated Circuits. In respect of performers, producers of phonograms and broadcasting organizations, this obligation only applies in respect of the rights provided under this Agreement. Any Member availing itself of the possibilities provided in Article 6 of the Berne Convention (1971) or paragraph 1(b) of Article 16 of the Rome Convention shall make a notification as foreseen in those provisions to the Council for TRIPS.

2. Members may avail themselves of the exceptions permitted under paragraph 1 in relation to judicial and administrative procedures, including the designation of an address for service or the appointment of an agent within the jurisdiction of a Member, only where such exceptions are necessary to secure compliance with laws and regulations which are not inconsistent with the provisions of this Agreement and where such practices are not applied in a manner which would constitute a disguised restriction on trade.

Footnote: 3 For the purposes of Articles 3 and 4 "protection" shall include matters affecting the availability, acquisition, scope, maintenance and enforcement of intellectual property rights as well as those matters affecting the use of intellectual property rights specifically addressed in this Agreement.

Given the different formulations of Article 3, Paris Convention, entailing the concept of *equal treatment*, and Article 3, TRIPS Agreement, entailing *treatment no less favorable*, it is unclear whether there is a difference in the substance of the national treatment obligation as between the two agreements. Under WTO standards, national treatment does not necessarily entail equal treatment of a Member's own nationals. The WTO concept theoretically allows, as under the GATT and GATS Agreement, as well as EU law, that particular privileges will be accorded to foreign nationals (*discrimination à rebours*). In the field of IPRs protection, privileges accorded to foreign nationals are extremely rare, but occasionally occur and will be discussed under the principle of most-favored nation treatment (MFN). Article 3, Paris Convention, on its face, may be read to exclude this possibility as equal treatment is required. An obligation to treat foreigners alike, however, may not necessarily entail equal treatment of domestic right holders, as the Paris Convention grants rights to foreign — and not to domestic — right holders. The Paris provision should probably be construed in accordance with Article 3 of the TRIPS Agreement, following the latter in time rule. As a practical matter, the difference, if any, is likely to remain of little importance as domestic constituencies normally will see to it that foreigners are not treated in a more favorable manner.

The principle of national treatment is anathema to the legal concept of reciprocity, which demands that rights and obligations as between states in respect to a subject matter be formally or informally equivalent. In a system of legal reciprocity, a first state will not grant rights to a second state unless the second state accords equivalent rights to the first state. Under a system of national treatment, however, formal or informal equivalence is not required.

If the term of copyright protection in two countries varies in duration (seventy v. fifty years, the latter being a minimum standard under Article 12, TRIPS Agreement), the principle of national treatment generally would not allow the country with the longer term to accord only the shorter term to the other's nationals. IPRs holders would equally enjoy a term of 70 years in one country, and fifty years in the other. The Berne Convention, it must be noted, deviates from the principle of national treatment in regard to the duration of copyright, stating that foreigners need only be accorded the term of their home country (cf. Article 7, Berne Convention), so that the foregoing illustration of national treatment in respect to copyright duration is only correct for cases where at least one country is not party to the Berne Convention. If both countries are party to the Berne Convention, then according to Article 3, TRIPS Agreement, the rule of Article 7, Berne Convention, is applicable. In a number of other areas as well, policies of reciprocity have prevailed over strict national treatment, and these policies are expressed in terms of exceptions to the principle of national treatment. As Article 3, TRIPS Agreement, indicates, these exceptions operate predominantly in the field of copyright and performance rights as a consequence of differing national policies and systems of remuneration.

The following excerpt by Paul Katzenberg discusses the rule-exception constellation regarding copyright. This discussion is not for the faint of heart, or for those who may yet be thinking that the TRIPS Agreement has resulted in a consistent approach to the national treatment principle.

TRIPs and Copyright Law

Paul Katzenberger*

4. National Treatment

a) One of the fundamental principles of TRIPs copyright protection is, as mentioned above, that of national treatment. It is laid down in Art. 3 of the TRIPs Agreement, in basic conformance with the traditional agreements and conventions, but derogating from the GATT (1947 and 1994). With reference to copyright proper this principle also derives from the incorporation into TRIPs of Art. 5, Revised Berne Convention, which determines national treatment as a rule in the Berne Convention, by means of Art 9(1), first sentence, TRIPs Agreement. Due to the fact that this incorporation gives rise to the applicability of the Revised Berne Convention rule for all

---

*In FROM GATT TO TRIPs 59 (F-K BEIER & G. SCHRICKER EDS.,1996).

TRIPs Members and because the Berne Convention is basically non-exhaustive as regards both new types of works and new rights, the provision in Art. 3, TRIPs Agreement, would not have been absolutely necessary, yet it serves to provide clarity and security in respect of the Berne-Plus elements of the TRIPs Agreement.

The view that the TRIPs establishment of national treatment was necessary with regard to the TRIPs provisions on the enforcement of rights, is obviously based on the opinion that the Berne Convention provision on national treatment does not relate to enforcement of rights. As regards protection of the author pursuant to Art. 5(2), Revised Berne Convention, with reference also to the exercise of his or her rights and the means of redress afforded to the author to protect his rights, this opinion applies, if at all, only with regard to procedures for enforcement of rights, which is confirmed e.g. by the explicit stipulation in Art. 2(3), Paris Convention; yet it does not hold true with respect to claims of an author in the case of an infringement of his or her rights, such claims also being regulated in the TRIPs Agreement by the provisions on enforcement of rights. Furthermore, application of TRIPs national treatment to the TRIPs provisions on the procedure for enforcement of rights is also questionable because these provisions in any case oblige the TRIPs Members and, together with the entire TRIPs Agreement, are not applicable to purely domestic relations anyway. However, these issues cannot be discussed in further detail within the current context.

b) The provision in Art. 3(1), first sentence, TRIPs Agreement, pursuant to which TRIPs national treatment is subject to the same exceptions as those laid down in the Berne Convention, at least provides clarification. This provision means, for example, that restrictions on national treatment permitted under the latter Convention by means of a comparison of the terms of protection apply under TRIPs not only in relation to the unequivocal protection standard of this Convention but also with regard to the Berne-Plus elements of the TRIPs Agreement. Apart from this, Art. 3(1), third sentence, TRIPs Agreement also concerns a possible exception from national treatment, namely retaliatory measures in the sense of Art. 6, Revised Berne Convention, for the uniform handling of which paragraph (3) of this provision prescribes notification to WIPO; within the scope of application of TRIPs such measures shall be notified to the TRIPs Council. As indicated above, another specific regulation in Art. 3(2) TRIPs regarding exceptions from national treatment obviously concerns the fact that in the traditional agreements and conventions national treatment does not extend to procedural law. It appears that this should apply to TRIPs as well, subject to the restrictions in Art. 3(2).

c) The TRIPs provisions on national treatment are necessary at least with respect to neighboring rights, owing to the fact that TRIPs does not adopt the Rome Convention, but standardizes the protection by means of its own provisions. According to Art. 3(1), first sentence, TRIPs Agreement, this protection is subject to the exceptions from national treatment as provided for in the Rome Convention. With respect to the possibility established in Art 16(1)(b) of that Convention for each contracting state to exclude protection of broadcasting organizations against public communication of their television programs against payment, albeit with the possible consequence of retaliatory measures being imposed by the other contracting states (Art. 13(d) Rome Convention), Art. 3(1), third sentence, TRIPs Agreement on its part requires notification to the TRIPs Council. Upon this is based the recognition of this protection anchored in Art. 14(3), first sentence, TRIPs Agreement.

The provision in Art. 3(1), second sentence, TRIPs Agreement, according to which the obligation to accord national treatment to performing artists, phonogram producers and broadcasting organizations only applies to rights granted by TRIPs itself, is particularly important: It means that TRIPs Members that are simultaneously bound to the Rome Convention and protect neighboring rights at a correspondingly high level lying above that of the TRIPs provisions, are not obliged *qua* national treatment to grant rights that are not foreseen in TRIPs to nationals of other TRIPs Members that on their part are not signatories of the Rome Convention.

Notes and Questions

1. In Chapter IV, we will review the various treaties referred to by Katzenberger, including the Rome Convention, and the more recently adopted WIPO Copyright Treaty (WCT) and WIPO Performances and Phonograms Treaty (WPPT). The WPPT, for example, contains a national treatment rule that is more or less consistent with the general principles

operating in the WTO, but which nevertheless permits certain reservations to be entered (Arts. 4 & 15, WPPT). The situation regarding national treatment in respect to copyright and neighboring rights remains complex and unsettled.

2. Article 1 of the TRIPS Agreement also addresses national treatment subject matter, and raises further issues concerning the scope of the TRIPS national treatment obligation. Article 1 provides:

Article 1, TRIPS Agreement

1. Members shall give effect to the provisions of this Agreement. Members may, but shall not be obliged to, implement in their law more extensive protection than is required by this Agreement, provided that such protection does not contravene the provisions of this Agreement. Members shall be free to determine the appropriate method of implementing the provisions of this Agreement within their own legal system and practice.

2. For the purposes of this Agreement, the term "intellectual property" refers to all categories of intellectual property that are the subject of Sections 1 through 7 of Part II.

3. Members shall accord the treatment provided for in this Agreement to the nationals of other Members.[1] In respect of the relevant intellectual property right, the nationals of other Members shall be understood as those natural or legal persons that would meet the criteria for eligibility for protection provided for in the Paris Convention (1967), the Berne Convention (1971), the Rome Convention and the Treaty on Intellectual Property in Respect of Integrated Circuits, were all Members of the WTO members of those conventions.[2] Any Member availing itself of the possibilities provided in paragraph 3 of Article 5 or paragraph 2 of Article 6 of the Rome Convention shall make a notification as foreseen in those provisions to the Council for Trade-Related Aspects of Intellectual Property Rights (the "Council for TRIPS").

Footnote: 1 When "nationals" are referred to in this Agreement, they shall be deemed, in the case of a separate customs territory Member of the WTO, to mean persons, natural or legal, who are domiciled or who have a real and effective industrial or commercial establishment in that customs territory.

Footnote: 2 In this Agreement, "Paris Convention" refers to the Paris Convention for the Protection of Industrial Property; "Paris Convention (1967)" refers to the Stockholm Act of this Convention of 14 July 1967. "Berne Convention" refers to the Berne Convention for the Protection of Literary and Artistic Works; "Berne Convention (1971)" refers to the Paris Act of this Convention of 24 July 1971. "Rome Convention" refers to the International Convention for the Protection of Performers, Producers of Phonograms and Broadcasting Organizations, adopted at Rome on 26 October 1961. "Treaty on Intellectual Property in Respect of Integrated Circuits" (IPIC Treaty) refers to the Treaty on Intellectual Property in Respect of Integrated Circuits, adopted at Washington on 26 May 1989. "WTO Agreement" refers to the Agreement Establishing the WTO.

Consider the effect of Article 1:2 which defines "intellectual property" by reference to the "categories" that are the subject of Part II. Does this definition exclude other forms of IPRs from national treatment and related obligations of the TRIPS Agreement? What if a WTO Member adopts legislation that prescribes a new *sui generis* form of IPR. Is that new form outside the scope of the national treatment obligation? What if that new form is "like," but not the same as, an existing form mentioned in Part II of the TRIPS Agreement?

3. Perhaps the most immediate unresolved problem relating to national treatment is found in the field of collection societies and exceptions under the Rome Convention. Collection societies, which are found in many countries, provide a mechanism by which artists may efficiently receive revenues arising out of the broadcast or public performance of their works. Collection societies act on behalf of artists to secure revenues in substantial geographic territories, and from many users of protected works. These societies distribute the revenues they collect based on varying formulae. EU collection societies follow a practice of admitting only EU national artists as members who are entitled to receive distributions. This excludes U.S. national artists (and others) from substantial streams of income. The United

595

States claims that national treatment should be extended for remuneration of artists by European collection societies. U.S. artists should benefit along with European artists, since the major portion of European collection society revenues are generated by U.S.-origin works. What would be the impact of granting national treatment? How would this affect cultural policies in Europe and other parts of the world?

2. Most Favored Nation Treatment

Most favored nation (MFN) treatment is a second mainstay of non-discrimination in international trade and investment regulation. It has been companion to national treatment in many bilateral agreements, and it became the main conceptual and legal pillar of the GATT 1947. This classical principle prescribes in Article I, GATT 1994, that "any advantage, favour, privilege or immunity granted by any contracting party to any product originating in or destined for any other country shall be accorded immediately and unconditionally to the like product originating or destined for the territories of all other contracting parties. " The MFN principle has been critical to the successful reduction of tariff barriers during the last fifty years. Unlike national treatment, this cornerstone of the international trading system did not apply to intellectual property under the Paris and Berne Conventions. Neither of them contained comparable rights and obligations.

There was an important political motive for adoption of an unconditional MFN rule for the international trading system. In the pre-Second World War environment, trade concessions were widely used as an instrument of diplomacy. Political alliances were created and maintained through economic preferences. Since diplomatic decisions were often made for reasons apart from improving world prosperity, an economic system in which trade concessions were used as political instruments would be unlikely to generate a global welfare-optimizing result. The MFN principle was and is intended to de-politicize the international economic system so as to reduce the chances of breakdown into a system of diplomacy-based alliances. The net effect should be to distribute the benefits of trade widely. The MFN principle was the key "multilateralism" provision in the GATT 1947, and it remains a cornerstone of the WTO system, including in the TRIPS context.

So far as the Paris and Berne Conventions were concerned, the MFN principle appeared to be dispensable as non-discrimination could be largely achieved on the basis of national treatment in the regulatory context of IPRs. As all foreign national IPRs holders are entitled to equal treatment with nationals, discrimination among foreign IPRs holders was unlikely to arise. In the 1980s and early 1990s, however, the United States pursued bilateral and regional agreements to obtain IPRs protection that went beyond national standards, particularly in the field of patent "pipeline" protection for pharmaceutical and chemical products.[1] This raised concerns during the Uruguay Round, and lead to the introduction of the MFN principle in the international IPRs system — Article 4, TRIPS Agreement. An intention to maintain consistency within the WTO system also played a role in the adoption of Article 4. This MFN rule is subject to a number of carefully drafted exceptions:

Article 4, TRIPS Agreement

With regard to the protection of intellectual property, any advantage, favour, privilege or immunity granted by a Member to the nationals of any other country shall be accorded immediately and unconditionally to the nationals of all other Members.

Exempted from this obligation are any advantage, favour, privilege or immunity accorded by a Member:

(a) deriving from international agreements on judicial assistance or law enforcement of a general nature and not particularly confined to the protection of intellectual property;

(b) granted in accordance with the provisions of the Berne Convention (1971) or the Rome Convention authorizing that the treatment

---

[1] "Pipeline" protection refers to several variations on a similar theme. Essentially, it connotes agreement by a country to provide patent (or equivalent) protection to products which already have been granted patent protection in a second country, or which are in the process of regulatory approval in that second country, even though patent (or equivalent) protection has not been available in the first country prior to expiration of the Paris Convention priority period.

accorded be a function not of national treatment but of the treatment accorded in another country;

(c) in respect of the rights of performers, producers of phonograms and broadcasting organizations not provided under this Agreement;

(d) deriving from international agreements related to the protection of intellectual property which entered into force prior to the entry into force of the WTO Agreement, provided that such agreements are notified to the Council for TRIPS and do not constitute an arbitrary or unjustifiable discrimination against nationals of other Members.

The following excerpt discusses the implications of MFN in the field of copyrights.

TRIPs and Copyright Law

Paul Katzenberger*

5. Most-Favored-Nation Treatment

a) The principle of most-favored-nation treatment as provided for in Art. 4 of the TRIPs Agreement represents a novum in the area of international copyright protection by means of multilateral conventions. Similarly to the manner in which the principle of national treatment aims to prevent discrimination against foreign authors and works and against foreign owners of neighboring rights or performances in comparison to nationals and their works or performances, the principle of most-favored-nation treatment intends to avoid discrimination in comparison with other foreign rights owners. The introduction of the most-favored-nation treatment into the TRIPs Agreement — adjusted to the conditions of international intellectual property protection — can be explained by the fact that it is one of the fundamental principles of GATT (1947 and 1994) and because the recent bilateralization of international copyright protection instigated in

---

*In FROM GATT TO TRIPS 59 (F-K BEIER & G. SCHRICKER EDS.,1996).

particular by the US meant that the problem of different treatment of foreigners from and in various countries gained in topicality.

Since national copyright law regimes do not tend to give preference to certain foreign states and nationals of such states of their own accord, international agreements constitute the natural source for privileges which, pursuant to the basic principle of the TRIPs most-favored-nation clause, should be accorded to the nationals of all other TRIPs Members in the contracting states of such agreements and conventions. If this principle were implemented without exception, it would mean that a TRIPs Member would participate in the highest protection standard of all existing and future copyright conventions and agreements, of which only one other TRIPs Member is a signatory state, without the former having to adhere to this convention or agreement and without having on its part to grant more than the minimum protection laid down in the TRIPs Agreement; in view of this possible free-rider effect it is imaginable that future agreements and conventions would only seldom be concluded.

b) Consequently, Art. 4, TRIPs Agreement, provides for several exceptions to the most-favored-nation clause with respect to certain other agreements and areas of law regulated in such agreements, such exceptions being correct yet possibly not far-reaching enough.

(1) The exceptions concern advantages ensuing from general international agreements on judicial assistance and law enforcement and, primarily, advantages that derive from the provisions of the Berne Convention or the Rome Convention, in which it is authorized that the treatment accorded be a function not of national treatment but of the treatment accorded in another country. This somewhat complex provision is obviously directed to exception clauses from national treatment contained in the conventions named and concerning material reciprocity of protection, such as, e.g. with regard to the comparison of the terms of protection, limit the protection to be granted in the country of protection to the extent of protection conferred in the country of origin of the work, or, e.g. with regard to *droit de suite*, render such protection contingent upon recognition of the right in the author's country of origin. An author who is a national of Switzerland, which does not recognize a *droit de suite*, should not be able to claim this right in Germany by referring to the fact that Germany accords this right to authors e.g. from France and Belgium, which on their part do grant a *droit*

de suite. A national of a country with a 50-year term of protection should not be able to enjoy the 70-year protection period in Germany for his works simply because German law grants this term of protection to works of foreigners from a country which accords a 70-year term of protection, e.g. in the meantime Switzerland.

(2) In addition, existing and future agreements and conventions on neighboring rights are concerned, inasfar as these relate to the rights of performers, phonogram producers and broadcasting organizations that are not regulated in the TRIPs Agreement itself. This corresponds to the limitation of national treatment under Art.3(1), second sentence of the TRIPs Agreement, and takes into account the particularly glaring differences in protection in this field in the various countries.

(3) A particularly significant exception from the most-favored-nation clause is that regarding "international agreements related to the protection of intellectual property which entered into force prior to the entry into force of the Agreement Establishing the WTO." This clause encompasses, e.g., the Rome Convention, but also the bilateral German-American Agreement on copyright dating from 1892, which contrary to the Berne Convention does not permit a comparison of the terms of protection and which remains valid next to both Berne and the TRIPs Agreement. Consequently, since the adherence of the US to Berne, US works enjoy a 70-year term of protection in Germany within the framework of Art. 18 of the Revised Berne Convention, although the US itself only recognizes a 50-year term of protection *p.m.a.* [*post mortem autoris*]**. However, other countries with the same 50-year term of protection are not able to claim the longer term in Germany by referring to the legal situation applicable to US works.

c) In particular, these limited exceptions from the TRIPs most-favored-nation clause do not encompass future further developments of the Berne Convention and future bilateral and regional agreements on copyrights proper, so that particularly in the latter regard a cementation of the current situation cannot be excluded. However, according to the widespread understanding of inter-state copyright protection in the Member States of the EC, this would not apply to their harmonization of copyright at a high

---

**Authors' note: the U.S. has now adopted a seventy-year term *post mortem autoris*.

level: according to this understanding, copyright relations among the EC Member States would be determined by the relevant binding conventions and agreements, in particular the Revised Berne Convention. Consequently, on the one hand the principle of national treatment would apply and, on the other hand, the Berne exceptions from this principle, such as regards e.g. the comparison of the terms of protection (Art. 7(8), Revised Berne Convention) and *droit de suite* (Art. 14ter (2), Revised Berne Convention). Within the context of European copyright law harmonization at a high level of protection, e.g. with respect to the 70-year protection period pursuant to Art. 1 of the Directive on Harmonizing the Term of Protection of Copyright and Certain Related Rights of October 29, 1993, this understanding would mean that nationals of other TRIPs Members would be able to participate in this protection in EC states either pursuant to the TRIPs principle of national treatment or, e.g. with regard to the term of protection or *droit de suite* as possible issues to be regulated in future EC Directives, would be bound to the corresponding Revised Berne Convention exceptions. The latter would also apply according to the perspective of TRIPs most-favored-nation treatment.

Notes and Questions

1. The TRIPs Agreement does not contain a general exception for regional integration arrangements (customs unions, free trade areas), such as are found in Article XXIV, GATT 1994, and Article V, GATS. How does this affect the EU, NAFTA, Mercosur and other regional arrangements? Are there privileges in the field of IPRs which are granted exclusively within and for the benefit of the member states of the EU, or other regional institutions? How does this relate to the problem of the intra-Union exhaustion rule which we examined in Ideal Standard?[1]

2. Why does Article 4, TRIPS Agreement contain an MFN exception for judicial assistance or law enforcement? How do governments ordinarily organize cooperation in these areas?

---

[1] *See supra*, Ch. I, § B, 6, c.

3. Territoriality

The concept of territoriality plays an enormously important role in the international IPRs system. From an historical perspective, IPRs are granted by the government of — and have effects only with respect to — the territory of a single nation-state. In order to secure IPRs protection for one invention, expressive work or indication of origin, the creator must obtain protection in each territory where protection is considered necessary. The grounding of the international IPRs system in the nation-state, and the principle of territoriality, was a logical consequence of the world political order of the late Nineteenth Century, when the Paris and Berne Conventions were negotiated and concluded. In that era, and to a large extent today, the sovereignty of each national government within its own territory was considered the paramount principle by which the international legal and political order was constituted.

The formation of regional institutions (such as the EU), and the development of regional and multilateral mechanisms that facilitate the granting of IPRs on a multi-country basis, have not so far fundamentally altered the reliance of the international IPRs system on the principle of territoriality. In Chapters IV and V, the rules and mechanisms by which IPRs are secured at the regional and multilateral levels will be presented in some detail. The major area in which an evolution away from strict reliance on territoriality can be seen is in the EU, where some forms of IPRs are now granted and regulated on a Union-wide level. Note, however, that the EU is somewhat exceptional in the sense of its organization as a quasi-federal polity.[1] An evolution away from the strict nation-state IPRs territoriality principle in the EU in some ways reflects a consolidation of that principle within a new and larger political unit.

The observation that IPRs are territorial should not be understood categorically. There is some jurisprudence in the United States, particularly in the field of trademarks, which suggests that holders of rights in one nation (e.g., the United States) may on that basis assert rights to protect against injury suffered in other nations or regions. In Chapter VI we will examine a decision of the U.S. Court of Appeals for the Eleventh Circuit (*Bab-*

---

[1] *See supra*, Ch. II, § B, 2, a.

bitt Electronics) in which such doctrine is invoked. Doctrines asserting so-called extra-territorial IPRs are controversial, and to date have been used in very limited contexts. We could not from this limited experience generalize a departure from the accepted territorial nature of IPRs.

Whether the principle of territoriality continues to serve well the international IPRs system, or the international economic and political systems, is another question entirely. Many important challenges to territoriality are already present, and more are on the horizon. The inherent tension between territorially-based IPRs, on one side, and the free movement of goods and services, on the other, is a subject which we address extensively in this book. Resolving this conflict may not necessarily involve a diminished stature for the basic principle of territoriality of IPRs, but may instead involve more adequately elaborating the goals which territoriality is expected to accomplish.

Another important challenge to the territoriality of IPRs is raised by the Internet and other forms of high speed data transmission, as well as the concomitant evolution of global electronic commerce. As it has become possible to simultaneously and instantaneously transmit copyrighted works to all countries of the world, the utility of maintaining different rule systems and bundles of rights in each country is called into question. The Internet domain name is a globally-employed identifier that has limited relevance as a creature of national law, and its regulation on a nation-to-nation basis raises a host of law and policy issues. We examine these phenomena and their potential impact in Chapter VIII.

While the territorial basis of the international IPRs system may be under challenge, for present purposes the principle of the territorial nature of IPRs remains basic to the system. Neither the Paris, Berne or Rome Conventions, nor any other instrument under the umbrella of WIPO, nor the TRIPS Agreement, creates a supranational system of IPRs protection. These international agreements are instruments to bring about minimum standards — to harmonize or approximate national and regional intellectual property law.

Notes and Questions

1. It seems apparent that more universal rules and mechanisms to grant and enforce IPRs protection would result in certain efficiency gains from an

economic standpoint. At the same time, there are a number of significant potential drawbacks to "universalization." Consider, for example, whether there is some utility to allowing national and regional governments to flexibly adopt rules adapted to local conditions. Does the progressive universalization of IPRs standards necessarily imply the loss of adaptability? Might there be mechanisms by which flexibility could be built into a universal IPRs system — or does this strike you as a contradiction, or as unrealistic? Who would be the likely winners and losers in a process of universalization?

2. Is it possible that some forms of IPRs would be better suited to universalization than others, based on their policy foundations? For example, might a trademark governed by a single set of global rules make more sense than a patent governed that way? Or not? Why?

3. What are the institutional prerequisites to global rights? Would it be necessary to have a world IPRs court if global IPRs were granted, or do you consider that countries would be prepared to envisage the invalidation of rights on the basis of decisions taken by other national courts? The USPTO employs over 5000 persons. Do you think that the United States, or other countries/regions with commensurately sized patent offices, would be prepared to see this employment go offshore to a global institution?

---

4. Ubiquity and Exhaustion of Rights

As we observed in Chapter I, intellectual property is characterized by a unique feature which clearly distinguishes it from real and tangible property. Ownership of IPRs is fundamentally different from ownership of a chair, a house or a car. IPRs are of a "ubiquitous" nature. They exist independently of the specific material good in which they are incorporated. Yet each and every copy of a protected product contains these IPRs. IPRs follow the product downstream, and potentially control the use of the product. In an age in which goods increasingly contain IPRs-protected components (such as a refrigerator with a silicon chip), the potential effects of IPRs are extremely far reaching.

Perhaps the most telling example is in the field of biotechnology. The patented technical rule in this field is an abstract idea. Yet it is incorporated in each and every copy of a product which, moreover, produces its own off-spring. Logically, the patent right could expand endlessly, interfering in downstream markets infinitely. It therefore is necessary, at some point, to put an end to the effect on the market of IPRs. This concept is called "exhaustion of rights" (*Erschöpfung, epuisement*). The following excerpt describes the point at which exhaustion of IPRs normally takes place, and discusses geographical concepts of exhaustion. While the latter concepts are controversial and were largely left unresolved by Article 6 of the TRIPS Agreement, it is important to stress that the principle of exhaustion of rights is a necessary ingredient in balancing exclusive rights and the needs of markets. In Chapter IV we will examine a number of judicial decisions which consider the exhaustion of IPRs in the trade context, and we will revert to the exhaustion issue at the WTO law and policy level in Chapter VII.

Article 6 of the TRIPS Agreement provides:

Article 6, TRIPS Agreement

For the purposes of dispute settlement under this Agreement, subject to the provisions of Article 3 and 4, nothing in this Agreement shall be used to address the issue of exhaustion of intellectual property rights.

Parallel Imports in Patent, Copyright and Industrial Design Law — The Scope of European and International Public Law

Thomas Cottier and Marc Stucki[*]

National, International and Regional Exhaustion

The question of parallel imports is one of the major problems to which solution still needs to be found on the international level. So far,

---

*In *Conflit entre importations parallèle et propriété intellectuelle?* Actes du colloque de Lausanne, Comparativa no. 60 (1996). Translated by Ingo Meitinger.

there are a considerable number of different solutions which vary from country to country. These have mainly been determined by the most influential economic interests.

The different national systems share, as a common basis, the so called doctrine of exhaustion of rights. First, this doctrine is a necessary response to the ubiquity of intellectual property. It defines the limits of its content, which is linked to the product, and would thus be permanent. In a national context the right is exhausted as soon as the product is put on the market by a right holder or with its consent. (e.g., by way of a license agreement). The right holder therefore no longer influences the fate and further disposition of the product on the market by legal means; the rights are "exhausted".

In international trade, we find three types of exhaustion: National, international and regional exhaustion. If the doctrine of exhaustion is primarily seen as a necessary tool in order to solve the problem of ubiquity of intangible intellectual property, the traditional view establishing a compulsory link between principle of territoriality and of (national) exhaustion of rights can no longer be upheld.

In international trade, the doctrine of exhaustion of rights answers the question whether the first sale of a product, protected by intellectual property in country A, leads to the result that the right holder retains exclusive rights to sale of the product in all other countries except country A, or whether the right holder loses ("exhausts") these rights. In the first case, he may keep and enforce his rights by activating the possibilities of defense in other countries, e.g., obtain an import ban against a parallel importer. The answer depends upon which doctrine of exhaustion applies.

*****

We may explain this by means of a case pending [at the time] before the ECJ:[61] A parallel trader buys a pharmaceutical product ("Capoten") in Greece and imports it to Denmark, where the right holder ("Brystol-Myers Squibb") tries to prevent the importation by claiming an infringement of its intellectual property right. The same enterprise, Bristol Myers had sold

---

[61]Taken from the Opinion of the Attorney General F.G. Jacobs ov December 14, 1995 in the joined Cases C-427/93, C-429/93, C-436/93, C-71/94, C-72/94, C-73/94 and C-232/94, pp. I-4.

the pharmaceutical in Greece. Does the fact that the first sale in Greece has already taken place influence the ability of the right holder in Denmark to prevent parallel imports of "Capoten" by means of intellectual property? This shows that exhaustion of rights deals with the issue as to whether acts taking place and producing effects abroad, i.e. the sale of the product, is of any legal consequence for intellectual property rights at home. The divergence from the proper principle of territoriality in intellectual property right is obvious, since territoriality is not about acts taking place abroad, but about the coordination of different rights. The question is answered differently in the three cases of national, regional and international exhaustion of rights.

National exhaustion has the effect that the sale of the pharmaceutical product in Greece is without any impact on Danish intellectual property rights. Only the sale on the national market (i.e. in Denmark) leads to the of exhaustion of the rights to resale. The result is the possibility of preventing of parallel imports.

International exhaustion, by contrast, means that it makes no difference whether a pharmaceutical product was first sold on the national market or abroad. Both cases are treated equally. Wherever the first sale took place, the right holder cannot prevent parallel imports by means of intellectual property rights.

Regional exhaustion does not apply globally, but is treaty-based and multilaterally agreed. Its territorial scope is limited to the respective signatory states. . . . Regional exhaustion is located between national and international exhaustion. It increases national exhaustion to two or more countries, but also leaves its effects limited to this group of countries.

It should be added that in all kinds of exhaustion it is not in itself the intellectual property (i.e. the patent, trademark, design or copyright) which is exhausted, even though the matter is generally referred to as the exhaustion of intellectual property. In fact, exhaustion only relates to one specific aspect of intellectual property rights: that is, the right of sale after first sale or, to be more precise, the right to control the resale of the protected product after first sale by means of intellectual property.

A holder of a copyright, patent or design right therefore may decide on its own, where, how and by whom the first sale of a protected product takes place. This is referred to, in this context, as the right of first marketing. After that, exhaustion applies. It affects the subsequent phase of worldwide distribution, also referred to as the right of subsequent marketing control. While the holder of the intellectual property right always has the right of first marketing, the issue of exhaustion depends on the fact whether this person also has a right of subsequent marketing control. This right again depends on the place of first sale. International exhaustion means that this right has vanished, i.e. it is exhausted, no matter where the first sale took place. National exhaustion, on the contrary, means that the right of resale is only exhausted in the specific country in which the product was first sold.

Note

1. While the doctrine of exhaustion of IPRs and the act of parallel importation are closely linked, IPRs law is not the only body of law which affects and regulates parallel importation. In Chapter VII, we will examine the link between competition law and parallel importation.

---

5. Right of Priority

The coexistence of national (or regional) systems of intellectual property, each based upon the principle of territoriality, requires appropriate tools of interconnection. One of the key instruments to bring about interconnection is the "right of priority." Because the validity of IPRs generally depends on an intellectual step,[1] the filing and registration of rights theoretically should take place simultaneously in all countries where protection

---

[1] *See infra*, § 7.

is sought. A failure to act simultaneously would risk that novelty, originality or creativity would be lost, either as a later act of creation rendered the earlier act non-original, or as disclosure or public use of a covered product in one country undermined novelty in another.

The international IPRs system guards against the undermining of intellectual step by means of the principle of right of priority. The principle prescribes the preservation of novelty, originality and creativity upon the filing of an application for the grant of protection in one country of the Paris Union — for a limited period of time of twelve months (patents) and six months (trademarks and industrial designs). During that limited period, a more recent invention, creation or disclosure cannot legally destroy novelty, and the creator may file in other countries of the Paris Union based upon the priority date. This right of interconnection is contained in Article 4 of the Paris Convention.

The right of priority as such is unknown in the field of copyright. Internationally, interconnection between the various national systems is achieved in the Berne Convention through the use of two concepts: nationality and publication. Under Article 3 of the Berne Convention, the protection established by the Convention extends to the works, whether published or not, of all authors who are nationals of one of the countries party to the Convention or who have their habitual residence in one of those countries, as well as to the works of any authors who are not a national of a contracting party, where the works are first published in one of the countries party to the Berne Convention. These are more appropriate tools of interconnection for copyright than a priority right, since most countries have no registration system for copyrighted works and the Berne Convention requires that the enjoyment and exercise of rights established under the Convention not be subject to any formality.

One of the purposes of the priority right is to allow time for the applicant to evaluate the commercial and geographical potential of the invention. In Chapter IV we examine the Paris Convention rule of priority in further detail. In Chapter V, as we study the Patent Cooperation Treaty mechanism for applying for patents in multiple jurisdictions, we will see how rules in addition to the basic priority principle allow for more methodical evaluation of the economic potential of patents — that is, how it is possible to delay national filings beyond the priority period without prejudice to patentability.

Notes and Questions

1. We have mentioned why the right of priority is not relevant to copyright. Why is it also not relevant to trade secret protection?

2. The TRIPS Agreement (Article 2:1) obligates WTO Members to comply with Paris Convention rules, including the rule establishing the right of priority (Article 4, Paris Convention). Does this mean that the right of priority may be the subject of WTO dispute settlement?

6. Duration of Intellectual Property Rights

The different disciplines of IPRs have in common that the duration of protection is — in general — limited. This principle is based, first, on the idea that IPRs are granted to allow the author or inventor to secure an appropriate return on investment, but that they should not unnecessarily impair the diffusion of knowledge. Second, limitations in time are motivated by competition policies which require a balancing of exclusive rights and open markets. Third, and related to the doctrine of exhaustion, IPRs inhering in products must at some point give way to legal security for the owner of the product.

Exceptions to the principle of limited duration are found in trademarks and trade secrets. The protection of trademarks generally can be indefinitely extended if certain conditions are met. Trade secrets are protected as long as the conditions of secrecy are satisfied. The unlimited duration of trademarks relates to their prime function, which is to allow consumers to distinguish between products of competitors, and to identify their origin.

Unlimited duration of trade secret protection is controversial. Some argue that unlimited duration is inherent to the concept of trade secret since a trade secret exists as long as valuable information is not disclosed. On the other hand, it is not so apparent why the trade secret is more worthy of restriction on the diffusion of knowledge than other forms of IPR. In practical terms, trade secrets will often be of a limited duration as conditions for protection are not easy to maintain. The protection of intellectual property as undisclosed information is a risky strategy. Once a secret is disclosed, protection no longer is afforded.

The duration of IPRs protection varies in different legal systems. Specific mechanisms for extending duration exist in the field of patents to offset time spent during government approvals and clinical trials.[1]

Efforts to harmonize the duration of protection at the international level historically have met with difficulty. The Paris Convention failed to regulate duration. The results achieved in the TRIPS Agreement were a major advance, particularly in the fields of copyright and patent law, and have lead — or will lead — to the substantial extension of protection in many countries.

However, while the TRIPS Agreement has resulted in harmonization of minimum terms of protection, the TRIPS Agreement does not specifically prescribe, and it has not led to, harmonized maximum terms of protection. There has been a persistent trend within the EU to extend the duration of IPRs protection beyond that mandated by the TRIPS Agreement, and the United States has largely followed the EU in this regard. In Chapter IV, we will focus on varying terms of protection in respect to copyright and related rights, and the implications both of longer duration of protection and lack of uniformity, for the international IPRs system.

TRIPS Agreement Norms on Duration

Copyright Art. 12

Whenever the term of protection of a work, other than a photographic work or a work of applied art, is calculated on a basis other than the life of a natural person, such term shall be no less than 50 years from the end of the calendar year of authorized publication, or, failing such

---

[1]*See, e.g.*, EC Council Regulation 1768/92 of 18 June 1992 on the creation of a supplementary protection certificate for medicinal products [1992] O.J. L182/1.

authorized publication within 50 years from the making of the work, 50 years from the end of the calendar year of making.[2]

Trademarks: Art. 18

Initial registration, and each renewal of registration, of a trademark shall be for a term of no less than seven years. The registration of a trademark shall be renewable indefinitely.

Industrial Designs: Art. 26:3

3. The duration of protection available shall amount to at least 10 years.

Patents: Art. 33

The term of protection available shall not end before the expiration of a period of twenty years counted from the filing date.[12]

Foonote: 12 It is understood that those Members which do not have a system of original grant may provide that the term of protection shall be computed from the filing date in the system of original grant.

Layout-designs: Art. 38

1. In Members requiring registration as a condition of protection, the term of protection of layout-designs shall not end before the expiration of a period of 10 years counted from the date of filing an application for registration or from the first commercial exploitation wherever in the world it occurs.

2. In Members not requiring registration as a condition for protection, layout-designs shall be protected for a term of no less than 10 years from the date of the first commercial exploitation wherever in the world it occurs.

---

[2]Recall that the TRIPS Agreement (Article 9) also incorporates by reference the basic Berne Convention rule on duration (Article 7).

3. Notwithstanding paragraphs 1 and 2, a Member may provide that protection shall lapse 15 years after the creation of the layout-design.

Notes and Questions

1. We will look at the terms of the various forms of IPRs in Chapter IV, and consider whether they are appropriate. Yet, at this early stage, can you identify the reasons why the different forms of IPRs should be subject to such wide variations in duration?

2. It has been proposed that duration should not be based on the field of law, but instead on the nature of the product or work that is protected. Computer programs, for example, might be protected for a different time period than paintings. Would such an approach be preferable? What are the potential drawbacks?

3. The duration of IPRs protection directly affects conditions of competition in the marketplace. In Chapter VII, we will explore the relationship between IPRs and competition law, and examine the provisions of the TRIPS Agreement relating to competition. Should the TRIPS Agreement attempt to limit the maximum duration of IPRs protection as a means for preserving competitive markets?

---

7. Intellectual Step

In historical terms, the systematic legal appropriation of knowledge and information is relatively recent. Societies, for centuries, evolved on the basis of informal transfers of knowledge and technological advances in know-how — from masters to students, from fathers to sons, from mothers to daughters. The advent of systematic legal entitlement — of exclusive rights to information — is mainly linked to the advent of modern capitalism, individualism, industrial organization and the technological age. IPRs contrast with informal modes and methods of progress in the traditional manner of rural societies, which were governed by customs and customary law, and in which knowledge and information for the greatest part were in the public domain. Fundamentally new technologies, in particular the printing press, were at the origin of copyright, which primarily served to control these new technologies in an authoritarian age. Later on, the concept shifted to promotion and protection of investment. IPRs were developed and became part of a legal structure favoring and accelerating progress. IPRs are inherently linked to the idea of societal and technological progress. In that respect they fundamentally differ from real property rights, originating in Roman law, which are mainly concerned with the allocation of wealth.

The fundamental purposes of intellectual property provide the foundation for an encompassing principle of *intellectual step* which is shared by all forms of intellectual property — at least until very recent actions of the EU in the field of database protection, and with the possible exception of trademarks, which serve more to appropriate identity than information and knowledge. Short of an intellectual step, short of novelty, originality, or newness of idea and information, a fundamental requirement for legal protection is lacking. The principle of intellectual step is perhaps the most important feature of intellectual property. As the principle is part of the explicit requirements which define different forms of intellectual property in statutory and international law, there has been no need to state the principle *in abstracto*. It did not emerge as a legal principle comparable to the principles of territoriality, exhaustion or priority. Nevertheless, it should be noted and observed as an underlying principle of the present international IPRs system, particularly as it is challenged by emerging claims to appropriation of information and knowledge.

With the advent of concepts of sustainable development and intergenerational equity, the principle of intellectual step and the overall foundation of the modern intellectual property system has been challenged. Efforts are underway to bring about better legal protection of traditional knowledge, in particular in the context of biotechnological advances. Leaving traditional knowledge in the informal sector risks bringing about substantial imbalances, and may jeopardize the legitimacy of the overall IPRs system. We will return to this subject in Chapter VII.

Another challenge to the principle of intellectual step emerged — and succeeded — in respect to claims of protection for databases. Producers of databases have argued that investments in assembling quantities of information, regardless of any creative contribution, should be protected by intellectual property law. This argument is contrary to the traditions and history of the IPRs field, and so far has been rejected at the multilateral level (e.g., in WIPO negotiations). However, it has succeeded in the EU, which adopted a high level of legal protection for the mechanical assembly of information in the form of the database (we will study this *sui generis* form of protection in Chapter IV). Database producers contend that advances in digital technology, which facilitate copying and extraction from databases, demand that a new form of protection emerge.

While the fundamental principle of intellectual step is under attack in the database field, and may need some rethinking in the context of sustainable development, for the time being, it still dominates the positive law of IPRs and the international IPRs system.

Norms on Intellectual Step

At the international level, the requirement of the intellectual step can be found explicitly and implicitly in the Berne Convention, the Treaty on Intellectual Property in respect of Integrated Circuits, and the TRIPS Agreement. (All italics are added.)

Copyright — Article 2, Berne Convention

(1) The expression "literary and artistic works" shall include every production in the literary, scientific and artistic domain, whatever may be the mode or form of its expression, . . .

Trademark — Article 15(1), TRIPS Agreement

Any sign, or any combination of signs, *capable of distinguishing* the goods or services of one undertaking from those of other undertakings, shall be capable of constituting a trademark. Such signs, in particular words including personal names, letters, numerals, figurative elements and combinations of colors as well as any combination of such signs, shall be eligible for registration as trademarks. Where signs are not inherently capable of distinguishing the relevant goods or services, Members may make registrability depend on distinctiveness acquired through use. Members may require, as a condition of registration, that signs be visually perceptible.

Industrial design — Article 25(1) TRIPS Agreement

Members shall provide for the protection of independently created industrial designs that are *new* or *original*. Members may provide that designs are not new or original if they do not significantly differ from known designs or combinations of known design features. Members may provide that such protection shall not extend to designs dictated essentially by technical or functional considerations.

Layout Designs (Topographies) and Integrated Circuits — Art. 3(2), Treaty on Intellectual Property in Respect of Integrated Circuits (Washington Agreement)

The obligation referred to in para. (1)(a) shall apply to layout-designs (topographies) that are *original* in the sense that they are the result of their creators' own *intellectual effort* and are not commonplace among creators of layout-designs (topographies) and manufacturers of integrated circuits at the time of their creation.

A layout-design (topography) that consists of a combination of elements and interconnections that are commonplace shall be protected only if the combination, taken as a whole, fulfills the conditions referred to in subparagraph (a).

Patents — Article 27(1), TRIPS Agreement

Subject to the provisions of paragraphs 2 and 3, patents shall be available for any inventions, whether products or processes, in all fields of technology, provided that they are *new*, involve an *inventive step* and are capable of industrial application. Subject to Article 65(4), Article 70(8) and paragraph 3 of this Article, patents shall be available and patent rights enjoyable without discrimination as to the place of invention, the field of technology and whether products are imported or locally produced.

Trade secrets — Article 39(2), TRIPS Agreement

Natural and legal persons shall have the possibility of preventing information lawfully within their control from being disclosed to, acquired by, or used by others without their consent in a manner contrary to honest commercial practices so long as such information:

(a) is secret in the sense that it is *not*, as a body or in the precise configuration and assembly of its components, *generally known* among *or readily accessible* to persons within the circles that normally deal with the kind of information in question;

*****

Notes and Questions

1. Compare the different formulations of intellectual step in the legal definitions set out above. Are these formulations compatible? How would you explain the conditions for trademarks and trade secrets in light of the principle of intellectual step? Does distinctiveness imply an intellectual step in trademarks? Does trade secret inherently entail an intellectual step as the information is not (yet) known in the public domain? Or, would you conclude that the principle of intellectual step is not applicable to trade secret, perhaps placing it outside the proper realm of intellectual property?

2. In the introduction to this subsection, we posited that intellectual step is an essential element of IPRs, and that it is rooted in the fundamental policies underlying the grant of IPRs protection. Do you agree, or do you think

617

this criterion of protection might be jettisoned? If intellectual step is important, and if databases do not embody intellectual step, how should databases be characterized? Are they intellectual property, or something else?

---

8. Dissemination of Protected Information

IPRs are characterized, on the one hand, by the grant of exclusive property rights to private persons and operators. This is the private side of the matter. The IPRs system, however, is equally characterized by the idea of bringing protected information and know-how into the realm of public knowledge. A creation must be properly disclosed. This is the public side of the matter. The fundamental trade-off between private rights and dissemination is particularly evident in the field of industrial property. Mandatory disclosure and publication of patented information is an important source of technological information for competitors. With the advent of electronic communications, data is more readily available and accessible worldwide. Indeed, patent searches (while often not undertaken systematically, in particular by small- and medium-sized companies or individual inventors) are important in the process of developing a new product, and they define the boundaries and scope of new patents. Modern patent information systems are available (including in CD-ROM format and through Internet connection), and these systems should be used regularly by those involved in the process of inventing and producing new products. Similarly, registered trademarks are published, and should be researched before marketing divisions design new brands and marks. An uninformed approach to the introduction of new marks may result in conflict with existing marks, leading to extensive costs and losses. The same arguments can be made regarding registered industrial designs and topographies.

The principle of dissemination or disclosure also applies to copyright. While copyright right exists *ab initio* and without registration, the scope of protection inherently applies to the form of information and data made available to the public, and prevents a third party from commercial use of the forms expressed. In the copyright jurisprudence of the U.S. Supreme Court, for example, there is very clear elucidation of the idea that promoting dissemination to the public of works of authorship is the primary function of copyright.

A clear exception to the dissemination principle, of course, is inherent in the nature of trade secret. In this case, legal protection is granted with a view to offering alternative strategies to formal protection by industrial property rights. A trade-off between legal security and disclosure is not present. Strategies relying upon trade secret bear considerable risks.

The following provisions indicate the disclosure policy underlying the patent grant at the international and regional level.

Article 21, Patent Cooperation Treaty (PCT) — International Publication

(1) The International Bureau shall publish international applications.

(2)(a) Subject to the exceptions provided for in subparagraph (b) and in Article 64(3), the international publication of the international application shall be effected promptly after the expiration of 18 months from the priority date of that application.

(b) The applicant may ask the International Bureau to publish his international application any time before the expiration of the time limit referred to in subparagraph (a). The International Bureau shall proceed accordingly, as provided in the Regulations.

(3) The international search report or the declaration referred to in Article 17(2)(a) shall be published as prescribed in the Regulations.

(4) The language and form of the international publication and other details are governed by the Regulations.

(5) There shall be no international publication if the international application is withdrawn or is considered withdrawn before the technical preparations for publication have been completed.

(6) If the international application contains expressions or drawings which, in the opinion of the International Bureau, are contrary to

morality or public order, or if, in its opinion, the international application contains disparaging statements as defined in the Regulations, it may omit such expressions, drawings, and statements, from its publications, indicating the place and number of words or drawings omitted, and furnishing, upon request, individual copies of the passages omitted.

Article 93 European Patent Convention — Publication of a European patent application

(1) A European patent application shall be published as soon as possible after the expiry of a period of eighteen months from the date of filing or, if priority has been claimed, as from the date of priority. Nevertheless, at the request of the applicant the application may be published before the expiry of the period referred to above. It shall be published simultaneously with the publication of the specification of the European patent when the grant of the patent has become effective before the expiry of the period referred to above.

(2) The publication shall contain the description, the claims and any drawings as filed and, in an annex, the European search report and the abstract, in so far as the latter are available before the termination of the technical preparations for publication. If the European search report and the abstract have not been published at the same time as the application, they shall be published separately.

Article 98 European Patent Convention — Publication of a specification of the European patent

At the same time as it publishes the mention of the grant of the European patent, the European Patent Office shall publish a specification of the European patent containing the description, the claims and any drawings.

The following article analyzes the advantages of patents as a source of technological information.

Patent Documents as a Source of Technological Information

International Bureau of WIPO*

20. Patent documents generally *convey the most recent information*. This is so because applicants are in a hurry; usually the applicant who, among several applicants applying in respect of a similar invention, was the first to apply will be granted the patent, whereas the application of the others will be denied; furthermore, only with a patent in his hand has an inventor the maximum legal means at his disposal for contesting the use of his invention by others against his will; finally, an inventor having a patent usually can stipulate a higher sales price or royalty for selling or licensing his invention than if he does not, or does not yet, have a patent. There are some well-known cases which show that important inventions were disclosed in patent documents several years before their appearance in other forms of literature, for example:

	Date of published patent	Date of first disclosure in other forms of literature
Hollerith (punched card)	1889	1914
Baird (television)	1923	1928
Whittle (jet engine)	1936	1946
Morrogh (ductile cast iron)	1939	1947
Ziegler, Natta (poly-merization catalysts)	1953	1960

21. Patent documents generally *have a fairly uniform structure:* the claims give the essence of what is new; the description gives the background to the invention (what was known *before* the invention, i.e., the "prior art"), and defines the difference between the pre-existent technology and what the invention contributes, as a new matter, as a step forward, in technology; this means, among other things, and, as distinct from scientific or technological articles, that the reader of patent documents does not first have to familiarize himself with, and adjust his mental processes to, the mental processes —

*WIPO/IP/MNL/89/1.

different for every author — of the author of a scientific article; in other words, this fairly uniform structure of patent documents makes their reading, once one gets accustomed to it, generally easier.

22. Patent documents generally *disclose technological information* by describing the inventions in accordance with the requirements of the applicable patent law and by indicating the claimed novelty and inventiveness by reference to the existing state of the art. They are thus sources of information not only on what is new (the invention) but also on what is already know (i.e. the state of the art) and in many cases furnish a history, in summary form, of the technological progress in the field to which they relate. Certain patent documents are published together with a search report showing a series of references found at the occasion of a documentary search made to establish in a first instance the level of novelty of the claimed invention.

23. Patent documents generally *cover most of what is new and most of what is worthwhile knowing* about technological advance; this is shown not only by the great number of patents but also by the fact that they cover every branch — big or small, relatively simple or sophisticated — of technology. Naturally there are certain inventions, mainly in the field of arms and warfare, which are not or cannot be patented or are patented but not published because their publication could be prejudicial to national security. But, on the whole, such inventions constitute a relatively small percentage of all the inventions made.

24. Patent documents generally *contain information which is not divulged in any other form of literature.* Thus it is wrong to consider that relevant information contained in patent documents will come to one's notice by other means. An investigation made by the U.S. Patent and Trademark Office shows that as much as 70% of the technology disclosed in U.S. patent documents from 1967 to 1972 had not been disclosed in non-patent literature.

25. Many patent documents *contain an abstract.* Abstracts allow a general idea to be formed of the contents of the document within a few minutes, and in any case a much shorter time than would be required to read the full text of the patent document.

26. Patent documents *bear "classification symbols."* For the purposes of maintaining search files and performing searches for the state of the art, Patent Offices classify patent documents according to the field or fields of technology to which their contents relate. A number of different classification systems exist. The International Patent Classification (IPC) has been established by an intergovernmental agreement, and is now applied by at least 50 Patent Offices.

27. The main part of the *high cost of processing and classifying patent documents* for building-up search files, and of keeping the classification system up to date, *is borne directly by the Patent Offices which publish large numbers of patent documents;* users other than the Patent Office itself thus have access to patent documentation without incurring, in addition to their costs as users, the cost of maintaining, developing and classifying their own patent documentation collections.

28. Patent documents belonging to a given classification subdivision *contain a highly concentrated supply of usually technically advanced information* on a given technological field.

29. Patent documents *bear a date* from which conclusions can be drawn as to the age of an invention and to the question of whether the inventions they describe are still under legal protection. If they are no longer legally protected, they can be used without the consent of the patentee.

30. Patent documents mostly *indicate the name and address of the applicant, the patentee, and the inventor,* or at least one or two of these persons. These indications allow any potential licensee to contact the persons concerned in order to find out under what conditions he may be authorized to exploit the invention.

31. Patent documents often disclose not only concepts concerning the general utility of the invention, but generally also give *detailed information on the possibility of its practical application in industry.*

32. Since the technological *information contained in patent documents is not secret,* it can be freely used to support research and development activities; if a given invention is not protected by a patent in the country of the

user (and it is obvious from the statistics that only a minority of inventions are ever protected in the majority of developing countries), the said invention can even be put to industrial application in that country, although the results of that industrial application cannot be exported to another country where the invention is protected by a patent.

33. The above-mentioned specific characteristics of patent documents make them eminently useful sources of technological information, with some clear advantages over other sources of information. There are, however, a certain number of limitations to this usefulness, which are the following:

(a) new technology is not always sufficiently inventive to be patentable;

(b) even where a patent has been granted by an examining Office, this is not a guarantee that the invention is absolutely new. Furthermore, the question of whether the invention is such that, in practice, it will be economically desirable to use it is one whose solution — particularly if the invention or the technical field to which it relates is a sophisticated one — requires great experience in the technical field concerned. Even highly specialized experts may make mistakes in judging this question. It is clear that purely technological information as contained in patent documents often needs to be complemented by information of other sorts (commercial or economic for instance);

(c) although patent documents should be and generally are, written in a way which allows the invention to be executed on the basis of them alone, it will frequently be necessary in practice to execute it with the cooperation of the inventor (for example, by acquiring his know-now and blueprints under a contract concluded with him).

Notes and Questions

1. The benefits granted to private operators by IPRs are often justified by accompanying obligations to disclose intellectual steps, in particular in the

fields of patents. Does one side of this equation justify the other or, instead, are both sides in the long-term public interest?

2. Does the inherent exclusion of trade secrets from the principle of dissemination of information render the protection, once again, outside the proper realm of IPRs? Or, does the exception rather confirm the rule?

9. Transparency of Rules

Another aspect of dissemination was added to the international IPRs system by obligations to provide transparency as set forth in Article 63 of the TRIPS Agreement. This provision reflects the general principles underlying "sunshine" laws established since the Second World War, as in Article X of the GATT 1947. The obligation to publish laws, regulations and leading cases would seem an apparent and necessary attribute of the rule of law. However, there are certain countervailing forces at work which have made positive legislation on transparency a necessity. A history of secretive Nineteenth Century trade diplomacy — which has its roots much farther back in secretive politico-military diplomacy — made such rules imperative, with a view to achieving an open and transparent multilateral trading system.

Similar history and concerns are relevant to IPRs regulation, albeit to a lesser degree. IPRs regulation has a long legal tradition, and is mainly framed by statutory law and judicial precedent. Nevertheless, the very first case relating to the TRIPS Agreement, the *India-Mailbox* case discussed earlier in this chapter, shows that IPRs regulation in national law needs to be accompanied by international disciplines ensuring transparency.

The international IPRs system does not merely impose obligations on national or regional systems. It also assists governments in bringing about transparency. WIPO publishes several collections of national IPRs laws, and it disseminates information to the public in other ways (e.g., over the Internet). An agreement between WIPO and the WTO promotes cooperation, *inter alia,* in the effort to assist governments in publishing pertinent rules and decisions. The WTO TRIPS Council, moreover, has authorized the public distribution, following a brief waiting period, of its reviews of national and regional IPRs laws over the Internet.

Norms on Transparency

Article 63, TRIPS Agreement

1. Laws and regulations, and final judicial decisions and administrative rulings of general application, made effective by any Member pertaining to the subject matter of this Agreement (the availability, scope, acquisition, enforcement and prevention of the abuse of intellectual property rights) shall be published, or where such publication is not practicable made publicly available, in a national language, in such a manner as to enable governments and right holders to become acquainted with them. Agreements concerning the subject matter of this Agreement which are in force between the government or a governmental agency of any Member and the government or a governmental agency of any other Member shall also be published.

2. Members shall notify the laws and regulations referred to in paragraph 1 above to the Council for Trade-Related Aspects of Intellectual Property Rights in order to assist that Council in its review of the operation of this Agreement. The Council shall attempt to minimize the burden on Members in carrying out this obligation and may decide to waive the obligation to notify such laws and regulations directly to the Council if consultations with the World Intellectual Property Organization on the establishment of a common register containing these laws and regulations are successful. The Council shall also consider in this connection any action required regarding notifications pursuant to the obligations under this Agreement stemming from the provisions of Article 6ter of the Paris Convention (1967).

3. Each Member shall be prepared to supply, in response to a written request from another Member, information of the sort referred to in paragraph 1 above. A Member, having reason to believe that a specific judicial decision or administrative ruling or bilateral agreement in the

area of intellectual property rights affects its rights under this Agreement, may also request in writing to be given access to or be informed in sufficient detail of such specific judicial decisions or administrative rulings or bilateral agreements.

4. Nothing in paragraphs 1 to 3 above shall require Members to disclose confidential information which would impede law enforcement or otherwise be contrary to the public interest or would prejudice the legitimate commercial interests of particular enterprises, public or private.

Pursuant to Article 63(2), TRIPS Agreement, the WTO and the WIPO signed an agreement for cooperation.

Notes and Questions

1. In the *India-Mailbox* case, the AB refused to accept one argument made by the United States on procedural grounds. According to the AB, the claim was introduced too late. However, the WTO panel had determined that a requirement of transparency is inherent in the TRIPS Agreement, based upon the doctrine of legitimate expectations and security of law. Does a requirement of transparency implicitly flow from the principle of legal security which is recognized to be inherent in the WTO system?

2. In civil law countries, not all court decisions are published. Courts generally are not fully aware of obligations under international law to publish leading cases and important precedents.

---

10. Enforceability of IPRs

The international IPRs system, for a long time, was mainly concerned with harmonization of substantive rules and standards, and the establishment of international systems of registration. With the exception of seizure of infringing goods, little attention was paid to the problem of enforcing rights abroad. Although the Paris and Berne Conventions include some explicit provisions regarding enforcement, and imply additional obligations,[1] enforcement matters were largely left to the discretion of national or regional IPRs legal systems. While international standards, to the extent they existed, were incorporated in national law, legal security and effective protection often failed due to lack of adequate tools and resources relating to the administration of justice and to the enforcement of rights.

This situation has been changing since the Uruguay Round negotiations and the adoption of the TRIPS Agreement. Part III of the TRIPS Agreement is devoted to procedural standards of a civil, administrative and criminal character, with a view to improving enforcement of IPRs. These provisions are surprisingly detailed, and emerged from an effort to combine common and civil law traditions. They have influenced other agreements, in particular the NAFTA. Given the post-Uruguay Round climate, and a substantive body of law dedicated to enforcement, it seems appropriate to include enforceability under the present heading of basic principles of the international IPRs system. The enforcement of IPRs is discussed in detail in Chapter VI.

TRIPs and the Enforcement of Intellectual Property Rights

Thomas Dreier*

*****

II. Point of Departure

In contrast to substantive provisions and principles, traditional international conventions and agreements on intellectual property protection contain very few regulations on enforcement of rights; in this respect they at most prescribe minimum obligations. It follows that until now the formal and practical aspects of enforcement of these rights have been left for the most part to the signatory states.

---

[1]See Chapter VI, *infra*.
*In FROM GATT TO TRIPs 244 (F-K BEIER & G. SCHRICKER EDS.,1996). Translated by Catriona Thomas.

In the face of the absence of explicit and general competence, the European Union has also given but fragmentary consideration to the harmonization of the legal consequences of infringement of intellectual property rights. So far, its attempts have been confined to customs regulations for the external borders of the Community and to a certain degree of harmonization in the fields of misleading advertising, computer programs, trademark law and utility model law. The situation is different, however, as regards the latest trade agreements, e.g., the Cartagena Agreement and especially the North American Free Trade Agreement (NAFTA), which do contain independent chapters regulating enforcement of rights — not least following the example of the TRIPs Agreement that was concluded at about the same time.

In contrast, existing international conventions and agreements do include provisions on the acquisition and maintenance of registered rights and for the most part on related inter-partes procedures. Hence, the point of departure in this respect is completely different from the situation regarding provisions on the enforcement of rights.

Enforcement and International Conventions

Article 9 of the Paris Convention for the Protection of Industrial Property provides for the seizure on importation of goods unlawfully bearing a trademark or trade name; pursuant to Art. 10 of the Convention this also applies with respect to the direct or indirect use of a false indication. However, adoption of this possibility of seizure is not mandatory, as becomes clear from Art. 9(6), Paris Convention. In this respect — and as regards acts of unfair competition pursuant to Art. 10bis — Article 10ter(1), Paris Convention, contains a general obligation of its signatory states to assure to nationals of the other countries of the Union "appropriate legal remedies" to repress such acts "effectively." In addition, the second paragraph of this provision obliges the signatory states to afford procedural national treatment to associations and organizations of businesses, manufacturers and retailers before courts and administrative authorities. Apart from this, Art. 6bis(1) and Art. 6septies(2), Paris Convention provide for explicit injunction claims in the case of a highly renowned trademark, to be asserted in favor of the trademark owner vis-à-vis an agent or representative who uses the mark without his consent.

A more recent international convention text, namely the

Washington Treaty on Intellectual Property in Respect of Integrated Circuits, once again confines itself to a description of substantive standards of protection.

Apart from the procedural alleviation of proof by means of the assumption of authorship pursuant to Art. 15, the Revised Berne Convention for the Protection of Literary and Artistic Works (RBC) contains a sparse reference in Art. 16 to an obligation to seize unlawful copies of works pursuant to the regulations of the relevant national law. Pursuant to Art. 13(3) of the RBC, phonograms that were produced under a compulsory license and that were imported without the permission of the right owners are subject to seizure in import countries in which they are prohibited. Article I of the Universal Copyright Convention (UCC) contains a general obligation to grant "adequate and effective protection." The International Convention for the Protection of Performers, Producers of Phonograms and Broadcasting Organizations, the so-called Rome Convention, does not contain any provisions on enforcement of rights; the Geneva Phonograms Convention merely includes a reference to the grant of protection by virtue of criminal law, i.e. it does not contain any provisions concerning the enforcement of rights.

*****

4. Point of Departure of TRIPs Negotiations

It is true that the national laws of all WTO Members, insofar as they grant substantive protection, contain provisions on the enforcement of these rights. Yet at the same time there are sometimes considerable differences in practice regarding numerous aspects of the implementation and hence the effectiveness of these provisions.

Corresponding to these considerations, the main problem in drafting rules for the enforcement of rights within the framework of TRIPs was the global applicability which was to be attributed to these rights. On the one hand, they had to fulfill the necessity of sufficiently effective protection in industrialized countries. On the other hand, they must not themselves lead to barriers to unrestricted trade in goods and services; however, the main hurdle was that they had to be accepted and adhered to by developing countries as well. It is true that in principle this also applies with respect to substantive protection standards yet it was apparently less difficult to achieve harmonization in that area. It may well be that the substantive protection is too far-reaching in the eyes of a certain Member, yet it can grant

630

this protection in principle. Procedural regulations and possibilities of enforcing rights can only be established with any hope of success if and where — and to the extent that — this is possible under the infrastructural and socio-economic circumstances prevailing in the country of the Member concerned.

Consequently, it did not seem feasible to adopt an approach of complete harmonization in the area of enforcement of rights. The approach of universal recognition and execution of court judgments was also rejected from the outset because this would probably only work in a relatively "homogenous" environment. Instead, an attempt was made to formulate a *minimum basic stock of procedural regulations*, guided by the intention to achieve the best possible "effectiveness," and to tie this stock of regulations to result-oriented criteria instead of setting out all the details. At the same time, this approach reflects a certain Anglo-American pragmatism, which need not necessarily always conform with Continental-European concepts of formal procedural fairness. This result-oriented approach is the reason why Part III, TRIPs Agreement and Part IV inasfar as similar problematic issues are concerned — contains such vague phrases as "effective," "reasonable," "undue," "unwarranted," "fair and equitable" and "not . . . unnecessarily complicated or costly."

Notes and Questions

1. Article 42.5, TRIPS Agreement, does not require WTO Members to allocate additional resources to the enforcement of IPRs, yet judicial systems remain bound to meet TRIPS standards, often with inadequate resources. At the time of the TRIPS negotiations, developing and transforming Members were not prepared to make commitments on the expenditure of resources for enforcement.

Who will mainly benefit from the effective enforcement of IPRs? Might industrialized countries, interested in effective protection, along with international institutions, such as the World Bank, actively assist countries in building more efficient administrative and judicial structures within policies of good governance and the promotion of the rule of law? What contributions might WIPO and the WTO make? In Chapter VIII, Carlos Primo

Braga, Carsten Fink and Claudia Sepulveda consider IPRs enforcement in the developing countries from the perspective of the World Bank.

2. Recall the *Hermès* decision of the ECJ discussed earlier in this Chapter. Did the ECJ have jurisdiction to review national enforcement rules in light of the TRIPS Agreement? What problems might international organizations and panels encounter in reviewing national enforcement regimes? This question is further explored in Chapter VI.

CHAPTER IV

Norms and Norm-Making in the International IPRs System

A. Introduction

So far we have introduced the forms of IPRs, the international institutions that make and enforce international IPRs rules and general principles of law applicable in the IPRs field. We now turn to a more detailed examination of the norms that have so far been adopted, as well as some of the ongoing efforts to make these norms more efficient and effective on a worldwide basis.

As we have previously noted, efforts to create an international IPRs system date back to the late 1800s when two treaties that continue to form the backbone of the system were agreed upon — The Paris Convention for the Protection of Industrial Property (1883) and the Berne Convention for the Protection of Literary and Artistic Works (1886). We will look first at the norm system regarding patents, and we will subsequently examine norm systems for other forms of IPRs.

We start with a historical perspective to better understand the context in which patent rules were made. Decisions as to whether particular rules continue to be appropriate to our turn-of-the-millennium setting may be influenced by an appreciation of why the rules were adopted in the first place. Of course, historical context will not alone provide answers to whether rules should be preserved or changed because the context in which rules are applied evolves continuously.

The Paris Convention has been subject to a series of revisions since its adoption in 1883. The most recent revision was undertaken at Stockholm in 1967 (and amended in 1979), and the Stockholm revision of the Paris Convention is the most widely adopted among its contracting parties. Only three of the 153 countries party to the Paris Convention are not party to the Stockholm Act. Nevertheless, the fact that different parties may be subject to different versions of the same convention does create confusion. It was in substantial part because of a similar situation in the GATT that countries decided during the Uruguay Round negotiations that the final result would take the form of a "single undertaking" to which all Members of the WTO must be party. This single undertaking approach applies to the TRIPS Agreement, which covers all WTO Members.

The TRIPS Agreement adds specific substantive rules to those of the Paris Convention in respect to patents. These new rules are set out and discussed following those of the Paris Convention.

As initially proposed a number of years ago and debated in a WIPO Committee of Experts group, a draft Patent Law Treaty would have harmonized or approximated substantive rules in relation to patents. These rules are of considerable sensitivity and importance to interest groups within different nations and regions. They included rules that would have required the United States to abandon its *first to invent* patent system (in favor of the *first to file system*), and rules that would have required continental European countries to modify their approaches to the grace periods following the disclosure of inventions. However, as it became increasingly clear that agreement on these significant substantive changes might not be realized for some time, the ambition of the Patent Law Treaty drafters shifted to the realm of procedural formalities in connection with obtaining and maintaining patent protection. While the importance of these formalities is not to be discounted, we leave consideration of the draft Patent Law Treaty for a later section of the book that deals with the mechanisms for obtaining patent protection.

After looking at the norms on patents at the broad multilateral level — the WIPO and WTO norms and norms-in-the-making — we turn to the rules of the European Patent Convention (EPC), undoubtedly the most widely used and important set of regional patent rules. After this, we look somewhat more briefly at other regional norm systems. Finally, we consider a few national systems, such as the Chinese and Japanese, to give us a more global perspective on patent norms and norm-making.

B. The Paris Convention

1. Historical Context

We previously studied Edith Tilton Penrose's economic analysis of the international patent system. In the same book from which that excerpt was drawn, Edith Penrose wrote about the negotiating history of the Paris Convention.

The Economics of the International Patent System

Edith Tilton Penrose*

Chapter III
The Development of the International Convention for the Protection of Industrial Property

As the patent system spread into one country after another in the 19th century, demands from various quarters for the adoption of international regulations increased. Commercial interests are no respecters of national boundaries and while the law of each country prevails only within the jurisdiction of that country, the interest of the patentees in the use of their inventions frequently extends beyond the jurisdiction of any one country. As might be expected, the patent laws adopted by the various countries, though designed broadly for the same purposes, varied considerably in their detailed provisions. Although few discriminated against foreigners specifically, the difficulty of complying with many different regulations made it almost impossible for a patentee to get protection in many countries.

The definition of what was considered a patentable invention differed between the laws of different countries and consequently a patent might be obtained on an invention in some countries while in others the invention was excluded from patent protection. This was — and is — particularly true with regard to medicines, foods, drugs and chemical products. Novelty of the invention was required in most countries and an invention was frequently not considered new if it had been published or publicly used abroad. When an inventor applied for a patent in his own country he had to disclose the nature of his invention, and the publication of the specification attached to this patent application was held by a few other countries to destroy the newness of the invention for patent purposes. In applying for a patent in several countries an inventor had to draw up applications conforming to widely different and extremely detailed rules; he had strictly to observe complicated procedures, and he had to do all of these things within short periods of time. In the meantime, others might learn of his invention through the patent application in his own country and patent the invention

---

*Johns Hopkins University Press (1951).

635

themselves, if permitted. Or they might simply use it, thus either destroying its novelty for patent purposes or acquiring a legal right to its use which could not be touched even if the original inventor succeeded eventually in obtaining a patent. Taxes had to be paid on time or the patent would be forfeited. In many countries the invention had to be put into commercial use within a limited period of time. Thus, to obtain and maintain patents in foreign countries, a patentee was usually forced to incur the expense of obtaining and maintaining patent agents in each country to defend his interests.

Hence a patentee who wished to exploit his invention abroad, or to obtain a revenue from its exploitation abroad by others, or to prevent others from using his invention to compete with him in foreign markets, had a strong incentive to press for international agreements which would eliminate the difficulties of obtaining protection in countries other than his own.

Patent lawyers, jurists and manufacturers joined in the demand for international legislation. The "rights of man" were freely invoked in the cause and at times the movement took on the tone of a religious crusade. One of the crusaders, for example, wrote:

> The striving of the individual human and the interest of the social organism join in a common cause to justify the juridical institution of the right of the inventor or of the creator.... But a right which has its source in a human aspiration as profound as that we have just revealed extends to the entire community of men who live and think.... How contain the explosion of a new principle in the narrow confines of a single country without permitting it to expand across the universe?

Nor was invention the only type of industrial property for which international arrangements were being asked. Trade marks, industrial designs and models were included. The only international protection existing when the International Convention for the Protection of Industrial Property was created in 1880 was such as had been written into bipartite treaties most of which were concerned primarily with other matters. Of these there were some 69 that included provisions affecting industrial property, but only two of them contained provisions for the protection of patents. This type of protection was generally considered to be unsatisfactory since it had no separate existence apart from the general commercial arrangements with which it was usually associated. Hence the protection was apt to be "*brève et précaire.*"

The Vienna Congress of 1873

The first conference to consider the protection of inventors on an international scale met in Vienna in 1873. An international Exposition under the auspices of the Austria-Hungarian Government was to be held in that year and the inventors in some countries, particularly the United States, feared that their inventions would be inadequately protected under Austrian law. The United States took the lead in pressing Austria to protect more adequately inventions exhibited at the Exposition and, in addition, to revise her patent laws to give more complete protection to foreign patentees in general. Among those provisions of the Austrian law which met the disapproval of the United States was the compulsory working requirement, under which a patented article had to be manufactured in Austria within a year from the issue of the patent. The American Minister in Vienna even referred the Austrian Foreign Ministry to an article in the Scientific American which complained of Austrian treatment of American inventors and ended with a veiled threat of refusal to join in the Exposition if the Austrian law were not changed.

The Austrians passed a special law protecting exhibited inventions. In addition, on the suggestion of the United States, it was decided to hold an international conference on patent reform immediately after the Exposition. Thus, the first international conference on patents was held while the controversy between the patent and anti-patent forces throughout Europe was still lively and bitter. It was not an official conference although representatives from 13 countries were included among the 158 participants. The majority of those attending the conference were from Germany and the acute difference of opinion in Germany as to whether a patent law was desirable and whether Germany should adopt one was reflected in the debates of the conference.

The resolutions were very general but clearly endorsed the principle of patent protection. The first resolution, consisting of seven reasons why "the protection of inventions should be guaranteed by the laws of all civilized nations under the condition of a complete publication of the same," was violently debated but was adopted by a vote of 80 to 4. The second resolution, setting out the principles on which an "effective and useful patent law should be based" was even more controversial. The most notable decision of the conference was paragraph (f) of this resolution which recommended compulsory licensing of patents "in cases in which the public interest should require it." This principle was not again to be accepted by an international conference for 50 years but the anti-patent movement in the 19th century had created such an awareness of the possible monopolistic and restrictive effects of the patent system that some limitation of the patent monopoly had to be conceded by the patent advocates. The official United States position was strongly opposed to any concessions but the resolution was carried by a vote of 42 to 17.

Finally the conference resolved that it was "of pressing moment that governments should endeavor to bring about an international understanding upon patent protection as soon as possible" and empowered a preparatory committee "to continue the work commenced by this first international congress, and to use all their influence that the principles adopted be made known as widely as possible, and carried into practice." Five years later the conference that was to establish the basis of an international agreement was called.

The Paris Conference of 1878

Under the auspices of the French Government, and again in connection with an international Exposition, a conference of nearly 500 participants, including eleven government delegates and delegates from 48 Chambers of Commerce and industrial and technical societies was called in Paris. Like the Vienna conference, this conference was an unofficial affair, although called by the French government and attended by some official delegates. More than three-fifths of the delegates were French industrialists and thus the French point of view completely dominated the conference. This is one of the reasons why the views of this conference in many respects contrasted strongly with those of the Vienna conference in which the German element was predominant. Malapert, a French jurist and patent authority, complained that, although invitations were widely sent out, the scope of the conference was so restricted by its promoters that people with a critical point of view did not attend:

> The acts of the organizing committee had restricted too much a field which ought to be open. There was no place where one could take account of the social position of different populations of the globe, although all were invited to engage in a common task. The radius of the

circle was too short, the circumference inscribed a cell in which it was not possible to breathe. It was for this reason that many jurists and economists, expert in the study of patent laws, refrained from attending the conference where they would have nothing to learn and nothing to do or teach, since limits had been set outside of which it was forbidden to go.

The stenographic report of the conference shows clearly that critics of the operation of the patent system were not well received. "Vice applandissements" occur after speeches in which the strongest and most far-reaching claims were made for inventors' rights, while "rumeurs" are reported when remarks such as the following were made:

> Messieurs, after the eloquent words which you have just heard, it takes great temerity on my part to mount this platform; but I consider it my duty to arise here to tell you of the dangers and inconveniences which result from the monopoly of exploitation granted by the French law to patentees for fifteen years. (Murmurs)

It is not surprising, therefore, that the resolutions of the conference reflect almost exclusively the patentees' point of view. In addition to the exaltation of the rights of inventors was the exaltation of the spirit of international union. The dream of many who attended the conference was complete uniformity of the laws protecting industrial property in all nations. At this time the formation of unions of many kinds was being discussed in conferences all over Europe. The most important of these referred to postal matters, the telegraph, weights and measures, and literary and artistic property. A patent union analogous to these other unions, with a uniform international law, was the goal.

There were a few participants, however, who were aware of the social implications of the patent law and who felt that some recognition of the interest of society should be explicitly stated other than the general assertion that society benefitted because of the encouragement of invention. The very first debate of the conference was on the nature of the inventor's right and the proposition before the conference was as follows:

> The right of inventors and of industrial creators in their work, or of manufacturers and business men in their marks is a right of property, the civil law does not create it, it only regulates it.

639

M. Clunet, a French jurist, presented a "counter-proposition";

> The right of inventors and of industrial creators is an equitable and use-
> ful creation of the civil law, which reconciles the rights of inventors and
> of society by the concession of a temporary monopoly.

The debate on this issue was heated and involved, but the conference
came out decisively in favor of the first proposition. It adopted in effect the
"natural property" theory of inventors' rights. Nonetheless, in spite of this
extreme position, it was not possible for the participants in the discussions
to escape the fact that at times there might be a serious interference with the
welfare of society if this "most sacred of all property" was subject to no limitations. Hence it was proposed that "the principle of expropriation in the
public interest is applicable to patents." The adoption of this proposal was
opposed on the ground that it was not necessary; if a matter of public
health or military necessity existed, the state obviously had the power to
override private interests. The majority of the conference, however, felt it
was worthwhile to make this principle explicit and adopted the proposal.

On the principle of expropriation in the public interest, the conference
admitted the right of the state to revoke a patent if manufacture was not
undertaken in the country in a specified time, at least if the patentee could
not justify his inaction. In other words, the conference approved what is
now known as compulsory working—revocation of the patent if it was not
worked. Even compulsory licensing as the sanction for failure to work was
rejected. In later conferences, revocation of the patent was considered to be
too harsh on the inventor, and its replacement by compulsory licensing was
fought for and obtained. The Vienna conference had rejected the principle
that a patent must be worked in the country granting it and had therefore
not even proposed compulsory licensing as a sanction for non-working although it had approved compulsory licensing whenever the public interest
required it. In both respects, the Vienna conference was far ahead of the
times.

It seems curious, however, that in the 1878 conference, where the
rights of inventors were upheld in the most extreme forms, the principle of
compulsory licensing for failure to work was rejected in favor of outright
revocation of the patent. This position was the direct result of the natural
property theory of patents adopted by the conference. M. Charles Lyon-
Caën, a prominent French lawyer, argued heatedly that compulsory licens-

ing was a derogation of the right of property and compared the inventor subject to such licensing to a man who owned his house but was required to allow all who requested it, to live with him on the payment of a rental. Compulsory licensing only aided other private groups and could not be tolerated, although he would accept expropriation "*pour cause d'utilité publique*" if necessary:

> If one thinks that industry would have to suffer because of the monopoly, the remedy should not be to impose the obligation on the patentee to concede licenses, but to eliminate patents. . . . It is to completely misunderstand the absolute character of the right of property of the inventor to impose on him the obligation to concede licenses.

The conference accepted M. Lyon-Caën's point of view and approved the resolution that:

> Patents ought to assure, during their entire duration, to inventors or their assigns, the exclusive right to the exploitation of the invention and not a mere right to a royalty paid to them by third parties.

The conference adopted a number of other resolutions which were much more practical than those so far discussed. Some of them were subsequently taken over as the basis of the international Convention when it was finally agreed. These included the principle that foreigners should be treated equally with nationals in each country; that the laws of each country should apply to its colonies; that the importation of patented products by a patentee should not cause revocation of his patent; and that the rights acquired for the same invention in different countries should be independent of each others. It was also agreed that it should be possible for a patent claim to be made simultaneously at the appropriate national office and at the consulates of the various foreign nations in which a patent was desired.

When it came, however, to the problem of devising the framework of uniform legislation, the conference was obliged to recognize the realism of those who had insisted that uniformity was impossible in a world of national states with different interests, different legal structures and different economic histories, aspirations and ideologies. The participants contested vigorously over their different positions, but it soon became clear that the ideal of uniformity of legislation would have to give way to lesser goals. To the orators the ideal was good but the practical problems of achieving it were too great, since no state would admit that its own legal framework was not the best from which to take the international model.

The biggest obstacle to agreement on uniform patent laws was the question of the "previous examination" of the invention. Under the law of France and some other countries a patent was issued on the claim of the inventor, without examination of the merits or validity of his claim or of the novelty of the invention. Many other countries, on the other hand, required that the novelty, utility, patentability, etc. of the invention be scrutinized before the patent could be issued. Although most of the non-French delegates supported the latter system, the French were in the majority and the conference passed a resolution that a patent should be delivered to all claimants at their own risk and thus without governmental examination.

Nor was there unanimous agreement on what products, should be patentable. "Batailles très chaudes" took place on whether chemical products, pharmaceutical preparations and foodstuffs should be patentable and, although the conference decided in the affirmative, an important minority was left dissatisfied.

These various differences prevented the conference from coming to any final agreement on the nature of an international patent law, and it was decided to charge a permanent international commission with the task of carrying out the resolutions of the conference and of arranging an official international conference called by a government to lay the basis for uniform international legislation. In spite of the violent differences of opinion, the promoters of the conference had not yet lost hope of seeing such uniform legislation adopted.

The First Draft Convention

The commission set up by the conference of 1878 set to work immediately after the conference was over and the French section, which formed the executive committee of the commission, produced a long draft which constituted in effect an extensive universal law. The French Minister of Commerce, to whom the draft was presented, recognized that such a far-reaching proposal could never command universal acceptance, and requested the section to draft a convention of more modest proportions. A "Projet d'une Union Internationale pour la protection de la propiété industrielle" was then drafted by the French delegate Jagerschmidt.

In the drafting of this project an eye was kept on existing national laws; uniform international legislation was no longer the goal and the convention was admittedly designed to encroach as little as possible on existing laws. Since the next step was a governmental one, it became necessary to produce specific proposals that would be politically viable. Thus the delegates had come down from the stars, and concentrated on provisions that they hoped would overcome the worst difficulties facing patentees with international interests, and would at the same time be politically practical. Gone was the talk of "natural property rights," or any attempt to define the nature of an inventor's right; gone were attempts to eliminate compulsory working, which was provided for in the laws of nearly all countries; and gone were attempts to impose a uniform standard of patentability devised in the interest of patentees. M. Jagerschmidt showed remarkable political acumen in the draft, most of the essentials of which were eventually accepted in the Convention.

The Conference at Paris in 1880

The draft together with an invitation to an international diplomatic conference, was sent by the French government to other governments. The response was favorable, and in 1880 the official conference met in Paris with representatives from 19 governments. The draft convention was adopted with some amendments and the amended draft was submitted to governments for their comment and approval. Provision was made for the protection of other forms of industrial property as well as for patents, for the organization of an International Bureau for the Protection of Industrial Property, for amendments to the Convention and for the adhesion of new member states.

The provisions on patents were confined to specific issues on which it was hoped sufficient agreement could be obtained to form a union. The important ones were as follows:

Art. 2. The subjects or citizens of each of the contracting states shall enjoy, in all of the other States of the Union, so far as patents, industrial designs or models, trade marks, and commercial names are concerned, the advantages that their respective laws now grant, or may hereafter grant to their own nationals. Consequently they shall have the same protection as the latter, and the same legal remedy against any infringement of their rights, provided they comply with the formalities and conditions imposed on nationals by the domestic legislation of each State.

Art. 3. The subjects of States not forming part of the Union who are domiciled or who have industrial or commercial establishments in the territory of one of the States of the Union are assimilated to the subjects or citizens of the contracting States.

Art. 4. Any person who has duly applied for a patent, the registration of an industrial design or model, or a trade mark in one of the contracting States, shall enjoy for the purpose of registration in other countries and subject to the rights of third parties, a right of priority during the periods hereinafter stated.

Consequently, subsequent filing in one of the other States of the Union, before the expiration of these periods shall not be invalidated through any acts accomplished in the interval, as, for instance, by another filing, by publication of the invention or the working thereof, by the sale of copies of the design or model, or by the use of the trade mark.

The above-mentioned periods of priority shall be six months for patents and three months for industrial designs or models and for trade marks they shall be increased by one month for countries overseas.

Art. 5. The introduction by the patentee into the country where the patent has been granted of objects manufactured in any of the countries of the Union shall not entail forfeiture.

Nevertheless the patentee is subject to the obligation to work his patent in accordance with the laws of the country into which he introduces the patented articles.

The International Union for the Protection of Industrial Property

In 1883 a brief conference was held at which the Convention was finally approved and signed. Ratifications were exchanged and in 1884 the International Union for the Protection of Industrial Property came into being. The Union was first composed of eleven countries, to which another twenty-nine were successively added.

Amendments to the Convention are made by Conferences of Revision, of which there have been six so far. These conferences meet periodically and are called when it seems desirable to the countries concerned. All amendments must have the unanimous approval of the members of the Union. If unanimity is not forthcoming Special Arrangements between the countries agreeing to the provisions under discussion may be adopted. The principle of special arrangements or "restricted unions" is not looked upon with favor, since it destroys the uniformity of the international regulations affecting members of the Union, and only three special arrangements have been established, none for patents.

The text of the Convention, as revised in the conferences of revision, comes into effect for each country when it deposits its ratification. The old text remains in force for countries that have not ratified the new text. Hence at any given time there may be several regimes in effect depending upon the progress of ratification of the latest revised texts.

Notes and Questions

1. Edith Penrose discusses the factors that underlay the negotiation of the Paris Convention for the Protection of Industrial Property. She attributes the motivation for the negotiations to concerns surrounding the Austria-Hungarian International Exposition of 1873. What were American inventors concerned about? How could the display of an invention affect their economic rights?

Generally speaking, disclosure of an invention would undermine its novelty, a critical element in determining patentability. Thus, disclosure of an invention in a country where a patent had not yet been granted may have prevented patent protection from ever being obtained there, or from being obtained in any other country whose patent office took into account foreign disclosures in determining novelty.

If disclosure did not preclude patentability, someone other than the inventor may nevertheless have sought a patent on the invention before the original inventor. Some patent systems would have awarded a patent only to the true inventor, but it may not always have been easy to disprove another party's claim to inventive activity.

2. Edith Penrose notes that during the negotiation of the Paris Convention, there were some proposals to adopt a far more ambitious system of harmonized rules than those which eventually resulted. She observes that each country was persuaded that its own rules were the best, and that this made harmonization efforts difficult. Are matters so different today?

3. The harmonization of patent rules would likely have been a useful innovation. Yet in the late 1800s many countries' patent systems did not provide for the pre-grant examination of patent applications (and some still do not, including the Swiss). These systems relied instead on post-grant opposition to patents by parties challenging the entitlement of the grantees. Such challenges may have taken the form of administrative or judicial proceedings seeking revocation of patents, or may have taken the form of defense against the enforcement of patents in civil litigation (claiming defects in the original patent grants).

The absence of a pre-grant examination procedure reduces the *ex ante* cost of administering a patent system, but might impose substantial *ex post* costs, particularly on the general public which may face a proliferation of product markets monopolized by patent holders. The typical consumer would not challenge the grant of a patent simply to reduce the cost of a single purchase. Only a party with a vested interest in the market, e.g. a potential competitor, might be willing to bear such costs.

4. The architects of the Paris Convention employed certain fundamental rules in the new international patent protection system. These were:

    1. National treatment;

    2. Independence of patents; and

    3. Right of priority

These fundamental principles continue to underlie the international patent protection system.

2. The Treaty Text Explored

Next is WIPO's summary of the terms of the Paris Convention, after which the text of the provisions relevant to patents are set out. Notes and questions follow the text.

WIPO — International Protection of Industrial Property*
Paris Convention for the Protection of Industrial Property (1883)

The following 153 States were party to this Convention on April 1, 1999**:
*****

---

*http://www.wipo.int.

**[note moved from text] Albania, Algeria, Argentina, Armenia, Australia, Austria, Azerbaijan, Bahrain, Bahamas, Bangladesh, Barbados, Belarus, Belgium, Benin, Bolivia, Bosnia and Herzegovina, Botswana, Brazil, Bulgaria, Burkina Faso, Burundi, Cambodia, Cameroon, Canada, Central African Republic, Chad, Chile, China, Colombia, Congo, Costa Rica, Côte d'Ivoire, Croatia, Cuba, Cyprus, Czech Republic, Democratic People's Republic of Korea, Democratic Republic of the Congo, Denmark, Dominican Republic, Ecuador, Egypt, El Salvador, Equatorial Guinea, Estonia, Finland, France, Gabon, Gambia, Georgia, Germany, Ghana, Greece, Grenada, Guatemala, Guinea, Guinea-Bissau, Guyana, Haiti, Holy See, Honduras, Hungary, Iceland, India, Indonesia, Iran (Islamic Republic of), Iraq, Ireland, Israel, Italy, Japan, Jordan, Kazakhstan, Kenya, Kyrgyzstan, Lao People's Democratic Republic, Latvia, Lebanon, Lesotho, Liberia, Libya, Liechtenstein, Lithuania, Luxembourg, Madagascar, Malawi, Malaysia, Mali, Malta, Mauritania, Mauritius, Mexico, Monaco, Mongolia, Morocco, Mozambique, Netherlands, New Zealand, Nicaragua, Niger, Nigeria, Norway, Panama, Papua New Guinea, Paraguay, Peru, Philippines, Poland, Portugal, Republic of Korea, Republic of Moldova, Romania, Russian Federation, Rwanda, Saint Kitts and Nevis, Saint Lucia, Saint Vincent and the Grenadines, San Marino, Sao Tome and Principe, Senegal, Sierra Leone, Singapore, Slovakia, Slovenia, South Africa, Spain, Sri Lanka, Sudan, Suriname, Swaziland, Sweden, Switzerland, Syria, Tajikistan, The former Yugoslav Republic of Macedonia, Togo, Trinidad and Tobago, Tunisia, Turkey, Turkmenistan, Uganda, Ukraine, United Arab Emirates, United Kingdom, United Republic of Tanzania, United States of America, Uruguay, Uzbekistan, Venezuela, Viet Nam, Yugoslavia, Zambia, Zimbabwe.

The Convention, concluded in 1883, was completed by an Interpretative Protocol in Madrid in 1891, was revised at Brussels in 1900, at Washington in 1911, at The Hague in 1925, at London in 1934, at Lisbon in 1958 and at Stockholm in 1967, and it was amended in 1979.

The Convention is open to all States. Instruments of ratification or accession must be deposited with the Director General of WIPO[1].

The Convention applies to industrial property in the widest sense, including inventions, marks, industrial designs, utility models (a kind of "small patent" provided for by the laws of some countries), trade names (designations under which an industrial or commercial activity is carried on), geographical indications (indications of source and appellations of origin) and the repression of unfair competition[2].

The substantive provisions of the Convention fall into three main categories: national treatment, right of priority, common rules.

(1) Under the provisions on national treatment, the Convention provides that, as regards the protection of industrial property, each contracting State must grant the same protection to nationals of the other contracting States as it grants to its own nationals. Nationals of noncontracting States are also protected by the Convention if they are domiciled or have a real and effective industrial or commercial establishment in a contracting State [3].

(2) The Convention provides for the right of priority in the case of patents (and utility models, where they exist), marks and industrial designs. This right means that, on the basis of a regular first application filed in one of the contracting States, the applicant may, within a certain period of time (12 months for patents and utility models; six months for industrial designs and marks), apply for protection in any of the other contracting States; these later applications will then be regarded as if they had been filed on the same day as the first application, in other words, these later applications will have priority (hence the expression "right of priority") over applications which may have been filed during the said period of time by other persons for the same invention, utility model, mark or industrial design. Moreover, these later applications, being based on the first application, will not be affected by

any event that may have taken place in the interval, such as any publication of the invention or sale of articles bearing the mark or incorporating the industrial design. One of the great practical advantages of this provision is that, when an applicant desires protection in several countries, he is not required to present all his applications at the same time but has six or 12 months at his disposal to decide in which countries he wishes protection and to organize with due care the steps he must take to secure protection [3].

(3) The Convention lays down a few common rules which all the contracting States must follow. The more important are the following:

(a) As to Patents: Patents granted in different contracting States for the same invention are independent of each other: the granting of a patent in one contracting State does not oblige the other contracting States to grant a patent; a patent cannot be refused, annulled or terminated in any contracting State on the ground that it has been refused or annulled or has terminated in any other contracting State.

The inventor has the right to be named as such in the patent.

The grant of a patent may not be refused, and a patent may not be invalidated, on the ground that the sale of the patented product, or of a product obtained by means of the patented process, is subject to restrictions or limitations resulting from the domestic law.

Each contracting State that takes legislative measures providing for the grant of compulsory licenses to prevent the abuses which might result from the exclusive rights conferred by a patent may do so only with certain limitations. Thus, a compulsory license (license not given by the owner of the patent but by a public authority of the State concerned) based on failure to work the patented invention may only be given pursuant to a request filed after three or four years of failure to work or insufficient working of the patented invention and it must be refused if the patentee gives legitimate reasons to justify his inaction. Furthermore, forfeiture of a patent may not be provided for, except in cases where the grant of a compulsory license would not have been sufficient to prevent the abuse. In the latter case, proceedings for forfeiture of a patent may be instituted, but only after the expiration of two years from the grant of the first compulsory license[4].

*****

(g) As to National Administrations: Each contracting State must maintain a special industrial property service and a central office for the communication to the public of patents (and utility models), marks and industrial designs. An official periodical journal must be published by this service. The journal must contain the names of the owners of the patents granted, with a brief description of the patented inventions, and the reproduction of every registered mark[10] [11].

* * *

The Paris Union has an Assembly and an Executive Committee. Every State member of the Union which has adhered to at least the administrative and final provisions of the Stockholm Act (1967) is a member of the Assembly. The members of the Executive Committee are elected from among the members of the Union, except for Switzerland, which is a member ex officio. On January 1, 1997, the Executive Committee had 35 members.

The establishment of the biennial program and budget of the International Bureau — as far as the Paris Union is concerned — is the task of its Assembly.

[1] It is to be noted that WTO Members, even if they are not party to the Paris Convention (e.g., Pakistan), must comply with the substantive law provisions of the Paris Convention (see TRIPS Agreement, Article 2.1). However, developing and "transition" countries may, at least until 2000, delay the application of most of the obligations provided for in the TRIPS Agreement (Article 65). Naturally, States party to the Paris Convention cannot delay the application of their obligations provided for in the Paris Convention.

[2] The TRIPS Agreement also mentions "undisclosed information" (commonly called "trade secrets") and "layout-designs (topographies) of integrated circuits" among the objects of intellectual property rights.

[3] Under the TRIPS Agreement, the principles of national treatment and right of priority also bind those WTO Members which are not party to the Paris Convention. In addition, the TRIPS Agreement imposes an obligation of "most-favored-nation treatment," under which advantages accorded by a WTO Member to the nationals of any other country must also be accorded to the nationals of all WTO Members. It is to be noted that the possibility of delayed application of the TRIPS Agreement mentioned above does not apply to national treatment and most-favored-nation treatment obligations.

[4] In the field of patents, the TRIPS Agreement contains additional obligations concerning, among others, minimum term of protection, protection for products and processes, patentable subject matter, allowable exclusions from protection, minimum exclusive rights, prohibition against certain types of discrimination, protection of plant varieties by patents or a sui generis system, guidelines for compulsory licenses, and certain forms of evidence of infringement.

*****

[10] In the field of administration, the TRIPS Agreement adds general obligations concerning procedures for acquiring or maintaining intellectual property rights and to ensure that unnecessary procedural difficulties do not impair the protection required by the Agreement.

[11] The TRIPS Agreement provides for obligations to ensure that effective enforcement of intellectual property rights is available to right holders, and that enforcement procedures do not create barriers to legitimate trade. These include the obligation that certain remedies be available, including injunctions, damages, forfeiture and provisional measures, that enforcement authorities meet certain performance requirements, and that border measures and criminal penalties be put in place for willful trademark counterfeiting and copyright piracy.

Paris Convention for the Protection of Industrial Property*

Article 1

[Establishment of the Union; Scope of Industrial Property][1]
1. The countries to which this Convention applies constitute a Union for the protection of industrial property.
2. The protection of industrial property has as its object patents, utility models, industrial designs, trademarks, service marks, trade names, indications of source or appellations of origin, and the repression of unfair competition.
3. Industrial property shall be understood in the broadest sense and shall apply not only to industry and commerce proper, but likewise to agricultural and extractive industries and to all manufactured or natural products, for example, wines, grain, tobacco leaf, fruit, cattle, minerals, mineral waters, beer, flowers, and flour.
4. Patents shall include the various kinds of industrial patents recognized by the laws of the countries of the Union, such as patents of importation, patents of improvements, patents and certificates of addition, etc.

Article 2

[National Treatment for Nationals of Countries of the Union]
1. Nationals of any country of the Union shall, as regards the protection of industrial property, enjoy in all the other countries of the Union the advantages that their respective laws now grant, or may hereafter grant, to nationals; all without prejudice to the rights specially provided for by this Convention. Consequently, they shall have the same protection as the latter, and the same legal remedy against any infringement of their rights, provided that the conditions and formalities imposed upon nationals are complied with.

---

*Source of text: World Intellectual Property Organization, Geneva 1981. Of March 20, 1883, as revised at Brussels on December 14, 1900, at Washington on June 2, 1911, at The Hague on November 6, 1925, at London on June 2, 1934, at Lisbon on October 31, 1958, and at Stockholm on July 14, 1967, and amended on October 2, 1979.
[1]Articles have been given titles to facilitate their identification. There are no titles in the signed (French) text.

2. However, no requirement as to domicile or establishment in the country where protection is claimed may be imposed upon nationals of countries of the Union for the enjoyment of any industrial property rights.

3. The provisions of the laws of each of the countries of the Union relating to judicial and administrative procedure and to jurisdiction, and to the designation of an address for service or the appointment of an agent, which may be required by the laws on industrial property are expressly reserved.

Article 3

[Same Treatment for Certain Categories of Persons as for Nationals of Countries of the Union]

Nationals of countries outside the Union who are domiciled or who have real and effective industrial or commercial establishments in the territory of one of the countries of the Union shall be treated in the same manner as nationals of the countries of the Union.

Article 4

[A to I — Patents, Utility Models, Industrial Designs, Marks, Inventors' Certificates: Right of Priority G — Patents: Division of the Application]

A. 1. Any person who has duly filed an application for a patent, or for the registration of a utility model, or of an industrial design, or of a trademark, in one of the countries of the Union, or his successor in title, shall enjoy, for the purpose of filing in the other countries, a right of priority during the periods hereinafter fixed.

2. Any filing that is equivalent to a regular national filing under the domestic legislation of any country of the Union or under bilateral or multilateral treaties concluded between countries of the Union shall be recognized as giving rise to the right of priority.

3. By a regular national filing is meant any filing that is adequate to establish the date on which the application was filed in the country concerned, whatever may be the subsequent fate of the application.

B. Consequently, any subsequent filing in any of the other countries of the Union before the expiration of the periods referred to above shall not be invalidated by reason of any acts accomplished in the interval, in particular, another filing, the publication or exploitation of the invention, the putting on sale of copies of the design, or the use of the mark, and such acts cannot give rise to any third-party right or any right of personal possession. Rights acquired by third parties before the date of the first application that serves as the basis for the right of priority are reserved in accordance with the domestic legislation of each country of the Union.

C. 1. The periods of priority referred to above shall be twelve months for patents and utility models, and six months for industrial designs and trademarks.

2. These periods shall start from the date of filing of the first application; the day of filing shall not be included in the period.

3. If the last day of the period is an official holiday, or a day when the Office is not open for the filing of applications in the country where protection is claimed, the period shall be extended until the first following working day.

4. A subsequent application concerning the same subject as a previous first application within the meaning of paragraph (2), above, filed in the same country of the Union, shall be considered as the first application, of which the filing date shall be the starting point of the period of priority, if, at the time of filing the subsequent application, the said previous application has been withdrawn, abandoned, or refused, without having been laid open to public inspection and without leaving any rights outstanding, and if it has not yet served as a basis for claiming a right of priority. The previous application may not thereafter serve as a basis for claiming a right of priority.

D. 1. Any person desiring to take advantage of the priority of a previous filing shall be required to make a declaration indicating the date of such filing and the country in which it was made. Each country shall determine the latest date on which such declaration must be made.

2. These particulars shall be mentioned in the publications issued by the competent authority, and in particular in the patents and the specifications relating thereto.

3. The countries of the Union may require any person making a declaration of priority to produce a copy of the application (description, drawings, etc.) previously filed. The copy, certified as correct by the authority which received such application, shall not require any authentication, and may in any case be filed, without fee, at any time within three months of the filing of the subsequent application. They may require it to be accompanied by a certificate from the same authority showing the date of filing, and by a translation.

4. No other formalities may be required for the declaration of priority at the time of filing the application. Each country of the Union shall deter-

mine the consequences of failure to comply with the formalities prescribed by this article, but such consequences shall in no case go beyond the loss of the right of priority.

5. Subsequently, further proof may be required.

Any person who avails himself of the priority of a previous application shall be required to specify the number of that application; this number shall be published as provided for by paragraph (2), above.

E. 1. Where an industrial design is filed in a country by virtue of a right of priority based on the filing of a utility model, the period of priority shall be the same as that fixed for industrial designs.

2. Furthermore, it is permissible to file a utility model in a country by virtue of a right of priority based on the filing of a patent application, and vice versa.

F. No country of the Union may refuse a priority or a patent application on the ground that the applicant claims multiple priorities, even if they originate in different countries, or on the ground that an application claiming one or more priorities contains one or more elements that were not included in the application or applications whose priority is claimed, provided that, in both cases, there is unity of invention within the meaning of the law of the country.

With respect to the elements not included in the application or applications whose priority is claimed, the filing of the subsequent application shall give rise to a right of priority under ordinary conditions.

G. 1. If the examination reveals that an application for a patent contains more than one invention, the applicant may divide the application into a certain number of divisional applications and preserve as the date of each the date of the initial application and the benefit of the right of priority, if any.

2. The applicant may also, on his own initiative, divide a patent application and preserve as the date of each divisional application the date of the initial application and the benefit of the right of priority, if any. Each country of the Union shall have the right to determine the conditions under which such division shall be authorized.

H. Priority may not be refused on the ground that certain elements of the invention for which priority is claimed do not appear among the claims formulated in the application in the country of origin, provided that the application documents as a whole specifically disclose such elements.

I. 1. Applications for inventors' certificates filed in a country in which applicants have the right to apply at their own option either for a patent or for an inventor's certificate shall give rise to the right of priority provided for by this article, under the same conditions and with the same effects as applications for patents.

2. In a country in which applicants have the right to apply at their own option either for a patent or for an inventor's certificate, an applicant for an inventor's certificate shall, in accordance with the provisions of this article relating to patent applications, enjoy a right of priority based on an application for a patent, a utility model, or an inventor's certificate.

Article 4bis

[Patents: Independence of Patents Obtained for the Same Invention in Different Countries]

1. Patents applied for in the various countries of the Union by nationals of countries of the Union shall be independent of patents obtained for the same invention in other countries, whether members of the Union or not.

2. The foregoing provision is to be understood in an unrestricted sense, in particular, in the sense that patents applied for during the period of priority are independent, both as regards the grounds for nullity and forfeiture, and as regards their normal duration.

3. The provision shall apply to all patents existing at the time when it comes into effect.

4. Similarly, it shall apply, in the case of the accession of new countries, to patents in existence on either side at the time of accession.

5. Patents obtained with the benefit of priority shall, in the various countries of the Union, have a duration equal to that which they would have, had they been applied for or granted without the benefit of priority.

Article 4ter

[Patents: Mention of the Inventor in the Patent]
The inventor shall have the right to be mentioned as such in the patent.

Article 4quater

[Patents: Patentability in Case of Restrictions of Sale by Law]
The grant of a patent shall not be refused and a patent shall not be invalidated on the ground that the sale of the patented product or of a product

obtained by means of a patented process is subject to restrictions or limitations resulting from the domestic law.

Article 5

[A — Patents: Importation of Articles; Failure to Work or Insufficient Working; Compulsory Licenses

B — Industrial Designs: Failure to Work; Importation of Articles

C — Marks: Failure to Use; Different Forms; Use by Co-Proprietors

D — Patents, Utility Models, Marks, Industrial Designs: Marking]

A. 1. Importation by the patentee into the country where the patent has been granted of articles manufactured in any of the countries of the Union shall not entail forfeiture of the patent.

2. Each country of the Union shall have the right to take legislative measures providing for the grant of compulsory licenses to prevent the abuses which might result from the exercise of the exclusive rights conferred by the patent, for example, failure to work.

3. Forfeiture of the patent shall not be provided for except in cases where the grant of compulsory licenses would not have been sufficient to prevent the said abuses. No proceedings for the forfeiture or revocation of a patent may be instituted before the expiration of two years from the grant of the first compulsory license.

4. A compulsory license may not be applied for on the ground of failure to work or insufficient working before the expiration of a period of four years from the date of filing of the patent application or three years from the date of the grant of the patent, whichever period expires last; it shall be refused if the patentee justifies his inaction by legitimate reasons. Such a compulsory license shall be non-exclusive and shall not be transferable, even in the form of the grant of a sub-license, except with that part of the enterprise or goodwill which exploits such license.

5. The foregoing provisions shall be applicable, mutatis mutandis, to utility models.

B. The protection of industrial designs shall not, under any circumstance, be subject to any forfeiture, either by reason of failure to work or by reason of the importation of articles corresponding to those which are protected.

C. 1. If, in any country, use of the registered mark is compulsory, the registration may be cancelled only after a reasonable period, and then only if the person concerned does not justify his inaction.

2. Use of a trademark by the proprietor in a form differing in elements which do not alter the distinctive character of the mark in the form in which it was registered in one of the countries of the Union shall not entail invalidation of the registration and shall not diminish the protection granted to the mark.

3. Concurrent use of the same mark on identical or similar goods by industrial or commercial establishments considered as co-proprietors of the mark according to the provisions of the domestic law of the country where protection is claimed shall not prevent registration or diminish in any way the protection granted to the said mark in any country of the Union, provided that such use does not result in misleading the public and is not contrary to the public interest.

D. No indication or mention of the patent, of the utility model, of the registration of the trademark, or of the deposit of the industrial design, shall be required upon the goods as a condition of recognition of the right to protection.

Article 5bis

[All Industrial Property Rights: Period of Grace for the Payment of Fees for the Maintenance of Rights; Patents: Restoration]

1. A period of grace of not less than six months shall be allowed for the payment of the fees prescribed for the maintenance of industrial property rights, subject, if the domestic legislation so provides, to the payment of a surcharge.

2. The countries of the Union shall have the right to provide for the restoration of patents which have lapsed by reason of non-payment of fees.

Article 5ter

[Patents: Patented Devices Forming Part of Vessels, Aircraft, or Land Vehicles]

In any country of the Union the following shall not be considered as infringements of the rights of a patentee:

(1) The use on board vessels of other countries of the Union of devices forming the subject of his patent in the body of the vessel, in the machin-

ery, tackle, gear and other accessories, when such vessels temporarily or accidentally enter the waters of the said country, provided that such devices are used there exclusively for the needs of the vessel;

(2) The use of devices forming the subject of the patent in the construction or operation of aircraft or land vehicles of other countries of the Union, or if accessories of such aircraft or land vehicles, when those aircraft or land vehicles temporarily or accidentally enter the said country.

Article 5quater

[Patents: Importation of Products Manufactured by a Process Patented in the Importing Country]

When a product is imported into a country of the Union where there exists a patent protecting a process of manufacture of the said product, the patentee shall have all the rights, with regard to the imported product, that are accorded to him by the legislation of the country of importation, on the basis of the process patent, with respect to products manufactured in that country.

*****

Article 11

[Inventions, Utility Models, Industrial Designs, Marks: Temporary Protection at Certain International Exhibitions]

1. The countries of the Union shall, in conformity with their domestic legislation, grant temporary protection to patentable inventions, utility models, industrial designs, and trademarks, in respect of goods exhibited at official or officially recognized international exhibitions held in the territory of any of them.

2. Such temporary protection shall not extend the periods provided by Article 4. If, later, the right of priority is invoked, the authorities of any country may provide that the period shall start from the date of introduction of the goods into the exhibition.

3. Each country may require, as proof of the identity of the article exhibited and of the date of its introduction, such documentary evidence as it considers necessary.

Article 12

[Special National Industrial Property Services]

1. Each country of the Union undertakes to establish a special industrial property service and a central office for the communication to the public of patents, utility models, industrial designs, and trademarks.

2. This service shall publish an official periodical journal. It shall publish regularly:

(a) the names of the proprietors of patents granted, with a brief designation of the inventions patented;

(b) the reproductions of registered trademarks.

*****

Article 28

[Disputes]

1. Any dispute between two or more countries of the Union concerning the interpretation or application of this Convention, not settled by negotiation, may, by any one of the countries concerned, be brought before the International Court of Justice by application in conformity with the Statute of the Court, unless the countries concerned agree on some other method of settlement. The country bringing the dispute before the Court shall inform the International Bureau; the International Bureau shall bring the matter to the attention of the other countries of the Union.

2. Each country may, at the time it signs this Act or deposits its instrument of ratification or accession, declare that it does not consider itself hound by the provisions of paragraph (1). With regard to any dispute between such country and any other country of the Union, the provisions of paragraph (1) shall not apply.

3. Any country having made a declaration in accordance with the provisions of paragraph (2) may, at any time, withdraw its declaration by notification addressed to the Director General.

Notes and Questions

1. In promoting the TRIPS Agreement, OECD country industries pointed to several weaknesses of the Paris Convention in respect to patents. One such weakness is that the Paris Convention does not prescribe the subject matter areas or fields of invention for which a government must offer patent protection. Observe that Article 1(3) prescribes a broad scope of subject matter coverage for "industrial property," but that this prescription does not extend specifically to patents. Why do you think that the drafters of the Paris Convention may have limited their subject matter definition to "industrial property"?

2. Note that the Paris Convention does not attempt to set forth any criteria of patentability. Edith Penrose has told us that efforts to harmonize substantive criteria for patenting proved too controversial. Do you think it is unusual to find a treaty (for example, this one on "patents") that does not establish a definition for its most basic element?

   In fact it is common for treaties to leave the meaning of basic terms open. The United Nations Charter allows the Security Council to take action after it has determined that a "threat to the peace" exists, but its does not attempt to define what a threat to the peace may be. Human rights treaties often (though certainly not always) refer to basic human rights in general terms. Reaching agreement on the specific content of rights may be quite difficult in a wide number of international contexts. Much of the Uruguay Round negotiations involved reducing broadly drafted GATT provisions to more precise rules.

3. Another provision of the Paris Convention criticized by OECD industry groups was the compulsory licensing provision which, as you will note in Article 5, refers only to preventing "abuses" of the patent right. There is no reference in Article 5 to compensation for the right holder.

4. Article 28 of the Paris Convention provides for dispute settlement before the International Court of Justice (ICJ). No complaint under the Paris (or Berne) Convention has ever been filed in the ICJ. In the TRIPS negotiations, OECD industry groups contended that referral to the ICJ is a "weak"

means of settling IPRs-related disputes. Why is the ICJ perceived as weak? International dispute settlement bodies almost always rely on the persuasive force of their decisions (and not on gunboats) to assure compliance. ICJ judges are certainly as capable as WTO panel members of understanding the issues at stake in an IPRs-related dispute. Might the real concern of OECD industry groups with the Paris Convention have been that the ICJ would have too much flexibility in interpreting the Paris Convention since its provisions are rather broad? The real key to the perceived weakness of the Paris Convention perhaps lay more in its lack of substantive definition.

---

3. The Independence of Patents

a. Independence in the Courts

In the *Cuno v. Pall* decision which follows, an American federal district court judge has occasion to give concrete effect to the principle of the *independence of patents* established by the Paris Convention. An English court had already ruled upon the validity of various competing patent claims after prolonged litigation, and the U.S. federal court is in essence asked to repeat the process, but in a different national jurisdiction. The party that succeeded in England would for obvious reasons prefer that the U.S. judge decide that there is no point to reconsidering the same issues, at what will undoubtedly be considerable cost both in terms of money and wasted time. The U.S. judge seems to share this perspective, but must consider the relevant provisions of the Paris Convention. Keep this decision in mind as we look at the decision of the Technical Board of Appeals of the European Patent Office in the *Procter & Gamble* case later in this chapter.

Cuno Incorporated v. Pall Corporation, et al.

United States District Court For The Eastern District of New York
729 F. Supp. 234; 1989 U.S. Dist. LEXIS 15241

December 19, 1989, Decided

*****

Opinion: Memorandum and Order Jack B. Weinstein, United States District Judge

The production of microporous nylon membrane filters generates hundreds of millions of dollars in worldwide revenues. It is vital to pharmaceutical, microchip and other industries requiring filtration of impurities the size of the smallest microbes. Plaintiff Cuno and defendants Pall and its associated companies are major competitors in this field. They press claims and counterclaims relating to the validity, infringement and enforceability of a number of key patents teaching methods of producing these filters.

Defendants move for partial summary judgment based on the collateral estoppel effect of factual findings made by a Justice of the United Kingdom Court of Chancery, Patent Division, in a prior adjudication between the parties. The European Patent Office's counterpart of defendants' United States patent at issue here was there found to be valid and non-infringing. Defendants argue that the findings of fact made by the foreign court are entitled to preclusive effect since the patent issued by the European Patent Office on behalf of the countries of the European Economic Community describes the same technological invention and makes claims that are in all material ways identical to those contained in defendants' United States patent.

Plaintiff argues that the traditional requirements for granting collateral estoppel are not present here and that the application of preclusive effect to findings made by a foreign court runs counter to policies underlying both domestic and foreign patent law. For the reasons noted below, the court denies defendants' motion.

I. Facts

At issue are six patents. Five of the patents — four of which are held by plaintiff — relate to the membrane filters themselves. One — also held by plaintiff — covers a process for producing microporous membrane filters. Closely analogous counterpart patents for the membranes have been issued to both plaintiff and defendants in a number of foreign countries.

In 1975 plaintiff Cuno was granted the first of the patents, U.S. Patent No. 3,876,738, known after its inventor as the Marinaccio patent. The Marinaccio patent describes a process for producing membrane filters, in part by mixing nylon with a solvent and a non-solvent and spreading the resultant liquid "dope solution" into sheet form under the surface of a quenching medium. Cuno did not utilize this process commercially to produce membranes — if it did so at all — until the early 1980s. Nor did plaintiff apply for any foreign counterpart patents for the Marinaccio process.

In the late 1970s defendants (referred to collectively as Pall) developed their own nylon membrane filters. Pall applied in 1978 for a patent from the United States Patent Office. The following year Pall applied for counterpart patents in approximately two dozen countries, primarily through the European Patent Office in Munich, Germany. Plaintiff opposed these foreign patent applications in the various patent offices. Opposition appears to have been largely unsuccessful. Defendants began to market their nylon membranes commercially in 1978. They were issued a patent, U.S. Patent No. 4,340,479 — the Pall patent — in 1982. A counterpart, Pall's European Patent Convention (EPC) Patent No. 5,536, was issued in 1987. To date domestic sales of the Pall membrane have generated approximately $300 million in revenues, considerably more than the amount generated by plaintiff's products.

In the early 1980s Cuno developed and introduced a line of membrane filters, known as Zetapor membranes. Cuno claims that these membranes can be distinguished from those produced by defendants by virtue of the application of a coating and a charge-modifying agent, additions designed to enhance the removal of bacteria. Beginning in 1981, and for several years thereafter, Cuno applied for and was subsequently issued patents for its Zetapor membranes. These patents are known collectively as the Ostreicher patents, and four are at issue in this action: U.S. Patent Nos. 4,473,474, 4,673,504, 4,708,803 and 4,711,973. Cuno successfully applied for counterpart patents in a number of foreign countries.

Pall developed and began to market its own charge-modified membranes in 1982, known as co-cast Posidyne membranes. Although the Posidyne membranes are not in suit here, plaintiff argues that they infringe its Ostreicher patents insofar as they do no more than modify the allegedly infringing basic Pall membrane.

In addition to opposing Pall's various patent applications abroad, Cuno brought the instant lawsuit in September of 1986. Plaintiff's complaint charged defendants' membranes with infringing two of the Cuno Ostreicher patents, U.S. Patent Nos. 4,473,474 and 4,673,504. In an amendment to the complaint a year later, Cuno charged that the Pall membrane also infringes the Marinaccio process patent, U.S. Patent No. 3,876,738. Cuno alleges that the 1975 Marinaccio patent claims disclosed Pall's later invention and thus constituted invalidating prior art both because they anticipated the Pall invention within the meaning of 35 U.S.C. §102 and because plaintiff's invention rendered the Pall product obvious and therefore unpatentable under 35 U.S.C. §103. Cuno also challenged the validity of Pall's patent, alleging that it had been anticipated by the prior public use at several companies of defendants' membranes over a year before Pall applied for a patent.

Pall counterclaimed for infringement of its U.S. Patent No. 4,340,479, and for a declaration that two additional Cuno Ostreicher patents, U.S. Patent Nos. 4,708,803 and 4,711,973, were invalid and not infringed by Pall's membrane. In response, Cuno counterclaimed for infringement of its remaining Ostreicher patents as well.

Briefly, the Marinaccio-Pall dispute focuses on the process by which the parties produce their respective membrane filters. Cuno asserts the Marinaccio process patent against claims made in the Pall patent, alleging that its earlier patent and the membranes produced by the Marinaccio process constitute invalidating prior art. Cuno also charges that Pall copied plaintiff's Marinaccio process without informing the United States Patent Office and subsequently responded to direct inquiries made in the early 1980's by Cuno's parent company by falsely denying use of an infringing process.

In response, Pall denies infringement, first on the grounds that its production process differs from plaintiff's since it involves two separate steps of casting and quenching, rather than the combined process disclosed in the Marinaccio process by which the dope solution is cast directly under the surface of the quenching medium. Second, defendants argue that the Marinaccio patent is invalid because it not only failed to produce a useful product as defined by 35 U.S.C. §101, but also because the process it describes had in fact been abandoned by Cuno — a fact plaintiff allegedly concealed from the patent office — for some time before the patent was granted in 1975. See 35 U.S.C. §102(c) (patent shall not be issued if applicant has abandoned the invention).

The Ostreicher-Pall claims and counterclaims relate to the charge-modified membranes produced by each of the parties. Cuno claims that Pall's Posidyne membranes infringe plaintiff's Ostreicher patents. Defendants counterclaim, alleging infringement insofar as Cuno's Zetapor membranes merely coat Pall's basic membrane. Defendants base this argument on the alleged invalidity of the Marinaccio patent, as well as on the ground that their own charge-modified membranes constitute invalidating prior art. Included in these claims are allegations and counterallegations of fraudulent failure to disclose information to the United States Patent Office.

While discovery was proceeding in the United States action, Pall initiated a lawsuit in Great Britain in 1987 against Cuno and two of its European subsidiaries, claiming that Cuno's Zetapor membranes infringed key claims made in Pall's newly-granted EPC patent. Discovery for the United States case was used in the British action. That case was tried in London for four weeks in the late spring and summer of 1989. Some of the testimony, and many of the witnesses from the British case are expected to be utilized in the upcoming United States trial.

On July 25, 1989 the British judge, Justice Falconer, ruled in Pall's favor, making extensive findings and construing critical terms in the claims made in Pall's EPC patent. In a 64-page opinion, he concluded, inter alia, 1) that Pall's patent was valid; 2) that Cuno's Zetapor membranes infringed claims in Pall's EPC patent; 3) that there was no merit to the anticipation defense raised by Cuno based on its United States Marinaccio patent; and 4) that there had been no invalidating prior public use when Pall utilized some of its filters in 1976 and 1977 in tests by prospective customers. An order enjoining Cuno from infringing the Pall EPC patent was entered on August 1, 1989. Shortly thereafter Cuno filed a notice of appeal.

Cuno continues to prosecute its opposition to the Pall EPC patent in the European Patent Office. It is unclear what, if any effect a decision revoking or modifying Pall's EPC patent would have on the British court's ruling should Cuno's opposition prove successful. The court's order contained a "liberty to apply" provision, which apparently allows either party to return to the court to make further applications in the event that matters are elicited "concerning or arising out of [Cuno's] Opposition in the [European Patent Office]." In any event, the parties have informed the court that the European Patent Office may not render a decision for years.

This court originally ordered a jury trial to begin in September. As a result of the United Kingdom decision, the court tentatively suggested that collateral estoppel might permit shortening of the trial. It became apparent, however, that the procedural and technical problems associated with a motion for application of collateral estoppel on the basis of findings made in the English judgment were so difficult and required so much further briefing and argument that it would be impossible to start the jury trial as scheduled.

In support and opposition to the motion for partial summary judgment, several days of hearings were conducted at which experts on patent and procedural law from the United States, the United Kingdom and Germany testified. Experts from both sides described the technology and development of a variety of patents in this field over the last 20 years. Extensive briefing and argument followed.

II. Law

A motion for summary judgment pursuant to Rule 56 of the Federal Rules of Civil Procedure is appropriate in a patent case. Johnston v. Ivac Corp., 885 F.2d 1574, 1577 (Fed.Cir. 1989) (citing the expansive view of power to grant summary judgment in Anderson v. Liberty Lobby, Inc., 477 U.S. 242, 248, 106 S. Ct. 2505, 91 L. Ed. 2d 202 (1986)); . . .

The application of collateral estoppel to patent cases is similarly appropriate. See, e.g., Blonder-Tongue Laboratories, Inc. v. University of Illinois Foundation, 402 U.S. 313, 333, 91 S. Ct. 1434, 28 L. Ed. 2d 788 (1971) (collateral estoppel effect applied to issue of validity of patent where patent was declared invalid in prior proceeding in which patentee had full and fair chance to litigate); Hartley v. Mentor Corp., 869 F.2d 1469, 1471 (Fed.Cir. 1989) ("Issue preclusion in patent litigation may arise under same conditions as in any litigation . . ."); Molinaro v. Fannon/Courier Corp., 745 F.2d 651, 655 (Fed.Cir. 1984) (granting summary judgment on basis of collateral estoppel); Mississippi Chemical Corp. v. Swift Agricultural Chemicals Corp., 717 F.2d 1374 (Fed.Cir. 1983) (where no evidence existed that patentee had been deprived of full and fair opportunity to litigate in earlier case, it was appropriate to issue writ of mandamus ordering district court judge to grant summary judgment based on application of collateral estoppel to prior finding of invalidity).

Nevertheless, the Federal Circuit has shown a general antipathy to applying collateral estoppel as a basis for a judgment in circumstances arguably similar to those present in this case. See, e.g., Ethicon, Inc. v. Quigg, 849 F.2d 1422, 1428-29 (Fed.Cir. 1988) ("[A] court's decision upholding a patent's validity is not ordinarily binding on another challenge to the patent's validity ... in ... the courts. ...") (citation omitted); A.B. Dick Co. v. Burroughs Corp., 713 F.2d 700 (Fed.Cir. 1983) (in order to apply collateral estoppel to judicial statements in prior proceeding regarding scope of patent claims, such statements must be narrowly construed and must have been essential to final judgment on question of either validity or infringement). Cf. Interconnect Planning Corp. v. Feil, 774 F.2d 1132, 1136 (Fed.Cir. 1985) (denying summary judgment sought on collateral estoppel ground); Young Engineers, Inc. v. United States International Trade Commission, 721 F.2d 1305, 1316 (Fed.Cir. 1983) (refusing to apply collateral estoppel); Plastic Container Corp. v. Continental Plastics, 607 F.2d 885, 894 (10th Cir. 1979) ("The public interest in upholding valid patents ... outweighs the public interest underlying collateral estoppel. ...").

Where the prior adjudication was by a foreign nation's court applying its patent law to its patents, the barriers to reliance on the foreign judgment for collateral estoppel purposes become almost insurmountable. Differences in the law of the two nations and in the detailed language of the patent are emphasized to avoid issue preclusion in a patent case pending in this country even where the invention, the technological and economic competition between the parties, and the consequences of the judgments are for all practical purposes the same. See, e.g., Medtronic, Inc. v. Daig Corp., 789 F.2d 903, 907-08 (Fed.Cir.), cert. denied, 479 U.S. 931, 107 S. Ct. 402, 93 L. Ed. 2d 355 (1986) (prior conclusion of German tribunal as to obviousness of counterpart German patent does not control issue of obviousness in action involving United States patent); Stein Associates, Inc. v. Heat and Control, Inc., 748 F.2d 653 (Fed.Cir. 1984) (denying motion to enjoin efforts to enforce British patent in Britain) (citing cases); In re Yarn Processing Patent Validity Litigation, 498 F.2d 271, 278-85 (5th Cir. 1974) (issue in United States of date of "reduction to practice" not the same as issue of "date of invention" decided in previous Canada case); Ditto, Inc. v. Minnesota Mining & Manufacturing Co., 336 F.2d 67, 70-71 (8th Cir. 1964) (prior adjudication in which West German Federal Patent Court found

German counterpart patent invalid is not controlling authority); Baracuda International Corp. v. F.N.D. Enterprises, Inc., 222 U.S.P.Q. 134, 135 (S.D.Fla. 1982) ("The South African courts' judgments are, of course, not binding upon our own where patent validity is at issue."). As Chief Judge Markey remarked in Stein Associates v. Heat and Control, Inc., 748 F.2d 653 (Fed.Cir. 1984):

> British law being different from our own, and British and United States courts being independent of each other, resolution of the question of whether the United States patents are valid could have no binding effect on the British court's decision.

Id. at 658. The converse is equally true.

Even if this court were to apply collateral estoppel to certain factual findings made by the British court — as opposed to importing its legal conclusions wholesale — it is not clear that trial time would be significantly shortened. Furthermore, the Federal Circuit's reluctance to give collateral estoppel effect to foreign judgments would seem to apply here to foreign findings of fact insofar as those findings involve mixed questions of fact and foreign law.

It is a quiddity of our law that a well and thoroughly reasoned decision reached by a highly skilled and scientifically informed justice of the Patent Court, Chancery Division, in the High Court of Justice of Great Britain after four weeks of trial must be ignored and essentially the same issues with the same evidence must now be retried by American jurors with no background in science or patents, whose average formal education will be no more than high school. This curious event is the result of the world's chauvinistic view of patents.

The law's absurdity as revealed by this case lends force to recommendations for a universal patent system that recognizes that ours is a worldwide technological and economic community. See, e.g., Note, International Patent Cooperation: The Next Step, 16 Cornell Int'l L. J. 229, 248-49, 252-68 (1983) (recommending unified international patent law); Beier, The European Patent System, Vand. J. Transnat'l L. 1, 14-15 (1981) (recommending greater cooperation along lines of European system). Obviously there are grave difficulties in devising a system that will not disadvantage the old fashioned single craftsman-inventor or citizens of countries with patent offices that are careful in investigating before issuing patents. But the European Patent Office furnishes a model that appears to be working. Perhaps paragraph (1) of Article 4bis of the Paris Convention, with its emphasis on nationality, needs to be reconsidered. It reads:

> (1) Patents applied for in the various countries of the Union by nationals of countries of the Union shall be independent of patents obtained for the same invention in other countries, whether members of the Union or not.

Convention of Paris for the Protection of Industrial Property, article 4bis (1), 21 U.S.T. 1583, 1635, T.I.A.S. No. 6923 (text), 24 U.S.T. 2140, T.I.A.S. No. 7727 (ratification).

There would appear to be no constitutional inhibition against a reconsideration of international patent policy. Clause 8 of Article I of the Constitution grants Congress power over patents. But, just as Congress delegates much of its patenting power to the patent office and the courts, the government may, under Article II, section 2, clause 2 of the Constitution, provide a role for international bodies through the treaty making powers. See, e.g., 39 U.S.C. § 407(a) (authorizing Postal Service, with consent of President, to negotiate and conclude postal treaties or conventions); Universal Postal Union, 16 U.S.T. 1291, T.I.A.S. 5881 (international treaty ratified and approved by United States Postmaster, approved by President). Cf. Casad, Issue Preclusion and Foreign Country Judgments: Whose Law?, 70 Iowa L.Rev. 53, 79-80 (1984) (suggesting treaty or exercise of federal common law power of Supreme Court to resolve issues of recognizing and enforcing foreign judgments).

III. Other Grounds for Summary Judgment

As an alternative ground for summary judgment the court could rely on the evidence produced on the motion for summary judgment. It includes extensive affidavits, testimony before this court of scientific and legal experts, the transcript of the trial in Great Britain, patent files and extensive materials for judicial notice. Taken together this mass of evidence still depends somewhat on evaluation of the credibility of prospective witnesses. The issue must be left for the jury.

Should the jury decide in a way inconsistent with the United Kingdom court's decision or the record, the court could, after the trial, grant what would be in effect a delayed summary judgment motion. See County of Suffolk v. Long Island Lighting Co., 710 F. Supp. 1387, 1393 (E.D.N.Y. 1989) (citing DeRosa v. Remington Arms Co., 509 F. Supp. 762 (E.D.N.Y. 1981)).

IV. Conclusion

The motion for summary judgment is denied. . . . The court does not believe that an immediate appeal from this order may materially advance the ultimate termination of the litigation.

So ordered.

Notes and Questions

1. Like the *Biogen*[1] case, *Cuno v. Pall* provides an illustration of the process by which an inventor secures international patent protection through the first filing in one national or regional patent office, using that first filing to secure a "priority date", then filing corresponding patent applications in other jurisdictions. We also observe Cuno's use of the EPC opposition procedure to object to the grant of Pall's European patent and to seek its revocation (or modification). Judge Weinstein says it is not clear what effect revocation of Pall's European patent would have on the British judge's finding of patent infringement in favor of Pall. Examine articles 68 and 99 of the EPC in section B.1 and Ch. V, § C, *infra*, and consider why the result may be unclear to Judge Weinstein. Is the result unclear to you?

2. Cuno claimed that Pall's patent was invalid because Pall had publicly used the patented product more than one year before applying for a patent in the United States. The rules in different jurisdictions vary on the extent to which an invention may be publicly disclosed prior to filing an application without undermining its patentability. In the United States, public disclosure within one year of filing does not affect patentability.[2] Under the EPC, public disclosure made within six months of an EPC filing does not

---

[1] *See supra*, Ch. I, § B, 2, c.
[2] 35 U.S.C. § 102(b).

affect novelty, but only in the limited cases of abuse in relation to the patent applicant or display at an officially recognized international exhibition.[3]

3. Judge Weinstein observes that it is a "quiddity" of U.S. patent law that the opinion of a specialized British judge must be ignored in favor of a decision by a jury with an average of high school education and no background in science. The question whether the U.S. patent system is adequately served by trying facts before lay juries is a long-standing one. What do you think?

4. The key to Judge Weinstein's decision is article 4bis of the Paris Convention. The drafters of the Paris Convention adopted the principle of independence, among other reasons, out of concern that national sentiment might cause administrators or courts in one country to refuse or revoke a foreigner's patent. The effects of such national sentiment would at least be limited if that decision applied only in one territory. Would such concerns about national sentiment be valid today? If so, how might a more efficient international patent system cope with such sentiment?

5. At the conclusion of his opinion, Judge Weinstein says that a jury decision inconsistent with the British judge's decision could be dealt with after trial by what would be in effect "a delayed summary judgment motion." Do you think that Judge Weinstein may have been sending a message to Cuno and its lawyers?

---

b. Independence of Patents and the Free Movement of Goods

As we just observed, the Paris Convention norm system with respect to patents assumes that each country party will grant and determine the validity of patents by itself. A patent may be ruled invalid by a court in Germany or Japan, but nevertheless be considered valid and enforceable in the United States. This rule precludes defects in procedural formalities in one Paris Convention country from leading to the wholesale invalidation of the inventor's patent throughout the international system. This rule, *inter alia*, reduces the risk that procedures in one country might be misused by an in-

---

[3]EPC, art. 55.

ventor's competitors to undercut the inventor's position in the global market.

An important question is whether the concept of independence of patents was also intended to codify the idea of the territorial nature of the patent grant, and with what consequences. This question becomes particularly important when considering the issue of the *parallel importation* of patented products. By parallel importation we refer to the importation into one country of a product which has been placed on the market in another country with the consent of its patent holder. Patent holders often attempt to preclude the movement of such products into a second or third country on the grounds that they hold a corresponding or "parallel" patent in that second or third country. This obviously inhibits the free movement of patented goods among countries. Patent holders seek to justify this inhibition on the grounds that every national or regional patent is independent of the other, and thus that they maintain a separate right to import and market their products under the patent monopoly in each country in which they hold a patent. At least one commentator has noted that the Paris Convention provision on the independence of patents was not intended to address the issue of territoriality, but was rather directed at the mechanics of the patent grant.[1]

We first examined the parallel imports issue in the intra-EU context in the *Ideal Standard*[2] case that was concerned with the free movement of trademarked goods. You will recall that in the *Ideal Standard* case the European Court of Justice differentiated between the situation in which a trademark is owned or controlled in different member states by parties with an economic link — in which case parallel importation must be permitted — and the situation in which a trademark is owned and controlled by independent economic operators, in which case parallel trademarks may be used to block imports. It is the consent of the holder to placing the trademarked goods on the market that exhausts its right to further control the movement of the goods.

The Supreme Court of Japan recently decided a case involving the parallel importation into Japan of a product patented both in Japan and Germany. The product was first sold in Germany with the consent of the German patent holder. A Japanese affiliate of the German patent holder

---

[1] *See* Christopher Heath, Parallel Imports and International Trade, 28 IIC 623, 627-28 (1997).

[2] *See supra*, Ch. I, § B, 6, c.

held a license under a parallel patent in Japan. The Japanese patent holder/licensee thereafter attempted to block importation into Japan of the product first sold in Germany. The Supreme Court of Japan held that the principle of independence of patents means that the first sale of the product in Germany did not exhaust the rights of the patent holder in Japan. However, it went on to hold that the close integration of the global economy leads to the presumption that a patent holder in Japan that consents to the placement of its product on the market in a foreign country does so with the expectation that such product may be exported to Japan or another third country. Consequently, unless the Japanese patent holder establishes a contractual obligation on the part of the first purchaser not to export the patented product to Japan, the Japanese patent holder may not block importation of the product into Japan. By entering into a restrictive agreement with the first purchaser, and by affixing a notice to the product itself declaring this restriction, the Japanese patent holder may apparently extend the restriction to subsequent purchasers. The Court says it is not relevant whether the product is patented in the country of first sale outside of Japan.

Following is an excerpt from the opinion of the Japanese Supreme Court in the *BBS* case.

BBS Kraftfahrzeugtechnik AG and BBS Japan, Inc. v. Rasimex Japan, Inc., Supreme Court Heisei 7 (o) No. 1988 (July 1, 1997), J. of S. Ct., No. 1198 (July 15, 1997), Pages 8-10.*

The following is the summary of the Supreme Court decision in the *BBS* case, Part 3, Chapter 4 which, according to the translator, is translated as accurately as possible even at the sacrifice of ease of reading:

The Judgment is in favor of the importer (Rasimex) of a patented product (aluminum wheels) rejecting an appeal made by the patent holder (BBS). Part 1 of the opinion relates the factual and procedural background of the case. Part 2 summarizes the arguments heretofore made by both parties. Part 3, occupying majority of pages of the decision, gives the opinion

---

*Translation with introductory synopsis by Tadayoshi Homma, Professor of Law, Chiba University, Japan.

of the court in reaching the decision. Chapter 1 of Part 3 concludes that the present case should be decided only in light of the Japanese Patent Act and not by the Paris Convention or by the doctrine of territoriality. Chapter 2 states that the doctrine of exhaustion is based on Article 1 of the Japanese Patent Act ("The purpose of the Act is to promote invention and thereby to contribute to the development of industries"). Chapter 3 denies so-called international exhaustion, saying that patent rights in Japan and in the exporting country are different rights. Chapter 5 is the conclusion of the opinion.

Brackets [ ] are added for contextual clarity.

4. Now, considering the balance between the distribution of products in international trade and the right of a patentee, it is safely to be said that, in light of the situation that international trade is progressing extremely widely and highly in modern society, the highest degree of respect to the freedom of distribution of products including importation is required, even where a Japanese trader imports into Japan the product [first] sold in other countries and puts the same into distribution into the [Japanese] market. And whereas, even in economic transactions in other countries, a transaction is achieved on the basis that a seller generally transfers all of his rights in the merchandise to the purchaser and the purchaser acquires all of the rights owned by the seller, it is naturally expected that, where a patentee has sold a patented product in other countries, the [first] purchaser or the third parties who purchased the same from the [first] purchaser may import into Japan, use or further sell to others as a business, in light of the abovementioned situation of international trade in modern society. Considering the above points, the patentee is not permitted to enforce his patent right in Japan [1] against the [first] purchaser of the product except where the patentee has agreed with the [first] purchaser to exclude Japan from the territories for sale or use or [2] against the third parties or subsequent purchasers who purchased the product from the [first] purchaser except where the patentee has agreed with the [first] purchaser as abovementioned and has explicitly indicated the same on the patented product. In other words, (1) in light of the abovementioned fact that a patented product sold in other countries is naturally expected to be imported into Japan subsequently, the sale of a product by the patentee in other countries without any reservation should be interpreted as a grant of

rights to the [first] and subsequent purchasers to control the product in Japan without any patent restriction. (2) Focusing upon the right of the patentee on the other hand, it should be permitted for a patentee to make a reservation of right upon the sale of a patented product in other countries, to enforce his patent right in Japan, and where the patentee has agreed with the [first] purchaser and has explicitly indicated the same on the patented product, the subsequent purchasers can recognize the attached restriction to that effect even if third parties have intervened during the distribution of the product and can decide at his free will whether or not to purchase the product in the face of such restriction. (3) And the sale of the patented product in other countries by subsidiaries or affiliates who can be regarded as same as the patentee should be interpreted as the sale of the product by the patentee himself, and (4) the need to protect the belief in free trade of the purchaser of a patented product does not differ depending upon whether or not the patentee has a parallel patent right at the place of first sale of the patented product.

Notes and Questions

1. The Japanese Supreme Court says that the rights of the Japanese patent holder are not exhausted by the first sale of the product outside Japan, but that the purchaser of the product outside Japan has a legitimate expectation that it will be able to resell the product in international commerce free of the patent restriction. Thus the Court accepts a basic territorial nature for the patent grant, but seeks to limit the consequences of this territorial nature for the free movement of goods in world trade. What changes in business practices might you expect as a consequence of this decision? Might these changes add transparency to the effects of the international patent system? Are they likely to materially affect the flow of goods in world commerce?

4. The Right of Priority

In Chapter III the right of priority was introduced as one of the basic principles of the international intellectual property system. The right of

BBS

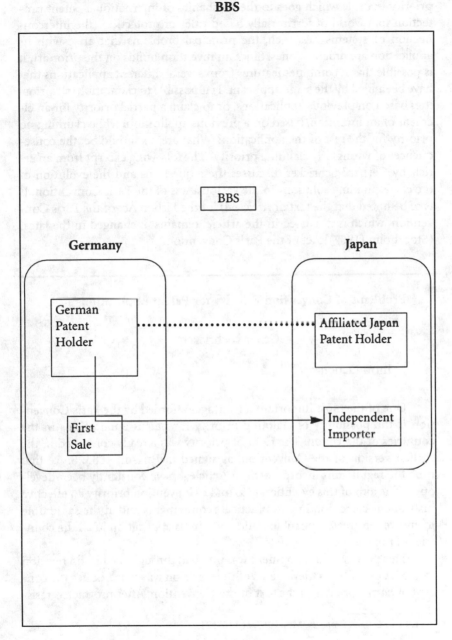

priority is a rule which goes to the mechanics of international patent protection in a world of territorially based titles of protection (the interconnection of systems). As such, the principal problems that arise with its application are practical ones. Since an invention builds on the prior art, it is possible that it combines features from several different applications that have been filed by the same applicant. Is it possible to claim multiple priorities based on previous applications, or to claim a partial priority for an element of an invention, based on a previous application, while claiming no priority for the rest of the application? What are, or should be, the consequences of wrongfully claiming priority? The following excerpt from an article by Gerhard Schricker discusses these questions and the evolution of the corresponding solutions in the various Acts of the Paris Convention. It is to be noted that the text of Article 4F of the Lisbon Act of the Paris Convention, which is discussed in the article, remains unchanged in the latest (Stockholm (1967)) Act of the Paris Convention.

Problems of Convention Priority for Patent Applications

Gehard Schricker*

I. Introduction

One of the most important advantages afforded by the Paris Convention is the possibility of claiming priority for patent applications in the countries of the Union. The right of priority was already contained in the earliest version of the Convention, as signed in Paris in 1883. Since that time the regulations incorporated in Article 4 have constantly been developed. The aim of this evolution is to make Convention priority an effective instrument corresponding to practical requirements and at the same time to ensure the greatest possible uniformity in its application in all the countries of the Union.

This process of development was pursued through the Lisbon revision in 1958. One of the achievements of that revision was to introduce the concept of *partial priority* in the text of the Convention. After protracted resis-

---

*WIPO, *Industrial Property,* May 1967, at 113-121.

tance from a small number of countries had been overcome, the principle of *multiple priority* had first been included in Article 4 as revised in London. The provisions were extended at Lisbon to cover partial priority also. The first purpose of the present article is to give a brief survey of these developments with regard to the provisions of the Convention . . .

It would be rash to imagine that the form of Article 4 of the Paris Convention as adopted in Lisbon will stand for good. There remain points on which it seems desirable for practice in the countries of the Union to be standardized by means of appropriate provisions in the Convention. I shall refer in section III to one such problem: the question of what consequences follow when it is discovered after a patent has been issued that the *material requirements do not exist for the Convention priority claimed.*

II. Multiple and Partial Convention Priorities

1. Concepts

If a patent application or a patent cannot be given uniform priority and there are different priority dates for the various parts of the application or the patent, irrespective of the cause of such differences, the term *partial priorities* is used in its *broadest meaning.* Partial priorities may be due to the fact that Convention priority was claimed for the various parts of the application on the basis of different prior applications in which the respective parts of the invention were first disclosed. These are known as *multiple priorities.*[1]

---

[1] *Cf.* Article 4F of the Paris Convention. Sepúlveda (in *Boletin de Instituto de derecho comparado de Mexico,* Tenth Year, 1956, No. 25, pp. 22 et *seq.*) regards the expression as misleading. He argues that the question is not one of different priority dates, but of deciding whether a single Convention priority can be recognized for a single Mexican deposit of an invention developed in stages and consequently filed abroad in several complementary first applications. Sepúlveda fails to recognize the character of multiple priority, as governed by Article 4F: this relates to an instance where several first applications — irrespective of whether they are filed in one or in more than one Union country, which Article 4F, paragraph 1 of the Lisbon version makes quite clear — to which, as a rule, different priority dates apply are then grouped in one subsequent application in such a manner that *different* Convention priorities are claimed for the various parts, in accordance with the date of the prior filing of the particular part. All that the various parts

Partial priorities may, however, also occur where Union priority is claimed for only one part of the application, while simple priority of filing exists in the case of the rest. In this connection the expression *partial priority in its narrower sense* is normally used.

2. The Development of Convention Law

The need to recognize claims to multiple priority in respect of one and the same application arose very early in connection with the Paris Convention. As early as 1911, at the *Washington Conference of Revision,* the International Bureau proposed, with the approval of the United States Government, to include an appropriate additional provision in Article 4 of the Paris Convention. The reasons—which, mutatis mutandis, apply similarly to the recognition of partial priorities—were described by the International Bureau in the following terms:

> It often happens that, after filing a first patent application, an inventor improves his invention while the period of priority is still valid and requests for these improvements either ordinary patents or additional patents or certificates. The problem has arisen of whether the inventor who patents his invention in one or more countries of the Union can combine all of their elements in the same application or whether he must on the contrary apply for as many foreign patents as he has successively obtained for his invention in the country of original deposit. The latter, and more stringent, solution is scarcely in harmony with the spirit of the Convention, which aims to favor and promote the inventive spirit. If the multiplicity of the successive patents in the country of original deposit is a consequence of the fact that they had been requested following the successive improvements, this is not true of the applications in other countries once the invention has been fully adapted. It is only natural for all the elements to be grouped within the same application at that point, provided that the character of the invention has remained unchanged and that it has only been improved and not basically transformed or modified in its principles.

The proposal met with the approval of all members of the competent Sub-committee except for Great Britain. The British representative ob-

---

have in common is that they are part of one and the same invention and that the twelve-month priority period has not expired for any of them.

jected that there would be practical difficulties owing to the different claims, and that it would be too complicated to establish whether the claims corresponded to the relevant prior applications. Although several delegates pointed out that certain countries were already practising the system without encountering any serious difficulties, the British opposition prevented the adoption of the proposed amendment to Article 4.

At the *Conference of Revision of The Hague,* in 1925, the question of multiple priorities was again discussed. There was a French proposal to allow claims to multiple priorities at least up to a total of four, subject to preservation of the unity of invention. It was further suggested that in the case of complex applications division should be allowed provided that the respective partial priorities were respected. The majority of member countries on the competent sub-committee were in favor of allowing multiple priorities, but a smaller group, including Great Britain, rejected the idea. It was finally agreed, however, that in the event of a claim for multiple priorities at least a division of the patent application must be allowed, without affecting the relevant right of priority. Article 4 of the Convention was amended by means of an appropriate section F.

Although this solution overcame the worst inconveniences of the previous situation, it did not constitute a thoroughly satisfactory settlement. The question was therefore placed on the agenda of the *London Conference of Revision* in 1934. The program drafted by the host country and the International Bureau noted that strict application of Article 4, according to which a second application could be based on only one of the applications filed in the first country, was an obstacle to inventors and required them unnecessarily to comply with additional formalities. It was therefore proposed that multiple priorities should be allowed, and the competent Subcommittee concurred in this view. An appropriate provision was approved in the plenary, and was incorporated as section F of Article 4, the previous section F concerning the filing of complex applications becoming Article 4G. Article 4F of the London version reads as follows:

> No country of the Union may refuse a patent application on the ground that it contains multiple priority claims, provided that there is unity of invention within the meaning of the law of the country.

At the *Lisbon Conference of Revision,* in 1958, Article 4F was again reworded. The initiative came from a suggestion made by the International

Bureau that the recognition of *partial priorities* should also be specifically covered, that is to say, instances where Convention priority is claimed for part of a subsequent application, whereas the rest of the application is not based on any Convention right of priority. Once multiple priorities had been introduced into Convention law and recognition had thereby been given to the fundamental possibility that different parts of one and the same application could have different priorities, it was a logical step forward to allow partial priorities as well; claims for partial priority are thus seen as a special case of multiple priority. It had already been proposed by the British national group at the Prague Congress of the IAPIP, in 1938, that a ruling on the recognition of partial priorities should be included in Article 4 of the Convention.

The Lisbon Conference unanimously agreed to the recognition of claims for partial priority. The new version of Article 4F lays down the clear obligation incumbent on member countries to recognize claims for both multiple and partial Union priority, provided that the general requirements of Article 4 are fulfilled and that there is unity of invention. For parts of the application which enjoy no Convention priority general criteria have to be used in regard to the question of priority, which means that the priority of filing the application is normally decisive. In the case of applications which contain more than one invention the applicant remains entitled to divide the applications, as after the London revision; irrespective of this, however, Article 4G(2) also allows division on the initiative of the applicant.

Article 4F of the Lisbon Act reads as follows:

> No country of the Union may refuse a priority or a patent application on the ground that the applicant claims multiple priorities, even originating in different countries, or on the ground that an application claiming one or more priorities contains one or more elements that were not included in the original application or applications whose priority is claimed, provided that, in both cases, there is unity of invention within the meaning of the law of the country.

> With respect to the elements not included in the original application or applications whose priority is claimed, the filing of the later application shall give rise to a right of priority under the usual conditions.

> ...

III. Legal Consequences in the Event of Wrongful Claim for Priority

1. Convention Law

The Paris Convention does not specify the legal consequences that will apply if it is discovered that the Convention priority claimed in respect of a patent that has already been issued is not materially founded, for example because the earlier application does not concern the same invention as the subsequent application.

With regard to omission of formalities it is laid down in Article 4D, paragraph 4, second sentence, that the consequences decided upon by the countries of the Union shall in no case go beyond the loss of the right of priority:

> Each of the countries of the Union shall decide what consequences shall follow the omission of the formalities prescribed by the present Article, but such consequences shall in no case go beyond the loss of the right of priority.

The consideration underlying this ruling is that Convention priority is conceived as an advantage for the applicant, providing him with definite advantages for the international protection of his invention, and that it is not a dangerous instrument in handling which he is liable to forfeit his patent owing to minor errors of form. If Convention priority were fraught with such perils it would lose much of its value. This was why, at the time of the Washington Revision of 1911, when formal requirements for claims to Convention priority were introduced, it was decided that errors of form should result in refusal of priority at the very most but not in loss of patent.

The same considerations must apply in the case of material shortcomings, for example if the previous Convention application on which the claim for priority is based does not contain the same invention. If every discrepancy, even of a trifling nature, led to loss of patent rights, priority would be affected by a serious factor of uncertainty. It is in keeping with both the spirit and the purpose of the Union that the applicant should not be penalized through revocation of the patent — provided in any case that he has not deliberately sought to deceive the authorities — but that Convention priority should be simply withheld for the part of the invention concerned, priority of application being given for the patent. The great majority of countries of the Union regard this solution as fair and proper and apply it in practice... However, the position is different in Great Britain..., while there is a division of opinion in Canada as to which solution should be followed ...

In the negotiations at the Lisbon Conference of Revision, the view was also expressed that the normal consequence of incorrect claims to priority should consist not in revocation of the patent but rather in refusal of priority. As a consequence of this idea, the obligation to recognize multiple and partial priorities stated in Article 4F, paragraph (1), of the Lisbon Act was worded primarily so as to preclude refusal of priority in such cases, whereas in the London Act it was merely mentioned that the patent application should not be rejected. The relevant amendment to the wording was proposed by the delegation of the Netherlands.

*****

3. Conclusions

As I have already stated in the first part of this section, revocation of patents in the event of incorrect claim for Convention priority does not appear to be a sanction in keeping with the spirit of the Paris Convention. It lays the inventor open to severe risks and deprives him of full enjoyment of the advantages that the right of Convention priority might represent for him. The survey of practice in the countries of the Union has shown that in certain States errors in priority are likely to incur complete forfeiture of the patent. It would therefore be desirable for a provision excluding such legal consequences to be included in the text of the Convention. Such a provision might be worded on the lines of Article 4D, paragraph (4), second sentence, of the Paris Convention and state in general terms that each of the Countries of the Union shall decide what consequences shall follow when Union priority is claimed without satisfying the formal or material requirements of the Convention, but that such consequences shall in no case go beyond the loss of the right of priority. The present second sentence of paragraph (4) of Article 4D could then be deleted.

Notes and Questions

1. Multiple priorities enable an applicant to claim different prior applications (within the preceding twelve months) in the same application, but the applicant has the advantage of priority for each "invention" or element of an invention only from the date of the corresponding earlier application. Suppose that an applicant claims A, B, C and D. Suppose that A and B were covered in an application twelve months (minus one day) ago, C was covered in an application ten months ago and D in an application nine months ago. For the purposes of assessing the novelty of C and D, the state of the art is considered as it was ten and nine months ago, respectively. The applicant does not need to file three applications. He or she can file one, provided that there is unity of invention. It is mainly a practical question: the inventor can take advantage of the development of an inventive concept over twelve months to include in a subsequent application all developments that hold together as one inventive concept, thus giving him or her the best expression of the invention. You might note that in the *Biogen*[1] case, the House of Lords refers to provisions of the UK Patents Act which govern applications claiming multiple priorities.

2. By allowing the patent applicant to claim partial priorities, the Paris Convention spares him or her from the necessity to make a new initial filing that would separate out that part of an invention for which priority is claimed.

C. The Patent Norms of the WTO TRIPS Agreement

We now turn our attention to the substantive provisions of the WTO TRIPS Agreement. The first article, by Thomas Cottier, was published two years before the conclusion of the Uruguay Round negotiations. In this article he lays out many of the issues that either were resolved during the long course of negotiations, or that remained to be resolved before the Agreement could be finalized. (Thomas Cottier was Switzerland's chief negotiator for the TRIPS Agreement, and this accounts for his "bird's eye" view of the negotiations.) In interpreting the TRIPS Agreement it may be quite use-

---

[1] *Supra* Ch. I, § B, 2, c.

ful to consider this negotiating history since many of the finally-concluded provisions represent a compromise among interests. It might be difficult to follow some of these provisions (e.g., consider the "mailbox" provision and its reference to "exclusive marketing rights") without this contextual background.

The Cottier contribution is followed by an article by Adrian Otten and Hannu Wager. This second article describes the results of the negotiations from the perspective of the WTO Secretariat. Adrian Otten played a direct role in the TRIPS negotiations on behalf of the GATT Secretariat, and he went on to serve as the first Director for Intellectual Property and Investment in the new (yet old!) WTO Secretariat.

The articles by Cottier and Otten and Wager are followed by the text of the TRIPS Agreement as it relates to substantive patent norms. There are then a substantial number of notes and questions intended to highlight some of the more interesting issues raised by the patent provisions of the TRIPS Agreement.

---

1. Negotiation of TRIPS Agreement Norms

The Prospects For Intellectual Property in GATT

Thomas Cottier*

*****

2. Changing attitudes and perceptions

A brief history of negotiations may indicate how attitudes have been changing during the last decade. Multilateral efforts to address the problem of counterfeit trademarked products and later of copyright piracy date back to the final stage of the Tokyo Round when the United States and the European Economic Community unsuccessfully submitted a draft Anti-Counterfeit Code (ACC). Continued work in GATT did not materialize due to opposition by newly industrialized countries, at the time. Equally, efforts

---

*28 CMLR 383 (1991).

made in the 1980-1984 Conference to revise the Paris Convention for the Protection of Industrial Property failed. The overall situation stimulated a reinforcement of national remedies by the United States, and efforts to include intellectual property beyond counterfeiting and piracy on the agenda of the upcoming eighth Round of multilateral trade negotiations in GATT. The United States initiative resulted in the inclusion of IPRs in the ministerial mandate of Punta del Este which coined, in terms of a political compromise, the notion of trade-related aspects of intellectual property rights (TRIPs). Two years of analysis and discussion in Negotiating Group 11 of the Trade Negotiations Committee (TNC) led to the expanded and refined Montreal mandate, achieved in Geneva in April 1989. The task ahead was enormous. A checklist prepared by the GATT Secretariat in early 1990 reflects the complexity. It listed a total of 161 conceptual and substantial problems to be settled. Up to spring 1990, discussions continued in a manner which often appeared to be a *dialogue des sourds.* In retrospect, this was not exactly the case. Changing attitudes began to appear when first legal texts were submitted on the basis of a great number of communications by industrialized and developing countries and conceptual papers were tested formally and informally. The draft proposals by the European Economic Community of March 1990 were a landmark. Additional, comprehensive submissions followed on the part of the United States, Switzerland and Japan. A group of fourteen developing countries elaborated detailed proposals focusing on enforcement against trademark counterfeiting and copyright piracy. Essentially based on these competing legal texts, negotiations started focusing on single items, working them over and over in numerous versions drafted on its own responsibility by the Chairman of NG 11, Ambassador Anell of Sweden, with the skillful assistance of the Secretariat. The process was conducted in a transparent manner. A group called Ten plus Ten did not exclude any contracting party interested in the matter. At a later stage, smaller drafting groups *à géométrie variable,* chaired by Director David Hartridge and Councellor Adrian Otten from the Secretariat, further refined the text. Although industrialized countries share overall interests, work and progress relied upon a constellation of flexible alliances, which, depending on the subject, brought about changing coalitions among industrialized and developing countries. Indeed, such dynamics, far from traditional block grouping in the U.N. system, have greatly catalysed the process and facilitated personal interaction among negotiators. On the eve of the Brussels Ministerial Meeting, a partly bracketed legal text was achieved, also including a separate draft agreement limited to trade in counterfeit and pirated goods as a formal alternative for decision on the ministerial level. Work continued at the Brussels Meeting until interrupted by the break-down of negotiations on agriculture. A number of politically sensitive issues remain to be solved and depend on the overall outcome of the Uruguay Round.

During the process of negotiations, attitudes changed and evolved in various ways. The European Economic Community, reluctant to endorse the GATT approach in the beginning, gradually emerged as major demandeur, perhaps stimulated by the ambitious submissions from the private sector and other participants. On the other hand, the United States delegation and constituencies indicated a gradually decreasing interest as the process moved foreword. Perhaps unexpected demands, such as the abolition of the first-to-invent principle and nondiscrimination in administrative patent procedures, the inclusion of moral rights and neighbouring rights in United States law, increased tensions within industrialized countries. Negotiations were not, and could not be, limited to what sometimes, in a simplified manner, are depicted as North-South problems. In many areas, successful progress requires changes in the laws of industrialized countries, such as geographical indications, non-discrimination, acquisition, government use and compulsory licensing. But there is no doubt that developing countries have come furthest in changing perceptions and attitudes to intellectual property in the four years of negotiations. There are a number of reasons, political and economic, for this.

Firstly, it is evident that the United States threats to use "Super 301" procedures and retaliate against what the U.S. administration unilaterally considers to be insufficient protection and unfair trade have greatly enhanced the attractiveness of an overall multilateral framework. Many consider it more beneficial to defend their interests in a multilateral system with well-defined standards rather than being exposed to unilateral determination. Moreover, a failure of negotiations could also lead to similar policies on the part of the European Economic Community and Japan. Secondly, it should not be underestimated that increased standards of protection in intellectual property also reinforce retaliatory powers of LDCs in trade disputes where their own export interests are affected. But beyond trade politics, the process also began to shift legal and economic attitudes towards the functions of IPRs for the benefit of long-term social and economic development. This is clearly linked to an increasing orientation towards less interventionist, open-market economies in many LDC's and in Eastern Europe which coincides with, and has been generally stimulated by, the Uruguay Round. It is evident that the positions of industrialized countries were primarily defined in order to defend their assets on export markets. But there are also increasing doubts whether a permissive network of IPR protection and the absence of higher standards inherently stimulate social and economic development in the Third World. In many instances, this form of protectionism tends to benefit vested interests and not the public at large.[23] The consensus found so far in the field of counterfeiting and piracy of trademarks and copyright (enforcement) — still impossible ten years ago — indicates that these doubts are increasing. More and more, it is acknowledged that adequate protection of IPRs is a beneficial factor in order to increase the flow of technology and know-how and to stimulate investment[24] by facilitating licensing agreements.

---

[23]For example, the exclusion of patentability of pharmaceutical products in 49 countries (1988) has been mainly justified in terms of lowering costs for the health system. It should be noted, however, that only a few products contained in the World Health Organization's list of essential drugs are still under patent protection (10 products in 1989 according to industry source, on file with author). A large majority (over 95 %) are off-patent and open to generic production. Cost-effective essential health service therefore does not exclude patentability. As to drugs under patent protection, it is doubtful whether reproduction without licensing and transfer of research experience related to the product is beneficial to public health at large since quality standards may not be reached and further research is impaired and frustrated, see also Jayasuriya, "Pharmaceuticals, Patents and the Third World", 22/6 Journal of World Trade (1988) 117-121. There is strong evidence that manufacturing of such products (often counterfeit) is inaccurate and dangerous, see "The Pill Pirates", Newsweek Nov. 5, 1990, 18-23. For essential drugs see World Health Organization, The Use of Essential Drugs (Technical Reports Series 796, 1990).

[24]The current rethinking of traditional perceptions, involving some ambivalence, to transfer of technology and IPR protection is well reflected in the present work of UNCTAD on transfer of technology: "Indeed, there appears to be widespread tendency to Governments world wide to grant stronger intellectual property protection. Although the granting of higher standards of protection may be justified on grounds of providing incentives and securing investment, returns for technology creators and innovators, other effects which may ensue from it, particularly in respect of international transfer and diffusion of technology, should not be overlooked; such effects would include

True, it is not established that increased protection per se brings about growth and equitable development. Empirical evidence is not conclusive. Much depends on other factors and policies, in particular to what extent governments (e.g. by financing licencing agreements in development programmes), industries and investors are willing to honour increased levels of protection and a more secure legal environment and establish fair terms of trade for developing countries in order to redress the global imbalance and avoid further capital drain to the North. IPRs are merely one aspect in a larger context. But is seems safe to say that adequate levels of protection are a necessary, albeit not sufficient, requirement for achieving successful integration in the world economy, to which contracting parties to the GATT are legally committed. They are necessary in order to increase substantially the level of foreign investment and to compete on private and public financial markets. They are equally necessary in order to secure market access of protected products on foreign markets. They are functional, once policies are directed towards an open-market economy based on fair competition. In other words, adequate IPRs protection is functional within GATT. There is no paradox or inherent conflict of free trade and adequate protection. Present efforts of Eastern European economies to introduce high standards of protection in order to attract investment and transfer of technology in an environment providing sufficient legal business security is significant in this context.

---

stronger incentives to maintain import monopolies rather than to work or license the technology locally, higher royalties and more restrictive practices in licensing contracts. On the other hand, given the importance attached by suppliers to the protection regimes of potential recipient countries, there is evidence that stronger protection could lead to greater willingness to transfer technology, particularly new technologies. However, although stronger protection may be considered a necessary condition for greater transfer, particularly of the more advanced technologies, it is far from being a sufficient condition, given the importance of several other factors", United Nations Conference on Trade and Development, Further Consultations on a Draft International Code of Conduct on the Transfer of Technology, Report by the Secretariat, TD/CODE TOT/56 (19 Nov. 1990) pare. 11 at 5. See also Commission on Transnational Cooperation, TradeRelated Aspects of Intellectual Property Rights and Trade-related Investment Measures, Report of the Secretary-Ceneral, E/C.10/1190/13 (7 March 1990) or ibid., New Issues in the Uruguay Round of Multilateral Trade Negotiations (UNCTC Current Studies Series A No. 19, 1190) 1 -7.

At the same time, it is equally necessary to provide for checks and balances and prevent excessive exploitation of enhanced protection by rightholders, such as import monopolies at excessive costs. It is remarkable that, perhaps for the first time, the TRIPs negotiations not only provided the ground for progress in the field of compulsory licensing, but also for that of abusive, anti-competitive licensing agreements.

3. Interfacing GATT and IPRs: Conceptual problems
*****

3.3 The relationship of TRIPs to existing agreements on intellectual property

From the very beginning, the relationship between a GATT agreement in intellectual property and existing international conventions, in particular the Paris Convention, the Berne Convention for the Protection of Literary and Artistic Works, the Rome Convention for the Protection of Performers, Producers of Phonograms and Broadcasting Organisations, and the Washington Treaty on Intellectual Property in Respect of Integrated Circuits has been controversial. Should the GATT draw from existing standards and enforce them, or build a system of its own, particularly addressing problems of trade distortions? Various approaches were offered, ranging from independence to an obligation to adhere to relevant agreements. An early Swiss proposal suggested the application of basic GATT principles and the elaboration of indicative lists subject to further evolution, stating situations which would be considered trade distortive. No formal links with existing systems were made. The European Economic Community, on the other hand, insisted for a long time on an obligation to adhere to the Berne, Rome, Paris and Washington Conventions. A solution finally found is the doctrine of incorporation by reference. A GATT agreement will not impair existing obligations of the Paris Convention (1967), the Berne Convention (1971) and the Washington Treaty. It would add so-called plus elements where a body of law to build upon already exists. As a result, existing conventions would be applied and construed in future dispute settlements and build a coherent body of case law, which has been missing so far.

691

*****

4. General operative principles
4.1 National and most-favoured nation treatment

The conceptual difference of directly protecting rightholders, not goods, excludes broad references to Articles I and III of GATT and requires specific principles applicable to IPRs. Moreover, it is necessary to achieve compatibility with existing principles in the Paris, Berne and Washington Conventions, and the Rome Convention as far as relevant. The draft contains a national treatment clause which is substance should produce the same effect as Article 2 of the Paris Convention and Article 3 of the Berne Convention. Equally, the scope of protection (definition of national) coincides (and was further extended to serve Hong Kong, which was not in a position to join the said agreements). The difference partly lies in exceptions. Efforts were made to narrow the scope of reciprocity. With a view to correcting the over-broad exclusion of procedural law from national treatment in Article 2(3) of the Paris Convention, exceptions were drawn in such a manner as to exclude disguised restrictions of trade — a lesson learnt from the EEC-US dispute on Sec. 337 Tariff Act.

Moreover, exceptions on the basis of reciprocity in Article 6 of the Berne Convention and Article 16.1 (a) (iii) or (iv) or Article 16.1 (b) of the Rome Convention are valid under the draft agreement only to the extent they are notified to the TRIPS Committee. In terms of principles, however, the major step consists in the application of the MFN principle to IPRs. This principle has been unknown to the existing network of IPR protection. The proliferation of bilateral or special agreements was encouraged with a view to improve the overall level of protection. Possible discrimination has not been a legal concern and no remedies were available. The issue of MFN in the negotiations again shows that TRIPs is by no means a matter limited to a North-South debate. Strict rules on MFN with clear and narrowly defined exceptions relating to judicial assistance, reciprocity treatment, grand-fathering of existing non-arbitrary privileges, are supported by smaller and medium sized parties, but have been opposed by the European Economic Community, which preferred to limit discipline to a mere prohibition of arbitrary discrimination, a concept which would further allow rather wide-open preferential treatment of rightholders of selected countries. A possible compromise, linking advantages of both philosophies, may consist in conditional MFN, i.e. an obligation to enter into good faith negotiations with a view to extend any additional advantages, favours, privileges or immunities exceeding this agreement to such other contracting party as is prepared and in a position to make similar commitments.

4.2 Exhaustion and parallel importation

Perhaps one of the most trade-related issues in the field of intellectual property is exhaustion of rights together with the issue of parallel importation. It would seem that regulation of this problem in the different fields of IPRs would be paramount in GATT negotiations. Quite the opposite is true. It almost remained untouched. No party was willing to make any commitment in this complex field, which is often left to national courts. Indeed, many participants thought it necessary to include an explicit guarantee of sovereignty in this area. As a corollary, the draft also implies, as a matter of GATT law, that there is no obligation to recognize national doctrines. Their application may result in nullification and impairment under conditions of unfair trade and competition, e.g. due to subsidized exports of licensed products to countries. Doctrines of exhaustion are therefore subject to Article XXIII(1)(b) of GATT and do not forfeit this right. The introduction of international exhaustion, after committing oneself to a TRIPs agreement, may amount to frustration of legitimate expectations created by increased protection of IPRs and may be estopped.

Existing GATT law also continues to govern other aspects of exhaustion and parallel importation. Article XX(d) of GATT provides the basis for exclusion of parallel importation whenever the doctrine of national exhaustion is applied by a contracting party. Equally, Article XXIV of GATT continues to provide the basis for regional exhaustion within customs unions or free-trade areas. It is for such reasons that the present draft text does not contain exceptions to MFN similar to Article XXIV of GATT.

4.3 Transitional arrangements

Transitional arrangements are worth discussing under the heading of general principles. They replace the application of doctrines of special and differential treatment of LDCs in trade regulation, which have not shown much economic benefit but have rather left LDCs without a great deal impact in GATT due to the absence of real commitments. The draft provides for special periods open to LDCs and Eastern European countries. During these periods, obligations on standards do not take effect, while general principles, benefits accruing under the agreement and obligations to abstain from unilateral action are operative. Additional, open-ended periods are available for least-developed countries. In addition, these countries would benefit from incentives provided by industrialized countries to promote and encourage transfer of technology. These transitional periods seek to provide sufficient time to undertake necessary structural adjustments of industries concerned and would be subject to monitoring. They are different from the general, initial period for legislative work required to make necessary adjustments in national law. Overall, the duration of transitional arrangements will depend on the level of standards achieved. It still has to be settled at a political level.

5. Substantive standards of intellectual property protection

The core of negotiations was dedicated to the elaboration of substantive standards in virtually all fields of intellectual property except the area of special plant breeders' rights. The draft includes standards on copyright and related rights, trademarks, geographical indications, industrial designs, patents, lay-out designs (topographies) of integrated circuits. It is completed by rules on undisclosed information which some would not yet consider a novel branch of intellectual property law. A brief survey may indicate issues which were informally settled and those, mainly of political importance, which still await further decision in the light of overall results of the Round. Of course, all results achieved are of a delicate, preliminary nature, and subject to further changes in the final stages of negotiations.

*****

5.6 Patents

From the beginning, patents ranged among the most contentious subjects of the Round, and negotiations are not at all limited to North-South issues, as was perhaps initially thought. They have addressed a number of key political issues: patentability, exclusions, nondiscrimination, patent term, burden of proof, novel perceptions on obligations on patent applicants and owners, rights conferred, compulsory licences and the problem of government use.

Considerable progress seems possible in a number of areas. Obligations to grant patents include both product and process patents. They include, subject to explicitly tolerated exceptions yet to be defined, basically all fields of technology. It is within possible reach that a patent term of twenty years from filing will carry the day. Rights conferred include the right to prevent importation of protected products (subject to international exhaustion, where applied), and at least of the products obtained from a process patent, which is essential to protect such inventions. In a long and arduous process, negotiations achieved the establishment of a common structure providing a fairly detailed list of fourteen, mostly innovative conditions on compulsory licences and government use. They considerably increase business security and remedies against unlawful use of these instruments. The list also contains provisions on the grant of licences for dependent patents. Finally, the reversal of the burden of proof in process patents, albeit a compromise, could considerably enhance effective protection of such inventions.

Major, politically sensitive issues remain to be settled. Final solutions in the field of exclusions of patentability are of a profoundly controversial nature. They depend, with respect to LDCs, on the overall outcome and balance of the Round. This is particularly true with respect to the proposed exclusion of pharmaceuticals which is firmly considered nonnegotiable on the part of many industrialized countries including the European Economic Community, the United States and Switzerland. Except for India, it seems that most parties are increasingly prepared to accept the inclusion of pharmaceuticals and foodstuffs at the end of the day. The debate has shifted instead to the complex problems involving biotechnological and genetically engineered products. In the long run, patentability of pharmaceuticals will depend on solutions found in this context since research and production increasingly rely upon new biotechnological and genetical methods. Existing patentability of such inventions in Australia, the United States and Japan create comparative advantages which partly assist in explaining the increasing exodus of research and know-how from Europe despite high investment. Present European law under Article 53(b) of the European Patent Convention, excluding animal and plant varieties, has created legal uncertainty. It is not favourable to sustained research efforts. Categorical classifications along these lines are hardly any longer in a position to draw meaningful lines between patentable and non-patentable subject matter under the precepts of modern science. Existing approaches need to be redirected by criteria which reflect ethical and legal considerations. This includes moral standards, but foremost is the fundamental principle of human dignity. A careful balance of reasonable conditions for research and investment and legitimate ethical concerns and barriers against abuse in this delicate field still needs to be found.

The second issue of fundamental controversy relates to compulsory licensing. It is of great impact on trade flows and competition. Developing countries and Canada argue in favour of an obligation to work the patent, excluding importation, even on normal commercial terms. Exporting countries argued in favour of importation fully satisfying the requirement of exploitation or working. GATT law may provide some guidance: requirements to produce locally where importation can satisfy local markets on normal business terms are difficult to justify under GATT, in particular where the licence amounts to an "other measure", non-tariff quantitative import restriction within Article XI of GATT. This provision contains an exhaustive list of justified restrictions. Further derogations would need to be justified under Article XX(d). This is extremely difficult because exceptions in favour of patent protection are clearly intended to protect the holder of the patent, and not the contracting party restricting importation. The argument in favour of local working is difficult to sustain, even more so since technology-importing participants strongly insist on keeping the freedom to import under the doctrine of international exhaustion. As to exportation of goods produced under compulsory licences, the draft contains provision that compulsory licences shall be authorized predominantly for the supply of the local market of the authorizing contracting party. The fragile compromise, much criticized, is clearly conditional and subject to the other provisions of the draft which considerably limit the scope for lawful compulsory licences, including a still controversial provision on non-discrimination between different fields of technology. These provisions will make it possible to challenge excessive licensing and thereby stop exportation to all countries, including those without patent protection, under Article XX(d) of the GATT. Moreover, the provision is also subject to substantially improved patent protection in contracting parties, which will make it possible to stop importation in most countries, since the rights of the patent owner are not exhausted by a compulsory licence.

*****

2. The Resulting Agreement

Compliance with TRIPS: The Emerging World View*

Adrian Otten** and Hannu Wager***

I. Intellectual Property Protection as an Integral Part of the Multilateral Trading System

As a result of the TRIPS Agreement (Agreement), the protection of intellectual property has become an integral part of the multilateral trading system, as embodied in the World Trade Organization (WTO). Indeed, the protection of intellectual property is one of the three pillars of the WTO, the other two being trade in goods (the area traditionally covered by the General Agreement on Tariffs and Trade (GATT)) and the new agreement on trade in services. The fact that the protection of intellectual property has thus moved to the center stage of international economic relations is not surprising given its major and growing importance to international competition in many areas of economic activity. In fact, the negotiation of the TRIPS Agreement was prompted by the perception that inadequate standards of protection and ineffective enforcement of intellectual property rights were often unfairly depriving the holders of such rights of the benefits of their creativity and inventiveness, and, as a result, prejudicing the legitimate commercial interests of their respective countries.

The new status of intellectual property protection in the international trading system has a number of important consequences, three of which will be discussed here. First, it explains why it was possible to negotiate, in the context of the Uruguay Round, such a major advance in the interna-

---

*29 Vand. J. Transnat'l L. 391 (1996).

**Director, Intellectual Property and Investment Division, the World Trade Organization. The views presented in this Article are the responsibility of the authors and should not be taken as necessarily those of the World Trade Organization or the World Trade Organization Secretariat.
***Legal Affairs Officer, Intellectual Property and Investment Division, the World Trade Organization.

tional protection of intellectual property. It became accepted, at least from the halfway point of the Uruguay Round negotiations, that a major agreement on intellectual property was a necessary component of a successful conclusion to the negotiations and therefore, in a certain sense, to the maintenance and strengthening of the multilateral trading system as a whole.

Second, due to the place of the TRIPS Agreement within the trading system it can be expected that over the coming years there will be something close to universal acceptance of its obligations. One of the important changes in the WTO, in contrast to the GATT, is that all countries wishing to be members, and to enjoy the market access it provides, will have to accept all the main WTO agreements, including the TRIPS Agreement. Of the 125 countries that were parties to the adoption of the Uruguay Round results in Marrakesh in April of 1994, 120 have already become members. Most of the remaining countries are expected to become members in the near future once they complete necessary domestic procedures. In addition, accession negotiations are under way with virtually all other governments of economic significance (twenty-nine at present), including China, Chinese Taipei, Vietnam, Russia, and the Ukraine.

Third, the dispute settlement procedures, as revised and strengthened in the Uruguay Round, will also apply to the TRIPS Agreement. Under the WTO, the failure of a country to meet its TRIPS obligations can put its market access rights and other benefits in jeopardy.

II. Certain General Provisions

Like the preexisting international intellectual property conventions, the TRIPS Agreement is a minimum standards agreement. It leaves members free to provide more extensive protection of intellectual property. Members may do so for purely domestic reasons or because they conclude international agreements in this regard, whether bilateral, regional (e.g., European Communities and North American Free Trade Agreement (NAFTA)), or multilateral (e.g., World Intellectual Property Organization (WIPO)). This is made clear in Article 1(1) of TRIPS, which provides that members may, but shall not be obliged to, implement in their law more extensive protection than is required by the Agreement, provided that such protection does not contravene the provisions of the Agreement. Article 1(1) also makes it clear that the Agreement is not intended to be a harmonization agreement — provided that members conform to the minimum requirements established by the Agreement, they are left free to determine the appropriate method of doing so within their own legal system and practice.

As in the main preexisting intellectual property conventions, the basic obligation on each member country is to accord the treatment in regard to the protection of intellectual property provided for under the Agreement to the persons of other members. Article1(3) defines who these persons are. These persons are referred to as "nationals," but include persons, natural or legal, who have a close attachment to other members without necessarily being nationals. The criteria for determining which persons will thus benefit from the treatment provided for under the Agreement are those laid down for this purpose in the main preexisting intellectual property conventions of WIPO, which are applied, of course, to all WTO members whether or not they are parties to those conventions.

Articles 3, 4, and 5 include the fundamental rules on national treatment and most-favored-nation treatment of foreign nationals, which are common to all categories of intellectual property covered by the Agreement. These obligations cover not only the substantive standards of protection but also matters affecting the availability, acquisition, scope, maintenance, and enforcement of intellectual property rights, as well as those matters affecting the use of intellectual property rights specifically addressed in the Agreement. While the national treatment clause forbids discrimination between a member's own nationals and the nationals of other members, the most-favored-nation treatment clause forbids discrimination between the nationals of other members. In respect of the national treatment obligation, the exceptions allowed under the preexisting intellectual property conventions of WIPO are also allowed under TRIPS. Where these exceptions allow material reciprocity, a consequential exception to most-favored-nation treatment is also permitted. TRIPS also provides certain other limited exceptions to the most-favored-nation obligation.

An issue that the Uruguay Round negotiations left unresolved is the question of "exhaustion." Article 6 provides that, for the purposes of dispute settlement under the TRIPS Agreement, nothing in the Agreement shall be used to address the issue of the exhaustion of intellectual property rights, provided that there is compliance with the national treatment and most-favored nation treatment obligations.

Article 7 of the Agreement is entitled "Objectives." It should be read in conjunction with the preamble, which reproduces the basic Uruguay Round negotiating objectives established in the TRIPS area by the 1986 Punta del Este Declaration and the 1988-89 Mid-Term Review. Also, Article 8, entitled "Principles," recognizes the rights of members to adopt measures for public health and other public interest reasons and to prevent the abuse of intellectual property rights, provided that such measures are consistent with the provisions of the TRIPS Agreement. Developing countries attach importance to these articles, which put emphasis on the transfer and dissemination of technology.

III. Substantive Standards of Protection

In respect of each of the main areas of intellectual property covered by the TRIPS Agreement, the Agreement sets out the minimum standards of protection to be provided by each member. These standards are set at a level comparable to those in the major industrial countries today. Each of the main elements of protection is defined, namely the subject matter to be protected, the rights to be conferred and permissible exceptions to those rights, and the minimum duration of protection.

The Agreement sets these standards by requiring, first, compliance with the substantive obligations of the main WIPO Conventions, the Paris Convention, and the Berne Convention, in their most recent versions. With the exception of the provisions of the Berne Convention on moral rights, all the main substantive provisions of these conventions are incorporated by reference and thus become obligations under the TRIPS Agreement. The relevant provisions are to be found in Articles 2(1) and 9(1) of the TRIPS Agreement, which relate to the Paris Convention and to the Berne Convention, respectively.

Second, the TRIPS Agreement adds a substantial number of additional obligations with respect to matters where the preexisting conventions were silent or were perceived as being inadequate. The TRIPS Agreement is thus sometimes referred to as a Berne and Paris-plus agreement. While the TRIPS Agreement adds new obligations, it also aims to make more effective the application of the main preexisting conventions.

The main features of the provisions concerning various categories of intellectual property covered by the TRIPS Agreement are summarized infra. The relevant provisions can be found in Part II of the Agreement.

700

*****

E. Patents[42]

In the area of patents, the Agreement requires member states to make patent protection available for inventions in all areas of technology without discrimination, the only substantial sectorial exceptions being for plants and animals other than microorganisms and for essentially biological processes for the production of plants and animals other than microbiological processes.[43]Any country opting to exclude plant varieties from patent protection, however, will be required to introduce an effective sui generis system of protection.[44] The Agreement does not address the first-to-file/first-to-invent debate directly, but will require member countries not to discriminate in the availability of patent protection according to the place of invention.

The basic patent rights are specified, including the requirement that process protection must extend to products obtained directly by the protected process.[45] Compulsory licensing and government use without the authorization of the right holder are allowed, but are made subject to fifteen conditions aimed at protecting the legitimate interests of the right holder.[46] These conditions include the obligation, as a general rule, to grant such licenses only if an unsuccessful attempt has been made to acquire a voluntary license on reasonable terms and conditions within a reasonable period of time; the requirement to pay adequate remuneration in the circumstances of each case, taking into account the economic value of the license; a requirement that decisions be subject to judicial or other independent review by a distinct higher authority; and the prohibition of discrimination in compulsory licensing as to the field of technology, the place of invention, and whether products are imported or locally produced.[47] Certain of these conditions are relaxed where compulsory licenses are employed to remedy practices that have been established as anticompetitive by a legal process.[48] The minimum term of protection is twenty years from the filing date.[49]

---

[42]See [TRIPS Agreement], arts. 27-34.
[43]Id. art. 27.
[44]Id. art. 27(3).
[45]Id. art. 28(9).
[46]Id. art. 31.
[47]Id. arts. 27(1), 31.

WTO Agreement on Trade-Related Aspects of Intellectual Property Rights

Part I
General Provisions and Basic Principles

*****

Article 2
Intellectual Property Conventions

1.   In respect of Parts II, III and IV of this Agreement, Members shall comply with Articles 1 through 12, and Article 19, of the Paris Convention (1967).

2.   Nothing in Parts I to IV of this Agreement shall derogate from existing obligations that Members may have to each other under the Paris Convention, the Berne Convention, the Rome Convention and the Treaty on Intellectual Property in Respect of Integrated Circuits.

*****

Article 7
Objectives

The protection and enforcement of intellectual property rights should contribute to the promotion of technological innovation and to the transfer and dissemination of technology, to the mutual advantage of producers and users of technological knowledge and in a manner conducive to social and economic welfare, and to a balance of rights and obligations.

Article 8
Principles

1.   Members may, in formulating or amending their laws and regulations, adopt measures necessary to protect public health and nutrition, and to promote the public interest in sectors of vital importance to their socio-economic and technological development, provided that such measures are consistent with the provisions of this Agreement.

---

[48]Id. art. 39(k).
[49]Id. art. 33.

2.   Appropriate measures, provided that they are consistent with the provisions of this Agreement, may be needed to prevent the abuse of intellectual property rights by right holders or the resort to practices which unreasonably restrain trade or adversely affect the international transfer of technology.

Part II

Standards Concerning the Availability, Scope
and Use of Intellectual Property Rights

*****

Section 5: Patents

Article 27
Patentable Subject Matter

1.   Subject to the provisions of paragraphs 2 and 3, patents shall be available for any inventions, whether products or processes, in all fields of technology, provided that they are new, involve an inventive step and are capable of industrial application.[5] Subject to paragraph 4 of Article 65, paragraph 8 of Article 70 and paragraph 3 of this Article, patents shall be available and patent rights enjoyable without discrimination as to the place of invention, the field of technology and whether products are imported or locally produced.

2.   Members may exclude from patentability inventions, the prevention within their territory of the commercial exploitation of which is necessary to protect ordre public or morality, including to protect human, animal or plant life or health or to avoid serious prejudice to the environment, provided that such exclusion is not made merely because the exploitation is prohibited by their law.

3.   Members may also exclude from patentability:
   (a) diagnostic, therapeutic and surgical methods for the treatment of humans or animals;

---

[5]For the purposes of this Article, the terms "inventive step" and "capable of industrial application" may be deemed by a Member to be synonymous with the terms "non-obvious" and "useful" respectively.

(b) plants and animals other than micro-organisms, and essentially biological processes for the production of plants or animals other than non-biological and microbiological processes. However, Members shall provide for the protection of plant varieties either by patents or by an effective sui generis system or by any combination thereof. The provisions of this subparagraph shall be reviewed four years after the date of entry into force of the WTO Agreement.

Article 28
Rights Conferred

1. A patent shall confer on its owner the following exclusive rights:

(a) where the subject matter of a patent is a product, to prevent third parties not having the owner's consent from the acts of: making, using, offering for sale, selling, or importing[6] for these purposes that product;

(b) where the subject matter of a patent is a process, to prevent third parties not having the owner's consent from the act of using the process, and from the acts of: using, offering for sale, selling, or importing for these purposes at least the product obtained directly by that process.

2. Patent owners shall also have the right to assign, or transfer by succession, the patent and to conclude licensing contracts.

Article 29
Conditions on Patent Applicants

1. Members shall require that an applicant for a patent shall disclose the invention in a manner sufficiently clear and complete for the invention to be carried out by a person skilled in the art and may require the applicant to indicate the best mode for carrying out the invention known to the inventor at the filing date or, where priority is claimed, at the priority date of the application.

2. Members may require an applicant for a patent to provide information concerning the applicant's corresponding foreign applications and grants.

---

[6]This right, like all other rights conferred under this Agreement in respect of the use, sale, importation or other distribution of goods, is subject to the provisions of Article 6.

Article 30
Exceptions to Rights Conferred

Members may provide limited exceptions to the exclusive rights conferred by a patent, provided that such exceptions do not unreasonably conflict with a normal exploitation of the patent and do not unreasonably prejudice the legitimate interests of the patent owner, taking account of the legitimate interests of third parties.

Article 31
Other Use Without Authorization of the Right Holder

Where the law of a Member allows for other use[7] of the subject matter of a patent without the authorization of the right holder, including use by the government or third parties authorized by the government, the following provisions shall be respected:

(a) authorization of such use shall be considered on its individual merits;

(b) such use may only be permitted if, prior to such use, the proposed user has made efforts to obtain authorization from the right holder on reasonable commercial terms and conditions and that such efforts have not been successful within a reasonable period of time. This requirement may be waived by a Member in the case of a national emergency or other circumstances of extreme urgency or in cases of public non-commercial use. In situations of national emergency or other circumstances of extreme urgency, the right holder shall, nevertheless, be notified as soon as reasonably practicable. In the case of public non-commercial use, where the government or contractor, without making a patent search, knows or has demonstrable grounds to know that a valid patent is or will be used by or for the government, the right holder shall be informed promptly;

(c) the scope and duration of such use shall be limited to the purpose for which it was authorized, and in the case of semi-conductor technology shall only be for public non-commercial use or to remedy a practice determined after judicial or administrative process to be anti-competitive;

---

[7] "Other use" refers to use other than that allowed under Article 30.

(d) such use shall be non-exclusive;

(e) such use shall be non-assignable, except with that part of the enterprise or goodwill which enjoys such use;

(f) any such use shall be authorized predominantly for the supply of the domestic market of the Member authorizing such use;

(g) authorization for such use shall be liable, subject to adequate protection of the legitimate interests of the persons so authorized, to be terminated if and when the circumstances which led to it cease to exist and are unlikely to recur. The competent authority shall have the authority to review, upon motivated request, the continued existence of these circumstances;

(h) the right holder shall be paid adequate remuneration in the circumstances of each case, taking into account the economic value of the authorization;

(i) the legal validity of any decision relating to the authorization of such use shall be subject to judicial review or other independent review by a distinct higher authority in that Member;

(j) any decision relating to the remuneration provided in respect of such use shall be subject to judicial review or other independent review by a distinct higher authority in that Member;

(k) Members are not obliged to apply the conditions set forth in subparagraphs (b) and (f) where such use is permitted to remedy a practice determined after judicial or administrative process to be anti-competitive. The need to correct anti-competitive practices may be taken into account in determining the amount of remuneration in such cases. Competent authorities shall have the authority to refuse termination of authorization if and when the conditions which led to such authorization are likely to recur;

(l) where such use is authorized to permit the exploitation of a patent ("the second patent") which cannot be exploited without infringing another patent ("the first patent"), the following additional conditions shall apply:

(i) the invention claimed in the second patent shall involve an important technical advance of considerable economic significance in relation to the invention claimed in the first patent;

(ii) the owner of the first patent shall be entitled to a cross-licence on reasonable terms to use the invention claimed in the second patent; and

(iii) the use authorized in respect of the first patent shall be non-assignable except with the assignment of the second patent.

Article 32
Revocation/Forfeiture

An opportunity for judicial review of any decision to revoke or forfeit a patent shall be available.

Article 33
Term of Protection

The term of protection available shall not end before the expiration of a period of twenty years counted from the filing date.[8]

Article 34
Process Patents: Burden of Proof

1. For the purposes of civil proceedings in respect of the infringement of the rights of the owner referred to in paragraph 1(b) of Article 28, if the subject matter of a patent is a process for obtaining a product, the judicial authorities shall have the authority to order the defendant to prove that the process to obtain an identical product is different from the patented process. Therefore, Members shall provide, in at least one of the following circumstances, that any identical product when produced without the consent of the patent owner shall, in the absence of proof to the contrary, be deemed to have been obtained by the patented process:

---

[8]It is understood that those Members which do not have a system of original grant may provide that the term of protection shall be computed from the filing date in the system of original grant.

(a) if the product obtained by the patented process is new;

(b) if there is a substantial likelihood that the identical product was made by the process and the owner of the patent has been unable through reasonable efforts to determine the process actually used.

2.   Any Member shall be free to provide that the burden of proof indicated in paragraph 1 shall be on the alleged infringer only if the condition referred to in subparagraph (a) is fulfilled or only if the condition referred to in subparagraph (b) is fulfilled.

3.   In the adduction of proof to the contrary, the legitimate interests of defendants in protecting their manufacturing and business secrets shall be taken into account.

Notes and Questions

1.   Recall that industrialized country industries considered one of the main drawbacks of the Paris Convention to be its failure to define the subject matter area or field of patent protection. Article 27 of the TRIPS Agreement defines the minimum scope of subject matter coverage that WTO Members now must provide. What range of subject matter is included? What range of subject matter is excluded? Governments retain some flexibility in determining the scope of protection. Which provisions provide this flexibility?

2.   Article 27:1 provides that patents shall be granted without discrimination as to the place of invention. This provision addressed a discriminatory feature of U.S. patent law that allowed a patent applicant to prove a date of invention based on inventive activity within the United States, but excluded evidence of inventive activity outside the United States. The U.S. Patent Act has been amended to allow evidence of inventive activity wherever it may take place in a NAFTA or WTO Member country (U.S. Patent Act, § 104(a), as amended effective January 1, 1996).

3.   You will recall that the Paris Convention envisages that parties may grant compulsory patent licenses for "non-working" of an invention. Article 27:1

of the TRIPS Agreement provides that "patents shall be available and patent rights enjoyable without discrimination as to . . . whether products are imported or locally produced." Would you conclude that WTO Members are precluded from granting compulsory licenses solely on the grounds that the local market is supplied by imports and not by local working of the invention? We will focus on the subject of compulsory licensing in the following section.

4. TRIPS Agreement Article 27:2 allows WTO Members to exclude patents for products as necessary to protect ordre public (public order) or morality, including to protect human health. Under this provision, might a government be justified in excluding certain critical health care products from patentability? If a government concluded that patenting of human genetic information was contrary to fundamental religious ideology or to basic secular moral norms, would it be permitted to exclude such subject matter from patentability?

5. Article 27:3 allows the exclusion of plants and animals, but not microorganisms, and allows the exclusion of essentially biological processes for producing plants and animals, but not microbiological processes. Why did negotiators draw these distinctions? What is the difference between a "biological" process and a "microbiological" process?

6. Article 28:1 includes among the patent holder's rights that of preventing those acting without consent from "importing" a covered product. This provision is relevant to the parallel imports question. Observe first that footnote 6 expressly refers back to Article 6, which reserves resolution of the parallel imports question. Observe also that the right to prevent imports refers to acts undertaken without the patent holder's "consent." The test employed by the ECJ in applying the intra-Union exhaustion doctrine is whether a product has been placed on the market with (or without) the IPRs holder's consent. Does the express text of Article 28:1 resolve the parallel imports question as it relates to patents?

7. Observe that TRIPS Article 29 accommodates the European concept of enabling disclosure and the U.S. concept of best known means disclosure.

8. Article 30 permits Members to provide limited exceptions to the rights of patent holders, provided those exceptions do not interfere with normal

exploitation of the patent. The terms of Article 30 are similar to those employed by the Berne Convention as it provides for "fair use' of copyrighted materials (Berne, art. 9(2)). What might constitute fair use of patented products or processes?

9. Article 31 addresses compulsory licensing and is addressed in the next section.

10. Article 33 establishes a minimum patent term of twenty years from the date of filing. Since the United States had previously computed its patent term as seventeen years from the date of grant, this provision required amendment of the U.S. Patent Act (section 154(2)).[1]

---

3. Compulsory Licensing and the Balance of Rights

Governments may act to grant patent licenses to private parties or governmental entities without the consent of patent holders. These grants are addressed in Article 5 of the Paris Convention and Article 31 of the TRIPS Agreement. This act is customarily referred to as "compulsory licensing." The Paris Convention places few restrictions on the right of governments to legislate on the grant of compulsory licenses, except in the limited area of "failure to work." With respect to "failure to work," a minimum time period of four years is required to elapse before a compulsory license may issue. Compulsory licenses are to be non-exclusive and in general non-transferable. The Paris Convention does not mandate the payment of compensation to the patent holder whose rights have been licensed under compulsion.

TRIPS Agreement Art. 31 adds conditions on the grant of the compulsory patent license. It notes that such licenses may be granted to governments or to "third parties authorized by the government." The proposed licensee must have made efforts "to obtain authorization from the right

---

[1] This amendment was made by the United States prior to the conclusion of the Uruguay Round in connection with a Japan-U.S. bilateral agreement on patents that contemplated successful conclusion of the TRIPS Agreement .

holder on reasonable commercial terms and conditions and that such efforts have not been successful within a reasonable period of time." This requirement may be waived in case of "national emergency," "other circumstances of extreme urgency" or "in cases of public non-commercial use." In the former two cases, the right holder "will be notified as soon as reasonably practicable." In the case of "public non-commercial use" ... "where the government or contractor, without making a patent search, knows or has demonstrable grounds to know that a valid patent is or will be used by or for the government, the right holder shall be informed promptly."

There are a number of additional conditions on compulsory licensing: (1) the scope should be limited to the purpose of the authorization (and semi-conductor patents may only be licensed for non-commercial purposes or to remedy anticompetitive practices); (2) the licensing shall be non-exclusive; (3) no assignment should be made except in connection with transfer of the business; (4) use should be predominantly to supply the domestic market; (5) the license should be terminated when the conditions which lead to its authorization cease; (6) "the right holder shall be paid adequate remuneration in the circumstances of each case, taking into account the economic value of the authorization"; and (7) decisions of government authorities should be subject to independent judicial review. The aforementioned conditions do not apply when anticompetive practices are being remedied.

You will recall that Edith Tilton Penrose favored the liberal granting of compulsory licenses to maintain a balance of interests among industrialized and developing countries. Though developing countries do not appear to grant compulsory licenses with any frequency, industry groups have argued that the mere possibility that a compulsory license may be granted affects negotiations on the transfer of technology. The following excerpt is an elaboration of the patent law of India and its compulsory licensing system under the Patents Act of 1970. Towards the end of 1998, the government of India was in the process of considering various proposals for revision of the Patents Act so as to bring that law into conformity with the TRIPS Agreement (note, however, that as a developing country WTO Member, India is not yet obligated to implement reforms in various areas in accordance with TRIPS transition provisions). Even if the Indian Patents Act is revised, it will be useful to have examined this alternative approach to a patent regime.

TRIPs and the Third World: The Example of Pharmaceutical Patents in India

Elizabeth Henderson*

The Patents Act 1970

To the West, particularly the United States, the Patents Act of 1970 does not go anywhere near far enough to protecting inventions, especially pharmaceuticals. Interestingly however, the Act has received criticism from within India for going too far, and for protecting foreign patent owners at the expense of the domestic economy. Critics point to the fact that the majority of Indian patents are owned by foreigners and that a large proportion of these are not commercially worked in India or are worked for the sole purpose of securing import monopolies or preventing imports. Although the compulsory licensing provisions are potentially harsh to patent owners they are rarely used and there is little evidence that the threat of compulsory licenses had induced patent owner to issue voluntary licences.

> There is every reason to suspect that the Patent Act 1970 has failed in its major objective of defending the public and India's interest.
> In spite of all this, although there are powerful lobbies arguing that the Indian Patents Act of 1970 is too restrictive and unfair to foreign patent holders, the contrapuntal voice that the Act has not succeeded in its primary purpose of defending and advancing the public interest is not heard.
> ... [B]ecause minds have absorbed and totally believed the complex rhetoric that the Act is onerous to the patent holder, an otherwise incredible and wholly inexplicable support seems to give impetus to the campaign for more rights to the foreign patent holder. This is all the more incredible because those who are responsible for making these decisions felt that every time a patent right is granted a slice of India's economy is handed over to foreign ownership and control.[68]

---

*19 European Intellectual Property Review 651, 658-59 (1997).

[68]Dhavan, Harris and Jain "Power without responsibility on aspects of the Indian Patents Legislation", (1991) 33 JILI 1 at 70.

Patentable inventions

Section 48 (2) provides for two kinds of patents;

- process patents — a patent for a method or process of manufacturing an article or substance whereby the patentee gains the "exclusive right . . . to use or exercise the method or process in India";
- product patents — a patent for an article or substance whereby the patentee gains the "exclusive right to make, use, exercise, sell or distribute such articles or substance in India."[69]

Both types of patents have a term of 14 years except for process patents in relation to food, medicine or drugs which have a term of only five years from the date of sealing or seven years from the date of the patent whichever is shorter.

In keeping with the traditional approach in the United Kingdom, in order to be patentable an invention must be new, capable of industrial application and relate to a machine, article, substance produced by manufacture, process of manufacture or be an improvement of an article or process of manufacture.

Section 5 provides that, in relation to certain categories of inventions, only process patents are available. Product patents are not available for inventions:

(a) claiming substances intended for use, or capable of being used, as food or medicine or drug; or

(b) relating to substances prepared or produced by chemical process (including alloys, optical glass, semiconductors and inter-metallic compounds).

Food is defined by section 2 (1) (g) to include "any article of nourishment and includes any substances intended for the use of babies, invalids or convalescents as an article of food or drink". Medicine and drugs are defined very widely in section 2 (1).[70]

---

[69]Patents Act, s. 2 (j).
[70]The definition encompasses:
    (1) medicines for external or internal uses of humans or animals;

It is therefore not possible to gain product patents in relation to food, medicine and drugs. This has caused the greatest amount of controversy at an international level. By comparison with the level of protection in developed countries, pharmaceutical patents are vastly underprotected in India.

Compulsory licenses, licenses of right and revocation

The patentee has a three year grace period from the sealing of the patent before a compulsory license can be granted. After this any person can apply for a compulsory license where:

> The reasonable requirements of the public with respect to the patented invention have not been satisfied or [where] the patented invention is not available to the public at a reasonable price. . .[71]

In deciding whether to grant a compulsory license the Controller of Patents must also consider such things as the nature of the invention and the measures taken to put it to use, the applicant's ability to work the patent to the public advantage and undertake the risk in providing capital and working the invention.[72]

The Central government may make an application under section 86 (1) that a patent be endorsed with a license of right. These are also determined according to the "reasonable requirements" criteria. Process patents for inventions relating to food, medicine, drugs or chemical processes are automatically endorsed with licenses of right three years after they are granted.[73]

Once an invention has been endorsed with a license of right, any person may request that they be granted a license to exploit it. They do not

---

(2) substances intended to be used
(a) in diagnosis, treatment, mitigation or prevention of diseases in humans or animals;
(b) for or in the maintenance of public health, or the prevention or control of epidemics among humans or animals;
(3) insecticides, germicides, fungicides, weedicides and all substances intended to be used for plant production or preservation;
(4) chemical substances ordinarily used as intermediates in the preparation or manufacture of any of the above substances.

[71]Dhavan, Harris and Jain n 68 above, at 13 citing s. 84 of the Patents Act 1970.
[72]ibid., at 13.
[73]ibid.

714

need to show that the patentee has failed to make full use of the patent or is unable to work the invention effectively.

The Central government may apply to the Controller to revoke a patent altogether if it feels that the reasonable requirements of the public have not been met or the invention is not available at a reasonable price. This may occur only after two years have passed from the date a compulsory license of right was granted. In determining whether to revoke a patent whether the patentee has failed to develop the related industry in India is relevant.[74] The Central government may also revoke a patent if "the mode of its exercise is mischievous to the state or generally prejudicial to the public".[75]

The granting of a license or revocation will depend on whether the reasonable requirements have been met. Section 90 lists five circumstances where the reasonable requirements are deemed to have not been met.[76] Notably, a patent owner may be subject to a license or revocation if it fails to work the invention in India or where demand for the invention is substantially being met by importation. Further, importation does not qualify as working the patent under the Act.[77] This limits the ability of a foreign

---

[74]McLeland and Toole, "Patent systems in less developed countries: the cases of Indian and the Andean pact countries" (1987) 2 (2) Journal of Law and Technology, at 235.
[75]Dhavan, Harris and Jain n 68 above, at 17.
[76]These are where:

1. As a result of the patentee's failure to manufacture or grant a reasonable license-
(a) trade or industry is prejudiced;
(b) demand for the patented article is not being met from manufacture in India to an adequate extent or on reasonable terms;
(c) an export market of the patented article manufactured in India is not being supplied or developed;
(d) Indian commercial activity is prejudiced.
2. The patentee imposes extraneous conditions on the grant of the patent so as to restrain manufacture, sale or use of other materials or prejudice the development of an Indian trade or industry.
3. The invention is not being worked to an adequate extent or to the fullest extent practicable in India.
4. When Indian demand for the invention is being substantially met by importation by the patentee, those directly or indirectly purchasing from him/her and those against whom s/he is not enforcing his/her monopoly.
[77]Ahjua "GATT and TRIPs — The impact on the Indian Pharmaceutical Industry" (1994) September, Patent World 28, 29.

patent owner to obtain a patent for the mere purpose of preventing importation by competitors or local production. The invention must be worked in India and Indian demand must be substantially met by local production to avoid failing the "reasonable requirements" criteria.

Licensing is an important feature of economic regulation in India. The government takes an interventionist approach in the terms and conditions of the licensing agreements and controls royalty payments.[78]

The Act also gives the government two types of rights and powers — condition precedent rights and acquisition powers. These allow the government to acquire or use a patent without the owner's consent in certain circumstances. Their powers are extensive but are generally used sparingly.

Underlying rationale

Essentially, the Patents Act of 1970 focuses on the public interest rather than on the protection of private property interests. Its underlying philosophy is expressed in section 83 which states:

> ... patents are granted to encourage inventions and to insure that the inventions are worked in India on a commercial scale and to the fullest extent that is reasonably practicable without undue delay
> ... they are not granted merely to enable patentees to enjoy a monopoly for the importation of the patented article.

The rationale underpinning Indian patent law is that the government grants exclusive rights to exploit an invention on a quid pro quo basis. In return for exclusive rights the patent owner works the invention in India leading to the establishment of a new industry, increased employment and capital. The patent owner must also disclose the invention so that the public can work it once the patent has expired. Patent law centers around this bargain — exclusive rights exchanged for knowledge and input into the local economy.

The Patents Act of 1970 substantially limits the range of patentable inventions and lists numerous categories of inventions which are not patentable. While the Act provides certain protection of the rights of the

---

[78]McLeland and Toole n 74 above, at 10-11.

patent owners, it also provides government with substantial powers to restrict those rights.

Notes and Questions

1. Recall that the TRIPS Agreement includes transition arrangements in respect to patents. In studying the WTO India-Mailbox decision, we reviewed the specific provisions regarding pharmaceuticals and agricultural chemicals. In addition to establishing a "mailbox" for pharmaceutical and agricultural chemical patent applications, what other changes do you think the TRIPS Agreement requires India to make to its patent law?

2. Elizabeth Henderson reports that India's rarely used compulsory licensing rules have not affected the business decisions of foreigners. One of the main contentions of OECD industry groups in the TRIPS negotiations was that even though developing country governments rarely grant compulsory licenses, the mere background presence of the permissive rules affects the bargaining dynamic between licensors and licensees, to the detriment of licensors. How does Elizabeth Henderson know that the decisions of foreign holders of patents in India have not been affected by liberal compulsory licensing rules? How might data on such a phenomenon be collected and analyzed?

3. The TRIPS Agreement requires that patent holders receive "adequate remuneration" in respect to the grant of a compulsory license. What method do you think should be used to determine adequate remuneration? Does the India Patents Act require the payment of adequate remuneration?

4. Compulsory licensing is one of the ideological questions that has attracted intense negotiations at various stages throughout the history of international relations over patents. Attempts to revise the Paris Convention throughout the 1970s and 1980s foundered on the lack of agreement over a revised text for Article 5. Yet, as has been pointed out, developing countries have rarely invoked the use of compulsory licenses. One explanation for this is the lack of a sufficiently sophisticated industrial and technological infrastructure in many developing countries to be able to take advantage of

a compulsory license. Another is that a patent discloses the skeleton of the new technology only. Disclosure is required to enable a person skilled in the relevant art to work the invention. Thus, much background information and technology is assumed. Furthermore, a great deal of know-how is usually accumulated as a consequence of the patent owner practicing the invention after the patent application has been filed and, thus, after the public disclosure of the invention has been made. This know-how is secret and is not available under a compulsory license, which covers only the patent. One might say, therefore, that developing countries have exaggerated the benefits that compulsory licenses might bring and, likewise, the industrialized countries have exaggerated the fear and the dangers of compulsory licenses. Do you consider that the issue of compulsory licenses justifies the attention that it has received? Do you consider the debate to be one about the ideology of the sanctity of property rights, or do you think that the issue is of real practical importance?

4. Interpreting the Patent Norms of the TRIPS Agreement

The TRIPS Agreement is unique in the WTO pantheon of agreements. It is the only agreement to date which requires WTO Members to adopt systems of national/regional legislative measures that meet certain minimum standards. It is also the only WTO agreement to date which incorporates major portions of treaties outside the WTO set of agreements. As such, the TRIPS Agreement raises a host of issues in the context of its potential application by dispute settlement panels and the Appellate Body. The following article by Frederick Abbott explores a number of the key issues surrounding interpretation of the TRIPS Agreement, and makes some suggestions concerning the interpretative avenues that might be followed in WTO dispute settlement.

WTO Dispute Settlement and the Agreement on Trade-Related Aspects of Intellectual Property Rights

Frederick M. Abbott*

The WTO Agreement on Trade-Related Aspects of Intellectual Property Rights (the "TRIPS Agreement") has ushered in a new generation of legal issues that may ultimately find their way into the WTO dispute settlement arena . . .

The TRIPS Agreement is unique in the WTO context. The TRIPS Agreement is the only WTO agreement that requires the Members to affirmatively (or positively) incorporate complex substantive legal standards into national laws that govern both domestically-produced and imported goods.[1] It relies for many of its rules on cross-reference to an existing body of multilateral conventions administered outside the WTO. The substantive rules imposed by the TRIPS Agreement are the subject of existing bodies of judicial opinion in the national and regional territories that are now subject to its discipline. Underlying the superficial certainty of the TRIPS Agreement substantive prescriptions are existing gulfs of interpretative difference regarding the meaning of many of its rules.

The TRIPS Agreement is unique in that it establishes minimum standards applicable to the enforcement of legislation by WTO Members. The establishment of minimum enforcement standards necessarily implies that

---

*In International Trade Law and the GATT-WTO Dispute Settlement System 415 (E.- U. Petersmann ed., 1997).

[1] There are many GATT, and now WTO/GATT, rules that impose negative or prohibitory requirements on Members. For example, the national treatment rule of GATT article III obligates Members to provide at least equivalent treatment to imported goods for purposes of internal sale. It does not, however, require the Members to maintain any particular internal system regulating the sale of goods; only one that is non-discriminatory. There are also WTO/GATT agreements, such as the Agreement on Article VII (Valuation for Customs Purposes), that may circumscribe fairly narrowly the regulatory system that a Member adopts. To some extent the Agreement on Customs Valuation might be considered an agreement that requires the Members to adopt minimum substantive standards, e.g., to use "transaction value" as the primary basis for customs valuation. But customs valuation rules are strictly trade-related, affecting only imported (and potentially, in limited circumstances, exported) goods.

claims alleging the maintenance of inadequate enforcement procedures can and may be brought before the WTO Dispute Settlement Body. Yet the TRIPS Agreement is silent on just how such a claim might be proven, e.g., where the threshold of inadequate enforcement might lie.

Identifying methods and sources of interpretation for TRIPS Agreement substantive requirements, as well as delimiting the appropriate threshold of adequate enforcement, are but two of the intriguing tasks facing the WTO Dispute Settlement Body.

*****

II. Interpretation of the TRIPS Agreement

The DSU states that the WTO dispute settlement system "serves to . . . clarify the existing provisions of [the covered agreements] in accordance with customary rules of interpretation of public international law."[15] The reference to customary rules should in general be understood as a reference to the rules of interpretation set forth in the Vienna Convention on the Law of Treaties.[16] The Members of the WTO also have agreed to "be guided by the decisions, procedures and customary practices followed" under the GATT 1947 regime, except as otherwise provided by the WTO agreements.[17] There is nothing in the TRIPS Agreement that seeks to modify these principles in their general application to dispute settlement in the TRIPS Agreement context.[18]

---

[15]DSU, art. 3:2.

[16]Vienna Convention on the Law of Treaties, May 23, 1969, 1155 UNTS 331 (entered into force Jan. 27, 1980; not in force for the United States, U.N. Doc. A/Conf. 39 (1969)), reprinted in 63 Am J. Int'l L. 875 (1969) [hereinafter Vienna Convention or VCLT]. Since the United States is not party to the VCLT, it was considered more appropriate to refer to customary rules than to the VCLT, particularly since it is the official position of the U.S. government that the VCLT largely restates custom. For references to official U.S. position regarding the VCLT, see Restatement (Third) of the Law of Foreign Relations, at Part III, Introductory Note. There is no indication in the WTO agreements that anything other than the rules of the VCLT are intended, except in the express case of the Antidumping Agreement.

[17]WTO Agreement, art. XVI:1.

[18]TRIPS Agreement Article 64:2-3 removes non-violation nullification and impairment complaints from the purview of dispute settlement for a five year period and, while this

The reference in the DSU to use of "customary rules of interpretation of international law" is rather important in respect to TRIPS Agreement dispute settlement. The unique character of the TRIPS Agreement will almost certainly result in a greater reliance by dispute settlement panels on sources of law outside the WTO/GATT texts, and outside WTO/GATT panel decisions, than has been the practice in regard to interpretation of the GATT 1947. The custom of GATT 1947 dispute settlement panels has been to rely principally on the text of the GATT agreement and its negotiating history, prior dispute settlement panel decisions regarding that agreement, and performance by the Members with respect to that agreement, as evidence of interpretation.[19] However, up until the coming into force of the WTO agreements, the GATT has been a largely self-contained system. The GATT 1947 established the fundamental rules governing the international trading system as of 1947, and its dispute settlement panels thereafter construed those rules. The TRIPS Agreement injects a decidedly new element into the dispute settlement equation. There is a body of multilateral conventions governing the international IPRs system that has been in the process of continual development and refinement since the end of the 19th century. Provisions of these conventions have been directly and indirectly incorporated into the TRIPS Agreement. National legislatures have long interpreted these conventions in adopting legislation compliant with them. National, subnational and regional courts have long construed these conventions and related national legislation. The IPRs field is one of unusual complexity and subtlety, and in which broad statements of governing law do not easily refine themselves into the details of practice. WTO dispute settlement panels may find it quite useful, and perhaps necessary, to refer to the existing body of relevant law in interpreting the TRIPS Agreement. If the GATT dispute settlement system has been insulated from external sources of law, it is unlikely that the situation will continue in the field of TRIPS dispute settlement.

There are two major categories of dispute that may arise under the TRIPS Agreement. The first is disputes concerning whether a Member has

---

is a rather important provision in its own right . . ., it should not affect the general operation of the dispute settlement process as discussed in this section.

[19]See, e.g., United States — Restrictions on Imports of Tuna, Report of the Panel, Sept. 3, 1991, DS21/R, not adopted, 30 I.L.M. 1594 (1991); United States — Restrictions on Imports of Tuna, June 1994, not adopted, 33 I.L.M. 839 (1994); United States — Section 337 of the Tariff Act of 1930, report of the panel adopted Nov. 7, 1989, BISD 36S/345.

adequately implemented TRIPS Agreement substantive standards of IPRs protection into national law.[20] The second is disputes concerning whether a Member has provided and given operational effect to adequate enforcement mechanisms for the substantive standards so provided.

For purposes of considering potentially relevant interpretative sources, the TRIPS Agreement substantive standards may usefully be divided into three subcategories. The first subcategory is substantive standards that are established by cross-reference to existing multilateral conventions. For example, Members undertake to comply with Articles 1 through 21 of the Berne Convention for the Protection of Literary and Artistic Works, subject to specified exception.[21] Berne Convention, Article 2, for example, generally defines the subject matter of copyright for purposes of the TRIPS Agreement. The second subcategory is substantive standards that are specific to the TRIPS Agreement. That is, substantive standards that are not established by cross-reference to other multilateral agreements. For example, the requirement that patents be available for inventions in all fields of technology, subject to specified exceptions,[22] is not established by cross-reference to the Paris Convention for the Protection of Industrial Property, which agreement does not define a scope of patent pro-

---

[20]Such implementation may take place though the direct operation of the TRIPS Agreement (i.e. through self-executing effect) in Members in which this is constitutionally permitted, or through the enactment of domestic legislation in any Member. The TRIPS Agreement states that "Members shall be free to determine the appropriate method of implementing the provisions of this Agreement within their own legal system and practice." TRIPS Agreement, art. 1:1. TRIPS Agreement provisions that are sufficiently precise to be applied in concretes case may nevertheless be directly applied by national courts. The Congress of the United States has denied the TRIPS Agreement, and all other WTO agreements, direct effect in the United States (in the sense of permitting private rights of action in the courts) by enactment of a statutory bar. See Uruguay Round Agreements Implementation Act, Pub. L. 103 — 465, 108 Stat. 4809, 103rd Cong., 2d Sess., Dec. 8, 1994, § 102(a)(1)&(c). Regarding the direct effect of treaties in national legal systems, *see generally* PARLIAMENTARY PARTICIPATION IN THE MAKING AND OPERATION OF TREATIES: A COMPARATIVE STUDY (Stefan A. Riesenfeld and Frederick M. Abbott eds. 1994).

[21]TRIPS Agreement, art. 9:1. The exception is in regards to moral rights as provided for in Berne Convention, art. 6bis.

[22]TRIPS Agreement, Article 27:1 establishes the rule. TRIPS Agreement, Article 27:1&2, establish the exceptions.

tection coverage.[23] The third subcategory of substantive standards is a hybrid of the first two subcategories. There are certain TRIPS Agreement substantive standards that operate to clarify or extend certain rights or obligations that are found in existing multilateral IPRs conventions. For example, TRIPS Agreement Article 10:1 provides that "[c]omputer programs, whether in source or object code, shall be protected as literary works under the Berne Convention (1971)." Berne Convention Article 2 may well have been understood to extend to such subject matter in the absence of the TRIPS Agreement, but there had been sufficient doubt on this point to prompt national legislatures (and the European Council) to adopt measures clarifying that computer programs are copyrightable subject matter.[24]

A. Multilateral Intellectual Property Rights (IPRs) Convention Rules Incorporated by Reference in the TRIPS Agreement

The relevance of sources of law outside the strict WTO/GATT context is most apparent in respect to the first subcategory of TRIPS Agreement substantive rules, i.e. those that are defined by cross-reference to existing multilateral IPRs conventions. Article 31 of the Vienna Convention provides that a treaty shall be construed in accordance with the ordinary meaning of its terms, and in its context.[25] Multilateral IPRs convention rules that are directly incorporated by reference in the TRIPS Agreement are pari passu with the terms of the TRIPS Agreement itself for purposes of Vienna Convention Article 31.[26] If these rules were not treated as part of the TRIPS Agreement, then the substantive provisions of the TRIPS Agreement

---

[23]...

[24]*See, e.g.,* U.S. Copyright Act of 1976, §§ 101 & 117 and Council Directive of 14 May 1991 on the legal protection of computer programs, 91/25/EEC, OJEC L 122/42, May 17, 1991.

[25]Also, in light of the object and purpose of the treaty. "Context" is defined to include "any agreement relating to the treaty which was made between all the parties in connection with the conclusion of the treaty," VCLT, art. 31(2)(a).

[26]These rules would at least have the status of interpretative "context" as an agreement made in connection with the treaty, VCLT, art. 31(2)(a). However, TRIPS Agreement Article 9 provides that "Members shall comply with Articles 1 through 21 of the Berne Convention (1971) and the Appendix thereto." The use of the terms "shall comply" in connection with reference to a legal text, and without qualification, appears to directly incorporate the rules of the text referred to as a legal obligation of the Members.

regarding copyright would be devoid of content.[27] This result could not have been intended by its drafters.

Vienna Convention Article 31 also provides that "there shall be taken into account, together with the context ... any subsequent practice in the application of the treaty which establishes the agreement of the of the parties regarding its interpretation."[28] Under Article 32 of the Vienna Convention, when recourse to the means of interpretation provided for in Article 31 leaves ambiguity, the "preparatory work of the treaty and the circumstances of its conclusion" may be used as interpretative sources.

Under a restrictive view of Vienna Convention Articles 31 and 32, interpretation of multilateral IPRs convention sources derived from state practice prior to the coming into force of the TRIPS Agreement on January 1, 1995 would not be taken into account in interpreting the TRIPS Agreement. This restrictive view might be justified on the basis that state practice prior to the coming into force of the TRIPS Agreement did not take into account the negotiation and new disciplines of the TRIPS Agreement regime. This view would assume that TRIPS Agreement drafters intended to take over multilateral IPRs rules only in their strict textual form, and without the surrounding context of state practice regarding those texts, which would include interpretive decision.

Under a more realistic view, pre-existing interpretations will be considered a source of interpretative evidence with respect to the TRIPS Agreement. The purpose of the TRIPS Agreement was to establish a minimum level of IPRs protection throughout the WTO system. WTO Members chose to accomplish this purpose in substantial part by adopting the most prevalent multilateral IPRs rule systems in force at the time of concluding the TRIPS Agreement, supplementing or amending such rules as appropriate. If the sole purpose of cross-reference to existing multilateral IPRs conventions was to incorporate the strict text of those conventions into the TRIPS Agreement, that purpose could have been easily accomplished by restating the textual formulae in the TRIPS text. WTO Members did not choose this option. In adopting Article 2 of the Berne Convention, for ex-

---

[27]Although these rules might alternatively be considered interpretative context, the fact that such "context" would have no substantive legal referent, argues against this alternative.

[28]*Id.* art. 31(3)(b).

ample, the Members chose to adopt a convention rule with 100 years of state practice that has elaborated the concept of copyrightable subject matter in great detail. It strains logic to suggest that the WTO Members instead may have intended to adopt only the bare language of Article 2, which language would furnish only a minimalist structure on which to rebuild the international system defining copyrightable subject matter.

There is not a specific rule in the Vienna Convention that governs whether parties incorporating by reference an existing treaty text into a new treaty do so subject to existing state practice regarding the existing treaty. However, Article 31 of the Vienna Convention provides that a treaty is to be interpreted "in the light of its object and purpose." The object and purpose of WTO Members in adopting the TRIPS Agreement was to create a reasonably clear set of international minimum IPRs standards, relying on existing multilateral treaty practice. It was not to begin a de novo exercise in creating basic IPRs standards. In adopting the rules of external IPRs conventions, the WTO Members took them subject to existing state practice, including interpretative decision.

A Member may not have been party to one of the relevant multilateral IPRs conventions prior to entry into force of the TRIPS Agreement. That Member might argue that it should not be subject to interpretation of the TRIPS Agreement based on state practice under the incorporated multilateral IPRs convention that occurred prior to entry into force of the TRIPS Agreement, which by extension applies the multilateral IPR convention rules. Such a Member is not in the same position as one which asserts that it cannot be subject to interpretation based on practice under a treaty to which it is not a party.[29] As discussed above, the Member parties to the TRIPS Agreement deliberately incorporated by reference the rules of multilateral IPRs conventions into the TRIPS text. Each Member became bound by those rules, as if they were parties to the incorporated agreements. In the ordinary case in which a country adheres to a treaty that is al-

---

[29]This reasoning was followed by the GATT panel in the second *Tuna* case which said that state practice under international environmental agreements to which all GATT members were not parties could not be used to interpret the GATT. See United States — Restrictions on Imports of Tuna, June 1994, not adopted, 33 I.L.M. 839 (1994), at para. 5.19. This may follow from Article 34 of the Vienna Convention that establishes the general rule that states are not obligated by rules of treaties to which they are not party.

ready in force for other parties, the adhering party is subject to the practice of the states already party to the agreement.[30] Members who were not parties to relevant multilateral IPRs conventions prior to entry into force of the TRIPS Agreement, or who elect not to become parties to these conventions, should nevertheless be subject to interpretation involving state practice under those conventions to the extent that the rules of those conventions are incorporated by reference in the TRIPS Agreement.

State practice with respect to the multilateral IPRs convention rules incorporated in the TRIPS Agreement include regional,[31] national, and subnational judicial decisions;[32] executive actions, including administrative regulations and decisions of administrative agencies; and legislative measures, including legislative debates.[33] There are good examples provided by

---

[30]This follows from the terms of Article 31(3)(b) of Vienna Convention which does not limit applicable state practice to practice only among states party to a specific dispute.

[31]The European Court of Justice has referred to the Berne Convention in a number of important decisions. *See, e.g.,* Phil Collins v. Imtrat Handelsgesellschaft, ECJ [1993] CMLR 773, 30 Oct. 1993; Volker Huber v Hauptzollamt (Main Customs Office), Frankfurt Am Main-Flughafen (Case 291/87), Court of Justice of the European Communities (2nd Chamber) [1988] ECR 6449, [1990] 2 CMLR 159, 14 December 1988 Coditel SA, Compagnie Generale pour la Diffusion de la Television, and Others v Cine-Vog Films SA and Others (reference for a preliminary ruling from the Cour de Cassation of the Kingdom of Belgium) (Case 262/81), European Court of Justice, [1982] ECR 3381, [1983] 1 CMLR 49, [1983] FSR 148, 6 October 1982.

[32]Decisions of national tribunals have long been recognized as a source of international law. *See, e.g.* I Oppenheim's International Law §§ 15-17 (H. Lauterpacht ed. 1955, 7th ed.). Reference to subsequent state practice as an interpretative device is not, of course, limited to judicial decision by the terms of the Vienna Convention.

Decisions of private arbitration bodies and customary commercial practices may also furnish evidence of customary interpretation, though not under the rubric of state practice as such. Thus, for example, the decision of the arbitrator in Texaco Overseas Petroleum Company/California Asiatic Oil Company v. Libyan Arab Republic (Dupuy arb., Award of 19 Jan. 1977, *reprinted in* 17 I.L.M. 1 (1978), is referred to by the Iran Claims Tribunal as evidencing the application of customary international law regarding compensation for takings of alien property. Sedco, Inc. v. National Iranian Oil Company and the Islamic Republic of Iran, Award No. ITL 59-129-3 (27 Mar. 1986), 10 IRAN-U.S. C.T.R. 180 at 186.

[33]*See generally* PARLIAMENTARY PARTICIPATION IN THE MAKING AND OPERATION OF TREATIES, supra note 20, in which the treaty interpretative practices of courts in Europe, Latin America and the United States are reviewed. There are, of course, differences in approach taken by courts in different jurisdictions. In the United States, for example, leg-

national and regional courts with respect to interpretation of national and international IPRs rules by reference to the practice of states.

For example, in SUISA v. Rediffusion AG,[34] the Swiss Federal Supreme Court had occasion to consider whether under national copyright law, the retransmission by a cable operator of broadcast programming constituted broadcast to the public (when the potential audience for both modes of transmission was roughly equivalent), and was therefore subject to copyright restriction. The court interpreted national copyright legislation in light of the Berne Convention because the legislature had intended to follow Berne Convention rules in adopting it. For interpretative guidance with respect to the Berne Convention, the court examined decisions by courts in Austria, Belgium, Germany and Holland, recognizing that such decisions were also in part based on national legislation. The court also looked to the negotiating history of the Berne Convention, and its revisions; to the legislative history of the national copyright act; to the opinion of scholarly writers; to interpretative activities under WIPO auspices, including the publication of guides and the work of expert groups; as well as to observations submitted by interest groups.

It should not be doubted that disputes will arise among TRIPS Agreement Members regarding interpretation of multilateral IPRs convention substantive rules, even if perhaps these disputes might be settled before recourse to a DSU panel. A dispute settlement panel will not be able to resolve all interpretative questions by reference to state practice.[35] There are significant questions regarding the interpretation of existing IPRs standards

---

islative materials may be more frequently referred to than in some other jurisdictions. Courts in the United Kingdom never consult the legislative record in the course of treaty interpretation. [Eds. Note: The U K recently changed its practice to permit such consultation.]

[34]SUISA v. Rediffusion AG, Bundesgericht (Switzerland), [1982] ECC 481, Jan. 20, 1981. See also, e.g., Re Cross-Border Copyright in Television Works (Case 4 Ob 19/91), Oberster Gerichtshof (Austrian Supreme Court), [1992] ECC 456, May 28, 1991. The Austrian Supreme Court interprets the national copyright act in light of the Berne Convention and with reference to German law. The question is whether the rights of a copyright holder to prohibit broadcasts are defined by the law of the country where the broadcasts originate, or whether the law of the country where transmissions are received is also applicable.

[35]Compare, for example, the approaches of the Supreme Court of the United States and the French Court of Appeal (Paris) regarding the originality requirement for copyright

among OECD countries that are not resolved by the TRIPS Agreement text.[36] The question has already been raised with this author by a senior WTO official to what extent the customary practices of developing countries which have not followed high standards of IPRs protection should be taken into account in interpreting the TRIPS Agreement. In respect to TRIPS standards that are established by reference to multilateral IPRs conventions, it may be recalled that developing country practices have been the subject of consistent objection by some industrialized countries, and that the refusal by some states to acknowledge prior developing country compliance with existing standards will influence the weight which DSU panels will accord to these developing country practices.

The text of an incorporated IPRs convention rule, such as Article 2 of the Berne Convention, is a rule of law binding on the panel without evidence of state practice.[37] State practice as an interpretative source is only one element used in the interpretative process. Nevertheless, if state practice becomes sufficiently widespread, and is accompanied by the necessary opinio juris, that practice will ripen into an independent customary rule of law that a tribunal, including a DSU panel, must apply as a rule supplementary to the treaty text, provided that it is not inconsistent with that

---

in a compilation. In Feist Publications v. Rural Telephone Service, 499 U.S. 340 (1991), the U.S. Supreme Court said that the "standard of originality is low," and that a "modicum of creativity" is necessary. In Societe Microfor v Sarl Le Monde, Cour D'Appel, Paris, [1987] ECC 205, 18 December 1985 the Paris Appeals Court, refusing to follow the judgment of the Cour de Cassation, rejected a copyright infringement defense of independent compilation on grounds that the compiler failed to adequately encapsulate the original copyright holder's ideas in a complete enough manner. The court also said that a poor job of extraction interferes with moral rights of the author.

[36]For example, the extent to which retransmission of satellite signals into hotel rooms constitutes broadcast to the public has been the subject of considerable controversy. See, e.g., Cable News Network Inc. and another v. Novotel SA, Tribunal de Grande Instance (District Court), Paris, [1991] ECC 492, 14 Feb. 1990, in which the court ruled that a hotel room is a "private" as opposed to "public" place, and that since relevant law (including the Berne Convention) prevents broadcast or retransmission only to the public, retransmission to hotel rooms is not restricted by copyright. This decision was subsequently overturned by the Cour de Cassation. Cable News Network and CNN International Sales Limited v. Novotel Paris-Les Halles SA, Cour de Cassation (Supreme Court)[1994 ECC 530], 6 Apr. 1994.

[37]A treaty rule binds the parties to the treaty upon its entry into force. Vienna Convention, arts. 24-26 & 28.

text.[38] It seems likely that in respect to most disputes to be decided under the TRIPS Agreement in the near to medium term, relevant IPRs-related practices will not have ripened into customary rules of international law.

In deciding whether a WTO Member has adequately fulfilled its obligation to implement TRIPS Agreement substantive standards that are established by cross-reference to WIPO-administered conventions such as the Berne Convention, a DSU panel will examine the text of the TRIPS Agreement, the text of the WIPO-administered convention, and state practice under both agreements as evidence of the WTO Members' agreed interpretation.

B. Newly Established TRIPS Agreement Substantive Rules

The second subcategory of rules that may be subject to interpretation and application by DSU panels is TRIPS Agreement rules that are specific to the TRIPS Agreement. In respect to disputes arising with respect to these rules, a dispute settlement panel will be less likely to refer to practice under pre-existing multilateral IPRs conventions, and will rely more strictly on the TRIPS Agreement text. This follows from the fact that these rules will not have been subject to prior state practice under a multilateral regime that is incorporated in the TRIPS Agreement. Nevertheless, reference to supplementary sources of interpretation, including reference to national and regional court decisions, may be difficult to avoid.

For example, although TRIPS Agreement Article 27:1 provides that patents are to be granted with respect to all fields of invention, patentability under national law may be excluded on the basis that it is contrary to ordre public or morality, pursuant to Article 27:2.[39] Assume Member A's legislature or court decides that the grant of patent protection for human

---

[38]*See generally* regarding the creation of customary international law, I Oppenheim's International Law §§ 15-17 (H. Lauterpacht ed. 1955, 7th ed.). *See* decision of the ICJ in the Nicaragua case in which it is held that custom and treaty coexist, and may apply to the same subject matter (Case Concerning Military and Paramilitary Activities in and Against Nicaragua, International Court of Justice, 1986 I.C.J. 14). Since a treaty may in general supersede customary international law (see North Sea Continental Shelf Cases, International Court of Justice, 1969, I.C.J. 1, at para. 72), for a rule of custom to be applicable it cannot be inconsistent with the treaty rule. Preemptory norms of international law may not be superseded by treaty. VCLT., art. 53.

[39]TRIPS Agreement, art. 27:2.

genetic information is contrary to ordre public or morality. Member B, whose legislature and courts permit the granting of such patents, may object to Member A's decision to prohibit such patenting, because this will deprive Member B's pharmaceutical exporters of protected marketing opportunities.[40]

If such a dispute is submitted to WTO dispute settlement, a panel would first turn to the text of Article 27 of the TRIPS Agreement to decide whether human genetic information may be excluded from patentability. Since the terms "ordre public" and "morality" in Article 27:2 are not self-defining, the panel will turn to other sources for interpretative guidance. The panel should examine state practice following entry into force of the TRIPS Agreement.[41] The panel should also examine prior state practice under GATT 1947 Article XX(a), the general "public morals" safeguard provision, which includes GATT dispute settlement panel rulings, since WTO Members have agreed to follow prior customary practices under the GATT 1947. If the terms of Article 27:2 remain ambiguous, the panel should examine the negotiating history of the TRIPS Agreement.[42] The panel should also seek to determine whether there exists a general principle of law among national legal systems that would furnish a customary international law rule of interpretation of the TRIPS Agreement ordre public/morality safeguard provision. The panel may examine decisions of regional, national and subnational courts, as well as other state practice, to decide whether such a rule might exist. That rule might be specific with respect to the patentability of human genetic information, or it might be of general application with respect to *ordre public*/morality and patents. At the present stage of the development of international IPRs standards, it is doubtful that rules of general application will be found regarding controversial issues, but in the course of examining related decisions, a panel may nevertheless be able to refine its own perspective.

The main difference between the approach that a panel should follow with respect to TRIPS Agreement rules established by reference to multilateral IPRs conventions, and rules newly established by the TRIPS Agree-

---

[40]The patentability of human genetic information is the subject of considerable controversy, and it is not unlikely that the governments of Members will divide on the issue of patentability.

[41]Vienna Convention, art. 31(3)(b).

[42]This is a subsidiary source under Vienna Convention Article 32.

ment, is that in the former case, prior state practice should be considered as an interpretative source, regardless whether that state practice has evolved into a rule of law. In the latter case, the panel may examine state practice prior to entry into force of the TRIPS Agreement for evidence of a rule of customary law that will govern its interpretation, but it should not use state practice outside the TRIPS Agreement for interpretative guidance unless that practice has indeed ripened into a rule of customary international law that does not conflict with the TRIPS Agreement text.

C. Hybrid Rules

The third subcategory of TRIPS Agreement substantive rules are those that supplement or amend existing rules found in multilateral IPRs conventions. The rule that computer software, whether in source or object code, is copyrightable subject matter is an example of such a rule. The fact that the WTO Members adopted an express rule that arguably may have been found in an existing IPRs convention (Berne Conv., art. 2) suggests that the Members may not have been satisfied with prior state practice regarding the interpretation of that provision. Therefore, in interpreting the relevant provision of the TRIPS Agreement (art. 10:1), it would not be appropriate to refer to prior state practice as to the general question whether computer software is the subject matter of copyright.

Unfortunately, the terse statement that "computer programs, whether in source or object code, shall be protected as literary works ... " answers very few of the important issues confronted by national courts in computer program copyright infringement cases.[43] Even in countries in which computer software has clearly been the subject of copyright protection, there has been a great deal of room for interpretation of the basic rule. Disputes may arise concerning whether WTO Members have adopted TRIPS compliant interpretations of that rule. A panel addressing the scope of copyright protection of computer software is not approaching a clean slate, and

---

[43]For example, the questions of the extent to which the visual output of a program is protected by copyright, and the extent to which literal copying of source code is required to constitute a copyright violation, have been the subject of extensive and inconclusive litigation in United States courts. *See, e.g.,* Apple Computer, Inc. v. Microsoft Corp., 799 F. Supp. 1006 (N.D. Cal. 1992); Computer Associates International, Inc. v. Altai, Inc., 982 F.2d 693 (2d Cir. 1992).

should refer to the existing body of law developed among national legal systems on this subject. If such an approach is not followed, established commercial practices could be upset without an adequate basis.

Panels confronting hybrid cases — those involving rules supplementing or amending the rules of multilateral IPRs conventions — may wish to follow an approach of using the existing body of state practice as an interpretative source, and then determining the extent to which the terms of the TRIPS Agreement were intended to modify that state practice. In the case of computer software, for example, a DSU panel may decide that the WTO Members did not intend to modify the general customary practice of the great majority of states, but intended to adopt the rule followed in those countries as a crystallized rule of international law. Specific questions regarding the scope of copyright protection of computer software may be difficult for a panel to answer, and until there is a greater consensus among national systems on specific rules of law, this may be an area in which wider deference to national decisions is appropriate.

Notes and Questions

1. A substantial portion of patent litigation involves the interpretation of patent claims. In an action for infringement, one issue that must be addressed is whether the alleged infringer's product (or process) in fact is the same as the patent holder's, and therefore within the scope of the patent holder's right to prevent making, using, etc. If the allegedly infringing product is not the same, it may nevertheless be sufficiently similar to the patent holder's invention to be considered its equivalent. Well developed national and regional patent systems have evolved sophisticated sets of rules to sort out claims of literal and equivalent patent infringement. Assume that the courts of one WTO Member consistently interpret patent claims very narrowly, i.e., those courts apply tests which make it very difficult to prove literal infringement and that virtually preclude proving equivalent infringement. This would operate to the disadvantage of foreign patent holders. Are there rules of the TRIPS Agreement under which another Member could successfully bring a claim that the courts of the first Member are applying overly strict tests of infringement? Would the general rule of customary international law that treaties be interpreted in good faith be

adequate to address this kind of issue? How much discretion are national and regional courts allowed?

2. Consider the previous question in light of the Appellate Body's decision in the India-Mailbox case. Recall the Panel ruled that Members and patent holders had certain legitimate expectations concerning implementation of the TRIPS Agreement and that India had an obligation to create a situation of legal security. The Appellate Body said that the Panel had overstepped its bounds and that India was required only to follow the strict terms of the Agreement. Would following one or the other of these two approaches affect the way in which the question is answered?

D. The European Patent Convention (EPC) Norms

1. The Establishment of EPC Norms

In Chapter II, Friedrich-Karl Beier introduced us to the European Patent Convention (EPC) system. In the EPC system, the application for a patent is examined by the search authority of the EPO located in the Hague. The EPC establishes the criteria of patentability, which are that the invention be new, capable of industrial application and involve an inventive step. If an EPC patent is granted, the inventor obtains a separate bundle of patent rights in each EPC country which was designated in the application. There are a number of important differences in the process by which patents are granted as between the United States and EPC-Europe. These differences are examined in the next Chapter, and include in respect to the EPC that the first applicant to file an application for the same invention is entitled to the patent, that EPC applications are published at the end of eighteen months, and that there is a post-grant opposition period in the EPC system which entitles third parties to seek revocation of a patent which has been granted. The EPC establishes an administrative and judicial system for resolving disputes that may arise throughout the patenting process, from the time the application is submitted until any opposition has run its course (and even after). At each stage, decisions of bureaucrats may be appealed to various Boards of Appeal.

We begin with another part of the article by Beier that describes the basic rules of the EPC concerning patentability. Next is the text of the relevant EPC rules. In the Procter & Gamble decision of a Technical Board of Appeal that follows, the relationship among the various examining and opposition divisions, and the Boards, is considered.

The European Patent System

Friedrich — Karl Beier*

*****

IV. The Munich Patent Convention

B. Conditions of Patentability

Part II of the Munich Convention contains the provisions of substantive patent law of which the chapter on patentability is the most important one. Under article 52(1), European patents shall be granted for inventions which are new, involve an inventive step, and are susceptible of industrial applications. Since the basic provisions on patentability mention only these four criteria, namely: invention, novelty, inventive step or nonobviousness, and industrial applicability, and are to be understood as containing an exhaustive enumeration, no other criteria of patentability can be applied to European patent applications, in particular the requirement that the invention achieve technical progress as was required in the Federal Republic of Germany and is still required in many other countries. At first glance, it seems contrary to the basic philosophy of patent protection to abandon the very requirement of technical progress whose promotion is the main purpose of the patent system. We must admit, however, that the requirement of technical progress as a separate object of examination, in addition to novelty and non-obviousness, is of minor importance in practice and that its proof in some fields leads to practical difficulties. It is, therefore, no great loss if European patent law relinquishes the requirement of technical

---

*14 Vand. J. Transnat'l L. 1 (1981).

progress as an independent examination criterion and proceeds from the general presumption that an invention which is susceptible of industrial application and which is not obvious to the average man skilled in the art constitutes an enrichment of technology and thus contributes to technical progress, without the applicant's having to prove in each case that the invention is more advantageous than all other known technical solutions. This does not mean, however, that we should totally forget that patents are granted to advance the art, stimulating not only technical but also economic and social progress. If, therefore, the invention actually achieves such progress, it should be taken into consideration as a positive criterion for patentability, be it as a general rule derived from the main objective of patent protection or as the most important indicia in proving an inventive step.

The Munich Convention avoids the questionable attempt to give a positive definition to the term "invention." Article 52(2) gives only a negative, non-exhaustive enumeration of subjects which should not be considered inventions. Excluded are discoveries, scientific theories, mathematical methods, aesthetic creations, presentations of information, and, in particular, non-technical mental processes, including computer programs. With that provision, the contracting states have, under the motto of "no experiments," adopted a very conservative concept of patentable inventions which leaves little room for the future adaptation of the European patent system to new scientific and technical developments. This is, in my opinion, a short-sighted view which can only be explained, not justified, by the administrative consideration that the newly-created EPO should not be burdened with additional and difficult problems of substantive patent law and search.

Much more forward looking is article 53, containing the other exceptions to patentability. The catalogue is, fortunately, very small. Only inventions whose publication or exploitation would be contrary to the *ordre public* or morality and inventions in the area of plant cultivation and animal breeding are excluded. The latter exclusion does not, however, apply to microbiological processes and the products thereof. Thus, the patentability of microbiological inventions, which play an important role in the field of antibiotics, is expressly acknowledged. Rule 28 of the Implementing Regulations contains specific provisions concerning the disclosure of such inventions and regulating the details of microorganism deposit, culture collection, and the release of samples to the public. Although the content of rule 28 was improved during the Munich Diplomatic Conference, the pharmaceutical industry was not completely satisfied. It therefore urged a further amendment, which, after an interesting discussion, was recently adopted by the Administrative Council.

The most important feature of article 53, however, is that it does not exclude or restrict patent protection for chemical and pharmaceutical inventions, foods, or agricultural products. This is a complete deviation from the existing national law of many contracting states, which, for reasons of economic, health, or agricultural policy, have restricted patent protection in these fields to the manufacturing process only or even, for pharmaceutical inventions, have granted no protection at all, as in Italy. In all these fields, full patent protection will be available at the end of a transition period. Exceptions may be claimed by the contracting states by way of reservation. Up to now, only Austria has used that possibility to maintain provisionally its existing restrictions for chemical products, medicines, and foods.

With respect to novelty, the basic patentability criterion, the French law concept of absolute novelty has been adopted. According to article 54, an invention is considered new if it does not belong to the state of the art. The state of the art comprises everything made available to the public before the priority date through written or oral description, use, or any other method. All substantive, temporal, and territorial limitations of the novelty concept, which are known from various national patent laws, have become obsolete. The European novelty examination is based on the strictest world wide novelty standard.

According to article 64(3), the content of prior applications, which on the priority date of a later publication have not yet been published, will also belong to the state of the art. Such a rule was necessary in order to prevent double patenting. But how this objective was to be accomplished has been extraordinarily controversial in the last twenty years. After a long discussion of the advantages and disadvantages of the traditional prior claim approach, its modern counterpart, the so-called whole contents approach, and many intermediate solutions, the contracting states adopted the whole contents approach to avoid a separate identity test by the simple inclusion of the prior application in the normal novelty test. Therefore, not only the claims, but the entire disclosure contained in the prior application, will hinder the grant of a subsequently filed patent application. These prior applications, however, are considered only as a bar to novelty; they will not be considered in deciding whether the later application involves an inventive step. To be patented, a subsequent application, in other words, can therefore be obvious in view of the contents of an earlier, not yet published application; it must not be fully anticipated. This solution constitutes a reasonable compromise which facilitates the granting procedure and meets the demands of patent practice.

Unfortunately, the same cannot be said with respect to article 55 dealing with non-prejudicial disclosures. In contrast to the German, Japanese, and United States patent laws, which provide a grace period of six or twelve months during which the inventor or his legal successor is protected against the anticipatory effects of his own disclosures, article 65 restricts that protection to disclosures by third parties which may be considered as evident abuse. This very narrowly defined exception, together with the introduction of the absolute novelty concept and the requirement of nonobviousness, will certainly lead to great disadvantages for independent inventors, scientists, and small and medium-sized enterprises which are used to test, exhibit, or give other information on their inventions before filing a patent application. The grace period accorded them sufficient time to evaluate the technical and economic value of the invention, and, if necessary, to improve the invention without fear of losing patent protection. If these possibilities no longer exist, serious disadvantages for many inventors will be the consequence. A more liberal solution which should preferably be an international, worldwide solution would be highly desirable.

My final comments on patentability concern the concept of nonobviousness, for which the Munich Convention utilizes the somewhat unfortunate expressions "inventive step," "*activité inventive*," and "*erfinderische Tätigkeit*" adopted by the Strasbourg Patent Convention of 1963. These terms, at least the German and French versions, are unfortunate since they mis-state the real meaning of this important criterion of patentability. It is not the activity of inventing which is decisive to the concept, but rather the product of that activity, the invention, and its distance from the state of the art. It is nevertheless a welcome development that this judge-made condition of patentability, whose practical importance is much greater than that of novelty, is now firmly anchored in the European patent law. According to the legal definition in article 56, an invention shall be considered to involve an inventive step if, having regard to the state of the art it is not obvious to a person skilled in the art. This definition corresponds to the definitions developed by United States and German courts for nonobviousness or *Erfindungshöhe* respectively. It is to be hoped that this criterion, upon which the quality of future European patent examination will largely depend, will find reasonable interpretation by the European Patent Office and the national courts. After thorough discussions within interested circles, the European Patent Office recently announced its intention to follow the middle line practiced by the German Patent Office rather than the too liberal English or too strict Dutch standard of evaluating nonobviousness.

V. The European Granting Procedures

Most of the remaining articles of the Munich Patent Convention deal with the European patent granting procedure. It is not possible in this article to comment on the details of that procedure. It will be sufficient to say that the European Patent Office will practice one of the most elaborate, modern examination procedures based on the experiences of large, national patent offices and provide all the necessary legal guarantees for the patent applicant as well as for competitors and the general public. This procedure contains the following steps:

(1) The filing of a European patent application designating the member states for which protection is sought, in one of the three official languages, English, French, or German;

(2) the examination on filing and formal requirements;

(3) the drawing up of a search report revealing the relevant state of the art

(4) the publication of the application, together with the search report, eighteen months after the date of priority;

(5) the examination of the published patent application as to patentability, dependent on a written request by the applicant which can be filed within six months after publication; otherwise the application will be deemed to be withdrawn;

(6) the grant of the European patent or its refusal, with the possibility of appeal; and

(7) a post-grant opposition procedure to give third parties the opportunity to raise objections against patentability; if the opposition is suc-

cessful, the patent will be revoked, with retroactive effect; if the opposition fails or no opposition is raised during the nine month period after publication of the grant, the European patent will be given full effect within the territories of all contracting states for which it has been granted.

Notes and Questions

1. In *Biogen*,[1] the House of Lords observed the conceptual difficulties surrounding attempts to define "invention" beyond the requirements of newness, commercial applicability and inventive step. Note that the drafters of the EPC did not overcome these conceptual difficulties.

2. The EPC expressly excludes computer software from the scope of patentable subject matter. The EPO has nevertheless found some room for patenting computer software that forms part of an otherwise patentable invention. This is consistent with the approach that the U.S. Supreme Court adopted in *Diamond v. Diehr*.[2] The U.S. Patent and Trademark Office now grants patents on computer software standing alone. Does the EPC give the EPO the flexibility to follow this lead, or would an amendment to the EPC be required?

3. Friedrich-Karl Beier is quite critical of the EPC rule on non-prejudicial disclosures, suggesting that it will substantially disadvantage small and medium-sized businesses. Recall that the U.S. Patent Act provides a broad one year grace period for prior public disclosure. At least part of the patent bargain between inventors and the public at large is that inventors receive a grant of exclusivity in exchange for disclosing their inventions to the public. If an inventor has already publicly disclosed an invention prior to filing a patent application, for what is the public bargaining? We will study the EPC patent application filing system further in Chapter V.

---

[1] *See supra*, Ch. I, § B, 2, c.
[2] 450 U.S. 175 (1981).

EPC
Convention
on the Grant of European Patents
(European Patent Convention)*

of October 1973
text as amended by the act revising Article 63 EPC of 17 December 1991
and by decisions of the Administrative Council of the European Patent Organisation of 21 December 1978, 13 December 1994, 20 October 1995 and
5 December 1996.

Preamble
The Contracting States,

Desiring to strengthen co-operation between the States of Europe in respect of the protection of inventions,
Desiring that such protection may be obtained in those States by a single
procedure for the grant of patents and by the establishment of certain stan-
dard rules governing patents so granted,
Desiring, for this purpose, to conclude a Convention which establishes a
European Patent Organisation and which constitutes a special agreement
within the meaning of Article 19 of the Convention for the Protection of
Industrial Property, signed in Paris on 20 March 1883 and last revised on 14
July 1967, and a regional patent treaty within the meaning of Article 45,
paragraph 1, of the Patent Cooperation Treaty of 19 June 1970,
HAVE AGREED on the following provisions:

Part I — General and Institutional Provisions

Chapter I — General provisions

Article 1 — European law for the grant of patents

A system of law, common to the Contracting States*, for the grant of
patents for invention is hereby established.

---

*As annotated by the European Patent Office with useful cross-references within the text
of the Agreement, and to decisions of the Boards of Appeal.

* Currently the 18 Contracting States are: AT, BE, CH, DE, DK, ES, FI, FR, GB, GR, IE, IT, LI, LU, MC, NL, PT, SE.

Article 2 — European patent

(1) Patents granted by virtue of this Convention shall be called European patents.
(2) The European patent shall, in each of the Contracting States for which it is granted, have the effect of and be subject to the same conditions as a national patent granted by that State, unless otherwise provided in this Convention.

Ref.: Art. 63-65, 68, 69, 70, 99-105, 142 R. 61

Article 3 — Territorial effect

The grant of a European patent may be requested for one or more of the Contracting States.

Ref.: Art. 79, 149

*****

Article 52 — Patentable inventions

(1) * European patents shall be granted for any inventions which are susceptible of industrial application, which are new and which involve an inventive step.
(2) The following in particular shall not be regarded as inventions within the meaning of paragraph 1:
(a) discoveries, scientific theories and mathematical methods;
(b) aesthetic creations;
(c) schemes, rules and methods for performing mental acts, playing games or doing business, and programs for computers;
(d) presentations of information.
(3) The provisions of paragraph 2 shall exclude patentability of the subject-matter or activities referred to in that provision only to the extent to which a European patent application or European patent relates to such subject-matter or activities as such.

(4) * Methods for treatment of the human or animal body by surgery or therapy and diagnostic methods practised on the human or animal body shall not be regarded as inventions which are susceptible of industrial application within the meaning of paragraph 1. This provision shall not apply to products, in particular substances or compositions, for use in any of these methods.

Ref.: Art. 54, 56, 57, 100, 138

* See decisions of the Enlarged Board of Appeal G 1/83, G 5/83, G 6/83 (Annex I).

Article 53 * — Exceptions to patentability

European patents shall not be granted in respect of:
(a) inventions the publication or exploitation of which would be contrary to "ordre public"' or morality, provided that the exploitation shall not be deemed to be so contrary merely because it is prohibited by law or regulation in some or all of the Contracting States;
(b) plant or animal varieties or essentially biological processes for the production of plants or animals; this provision does not apply to microbiological processes or the products thereof.

Ref.: Art.100, 138, 167

* See decision of the Enlarged Board of Appeal G 3/95 (Annex I)

Article 54 * — Novelty
(1) An invention shall be considered to be new if it does not form part of the state of the art.
(2) The state of the art shall be held to comprise everything made available to the public by means of a written or oral description, by use, or in any other way, before the date of filing of the European patent application.
(3) Additionally, the content of European patent applications as filed, of which the dates of filing are prior to the date referred to in paragraph 2 and which were published under Article 93 on or after that date, shall be considered as comprised in the state of the art.

(4) Paragraph 3 shall be applied only in so far as a Contracting State designated in respect of the later application, was also designated in respect of the earlier application as published.

(5) The provisions of paragraphs 1 to 4 shall not exclude the patentability of any substance or composition, comprised in the state of the art, for use in a method referred to in Article 52, paragraph 4, provided that its use for any method referred to in that paragraph is not comprised in the state of the art.

Ref.: Art. 52, 55, 56, 80, 85, 89, 100, 138, 158 R. 27, 44, 87

* See decisions of the Enlarged Board of Appeal G 1/83, G 5/83, G 6/83, G 2/88, G 6/88, G 1/92, G 3/93 (Annex I).

Article 55 — Non-prejudicial disclosures

(1) For the application of Article 54 a disclosure of the invention shall not be taken into consideration if it occurred no earlier than six months preceding the filing of the European patent application and if it was due to, or in consequence of:

(a) an evident abuse in relation to the applicant or his legal predecessor, or

(b) the fact that the applicant or his legal predecessor has displayed the invention at an official, or officially recognised, international exhibition falling within the terms of the Convention on international exhibitions signed at Paris on 22 November 1928 and last revised on 30 November 1972.

(2) In the case of paragraph 1 (b), paragraph 1 shall apply only if the applicant states, when filing the European patent application, that the invention has been so displayed and files a supporting certificate within the period and under the conditions laid down in the Implementing Regulations.

Ref.: Art.100, 138 R. 23, 104b/ter

Article 56 — Inventive step

An invention shall be considered as involving an inventive step if, having regard to the state of the art, it is not obvious to a person skilled in the art.

If the state of the art also includes documents within the meaning of Article 54, paragraph 3, these documents are not to be considered in deciding whether there has been an inventive step.

Ref.: Art. 52, 100, 138 R. 27, 27a/bis, 44

Article 57 * — Industrial application

An invention shall be considered as susceptible of industrial application if it can be made or used in any kind of industry, including agriculture.

Ref.: Art. 52, 100, 138 R. 27, 27a/bis

* See decisions of the Enlarged Board of Appeal G 1/83, G 5/83, G 6/83 (Annex I).

Chapter II — Persons entitled to apply for and obtain European patents — Mention of the inventor

Article 58 — Entitlement to file a European patent application

A European patent application may be filed by any natural or legal person, or any body equivalent to a legal person by virtue of the law governing it.

*****

Article 62 — Right of the inventor to be mentioned

The inventor shall have the right, vis à vis the applicant for or proprietor of a European patent, to be mentioned as such before the European Patent Office.

Ref.: Art. 81 R. 17-19, 42, 92

Chapter III — Effects of the European patent and the European patent application

Article 63 * — Term of the European patent

(1) The term of the European patent shall be 20 years as from the date of filing of the application.

(2) Nothing in the preceding paragraph shall limit the right of a Contracting State to extend the term of a European patent, or to grant corresponding protection which follows immediately on expiry of the term of the patent, under the same conditions as those applying to national patents:

(a) in order to take account of a state of war or similar emergency conditions affecting that State;

(b) if the subject-matter of the European patent is a product or a process of manufacturing a product or a use of a product which has to undergo an administrative authorisation procedure required by law before it can be put on the market in that State.

(3) Paragraph 2 shall apply mutatis mutandis to European patents granted jointly for a group of Contracting States in accordance with Article 142.

(4) A Contracting State which makes provision for extension of the term or corresponding protection under paragraph 2 (b) may, in accordance with an agreement concluded with the Organisation, entrust to the European Patent Office tasks associated with implementation of the relevant provisions.

Ref.: Art. 2, 167

* Amended by act revising Article 63 EPC of 17.12.1991, which entered into force on 04.07.1997 (OJ EPO 1992, 1 ff).

Article 64 */** — Rights conferred by a European patent

(1) A European patent shall, subject to the provisions of paragraph 2, confer on its proprietor from the date of publication of the mention of its grant, in each Contracting State in respect of which it is granted, the same rights as would be conferred by a national patent granted in that State.

(2) If the subject-matter of the European patent is a process, the protection conferred by the patent shall extend to the products directly obtained by such process.

(3) Any infringement of a European patent shall be dealt with by national law.

Ref.: Art.2, 67, 68, 97

* See Legal advice No. 2/79 (Annex II).

** See decision of the Enlarged Board of Appeal G 2/88 (Annex I).

*****

Article 66 * — Equivalence of European filing with national filing
A European patent application which has been accorded a date of filing shall, in the designated Contracting States, be equivalent to a regular national filing, where appropriate with the priority claimed for the European patent application.

Ref.: Art. 80, 87, 88, 135, 136, 140

* See Legal advice No. 2/79 (Annex II).

Article 67 * — Rights conferred by a European patent application after publication

(1) A European patent application shall, from the date of its publication under Article 93, provisionally confer upon the applicant such protection as is conferred by Article 64, in the Contracting States designated in the application as published.
(2) Any Contracting State may prescribe that a European patent application shall not confer such protection as is conferred by Article 64. However, the protection attached to the publication of the European patent application may not be less than that which the laws of the State concerned attach to the compulsory publication of unexamined national patent applications. In any event, every State shall ensure at least that, from the date of publication of a European patent application, the applicant can claim compensation reasonable in the circumstances from any person who has used the invention in the said State in circumstances where that person would be liable under national law for infringement of a national patent.
(3) Any Contracting State which does not have as an official language the language of the proceedings, may prescribe that provisional protection in

accordance with paragraphs 1 and 2 above shall not be effective until such time as a translation of the claims in one of its official languages at the option of the applicant or, where that State has prescribed the use of one specific official language, in that language:

(a) has been made available to the public in the manner prescribed by national law, or

(b) has been communicated to the person using the invention in the said State.

(4) The European patent application shall be deemed never to have had the effects set out in paragraphs 1 and 2 above when it has been withdrawn, deemed to be withdrawn or finally refused. The same shall apply in respect of the effects of the European patent application in a Contracting State the designation of which is withdrawn or deemed to be withdrawn.

Ref.: Art. 68, 70, 93, 158

* See Legal advice No. 2/79 (Annex II).

Article 68 * — Effect of revocation of the European patent

The European patent application and the resulting patent shall be deemed not to have had, as from the outset, the effects specified in Articles 64 and 67, to the extent that the patent has been revoked in opposition proceedings.

Ref.: Art. 2, 102

* See Legal advices No. 2/79 and No. 11/82 (Annex II).

Article 69 */**/*** — Extent of protection

(1) The extent of the protection conferred by a European patent or a European patent application shall be determined by the terms of the claims. Nevertheless, the description and drawings shall be used to interpret the claims.

(2) For the period up to grant of the European patent, the extent of the protection conferred by the European patent application shall be determined by the latest filed claims contained in the publication under Article

93. However, the European patent as granted or as amended in opposition proceedings shall determine retroactively the protection conferred by the European patent application, in so far as such protection is not thereby extended.

Ref.: Art.2, 164

* See Protocol on the Interpretation of Article 69 of the Convention, adopted at the Munich Diplomatic Conference for the setting up of a European System for the Grant of Patents on 5 October 1973, as set out below: "Article 69 should not be interpreted in the sense that the extent of the protection conferred by a European patent is to be understood as that defined by the strict, literal meaning of the wording used in the claims, the description and drawings being employed only for the purpose of resolving an ambiguity found in the claims. Neither should it be interpreted in the sense that the claims serve only as a guideline and that the actual protection conferred may extend to what, from a consideration of the description and drawings by a person skilled in the art, the patentee has contemplated. On the contrary, it is to be interpreted as defining a position between these extremes which combines a fair protection for the patentee with a reasonable degree of certainty for third parties."

(The Protocol shall be an integral part of the Convention pursuant to Article 164, paragraph 1.)

** See Legal advice No. 2/79 (Annex II).

*** See decisions of the Enlarged Board of Appeal G 2/88, G 6/88 (Annex I).

Notes and Questions

1. Article 2(2) EPC establishes the fundamental rule that European patents will have the effect of national patents granted by the EPC contracting states. Note that the European patent only has effect in the contracting states designated by the patent applicant (art. 3 EPC), and that in practice most applications are limited in the designation of states. This reflects the

high fees and translation costs associated with securing European patents, and is the subject of a European Commission study that is included later in this Chapter.[1]

2. EPC patent applications are published eighteen months after the filing or priority date (art. 93(1) EPC). This is different than the U.S. patent system, in which patent applications are published only if and when a patent issues. The applicant for a European patent thus discloses to the public prior to learning whether a patent will be granted, unless it withdraws its application prior to publication. What happens if another party uses the information in the patent application after publication yet prior to a grant? This eventuality is addressed in Article 67. What rights does the patent applicant have?

3. In discussing interpretation of the WTO TRIPS Agreement, we observed that one major issue in patent infringement cases is how broadly or narrowly patent claims are to be construed. The rules on this question have varied widely among national legal systems, and the drafters of the EPC attempted to set some guidelines in Article 69 EPC and a Protocol to that article adopted in connection with the Diplomatic Conference that approved the agreement.

There is a folk tale called "Goldilocks and the Three Bears." In this tale, a young girl (Goldilocks) enters a house where live a Mama Bear, Papa Bear and Baby Bear. Goldilocks disdains the porridge of the Papa Bear (too hot) and the Mama Bear (too cold), but finds the porridge of the Baby Bear to her liking (just right!). Her attitude is the same toward the beds (too hard, too soft, just right!). Do you detect a similarity between the folk tale and the Protocol to Article 69 EPC?

2. Case Law of the European Patent Office

The EPC establishes a number of divisions at the European Patent Office, which are the Receiving Section, Search Divisions, Examining Divisions, Opposition Divisions, Legal Division, Boards of Appeal and Enlarged

---

[1]*See infra,* § D, 3.

Board of Appeals (art. 15 EPC). The Boards of Appeal, as their name suggests, review the decisions of the various divisions. The Boards of Appeal and the President of the EPO may refer questions of law to the Enlarged Board of Appeals. In deciding a case, a Board of Appeal may exercise any of the powers conferred by the EPC on the department from which an appeal is taken, or it may remit a case back to that department for further action consistent with its decision (art. 111 EPC).

The Boards of Appeal and Enlarged Board of Appeals have developed a substantial case law regarding the interpretation and application of the EPC. Two such cases follow. The first is intended to illustrate how the legal system of the EPO functions.

The second decision bears relation to *Biogen*[2] in that it concerns the extent to which disclosure must enable practice of the invention across the scope of the patent claims. The *Mycogen* decision nicely illustrates how the rules of the EPC regarding the criteria for patenting are applied in a concrete situation. This decision involves an opposition proceeding. An EPC patent has been granted to Mycogen, and parties opposing this grant have filed their complaints within the time period specified in the EPC. If the Board of Appeal decides to revoke the patent, it ceases to have effect throughout the contracting states of the EPC which were designated in the patent application. Once the period for filing oppositions has passed, a party wishing to challenge the patent must do so within the national court systems of the EPC contracting states, and a decision of a national court would be binding only in respect of one state. Since patent litigation often lasts for a number of years, it may happen (as in *Biogen*) that an opposition proceeding within the EPO (based on a complaint filed within the opposition period) and litigation in the national courts (for example, claiming patent infringement) proceed at the same time.

---

[2] *See supra,* Ch. I, § B, 2, c.

Decision of Technical Board of Appeal 3.3.1

dated 3 May 1996
T 167/93 — 3.3.1
Composition of the board:
Chairman: A. J. Nuss
Members: J. M. Jonk, S. C. Perryman

Patent proprietor/Appellant: **The Procter & Gamble Company**

Opponent/Respondent: Unilever PLC / Unilever N.V.

*****

Article: 54, 56, 111(2), 113(1), 125 EPC

*****

Headnote

A decision of a Board of Appeal on appeal from an Examining Division has no binding effect in subsequent opposition proceedings or on appeal therefrom, having regard both to the EPC and 'res judicata' principle(s).

Summary of Facts and Submissions
I. The Appellant (proprietor of the patent) lodged an appeal against the decision of the Opposition Division by which European patent No. 0 098 021 was revoked in response to an opposition, based on Article 100(a) EPC, which had been filed against the patent as a whole.

*****

IV. The Opposition Division held that the subject matter of Claim 1 as granted lacked novelty and that of the claims of the auxiliary request did not involve an inventive step in the light of the document (3).

*****

V. Oral proceedings were held on 3 May 1996.

VI. The Appellant argued in view of the decision T 298/87 of another Board of Appeal, setting aside the decision of the Examining Division refusing the present patent application, in which the then deciding Board concluded that neither of the documents considered (i.e. the present documents (3) and (9)), taken alone or in combination, had been shown to lead in an obvious manner to the subject matter claimed . . . , that the issues considered by the Opposition Division on which their decision was based were res judicata. In support of this view he referred to the decisions T 934/91 and T 843/91.

The Appellant also argued that the subject matter of Claim 1 of the disputed patent was novel in view of document (3), since . . .

VII. The Respondents disputed that the issues considered by the Opposition Division would be res judicata. In their view an Opposition Division was entitled to disagree with a Board's decision in examining proceedings. Moreover, res judicata could only apply in cases involving the same parties. Furthermore, the Respondents fully agreed with the reasoning of the Opposition Division regarding lack of novelty for the main request and lack of inventive step for the auxiliary request.

IX. At the conclusion of the oral proceedings the Board's decision to allow the Appellant's auxiliary request was pronounced.

Reasons for the Decision
1. The appeal is admissible.

2. The first issue to be dealt with is the Appellant's submission on res judicata. The Appellant was arguing that the Opposition Division was bound by the ratio decidendi of the remitting decision T 298/87 of the Board of Appeal, setting aside the decision of the Examining Division refusing the present patent application on the ground of lack of inventive step in view of document (3). In the Appellant's view, this also meant that

all findings of facts from document (3) on which the binding part of the decision rested were not open to reconsideration and thus equally binding.

2.1 This issue requires a preliminary investigation of whether there is any legal basis under the European Patent Convention for such a binding effect.

The only explicit reference to any binding effect of a decision of a Board of Appeal (other than the Enlarged Board) is in Article 111(2) EPC stating:

> If the Board of Appeal remits the case for further prosecution *to the department whose decision was appealed, that department shall be bound* by the ratio decidendi of the Board of Appeal, in so far as the facts are the same. If the decision which was appealed emanated from the Receiving Section, the Examining Division shall similarly be bound by the ratio decidendi of the Board of Appeal. (Emphasis by the Board)

2.2 There is no reference here to an Opposition Division being bound by a decision of a Board of Appeal on appeal from an Examining Division. The basis, if any, for such binding effect could thus only be under Article 125 EPC stating

> In the absence of procedural provisions in this Convention, the European Patent Office shall take into account the principles of procedural law generally recognized in the Contracting States,

or some principle developed by interpretation of the European Patent Convention.

2.3 To discover principles of procedural law generally recognized in the Contracting States it is useful first to turn to maxims of Roman Law, as these have proved themselves in practice over many centuries, have fundamentally influenced the laws of all Contracting States, and survive, though possibly in slightly modified form, in these laws today. In this case, where the Appellant has referred to a principle of res judicata to support his argument, relevant maxims are:

(1) Res inter alios judicata alii non praejudicat.

(Dig, 2, 7, §2 in Corpus iuris civilis, editio stereotypa, Bd. 1, Berlin 1908)

A matter adjudged between others does not prejudice third parties.

(2) Res judicata pro veritate accipitur. (Digest 1, 5, 25 in Op. cit.)

The adjudged matter is to be accepted as truth.

(3) Res judicatas restaurari exemplo grave est.

(Codex Just. 7, 52, 4 in Corpus iuris civilis, editio stereotypa, Bd. 2, Berlin 1877)

To reopen adjudged matters is undesirable because of the [bad] example set.

(4) Expedit rei publicae, ut finis sit litium.

(Cod. Just. 7, 52, 2 (Caracalla); 2, 4, 10 (Philipp); 3, 1, 16 (Justinian) in Corpus iuris civilis, editio stereotypa, Bd. 1, Berlin 1908)

It is in the public interest that there be an end to litigation.

The principle of res judicata is thus a compromise between the right of all parties to a fair hearing (maxim (1)), and a desire to bring litigation to a speedy end (maxims (2) to (4)).

2.4 This is also accepted under the national laws of at least certain Contracting States as set out below:

2.4.1 For the purpose of English law it is useful to quote the following definitions taken from Halsbury's Laws of England, Fourth Edition Reissue 1992, Volume 16:

> There is said to be an estoppel where a party is not allowed to say that a certain statement of fact is untrue, whether in reality it is true or not. Estoppel may therefore be defined as a disability whereby a party is pre-

cluded from alleging or proving in legal proceedings that a fact is otherwise than it has been made to appear by the matter giving rise to that disability. (§ 951)

Estoppel per rem judicatam arises:

(1) where an issue of fact has been judicially determined in a final manner between the parties by a tribunal having jurisdiction, concurrent or exclusive in the matter, and the same issue comes directly in question in subsequent proceedings between the same parties (this is sometimes known as cause of action estoppel);

(2) where the first determination was by a court having exclusive jurisdiction, and the same issue comes incidentally in question in subsequent proceedings between the same parties (this is sometimes known as issue estoppel)" (§ 953)

2.4.2 For French law, the Code Civil Art. 1351 states:

L'autorité de la chose jugée n'a lieu qu'à l'égard de ce qui a fait l'objet du jugement. Il faut que la chose demandée soit fondée sur la même cause; que la demande soit entre les mêmes parties, et formée par elles et contre elles en la même qualité.

The binding effect of the adjudged matter only exists for what was the object of the judgment. It is necessary that the relief sought is based on the same cause of action; that the suit is between the same parties, and for and against them in the same legal capacity.

2.4.3 In respect of German law § 325 Zivilprozeßordnung (Rechtskraft und Rechtsnachfolge) states that:

Das rechtskräftige Urteil wirkt für und gegen die Parteien und die Personen, die nach dem Eintritt der Rechtshängigkeit Rechtsnachfolger der Parteien geworden sind oder den Besitz der in Streit befangenen Sache in solcher Weise erlangt haben, daß eine der Parteien oder ihr Rechtsnachfolger mittelbarer Besitzer geworden ist.

A legally binding judgment has force for and against the parties and persons, who after the start of litigation became successors of the parties or obtained possession of the thing in dispute in such a manner, that one of the parties or its successors has become the mediate owner.

2.5 Without needing to consider the laws of the Contracting States in more detail, in the Board's judgment, it can be seen from the above that any generally recognized principle of estoppel by rem judicatam for the Contracting States is of extremely narrow scope as it will involve something that has been:

(a) judicially determined

(b) in a final manner

(c) by a tribunal of competent jurisdiction,

(d) where the issues of fact are the same,

(e) the parties (or their successors in title) are the same, and

(f) the legal capacities of the parties are the same.

2.6 In cases T 843/91 (OJ EPO 1994, 832) and T 934/91 (OJ EPO 1994, 184) relied on by the Appellant, all criteria (a) to (f) were met, as the proceedings in both cases involved a second appeal in the same opposition proceedings. Here, however at least criterion (e) is not met, as the Respondent was not a party to the application proceedings in which decision T 298/87 issued.

2.7 As stated above, the principle of res judicata is based on public policy that there should be an end to litigation. But the European Patent Convention specifically provides that the grant of a patent should be considered both at a first examination stage (Articles 96 and 97) and at an opposition stage (Articles 99 to 102), and Article 113(1) EPC provides that "The decisions of the European Patent Office may only be based on grounds or evidence on which the parties concerned have had an opportunity to present their comments". In the Board's view these explicit provisions of the Convention preclude any implicit public policy preventing a matter being considered a second time in judicial proceedings, that is estoppel per rem judicatam, from being applicable. Further, to consider in opposition proceedings whether certain lines of argument are precluded on some principle of res judicata, would itself be an undue complication. As a party in opposition proceedings is free to adopt as its own argument the reasons given in a decision of a Board of Appeal in ex parte proceedings, it is this Board's view that the aim of speedy proceedings is best served, if all the issues in opposition proceedings are decided by the relevant tribunal on its own view of the facts, free from res judicata considerations relating to decisions made during the examination proceedings.

2.8 It should be stated that until the beginning of 1996 it was the generally accepted view that Boards of Appeal are not in inter partes proceedings bound by decisions in ex parte proceedings (see, for example, the categoric statement to this effect in the commentary on the basis of German and European jurisprudence, Schulte, "Patentgesetz mit EPÜ, 5. Auflage" (Carl Heymanns Verlag KG 1994), last sentence on page 710). This could have been justified as consistent with the above criteria for res judicata not only on the basis of criterion (e), but also on criterion (c) since an examining division has no jurisdiction to decide an inter partes case, its decision could not bind the opposition division.

2.9 However in decision T 386/94 of 11 January 1996 (OJ EPO 1996, 658), it has been said by Board 3.3.4 that a document may not be taken into account when assessing novelty under Article 54(3)(4) EPC (in circumstances where this document was an application in the name of an opponent, who was arguing that it was entitled to its priority and therefore destroyed the novelty of the opposed patent) because in two earlier appeal proceedings on the opponent's application firstly Board 3.3.2 had decided (T 269/87 of 24 January 1989 (not published in the OJ EPO))that the application was not entitled to such priority and secondly Board 3.3.4 in decision T 690/91 of 10 January 1996 (not published in the OJ EPO) had reached the conclusion that the findings of T 269/87 with regard to priority were res judicata and not amenable to being reinvestigated.

2.9.1 It is worth observing that the patent under consideration in T 386/94 was in fact revoked for lack of inventive step over other prior art, so the part of this decision (points 19, 21 and 22) stating that this opponent was precluded by earlier decisions from relying on his own application to destroy novelty of the opposed patent was not necessary to support the order made.

2.9.2 There is no discussion in decision T 386/94 of why the matter is res judicata in the opposition proceedings, or whether the change in capacity from applicant to opponent might not require that the merits of the argument be looked at afresh. Other opponents could have raised the same argument, so it is not clear why in the public interest the allegation should not be considered on its merits. Further, while on the facts of T 386/94 the opponent had at least been heard in some proceedings, this Board would not agree that this is sufficient to invoke the principle of res judicata to preclude an opponent raising a particular issue which he has lost in the capacity of applicant in different proceedings.

2.10 Thus, this Board can see no basis for res judicata in the present case, either under the wording of Article 111 or 125 EPC, or on the basis of any interpretation of the European Patent Convention.

2.11 This is a situation where in accordance with the Enlarged Board Decision G 5/83 (OJ EPO 1985, 64, point 5), it is legitimate to take into account the preparatory documents and the circumstances of the conclusion of the treaty in order to confirm the meaning that the Board believes correct.

2.11.1 The penultimate version of what is now Article 111(2) EPC read:

"All further decisions on the same application or patent involving the same facts shall be based on the ratio decidendi of the Board of Appeal" (see document BR/184 e/72 of the Historical documentation relating to the European Patent Convention).

2.11.2 The reason for the change from that version to the present one appears from document BR/209 e/72 zat/QU/K of the Historical documentation relating to the European Patent Convention. This shows that it resulted from a joint proposal of the German, British, French and Dutch delegations, in which the committee agreed basically with their suggestion to avoid having a decision of a Board of Appeal from being binding on the Opposition Division or the courts of the individual states or the revocation divisions of the second convention. The committee however approved a change to make clear that the department to which the matter is remitted is bound by the ratio decidendi in so far as the facts are the same.

2.11.3 The Board thus concludes that a decision of a Board of Appeal on appeal from an Examining Division has no binding effect in subsequent Opposition proceedings or on appeal therefrom, having regard both to the European Patent Convention and 'res judicata' principle(s).

2.12 The question of the circumstances, if any, in which the principle of res judicata can be relied on to achieve a binding effect of an Appeal Board Decision going beyond that specifically provided for by Article 111(2) EPC is one which may at some time have to be considered by the Enlarged Board. However in decision T 298/87, on which the res judicata argument of the appellant is based and which was a decision on appeal from the Examining Division, while the Board concerned had admittedly considered that inventive step was established for the Claim 1 before it, it also considered that feature (a) of this Claim 1, introduced during the examination procedure to remove an objection of lack of novelty, and which had been accepted without comment by the Examining Division, did not seem, on closer review, to meet the formal requirements of Article 123(2) EPC. As that Board was unable to trace any explicit disclosure of feature (a) in the originally filed documents, it found it necessary to remit the matter to the Examining Division for a full examination of the matter of the amended claims, especially as regards Article 123 EPC, on which the decision of the Examining Division then under appeal was completely silent. The Examining Division on the referral then found these claims unallowable under Article 123(2) EPC, but granted the patent on the basis of a different set of claims. The claims considered by the Board of Appeal in T 298/87 thus differed significantly from the claims before the Opposition Division, and now before this Board, so that on any view of the law no estoppel arises, and an independent consideration of novelty and inventive step is necessary. In these circumstances, this Board does not consider that a referral to the Enlarged Board relating to an issue of estoppel by rem judicatam is necessary in the present case.

2.13 The Board accordingly holds that the Respondent's arguments on all issues must be decided anew on the facts as determined.

3. Main request

3.1 The first substantive issue to be dealt with is whether the subject matter of the claims of the patent in suit as granted is novel in view of the novelty objections indicated above under points IV and VII.

4. Auxiliary request

. . .

Order

For these reasons it is decided that:

1. The decision under appeal is set aside.

2. The case is remitted to the first instance with the order to maintain the patent on the basis of the set of claims submitted as auxiliary request at the oral proceedings on 3 May 1996, and a description to be adapted.

Notes and Questions

1. The Board of Appeal invokes maxims of Roman law since, according to the Board, these maxims "have fundamentally influenced the law of all Contracting States, and survive, though possibly in slightly modified form, in these laws today." Do you think this was an appropriate way for the Board to determine the procedural rules common to the contracting states of the EPC? What other method(s) might you have suggested?

2. It is interesting to note that the drafters of the EPC finally undertook to narrow the effect of decisions of the Boards of Appeal. Consider the House of Lords decision in *Biogen,* in which it was held that the decision of the EPO Board of Appeal regarding the same patent was not binding on the U.K. courts. If the penultimate version of Article 111(2) EPC referred to by the Board of Appeal (in *Procter & Gamble*) had been adopted, do you think the result in Biogen would have been different? Would it be preferable that

national courts in EPC states be required to follow the decisions of Boards of Appeal?

Decision of Technical Board of Appeal 3.3.4

dated 8 May 1996
T 694/92 — 3.3.4
Composition of the board:
Chairman: U. M. Kinkeldey
Members: L. Galligani, W. Moser, F. Davison-Brunel, J.-C. Saisset

Patent proprietor/Respondent:
Mycogen Plant Science, Inc.

Opponent/Appellant:
Unilever N.V. Centerns Ungdomsförbund, Sandoz Ltd., Monsanto Company, Max-Planck-Gesellschaft zur Förderung der Wissenschaften e.V.

Opponent/Other party:
Koninklijk Kweekbedrijf en Zaad-handel, D.J. van der Have B.V., Stichting Oppositie Plantoctrooi p/a Studium Generale, Gen-Ethisches Netzwerk, Godehard Graf Hoensbroech, Die Grüne Alternative (Grüne)

*****

Headnote
I. Where an invention relates to the actual realization of a technical effect anticipated at a theoretical level in the prior art, a proper balance must be found between, on the one hand, the actual technical contribution to the state of the art by said invention, and, on the other hand, the terms in which it is claimed, so that, if patent protection is granted, its scope is fair and adequate (see point 3 of the Reasons).

II. In cases where the gist of the claimed invention consists in the achievement of a given technical effect by known techniques in different areas of application and serious doubts exist as to whether this effect can readily be obtained for the whole range of applications claimed, ample technical details and more than one example may be necessary in order to support claims of a broad scope. Accordingly, claims of broad scope are not allowable, if the skilled person, after reading the description, is not able to readily perform the invention over the whole area claimed without undue burden and without needing inventive skill (see points 5 and 19 of the Reasons).

Summary of Facts and Submissions

I. European patent No. 0 122 791 was granted on 29 March 1989 with twenty claims for eleven contracting states. It was based on European patent application No. 84 302 533.9, claiming US priority of 15 April 1983.

II. Opposition was filed against the grant of the patent by eleven parties (opponents 1 to 11) all requesting its revocation in part or in toto on the grounds of lack of novelty, lack of inventive step, lack of sufficiency of disclosure and noncompliance with Articles 52(2)(a) and 53 EPC. The opposition by opponent 9 was deemed not to have been filed since the opposition fee was not paid. During the proceedings before the opposition division, the parties relied upon a large number of documents, including in particular the following (numbering as used by the opposition division): . . .

III. On 5 June 1992 the opposition division issued an interlocutory decision within the meaning of Article 106(3) EPC in which the patent was maintained in amended form on the basis of claims 1 to 11 filed on 31 March 1992. Claims 1, 10 and 11 therein read as follows:

> 1. A method for genetically modifying a plant cell, comprising the steps of:

> (a) inserting a plant gene comprising a plant promoter and a plant structural gene into T-DNA, thereby forming a T-DNA/plant gene combination, the plant promoter being adjacent to the 5' end of the plant structural gene and the plant structural gene being downstream from the plant promoter in the direction of transcription; and

(b) transferring the T-DNA/plant gene combination into a plant cell, such that expression of the protein encoded by the said plant structural gene is detectable in said plant cell.

10. A plant cell produced according to the method of any of Claims 1 — 9.

11. A plant or plant tissue grown from a plant cell according to Claim 10.

*****

VIII. Oral proceedings were held on 7 and 8 May 1996. During the proceedings, the respondents filed three new auxiliary requests to replace the four previous auxiliary requests. An amended page 9 of the description was also filed in connection with the third new auxiliary request.

*****

Claims 1 and 7 of the third auxiliary request read as follows:

1. A method for genetically modifying a dicotyledonous plant cell, comprising the steps of:

(a) inserting a plant gene comprising a phaseolin promoter and a phaseolin structural gene into T-DNA, thereby forming a T-DNA/plant gene combination, the promoter being adjacent to the 5' end of the structural gene and the structural gene being downstream from the plant promoter in the direction of transcription; and

(b) transferring the T-DNA/plant gene combination into a dicotyledonous plant cell, such that expression of the protein encoded by said structural gene is detectable in said plant cell.

7. A plant cell produced according to the method of any of claims 1-6.

This request no longer contains a claim directed to a plant (see claim 11 in section III above).

*****

XI. The appellants requested that the decision under appeal be set aside and the patent be revoked. The respondents requested that the appeals be dismissed or, alternatively, that the decision under appeal be set aside and the patent be maintained (a) with claims 1 to 10 according to the first auxiliary request, or (b) with claims 1 to 10 according to the second auxiliary request, or (c) with claims 1 to 7 according to the third auxiliary request and amended page 9 of the description, as submitted during oral proceedings.

Reasons for the Decision
1. The appeals are admissible.

The main request
2. No objections have been raised by the appellants under Article 123(2) and (3) EPC in respect of this request.

3. The present case is a typical example of a not uncommon situation especially in the context of inventions in the field of biotechnology in which the contribution to the state of the art by the invention disclosed in a patent or patent application resides in the actual realization of a technical effect anticipated at a theoretical level in the prior art. In such a situation, a proper balance must be found between, on the one hand, the actual technical contribution to the state of the art by the invention disclosed in said patent or patent application, if any, and, on the other hand, the manner of claiming so that, if patent protection is granted, its scope is fair and adequate. This need for fair and adequate protection has been emphasized in several decisions of the boards of appeal (see, for example, T 292/85 above, and T 301/87, OJ EPO 1990, 335). The board deems it appropriate to consider the interrelation between the requirements of Articles 84, 83 and 56 EPC in order to find a fair balance in the present case.

4. Article 84 EPC requires that the matter for which protection is sought be defined in the claims in a clear and concise manner and that the claims be supported by the description. This means not only that a claim must be nonambiguous and comprehensible, but also that all the essential features of the claimed invention have to be indicated in the claim, these being the

features which are necessary in order to obtain the desired effect (see, for example, T 32/82, OJ EPO, 1984, 354, and T 1055/92, OJ EPO 1995, 214). The essential technical features may also be expressed in general functional terms, if, from an objective point of view, such features cannot otherwise be defined more precisely without restricting the scope of the claim, and if these features provide instructions which are sufficiently clear for the skilled person to reduce them to practice without undue burden, i.e. with no more than a reasonable amount of experimentation, and without applying inventive skill (see, for example, T 68/85 above). Although Article 84 EPC is not open to objection under the terms of Article 100 EPC, it may nevertheless constitute a proper ground for revoking a patent if objections to either clarity or support arise out of amendments to the patent as granted (see G 10/91, OJ EPO 1993, 420, point 19 of the Reasons). Furthermore, questions of clarity or support may affect the decision on issues under Article 100 EPC such as novelty (Article 54 EPC), inventive step (Article 56 EPC) or sufficiency of disclosure (Article 83 EPC) (see, for example, T 435/91, OJ EPO 1995, 188, and T 626/91 of 5 April 1995).

5. Article 83 EPC requires an invention to be disclosed in a manner sufficiently clear and complete for it to be carried out by a person skilled in the art. As made clear in T 409/91 (OJ EPO 1994, 653, see in particular points 3.3 to 3.5 of the Reasons), the extent to which an invention is sufficiently disclosed is highly relevant when considering the issue of support within the meaning of Article 84 EPC, because both these requirements reflect the same general principle, namely that the scope of a granted patent should correspond to its technical contribution to the state of the art.

Hence it follows that, despite being supported by the description from a purely formal point of view, claims may not be considered allowable if they encompass subject matter which in the light of the disclosure provided by the description can be performed only with undue burden or with application of inventive skill. As for the amount of technical detail needed for a sufficient disclosure, this is a matter which depends on the correlation of the facts of each particular case with certain general parameters, such as the character of the technical field, the date on which the disclosure was presented and the corresponding common general knowledge, and the amount of reliable technical detail disclosed in a document (see decision T 158/91 of 30 July 1991).

In certain cases a description of one way of performing the claimed invention may be sufficient to support broad claims with functionally defined features, for example where the disclosure of a new technique constitutes the essence of the invention and the description of one way of carrying it out enables the skilled person to obtain without undue burden the same effect of the invention in a broad area by use of suitable variants of the component features (see T 292/85 above). In other cases, more technical details and more than one example may be necessary in order to support claims of a broad scope, for example where the achievement of a given technical effect by known techniques in different areas of application constitutes the essence of the invention and serious doubts exist as to whether the said effect can readily be obtained for the whole range of applications claimed (see T 612/92 of 28 February 1996). However, in all these cases, the guiding principle is always that the skilled person should, after reading of the description, be able to readily perform the invention over the whole area claimed without undue burden and without needing inventive skill (see T 409/91 and T 435/91 above). On the other hand, the objection of lack of sufficient disclosure presupposes that there are serious doubts, substantiated by verifiable facts, in this respect, see T 19/90 (OJ EPO 1990, 476, see point 3.3 of the Reasons).

6. Article 56 EPC requires the claimed invention, i.e. the proposed technical solution for a given technical problem, not to be obvious to a person skilled in the art. If the non-obviousness of a claimed invention is based on a given technical effect, the latter should, in principle, be achievable over the whole area claimed (see, for example, T 939/92, OJ EPO 1996, 309).

7. For the purposes of Articles 56 and 83 EPC the same level of skill is required from the person skilled in the art (see T 60/89, OJ EPO 1992, 268) in two different technical situations: whereas for the purpose of evaluating inventive step the skilled person has knowledge of the prior art only, for the purpose of evaluating sufficiency of disclosure (and, hence, support) he or she has knowledge of the prior art and of the invention as disclosed.

8. The above considerations show how closely interrelated and how critical the issues of support of the claims, sufficiency of disclosure and inventive step are in cases such as the present one where it is particularly difficult to find a proper balance between the breadth of the claims and the actual contribution to the state of the art by the disclosure of the patent in suit.

9. In the present case, the closest prior art is represented by document (5a). This document is a transcript of an oral disclosure by Dr J.D. Kemp which was made before the priority date. This disclosure included inter alia the construction of a DNA vector comprising T-DNA having inserted therein "the entire phaseolin gene including its own promoter regions" (see page 4, lines 7 to 8). Dr Kemp also stated: "But as you've heard, this has been done by a number of people now and nobody has shown a functional gene when one includes the endogenous promoter" (see page 4, lines 8 to 10). Although it is not immediately evident which reports Dr Kemp was referring to, it was known in the art that previous attempts to transfer a variety of bacterial, yeast and animal genes into plant cells did not lead to expression of the foreign genes because their own control sequences were not recognized by the plant machinery (see document (31)). Dr Kemp stated that he could not report the final experiment because "it hasn't been completed" (see page 4, lines 3 to 4). As it can be inferred from document (5a) (see passage starting on page 3 and continuing on page 4), this experiment consisted in the determination of whether transcription and translation would take place in plant cells subsequent to the transfer into them of the vector.

*****

11. Thus the actual technical contribution to the state of the art by the disclosure of the patent in suit essentially consists of providing experimental support for the transfer and expression into plant cells of a DNA sequence encoding phaseolin under the control of its own promoter. In other words, the technical contribution is not a new general technique for achieving expression of a plant structural gene in a plant cell, but the successful completion of the experiment anticipated by Dr Kemp in his oral disclosure by testing the effect of the transfer into plant cells of the known vector construct comprising the phaseolin gene including its own promoter regions (see point 9 above). *****

12. Claim 1 at issue is generally directed to a method for genetically modifying a plant cell by transferring into it a combination T-DNA/plant promoter plant gene, such that expression of the protein encoded by the said plant structural gene is detectable in said plant cell (feature "such that . . .").
*****

13. Formal support for this broadly formulated claim can indeed be found in the general statements in the description (see point 11 above). However,

the question is whether the skilled person, on the basis of the description of the patent in suit (see point 10 above) and of the prior art, would have been in a position at the priority date to carry out the method for the whole range of applications claimed without finding himself/herself in a situation where, despite using reasonable effort to make the method work, he or she would not have achieved the technical effect for some applications or would have achieved it only with undue burden.

14. The present case is a delicately balanced one because:

— If it is maintained that the achievement of the technical effect (expression) is the inevitable result of the technical measure of placing a plant structural gene into a T-DNA vector adjacent and downstream from a plant promoter, then substantiation by way of one example could be considered sufficient, but there would indeed be little merit in such a proposition because this measure had already been anticipated in explicit, though predictive terms by document (5a);

— If, however, it can be inferred that the achievement of the technical effect is by no means certain, especially when working in areas of application other than the one given by way of example, and possibly requires more work than the simple placing of a plant structural gene downstream from a plant promoter, then, although merit could possibly be seen in the specific achievement concerned, more technical details would be required to support a claim to the whole range of envisaged applications.

15. The board notes that, in their arguments in favor of inventive step ..., the respondents submitted that major research was needed in order to test whether the vector construction disclosed in document (5a) was capable of bringing about expression of phaseolin. If this is accepted to be the case notwithstanding the explicit indications already provided in document (5a), then there must be serious doubts as to whether the mere completion of the experiment announced by Dr Kemp, this being the actual contribution to the state of the art by the patent in suit (see point 11 above), can give the proper technical support to a claim with such a wide range of applications as present claim 1. This is because it can reasonably be expected that the skilled person would face similar difficulties when trying to obtain the same technical effect with the whole range of different combinations of

plant structural gene/plant promoter claimed. In fact, these comprise not simply suitable variants of the exemplified component features, e.g. variant forms of the phaseolin gene and/or phaseolin promoter, but also a wealth of structurally and functionally different entities, e.g. plant structural genes encoding a protein other than phaseolin or promoters other than the phaseolin promoter, or technical situations, e.g. monocotyledonous or other dicotyledonous plants, in respect of which difficulties and uncertainties in achieving the claimed technical effect still remain, in spite of the reported specific example of phaseolin with its own promoter. Confirmation of the fact that success can be achieved with phaseolin with its own promoter is not necessarily of any help to the skilled person trying to obtain the same effect with totally different plant gene/ promoter combinations.

*****

17. In a technically similar case relating to a patent with generic claims directed to a method for incorporating foreign DNA into the genome of monocotyledonous plants via a T-DNA, the then competent board of appeal decided that the requirements of Article 83 were not fulfilled because there were serious doubts as to whether such a method could be performed over the whole range that was claimed, namely with any monocotyledonous plant (see T 612/92 above).

18. In summary, the following observations can be made:

(a) the art of genetically modifying plant cells so as to achieve detectable levels of expression of a transferred foreign gene was not very well established at the priority date of the patent in suit and was faced with a number of uncertainties and problems such as stability of alien DNA into T-DNA and into the plant genome, presence of introns, stability of the proteins, effects of regulatory controls, etc. (see document (5a), in particular page 1);

(b) While confirming the validity of the technical indications given in document (5a), the patent in suit, by providing the single example of successful expression of phaseolin in plant cells following transfer via T-DNA of a phaseolin coding DNA with its own promoter, did not generally remove the problems and uncertainties mentioned under (a) above. The patent in suit did not make it plausible that the same effect would be obtained routinely in any plant cell by operating in an analogous manner with any combination of any plant structural gene with any plant promoter. In fact, the specification of the patent in suit leaves to the skilled person the whole burden of finding out and testing how and whether the transfer of any such combination into a plant cell is such that expression of the protein encoded by the plant structural gene is detectable in said plant cell. Under these circumstances, the feature "such that . . ." in claim 1 is seen as being not more than an invitation to perform a research program in order to find the combinations which, if successful, are stated by the claim to fall under its scope (see T 435/91 above, in particular point 2.2.1 of the Reasons); (c) later publications (see point 16 above) indeed show that the transfer of foreign DNA via T-DNA into some classes of plants, e.g. monocotyledonous plants, as well as the expression of the transferred gene under its own signals, were largely empirical and thus involved a large amount of trial and error with a high risk of failure.

19. In view of the above considerations, the board has decided that the experimental evidence and technical details in the description of the patent in suit are not sufficient for the skilled person to reliably achieve without undue burden the technical effect of expression in any plant cell of any plant structural gene under the control of any plant promoter and that, consequently, they do not provide sufficient support for a claim, such as present claim 1, broadly directed to such a method

20. For these reasons the main request, of which claim 1 is part, is refused under the provisions of Articles 83 and 84 EPC.

First auxiliary request

*****

23. For these reasons the first auxiliary request has also to be refused under the provisions of Articles 83 and 84 EPC.

Second auxiliary request
*****
Third auxiliary request
25. Compared with claim 10 as granted, claim 1 of this request, apart from the feature "such that . . ." (see point 2 above), contains a limitation of the

method to the modification of a dicotyledonous plant cell by transfer of a phaseolin promoter with a phaseolin structural gene. By way of this amendment the scope of protection is narrowed over the claims as granted so that no objection under Article 123(3) EPC arises. The combination of the phaseolin structural gene with its own promoter is disclosed in the examples of the application as filed (see Example 1). This application also refers on page 13 to the homology of the molecular species of phaseolin and on page 16 to the naturally or artificially induced modifications of the promoter and/or coding regions of plant genes. This constitutes direct and unambiguous support not only for the combination of a specific phaseolin structural gene with its own promoter, but also for various combinations of variant forms of both. For these reasons it is considered that the amendments in question do not result in the creation of subject-matter extending beyond the content of the application as filed and, consequently, that no objection under Article 123(2) EPC arises.

26. The limitation of claim 1 of this request to a dicotyledonous plant cell into which a phaseolin promoter with a phaseolin structural gene is transferred brings the subject matter of this claim into compliance with the requirements of Articles 83 and 84 EPC. In fact, the description of how expression at detectable levels was achieved in respect of the phaseolin gene with its own promoter provides the skilled person with sufficient guidance for performing the invention as claimed in claim 1 without undue burden and for reliably obtaining the same technical effect, including when suitable variants of the component features concerned are used (e.g. variant forms of the phaseolin gene or phaseolin promoter) (see T 292/85, above; see point 5 above). The board considers that, unlike the case with genes and promoters other than phaseolin, the technical circumstances in the case of variants of the phaseolin gene and promoter are so similar that it is plausible that the claimed invention can be put into practice routinely within this framework. In the light of the contribution to the state of the art by the patent in suit, this is considered by the board to be a fair generalization.

27. In his oral disclosure, Dr J.D. Kemp (see document (5a)), while making reference to the construction of a DNA vector comprising T-DNA having inserted into it "the entire phaseolin gene including its own promoter regions" (see page 4, lines 7 to 8; compare with feature (a) in claim 1), stated that he could not report on the final experiment because this had not yet

been completed (see page 4, lines 3 to 4). Thus, the transfer of said DNA vector construct into a dicotyledonous plant cell and/or the tests of the level of expression of the protein encoded by the inserted plant gene (see feature (b) in claim 1) were not disclosed by Dr Kemp. In the board's judgment, these cannot be considered to be an implicit part of his disclosure as inevitably derivable from the description of the DNA vector. In fact, failing any further details and reports of experimental data, the skilled person at the priority date was not in a position to inevitably derive from document (5a) the technical effect produced by the DNA vector in a dicotyledonous plant cell, in view of the many uncertainties and problems of this technical area. Thus the difference between the statements in document (5a) and the claimed subject matter is not merely in the wording, but in the technical teaching. For these reasons the subject matter of claims 1 to 7 of the present request is novel having regard to document (5a). Novelty over the other documents on file is undisputed.

28. Inventive step (Article 56 EPC)

*****

28.2 In the light of this document, the technical problem to be solved is the achievement of detectable levels of expression of phaseolin in a dicotyledonous plant cell.

*****

28.4 In view of the examples disclosed in the patent in suit, in particular Examples 1 and 2, the board is satisfied that the above stated technical problem has been solved since it has been shown that detectable levels of phaseolin are measured in sunflower plant cells when the proposed method is applied.

28.5 The relevant question in respect of inventive step is whether the skilled person, starting from the oral disclosure of Dr Kemp (document (5a)), would have carried out the experiment referred to in it with a reasonable expectation of success. In this respect, the statement in decision T 296/93 (above) that "a reasonable expectation of success" should not be confused with the understandable "hope to succeed" (see loc.cit., point 7.4.4 of the Reasons) is of relevance. In fact, while it can be said that, in the light of document (5a), the experiment in question was "obvious to try" for the skilled person, it is not necessarily true that this person would have had any reasonable expectation of success when embarking on it. The announcement by Dr Kemp that such an experiment was in progress in his laboratory was not in itself a guarantee in this respect, especially in view of the warning given by the same Dr Kemp that ". . . this has been done by a number of people now and nobody has shown a functional gene when one includes the endogenous promoter". Thus, the outcome of the said experiment was still uncertain. The question to be decided is therefore whether the average skilled person was in a position to reasonably predict its successful conclusion, on the basis of the existing knowledge, before starting the experiment.

28.6 As stated above (see point 18, item (a)), in early 1983 the art of genetically modifying plant cells so as to achieve detectable levels of expression of a transferred foreign gene was not yet routinely established. Although some success had been reported in respect of T-DNA vector constructs where the foreign gene was placed under the control of Ti promoters (see, for example, documents (9a) and (31)), the skilled person still faced a number of uncertainties and problems, such as stability of alien DNA into T-DNA and into the plant genome, presence of introns, stability of the proteins, effects of regulatory controls, etc. (see document (5a), in particular page 1). This should be taken into account when making an objective analysis of the degree of confidence of the skilled person on the priority date that he or she would have succeeded in solving the underlying technical problem by embarking on the experiment referred to by Dr Kemp.

28.7 When trying to make a reasonable prediction of the prospects of success for the experiment indicated in document (5a), the skilled person would have had to have taken the following facts into account:

(a) the uncertainties and difficulties of the technical field (see point 28.6 above);

(b) while there were reports of expression in a plant cell of a foreign gene inserted into T-DNA downstream from Ti regulatory sequences (see documents (9a) and (31)), there were no positive reports of functional genes when the endogenous promoter was included (see document (5a));

(c) although from a theoretical point of view it was conceivable that a plant promoter could be recognized by the plant transcription machinery, no prediction could have been made as to whether it would be actually recognized when placed into a T-DNA (see item (b) above). Moreover, in view of the highly specialized nature and regulation of the phaseolin promoter a seed promoter (see the general background information as reported on page 8, lines 5 to 20, of the patent specification), it was difficult to predict whether it would operate in dicotyledonous plant tissues other than the seed;

(d) although the isolation and partial nucleotide sequence of a phaseolin genomic clone containing the entire gene together with extensive sequences flanking its 3' and 5' ends and of a cloned cDNA had been reported (see document (49)), the expression of phaseolin in a recombinant organism had not yet been disclosed. An indirect report in the literature (see document (3), in particular page 266, left-hand column, fifth paragraph) referred to an experiment in which, using Agrobacterium with a gene of unspecified structure coding for phaseolin inserted into its T-DNA, transcription of bean globulin mRNA in tissue cultures from sunflower tumors had been obtained, but not its translation.

28.8 All the above factors and considerations would have negatively influenced the degree of confidence of the skilled person in the successful outcome of the experiment referred to in document (5a). He or she would therefore not have reasonably expected that expression of detectable levels of phaseolin in a dicotyledonous plant cell would be easily achievable and, owing to this, would have received the results of the patent in suit with some surprise.

28.9 For these reasons the board concludes that the subject matter of claim 1 of the request at issue involves an inventive step (Article 56 EPC). The same applies to claims 2 to 6 of this request, which represent embodiments of the invention as claimed in claim 1, as well as to the subject matter of claim 7, i.e. the plant cell produced according to the method of claims 1 to 6.

Conclusion

29. From the above it follows that the patent in suit can be maintained on the basis of claims 1 to 7 of the third auxiliary request.

Order

For these reasons it is decided that:

1. The decision under appeal is set aside.

2. The case is remitted to the first instance with the order to maintain the patent on the basis of claims 1 to 7 according to the third auxiliary request and the amendment on page 9, line 21, of the description, both submitted during oral proceedings.

Notes and Questions

1. According to the Board, this case illustrates "how closely interrelated and how critical the issues of support of the claims, sufficiency of disclosure and inventive step are in cases such as the present one . . ." This suggests that the claims and description must be adequately precise to allow the invention to be practiced over the full range of the claims, and that the extent to which an inventor provides precise disclosure may determine whether a claimed technical advance is a step over prior art.

2. The Board finds that an invention should be disclosed in such a manner that it may be practiced by a person reasonably skilled in the art without engaging in an inventive act.

3. The Board rejects the claims initially filed by Mycogen. On what basis? How does this decision compare with the House of Lords' decision in *Biogen*?

4. A transcript of Dr. Kemp's oral remarks constitutes the most directly relevant prior art in this case. The claimed invention is within a broad category of work which Dr. Kemp describes. What distinguishes the invention from the prior art?

5. The Board finds that whether there is an inventive step when a prior broad disclosure has been made depends on whether a skilled person would have undertaken an "obvious to try" experiment with a "reasonable expectation of success." If yes, there is no inventive step. If there is only a "hope to succeed," there may be an inventive step. Does this suggest that the EPC system is designed to reward risk-taking? Recall the House of Lords suggestion in *Biogen* that the reward of a patent should not be dependent on the extent of the gamble. Are these two perspectives consistent?

---

3. The EPC, the European Union and the
Community Patent Convention

In Chapter II we observed that the EU is rapidly developing a harmonized system of laws in the IPRs field. It is mainly a historical curiosity that the EPC system stands apart from the general EU regional institution framework. The European Commission is proposing that field of patents be taken over more completely by the Union, and the main starting point of this proposal is the Commission Green Paper that follows.

As Beier discussed, a second tier of the European patent system was envisaged by the Community Patent Convention (CPC) which was initially proposed to enter into force shortly after the EPC. However, various parliaments of EU members refused to approve that treaty, and it has still not entered into force. The CPC is an international agreement that would be open only to member states of the EU. As will be seen, the Commission now proposes that the Union adopt a new patent system in the form of a "regulation" emanating from the Union organs under their general powers to complete the internal market. At the heart of this system would remain the European Patent Office, albeit under new direction (though largely as a technical matter since the contracting states of the EPC are almost all EU members).

The Green Paper provides a very useful overview of the European patent system, and highlights the impediments to patenting at the European level that arise from high fees and translation costs. It also addresses some substantive issues — such as whether computer software should be patented and whether the rights of employees in inventions should be made uniform — affecting all EU member states.

Promoting innovation through patents
Green Paper on the Community patent and the patent system in Europe

(presented by the Commission)*

1. Introduction

Innovation is vital for the viability and success of a modern economy. In this regard, Europe seems less well placed than its main competitors. It has an excellent scientific base but is less successful than other regions of the world at converting its skills into new products and market share, especially in high-technology sectors.[1] Despite certain notable success stories, such as the French high-speed train (TGV) and the GSM mobile phone system, Europe is lagging behind in many of the new technical fields, especially information and communications technology. Concern has been voiced about the extent to which European industry is taking part in the development of the information society and electronic commerce; a special effort needs to be made to improve the situation.[2]

It is vital to protect the fruits of innovation. In economic terms, it has been clearly established that companies with specialized know-how which sell branded products and patented products or processes have a competitive advantage when it comes to maintaining or expanding their market share.

---

*June 1997.
[1]Green Paper on innovation (COM(95) 688 final, 20.12.1995).
[2]Commission communication entitled "A European initiative in electronic commerce" (COM(97) 157 final, 16.4.1997).

We are now witnessing the globalization of our economies. At the same time, the value of what is produced lies more in the intangible investment component. Despite this, in a number of key indicators of research effort (the percentage of GDP allocated to research, research costs in industry, research expenditure per capita and the total number of researchers as a proportion of the labour force) the European Union trails behind Japan and the United States. Improving the patent system in Europe is not, in itself, going to reverse this trend; this can be achieved only by a fundamental reorganization of European research, as is currently under consideration. However, the patent system must under no circumstances act as a further brake on the competitiveness of European companies. Ease of obtaining patents, legal certainty, appropriate geographic coverage: these are all essential criteria for the effective protection of innovation in the European Union.

It must be noted that today, almost forty years after the Treaty of Rome was signed, companies doing business within the Community still do not have access to a single system of patent protection. Although the advantages of such a system speak for themselves (enabling rights to be managed centrally and affording greater transparency for competitors), the 1975 Luxembourg Convention, which was supposed to establish such a system, has never been applied.

The Community must seek to remove the political and practical obstacles that remain, preventing the single market from realizing its full potential. It is currently faced with an array of challenges, such as the need to create more jobs by increasing the international competitiveness of European companies, the globalization of the economy (in the face of which the single market is an essential condition of success) and the commitment of the Union to strengthening ties with the countries of central and eastern Europe.

2.   The patent system and the single market

2.1 History

Patent protection is ensured in the European Union by two systems, neither of which is based on a Community legislative instrument: the national patent systems and the European patent system.

The national patent was the first to appear. It must be stressed that, in the Member States of the European Community, the national patent was harmonized *de facto* as, one by one, all the Member States acceded to the Munich Convention on the European Patent.[3]

The European patent system is based on two international agreements, the 1973 Munich Convention on the European Patent, or European Patent Convention, and the 1975 Luxembourg Convention on the Community Patent, or Community Patent Convention, which is an integral part of the Agreement relating to Community patents, signed in 1989.[4] It was the Member States' intention in 1975 to ensure that the time-lag between the entry into force of the two Conventions was as short as possible.

The European Patent Convention does not create a uniform protection right but it does provide the applicant with protection in as many of the Signatory States as he wishes. Although this system has the advantage of being extremely flexible, it also has certain drawbacks associated with its complexity and cost. What is more, there is no provision within this system for a court with powers to settle patent disputes at European level; there is the risk here that the competent courts in the Member States will hand down contradictory judgments.

The Community patent (introduced by the Community Patent Convention) is intended to bring together the bundle of protection rights resulting from the grant of a European patent and merge them into a single, unitary and autonomous, protection right valid throughout the Community of Twelve and governed only by the provisions of the 1989 Agreement relating to Community patents. However, this Convention has yet to take effect owing to delays in ratification by the twelve signatory Member States.

The aims of the European Patent Convention and the Agreement relating to Community patents differ but complement each other. The European Patent Convention is intended to rationalize the grant of patents by establishing a centralized procedure managed by the European Patent Office in Munich. It is thus open to accession by any European State, in some

---

[3]All the Member States of the European Community are members of the Munich Convention on the European Patent, as are also three non-member countries: Switzerland, Liechtenstein and the Principality of Monaco.

[4]Agreement relating to Community patents, done at Luxembourg on 15 December 1989 (OJ No L 401, 30.12.1989, p. 1).

cases at the invitation of the Administrative Council of the European Patent Organization.[5] The Agreement relating to Community patents is designed to contribute to the achievement of the aims of the single market, with special reference to fair competition and the free movement of goods.

2.2 The need for further Community action on the Community patent

The first question that needs to be addressed is whether and to what extent interested parties would be prepared to use the Community patent system as devised in the Luxembourg Convention if it were at last to come into effect following ratification by the 12 Signatory States. Would industry be attracted towards the new system or would, on the contrary, the existing system of the European patent and national patents prove sufficient to meet its needs? In the latter eventuality, use of the Community patent would be extremely limited, if not marginal.

In 1975 the nine Member States which then made up the European Community, "desiring to give unitary and autonomous effect to European patents granted in respect of their territories",[6] concluded the first version of the Luxembourg Convention. The definitive version of the Convention was adopted in 1989. The Agreement relating to Community patents signed in Luxembourg on 15 December 1989 concerns the Community of Twelve but does not deal with the 1995 enlargement in which Austria, Finland and Sweden joined the Community; the three new Member States are not directly concerned by the 1989 Agreement, although they are legally required to accede to it. In accordance with the provisions of the 1989 Agreement, a special agreement may be concluded between the Contracting States and the acceding State to determine the details of application of the Agreement necessitated by the accession of that State.[7] This would require such a special agreement to be negotiated, signed and then ratified by all the signatories to the 1989 Agreement: obviously an extremely cumbersome and

---

[5]Article 166 of the Convention.
[6]Preamble to the Convention for the European patent for the common market (Community Patent Convention) (OJ No L 17, 26.1.1976, p. 1).
[7]Article 7(4) of the Agreement.

complicated procedure, which could only become more so as further countries join the European Union.

The patent system was set up in Europe by means of international agreements. This is because, at the time, the Community's competence in this field was not clearly established. Times have changed, however, and the Court of Justice of the European Communities has repeatedly recognized that the Community is competent to take action in the field of patents if this contributes to the attainment of one of the objectives of the Treaty (in this case, either the free movement of goods or a system ensuring that competition is not distorted).[8] It should, however, be stressed that, in accordance with Article 235 of the EC Treaty, the creation of a new Community system of protection by means of a regulation would require unanimity, in turn necessitating a consensus between Member States on all the technical issues involved. Adoption of a Community regulation would offer the following advantages: the date of entry into force of the provisions would be known for certain, since it would be fixed irrevocably by the text itself (whereas the entry into force of a convention is uncertain, depending as it does on the speed with which the signatory countries ratify it), and matters would be greatly simplified when it came to future enlargements of the Community since the regulation would automatically form part of the acquis communautaire and would not have to be amended or renegotiated.

Whether or not the Luxembourg Convention should be turned into a legal instrument covered by the Treaty and adopted under Article 235 is therefore a fundamental question to be addressed.

As soon as strategic discussions began at Community level on innovation and how to protect it and on its effects on employment, the Commission deemed it necessary to take stock of the situation concerning the Community patent and the patent system in Europe.[9] Hence this Green Paper, which first tackles the shortcomings resulting from the absence of

---

[8]Paragraph 27 of the Court's judgment of 13 July 1995 in Case C-350/92 *Spain v Council* [1995] ECR I-1985 and paragraph 59 of its Opinion 1/94 of 15 November 1994 [1994] ECR I-5267 (request submitted by the Commission for an opinion on whether or not the Community had exclusive competence to conclude the GATT Agreements).
[9]First Action Plan for Innovation in Europe, presented by the Commission on 20 November 1996 (COM(96) 589 final).

the Community dimension in the European patent system and the obstacles preventing the Community system from coming into operation, before going on to look into the related technical, legal and political questions, such as further harmonization of patent law at Community level.

The Green Paper has three main objectives:

— *to gain as full a picture as possible of the situation as regards the protection of innovation by the patent system in the European Community;*

— *to examine whether new Community measures are necessary and/or whether existing arrangements need to be adjusted; and*

— *to consider what these new measures could involve and what form they could take.*

The Commission invites all interested parties to take part in a wide-ranging consultation on the topic and to respond to the questions set out in this Green Paper.

3. The Community patent

   3.1 The need for a unitary patent system

The Munich Convention ushered in major improvements in the patent system, such as a centralized procedure for the grant of patents based on uniform patent law and conducted in a single language, a reduction in the costs of protection where it is sought in more than one Member State, a high quality protection right and *de facto* harmonization of the provisions of national patent law governing patentability, validity and the extent of protection.

But, because it is not supplemented by the unitary Community patent, the system also has its limitations:

— once a European patent has been granted, its entry into the national phase gives rise to considerable costs and complicates the management of rights, since translations of the specification have to be filed with the national patent office of each designated country and renewal fees have to be paid for each of those countries;

— the management of proceedings for infringement or revocation is complex, since actions have to be brought before the national courts of each country for which the European patent has been granted;

— in the absence of a common court, the emergence of different interpretations of European patent law by national courts is liable to undermine the value of the European patent;

— the sum total of the national fees payable for renewal of a European patent constitutes a heavy burden for patentees, especially since only part of the proceeds (currently 50%) is used to defray the costs incurred by the European Patent Office in managing the procedure for granting patents;

— the additional costs of protection for each designated country are prompting businesses to be selective in their choice of countries, with effects that run counter to the aims of the single market. The fact that requests for protection are concentrated on the larger Member States disadvantages the smaller ones in terms of both technology transfer and their attractiveness to investors. And the limitation of protection to only part of the single market reduces its commercial value.

If the Community patent system was brought into operation, it would have the essential feature of granting patents with a unitary character that would have equal effect throughout the Community and could be granted, transferred, revoked or allowed to lapse only in respect of the whole of the Community.[10] The more Member States that joined the Community, the wider the geographic coverage of the protection afforded by the Community patent.

Although the Agreement relating to Community patents could have been expected to be ratified reasonably soon after it was signed in Luxembourg in 1989, this is still not the case more than seven years later,[11] and it

---

[10]Article 2(2) of the Community Patent Convention.
[11]Only seven Member States have so far completed ratification procedures: Denmark, Germany, Greece, France, Luxembourg, the Netherlands and the United Kingdom (source: Council memorandum of 22 November 1996).

is debatable whether, in its present form, the Convention still attains the objectives assigned to it at the time.

Some commentators — in academic circles more than in industry — have taken up a stance which they claim to be based on logic: they argue that the approach taken towards trade marks and proposed for designs, which involves setting in place a unitary protection right by means of a Community regulation, must necessarily be followed in the case of patents. This argument is not strong enough on its own to justify such an approach. It is, however, easy to imagine the advantages of a unitary patent system:

— the management of rights would be greatly facilitated, since there would no longer be any national phase, which should also have the effect of reducing costs (no fees for entry into the national phase, savings in the use of professional representatives, etc.);

— the system would avoid the need for infringement actions to be brought in each Member State since the plaintiff could bring all the actions before the courts of the Member State in which the defendant is domiciled;[12]

— it would offer greater legal certainty through the creation of a central court competent to hand down decisions on interpretation and validity of Community patents.

In response to this Green Paper, potential users are invited to give their views on the advantages and disadvantages of unitary patent protection, having due regard to the essential features of such a system: wide geographic coverage, necessary costs, application of the Community principle of the exhaustion of rights, etc.

Two questions will then have to be addressed:

— the size of the need expressed by users for a unitary patent system will first have to be assessed;

---

[12]Article 14(1) of the Protocol on the settlement of litigation concerning the infringement and validity of Community patents.

— it will then have to be seen whether the objectives to be set for such a unitary system can be attained by means of the Luxembourg Convention, either in its present form or after amendment.

*****

3.2 Apparent weaknesses of the Luxembourg Convention

The elimination, as far as the single market is concerned, of all the disadvantages and imperfections of the European patent system as outlined in point 3.1 is the very purpose of the Community patent. But, according to information in the Commission's possession, two fundamental aspects of the Community patent, as devised in the 1989 Agreement, are seen as detracting from its usefulness and practical attractiveness.

For one thing, there are the extremely high translation costs due to the need to have the entire patent specification translated into the languages of all the Member States.[13] A Community patent granted in the Community of Fifteen would require ten translations. As the average cost of a page of translation is DM 128[14] and patent specifications run on average to 20 pages, total expenditure on translation would be in the region of DM 25 000, which is clearly a huge cost for firms to bear, particularly SMEs. That cost is, however, to be compared with the major advantage conferred by the unitary nature of the Community patent, which offers uniform protection throughout a market of over 340 million people.[15]

The second problem posed by the Luxembourg Convention appears to be that of the judicial arrangements set in place. The Convention provides for two procedures that can result in revocation of a Community patent.

Firstly, an application for revocation may be filed direct with the European Patent Office. If the Revocation Division finds that the grounds for revocation laid down in the Convention are met, it revokes the patent with effect throughout the Community.[16]

---

[13]Article 30(1) and (2) of the Community Patent Convention.
[14]Figures are taken from documents produced by the European Patent Office in Munich, which uses the German mark as its reference currency.
[15]In the Community of Twelve.
[16]Articles 55 to 58 of the Community Patent Convention.

There is, however, a second means of obtaining revocation of a patent: it is to bring a counterclaim for revocation before a national court in which an infringement action has already been initiated. In such cases, if the court finds that any of the grounds for revocation laid down in the Convention prejudices the maintenance of the Community patent, it orders the revocation of the patent.[17] A judgment by a national court of first instance which has become final and orders the revocation of a Community patent has the same effects in all Contracting States. Notwithstanding the possibility of bringing the matter before the Common Appeal Court in such cases,[18] the powers which are conferred by the Convention on a single national court to order the revocation of a Community patent throughout the Community is considered by some to be a potential source of legal uncertainty. Some potential users of the Community patent system take the view that there is too great a risk of a patent covering a territory as vast and economically important as the Community being revoked by a judgment handed down by a single national court.

This is compounded by a further difficulty: once the validity of a Community patent has been challenged by a counterclaim before a national court following an infringement action, any other national court in which another infringement action has been brought must normally stay the proceedings.[19] In view of the length of proceedings, which are often pursued up to a third judicial tier, the criticism is levelled against this rule that it is liable to result in implementation of the legal protection conferred by the Community patent being held in check.

*****

3.3 The problem of the cost of translations and possible solutions

If the view is taken that the cost of translating the Community patent specification into all Community languages constitutes a major stumbling-block to the success of the Community patent, then solutions must be con-

---

[17]Articles 15(2) and 19(1) of the Protocol on the settlement of litigation.
[18]Articles 21 and 22 of the Protocol on the settlement of litigation.
[19]Article 34 of the Protocol on the settlement of litigation.

templated. But we must acknowledge from the outset that it is a thorny problem.

One solution that can be contemplated is that envisaged by the original version of the Luxembourg Convention, which dates back to 1975. The general idea was to limit the translation requirement to the patent claims (Article 33). But this limited translation requirement could be extended by means of the reservation provided for in Article 88, whereby any Member State could declare that, if the patent specification was not published in one of the official languages of that State, the proprietor of the patent could not avail himself in that State of the rights conferred by the patent. The system established by the 1975 Luxembourg Convention thus involved compulsory translation of the patent claims only, either at the time the patent was granted or shortly afterwards. Any Contracting State also had the right to demand a translation of the patent specification, the proprietor of the patent being free to decide when to file the translation, according to his protection needs.

This solution would enable the patentee to decide how urgently he needs protection in a particular Member State and would allow him flexibility in choosing the point when he files a translation of the patent specification. The provision draws a distinction between cases where the patentee files the translation of the patent specification within three months of the date of publication of the mention of the grant of the patent, more than three months but less than three years later, or after three years have elapsed. In the first case, the patentee can avail himself of the rights conferred by the patent as soon as the translation is filed. In the second case, he can do so from the same point in time but, in respect of use of the invention without his consent before the translation is filed, he can avail himself of the rights conferred by the patent only to the extent of claiming reasonable compensation. In the third case, any person who has used or made effective and serious preparations for using the invention before the translation is filed may continue to use it on reasonable terms.

A second solution was discussed at the 1989 Conference on revising the Convention and appeared to meet with fairly broad agreement. It involved leaving the requirement for translation of the full specification intact, but failure to file the translation in one or more languages was not to result in revocation of the Community patent: its sole consequence would be that the patent would not take effect in the Member State(s) concerned.

This would constitute an exception to the unitary character of the Community patent and would make it similar in that respect to the European patent.

A third solution that can be considered with a view to reducing translation costs is the "package solution" developed by the European Patent Office for the European patent.[20] The three main features of this solution are:

— publication, at the same time as publication of the application or as soon as possible thereafter, of an enhanced abstract in the language of the proceedings and, subsequently, of translations into the languages of all Member States;

— translation of the patent claims only at the time the patent is granted;

— translation of the full patent specification before any action is brought by the patentee with a view to enforcing the rights created by the patent.

The aim of the package solution is to improve the supply of information on patents and to eliminate the serious disadvantages inherent in the existing system while alleviating the financial burden on applicants.

On the basis of the projections established by the EPO it can be estimated that, if it were transposed to the Community patent, the package solution would involve the preparation of the enhanced abstract, at a cost of approximately DM 100, and its translation into ten languages at DM 120 per language, i.e. a total translation cost for the new abstract of some DM 1 300. Since a patent contains on average 3.5 pages of claims, and assuming that the translation of claims would cost DM 500 per language, the average translation costs for the claims would work out at DM 5 000.

Total translation costs would therefore be in the region of DM 6 300 per patent application, which would represent a saving of some DM 18 700 per application in comparison with a situation in which the complete patent specification had to be translated into all Community languages.

---

[20]Document No CA/46/96 of 19 November 1996 presented to the Administrative Council of the European Patent Organization.

Other solutions to the translation problem can be contemplated:

- doing away with the requirement for translations altogether or requiring translation of the claims only;

- establishing a system of translation "on demand", whereby a translation would have to be provided only if a third party were to demand one. To finance such a system, it would be necessary either to set up a reserve fund to cover the cost of any translations that were demanded or to introduce a levy to cover the costs of insuring against such an eventuality;

- the patent specification could comprise a summary description, which would contain the information essential to an understanding of the invention and interpretation of the claims and would be translated, together with an annex containing a more comprehensive description that would not normally have to be translated. A variation on this idea was recently made public: the shortened version of the description. This would involve the description being condensed, at the initiative of the applicant but with the cooperation of the examiner, on completion of the substantive examination of the application.

Whatever the scenario chosen, it appears to have been accepted that, in the interests of optimum efficiency, the filing of translations should not be devolved to the national patent offices but should be centralized at the European Patent Office. This is the approach taken in the Luxembourg Convention.

*****

3.4 The problem of the judicial arrangements and possible solutions

The problem posed by the judicial arrangements set in place by the Luxembourg Convention was described in point 3.2 above. To remedy the

789

presumed disadvantages of these arrangements, it should be seen whether adjustments can be made to the machinery[21] in the context of a Community initiative aimed at integrating the Community patent more effectively into the legal system covered by the Treaty.

One solution would be to give Member States' national courts jurisdiction for infringement actions, actions for a declaration of non-infringement and all actions in respect of the use made of the invention prior to publication of the mention of the grant of the patent. On the other hand, actions for revocation of Community patents could fall within the exclusive jurisdiction of a new revocation division to be set up within the European Patent Office. In other words, contrary to the provisions of the existing Convention,[22] the national courts would not have jurisdiction for counterclaims for revocation of Community patents.

If a counterclaim for revocation were brought before a national court in response to an infringement action, the court would have to stay the infringement proceedings until the competent revocation division at the EPO had decided on the validity of the patent. In other words, questions to do with the validity and revocation of Community patents could no longer be decided by national courts, but only by bodies operating at Community level. To prevent any proliferation of counterclaims for revocation by alleged infringers, it would no doubt be necessary to limit the obligation to stay the proceedings to cases where the court hearing the infringement action considers that there are serious grounds affecting the validity of the Community patent.

Starting from two separate lines of action, jurisdiction for validity and revocation questions would be exclusively conferred on a body operating within the EPO and, thereafter, the Court of First Instance of the European Communities. Two avenues would thus be open for securing the revocation of a Community patent:

— filing an application for revocation direct with the European Patent Office;[23] or

---

[21]Chiefly to avoid the consequences of Article 20 of the Protocol on the settlement of litigation.

[22]Article 15(1)(d) of the Protocol on the settlement of litigation.

[23]Article 55 of the Community Patent Convention.

— bringing a counterclaim for revocation before a national court, which would have to stay the proceedings until the revocation division had taken its decision. Having due regard for that decision, the national court could then settle the dispute over infringement.

As regards the conditions in which an application for revocation may be filed, the grounds for revocation, examination of the application, revocation or maintenance of the patent, and publication of a new specification following revocation proceedings, the present wording of Articles 55 to 59 of the Luxembourg Convention could probably be maintained.

To allow appeals against decisions on the validity of Community patents, an appeal to the Court of First Instance of the European Communities (CFI) would lie from decisions taken by the revocation divisions. Appeals could be brought on grounds of lack of competence, infringement of an essential procedural requirement, infringement of the Treaty or of the legal instrument establishing the Community patent or of any rule of law relating to their application, or misuse of powers. The CFI would be competent both to revoke and to reverse the decision challenged. Certain questions to do with the organization of the CFI's work could arise in this context, and the possibility of setting up within the CFI a specialized chamber for dealing with Community patent issues could be considered.[24]

A final appeal would lie from decisions on Community patents by the Court of First Instance to the Court of Justice of the European Communities. This right of appeal would be restricted to points of law.[25]

To ensure that these arrangements are fully effective, it would have to be clearly stipulated that decisions which have become final and which order the revocation or amendment of a Community patent have the same effects in all Member States.

Another possible solution would be based more closely on the architecture of the 1975 Convention. Under the Convention, a national court in which an action for infringement had been brought would retain jurisdiction to decide on a counterclaim for revocation; however, its decision on

---

[24]If this suggestion were accepted, the detailed arrangements for setting up the new revocation division at the EPO and the possibility of appealing against its decisions before the Community Courts would be the subject of detailed study; this would hinge chiefly on the nature of the legal instrument chosen for setting these procedures in place.
[25]Article 168a(1) of the EC Treaty.

that counterclaim would affect the Community patent only in the Member State in which the court was located. An exception to this limitation of the effect of the decision could be contemplated in cases where an action for infringement brought before a court in the Member State of the alleged infringer's domicile related to infringements committed in another Member State. In such cases, the revocation order would affect the Community patent in that other Member State too. Such a solution would shield the proprietor of the patent from the risk of generalized and immediate revocation of his right.

A general point needs to be made here. It is not possible to create new courts under legal arrangements which are covered by the Treaty, unlike the arrangements established by the Luxembourg Convention, which involve setting up a common appeal court for Community patents. Under legal arrangements covered by the Treaty, cases can be heard only by the Court of First Instance or the Court of Justice of the European Communities; the solution outlined here therefore does not envisage the creation of a common appeal court for patents.

*****

3.5 Fees

It should first be stressed that the European Patent Office should be in charge of technical operation of the Community patent, whether the latter comes into existence in the manner provided for by the Luxembourg Convention or in a legal form that is covered by the Treaty. The procedural fees (filing fee, search fee, examination fees, etc.) levied in the case of the European patent will therefore likewise apply to the Community patent. At its December 1996 meeting, the Administrative Council of the European Patent Organization took two major decisions designed to reduce procedural fees significantly. One of those decisions reduces the amount of the filing, search and designation fees,[26] while the other postpones the date on

---

[26]The filing fee is to be reduced from DM 600 to DM 250, the European search fee from DM 1 900 to DM 1 700, the international search fee from DM 2 400 to DM 2 200 and the designation fee from DM 350 to DM 150. The reductions will represent a total saving of DM 124 million in a full year.

which designation fees fall due to six months after publication of the search report.

These new procedural fees, which are to come into effect from 1 July 1997, would also apply to the Community patent. There should be no designation fee for the Community patent since it is unitary and affords uniform protection throughout the Community; no particular Member State is, strictly speaking, "designated". If a designation fee or its equivalent were nevertheless applied, it would at the very least have to be capped so that it did not exceed the amount paid for a limited number of designations in the case of the European patent.

If the Community patent were to migrate towards a legal system covered by the Treaty, the financial provisions relating to renewal fees would have to be revised. The 1989 version of the Luxembourg Convention provides that revenue derived from fees, less the payments to the European Patent Organization by way of renewal fees, are to be distributed among the States parties to the Convention in accordance with a scale laid down therein.[27] Under a legal system covered by the Treaty, such a system could not work and would have to be abolished.

The body in charge of operation of the Community patent system should be financially in balance, which means that it should retain all the different fees paid by users. The revenue side of its budget should therefore comprise, without prejudice to other items, the revenue from fees payable under the fees regulation and, if necessary, a contribution charged to the general budget of the European Communities. The regulation on fees for the Community patent should, for its part, be adopted by way of the committee procedure, on a proposal from the Commission.

Fees should be set such that the corresponding revenue normally enables the budget to be balanced. This means that, as a general rule, the body operating the system would not be able to make over any share of the revenue to other national or international bodies.

Lastly, given the unitary character of the Community patent and therefore the absence of any choice as regards the geographic extent of the protection it confers, thought should be given to the question of whether additional measures should be taken on the fees front in order to make the system attractive to users. The possibility should be discussed of setting the

---

[27]Article 20 of the Community Patent Convention.

renewal fees for the Community patent payable to the European Patent Office such that they amount to less than the total amount of the renewal fees for a European patent covering the whole of the Community.

It has also been suggested that the proprietor of a Community patent should have the option of not paying a share of the annual renewal fee corresponding to certain Member States; this would make the system more flexible and would enable the Community patent to be renewed in respect of some Member States only. This system, which is sometimes referred to as the "*à la carte* Community patent", would introduce a form of partial waiver of rights, restricted to certain Member States, through non-payment of a proportion of the annual renewal fees.[28]

*****

3.6 Links to be established between the Community patent and the European patent

The Community patent should be a unitary system conferring rights that can be relied on throughout the Community. The larger the Community becomes, the wider the geographic coverage of the protection. This will no doubt be an advantage, but it could also prove problematic for some businesses, which might find it difficult to assess, at an early stage in the procedure, the need for such extensive protection. In addition to the possible need for protection in certain countries that are not Member States of the European Community, the European patent will retain its usefulness in that it enables the firm concerned to designate certain countries and not necessarily all the Member States.

There is therefore undoubtedly a need to introduce some flexibility into the patent system in Europe, and this could possibly be achieved by establishing links between the Community patent and the European patent. The advantage of allowing such conversion would be that it would make it possible initially to cover the whole of the single market and then to limit the geographic coverage only during or towards the end of the procedure for the grant of the patent.

---

[28]This would require the amendment of Articles 48 and 49 of the Community Patent Convention.

An applicant for a Community patent would thus be able to ask for his application to be converted into a European patent application as long as the application existed in legal terms (which would not be the case if the application had been withdrawn or was deemed to have been withdrawn or if it had been refused). A European patent application deriving from the conversion of a Community patent application would have the same date of filing or priority as the Community patent application it replaces.

The opposite situation, in which a European patent application could be converted into a Community patent application, would be more difficult to envisage, except in cases where the European patent application designated all the Member States of the European Community.

It should furthermore be borne in mind that the possibility of converting a Community patent (once it has been granted) is already provided for by the second sentence of Article 30(6) of the 1989 Luxembourg Convention.

*****

3.7 Other questions

The Annexes to the Agreement relating to Community patents signed in Luxembourg in 1989 contain several declarations and resolutions on certain substantive points of patent law.

In the context of a new initiative regarding the Community patent, thought could be given to the question of whether action should be taken on some of these resolutions.

The resolution on common rules on the granting of compulsory licences in respect of Community patents has become largely irrelevant since a comprehensive set of rules governing compulsory licences has been incorporated in the GATT/WTO Agreement on trade-related aspects of intellectual property rights (TRIPs).[29] If a new initiative covered by the Treaty were taken in the field of the Community patent, all the provisions of the TRIPs Agreement could be either reproduced in full or explicitly referred to in the legal instrument used.

---

[29]Article 31(a) to (l) of the TRIPs Agreement.

According to the resolution concerning prior use or possession, a procedure is to be initiated for revising the Convention in order to create a right, based on prior use or possession of an invention which is the subject-matter of a Community patent, which will have uniform effect throughout the territories of the Member States. The right of prior use or possession depends on good faith. It is debatable whether there is any need for further action in this area in order to ensure that the effects of prior use or possession are uniform throughout the Community. It should be borne in mind that all European countries agreed on rules governing prior use in the context of the first part of the diplomatic conference for the conclusion of the treaty on patent harmonization (The Hague, 1991).

4. Further harmonization at Community level

4.1 The need for further harmonization at Community level

The European Community has been able to use its powers to legislate in the patents field, notably in order to take account of technological progress in sectors with high value added. Two Parliament and Council Regulations have thus been adopted creating a supplementary protection certificate for pharmaceutical and plant-health products with a view to plugging the gap in protection that was penalizing research into those products. In another field, the Commission has proposed an instrument specifying the conditions in which a patent may be obtained for a biotechnological invention.[30]

These examples demonstrate that if the need is clearly established, the Community is capable of proposing and adopting appropriate legislation. The question arises whether further harmonization, at Community level, of patent law in other areas of technology or on other aspects would be desirable.

4.2 The patentability of computer programs and software-related inventions

---

[30]Proposal for a European Parliament and Council Directive on the legal protection of biotechnological inventions (COM(95) 661 final, 13.12.1995; OJ No C 296, 8.10.1996).

The development of the information society and electronic commerce offers the European economy a genuine opportunity but also confronts it with new challenges. The design and constant improvement of new computer programs and software is set to play a major role in the development of the information society and electronic commerce since the programs concerned have to afford swift, reliable and accurate access to the information and interactive services sought. The Commission has already taken certain steps with a view to setting in place legislation ensuring, throughout the Union, an adequate level of protection of innovation linked to the information society. In November 1996 it thus adopted a communication on follow-up to the Green Paper on copyright and related rights in the information society.[31] Rules on copyright and related rights are essential if the information society and electronic commerce are to function properly in the European Union, since the content of most of the new services lends itself to protection by intellectual property rights.

In the European Community today, computer programs can enjoy copyright protection as literary works[32] but cannot be protected "as such" by patents. The patentability of software-related inventions does not call into question the existing protection of software by copyright law. Faced with the increasing importance of software, the European Patent Office and the national patent offices of some Member States have in recent years granted thousands of patents protecting logical models composed of basic ideas and principles that constitute "technical solutions to technical problems". These patents were not granted for the software per se but in respect of software-related inventions consisting of hardware and specific software.

At international level, Article 27 of the TRIPs Agreement does not rule out the patentability of computer programs, and some non-member countries do allow them to be the subject-matter of patents. On 28 February 1996 the United States published new guidelines for examiners concerning software-related inventions: whereas a claim relating to a mathematical algorithm was accepted in the past only if a physical transformation was present, a more pragmatic approach is advocated today based on the necessary "utility" of the invention. This has the effect of broadening the scope of

---

[31]COM(96) 568 final, 20.11.1996.
[32]Council Directive 91/250/EEC of 14 May 1991 on the legal protection of computer programs (OJ No L 122, 17.5.1991, p. 42).

software-related inventions that are patentable. Software was, however, already extensively patented in the United States: a computer program carried on a tangible medium, e.g. a diskette, was patentable even before the new guidelines were published.[33]

Japan is also examining whether the guidelines issued to examiners on this question need to be amended. On 8 August 1996 the Japanese Patent Office thus published new draft guidelines in accordance with which computer programs would not be patentable as such, but inventions would be patentable where they involved a high degree of "technological" creativeness using the laws of nature.

In the Community, interested parties have already been consulted on these matters via the questionnaire on industrial property rights in the information society drawn up by the Commission in July 1996. The answers received vary widely: some respondents wished to see the present balance maintained between copyright (for programs as such) and patent protection (for software-related inventions) and action limited to ensuring that the relevant provisions are applied uniformly in the different Member States; others felt, on the contrary, that the time had come to reshape the system and, in particular, to consider deleting Article 52(2) of the European Patent Convention so as to allow the patentability of computer programs as such. In the opinion of those advocating such an approach, the requirement that the invention be of a "technical" nature should be maintained but once such a feature was present, a program which is recorded on a medium and puts the invention into effect once it is loaded and started up would become patentable.

Given the position taken by some interested parties, who advocate deleting Article 52(2) of the European Patent Convention, the possible practical consequences of such a step need to be examined, with special reference to the simultaneous application of copyright law and patent law to the same work or invention.

*****

4.3 Employees' inventions

---

[33]Decision of the US Patent and Trademark Office of 26 April 1996 in *re Beauregard.*

There are at present great differences between Member States' rules governing inventions by employees. Employees' inventions are inventions made by research staff or technical staff (researchers, engineers, etc.) under an employment contract with a firm or laboratory. In some Member States the question is dealt with in general terms by patent law (e.g. in France[34] and the United Kingdom[35]); in others a specific law has been enacted, as in Germany and Sweden. The general rule which is common to all such legislation is that if an invention is made in the course of the employee's normal duties under his employment contract (i.e. if the employee has an inventive role), the patent belongs to the employer. For the rest, the precision of the legislation varies greatly from one Member State to another. Some laws contain procedural provisions on the filing of patent applications by the inventor, stipulate whether the inventor can or must have his name mentioned on the patent, etc. Other laws distinguish between "permanent", "temporary" and "occasional" inventive roles, with different rules for determining ownership of the patent in each case. Other laws, such as the German act, contain a long series of provisions relating to the remuneration of employees with an inventive role and lay down the precise method for calculating additional remuneration.

Clearly, the application of these different rules by businesses has an impact on research work and management. The more the legislation is detailed and complex, the more human resources the firm has to devote to the management of such matters. It could be that differences between national laws on employees' inventions are having an effect on the freedom to provide services in the single market and/or on the conditions of competition.

*****

4.4 Formalities, use of patent agents and recognition of professional qualifications

4.4.1 Formalities

---

[34]Article L.611-7 of the Intellectual Property Code.
[35]Sections 39 to 43 of the Patents Act ("Employees' inventions").

Formalities currently differ between Member States as regards the forms to be completed, time-limits to be observed, information to be provided, the way in which information has to be presented and legalization of documents. Procedures also occasionally differ following the grant of a patent. This means that detailed knowledge of each national system is necessary in order to be able to give valid advice to applicants or patentees. Work currently in progress within the World Intellectual Property Organization (WIPO) with a view to concluding a treaty harmonizing patent law with regard to such formalities shows the way forward. It is questionable whether, once such a treaty were adopted, there would be any need to engage in further harmonization of formalities at Community level, for example with regard to the information required on the invention, the inventor and the applicant, the way in which the information is to be presented and the degree of authentication required, and the number of forms to be completed, so that the application is treated in the same manner throughout the Community.

4.4.2 Use of patent agents

Most Member States' laws contain provisions which, in one way or another, require applicants for or proprietors of patents to have a domicile or address for service in their territory insofar as the protection requested there is granted. The applicant, or his representative, is not usually allowed to deal direct, from his home Member State, with the patent offices of the other Member States without having a domicile or address for service in those Member States.

Some national rules also make it mandatory to use the services of a qualified representative who is domiciled in the national territory. These rules prevent a single representative, domiciled in one Member State, acting for his client vis-à-vis the patent offices of the other Member States.

In connection with this question, the Court has stated in *Säger v Dennemeyer*[36] that, having regard to the particular characteristics of the provision of services in certain sectors of activity, specific requirements imposed on the service provider cannot be regarded as incompatible with the Treaty, particularly where they are intended to protect the recipients of the services in question against the harm which they could suffer as a result of legal ad-

---

[36]Judgment of 25 July 1991 in Case C-76/90 [1991] ECR I-4221.

vice given to them by persons who did not possess the necessary professional or personal qualifications. However, as a fundamental principle of the Treaty, the freedom to provide services may be limited only by rules which are justified by imperative reasons relating to the public interest and which apply to all persons or undertakings pursuing an activity in the State of destination, insofar as that interest is not already protected by the rules to which the service provider is subject in the Member State in which he is established. In the case of the monitoring and renewal of patents through the payment of fees, the service provider does not advise his clients but confines himself to alerting them when the renewal fees have to be paid. The Court held that rules reserving such services for persons holding a special professional qualification, such as lawyers or patent agents, were disproportionate in relation to the objective sought.

It is worth considering whether the consequences of this judgment should be codified in some way at Community level, either through legislative harmonization or by means of an interpretative communication, and whether any such instrument should also cover other procedural aspects such as addresses for service and requirements regarding domicile. In any event, such codification would not affect the possibility of initiating infringement proceedings if certain national rules were to prove incompatible with the freedom to provide services (Article 59 of the EC Treaty) or the right of establishment (Article 52 of the EC Treaty).

4.4.3 Professional qualifications

As far as professional qualifications are concerned, the scope of Directive 89/48/EEC includes qualifications in the field of patents. Under that Directive, professional qualifications acquired in one Member State must be recognized throughout the Community, but the Member States are entitled to require the person concerned either to undergo an adaptation period or to take an aptitude test. The form this aptitude test is to take and the topics covered have so far not been finally decided in several Member States.

In accordance with the Directive (see in particular Article 1(g)), and indeed with the proportionality principle, the aptitude test should be limited to what is necessary. Since the substantive law practised by the professional has already been to a great extent harmonized and transposed by the Member States, the aptitude test should be limited to cases where the matters covered by the applicant's education and training "differ substantially from those covered by the diploma required in the host Member State".[37] The European qualifying examination (Article 134(2)(c) of the European Patent Convention) could also be deemed, as far as patents are concerned, an adequate qualification for making representations to the national offices.

In its judgment in *Gebhard*[38] the Court of Justice held that the possibility for a national of a Member State of exercising his right of establishment, and the conditions for his exercise of that right, must be determined in the light of the activities which he intends to pursue on the territory of the host Member State. Where the taking-up or the pursuit of a specific activity is subject to certain conditions, such as the obligation to hold particular diplomas, those conditions must satisfy four fundamental requirements: they must be applied in a non-discriminatory manner; they must be justified by imperative requirements in the general interest; they must be suitable for securing the attainment of the objective which they pursue; and they must not go beyond what is necessary in order to attain it (principle of proportionality).

*****

4.5 Additional measures to make the patent system more attractive

It is clear that one of the obstacles to optimum use of the patent system in Europe is the cost involved not only in obtaining protection, but also in enforcing it before the courts. Suggestions have been made for facilitating use of the patent system by businesses, and in particular SMEs.

One line of action could be to harmonize national laws on utility models, a particular form of protection for technical innovation that can be obtained swiftly and cheaply and is well-suited to the needs of many SMEs.[39] In the patents field, consideration could be given to the possibility of setting up a system of legal costs insurance that would be financed individually by each patent holder. If a business which had taken out an insurance policy of this type had to take court action in order to enforce the

---

[37] Article 4(1)(b) of the Directive 89/48/EEC.
[38] Judgment of 30 November 1995 in Case C-55/94 [1995] ECR I-4165.
[39]Green Paper on the protection of utility models in the single market (COM(95) 370 final, 19.7.1995).

rights conferred on it by a patent, it would be entitled to submit a claim to the insurance company for reimbursement of its costs. Various alternative arrangements could be considered: either individual policies taken out by firms, or an insurance pool that could be joined, on a voluntary basis, by all businesses in a given sector, in order to spread the risks more evenly. In the case of SMEs in particular and given the difficulties they usually face in securing protection for their innovations, some form of public financing (or part-financing) of the system of legal costs insurance could be considered.

Since the idea would be to enable private initiatives to develop (such as the insurance pool) or to allow action at national level (such as public financing), care would clearly have to be taken to ensure that such measures were compatible with Articles 85 and 92 of the EC Treaty.

5. The European patent

5.1 General structure of the European patent

The European patent came into existence following the conclusion of the European Patent Convention, which was signed in Munich on 5 October 1973. The Convention establishes a single procedure for the grant of patents, which, once granted, are subject to the national rules of the Contracting States designated in the application. The number of member countries of the European Patent Organization is currently 18. It is worth noting that, under the Europe Agreements concluded between the European Community and its Member States, on the one hand, and the countries of central and eastern Europe, on the other, the central and eastern European countries have undertaken to be ready within five years to apply to join the Munich Convention.

According to opinions voiced by users of the patent system in Europe, the European patent is giving ample satisfaction both in terms of the calibre of the work carried out by the European Patent Office and in terms of the value of the protection right which it confers. Two major improvements are, however, eagerly awaited by users. One concerns the patentability of biotechnological inventions, an area in which the present uncertainties should be resolved through early adoption of the new proposal for a Directive presented by the Commission in late 1995. The other relates to reductions in the fees charged by the European Patent Office and changes to the rules governing translations of the European patent; the first issue has been settled and the second is currently under discussion within the Office.

For the rest, the current structure of the patent system in Europe, in which the European Patent Office is an international organization set up by treaty and is therefore independent of the Community, does not appear to pose the slightest problem for users. It should be stressed that the European Commission is entitled to attend meetings of the Administrative Council of the European Patent Organization as an observer and that it decided, three years ago, to avail itself fully of the opportunities thus available to it for making its views known on issues of common interest to both organizations.

5.2 The problem of the cost of the European patent

5.2.1 Fees

In 1996 the Administrative Council of the European Patent Organization, supported by the Commission, came to the conclusion that, in view of the Organization's revenue and the persistent level of its surpluses, a reduction in the cost of patents should be considered and a signal given to users of the system.

The thrust of the decision on the level of fees taken by the Administrative Council on 6 December 1996 was explained in point 3.5 above. This was a highly significant decision, which demonstrated that the European Patent Organization had taken on board the criticisms voiced by users and was able, in the prevailing circumstances, to respond positively. The Administrative Council also decided on that date that applicants for European patents would no longer have to pay the designation fees when filing the application but could do so up to six months after publication of the search report.

These decisions are in line with the wishes of users. On the assumption that the European Patent Office will at some time in the future again have some room for manoeuvre financially, it is worth considering which fees should be reduced as a matter of priority.

Another question which is repeatedly raised in Europe is whether it would be desirable to introduce, as has been done in the United States, a special scale of fees — e.g. 50% lower — for SMEs. Such an approach, which could be applied not only to SMEs but also to individual inventors and universities, would involve reducing all the fees payable by a uniform rate. The problems to do with the definition of small and medium-sized enterprises have been resolved by the Commission Recommendation of 3 April 1996,[40] which standardizes the definitions of SMEs, small enterprises and micro-enterprises used at Community and national level. But it should be examined whether all SMEs would automatically qualify for reduced fees, and the effects that reduced fees for SMEs would have should also be studied in detail. At the present time, some 41% of European patent applications originating in Europe are filed by SMEs (i.e. businesses with fewer than 250 employees); consequently, in a balanced budget situation, a 50% reduction for SMEs would have to be offset by a general increase in fees of approximately 22%. It could also prove necessary to stipulate that any false representations in this connection would lead to the loss of protection, along the lines of the system in place in the United States ("fraud on the Office").

5.2.2 The distribution of revenue from renewal fees

Under the Munich Convention, the amounts of the procedural fees collected by the Organization and the share of revenue from renewal fees for European patents paid to the Organization by Contracting States must be fixed such that the corresponding income enables the budget to be balanced. Since, once they have been granted, European patents are governed by national law, it is stipulated that the Organization is to receive revenue from the Contracting States by way of a share of the annual renewal fees they collect. Although the Convention stipulates that the proportion of renewal fees to be paid to the Organization may be fixed at up to 75%, the Administrative Council decided in 1984 to reduce it to 50%.

According to estimates that have been made, the result of this share-out formula is that the total revenue of the national offices has on average remained unchanged in comparison with the situation prevailing before the European patent system was introduced, although their workload has on average fallen by half.

Interested parties have repeatedly voiced their opposition to any further reduction in the share of revenue from renewal fees accruing to the Organization and called for the Organization's surplus income over its expenditure to be used in its entirety in order to reduce procedural fees.

---

[40]OJ No L 107, 30.4.1996.

The way in which revenue from renewal fees is used varies greatly between the Contracting States. In some States, the share of renewal fees for European patents retained by the national authorities is not allocated to activities linked to the operation of the patent office or intended to promote innovation since it is paid straight into the general government budget; some commentators have even described such a situation as a "tax on innovation" insofar as the revenue from renewal fees is not earmarked for innovation-related activities. In these circumstances, thought should be given to the allocation and use of revenue from annual fees.

One last point should be made on the question of fees: the total cost of a European patent is also due to the procedures for validating European patents in the different Contracting States and the fees charged in connection with those procedures. The mere cost of publishing a European patent in the different countries thus amounts to DM 4 762.

*****

5.2.3 Translations

One item that looms large in the total cost of patent protection is the extremely high cost of having European patents translated/validated. It is estimated that European industry alone spends some DM 430 million per year on this item, which means that an "average" European patent granted for the eight most commonly designated Member States costs more than DM 20 000 merely to be translated/validated. Aware of this problem, the Administrative Council of the European Patent Organization has looked into several solutions, and these were outlined in point 3.3 above.

*****

Notes and Questions

1. One solution to the translation problem proposed by a senior German official of the EPO is that English be adopted as the common language for patent applications in Europe, since English is the common language of sci-

ence. Do you think it likely that such a solution might be accepted among the EU member states? Even if it resulted in substantial cost savings?

The problem of translations (and their cost) is of course not limited to Europe. Generally speaking, obtaining a patent in any country requires translating the application, claims and description into the local language. After forty years, the EU seems no closer to agreement on language simplification for government business than it was at its formation. Is it likely that progress on language simplification will be any easier in the WIPO Patent Cooperation Treaty system which involves 100 states? In 1998, 67,007 international applications were filed under the PCT. The languages in which they were filed were as follows:

Language of filing	Number of applications		Percentage	
	1998	(1997)	1998	(1997)
English	44,458	(35,953)	66.3	(66.1)
German	10,086	(8,304)	15.1	(15.3)
Japanese	5,689	(4,521)	8.5	(8.3)
French	3,392	(2,618)	5.1	(4.8)
Swedish	899	(968)	1.3	(1.8)
Finnish	523	(419)	0.8	(0.8)
Dutch	476	(349)	0.7	(0.6)
Russian	434	(404)	0.6	(0.7)
Spanish	422	(370)	0.6	(0.7)
Norwegian	236	(209)	0.3	(0.4)
Danish	178	(173)	0.3	(0.3)
Chinese	177	(134)	0.3	(0.2)
Other languages	37	n.a.	<0.1	n.a.
Total	67,007	(54,422)	100.0	(100.0)

2. When studying the Paris Convention rule on independence of patents, we noted that it was adopted at least in part to prevent national sentiments from undermining the worldwide rights of patent holders. Objections to the Community Patent Convention focus on the proposed right of each national court to revoke patents with effects throughout the EU. Does this reflect the same kinds of concern that prompted the rule of independence in the Paris Convention?

3. For many years it was debated whether the EU had the power to harmonize the IPRs laws of its member states. Significant actions have so far been taken by the EU in the fields of copyright, design, neighboring rights, database and trademark. Patents are a "final frontier." Has the EU moved slowly into the field of patents because the public is more sensitive to common regulation in this area? Alternatively, has the EU been comfortable to stay out of the patent field because of the success of the EPC/EPO system which predates EU regulation in the fields of copyright and trademark?

E. The NAFTA Patent Norms

In Chapter II we reviewed the basic NAFTA framework for IPRs protection. Following is the text of the NAFTA patent norms. Recall that the NAFTA patent norms were agreed upon before the WTO TRIPS Agreement was finalized, and that the NAFTA norms were based on a working draft of the TRIPS Agreement. There was not a significant difference between the 1991 working draft of the TRIPS Agreement (the so-called "Dunkel draft" text) and the final text of that Agreement insofar as patents are concerned. Nevertheless, several of the differences between the NAFTA text and the TRIPS Agreement text on patents exist as a result of changes to the TRIPS Agreement made just before the Uruguay Round ended.

Canada, Mexico and the United States (the NAFTA "Parties") are Members of the WTO and parties to the TRIPS Agreement. They are bound in their relations among themselves both to the terms of the NAFTA and to the terms of the TRIPS Agreement. The legal relationship between the NAFTA and the WTO Agreement is a complex one. For the limited purposes of the TRIPS Agreement, it is likely that priority would be given to a TRIPS Agreement rule over a NAFTA rule in the event of a conflict between the two agreements. The TRIPS Agreement post-dates the NAFTA, and it is a "new area" agreement and thus outside the scope of pre-existing GATT rules (which might otherwise be included in a general rule of NAFTA priority over pre-existing GATT rules under a broad construction of NAFTA Article 103). The TRIPS Agreement provides an exception from its MFN requirement based on pre-existing agreements among its Members (TRIPS art. 4(d)). The differences between the NAFTA and TRIPS Agreement on the subject of patents are fairly minor, and it is doubtful that the question of priority is of much importance as matters now stand.

The most significant difference between the NAFTA patent norms and TRIPS patent norms concerns the scope of so-called "pipeline protection" (see Articles 1709(4) and 1720). A few general NAFTA IPRs provisions are included below to facilitate understanding of the relevant patent norms.

NAFTA Patent Provisions

Chapter 17

Article 1701: Nature and Scope of Obligations

1. Each Party shall provide in its territory to the nationals of another Party adequate and effective protection and enforcement of intellectual property rights, while ensuring that measures to enforce intellectual property rights do not themselves become barriers to legitimate trade.

2. To provide adequate and effective protection and enforcement of intellectual property rights, each Party shall, at a minimum, give effect to this Chapter and to the substantive provisions of:

*****

(c) the Paris Convention for the Protection of Industrial Property, 1967 (Paris Convention); and

(d) the International Convention for the Protection of New Varieties of Plants, 1978 (UPOV Convention), or the International Convention for the Protection of New Varieties of Plants, 1991 (UPOV Convention).

If a Party has not acceded to the specified text of any such Conventions on or before the date of entry into force of this Agreement, it shall make every effort to accede.

3. Annex 1701.3 applies to the Parties specified in that Annex.

Article 1702: More Extensive Protection

A Party may implement in its domestic law more extensive protection of intellectual property rights than is required under this Agreement, provided that such protection is not inconsistent with this Agreement.

Article 1703: National Treatment

1. Each Party shall accord to nationals of another Party treatment no less favorable than that it accords to its own nationals with regard to the protection and enforcement of all intellectual property rights. In respect of sound recordings, each Party shall provide such treatment to producers and performers of another Party, except that a Party may limit rights of performers of another Party in respect of secondary uses of sound recordings to those rights its nationals are accorded in the territory of such other Party.

2. No Party may, as a condition of according national treatment under this Article, require right holders to comply with any formalities or conditions in order to acquire rights in respect of copyright and related rights.

3. A Party may derogate from paragraph 1 in relation to its judicial and administrative procedures for the protection or enforcement of intellectual property rights, including any procedure requiring a national of another Party to designate for service of process an address in the Party's territory or to appoint an agent in the Party's territory, if the derogation is consistent with the relevant Convention listed in Article 1701(2), provided that such derogation:

   (a) is necessary to secure compliance with measures that are not inconsistent with this Chapter; and

   (b) is not applied in a manner that would constitute a disguised restriction on trade.

4. No Party shall have any obligation under this Article with respect to procedures provided in multilateral agreements concluded under the auspices of the World Intellectual Property Organization relating to the acquisition or maintenance of intellectual property rights.

Article 1704: Control of Abusive or Anticompetitive Practices
or Conditions

Nothing in this Chapter shall prevent a Party from specifying in its domestic law licensing practices or conditions that may in particular cases constitute an abuse of intellectual property rights having an adverse effect on competition in the relevant market. A Party may adopt or maintain, consistent with the other provisions of this Agreement, appropriate measures to prevent or control such practices or conditions.

*****

Article 1709: Patents
1. Subject to paragraphs 2 and 3, each Party shall make patents available for any inventions, whether products or processes, in all fields of technology, provided that such inventions are new, result from an inventive step and are capable of industrial application. For purposes of this Article, a Party may deem the terms "inventive step" and "capable of industrial application" to be synonymous with the terms "non-obvious" and "useful", respectively.

2. A Party may exclude from patentability inventions if preventing in its territory the commercial exploitation of the inventions is necessary to protect ordre public or morality, including to protect human, animal or plant life or health or to avoid serious prejudice to nature or the environment, provided that the exclusion is not based solely on the ground that the Party prohibits commercial exploitation in its territory of the subject matter of the patent.

3. A Party may also exclude from patentability:

(a) diagnostic, therapeutic and surgical methods for the treatment of humans or animals;

(b) plants and animals other than microorganisms; and

(c) essentially biological processes for the production of plants or animals, other than non-biological and microbiological processes for such production. Notwithstanding subparagraph (b), each Party shall provide for the protection of plant varieties through patents, an effective scheme of sui generis protection, or both.

4. If a Party has not made available product patent protection for pharmaceutical or agricultural chemicals commensurate with paragraph 1:

(a) as of January 1, 1992, for subject matter that relates to naturally occurring substances prepared or produced by, or significantly derived from, microbiological processes and intended for food or medicine, and

(b) as of July 1, 1991, for any other subject matter, that Party shall provide to the inventor of any such product or its assignee the means to obtain product patent protection for such product for the unexpired term of the patent for such product granted in another Party, as long as the product has not been marketed in the Party providing protection under this paragraph and the person seeking such protection makes a timely request.

5. Each Party shall provide that:

(a) where the subject matter of a patent is a product, the patent shall confer on the patent owner the right to prevent other persons from making, using or selling the subject matter of the patent, without the patent owner's consent; and

(b) where the subject matter of a patent is a process, the patent shall confer on the patent owner the right to prevent other persons from using that process and from using, selling, or importing at least the product obtained directly by that process, without the patent owner's consent.

6. A Party may provide limited exceptions to the exclusive rights conferred by a patent, provided that such exceptions do not unreasonably conflict with a normal exploitation of the patent and do not unreasonably prejudice the legitimate interests of the patent owner, taking into account the legitimate interests of other persons.

7. Subject to paragraphs 2 and 3, patents shall be available and patent rights enjoyable without discrimination as to the field of technology, the

territory of the Party where the invention was made and whether products are imported or locally produced.

8. A Party may revoke a patent only when:

(a) grounds exist that would have justified a refusal to grant the patent; or

(b) the grant of a compulsory license has not remedied the lack of exploitation of the patent.

9. Each Party shall permit patent owners to assign and transfer by succession their patents, and to conclude licensing contracts.

10. Where the law of a Party allows for use of the subject matter of a patent, other than that use allowed under paragraph 6, without the authorization of the right holder, including use by the government or other persons authorized by the government, the Party shall respect the following provisions:

(a) authorization of such use shall be considered on its individual merits;

(b) such use may only be permitted if, prior to such use, the proposed user has made efforts to obtain authorization from the right holder on reasonable commercial terms and conditions and such efforts have not been successful within a reasonable period of time. The requirement to make such efforts may be waived by a Party in the case of a national emergency or other circumstances of extreme urgency or in cases of public non-commercial use. In situations of national emergency or other circumstances of extreme urgency, the right holder shall, nevertheless, be notified as soon as reasonably practicable. In the case of public non-commercial use, where the government or contractor, without making a patent search, knows or has demonstrable grounds to know that a valid patent is or will be used by or for the government, the right holder shall be informed promptly;

(c) the scope and duration of such use shall be limited to the purpose for which it was authorized;

(d) such use shall be non-exclusive;

(e) such use shall be non-assignable, except with that part of the enterprise or goodwill that enjoys such use;

(f) any such use shall be authorized predominantly for the supply of the Party's domestic market;

(g) authorization for such use shall be liable, subject to adequate protection of the legitimate interests of the persons so authorized, to be terminated if and when the circumstances that led to it cease to exist and are unlikely to recur. The competent authority shall have the authority to review, on motivated request, the continued existence of these circumstances;

(h) the right holder shall be paid adequate remuneration in the circumstances of each case, taking into account the economic value of the authorization;

(i) the legal validity of any decision relating to the authorization shall be subject to judicial or other independent review by a distinct higher authority;

(j) any decision relating to the remuneration provided in respect of such use shall be subject to judicial or other independent review by a distinct higher authority;

(k) the Party shall not be obliged to apply the conditions set out in sub-paragraphs (b) and (f) where such use is permitted to remedy a practice determined after judicial or administrative process to be anticompetitive. The need to correct anticompetitive practices may be taken into account in determining the amount of remuneration in such cases. Competent authorities shall have the authority to refuse termination of authorization if and when the conditions that led to such authorization are likely to recur;

(l) the Party shall not authorize the use of the subject matter of a patent to permit the exploitation of another patent except as a remedy for an adjudicated violation of domestic laws regarding anticompetitive practices.

11. Where the subject matter of a patent is a process for obtaining a product, each Party shall, in any infringement proceeding, place on the defendant the burden of establishing that the allegedly infringing product was made by a process other than the patented process in one of the following situations:

(a) the product obtained by the patented process is new; or

(b) a substantial likelihood exists that the allegedly infringing product was made by the process and the patent owner has been unable through reasonable efforts to determine the process actually used.

In the gathering and evaluation of evidence, the legitimate interests of the defendant in protecting its trade secrets shall be taken into account.

12. Each Party shall provide a term of protection for patents of at least 20 years from the date of filing or 17 years from the date of grant. A Party may extend the term of patent protection, in appropriate cases, to compensate for delays caused by regulatory approval processes.

*****

Article 1720: Protection of Existing Subject Matter
1. Except as required under Article 1705(7), this Agreement does not give rise to obligations in respect of acts that occurred before the date of application of the relevant provisions of this Agreement for the Party in question.

2. Except as otherwise provided for in this Agreement, each Party shall apply this Agreement to all subject matter existing on the date of application of the relevant provisions of this Agreement for the Party in question and that is protected in a Party on such date, or that meets or subsequently meets the criteria for protection under the terms of this Chapter. In respect of this paragraph and paragraphs 3 and 4, a Party's obligations with respect to existing works shall be solely determined under Article 18 of the Berne

Convention and with respect to the rights of producers of sound recordings in existing sound recordings shall be determined solely under Article 18 of that Convention, as made applicable under this Agreement.

3. Except as required under Article 1705(7), and notwithstanding the first sentence of paragraph 2, no Party may be required to restore protection to subject matter that, on the date of application of the relevant provisions of this Agreement for the Party in question, has fallen into the public domain in its territory.

4. In respect of any acts relating to specific objects embodying protected subject matter that become infringing under the terms of laws in conformity with this Agreement, and that were begun or in respect of which a significant investment was made, before the date of entry into force of this Agreement for that Party, any Party may provide for a limitation of the remedies available to the right holder as to the continued performance of such acts after the date of application of this Agreement for that Party. In such cases, the Party shall, however, at least provide for payment of equitable remuneration.

5. No Party shall be obliged to apply Article 1705(2)(d) or 1706(1)(d) with respect to originals or copies purchased prior to the date of application of the relevant provisions of this Agreement for that Party.

6. No Party shall be required to apply Article 1709(10), or the requirement in Article 1709(7) that patent rights shall be enjoyable without discrimination as to the field of technology, to use without the authorization of the right holder where authorization for such use was granted by the government before the text of the Draft Final Act Embodying the Results of the Uruguay Round of Multilateral Trade Negotiations became known.

7. In the case of intellectual property rights for which protection is conditional on registration, applications for protection that are pending on the date of application of the relevant provisions of this Agreement for the Party in question shall be permitted to be amended to claim any enhanced

protection provided under this Agreement. Such amendments shall not include new matter.

Notes and Questions

1. Recall from Chapter III (section E, 2) that the TRIPS Agreement (art. 4) requires that WTO Members grant each other most favored nation (MFN) treatment, although privileges "deriving from" pre-existing international agreements related to IPRs protection are exempted from this obligation (art. 4(d)). What effect will the TRIPS Agreement MFN obligation have on NAFTA patent standards? If the MFN principle is fundamental to the international trade and IPRs systems, what is the purpose of regional IPRs agreements?

2. NAFTA Article 1704 permits Parties to act to prevent abuses of IPRs in connection with licensing practices, as does the TRIPS Agreement (art. 40). We will study competition law aspects of the international IPRs system in Chapter VII. Since the patent by definition confers a limited monopoly on its holders, there is naturally a tension between patent rights and rules on anticompetitive practices.

3. Compare the NAFTA rule on pipeline protection for pharmaceutical and agricultural chemical products (art. 1709(4)) with the TRIPS Agreement special transition provision regarding the same subject matter (art. 70:8) (the "mailbox" rule). How do these provisions differ? Since the NAFTA rule requires that the holder of an existing patent make a "timely" request for protection, and since the NAFTA entered into force on January 1, 1994, has the operational significance of the NAFTA pipeline rule come to an end?

4. NAFTA Article 1709(5)(a) lists the rights conferred on product patent holders. The list does not include the right to import as does the corresponding TRIPS Agreement provision (art. 28:1(a)). Do you think that this difference is an important one?

5. Article 31(c) of the TRIPS Agreement (compulsory licensing) contains a special rule in respect to integrated circuits. There is no corresponding special rule in the NAFTA. The TRIPS Agreement rule reflects one of the Uruguay Round end-game changes based on demands of the U.S. semiconductor industry.

6. NAFTA Article 1720(4) provides a basis for limiting remedies as against private parties whose actions become infringing as a consequence of changes brought about by the NAFTA. What conditions must be fulfilled in the application of this provision?

F. The Andean Pact Patent and Technology Transfer Provisions

1. The Andean Experiment

From the early 1970s through the early 1980s, there was a movement among developing countries to readjust the international economic system in their favor. This movement foresaw a New International Economic Order (NIEO). One of the most innovative actions taken by any group of developing countries during this period was the adoption by the Andean Pact regional group of Decision 24. This regional legislation generally required foreign investors to reduce their percentage of ownership in Andean enterprises. In addition to mandating changes to the structure of foreign direct investment holdings, the Andean Pact countries sought to strictly limit the ways in which patents, patent licenses and other technology-related agreements could be used to exploit the Andean region. This policy was implemented in Decisions 84 and 85 of the Andean Commission.

Whether the Andean Group could successfully force a major change in the relationship between itself and industrialized country investors/IPRs holders was the subject of an article written by Frederick Abbott in 1975. In that article he observed that the ability of the Andean Group to influence foreign investors would largely depend on the alternative opportunities open to those investors. Why would an investor bear the brunt of harsh policies in the Andean region if it could pursue alternative investment opportunities in more hospitable environments? Decision 24 has long ceased to generally require "disinvestment" by foreign investors, and Decisions 84 and 85 have been repealed and are now replaced by Decision 344, the patent provisions of which follow excerpts from Abbott's article. Today developing countries often race to provide incentives to attract foreign investors, instead of seeking to impose harsh conditions. The Andean experiment turned out to be an unsuccessful one. Was the policy perspective of the architects of the Andean plan so misguided?

Bargaining Power and Strategy in the Foreign Investment Process: A Current Andean Code Analysis

Frederick M. Abbott*

I. Introduction

Significant changes in the global economic balance of power have taken place during the last several years. Japan and the Western European nations have made substantial progress in achieving technological equality with the United States, and many developing countries have taken or are now taking steps to improve their bargaining position relative to the developed countries.

In addition, the past few decades have produced an enormous growth in the amount of direct equity investment made by companies in countries other than their home country. In order to maintain control over their domestic economies, developing country governments have come to rely on foreign investment laws, tariffs, quotas, and other means of regulating foreign economic influence.

In 1970, the countries of the Andean Common Market (the Andean Pact or ANCOM), adopted uniform foreign investment regulations. The Andean Foreign Investment Code, as Decision 24 of the Andean Commission is called, regulates both the treatment of foreign capital entering or within ANCOM, and related agreements on the transfer of technology,

---

*3 Syr. J. Int'l L. & Com. 319 (1975).

patents, licenses, and royalties. The member countries of ANCOM were required by Decision 24 to implement this Code as domestic legislation following its adoption by the Andean Commission.

The governments of the ANCOM members were motivated by both common and individual interests when they adopted the Andean Code. Among these were the desire to achieve a reduction in foreign economic influence, and to be able to plan more efficiently a regional industrial structure. This was to be done in a way which would give no individual member country a significant economic advantage over the others.

Since the adoption of the Andean Foreign Investment Code, there have been important changes in the political and economic situations of the member countries (for example, the quadrupling of oil prices which has made Venezuela a new economic power in the Western Hemisphere), and there have been several important developments in the Code's local implementation. This Article is designed to apprize the practitioner concerned with Latin America of progress in the implementation of the Andean Code and related regulations in the six ANCOM countries, and to discuss implications for the investment lawyer. It examines the progress of the Andean Pact's efforts in the field of foreign investment regulation in terms of bargaining theories previously used solely by economists, political scientists, and military strategists, but which have recently begun to receive attention from international lawyers. It is the premise of this Article that both international lawyers and government officials should begin to see the forces which influence the foreign investment process in a general theoretical framework in order to fully understand and perhaps better control these forces . . .

Provisions Regulating the Transfer of Technology

The ANCOM countries attach great value to the role of modern technology in the industrial development process.[130] The goal of ANCOM technology policy is to acquire necessary technology from abroad at the least

---

[130]The introductory portion of Decision 84 of the Andean Commission reads in part: "Our contemporary world is characterized by the controlling influence that is inherent in the possession of know-how and the capacity to utilize it in economic and social orientation."

possible cost and with the fewest strings attached,[131] and simultaneously to improve local research and development capabilities.

The ANCOM countries have developed a new attitude towards the transfer of technology from abroad, whose impact is only beginning to be felt by foreign direct investors.[133] In essence, the attitude derives from the belief that technology should not be commercialized, but that developed country industries should make it freely or cheaply available to developing countries. Research and development costs involved in the generation of new commercial technology are fixed costs of the enterprise involved. This fixed cost is recovered by the enterprise when its product is marketed—that is, the product incorporates the technology, and the technology costs are reflected in the selling price of the product. For a parent company to sell this technology to its own subsidiary is to profit twice from the technology: once from the sale of the product itself, and once from the sale of the technology.

The ANCOM countries have created legal mechanisms for implementing their policy relating to technology transfer in the Andean Code and in the recently enacted Decisions 84 and 85 of the Andean Commission. The Andean Code provides broad rules on several aspects of the technology transfer (or "commercialization") process, and Decisions 84 and 85 supplement the Code with detailed provisions relating both to the creation of a regional technological infrastructure and to the legal treatment of patents, licenses, and trademarks within ANCOM.

---

[131]The ANCOM countries relate their previous relation to technology transfer as following:

Member Nations have had recourse to external services in a preponderant form to satisfy the needs of technical development, with such undesirable results as the following solutions inadequate to the characteristics of economic development of the Member Nations and to the availability of productive factors; extremely elevated costs; limited possibility to exercise a choice among various alternative solutions; the displacement of local operations and elements, and the underutilization of local scientific and technological resources; a conditioning of political and economic decisions to technological solution imposed from abroad; and a miscellany of unsatisfied needs due to the inadequacy of technological solutions. . . . Decision 84.

[133]This impact comes as the ANCOM countries gradually require investors to conform their technology agreements to the Andean Code's regulations. Venezuela has, for example, given foreign investors until December 31, 1975, to have their contracts approved by the Superintendency of Foreign Investments; after which, contracts which do not conform will cease to have legal effect. Decree 63, arts. 61 & 63. . . .

The Andean Code provides that technological agreements may not be capitalized as foreign direct investments. In addition, parent companies or their affiliates are prohibited from receiving royalty payments from their subsidiaries incorporated in ANCOM countries for the use of patents, trademarks, licenses, and in some cases, even technical assistance in the form of personnel. All technological agreements, whether between parent and subsidiary, or between an ANCOM incorporated firm and unrelated foreign firm, must be approved by the competent authority of the receiving member country.

Patent and trademark licensing agreements are prohibited from incorporating a variety of restrictive clauses which might tend to limit the flexibility of the receiving ANCOM company in the use of the license (for example, export restricting clauses, tie-in clauses, and the like). The recent Decisions 84 and 85 of the Andean Commission, however, establish in detail the guidelines for the registration and authorization of patents, trademarks, and licenses within ANCOM, and the uniform legal treatment which such registration will confer.

Decision 85 provides regulations for the registration of patents in the receiving ANCOM country and delineates the legal rights which ownership of a patent may confer. Patents may not be granted for certain types of products.[142] The application for a patent must include a technical description of the invention complete enough to allow duplication. Patents may be granted for a maximum period of ten years, with renewal and proof of exploitation required after five years. Subject to the limitations expressed in other areas of Decision 85, a patent confers on the owner the exclusive right to exploit it in the recipient country, to grant licenses for its exploitation, and to receive royalties or compensation for its exploitation. Patents do not confer an exclusive right to import the patented product or one manufactured under the patented process. Filing a patent application in one ANCOM country gives the applicant a (one-year) priority right to file for patent in the other member countries.

The more interesting regulations of Decision 85 have to do with the licensing of patents. Patents may only be exploited in ANCOM pursuant to authorization by competent national authorities. Licensed patents must be exploited within the country of registration according to conditions estab-

---

[142]This includes, inter alia, pharmaceutical products and beverages. Decision 85, art. 5. . . .

lished in Decision 85.[148] After a period of three years from the date that the patent is granted, any person may apply to the competent authority for the granting of a "compulsory license" if the patent has not been exploited adequately within the member country. After a period of five years the competent authority may grant a compulsory license regardless of whether or not conditions of exploitation have been satisfied. The holder of a compulsory license must pay an "adequate compensation" to a patent holder. The government of the country in which the patent is registered may at any time grant a compulsory license in view of national development needs or interest in the public health. Licenses which do not comply with the regulations established in Decision 85 will be considered void.

Trademarks must be approved and registered by the competent national authority as well, and registration of a trademark grants the right of exclusive use for continuously renewable periods of five years. Likewise, trademark licensing agreements must be approved and registered. Trademark licensing agreements may not include a variety of export-restrictive clauses, which were earlier prohibited by Article 25 of the Andean Code. Trademarks are not subject to "compulsory licensing" as are patents.

The new ANCOM regulations governing patents, licensing, and trademarks represent an attempt by the member countries to make modern technology more freely accessible to commercial enterprises in the region. The regulations provided by Decision 85 represent a radical departure from the traditional concept that patent ownership rights should be afforded the highest degree of protection. In effect, the patent licensing rules provided by Decision 85 mean that ANCOM country governments are free to give away a registered patent to any enterprise which desires it, so long as this procedure is considered in the interests of the member countries' development plans, and so long as some unspecified form of compensation is provided to the patent owner. The rules do not specify that "compulsory licenses" may be issued solely to ANCOM national investors, and it appears that a foreign investor's registered patents may even be licensed to other foreign enterprises in ANCOM.

Decision 85 was designed to be implemented in the domestic law of the ANCOM members within six months following its approval by the

---

[148]The exploitation of a patent may not be suspended for more than one year; production of the patented product must meet the demands of the national market re quality, quantity, and price; and the patent owner must grant licenses under reasonable conditions to satisfy the market. Decision 85, art. 34. . . .

Commission. No information has yet been made available on the process of implementation and, as was the case with the Andean Code, the time limit on implementation may be exceeded by the member countries. However, when the Decision is implemented its rules will apply to patents, licenses, and trademarks already registered in the region. In addition, the rule established in Article 21 of the Andean Code which provides that subsidiaries may not pay royalties to their parent companies is already being enforced in at least some of the member countries; and while technology supply costs may to some extent be added to the selling price of products and thereby returned as profit, these profits are limited to 14 percent per annum on the registered value of the investment (which cannot include technology).

The impact of the new technology transfer regulations on foreign direct investor behavior can only be speculated upon, as they have no precedent in modern investment regulation. It might be expected that for foreign firms whose research and development costs are high (for whom innovative technology represents a primary competitive advantage over their international rivals), the ANCOM technology regulations will represent a major disincentive to new investment. Or, at least, these firms may wait a period of several years after the development of a new technology before bringing it into the Andean region. For firms whose products embody technology which is widely dispersed and whose investment advantages lay more in the access to capital, marketing, or managerial skills, the technology regulations should have little impact at all.

The ANCOM countries are betting that foreign investors will be willing to trade their technology for access to the expanded ANCOM market. The outcome of this gamble remains to be seen. If successful, the ANCOM policy may improve their technological infrastructure and increase their industrial self-sufficiency. If unsuccessful, the result may be another period of years in which ANCOM industries fall farther behind those of the developed countries in technological development. It remains to be seen how far the ANCOM countries can proceed in extracting concessions from foreign direct investors before disincentives overshadow opportunities.

Notes and Questions

1. Decisions 84 and 85 are no longer in force. What concerns would these Decisions have raised under the TRIPS Agreement?

2. As it turns out, the Andean Pact countries did not have the bargaining power to force a major realignment of their economic relations with the industrialized countries. Might the result have been different if 100 developing countries had adopted the same rules? If such rules had been widely adopted, would the result have been more technology transfer from the industrialized countries, greater innovation within the developing countries, or economic stagnation in the developing (and industrialized countries)?

2. Adapting to a New Reality

Decision 344 takes the place of Decisions 84 and 85. It represents a substantial shift toward providing levels of patent protection consistent with TRIPS Agreement standards. Yet there remain a number of elements embodying the perspective on IPRs and technology transfer developed by the Andean Pact countries in the 1970s, and some of these elements are criticized by the U.S. Trade Representative's Office and U.S. business groups. Look closely at the rules on compulsory licensing.

Andean Pact: Decision 344 Regarding Common Provisions on Industrial Property*

Chapter I

Patents

Section I

Patentability Requirements

1. The Member Countries shall grant patents for inventions in all areas of technology, whether goods or processes, that are new, involve an inventive step and are industrially applicable.

---

*Reproduced from the English translation provided by the International Bureau of the World Intellectual Property Organization. The official Spanish text can be found in Gaceta Oficiel del Acuerdo de Cartagena, X-No. 142, of October 29, 1993. This Decision replaces Decision 313, Common Code on Intellectual Property of February 6, 1992, which is reproduced at 32 I.L.M. 180 (1993). There are currently five members of the Andean Group: Bolivia, Colombia, Ecuador, Peru and Venezuela.
DATE: October 21, 1993; in effect from January 1, 1994

2. An invention is new when it is not included in the state of the art.

The state of the art comprises everything that has been made available to the public by written or oral description, by use or by any other means prior to the filing date of the patent application or, where appropriate, of the priority claimed.

Solely for the purpose of determining novelty, the contents of a patent application pending before the competent national office and having a filing date or priority date earlier than the priority date of the patent application under examination shall likewise be considered part of the state of the art, provided that the said contents are published.

3. For the purposes of determining patentability, no account shall be taken of any disclosure of the contents of the patent during the year prior to the filing date of the application in the country, or during the year before the priority date if priority has been claimed, provided that such disclosure is attributable to:

   (a) the inventor or his successor in title;

   (b) a competent national office which, in violation of the provisions applicable, publishes the contents of the patent application filed by the inventor or his successor in title;

   (c) a third party who has obtained the information directly or indirectly from the inventor or his successor in title;

   (d) manifest abuse to the detriment of the applicant or his successor in title;

   (e) the fact that the applicant or his successor in title has displayed the invention at officially recognized exhibitions or fairs, or where for academic or research purposes it has been necessary to make it public in order to proceed with its development. In that case the person concerned shall submit, on filing the application, a statement attesting that the invention has actually been so displayed, and shall submit the appropriate certification.

4. An invention shall be regarded as involving an inventive step if, for a person in the trade with average skills in the technical field concerned, the said invention is neither obvious nor obviously derived from the state of the art.

5. An invention shall be regarded as industrially applicable when its subject matter may be produced or used in any type of industry, industry being understood as that involving any productive activity, including services.

6. The following shall not be considered inventions:

(a) discoveries, scientific theories and mathematical methods;

(b) subject matter that already exists in nature or is a reproduction thereof;

(c) literary and artistic works or any other aesthetic creation, and also scientific works;

(d) plans, rules and methods for the pursuit of intellectual activities, for the playing of games or for economic and business activities, and also computer programs or software;

(e) methods of presenting information;

(f) therapeutic or surgical methods for the treatment of human beings or animals, and methods of diagnosis.

7. The following shall not be patentable:

(a) inventions contrary to public policy, morality or proper practice;

(b) inventions that are clearly prejudicial to human or animal health, the preservation of plants or the conservation of the environment;

(c) animal species and breeds and essentially biological processes for the production or breeding thereof;

(d) inventions relating to matter that makes up the human body and to the genetic identity thereof;

(e) inventions relating to pharmaceutical products appearing in the List of Essential Drugs of the World Health Organization.

Section II

Owners of Patents

8. The right to the patent shall belong to the inventor or to his successor in title.

The owners of patents may be natural persons or legal entities.

If two or more persons have made an invention jointly, the right shall be jointly held by both or all of them.

If two or more persons make the same invention independently of each other, the patent shall be granted to the person, or to the successor in title, who files the first application in respect of it or claims the earliest priority.

9. Where a patent application relates to an invention that has been unlawfully obtained from the inventor or from his successors in title, or where, by virtue of contractual or legal obligations, the owner of the patent has to be a person other than the applicant, any person having a legitimate interest may, up to three years following the grant of the patent, claim the status of true owner before the competent judicial authority.

10. Without prejudice to the provisions of the national legislation of each Member Country, in the case of inventions occurring in the course of employment relations, the State employer, whatever its form and nature, may transfer part of the economic benefit deriving from the innovations to the employee inventors with a view to promoting research activity, as provided in the laws of the country concerned.

Entities that receive State funding for their research shall reinvest part of the royalties received from the marketing of inventions, with a view to accumulating a continuous supply of research funds and stimulating researchers by giving them a share in the proceeds from innovations, in accordance with the legislation of each Member Country.

11. The inventor shall have the right to be mentioned as such in the patent, and may likewise object to being so mentioned.

*****

Section IV

Processing of the Application

*****

30. The patent shall have a term of 20 years following the filing date of the corresponding application.

*****

Section V

Rights Conferred by the Patent

34. The scope of the protection conferred by the patent shall be determined by the wording of the claims. The description and drawings or plans, or the deposit of biological material where applicable, shall be used for the interpretation of the claims.

35. The patent shall confer on its owner the right to prevent third parties from exploiting the patented invention without his consent.

The owner may not exercise that right in any of the following cases:

(a) when the case concerns the importation of the patented product that has been marketed in any country with the consent of the owner, a licensee or any other authorized person;

(b) where the use takes place in a private circle and on a non-commercial scale;

(c) where the use is made at an experimental, academic or scientific level and for non-profit-making purposes.

36. The rights conferred by a patent may not be asserted against a third party who, in good faith and before the priority date or the filing date of the application on which the patent was granted, was already using the invention in a private circle, or had made real or effective preparations for such use.

In such a case, the said third party shall have the right to start or continue, within any Member Country, the manufacture of the product or use of the process, as the case may be, but that right may only be assigned or transferred together with the establishment or business in which the manufacture or use was taking place.

Section VI

Obligations on the Owner of the Patent

37. The owner of the patent shall be under the obligation to exploit the patented invention in any Member Country, either directly or through any person authorized by him.

38. For the purposes of this Decision, exploitation shall be understood to mean the industrial manufacture of the patented product or the full use of the patented process, including the distribution and marketing of the results thereof. Exploitation shall also be understood to mean the importation of the patented product, including distribution and marketing, of the patented product, where this is done on a scale sufficient to satisfy the demands of the market.

39. The owner of the patent shall register with the competent national office any contract for the assignment or licensing of the patent or any other form of use thereof by third parties in whatever capacity.

This obligation shall be met by the patentee or his successors in title, assignees, licensees or any other person who holds a right deriving from the patent.

Section VII

Licensing

40. The patentee may license another person to work the patent, but only by written contract.

License agreements shall be registered with the competent national office, failing which they shall not be binding on third parties.

41. The competent national office shall not register license agreements for the working of patents that do not conform to the provisions of the Common System for the Treatment of Foreign Capital and for Trademarks, Patents, Licenses and Royalties.

42. On expiration of a period of three years following the grant of the patent, or four years following the application for the patent, whichever is the longer, the competent national office may grant a compulsory license for the industrial manufacture of the product to which the patent relates, or for the full use of the patented process, at the request of any interested party who has failed to secure a contractual license on reasonable terms, but only if, at the time of the request, the patent has not been worked in the manner specified in Articles 37 and 38 of this Decision in the Member Country in which the license is sought, or if exploitation of the invention has been suspended for more than one year.

A compulsory license shall not be granted if the owner of the patent provides legitimate justification of his failure to act, which may be reasons of force majeure, in accordance with the domestic provisions of each Member Country.

The compulsory licensee shall pay appropriate compensation to the owner of the patent.

Any person who applies for a compulsory license shall prove that he has the technical and economic capability to carry out the industrial manufacture of the product to which the patent relates or the full use of the patented process.

43. The decision on the grant of compulsory licenses referred to in the foregoing Article shall be taken after the owner of the patent has been notified, so that, within 60 working days following the said decision, he may, if he sees fit, present his arguments.

The said grant decision shall specify the scope or extent of the license, and in particular shall specify the period for which it is granted, the subject matter of the license, the amount of the royalties and the conditions for the payment thereof.

The competent national office shall determine the amount of the consideration, after hearing the parties, in relation to the scale of the exploitation of the licensed invention and the cooperation that the patentee may have obtained to facilitate the said exploitation especially in terms of the provision of the necessary technical skills and whatever other conditions the office considers relevant thereto.

A complaint shall not prevent working or have any effect on periods that may be running. The making of a complaint shall not prevent the owner of the patent from collecting, among other things, the royalties specified by the office in respect of the part unaffected by the said complaint.

44. At the request of the owner of the patent or his licensee, the licensing conditions may be altered by the body that approved them, after the parties have been heard, where new circumstances dictate and in particular where the owner of the patent grants another license on terms more favorable than those previously granted.

45. The licensee shall be bound to exploit the licensed invention, which, unless the licensee justifies his inaction with legitimate reasons, shall occur within a period of two years following the date of grant of the license, failing which the license shall be revoked.

46. Following a declaration by the Government of the Member Country concerned regarding the existence of public interest, emergency or national security considerations, and only for as long as those considerations obtain, the said Government may make the patent subject to compulsory licensing at any time, in which case the competent national office may grant such licenses as are applied for. The owner of the patent so licensed shall be notified where reasonably possible.

The decision to grant a compulsory license shall specify the scope or extent of the license, and in particular the term for which it is granted, the subject matter of the license and the amount of royalties and the conditions for the payment thereof, without prejudice to the provisions of Article 49 of this Decision.

In the cases provided for in this Article, licenses may be granted for working according to the provisions of Articles 37 and 38 of this Decision.

The grant of a compulsory license for reasons of public interest shall not diminish the right of the owner of the patent to continue to work the said patent.

47. The competent national office may, either ex officio or at the request of a party, and after having obtained the consent of the national authority on free competition, grant compulsory licenses where practices are noted that are not in keeping with the proper exercise of industrial property rights and adversely affect free competition, especially when they constitute an abuse by the owner of the patent of his dominant position on the market.

In the decision on the appropriateness and the possible amount of economic compensation, due account shall be taken of the assessment made by the competent national authority.

48. The competent national office may grant a license at any time where it is applied for by the owner of a patent the exploitation of which requires the use of another, and where the said owner has been unable to secure a contractual license on reasonable terms. Such a license shall, without prejudice to the provisions of Article 49 of this Decision, be subject to the following:

(a) the invention claimed in the second patent must embody substantial technological progress in relation to that claimed in the first;

(b) the owner of the first patent shall have the right to a cross-license on reasonable terms for the exploitation of the invention claimed in the second;

(c) the license under the first patent may not be assigned without assignment also of the second.

49. Compulsory licenses shall be subject to the following:

(a) the compulsory license shall not be exclusive and may not be transferred or sublicensed except with the part of the enterprise within which it is exploited and with the consent of the owner of the patent; it shall be evidenced in writing and registered with the competent national office;

(b) the compulsory license shall be granted mainly to supply the domestic market of the Member Country that grants it; the Member Country shall be under no obligation to apply the provisions of this subparagraph where the compulsory license was issued pursuant to the provisions of Article 47 of this Decision;

(c) the compulsory license may be revoked, subject to the adequate protection of the legitimate interests of the licensee, where the circumstances that gave rise to it no longer obtain.

50. Except as provided in Article 40, licenses that do not conform to the provisions of this Section shall be devoid of legal effect.

Without prejudice to the provisions of this Section, the procedure for the grant of compulsory licenses shall be that laid down in the domestic legislation of the Member Countries.

Section VIII

Legal Protection of the Patent

51. The owner of the patent or the person who considers himself entitled to a patent by virtue of this Decision may institute any actions claiming ownership or indemnification that are available to him under the national legislation of the Member Country concerned.

Without prejudice to any other action that may be available to him, the owner of the patent may, after the patent has been granted, bring action for damages against any person who, without his consent, has exploited the patented process or product, where such exploitation took place after the publication date of the patent application.

In cases of alleged infringement of a patent relating to a process for the manufacture of a product, the defendant shall be responsible for proving that the process used by him to manufacture the product is different from that protected by the patent allegedly infringed. To that end it shall be assumed, in the absence of proof to the contrary, that any identical product manufactured without the consent of the owner of the patent has been manufactured by means of the patented process if:

(a) the product manufactured by means of the patented process is new;

(b) there is a reasonable likelihood that the identical product was manufactured by means of the process, and the owner of the process patent is not able to establish, after reasonable effort, what process actually was used.

In the submission of proof to the contrary, due account shall be taken of the legitimate interests of the defendant with respect to the protection of his trade and manufacturing secrets.

Section IX

Invalidation of the Patent

52. The competent national authority may, either ex officio or at the request of a party, declare the patent null and void, after the parties concerned have been heard, where:

(a) it has been granted in contravention of any of the provisions of this Decision;

(b) it has been granted on the basis of false or inaccurate particulars contained in the application which are essential.

Invalidation actions under this Article may be brought at any time.

Where the grounds specified above are applicable only to some of the claims or some parts of a claim, invalidation shall be pronounced only in respect of those claims or those parts of the said claim, as the case may be.

The patent, claim or part of a claim that has been invalidated shall be deemed null and void as from the filing date of the patent application.

Section X

Lapse of the Patent

53. In order to keep the patent in force or maintain a pending patent application, as the case may be, periodical fees shall be paid as provided by the competent national office.

Before the patent is declared lapsed, the Member Countries shall allow the person concerned a period of six months within which to effect payment of the fees referred to in the foregoing paragraph. The patent or pending application shall remain in full force during the periods referred to.

*****

Transitional Provisions

First. Any industrial property right validly granted under the legislation existing prior to the date of entry into force of this Decision shall subsist throughout the period for which it was granted. With respect to its use and enjoyment, and also obligations, licensing, renewals and prolongations, the provisions laid down in this Decision shall apply.

Second. This Decision shall be applicable in the Member Countries as from January 1, 1994.

Note and Questions

1. Article 7(d) and (e) of Decision 344 provide exclusions from patentability for inventions "relating to matter that makes up the human body and to the genetic identity thereof," and for pharmaceutical products "appearing in the List of Essential Drugs of the World Health Organization." Consider whether these exclusions are consistent with the exceptions in the TRIPS Agreement. Note that there is a growing industry that produces synthetic biological replacement parts for the human body.

2. Observe that regional policy on R & D generation is reflected in Article 10 (Dec. 344). Does this article mandate any specific commitments?

3. Article 35(a), Dec. 344, establishes a rule of international exhaustion in respect to patent rights for the Andean Pact countries. Keep this provision

in mind as we continue our study of the issue of international exhaustion of IPRs.

4. Article 36, Dec. 344, establishes rights in favor of good faith prior users of patented technology. A provision of this type was included in drafts of the WIPO Patent Law Treaty when it was still contemplated to address substantive patent law issues. Is it consistent with a patent system according rights to the first-to-invent, or is it a principle that only has an application in a first-to-file system?

5. Articles 37-38, Dec. 344, impose affirmative obligations on patent holders. What are these obligations? What are the consequences to the patent holder of failing to fulfill these obligations? Are these obligations consistent with the terms of the TRIPS Agreement?

6. Note that patent holders must register their license agreements with relevant authorities, and that such licenses will not be registered if they fail to conform with common rules on the treatment of capital and patents (Dec. 344, art. 41).

7. Compare the Andean Pact rules on compulsory patent licensing (Dec. 344, arts. 42-50) with the rules on compulsory licensing in the TRIPS Agreement (art. 31). Do you detect any significant inconsistencies?

8. Article 52, Dec. 344, permits the competent authorities to revoke a patent that has been granted "in contravention of any of the provisions of this Decision" at any time during the term of the patent. Do you think the potential grounds for revocation under this provision may be too broad?

G. National Patent Norms

1. Comparison of U.S. PTO, EPO and Japan Patent Office Rules

We have emphasized at a number of points throughout the book that national IPRs rules contain important variations at a number of levels, ranging from variations in broad constitutional frameworks, to ordinary legislative enactments, and to administrative rules and procedures. Yet as international economic integration continues at a rapid pace, and as information exchange is facilitated through mechanisms such as the Internet, governments become increasingly interested in cooperation. The U.S. Patent and Trademark Office (PTO), EPO and Japan Patent Office (JPO) have developed a trilateral program of cooperation which is significantly improving the transparency (*i.e.* openness) and efficiency of the international patenting framework. It seems reasonable to expect that as governments closely cooperate in the comparison of their rules, they will come to identify ways in which the national and regional systems may be made more compatible and efficient. The following is part of a trilateral study of biotechnology patent practices of the three offices. This excerpt addresses a number of concepts which by now should be familiar to us, including the requirement of enabling disclosure and the inventive step.

Trilateral Project 24.1 — Biotechnology*
Comparative Study on Biotechnology Patent Practices

Comparative Study Report

1.1.2 Relationship between Claims and Description of the Invention . . .

Please discuss those issues mentioned below in "1.2.1 Enablement Requirement" in this paragraph, if the USPTO or the EPO finds it more proper to handle those issues as a matter of "support" or "adequate written description" for the invention described in the claims.

(For example, if those issues mentioned below are considered under EPC Article 84 rather than EPC Article 83, it might be reasonable to handle them in this paragraph.)

The different thinking around this question is recognized between the EPO and the JPO.

In the JPO, it is enough to satisfy a requirement for the Patent Law Section 36(6)(i) that the matter corresponding to what is claimed is formally writ-

---

*Japan Patent Office, http://www.jpo-miti.go.ip (visited May 1998). Syntax is as it appears in the original text.

ten in the detailed description of the invention. Consequently, it is usually discussed as the matter of "enablement requirement."

On the other hand, the EPO explains that an objection of lack of support under Article 84 EPC can often also be considered as an objection of insufficient disclosure under Article 83 EPC.

The USPTO gives answers that the specification must provide both a written description of the invention and sufficient enablement to practice the invention as claimed. These are separate and distinct requirements of the statute 35 U.S.C.112, first paragraph.

1.2 Description of the invention

1.2.1 Enablement Requirement (Adequacy of Disclosure)

1.2.1.1 General rules

The report "Consolidated Comparative Study of Patent Practices in the Field of Biotechnology Related Mainly to Microbiological Inventions"(1990.1) of Project 12.3 and the report "Comparative Study Report on Requirements for Disclosure and Claims"(1990) of Project 12.6 have been made. Considering these reports, please explain the following items.

(1) Please explain the examining practice related to "Enablement Requirement (Adequacy of Disclosure)" in detail.

For example, please refer to "how to make" and "how to use".

The three Offices coincide that enough or sufficient information is needed to carry out the claimed invention by a person skilled in the art, without undue experimentation and using his common general knowledge as of the filing.

In addition, the EPO states that the description must disclose any feature essential for carrying out the invention in sufficient detail to render it obvious to the skilled person how to put the invention into practice. Also, the JPO explains that normally one or more representative embodiments or working examples are necessary in the case of inventions in technical fields where it is generally difficult to infer how to make and use a product on the basis of its structure.

(2) Is there difference in the definition (level) of the "person skilled in the art" between the assessing inventive step and the assessing sufficiency of description?

The three Offices show that there may be no practical difference about the term "person skilled in the art" itself, between the assessing inventive step and the assessing sufficiency of description.

The three Offices agree that the range of knowledge is limited only to the "common general knowledge" as of the filing, not to all the "state of the art" as of the filing including common general knowledge for assessing sufficiency of description.

(3) In determining whether claimed invention *not accompanied by sufficient description in the specification* can be carried out by a person skilled in the art, should an examiner take into consideration either the common general knowledge (such as well-known or commonly used art) or all the relevant documents in the state of the art?

In general, an examiner should take into consideration the "common general knowledge" in all the three Offices.

The EPO notices that patent specifications may exceptionally be considered as forming part of common general knowledge in a field of, for example, biotechnology, which field is so new that the relevant technical knowledge is not yet available from textbooks.

(4) If the applicant presents the written Argument (or the certificate on the result of experiment) which includes the explanation of how to make and how to use without amending the specification, may the reason for rejection related to the enablement requirement be overcome? Is it possible to take into consideration those relevant documents which were published after the filing date?

The three Offices give the same answer to this question, that is, the reasons for rejection related to the enablement requirement shall be overcome if the examiner determine that the claimed invention can be carried out by a person skilled in the art based on what is described in the specification and common general knowledge as of the filing, when the applicant presents literature that is clearly establishing the common general knowledge as of the filing in a written argument. The literature published after the filing may be also available if the contents of this literature clearly represents the common general knowledge as of the filing.

(5) What kind of factors may be taken into account in determining whether the experimentation required is undue (or unreasonable)?

The USPTO and the JPO point out the same several factors listed below;

— quantity of experimentation needed

— amount of direction or guidance given in the specification

— the presence or absence of working examples (showed only by the USPTO)

— the nature of the invention

— state of the prior art

— relative skill levels present in the technical area

— predictability of that particular art

— the breadth of the claims

The EPO explains that the sufficiency requirement would not be fulfilled if the successful performance of the invention is dependent on chance and is achieved in a totally unreliable way; however if repeated success is assured even though accompanied by a proportion of failures, this would not be considered as undue experimentation.

(6) Which one has the burden of giving reasons why the specification is (not) enabling, an examiner or an applicant?

The practices of the three Offices are common in that the initial burden of pointing out the reason of rejection is on the examiner. However, though the JPO and the EPO find that the burden of proof (the burden of persuasion) is finally on the applicant throughout prosecution, the USPTO must always shoulder the burden of proving that the specification is not enabled.

(7) Where there are well-founded reasons to believe that a skilled person would not be able to extend teaching of the description to the whole of the field claimed, what kind of evidences should an examiner prepare necessarily? Should such reasons be supported by a published document?

Please explain other examination practices related to "well-founded reasons" in detail, if any.

The USPTO explains that unpredictability in the art and lack of working examples are important in questioning whether the invention is enabled throughout the scope of the claim.

The EPO gives two examples that 1) a specific microorganism isolated by chance and not deposited is being claimed or 2) common general knowledge suggests a claimed invention would not be repeatable.

According to the answer of the JPO, among the concrete reasons is the reasoning that a skilled person would be unable to extend the particular enabling description in the detailed description of the invention to the whole of the field within the extent (or the metes and bounds) of the claimed invention.

Furthermore, the three Offices mention that the reasons of rejection should preferably be supported by reference documents.

(8) Where there was no variant of means to solve the problems in a claim other than the only one means used in the working example as of filing,

should functional expression be accepted taking into account the other later developed means to achieve the same effect?

The answers of the EPO and the JPO to this question are similar to the question 1.1.1.1(1).

In particular, the JPO states that, with respect to an application having a claim defined by a result to be achieved and a disclosure of only one specific means to achieve the result, the enablement requirement is judged regardless of the existence or absence of other later developed means.

On the other hand, the EPO points out that a claim may be allowed covering all means later developed if the invention is major one opening up a new field and the teaching of the invention leads the later development.

Also, the JPO shows that inventive step of the claimed invention which defines a product solely by a result to be achieved should be denied when the result to be achieved is a well-known technical problem and a certain product to be defined by the result is either known to or easy-to-invent to a person skilled in the art as of the filing, unless otherwise inventive step can be positively inferred by other facts, even if a specific means to solve the technical problem is not known as of the filing.

The USPTO states that such claims reciting means plus function are authorized, if the claim is drawn to a combination of elements.

Notes and Questions

1. In *Biogen*,[1] we observed a microbiological process for producing antigens that was based on repeated trial, and in *Mycogen*[2] we observed patent claims whose working may have required independent invention on the

---

[1] *See supra,* Ch. I, § B, 2, c.
[2] *See supra,* § D, 2.

part of persons reasonably skilled in the art. Consider these cases in the light of items 1, 5 and 7 above.

2. Based solely on the comparative analysis of patenting practices discussed above, do you think it might be feasible to harmonize the patenting practices of the United States, Europe and Japan? There are a number of similar studies being conducted by the USPTO, EPO and JPO. Might these studies provide the foundation for such harmonization efforts?

3. Be aware that the foregoing excerpts are limited to the non-technical aspects of this comparative report. The complete report is suffused with scientific/technical detail. The impression of similarity reflected in the excerpt may not be fully reflected at the technical level.

---

2. The Patent System of China

Over the past decade, most governments which had followed a central-planning economy model have moved toward a market economy model. Prior to this recent development, many of the centrally-planned and social-market economy countries maintained a variant of the patent system based on so-called "inventors' certificates." These certificates were granted to inventors as a form of reward for their contribution to society, and they generally entitled the inventor to some form of monetary (or standard of living) reward. At the same time, the government, as owner and manager of the means of production, exploited the invention. Inventors' certificate systems have been widely replaced, and are of interest today mainly from a historical perspective.

Since the late 1970s, China has been in the process of transforming from a centrally-planned economy country to a market economy country. As part of this transformation, China has gradually been implementing a system for the granting and enforcement of IPRs. The U.S. and other OECD governments have not always been satisfied with China's progress in this regard, though it may be worthwhile to note that there has never before been a comparable attempt to transform an economy of such size. The risks inherent in this process are substantial. (In Chapter VI we will examine the bilateral relationship between the United States and China.)

Gao Lulin was Commissioner of the China Patent Office. In the following article he describes China's new attitude toward IPRs protection, and the steps taken so far to implement a modern patent system.

China's Intellectual Property Protection System in Progress

Dr. Gao Lulin*

Since the opening-up and reform policy in the late 1970s, the system for the protection of the intellectual property has been gradually established in China. As the reform policy is further deepened and society strides forward, China has developed and improved the system for effective protection of intellectual property rights and the laws related to intellectual property. The enforcement procedures have been further enhanced and public awareness of the procedures is being promoted. The intellectual property protection system in China has developed rapidly over the decades. On the whole, due to the efforts and coordination of the administrative, legislative and judicial organs, it should be noted that China has come in line ahead of schedule with the international system for the protection of the intellectual property with respect to scope, standards and enforcement. The progress not only meets the needs of the reform and opening-up policy, but matches world economic development. What is more, it will also lead to the encouragement of inventive and creative activities, the promotion and application of inventions and creations, as well as scientific and technological progress, cultural prosperity and the development of the economy.

Since the implementation of the intellectual property system in China, great achievement has been made in patent, trademark, and cultural and artistic works, in particular patent which is closely connected to science and technology. In 1993, the Patent Law was revised, and in 1994, China acceded to the Patent Cooperation Treaty (PCT), which further perfected the patent system and resulted in the increase of patent applications. It is estimated that from 1982 to 1992, applications increased from over 10,000 to

---

*In China in the World Trading System 127 (F. M. Abbott ed. 1998).

67,000. In 1996, the Chinese Patent Office (CPO) received more than 102,000 patent applications. Among them, foreign applications increased from more than 4,900 in 1985 to over 20,000 in 1996. This indicates that the Chinese patent system not only encourages inventive and creative activities at home, but actively facilitates foreign applications, technology transfer and investment in China. Patents, in turn, have become the key stimulus in pushing forward the development of trade and economy.

Let me give you some statistics. The import and export volume in China increased from 20.6 billion USD in 1978 and 165.5 billion USD in 1992 to 289 billion USD in 1996, the average increase rate being 16.4% from 1991 to 1996. Imports and exports were balanced. The ranking in world trade was 32nd in 1978, 15th in 1992, and the 11th in 1996. It is worth mentioning that the export volume by foreign investment companies increased from 20.4% in 1992 to 40.6% in 1996. During that period, actual foreign capital worth 200 billion USD was invested. This ranks first among the developing countries with respect to annual investment, being the second after the USA. From the view point of economic growth, the GDP increased from 2166.25 billion RMB in 1991 to 6779.5 billion RMB in 1996; the annual growth rate was 12.1%. China was at that time the region with the fastest economic development in the world. It can be seen from the above statistics that as the national economy grew, the number of patent applications also increased. Though there is no doubt that many factors contributed to the rapid development of Chinese economy, the favorable legal situation for intellectual property assumes an ever-increasing importance in stimulating economic development.

I. Legal System for the Protection of Intellectual Property

Before 1985, the laws concerning intellectual property mainly covered trademarks (1982), patents (1984) and copyright in General Principles of Civil Law (1986). Generally speaking, protection for intellectual property was not highly guaranteed. In the field of international IP treaties China only acceded to the World Intellectual Property Organization (WIPO). In 12 years, a well-established system for the effective protection of intellectual property has come into being in China. China has become member of almost all the important international treaties and has met the requirements for the protection of intellectual property around the world. At present,

China plays a more important role in the international intellectual property system.

1. Revision of the Trademark and Patent Law and Enhancement of Protection

The problems arising out of the trademark and patent laws led to the revision of the laws in China. The revised trademark and patent laws came into force in 1993 and 1994 respectively. According to the revision, (1) the scope for protection has extended to service marks, chemical substances such as pharmaceuticals and agrochemicals, food, beverages, flavorings and microorganisms; (2) the term has extended from 15 years to 20 years for patents, 8 to 10 years for utility models and designs; (3) process patents have been extended to products directly made by the process; (4) protection has been enhanced to the extent that import right is included; (5) in the process patent case, where the product is new the burden of proof is reversed. . . .

2. Formulation of New IP Laws and Improvement of IP Protection

***** In 1997, "Regulations for the Protection of Plant Varieties" were promulgated in which for the first time the plant varieties are clearly protected. . . .

3. Fulfillment of Obligations under International IP Treaties

Since its accession to WIPO in 1980 and for the purpose of better meeting the needs of the opening-up and reform policy, China acceded to the "Paris Convention for the Protection of Industrial Property" in 1985, the "Berne Convention for the Protection of Literary and Artistic Works" in 1992, and "Universal Copyright Convention" in the same year. At present, China is member of almost all important international treaties related to intellectual property.

(1) China insistently commits itself to the obligations set fourth in the treaties of which China is a member. Wherever the international treaty contains provisions differing from those in civil laws, the provisions of the international treaty shall apply according to Article 142 of the "General

Principles of Civil Law". For instance, the Chinese "Regulations for the Protection of Computer Software" stipulate that registration of computer software is a condition precedent to initiation of any administrative dispute resolution or legal proceedings in China. Obviously, this is not in conformity with the Berne Convention's requirement. In this case, according to Article 142 of "General Principles of Civil Law", the foreigners may obtain protection for their computer software works without registration.

*****

(3) In order to simplify the procedures for international applications so that foreigners may apply for trademarks and patents in China, China acceded to the "Madrid Agreement Concerning the International Registration of Marks" in 1989; the "Protocol Relating to the Madrid Agreement" in 1995; the "Patent Cooperation Treaty" (PCT) on January 1, 1994; the "Budapest Treaty on the International Recognition of the Deposit of Microorganisms for the Purpose of Patent Procedure" in 1995. For PCT applications, CPO serves as the International Searching Authority and International Preliminary Examining Authority not only for Chinese but also for citizens of several other countries, and both Chinese and English can be used for application.

(4) The Chinese government has formally made the claim that after the return of Hong Kong on July 1, 1997, treaties such as the Paris Convention, the Berne Convention and PCT shall apply in Hong Kong.

(5) Though China is not member of World Trade Organization (WTO), China has always taken an active part in the international negotiations, but also looks at methods of implementation. With regard to the current mechanism for the protection of intellectual property, we have on the whole met the requirements set for the developing countries in TRIPS Agreement ahead of time. Meanwhile, China also participates actively in discussions for and the formulation of the new international treaties in the field of patent, trademark and copyright, and it has made significant contributions to the world in respect of international cooperation.

II. Enforcement of Intellectual Property

Although it is generally agreed that the legal system for the protection of intellectual property in China is acceptable, enforcement of IP law in

China is viewed differently, and has been subject to some harsh criticisms. The following will attempt to look at aspects of the enforcement.

1. Administrative Approach

In addition to judicial procedures similar to those of other nations, the relevant administrative organs in China have the right to settle the IP related civil disputes within the enforcement framework of IP. Administrative settlement is to be in accordance with civil procedures. In the case where IP disputes happen, the concerned parties may be faced with two choices of either asking for administrative settlement or taking an action before court. As far as the first choice is concerned, a party concerned may, within a limited time, apply for judicial procedures if he is not satisfied with the decision. The administrative approach is convenient, timesaving, and efficient, and it is therefore more acceptable. It is estimated that of more than 6,000 cases concerning patent disputes since 1985, half of them were settled through administrative action; of the copyright cases, more than half were settled by administrative action and on their own initiative; of the trademark cases, approximately 90% were administratively settled. The concerned parties in China have been faced with additional choices beyond the judicial one in settling disputes compared with the counterparts of the rest of the world.

2. Improved Remedies and Injunction

According to Chinese intellectual property laws, the administrative organs shall have the authority to stop the infringement and order infringers to pay compensation for damages in settling IP disputes. Moreover, the local branches of State Administration of Industry and Commerce and the copyright administrative organs are authorized to seize illegal income and fine the infringers. In addition to the above remedies, the courts may take other remedies like provisional or permanent injunctions upon the request of the applicant or at its own discretion.

The court shall have the authority to adopt provisional measures to preserve the relevant evidence in regard to infringement, in particular where any delay is likely to cause irreparable harm to the holder of the rights. According to Articles 92 and 93 of the Civil Procedures, the court shall have the right, upon the request of the applicant, to take the measure of property preservation. But in order to prevent abuse, the court shall require the applicant to provide security or equivalent assurance. When the party concerned does not apply, the court may upon its own initiative take the measure of property preservation. In order to improve the standard of settling IP disputes, the court also organized specialized groups. At present, IP tribunals have been established in over 20 higher and intermediate people's courts, responsible for the settlement of IP related infringements.

3. Severe Criminal Penalties

According to Chinese IP laws, criminal penalties may be imposed for severe infringement in addition to the civil remedies. The new Criminal Law which came into force on October 1, 1997, provides for imprisonment together with fines, of which the highest imprisonment has been raised from previous 5 years to 7 years for counterfeiting and piracy, the highest for patent infringement being 3 years, and 7 years for infringing business secrets.

4. Efficient Border Measures

On July 5, 1995, the "Regulations Concerning the Protection of IP in Customs" were issued in China. These are characterized by three features: (1) The scope for seizures includes not only counterfeit and pirated products but infringing patent products; (2) both imports and exports are inspected; (3) this can be done either by Custom's authority or upon the request of the applicant. Since the implementation of the regulations until the end of 1996, more than 700 cases had been stopped, of which 18% related to foreign holder of rights; 56% related to export; 93% by Customs own authority; of the infringed products, 94% are pirated products, 5% counterfeited, 1% patent infringing products.

5. Irregular Raids on the Market

With the joint efforts of the administrative, inspection and security authorities, irregular raids on the market are organized each year to seize pirated and counterfeit products. For two years, more than 4,000 places were closed down for showing illegal video compact disks. Over 10 assembly lines producing illegal disk were closed, and millions of various illegal pirated and counterfeited products were destroyed.

It should be pointed out that not only do the principles and measures in the enforcement of Chinese IP accord with IP Enforcement in Part III, General Obligations in Chapter 1 and Article 41 of TRIPS Agreement, but in some aspects are more strict and concrete. Therefore it is more efficient. However, due to the large population and unbalanced development of economy and culture in different regions, as well as the short period of implementation of the IP system in China, there might be some infringement cases, which is unavoidable for the moment. Chinese administrative, legislative and judicial organs are fully aware of the importance for the effective protection of the intellectual property. It is my sincere belief that through constant efforts, the IP system will be better improved and people will highly realize the importance of IP. The problems will be finally solved.

III. Future Tasks

We are now coming into the 21st century and we are faced with challenges in the new century: (1) the liberalization and globalization of world trade will lead to the inevitable dependence upon the progress of science and technology as well as knowledge of intellectual property; (2) this also requires the establishment of unified standards and efficient enforcement systems for the protection of intellectual property and; (3) the new technology revolution symbolized by information technology will bring us new challenges in two ways. On the one hand, new issues will arise for the protection of intellectual property; on the other hand, the application of new information technology will improve the infrastructure of the patent, administration of trademarks, searching and communication, etc. In order to meet the challenge of the 21st century, we face with the following tasks:

1. Continuous Improvement of IP Legislation

*****China plans to adapt itself to the requirements of the world by revising its patent and trademark laws to simplify the procedures for the applicants and improve efficiency. In addition, where the Internet is widely used, it could become the key issue to further perfect the copyright law and settle the problems for the protection of the IP arising from rapid development of information technology. In this event, China will cooperate with the rest of the world to jointly solve the problems by research and formulation of new international laws. In summary, we will meet all the requirements set out in the TRIPS Agreement for the protection of the intellectual property and we will actively participate in the new international treaties for the harmonization of IP standards.

2. Automation Plan for Patent

Before the year 2000, China plans to cooperate with the rest of the world for patent automation to solve the issues of searching, examination process management, and electronic applications and publications. Through joint efforts across the world, we will solve the problem of electronic information transmission with WIPO and other large patent offices. The Chinese Patent Office plans to finish the automation of the office by the year 1998 to meet international standards using governmental loans from Germany in cooperation with EPO (European Patent Office) and with the help of JPO (Japan Patent Office) and USPTO.

3. Strategic Position of the Development of Human Resources

Innovation is the soul of a nation's advance and the eternal driving force for national prosperity. A highly qualified innovative group should be trained for the purpose of innovation and protection of intellectual property. Under these circumstances, the Chinese Patent Office was authorized to establish China Intellectual Property Training Center in Beijing, with the aim to train service personnel in the fields of administration, enforcement, judiciary, examination, as well as agents and lawyers. We hope to make the center a Regional Center of World-Wide WIPO Academy to train the personnel specialized in IP for Asia and the rest of developing countries. At the same time, with the challenge of the 21st century, we will not only disseminate the IP knowledge, but also improve the awareness of people of intellectual property through the mass media. Generally speaking, the training of personnel is the key factor through which the future needs can be met and the new issues in the field of the intellectual property can be then settled.

4. Further Strengthening International Cooperation in the field of IP

We can never forget the speech by Mr. Bogsch, Director-General of WIPO for almost 25 years. He said: "Human genius is the source of all works of art and inventions. These works are the guarantee of a life worthy of men. It is the duty of the state to ensure with diligence the protection of the arts and inventions". We also realize that the protection of intellectual property is far beyond the limit of a nation and that it has become a common issue for the whole world. However, from another point of view, due to unbalanced development, there is still a big gap among the developed countries, developing countries and the transitional countries, which in turn leads to differences in the protection standards of intellectual property. There is still a long way to go to reach common standards of protection all over the world. We shall continue to cooperate with the rest of the world in the field of the personnel training, application of information technology, automatization, legislation for the protection of IP and implementation of the TRIPS Agreement. China is much concerned in this respect, and is willing to further strengthen its cooperation with other countries. In the past, China has received much help from other nations. Now it is willing to make every effort to offer help to other developing countries in this field so as to share the efforts for effective protection of intellectual property.

Conclusion

China is the biggest developing country in the world. For decades since the reform and opening-up policy, not only have we created the miracle of annual economic growth of 10%, but much has been achieved for the protection of the intellectual property. In order to meet the challenges of the 21st century, we will on the one hand continue to well protect intellectual property; on the other hand, we hope to continue to develop and maintain good relationships with friendly countries to promote cooperation in the international intellectual property field and create a better and beautiful world.

Notes and Questions

1. For inventors of new products and processes, the opportunity to obtain a patent monopoly in a market of 1.2 billion consumers should prove attractive. For the time being, the challenge for inventors entering the Chinese market lies not so much in securing a patent as in enforcing it. China's law enforcement system as a whole is at an early stage of development as compared with the systems of Europe and the United States, and it should perhaps not be surprising that the system for enforcing patents is weak.

2. It has been suggested that a number of countries which rapidly industrialized over the past few decades used their patent systems as a tool to extract technology from foreign inventors, without offering them meaningful protection. The governments of these countries instead encouraged local enterprises to exploit foreign technology. There is no reason to believe that the Chinese government intends to pursue this route and to discriminate in favor of local enterprises. It is certain that industry groups in other countries will be paying close attention to the way in which the Chinese patent system is administered.

3. The Japanese Patent Experience

The patent law was one of the very first laws that China adopted after espousing an open-door policy. The patent law preceded most of the laws that together lay the foundation for the economic and commercial development of a country. Compare, in this respect, the approach of China to that of Japan, one century earlier following the Meiji Restoration, as described in the following excerpt.

Japanese Experience of the Relation Between
Industrial Property and Development

Guntram Rahn*

I. Historical Development

1. The Meiji Period (1868-1911)

(a) Industrial Development

The year 1868 in Japanese history is commonly known in the West as the year of the Meiji Restoration, that is, the return to Imperial rule under the Emperor Meiji. In Japan, however, it is known as *Meiji ishin* (literally, Meiji Renovation) and this justly emphasizes the innovating policies which were adopted at that time and which were to make the country change more profoundly than it had done during the preceding millennium.

A period of sweeping reforms and extensive modernization began. Taking the United States and Europe as their model, the Japanese embarked on a feat of learning by borrowing, which gave new opportunities to their traditional eagerness for foreign ideas.

At this time, what now has become a fixed tradition was started on a grand scale: young Japanese by the thousands were sent to study abroad (*ryugaku*). They studied American railways, British textiles and metallurgy, French and German law, German military sciences.

On the other hand, hundreds of foreigners came to Japan — as technical experts hired by the new Government, as foreign traders, as missionaries and educators. Already by 1876 some 400 foreigners (*o-yatoi gaikokujin*) were in the service of the Japanese Government. British technicians built pilot factories and trained the Navy, German advisers helped draft the Constitution and staffed the new medical schools. A French jurist was responsible for the Criminal Code. Americans took a hand in everything from agricultural science to seismology. However, these foreigners were always dismissed as soon as the Japanese were able to do without them.

---

*WIPO-CEIPI/IP/SB/88/3, Sept. 1988.

It was also the policy of the Government virtually to exclude foreign business investment, except in trading activity. Only after the turn of the century was there a small amount of foreign investment in the equipment industries, where, however, they played a strategic role in technology transfer out of proportion to their size.

Moreover, Western imports of a great variety of goods were not only put to their intended use in Japanese industry, but also served as transmitters of ideas. Thus, although annual imports of machinery, instruments and vehicles never even reached ten per cent of Japan's total imports, this gives no measure of their catalytic effect on development. New, small Japanese industries sprang up on every side to copy foreign goods—soap, matches, shoes, umbrellas and the like. "The foreign mania raged everywhere," says one official report, "and everything was manufactured in imitation of foreign articles."

Japan's technological learning method during these decades thus generally began with the imported product, which after some time was copied, usually resulting in inferior quality, and then improved upon as experience grew. In the meantime imports would change to finer grades and specialities, and finally be replaced entirely.

It was the growth mainly of Japan's agriculture, and also that of other basic industries, through a steady process of modernization, that provided the rising national income to carry the country through these first stages of economic development. The eighteen-nineties finally marked a turning point in the evolution of the Japanese economy. An industrial system began to take shape. Two victorious wars, the Sino-Japanese war of 1894-1895 and the Russo-Japanese war of 1904-1905 lent additional impetus to development in transport, banking and strategic industries.

At the end of the Meiji Period Japan was only a third-rate industrial nation by world standards. But its development continued and it had already made substantial progress, which was already apparent in national income and political power.

(b) Industrial Property Development

The first legal system Japan introduced from the West was the patent system. As early as 1867, Yukichi Fukuzawa, an influential and widely read proponent of Western civilization, reported the existence of such things as patents in one of his travelogues, and other authors soon emphatically rec-ommended that Japan should have them too.

The Meiji government lost no time. In 1871, only three years after the Restoration, it introduced the Summary Rules of Monopoly, (*Sembai ryaku kisoku*), a code of 19 articles, which began with the words, "He who makes a new invention of anything whatsoever, will from that time on receive per-mission to sell it exclusively."

However, this enthusiastic attempt at introducing patents was doomed to failure. It proved impossible to create a functioning patent system out of nothing by just promulgating a law. Although patents were to be granted upon examination, there was no competent authority or qualified person-nel to prosecute applications. And since the turnabout from prohibition of innovation under the Tokugawa to encouragement of invention under Meiji had come so fast, the new system seemed to be beyond the compre-hension of the people at that time. In any event, when there had not been a single application for a patent in a whole year, the Summary Rules of Mo-nopoly were repealed.

It was 13 years before the second try at introducing the patent system in Japan was made. But the era was still one in which machinery, technol-ogy and know-how were freely available from the advanced industrial na tions. Business came first for the West, and the lack of an industrial property system meant that there was nothing to inhibit the influx of im-ports into Japan.

Japan's history of industrial property law got off to a successful start when in 1874 an American named Morley, who was in the service of the Japanese Government as an advisor to the Ministry of Education, lectured a young Government official on the "three intellectual properties." "Inven tions, trademarks, and copyright," he said, "are the most prized properties in the United States."

The young Government official, by the name of Korekiyo Takahashi, was to become the founder of the Japanese industrial property system. Takahashi was immediately fascinated by the idea of intellectual property, began to study it, and enthusiastically promoted its cause. This extraordi-nary man almost single-handedly devised Japan's first effective industrial property laws. At 32 he was appointed Director General of the newly estab-lished Japanese Patent Office. He later served also as Finance Minister and Prime Minister. From a very early date Takahashi held the firm conviction that the industrial property system was indispensable for Japan's rise to the position of great industrial power. The most splendid and imposing Government building of the Meiji Period, which housed the Ministry of Agriculture and Commerce, had actually been designed by him to become the Japanese Patent Office building. "It must come to pass that, when people visit Tokyo," he is said to have remarked once, "second only to the Asakusa Temple they will want to see the Patent Office." Today, a hundred years later, Takahashi's wish seems to be coming true.

After extensive preparations by Takahashi, the Patent Monopoly Ordinance (*Sembai Tokkyo Jorei*) was finally promulgated on April 18, 1885. That day is commemorated as Invention Day (*Hatsumei no hi*) in Japan today. The Ordinance was modeled on American and French law. Four hundred and twenty-five applications were filed in its first year and 99 patents granted. In 1886 already, 1,384 applications were filed and 205 patents granted.

Preceding the Patent Law by a year, the first Japanese trademark law, the Trademark Ordinance (*Shohyo Jorei*), was promulgated in 1884. The copying of foreign goods in Japan did not stop short of trademarks, and this had led to trouble when the imitations were exported. The German first-to-register principle was embodied in the new law, and thus imitators could at least legalize their practice in Japan by having the foreign trademarks registered in their name.

In 1888 the first ordinances were replaced by improved patent and trademark laws. The grant of a patent, which before was considered to be an act of grace, was now recognized as the subject of a right. Also in 1888, because of the increase export of Japanese handicraft articles, a Design Ordinance (*Isho Jorei*), modeled on English law, was promulgated. At that time, foreigners were barred from obtaining industrial property rights. There was some fear in Japan that, if they were allowed to obtain patents, the development of Japanese industry would be obstructed, but the Patent Office under Korekiyo Takahashi called this a cowardly attitude not befitting the promotion of innovation. Meanwhile, the Paris Convention for the Protection of Industrial Property had entered into force in 1883, and foreign governments were beginning to press Japan to open its industrial property system to foreigners and become party to the Convention.

The access of foreigners to industrial property thus became a bargaining factor in Japan's endeavors to bring about revision of the "Unequal Treaties" of 1858. The Tokugawa had signed treaties with the Western Powers which excluded their nationals from Japanese jurisdiction and imposed a tariff limit of 5 per cent on imports. The repeal of these "humiliating" treaties was one of the overriding political objectives of the Meiji State during its early decades. Only when this objective was realized in 1899 were foreigners finally admitted to the Japanese industrial property system, and Japan became party to the Paris Convention in the same year. Foreigners filed 224 applications for patents in 1899, and 98 patents were granted to them.

With Japan's industry burgeoning at the turn of the century, a need was felt to protect also the numerous "small innovations," which were not patentable because of their low inventive level. Thus a Utility Model Law, inspired by the German *Gebrauchsmustergesetz*, was enacted in 1905. It became an immediate success, with 2,011 applications filed in its first year, 7,952 in the second, and 14,057 in 1909.

The additional impetus given to economic development by the Russo-Japanese War in 1909 led to a revision of the now complete set of four industrial property laws, the patent law, the utility model law, the design law and the trademark law. In the patent law, a section on employee inventions was introduced for the first time, stating that the right to the patent belonged to the employer.

Notes and Questions

1. What conclusions about the Japanese experience is Rahn suggesting? The Japanese economy remained largely agriculture-based throughout much of the Nineteenth Century, but it fairly rapidly evolved into a burgeoning industrial one at the beginning of the Twentieth Century. According to Rahn, the transition is more or less coincident with Japan's introduction of an effective patent system and other IPRs rules. Would you conclude that the introduction of a patent system led to the rapid industrialization of Japan? Does this validate China's decision to introduce a patent system early in its market opening process?

2. It is not infrequently suggested that Japan's rapid re-industrialization after 1945 was aided by the acquisition of foreign technology on terms that

were very favorable to Japan. If a country's economic development is undermined by political events, does this justify a temporary respite from providing patent protection at the same level as other countries? Is there anything in the TRIPS Agreement that might provide a basis for different levels of protection, or a mechanism for acquiring technology other than on usual commercial terms, in such circumstances?

H. International Copyright Norms

International norms on copyright are rooted in the Berne Convention for the Protection of Literary and Artistic Work, dating back in its initial form to 1886. The main substantive provisions of the Berne Convention were supplemented by the copyright provisions of the TRIPS Agreement, which incorporates by reference the Berne text. In addition to the TRIPS Agreement, the so-called "neighboring rights" to copyright are the subject of several separate international agreements, including the Rome Convention for the Protection of Performers, Producers of Phonograms and Broadcasting Organisations and the Geneva Convention for the Protection of Producers of Phonograms Against Unauthorized Duplication of Their Phonograms. Neighboring rights subject matter that is covered by the Rome and Geneva Conventions is the subject of new rules of the TRIPS Agreement. Moreover, subsequent to entry into force of the TRIPS Agreement, two important new treaties — the WIPO Copyright Treaty and the WIPO Performances and Phonograms Treaty — were concluded.[1] These treaties supplement the rules of the Berne and Rome Conventions. One objective of the negotiators of these new treaties was to create consistency between WTO and WIPO rules. The new WIPO treaties also create rules for the "digital environment"which are not found in the TRIPS Agreement. This is a complex system of agreements.

As with other areas of international IPRs regulation, the rules of the Berne Convention, TRIPS Agreement and other multilateral treaties are transformed into regional, national and subnational law, and in this process are often supplemented by additional rules.

The following excerpt provides a historical perspective on international copyright protection, including the background of the Berne Con-

---

[1]As of April 1999 these two treaties had not yet entered into force.

vention negotiations. It is of some interest that a number of the countries which today are the main advocates of strong copyright protection went through long periods as copyright "pirates." These countries discovered the virtues of copyright protection only after developing a strong local creative community interested in securing copyright protection abroad. The United States maintained a "manufacturing clause" in its copyright statute and effectively offered copyright protection only to materials printed in the United States until the 1950s.[2]

The Birth of the Berne Union

Sam Ricketson*

We are celebrating today the centenary of the first true multilateral convention on copyright, the Berne Convention for the Protection of Literary and Artistic Works. I use the adjective "true" advisedly, as prior to the Berne Convention there had been other multilateral conventions on copyright. However, these had been of limited territorial effect and had been entered into in order to overcome particular political problems, such as those that existed in Germany and Italy prior to the unification of those countries. The Berne Convention, on the other hand, was open to all states without restriction, as long as they were prepared to comply with the obligations embodied therein. It is also important to see the Convention in a broader context as it was only one of series of impressive multilateral conventions that came into existence during this period. Of these, the International Telegraph Convention, the Universal Postal Convention, and, of course, the Paris Convention for the Protection of Industrial Property still remain in force today. The Berne Convention, then, can be seen as a manifestation of

---

[2]*See* Hamish R. Sandison, *The Berne Convention and the Universal Copyright Convention: The American Experience, in* THE CENTENARY OF THE BERNE CONVENTION, CONFERENCE, at 11-22 at 11-22 (Intellectual Property Law Unit, Queen Mary College, University of London and British Literary and Artistic Copyright Association, London, April 17-18, 1986).
*In THE CENTENARY OF THE BERNE CONVENTION, CONFERENCE (Intellectual Property Law Unit, Queen Mary College, University of London and British Literary and Artistic Copyright Association London, April 17-18, 1986).

a period when human society was attempting, in a high-minded but practical spirit, to bring about change and development across a whole range of matters through international cooperation. While most of this conference will be devoted to the present status and future prospects of this Convention, my task here is to outline the circumstances and events that led to its formation. In 1886, most national copyright laws were not much more than a few decades old. The United Kingdom was, of course, an exception as it had enacted the first modern copyright statute as far back as 1709 (the "Act of Anne"). The scope of this Act was quite limited, and it was restricted to books, but during the next hundred years protection was extended in piecemeal fashion to other kinds of works, including engravings, sculptures and dramatic works. In most other European countries, however, the situation as regarded the protection of authors was similar to that which had obtained in the United Kingdom prior to 1709: there was no express recognition of authors' rights, and the only protection available was that accorded through the grant of privileges or monopolies for the printing of particular books. These privileges were usually granted by governments to publishers and printers, rather than authors. It is ironic, perhaps, that we should today be meeting in the Hall of the Stationers' Company as this was the trade association whose members traditionally exercised the printing monopolies that were granted by the Crown in the sixteenth and seventeenth centuries in this country. A similar situation prevailed for longer in most European countries, in particular France, the German and Italian states and Spain. Even in this country, the members of the Stationers' Company strove long and hard throughout the eighteenth century to retain their traditional privileges with respect to the printing of books. Thus, it was not until the end of that century that it was firmly established that the rights accorded under the Act of Anne were authors' rights, rather than publishers' or printers' rights. In France, on the other hand, completely new ground was broken when the ancien regime was swept away by the Revolution of 1789. The rights of man, now enshrined in the new revolutionary laws, were soon recognised to include the rights of authors in their works. A Law of 1791 therefore accorded an exclusive right of public performance to the authors of dramatic and musical works for a period lasting five years after their deaths. A second Law of 1793 granted, in respect of all works, what we would now call an "exclusive reproduction right", enduring for the life of the author. There was a conscious philosophical basis to these laws that was lacking in the Act of Anne, in that the former conceived of the rights of authors as being rooted in natural law, with the consequence that these laws were simply according formal recognition to rights that were already in existence. In the years following the French Revolution this new conception of authors' rights spread to other continental European countries, in particular Belgium, the Netherlands and the Italian states. It also influenced the adoption of copyright laws in the various German states after the dissolution of the Holy Roman Empire brought an end to the system of imperial privileges that had formerly applied in those states. Other European countries followed suit, and by 1886 almost all the European states, including the newly unified states of Italy and Germany, had enacted their own copyright laws. Outside of Europe, the United States had had a copyright law since 1791, and laws on copyright were to be found in seven other states of Latin America. A number of other countries, such as Greece, Bulgaria and Turkey, protected authors' rights in a partial or incidental fashion through provisions in their general civil, criminal or press laws.

Many of these new laws drew on the models provided by the two French Laws of 1791 and 1793, although it should be noted that French copyright law continued to develop rapidly throughout the nineteenth century and to do so as much through the jurisprudence as through legislative enactments. Nevertheless, while the principal issues addressed by national laws were the same, the solutions adopted were often quite different. Most laws extended protection to a wide range of productions of a literary and artistic character, including works intended for public presentation, such as musical and dramatic works. But some categories of works, such as architectural, oral and choreographic works, were protected only in a few countries, and there were widely differing approaches to the protection of photographic works. Great diversity also existed in relation to the matter of duration of protection. In two Latin American countries, Guatemala and Mexico, this was perpetual, but in all other countries protection was limited in time. This was usually for a period comprising the life of the author together with a fixed period after his death. France had led the way here with a post mortem autoris term of 50 years, but 1879 Spain adopted a period of 80 years, and other nations had terms ranging between 5 and 50. A few other countries, such as the United States of America had terms that were not fixed to the life of the author, and some, including the United Kingdom, accorded different terms of protection to different categories of works. Finally, in Italy there was a system of paying public domain, under which works were protected absolutely for a given period (the author's life or 40 years after publication), and this was followed by a further period of 40 years during which the work might be used by third parties subject to a payment of a compulsory royalty to the author.

The rights protected under these early national laws also varied considerably although the principal ones recognised were those of reproduction and public performance. The right to make translations was recognised to differing degrees and was often of far shorter duration than the other rights, particularly in case of foreign authors. The scope of the reproduction right was also variously interpreted: some countries, for example, did not consider that artistic work in one dimension was infringed by the making of a reproduction in another dimension and the matter of adaptation of works was treated in widely different ways. Again, the reproduction of musical works by mechanical devices, such as piano rolls and music boxes, was not considered as an infringement in certain countries. Most national laws recognised exceptions and limitations to the exercise of rights, for example, for educational or religious purposes, but once again, there were great variations here. Finally, most laws required that the author comply with some kind of formality before protection would be accorded. The nature and effect of these formalities differed widely from country to country, but the chief ones were registration, the deposit of copies and the making of declarations. In some cases, failure to comply with formalities was fatal, meaning that the work fell into the public domain; in other cases, it meant merely that the copyright owner was unable to enforce his rights until he rectified the omission. By 1886, only a few countries, including Belgium, Germany and Switzerland (but not France), had abolished formalities altogether.

*****

The above sketch has concentrated on the contents of national copyright laws in the pre-1886 period. However, it will be clear that there is an equally important international dimension to the protection of authors' works. Literary and artistic works and musical compositions recognise no national boundaries, even where translation into another language is required for a work to be fully appreciated in a particular country. Thus it was that after the need for protection of authors by national laws had been recognised, the works of these authors still remained vulnerable to copying and exploitation abroad. These activities, commonly referred to as " piracy", had been a long-established feature of European social and cultural life, and this continued to be the case for a considerable time after the enactment of national copyright laws. The attitudes of many countries to these practices were highly anomalous: whilst prepared to protect their own authors, they did not always regard the piracy of foreign authors' works as unfair or immoral. Some countries, in fact, openly countenanced piracy as contributing to their educational and social needs and as reducing the prices of books for their citizens. The particular victims of these practices were the United Kingdom and France. During the eighteenth century English authors suffered from the activities of Irish pirates who could flood both the English and other markets with cheap reprints; after the Act of Union with Ireland in 1800, the chief threat came from the publishing houses of the United States and this continued to be a major problem for the rest of the century. French authors, in turn, suffered from the activities of pirates located in Switzerland, Germany, Holland, and, in particular, Belgium. By the early nineteenth century, Brussels was a major centre for the piracy of French books, and this led to considerable strains in the relations between France and Belgium. Piracy was likewise rampant between the different German and Italian states.

This widespread piracy of foreign works was the principal reason for the development of international copyright relations in the mid-nineteenth century. The arguments that raged both for and against the protection of foreign authors at this time have a surprisingly modern ring to them. On the one hand, it could be said that the activities of the pirates resulted in cheaper copies and the greater availability of the work in question. In countries hungry for knowledge and enlightenment, this could only be to the advantage of the public interest and this, indeed, was the reason for the persistent refusal of the United States to protect foreign works throughout the nineteenth century. On the other hand the moral and practical arguments in the author's favour were obvious: not only was he being robbed of the fruits of his creativity, but this would discourage him from continuing to create, with resultant loss to his own, and other, countries.

It is hard to identify the point at which a country no longer sees advantage in the piracy of foreign works, and decides to extend protection to the authors of such works. It may be that the activities of its own authors have increased, and that the latter now desire protection for their own works abroad. It may also be that, after a while, a country wishes to obtain some kind of international respectability, and to avoid the opprobrium of being labelled as a nation of pirates. Another factor may be that countries with large literary and artistic outputs bring pressure to bear on their more recalcitrant neighbours, promising various forms of trade advantage in return for copyright protection for their authors. Finally, pirate nations may come to recognise that the rights of authors in their works are of a proprietary nature, and that they should therefore be protected internationally in the same way as other property of foreigners. All these factors were certainly applicable in the case of Belgium, which, in the mid-nineteenth century, switched suddenly from being the chief centre of piracy for French works to being one of the most zealous defenders of authors' rights. The same factors applied to many other countries as they began to enter into international copyright relations with each other. Indeed, agreements between states and the formal sanctions of copyright law were not always necessary to achieve protection for foreign authors, at least in a limited form, as systems of "courtesy" copyright operated with some effect during this time and sometimes predated formal international agreements. This was particularly so in the United States, where the major publishing houses observed an unwritten custom whereby each would refrain from publishing editions of foreign works in respect of which another had reached a publishing agreement with the author. This system of mutual self-restraint had several advantages for the parties concerned: it protected the first American publisher of a foreign work from the unfettered copying of his edition, and gave the author the opportunity of earning some remuneration, even if he were unable to prevent the American publication of his work in the first place. As a consequence, authors such as Dickens and Trollope received large sums in respect of the American sales of their works, although they did not enjoy protection under United States copyright law.

"Courtesy copyright", however, is only a partial substitute for full copyright protection, and, in any case, it was not really of great significance outside the American market. Many European countries therefore began to take more formal steps to secure the protection of their authors abroad. In a bold move in 1852, France passed a decree extending the protection of its laws to all works published abroad, irrespective of whether the law of the country in question accorded corresponding protection to the works of French authors. This measure was consistent with the philosophical basis of French copyright law, according to which authors' rights, being natural rights of property, should not be subject to artificial restraints such as nationality and political boundaries. Nevertheless, a practical motivation also lay behind the decree. Up to this time, France had found other nations reluctant to enter agreements for the protection of French works on a reciprocal basis. She therefore hoped that unilateral grant of protection to authors from these countries in France would "shame" them into responding in like manner. Whether or not there is a causal connection is hard to say, but the fact remains that after 1852 the blockage cleared, and France entered agreement with a large number of other nations under which each agreed to accord protection to the works of the other.

Bilateral copyright agreements of this kind had, in fact, become quite common by the middle of the century. The first country to enter such agreements was the Kingdom of Prussia which made 32 of these with the other German states in the years 1827 to 1829. The basis of these agreements was simple or formal reciprocity, under which each state undertook to accord to the works of the other state the same treatment that it accorded to its own works (the principle of "national treatment"). These early German agreements, however, were of a special character, as their purpose was to fill the gap left by the failure of the legislature of the Germanic Confederation to enact a federal copyright law. Subsequent bilateral agreements between fully autonomous states tended to include more substantive provisions embodying common rules that each country undertook to apply to the works of the other, in addition to the basic principle of national treatment. The basis of these agreements thus came closer to what is called "material" or substantive reciprocity under which there is approximate parity between the level of protection accorded by each state to the works of the other. The first example of such a treaty was that between Austria and the Kingdom of Sardinia in May 1840, and France and the United Kingdom, the two leading literary countries of the period, were not far behind. By 1886, there was an intricate network of bilateral copyright conventions in force between the majority of European states, as well as with several Latin American countries. Of these, France was party to the most agreements (13), followed closely by Belgium (9), Italy and Spain (8 each), the United Kingdom (5) and Germany (5).

The basis of the majority of these conventions was national treatment, but, as stated above, they also contained a number of common rules which each country undertook to apply in its protection of works from the other country. There was usually a statement of the categories of works covered by the agreement, and specific provision was generally made for the protection of translation and performing rights. Restrictions in respect of particular kinds of use were also often allowed relating, for example, to education or the reproduction of newspaper articles. The scope and detail of these provisions differed considerably from one convention to another, but the most "advanced", in terms of protection of authors' interests, were to be found in the conventions made by France, Germany and Italy in the early 1880s. With regard to duration of protection, most of the pre-1886 conventions required material reciprocity, providing that country A was not obliged to protect the works of country B for any longer period than that accorded by state B to its own works, and in any event for no longer than country A protected its own nationals.

There were wider discrepancies with respect to formalities: under some conventions, compliance with the formalities of the country of origin of the work was sufficient to obtain protection in the other state; in other conventions, it was necessary for an author to comply with the formalities of both states. Matters were further complicated by the fact that the duration of many conventions was uncertain, in that they were linked to some wider treaty of trade or commerce between the countries in question and might suddenly fall to the ground if the latter was revoked or renegotiated. Another source of uncertainty arose from the insertion of "most favoured nation" clauses in many copyright conventions. The effect of these was that the contracting parties agreed to admit each other to the benefits that might be accorded to a third state under another treaty that was made by one of them with that state. The effect of such clauses was that a copyright convention between countries A and B might be abrogated, in whole or in part, by the terms of another convention made by either country A or B with country C if this agreement contained additional measures for the protection of copyright. While these clauses did not mean any loss or protection for authors, they obviously made it difficult for an author from country A to know, at any one time, what level of protection he was entitled to in country B, and vice versa.

It will be clear that this network of bilateral agreements meant that there was little uniformity in the protection that an author might expect to receive in countries other than his own. As far as Europe was concerned, the threat posed by international piracy earlier in the century had largely disappeared by 1886, but quite a number of European states still remained reluctant to enter bilateral agreements on copyright. These included the Scandinavian countries, the Netherlands, Greece, the newly independent Balkan states, and, most importantly, the Russian and Austro-Hungarian empires. Outside Europe, much of the world's surface was then controlled by one of the chief European colonial powers. Of those states which were independent, very few had entered any international copyright agreements, and many, in fact, had no internal copyright laws. The most important of these countries was the United States, which throughout the nineteenth century continued to be a major centre for pirated works and resisted efforts by other countries, in particular the United Kingdom, to draw it into bilateral agreements. Several such attempts were made, but the vested interests of publishers and printers, on the one hand, and the voracious appetite for cheap books from the rapidly growing American population, on the other, doomed them to failure.

* * * * *

In the light of the above, it was not surprising that moves for a more widely based and uniform kind of international copyright protection began in the middle of the nineteenth century.

Notes and Questions

1. The early forms of protection granted for books and other printed material were generally in favor of publishers, and not in favor of authors. Today the largest streams of copyright revenue flow to the producers of films and television programs like Walt Disney and General Electric, and to the large publishing houses like Time-Warner. The rights of authors are certainly the subject of copyright protection, yet have the basic economics of the copyright industries changed very much from the Middle Ages?

2. Is it possible that the Internet and related digital delivery systems will allow authors to bypass large producer/publishers and benefit more directly from their creative acts? If booksellers like Amazon.com already index and allow book buyers to search for copyrighted material in cyberspace, how far is it to routine text delivery (including at-home or office printout systems) over the Web? Will producers and publishers be needed in this new digital environment? Are we in the midst of the next French Revolution in copyright?

3. Consider the copyright "pirates" of today's China and the copyright pirates of the Industrial Age in the United States. British publishers were unhappy with American pirates in 1870, and U.S. publishers are unhappy with Chinese pirates in 1998. Did the American pirates have a better justification for their conduct than the Chinese pirates?

I. The Berne Convention

1. Terms of the Berne Convention

Next is a description of the terms of the Berne Convention by the International Bureau of WIPO. After this description, the text of relevant provisions of the Berne Convention are set out, followed by Notes and Questions.

International Protection of Copyright and Neighboring Rights
Berne Convention
for the Protection of Literary and Artistic Works (1886)

International Bureau of WIPO*

The Convention, concluded in 1886, was revised at Paris in 1896 and at Berlin in 1908, completed at Berne in 1914, revised at Rome in 1928, at Brussels in 1948, at Stockholm in 1967 and at Paris in 1971, and was amended in 1979.**

---

*http://www.wipo.int (Footnote references are renumbered).
**The following 138 States were party to this Convention on April 1, 1999:
Albania, Algeria, Argentina, Australia, Austria, Azerbaijan, Bahamas, Bahrain, Bangladesh, Barbados, Belarus, Belgium, Benin, Bolivia, Bosnia and Herzegovina, Botswana, Brazil, Bulgaria, Burkina Faso, Cameroon, Canada, Cape Verde, Central African Republic, Chad, Chile, China, Colombia, Congo, Costa Rica, Côte d'Ivoire, Croatia, Cuba, Cyprus, Czech Republic, Democratic Republic of the Congo, Denmark, Dominican Republic, Ecuador, Egypt, El Salvador, Equatorial Guinea, Estonia, Fiji, Finland, France, Gabon, Gambia, Georgia, Germany, Ghana, Greece, Grenada, Guatemala, Guinea, Guinea-Bissau, Guyana, Haiti, Holy See, Honduras, Hungary, Iceland, India, In-

The Convention is open to all States. Instruments of ratification or accession must be deposited with the Director General of WIPO.[1]

The Convention rests on three basic principles and contains a series of provisions determining the minimum protection to be granted, as well as special provisions available to developing countries which want to make use of them.

(1) The three basic principles are the following:

(a) Works originating in one of the contracting States (that is, works the author of which is a national of such a State or works which were first published in such a State) must be given the same protection in each of the other contracting States as the latter grants to the works of its own nationals (principle of "national treatment").[2]

---

donesia, Ireland, Israel, Italy, Jamaica, Japan, Kazakhstan, Kenya, Kyrgyzstan, Latvia, Lebanon, Lesotho, Liberia, Libya, Liechtenstein, Lithuania, Luxembourg, Madagascar, Malawi, Malaysia, Mali, Malta, Mauritania, Mauritius, Mexico, Monaco, Mongolia, Morocco, Namibia, Netherlands, New Zealand, Niger, Nigeria, Norway, Oman, Pakistan, Panama, Paraguay, Peru, Philippines, Poland, Portugal, Republic of Korea, Republic of Moldova, Romania, Russian Federation, Rwanda, Saint Kitts and Nevis, Saint Lucia, Saint Vincent and the Grenadines, Senegal, Singapore, Slovakia, Slovenia, South Africa, Spain, Sri Lanka, Suriname, Swaziland, Sweden, Switzerland, Thailand, The former Yugoslav Republic of Macedonia, Togo, Trinidad and Tobago, Tunisia, Turkey, Ukraine, United Kingdom, United Republic of Tanzania, United States of America, Uruguay, Venezuela, Yugoslavia, Zambia, Zimbabwe. [text moved to footnote]

[1] It is to be noted that WTO Members, even if they are not party to the Berne Convention (e.g., Indonesia), must comply with the substantive law provisions of the Berne Convention, except that WTO Members not party to the Berne Convention are not bound by the moral rights provisions of the Berne Convention.

It is to be noted that developing and "transition" countries may, at least until 2000, delay the application of most of the obligations provided for in the TRIPS Agreement (Article 65). Naturally, States party to the Berne Convention cannot delay the application of their obligations provided for in the Berne Convention.

[2] Under the TRIPS Agreement, the principles of national treatment, automatic protection and independence of protection also bind those WTO Members which are not party to the Berne Convention. In addition, the TRIPS Agreement imposes an obligation of "most-favored-nation treatment," under which advantages accorded by a WTO Member to the nationals of any other country must also be accorded to the nationals of all WTO Members. It is to be noted that the possibility of delayed application of the

(b) Such protection must not be conditional upon compliance with any formality (principle of "automatic" protection).[3]

(c) Such protection is independent of the existence of protection in the country of origin of the work (principle of the"independence" of protection). If, however, a contracting State provides for a longer term than the minimum prescribed by the Convention and the work ceases to be protected in the country of origin, protection may be denied once protection in the country of origin ceases.[4]

(2) The minimum standards of protection relate to the works and rights to be protected, and the duration of the protection:

(a) As to works, the protection must include "every production in the literary, scientific and artistic domain, whatever may be the mode or form of its expression" (Article 2(1) of the Convention).

(b) Subject to certain permitted reservations, limitations or exceptions, the following are among the rights which must be recognized as exclusive rights of authorization:

the right to translate,

the right to make adaptations and arrangements of the work,

the right to perform in public dramatic, dramatico-musical and musical works,

the right to recite in public literary works,

the right to communicate to the public the performance of such works,

---

TRIPS Agreement mentioned above does not apply to national treatment and most-favored-nation treatment obligations.
[3]*Id.*
[4]*Id.*

the right to broadcast (with the possibility of a contracting State to provide for a mere right to equitable remuneration instead of a right of authorization),

the right to make reproduction in any manner or form (with the possibility of a contracting State to permit, in certain special cases, reproduction without authorization provided that the reproduction does not conflict with the normal exploitation of the work and does not unreasonably prejudice the legitimate interests of the author, and with the possibility of a contracting State to provide, in the case of sound recordings of musical works, for a right to equitable remuneration),

the right to use the work as a basis for an audiovisual work, and the right to reproduce, distribute, perform in public or communicate to the public that audiovisual work[5]

The Convention also provides for "moral rights," that is, the right to claim authorship of the work and the right to object to any mutilation or deformation or other modification of, or other derogatory action in relation to, the work which would be prejudicial to the author's honor or reputation.

(c) As to the duration of protection, the general rule is that protection must be granted until the expiration of the 50th year after the author's death. There are, however, exceptions to this general rule. In the case of anonymous or pseudonymous works, the term of protection expires 50 years after the work has been lawfully made available to the public, except if the pseudonym leaves no doubt as to the author's identity or if the author discloses his identity during that period; in the latter case, the general rule applies. In the case of audiovisual (cinematographic) works, the minimum term of protection is 50 years after the making available of the work to the public ("release") or — failing such an event — from the creation of the work. In the case of works of applied art and photographic works, the minimum term is 25 years from the creation of such a work.[6]

---

[5]Under the TRIPS Agreement, an exclusive right of rental must be recognized in respect of computer programs and, under certain conditions, audiovisual works.

(3) Countries regarded as developing countries in conformity with the established practice of the General Assembly of the United Nations may, for certain works and under certain conditions, depart from these minimum standards of protection with regard to the right of translation and the right of reproduction.

The Berne Union has an Assembly and an Executive Committee. Every country member of the Union which has adhered to at least the administrative and final provisions of the Stockholm Act is a member of the Assembly. The members of the Executive Committee are elected from among the members of the Union, except for Switzerland, which is a member ex officio. On January 1, 1997, the Executive Committee had 30 members.

The establishment of the biennial program and budget of the International Bureau — as far as the Berne Union is concerned — is the task of its Assembly.

Berne Convention for the Protection of Literary and Artistic Works

Paris Act of July 24, 1971,
as amended on September 28, 1979*

The countries of the Union, being equally animated by the desire to protect, in as effective and uniform a manner as possible, the rights of authors in their literary and artistic works,

---

[6]Under the TRIPS Agreement, any term of protection which is calculated on a basis other than the life of a natural person, must be at least 50 years from the first authorized publication of the work, or—failing such an event—50 years from the making of the work. However, this rule does not apply to photographic works, or works of applied art.
*Berne Convention for the Protection of Literary and Artistic Works of September 9, 1886, completed at Paris on May 4, 1896, revised at Berlin on November 13, 1908, completed at Berne on March 20, 1914, revised at Rome on June 2, 1928, at Brussels on June 26, 1948, at Stockholm on July 14, 1967, and at Paris on July 24, 1971, and amended on September 28, 1979.

Recognizing the importance of the work of the Revision Conference held at Stockholm in 1967,

Have resolved to revise the Act adopted by the Stockholm Conference, while maintaining without change Articles 1 to 20 and 22 to 26 of that Act.

Consequently, the undersigned Plenipotentiaries, having presented their full powers, recognized as in good and due form, have agreed as follows:

Article 1
[Establishment of a Union][1]

The countries to which this Convention applies constitute a Union for the protection of the rights of authors in their literary and artistic works.

Article 2
[Protected Works: 1. "Literary and artistic works"; 2. Possible requirement of fixation; 3. Derivative works; 4. Official texts; 5. Collections; 6. Obligation to protect; beneficiaries of protection; 7. Works of applied art and industrial designs; 8. News]

(1) The expression "literary and artistic works" shall include every production in the literary, scientific and artistic domain, whatever may be the mode or form of its expression, such as books, pamphlets and other writings; lectures, addresses, sermons and other works of the same nature; dramatic or dramatico-musical works; choreographic works and entertainments in dumb show; musical compositions with or without words; cinematographic works to which are assimilated works expressed by a process analogous to cinematography; works of drawing, painting, architecture, sculpture, engraving and lithography; photographic works to which are assimilated works expressed by a process analogous to photography; works of applied art; illustrations, maps, plans, sketches and three-dimensional works relative to geography, topography, architecture or science.

---

[1] Each Article and the Appendix have been given titles to facilitate their identification. There are no titles in the signed (English) text.

(2) It shall, however, be a matter for legislation in the countries of the Union to prescribe that works in general or any specified categories of works shall not be protected unless they have been fixed in some material form.

(3) Translations, adaptations, arrangements of music and other alterations of a literary or artistic work shall be protected as original works without prejudice to the copyright in the original work.

(4) It shall be a matter for legislation in the countries of the Union to determine the protection to be granted to official texts of a legislative, administrative and legal nature, and to official translations of such texts.

(5) Collections of literary or artistic works such as encyclopaedias and anthologies which, by reason of the selection and arrangement of their contents, constitute intellectual creations shall be protected as such, without prejudice to the copyright in each of the works forming part of such collections.

(6) The works mentioned in this Article shall enjoy protection in all countries of the Union. This protection shall operate for the benefit of the author and his successors in title.

(7) Subject to the provisions of Article 7(4) of this Convention, it shall be a matter for legislation in the countries of the Union to determine the extent of the application of their laws to works of applied art and industrial designs and models, as well as the conditions under which such works, designs and models shall be protected. Works protected in the country of origin solely as designs and models shall be entitled in another country of the Union only to such special protection as is granted in that country to designs and models; however, if no such special protection is granted in that country, such works shall be protected as artistic works.

(8) The protection of this Convention shall not apply to news of the day or to miscellaneous facts having the character of mere items of press information.

Article 2bis
[Possible Limitation of Protection of Certain Works: 1. Certain speeches;
2. Certain uses of lectures and addresses; 3. Right to make
collections of such works]

(1) It shall be a matter for legislation in the countries of the Union to exclude, wholly or in part, from the protection provided by the preceding Article political speeches and speeches delivered in the course of legal proceedings.

(2) It shall also be a matter for legislation in the countries of the Union to determine the conditions under which lectures, addresses and other works of the same nature which are delivered in public may be reproduced by the press, broadcast, communicated to the public by wire and made the subject of public communication as envisaged in Article 1bis(1) of this Convention, when such use is justified by the informatory purpose.

(3) Nevertheless, the author shall enjoy the exclusive right of making a collection of his works mentioned in the preceding paragraphs.

Article 3
[Criteria of Eligibility for Protection: 1. Nationality of author; place of
publication of work; 2. Residence of author; 3. "Published" works;
4. "Simultaneously published" works]

(1) The protection of this Convention shall apply to:

(a) authors who are nationals of one of the countries of the Union, for their works, whether published or not;

(b) authors who are not nationals of one of the countries of the Union, for their works first published in one of those countries, or simultaneously in a country outside the Union and in a country of the Union.

(2) Authors who are not nationals of one of the countries of the Union but who have their habitual residence in one of them shall, for the purposes of this Convention, be assimilated to nationals of that country.

(3) The expression "published works" means works published with the consent of their authors, whatever may be the means of manufacture of the copies, provided that the availability of such copies has been such as to satisfy the reasonable requirements of the public, having regard to the nature of the work. The performance of a dramatic, dramatico-musical, cinematographic or musical work, the public recitation of a literary work, the communication by wire or the broadcasting of literary or artistic works, the exhibition of a work of art and the construction of a work of architecture shall not constitute publication.

(4) A work shall be considered as having been published simultaneously in several countries if it has been published in two or more countries within thirty days of its first publication.

Article 4
[Criteria of Eligibility for Protection of Cinematographic Works, Works of Architecture and Certain Artistic Works]

The protection of this Convention shall apply, even if the conditions of Article 3 are not fulfilled, to:

(a) authors of cinematographic works the maker of which has his headquarters or habitual residence in one of the countries of the Union;

(b) authors of works of architecture erected in a country of the Union or of other artistic works incorporated in a building or other structure located in a country of the Union.

Article 5
[Rights Guaranteed: 1. and 2. Outside the country of origin; 3. In the country of origin; 4. "Country of origin"]

(1) Authors shall enjoy, in respect of works for which they are protected under this Convention, in countries of the Union other than the country of

origin, the rights which their respective laws do now or may hereafter grant to their nationals, as well as the rights specially granted by this Convention.

(2) The enjoyment and the exercise of these rights shall not be subject to any formality; such enjoyment and such exercise shall be independent of the existence of protection in the country of origin of the work. Consequently, apart from the provisions of this Convention, the extent of protection, as well as the means of redress afforded to the author to protect his rights, shall be governed exclusively by the laws of the country where protection is claimed.

(3) Protection in the country of origin is governed by domestic law. However, when the author is not a national of the country of origin of the work for which he is protected under this Convention, he shall enjoy in that country the same rights as national authors.

(4) The country of origin shall be considered to be:

(a) in the case of works first published in a country of the Union, that country; in the case of works published simultaneously in several countries of the Union which grant different terms of protection, the country whose legislation grants the shortest term of protection;

(b) in the case of works published simultaneously in a country outside the Union and in a country of the Union, the latter country;

(c) in the case of unpublished works or of works first published in a country outside the Union, without simultaneous publication in a country of the Union, the country of the Union of which the author is a national, provided that:

(i) when these are cinematographic works the maker of which has his headquarters or his habitual residence in a country of the Union, the country of origin shall be that country, and

(ii) when these are works of architecture erected in a country of the Union or other artistic works incorporated in a building or other structure located in a country of the Union, the country of origin shall be that country.

Article 6
[Possible Restriction of Protection in Respect of Certain Works of Nationals of Certain Countries Outside the Union: 1. In the country of the first publication and in other countries; 2. No retroactivity; 3. Notice]

(1) Where any country outside the Union fails to protect in an adequate manner the works of authors who are nationals of one of the countries of the Union, the latter country may restrict the protection given to the works of authors who are, at the date of the first publication thereof, nationals of the other country and are not habitually resident in one of the countries of the Union. If the country of first publication avails itself of this right, the other countries of the Union shall not be required to grant to works thus subjected to special treatment a wider protection than that granted to them in the country of first publication.

(2) No restrictions introduced by virtue of the preceding paragraph shall affect the rights which an author may have acquired in respect of a work published in a country of the Union before such restrictions were put into force.

(3) The countries of the Union which restrict the grant of copyright in accordance with this Article shall give notice thereof to the Director General of the World Intellectual Property Organization (hereinafter designated as "the Director General") by a written declaration specifying the countries in regard to which protection is restricted, and the restrictions to which rights of authors who are nationals of those countries are subjected. The Director General shall immediately communicate this declaration to all the countries of the Union.

Article 6bis
[Moral Rights: 1. To claim authorship; to object to certain modifications and other derogatory actions; 2. After the author's death; 3. Means of redress]

(1) Independently of the author's economic rights, and even after the transfer of the said rights, the author shall have the right to claim authorship of

the work and to object to any distortion, mutilation or other modification of, or other derogatory action in relation to, the said work, which would be prejudicial to his honor or reputation.

(2) The rights granted to the author in accordance with the preceding paragraph shall, after his death, be maintained, at least until the expiry of the economic rights, and shall be exercisable by the persons or institutions authorized by the legislation of the country where protection is claimed. However, those countries whose legislation, at the moment of their ratification of or accession to this Act, does not provide for the protection after the death of the author of all the rights set out in the preceding paragraph may provide that some of these rights may, after his death, cease to be maintained.

(3) The means of redress for safeguarding the rights granted by this Article shall be governed by the legislation of the country where protection is claimed.

Article 7
[Term of Protection: 1. Generally; 2. For cinematographic works; 3. For anonymous and pseudonymous works; 4. For photographic works and works of applied art; 5. Starting date of computation; 6. Longer terms; 7. Shorter terms; 8. Applicable law; "comparison" of terms]

(1) The term of protection granted by this Convention shall be the life of the author and fifty years after his death.

(2) However, in the case of cinematographic works, the countries of the Union may provide that the term of protection shall expire fifty years after the work has been made available to the public with the consent of the author, or, failing such an event within fifty years from the making of such a work, fifty years after the making.

(3) In the case of anonymous or pseudonymous works, the term of protection granted by this Convention shall expire fifty years after the work has been lawfully made available to the public. However, when the pseudonym adopted by the author leaves no doubt as to his identity, the term of protection shall be that provided in paragraph (1). If the author of an anonymous or pseudonymous work discloses his identity during the above-mentioned

period, the term of protection applicable shall be that provided in paragraph (1). The countries of the Union shall not be required to protect anonymous or pseudonymous works in respect of which it is reasonable to presume that their author has been dead for fifty years.

(4) It shall be a matter for legislation in the countries of the Union to determine the term of protection of photographic works and that of works of applied art in so far as they are protected as artistic works; however, this term shall last at least until the end of a period of twenty-five years from the making of such a work.

(5) The term of protection subsequent to the death of the author and the terms provided by paragraph (2), paragraph (3) and paragraph (4) shall run from the date of death or of the event referred to in those paragraphs, but such terms shall always be deemed to begin on the first of January of the year following the death or such event.

(6) The countries of the Union may grant a term of protection in excess of those provided by the preceding paragraphs.

(7) Those countries of the Union bound by the Rome Act of this Convention which grant, in their national legislation in force at the time of signature of the present Act, shorter terms of protection than those provided for in the preceding paragraphs shall have the right to maintain such terms when ratifying or acceding to the present Act.

(8) In any case, the term shall be governed by the legislation of the country where protection is claimed; however, unless the legislation of that country otherwise provides, the term shall not exceed the term fixed in the country of origin of the work.

Article 7bis
[Term of Protection for Works of Joint Authorship]

The provisions of the preceding Article shall also apply in the case of a work of joint authorship, provided that the terms measured from the death of the author shall be calculated from the death of the last surviving author.

Article 8
[Right of Translation]

Authors of literary and artistic works protected by this Convention shall enjoy the exclusive right of making and of authorizing the translation of their works throughout the term of protection of their rights in the original works.

Article 9
[Right of Reproduction: 1. Generally; 2. Possible exceptions;
3. Sound and visual recordings]

(1) Authors of literary and artistic works protected by this Convention shall have the exclusive right of authorizing the reproduction of these works, in any manner or form.

(2) It shall be a matter for legislation in the countries of the Union to permit the reproduction of such works in certain special cases, provided that such reproduction does not conflict with a normal exploitation of the work and does not unreasonably prejudice the legitimate interests of the author.

(3) Any sound or visual recording shall be considered as a reproduction for the purposes of this Convention.

Article 10
[Certain Free Uses of Works: 1. Quotations; 2. Illustrations for teaching;
3. Indication of source and author]

(1) It shall be permissible to make quotations from a work which has already been lawfully made available to the public, provided that their making is compatible with fair practice, and their extent does not exceed that justified by the purpose, including quotations from newspaper articles and periodicals in the form of press summaries.

(2) It shall be a matter for legislation in the countries of the Union, and for special agreements existing or to be concluded between them, to permit the utilization, to the extent justified by the purpose, of literary or artistic works by way of illustration in publications, broadcasts or sound or visual

recordings for teaching, provided such utilization is compatible with fair practice.

(3) Where use is made of works in accordance with the preceding paragraphs of this Article, mention shall be made of the source, and of the name of the author if it appears thereon.

Article 10bis
[Further Possible Free Uses of Works: 1. Of certain articles and broadcast works; 2. Of works seen or heard in connection with current events]

(1) It shall be a matter for legislation in the countries of the Union to permit the reproduction by the press, the broadcasting or the communication to the public by wire of articles published in newspapers or periodicals on current economic, political or religious topics, and of broadcast works of the same character, in cases in which the reproduction, broadcasting or such communication thereof is not expressly reserved. Nevertheless, the source must always be clearly indicated; the legal consequences of a breach of this obligation shall be determined by the legislation of the country where protection is claimed.

(2) It shall also be a matter for legislation in the countries of the Union to determine the conditions under which, for the purpose of reporting current events by means of photography, cinematography, broadcasting or communication to the public by wire, literary or artistic works seen or heard in the course of the event may, to the extent justified by the informatory purpose, be reproduced and made available to the public.

Article 11
[Certain Rights in Dramatic and Musical Works: 1. Right of public performance and of communication to the public of a performance; 2. In respect of translations]

(1) Authors of dramatic, dramatico-musical and musical works shall enjoy the exclusive right of authorizing:

(i) the public performance of their works, including such public performance by any means or process;

(ii) any communication to the public of the performance of their works.

(2) Authors of dramatic or dramatico-musical works shall enjoy, during the full term of their rights in the original works, the same rights with respect to translations thereof.

Article 11bis

[Broadcasting and Related Rights: 1. Broadcasting and other wireless communications, public communication of broadcast by wire or rebroadcast, public communication of broadcast by loudspeaker or analogous instruments; 2. Compulsory licenses; 3. Recording; ephemeral recordings]

(1) Authors of literary and artistic works shall enjoy the exclusive right of authorizing:

(i) the broadcasting of their works or the communication thereof to the public by any other means of wireless diffusion of signs, sounds or images;

(ii) any communication to the public by wire or by rebroadcasting of the broadcast of the work, when this communication is made by an organization other than the original one;

(iii) the public communication by loudspeaker or any other analogous instrument transmitting, by signs, sounds or images, the broadcast of the work.

(2) It shall be a matter for legislation in the countries of the Union to determine the conditions under which the rights mentioned in the paragraph 1 may be exercised, but these conditions shall apply only in the countries where they have been prescribed. They shall not in any circumstances be prejudicial to the moral rights of the author, nor to his right to obtain equitable remuneration which, in the absence of agreement, shall be fixed by competent authority.

(3) In the absence of any contrary stipulation, permission granted in accordance with paragraph (1) of this Article shall not imply permission to

record, by means of instruments recording sounds or images, the work broadcast. It shall, however, be a matter for legislation in the countries of the Union to determine the regulations for ephemeral recordings made by a broadcasting organization by means of its own facilities and used for its own broadcasts. The preservation of these recordings in official archives may, on the ground of their exceptional documentary character, be authorized by such legislation.

Article 11ter
[Certain Rights in Literary Works: 1. Right of public recitation and of communication to the public of a recitation; 2. In respect of translations]

(1) Authors of literary works shall enjoy the exclusive right of authorizing:

(i) the public recitation of their works, including such public recitation by any means or process;

(ii) any communication to the public of the recitation of their works.

(2) Authors of literary works shall enjoy, during the full term of their rights in the original works, the same rights with respect to translations thereof.

Article 12
[Right of Adaptation, Arrangement and Other Alteration]
Authors of literary or artistic works shall enjoy the exclusive right of authorizing adaptations, arrangements and other alterations of their works.

Article 13
[Possible Limitation of the Right of Recording of Musical Works and Any Words Pertaining Thereto: 1. Compulsory licenses; 2. Transitory measures; 3. Seizure on importation of copies made without the author's permission]

(1) Each country of the Union may impose for itself reservations and conditions on the exclusive right granted to the author of a musical work and to the author of any words, the recording of which together with the musical work has already been authorized by the latter, to authorize the sound recording of that musical work, together with such words, if any; but all

such reservations and conditions shall apply only in the countries which have imposed them and shall not, in any circumstances, be prejudicial to the rights of these authors to obtain equitable remuneration which, in the absence of agreement, shall be fixed by competent authority.

(2) Recordings of musical works made in a country of the Union in accordance with Article 13(3) of the Conventions signed at Rome on June 2, 1928, and at Brussels on June 26, 1948, may be reproduced in that country without the permission of the author of the musical work until a date two years after that country becomes bound by this Act.

(3) Recordings made in accordance with paragraph (1) and paragraph (2) of this Article and imported without permission from the parties concerned into a country where they are treated as infringing recordings shall be liable to seizure.

Article 14
[Cinematographic and Related Rights: 1. Cinematographic adaptation and reproduction; distribution; public performance and public communication by wire of works thus adapted or reproduced; 2. Adaptation of cinematographic productions; 3. No compulsory licenses]

(1) Authors of literary or artistic works shall have the exclusive right of authorizing:

(i) the cinematographic adaptation and reproduction of these works, and the distribution of the works thus adapted or reproduced;

(ii) the public performance and communication to the public by wire of the works thus adapted or reproduced.

(2) The adaptation into any other artistic form of a cinematographic production derived from literary or artistic works shall, without prejudice to the authorization of the author of the cinematographic production, remain subject to the authorization of the authors of the original works.

(3) The provisions of Article 13(1) shall not apply.

Article 14bis
[Special Provisions Concerning Cinematographic Works: 1. Assimilation to "original" works; 2. Ownership; limitation of certain rights of certain contributors; 3. Certain other contributors]

(1) Without prejudice to the copyright in any work which may have been adapted or reproduced, a cinematographic work shall be protected as an original work. The owner of copyright in a cinematographic work shall enjoy the same rights as the author of an original work, including the rights referred to in the preceding Article.

(2)

(a) Ownership of copyright in a cinematographic work shall be a matter for legislation in the country where protection is claimed.

(b) However, in the countries of the Union which, by legislation, include among the owners of copyright in a cinematographic work authors who have brought contributions to the making of the work, such authors, if they have undertaken to bring such contributions, may not, in the absence of any contrary or special stipulation, object to the reproduction, distribution, public performance, communication to the public by wire, broadcasting or any other communication to the public, or to the subtitling or dubbing of texts, of the work.

(c) The question whether or not the form of the undertaking referred to above should, for the application of the preceding subparagraph (b), be in a written agreement or a written act of the same effect shall be a matter for the legislation of the country where the maker of the cinematographic work has his headquarters or habitual residence. However, it shall be a matter for the legislation of the country of the Union where protection is claimed to provide that the said undertaking shall be in a written agreement or a written act of the same effect. The countries whose legislation so provides shall notify the Director General by means of a written declaration, which will be immediately communicated by him to all the other countries of the Union.

(d) By "contrary or special stipulation" is meant any restrictive condition which is relevant to the aforesaid undertaking.

(3) Unless the national legislation provides to the contrary, the provisions of paragraph (2)(b) above shall not be applicable to authors of scenarios, dialogues and musical works created for the making of the cinemato-graphic work, or to the principal director thereof. However, those countries of the Union whose legislation does not contain rules providing for the ap-plication of the said paragraph (2)(b) to such director shall notify the Director General by means of a written declaration, which will be immediately communicated by him to all the other countries of the Union.

Article 14ter
["Droit de suite" in Works of Art and Manuscripts: 1. Right to an interest in resales; 2. Applicable law; 3. Procedure]

(1) The author, or after his death the persons or institutions authorized by national legislation, shall, with respect to original works of art and original manuscripts of writers and composers, enjoy the inalienable right to an in-terest in any sale of the work subsequent to the first transfer by the author of the work.

(2) The protection provided by the preceding paragraph may be claimed in a country of the Union only if legislation in the country to which the author belongs so permits, and to the extent permitted by the country where this protection is claimed.

(3) The procedure for collection and the amounts shall be matters for de-termination by national legislation.

Article 15
[Right to Enforce Protected Rights: 1. Where author's name is indicated or where pseudonym leaves no doubt as to author's identity; 2. In the case of cinematographic works; 3. In the case of anonymous and pseudonymous works; 4. In the case of certain unpublished works of unknown author-ship]

(1) In order that the author of a literary or artistic work protected by this Convention shall, in the absence of proof to the contrary, be regarded as such, and consequently be entitled to institute infringement proceedings in the countries of the Union, it shall be sufficient for his name to appear on

the work in the usual manner. This paragraph shall be applicable even if this name is a pseudonym, where the pseudonym adopted by the author leaves no doubt as to his identity.

(2) The person or body corporate whose name appears on a cinematographic work in the usual manner shall, in the absence of proof to the contrary, be presumed to be the maker of the said work.

(3) In the case of anonymous and pseudonymous works, other than those referred to in paragraph (1) above, the publisher whose name appears on the work shall, in the absence of proof to the contrary, be deemed to represent the author, and in this capacity he shall be entitled to protect and enforce the author's rights. The provisions of this paragraph shall cease to apply when the author reveals his identity and establishes his claim to authorship of the work.

(4)

(a) In the case of unpublished works where the identity of the author is unknown, but where there is every ground to presume that he is a national of a country of the Union, it shall be a matter for legislation in that country to designate the competent authority which shall represent the author and shall be entitled to protect and enforce his rights in the countries of the Union.

(b) Countries of the Union which make such designation under the terms of this provision shall notify the Director General by means of a written declaration giving full information concerning the authority thus designated. The Director General shall at once communicate this declaration to all other countries of the Union.

Article 16
[Infringing Copies: 1. Seizure; 2. Seizure on importation; 3. Applicable law]

(1) Infringing copies of a work shall be liable to seizure in any country of the Union where the work enjoys legal protection.

(2) The provisions of the preceding paragraph shall also apply to reproductions coming from a country where the work is not protected, or has ceased to be protected.

(3) The seizure shall take place in accordance with the legislation of each country.

Article 17
[Possibility of Control of Circulation, Presentation and Exhibition of Works]

The provisions of this Convention cannot in any way affect the right of the Government of each country of the Union to permit, to control, or to prohibit, by legislation or regulation, the circulation, presentation, or exhibition of any work or production in regard to which the competent authority may find it necessary to exercise that right.

Article 18
[Works Existing on Convention's Entry Into Force: 1. Protectable where protection not yet expired in country of origin; 2. Non-protectable where protection already expired in country where it is claimed; 3. Application of these principles; 4. Special cases]

(1) This Convention shall apply to all works which, at the moment of its coming into force, have not yet fallen into the public domain in the country of origin through the expiry of the term of protection.

(2) If, however, through the expiry of the term of protection which was previously granted, a work has fallen into the public domain of the country where protection is claimed, that work shall not be protected anew.

(3) The application of this principle shall be subject to any provisions contained in special conventions to that effect existing or to be concluded between countries of the Union. In the absence of such provisions, the respective countries shall determine, each in so far as it is concerned, the conditions of application of this principle.

(4) The preceding provisions shall also apply in the case of new accessions to the Union and to cases in which protection is extended by the application of Article 7 or by the abandonment of reservations.

Article 19
[Protection Greater than Resulting from Convention]

The provisions of this Convention shall not preclude the making of a claim to the benefit of any greater protection which may be granted by legislation in a country of the Union.

Article 20
[Special Agreements Among Countries of the Union]

The Governments of the countries of the Union reserve the right to enter into special agreements among themselves, in so far as such agreements grant to authors more extensive rights than those granted by the Convention, or contain other provisions not contrary to this Convention. The provisions of existing agreements which satisfy these conditions shall remain applicable.

Article 21
[Special Provisions Regarding Developing Countries: 1. Reference to Appendix; 2. Appendix part of Act]

(1) Special provisions regarding developing countries are included in the Appendix.

(2) Subject to the provisions of Article 28(1)(b), the Appendix forms an integral part of this Act.

*****

Article 33
[Disputes: 1. Jurisdiction of the International Court of Justice; 2. Reservation as to such jurisdiction; 3. Withdrawal of reservation]

(1) Any dispute between two or more countries of the Union concerning the interpretation or application of this Convention, not settled by negoti-

ation, may, by any one of the countries concerned, be brought before the International Court of Justice by application in conformity with the Statute of the Court, unless the countries concerned agree on some other method of settlement. The country bringing the dispute before the Court shall inform the International Bureau; the International Bureau shall bring the matter to the attention of the other countries of the Union.

(2) Each country may, at the time it signs this Act or deposits its instrument of ratification or accession, declare that it does not consider itself bound by the provisions of paragraph (1). With regard to any dispute between such country and any other country of the Union, the provisions of paragraph (1) shall not apply.

(3) Any country having made a declaration in accordance with the provisions of paragraph (2) may, at any time, withdraw its declaration by notification addressed to the Director General.

*****

Appendix
[Special Provisions Regarding Developing Countries]

Article I
[Faculties Open to Developing Countries: 1. Availability of certain faculties; declaration: 2. Duration of effect of declaration, 3. Cessation of developing country status; 4. Existing stocks of copies; 5. Declarations concerning certain territories; 6. Limits of reciprocity]

(1) Any country regarded as a developing country in conformity with the established practice of the General Assembly of the United Nations which ratifies or accedes to this Act, of which this Appendix forms an integral part, and which, having regard to its economic situation and its social or cultural needs, does not consider itself immediately in a position to make provision for the protection of all the rights as provided for in this Act, may, by a notification deposited with the Director General at the time of depositing its instrument of ratification or accession or, subject to Article V(1)(c), at any time thereafter, declare that it will avail itself of the faculty provided for. . . .

Notes and Questions

1. You will recall that OECD industry groups criticized the Paris Convention for its lack of adequate subject matter coverage with respect to patents. By contrast, Article 2 of the Berne Convention provides broad subject matter coverage for copyright. In light of Article 2, were the provisions of the TRIPS Agreement on computer programs and compilations necessary? Is there a risk associated with adding express subject matter coverage for new technologies? In other words, if some new subject matter is expressly covered, might it be implied that other new subject matter is not covered absent an express reference?

2. Article 2(2), Berne, permits members to require that a copyrighted work be fixed in some material form. By way of illustration, the U.S. Copyright Act refers to "original works of expression fixed in any tangible medium of expression, now known or later developed, from which they can be perceived, reproduced, or otherwise communicated, either directly or with the aid of a machine or device."[1] What types of expressive works are not fixed in a tangible medium of expression?

3. Article 2(3), Berne, extends copyright protection to translations (as well as to adaptations, arrangements and other alterations). In the highly integrated global economy, the economic value of translation rights should be apparent. Article 21, Berne and the referenced Appendix authorize developing countries to grant compulsory licenses for the translation and reproduction of copyrighted works under specified terms and conditions. The Appendix generally requires that a work has not been translated and made available at a reasonable cost. Berne Article 21 and the Appendix are incorporated by reference in the TRIPS Agreement (TRIPS Agreement, art. 9:1).

4. Note that pursuant to Berne Article 3(1)(a), unpublished works are protected. Article 3(1)(b) provides Berne protection to works first published in a Berne member even if the author is not a national of a Berne member. This article provides a mechanism which permits Berne protection to be se-

---

[1] 17 U.S.C §102.

cured "through the back door," and this provision was quite important for American authors so long as the United States had not adhered to the Berne Convention. Now that Berne Convention membership has become virtually universal, this provision is of lesser importance.

5. Article 6bis addresses the subject of "moral rights" of authors, a topic we will consider in detail later in this Chapter. The TRIPS Agreement expressly excludes article 6bis, Berne, from its incorporated provisions (TRIPS Agreement, art. 9:1).

6. The term of copyright protection generally required by article 7(1), Berne, is the life of the author plus fifty years. However, members may grant a longer term of protection (art. 7(6)) and, as we will see, the European Union and the United States have extended the term to the author's life plus seventy years. Article 7(8) is of particular importance in the context of nations and regions with differing durations of copyright protection. What is the effect of Article 7(8), Berne?

7. The basic protection of the Berne Convention is set out in Article 9(1), i.e., the "exclusive right of authorizing the reproduction of these works, in any manner or form." The most important exceptions to the author's exclusive rights are in Article 9(2), which generally establishes the rights referred to as "fair use" rights. Specific embodiments of fair use rights are set forth in Articles 10 and 10bis.

8. Article 11bis establishes the rights to broadcast "to the public" by wireless means (11bis(1)(i)), and by wire or by rebroadcasting when the communication is made by an organization other than the "original one" 11bis(1)(ii). The meaning of the various phrases in Article 11bis has been the subject of considerable litigation in national and regional courts. For example, Cable News Network (CNN) fought a long court battle in France against a Paris hotel which claimed that its guest rooms were not public areas, and that it was thus entitled to retransmit CNN satellite signals to its guests without payment. CNN eventually prevailed.[1]

---

[1]*See, e.g.,* Cable News Network Inc. v. Novotel SA, Tribunal de Grande Instance, Paris, [1991] ECC 492, 14 Feb. 1990, holding that a hotel room is a "private" as opposed to "public" place, subsequently overturned by the Cour de Cassation. Cable News Network and CNN International Sales Limited v. Novotel Paris-Les Halles SA, Cour de Cassation [1994 ECC 530], 6 Apr. 1994.

9. Article 14ter(1) refers to the *droit de suite* which requires that an author (and his or her heirs) collect an interest in the sale of a work of art or original manuscript in any sale after its first transfer. However, this right only extends in Berne members which choose to prescribe it by legislation, and it only benefits foreign authors whose home country also prescribes such rights (art. 14ter(2), Berne).

10. We have previously observed that copyright and other IPRs do not afford market access rights. Article 17, Berne, establishes a right in favor of governments to prohibit the distribution of any copyrighted work. Does the fact that governments exercise that right as they "may find it necessary" suggest any meaningful limitation on the right?

11. Might you have foreseen that Article 18, concerning the retroactive application of Berne protection, would be the subject of a major trade dispute? It was. Article 70:2 of the TRIPS Agreement provides that questions relating to copyright in existing works will be governed solely by the terms of Article 18, Berne. Article 14 of the TRIPS Agreement extended the term of protection for performers and producers of phonograms to fifty years from the calendar year of fixation, well beyond the twenty-year term prescribed by the Rome Convention for such subject matter. When Japan implemented the TRIPS Agreement provisions with respect to performers and producers of phonograms, it presumed that works existing for more than twenty years had fallen into the public domain, and therefore were not subject to TRIPS protection (per art. 18(2), Berne). The United States vehemently objected, arguing that the TRIPS Agreement specifically contemplated the extension of copyright to existing works. Japan eventually conceded and adopted legislation extending protection, though not because it was convinced of the soundness of any U.S. legal argument. What do you think?

12. Note again, as in the Paris Convention, the possibility of referral of a dispute to the International Court of Justice (art. 33, Berne).

---

2. The Berne Convention in National Law

The Berne Convention may be applied directly by the courts of a contracting state when the constitution of that state permits the direct application of treaties. The Convention may also be transformed into national law by the legislature or parliament of a contracting state. Even when a national legislature has adopted copyright legislation specifically to implement the provisions of the Berne Convention, the Convention may be referred to by courts either to aid in the interpretation of that national legislation, or to fill a gap in the legislation. The extent to which a court may directly rely on the provisions of the Convention (for example, to fill a gap) will depend on the way in which the national constitution regards treaty law.

In *SUISA v. Rediffusion*, the Swiss Federal Court applies the Berne Convention in a case involving a cable television company which picks up over-air broadcast signals and retransmits the signals via cable to paying subscribers. The cable company (Rediffusion) contends that it need not pay a copyright fee for its retransmissions because it is reaching roughly the same audience as by the over-air broadcaster which already is paying copyright fees.

SUISA (Swiss Society of Authors and Publishers) v. Rediffusion AG

Bundesgericht (Swiss Federal Supreme Court)

[1982] ECC 481
20 January 1981

Panel: The President, Judge Chatelain; Judges Ruedi, Stoffel, Messmer and Weyermann

Headnote:
Appeal from the Tribunal Cantonal (Cantonal Court), Zurich.

Copyright. Foreign broadcasts. Locus standi. A Swiss collecting society may properly sue in a Swiss court for infringement in Switzerland of copyrights or performing rights deriving from foreign broadcasts, its standing being based on reciprocal agency agreements with foreign copyright management societies.

Copyright. Cable television. Article 11bis (2) of the Berne Convention may apply to rediffusion services even where the rediffusion does not reach a new public but merely improves the reception of users who might also receive over the air.

Interpretation. Precedent. Foreign case law. Copyright. Judgments of foreign courts, in so far as they refer to the Berne Copyright Convention, may be used by Swiss courts to assist in the interpretation of the Convention, so long as allowance is made for the fact that they are based partly on national law which takes priority over the Convention when the Contracting State has made use of the proviso in Article 11bis (2) of the Convention.

Interpretation. Treaties. Copyright. As the Swiss Copyright Act was amended in 1955 with the specific purpose of harmonising it with the Brussels version of the Berne Convention, Swiss courts may, when interpreting provisions of the Act, pay attention to international and foreign interpretations of the equivalent provisions of the Convention.

Copyright. Broadcasting. Cable transmission. Where works originally broadcast over the air are rediffused by cable, the act of rediffusion will be a new act requiring copyright permissions if there is a public communication by a body other than the originating (broadcasting) body, irrespective of whether the direct reception area is enlarged or not.

Copyright. Broadcasting. Cable rediffusion. Community aerials. Rediffusion of broadcast signals by cable may constitute a new copyright act if it is a "public communication". It will be "public" if the signals are retransmitted to 60,000 subscribers in the Zurich region, as opposed to ordinary private reception through a building aerial or a residential unit aerial serving buildings or groups of buildings.

Copyright. Cable rediffusion. Separate identity. The separate identity from the original broadcaster which is required of a cable rediffusion service if the latter is to require a separate copyright clearance does not apply to the public telecommunications service in so far as it relays broadcasts from the public broadcasting service.

The Court, allowing the appeal, held that the defendant cable rediffusion company was entitled to retransmit to its 60,000 subscribers in the Zurich region broadcasts received over the air from both Swiss and foreign broadcasting companies only with the authorisation of the plaintff, the Swiss copyright collecting society.

*****

Decision:

*****

The issue between the parties is essentially the extent to which the simultaneous retransmission of unaltered broadcasts with the aid of collective aerials requires authorisation from the authors and payment of their royalties. The decision would be the same whether it related only to radio broadcasts or also to television programmes. On the other hand, what must be clarified from the beginning is the meaning to be attached to the term "collective aerial". Indeed it may refer to installations of very different sizes, from the external aerial of an apartment block to a giant network serving an entire town or even region and, in between, a common aerial for several neighbouring houses or a number of districts. (HJ Stern, Die Weiterverbreitung von Radio und Fernsehsendungen, Thesis, Zurich 1970, p 36.) In this case there is a large network with wide-spread branches offering some 60,000 subscribers in the Zurich region the broadcasts which are the subject of the dispute.

Section 12 of the Federal Copyright Act (LDA) gives an author the exclusive right to broadcast his work by radio (sub-section (1) no 5) and, in addition, to "communicate [it] publicly either by cable or wireless, if such communication is made by a body other than that which originated it" (no 6), television being treated in the same way as radio broadcasting (sub-section 2). Any person who infringes copyright in respect of any of these provisions is liable, according to section 42, no 1(f) LDA, to civil procedings and prosecution.

In the opinion of the cantonal Court, no such contravention can be found to have occurred in the present case because the defendant does not itself broadcast and confines itself to making technical improvements to reception conditions. The Court's decision argument is that the defendant simultaneously transmits, without alteration, programmes which its subscribers could just as easily receive directly with the aid of private aerials and that, in either case, the user must apply for a licence from the Post Office and pay a fee a share of which intended for authors is already collected by SUISA through the Swiss Radio and Television Corporation (SSR), so that the plaintiff would be seeking to obtain double payment for one and the same service, which constitutes an abuse.

With this reasoning the cantonal Court takes account only of the Federal Copyright Act and neglects, even with regard to foreign broadcasts, the Berne Convention for the protection of literary and artistic works, revised in Brussels on 26 June 1948. The plaintiff submits, on the other hand, that the Convention applies directly to the present case by virtue of Article 4(1) and section 68bis of the Federal Copyright Act. The defendant appears to draw a different conclusion from the restrictive clause of Article 11bis (2) of the Berne Convention, although it admits that Switzerland has not made use of this proviso and that a derogation is therefore excluded. In addition the defendant has not failed to observe that legal theory and case law on the Berne Convention are also valid for interpreting section 12(1), nos 5 and 6 of the Federal Copyright Act because the legislature deliberately and literally repeated the provisions of Article 11bis, nos 1 and 2 of the Convention. (Official Memorandum of 12 October 1954 on the revision of the Federal Copyright Act, BB 1 1954, II, 654.)

This is why, after all, the parties refer to the origin of the rules adopted by Swiss law, to foreign case law and international attempts to interpret the Convention on these points and to adopt it to technical progress.

(a) In the Rome version of 1928 the Convention reserves to the author the initial radio broadcasting right, and this had to be reconsidered later when it became technically possible to retransmit broadcasts. During the preparatory work of the Brussels Conference on Article 11bis of the Berne Convention, there was a proposal to subject any new public communication of the broadcast work, whether by cable or wireless, to a fresh authorisation from the author. This requirement seemed excessive to some delegations, insufficient to others, and was also considered too vague. On a proposal from Belgium, agreement was finally reached on the wording "any public communication", but making the author's authorisation subject to the additional condition: "when this communication is made by a body other than that which originated it" (A Baum, [1949] GRUR 18).

In the plaintiff's opinion this means that there is no requirement for a "new public", but this is disputed by the defendant which considers that the specific words "a body other . . ." aimed, on the contrary, to restrict the author's right even more. However, it does not appear from the proceedings cited by the defendant that the Conference really had this intention. Even in the general report of 25 June 1948, which served as a basis for the revision of 26 June 1948, the only remaining question is the requirement for another body. (Text cited by Mestmacker/Schulze, Urheberrechtskommentar, Vol II, annex B/2.) If, as the defendant alleges, the Conference had regarded this requirement merely as a limitation of the first version, it could have abided by it. However, this was not the case because the Conference replaced the former "new public communication" merely by "public communication". Consequently Article 11bis, no 2 of the Berne Convention may apply in cases where the retransmission does not reach a new public, so that it is unnecessary for the reception area of the original broadcast to be enlarged.

Moreover, this is the interpretation given to the preparatory work for the Brussels revision by several writers, particularly M Walter who has made the most systematic study (In [1974] GRUR Int 120-21 and in [1975] Film und Recht 754/5). The same view point is defended by D Gaudel (La teledistribution, Paris 1976, p 23 ff with references to other French writers). R Dittrich (Kabelfernsehen und Probleme des Urheberrechts, in Internationale Gesellschaft fur Urheberrecht 1979, p 381 et seq and in [1979] Le droit d'auteur 27 et seq) does not dispute it, although he considers, on other grounds which are essentially technical and legal, that the area served by the original transmitter should be excluded. J von Ungern-Sternberg (Die Rechte der Urheber an Rundfunk und Drahtfunksendungen, Munich 1973, pp 36 et seq and 50; likewise in [1973] GRUR 18-19) also concurs in the accepted interpretation, together with Nordemann/Vinck/Hertin (Internationales Urheberrecht, Dusseldorf 1977, note 4 on Article 11bis of the Convention) and E Ulmer (In [1980] GRUR 582 et seq). Even D Reimer (In [1979] GRUR Int 93) does not interpret the disputed clause any differently in the final analysis, although he considers that it should be revised so as to except the area served by the original transmitter, in the manner suggested by Dittrich.

Among Swiss writers, Stern (Thesis, p 58 et seq and in [1975] Film und Recht 773) also accepts that Article 11bis, no 2 of the Berne Convention does not presuppose either a new public or an enlargement of the reception area. This is also the opinion of K Govoni (Urheberrechtliche Probleme des Kabelfernsehens, p 10). According to MJ Lutz (Die Schranken des Urheberrechts nach schweizerischem Recht, Thesis, Zurich 1964, pp 133/4), the theory of the new public played an important role in Switzerland until the adoption of the Brussels version. The defendant's point of view is, on the other hand, shared by R Gillard (L'antenne collective et la communication par fil au public en droit de propriete intellectuelle, Thesis, Fribourg 1976, pp 40 et seq), A Tritten (Antenne commune et droit d'auteur, p 6 et seq), Pedrazzini (In ZSR 96/1977 II, p 90), and, by analogy, D Barrelet (Droit suisse des mass media, 1980, p 163). In the case of all these writers, however, the striking fact is that they state no grounds for their proposition and they take even less account of the opposite opinion. On the other hand, the defendant is wrong to invoke JF Egli ("Le droit de radiodiffusion en Suisse," in ZSR 87/1968, p 303) because he expressly rejects the criterion of a new public.

(b) The cantonal Court has not taken account of the judgments of foreign courts cited by the parties on the pretext that they cannot constitute precedents in Switzerland. However, in so far as they refer to the Berne Convention they may very well assist in its interpretation. It is true that allowance must be made for the fact that these judgments are based partly on national law which takes priority over the Berne Convention when a contracting State uses the proviso stipulated in Article 11bis (2) of the Convention.

The legal situation in Belgium, where the Convention applies as it stands, is instructive. In an action against Coditel, a cable television company, a contravention of Article 11bis (1), no 1 of the Berne Convention was sanctioned on 19 June 1979 by the Brussels Appeal Court. Both courts adhered strictly to the letter of the Convention without entering into technical details or into the theory of a new public. The defendant is wrong in invoking an allegedly contradictory judgment by the Antwerp Appeal Court dated 3 December 1980. This decision in fact rejected a claim by a radio broadcasting organisation within the meaning of Article 11bis (1), no 1 of the Berne Convention, which according to the decision was to be distinguished from the rediffusion enterprises referred to by no 2. Moreover, no allusion was made to the Brussels decision.

In a case in Feldkirch in Austria judgment was given against a cable television enterprise for infringing copyright. Although the lower courts found that there had only been an enlargement, though only in part, of the direct reception area, the Austrian Supreme Court, in its judgment of 25 June 1974, refused to consider this distinction ([1975] GRUR Int 68-69). In another action against Telesystem, a cable television enterprise, the same Court reached a similar decision on 12 November 1979. The criticism to which these judgments gave rise led to an amendment of the Austrian Act on 2 July 1980. Section 17(3) exempts cable relays of broadcasts by Austrian Radio (ORF) and small collective aerials serving not more than 500 users from authorisation by the author. Section 59 lays down a statutory licence for the rediffusion of foreign broadcasts. These new provisions clearly differ from the Swiss legislation and are therefore of no assistance to the defendant.

On the other hand the defendant can invoke the case law of Holland, where two actions against Amstelveen, a cable television enterprise, were dismissed. It is true that the Amsterdam District Court accepts that there was "public communication" within the meaning of the Berne Convention, without it being necessary for it to involve a public other than the original public. The Court merely found that there was no "own" publication for the purpose of the Dutch Act. On appeal, the Amsterdam Court of Justice rejected this distinction on 12 June 1980 and upheld the decision of the court of first instance, without taking the Berne Convention into consideration, on the ground that the broadcasts in question could have been just as well received direct with the aid of private aerials.

Two decisions by German courts also provide grist for the defendant's mill because they dismiss actions by GEMA, a copyright management society, against the German Post Office concerning its cable networks in Hamburg and Nuremberg. These judgments, which are said to have been affirmed in the meantime by the German Federal Supreme Court, do not however refer to the Berne Convention. They are more concerned with establishing whether, from the viewpoint of national law, a rediffusion network must be considered as a means of broadcasting or of reception. In its judgment of 6 January 1978 the Hamburg District Court stated that the mere fact that such a network did not involve a new public did not prevent it from being considered as a broadcasting body, but that a distinction should be made between enterprises with collective aerials and genuine cable distribution networks. The Hamburg Appeal Court upheld this judgment on 14 December 1978, finding that only retransmissions "of a broadcasting nature" (rundfunkgemab) gave rise to copyright. The Court found that the retransmissions were not of this kind because the German Post Office did not produce a programme of its own, nor did it offer a range of broadcasts considerably exceeding the possibilities of direct reception. Therefore the Court held that only a considerable installation serving a large number of subscribers could be considered as a "cable transmitter", which could not be said of a network with only approximately 3,000 to 6,000 connections. It seems, therefore that larger installations could be judged differently.

When these foreign judgments do not simply ignore the Berne Convention, as in Germany or Holland, they all interpret Article 11bis, no 2 in the manner described above, as moreover E Ulmer agrees (In [1980] GRUR 584). Consequently foreign case law does not permit this Article to be interpreted contrary to its literal meaning by subjecting its effects to the existence of a new public or an enlarged reception area. Furthermore the decisions of the German courts clearly show how difficult it is to find criteria permitting a distinction to be made between cable television enterprises which come within copyright law and those which do not.

(c) Finally, important guidelines will be found in the international efforts at interpretation and adjustment of the controversial provisions of the Berne Convention. First of all we may cite the Guide de la Convention de Berne published in 1978 by the World Intellectual Property Organisation (WIPO). Here again, mention is made only of the criteria listed in Article 11bis, no 2 of the Convention, and not of the additional requirement for a new public, although it is stated that it is a matter for national legislation to lay down the demarcation line between communication within the meaning of the Convention and ordinary reception (note 10 on Article 11bis). During the discussions by experts who prepared the Strasbourg Agreement on television in January 1979, it became clear that exception of the direct reception zone, or of the service zone, was not a satisfactory solution in the absence of technical criteria which were legally certain. The harmonisation of national legislation appeared necessary. In June 1977 a group of experts appointed by UNESCO and WIPO had already decided that the concept of a direct reception area was unknown by Article 11bis of the Berne Convention. The same criterion was rejected once again by the same experts in 1980 for the additional reason that cable distribution enterprises always appeal to a different public, even if it remains partly identical, because what use would they have otherwise?

The observations by interest groups are, on the other hand, less convincing. Nevertheless it is clear from their documentation that already for a very long time the international associations of authors' societies of copyright management societies, radio broadcasting organisations and cable distribution enterprises have been conferring together. From this it may be deduced that the rediffusion organisations accept the principle of a copyright fee although, it is true, disputing it in respect of the direct reception area.

As the Federal Copyright Act was amended in 1955 with the specific purpose of harmonising it with the Brussels version of the Berne Convention, which has been said of the latter also applies to the interpretation of section 12(1), no 6 of the Act. In its memorandum on ratification of the Berne Convention, the Federal Council explained that, pursuant to Article 11bis, no 2 of the Convention, retransmission as well as radio distribution require authorisation from the author if they are made by a body other than the originating body because the transmission is then received by a circle of listeners which the original transmission could not have reached (BB 1, 1954, II 608). The defendant, which alleges that the parallel memorandum on the Federal Copyright Act is inaccurate, is wrong in regarding this explanation by the Federal Council as a decisive interpretation of the Convention. The defendant forgets that the memorandum merely explains the reasons for the amendment without intending to add to it an additional restriction. The possibility of reaching a new public is a permanent feature of cable television. Finally it is striking that, in order to dispose of the fears created in the minds of Rediffusion, Radibus and the Post Office by the new provision taken from the Berne Convention, the Federal Council did not invoke the argument that these enterprises would not come within the ambit of the Act in the absence of a new public, but that it rather emphasised the fact that the Swiss Radio and Television Corporation was then paying the authors' royalties on behalf of the three organisations.

In addition the defendant seeks support in the current proposals for amending the Federal Copyright Act to try to show how the legislature would, according to the defendant, settle the question now by reference to the Convention. . . . Therefore the expert commissions never once decided that the Berne Convention required fresh authorisation from an author only in the case of a "new public", since otherwise it would not have failed to say so specifically.

The cantonal Court has not borrowed its theory of the "new public" from the substantive provisions of the Berne Convention, because the point is not referred to at all by the Convention. The Court merely sees it as a suitable opportunity for filling a gap. The defendant also starts from the idea of a gap but the plaintiff, with good reason, denies the gap's existence. The Brussels Conference regulated the retransmission by cable of radio broadcasts without ambiguity. At that date, however, rediffusion networks like those of Radibus and Rediffusion SA were already in service. The fact that the rapid spread of this technique was not foreseen at the time is of as little account as the fact that the above-mentioned enterprises generally broadcast their own programmes.

Under no circumstances, therefore, is there any question of providing for a new legal situation which was not regulated either by the Convention or the Federal Copyright Act. What is much more important to decide is whether the protection guaranteed by section 12, no 6 of the Act can be coupled with a new restriction at the expense of authors. As the reply is in the negative, this Court will abide by the Berne Convention and Swiss legislation which, for the retransmission of a work broadcast by radio, lay down no other condition for the exercise of copyright than a public communication by a body other than the originating body, irrespective of whether the direct reception area is enlarged or not.

*****

Notes and Questions

1. The cable company argues that by requiring it to pay a copyright fee, the Court will award the copyright holder a double-payment. The Court accepts that this may be true, but says this is a legislative determination already made by the drafters of the Berne Convention. What do you think will be the economic impact of the Court's decision? Are authors and artists likely to see a significant increase in their income?

2. The Court refers to decisions in other countries in which the courts have distinguished between larger and smaller scale retransmission enterprises. An apartment building owner may install equipment which boosts signal reception from an antenna and retransmits that signal to individual apartments. On what legal basis, if any, might a court or legislature differentiate such small-scale retransmissions from those that require payment of a copyright fee? (The U.S. Copyright Act, for example, makes specific provision for small scale retransmissions at 17 USC §111.)

J. The WIPO Copyright Treaty

As technologies evolve, the rules of the international IPRs system likewise evolve to govern their protection and use. In the late 1980s and early

1990s, the attention of government IPRs negotiators and other international IPRs specialists was focused on negotiation of the TRIPS Agreement and its implementation into national/regional law. Once the TRIPS Agreement negotiations were concluded, attention was soon directed toward new matters.

The TRIPS Agreement had put into place new rules for copyright, and it had extended coverage in the areas of neighboring rights. One matter on the WIPO agenda would be to bring its rules at least up to date with those of the WTO.

Only late in the TRIPS negotiations did it appear that development of the Internet and other digital media might play a significant role in international commerce. In this regard, the TRIPS Agreement was a step behind developments in the global economic arena even before the "ink had dried." An important step following the TRIPS Agreement would be the negotiation of new rules for the digital environment. The first tranche of these negotiations took place within WIPO.

In the following article, Pamela Samuelson describes and analyzes the final stage of negotiation of the WIPO Copyright Treaty (WCT) in 1996. She refers to former U.S. Patent Commissioner Bruce Lehman, and to some other IPRs protection advocates, as "high-protectionists." For the individual private business enterprise — the goal of which is usually to maximize return on investment — the perspective of the "high-protectionist" often resonates favorably. It is not surprising to hear the chief legal officer of a computer software or biotechnology firm speak in the manner of the high protectionist. As a lawyer in private practice, one is also generally expected to advocate the specific interests of his or her clients, and in a specific transaction this will often mean advocating the highest level of IPRs protection obtainable.

Government officials are elected or appointed to act in the public interest, and we might generally expect these officials to take more moderate positions — seeking to balance the rights of creators to achieve a reasonable return on investment with the interests of the general public in the diffusion of knowledge and information. Law professors and other academics have traditionally enjoyed a wider freedom of expression than private practitioners and government officials, and it should not be surprising that many of the challenges to the high-protectionist agenda emanate from the academic community.

The U.S. Digital Agenda at WIPO

Pamela Samuelson*

I. Introduction

In December 1996, the World Intellectual Property Organization (WIPO) hosted a diplomatic conference in Geneva to consider three proposals to update world intellectual property law. The conferees considered draft treaties to revise treatment of copyright issues, legal protection for sound recordings, and legal protection for the contents of databases. Each contained provisions intended to respond to challenges that global digital networks pose for intellectual property law. This article will trace the fate of the U.S. digital agenda for these treaties. It will show that the treaties which were eventually concluded in Geneva, particularly the copyright treaty, are more compatible with traditional principles of U.S. copyright law than was the high-protectionist agenda that U.S. officials initially sought to promote in Geneva.

The digital agenda was not the only, or even the most pressing, part of the U.S. agenda in Geneva. Of more immediate importance to U.S. copyright industries were provisions in the draft treaty (generally known as "the New Instrument") that concerned the rights of performers and producers of sound recordings. Weaknesses in earlier international accords on rights in sound recordings had made it difficult for the U.S. recording industry to control large-scale unauthorized reproductions and distributions of their products in markets outside the United States. A treaty to strengthen and harmonize international rules about rights of producers of sound recordings was thus of great concern to this sector of the U.S. entertainment industry.

Also of importance to the U.S. entertainment industry were draft treaty provisions that would have accorded certain rights to performers of audiovisual works. Although the U.S. and European delegations were allied on almost all other intellectual property issues at the diplomatic confer-

---

*37 Va. J. Int'l L. 369 (1997).

ence, they were bitterly divided on a proposal to universalize European norms about rights of performers of audiovisual works which the U.S. motion picture industry regarded as an anathema. After the Europeans finally agreed to put off to another day the debate over international rights for audiovisual performers, the New Instrument could be finalized. The final treaty provides a much improved framework for protecting the rights of producers and performers of sound recordings.

As interesting and important as were the WIPO New Instrument negotiations, this Article does not focus on these negotiations as they mainly concern the present day struggles of a sector of the entertainment industry. Rather, the digital agenda negotiations warrant attention because they were a battle about the future of copyright in the global information society. To use that awful, shopworn metaphor just this once, the U.S. digital agenda at WIPO aimed to write the rules of the road for the emerging global information superhighway. Under these rules, copyright owners would have considerably stronger rights than ever before, and the rights of users of protected works would largely be confined to those for which they had specifically contracted and paid.

More specifically, Clinton administration officials sought approval in Geneva for international norms that would have (1) granted copyright owners an exclusive right to control virtually all temporary reproductions of protected works in the random access memory of computers; (2) treated digital transmissions of protected works as distributions of copies to the public; (3) curtailed the power of states to adopt exceptions and limitations on the exclusive rights of copyright owners, including fair use and first sale privileges; (4) enabled copyright owners to challenge the manufacture and sale of technologies or services capable of circumventing technological protection for copyrighted works; (5) protected the integrity of rights management information attached to protected works in digital form; and (6) created a sui generis form of legal protection for the contents of databases. U.S. negotiators worked with their European counterparts in pursuit of high-protectionist norms that these delegations believed would enable their industries to flourish in the growing global market for information products and services.

The digital agenda that Clinton administration officials pursued in Geneva was almost identical to the digital agenda they had put before the U.S. Congress during roughly the same time period. Notwithstanding the fact that this digital agenda had proven so controversial in the U.S. Congress that the bills to implement it were not even reported out of committee, Clinton administration officials persisted in promoting these proposals in Geneva and pressing for an early diplomatic conference to adopt them. For a time, it appeared that administration officials might be able to get in Geneva what they could not get from the U.S. Congress, for the draft treaties published by WIPO in late August 1996 contained language that, if adopted without amendment at the diplomatic conference in December, would have substantially implemented the U.S. digital agenda, albeit with some European gloss. Had this effort succeeded in Geneva, Clinton administration officials would almost certainly have then argued to Congress that ratification of the treaties was necessary to confirm U.S. leadership in the world intellectual property community and to promote the interests of U.S. copyright industries in the world market for information products and services.

Realizing the potential for an end run around Congress, many of those who had argued before Congress that the Clinton administration's digital agenda was an unwise and unbalanced extension of rights to information publishers redirected their efforts toward lobbying the administration about the WIPO negotiations. They not only successfully lobbied the Clinton administration, persuading it to moderate or abandon parts of its digital agenda at WIPO, they also attended WIPO-sponsored regional meetings to acquaint other states with their concerns about the draft treaties, and went to Geneva in large numbers to participate informally in the diplomatic conference as observers and lobbyists. These expressions of concern found a receptive audience among many national delegations to the diplomatic conference. In the end, none of the original U.S.-sponsored digital agenda proposals emerged unscathed from the negotiation process, and at least one — the proposed database treaty — did not emerge at all.

Insofar as the copyright treaty emanating from the diplomatic conference contains provisions addressing digital agenda issues, these provisions reflect an approach that strongly resembles the balancing-of-interests approach that has been traditional in U.S. copyright law. The WIPO Copyright Treaty even affirms "the need to maintain a balance between the interests of authors and the larger public interest, particularly education, research and access to information." This expression of renewed faith in the abiding value of a balanced public policy approach to copyright in the digital environment suggests that predictions of the end of copyright — that is, its displacement by trade policy in the aftermath of the Agreement on Trade-Related Aspects of Intellectual Property Rights (TRIPS) — may have been premature. Still, defeat of the high-protectionist digital agenda at WIPO was a close enough call that its story deserves to be told in some detail.

II. Origins of the U.S. Digital Agenda at WIPO

Shortly after the United States finally acceded to the major international copyright treaty, known as the Berne Convention, in 1989, the governing body of the Berne Union called upon WIPO to form a Committee of Experts concerning a possible supplementary agreement (or "protocol") to the Berne Convention "to clarify the existing, or establish new, international norms where, under the present text of the Berne Convention, doubts may exist as to the extent to which that Convention applies." Given that the Berne Convention had last been revised in 1971, and that it had typically been amended or supplemented every ten to twenty years, the decision to form a Committee of Experts to consider a supplemental agreement to the Berne Convention was, in a sense, a relatively routine matter.

However, the decision in this case was also a product of a growing awareness within the international intellectual property policymaking community that advances in digital technologies raised some challenging questions for copyright law. Many of these had been surveyed in the European Commission's 1988 Green Paper on Copyright and the Challenge of Technology. If any one document can be credited with formulating the questions whose answers came to comprise the digital agenda at WIPO, it was this Green Paper.

Insofar as the United States had a digital agenda at WIPO in the early period of Berne protocol negotiations, it was to persuade the international community to use copyright law to protect computer programs. Under pressure from the United States, Japan had already acceded to this demand. In view of an earlier WIPO proposal for a sui generis form of legal protection for computer programs and the European Commission's expressed willingness to consider something other than copyright as a means by which to protect computer programs, there was, for a time, some reason to doubt that the United States would succeed in convincing the international community to make copyright protection for computer programs an accepted norm.

911

After the European Council of Ministers directed member states of the European Community to protect computer programs by means of copyright law, the prospects for eventual success of this U.S. digital agenda improved substantially. Even so, copyright protection for computer programs remained a high priority for the United States in the negotiations that followed formation of the Committee of Experts on a possible Berne Protocol, as well as during the negotiations that eventually led to the successful conclusion of the TRIPS Agreement which the World Trade Organization (WTO) administers. Because the TRIPS Agreement now obliges states to protect computer programs and databases by means of copyright law, this part of the U.S. digital agenda at WIPO became less urgent. Nevertheless, it is worth mentioning that the copyright treaty recently concluded in Geneva contains provisions requiring the use of copyright law to protect original computer programs and databases in line with draft treaty language previously submitted by the United States.

The more recent U.S. digital agenda grew out of work done under the auspices of the Clinton administration's Information Infrastructure Task Force (IITF). The principal goal of the IITF was to make policy recommendations that would promote optimal development of the emerging information infrastructure, which held considerable promise as an enabler of commerce, education, and a host of other communication functions. Formation of the IITF was hailed at the time as a forward-looking step that would prepare the United States for the twenty-first century. The IITF established a number of working groups to focus on specific policy areas. Bruce Lehman, a former copyright industry lobbyist who had become the Commissioner of Patents and Trademarks, was named chair of the Working Group on Intellectual Property Rights. That group produced a "Green Paper" in July 1994[64] and a "White Paper" in September 1995,[65] which analyzed existing copyright law as applied to works in digital form. It also rec-

---

[64]See Information Infrastructure Task Force Working Group on Intellectual Property Rights, Intellectual Property Rights and the National Information Infrastructure (Preliminary Draft, July 1994) [hereinafter U.S. Green Paper].
[65]Information Infrastructure Task Force Working Group on Intellectual Property Rights, Intellectual Property Rights and the National Information Infrastructure, app. (Sept. 1995), http://www.uspto.gov/web/offices/com/doc/ipnii/lawcopy.pdf [hereinafter White Paper]. This report contains substantially the same analysis and recommendations as the U.S. Green Paper, [id.]. . . .

ommended some changes to the law, which it found to be necessary to induce copyright owners to make their commercially valuable works available in digital networked environments.

Although the main focus of these reports was domestic law, the White Paper also saw in the ongoing WIPO negotiations about a possible Berne Protocol an opportunity to gain international acceptance for the copyright rules that the White Paper was urging for the United States. The global nature of the emerging information infrastructure contributed to the importance of seizing this opportunity to gain international consensus on digital copyright issues. Facilitating the internationalization of the White Paper's digital agenda was the fact that Commissioner Lehman was head of the Clinton administration's delegation to the WIPO negotiations on a possible Berne Protocol and New Instrument.

III. Components of the U.S. Digital Agenda and How They Fared at WIPO

The U.S. White Paper's digital agenda aimed to:

(1) give copyright owners control over every use of copyrighted works in digital form by interpreting existing law as being violated whenever users make even temporary reproductions of works in the random access memories of their computers;

(2) give copyright owners control over every transmission of works in digital form by amending the copyright statute so that digital transmissions will be regarded as distributions of copies to the public;

(3) eliminate fair-use rights whenever a use might be licensed . . . ;

(4) deprive the public of the 'first sale' rights it has long enjoyed in the print world . . . because the White Paper treats electronic forwarding as a violation of both the reproduction and distribution rights of copyright law;

(5) attach copyright management information to digital copies of a work, ensuring that publishers can track every use made of digital copies and trace where each copy resides on the network and what is being done with it at any time;

(6) protect every work technologically (by encryption, for example) and make illegal any attempt to circumvent that protection; [and]

(7) force online service providers to become copyright police. . . .

The only new element in the U.S. digital agenda at WIPO, as compared with the digital agenda reflected in the White Paper, was a late-added proposal by the U.S. delegation calling for a treaty to create a new form of legal protection for the contents of databases. U.S. officials submitted this in reaction to a European proposal that they apparently thought needed improvement.

In analyzing the U.S. digital agenda at WIPO, this Article will discuss in separate subsections how U.S. officials sought to accomplish this agenda internationally by proposing or supporting draft treaty provisions concerning temporary reproductions in computer memory, digital transmissions, curtailment of user rights, regulation of technologies capable of circumventing technological protection, rights management information, and protection of database contents. By tracing the evolution of the U.S. proposals, the draft treaty prepared by Jukka Liedes (who chaired the WIPO Committee of Experts), alternative treaty language proposed at the diplomatic conference, and the provisions contained in the final treaty, we will see that the White Paper's high-protectionist digital agenda met with limited favor at the diplomatic conference, even though it had been substantially embodied in the draft treaties considered at that conference.

A. Temporary Copies as Reproductions

Echoing the White Paper's views on U.S. copyright law, a key component of the U.S. digital agenda at WIPO was the establishment of an international right in copyright owners to control temporary copies of their works in computer memory. If successful, adoption of this norm would not only lay the groundwork for giving copyright owners the right to control every access, viewing, and use of protected works in digital form; it would also help accomplish another goal set forth in the White Paper: to make intermediate institutions, such as online service providers, strictly liable for user infringements. This would, conveniently for copyright industries, have placed the bulk of the responsibility for enforcing copyright interests on these intermediate institutions.

Although representatives of the European Union (E.U.) strongly supported this aspect of the U.S. digital agenda, neither U.S. nor E.U. delegations initially submitted draft treaty language to implement this agenda item. E.U. representatives proposed only that a statement should accompany the final treaty, saying that a treaty provision on temporary copying was unnecessary because article 9(1) of the Berne Convention already recognized the rights of authors to control reproductions of their works "in any manner or form."

However, Chairman Liedes decided to include a provision on temporary copying in the draft treaty he prepared for consideration at the diplomatic conference. Article 7(1) of the draft copyright treaty provided:

> The exclusive right accorded to authors of literary and artistic works in Article 9(1) of the Berne Convention of authorizing the reproduction of their works shall include direct and indirect reproduction of their works, whether permanent or temporary, in any manner or form.

Commentary on this provision explained that such a treaty provision was desirable because diverse opinions existed in the international community about whether ephemeral copies were reproductions of copyrighted works within the meaning of article 9(1) of the Berne Convention. Because "some relevant uses may, now or in the future, become totally based on a temporary reproduction," the commentary went on to say that the right to control temporary copies was of such importance that a rule on it "should be in fair and reasonable harmony all over the world."

Instead of leaving to member states the task of articulating circumstances in which temporary copies could reasonably be privileged in national laws, the draft treaty proposed a special limitation provision as article 7(2):

> Subject to the provisions of Article 9(2) of the Berne Convention, it shall be a matter for legislation in Contracting Parties to limit the right of reproduction in cases where a temporary reproduction has the sole purpose of making the work perceptible or where the reproduction is of a transient or incidental nature, provided that such reproduction takes place in the course of use of the work that is authorized by the author or permitted by law.

It is reasonable to infer that this provision was added to the draft treaty in anticipation of concerns that without it, the reproduction right would be overbroad.

Draft article 7(2) would certainly have enabled states to exempt from infringement the making of temporary copies necessary to enable a computer to "read" data on a lawfully purchased CD-ROM or to view content on an unrestricted website. However, it was sufficiently narrowly drawn that it would not, for example, have relieved telephone companies or online service providers from potential liability for temporary copies of infringing material made in company equipment as the material passed through their systems en route from sender to recipient. Such copies would, of course, meet the transient or incidental standard of draft article 7(2), but they would not have "taken place in the course of use of the work that was authorized by the author or permitted by law."

A number of telephone and high technology companies were among those who objected to the breadth of draft article 7(1) and the narrowness of draft article 7(2). Some of them formed the Ad Hoc Alliance for a Digital Future to lobby against it.

*****

These industry concerns about article 7(2) might have seemed unwarranted, and possibly even paranoid, but for two things: first, by setting forth only two extremely limited situations in which privileges for temporary copying were permissible, draft article 7(2) implicitly questioned the viability of any additional exceptions for temporary copies; and second, the White Paper had already taken the position that intermediate institutions, such as online service providers, were and should be strictly liable for user infringements, both directly (on account of the copies made or distributed in their systems) and indirectly (as vicarious infringers because they benefited financially from infringing activities). It was reasonable to expect that the U.S. delegation would want intermediate institutions outside the United States to be treated in the same manner as the White Paper had sought to treat them in the United States. A number of U.S. telephone and online service executives were so concerned about draft article 7 that they wrote a letter to President Clinton shortly before the diplomatic conference stating that they would oppose ratification of any copyright treaty containing a provision such as article 7.

The high-protectionist position reflected in draft article 7 initially seemed to be on its way to acceptance at the diplomatic conference. Not only had the Chairman of the Committee of Experts endorsed it by including it in the draft treaty, but it also had the support of WIPO officials, the

916

U.S. and E.U. delegations, and some allies of the United States and the European Union. However, considerable opposition to article 7 emerged at the diplomatic conference.

Some countries, such as Australia, questioned the need for a provision covering temporary copying in the copyright treaty. As the Ad Hoc Alliance for a Digital Future had pointed out, the notion that article 9(1) already covered temporary copies in computer memory was doubtful given that "computers did not exist in any great numbers in 1971 when the reproduction right was expressly included in the Berne Convention, and computer networks had hardly been imagined." Others objected to the seeming preclusionary character of article 7(2). Still others, including Singapore, South Africa, and Denmark, favored redrafts of article 7(2) akin to those proposed by the Ad Hoc Alliance for a Digital Future to weed out economically insignificant temporary copies and preserve fair uses.

Different people have different theories about what turned the tide on the temporary copying issue at the diplomatic conference. Some say it was due to prominent copyright scholars making their reservations about article 7's overbreadth known at the diplomatic conference. Others thought that the explanation lay in no one proposal attracting enough support to become a consensus position. Still others suggest that it may have been the result of a faux pas committed by Chairman Liedes when he published African Bloc and some other national proposals as separate documents, rather than including them as alternative treaty language proposals in his redraft of the treaty.

*****

Following the eruption of dissatisfaction with the Chairman's redraft, negotiations over the copyright treaty went into closed sessions. Chairman Liedes must have hoped these sessions would result in a consensus provision on temporary copying. However, no such consensus was achieved. On the final day of the diplomatic conference, a motion was made and carried to delete article 7 from the copyright treaty. The WIPO Copyright Treaty, as a consequence, contains no provision on temporary copying.

There are, however, some who will argue that the WIPO Copyright Treaty should be understood as regarding temporary copies as copyright-significant acts owing to a last-minute resolution that the U.S. delegation insisted be voted on in the final hour of the diplomatic conference. Like Cinderella at the fancy ball, the diplomatic conference had to end before

12:00 a.m. on December 21, 1996. Sometime after 10:30 p.m., many hours after the text of the copyright treaty had been finalized, after the unanimously acceptable agreed-upon statements of interpretation had been voted on, at a time when nearly half of the delegates had already gone home and those who remained were near exhaustion from more than twelve hours of work that day, the U.S. delegation called for a vote on a proposed three sentence statement about digital reproductions. The U.S. agreement to the deletion of article 7 from the copyright treaty, it asserted, had been contingent on the conference's acceptance of a statement on the reproduction right.

The first sentence of the U.S. proposal affirmed that article 9 of the Berne Convention and exceptions thereto applied in the digital environment. More controversial and hotly debated was a second sentence of the U.S. proposal which read: "It is understood that the storage of a protected work in digital form in an electronic medium constitutes a reproduction within the meaning of Article 9 of the Berne Convention." In an attempt to quell questions about and budding opposition to this part of the U.S. proposal, Mihaly Ficsor, a senior WIPO official, asserted that it reflected a long-standing, well-accepted principle that could not be questioned. Yet many did question it, partly because they were unsure what the term "storage" might mean. Some did so by abstaining from the vote on this statement, and others by voting against it. Still, a majority of those in attendance at that late hour did vote in favor of this second sentence. A third sentence saying that up — and downloading of works by computer was a reproduction within the meaning of the Berne Convention was, however, voted down.

Even at the time, some delegates asserted that the U.S. resolution could not be an agreed-upon statement of interpretation of the WIPO Copyright Treaty because it did not satisfy the standards for binding treaty interpretation statements set forth in the Vienna Convention on the Law of Treaties.[127] WIPO may have wrangled internally about this question for, although the Copyright Treaty went up on the WIPO website within days of the diplomatic conference's conclusion, it was almost a month before the agreed-

---

[127]Vienna Convention on the Law of Treaties, opened for signature May 23, 1969, U.N. Doc. A/Conf./39/27, 8 I.L.M. 679 (entered into force Jan. 27, 1980). The argument that a mere majority resolution can serve as an agreed-upon statement of interpretation relies upon the notion that the diplomatic conference's own rules may permit resolutions supported by a bare majority as being agreed-upon statements. Such a rule had been adopted at the WIPO diplomatic conference.

upon statements of interpretation to the Treaty were to be found there. When finally they were, the first two sentences of the U.S.-sponsored resolution were included as an agreed-upon statement of interpretation to article 1(4) of the treaty.

Exactly what weight and scope should be given to this statement will likely be a source of contentious debate and discussion in coming years. Commissioner Lehman and others who supported article 7 will likely regard these two statements and article 9(1) of the Berne Convention as sufficient to establish that temporary copies are reproductions that copyright owners have the right to control. Others will see in the defeat of article 7 and the "up — and downloading" part of the U.S. resolution an international repudiation of the position that temporary copying is a reproduction. The most honest thing that can be said about the temporary copying of works in computer memory is that there is no international consensus on this subject. Still, it is significant that the copyright treaty signed in Geneva does not include a provision on temporary copying given how intent the U.S. and E.U. delegations had been about getting such a treaty provision.

B. Digital Transmissions

A second component of the U.S. digital agenda at WIPO was the attainment of international recognition of a right in copyright owners to control digital transmissions of their works. In line with the approach taken in the U.S. White Paper, the U.S. delegation to the WIPO negotiations submitted draft treaty language calling for digital transmissions to be treated as distributions of copies to the public. Although the E.U. delegation agreed about the need for an international accord on the right of authors to control digital transmissions of their works, it proposed to accomplish this goal in a different manner. The E.U. draft treaty language called for digital transmissions to be regulated as communications of protected works to the public.

At first glance, it might seem that differences in these two characterizations of digital transmissions were of little import. However, there was at least some symbolic significance in this U.S.-E.U. divide. Within the international copyright policymaking community, there is a struggle underway over whose conceptions about copyright should have ascendance in the international arena. The United States and the European Union are the leading contenders for this hegemony. It is worth noting that U.S. copyright law grants authors an exclusive right to distribute copies to the public, but not an exclusive right to communicate works to the public. In contrast, the laws of most other states, including many member states of the European Union, contain no exclusive distribution right as such, but do grant authors rights to control communications of protected works to the public. Also noteworthy is the fact that the United States has been a member of the Berne Union for less than a decade, whereas the Europeans have been the dominant players in Berne Convention treaty negotiations since its inception. As welcome as the belated U.S. conversion to high-protectionist norms might be, many Europeans remember the errant nature of earlier U.S. ways. For such a latecomer to Berne, the United States was behaving in the WIPO Copyright Treaty negotiations in a very aggressive manner, especially in regard to its digital agenda.

Chairman Liedes took a Solomonic approach to resolving these differences in national approaches in the draft copyright treaty. The draft treaty contained a provision to require all states to confer on copyright owners an exclusive right to control distributions of copies of protected works to the public, as well as to confer on them an exclusive right to control communications of protected works to the public. Although granting the wish of the U.S. delegation for international recognition of a distribution right as such, the draft treaty favored the E.U. proposal and treated digital transmissions as communications to the public.

The Chairman's commentary to the draft treaty did not explain why it opted for the communication right approach to digital transmissions, so it is difficult to judge whether the Chairman believed there was any substantive difference between the communication and distribution approaches to regulating digital transmissions. Insofar as there is no substantive difference between the two proposals, the Chairman's decision may simply have been a gesture in deference to European sensibilities or a demonstration of the Chairman's independence from the U.S. delegation to fend off potential criticism that his draft was unduly deferential to that state's proposals.

However, from both European and U.S. sources, there is reason to believe that the decision to treat digital transmissions as communications to the public, instead of as distributions of copies to the public, may have important practical effects. European scholars who studied this issue contemporaneous with the WIPO Expert meetings leading up to the diplomatic conference had argued for treating digital transmissions as communications to the public rather than as distributions of copies. They did so partly because of similarities between digital transmissions and broadcast transmissions which Europeans have long regulated as communications to the public. Some also favored the digital-transmission-as-communication approach because it would more clearly permit users to make occasional private transmissions of digital works (for example, an exchange between two friends).

Some might question that there might be a substantive difference between public distributions and public communications under U.S. law. It, after all, grants copyright owners an exclusive right to control distribution of copies "to the public." An untutored reading of this provision might suggest that U.S. law would distinguish between private and public distributions of copies, perhaps leaving the former unregulated. There is, however, some authority in U.S. caselaw for treating the transfer of a single unauthorized copy to a single member of the public as a distribution to the public. This contrasts with the U.S. public performance right, which grants copyright owners the right to control performances only if they occur outside of a circle of family members or a small group of friends. As experienced copyright lawyers, Commissioner Lehman and his staff would have been aware of this difference. Their preference for treating digital transmissions as distributions of copies, rather than as communications or performances, likely stemmed from the greater control that they thought copyright owners would have if the first characterization became the norm.

Although controversies abounded at the December 1996 diplomatic conference, the proposal to treat digital transmissions as communications to the public was not among them. The U.S. delegation apparently found this approach acceptable as long as the United States could satisfy such a treaty obligation without amending U.S. law to add another exclusive rights provision. Hence, the final treaty includes as article 8 a provision that authors of literary and artistic works shall enjoy the exclusive right of authorizing any communication to the public of their works, by wire or wireless means, including the making available to the public of their works in such a way that members of the public may access these works from a place and at a time individually chosen by them. This article contains no specific reference to digital transmissions, but will nonetheless be understood as encompassing them.

Telephone companies and online service providers had many of the same concerns about the draft treaty provision on the communication right as they had about the draft treaty provision on temporary copying.

Under one interpretation, these firms could be viewed as communicating protected works to the public whenever they provided users with facilities for transmitting works. In response to these concerns, delegates to the diplomatic conference adopted an agreed-upon statement of interpretation to the WIPO Copyright Treaty which said that merely providing services for transmission of digital works should not be construed as a communication to the public. This, along with the omission of article 7 from the final treaty, meant that telephone companies and online service providers could finally breathe easily about the copyright treaty that would emanate from Geneva.

*****

C. Curtailing User Rights

Expansion of the rights of copyright owners over temporary copies and digital transmissions would not have been complete without achievement of a third component of the U.S. digital agenda at WIPO: a substantial curtailment of national authority to limit the rights accorded to copyright owners (for example, by providing that a particular exclusive right could only be infringed by literal copying) or to grant exceptions to those rights for certain classes of users or classes of uses (for example, enabling veteran groups to perform dramatic works without permission).

The initial aim of the U.S. delegation was not only to prevent the adoption of new limitations and exceptions to the expanded rights that the copyright treaty would recognize, but also to call into question the viability of existing limitations and exceptions, particularly as they might apply to digital works. The principal targets of this effort were the so-called "first sale" rule, under which consumers are generally free to redistribute their own copies of a protected work, and fair use and kindred privileges and doctrines, under which private or personal copying of protected works has often found shelter.

Although the U.S. delegation to WIPO did not formally propose draft treaty language to curtail user rights, its submissions to WIPO and the Committee of Experts expressed concern about the potential for limitations and exceptions to undermine the legitimate interests of rights holders. It also opposed a private copying proposal made by the Uruguay delegation. Given the hostility that the White Paper had expressed towards first sale, fair use, and similar privileges in digital networked environments, as well as statements by U.S. officials about the desirability of harmonizing norms at higher levels of protection, there was reason to expect that the U.S. delegation to WIPO would favor a treaty provision curtailing authority to create limitations and exceptions in the WIPO treatymaking process.

Although its origins are something of a mystery — there having been no counterpart to it in national submissions to the Committee of Experts and no explanation of its genesis in the Chairman's commentary — the following was proposed in the draft treaty as article 12:

(1) Contracting Parties may, in their national legislation, provide for limitations of or exceptions to the rights granted to authors of literary and artistic works under this Treaty only in certain special cases that do not conflict with the normal exploitation of the work and do not unreasonably prejudice the legitimate interests of the author.

(2) Contracting Parties shall, when applying the Berne Convention, confine any limitations of or exceptions to rights provided for therein to certain special cases which do not conflict with the normal exploitation of the work and do not unreasonably prejudice the legitimate interests of the author.

Although draft article 12 was the main focus of the debate about national authority to create or maintain limitations and exceptions, it was not the only provision in the draft treaty that would have affected user rights. A significant — and intended — consequence of the draft treaty's characterization of digital transmissions as communications to the public was to ensure that no "exhaustion of rights" would occur as to digital transmissions.

Although the U.S. delegation would have preferred to characterize digital transmissions as distributions of copies, this did not mean that the U.S. delegation supported application of "first sale" (or the European equivalent, "exhaustion of rights") principles to allow recipients of digitally transmitted copies to redistribute their copies.[176] Consistent with the White Paper's assertions, the U.S. position was that first sale privileges did not

---

[176]See White Paper, at 90-95. The White Paper argued against the existence of first sale rights in digital copies on account of the potential for infringement that would arise from recognition of such a right. Id. at 91.

apply to digitally transmitted copies because, in contrast with secondary transfers of physical copies, the secondary transfer of a digital copy could not be accomplished without making additional copies of the work for which there would be no authorization from the copyright owner or the law.[177]

The curtailment of fair use and kindred privileges was a somewhat more subtle and indirect project. Proponents of draft article 12 argued that it merely restated international treaty obligations already embodied in article 9(2) of the Berne Convention and article 13 of the TRIPS Agreement. Because there had been no challenges to fair use or other existing privileges under these treaties, proponents of article 12 assured fair use advocates that there was no cause for worrying about such a provision in the WIPO Copyright Treaty.

There were a number of reasons why it was difficult for fair use advocates to take heart from these assurances. Some arose from textual differences between draft article 12 and its predecessor provisions, some from the Chairman's commentary to draft article 12, and some from contextual differences between draft article 12 and its predecessors.

On its face, draft article 12 was more restrictive than its ancestors. There was, for example, no antecedent in the Berne Convention to draft article 12(2) which provided that states "shall, when applying the Berne Convention, confine any limitations of or exceptions" to those meeting the three-step test. In addition, article 9(2) of the Berne Convention and article 13 of the TRIPS Agreement provided that states could grant limitations or exceptions "in certain special cases." Draft article 12(1) would have inserted the word "only" just before this clause, an insertion that would almost certainly have been construed as strengthening the potential bite that such an

---

[177]The U.S. Green Paper had initially recommended amending copyright law in order to deprive owners of digital copies of their first sale rights. See U.S. Green Paper, supra note 64, at 53-56, 124-25. When they discerned that it was necessary to make a copy of a digital work in order to redistribute it, the drafters of the White Paper realized they could achieve their goal by statutory interpretation. The first sale rule, after all, only limits the exclusive distribution right, not the reproduction right. See White Paper, supra note 29, at 92-94. Other commentators argue that temporary copies necessary to effectuate first sale rights are fair uses under precedents such as Sega Enters., Ltd. v. Accolade, Inc., 977 F.2d 1510, 1527 (9th Cir. 1992) (incidental copying necessary to get access to unprotected ideas in a computer program held fair use).

article might have in subsequent challenges to national exceptions or limitations before WTO panels.

*****

Adoption of draft article 12 in the WIPO copyright treaty would have significantly advanced the potential for a successful WTO challenge to national exceptions or limitations. This was partly because of the more restrictive text of draft article 12 and the Chairman's commentary indicating that exceptions "must never" fail any part of the three-step test. Without article 12, it would have been difficult for states to challenge the application of fair use and kindred doctrines in the digital environment because article 13 had become part of TRIPS before international policymakers had given any thought about the appropriate scope of intellectual property rights in the digital networked environments. Moreover, draft article 12 appeared in a document that explicitly aimed to protect copyright owner interests in markets they were not currently exploiting. Indeed, this was the very reason for the proposal to grant broad rights to control temporary copying. The document's goal suggested that article 12 would be interpreted as broadening the conventional understanding of what constituted "normal exploitation."

*****

Fairly soon after the diplomatic conference got down to business, considerable support emerged for conforming the text of article 12 to that of article 13 of TRIPS, as well as for an agreed upon statement to accompany it that would preserve existing fair use-like privileges in national laws and permit evolution of new exceptions in the digital environment.

*****

Not only was there support at the diplomatic conference for recognition of national authority to grant exceptions and limitations as a means of balancing the interests of copyright owners and the public, there was also support for making the principle of balance a fundamental purpose of the treaty by adding a new clause to the treaty's preamble. The preamble to the Chairman's original draft treaty had three parts:

Desiring to develop and maintain the protection of the rights of authors in their literary and artistic works in a manner as effective and uniform as possible,

Recognizing the need to introduce new international rules and clarify the interpretation of certain existing rules in order to provide adequate solutions to the questions raised by new economic, social, cultural and technological developments,

Recognizing the profound impact of the development and convergence of information and communication technologies on the creation and use of literary and artistic works[.]

To these, the final treaty added another purpose:

Recognizing the need to maintain a balance between the rights of authors and the larger public interest, particularly education, research and access to information, as reflected in the Berne Convention[.]

This new preamble provision represents a major development in international copyright policy.[226]

If copyright policy on an international scale had seemed to be veering away from traditional purposes such as the promotion of knowledge in the public interest and toward a solely trade-oriented set of purposes, this treaty can be seen as a timely correction in the course of international copyright policy. Though the Chairman's initial draft was consistent with a trade-based approach to copyright policy, the final treaty reaffirms faith in the concept of maintaining a balance between private and public interests in copyright policymaking and of recognizing that education, research, and

---

[226]Another significant, although not much heralded, aspect of the WIPO Copyright Treaty is article 2, which states: "Copyright protection extends to expressions and not to ideas, procedures, methods of operation or mathematical concepts as such." Oddly enough, the idea/expression distinction as such had not been embodied in the Berne Convention or supplemental agreements to it. Agreed-upon statements of interpretation to the WIPO Copyright Treaty make it clear that article 2's proscriptions apply to computer programs and databases.

access to information are among the important social values that a well-formed copyright law should serve.

D. Regulating Circumvention Technologies

An important part of the U.S. digital agenda at WIPO was establishment of a new international norm to regulate technologies and services likely to be used to circumvent technological protection for copyrighted works. The electronic future envisioned in the U.S. White Paper, as well as that for which many major content providers seem to be planning, contemplates broad use of technological measures, such as encryption, to protect content in digital form. As promising as such technologies are, they too pose a problem: what one technology can do, another can generally undo. Hence, the perceived need for law to regulate infringement-enabling technologies and services.

The impetus for this provision came largely from the U.S. motion picture industry, which has for many years been keen on the idea of regulating technologies that enable infringement. Although unsuccessful in previous efforts to persuade Congress to pass a broad law to allow them to sue makers of circumvention technologies, the motion picture industry saw in the Clinton administration's National Information Infrastructure (NII) intellectual property initiative a new opportunity for getting the desired legislation. As other content owners came to understand the desirability of technological solutions to the problem of protecting digital content, the motion picture industry gained new allies to support stronger regulation of circumvention technologies and services. . . ."

*****

Article 13 of Chairman Liedes' draft copyright treaty was closely modeled on the U.S. proposal:

> Contracting parties shall make unlawful the importation, manufacture or distribution of protection-defeating devices, or the offer or performance of any service having the same effect, by any person knowing or having reasonable grounds to know that the device or service will be used for, or in the course of, the exercise of rights provided under this Treaty that is not authorized by the rightholder or the law.

It defined the term "protection-defeating device" — in terms that closely track the U.S. proposal — as "any device, product or component incorporated into a device or product, the primary purpose or primary effect of which is to circumvent any process, treatment, mechanism or system that prevents or inhibits any of the acts covered by the rights under this Treaty." Draft article 13 would have required "appropriate and effective remedies" for violations of this provision.

*****

The principal difference between draft article 13 and the U.S. White Paper provision was the knowledge requirement in the former, which had no counterpart in the latter. The Chairman's commentary to draft article 13 explained that the knowledge requirement "focuses on the purpose for which the device or service will be used." This knowledge requirement responded to a common criticism of the White Paper proposal, which asserted the unfairness of imposing strict liability on manufacturers who had expected their equipment to be used in a lawful manner.

Recognizing that a provision on circumvention technologies would be a new feature for copyright laws of many countries, Chairman Liedes tried to alleviate potential concerns about the breadth of his proposal by indicating that there would be substantial latitude for national implementations of this norm. States would, for example, be "free to choose appropriate remedies according to their own legal traditions," and they could "design the exact field of application of the provision . . . taking into consideration the need to avoid legislation that would impede lawful practices and the lawful use of subject matter that is in the public domain."

Neither the insertion of a knowledge requirement nor the Chairman's assurances regarding latitude in national implementations sufficed to overcome serious concerns about draft article 13. Many delegates to the diplomatic conference expressed deep concerns about the implications of such regulation for the public domain and for fair use. Even a knowledge-based standard for regulating technologies with infringing uses represented a dramatic change in policy. Under existing U.S. law, for example, firms have been free to sell a device (or presumably to provide a service) to customers as long as it had a substantial noninfringing use.

There was also reason to doubt whether a provision with a "knowing or having reason to know" requirement would, in practice, have been meaningfully different from the U.S. White Paper standard. Rights holders could surely be expected to argue that people intend the natural consequences of their actions. In addition, the commentary to draft article 13 made clear that the anti-circumvention provision could be employed to challenge the sale of technologies based on predictions about their primary uses, which meant that technologies could be challenged before the opportunity arose to see what the primary uses of the product would actually be.

At the diplomatic conference, there was little support for the Chairman's proposal. Some countries, such as Korea, opposed inclusion of any anti-circumvention provision in the treaty. Others, such as Singapore, proposed a "sole purpose" or "sole intended purpose" standard for regulating circumvention technologies. Some delegations wanted an explicit statement that carved out circumvention for fair use and public domain materials. The European Union emphasized the importance of a knowledge of infringement requirement in any provision regulating devices and services possessing technology-defeating purposes.

Facing the prospect of little support for the Chairman's watered-down version of the U.S. White Paper proposal, the U.S. delegation was in the uncomfortable position of trying to find a national delegation willing to introduce a compromise provision brokered by U.S. industry groups that would simply require states to have adequate and effective legal protection against circumvention technologies and services. In the end, such a delegation was found, and the final treaty embodied this provision in article 11.

This compromise was, of course, a far cry from the provision that the United States had initially promoted. Still, it was an accomplishment to get any provision on this issue in the final treaty. The inclusion of terms like "adequate" and "effective" protection in the treaty means that U.S. firms will be able to challenge national regulations that they deem deficient.

F. Protecting Rights Management Information

A fifth component of the U.S. digital agenda at WIPO was acceptance of a second unprecedented norm for an international copyright treaty, namely, an agreement to protect the integrity of copyright management information (CMI) that might be attached to digital copies of protected works. In keeping with the White Paper's proposal to amend U.S. copyright law to protect CMI from depredations by would-be pirates who might strip the CMI from distributed copies of digital content, falsify, or otherwise tamper with CMI in aid of infringing activities, the U.S. delegation to WIPO recommended a virtually identical provision to the Committee of Experts for inclusion in the WIPO copyright treaty.

*****

As with the anti-circumvention provision, Chairman Liedes modeled the draft treaty provision on rights management information on the U.S. proposal, albeit with some differences in terminology and reorganization of its structure. Subsection (1) of article 14 of the draft treaty read:

> Contracting parties shall make it unlawful for any person knowingly to perform any of the following acts:
>
> (i) to remove or alter any electronic rights management information without authority;
>
> (ii) to distribute, import for distribution or communicate to the public, without authority, copies of works from which electronic rights management information has been removed or altered without authority.

Subsection (2) defined "rights management information" [RMI] as information which identifies the work, the author of the work, the owner of any right in the work, and any numbers or codes that represent such information, when any of these items of information are attached to a copy of a work or appear in connection with the communication of a work to the public.

The commentary accompanying this subsection stated the Chairman's expectation that criminal as well as civil penalties should be available for violations of this provision.

*****

The RMI provision of the draft treaty proved to be one of the least controversial parts of the digital agenda at WIPO. But even this limited version of the U.S. proposal was further trimmed in the course of diplomatic negotiations. Concerns had arisen that the U.S. proposal would inadvertently make illegal some alterations to RMI that presented no threat to the legitimate interests of rights holders. An alteration to RMI attached to licensed copies to correct RMI after a change in copyright ownership should not be illegal, but would have been under the Chairman's original draft. To overcome this problem, the RMI provision was amended so that alterations to RMI and distributions of copies with altered RMI would only be illegal insofar as they facilitated or concealed infringing activities.

As with the anti-circumvention provision in the WIPO Copyright Treaty, the U.S. delegation did not get exactly what it had originally sought. However, it was no small achievement to get as article 12 of the final treaty a provision that will significantly protect rights management information attached to digital copies of protected works transmitted via global networks.

F. Protecting the Contents of Databases

A late-added component of the U.S. digital agenda at WIPO was acceptance of the U.S. proposal for an international treaty to protect investments in database development by granting database makers exclusive rights to authorize or prevent extractions and uses of database contents. Had the European Union not included a material reciprocity provision in a recent directive calling for the creation of a new form of intellectual property protection for the contents of databases, and had the Europeans not proposed a draft treaty to universalize this new norm in the ongoing round of WIPO treaty negotiations, the United States might have been content to let this agenda item simmer somewhat longer. The U.S. White Paper had expressed only general support for the idea of protecting database contents, but made no specific proposal about it.

Because of substantial U.S. industry objections to some parts of the European approach to database protection, including its reciprocity provision, the U.S. delegation decided to submit a counterproposal so that the United States could have some influence on the text of whatever database treaty might emerge from Chairman Liedes' word processor. Once the Chairman decided to propose a database contents treaty, members of the U.S. delegation pledged their "unswerving support" for such a treaty.

As the concept of a database contents law is sufficiently new, it may aid understanding to examine the origins and essential contours of the European directive. In planning for the future of the information society, the

Commission of the European Communities noticed that there was an uneven level of investment in database development in E.U. states. It noticed, as well, that there was considerable disharmony, as well as some uncertainty, about the extent of legal protection available to database makers in the European Union. The database market, both domestically and internationally, was already substantial and its potential for growth was considerable. The Commission was quite frank in expressing its desire for Europe to become a more substantial player in the world database market. Seemingly trying to explain the generally low level of investment in databases in the European Union (with the exception of the United Kingdom, where copyright protection had long been available to data compilers on a "sweat of the brow" basis), the Commission observed that many commercially valuable electronic databases were vulnerable to market-destructive appropriations. Existing law provided no or uncertain remedies for such appropriations, either because some of these databases could not be copyrighted or because even when copyright protection was available, this law did not protect the data they contained. Reselections and rearrangements of these data might not infringe copyright, but they could undermine the commercial viability of the databases from which the data came.

To induce higher levels of investment in databases, the Commission proposed a directive to create a new law to protect databases against appropriations of the whole or substantial parts of their contents. As finally adopted, the European directive gave database makers who had made substantial investments in the development or maintenance of databases fifteen years of protection for their contents. These rights could be renewed by making additional substantial investments in the database. To prod other states to adopt similar laws, the E.U. directive mandated that this new form of legal protection would be available to databases of non-E.U. nationals only if their country of origin had an equivalent law.

Although the reciprocity clause of the European directive was probably the most immediate cause for database protection becoming part of the U.S. digital agenda at WIPO, it was not the only cause. U.S. database developers were, of course, upset at the prospect that European database makers would be able to extract and reuse data from U.S. databases because the United States had no equivalent law. It was also true, however, that some U.S. database developers were unhappy with other provisions of the E.U. directive. In addition, some worried about Asian competitors who were taking advantage of the "gap" in existing international intellectual property law that permitted extraction of the whole or substantial parts of unoriginal databases, such as telephone directories, to develop databases to compete with U.S. producers.

Once the European Union submitted its proposed treaty language to the WIPO Committee of Experts, U.S. officials saw a way to kill three birds with one stone. By submitting its own proposal for a database treaty, the United States could cure a number of perceived deficiencies in the European proposal, ensure that the United States would adopt an equivalent law to the E.U. directive, and protect U.S.-originated databases from unfair competition outside the United States by universalizing norms that seemed likely to maintain U.S. dominance in the world market for databases.

It was a major victory for the U.S. delegation when Chairman Liedes issued a draft treaty on database protection that was an amalgam of the European and U.S. proposals. Where the U.S. and E.U. proposals were in agreement, such as in making eligibility for protection depend on a substantial investment in the collection, assembly, verification, organization or presentation of database contents, and in enabling a renewal of rights upon substantial additional investments in the database, the draft treaty unsurprisingly adopted the same approach. On one issue about which the two proposals differed, namely, the duration of protection, the draft treaty took no position, offering as alternative A, the U.S. proposal of twenty-five years, and as alternative B, the E.U. proposal of fifteen years.

In a number of respects, however, the draft treaty more closely resembled the U.S. than the E.U. proposal. This too represented a victory for the U.S. delegation. For example, the draft treaty would have required contracting states to grant makers of databases the right to authorize or prohibit the extraction and utilization of database contents. The use right had been proposed for the first time in the U.S submission. In line with the U.S proposal, the draft treaty would also have accorded protection to databases of foreign nationals on a national treatment basis, that is, states would protect the databases of foreign nationals in the same manner as they did the databases of their own nationals. The draft database treaty also had a provision to regulate circumvention technologies derived from the U.S. database treaty proposal.

Within weeks, similar expressions of concern or opposition to the database treaty emanated from a number of quarters, including in a letter from Jack Gibbons, President Clinton's Science Advisor, to Laura Tyson, the head of the National Economic Council, which was then reviewing U.S. positions on treaty matters in anticipation of the December diplomatic conference. These outpourings of concern finally sparked media interest in the

WIPO negotiations. Patent & Trademark Office (PTO) officials initially sought to avert scientific opposition to the database treaty by proposing changes to the draft treaty to address concerns raised by the science agencies and by offering to have a representative of the science agencies join the U.S. delegation in Geneva in an advisory capacity. This did not suffice to stem the tide of concern over the database treaty. Even so, on the eve of their departure for Geneva, PTO officials were still saying publicly that they were going to Geneva with the intention of negotiating and concluding a database treaty.

There is, of course, ample reason to doubt whether a database treaty would have been concluded in Geneva in December 1996, even without the substantial U.S.-based opposition to the treaty. After all, the European Union was the only governmental entity that had adopted such a law, and its adoption was so recent that no member state of the European Union had actually implemented the directive by the time of the diplomatic conference. Given that the norms of the treaty were vague (for example, forbidding unauthorized use of a substantial part of a database), that the idea of such a law was still very new, and that some delegations to WIPO meetings had previously expressed reservations about it, it would have been somewhat surprising if a database treaty had been concluded in December 1996.

It is unquestionably true, however, that as news of substantial U.S.-based opposition to the database treaty spread among the delegations to the WIPO negotiations, it valorized expressions of doubt about the database treaty. In the cloister of copyright specialists at WIPO, proposals of E.U. and U.S. delegations are generally accorded considerable deference. When it came to assessing the impact of digital technologies on intellectual property law, most WIPO delegates knew little more than that these technologies did pose challenges for content owners. If the U.S. and E.U. authorities had studied these issues carefully and come to the conclusion that the additional legal norms they proposed were needed, who were they to say that these norms would be a bad idea?

There is also peer pressure among copyright specialists at gatherings such as WIPO meetings constraining somewhat their willingness to express doubts about strong protectionist positions. Amidst a flock of copyright fundamentalists, delegates do not want to find themselves cast as agnostics or atheists. Even less do they want to appear to be contributing, wittingly or unwittingly, to international piracy of copyrighted works. The U.S. and E.U. delegations would naturally be inclined to take advantage of this reluctance. News of scientific opposition to the database treaty changed the dynamics of the diplomatic conference. Suddenly, delegates who had doubts about the database treaty could feel that they were standing up for science.

Widespread criticism of the Chairman's draft database treaty caused its quick removal from the conference agenda. Consideration of the draft database treaty has, however, not merely been postponed or sent back to the Committee of Experts for further refinement; it has been taken off the table. In order for database protection issues to be raised again at WIPO, the governing body of WIPO will have to constitute a new Committee of Experts to study the matter. This new committee should be charged, as the previous Committee of Experts did not believe itself to be, with first inquiring whether any such treaty is actually needed. Only after concluding that a treaty is necessary should the Committee consider proposals for new treaty language to protect database contents, and even then, it should consider other alternative solutions to any database protection problem that exists. Although this aspect of the U.S. digital agenda at WIPO was not successful at the December 1996 diplomatic conference, database protection will unquestionably be part of the international digital agenda in years to come.

*****

IV. Reflections on the Outcome in Geneva

*****

The principal fly in the ointment — first in the U.S. Congress, then inside the administration, and finally in Geneva — was the openness of the democratic process. Commissioner Lehman may have been convinced that he had charted an appropriate digital future for copyright law, but others were not. When the White Paper's legislative package encountered such substantial opposition in the U.S. Congress that it did not even get reported out of the relevant subcommittees, Lehman's reaction was not to reconsider what the U.S. position in Geneva should be or to slow down the treaty making process on these issues until domestic consensus could be achieved. Rather, his response was to redouble efforts to put the international treaty making process on as fast a track as possible to take advantage of the momentum toward international adoption of the White Paper proposals that he had been striving to achieve. Perhaps he could get in Geneva an implementation of the digital agenda that he had not yet been able to get from Congress. This, then, became Lehman's second order strategy for accomplishing the White Paper's digital agenda.

*****

In addition, the early and complete failure of the database treaty profoundly changed the dynamics at the WIPO conference. It hurt the credibility of U.S. negotiators who had been pushing as earnestly for the database treaty as for the other two treaties. They hoped to have three treaties to take back to please the information industries in the United States, which had so strongly supported President Clinton in his re-election bid. Failure of the database treaty also tarnished the image that the U.S. delegation had previously tried to project as farsighted and disinterested futurists who had studied the complex issues in depth and arrived at the right solution for the future. And it made it easier for delegates to express broad concerns about the implications for science, research, and education likely to flow from the high-protectionist norms that the U.S. and E.U. delegations had been promoting in both the copyright and database treaties. These concerns spilled over to affect negotiations on draft articles 7 and 12 of the draft treaty, as well as on the preamble to the copyright treaty affirming the treaty's aim to balance the rights of authors and rights of users with due consideration to the needs and concerns of science and education.

B. Measures of Success for the U.S. Digital Agenda at WIPO

Whether one judges U.S. efforts to promote a digital agenda at WIPO as a success or a failure depends on what one decides to measure. By comparison with the high-protectionist agenda reflected in the White Paper and the U.S. submissions to WIPO, one would have to say that the U.S. efforts were largely unsuccessful. The conference rejected the temporary copying proposals that had initially had U.S. support. It decided to treat digital transmissions as communications to the public, rather than as distributions of copies (which may bring with it a widened possibility for some private transmissions of works). The treaty not only preserved existing user right privileges in national laws; it recognized that new exceptions might appropriately be created. The Chairman's variant on the U.S. White Paper's anti-circumvention provision garnered almost no support. Even though the treaty contains a rights management information provision, it is watered down by comparison with what the U.S. delegation had sought. Moreover, the U.S. model for a database treaty was so objectionable that it was dropped virtually without discussion from the agenda in Geneva.

Seen from another perspective, however, the U.S. digital agenda had considerable success. It is now clear that copyright law applies in the digital environment, and that storage of protected works is a reproduction that can be controlled by copyright owners. The treaty also protects copyright owners from digital transmissions insofar as they constitute communications to the public. The treaty reaffirms the three-step test that limits national authority to adopt exceptions or limitations to certain special cases that do not conflict with a normal exploitation of the work or unreasonably prejudice the legitimate interests of the author. It also requires states to have adequate protection and effective remedies against circumvention technologies and services, and to protect rights management information from alteration and removal insofar as these conceal or facilitate infringement. Finally, WIPO is to sponsor further discussions concerning a database treaty.

The copyright treaty that emerged from the diplomatic conference was a real success for the United States in part because that treaty is actually more consistent with the letter and spirit of U.S. copyright law than the digital agenda that Commissioner Lehman initially sought to promote in Geneva. For example, the conference decision not to overstretch the reproduction right of copyright law by insisting that it gives rights over all temporary copies, as draft article 7 would have done, is consistent with the general trend in U.S. caselaw which has thus far treated some temporary copies, but not others, as reproductions. Insofar as the original draft of article 7 would have made online service providers and other intermediate institutions liable for all user infringements, including those of which they knew nothing, the treaty's rejection of article 7 is consistent with U.S. caselaw. U.S. courts lately have been holding intermediate institutions liable only when they knew of infringement and took no action to control it.

U.S. copyright law has long accorded copyright owners the right to transmit their works to the public. Hence, the treaty's endorsement of treating digital transmissions as communications to the public is consistent with U.S. copyright law. Now that the treaty has confirmed that copyright owners do have rights to control digital transmissions that communicate their works to the public, perhaps they will feel sufficiently protected and will begin digitally transmitting more of their commercially valuable works to the public.

The treaty's endorsement of balancing principles in copyright law, in particular, the importance of considering the impact of copyright rules on education, research, and access to information, is consistent with long-standing principles of U.S. copyright law. The treaty's confirmation of the viability of existing exceptions and limitations preserves the U.S. fair use defense, as well as other privileges embodied in the U.S. copyright statute. Also consistent with U.S. copyright principles is the treaty's stated expectation that new exceptions and limitations may emerge or evolve in digital networked environments.

Insofar as the U.S. copyright law already has a number of rules that regulate circumvention technologies, the treaty's provision on this subject is also consistent with U.S. law. The overbroad provision that the U.S. delegation to WIPO had wanted to include in the treaty would have been a break from the general thrust of U.S. law. Even the RMI provision has some counterpart in existing U.S. copyright rules on removal and falsification of copyright notices. The more narrowly tailored treaty provision on RMI, as compared with the provision initially sought by the U.S. delegation, is also consistent with balancing principles of U.S. law.

Finally, the repudiation of the database treaty is consistent with the preservation of freedom of information principles that also have a long history in U.S. copyright law. The Supreme Court's decision in Feist Publications, Inc. v. Rural Telephone Service Co. recognized that the constitutional purposes of copyright law are promoted when second comers are free to extract and reuse data from one work in order to make another work. This does not mean that a well-crafted database treaty to protect data compilers from market-destructive appropriations of the whole or substantial parts of their data compilations would not also be consistent with the U.S. legal tradition. There is general agreement in the United States that market-destructive appropriations of information, such as that which occurred in International News Service, Inc. v. Associated Press, can and should be regulated. The problem with the draft database treaty was that its overbreadth threatened to unduly interfere with many socially desirable extractions and reuses of data. The diplomatic conference in Geneva rightly refused to endorse it.

Although this Article has depicted the outcome of the digital agenda at WIPO in relatively rosy terms, this success should not be seen for more than it is. Just because balancing principles found their way into the recent copyright treaty does not mean that there will cease to be pressure to grant more extensive protection to copyright owners. Clinton administration officials may still choose to pursue the same legislative package in the U.S. Congress as they sought before. The Berne Convention, after all, only establishes minimum rules for national laws, not maximum rules. Moreover, other developments, such as widespread use of shrinkwrap licenses or electronic equivalents that substantially limit user rights, as well as emerging use of encryption and other technological protections may make the balancing principles of copyright law something of an historical anachronism.

However, there is still reason to cheer the digital agenda reflected in the copyright treaty signed in Geneva on December 20, 1996. Confidence in balancing principles, such as those reflected in the copyright treaty, may yet be carried over to other legal rules regulating digital information, such as those that will govern electronic commerce in digital information products and services. Moreover, consumer preference for unrestricted or more lightly restricted copies of digital works over the highly protected copies may cause many publishers to abandon the otherwise appealing mindset that would seek ever stronger technological protection for digital content. The right motto for the digital future may be: "protect revenues, not bits."

The phenomenal success of the software industry has, after all, occurred notwithstanding the unprotected nature of most copies sold in the mass-market. This should hearten traditional copyright industries which are now trying to retool their products and processes so they can commercially distribute works in digital networked environments. The market for copyrighted works in digital form is already very substantial, and it will continue to grow. Copyright owners cannot expect a digital future in which no unauthorized copies will be made. What they can expect, and what the digital agenda in the just-completed WIPO Copyright Treaty will bring, is enough protection so that the leakage that occurs does not become a hemorrhage.

Notes and Questions

1. Pamela Samuelson calls attention to a provision added to the WIPO Copyright Treaty preamble at the diplomatic conference which recognizes the need to maintain a balance among interests. Why might a provision in

the preamble of a treaty be important? The preamble does not create specific rights or obligations. How might it be used?

2. Samuelson's article does not deal with the question of exhaustion of rights (other than in the context of temporary reproductions). Yet negotiation of the WCT illustrated — as does Article 6 of the TRIPS Agreement — that governments do not agree on an approach to exhaustion of rights in the international context. It was once again made clear in the WCT and WPPT negotiations that the subject matter remains sufficiently controversial that an attempt to find common ground might have impeded the successful conclusion of these treaties. The Chairman's drafts of the Copyright Treaty and the Performances and Phonograms Treaty included alternatives that would either have precluded international exhaustion, or reserved discretion to the contracting states. The Chairman's drafts did not propose an alternative in favor of international exhaustion.[1] Examine article 6(2) of the WCT and article 8(2) and 12(2) of the Performances and Phonograms Treaty (*infra* this section). What do these provisions accomplish?

3. Telecommunications service providers played a major role in the WCT negotiations. These providers were greatly concerned over potential liability for content carried over the Internet and other digital transmission media to which they provide access. Do you think that the "phone company" should be responsible for what individuals say on the telephone? Do you think that the "phone company" should be responsible for what individuals post on the Internet? What is the difference between the two contexts?

---

[1] *See* Chairman of the Committee of Experts, Basic Proposal for the Substantive Provisions of the Treaty on Certain Questions Concerning the Protection of Literary and Artistic Works to be Considered by the Diplomatic Conference, WIPO Doc. CRNR/DC/4, Aug. 30, 1996, at art. 8.

WIPO Copyright Treaty (WCT) (1996)

International Bureau of WIPO*

This Treaty was concluded in Geneva on December 20, 1996. It is open for signature at the headquarters of WIPO until December 31, 1997.

This Treaty is open to States members of WIPO and to the European Community. The Assembly constituted by the Treaty may, once the Treaty enters into force, decide to admit other intergovernmental organizations to become party to the Treaty.

This Treaty will come into force after 30 instruments of ratification or accession by States have been deposited. Such instruments must be deposited with the Director General of WIPO, who is the depositary of the Treaty.

* * *

Any Contracting Party (even if it is not bound by the Berne Convention) must comply with the substantive provisions of the 1971 (Paris) Act of the Berne Convention.

* * *

As to the subject matters to be protected by copyright, the Treaty mentions two:

(i) computer programs, whatever may be the mode or form of their expression, and

(ii) compilations of data or other material ("databases"), in any form, which by reason of the selection or arrangement of their contents constitute intellectual creations. (Where a database does not constitute such a creation, it is outside the scope of this Treaty.)

* * *

---

*http://www.wipo.int.

As to the rights of authors, the Treaty deals with three:

(i) the right of distribution,

(ii) the right of rental, and

(iii) the right of communication to the public.

Each of them is an exclusive right, subject to certain limitations and exceptions. Not all of the limitations or exceptions are mentioned in the following:

the right of distribution is the right to authorize the making available to the public of the original and copies of a work through sale or other transfer of ownership,

the right of rental is the right to authorize commercial rental to the public of the original and copies of three kinds of works:

(i) computer programs (except where the computer program itself is not the essential object of the rental),

(ii) cinematographic works (but only in cases where commercial rental has led to widespread copying of such works materially impairing the exclusive right of reproduction), and

(iii) works embodied in phonograms as determined in the national law of the Contracting Parties (except for countries that since April 15, 1994, have in force a system of equitable remuneration for such rental),

the right of communication to the public is the right to authorize any communication to the public, by wire or wireless means, including "the making available to the public of works in a way that the members of the public may access the work from a place and at a time individually chosen by them." The quoted expression covers in particular on-demand, interactive communication through the Internet.

* * *

The Treaty obliges the Contracting Parties to provide legal remedies against the circumvention of technological measures (e.g., encryption) used by authors in connection with the exercise of their rights and against the removal or altering of information, such as certain data that identify the work or their authors, necessary for the management (e.g., licensing, collecting and distribution of royalties) of their rights ("rights management information").

* * *

The Treaty obliges each Contracting Party to adopt, in accordance with its legal system, the measures necessary to ensure the application of the Treaty. In particular, the Contracting Party must ensure that enforcement procedures are available under its law so as to permit effective action against any act of infringement of rights covered by the Treaty. Such action must include expeditious remedies to prevent infringement and remedies which constitute a deterrent to further infringements.

* * *

The Treaty establishes an Assembly of the Contracting Parties whose main task is to deal with matters concerning the maintenance and development of the Treaty, and it entrusts to the International Bureau of WIPO the administrative tasks concerning the Treaty.

WIPO Copyright Treaty*

Preamble

The Contracting Parties,

Desiring to develop and maintain the protection of the rights of authors in their literary and artistic works in a manner as effective and uniform as possible,

---

*Adopted by the Diplomatic Conference on December 20, 1996.

Recognizing the need to introduce new international rules and clarify the interpretation of certain existing rules in order to provide adequate solutions to the questions raised by new economic, social, cultural and technological developments,

Recognizing the profound impact of the development and convergence of information and communication technologies on the creation and use of literary and artistic works,

Emphasizing the outstanding significance of copyright protection as an incentive for literary and artistic creation,

Recognizing the need to maintain a balance between the rights of authors and the larger public interest, particularly education, research and access to information, as reflected in the Berne Convention,

Have agreed as follows:

Article 1
Relation to the Berne Convention

(1) This Treaty is a special agreement within the meaning of Article 20 of the Berne Convention for the Protection of Literary and Artistic Works, as regards Contracting Parties that are countries of the Union established by that Convention. This Treaty shall not have any connection with treaties other than the Berne Convention, nor shall it prejudice any rights and obligations under any other treaties.

(2) Nothing in this Treaty shall derogate from existing obligations that Contracting Parties have to each other under the Berne Convention for the Protection of Literary and Artistic Works.

(3) Hereinafter, "Berne Convention" shall refer to the Paris Act of July 24, 1971 of the Berne Convention for the Protection of Literary and Artistic Works.

(4) Contracting Parties shall comply with Articles 1 to 21 and the Appendix of the Berne Convention.

Article 2
Scope of Copyright Protection

Copyright protection extends to expressions and not to ideas, procedures, methods of operation or mathematical concepts as such.

Article 3
Application of Articles 2 to 6 of the Berne Convention

Contracting Parties shall apply mutatis mutandis the provisions of Articles 2 to 6 of the Berne Convention in respect of the protection provided for in this Treaty.

Article 4
Computer Programs

Computer programs are protected as literary works within the meaning of Article 2 of the Berne Convention. Such protection applies to computer programs, whatever may be the mode or form of their expression.

Article 5
Compilations of Data (Databases)

Compilations of data or other material, in any form, which by reason of the selection or arrangement of their contents constitute intellectual creations, are protected as such. This protection does not extend to the data or the material itself and is without prejudice to any copyright subsisting in the data or material contained in the compilation.

Article 6
Right of Distribution

(1) Authors of literary and artistic works shall enjoy the exclusive right of authorizing the making available to the public of the original and copies of their works through sale or other transfer of ownership.

(2) Nothing in this Treaty shall affect the freedom of Contracting Parties to determine the conditions, if any, under which the exhaustion of the right in

paragraph (1) applies after the first sale or other transfer of ownership of the original or a copy of the work with the authorization of the author.

Article 7
Right of Rental

(1) Authors of

(i) computer programs;

(ii) cinematographic works; and

(iii) works embodied in phonograms, as determined in the national law of Contracting Parties, shall enjoy the exclusive right of authorizing commercial rental to the public of the originals or copies of their works.

(2) Paragraph (1) shall not apply

(i) in the case of computer programs, where the program itself is not the essential object of the rental; and

(ii) in the case of cinematographic works, unless such commercial rental has led to widespread copying of such works materially impairing the exclusive right of reproduction.

(3) Notwithstanding the provisions of paragraph (1), a Contracting Party that, on April 15, 1994, had and continues to have in force a system of equitable remuneration of authors for the rental of copies of their works embodied in phonograms may maintain that system provided that the commercial rental of works embodied in phonograms is not giving rise to the material impairment of the exclusive right of reproduction of authors.

Article 8
Right of Communication to the Public

Without prejudice to the provisions of Articles 11(1)(ii), 11bis(1)(i) and (ii), 11ter(1)(ii), 14(1)(ii) and 14bis(1) of the Berne Convention, authors of literary and artistic works shall enjoy the exclusive right of authorizing any communication to the public of their works, by wire or wireless means, including the making available to the public of their works in such a way that members of the public may access these works from a place and at a time individually chosen by them.

Article 9
Duration of the Protection of Photographic Works

In respect of photographic works, the Contracting Parties shall not apply the provisions of Article 7(4) of the Berne Convention.

Article 10
Limitations and Exceptions

(1) Contracting Parties may, in their national legislation, provide for limitations of or exceptions to the rights granted to authors of literary and artistic works under this Treaty in certain special cases that do not conflict with a normal exploitation of the work and do not unreasonably prejudice the legitimate interests of the author.

(2) Contracting Parties shall, when applying the Berne Convention, confine any limitations of or exceptions to rights provided for therein to certain special cases that do not conflict with a normal exploitation of the work and do not unreasonably prejudice the legitimate interests of the author.

Article 11
Obligations concerning Technological Measures

Contracting Parties shall provide adequate legal protection and effective legal remedies against the circumvention of effective technological measures that are used by authors in connection with the exercise of their rights under this Treaty or the Berne Convention and that restrict acts, in respect of their works, which are not authorized by the authors concerned or permitted by law.

Article 12
Obligations concerning Rights Management Information

(1) Contracting Parties shall provide adequate and effective legal remedies against any person knowingly performing any of the following acts knowing, or with respect to civil remedies having reasonable grounds to know, that it will induce, enable, facilitate or conceal an infringement of any right covered by this Treaty or the Berne Convention:

(i) to remove or alter any electronic rights management information without authority;

(ii) to distribute, import for distribution, broadcast or communicate to the public, without authority, works or copies of works knowing that electronic rights management information has been removed or altered without authority.

(2) As used in this Article, "rights management information" means information which identifies the work, the author of the work, the owner of any right in the work, or information about the terms and conditions of use of the work, and any numbers or codes that represent such information, when any of these items of information is attached to a copy of a work or appears in connection with the communication of a work to the public.

Article 13
Application in Time

Contracting Parties shall apply the provisions of Article 18 of the Berne Convention to all protection provided for in this Treaty.

Article 14
Provisions on Enforcement of Rights

(1) Contracting Parties undertake to adopt, in accordance with their legal systems, the measures necessary to ensure the application of this Treaty.

(2) Contracting Parties shall ensure that enforcement procedures are available under their law so as to permit effective action against any act of in-

fringement of rights covered by this Treaty, including expeditious remedies to prevent infringements and remedies which constitute a deterrent to further infringements.

Notes and Questions

1. There are certain differences in the language used in the WIPO Copyright Treaty and in the TRIPS Agreement on the same subject matter. For example, the language used to make clear that computer software is copyrightable subject matter is different in the two agreements. Do you find any differences that you think may be material? It would seem logical that the same governments negotiating in the WTO and WIPO would strive for consistency in the resulting legal rules. Assuming that small differences in language might lead to large differences in result, why do you think that these governments did not employ uniform language?

2. Rental rights are expressly limited to computer programs, videos and phonograms (which include CDs). Why is the rental right limited to these three subject matters? Why is the video rental right only applicable when such rental has led to widespread copying of videos to the detriment of the author?

3. The United States implemented the provisions of the WCT and WIPO Performances and Phonograms Treaty (WPPT) into domestic law in the Digital Millennium Copyright Act (DMCA), enacted October 28, 1998.[1] The DMCA is a detailed statute that includes provisions making it unlawful to remove or alter copyright management information,[2] and provisions by which copyright holders may at least temporarily require Internet service providers to remove allegedly infringing materials by giving notice of alleged infringement (the so-called "notice and take-down" procedure).[3] The DMCA includes a number of rules that are not mandated by the WCT or the WPPT, but reflect instead the U.S. Congress' legislative balancing of the competing interests at stake in regulation of the digital environment.

---

[1] Public Law 105-304.
[2] 17 U.S.C. §1201 et seq.
[3] 17 U.S.C. §512.

K. The WIPO Performances and Phonograms Treaty (WPPT)

1. Introduction

Pam Samuelson observed that one of the main reasons for the 1996 diplomatic conference at WIPO was to strengthen protection for performers. We turn now to a decision by the Swiss Federal Court that helps to illustrate why performers sought new standards of protection.

At the time this case was decided, neither the TRIPS Agreement nor the WPPT had entered into force. Moreover, though Switzerland had signed the Rome Convention in 1961, it did not ratify the Convention until September 1993, after adopting new domestic legislation protecting neighboring rights, including performance rights. Title 3 of the 1992 Federal Law on Copyright and Neighboring Rights Protection (Bundesgesetz über das Urheberrecht und verwandte Schutzrechte) concerns neighboring rights, and Article 33 grants performance rights to artists, including the right to authorize sound recordings (art. 33(c)). Article 34 concerns the distribution of rights among performing groups, and provides that in the case of a choral, orchestral or theatrical performance, the rights are shared among soloists, producers, conductors and the representative of the artists' group. It would appear that all of the aforementioned parties must consent to authorize a sound recording.

Schweizerische Interpreten-Gesellschaft and Others v. X and Z

Bundesgericht (Swiss Federal Court)
[1986] ECC 384
2 OCTOBER 1984

Headnote:
Appeal from the Obergericht (Cantonal Court of Appeal), Zurich.

*****

Facts:

A

On the evening of 2 November 1980 the Zurich Opera gave a gala performance of the opera 'Tosca' by Giacomo Puccini. At that time X was still a member of the Opera chorus. That evening he sat for almost the entire performance in the second row of a so-called relatives' box, where he made sound recordings with a cassette recorder. He was seen doing this, allegedly accompanied by Mrs. Z. In January 1981 he was reported by the Schweizerische Interpreten-Gesellschaft for infringement of copyrights.

In the criminal investigation, which was extended to Mrs. Z, X admitted that he had made sound recordings of approximately 15 musical stage works between the middle of 1979 and December 1980 in the Zurich Opera, and had sold approximately the same number of cassettes at cost price. Mrs. Z stated, as an accused, that she had advertised in the October 1980 issue of the magazine Opernwelt for people who wanted to exchange opera recordings, but only a few prospective purchasers had replied and she had sold them recordings of the opera "Tristan und Isolde" at cost price. Both accused denied that they had commercial intentions. The District Prosecutor's Office, Zurich, and, following an appeal, on 8 October 1982 the State Prosecutor of the Canton of Zurich discontinued the criminal proceedings because performances by performing artists (performers) are not protected by copyright.

Thereupon the Interpreten-Gesellschaft applied to the Single Judge of the District Court, Zurich, who on 20 October 1982 prohibited the accused, as a precautionary measure, from re-selling sound recordings of the Zurich Opera, subject to a penalty, and provisionally impounded the recordings, which had been placed in the criminal files.

B

In October 1983 the Society, together with seven musicians who had sung at the gala performance of 2 November 1980, brought an action against X and Mrs. Z in the Appeal Court of the Canton of Zurich. The plaintiffs sought an injunction prohibiting the defendants from selling and exploiting commercially sound recordings originating from the Opera

House, subject to a penalty; an order requiring them to disclose the volume of their sales and to surrender all receipts; and an order for the destruction of the impounded tapes and cassettes.

The defendants opposed these applications.

By judgment of 26 January 1984 the Appeal Court dismissed the action and rescinded the precautionary measures ordered by the Single Judge.

C

The plaintiffs have appealed against that judgment, maintaining their original applications. The defendants ask the Court to dismiss the appeal and to uphold the judgment appealed against.

Decision:

Before the Federal Court the plaintiffs have also pleaded copyright, unfair competition and general personal rights. In disputes concerning copyrights in works of literature and art an appeal is admissible, pursuant to section 45(a) of the Federal Administration of Justice Act, irrespective of the value of the subject matter. If a copyright claim is connected with a claim arising from unfair competition, this also applies to the latter (section 5(2), sentence 2 of the Unfair Competition Act). A dispute concerning the infringement of personal rights is not a matter of the law of property and may therefore be the subject of an appeal pursuant to section 44 of the Federal Administration of Justice Act (Se BGE 102 II 165 para 1). The appeal must therefore be admitted, regardless of whether the value of the subject matter exceeds 15,000 SFr, as the plaintiffs allege, or whether this limit is far from being reached as the defendants contend.

The plaintiffs maintain that performers also create works within the meaning of the Copyright Act and can therefore invoke the protection of the Act if their performances are to be regarded as artistic. In particular, a musical stage work is achieved only by the activity of all the performers, including the musicians of an orchestra. To refuse them protection for their performance is clearly contrary to the words and meaning of section 4(1)(2) and 4(2) of the Copyright Act, which lays down mandatory protection providing that the other requirements of copyright law are met. The Appeal Court, on the other hand, agrees with the defendants that a new work is not created by the performance of an orchestra or chorus, so that its members cannot be regarded as creators within the meaning of the Act; this applies in cases where, as here, we are not concerned with an interpretative achievement of a work, but the performance of a famous opera.

The Federal Court originally assumed that section 4(2) of the Copyright Act gives copyright protection to performing artists who take part in the staging of an original work (See BGE 62 II 247 para 4). In 1959 this view was discarded after serious objections to it had been raised, and the court stated that the presumption of copyright in favour of performing artists ran counter to the basic ideology of the Act. According to the court, this was clear from the object and position of the abovementioned provision, and from the definition of the work capable of copyright protection. No doubt the contribution by the performing artist was necessary to give an existing work its form and complete expression; however, the contribution was not of a creative nature and, even it it revealed considerable artistic qualities or gifts, was neither a work of art nor a secondhand work within the meaning of section 4(1) of the Copyright Act. (See BGE 85 II 433 para 2). This judgment was upheld two years later (See BGE 87 II 322 para 1).

These decisions related primarily, of course, to the rights given by section 4(2) of the Act to record manufacturers, who thought they derived these rights from the copyrights of the artists whose performances were being recorded. Consequently in each case the Federal Court considered firstly the question whether a performing artist could claim copyright protection for his own performance. In the second decision this question was answered in the negative on detailed grounds (See BGE 85 II 434 et seq) and, in the third, the court added that record manufacturers were not owners of copyrights, ie the right to public performance, but could only invoke protection under competition law. The court also set out its reasons (See BGE 87 II 323 et seq). In the present case the plaintiffs do not regard as decisive the reasoning for these devisions, which related solely to the assessment of the performance as a work. They argue that the criterion of individuality, meaning statistical uniqueness, is satisfied in every case with regard to musicians who perform an opera, because each musician plays a particular piece differently; in effect, therefore, BGE 62 II 247 paragraph 4 should be followed, also to the extent that section 4(1)(2) of the Copyright Act applies.

However, the plaintiffs' submissions in support of their argument fail owing to the definition of a copyright-protected work. This is true even if the Federal Court decisions of 1959 and 1961 which they criticise could have been based on other grounds, without enquiring firstly into the copyright, if any, of the participating artist. A work capable of copyright protection, within the meaning of section 1(2) of the Copyright Act, presupposes an original creation, ie an achievement of creative intellectual activity with a minimum degree of its own personal character. (See BGE 105 II 299 and 85 II 123 para 3, with references). The plaintiffs appreciate that this also applies to the individual performance of a performer. Contrary to their objections, however, protection for a performance cannot be inferred from the wording of the Act, nor can it be acknowledged regardless of the latitude which an individual performer has within a group of musicians or singers who are attuned to each other. There can be no serious question of this at least in relation to a classical opera, as here, the performance of which is predetermined in every detail by the composer, the producer and the conductor. In such a case an exception is justified at the most in relation to the conductor and soloists, but not other participants who are members of an orchestra or choir. It is unnecessary to decide here what the position would be with regard to so-called aleatoric works by modern composers, which give the performer wide latitude, which is not the same thing, or in the case of improvisations and variations.

(b) This is also the prevailing view of legal theorists. M Pedrazzini (In Uber den Leistungsschutz der Interpreten, der Ton-und Tonbildtragerhersteller und der Sendenunternehmen, ZSR 96/1977 II p 1 et seq) makes the fundamental assumption that the performance cannot normally be regarded as work (At p 25 et seq). Kummer (In Das urheberrechtlich schutzbare Werk, p 159) finds that it is impossible to deal with the performance by means of the criteria applying to copyright because the performer and the creator by nature contribute different things. He states that if the performer is intended to be given protection in addition to personal rights and those under the Unfair Competition Act this would have to be done in a special Act. However, he concedes that in particular cases a performance may have its own character as a work (See pp 160 and 162 et seq). Troller (In Immaterialguterrecht 1, 3rd edition, pp 391-2) likewise now (differing from the second edition (at p 501 et seq) accepts that conductors and soloists are able to fashion musical works individually but that orchestras and choruses cannot take part in this process because they have to subordinate their view of the work to that of the conductor. He regrets that the legislature and certain theorists do not include protection for creative performers in the ambit of the Copyright Act, regardless of the power to fash-

954

ion a work, and that neither the revised Berne Convention nor the Universal Copyright Convention mentions such protection, but leaves it to State Parties.

Attempts by these States to reach an objectively satisfactory solution show similar tendencies. In several European countries the rights of performing artists are protected by special legislation on the assumption that the performance does not give them a copyright in the work performed. (See Frank Gotzen, Das Recht des Interpreten in der Europaischen Wirtschaftsgemeinschaft, p 49 et seq). In other countries, by contrast, such protection is not given in any legislation but is left to the courts in individual cases. This applies to Switzerland, where neither the current law nor the new Copyright Bill contains, provisions for the protection of performing artists; on the contrary, according to the explanatory memorandum to the Bill, such provisions are to remain separate from copyright and incorporated in another field of law or a separate Act if necessary. (See BB1 [1984] III p 198 et seq).

In the present case, however, it is unnecessary to give a final answer to the question whether and, if so, to what extent qualified performers can invoke copyright protection. No doubt, there is much to be said for the proposition that conductors and soloists in particular fashion musical works individually in performance and may thereby create a work at second hand if they have enough latitude. However, this cannot be said in general of any performance of a work of classical music by elite participants, however high the qualitative level. The Court does not wish to diminish their contributions in any way, but the plaintiff members of the orchestra cannot claim copyright protection for their own contribution for this reason.

The other plaintiff, the Interpreten-Gesellschaft, must according to its by-laws safeguard and administer its members' rights when their performances are associated with the production, publication and utilisation of sound and visual recordings or used for radiophonic or similar purposes. It is unnecessary to decide whether the society covers qualified performers and whether the Court should by way of unfettered application of the law, grant it an independent right of action, as was done in BGE 103 II 294 et seq for cartel law. It must be assumed from the judgment appealed against that the society is, either way, merely a body responsible for performer's rights and is not asserting greater rights than can the other plaintiffs. It is therefore unnecessary to consider the position with regard to the overall contribution of an orchestra or chorus. (See BGE 107 II 87 para 3a, with references, and Pedrazzini p 32).

The plaintiff members of the orchestra also invoke their personal rights (droit moral) which they allege to have been infringed, within the meaning of section 28 of the Civil Code, by the fact that the defendants made sound recordings in the Opera House of performances in which they took part as musicians, and marketed cassettes of the recordings. According to these plaintiffs, the lower court failed to take notice that a bad recording could affect the reputation of a performing artist even if his individual contribution cannot be heard, because the bad reputation is automatically transferred from the orchestra to the individual member.

The immediate reply to this, in which this Court agrees with the Appeal Court, is that in principle it is not right to attempt to fill gaps in copyright or performing rights law indirectly by means of a general rule. (See BGE 107 II 88 para 3b). Under certain circumstances, no doubt, a performing artist may be protected by section 28 against the use of his performance without himself being the owner of a copyright. This form of protection has been allowed, for example, so that he can require an unsuccessful recording to be replaced by a new one or at least not marketed. (See BGE 85 II 436/37, with references). However, when recourse to the general provision is permissible and objectively justified is a question which is not decided once and for all, but depends on the circumstances of the particular case and, furthermore, it cannot be answered without regard to the purposes of copyright and the fundamental reasons for section 28.

The Copyright Act primarily aims to ensure that the creator can use his work as an asset and to protect him against illegal use of his rights by third parties. (See BGE 64 II 167). In addition to his powers in respect of the work by virtue of the law of property, he is protected in his relationship to the work, ie in his personal right as a creator, which is interpreted as a part of a particular aspect of general personal rights and remains attached to his person even if the rights to use the work are assigned. (See BGE 96 II 420 para 6 and 84 II 573). Claims arising from personal rights (droit moral) presuppose, according to section 28 of the Civil Code, unlawful interference in personal matters which, to be specific, means the private, confidential sphere as well as professional and private reputation. (See BGE 108 II 143 para 6, 107 II 4 para 2, 97 II 100 et seq and the academic works referred to therein). This does not mean that any kind of relationship between the creator and work or between the interpreter and performance is sufficient to pass off an alleged interference as infringement of a personal right. The general rule gives neither of them a claim to an exclusive right of disposition unless their reputation is affected. To accept this view would amount to using section 28 of the Civil Code to create a monopoly of what, according to the specific law, must be described as not subject to copyright.

This is why more recent academic texts give warnings, particularly in the field of performing rights, against trying to see section 28 as a legal basis for monetary payments. According to Pedrazzini (See ZSR 96/1977 II p 33 n 50 and p 40 n 69), this would amount to improper use of the personal right (droit moral), which would be given a different function and degraded to a source of claims in property law; he is of the opinion that the personal right with the object of protecting the interpreter should be limited to cases where the personal connection between the interpreter and the performance is really damaged. Similarly R Frank (Personlichkeitsschutz Heute, p 198) explains that, for the application of section 28 to performing artists, a stronger bond of a more intensively personal nature between performer and performance should be required than is the case with normal performance; he adds that where section 28 is obviously being used to serve financial interests and there is no genuine infringement of droit moral, it is not applicable.

The plaintiff musicians took part in public opera performances. Therefore they cannot plead their private or confidential sphere of life in order to have the acts in question judged by reference to section 28 of the Civil Code. This is clear from the parallel with the right to one's own picture, even if this right cannot be compared in every respect with the right to one's own voice or even to the sound of a musical instrument. In general, an orchestra can be photographed on a public appearance without individual members being able to assert their right to their own picture. Likewise it cannot seriously be said that the personal rights of an individual musician in the orchestra are affected by the risk that a sound recording may be abused or is likely, because of technical defects, to cause his abilities or gifts to appear in a poor light. In such cases it is not a question of diminishing the performer's performance in the eyes of other people, but of recording it in order to enjoy it again. In disputes concerning encroachment on personal matters careful consideration is also always given to the question whether personal rights really could have been jeopardised in any way or whether a person's professional or social reputation really could have been diminished. (See BGE 108 II 245 et seq. and 107 II 4 et seq). This also depends in turn on the circumstances under the which a performance is alleged to have been criticised or a sound recording of defective quality published.

In some respects the plaintiffs' submissions go beyond the Appeal Court's factual findings and are spent in mere allegations or assumptions. According to the judgment appealed against, it has been proved that the defendants made tape recordings of a number of musical performances at the Opera House, advertised the recordings once and thereupon sold a number of cassette recordings to third parties at cost price. The defendants have never denied this and even furnished more details during the criminal proceedings, the outcome of which they have pleaded in their defence. They also accepted the charge that they acted without the plaintiffs' consent. As the Appeal Court adds, however, they recorded the different performances solely for purposes of study and exchange and never thought of using them commercially. This finding by the Appeal Court regarding the defendants' actual intentions is binding on the Federal Court (See BGE 107 II 229 para 4 with references), so that it cannot be said that the defendants deliberately wished to create a bad impression by making and publishing defective recordings and thereby to destroy the considerable reputation of the orchestra or its members. On the contrary, according to the judgment appealed against, the plaintiffs themselves have never alleged any such thing, nor have they tried to show to what extent the personal rights (droit moral) of a member of the orchestra are infringed by the quality of a sound recording. In this connection also they are primarily concerned, on closer examination to safeguard their own opportunities for earning money at public performances, but for this purpose they cannot invoke section 28 of the Civil Code.

The plaintiffs also criticise the Appeal Court for having concluded wrongly that there was no competition between the parties, because it must be presumed that both parties sought to gain revenue by offering opera recordings for sale. This is said to arise from the fact that the defendants successfully advertised recordings and the plaintiff musicians were in the habit of commercialising their rights through the Interpreten-Gesellschaft. If record pirates like the defendants market opera recordings, record manufacturers are said usually to lose interest in contracts with performers. Therefore, they say, their action should be allowed on the basis of the Unfair Competition Act.

On this point it must be observed, firstly, that gaps in a particular Act relating to intangible property rights cannot be closed by means of the general clause in section 1(1) of the Unfair Competition Act, because in principle the results of effort and labour which, according to the special Act, are no longer protected or cannot be protected at all may be used by anyone, even competitors. Otherwise application of the clause would likewise amount to monopolisation of non-copyright property. (See BGE 107 II 89 and 105 II 301 para 4b with references). This must also apply to performances by performers who cannot invoke copyright protection because their performance is not in the nature of an individual intellectual creation. The only exception allowed by case law is where special circumstances show that particular conduct or measures are nevertheless anti-competitive and therefore justify application of the general cause. (See BGE 108 II 332-333 with references).

The plaintiffs do not allege that circumstances such as those in the above case exist here, nor should this be presumed from the established facts concerning the purpose of the recordings in question. In particular there can be no question of infringing the principles of good faith pursuant to section 1(1) of the Unfair Competition Act when it borne in mind that the defendant X was a member of the Opera chorus from mid-August 1975 to the end of 1980, that other musicians belonging to the Opera House were also in the habit of making recordings for private use, which the plaintiffs do not deny in their reply, and the defendants' allegation that they never intended to make a profit was not refuted. According to the judgment appealed against, the plaintiffs were unable to identify a single sale by the defendants or a purchase by third parties. Therefore, however understandable and however justified the performers' need, in view of modern technology, to resist unauthorised recordings and their commercial use, recourse to the general clause must be refused.

(b) Having reached this conclusion, it is unnecessary to decide whether the Appeal Court was wrong in finding there was no competition between the parties. In any case it should be observed that the plaintiffs can rely only on the potential opportunity to have recordings made together with all the participants in an opera and to share in the profit obtained by the sellers of the recordings. Whether such an opportunity is sufficient for the application of competition law is questionable and is doubted by certain theorists. (See Pedrazzini, ZSR 96/1977 II p 37 n 62; Gastiger, [1965] 67 GRUR p 181 et seq).

It should also be borne in mind that economic competition presupposes activity aiming at a financial profit, even though the desired pecuniary benefits need not be the only or the main object. (See BGE 80 II 170 para 3; Troller, Immaterialgutterrecht II, 2nd ed, p 1037 et seq). According to what the defendants have admitted and what the lower court finds to have been proved, it is also doubtful whether these conditions are fulfilled here, but it is unnecessary to decide this point because, either way, there can be no question of a manifest overight or of excessive demands regarding the obligation to allege the facts on which a party bases its case and regarding the burden of proof. On the contrary, this is mere criticism of the Appeal Court's assessment of the evidence, with which the plaintiffs cannot be heard in an appeal to the Federal Court. (See BGE 107 II 274 para 2b with references).

Accordingly the Federal Court dismisses the appeal and upholds the judgment by the Cantonal Appeal Court, Zurich, of 26 January 1984.

Appeal dismissed. Order of the court below reaffirmed.

Notes and Questions

1. It is not so uncommon for individuals or groups to initiate litigation to vindicate what they consider important matters of principle. In the preceding case, the plaintiffs are contesting a seemingly trivial act by a former member of the Opera Chorus and a co-defendant. What rights are the plaintiffs attempting to vindicate? Is there perhaps more to this case than meets the eye?

2. The Rolling Stones first recorded "Satisfaction" in 1965. How many times do you think the group has performed that song live over the past three decades? When they performed it live during their world tour in 1998, was there a creative element in the numerous performances? Under the rules applied by the Swiss Federal Court in the preceding case, would the group have been able to prevent its audiences from making sound recordings of "Satisfaction"?

3. Can we assume that the result in the preceding case would be different after the changes to Swiss law brought about by the 1992 law referred to in the introduction? What aspects of the decision would be changed?

---

2. The WPPT and the Rome Convention

The International Bureau of WIPO describes the new WPPT. This is followed by the text of the Treaty, and by provisions of the Rome Convention. The Rome Convention is included because various provisions of that Convention are referenced both in WPPT and the TRIPS Agreement.

WIPO Performances and Phonograms Treaty (WPPT) (1996)
International Bureau of WIPO*

This Treaty was concluded on December 20, 1996. It is open for signature at the headquarters of WIPO until December 31, 1997.

This Treaty is open to States members of WIPO and to the European Community. The Assembly constituted by the Treaty may, once the Treaty enters into force, decide to admit other intergovernmental organizations to become party to the Treaty.

The Treaty will come into force after 30 instruments of ratification or accession by States have been deposited. Such instruments must be deposited with the Director General of WIPO, who is the depositary of the Treaty.

* * *

The Treaty deals with intellectual property rights of two kinds of beneficiaries:

(i) performers (actors, singers, musicians, etc.), and
(ii) producers of phonograms (the persons or legal entities who or which take the initiative and have the responsibility for the fixation of the sounds).

They are dealt with in the same instrument because most of the rights granted by the Treaty to performers are rights connected with their fixed, purely aural performances (which are the subject matter of phonograms).

* * *

---

*http://www.wipo.int.

As far as performers are concerned, the Treaty grants performers four kinds of economic rights in their performances fixed in phonograms (not in audiovisual fixations, such as motion pictures):

(i) the right of reproduction,
(ii) the right of distribution,
(iii) the right of rental, and
(iv) the right of making available.

Each of them is an exclusive right, subject to certain limitations and exceptions. Not all of those limitations and exceptions are mentioned in the following:

the right of reproduction is the right to authorize direct or indirect reproduction of the phonogram in any manner or form,

the right of distribution is the right to authorize the making available to the public of the original and copies of the phonogram through sale or other transfer of ownership,

the right of rental is the right to authorize the commercial rental to the public of the original and copies of the phonogram as determined in the national law of the Contracting Parties (except for countries that since April 15, 1994, have in force a system of equitable remuneration for such rental),

the right of making available is the right to authorize the making available to the public, by wire or wireless means, of any performance fixed in a phonogram, in such a way that members of the public may access the fixed performance from a place and at a time individually chosen by them. This right covers, in particular, on-demand, interactive making available through the Internet.

* * *

The Treaty grants three kinds of economic rights to performers in respect of their unfixed (live) performances:

(i) the right of broadcasting (except in the case of rebroadcasting),

(ii) the right of communication to the public (except where the performance is a broadcast performance),

(iii) the right of fixation.

* * *

The Treaty also grants performers moral rights: the right to claim to be identified as the performer and the right to object to any distortion, mutilation or other modification that would be prejudicial to the performer's reputation.

* * *

As far as producers of phonograms are concerned, the Treaty grants them four kinds of rights (all economic) in their phonograms:

(i) the right of reproduction,
(ii) the right of distribution,
(iii) the right of rental, and
(iv) the right of making available.

Each of them is an exclusive right, subject to certain limitations and exceptions. Not all of those limitations and exceptions are mentioned in the following:

the right of reproduction is the right to authorize direct or indirect reproduction of the phonogram in any manner or form,

the right of distribution is the right to authorize the making available to the public of the original and copies of the phonogram through sale or other transfer of ownership,

the right of rental is the right to authorize the commercial rental to the public of the original and copies of the phonogram as determined in the national law of the Contracting Parties (except for countries that since April 15,1994, have in force a system of equitable remuneration for such rental), the right of making available is the right to authorize making available to the public the phonogram, by wire or wireless means, in such a way that members of the public may access the phonogram from a place and at a time individually chosen by them. This right covers, in particular, on-demand, interactive making available through the Internet.

* * *

As far as both performers and phonogram producers are concerned, the Treaty obliges — subject to various exceptions and limitations not mentioned here — each Contracting Party to accord to nationals of the other Contracting Parties with regard to the rights specifically granted in the Treaty the treatment it accords to its own nationals ("national treatment").

Furthermore, the Treaty provides that performers and producers of phonograms enjoy the right to a single equitable remuneration for the direct or indirect use of phonograms, published for commercial purposes, for broadcasting or for communication to the public. However, any Contracting Party may restrict or — provided that it makes a reservation to the Treaty — deny this right. In the case and to the extent of a reservation by a Contracting Party, the other Contracting Parties are permitted to deny, vis-à-vis the reserving Contracting Party, national treatment ("reciprocity").

The term of protection must be at least 50 years.

The enjoyment and exercise of the rights provided in the Treaty cannot be subject to any formality.

The Treaty obliges the Contracting Parties to provide legal remedies against the circumvention of technological measures (e.g., encryption) used by performers or phonogram producers in connection with the exercise of their rights and against the removal or altering of information, such as the indication of certain data that identify the performer, the performance, the producer of the phonogram and the phonogram, necessary for the management (e.g., licensing, collecting and distribution of royalties) of the said rights ("rights management information").

The Treaty obliges each Contracting Party to adopt, in accordance with its legal system, the measures necessary to ensure the application of the Treaty. In particular, the Contracting Party must ensure that enforcement procedures are available under its law so as to permit effective action against any act of infringement of rights covered by the Treaty. Such action must include expeditious remedies to prevent infringement and remedies which constitute a deterrent to further infringements.

* * *

The Treaty establishes an Assembly of the Contracting Parties whose main task is to deal with matters concerning the maintenance and development of the Treaty, and it entrusts to the International Bureau of WIPO the administrative tasks concerning the Treaty.

WIPO Performances and Phonograms Treaty*

Preamble

The Contracting Parties,

Desiring to develop and maintain the protection of the rights of performers and producers of phonograms in a manner as effective and uniform as possible,

Recognizing the need to introduce new international rules in order to provide adequate solutions to the questions raised by economic, social, cultural and technological developments,

Recognizing the profound impact of the development and convergence of information and communication technologies on the production and use of performances and phonograms,

---

*Adopted by the Diplomatic Conference on December 20, 1996.

Recognizing the need to maintain a balance between the rights of performers and producers of phonograms and the larger public interest, particularly education, research and access to information,

Have agreed as follows:

Chapter I
General Provisions

Article 1
Relation to Other Conventions

(1) Nothing in this Treaty shall derogate from existing obligations that Contracting Parties have to each other under the International Convention for the Protection of Performers, Producers of Phonograms and Broadcasting Organizations done in Rome, October 26, 1961 (hereinafter the "Rome Convention").

(2) Protection granted under this Treaty shall leave intact and shall in no way affect the protection of copyright in literary and artistic works. Consequently, no provision of this Treaty may be interpreted as prejudicing such protection.

(3) This Treaty shall not have any connection with, nor shall it prejudice any rights and obligations under, any other treaties.

Article 2
Definitions

For the purposes of this Treaty:

(a) "performers" are actors, singers, musicians, dancers, and other persons who act, sing, deliver, declaim, play in, interpret, or otherwise perform literary or artistic works or expressions of folklore;

(b) "phonogram" means the fixation of the sounds of a performance or of other sounds, or of a representation of sounds, other than in the form of a fixation incorporated in a cinematographic or other audiovisual work;

(c) "fixation" means the embodiment of sounds, or of the representations thereof, from which they can be perceived, reproduced or communicated through a device;

(d) "producer of a phonogram" means the person, or the legal entity, who or which takes the initiative and has the responsibility for the first fixation of the sounds of a performance or other sounds, or the representations of sounds;

(e) "publication" of a fixed performance or a phonogram means the offering of copies of the fixed performance or the phonogram to the public, with the consent of the rightholder, and provided that copies are offered to the public in reasonable quantity;

(f) "broadcasting" means the transmission by wireless means for public reception of sounds or of images and sounds or of the representations thereof; such transmission by satellite is also "broadcasting"; transmission of encrypted signals is "broadcasting" where the means for decrypting are provided to the public by the broadcasting organization or with its consent;

(g) "communication to the public" of a performance or a phonogram means the transmission to the public by any medium, otherwise than by broadcasting, of sounds of a performance or the sounds or the representations of sounds fixed in a phonogram. For the purposes of Article 15, "communication to the public" includes making the sounds or representations of sounds fixed in a phonogram audible to the public.

Article 3
Beneficiaries of Protection under this Treaty

(1) Contracting Parties shall accord the protection provided under this Treaty to the performers and producers of phonograms who are nationals of other Contracting Parties.

(2) The nationals of other Contracting Parties shall be understood to be those performers or producers of phonograms who would meet the criteria for eligibility for protection provided under the Rome Convention, were all

the Contracting Parties to this Treaty Contracting States of that Convention. In respect of these criteria of eligibility, Contracting Parties shall apply the relevant definitions in Article 2 of this Treaty.

(3) Any Contracting Party availing itself of the possibilities provided in Article 5(3) of the Rome Convention or, for the purposes of Article 5 of the same Convention, Article 17 thereof shall make a notification as foreseen in those provisions to the Director General of the World Intellectual Property Organization (WIPO).

Article 4
National Treatment

(1) Each Contracting Party shall accord to nationals of other Contracting Parties, as defined in Article 3(2), the treatment it accords to its own nationals with regard to the exclusive rights specifically granted in this Treaty, and to the right to equitable remuneration provided for in Article 15 of this Treaty.

(2) The obligation provided for in paragraph (1) does not apply to the extent that another Contracting Party makes use of the reservations permitted by Article 15(3) of this Treaty.

Chapter II
Rights of Performers

Article 5
Moral Rights of Performers

(1) Independently of a performer's economic rights, and even after the transfer of those rights, the performer shall, as regards his live aural performances or performances fixed in phonograms, have the right to claim to be identified as the performer of his performances, except where omission is dictated by the manner of the use of the performance, and to object to any distortion, mutilation or other modification of his performances that would be prejudicial to his reputation.

(2) The rights granted to a performer in accordance with paragraph (1) shall, after his death, be maintained, at least until the expiry of the eco-

nomic rights, and shall be exercisable by the persons or institutions authorized by the legislation of the Contracting Party where protection is claimed. However, those Contracting Parties whose legislation, at the moment of their ratification of or accession to this Treaty, does not provide for protection after the death of the performer of all rights set out in the preceding paragraph may provide that some of these rights will, after his death, cease to be maintained.

(3) The means of redress for safeguarding the rights granted under this Article shall be governed by the legislation of the Contracting Party where protection is claimed.

Article 6
Economic Rights of Performers in their Unfixed Performances

Performers shall enjoy the exclusive right of authorizing, as regards their performances:

(i) the broadcasting and communication to the public of their unfixed performances except where the performance is already a broadcast performance; and

(ii) the fixation of their unfixed performances.

Article 7
Right of Reproduction

Performers shall enjoy the exclusive right of authorizing the direct or indirect reproduction of their performances fixed in phonograms, in any manner or form.

Article 8
Right of Distribution

(1) Performers shall enjoy the exclusive right of authorizing the making available to the public of the original and copies of their performances fixed in phonograms through sale or other transfer of ownership.

(2) Nothing in this Treaty shall affect the freedom of Contracting Parties to determine the conditions, if any, under which the exhaustion of the right in

paragraph (1) applies after the first sale or other transfer of ownership of the original or a copy of the fixed performance with the authorization of the performer.

Article 9
Right of Rental

(1) Performers shall enjoy the exclusive right of authorizing the commercial rental to the public of the original and copies of their performances fixed in phonograms as determined in the national law of Contracting Parties, even after distribution of them by, or pursuant to, authorization by the performer.

(2) Notwithstanding the provisions of paragraph (1), a Contracting Party that, on April 15, 1994, had and continues to have in force a system of equitable remuneration of performers for the rental of copies of their performances fixed in phonograms, may maintain that system provided that the commercial rental of phonograms is not giving rise to the material impairment of the exclusive right of reproduction of performers.

Article 10
Right of Making Available of Fixed Performances

Performers shall enjoy the exclusive right of authorizing the making available to the public of their performances fixed in phonograms, by wire or wireless means, in such a way that members of the public may access them from a place and at a time individually chosen by them.

Chapter III
Rights of Producers of Phonograms

Article 11
Right of Reproduction

Producers of phonograms shall enjoy the exclusive right of authorizing the direct or indirect reproduction of their phonograms, in any manner or form.

Article 12
Right of Distribution

(1) Producers of phonograms shall enjoy the exclusive right of authorizing the making available to the public of the original and copies of their phonograms through sale or other transfer of ownership.

(2) Nothing in this Treaty shall affect the freedom of Contracting Parties to determine the conditions, if any, under which the exhaustion of the right in paragraph (1) applies after the first sale or other transfer of ownership of the original or a copy of the phonogram with the authorization of the producer of the phonogram.

Article 13
Right of Rental

(1) Producers of phonograms shall enjoy the exclusive right of authorizing the commercial rental to the public of the original and copies of their phonograms, even after distribution of them by or pursuant to authorization by the producer.

(2) Notwithstanding the provisions of paragraph (1), a Contracting Party that, on April 15, 1994, had and continues to have in force a system of equitable remuneration of producers of phonograms for the rental of copies of their phonograms, may maintain that system provided that the commercial rental of phonograms is not giving rise to the material impairment of the exclusive rights of reproduction of producers of phonograms.

Article 14
Right of Making Available of Phonograms

Producers of phonograms shall enjoy the exclusive right of authorizing the making available to the public of their phonograms, by wire or wireless means, in such a way that members of the public may access them from a place and at a time individually chosen by them.

Chapter IV
Common Provisions

Article 15
Right to Remuneration for Broadcasting and Communication
to the Public

(1) Performers and producers of phonograms shall enjoy the right to a single equitable remuneration for the direct or indirect use of phonograms published for commercial purposes for broadcasting or for any communication to the public.

(2) Contracting Parties may establish in their national legislation that the single equitable remuneration shall be claimed from the user by the performer or by the producer of a phonogram or by both. Contracting Parties may enact national legislation that, in the absence of an agreement between the performer and the producer of a phonogram, sets the terms according to which performers and producers of phonograms shall share the single equitable remuneration.

(3) Any Contracting Party may in a notification deposited with the Director General of WIPO, declare that it will apply the provisions of paragraph (1) only in respect of certain uses, or that it will limit their application in some other way, or that it will not apply these provisions at all.

(4) For the purposes of this Article, phonograms made available to the public by wire or wireless means in such a way that members of the public may access them from a place and at a time individually chosen by them shall be considered as if they had been published for commercial purposes.

Article 16
Limitations and Exceptions

(1) Contracting Parties may, in their national legislation, provide for the same kinds of limitations or exceptions with regard to the protection of performers and producers of phonograms as they provide for, in their national legislation, in connection with the protection of copyright in literary and artistic works.

(2) Contracting Parties shall confine any limitations of or exceptions to rights provided for in this Treaty to certain special cases which do not conflict with a normal exploitation of the performance or phonogram and do not unreasonably prejudice the legitimate interests of the performer or of the producer of the phonogram.

Article 17
Term of Protection

(1) The term of protection to be granted to performers under this Treaty shall last, at least, until the end of a period of 50 years computed from the end of the year in which the performance was fixed in a phonogram.

(2) The term of protection to be granted to producers of phonograms under this Treaty shall last, at least, until the end of a period of 50 years computed from the end of the year in which the phonogram was published, or failing such publication within 50 years from fixation of the phonogram, 50 years from the end of the year in which the fixation was made.

Article 18
Obligations concerning Technological Measures

Contracting Parties shall provide adequate legal protection and effective legal remedies against the circumvention of effective technological measures that are used by performers or producers of phonograms in connection with the exercise of their rights under this Treaty and that restrict acts, in respect of their performances or phonograms, which are not authorized by the performers or the producers of phonograms concerned or permitted by law.

Article 19
Obligations concerning Rights Management Information

(1) Contracting Parties shall provide adequate and effective legal remedies against any person knowingly performing any of the following acts knowing, or with respect to civil remedies having reasonable grounds to know, that it will induce, enable, facilitate or conceal an infringement of any right covered by this Treaty:

(i) to remove or alter any electronic rights management information without authority;

(ii) to distribute, import for distribution, broadcast, communicate or make available to the public, without authority, performances, copies of fixed performances or phonograms knowing that electronic rights management information has been removed or altered without authority.

(2) As used in this Article, "rights management information" means information which identifies the performer, the performance of the performer, the producer of the phonogram, the phonogram, the owner of any right in the performance or phonogram, or information about the terms and conditions of use of the performance or phonogram, and any numbers or codes that represent such information, when any of these items of information is attached to a copy of a fixed performance or a phonogram or appears in connection with the communication or making available of a fixed performance or a phonogram to the public.

Article 20
Formalities

The enjoyment and exercise of the rights provided for in this Treaty shall not be subject to any formality.

Rome Convention, 1961
International Convention for the Protection of Performers, Producers of Phonograms and Broadcasting Organisations

Done at Rome on October 26, 1961

The Contracting States, moved by the desire to protect the rights of performers, producers of phonograms, and broadcasting organisations,

Have agreed as follows:

Article 1
[Safeguard of Copyright Proper]

Protection granted under this Convention shall leave intact and shall in no way affect the protection of copyright in literary and artistic works. Consequently, no provision of this Convention may be interpreted as prejudicing such protection.

Article 2
[Protection given by the Convention. Definition of National Treatment]

1. For the purposes of this Convention, national treatment shall mean the treatment accorded by the domestic law of the Contracting State in which protection is claimed:

(a) to performers who are its nationals, as regards performances taking place, broadcast, or first fixed, on its territory;

(b) to producers of phonograms who are its nationals, as regards phonograms first fixed or first published on its territory;

(c) to broadcasting organisations which have their headquarters on its territory, as regards broadcasts transmitted from transmitters situated on its territory.

2. National treatment shall be subject to the protection specifically guaranteed, and the limitations specifically provided for, in this Convention.

Article 3
[Definitions: (a) Performers; (b) Phonogram; (c) Producers of Phonograms; (d) Publication; (e) Reproduction; (f) Broadcasting; (g) Rebroadcasting]

For the purposes of this Convention:

(a) "performers" means actors, singers, musicians, dancers, and other persons who act, sing, deliver, declaim, play in, or otherwise perform literary or artistic works;

975

(b) "phonogram" means any exclusively aural fixation of sounds of a performance or of other sounds;

(c) "producer of phonograms" means the person who, or the legal entity which, first fixes the sounds of a performance or other sounds;

(d) "publication" means the offering of copies of a phonogram to the public in reasonable quantity;

(e)"reproduction" means the making of a copy or copies of a fixation;

(f)"broadcasting" means the transmission by wireless means for public reception of sounds or of images and sounds;

(g)"rebroadcasting" means the simultaneous broadcasting by one broadcasting organisation of the broadcast of another broadcasting organisation.

Article 4
[Performances Protected. Points of Attachment for Performers]

Each Contracting State shall grant national treatment to performers if any of the following conditions is met:

(a) the performance takes place in another Contracting State;

(b) the performance is incorporated in a phonogram which is protected under Article 5 of this Convention;

(c) the performance, not being fixed on a phonogram, is carried by a broadcast which is protected by Article 6 of this Convention.

Article 5
[Protected Phonograms: 1. Points of Attachment for Producers of Phonograms; 2. Simultaneous Publication; 3. Power to exclude certain Criteria]

1. Each Contracting State shall grant national treatment to producers of phonograms if any of the following conditions is met:

(a) the producer of the phonogram is a national of another Contracting State (criterion of nationality);

(b) the first fixation of the sound was made in another Contracting State (criterion of fixation);

(c) the phonogram was first published in another Contracting State (criterion of publication).

2. If a phonogram was first published in a non-contracting State but if it was also published, within thirty days of its first publication, in a Contracting State (simultaneous publication), it shall be considered as first published in the Contracting State.

3. By means of a notification deposited with the Secretary-General of the United Nations, any Contracting State may declare that it will not apply the criterion of publication or, alternatively, the criterion of fixation. Such notification may be deposited at the time of ratification, acceptance or accession, or at any time thereafter; in the last case, it shall become effective six months after it has been deposited.

Article 6
[Protected Broadcasts: 1. Points of Attachment for Broadcasting Organizations; 2. Power to Reserve]

1. Each Contracting State shall grant national treatment to broadcasting organisations if either of the following conditions is met:

(a) the headquarters of the broadcasting organisation is situated in another Contracting State;

(b) the broadcast was transmitted from a transmitter situated in another Contracting State.

2. By means of a notification deposited with the Secretary-General of the United Nations, any Contracting State may declare that it will protect

broadcasts only if the headquarters of the broadcasting organisation is situated in another Contracting State and the broadcast was transmitted from a transmitter situated in the same Contracting State. Such notification may be deposited at the time of ratification, acceptance or accession, or at any time thereafter; in the last case, it shall become effective six months after it has been deposited.

Article 7
[Minimum Protection for Performers: 1. Particular Rights; 2. Relations between Performers and Broadcasting Organizations]

1. The protection provided for performers by this Convention shall include the possibility of preventing:

(a) the broadcasting and the communication to the public, without their consent, of their performance, except where the performance used in the broadcasting or the public communication is itself already a broadcast performance or is made from a fixation;

(b) the fixation, without their consent, of their unfixed performance;

(c) the reproduction, without their consent, of a fixation of their performance:

(i) if the original fixation itself was made without their consent;

(ii) if the reproduction is made for purposes different from those for which the performers gave their consent;

(iii) if the original fixation was made in accordance with the provisions of Article 15, and the reproduction is made for purposes different from those referred to in those provisions.

2.

(1) If broadcasting was consented to by the performers, it shall be a matter for the domestic law of the Contracting State where protection is claimed to regulate the protection against rebroadcasting, fixation for

broadcasting purposes and the reproduction of such fixation for broadcasting purposes.

(2) The terms and conditions governing the use by broadcasting organisations of fixations made for broadcasting purposes shall be determined in accordance with the domestic law of the Contracting State where protection is claimed.

(3) However, the domestic law referred to in sub-paragraphs (1) and (2) of this paragraph shall not operate to deprive performers of the ability to control, by contract, their relations with broadcasting organisations.

Article 8
[Performers acting jointly]

Any Contracting State may, by its domestic laws and regulations, specify the manner in which performers will be represented in connection with the exercise of their rights if several of them participate in the same performance.

Article 9
[Variety and Circus Artists]

Any Contracting State may, by its domestic laws and regulations, extend the protection provided for in this Convention to artists who do not perform literary or artistic works.

Article 10
[Right of Reproduction for Phonogram Producers]

Producers of phonograms shall enjoy the right to authorise or prohibit the direct or indirect reproduction of their phonograms.

Article 11
[Formalities for Phonograms]

If, as a condition of protecting the rights of producers of phonograms, or of performers, or both, in relation to phonograms, a Contracting State, under its domestic law, requires compliance with formalities, these shall be considered as fulfilled if all the copies in commerce of the published phonogram or their containers bear a notice consisting of the symbol (P), accompanied by the year date of the first publication, placed in such a manner as to give reasonable notice of claim of protection; and if the copies or their containers do not identify the producer or the licensee of the producer (by carrying his name, trade mark or other appropriate designation), the notice shall also include the name of the owner of the rights of the producer; and, furthermore, if the copies or their containers do not identify the principal performers, the notice shall also include the name of the person who, in the country in which the fixation was effected, owns the rights of such performers.

Article 12
[Secondary Uses of Phonograms]

If a phonogram published for commercial purposes, or a reproduction of such phonogram, is used directly for broadcasting or for any communication to the public, a single equitable remuneration shall be paid by the user to the performers, or to the producers of the phonograms, or to both. Domestic law may, in the absence of agreement between these parties, lay down the conditions as to the sharing of this remuneration.

Article 13
[Minimum Rights for Broadcasting Organizations]

Broadcasting organisations shall enjoy the right to authorise or prohibit:

(a) the rebroadcasting of their broadcasts;

(b) the fixation of their broadcasts;

(c) the reproduction:

(i) of fixations, made without their consent, of their broadcasts;

(ii) of fixations, made in accordance with the provisions of Article 15, of their broadcasts, if the reproduction is made for purposes different from those referred to in those provisions;

(d) the communication to the public of their television broadcasts if such communication is made in places accessible to the public against payment of an entrance fee; it shall be a matter for the domestic law of the State where protection of this right is claimed to determine the conditions under which it may be exercised.

Article 14
[Minimum Duration of Protection]

The term of protection to be granted under this Convention shall last at least until the end of a period of twenty years computed from the end of the year in which:

(a) the fixation was made — for phonograms and for performances incorporated therein;

(b) the performance took place — for performances not incorporated in phonograms;

(c) the broadcast took place — for broadcasts.

Article 15
[Permitted Exceptions: 1. Specific Limitations; 2. Equivalents with copyright]

1. Any Contracting State may, in its domestic laws and regulations, provide for exceptions to the protection guaranteed by this Convention as regards:

(a) private use;

(b) use of short excerpts in connexion with the reporting of current events;

(c) ephemeral fixation by a broadcasting organisation by means of its own facilities and for its own broadcasts;

(d) use solely for the purposes of teaching or scientific research.

2. Irrespective of paragraph 1 of this Article, any Contracting State may, in its domestic laws and regulations, provide for the same kinds of limitations

with regard to the protection of performers, producers of phonograms and broadcasting organisations, as it provides for, in its domestic laws and regulations, in connexion with the protection of copyright in literary and artistic works. However, compulsory licences may be provided for only to the extent to which they are compatible with this Convention.

Article 16

[Reservations]

1. Any State, upon becoming party to this Convention, shall be bound by all the obligations and shall enjoy all the benefits thereof. However, a State may at any time, in a notification deposited with the Secretary-General of the United Nations, declare that:

(a) as regards Article 12:

(i) it will not apply the provisions of that Article;

(ii) it will not apply the provisions of that Article in respect of certain uses;

(iii) as regards phonograms the producer of which is not a national of another Contracting State, it will not apply that Article;

(iv) as regards phonograms the producer of which is a national of another Contracting State, it will limit the protection provided for by that Article to the extent to which, and to the term for which, the latter State grants protection to phonograms first fixed by a national of the State making the declaration; however, the fact that the Contracting State of which the producer is a national does not grant the protection to the same beneficiary or beneficiaries as the State making the declaration shall not be considered as a difference in the extent of the protection;

(b) as regards Article 13, it will not apply item 13(d); if a Contracting State makes such a declaration, the other Contracting States shall not be obliged to grant the right referred to in Article 13(d), to broadcasting organisations whose headquarters are in that State.

2. If the notification referred to in paragraph 1 of this Article is made after the date of the deposit of the instrument of ratification, acceptance or accession, the declaration will become effective six months after it has been deposited.

Article 17
[Certain countries applying only the "fixation" criterion]

Any State which, on October 26, 1961, grants protection to producers of phonograms solely on the basis of the criterion of fixation may, by a notification deposited with the Secretary-General of the United Nations at the time of ratification, acceptance or accession, declare that it will apply, for the purposes of Article 5, the criterion of fixation alone and, for the purposes of paragraph 16.1(a)(iii) and 16.1(a)(iv), the criterion of fixation instead of the criterion of nationality.

Notes and Questions

1. The WIPO Performances and Phonograms Treaty (WPPT) grants rights to performers and producers of phonograms that in some respects are more extensive than the rights afforded by the Rome Convention. It also addresses new technologies which enable the delivery of sound recordings over the Internet and other digital networks. The United States did not join the Rome Convention because, *inter alia,* the U.S. did not recognize performers rights, but it is a party to the Geneva Convention for the Protection of Producers of Phonograms of 1971. The Geneva Convention provides protection to producers against unauthorized duplication of phonograms. The United States amended its copyright legislation in connection with implementation of the Uruguay Round Agreements to recognize the rights of performers.[1]

---

[1] 17 U.S.C. §1101.

The term of protection under the WPPT is fifty years as compared with the Rome term of twenty years. The fifty year-term is consistent with the provisions of the TRIPS Agreement. The Rome Convention to some extent favors the interests of phonogram producers over the interests of performers. The WPPT Treaty appears to carry forward territorial limitations with respect to the rights of performers by making their treatment subject to qualifications of the Rome Convention.[2] These qualifications are incorporated by reference in the TRIPS Agreement, which permits WTO Members to provide conditions and limitations on the rights of performers and producers consistent with the Rome Convention.[3] The rights of performers may still fall short of the rights of producers.

2. In the United States, sound recordings (e.g., phonograms) are defined by the Copyright Act as copyright subject matter.[4] When the U.S. Congress in 1998 extended the term of copyright to the life of author plus seventy years, this extended the copyright term applicable to sound recordings.[5] However, exclusive rights in sound recordings are less extensive than those generally applicable to copyrighted works,[6] and are subject to compulsory licensing upon payment of prescribed royalties.[7] The scope of rights in sound recordings in the digital environment are dealt with in the Digital Millennium Copyright Act.

L. TRIPS Agreement Copyright Provisions

As we did for the TRIPS Agreement norms on patents, we introduce the TRIPS Agreement norms with respect to copyright with Thomas Cottier's insights into the negotiating process. We then turn to a description of the resulting norms by Adrian Otten and Hannu Wager, succeeded by the relevant TRIPS Agreement text, and Notes and Questions.

---

[2]See art. 3(2), WPPT in conjunction with art. 4, Rome Convention.
[3]Art. 14:6, TRIPS Agreement.
[4]17 U.S.C. §102(7).
[5]See Sonny Bono Copyright Term Extension Act, Pub. L. 105-298, Oct. 27, 1998, §102.
[6]See 17 U.S.C. § 114, with attention to §114(c) (protecting the right to publicly perform copyrighted works by means of phonogram).
[7]17 U.S.C. §115.

The Prospects For Intellectual Property in GATT

Thomas Cottier*

*****

5.1 Copyright

The task of interfacing common law concepts of copyright, in particular United States' law and practices, with the continental system including neighbouring rights, has been extremely difficult to achieve in the draft. There is general consensus that the provisions of the Berne Convention (1971) should apply. From the United States point of view, however, this should not include entitlement based on moral rights in a GATT context. Subjecting moral rights to the GATT, it is argued, could upset the existing balance of negotiating powers within the industry and stir the national debate on this contentious subject. Referring to Berne, but making such exclusions, hardly seems consistent, quite apart from the fact that moral rights indeed include trade issues. On the other hand, it may be doubtful whether inclusion or exclusion makes a strong practical difference, since jurisdiction to challenge the use of moral rights for protectionist purposes already exists under Article XX(d) of GATT.

The draft completes developments towards protection of computer programs and electronic data compilation by means of copyright. Duration of protection is still pending and depends whether or not such works will be defined as literary works or not. Some developing countries favour the inclusion of alternative systems of protection and shorter periods of protection. Progress was made with respect to rental rights in the field of computer programs, cinematographic works, as well as phonograms. It is likely that a compromise will establish an obligation to introduce rental rights only to the extent that exclusive rights are substantially impaired and nullified. This case-by-case approach, possibly, in the end, not excluding other systems of equitable remuneration, is a typical fruit of interfacing GATT and IPRs. It borrows from the concept of material injury applied in antidumping, subsidy and safeguard regulation under GATT. Given the conceptual differences in the field of what are called neighbouring rights,

---

*28 CMLR 383 (1991).

between the United States and Europe as well as Japan, little progress was achieved in this area beyond the protection of phonogram producers which are likely to enjoy not only potential rental rights but also a fifty year term of protection. While performers and broadcasters are explicitly named, their rights do not go beyond those allocated to phonogram producers. In fact, they do not go beyond what is necessary to keep their rights in line with a strongly improved position of phonogram producers for the purpose of maintaining the balance in contractual relations.

Compliance with TRIPS: The Emerging World View*

Adrian Otten** and Hannu Wager***

*****

III. Substantive Standards of Protection

*****

The main features of the provisions concerning various categories of intellectual property covered by the TRIPS Agreement are summarized infra. The relevant provisions can be found in Part II of the Agreement.

A. Copyright and Related Rights

During the Uruguay Round negotiations, it was recognized that the Berne Convention already, for the most part, provided adequate basic standards of copyright protection. Thus, it was agreed that the point of depar-

---

*29 VAND. J. TRANSNAT'L L. 391 (1996).

**Director, Intellectual Property and Investment Division, the World Trade Organization. The views presented in this Article are the responsibility of the authors and should not be taken as necessarily those of the World Trade Organization or the World Trade Organization Secretariat. (c) 1996 Adrian Otten and Hannu Wager.

***Legal Affairs Officer, Intellectual Property and Investment Division, the World Trade Organization.

ture should be the existing level of protection under the latest Act of the Convention, the Paris Act of 1971. In the area of copyright, therefore, the TRIPS Agreement confines itself to clarifying or adding obligations on a number of specific points.

The Agreement clarifies two important points relating to new technology. First, it provides that computer programs, whether in source or in object code, shall be protected as literary works under the Berne Convention. Second, it clarifies that a database or other compilation of data or other material shall be protected under copyright even where it includes data or other material that, as such, is not protected under copyright, provided that, by reason of the selection or arrangement of its contents, the database or other compilation constitutes an intellectual creation.

The other main provisions include an obligation to provide exclusive rental rights to the authors of computer programs and, in certain situations, of cinematographic works. The provisions also require members to ensure that any limitations or exceptions to exclusive rights, including those permitted under the Berne Convention, are confined to special cases that do not conflict with the normal exploitation of the work or unreasonably prejudice the legitimate rights of the right holder.

The section of the TRIPS Agreement on copyright and related rights is intended to be strictly neutral as between the authors' rights and copyright traditions in this area, providing more effective protection in both respects. One example of this neutrality is in the treatment of the rights of performers, producers of phonograms, and broadcasting organizations. Here the focus is on the substance of the protection that should be granted, without prejudging the form that a member state might choose to use for this purpose. In contrast to the Berne Convention, there is no requirement in the TRIPS Agreement to comply with the substantive provisions of the Rome Convention. However, the provisions of the TRIPS Agreement in these areas are substantially inspired by the Rome Convention and certain provisions of the Rome Convention are referred to for the sake of economy in legal drafting. The standards in the TRIPS Agreement are in some respects higher than those in the Rome Convention and in other respects less so.

Under the TRIPS Agreement, performers must have the possibility of preventing the unauthorized fixation of their performances on phonograms as well as the reproduction of such fixations. They must also have the possibility of preventing the unauthorized broadcast by wireless means and the unauthorized communication to the public of their live performances.

The producers of phonograms must have exclusive rights over the reproduction of their phonograms and also exclusive rental rights. Broadcasting organizations must have the right to prohibit the unauthorized fixation, reproduction of fixations, and rebroadcasting by wireless means of broadcasts, as well as communication to the public of their television broadcasts. It is not necessary, however, to grant such rights to broadcasting organizations if owners of copyright in the subject matter of broadcasts are provided with the possibility of preventing these acts, subject to the provisions of the Berne Convention. One of the main improvements to the level of protection provided for in the Rome Convention is that the term of protection of both performers and producers of phonograms must be at least fifty years

---

Agreement on Trade-Related Aspects of Intellectual Property Rights

Section 1: Copyright and Related Rights

Article 9
Relation to the Berne Convention

1. Members shall comply with Articles 1 through 21 of the Berne Convention (1971) and the Appendix thereto. However, Members shall not have rights or obligations under this Agreement in respect of the rights conferred under Article 6bis of that Convention or of the rights derived therefrom.

2. Copyright protection shall extend to expressions and not to ideas, procedures, methods of operation or mathematical concepts as such.

Article 10
Computer Programs and Compilations of Data

1. Computer programs, whether in source or object code, shall be protected as literary works under the Berne Convention (1971).

2. Compilations of data or other material, whether in machine readable or other form, which by reason of the selection or arrangement of their contents constitute intellectual creations shall be protected as such. Such protection, which shall not extend to the data or material itself, shall be without prejudice to any copyright subsisting in the data or material itself.

Article 11
Rental Rights

In respect of at least computer programs and cinematographic works, a Member shall provide authors and their successors in title the right to authorize or to prohibit the commercial rental to the public of originals or copies of their copyright works. A Member shall be excepted from this obligation in respect of cinematographic works unless such rental has led to widespread copying of such works which is materially impairing the exclusive right of reproduction conferred in that Member on authors and their successors in title. In respect of computer programs, this obligation does not apply to rentals where the program itself is not the essential object of the rental.

Article 12
Term of Protection

Whenever the term of protection of a work, other than a photographic work or a work of applied art, is calculated on a basis other than the life of a natural person, such term shall be no less than 50 years from the end of the calendar year of authorized publication, or, failing such authorized publication within 50 years from the making of the work, 50 years from the end of the calendar year of making.

Article 13
Limitations and Exceptions

Members shall confine limitations or exceptions to exclusive rights to certain special cases which do not conflict with a normal exploitation of the work and do not unreasonably prejudice the legitimate interests of the right holder.

Article 14
Protection of Performers, Producers of Phonograms (Sound Recordings) and Broadcasting Organizations

1. In respect of a fixation of their performance on a phonogram, performers shall have the possibility of preventing the following acts when undertaken without their authorization: the fixation of their unfixed performance and the reproduction of such fixation. Performers shall also have the possibility of preventing the following acts when undertaken without their authorization: the broadcasting by wireless means and the communication to the public of their live performance.

2. Producers of phonograms shall enjoy the right to authorize or prohibit the direct or indirect reproduction of their phonograms.

3. Broadcasting organizations shall have the right to prohibit the following acts when undertaken without their authorization: the fixation, the reproduction of fixations, and the rebroadcasting by wireless means of broadcasts, as well as the communication to the public of television broadcasts of the same. Where Members do not grant such rights to broadcasting organizations, they shall provide owners of copyright in the subject matter of broadcasts with the possibility of preventing the above acts, subject to the provisions of the Berne Convention (1971).

4. The provisions of Article 11 in respect of computer programs shall apply mutatis mutandis to producers of phonograms and any other right holders in phonograms as determined in a Member's law. If on 15 April 1994 a Member has in force a system of equitable remuneration of right holders in respect of the rental of phonograms, it may maintain such system provided that the commercial rental of phonograms is not giving rise to the material impairment of the exclusive rights of reproduction of right holders.

5. The term of the protection available under this Agreement to performers and producers of phonograms shall last at least until the end of a period of 50 years computed from the end of the calendar year in which the fixation

was made or the performance took place. The term of protection granted pursuant to paragraph 3 shall last for at least 20 years from the end of the calendar year in which the broadcast took place.

6. Any Member may, in relation to the rights conferred under paragraphs 1, 2 and 3, provide for conditions, limitations, exceptions and reservations to the extent permitted by the Rome Convention. However, the provisions of Article 18 of the Berne Convention (1971) shall also apply, mutatis mutandis, to the rights of performers and producers of phonograms in phonograms.

Notes and Questions

1. By way of contrast with the patent provisions of the TRIPS Agreement, the copyright section devotes little attention to the subject matter of protection — addressing computer software and compilations. The main focus of the TRIPS provisions is granting an additional form of distribution right (i.e. the rental right), and enhancing the rights of performers, producers and broadcast organizations — the traditional beneficiaries of neighboring rights.

From the standpoint of the copyright industries, the TRIPS Agreement was needed not so much to enhance or clarify the scope of rights, but to provide the leverage by which enforcement of these rights could be secured, particularly in developing countries.

2. The copyright norms of the TRIPS Agreement are already somewhat dated in light of the WCT and WPPT. In Chapter II we studied the process by which the TRIPS Agreement may be amended to incorporate new rules. Do you think it important that the TRIPS Agreement be amended in line with the provisions of the new WIPO treaties? Might developing countries be in compliance with the TRIPS Agreement copyright provisions, but fail to comply (or not be a party to) the new WIPO provisions? Should a WTO Millennium Round include on its agenda the harmonization of WTO and WIPO IPRs rules?

M. Copyright in the European Union and the United States

1. The Path of Approximation

We have previously referred to a decade-long trend in the EU toward the adoption of directives and other harmonization or approximation legislation directed at achieving higher levels of protection for innovators and creators of artistic works. The *Warner Brothers v. Christiansen* case raised awareness in the EU regarding the potential for varying levels of IPRs protection to lead to distortions in patterns of trade. This case identified the emergence of a new form of right pertaining to the copyright — the right to control the renting out of the copyrighted work — distinct from the right to distribute or communicate to the public. The *Warner Brothers v. Christiansen* case helped form the background for the rental right embodied in the TRIPS Agreement.

Warner Brothers Inc. and Metronome Video ApS
v. Erik Viuff Christiansen

Reference for a preliminary ruling: OEstre Landsret — Denmark
Copyright — Objection to the hiring-out of video-cassettes
Case 158/86, 686J0158

Court of Justice of The European Communities
1988 ECJ CELEX LEXIS 2016

Judgment of the Court of 17 May 1988.

Introduction:
In Case 158/86

Reference to the Court under Article 177 of the EEC Treaty by the OEstre Landsret, Copenhagen, for a preliminary ruling in the action pending before that court between

Warner Brothers Inc.,
Metronome Video ApS

and

Erik Viuff Christiansen

on the interpretation of Articles 30, 36 and 222 of the EEC Treaty with regard to the action taken by an owner of exclusive rights in Denmark to restrain hiring-out in Denmark of a video-recording marketed in another Member State by the same owner of the exclusive rights or with his consent.

The Court composed of : G. Bosco, President of Chamber, for the President, O. Due and J. C. Moitinho de Almeida (Presidents of Chambers), T. Koopmans, U. Everling, K. Bahlmann, Y. Galmot, R. Joliet and F. Schockweiler, Judges,
Advocate General : G. F. Mancini

*****

Judgment-by: Galmot

Judgment:

1. By order dated 11 June 1986, which was received at the Court on 1 July 1986, the OEstre Landsret referred to the Court for a preliminary ruling under Article 177 of the EEC Treaty a question on the interpretation of Articles 30 and 36 of the EEC Treaty, with a view to establishing the extent to which national copyright legislation regarding the hiring-out of video-cassettes is compatible with the free movement of goods.

2. The question was raised in the context of proceedings brought by two companies, Warner Brothers Inc . (hereinafter referred to as "Warner") and Metronome Video ApS (hereinafter "Metronome"), against Mr Erik Viuff Christiansen.

3. Warner, the owner in the United Kingdom of the copyright of the film "Never Say Never Again", which it produced in that country, assigned the management of the video production rights in Denmark to Metronome.

4. The video-cassette of the film was on sale in the United Kingdom with Warner's consent. Mr Christiansen, who manages a video shop in Copenhagen, purchased a copy in London with a view to hiring it out in Denmark and imported it into that Member State for that purpose.

5. On the basis of Danish legislation, which enables the author or producer of a musical or cinematographic work to take action to restrain the hiring-out of videograms of that work until such time as he gives his consent, Warner and Metronome obtained an injunction from the Copenhagen City Court prohibiting the defendant from hiring out the video-cassette in Denmark.

6. In the context of the proceedings referred to it, the OEstre Landsret (Eastern Division of the High Court) decided to request the Court of Justice to give a preliminary ruling on the following question:

> Must the provisions of Chapter 2 in Title I of Part 2 of the EEC Treaty, on the elimination of quantitative restrictions between Member States, namely Articles 30 and 36, in conjunction with Article 222 of the Treaty, be interpreted as meaning that the owner of exclusive rights (copyright) in a video-recording which is lawfully put into circulation by the owner of the exclusive right or with his consent in a Member State under whose domestic copyright law it is not possible to prohibit the (resale and) hiring-out of the recordings is prevented from restraining the hiring-out of the video-recording in another Member State into which it has been lawfully imported, where the copyright law of that State allows such prohibition without distinguishing between domestic and imported video-recordings and without impeding the actual importation of video-recordings?

7. Reference is made to the Report for the Hearing for a fuller account of the facts of the main proceedings, the applicable national legislation and the observations submitted to the Court, which are mentioned or discussed hereinafter only in so far as is necessary for the reasoning of the Court.

8. In submitting the question the national court seeks to ascertain, in essence, whether Articles 30 and 36 of the EEC Treaty preclude the application of national legislation which gives an author the right to make the hiring-out of video-cassettes conditional on his authorization, where those

video-cassettes have already been put into circulation with his consent in another Member State whose legislation allows the author to control their initial sale without giving him the right to prohibit them from being hired out.

9. It should be noted that, unlike the national copyright legislation which gave rise to the judgment of 20 January 1981 in Joined Cases 55 and 57/80 Musik Vertrieb Membran v. GEMA (1981) ECR 147, the legislation which gives rise to the present preliminary question does not enable the author to collect an additional fee on the actual importation of recordings of protected works which are marketed with his consent in another Member State, or to set up any further obstacle whatsoever to importation or resale. The rights and powers conferred on the author by the national legislation in question comes into operation only after importation has been carried out.

10. Nonetheless, it must be observed that the commercial distribution of video-cassettes takes the form not only of sales but also, and increasingly, that of hiring-out to individuals who possess video-tape recorders. The right to prohibit such hiring-out in a Member State is therefore liable to influence trade in video-cassettes in that State and hence, indirectly, to affect intra-Community trade in those products. Legislation of the kind which gave rise to the main proceedings must therefore, in the light of established case-law, be regarded as a measure having an effect equivalent to a quantitative restriction on imports, which is prohibited by Article 30 of the Treaty.

11. Consideration should therefore be given to whether such legislation may be considered justified on grounds of the protection of industrial and commercial property within the meaning of Article 36 — a term which was held by the Court, in its judgment of 6 October 1982 in Case 262/81 Coditel v. Cine-Vog (1982) ECR 3381, to include literary and artistic property.

12. In that connection it should first be noted that the Danish legislation applies without distinction to video-cassettes produced in situ and video-cassettes imported from another Member State. The determining factor for the purposes of its application is the type of transaction in video-cassettes which is in question, not the origin of those video-cassettes. Such legislation does not therefore, in itself, operate any arbitrary discrimination in trade between Member States.

13. It should further be pointed out that literary and artistic works may be the subject of commercial exploitation, whether by way of public performance or of the reproduction and marketing of the recordings made of them, and this is true in particular of cinematographic works. The two essential rights of the author, namely the exclusive right of performance and the exclusive right of reproduction, are not called in question by the rules of the Treaty.

14. Lastly, consideration must be given to the emergence, demonstrated by the Commission, of a specific market for the hiring-out of such recordings, as distinct from their sale. The existence of that market was made possible by various factors such as the improvement of manufacturing methods for video-cassettes which increased their strength and life in use, the growing awareness amongst viewers that they watch only occasionally the video-cassettes which they have bought and, lastly, their relatively high purchase price. The market for the hiring-out of video-cassettes reaches a wider public than the market for their sale and, at present, offers great potential as a source of revenue for makers of films.

15. However, it is apparent that, by authorizing the collection of royalties only on sales to private individuals and to persons hiring out video-cassettes, it is impossible to guarantee to makers of films a remuneration which reflects the number of occasions on which the video-cassettes are actually hired out and which secures for them a satisfactory share of the rental market. That explains why, as the Commission points out in its observations, certain national laws have recently provided specific protection of the right to hire out video-cassettes.

16. Laws of that kind are therefore clearly justified on grounds of the protection of industrial and commercial property pursuant to Article 36 of the Treaty.

17. However, the defendant in the main proceedings, relying on the judgments of 22 January 1981 in Case 58/80 Dansk Supermarked v. Imerco (1981) ECR 181 and of 20 January 1981 Musik Vertrieb Membran v. GEMA, cited above, contends that the author is at liberty to choose the Member State in which he will market his work. The defendant in the main proceedings emphasizes that the author makes his choice according to his own interests and must, in particular, take into consideration the fact that

the legislation of certain Member States, unlike that of certain others, confers on him an exclusive right enabling him to restrain the hiring-out of the recording of the work even when that work has been offered for sale with his consent. That being so, a maker of a film who has offered the video-cassette of that film for sale in a Member State whose legislation confers on him no exclusive right of hiring it out (as in the main proceedings) must accept the consequences of his choice and the exhaustion of his right to restrain the hiring-out of that video-cassette in any other Member State.

18. That objection cannot be upheld. It follows from the foregoing considerations that, where national legislation confers on authors a specific right to hire out video-cassettes, that right would be rendered worthless if its owner were not in a position to authorize the operations for doing so. It cannot therefore be accepted that the marketing by a film-maker of a video-cassette containing one of his works, in a Member State which does not provide specific protection for the right to hire it out, should have repercussions on the right conferred on that same film-maker by the legislation of another Member State to restrain, in that State, the hiring-out of that video-cassette.

19. In those circumstances, the answer to be given to the question submitted by the national court is that Articles 30 and 36 of the Treaty do not prohibit the application of national legislation which gives an author the right to make the hiring-out of video-cassettes subject to his permission, when the video-cassettes in question have already been put into circulation with his consent in another Member State whose legislation enables the author to control the initial sale, without giving him the right to prohibit hiring-out.

*****

Notes and Questions

1. Christiansen points out that Warner Brothers elected to put its video cassette on the market in the U.K. where the law provided that a first sale exhausted the copyright holder's right to control further distribution of the cassette. Warner Brothers profited from the first sale in the U.K. By enabling

Warner Brothers to control the rental in Denmark, the Court is allowing Warner Brothers to obtain additional profits from the same video cassette. Has the Court persuaded you that Warner Brothers needed the additional right to control the rental of the cassette in Denmark?

2. Computer software vendors tend to characterize their transactions with consumers as "licenses." In essence, software vendors assert that their transactions with consumers are not sales, but rather rentals under restrictive conditions. As we review the EU Rental Rights Directive and Computer Software Directive, consider the potential impact of these directives on the typical vendor to end-user consumer software transaction.

---

a. The Rental Rights Directive

In *Warner Brothers*, the ECJ allowed differences in member state IPRs policies and laws to create a barrier to the free movement of goods. Since the objective of the EU is to create a "single market" for goods and services in Europe, it would be a logical next step for Union authorities to seek to remove this barrier. How would this be done? By approximation of the laws of the member states. The Rental Rights Directive seeks to approximate the laws of the member states in the field of rental rights, and it also addresses the rights of performers, producers and broadcasters.

Council Directive 92/100/EEC of 19 November 1992 on rental right and lending right and on certain rights related to copyright in the field of intellectual property*

COUNCIL DIRECTIVE 92/100/EEC of 19 November 1992 on rental right and lending right and on certain rights related to copyright in the field of intellectual property

The Council of the European Communities, [Recitals Omitted]
Has Adopted this Directive:

---

*1992 OJ L 346, Doc. Date, Nov. 19, 1992.

Chapter I Rental and Lending Right

Article 1
Object of harmonization

1. In accordance with the provisions of this Chapter, Member States shall provide, subject to Article 5, a right to authorize or prohibit the rental and lending of originals and copies of copyright works, and other subject matter as set out in Article 2(1).

2. For the purposes of this Directive, "rental" means making available for use, for a limited period of time and for direct or indirect economic or commercial advantage.

3. For the purposes of this Directive, "lending" means making available for use, for a limited period of time and not for direct or indirect economic or commercial advantage, when it is made through establishments which are accessible to the public.

4. The rights referred to in paragraph 1 shall not be exhausted by any sale or other act of distribution of originals and copies of copyright works and other subject matter as set out in Article 2(1).

Article 2
Rightholders and subject matter of rental and lending right

1. The exclusive right to authorize or prohibit rental and lending shall belong:
— to the author in respect of the original and copies of his work,
— to the performer in respect of fixations of his performance,
— to the phonogram producer in respect of his phonograms, and
— to the producer of the first fixation of a film in respect of the original and copies of his film. For the purposes of this Directive, the term "film" shall designate a cinematographic or audiovisual work or moving images, whether or not accompanied by sound.

2. For the purposes of this Directive the principal director of a cinematographic or audiovisual work shall be considered as its author or one of its authors. Member States may provide for others to be considered as its co-authors.

3. This Directive does not cover rental and lending rights in relation to buildings and to works of applied art.

4. The rights referred to in paragraph 1 may be transferred, assigned or subject to the granting of contractual licences.

5. Without prejudice to paragraph 7, when a contract concerning film production is concluded, individually or collectively, by performers with a film producer, the performer covered by this contract shall be presumed, subject to contractual clauses to the contrary, to have transferred his rental right, subject to Article 4.

6. Member States may provide for a similar presumption as set out in paragraph 5 with respect to authors.

7. Member States may provide that the signing of a contract concluded between a performer and a film producer concerning the production of a film has the effect of authorizing rental, provided that such contract provides for an equitable remuneration within the meaning of Article 4. Member States may also provide that this paragraph shall apply mutatis mutandis to the rights included in Chapter II.

Article 3
Rental of computer programs

This Directive shall be without prejudice to Article 4(c) of Council Directive 91/250/EEC of 14 May 1991 on the legal protection of computer programs.

Article 4
Unwaivable right to equitable remuneration

1. Where an author or performer has transferred or assigned his rental right concerning a phonogram or an original or copy of a film to a phonogram or film producer, that author or performer shall retain the right to obtain an equitable remuneration for the rental.

2. The right to obtain an equitable remuneration for rental cannot be waived by authors or performers.

3. The administration of this right to obtain an equitable remuneration may be entrusted to collecting societies representing authors or performers.

4. Member States may regulate whether and to what extent administration by collecting societies of the right to obtain an equitable remuneration may be imposed, as well as the question from whom this remuneration may be claimed or collected.

Article 5
Derogation from the exclusive public lending right

1. Member States may derogate from the exclusive right provided for in Article 1 in respect of public lending, provided that at least authors obtain a remuneration for such lending. Member States shall be free to determine this remuneration taking account of their cultural promotion objectives.
2. When Member States do not apply the exclusive lending right provided for in Article 1 as regards phonograms, films and computer programs, they shall introduce, at least for authors, a remuneration.
3. Member States may exempt certain categories of establishments from the payment of the remuneration referred to in paragraphs 1 and 2.
4. The Commission, in cooperation with the Member States, shall draw up before 1 July 1997 a report on public lending in the Community. It shall forward this report to the European Parliament and to the Council.

Chapter II Rights Related to Copyright

Article 6
Fixation right

1. Member States shall provide for performers the exclusive right to authorize or prohibit the fixation of their performances.
2. Member States shall provide for broadcasting organizations the exclusive right to authorize or prohibit the fixation of their broadcasts, whether these broadcasts are transmitted by wire or over the air, including by cable or satellite.
3. A cable distributor shall not have the right provided for in paragraph 2 where it merely retransmits by cable the broadcasts of broadcasting organizations.

Article 7
Reproduction right

1. Member States shall provide the exclusive right to authorize or prohibit the direct or indirect reproduction:
— for performers, of fixations of their performances,
— for phonogram producers, of their phonograms,

— for producers of the first fixations of films, in respect of the original and copies of their films, and
— for broadcasting organizations, of fixations of their broadcasts, as set out in Article 6 (2).
2. The reproduction right referred to in paragraph 1 may be transferred, assigned or subject to the granting of contractual licences.

Article 8
Broadcasting and communication to the public

1. Member States shall provide for performers the exclusive right to authorize or prohibit the broadcasting by wireless means and the communication to the public of their performances, except where the performance is itself already a broadcast performance or is made from a fixation.
2. Member States shall provide a right in order to ensure that a single equitable remuneration is paid by the user, if a phonogram published for commercial purposes, or a reproduction of such phonogram, is used for broadcasting by wireless means or for any communication to the public, and to ensure that this remuneration is shared between the relevant performers and phonogram producers. Member States may, in the absence of agreement between the performers and phonogram producers, lay down the conditions as to the sharing of this remuneration between them.
3. Member States shall provide for broadcasting organizations the exclusive right to authorize or prohibit the rebroadcasting of their broadcasts by wireless means, as well as the communication to the public of their broadcasts if such communication is made in places accessible to the public against payment of an entrance fee.

Article 9
Distribution right

1. Member States shall provide
— for performers, in respect of fixations of their performances,
— for phonogram producers, in respect of their phonograms,
— for producers of the first fixations of films, in respect of the original and copies of their films,
— for broadcasting organizations, in respect of fixations of their broadcast as set out in Article 6(2), the exclusive right to make available these objects,

including copies thereof, to the public by sale or otherwise, hereafter referred to as the "distribution right".

2. The distribution right shall not be exhausted within the Community in respect of an object as referred to in paragraph 1, except where the first sale in the Community of that object is made by the rightholder or with his consent.

3. The distribution right shall be without prejudice to the specific provisions of Chapter I, in particular Article 1(4).

4. The distribution right may be transferred, assigned or subject to the granting of contractual licences.

Article 10
Limitations to rights

1. Member States may provide for limitations to the rights referred to in Chapter II in respect of:
(a) private use;
(b) use of short excerpts in connection with the reporting of current events;
(c) ephemeral fixation by a broadcasting organization by means of its own facilities and for its own broadcasts;
(d) use solely for the purposes of teaching or scientific research.

2. Irrespective of paragraph 1, any Member State may provide for the same kinds of limitations with regard to the protection of performers, producers of phonograms, broadcasting organizations and of producers of the first fixations of films, as it provides for in connection with the protection of copyright in literary and artistic works. However, compulsory licences may be provided for only to the extent to which they are compatible with the Rome Convention.

3. Paragraph 1(a) shall be without prejudice to any existing or future legislation on remuneration for reproduction for private use.

Chapter III Duration

Article 11
Duration of authors' rights

Without prejudice to further harmonization, the authors' rights referred to in this Directive shall not expire before the end of the term provided by the Berne Convention for the Protection of Literary and Artistic Works.

Article 12
Duration of related rights

Without prejudice to further harmonization, the rights referred to in this Directive of performers, phonogram producers and broadcasting organizations shall not expire before the end of the respective terms provided by the Rome Convention. The rights referred to in this Directive for producers of the first fixations of films shall not expire before the end of a period of 20 years computed from the end of the year in which the fixation was made.

Chapter IV Common Provisions

Article 13
Application in time

1. This Directive shall apply in respect of all copyright works, performances, phonograms, broadcasts and first fixations of films referred to in this Directive which are, on 1 July 1994, still protected by the legislation of the Member States in the field of copyright and related rights or meet the criteria for protection under the provisions of this Directive on that date.

2. This Directive shall apply without prejudice to any acts of exploitation performed before 1 July 1994.

3. Member States may provide that the rightholders are deemed to have given their authorization to the rental or lending of an object referred to in Article 2(1) which is proven to have been made available to third parties for this purpose or to have been acquired before 1 July 1994. However, in particular where such an object is a digital recording, Member States may provide that rightholders shall have a right to obtain an adequate remuneration for the rental or lending of that object.

4. Member States need not apply the provisions of Article 2(2) to cinematographic or audiovisual works created before 1 July 1994.

5. Member States may determine the date as from which the Article 2(2) shall apply, provided that that date is no later than 1 July 1997.

6. This Directive shall, without prejudice to paragraph 3 and subject to paragraphs 8 and 9, not affect any contracts concluded before the date of its adoption.

7. Member States may provide, subject to the provisions of paragraphs 8 and 9, that when rightholders who acquire new rights under the national provisions adopted in implementation of this Directive have, before 1 July 1994, given their consent for exploitation, they shall be presumed to have transferred the new exclusive rights.

8. Member States may determine the date as from which the unwaivable right to an equitable remuneration referred to in Article 4 exists, provided that that date is no later than 1 July 1997.

9. For contracts concluded before 1 July 1994, the unwaivable right to an equitable remuneration provided for in Article 4 shall apply only where authors or performers or those representing them have submitted a request to that effect before 1 January 1997. In the absence of agreement between rightholders concerning the level of remuneration, Member States may fix the level of equitable remuneration.

Article 14
Relation between copyright and related rights

Protection of copyright-related rights under this Directive shall leave intact and shall in no way affect the protection of copyright.

Article 15
Final provisions

1. Member States shall bring into force the laws, regulations and administrative provisions necessary to comply with this Directive not later than 1 July 1994. They shall forthwith inform the Commission thereof. When Member States adopt these measures, they shall contain a reference to this Directive or shall be accompanied by such reference at the time of their official publication. The methods of making such a reference shall be laid down by the Member States.

2. Member States shall communicate to the Commission the main provisions of domestic law which they adopt in the field covered by this Directive

Article 16
This Directive is addressed to the Member States. Done at Brussels, 19 November 1992.

Notes and Questions

1. Member states were directed to comply with the Rental Rights Directive by July 1, 1994. Assume that Christiansen again travels to the U.K. and purchases a video cassette that includes a rental right. He again brings it back to Denmark and commences to rent it out. May Warner Brothers block the renting out on the basis of a separate Danish rental right? What if the rental right in Denmark differs in some respects from the rental right in the U.K.? Recall that directives generally leave EU members with some flexibility in implementation.

2. Recall our question whether software vendors may treat the ordinary end-user purchase as a license or rental. How are computer programs treated by the Rental Rights Directive? Examine article 4(c) of the Software Directive.[1] Does this answer the question?

3. The Rental Rights Directive provides that authors and performers who assign their rental right retain an "unwaivable" right to equitable remuneration for the rental. In the United States, by way of contrast, it is rare to find an economic right that may not be transferred or waived.

---

b. The Copyright Directive

One of the most significant steps taken by the EU in respect to copyright was to extend the general term of protection to the life of the author plus seventy years. According to the recitals of the Copyright Directive, the Berne Convention term of the author's life plus fifty years was intended to cover the average life span of an author, plus the life span of a second generation. According to the recitals, since the average life span is now longer than when the Berne norms were adopted, the copyright term should be extended. The Copyright Directive also extends the terms of protection for performers, producers and broadcasters in line with those mandated by the TRIPS Agreement.

---

[1]*Infra*, § Q, 1, b.

Council Directive 93/98/EEC of 29 October 1993 harmonizing the term of protection of copyright and certain related rights*

COUNCIL DIRECTIVE 93/98/EEC of 29 October 1993 harmonizing the term of protection of copyright and certain related rights

The Council of The European Communities, [recitals omitted]
Has Adopted this Directive:

Article 1
Duration of authors' rights

1. The rights of an author of a literary or artistic work within the meaning of Article 2 of the Berne Convention shall run for the life of the author and for 70 years after his death, irrespective of the date when the work is lawfully made available to the public.

2. In the case of a work of joint authorship the term referred to in paragraph 1 shall be calculated from the death of the last surviving author.

3. In the case of anonymous or pseudonymous works, the term of protection shall run for seventy years after the work is lawfully made available to the public. However, when the pseudonym adopted by the author leaves no doubt as to his identity, or if the author discloses his identity during the period referred to in the first sentence, the term of protection applicable shall be that laid down in paragraph 1.

4. Where a Member State provides for particular provisions on copyright in respect of collective works or for a legal person to be designated as the rightholder, the term of protection shall be calculated according to the provisions of paragraph 3, except if the natural persons who have created the work as such are identified as such in the versions of the work which are made available to the public. This paragraph is without prejudice to the rights of identified authors whose identifiable contributions are included in such works, to which contributions paragraph 1 or 2 shall apply.

5. Where a work is published in volumes, parts, instalments, issues or episodes and the term of protection runs from the time when the work was

---

*1993 OJ L 290, Doc. Date, Oct. 29, 1993.

lawfully made available to the public, the term of protection shall run for each such item separately.

6. In the case of works for which the term of protection is not calculated from the death of the author or authors and which have not been lawfully made available to the public within seventy years from their creation, the protection shall terminate.

Article 2
Cinematographic or audiovisual works

1. The principal director of a cinematographic or audiovisual work shall be considered as its author or one of its authors. Member States shall be free to designate other co-authors.

2. The term of protection of cinematographic or audiovisual works shall expire 70 years after the death of the last of the following persons to survive, whether or not these persons are designated as co-authors: the principal director, the author of the screenplay, the author of the dialogue and the composer of music specifically created for use in the cinematographic or audiovisual work.

Article 3
Duration of related rights

1. The rights of performers shall expire 50 years after the date of the performance. However, if a fixation of the performance is lawfully published or lawfully communicated to the public within this period, the rights shall expire 50 years from the date of the first such publication or the first such communication to the public, whichever is the earlier.

2. The rights of producers of phonograms shall expire 50 years after the fixation is made. However, if the phonogram is lawfully published or lawfully communicated to the public during this period, the rights shall expire 50 years from the date of the first such publication or the first such communication to the public, whichever is the earlier.

3. The rights of producers of the first fixation of a film shall expire 50 years after the fixation is made. However, if the film is lawfully published or lawfully communicated to the public during this period, the rights shall expire 50 years from the date of the first such publication or the first such communication to the public, whichever is the earlier. The term "film" shall des-

ignate a cinematographic or audiovisual work or moving images, whether or not accompanied by sound.

4. The rights of broadcasting organizations shall expire 50 years after the first transmission of a broadcast, whether this broadcast is transmitted by wire or over the air, including by cable or satellite.

Article 4
Protection of previously unpublished works

Any person who, after the expiry of copyright protection, for the first time lawfully publishes or lawfully communicates to the public a previously unpublished work, shall benefit from a protection equivalent to the economic rights of the author. The term of protection of such rights shall be 25 years from the time when the work was first lawfully published or lawfully communicated to the public.

Article 5
Critical and scientific publications

Member States may protect critical and scientific publications of works which have come into the public domain. The maximum term of protection of such rights shall be 30 years from the time when the publication was first lawfully published.

Article 6
Protection of photographs

Photographs which are original in the sense that they are the author's own intellectual creation shall be protected in accordance with Article 1. No other criteria shall be applied to determine their eligibility for protection. Member States may provide for the protection of other photographs.

Article 7
Protection vis-à-vis third countries

1. Where the country of origin of a work, within the meaning of the Berne Convention, is a third country, and the author of the work is not a Community national, the term of protection granted by the Member States shall

expire on the date of expiry of the protection granted in the country of origin of the work, but may not exceed the term laid down in Article 1.

2. The terms of protection laid down in Article 3 shall also apply in the case of rightholders who are not Community nationals, provided Member States grant them protection. However, without prejudice to the international obligations of the Member States, the term of protection granted by Member States shall expire no later than the date of expiry of the protection granted in the country of which the rightholder is a national and may not exceed the term laid down in Article 3.

3. Member States which, at the date of adoption of this Directive, in particular pursuant to their international obligations, granted a longer term of protection than that which would result from the provisions, referred to in paragraphs 1 and 2 may maintain this protection until the conclusion of international agreements on the term of protection by copyright or related rights.

Article 8
Calculation of terms

The terms laid down in this Directive are calculated from the first day of January of the year following the event which gives rise to them.

Article 9
Moral rights

This Directive shall be without prejudice to the provisions of the Member States regulating moral rights.

Article 10
Application in time

1. Where a term of protection, which is longer than the corresponding term provided for by this Directive, is already running in a Member State on the date referred to in Article 13 (1), this Directive shall not have the effect of shortening that term of protection in that Member State.

2. The terms of protection provided for in this Directive shall apply to all works and subject matter which are protected in at least one Member State, on the date referred to in Article 13 (1), pursuant to national provisions on copyright or related rights or which meet the criteria for protection under Directive 92/100/EEC.

3. This Directive shall be without prejudice to any acts of exploitation performed before the date referred to in Article 13 (1). Member States shall adopt the necessary provisions to protect in particular acquired rights of third parties.

4. Member States need not apply the provisions of Article 2 (1) to cinematographic or audiovisual works created before 1 July 1994.

5. Member States may determine the date as from which Article 2 (1) shall apply, provided that date is no later than 1 July 1997.

Article 11
Technical adaptation

*****

Article 12
Notification procedure

Member States shall immediately notify the Commission of any governmental plan to grant new related rights, including the basic reasons for their introduction and the term of protection envisaged.

Article 13
General provisions

1. Member States shall bring into force the laws, regulations and administrative provisions necessary to comply with Articles 1 to 11 of this Directive before 1 July 1995.

When Member States adopt these provisions, they shall contain a reference to this Directive or shall be accompanied by such reference at the time of their official publication. The methods of making such a reference shall be laid down by the Member States.

Member States shall communicate to the Commission the texts of the pro visions of national law which they adopt in the field governed by this Directive.

2. Member States shall apply Article 12 from the date of notification of this Directive.

Article 14
This Directive is addressed to the Member States.

Done at Brussels, 29 October 1993.

Notes and Questions

1. Article 7 addresses the rights of third country nationals. As noted earlier in this chapter, the United States followed the lead of the EU and, in October 1998, extended its copyright term to the life of author plus seventy years. For non-nationals of the EU that maintain an author's life plus fifty year term of copyright protection, what will be their term of protection in the EU? Note that obligations with respect to foreign performers, producers and broadcast organizations may be limited by existing member state legislation (art. 7(2), Copyright Directive).

2. U.S. industry groups pointed to the copyright term in the EU Directive as evidence of a "gap" in U.S. legislation that would ultimately provide a competitive advantage to EU industry and weaken the United States. (The Walt Disney Company was an active proponent of extending the term of copyright protection in the United States since the term of protection for several of its major properties (e.g., Mickey Mouse) was due to expire in the near future.) How would a longer term of copyright protection in the EU enhance industrial competitiveness there?

3. Consider that computer software will now be protected in the EU for more than 100 years (in many cases). Do you think that this term of protection appropriately balances the interests of authors and the public? Since computer programming technologies evolve rapidly, how likely is it that the copyrighted expression found in today's computer software will be economically significant in fifty years? Should Microsoft care whether the term of copyright protection for Windows 98 is twenty years, fifty years or 100 years?

---

c. Database Protection and the Database Directive

In her article on the digital agenda at WIPO, Pamela Samuelson referred to EU and U.S. efforts to promote an international agreement on the protection of databases. The Berne Convention included collections of literary and artistic works, which by reason of their selection and arrangement constitute intellectual creations, within the scope of copyrightable subject matter (art. 2(5) Berne). The TRIPS Agreement (art. 10:2) and WIPO Copyright Treaty (art. 5) went on to clarify that compilations of data (including in digital form) which constitute intellectual creations are copyrightable subject matter. This does not put an end to the database debate for reasons which are illustrated by the U.S. Supreme Court decision, *Feist v. Rural Telephone*. In this decision, the Supreme Court emphasizes the public policy considerations (including the constitutional basis) underlying U.S. copyright legislation, and the importance of balancing interests among various constituencies.

---

i. Databases in U.S. Law

Feist Publications v. Rural Telephone Service

Supreme Court of The United States
499 U.S. 340; 1991 U.S. LEXIS 1856
March 27, 1991, Decided

Judges: O'Connor, J., delivered the opinion of the Court, in which Rehnquist, C. J., and White, Marshall, Stevens, Scalia, Kennedy, and Souter, JJ., joined. Blackmun, J., concurred in the judgment.

Opinion: This case requires us to clarify the extent of copyright protection available to telephone directory white pages.

I

Rural Telephone Service Company, Inc., is a certified public utility that provides telephone service to several communities in northwest Kansas. It is subject to a state regulation that requires all telephone companies operating in Kansas to issue annually an updated telephone directory. Accordingly, as a condition of its monopoly franchise, Rural publishes a typical telephone directory, consisting of white pages and yellow pages. The white pages list in alphabetical order the names of Rural's subscribers, together with their towns and telephone numbers. The yellow pages list Rural's business subscribers alphabetically by category and feature classified advertisements of various sizes. Rural distributes its directory free of charge to its subscribers, but earns revenue by selling yellow pages advertisements.

Feist Publications, Inc., is a publishing company that specializes in area-wide telephone directories. Unlike a typical directory, which covers only a particular calling area, Feist's area-wide directories cover a much larger geographical range, reducing the need to call directory assistance or consult multiple directories. The Feist directory that is the subject of this litigation covers 11 different telephone service areas in 15 counties and contains 46,878 white pages listings — compared to Rural's approximately 7,700 listings. Like Rural's directory, Feist's is distributed free of charge and includes both white pages and yellow pages. Feist and Rural compete vigorously for yellow pages advertising.

As the sole provider of telephone service in its service area, Rural obtains subscriber information quite easily. Persons desiring telephone service must apply to Rural and provide their names and addresses; Rural then assigns them a telephone number. Feist is not a telephone company, let alone one with monopoly status, and therefore lacks independent access to any subscriber information. To obtain white pages listings for its area-wide directory, Feist approached each of the 11 telephone companies operating in northwest Kansas and offered to pay for the right to use its white pages listings.

Of the 11 telephone companies, only Rural refused to license its listings to Feist. Rural's refusal created a problem for Feist, as omitting these listings would have left a gaping hole in its area-wide directory, rendering it less attractive to potential yellow pages advertisers. In a decision subsequent to that which we review here, the District Court determined that this was precisely the reason Rural refused to license its listings. The refusal was motivated by an unlawful purpose "to extend its monopoly in telephone service to a monopoly in yellow pages advertising." Rural Telephone Service Co. v. Feist Publications, Inc., 737 F. Supp. 610, 622 (Kan. 1990).

Unable to license Rural's white pages listings, Feist used them without Rural's consent. Feist began by removing several thousand listings that fell outside the geographic range of its area-wide directory, then hired personnel to investigate the 4,935 that remained. These employees verified the data reported by Rural and sought to obtain additional information. As a result, a typical Feist listing includes the individual's street address; most of Rural's listings do not. Notwithstanding these additions, however, 1,309 of the 46,878 listings in Feist's 1983 directory were identical to listings in Rural's 1982-1983 white pages. . . . Four of these were fictitious listings that Rural had inserted into its directory to detect copying.

Rural sued for copyright infringement in the District Court for the District of Kansas taking the position that Feist, in compiling its own directory, could not use the information contained in Rural's white pages. Rural asserted that Feist's employees were obliged to travel door-to-door or conduct a telephone survey to discover the same information for themselves. Feist responded that such efforts were economically impractical and, in any event, unnecessary because the information copied was beyond the scope of copyright protection. The District Court granted summary judgment to Rural, explaining that "courts have consistently held that telephone directories are copyrightable" and citing a string of lower court decisions. 663 F. Supp. 214, 218 (1987). In an unpublished opinion, the Court of Appeals for the Tenth Circuit affirmed "for substantially the reasons given by the district court." . . . We granted certiorari, 498 U.S. 808 (1990), to determine whether the copyright in Rural's directory protects the names, towns, and telephone numbers copied by Feist.

II

A

This case concerns the interaction of two well-established propositions. The first is that facts are not copyrightable; the other, that compilations of facts generally are. Each of these propositions possesses an impeccable pedigree. That there can be no valid copyright in facts is universally understood. The most fundamental axiom of copyright law is that "no author may copyright his ideas or the facts he narrates." Harper & Row, Publishers, Inc. v. Nation Enterprises, 471 U.S. 539, 556 (1985). Rural wisely concedes this point, noting in its brief that "facts and discoveries, of course, are not themselves subject to copyright protection." Brief for Respondent 24. At the same time, however, it is beyond dispute that compilations of facts are within the subject matter of copyright. Compilations were expressly mentioned in the Copyright Act of 1909, and again in the Copyright Act of 1976.

There is an undeniable tension between these two propositions. Many compilations consist of nothing but raw data — i. e., wholly factual information not accompanied by any original written expression. On what basis may one claim a copyright in such a work? Common sense tells us that 100 uncopyrightable facts do not magically change their status when gathered together in one place. Yet copyright law seems to contemplate that compilations that consist exclusively of facts are potentially within its scope.

The key to resolving the tension lies in understanding why facts are not copyrightable. The sine qua non of copyright is originality. To qualify for copyright protection, a work must be original to the author. See Harper & Row, supra, at 547-549. Original, as the term is used in copyright, means only that the work was independently created by the author (as opposed to copied from other works), and that it possesses at least some minimal degree of creativity. 1 M. Nimmer & D. Nimmer, Copyright §§ 2.01[A], [B] (1990) (hereinafter Nimmer). To be sure, the requisite level of creativity is extremely low; even a slight amount will suffice. The vast majority of works make the grade quite easily, as they possess some creative spark, "no matter how crude, humble or obvious" it might be. Id., § 1.08[C][1]. Originality does not signify novelty; a work may be original even though it closely resembles other works so long as the similarity is fortuitous, not the result of copying. To illustrate, assume that two poets, each ignorant of the other, compose identical poems. Neither work is novel, yet both are original and, hence, copyrightable. See Sheldon v. Metro-Goldwyn Pictures Corp., 81 F. 2d 49, 54 (CA2 1936).

Originality is a constitutional requirement. The source of Congress' power to enact copyright laws is Article I, § 8, cl. 8, of the Constitution, which authorizes Congress to "secure for limited Times to Authors . . . the exclusive Right to their respective Writings." In two decisions from the late 19th century — The Trade-Mark Cases, 100 U.S. 82 (1879); and Burrow-Giles Lithographic Co. v. Sarony, 111 U.S. 53 (1884) — this Court defined the crucial terms "authors" and "writings." In so doing, the Court made it unmistakably clear that these terms presuppose a degree of originality.

In The Trade-Mark Cases, the Court addressed the constitutional scope of "writings." For a particular work to be classified "under the head of writings of authors," the Court determined, "originality is required." 100 U.S., at 94. The Court explained that originality requires independent creation plus a modicum of creativity: "While the word writings may be liberally construed, as it has been, to include original designs for engraving, prints, &c., it is only such as are original, and are founded in the creative powers of the mind. The writings which are to be protected are the fruits of intellectual labor, embodied in the form of books, prints, engravings, and the like." Ibid. (emphasis in original).

In Burrow-Giles, the Court distilled the same requirement from the Constitution's use of the word "authors." The Court defined "author," in a constitutional sense, to mean "he to whom anything owes its origin; originator; maker." 111 U.S., at 58 (internal quotation marks omitted). As in The Trade-Mark Cases, the Court emphasized the creative component of originality. It described copyright as being limited to "original intellectual conceptions of the author," 111 U.S., at 58, and stressed the importance of requiring an author who accuses another of infringement to prove "the existence of those facts of originality, of intellectual production, of thought, and conception." Id., at 59-60.

The originality requirement articulated in The Trade-Mark Cases and Burrow-Giles remains the touchstone of copyright protection today. See Goldstein v. California, 412 U.S. 546, 561-562 (1973). It is the very "premise of copyright law." Miller v. Universal City Studios, Inc., 650 F. 2d 1365, 1368 (CA5 1981). Leading scholars agree on this point. As one pair of commentators succinctly puts it: "The originality requirement is constitutionally mandated for all works." Patterson & Joyce, Monopolizing the Law: The Scope of Copyright Protection for Law Reports and Statutory Compilations, 36 UCLA L. Rev. 719, 763, n. 155 (1989) (emphasis in original) (hereinafter Patterson & Joyce). Accord, id., at 759-760, and n. 140; Nimmer § 1.06[A] ("Originality is a statutory as well as a constitutional requirement"); id., § 1.08[C][1] ("[A] modicum of intellectual labor . . . clearly constitutes an essential constitutional element").

It is this bedrock principle of copyright that mandates the law's seemingly disparate treatment of facts and factual compilations. "No one may claim originality as to facts." Id., § 2.11[A], p. 2-157. This is because facts do not owe their origin to an act of authorship. The distinction is one between creation and discovery: The first person to find and report a particular fact has not created the fact; he or she has merely discovered its existence. To borrow from Burrow-Giles, one who discovers a fact is not its "maker" or "originator." 111 U.S., at 58. "The discoverer merely finds and records." Nimmer § 2.03[E]. Census takers, for example, do not "create" the population figures that emerge from their efforts; in a sense, they copy these figures from the world around them. Denicola, Copyright in Collections of Facts: A Theory for the Protection of Nonfiction Literary Works, 81 Colum. L. Rev. 516, 525 (1981) (hereinafter Denicola). Census data therefore do not trigger copyright because these data are not "original" in the constitutional sense. Nimmer § 2.03[E]. The same is true of all facts — scientific, historical, biographical, and news of the day. "They may not be copyrighted and are part of the public domain available to every person." Miller, supra, at 1369.

Factual compilations, on the other hand, may possess the requisite originality. The compilation author typically chooses which facts to include, in what order to place them, and how to arrange the collected data so that they may be used effectively by readers. These choices as to selection and arrangement, so long as they are made independently by the compiler and entail a minimal degree of creativity, are sufficiently original that Congress may protect such compilations through the copyright laws. Nimmer §§ 2.11[D], 3.03; Denicola 523, n. 38. Thus, even a directory that contains absolutely no protectible written expression, only facts, meets the constitutional minimum for copyright protection if it features an original selection or arrangement. See Harper & Row, 471 U.S., at 547. Accord, Nimmer § 3.03.

This protection is subject to an important limitation. The mere fact that a work is copyrighted does not mean that every element of the work may be protected. Originality remains the sine qua non of copyright; accordingly, copyright protection may extend only to those components of a work that are original to the author. Patterson & Joyce 800-802; Ginsburg, Creation and Commercial Value: Copyright Protection of Works of Information, 90 Colum. L. Rev. 1865, 1868, and n. 12 (1990) (hereinafter Ginsburg). Thus, if the compilation author clothes facts with an original collocation of words, he or she may be able to claim a copyright in this written expression. Others may copy the underlying facts from the publication, but not the precise words used to present them. In Harper & Row, for example, we explained that President Ford could not prevent others from copying bare historical facts from his autobiography, see 471 U.S., at 556-557, but that he could prevent others from copying his "subjective descriptions and portraits of public figures." Id., at 563. Where the compilation author adds no written expression but rather lets the facts speak for themselves, the expressive element is more elusive. The only conceivable expression is the manner in which the compiler has selected and arranged the facts. Thus, if the selection and arrangement are original, these elements of the work are eligible for copyright protection. See Patry, Copyright in Compilations of Facts (or Why the "White Pages" Are Not Copyrightable), 12 Com. & Law 37, 64 (Dec. 1990) (hereinafter Patry). No matter how original the format, however, the facts themselves do not become original through association. See Patterson & Joyce 776.

This inevitably means that the copyright in a factual compilation is thin. Notwithstanding a valid copyright, a subsequent compiler remains free to use the facts contained in another's publication to aid in preparing a competing work, so long as the competing work does not feature the same selection and arrangement. As one commentator explains it: "No matter how much original authorship the work displays, the facts and ideas it exposes are free for the taking. . . . The very same facts and ideas may be divorced from the context imposed by the author, and restated or reshuffled by second comers, even if the author was the first to discover the facts or to propose the ideas." Ginsburg 1868.

It may seem unfair that much of the fruit of the compiler's labor may be used by others without compensation. As Justice Brennan has correctly observed, however, this is not "some unforeseen byproduct of a statutory scheme." Harper & Row, 471 U.S., at 589 (dissenting opinion). It is, rather, "the essence of copyright," ibid., and a constitutional requirement. The primary objective of copyright is not to reward the labor of authors, but "to promote the Progress of Science and useful Arts." Art. I, § 8, cl. 8. Accord, Twentieth Century Music Corp. v. Aiken, 422 U.S. 151, 156 (1975). To this end, copyright assures authors the right to their original expression, but encourages others to build freely upon the ideas and information conveyed by a work. Harper & Row, supra, at 556-557. This principle, known as the idea/expression or fact/expression dichotomy, applies to all works of authorship. As applied to a factual compilation, assuming the absence of original written expression, only the compiler's selection and arrangement may be protected; the raw facts may be copied at will. This result is neither unfair nor unfortunate. It is the means by which copyright advances the progress of science and art.

This Court has long recognized that the fact/expression dichotomy limits severely the scope of protection in fact-based works. More than a century ago, the Court observed: "The very object of publishing a book on science or the useful arts is to communicate to the world the useful knowledge which it contains. But this object would be frustrated if the knowledge could not be used without incurring the guilt of piracy of the book." Baker v. Selden, 101 U.S. 99, 103 (1880). We reiterated this point in Harper & Row:

> No author may copyright facts or ideas. The copyright is limited to those aspects of the work — termed "expression" — that display the stamp of the author's originality.

> Copyright does not prevent subsequent users from copying from a prior author's work those constituent elements that are not original — for example . . . facts, or materials in the public domain — as long as such use does not unfairly appropriate the author's original contributions. 471 U.S., at 547-548 (citation omitted).

This, then, resolves the doctrinal tension: Copyright treats facts and factual compilations in a wholly consistent manner. Facts, whether alone or as part of a compilation, are not original and therefore may not be copyrighted. A factual compilation is eligible for copyright if it features an original selection or arrangement of facts, but the copyright is limited to the particular selection or arrangement. In no event may copyright extend to the facts themselves.

B

As we have explained, originality is a constitutionally mandated prerequisite for copyright protection. The Court's decisions announcing this rule predate the Copyright Act of 1909, but ambiguous language in the 1909 Act caused some lower courts temporarily to lose sight of this requirement.

The 1909 Act embodied the originality requirement, but not as clearly as it might have. See Nimmer § 2.01. . . .

Most courts construed the 1909 Act correctly, notwithstanding the less-than-perfect statutory language. They understood from this Court's decisions that there could be no copyright without originality. . . .

But some courts misunderstood the statute. . . .

Making matters worse, these courts developed a new theory to justify the protection of factual compilations. Known alternatively as "sweat of the brow" or "industrious collection," the underlying notion was that copyright was a reward for the hard work that went into compiling facts. The classic formulation of the doctrine appeared in Jeweler's Circular Publishing Co., 281 F., at 88:

> The right to copyright a book upon which one has expended labor in its preparation does not depend upon whether the materials which he has collected consist or not of matters which are publici juris, or whether such materials show literary skill *or originality*, either in thought or in language, or anything more than industrious collection. The man who goes through the streets of a town and puts down the

names of each of the inhabitants, with their occupations and their street number, acquires material of which he is the author (emphasis added).

The "sweat of the brow" doctrine had numerous flaws, the most glaring being that it extended copyright protection in a compilation beyond selection and arrangement — the compiler's original contributions — to the facts themselves. Under the doctrine, the only defense to infringement was independent creation. A subsequent compiler was "not entitled to take one word of information previously published," but rather had to "independently work out the matter for himself, so as to arrive at the same result from the same common sources of information." Id., at 88-89 (internal quotations omitted). "Sweat of the brow" courts thereby eschewed the most fundamental axiom of copyright law — that no one may copyright facts or ideas. See Miller v. Universal City Studios, Inc., 650 F. 2d, at 1372 (criticizing "sweat of the brow" courts because "ensuring that later writers obtain the facts independently . . . is precisely the scope of protection given . . . copyrighted matter, and the law is clear that facts are not entitled to such protection").

Decisions of this Court applying the 1909 Act make clear that the statute did not permit the "sweat of the brow" approach. The best example is International News Service v. Associated Press, 248 U.S. 215 (1918). In that decision, the Court stated unambiguously that the 1909 Act conferred copyright protection only on those elements of a work that were original to the author. International News Service had conceded taking news reported by Associated Press and publishing it in its own newspapers. Recognizing that § 5 of the Act specifically mentioned "'periodicals, including newspapers,'" § 5(b), the Court acknowledged that news articles were copyrightable. Id., at 234. It flatly rejected, however, the notion that the copyright in an article extended to the factual information it contained: "The news element — the information respecting current events contained in the literary production — is not the creation of the writer, but is a report of matters that ordinarily are publici juris; it is the history of the day." Ibid.*[Ftnt: The Court ultimately rendered judgment for Associated Press on non-copyright grounds that are not relevant here. See 248 U.S., at 235, 241-242.]

Without a doubt, the "sweat of the brow" doctrine flouted basic copyright principles. Throughout history, copyright law has "recognized a greater need to disseminate factual works than works of fiction or fantasy."

Harper & Row, 471 U.S., at 563. Accord, Gorman, Fact or Fancy: The Implications for Copyright, 29 J. Copyright Soc. 560, 563 (1982). But "sweat of the brow" courts took a contrary view; they handed out proprietary interests in facts and declared that authors are absolutely precluded from saving time and effort by relying upon the facts contained in prior works. In truth, "it is just such wasted effort that the proscription against the copyright of ideas and facts . . . [is] designed to prevent." Rosemont Enterprises, Inc. v. Random House, Inc., 366 F. 2d 303, 310 (CA2 1966), cert. denied, 385 U.S. 1009 (1967). "Protection for the fruits of such research . . . may in certain circumstances be available under a theory of unfair competition. But to accord copyright protection on this basis alone distorts basic copyright principles in that it creates a monopoly in public domain materials without the necessary justification of protecting and encouraging the creation of 'writings' by 'authors.'" Nimmer § 3.04, p. 3-23 (footnote omitted).

C

"Sweat of the brow" decisions did not escape the attention of the Copyright Office. When Congress decided to overhaul the copyright statute and asked the Copyright Office to study existing problems, see Mills Music, Inc. v. Snyder, 469 U.S. 153, 159 (1985), the Copyright Office promptly recommended that Congress clear up the confusion in the lower courts as to the basic standards of copyrightability. The Register of Copyrights explained in his first report to Congress that "originality" was a "basic requisite" of copyright under the 1909 Act, but that "the absence of any reference to [originality] in the statute seems to have led to misconceptions as to what is copyrightable matter." Report of the Register of Copyrights on the General Revision of the U.S. Copyright Law, 87th Cong., 1st Sess., p. 9 (H. Judiciary Comm. Print 1961). The Register suggested making the originality requirement explicit. Ibid.

Congress took the Register's advice. In enacting the Copyright Act of 1976, Congress dropped the reference to "all the writings of an author" and replaced it with the phrase "original works of authorship." 17 U. S. C. § 102(a). In making explicit the originality requirement, Congress announced that it was merely clarifying existing law: "The two fundamental criteria of copyright protection [are] originality and fixation in tangible form. . . . The phrase 'original works of authorship,' which is purposely left undefined, is intended to incorporate without change the standard of originality established by the courts under the present [1909] copyright statute." H. R. Rep. No. 94-1476, p. 51 (1976) (emphasis added) (hereinafter H. R. Rep.); S. Rep. No. 94-473, p. 50 (1975) (emphasis added) (hereinafter S. Rep.). This sentiment was echoed by the Copyright Office: "Our intention here is to maintain the established standards of originality...." Supplementary Report of the Register of Copyrights on the General Revision of U.S. Copyright Law, 89th Cong., 1st Sess., pt. 6, p. 3 (H. Judiciary Comm. Print 1965) (emphasis added).

To ensure that the mistakes of the "sweat of the brow" courts would not be repeated, Congress took additional measures. For example, § 3 of the 1909 Act had stated that copyright protected only the "copyrightable component parts" of a work, but had not identified originality as the basis for distinguishing those component parts that were copyrightable from those that were not. The 1976 Act deleted this section and replaced it with § 102(b), which identifies specifically those elements of a work for which copyright is not available: "In no case does copyright protection for an original work of authorship extend to any idea, procedure, process, system, method of operation, concept, principle, or discovery, regardless of the form in which it is described, explained, illustrated, or embodied in such work." Section 102(b) is universally understood to prohibit any copyright in facts. Harper & Row, supra, at 547, 556. Accord, Nimmer § 2.03[E] (equating facts with "discoveries"). As with § 102(a), Congress emphasized that § 102(b) did not change the law, but merely clarified it: "Section 102(b) in no way enlarges or contracts the scope of copyright protection under the present law. Its purpose is to restate ... that the basic dichotomy between expression and idea remains unchanged." H. R. Rep., at 57; S. Rep., at 54.

Congress took another step to minimize confusion by deleting the specific mention of "directories ... and other compilations" in § 5 of the 1909 Act. As mentioned, this section had led some courts to conclude that directories were copyrightable per se and that every element of a directory was protected. In its place, Congress enacted two new provisions. First, to make clear that compilations were not copyrightable per se, Congress provided a definition of the term "compilation." Second, to make clear that the copyright in a compilation did not extend to the facts themselves, Congress enacted § 103.

The definition of "compilation" is found in § 101 of the 1976 Act. It defines a "compilation" in the copyright sense as "a work formed by the collection and assembling of preexisting materials or of data that are selected, coordinated, or arranged in such a way that the resulting work as a whole constitutes an original work of authorship" (emphasis added).

The purpose of the statutory definition is to emphasize that collections of facts are not copyrightable per se. It conveys this message through its tripartite structure, as emphasized above by the italics. The statute identifies three distinct elements and requires each to be met for a work to qualify as a copyrightable compilation: (1) the collection and assembly of pre-existing material, facts, or data; (2) the selection, coordination, or arrangement of those materials; and (3) the creation, by virtue of the particular selection, coordination, or arrangement, of an "original" work of authorship. "This tripartite conjunctive structure is self-evident, and should be assumed to 'accurately express the legislative purpose.'" Patry 51, quoting Mills Music, 469 U.S., at 164.

At first glance, the first requirement does not seem to tell us much. It merely describes what one normally thinks of as a compilation — a collection of pre-existing material, facts, or data. What makes it significant is that it is not the sole requirement. It is not enough for copyright purposes that an author collects and assembles facts. To satisfy the statutory definition, the work must get over two additional hurdles. In this way, the plain language indicates that not every collection of facts receives copyright protection. Otherwise, there would be a period after "data."

The third requirement is also illuminating. It emphasizes that a compilation, like any other work, is copyrightable only if it satisfies the originality requirement ("an original work of authorship"). Although § 102 states plainly that the originality requirement applies to all works, the point was emphasized with regard to compilations to ensure that courts would not repeat the mistake of the "sweat of the brow" courts by concluding that fact-based works are treated differently and measured by some other standard. As Congress explained it, the goal was to "make plain that the criteria of copyrightable subject matter stated in section 102 apply with full force to works . . . containing preexisting material." H. R. Rep., at 57; S. Rep., at 55.

The key to the statutory definition is the second requirement. It instructs courts that, in determining whether a fact-based work is an original work of authorship, they should focus on the manner in which the collected facts have been selected, coordinated, and arranged. This is a straight-forward application of the originality requirement. Facts are never original, so the compilation author can claim originality, if at all, only in the way the facts are presented. To that end, the statute dictates that the principal focus should be on whether the selection, coordination, and arrangement are sufficiently original to merit protection.

Not every selection, coordination, or arrangement will pass muster. This is plain from the statute. It states that, to merit protection, the facts must be selected, coordinated, or arranged "in such a way" as to render the work as a whole original. This implies that some "ways" will trigger copyright, but that others will not. See Patry 57, and n. 76. Otherwise, the phrase "in such a way" is meaningless and Congress should have defined "compilation" simply as "a work formed by the collection and assembly of preexisting materials or data that are selected, coordinated, or arranged." That Congress did not do so is dispositive. In accordance with "the established principle that a court should give effect, if possible, to every clause and word of a statute," Moskal v. United States, 498 U.S. 103, 109-110 (1990) (internal quotation marks omitted), we conclude that the statute envisions that there will be some fact-based works in which the selection, coordination, and arrangement are not sufficiently original to trigger copyright protection.

As discussed earlier, however, the originality requirement is not particularly stringent. A compiler may settle upon a selection or arrangement that others have used; novelty is not required. Originality requires only that the author make the selection or arrangement independently (i. e., without copying that selection or arrangement from another work), and that it display some minimal level of creativity. Presumably, the vast majority of compilations will pass this test, but not all will. There remains a narrow category of works in which the creative spark is utterly lacking or so trivial as to be virtually nonexistent. See generally Bleistein v. Donaldson Lithographing Co., 188 U.S. 239, 251 (1903) (referring to "the narrowest and most obvious limits"). Such works are incapable of sustaining a valid copyright. Nimmer § 2.01[B].

Even if a work qualifies as a copyrightable compilation, it receives only limited protection. This is the point of § 103 of the Act. Section 103 explains that "the subject matter of copyright . . . includes compilations," § 103(a), but that copyright protects only the author's original contributions — not the facts or information conveyed:

> The copyright in a compilation . . . extends only to the material contributed by the author of such work, as distinguished from the preexisting material employed in the work, and does not imply any exclusive right in the preexisting material. § 103(b).

As § 103 makes clear, copyright is not a tool by which a compilation author may keep others from using the facts or data he or she has collected.

"The most important point here is one that is commonly misunderstood today: copyright . . . has no effect one way or the other on the copyright or public domain status of the preexisting material." H. R. Rep., at 57; S. Rep., at 55. The 1909 Act did not require, as "sweat of the brow" courts mistakenly assumed, that each subsequent compiler must start from scratch and is precluded from relying on research undertaken by another. See, e. g., Jeweler's Circular Publishing Co., 281 F., at 88-89. Rather, the facts contained in existing works may be freely copied because copyright protects only the elements that owe their origin to the compiler — the selection, coordination, and arrangement of facts.

In summary, the 1976 revisions to the Copyright Act leave no doubt that originality, not "sweat of the brow," is the touchstone of copyright protection in directories and other fact-based works. Nor is there any doubt that the same was true under the 1909 Act. The 1976 revisions were a direct response to the Copyright Office's concern that many lower courts had misconstrued this basic principle, and Congress emphasized repeatedly that the purpose of the revisions was to clarify, not change, existing law. The revisions explain with painstaking clarity that copyright requires originality, § 102(a); that facts are never original, § 102(b); that the copyright in a compilation does not extend to the facts it contains, § 103(b); and that a compilation is copyrightable only to the extent that it features an original selection, coordination, or arrangement, § 101.

The 1976 revisions have proven largely successful in steering courts in the right direction. A good example is Miller v. Universal City Studios, Inc., 650 F. 2d, at 1369-1370: "A copyright in a directory . . . is properly viewed as resting on the originality of the selection and arrangement of the factual material, rather than on the industriousness of the efforts to develop the information. Copyright protection does not extend to the facts themselves, and the mere use of information contained in a directory without a substantial copying of the format does not constitute infringement" (citation omitted). Additionally, the Second Circuit, which almost 70 years ago issued the classic formulation of the "sweat of the brow" doctrine in Jeweler's Circular Publishing Co., has now fully repudiated the reasoning of that decision. See, e. g., Financial Information, Inc. v. Moody's Investors Service, Inc., 808 F. 2d 204, 207 (CA2 1986), cert. denied, 484 U.S. 820 (1987); Financial Information, Inc. v. Moody's Investors Service, Inc., 751 F. 2d 501, 510 (CA2 1984) (Newman, J., concurring); Hoehling v. Universal City Studios, Inc., 618 F. 2d 972, 979 (CA2 1980). Even those scholars who believe that "industrious collection" should be rewarded seem to recognize that this is beyond the scope of existing copyright law. See Denicola 516 ("The very vocabulary of copyright is ill suited to analyzing property rights in works of nonfiction"); id., at 520-521, 525; Ginsburg 1867, 1870.

III

There is no doubt that Feist took from the white pages of Rural's directory a substantial amount of factual information. At a minimum, Feist copied the names, towns, and telephone numbers of 1,309 of Rural's subscribers. Not all copying, however, is copyright infringement. To establish infringement, two elements must be proven: (1) ownership of a valid copyright, and (2) copying of constituent elements of the work that are original. See Harper & Row, 471 U.S., at 548. The first element is not at issue here; Feist appears to concede that Rural's directory, considered as a whole, is subject to a valid copyright because it contains some foreword text, as well as original material in its yellow pages advertisements. See Brief for Petitioner 18; Pet. for Cert. 9.

The question is whether Rural has proved the second element. In other words, did Feist, by taking 1,309 names, towns, and telephone numbers from Rural's white pages, copy anything that was "original" to Rural? Certainly, the raw data does not satisfy the originality requirement. Rural may have been the first to discover and report the names, towns, and telephone numbers of its subscribers, but this data does not "'owe its origin'" to Rural. Burrow-Giles, 111 U.S., at 58. Rather, these bits of information are uncopyrightable facts; they existed before Rural reported them and would have continued to exist if Rural had never published a telephone directory. The originality requirement "rules out protecting . . . names, addresses, and telephone numbers of which the plaintiff by no stretch of the imagination could be called the author." Patterson & Joyce 776.

Rural essentially concedes the point by referring to the names, towns, and telephone numbers as "preexisting material." Brief for Respondent 17. Section 103(b) states explicitly that the copyright in a compilation does not extend to "the preexisting material employed in the work."

The question that remains is whether Rural selected, coordinated, or arranged these uncopyrightable facts in an original way. As mentioned, originality is not a stringent standard; it does not require that facts be presented in an innovative or surprising way. It is equally true, however, that the selection and arrangement of facts cannot be so mechanical or routine as to require no creativity whatsoever. The standard of originality is low, but it does exist. See Patterson & Joyce 760, n. 144 ("While this requirement is sometimes characterized as modest, or a low threshold, it is not without effect") (internal quotation marks omitted; citations omitted). As this Court has explained, the Constitution mandates some minimal degree of creativity, see The Trade-Mark Cases, 100 U.S., at 94; and an author who claims infringement must prove "the existence of . . . intellectual production, of thought, and conception." Burrow-Giles, supra, at 59-60.

The selection, coordination, and arrangement of Rural's white pages do not satisfy the minimum constitutional standards for copyright protection. As mentioned at the outset, Rural's white pages are entirely typical. Persons desiring telephone service in Rural's service area fill out an application and Rural issues them a telephone number. In preparing its white pages, Rural simply takes the data provided by its subscribers and lists it alphabetically by surname. The end product is a garden-variety white pages directory, devoid of even the slightest trace of creativity.

Rural's selection of listings could not be more obvious: It publishes the most basic information — name, town, and telephone number — about each person who applies to it for telephone service. This is "selection" of a sort, but it lacks the modicum of creativity necessary to transform mere selection into copyrightable expression. Rural expended sufficient effort to make the white pages directory useful, but insufficient creativity to make it original.

We note in passing that the selection featured in Rural's white pages may also fail the originality requirement for another reason. Feist points out that Rural did not truly "select" to publish the names and telephone numbers of its subscribers; rather, it was required to do so by the Kansas Corporation Commission as part of its monopoly franchise. See 737 F. Supp., at 612. Accordingly, one could plausibly conclude that this selection was dictated by state law, not by Rural.

Nor can Rural claim originality in its coordination and arrangement of facts. The white pages do nothing more than list Rural's subscribers in alphabetical order. This arrangement may, technically speaking, owe its origin to Rural; no one disputes that Rural undertook the task of alphabetizing the names itself. But there is nothing remotely creative about arranging names alphabetically in a white pages directory. It is an age-old practice, firmly rooted in tradition and so commonplace that it has come to be expected as a matter of course. See Brief for Information Industry Association et al. as Amici Curiae 10 (alphabetical arrangement "is universally observed in directories published by local exchange telephone companies"). It is not only unoriginal, it is practically inevitable. This time-honored tradition does not possess the minimal creative spark required by the Copyright Act and the Constitution.

We conclude that the names, towns, and telephone numbers copied by Feist were not original to Rural and therefore were not protected by the copyright in Rural's combined white and yellow pages directory. As a constitutional matter, copyright protects only those constituent elements of a work that possess more than a de minimis quantum of creativity. Rural's white pages, limited to basic subscriber information and arranged alphabetically, fall short of the mark. As a statutory matter, 17 U. S. C. § 101 does not afford protection from copying to a collection of facts that are selected, coordinated, and arranged in a way that utterly lacks originality. Given that some works must fail, we cannot imagine a more likely candidate. Indeed, were we to hold that Rural's white pages pass muster, it is hard to believe that any collection of facts could fail.

Because Rural's white pages lack the requisite originality, Feist's use of the listings cannot constitute infringement. This decision should not be construed as demeaning Rural's efforts in compiling its directory, but rather as making clear that copyright rewards originality, not effort. As this Court noted more than a century ago, "'great praise may be due to the plaintiffs for their industry and enterprise in publishing this paper, yet the law does not contemplate their being rewarded in this way.'" Baker v. Selden, 101 U.S., at 105.

The judgment of the Court of Appeals is

Reversed.

Notes and Questions

1. The Supreme Court says that the originality requirement for copyright protection is constitutionally mandated. The U.S. Congress is considering legislation to grant protection to databases that do not meet the originality

requirement articulated in *Feist*. Is it constitutionally permissible for Congress to adopt such legislation?

2. The Court observes that the decision by Congress embodied in the Copyright Act to deprive compilers of the fruits of their work in certain contexts was the result of deliberate policy choice. The EU, as we will next see, has made a different choice, and perhaps the U.S. Congress will itself reverse direction in the next year or two. Has some change in the environment in which compilers of data operate influenced the perspective of governments? What has changed?

3. The Supreme Court does not address whether Rural might have more successfully pursued a claim based in unfair competition law. Has Feist engaged in a systematic effort to deprive Rural of the results of its labor in a way that might be considered tortious? Might the fact that Feist attempted to license the information from Rural influence whether Fiest's actions were unfair? Does the notion that a general claim of unfair competition should not govern a claim falling under specific IPRs legislation bear on this possibility? If database compilers could fairly readily pursue claims of unfair competition, would new legislation governing databases be required?

---

ii. The EU Database Directive

Advances in digital technology have greatly facilitated the extraction and reproduction of information contained in databases. On-line databases may be downloaded or captured from a video screen. Database compilers contend that investment in the creation of new databases will be curtailed unless the products of this investment are granted protection. The U.S. Supreme Court in *Feist* illustrated the legal obstacles confronting database compilers. A party seeking to extract information from a database will often have little interest in the creative arrangement of that database. Rather, the information contained in the database is being sought, and reused.

The EU sought to address the concerns of database compilers by adoption of the Database Directive (DBD). The DBD is comprised of two principal parts. The first part addresses, clarifies and supplements traditional copyright protection accorded to database compilers under the general principles of the Berne Convention. The second and more important part of the directive creates a *sui generis* form of protection for the producers of databases. This is an extensive right that attaches to a database on the basis of the level of investment by the compiler, measured by whether there has been a "substantial investment" in "qualitative" and/or "quantitative" terms in the "obtaining, verification or presentation of the contents." The holder of the *sui generis* right may prevent acts of "extraction and/or re-utilization of the whole or of a substantial part, evaluated qualitatively and/or quantitatively" (art. 7(1)). The directive contains some exceptions for fair use.

The overall perspective of the EU organs with respect to Internet and related on-line services is encapsulated in a recital to the Database Directive which provides that "every on-line service is in fact an act which will have to be subject to authorization where the copyright so provides" (para. 33, recitals, DBD).

COMMON POSITION (EC) No 20/95 adopted by the Council on 10 July 1995 with a view to adopting Directive 95/ /EC of the European Parliament and of the Council . . . on the legal protection of databases (95/C 288/02)*

The European Parliament and the Council of the European Union, Having regard to the Treaty establishing the European Community, and in particular Articles 57(2), 66 and 100a thereof, [recitals omitted]
Have Adopted this Directive:

Chapter I Scope

Article 1
Scope

1. This Directive concerns the legal protection of databases in any form.
2. For the purposes of this Directive, 'database' shall mean a collection of works, data or other independent materials arranged in a systematic or methodical way and capable of being individually accessed by electronic or other means.

---

*1995 OJ C 288, Doc. Date, July 10, 1995.

3. Protection under this Directive shall not apply to computer programs used in the manufacture or operation of databases which can be accessed by electronic means.

Article 2
Limitations of the scope

This Directive shall apply without prejudice to Community provisions relating to:

(a) the legal protection of computer programs;
(b) rental right, lending right and certain rights related to copyright in the field of intellectual property;
(c) the term of protection of copyright and certain related rights.

Chapter II Copyright

Article 3
Object of protection

1. In accordance with this Directive, databases which, by reason of the selection or arrangement of their contents, constitute the author's own intellectual creation shall be protected as such by copyright. No other criteria shall be applied to determine their eligibility for that protection.

2. The copyright protection of databases provided for by this Directive shall not extend to their contents and shall be without prejudice to any rights subsisting in those contents themselves.

Article 4
Authorship

1. The author of a database shall be the natural person or group of natural persons who created the base or, where the legislation of the Member States so permits, the legal person designated as the rightholder by that legislation.
2. Where collective works are recognized by the legislation of a Member State, the economic rights shall be owned by the person holding the copyright.

3. In respect of a database created by a group of natural persons jointly, the exclusive rights shall be owned jointly.

Article 5
Restricted acts

The author of a database shall have the exclusive right to do or to authorize in respect of the expression of the database which is protectable by copyright:
(a) temporary or permanent reproduction by any means and in any form, in whole or in part;
(b) translation, adaptation, arrangement and any other alteration;
(c) any form of distribution to the public of the database or of copies thereof. The first sale in the Community of a copy of the database by the rightholder or with his consent shall exhaust the right to control resale within the Community of that copy;
(d) any communication, display or performance to the public;
(e) any reproduction, distribution, communication, display or performance to the public of the results of the acts referred to in (b).

Article 6
Exceptions to the restricted acts

1. The performance by the lawful user of a database or of a copy thereof of any of the acts listed in Article 5 which is necessary for the purposes of access to the contents of the database and normal use of the contents by the lawful user shall not require the authorization of the author of the database. Where the lawful user is authorized to use only part of the database, this provision shall apply only to that part.
2. Member States shall have the option of providing for limitations on the rights set out in Article 5 in the following cases:
(a) in the case of reproduction for private purposes of a non-electronic database;
(b) where there is use for the sole purposes of illustration for teaching or scientific research, to the extent justified by the non-commercial purpose;
(c) where there is use for the purposes of public security or for the purposes of the proper performance of an administrative or judicial procedure;

(d) where other exceptions to copyright which are traditionally permitted by the Member State concerned are involved, without prejudice to points (a), (b) and (c).

3. In accordance with the Berne Convention for the Protection of Literary and Artistic Works, this article may not be interpreted in such a way as to allow its application to be used in a manner which unreasonably prejudices the rightholder's legitimate interests or conflicts with a normal exploitation of the database.

Chapter III Sui Generis Right

Article 7
Object of protection

1. Member States shall provide for a right for the maker of a database which shows that there has been qualitatively and/or quantitatively a substantial investment in either the obtaining, verification or presentation of the contents, to prevent acts of extraction and/or re-utilization of the whole or of a substantial part, evaluated qualitatively and/or quantitatively, of the contents of that database.
2. For the purposes of this chapter:
(a) 'extraction' shall mean the permanent or temporary transfer of all or a substantial part of the contents of a database to another medium by any means or in any form;
(b) 're-utilization' shall mean any form of making available to the public all or a substantial part of the contents of a database by the distribution of copies, by renting, by on-line or other forms of transmission. The first sale of a copy of a database within the Community by the rightholder or with his consent shall exhaust the right to control resale within the Community of that copy. Public lending is not an act of extraction or re-utilization.
3. The right referred to in paragraph 1 may be transferred, assigned or granted under contractual licence.
4. The right provided for in paragraph 1 shall apply irrespective of the eligibility of that database for protection by copyright or by other rights. Moreover, it shall apply irrespective of the eligibility of the contents of that database for protection by copyright or by other rights. Protection of data-

bases under the right referred to in paragraph 1 shall be without prejudice to rights existing in respect of their contents.

5. The repeated and systematic extraction and/or re-utilization of insubstantial parts of the contents of the database which would have the result of performing acts which conflict with a normal exploitation of that database or which unreasonably prejudice the legitimate interests of the maker of the database shall not be permitted.

Article 8
Rights and obligations of legitimate users

1. The maker of a database which is made available to the public in whatever manner may not prevent a lawful user of the database from extracting and/or re-utilizing insubstantial parts of its contents, evaluated qualitatively and/or quantitatively, for any purposes whatsoever. Where the lawful user is authorized to extract and/or re-utilize only part of the database, this paragraph shall apply only to that part.

2. A lawful user of a database which is made available to the public in whatever manner may not perform acts which conflict with a normal exploitation of the database or unreasonably prejudice the legitimate interests of the maker of the database.

3. A lawful user of a database which is made available to the public in any manner may not cause prejudice to the holder of a copyright or related right in respect of the works or services contained in the database.

Article 9
Exceptions to the sui generis right

Member States shall have the option to lay down that lawful users of a database which is made available to the public in whatever manner may, without the authorization of its maker, extract or re-utilize a substantial part of its contents:

(a) in the case of extraction for private purposes of the contents of a non-electronic database;

(b) in the case of extraction for the purposes of illustration for teaching or scientific research, as long as the source is indicated and to the extent justified by the non-commercial purpose to be attained;

(c) in the case of extraction and/or re-utilization for the purposes of public security or the proper performance of an administrative or judicial procedure.

Article 10
Term of protection

1. The right provided for in Article 7 shall run from the date of completion of the making of the database. It shall expire 15 years from 1 January of the year following the date of completion.

2. In the case of a database which is made available to the public in whatever manner before expiry of the period provided for in paragraph 1, the term of protection by that right shall expire 15 years from 1 January of the year following the date when the database was first made available to the public.

3. Any substantial change, evaluated qualitatively or quantitatively, to the contents of a database, including any substantial change resulting from the accumulation of successive additions, deletions or alterations, which would result in the database being considered to be a substantial new investment, evaluated qualitatively or quantitatively, shall qualify the database resulting from that investment for its own term of protection.

Article 11
Beneficiaries of protection under the sui generis right

1. The right provided for in Article 7 shall apply to databases whose makers or successors in title are nationals of a Member State or who have their habitual residence in the territory of the Community.

2. Paragraph 1 shall also apply to companies and firms formed in accordance with the law of a Member State and having their registered office, central administration or principal place of business within the Community; however, where such a company or firm has only its registered office in the territory of the Community, its operations must possess an effective and continuous link with the economy of one of the Member States.

3. Agreements extending the right provided for in Article 7 to databases manufactured in third countries and falling outside the provisions of paragraphs 1 and 2 shall be concluded by the Council acting on a proposal from the Commission. The term of any protection extended to databases by

virtue of that procedure shall not exceed that available pursuant to Article 10.

Chapter IV Common Provisions

Article 12
Remedies

Member States shall provide appropriate remedies in respect of infringements of the rights provided for in this Directive.

Article 13
Continued application of other legal provisions

This Directive shall be without prejudice to provisions concerning in particular copyright, rights related to copyright or any other rights or obligations subsisting in the data, works or other materials incorporated into a database, patent rights, trade marks, design rights, the protection of national treasures, laws on restrictive practices and unfair competition, trade secrets, security, confidentiality, data protection and privacy, access to public documents, and the law of contract.

Article 14
Application in time

1. Protection pursuant to this Directive as regards copyright shall also be available in respect of databases created prior to the date referred to in Article 16 (1) which on that date fulfil the requirements laid down in this Directive as regards copyright protection of databases.
2. Notwithstanding paragraph 1, where a database protected under a copyright system in a Member State on the date of publication of this Directive does not fulfil the eligibility criteria for copyright protection laid down in Article 3 (1), this Directive shall not result in any curtailing in that Member State of the remaining term of protection afforded under that system.
3. Protection pursuant to the provisions of this Directive as regards the right provided for in Article 7 shall also be available in respect of databases the manufacture of which was completed not more than 15 years prior to

the date referred to in Article 16(1) and which on that date fulfil the requirements laid down in Article 7.

4. The protection provided for in paragraphs 1 and 3 shall be without prejudice to any acts accomplished and rights acquired before the date referred to in those paragraphs.

5. In the case of a database the manufacture of which was completed not more than 15 years prior to the date referred to in Article 16(1), the term of protection by the right provided for in Article 7 shall expire 15 years from 1 January following that date.

Article 15
Binding nature of certain provisions

Any contractual provision contrary to Articles 6 (1) and 8 shall be null and void.

Article 16
Final provisions

1. Member States shall bring into force the laws, regulations and administrative provisions necessary to comply with this Directive before 1 January 1998. When Member States adopt these provisions, they shall contain a reference to this Directive or shall be accompanied by such reference on the occasion of their official publication. The methods of making such reference shall be laid down by Member States.

2. Member States shall communicate to the Commission the text of the provisions of domestic law which they adopt in the field governed by this Directive.

3. Not later than at the end of the third year after the date referred to in paragraph 1, and every three years thereafter, the Commission shall submit to the European Parliament, the Council and the Economic and Social Committee a report on the application of this Directive, in which, inter alia on the basis of specific information supplied by the Member States, it shall examine in particular the application of the sui generis right, including Articles 8 and 9, and especially whether the application of this right has led to abuse of a dominant position or other interference with free competition which would justify appropriate measures being taken, in particular the es-

tablishment of non-voluntary licensing arrangements. Where necessary, it shall submit proposals for adjustment of this Directive in line with developments in the area of databases.

Article 17
This Directive is addressed to the Member States.

Notes and Questions

1. The test for whether investment in a database is adequate is stated in qualitative and quantitative terms. Do you foresee any difficulties in the application of this test? Does this test favor large commercial database compilers, or does the qualitative measure appear to provide sufficient coverage for independent producers?

2. Permitted uses by "lawful users" include the extraction and reuse "for any purposes whatsoever" of "insubstantial parts" of the database (based on qualitative and/or quantitative assessment) (art.8(1), DBD). Additional permitted uses include extraction for teaching or scientific research for non-commercial purposes (art. 9(b)). Do you think these exceptions to the rights of database producers are sufficient to protect the interests of the public, including the scientific research community?

3. One of the most controversial provisions of the Database Directive is article 11. Under article 11, *sui generis* database protection is afforded only to EU nationals, including companies with a commercial presence in the EU. If a database is produced outside the EU by a non-EU person, it will be protected within the EU only pursuant to an agreement entered into between the EU and the country where the database is produced. The *sui generis* right established by the directive is presumably outside the scope of the national treatment rule of the Berne Convention (because the *sui generis* database is not copyrightable subject matter, though of course many databases will be covered by both copyright and the *sui generis* right). Nevertheless, is

the EU directive denying national treatment compatible with the national treatment rule of the TRIPS Agreement (art. 3:1)? Examine Article 1:2 of the TRIPS Agreement in this connection.

4. The nominal term of protection for the *sui generis* database right is fifteen years. However, examine article 10(3) which addresses ways in which this term may be extended. Does this approximate a perpetual right?

---

2. Free Movement and Copyrighted Works

a. Films and Broadcasts Within the EU

In the *Ideal Standard*[1] case we were introduced to the doctrine of intra-Union exhaustion. As a general rule, when goods and services are placed on the market by an IPRs holder or with its consent, that IPRs holder may not block the free movement of the goods and services to another member state on the basis of the IPR. In the *Ideal Standard* case, the ECJ held that the intra-Union exhaustion doctrine does not apply if there is no economic link between the holders of IPRs in different member states. In *Warner Brothers v. Christiensen*,[2] the Court held that differences in the substantive rights granted among the member states could also lead to disapplication of the intra-Union exhaustion doctrine (though it must be noted that the Court has applied this reasoning in very limited contexts). In *Coditel v. Cine Vog* which follows, the Court confronts certain special characteristics of the film distribution and television broadcast industries. A film differs from a book or newspaper in that the film depends on repeated showings to generate an adequate economic return. If the initial showing of a film is treated as a "first sale" for exhaustion purposes, artists and producers of films may not recover their investments. The *Coditel* case is thus of great interest to the film and broadcast industries.

---

[1] *See supra*, Ch. I, § B, 6, c.
[2] *See supra*, § M, 1.

Coditel v Cine Vog Films

(preliminary ruling requested by the Court d'Appel, Brussels)
(Case 62/79)

European Court of Justice
[1980] ECR 881, [1981] 2 CMLR 362
18 MARCH 1980

Panel: H. Kutscher, President, A. O'Keeffe and A. Touffait, (Presidents of Chambers), J. Mertens de Wilmars, P. Pescatore, Lord Mackenzie Stuart, G. Bosco, T. Koopmans and O. Due, Judges

Decision:

By a judgment of March 1979, which was received at the Court on 17 April 1979, the Cour d'Appel, Brussels, referred two questions to the Court under Article 177 of the EEC Treaty for a preliminary ruling on the interpretation of Article 59 and other provisions of the Treaty on freedom to provide services.

Those questions were raised during an action brought by a Belgian cinematographic film distribution company, Cine Vog Films S.A., the respondent before the Cour d'Appel, for infringement of copyright. The action is against a French company, Les Films la Boetie, and three Belgian cable television diffusion companies, which are hereafter referred to collectively as the Coditel companies. Compensation is sought for the damage allegedly caused to Cine Vog by the reception in Belgium of a broadcast by German television of the film "Le Boucher" for which Cine Vog obtained exclusive distribution rights in Belgium from Les Films la Boetie.

It is apparent from the file that the Coditel companies provide, with the authority of the Belgian administration, a cable television diffusion service covering part of Belgium. Television sets belonging to subscribers to the service are linked by cable to a central aerial having special technical features which enable Belgian broadcasts to be picked up as well as certain foreign broadcasts which the subscriber cannot always receive with a private aerial, and which furthermore improve the quality of the pictures and sound received by the subscribers.

The court before which the claim was made, the Tribunal de Premiere Instance, Brussels, declared that it was unfounded as against Les Films le Boetie, but it ordered the Coditel companies to pay damages to Cine Vog. The Coditel companies appealed against that judgment. That appeal was declared inadmissible by the Cour d'Appel to the extent to which it was brought against the company Les Films la Boetie, which is not now therefore a party to the dispute.

The facts of the case bearing upon the outcome of the dispute were summarized by the Cour d'Appel as follows. By an agreement of 8 July 1969 Les Films la Boetie, acting as the owner of all the proprietary rights in the film "Le Boucher", gave Cine Vog the "exclusive right" to distribute the film in Belgium for seven years. The film was shown in cinemas in Belgium starting on 15 May 1970. However, on 5 January 1971 German television's first channel broadcast a German version of the film and this broadcast could be picked up in Belgium. Cine Vog considered that the broadcast had jeopardized the commercial future of the film in Belgium. It relied upon this ground of complaint both against Les Films la Boetie, for not having observed the exclusivity of the rights which it had transferred to it, and against the Coditel companies for having relayed the relevant broadcast over their cable diffusion networks.

The Cour d'Appel first of all examined the activities of the cable television diffusion companies from the point of view of copyright infringement. It considered that those companies had made a "communication to the public" of the film within the meaning of the provisions applying in this field and that, as regards copyright law and subject to the effect thereon of Community law, they therefore needed the authorization of Cine Vog to relay the film over their networks. The effect of this reasoning by the Cour d'Appel is that the authorization given by the copyright owner to German television to broadcast the film did not include authority to relay the film over cable diffusion networks outside Germany, or at least those existing in Belgium.

The Cour d'Appel then went on to examine in the light of Community law the argument of the Coditel companies that any prohibition on the transmission of films, the copyright in which has been assigned by the producer to a distribution company covering the whole of Belgium, is contrary to the provisions of the EEC Treaty, in particular to Article 85 and Articles

59 and 60. After rejecting the argument based on Article 85, the Cour d'Appel wondered if the action undertaken against the cable television diffusion companies by Cine Vog infringed Article 59 "in so far as it limits the possibility for a transmitting station established in a country which borders on Belgium, and which is the country of the persons for whom a service is intended, freely to provide that service".

In the opinion of the appellant companies, Article 59 must be understood to mean that it prohibits restrictions on freedom to provide services and not merely restrictions on the freedom of activity of those providing services, and that it covers all cases where the provision of a service involves or has involved at an earlier stage or will involve at a later stage the crossing of intra-Community frontiers.

Believing that that submission bears upon the interpretation of the Treaty, the Cour d'Appel referred to the Court of Justice the following two questions:

> 1. Are the restrictions prohibited by Article 59 of the Treaty establishing the European Economic Community only those which prejudice the provision of services between nationals established in different Member States, or do they also comprise restrictions on the provision of services between nationals established in the same Member State which however concern services the substance of which originates in another Member State?

> 2. If the first limb of the preceding question is answered in the affirmative, is it in accordance with the provisions of the Treaty on freedom to provide services for the assignee of the performing right in a cinematographic film in one Member State to rely upon his right in order to prevent the defendant from showing that film in that State by means of cable television where the film thus shown is picked up by the defendant in the said Member State after having been broadcast by a third party in another Member State with the consent of the original owner of the right?

According to its wording the second question is asked in case the answer to the first limb of the first question should be in the affirmative; but the Cour d'Appel evidently had in mind an answer stating that in principle Article 59 et seq. of the Treaty apply to the provision of the services concerned because only in that case can the second question have any meaning.

The Court of Justice will first of all examine the second question. If the answer to this question is in the negative because the practice it describes is not contrary to the provisions of the Treaty on freedom to provide services — on the assumption that those provisions are applicable — the national court will have all the information necessary for it to be able to resolve the legal problem before it in conformity with Community law.

The second question raises the problem of whether Articles 59 and 60 of the Treaty prohibit an assignment, limited to the territory of a Member State, of the copyright in a film, in view of the fact that a series of such assignments might result in the partitioning of the Common Market as regards the undertaking of economic activity in the film industry.

A cinematographic film belongs to the category of literary and artistic works made available to the public by performances which may be infinitely repeated. In this respect the problems involved in the observance of copyright in relation to the requirements of the Treaty are not the same as those which arise in connection with literary and artistic works the placing of which at the disposal of the public is inseparable from the circulation of the material form of the works, as in the case of books or records.

In these circumstances the owner of the copyright in a film and his assigns have a legitimate interest in calculating the fees due in respect of the authorization to exhibit the film on the basis of the actual or probable number of performances and in authorizing a television broadcast of the film only after it has been exhibited in cinemas for a certain period of time. It appears from the file on the present case that the contract made between Les Films la Boetie and Cine Vog stipulated that the exclusive right which was assigned included the right to exhibit the film "Le Boucheur" publicly in Belgium by way of projection in cinemas and on television but that the right to have the film diffused by Belgian television could not be exercised until 40 months after the first showing of the film in Belgium.

These facts are important in two regards. On the one hand, they highlight the fact that the right of a copyright owner and his assigns to require fees for any showing of a film is part of the essential function of copyright in this type of literary and artistic work. On the other hand, they demonstrate that the exploitation of copyright in films and the fees attaching thereto cannot be regulated without regard being had to the possibility of television broadcasts of those films. The question whether an assignment of copyright limited to the territory of a Member State is capable of constituting a restriction on freedom to provide services must be examined in this context.

Whilst Article 59 of the Treaty prohibits restrictions upon freedom to provide services, it does not thereby encompass limits upon the exercise of certain economic activities which have their origin in the application of national legislation for the protection of intellectual property, save where such application constitutes a means of arbitrary discrimination or a disguised restriction on trade between Member States. Such would be the case if that application enabled parties to an assignment of copyright to create artificial barriers to trade between Member States.

The effect of this is that, whilst copyright entails the right to demand fees for any showing or performance, the rules of the Treaty cannot in principle constitute an obstacle to the geographical limits which the parties to a contract of assignment have agreed upon in order to protect the author and his assigns in this regard. The mere fact that those geographical limits may coincide with national frontiers does not point to a different solution in a situation where television is organized in the Member States largely on the basis of legal broadcasting monopolies, which indicates that a limitation other than the geographical field of application of an assignment is often impracticable.

The exclusive assignee of the performing right in a film for the whole of a Member State may therefore rely upon his right against cable television diffusion companies which have transmitted that film on their diffusion network having received it from a television broadcasting station established in another Member State, without thereby infringing Community law.

Consequently the answer to the second question referred to the Court by the Cour d'Appel, Brussels, should be that the provisions of the Treaty relating to the freedom to provide services do not preclude an assignee of the performing right in a cinematographic film in a Member State from relying upon his right to prohibit the exhibition of that film in that State, without his authority, by means of cable diffusion if the film so exhibited is picked up and transmitted after being broadcast in another Member State by a third party with the consent of the original owner of the right.

It is clear from the answer given to the second question that Community law, on the assumption that it applies to the activities of the cable diffusion companies which are the subject-matter of the dispute brought before the national court, has no effect upon the application by that court of the provisions of copyright legislation in a case such as this. Therefore there is no need to answer the first question.

*****

On those grounds,

THE COURT, in answer to the questions referred to it by the Cour d'Appel, Brussels, by judgment of 30 March 1979, hereby rules:

The provisions of the Treaty relating to the freedom to provide services do not preclude an assignee of the performing right in a cinematographic film in a Member State from relying upon his right to prohibit the exhibition of that film in that State, without his authority, by means of cable diffusion if the film so exhibited is picked up and transmitted after being broadcast in another Member State by a third party with the consent of the original owner of the right.

Notes and Questions

1. The special characteristics of the film and broadcast industries make it necessary to provide limitations on the exhaustion of copyright for these media. In what other copyright contexts do you think that limitations on the principle of exhaustion might be necessary?

2. The *Coditel* decision is addressed only to the intra-Union context. Do you think that the same policy considerations which motivated the ECJ in this decision should also apply in the international exhaustion of copyright context?

---

b. Copyright and International Trade

The question of the extent to which IPRs should be exhausted by first sale or transfer at the international level continues to be controversial. In

1998, the U.S. Supreme Court once again entered the debate with a decision that at a policy level strongly endorses the principle of international exhaustion. The *Quality King v. L'anza* decision specifically addresses copyrighted material — in this case the labeling on shampoo bottles. Since the Supreme Court previously limited the circumstances in which U.S. trademark holders may use their marks to block the parallel importation of goods, U.S. producers have increasingly turned to the copyright laws for protection. It might seem that the copyright in a shampoo label is a peculiar subject matter on which to hinge a demand for protection against imports. However, since copyright law (*see Feist supra*) provides a very low threshold of originality, this seemingly "industrial property" use of copyright has generally been permitted.

The holding of the *Quality King* decision directly applies to copyrighted subject matter produced within the United States, exported and subsequently imported into the United States. Because of the complex construction of the U.S. Copyright Act, it cannot be assumed that the rule of exhaustion announced by the Court in *Quality King* would govern in the situation in which copyrighted goods were produced outside the United States. Nevertheless, more important than the limited holding of this case is the statement of principles announced by the Court toward the end of its opinion in response to argumentation concerning the "pure" parallel imports context.

Quality King Distributors v. L'anza Research International

Supreme Court of The United States
1998 U.S. LEXIS 1606
March 9, 1998, Decided

Judges: Stevens, J., delivered the opinion for a unanimous Court. Ginsburg, J., filed a concurring opinion.

Section 106(3) of the Copyright Act of 1976 (Act), 17 U.S.C. § 106(3), gives the owner of a copyright the exclusive right to distribute copies of a copyrighted work. That exclusive right is expressly limited, however, by the provisions of §§ 107 through 120. Section 602(a) gives the copyright owner the right to prohibit the unauthorized importation of copies. The question presented by this case is whether the right granted by § 602(a) is also limited by §§ 107 through 120. More narrowly, the question is whether the "first sale" doctrine endorsed in § 109(a) is applicable to imported copies.

I

Respondent, L'anza Research International, Inc. (L'anza), is a California corporation engaged in the business of manufacturing and selling shampoos, conditioners, and other hair care products. L'anza has copyrighted the labels that are affixed to those products. In the United States, L'anza sells exclusively to domestic distributors who have agreed to resell within limited geographic areas and then only to authorized retailers such as barber shops, beauty salons, and professional hair care colleges. L'anza has found that the American "public is generally unwilling to pay the price charged for high quality products, such as L'anza's products, when they are sold along with the less expensive lower quality products that are generally carried by supermarkets and drug stores." App. 54 (declaration of Robert Hall). L'anza promotes the domestic sales of its products with extensive advertising in various trade magazines and at point of sale, and by providing special training to authorized retailers.

L'anza also sells its products in foreign markets. In those markets, however, it does not engage in comparable advertising or promotion; its prices to foreign distributors are 35% to 40% lower than the prices charged to domestic distributors. In 1992 and 1993, L'anza's distributor in the United Kingdom arranged the sale of three shipments to a distributor in Malta; each shipment contained several tons of L'anza products with copyrighted labels affixed. The record does not establish whether the initial purchaser was the distributor in the United Kingdom or the distributor in Malta, or whether title passed when the goods were delivered to the carrier or when they arrived at their destination, but it is undisputed that the goods were manufactured by L'anza and first sold by L'anza to a foreign purchaser.

It is also undisputed that the goods found their way back to the United States without the permission of L'anza and were sold in California by unauthorized retailers who had purchased them at discounted prices from Quality King Distributors, Inc. (petitioner). There is some uncertainty about the identity of the actual importer, but for the purpose of our decision we assume that petitioner bought all three shipments from the Malta distributor, imported them, and then resold them to retailers who were not in L'anza's authorized chain of distribution.

After determining the source of the unauthorized sales, L'anza brought suit against petitioner and several other defendants. The complaint alleged that the importation and subsequent distribution of those products bearing copyrighted labels violated L'anza's "exclusive rights under 17 U.S.C. §§ 106, 501 and 602 to reproduce and distribute the copyrighted material in the United States." App. 32. The District Court rejected petitioner's defense based on the "first sale" doctrine recognized by § 109 and entered summary judgment in favor of L'anza. Based largely on its conclusion that § 602 would be "meaningless" if § 109 provided a defense in a case of this kind, the Court of Appeals affirmed. 98 F.3d 1109, 1114 (CA9 1996). Because its decision created a conflict with the Third Circuit, see Sebastian Int'l, Inc. v. Consumer Contacts (PTY) Ltd., 847 F.2d 1093 (1988), we granted the petition for certiorari. 520 U.S. (1997).

II

This is an unusual copyright case because L'anza does not claim that anyone has made unauthorized copies of its copyrighted labels. Instead, L'anza is primarily interested in protecting the integrity of its method of marketing the products to which the labels are affixed. Although the labels themselves have only a limited creative component, our interpretation of the relevant statutory provisions would apply equally to a case involving more familiar copyrighted materials such as sound recordings or books. Indeed, we first endorsed the first sale doctrine in a case involving a claim by a publisher that the resale of its books at discounted prices infringed its copyright on the books. Bobbs-Merrill Co. v. Straus, 210 U.S. 339, 52 L. Ed. 1086, 28 S. Ct. 722 (1908).[4]

---

[4]The doctrine had been consistently applied by other federal courts in earlier cases. See Kipling v. G. P. Putnam's Sons, 120 F. 631, 634 (CA2 1903); Doan v. American Book Co., 105 F. 772, 776 (CA7 1901); Harrison v. Maynard, Merrill & Co., 61 F. 689, 691 (CA2 1894); Bobbs-Merrill Co. v. Snellenburg, 131 F. 530, 532 (ED Pa. 1904); Clemens v. Estes,

In that case, the publisher, Bobbs-Merrill, had inserted a notice in its books that any retail sale at a price under $1.00 would constitute an infringement of its copyright. The defendants, who owned Macy's department store, disregarded the notice and sold the books at a lower price without Bobbs-Merrill's consent. We held that the exclusive statutory right to "vend"[5] applied only to the first sale of the copyrighted work:

> What does the statute mean in granting "the sole right of vending the same"? Was it intended to create a right which would permit the holder of the copyright to fasten, by notice in a book or upon one of the articles mentioned within the statute, a restriction upon the subsequent alienation of the subject-matter of copyright after the owner had parted with the title to one who had acquired full dominion over it and had given a satisfactory price for it? It is not denied that one who has sold a copyrighted article, without restriction, has parted with all right to control the sale of it. The purchaser of a book, once sold by authority of the owner of the copyright, may sell it again, although he could not publish a new edition of it.
>
> In this case the stipulated facts show that the books sold by the appellant were sold at wholesale, and purchased by those who made no agreement as to the control of future sales of the book, and took upon themselves no obligation to enforce the notice printed in the book, undertaking to restrict retail sales to a price of one dollar per copy. Id., at 349-350.

The statute in force when Bobbs-Merrill was decided provided that the copyright owner had the exclusive right to "vend" the copyrighted work. Congress subsequently codified our holding in Bobbs-Merrill that the exclusive right to "vend" was limited to first sales of the work.[7] Under the 1976 Act, the comparable exclusive right granted in 17 U.S.C. § 106(3)

---

22 F. 899, 900 (Mass. 1885); Stowe v. Thomas, 2 Wall. Jr. 547, 23 F. Cas. 201, 206-207 (ED Pa. 1853).

[5]In 1908, when Bobbs-Merrill was decided, the copyright statute provided that copyright owners had "the sole liberty of printing, reprinting, publishing, completing, copying, executing, finishing, and vending" their copyrighted works. Copyright Act of 1891, § 4952, 26 Stat. 1107 (emphasis added).

[7]Congress codified the first sale doctrine in § 41 of the Copyright Act of 1909, ch. 320, 35 Stat. 1084, and again in § 27 of the 1947 Act, ch. 391, 61 Stat. 660.

is the right "to distribute copies . . . by sale or other transfer of ownership."[8] The comparable limitation on that right is provided not by judicial interpretation, but by an express statutory provision. Section 109(a) provides:

> Notwithstanding the provisions of section 106(3), the owner of a particular copy or phonorecord lawfully made under this title, or any person authorized by such owner, is entitled, without the authority of the copyright owner, to sell or otherwise dispose of the possession of that copy or phonorecord . . .[9]

The Bobbs-Merrill opinion emphasized the critical distinction between statutory rights and contract rights. In this case, L'anza relies on the terms of its contracts with its domestic distributors to limit their sales to authorized retail outlets. Because the basic holding in Bobbs-Merrill is now codified in § 109(a) of the Act, and because those domestic distributors are owners of the products that they purchased from L'anza (the labels of which were "lawfully made under this title"), L'anza does not, and could not, claim that the statute would enable L'anza to treat unauthorized resales

---

[8]The full text of § 106 reads as follows:

§ 106. Exclusive rights in copyrighted works

Subject to sections 107 through 120, the owner of copyright under this title has the exclusive rights to do and to authorize any of the following:

(1) to reproduce the copyrighted work in copies or phonorecords;

(2) to prepare derivative works based upon the copyrighted work;

(3) to distribute copies or phonorecords of the copyrighted work to the public by sale or other transfer of ownership, or by rental, lease, or lending;

(4) in the case of literary, musical, dramatic, and choreographic works, pantomimes, and motion pictures and other audiovisual works, to perform the copyrighted work publicly;

(5) in the case of literary, musical, dramatic, and choreographic works, pantomimes, and pictorial, graphic, or sculptural works, including the individual images of a motion picture or other audiovisual work, to display the copyrighted work publicly; and

(6) in the case of sound recordings, to perform the copyrighted work publicly by means of a digital audio transmission. 17 U.S.C. § 106 (1994 ed., Supp. I).

[9]The comparable section in the 1909 and 1947 Acts provided that "nothing in this Act shall be deemed to forbid, prevent, or restrict the transfer of any copy of a copyrighted work the possession of which has been lawfully obtained." Copyright Act of 1909, ch. 320, § 41, 35 Stat. 1084; see also Copyright Act of 1947, ch. 391, § 27, 61 Stat. 660. It is noteworthy that § 109(a) of the 1978 Act does not apply to "any copy"; it applies only to a copy that was "lawfully made under this title."

by its domestic distributors as an infringement of its exclusive right to distribute copies of its labels. L'anza does claim, however, that contractual provisions are inadequate to protect it from the actions of foreign distributors who may resell L'anza's products to American vendors unable to buy from L'anza's domestic distributors, and that § 602(a) of the Act, properly construed, prohibits such unauthorized competition. To evaluate that submission, we must, of course, consider the text of § 602(a).

III

The most relevant portion of § 602(a) provides:

> Importation into the United States, without the authority of the owner of copyright under this title, of copies or phonorecords of a work that have been acquired outside the United States is an infringement of the exclusive right to distribute copies or phonorecords under section 106, actionable under section 501 . . . [11]

It is significant that this provision does not categorically prohibit the unauthorized importation of copyrighted materials. Instead, it provides that such importation is an infringement of the exclusive right to distribute copies "under section 106." Like the exclusive right to "vend" that was construed in Bobbs-Merrill, the exclusive right to distribute is a limited right. The introductory language in § 106 expressly states that all of the exclusive

---

[11]The remainder of § 602(a) reads as follows:

This subsection does not apply to —

(1) importation of copies or phonorecords under the authority or for the use of the Government of the United States or of any State or political subdivision of a State, but not including copies or phonorecords for use in schools, or copies of any audiovisual work imported for purposes other than archival use;

(2) importation, for the private use of the importer and not for distribution, by any person with respect to no more than one copy or phonorecord of any one work at any one time, or by any person arriving from outside the United States with respect to copies or phonorecords forming part of such person's personal baggage; or

(3) importation by or for an organization operated for scholarly, educational, or religious purposes and not for private gain, with respect to no more than one copy of an audiovisual work solely for its archival purposes, and no more than five copies or phonorecords of any other work for its library lending or archival purposes, unless the importation of such copies or phonorecords is part of an activity consisting of systematic reproduction or distribution, engaged in by such organization in violation of the provisions of section 108(g)(2).

rights granted by that section — including, of course, the distribution right granted by subsection (3) — are limited by the provisions of §§ 107 through 120. One of those limitations, as we have noted, is provided by the terms of § 109(a), which expressly permit the owner of a lawfully made copy to sell that copy "notwithstanding the provisions of section 106(3)."

After the first sale of a copyrighted item "lawfully made under this title," any subsequent purchaser, whether from a domestic or from a foreign reseller, is obviously an "owner" of that item. Read literally, § 109(a) unambiguously states that such an owner "is entitled, without the authority of the copyright owner, to sell" that item. Moreover, since § 602(a) merely provides that unauthorized importation is an infringement of an exclusive right "under section 106," and since that limited right does not encompass resales by lawful owners, the literal text of § 602(a) is simply inapplicable to both domestic and foreign owners of L'anza's products who decide to import them and resell them in the United States.[14]

Notwithstanding the clarity of the text of §§ 106(3), 109(a), and 602(a), L'anza argues that the language of the Act supports a construction of the right granted by § 602(a) as "distinct from the right under Section 106(3) standing alone," and thus not subject to § 109(a). Brief for Respondent 15. Otherwise, L'anza argues, both the § 602(a) right itself and its exceptions would be superfluous. Moreover, supported by various amici curiae, including the Solicitor General of the United States, L'anza contends that its construction is supported by important policy considerations. We consider these arguments separately.

IV

L'anza advances two primary arguments based on the text of the Act: (1) that § 602(a), and particularly its three exceptions, are superfluous if limited by the first sale doctrine; and (2) that the text of § 501 defining an "infringer" refers separately to violations of § 106, on the one hand, and to imports in violation of § 602. The short answer to both of these arguments

---

[14]Despite L'anza's contention to the contrary, see Brief for Respondent 26-27, the owner of goods lawfully made under the Act is entitled to the protection of the first sale doctrine in an action in a United States court even if the first sale occurred abroad. Such protection does not require the extraterritorial application of the Act any more than § 602(a)'s "acquired abroad" language does.

is that neither adequately explains why the words "under section 106" appear in § 602(a). The Solicitor General makes an additional textual argument: he contends that the word "importation" in § 602(a) describes an act that is not protected by the language in § 109(a) authorizing a subsequent owner "to sell or otherwise dispose of the possession of" a copy. Each of these arguments merits separate comment.

The Coverage of § 602(a)

Prior to the enactment of § 602(a), the Act already prohibited the importation of "piratical," or unauthorized, copies. Moreover, that earlier prohibition is retained in § 602(b) of the present act.[17] L'anza therefore argues (as do the Solicitor General and other amici curiae) that § 602(a) is superfluous unless it covers non-piratical ("lawfully made") copies sold by the copyright owner, because importation nearly always implies a first sale. There are several flaws in this argument.

First, even if § 602(a) did apply only to piratical copies, it at least would provide the copyright holder with a private remedy against the importer, whereas the enforcement of § 602(b) is vested in the Customs Service. Second, because the protection afforded by § 109(a) is available only to the "owner" of a lawfully made copy (or someone authorized by the owner), the first sale doctrine would not provide a defense to a § 602(a) action against any non-owner such as a bailee, a licensee, a consignee, or one whose possession of the copy was unlawful.[19] Third, § 602(a) applies to a

---

[17]Section 602(b) provides in relevant part: "In a case where the making of the copies or phonorecords would have constituted an infringement of copyright if this title had been applicable, their importation is prohibited . . . ." The first sale doctrine of § 109(a) does not protect owners of piratical copies, of course, because such copies were not "lawfully made."

[19]In its opinion in this case, the Court of Appeals quoted a statement by a representative of the music industry expressing the need for protection against the importation of stolen motion picture prints: "We've had a similar situation with respect to motion picture prints, which are sent all over the world — legitimate prints made from the authentic negative. These prints get into illicit hands. They're stolen, and there's no contractual relationship . . . . Now those are not piratical copies." Copyright Law Revision Part 2: Discussion and Comments on Report of the Register of Copyrights on General Revision of the U.S. Copyright Law, 88th Cong., 1st Sess., 213 (H. R. Judiciary Comm. Print 1963) (statement of Mr. Sargoy), quoted in 98 F.3d 1109, 1116 (CA9 1996).

category of copies that are neither piratical nor "lawfully made under this title." That category encompasses copies that were "lawfully made" not under the United States Copyright Act, but instead, under the law of some other country.

The category of copies produced lawfully under a foreign copyright was expressly identified in the deliberations that led to the enactment of the 1976 Act. We mention one example of such a comment in 1961 simply to demonstrate that the category is not a merely hypothetical one. In a report to Congress, the Register of Copyrights stated, in part:

> When arrangements are made for both a U.S. edition and a foreign edition of the same work, the publishers frequently agree to divide the international markets. The foreign publisher agrees not to sell his edition in the United States, and the U.S. publisher agrees not to sell his edition in certain foreign countries. It has been suggested that the import ban on piratical copies should be extended to bar the importation of the foreign edition in contravention of such an agreement. Copyright Law Revision: Report of the Register of Copyrights on the General Revision of the U.S. Copyright Law, 87th Cong., 1st Sess., 125-126 (H. R. Judiciary Comm. Print 1961).

Even in the absence of a market allocation agreement between, for example, a publisher of the U.S. edition and a publisher of the British edition of the same work, each such publisher could make lawful copies. If the author of the work gave the exclusive U.S. distribution rights — enforceable under the Act — to the publisher of the U.S. edition and the exclusive British distribution rights to the publisher of the British edition,[20] however, presumably only those made by the publisher of the U.S. edition would be "lawfully made under this title" within the meaning of § 109(a). The first sale doctrine would not provide the publisher of the British edition who decided to sell in the American market with a defense to an action under § 602(a) (or,

---

[20]A participant in a 1964 panel discussion expressed concern about this particular situation. Copyright Law Revision Part 4: Further Discussion and Comments on Preliminary Draft for Revised U.S. Copyright Law, 88th Cong., 2d Sess., 119 (H. R. Judiciary Comm. Print 1964) (statement of Mrs. Pilpel) ("For example, if someone were to import a copy of the British edition of an American book and the author had transferred exclusive United States and Canadian rights to an American publisher, would that British edition be in violation so that this would constitute an infringement under this section?"); see also id., at 209 (statement of Mr. Manges) (describing similar situation as "a troublesome problem that confronts U.S. book publishers frequently").

for that matter, to an action under § 106(3), if there was a distribution of the copies).

The argument that the statutory exceptions to § 602(a) are superfluous if the first sale doctrine is applicable rests on the assumption that the coverage of that section is co-extensive with the coverage of § 109(a). But since it is, in fact, broader because it encompasses copies that are not subject to the first sale doctrine — e.g., copies that are lawfully made under the law of another country — the exceptions do protect the traveler who may have made an isolated purchase of a copy of a work that could not be imported in bulk for purposes of resale. As we read the Act, although both the first sale doctrine embodied in § 109(a) and the exceptions in § 602(a) may be applicable in some situations, the former does not subsume the latter; those provisions retain significant independent meaning.

Section 501's Separate References to §§ 106 and 602

The text of § 501 does lend support to L'anza's submission. In relevant part, it provides:

> (a) Anyone who violates any of the exclusive rights of the copyright owner as provided by sections 106 through 118 or of the author as provided in section 106A(a), or who imports copies or phonorecords into the United States in violation of section 602, is an infringer of the copyright or right of the author, as the case may be . . . .

The use of the words "or who imports," rather than words such as "including one who imports," is more consistent with an interpretation that a violation of § 602 is distinct from a violation of § 106 (and thus not subject to the first sale doctrine set out in § 109(a)) than with the view that it is a species of such a violation. Nevertheless, the force of that inference is outweighed by other provisions in the statutory text.

Most directly relevant is the fact that the text of § 602(a) itself unambiguously states that the prohibited importation is an infringement of the exclusive distribution right "under section 106, actionable under section 501." Unlike that phrase, which identifies § 602 violations as a species of § 106 violations, the text of § 106A, which is also cross-referenced in § 501, uses starkly different language. It states that the author's right protected by § 106A is "independent of the exclusive rights provided in Section 106." The contrast between the relevant language in § 602 and that in § 106A strongly implies that only the latter describes an independent right.[21]

Of even greater importance is the fact that the § 106 rights are subject not only to the first sale defense in § 109(a), but also to all of the other provisions of "sections 107 through 120." If § 602(a) functioned independently, none of those sections would limit its coverage. For example, the "fair use" defense embodied in § 107[22] would be unavailable to importers if § 602(a) created a separate right not subject to the limitations on the § 106(3) distribution right. Under L'anza's interpretation of the Act, it presumably would be unlawful for a distributor to import copies of a British newspaper that contained a book review quoting excerpts from an American novel protected by a United States copyright.[23] Given the importance of the fair use defense to publishers of scholarly works, as well as to publishers of periodicals, it is difficult to believe that Congress intended to impose an absolute

---

[21]The strength of the implication created by the relevant language in § 106A is not diminished by the fact that Congress enacted § 106A more recently than § 602(a), which is part of the Copyright Act of 1976. Section 106A was passed as part of the Visual Artists Rights Act of 1990 in order to protect the moral rights of certain visual artists. Section 106A is analogous to Article 6bis of the Berne Convention for the Protection of Literary and Artistic Works, but its coverage is more limited. See 2 P. Goldstein, Copyright § 5.12, p. 5:225 (2d ed. 1996) (§ 106A encompasses aspects of the moral rights guaranteed by Article 6bis of the Berne Convention, "but effectively gives these rights a narrow subject matter and scope").

[22]Title 17 U.S.C. § 107 provides as follows:

§ 107. Limitations on exclusive rights: Fair use

Notwithstanding the provisions of sections 106 and 106A, the fair use of a copyrighted work, including such use by reproduction in copies or phonorecords or by any other means specified by that section, for purposes such as criticism, comment, news reporting, teaching (including multiple copies for classroom use), scholarship, or research, is not an infringement of copyright. In determining whether the use made of a work in any particular case is a fair use the factors to be considered shall include —

(1) the purpose and character of the use, including whether such use is of a commercial nature or is for nonprofit educational purposes;

(2) the nature of the copyrighted work;

(3) the amount and substantiality of the portion used in relation to the copyrighted work as a whole; and

(4) the effect of the use upon the potential market for or value of the copyrighted work.

The fact that a work is unpublished shall not itself bar a finding of fair use if such finding is made upon consideration of all the above factors.

[23]The § 602(a) exceptions, which are substantially narrower than § 107, would not permit such importation. See n. 11, supra.

ban on the importation of all such works containing any copying of material protected by a United States copyright.

In the context of this case, involving copyrighted labels, it seems unlikely that an importer could defend an infringement as a "fair use" of the label. In construing the statute, however, we must remember that its principal purpose was to promote the progress of the "useful Arts," U.S. Const., Art. I, § 8, cl. 8, by rewarding creativity, and its principal function is the protection of original works, rather than ordinary commercial products that use copyrighted material as a marketing aid. It is therefore appropriate to take into account the impact of the denial of the fair use defense for the importer of foreign publications. As applied to such publications, L'anza's construction of § 602 "would merely inhibit access to ideas without any countervailing benefit." Sony Corp. of America v. Universal City Studios, Inc., 464 U.S. 417, 450-451, 78 L. Ed. 2d 574, 104 S. Ct. 774 (1984).[24]

Does an importer "sell or otherwise dispose" of copies as those words are used in § 109(a)?

Whether viewed from the standpoint of the importer or from that of the copyright holder, the textual argument advanced by the Solicitor General — that the act of "importation" is neither a sale nor a disposal of a copy under § 109(a) — is unpersuasive. Strictly speaking, an importer could, of course, carry merchandise from one country to another without surrendering custody of it. In a typical commercial transaction, however, the shipper transfers "possession, custody, control and title to the products" to a different person, and L'anza assumes that petitioner's importation of the L'anza shipments included such a transfer. An ordinary interpretation of the statement that a person is entitled "to sell or otherwise dispose of the possession" of an item surely includes the right to ship it to another person in another country.

More important, the Solicitor General's cramped reading of the text of the statutes is at odds not only with § 602(a)'s more flexible treatment of unauthorized importation as an infringement of the distribution right

---

[24]L'anza's reliance on § 602(a)(3)'s reference to § 108(g)(2), see n. 11, supra, to demonstrate that all of the other limitations set out in §§ 107 through 120 — including the first sale and fair use doctrines — do not apply to imported copies is unavailing for the same reasons.

(even when there is no literal "distribution"), but also with the necessarily broad reach of § 109(a). The whole point of the first sale doctrine is that once the copyright owner places a copyrighted item in the stream of commerce by selling it, he has exhausted his exclusive statutory right to control its distribution. As we have recognized, the codification of that doctrine in § 109(a) makes it clear that the doctrine applies only to copies that are "lawfully made under this title," but that was also true of the copies involved in the Bobbs-Merrill case, as well as those involved in the earlier cases applying the doctrine. There is no reason to assume that Congress intended either § 109(a) or the earlier codifications of the doctrine to limit its broad scope.

In sum, we are not persuaded by either L'anza's or the Solicitor General's textual arguments.

V

The parties and their amici have debated at length the wisdom or unwisdom of governmental restraints on what is sometimes described as either the "gray market" or the practice of "parallel importation."[28] In K mart Corp. v. Cartier, Inc., 486 U.S. 281, 100 L. Ed. 2d 313, 108 S. Ct. 1811 (1988), we used those terms to refer to the importation of foreign-manufactured goods bearing a valid United States trademark without the consent of the trademark holder. Id., at 285-286. We are not at all sure that those terms appropriately describe the consequences of an American manufacturer's decision to limit its promotional efforts to the domestic market and to sell its products abroad at discounted prices that are so low that its foreign distributors can compete in the domestic market.[29] But even if they do, whether or not we think it would be wise policy to provide statutory protection for such price discrimination is not a matter that is relevant to our duty to interpret the text of the Copyright Act.

---

[28]Compare, for example, Gorelick & Little, The Case for Parallel Importation, 11 N. C. J. Int'l L. & Comm. Reg. 205 (1986), with Gordon, Gray Market Is Giving Hair-Product Makers Gray Hair, N. Y. Times, July 13, 1997, section 1, p. 28, col. 1.

[29]Presumably L'anza, for example, could have avoided the consequences of that competition either (1) by providing advertising support abroad and charging higher prices, or (2) if it was satisfied to leave the promotion of the product in foreign markets to its foreign distributors, to sell its products abroad under a different name.

Equally irrelevant is the fact that the Executive Branch of the Government has entered into at least five international trade agreements that are apparently intended to protect domestic copyright owners from the unauthorized importation of copies of their works sold in those five countries.[30] The earliest of those agreements was made in 1991; none has been ratified by the Senate. Even though they are of course consistent with the position taken by the Solicitor General in this litigation, they shed no light on the proper interpretation of a statute that was enacted in 1976.[31]

The judgment of the Court of Appeals is reversed.
It is so ordered.

Concur: Justice Ginsburg, concurring.

This case involves a "round trip" journey, travel of the copies in question from the United States to places abroad, then back again. I join the Court's opinion recognizing that we do not today resolve cases in which the allegedly infringing imports were manufactured abroad. See W. Patry, Copyright Law and Practice 166-170 (1997 Supp.) (commenting that provisions of Title 17 do not apply extraterritorially unless expressly so stated, hence the words "lawfully made under this title" in the "first sale" provision, 17 U.S.C. § 109(a), must mean "lawfully made in the United States"); see generally P. Goldstein, Copyright § 16.0, pp. 16:1-16:2 (2d ed. 1998) ("Copyright protection is territorial. The rights granted by the United States Copyright Act extend no farther than the nation's borders.").

Notes and Questions

1. In *K mart v. Cartier*, the Supreme Court generally allowed holders of U.S. trademarks to block parallel imports of goods manufactured abroad, but

---

[30]The Solicitor General advises us that such agreements have been made with Cambodia, Trinidad and Tobago, Jamaica, Ecuador, and Sri Lanka.
[31]We also note that in 1991, when the first of the five agreements was signed, the Third Circuit had already issued its opinion in Sebastian Int'l, Inc. v. Consumer Contacts (PTY) Ltd., 847 F.2d 1093 (1988), adopting a position contrary to that subsequently endorsed by the Executive Branch.

Quality King v. L'anza

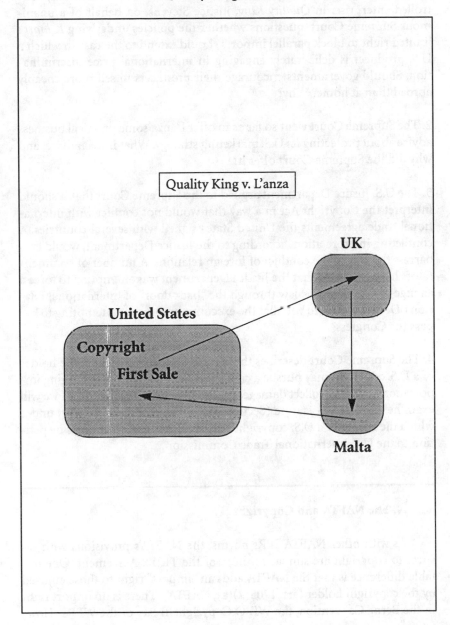

denied this right when the goods are produced abroad by a commonly controlled enterprise. In *Quality King*, Justice Stevens, on behalf of a unanimous Supreme Court, questions whether the policies underlying *K mart's* limited right to block parallel imports should extend to the case in which a U.S. producer is deliberately engaging in international price discrimination. Should governments encourage their producers to sell more cheaply abroad than at home? Why?

2. The Supreme Court went so far as to offer L'anza some practical business advice about protecting its U.S. marketing strategy. What is that advice, and why did the Supreme Court offer it?

3. The U.S. Justice Department argued to the Supreme Court that it should interpret the Copyright Act in a way that would not conflict with international trade agreements the United States signed with several countries. A conflicting interpretation, according to the Justice Department, would embarrass the U.S. in the conduct of foreign relations. A number of commentators have suggested that the Justice Department was attempting to force a change in U.S. domestic law through the "back door" of international relations. Does it appear to you that the executive branch was attempting to bypass the Congress?

4. The Supreme Court describes the statutory scheme by which the holder of a U.S. copyright may pursue a civil court action to enjoin infringing importation and/or to collect damages for infringement. In Chapter VI we will examine another U.S. statute (Section 337 of the Tariff Act of 1930) under which the holder of a U.S. copyright may block infringing imports by petition to the U.S. International Trade Commission.

N. The NAFTA and Copyright

As with other NAFTA IPRs norms, the NAFTA's provisions with respect to copyright are similar to those of the TRIPS Agreement. One notable difference is that the NAFTA adds an "import" right to those enjoyed by the copyright holder (art. 1705(2)(a), NAFTA). There is no import right in the Berne Convention, the WIPO Copyright Treaty or the WPPT. However, observe that the NAFTA import right applies only to works placed on a market without the consent of the right holder, so that the import right does not obligate a NAFTA Party to block parallel imports of copyrighted works.

NAFTA Copyright Provisions

Article 1705: Copyright

1. Each Party shall protect the works covered by Article 2 of the Berne Convention, including any other works that embody original expression within the meaning of that Convention. In particular:

   (a) all types of computer programs are literary works within the meaning of the Berne Convention and each Party shall protect them as such; and

   (b) compilations of data or other material, whether in machine readable or other form, which by reason of the selection or arrangement of their contents constitute intellectual creations, shall be protected as such.

The protection a Party provides under subparagraph (b) shall not extend to the data or material itself, or prejudice any copyright subsisting in that data or material.

2. Each Party shall provide to authors and their successors in interest those rights enumerated in the Berne Convention in respect of works covered by paragraph 1, including the right to authorize or prohibit:

   (a) the importation into the Party's territory of copies of the work made without the right holder's authorization;

   (b) the first public distribution of the original and each copy of the work by sale, rental or otherwise;

   (c) the communication of a work to the public; and

(d) the commercial rental of the original or a copy of a computer program.

Subparagraph (d) shall not apply where the copy of the computer program is not itself an essential object of the rental. Each Party shall provide that putting the original or a copy of a computer program on the market with the right holder's consent shall not exhaust the rental right.

3. Each Party shall provide that for copyright and related rights:

(a) any person acquiring or holding economic rights may freely and separately transfer such rights by contract for purposes of their exploitation and enjoyment by the transferee; and

(b) any person acquiring or holding such economic rights by virtue of a contract, including contracts of employment underlying the creation of works and sound recordings, shall be able to exercise those rights in its own name and enjoy fully the benefits derived from those rights.

4. Each Party shall provide that, where the term of protection of a work, other than a photographic work or a work of applied art, is to be calculated on a basis other than the life of a natural person, the term shall be not less than 50 years from the end of the calendar year of the first authorized publication of the work or, failing such authorized publication within 50 years from the making of the work, 50 years from the end of the calendar year of making.

5. Each Party shall confine limitations or exceptions to the rights provided for in this Article to certain special cases that do not conflict with a normal exploitation of the work and do not unreasonably prejudice the legitimate interests of the right holder.

6. No Party may grant translation and reproduction licenses permitted under the Appendix to the Berne Convention where legitimate needs in that Party's territory for copies or translations of the work could be met by the right holder's voluntary actions but for obstacles created by the Party's measures.

7. Annex 1705.7 applies to the Parties specified in that Annex. [Requiring the United States to protect certain films produced in Canada and Mexico

that had fallen into the public domain in the U.S. as a result of failure to comply with formalities.]

Article 1706: Sound Recordings

1. Each Party shall provide to the producer of a sound recording the right to authorize or prohibit:

(a) the direct or indirect reproduction of the sound recording;

(b) the importation into the Party's territory of copies of the sound recording made without the producer's authorization;

(c) the first public distribution of the original and each copy of the sound recording by sale, rental or otherwise; and

(d) the commercial rental of the original or a copy of the sound recording, except where expressly otherwise provided in a contract between the producer of the sound recording and the authors of the works fixed therein.

Each Party shall provide that putting the original or a copy of a sound recording on the market with the right holder's consent shall not exhaust the rental right.

2. Each Party shall provide a term of protection for sound recordings of at least 50 years from the end of the calendar year in which the fixation was made.

3. Each Party shall confine limitations or exceptions to the rights provided for in this Article to certain special cases that do not conflict with a normal exploitation of the sound recording and do not unreasonably prejudice the legitimate interests of the right holder.

Article 1707: Protection of Encrypted Program-Carrying Satellite Signals

Within one year from the date of entry into force of this Agreement, each Party shall make it:
(a) a criminal offense to manufacture, import, sell, lease or otherwise make available a device or system that is primarily of assistance in decoding

an encrypted program-carrying satellite signal without the authorization of the lawful distributor of such signal; and

(b) a civil offense to receive, in connection with commercial activities, or further distribute, an encrypted program-carrying satellite signal that has been decoded without the authorization of the lawful distributor of the signal or to engage in any activity prohibited under subparagraph (a).

Each Party shall provide that any civil offense established under subparagraph (b) shall be actionable by any person that holds an interest in the content of such signal.

Notes and Questions

1. As discussed in Chapter II, the NAFTA achieves IPRs protection standards comparable to those found in the TRIPS Agreement. However, the government of Mexico has included in its Schedules of Reservations (Annexes I and II) to its commitments in regard to investment and services market access (arts. 1108 and 1206, NAFTA) a number of preferences in favor of Mexican nationals (for example, thirty percent of the screen time of every Mexican theater may be reserved for films produced by Mexican persons). In addition, the government of Canada has reserved its right to adopt measures to protect its cultural industries (Annex 2106, NAFTA). Does a copyright entitle its holder to unrestricted market access? Are measures to protect cultural industries a reasonable response to an increasingly integrated global economy?

O. Copyright Law of China

In section G, 2, *supra*, Gao Lulin discussed the progress made in China in the field of patents. He also reported that in 1992 China acceded to the Berne Convention. The following article by Adolph Dietz of the Max-Planck-Institute in Munich describes and analyzes China's 1991 Copyright Law. Though this article precedes China's accession to Berne, it provides a most useful introduction to the Chinese legislation from the perspective of an adviser to the Chinese government during the drafting process. In light of China's importance in the world economy, and the controversy that has surrounded its implementation of IPRs legislation, we think it is appropriate to focus here on the development of Chinese copyright law.

The New Copyright Law of the People's Republic of China — An Introduction

Adolf Dietz*

1. Origins and Title of the Law

The long-promised, and no doubt eagerly awaited, Copyright Law of the People's Republic of China (hereinafter: CCL) was approved on September 7, 1990 at the 15th Session of the Standing Committee of the VIIth National People's Congress, and was promulgated on the same day by Decree No. 31 of the President of the People's Republic of China. It represents the first comprehensive legislation on copyright in the People's Republic of China, and is thus of considerable historical interest. Despite certain potential points of conflict, which will be discussed below, the overall regulation in this Law reveals that the legislation it contains is intended to conform to the standards of international copyright agreements, in particular the Revised Berne Convention (RBC); this applies in particular to the standard protected period of 50 years post mortem autoris.

As was the case with the revision of Chinese patent law, the new Chinese Copyright Law is also the result of many years of consultations and discussions with domestic and foreign specialists, international organizations and institutions; these include for instance WIPO and the German Patent Office, but also the Max Planck Institute in Munich. The various stages of development, as well as the initial and later drafts of the CCL, not all of which were published, reveal a growing awareness of the problems,

---

*22 IIC 441(1991).

but cannot be interpreted as a direct progression towards ever improving solutions in every aspect.

There is no doubt that wherever the preparatory work for the CCL concerned more than domestic considerations and discussions, it was influenced by the international rivalry between the two prevalent systems of today, the Anglo-American copyright system, and the continental "*droit d'auteur*" system. Leaving aside the question of content, which will be dealt with below, this rivalry also found expression in the terminological issue, namely whether the word to be used for "copyright" should be "*zhuzuo-quan*" (lit., "writer's right" or "work right"), as also used in Taiwan and Japan, or the term "*banquan*" (lit., "printing right" or "publishing right").

On this issue, the Chinese literature pointed out that both terms can claim a long history of use dating back to the times before the establishment of the People's Republic of China, and moreover that the terms "*zhuzuo-quan*" and "author's right" were not absolutely identical; the latter actually ought to be rendered by the term "*zuozhequan*," especially in the light of the term used in the law for "author," "*zuozhe*"; however "*zuozhequan*" is not usual. The supporters of the Anglo-American solution tend towards the term "*banquan*," whilst those who prefer the continental European emphasis on the author's moral rights, give expression to this preference by their choice of the term "*zhuzuoquan*."

Thus the use in the title of the Law and in the whole of the provisions of the 1990 CCL of the term "*zhuzuoquan*" can be seen as expressing a preference on the part of the legislature, which is also embodied in certain elements of the contents (such as the express provision of author's moral rights, and the separate regulation of neighboring rights). However, it is no doubt due to the Chinese desire for harmony and their pragmatic approach that this terminological preference, insofar as it was indeed deliberate, was ultimately withdrawn; Art. 51 of the CCL, as part of the concluding provisions ("Supplementary Provisions") clearly lays down that the term "*zhuzuoquan*" as used in the Law is synonymous with the term "*banquan*."

This synonymy of the two customary expressions was also a feature of a similar provision in Sec. 94 of the General Principles of Civil Law in the People's Republic of China, dated April 12, 1986, which contained several basic principles of copyright law. Hence one should not read too much into the mere use of the term "*zhuzuoquan*" and its similarity to the continental European approach. Nevertheless, the structural and contentual elements of the law, which will be discussed below, also reveal a certain affinity to the European notion of author's rights.

2. Structure and Contents of the Law

The CCL contains a total of 56 Articles organized in six Chapters, and is thus relatively short. The compactness of the legislation is no doubt a result of the Chinese tendency to lay down only the most important and fundamental provisions in the text of the law, and to leave the details to the executive orders. Article 54 of the CCL expressly empowers the State Council or its department responsible for administering copyright to issue implementing regulations; moreover, Art. 6 and Art. 53 contain specific power to issue regulations concerning "the method of protection of copyright in expressions of folklore" and "the method of protection for computer software" respectively, on which there are more details later.

Another instance of the legislative tendency towards compactness can be found in the fourth Chapter headed "Publication, Performance, Sound Recording, Video Recording and Broadcasting;" this combines the regulation of specific types of contract with the regulation of neighboring rights in a manner that is almost unique. The approach rightly deserves to be called original and makes particularly clear the historical development of neighboring rights from the exploitation of the work and the consequent justification for regulating these rights in the context of copyright.

Thus, whilst substantive copyright law, copyright contract law and neighboring rights are provided for, the provisions on collecting societies are remarkable by their absence; however, Art. 8, which regulates the responsibility for the administration of copyright at the national and provincial level, seems to assume that a comprehensive system of copyright administration bodies will be set up in the People's Republic of China. Given the socialist structures of the Chinese economy and society, we may expect that this administration will be entrusted with functions like for instance those of the Soviet Copyright Agency, "VAAP", which are traditionally carried out by collecting societies of the western type. Article 46 of the CCL also grants the copyright administration authorities certain powers of intervention and sanction in the prosecution of copyright infringements.

The term "neighboring rights" as used above is of course not without its problems, since the Law, not least because of the above-mentioned combination with the provisions on the individual exploitation of contracts, does not use the term as a Chapter heading. This is in marked contrast to the 1988 and 1989 draft versions of the legislation, both of which included in Chapter 3 a separate section on neighboring rights ("Rights related to copyright" — in Chinese "*yu zhuzuoquan youguan de quanli*"). As in the final text of the Law, the two drafts provided for a regulation both for publishers, performing artists, and video and/or sound recording producers, and for broadcasting organizations, but without the definitive text's combination of these provisions with the relevant types of exploitation contracts.

In the Law itself, by contrast, the heading of the relevant fourth Chapter simply reads: "Publication, Performance, Sound Recording, Video Recording and Broadcasting." It is interesting that the Chinese term for "neighboring rights" mentioned above and as used as a chapter heading in the drafts, is used almost identically in Art. 1, the policy article of the Law. The "rights and interests related to copyright" ("*yu zhuzuoquan youguan de quanyi*") are, alongside "the copyright of authors in their literary, artistic and scientific works", unequivocally declared to be the protected interest and the object of protection of the Law. This aspect of the Law ultimately justifies the assumption that the CCL regulates neighboring rights in a manner separate from but closely related to copyright in the narrow sense, and which can be classified in terms of both contents and structure as a more European type of copyright law. In particular the internationally disputed categorization of the protection of sound recordings is regulated in the People's Republic of China — as in Japan — by a continental European type of solution, i.e. not by means of the inclusion in a catalog of works, but rather as a neighboring right of the producer of sound recordings.

3. The Copyright Owner

One of the most difficult problems facing the Chinese legislature was without doubt that of the owners of copyright, as is revealed in the different approaches of the various drafts made public. The socialist ideas on the importance of the so-called units in Chinese society and economy no doubt played an influential role in the discussions. Nevertheless, it is also true that an approach that grants copyright to employers and legal entities has been adopted by a number of countries that would emphatically reject the name "socialist."

According to the express provision in Art. 9 CCL, the term "copyright owner" (lit. "copyright person") includes both the author himself and other citizens or entities who are entitled to copyright under this act. The Chinese term for "entitled to" ("*xiangyou*," lit. "enjoy") does not immediately reveal whether, in the case of persons other than the author himself, originating or derivative acquisition of copyright is meant. Apparently Art. 9 is intended to cover both cases. A more precise answer to the question of the (originating) source of copyright must therefore be sought in the 2nd Section of Chapter 2 of the Law, which deals specifically with this issue. According to this provision, copyright "belongs" (in Chinese: "*shuyu*") to the author unless this Law provides otherwise, whereby the author is defined as the citizen who created the work (Art. 11(1) and (2) CCL).

This, of course, is only the basic principle; the same Section also provides for a number of more or less significant exceptions, which, given the features of the socialist economic and social order in the People's Republic of China, will make the individual author as (originating) copyright owner more the exception than the rule.

First of all, Art. 11(3) provides that an entity is "deemed to be the author" if a work is created according to the intention and under its supervision and responsibility. This seems to be a wide-ranging replacement and displacement of the author, since, unlike the provision on employed authors in Art. 16, this provision does not even leave a residual moral right status. The influence of American copyright law is very noticeable here.

The difficulty in this very wide-reaching provision in Art. 11(3) lies in delimiting it from the "usual" cases of employed authors regulated in more detail in Art. 16, since it is difficult to conceive of cases under Art. 11(3) where the author is anything other than an employee who creates a work in the service of the entity. Consequently Art. 11(3) seems to deal with a qualified form of an employed author's creation that is to be fully ascribed to the entity in question, thus in a way totally eliminating the author behind the creation. Apparently in order to avoid an undesirable determinism, a possible escape route was inserted: a necessary precondition, *inter alia*, is that the unit assumes the responsibility for the work, a condition that will probably be met if its name (and its name only) is given at the publication of the work.

In addition, Art. 16 CCL also regulates two further cases of works made in the course of employment, which are defined as works created by a citizen in fulfilment of tasks assigned to him by an entity. According to Art. 16(1) the author is in principle entitled to copyright, but the entity has a priority right to exploit the work within the scope of its professional activities. During the first two years after the completion of the work, the author shall not without the consent of the entity authorize a third party to exploit the work in the same way as the entity does.

This essentially author-friendly principle is however restricted by an exception for certain categories of works in Art. 16(2); thus the author only retains the right of authorship and, by virtue of a discretionary provision, the possibility of a "reward," whilst the entity is entitled to all other powers deriving from copyright. The categories of works in question include drawings of engineering designs or product designs, computer software and maps, i. e. works where the practical purpose is the center of interest. In addition the Law provides that these works be made using the material and technical resources of the relevant entity, and, significantly, that the entity has assumed the responsibility for the work in question. Works made in the course of employment, within the meaning of para. (2), can of course also be works with respect to which laws, administrative regulations or contracts grant the copyright to the entity. As in the entire provision, the wording here does not make it absolutely clear whether the intention is the grant of the original (first) ownership of copyright, or a *cessio legis*, or even a transfer by contract.

In a like manner to these special cases of works made in the course of employment, pursuant to Art. 16(2), in the case of cinematographic, television or videographic works, Art. 15 only allows the actual film authors (director, scriptwriter, etc.) the right of authorship, while the producer is entitled to all the other rights. Although according to Art. 15(2), the copyright in works that can be exploited independently is reserved to the author, this is of little use to the director as actual author of the film, since, unlike the other authors, his creative contribution is inseparably linked with the film. As in many other countries, the legal position of the film director is extremely precarious in China, which is hardly a satisfactory position. Finally, according to Art. 17 CCL, copyright in the case of commissioned works is determined by the contractual agreement — which is also one of the alternatives in the case of "employment" works under [Art. 16(2)(2)]; however, in cases of doubt the right is granted to the commissioned party.

Although similar regulations awarding copyright to employers, commissioners and producers are also to be found in other countries, in particular in the Anglo-American world, in this Law these provisions amount to a transition point from one system to another, a transition in which an "author's right without authors" marks the step from classical copyright to industrial property. It is however too early for a definitive assessment of these provisions; other decisive factors will be the caution with which they are applied in practice, and their ultimately dogmatic interpretation.

For the rest, Art. 2 of the Law also contains a brief regulation of rights of foreigners, granting copyright to foreigners for works published for the first time in the territory of China. For other cases, the Law refers to the contents of bilateral agreements and international conventions. On the other hand, Chinese citizens or entities are granted copyright irrespective of whether (and no doubt where) their works are published. However, the Law does not contain any similar provision with respect to neighboring rights.

4. Catalog of Protected Works

Article 1 of the CCL uses the general concept of "literary, artistic and scientific works," as also found in German copyright law. The term "science" is subdivided at the beginning of Art. 3 into "natural science, social science and engineering technology. " The catalog of protected works, which is stated not to be definitive ("and the like") in Art. 3, follows the usual lines and takes into account recent developments by expressly including computer software in the list of protected works not as a subcategory of literary works but as an independent category. However, the consequences of this inclusion are difficult to predict, since Art. 53 CCL, as mentioned above, lays down that the method of protecting computer software is to be regulated separately by the State Council. Thus a system could develop in China along the lines of the French model, under which computer programs — no doubt in consideration of the application of convention law — are in principle included among the works protected, but special regulations are established for individual aspects (e.g. the protected period, the question of the author's moral rights, or the copyright awarded to the employer).

In the catalog of protected works of Art. 3, Nos. 1-5, 7 and 9 expressly require the existence of a "work" ("*zuopin*"), whilst Nos. 6 and 8, in respect of drawings of engineering designs and product designs and descriptions thereof, and computer software, do not expressly mention this criterion. Of course, both the opening phrase of Art. 3, and the text of No. 9 which enables the addition of further works by means of legal or administrative provisions, are entirely based on the concept of the work. Hence the absence of this term with respect to computer software does not necessarily lead to the conclusion that any and every computer program will now be protected in the People's Republic of China.

However, in this context it is important to note that the Law, apart from the concept of "literary, artistic and scientific works," and the requirement that the works must be "expressed in a form," does not lay down any express minimum standard for a protected work. Thus the delineation between protectable and unprotectable works will only be determined by practice.

In the case of drawings of engineering designs and product designs, it is interesting to note that neither the works of architecture nor the products of the design are themselves named as protected works, and indeed that works of applied art can only be subsumed under the term "drawings for product designs," unless the intention is to include them directly under "works of fine art" (No. 4). That this formulation reflects a specific intention on the part of the legislature can be seen in Art. 52(2) of the Law; this provision expressly lays down within the definition of the term "reproduction" that the construction of a building on the basis of drawings of engineering designs, or the manufacture of an industrial product using product designs does not amount to a reproduction within the meaning of the Law. It must therefore be assumed that these derivative forms of exploitation in this sector are not included in the scope of protection.

To the extent that works of architecture as such are excluded from protection, and that such works are not to be protected by means of the general term of "works of fine art" of Art. 3(4), the provisions do not fully conform with Art. 2(1) of the Revised Berne Convention. Moreover, it should be noted that, according to Art. 5 CCL, official works and current news, calendars, numerical tables and the like are excluded from protection. Furthermore, Art. 7 CCL contains a rather imprecise provision to the effect that where any scientific or technological work "is protected under the Patent Law, the Law on Technology Contracts or similar laws," the provisions of those Laws shall apply. Again, it will be for practice to decide whether this amounts to a defining rule, or whether it merely expresses what is obvious. As already mentioned, a special regulation is planned for works of folklore, as is the case with computer software.

5. The Contents of Copyright

The contents of copyright are regulated in a very compact form in a single provision (Art. 10); the author's moral rights are regulated in Nos. 1-4, whilst the author's pecuniary rights are contained in a very comprehensive formulation in No. 5. Article 10 begins by stating that copyright comprises "the following personality rights and property rights." Specifically, these are the right of publication, the right of authorship, the right of alteration and the right of integrity, on the one hand, and the exploitation right and the right to remuneration on the other hand. The right of exploitation (alongside the claim to remuneration) is then defined as the right to exploit or authorize others to exploit in the various forms named (reproduction, performance, broadcasting, exhibition, distribution, etc.) and to receive a remuneration therefor. The emphasis on the right to remuneration along with the comprehensive exploitation rights has to be understood in its Chinese and socialist context; it also has a pedagogical function as an authoritative "instruction" to the national user organization. Thus it is only logical that the claim to remuneration also plays an appropriate role in the regulation of copyright contract law. From the purely dogmatic point of view there is no need to emphasize the claim to remuneration when granting an exclusive right of exploitation, but, given the realities of copyright exploitation (not only in China), there is nothing to be criticized in such emphasis of the claim to remuneration.

As already mentioned, the term "reproduction" is defined in detail in Art. 52. Article 10 contains a closer definition of the author's moral rights (the right of publication, the right of authorship, the right of alteration and the right of integrity). Regrettably, the Law does not contain any further individual definitions of the individual exploitation powers listed in Art. 10(5) under exploitation rights, a lack which will no doubt cause certain problems of construction.

Although this is not the place to go into detail, a few questions should at least be raised. Firstly, it is not possible to determine the scope of the term "dissemination" (in Chinese "*faxing*," literally roughly equivalent to "issue, put into circulation, sell, publish, circulate"). If it is to be understood in the sense of the right "to issue copies" as for instance in the new British Copyright Act, then this would involve — to some extent automatically — an exhaustion of the right after the first putting into circulation. A rental right, as is expressly available only in specific instances (sound recordings, films and computer programs) in the British Act, does not automatically follow from the Chinese Law.

The second problem concerns the rights to use the work by means of adaptation, translation, annotation or arrangement and the like, which are named in the Law as subcategories of the exploitation right. This provision has to be seen in conjunction with Art. 12, which, in the case of a work that is created by means of the adaptation, translation, annotation or arrangement of a work that already exists, ascribes the copyright in the new work to the adapter, translator etc., whereby the latter, in the exercise of his copyright, may not prejudice the copyright in the original work. This provision also amounts to the regulation of adaptations, translations and the like as the *object* of copyright protection, since astonishingly the provisions on the object of copyright (Arts. 3 *et seq.*) do not directly contain any such regulation.

A further noteworthy provision is the granting of the right of exhibition, which must of course be considered in conjunction with Art. 18; despite the fact that the latter provision lays down the usual strict separation between ownership of the original work and copyright, nevertheless the right of exhibition with respect to the original of a work of fine art — similarly to the provisions of Sec. 44 of the German Copyright Act — lies with the owner of the original. However, the Chinese Law goes a step further in favor of the author than does the German Act, in that it does not link the right of exhibition to the fact that the work has not yet been publicly communicated. Thus, the right of exhibition in the CCL can rightly be regarded as a residual form of economic exploitation, even if this form of exploitation is not applicable to the author once the original has been disposed of.

Finally, the apparently comprehensive broadcasting right must also be seen in conjunction with Art. 40(2); the latter lays down that where a work has already been published, it may be exploited without permission for the "production" of a radio or television program in return for payment of remuneration unless the copyright owner has declared that he does not permit such exploitation. (Similar regulations are contained in Art. 35(2) with respect to commercial performances, and Art. 37(2) with respect to the use of published works for the production of sound recordings). The intention of the legislature here seems to be a type of expressly stated reservation of rights as was usual for performance rights at an earlier stage in the development of copyright law in Europe. Particularly critical is the allowability to transmit published sound recordings, according to Art. 43, without permission, even from the copyright owner, in instances of transmissions for non-commercial purposes.

6. Period of Protection

The fact that Art. 21(1) of the CCL provides for a period of protection of 50 years *post mortem autoris* is a clear sign that the Chinese government does not exclude the possibility of accession to the Revised Berne Convention at a later date. Since, according to Art. 20, the three moral rights of authorship, alteration and integrity are of unlimited duration as a "droit moral perpétuel", the 50-year term of protection of Art. 21 is restricted to

the right of publication, the right of exploitation and the right to remuneration. Correspondingly, Art. 21(2) provides that the rights of publication,
exploitation and remuneration with respect to works accredited to an entity — either through the "qualified" regulation of Art. 11(3), or as one of
the special cases of "employment" works under Art. 16(2) — shall last for
50 years after the first publication of the work (alternatively, for 50 years
after completion of the work). The same applies under Art. 21(3) to photographic and cinematographic or videographic works.

The Law contains no precise provisions on the enforcement of claims
under "*droit moral perpétuel*" (Art. 20) after the death of the author, especially since Art. 19 provides an express inheritance only with respect to the
right of exploitation and the right to remuneration. A point of official intervention may result from Art. 46, which not only applies civil liability to
certain infringements of copyright, but also, as already noted, permits the
imposition of administrative sanctions; the offenses in question also include infringements of moral rights (such as Art. 46(1) and (7)). It is possible that the planned implementing regulations will throw more light on
this issue.

For the sake of completeness it should be noted here that the term of
protection for the neighboring rights of producers of sound and video
recordings and of broadcasting organizations under Art. 39(1) and Art.
42(2) respectively is also 50 years starting from the date of first publication
or broadcast. On the other hand, no particular term of protection is provided for performing artists, no doubt because of their reduced neighboring right status deriving from the individual performances (Art. 36). The
book publisher's right, a right which is dogmatically difficult to interpret
and which is linked to the transfer of exclusive publication rights, lasts for a
maximum of 10 years under Art. 30, but can be renewed.

7. Limitations on Copyright

The limitations on copyright as set out in Art. 22 CCL are mainly
within the limits of what is internationally usual, whereby the absence of
any regulation on remuneration for reproductions or uses of a work for private purposes (Art. 22(1)) or for teaching purposes (Art. 22(6)) is to be re-
gretted, particularly from the German point of view. Here too the question
arises whether the limits under convention law (in particular Art. 9(2) of
the Revised Berne Convention) have been observed throughout.

A particularly important limitation is also to be found in Art. 22(9), which provides that as a general rule it is not necessary to pay remuneration with respect to free-of-charge live performances of published works. It has already been mentioned that, in addition, Arts. 35(2), 37(2) and 40(2) — outside the context of the limitations on copyright — permit the use, without permission but in return for remuneration, of a published work in order to achieve a commercial performance or to produce a sound recording or a radio or television broadcast, unless the copyright holder has expressly reserved these rights. The term "produce" in this context presumably means not only the production of the broadcasting material but also its use for the purposes of the broadcast itself, an interpretation that offers itself in the context of the provision, namely the requirement to obtain permission for the exploitation of unpublished works for the "production" of a program (Art. 40(1)). Further, according to Art. 43, the broadcast of published sound recordings for non-commercial purposes is permissible without authorization and payment of remuneration.

8. Copyright Contract Law

Leaving aside inheritance (Art. 19), the only conveyance of rights between living persons provided for by the CCL, like the German Copyright Act, is the granting of a license to use the work; thus copyright in its entirety may not be assigned *inter vivos*. In addition to this significant basic principle, the function of which is to protect the author, the third Chapter of the Law (Arts. 23-28) also contains general provisions concerning exploitation contracts and general copyright contract law; these provisions, although few in number, are of considerable importance as a means for protecting authors. This is particularly true of Art. 25, which is the Chinese version of the principle of interpretation of a copyright contract according to its purpose and the specification principle, and of the rule that an exploitation contract shall not exceed 10 years; of course, the contract can be renewed.

For the rest, Art. 27 provides for the possibility that the competent state departments may issue remuneration tariffs, whereby contractual provisions to the contrary are permitted. Finally, Art. 28 expressly imposes upon the author's contractual partner the duty to respect both the author's moral rights and his claim to remuneration. As will be discussed below, the fourth Chapter contains rudimentary provisions concerning specific types of exploitation contracts in connection with neighboring rights.

9. Neighboring Rights

As already frequently mentioned, the regulations on neighboring rights contained in the fourth Chapter of the Law are distinguished by what can only be described as an original mixture of items whose common factor is that they are linked to the regulation of different types of contract. In a structurally comparable manner, four Sections regulate publishing contracts, performance contracts, sound and/or video recording contracts and broadcasting contracts, whereby in the direct context of each case the rights granted to the copyright owner's contractual partner in the result or the product produced on the basis of the contract are also regulated. This structurally curious regulation, which naturally has its weak points, is no doubt the reason why the term "neighboring rights," which is used in Art. 1 of the Law, was not used in the Chapter heading. It is not clear whether these provisions mean that protection of the work and the neighboring rights are strictly collateral, or whether neighboring rights can also arise in cases that do not involve the contractually negotiated exploitation of works or the exploitation of works that are not or no longer protected. While the wording of Arts. 36, 39 and 42 does not exclude an interpretation independent of the protection of the work, the final answer will of course have to be left to Chinese practice.

Let us now examine the structure of this regulation in more detail, taking as our example the provision concerning the protection of the performing artist (who appears in the Law, together with the "performing group," as a subcategory of the term "performer"). Article 35 first of all lays down that a "performer" who exploits the unpublished work of another for his performance must obtain the permission of the copyright owner and pay remuneration. Article 36 then lays down that the performer himself is entitled to rights with respect to his performance, namely the right to claim performership, to protection of the image inherent in his performance from distortion and the right to authorize others to make live broadcasts and sound and/or video recordings (the latter, for commercial purposes).

Similarly, Arts. 37 and 38 regulate the obligations of the producer of sound and/or video recordings towards the copyright owner and the performing artists, while Art. 39 regulates the producer's rights (the right of reproduction and distribution, and a right to remuneration for 50 years); Arts. 40 and 41 regulate the obligations of broadcasting organizations towards the copyright owner and performing artists, while Art. 42 lays down the broadcasting organization's rights (the right to broadcast and the right of reproduction and distribution of the radio or television program, as well as a right to remuneration for 50 years).

In contrast, the publisher's right under Art. 30 does not amount to a neighboring right in the strict sense of the term, since its object is the exclusive right of publication deriving from copyright. The other neighboring rights, the three "Rome" rights plus the right of the producer of video recordings, on the other hand, are indeed independent neighboring rights with their own objects, namely the "performance" in the case of (performing artists), the "sound or video recording produced by" the producer of sound or video recordings, and finally the "radio or television program produced by" a broadcasting station or organization.

It has already been noted that in its regulation of the broadcasting contract (in the absence of a reservation of the right on the part of the copyright owner), Art. 40 provides for a sort of compulsory license, on payment of remuneration, for the exploitation of published works for the production of a radio or television program. However, Art. 43 goes further than this and provides that the broadcasting of published sound recordings for non-commercial purposes (which will no doubt continue to be the rule in China) requires neither permission nor the payment of remuneration. In contrast to this, Art. 44 expressly lays down that the broadcasting of cinematographic and videographic works requires both permission and the payment of remuneration.

As also previously mentioned, the provision on the limitations on copyright (Art. 22(9)) generally permits the free-of-charge live performance of a previously published work. In addition, however, Art. 35(2) also provides that the commercial performance of a previously published work is also allowed without the permission of the copyright owner on payment of remuneration, unless the copyright owner has expressly reserved this right. A parallel regulation with the same import is contained in Art. 37(1) with respect to the producer of sound recordings. However, according to Art. 37(2) this regulation does not apply to the producer of video recordings. It is doubtful whether this regulation conforms to convention law in every respect, particularly in the light of Art. 13(1) of the Revised Berne Convention; the question will have to be examined in more detail in the event of China's accession to the Revised Berne Convention.

10. Civil and Penal Sanctions

Under the heading "legal liability," the fifth Chapter contains a number of provisions concerning civil and penal liability. Article 45 lays down civil law liability (ceasing the infringing act, elimination of its effect, apology and damages) for certain cases of the infringement of the author's moral rights as well as of his right of exploitation and of neighboring rights. Article 46 on the other hand lays down the imposition of penal sanctions (confiscation and fines) in addition to the appropriate form of civil liability for infringements apparently deemed to be more serious.

A comparison of Arts. 45 and 46 shows that apparently the infringement of mere performance and broadcasting rights is deemed to be less serious than the infringement of the right of reproduction and distribution (for commercial purposes) and the infringement of the neighboring rights of the producer of sound and/or video recordings or of the broadcasting organization. Behind this approach, no doubt, lies the attempt to prosecute and punish piracy more severely, although this is to be by means of the intervention of the administrative authorities.

The remaining provisions in this Chapter are devoted to the possibility of arbitration (mediation) of disputes concerning the infringement of copyright and disputes arising out of contracts (Arts. 48 and 49). An alternative to mediation or arbitration is the recourse to the people's court. Moreover, according to Art. 50, an appeal against administrative penalties imposed by the copyright administration authorities can be made to the people's court.

In the light of Chinese traditions and circumstances, the fact that, as noted above. Art. 46 subjects certain serious infringements of copyright to prosecution by the copyright administration authorities (subject to an appeal against such sanctions to the people's court), leads to the assumption that, as in patent and trademark law, the primary intention is the official prosecution of infringements of intellectual property, which will certainly also be possible at the request of the injured party.

Final Assessment

A first analysis of the new Chinese Copyright Law shows that the Chinese legislature has taken considerable pains to present at the first attempt a copyright law that to an average degree meets international standards in content and in form. It cannot of course be compared with the leading modern European copyright laws such as those of France, Germany and Spain. The attempt to draft the regulations in such a manner as to prevent in advance any conflict with the Berne Convention has not always been successful. In particular, doubt must be expressed whether certain provisions (such as the absence of protection for works of architecture and the general exemption of unpaid performances of published works and of the non-commercial transmission of published sound recordings) concurs entirely with the law of this Convention. The same is true for the Rome Convention; in this connection, a particular problem is the fact that the performing artists are not granted the right of reproduction of recorded performances at all, although Art. 7(1)(c) of the Rome Convention does permit certain restrictions.

This very compact regulation will, as announced, shortly be supplemented by implementing regulations; these will not only concern the special cases of the protection of computer software and of works of folklore, as expressly mentioned in the Law, but also other issues. This is no doubt the reason why the Law is to enter into effect on the relatively late date of June 1, 1991 (Art. 56). Only when the whole legislative complex has been completed will it be possible to make a final judgment on the new Copyright Act of the People's Republic of China. But it can already be stated that the People's Republic of China has now definitely entered the ranks of copyright law countries.

Notes and Questions

1.Gao Lulin[1] indicates that China's "Regulations for the Protection of Computer Software" require the registration of software as a condition precedent to initiation of administrative dispute resolution or legal proceedings in China. He indicates that while this is contrary to Berne Convention norms, the terms of China's General Principles of Civil Law would mandate the application of Berne norms over the terms of the Regulations, and thus would assure that software authored by foreigners is protected without reg-

---

[1]*Supra*, §G, 2.

istration. Note that the United States still requires authors to register their works prior to initiation of actions for copyright infringement, but it provides an exception for Berne Convention works not of U.S. origin.[2]

2. In Chapter VI we will examine bilateral agreements between China and the United States which impose wide ranging obligations on the Chinese government in respect to the protection of copyrighted works, including works in digital format. From the standpoint of foreigners doing business in China, the Copyright Law must be read with such bilateral agreements in mind.

3. Adolph Dietz focuses attention on the ownership of copyrighted works, and refers to the special situation faced by socialist economies in which property is frequently owned by a collective (or "unit"). The trend toward "marketization" of the Chinese economy, which certainly accelerated after 1991, will likely produce reforms in favor of concrete recognition of individual rights in copyrighted works. Yet even in Europe and the United States, the large scale exploitation of copyrighted works is rarely within the province of individual authors or artists. The "collective" interest in copyrighted works may not be unique to the "socialist" economy. The difference between the socialist system and the market system may lie mainly in the direction to which the profits flow (i.e. to the government or to shareholders, managers and directors).

P. Moral Rights

It is often said that one of the greatest differences between Continental European and Anglo-American copyright law is the treatment of *"droit moral"* ("moral rights") of authors. These differences are often attributed to the different philosophical foundations of the two systems. The difference can be seen in terminology. In French, copyright is referred to as *le droit d'auteur*, that is, the author's rights, and those rights are directed at protecting the expressions of the author's personality. The English term, copyright, refers directly to the economic activity of copying and not to the author's

---

[2] 17 U.S.C. §§101, 411(a).

rights. Thus, Anglo-American systems have little difficulty in considering the rights of performers, the producers of sound recordings and broadcasters under the notion of copyright, whereas these rights, in Continental Europe, are considered to be "neighboring rights," that is, rights that are neighboring to those of an author. Moreover, the lack of attention to the moral rights of artists, at least in the United States, is often attributed to the free market capitalist philosophy which emphasizes the right of individuals to dispose of their possessions as they please.

Whether or not differences arise from profound cultural disparities, it is true that American businesses worry that allowing authors to retain residual rights in copyrighted works may lead to financial uncertainty. A business which contracts for the development of a computer program, and which by contract obtains the copyright to the resulting work, does not want to be faced with demands from the programmer that the work not be altered lest his or her reputation be injured. Likewise, the film producer who invests tens (or hundreds) of millions of dollars in a work does not want the screenwriter or the director objecting to the way the film is marketed on the basis of residual moral rights.

The tension between economics and art is not a new one. We might safely assume that since the very first commercial performances by singers, storytellers and actors, there has been conflict between artists desiring to perform in their own style, and producers of works (e.g, tavern or theater owners) seeking to please the general public and earn a greater return on investment. In a world in which a film studio may invest $200 million in a film and earn a gross return of $1 billion, the potential for conflict is heightened.

As we noted earlier in this Chapter, the Berne Convention requires that artists and authors enjoy certain moral rights.

The first decision below is by the French Cour de Cassation, the highest civil court in France. The decision involves a widely-reported dispute between the corporate owner of the copyright to a film "Asphalt Jungle," co-directed by John Huston, and the heirs to Huston's estate.

1. Moral Rights in Continental Europe

Angelica Huston v. Turner Entertainment Co.
French Cour de Cassation
[1992] ECC 334
28 MAY 1991

Panel: Presiding, M Massip; MM Gregoire, Zennaro, Bernard de Sainte-Affrique, Thierry, Averseng, Lemontey and Gelineau-Larrivet, Judges; M Savatier, Associate Judge

Headnote:

Appeal from the Cour d'Appel (Court of Appeal), Paris.
Copyright. Literary or artistic works. Foreign works. Copyright legislation provides that the integrity of a literary or artistic work must not be violated in France. These provisions are mandatory and apply no matter where in the world the work in question was published for the first time.

The Court allowed the appeal by the plaintiff and others, as heirs to John Huston, against the order of the court below, which refused to enjoin the television company La Cinq from transmitting a coloured version of the film, Asphalt Jungle, made by the defendant, which had succeeded to the producer's rights to the film.

Introduction:

*****

No cases were cited.

Decision:

Second ground of appeal, first limb, by Mrs. Angelica Huston, Mr. Daniel Huston and Mr. Walter Huston, and third ground of appeal by SFAI and other legal persons.

The court referred to section 1(2) of Act 64-689 of 8 July 1964, together with section 6 of the Copyright Act of 11 March 1957.

According to the former provision, the integrity of a literary or artistic work must not be violated, irrespective of the State in which the work is published for the first time. The person who is the author by the mere fact of creating it is invested with the droit moral granted to him by the latter provision. The application of these rules is mandatory.

Mrs Angelica Huston, Mr Daniel Huston and Mr Walter Huston are the heirs of John Huston, co-director of the film Asphalt Jungle (the French title being Quand laVille Dort), which was made in black and white, but a colour version of which was made by Turner Entertainment Co, which has succeeded to the producer's rights. Relying on their right to compel respect for the integrity of John Huston's work, the appellant heirs, who have been joined in this appeal on a point of law by the various other appellants which are legal persons, asked the courts dealing with the main issue to prohibit the television company La Cinq from showing this new version. The appeal court dismissed the application on the ground that the factual matters and points of law raised by them 'precluded the ouster of American law and setting aside of the contracts' between the producer and directors, which do not acknowledge that the latter are the authors of the film Asphalt Jungle.

In reaching its decision the appeal court infringed the abovementioned provisions by refusing to apply them.

Appeal allowed. Case remitted to the Cour d'Appel, Versailles for rehearing.

Notes and Questions

1. The decision of the Cour de Cassation is to the point: French legislation on the question of moral rights is mandatory — it is not waived by the U.S. contract which transferred the copyright to the film producer. The French rule applies despite the fact that the film is of U.S. origin, and despite the fact that the French Cour d'Appel found that the contract should otherwise be governed by U.S. law. Do you think that this result is unusual from a general conflict of laws standpoint? In other words, do countries commonly mandate the application of their own rules to activities taking place within

their territory, despite contractual provisions that might generally call for the application of another country's law?

In fact, it is not so uncommon for states to mandate the application of their own rules in cases in which important public policy considerations are at stake. A court in one state may, for example, refuse to enforce a judgment rendered by a court in another state if the court in the second state failed to follow a due process rule which is considered essential under the law of the first state.

2. Moral Rights in the United States

a. The Copyright Act and the Lanham Act

In the 1976 *Monty Python* decision which follows, the U.S. Court of Appeals for the Second Circuit elaborated a basis under the copyright statute of the United States, as well as under a statute on unfair competition, for the attribution of certain moral rights to authors.

Terry Gilliam, Graham Chapman, Terry Jones, Michael Palin, John Cleese and Eric Idle, individually and collectively performing as the professional group known as "Monty Python" v. American Broadcasting Companies, Inc.

United States Court of Appeals for the Second Circuit
538 F.2d 14; 1976 U.S. App. LEXIS 8225
June 30, 1976, Decided

Prior History:
Appeal from a denial of a preliminary injunction to enjoin broadcast of edited television programs that allegedly infringed appellants' copyright and violated the Lanham Act § 43(a), 15 U.S.C. § 1125(a).
Disposition: Reversed and remanded.

*****

Judges: Lumbard, Hays, and Gurfein, Circuit Judges. Gurfein, Circuit Judge (concurring).

Opinion: Lumbard, Circuit Judge:

Plaintiffs, a group of British writers and performers known as "Monty Python,"[1] appeal from a denial by Judge Lasker in the Southern District of a preliminary injunction to restrain the American Broadcasting Company (ABC) from broadcasting edited versions of three separate programs originally written and performed by Monty Python for broadcast by the British Broadcasting Corporation (BBC). We agree with Judge Lasker that the appellants have demonstrated that the excising done for ABC impairs the integrity of the original work. We further find that the countervailing injuries that Judge Lasker found might have accrued to ABC as a result of an injunction at a prior date no longer exist. We therefore direct the issuance of a preliminary injunction by the district court.

Since its formation in 1969, the Monty Python group has gained popularity primarily through its thirty-minute television programs created for BBC as part of a comedy series entitled "Monty Python's Flying Circus." In accordance with an agreement between Monty Python and BBC, the group writes and delivers to BBC scripts for use in the television series. This scriptwriters' agreement recites in great detail the procedure to be followed when any alterations are to be made in the script prior to recording of the program. The essence of this section of the agreement is that, while BBC retains final authority to make changes, appellants or their representatives exercise optimum control over the scripts consistent with BBC's authority and only minor changes may be made without prior consultation with the writers. Nothing in the scriptwriters' agreement entitles BBC to alter a program once it has been recorded. The agreement further provides that, subject to the terms therein, the group retains all rights in the script.

Under the agreement, BBC may license the transmission of recordings of the television programs in any overseas territory. The series has been broadcast in this country primarily on non-commercial public broadcast-

---

[1] Appellant Gilliam is an American citizen residing in England.

ing television stations, although several of the programs have been broadcast on commercial stations in Texas and Nevada. In each instance, the thirty-minute programs have been broadcast as originally recorded and broadcast in England in their entirety and without commercial interruption.

In October 1973, Time-Life Films acquired the right to distribute in the United States certain BBC television programs, including the Monty Python series. Time-Life was permitted to edit the programs only "for insertion of commercials, applicable censorship or governmental . . . rules and regulations, and National Association of Broadcasters and time segment requirements." No similar clause was included in the scriptwriters' agreement between appellants and BBC. Prior to this time, ABC had sought to acquire the right to broadcast excerpts from various Monty Python programs in the spring of 1975, but the group rejected the proposal for such a disjoined format. Thereafter, in July 1975, ABC agreed with Time-Life to broadcast two ninety-minute specials each comprising three thirty-minute Monty Python programs that had not previously been shown in this country.

Correspondence between representatives of BBC and Monty Python reveals that these parties assumed that ABC would broadcast each of the Monty Python programs "in its entirety." On September 5, 1975, however, the group's British representative inquired of BBC how ABC planned to show the programs in their entirety if approximately 24 minutes of each 90 minute program were to be devoted to commercials. BBC replied on September 12, "we can only reassure you that ABC have decided to run the programmes 'back to back,' and that there is a firm undertaking not to segment them."

ABC broadcast the first of the specials on October 3, 1975. Appellants did not see a tape of the program until late November and were allegedly "appalled" at the discontinuity and "mutilation" that had resulted from the editing done by Time-Life for ABC. Twenty-four minutes of the original 90 minutes of recording had been omitted. Some of the editing had been done in order to make time for commercials; other material had been edited, according to ABC, because the original programs contained offensive or obscene matter.

In early December, Monty Python learned that ABC planned to broadcast the second special on December 26, 1975. The parties began negotiations concerning editing of that program and a delay of the broadcast until Monty Python could view it. These negotiations were futile, however, and on December 15 the group filed this action to enjoin the broadcast and for damages. Following an evidentiary hearing, Judge Lasker found that "the plaintiffs have established an impairment of the integrity of their work" which "caused the film or program . . . to lose its iconoclastic verve." According to Judge Lasker, "the damage that has been caused to the plaintiffs is irreparable by its nature." Nevertheless, the judge denied the motion for the preliminary injunction on the grounds that it was unclear who owned the copyright in the programs produced by BBC from the scripts written by Monty Python; that there was a question of whether Time-Life and BBC were indispensable parties to the litigation; that ABC would suffer significant financial loss if it were enjoined a week before the scheduled broadcast; and that Monty Python had displayed a "somewhat disturbing casualness" in their pursuance of the matter.

Judge Lasker granted Monty Python's request for more limited relief by requiring ABC to broadcast a disclaimer during the December 26 special to the effect that the group dissociated itself from the program because of the editing. A panel of this court, however, granted a stay of that order until this appeal could be heard and permitted ABC to broadcast, at the beginning of the special, only the legend that the program had been edited by ABC. We heard argument on April 13 and, at that time, enjoined ABC from any further broadcast of edited Monty Python programs pending the decision of the court.

I

In determining the availability of injunctive relief at this early stage of the proceedings, Judge Lasker properly considered the harm that would inure to the plaintiffs if the injunction were denied, the harm that defendant would suffer if the injunction were granted, and the likelihood that plaintiffs would ultimately succeed on the merits. See Hamilton Watch Co. v. Benrus Watch Co., 206 F.2d 738 (2d Cir. 1953). We direct the issuance of a preliminary injunction because we find that all these factors weigh in favor of appellants.

There is nothing clearly erroneous in Judge Lasker's conclusion that any injury suffered by appellants as a result of the broadcast of edited versions of their programs was irreparable by its nature. ABC presented the appellants with their first opportunity for broadcast to a nationwide network audience in this country. If ABC adversely misrepresented the quality of Monty Python's work, it is likely that many members of the audience, many of whom, by defendant's admission, were previously unfamiliar with appellants, would not become loyal followers of Monty Python productions. The subsequent injury to appellants' theatrical reputation would imperil their ability to attract the large audience necessary to the success of their venture. Such an injury to professional reputation cannot be measured in monetary terms or recompensed by other relief. See Coca-Cola Co. v. Gemini Rising, Inc., 346 F. Supp. 1183, 1189 (E.D.N.Y. 1972); Estee Lauder, Inc. v. Watsky, 323 F. Supp. 1064, 1067 (S.D.N.Y. 1970).

In contrast to the harm that Monty Python would suffer by a denial of the preliminary injunction, Judge Lasker found that ABC's relationship with its affiliates would be impaired by a grant of an injunction within a week of the scheduled December 26 broadcast. The court also found that ABC and its affiliates had advertised the program and had included it in listings of forthcoming television programs that were distributed to the public. Thus a last minute cancellation of the December 26 program, Judge Lasker concluded, would injure defendant financially and in its reputation with the public and its advertisers.

However valid these considerations may have been when the issue before the court was whether a preliminary injunction should immediately precede the broadcast, any injury to ABC is presently more speculative. No rebroadcast of the edited specials has been scheduled and no advertising costs have been incurred for the immediate future. Thus there is no danger that defendant's relations with affiliates or the public will suffer irreparably if subsequent broadcasts of the programs are enjoined pending a disposition of the issues.

We then reach the question whether there is a likelihood that appellants will succeed on the merits. In concluding that there is a likelihood of infringement here, we rely especially on the fact that the editing was substantial, i.e., approximately 27 per cent of the original program was omitted, and the editing contravened contractual provisions that limited the right to edit Monty Python material. It should be emphasized that our discussion of these matters refers only to such facts as have been developed upon the hearing for a preliminary injunction. Modified or contrary findings may become appropriate after a plenary trial.

Judge Lasker denied the preliminary injunction in part because he was unsure of the ownership of the copyright in the recorded program. Appellants first contend that the question of ownership is irrelevant because the recorded program was merely a derivative work taken from the script in which they hold the uncontested copyright. Thus, even if BBC owned the copyright in the recorded program, its use of that work would be limited by the license granted to BBC by Monty Python for use of the underlying script. We agree.

Section 7 of the Copyright Law, 17 U.S.C. § 7, provides in part that "adaptations, arrangements, dramatizations . . . or other versions of . . . copyrighted works when produced with the consent of the proprietor of the copyright in such works . . . shall be regarded as new works subject to copyright. . . ." Manifestly, the recorded program falls into this category as a dramatization of the script, and thus the program was itself entitled to copyright protection. However, section 7 limits the copyright protection of the derivative work, as works adapted from previously existing scripts have become known, to the novel additions made to the underlying work, Reyher v. Children's Television Workshop, 533 F.2d 87 (2d Cir. 1976), and the derivative work does not affect the "force or validity" of the copyright in the matter from which it is derived. See Grove Press, Inc. v. Greenleaf Publishing Co., 247 F. Supp. 518 (S.D.N.Y. 1965). Thus, any ownership by BBC of the copyright in the recorded program would not affect the scope or ownership of the copyright in the underlying script.

Since the copyright in the underlying script survives intact despite the incorporation of that work into a derivative work, one who uses the script, even with the permission of the proprietor of the derivative work, may infringe the underlying copyright. See Davis v. E.I. DuPont deNemours & Co., 240 F. Supp. 612 (S.D.N.Y. 1965) (defendants held to have infringed when they obtained permission to use a screenplay in preparing a television script but did not obtain permission of the author of the play upon which the screenplay was based).

If the proprietor of the derivative work is licensed by the proprietor of the copyright in the underlying work to vend or distribute the derivative work to third parties, those parties will, of course, suffer no liability for their use of the underlying work consistent with the license to the proprietor of the derivative work. Obviously, it was just this type of arrangement that was contemplated in this instance. The scriptwriters' agreement between Monty Python and BBC specifically permitted the latter to license the transmission of the recordings made by BBC to distributors such as Time-Life for broadcast in overseas territories.

One who obtains permission to use a copyrighted script in the production of a derivative work, however, may not exceed the specific purpose for which permission was granted. Most of the decisions that have reached this conclusion have dealt with the improper extension of the underlying work into media or time, i.e., duration of the license, not covered by the grant of permission to the derivative work proprietor.[4] ... Appellants herein do not claim that the broadcast by ABC violated media or time restrictions contained in the license of the script to BBC. Rather, they claim that revisions in the script, and ultimately in the program, could be made only after consultation with Monty Python, and that ABC's broadcast of a program edited after recording and without consultation with Monty Python exceeded the scope of any license that BBC was entitled to grant.

The rationale for finding infringement when a licensee exceeds time or media restrictions on his license — the need to allow the proprietor of the underlying copyright to control the method in which his work is presented to the public — applies equally to the situation in which a licensee makes an unauthorized use of the underlying work by publishing it in a truncated version. Whether intended to allow greater economic exploitation of the work, as in the media and time cases, or to ensure that the copyright proprietor retains a veto power over revisions desired for the derivative work, the ability of the copyright holder to control his work remains paramount in our copyright law. We find, therefore, that unauthorized editing of the underlying work, if proven, would constitute an infringement of the copyright in that work similar to any other use of a work that exceeded the license granted by the proprietor of the copyright.

If the broadcast of an edited version of the Monty Python program infringed the group's copyright in the script, ABC may obtain no solace from

---

[4]Thus, a leading commentator on the subject concludes:

If the copyright owner of an underlying work limits his consent for its use in a derivative work to a given medium (e.g. opera), the copyright owner of the derivative work may not exploit such derivative work in a different medium (e.g. motion pictures) to the extent the derivative work incorporates protectible material from the underlying work. 1 M. Nimmer, Copyright § 45.3.

the fact that editing was permitted in the agreements between BBC and Time-Life or Time-Life and ABC. BBC was not entitled to make unilateral changes in the script and was not specifically empowered to alter the recordings once made; Monty Python, moreover, had reserved to itself any rights not granted to BBC. Since a grantor may not convey greater rights than it owns, BBC's permission to allow Time-Life, and hence ABC, to edit appears to have been a nullity. See Hampton v. Paramount Pictures Corp., 279 F.2d 100 (9th Cir. 1960), cert. denied, 364 U.S. 882, 5 L. Ed. 2d 103, 81 S. Ct. 170 (1970); Ilyin v. Avon Publications, 144 F. Supp. 368, 372 (S.D.N.Y. 1956).

ABC answers appellants' infringement argument with a series of contentions, none of which seems meritorious at this stage of the litigation. The network asserts that Monty Python's British representative, Jill Foster, knew that ABC planned to exclude much of the original BBC program in the October 3 broadcast. ABC thus contends that by not previously objecting to this procedure, Monty Python ratified BBC's authority to license others to edit the underlying script.

Although the case of Ilyin v. Avon Publications, Inc., 144 F. Supp. 368, 373 (S.D.N.Y. 1956), may be broadly read for the proposition that a holder of a derivative copyright may obtain rights in the underlying work through ratification, the conduct necessary to that conclusion has yet to be demonstrated in this case. It is undisputed that appellants did not have actual notice of the cuts in the October 3 broadcast until late November. Even if they are chargeable with the knowledge of their British representative, it is not clear that she had prior notice of the cuts or ratified the omissions, nor did Judge Lasker make any finding on the question. While Foster, on September 5, did question how ABC was to broadcast the entire program if it was going to interpose 24 minutes of commercials, she received assurances from BBC that the programs would not be "segmented." The fact that she knew precisely the length of material that would have to be omitted to allow for commercials does not prove that she ratified the deletions. This is especially true in light of previous assurances that the program would contain the original shows in their entirety. On the present record, it cannot be said that there was any ratification of BBC's grant of editing rights. ABC, of course, is entitled to attempt to prove otherwise during the trial on the merits.

*****

Aside from the question of who owns the relevant copyrights, ABC asserts that the contracts between appellants and BBC permit editing of the programs for commercial television in the United States. ABC argues that the scriptwriters' agreement allows appellants the right to participate in revisions of the script only prior to the recording of the programs, and thus infers that BBC had unrestricted authority to revise after that point. This argument, however, proves too much. A reading of the contract seems to indicate that Monty Python obtained control over editing the script only to ensure control over the program recorded from that script. Since the scriptwriters' agreement explicitly retains for the group all rights not granted by the contract, omission of any terms concerning alterations in the program after recording must be read as reserving to appellants exclusive authority for such revisions.

Finally, ABC contends that appellants must have expected that deletions would be made in the recordings to conform them for use on commercial television in the United States. ABC argues that licensing in the United States implicitly grants a license to insert commercials in a program and to remove offensive or obscene material prior to broadcast. According to the network, appellants should have anticipated that most of the excised material contained scatological references inappropriate for American television and that these scenes would be replaced with commercials, which presumably are more palatable to the American public.

The proof adduced up to this point, however, provides no basis for finding any implied consent to edit. Prior to the ABC broadcasts, Monty Python programs had been broadcast on a regular basis by both commercial and public television stations in this country without interruption or deletion. Indeed, there is no evidence of any prior broadcast of edited Monty Python material in the United States. These facts, combined with the persistent requests for assurances by the group and its representatives that the programs would be shown intact belie the argument that the group knew or should have known that deletions and commercial interruptions were inevitable.

Several of the deletions made for ABC, such as elimination of the words "hell" and "damn," seem inexplicable given today's standard television fare.[8] If, however, ABC honestly determined that the programs were obscene in substantial part, it could have decided not to broadcast the spe-

---

[8] We also note that broadcast of the Monty Python specials was scheduled by ABC for an 11:30 p.m. to 1:00 a.m. time slot.

cials at all, or it could have attempted to reconcile its differences with appellants. The network could not, however, free from a claim of infringement, broadcast in a substantially altered form a program incorporating the script over which the group had retained control.

Our resolution of these technical arguments serves to reinforce our initial inclination that the copyright law should be used to recognize the important role of the artist in our society and the need to encourage production and dissemination of artistic works by providing adequate legal protection for one who submits his work to the public. See Mazer v. Stein, 347 U.S. 201, 98 L. Ed. 630, 74 S. Ct. 460 (1954). We therefore conclude that there is a substantial likelihood that, after a full trial, appellants will succeed in proving infringement of their copyright by ABC's broadcast of edited versions of Monty Python programs. In reaching this conclusion, however, we need not accept appellants' assertion that any editing whatsoever would constitute infringement. Courts have recognized that licensees are entitled to some small degree of latitude in arranging the licensed work for presentation to the public in a manner consistent with the licensee's style or standards. See Stratchborneo v. Arc. Music Corp., 357 F. Supp. 1393, 1405 (S.D.N.Y. 1973); Preminger v. Columbia Pictures Corp., 49 Misc.2d 363, 267 N.Y.S.2d 594 (Sup.Ct.), aff'd 25 A.D.2d 830, 269 N.Y.S.2d 913 (1st Dept.), aff'd 18 N.Y.2d 659, 273 N.Y.S.2d 80, 219 N.E.2d 431 (1966). That privilege, however, does not extend to the degree of editing that occurred here especially in light of contractual provisions that limited the right to edit Monty Python material.

II

It also seems likely that appellants will succeed on the theory that, regardless of the right ABC had to broadcast an edited program, the cuts made constituted an actionable mutilation of Monty Python's work. This cause of action, which seeks redress for deformation of an artist's work, finds its roots in the continental concept of droit moral, or moral right, which may generally be summarized as including the right of the artist to have his work attributed to him in the form in which he created it. See 1 M. Nimmer, supra, at § 110.1.

American copyright law, as presently written, does not recognize moral rights or provide a cause of action for their violation, since the law seeks to vindicate the economic, rather than the personal, rights of authors. Nevertheless, the economic incentive for artistic and intellectual creation that serves as the foundation for American copyright law, Goldstein v. California, 412 U.S. 546, 37 L. Ed. 2d 163, 93 S. Ct. 2303 (1973); Mazer v. Stein, 347 U.S. 201, 98 L. Ed. 630, 74 S. Ct. 460 (1954), cannot be reconciled with the inability of artists to obtain relief for mutilation or misrepresentation of their work to the public on which the artists are financially dependent. Thus courts have long granted relief for misrepresentation of an artist's work by relying on theories outside the statutory law of copyright, such as contract law, Granz v. Harris, 198 F.2d 585 (2d Cir. 1952) (substantial cutting of original work constitutes misrepresentation), or the tort of unfair competition, Prouty v. National Broadcasting Co., 26 F. Supp. 265 (Mass. 1939). See Strauss, The Moral Right of the Author 128-138, in Studies on Copyright (1963). Although such decisions are clothed in terms of proprietary right in one's creation, they also properly vindicate the author's personal right to prevent the presentation of his work to the public in a distorted form. See Gardella v. Log Cabin Products Co., 89 F.2d 891, 895-96 (2d Cir. 1937); Roeder, The Doctrine of Moral Right, 53 Harv. L. Rev. 554, 568 (1940).

Here, the appellants claim that the editing done for ABC mutilated the original work and that consequently the broadcast of those programs as the creation of Monty Python violated the Lanham Act § 43(a), 15 U.S.C. § 1125(a).[10] This statute, the federal counterpart to state unfair competition laws, has been invoked to prevent misrepresentations that may injure plaintiff's business or personal reputation, even where no registered trademark is concerned. See Mortellito v. Nina of California, 335 F. Supp. 1288, 1294 (S.D.N.Y. 1972). It is sufficient to violate the Act that a representation of a product, although technically true, creates a false impression of the product's origin. See Rich v. RCA Corp., 390 F. Supp. 530 (S.D. N.Y. 1975) (recent picture of plaintiff on cover of album containing songs recorded in distant

---

[10]That statute provides in part:

Any person who shall affix, apply, or annex, or use in connection with any goods or services, ... a false designation of origin, or any false description or representation ... and shall cause such goods or services to enter into commerce ... shall be liable to a civil action by any person ... who believes that he is or is likely to be damaged by the use of any such false description or representation.

past held to be a false representation that the songs were new); Geisel v. Poynter Products, Inc., 283 F. Supp. 261, 267 (S.D.N.Y. 1968).

These cases cannot be distinguished from the situation in which a television network broadcasts a program properly designated as having been written and performed by a group, but which has been edited, without the writer's consent, into a form that departs substantially from the original work. "To deform his work is to present him to the public as the creator of a work not his own, and thus makes him subject to criticism for work he has not done." Roeder, supra, at 569. In such a case, it is the writer or performer, rather than the network, who suffers the consequences of the mutilation, for the public will have only the final product by which to evaluate the work. Thus, an allegation that a defendant has presented to the public a "garbled," Granz v. Harris, supra (Frank, J., concurring), distorted version of plaintiff's work seeks to redress the very rights sought to be protected by the Lanham Act, 15 U.S.C. § 1125(a), and should be recognized as stating a cause of action under that statute. See Autry v. Republic Productions, Inc., 213 F.2d 667 (9th Cir. 1954); Jaeger v. American Intn'l Pictures, Inc., 330 F. Supp. 274 (S.D. N.Y. 1971), which suggest the violation of such a right if mutilation could be proven.

During the hearing on the preliminary injunction, Judge Lasker viewed the edited version of the Monty Python program broadcast on December 26 and the original, unedited version. After hearing argument of this appeal, this panel also viewed and compared the two versions. We find that the truncated version at times omitted the climax of the skits to which appellants' rare brand of humor was leading and at other times deleted essential elements in the schematic development of a story line.[12] We therefore agree with Judge Lasker's conclusion that the edited version broadcast by ABC impaired the integrity of appellants' work and repre-

---

[12]A single example will illustrate the extent of distortion engendered by the editing. In one skit, an upper class English family is engaged in a discussion of the tonal quality of certain words as "woody" or "tinny." The father soon begins to suggest certain words with sexual connotations as either "woody" or "tinny," whereupon the mother fetches a bucket of water and pours it over his head. The skit continues from this point. The ABC edit eliminates this middle sequence so that the father is comfortably dressed at one moment and, in the next moment, is shown in a soaked condition without any explanation for the change in his appearance.

sented to the public as the product of appellants what was actually a mere caricature of their talents. We believe that a valid cause of action for such distortion exists and that therefore a preliminary injunction may issue to prevent repetition of the broadcast prior to final determination of the issues.[13]

III

We do not share Judge Lasker's concern about the procedures by which the appellants have pursued this action. The district court indicated agreement with ABC that appellants were guilty of laches in not requesting a preliminary injunction until 11 days prior to the broadcast. Our discussion above, however, suggests that the group did not know and had no reason to believe until late November that editing would take place. Several letters between BBC and Monty Python's representative indicate that appellants believed that the programs would be shown in their entirety. Furthermore, the group did act to prevent offensive editing of the second program immediately after viewing the tape of the first edited program. Thus we find no undue delay in the group's failure to institute this action until they were sufficiently advised regarding the facts necessary to support the action. In any event, ABC has not demonstrated how it was prejudiced by any delay. See Emle Industries, Inc. v. Patentex, Inc., 478 F.2d 562, 574 (2d Cir. 1973).

*****

[13]Judge Gurfein's concurring opinion suggests that since the gravamen of a complaint under the Lanham Act is that the origin of goods has been falsely described, a legend die claiming Monty Python's approval of the edited version would preclude violation of that Act. We are doubtful that a few words could erase the indelible impression that is made by a television broadcast, especially since the viewer has no means of comparing the truncated version with the complete work in order to determine for himself the talents of plaintiffs. Furthermore, a disclaimer such as the one originally suggested by Judge Lasker in the exigencies of an impending broadcast last December would go unnoticed by viewers who tuned into the broadcast a few minutes after it began.

We therefore conclude that Judge Gurfein's proposal that the district court could find some form of disclaimer would be sufficient might not provide appropriate relief.

For these reasons we direct that the district court issue the preliminary injunction sought by the appellants.

Concur: Gurfein, Circuit Judge, concurring:

I concur in my brother Lumbard's scholarly opinion, but I wish to comment on the application of Section 43(a) of the Lanham Act, 15 U.S.C. § 1125(a).

I believe that this is the first case in which a federal appellate court has held that there may be a violation of Section 43(a) of the Lanham Act with respect to a common-law copyright. The Lanham Act is a trademark statute, not a copyright statute. Nevertheless, we must recognize that the language of Section 43(a) is broad. It speaks of the affixation or use of false designations of origin or false descriptions or representations, but proscribes such use "in connection with any goods or services." It is easy enough to incorporate trade names as well as trademarks into Section 43(a) and the statute specifically applies to common law trademarks, as well as registered trademarks. Lanham Act § 45, 15 U.S.C. § 1127.

In the present case, we are holding that the deletion of portions of the recorded tape constitutes a breach of contract, as well as an infringement of a common-law copyright of the original work. There is literally no need to discuss whether plaintiffs also have a claim for relief under the Lanham Act or for unfair competition under New York law. I agree with Judge Lumbard, however, that it may be an exercise of judicial economy to express our view on the Lanham Act claim, and I do not dissent therefrom. I simply wish to leave it open for the District Court to fashion the remedy.

The Copyright Act provides no recognition of the so-called droit moral, or moral rights of authors. Nor are such rights recognized in the field of copyright law in the United States. See 1 Nimmer on Copyright, § 110.2 (1975 ed.). If a distortion or truncation in connection with a use constitutes an infringement of copyright, there is no need for an additional cause of action beyond copyright infringement. Id. at § 110.3. An obligation to mention the name of the author carries the implied duty, however, as a matter of contract, not to make such changes in the work as would render the credit line a false attribution of authorship, Granz v. Harris, 198 F.2d 585 (2 Cir. 1952).

So far as the Lanham Act is concerned, it is not a substitute for droit moral which authors in Europe enjoy. If the licensee may, by contract, distort the recorded work, the Lanham Act does not come into play. If the licensee has no such right by contract, there will be a violation in breach of contract. The Lanham Act can hardly apply literally when the credit line correctly states the work to be that of the plaintiffs which, indeed it is, so far as it goes. The vice complained of is that the truncated version is not what the plaintiffs wrote. But the Lanham Act does not deal with artistic integrity. It only goes to misdescription of origin and the like. See Societe Comptoir De L'Industrie Cotonniere Etablissements Boussac v. Alexander's Dept. Stores, Inc., 299 F.2d 33, 36 (2 Cir. 1962).

The misdescription of origin can be dealt with, as Judge Lasker did below, by devising an appropriate legend to indicate that the plaintiffs had not approved the editing of the ABC version.[1] With such a legend, there is no conceivable violation of the Lanham Act. If plaintiffs complain that their artistic integrity is still compromised by the distorted version, their claim does not lie under the Lanham Act, which does not protect the copyrighted work itself but protects only against the misdescription or mislabeling.

So long as it is made clear that the ABC version is not approved by the Monty Python group, there is no misdescription of origin. So far as the content of the broadcast itself is concerned, that is not within the proscription of the Lanham Act when there is no misdescription of the authorship.

I add this brief explanation because I do not believe that the Lanham Act claim necessarily requires the drastic remedy of permanent injunction. That form of ultimate relief must be found in some other fountainhead of equity jurisprudence.

Notes and Questions

1. The majority opinion adopts two distinct theories for recognizing Monty Python's right to prevent the broadcast of an edited version of its work. The

---

[1] I do not imply that the appropriate legend be shown only at the beginning of the broadcast. That is a matter for the District Court.

first theory is based in traditional copyright law principles. What is that theory?

2. In discussing the traditional U.S. reluctance to recognize moral rights, the Second Circuit observes that it is difficult to reconcile the economic incentive for creation that American copyright law is intended to provide, on the one hand, with a lack of attention to the reputation of authors and artists. A good reputation, the Court suggests, is a predicate of economic success. Do you agree with the Court's perspective?

3. The second theory of the Court of Appeals is grounded in misrepresentation of origin and unfair competition. The Swiss Federal Court has suggested to us that general civil law principles should not be used as a substitute for specific IPRs.[1] Does the concurring opinion of Judge Gurfein appear to reflect a similar legal philosophy?

---

b. The Visual Artists Rights Act of 1990

Some twenty years after *Monty Python*, the U.S. Court of Appeals for the Second Circuit again addressed the subject of moral rights in *Carter v. Helmsley-Spear*. In this case, the court is called upon to interpret and apply a recent amendment to the U.S. Copyright Act which expressly incorporates moral rights into federal law though, as we will see, in a limited way.

---

[1]*See, e.g.*, Frau X v. Frau Y and Z Publishing, *supra*, Ch. I, § B, 4, b.

John Carter, et al. v. Helmsley-Spear

United States Court of Appeals For The Second Circuit
71 F.3d 77; 1995 U.S. App. LEXIS 33708
December 1, 1995, Decided

Subsequent History: Certiorari Denied May 20, 1996, Reported at: 1996 U.S. LEXIS 3277.

Prior History: Defendants, owner and managing agent of a building, appeal from an order of the United States District Court for the Southern District of New York (Edelstein, J.) enjoining them from modifying, destroying, and removing a work of visual art incorporated into the building by plaintiffs, artists commissioned by a former tenant to install the work, and dismissing defendants' counterclaim for waste. Plaintiffs cross-appeal the dismissal of their claim for tortious interference with contractual relations and denial of their requests to complete the work and for attorney's fees and costs.

Disposition: Reversed and vacated, in part, affirmed, in part.

Judges: Before: Meskill, Cardamone, and Altimari Circuit Judges.

Opinion: Cardamone, Circuit Judge:

Defendants 474431 Associates and Helmsley-Spear, Inc. (defendants or appellants), as the owner and managing agent respectively, of a commercial building in Queens, New York, appeal from an order of the United States District Court for the Southern District of New York (Edelstein, J.), entered on September 6, 1994 following a bench trial. The order granted plaintiffs, who are three artists, a permanent injunction that enjoined defendants from removing, modifying or destroying a work of visual art that had been installed in defendants' building by plaintiffs-artists commissioned by a former tenant to install the work. See Carter v. Helmsley-Spear, Inc., 861 F. Supp. 303 (S.D.N.Y. 1994). Defendants also appeal from the dismissal by the trial court of their counterclaim for waste. Plaintiffs cross-appeal from the dismissal of their cause of action for tortious interference with contractual relations and from the denial of their requests to complete the work and for an award of attorney's fees and costs.

On this appeal we deal with an Act of Congress that protects the rights of artists to preserve their works. One of America's most insightful thinkers observed that a country is not truly civilized "where the arts, such as they have, are all imported, having no indigenous life." 7 Works of Ralph Waldo Emerson, Society and Solitude, Chapt. II Civilization 34 (AMS. ed. 1968). From such reflection it follows that American artists are to be encouraged by laws that protect their works. Although Congress in the statute before us did just that, it did not mandate the preservation of art at all costs and without due regard for the rights of others.

For the reasons that follow, we reverse and vacate the grant of injunctive relief to plaintiffs and affirm the dismissal by the district court of plaintiffs' other claims and its dismissal of defendants' counterclaim for waste.

Background

Defendant 474431 Associates (Associates) is the owner of a mixed use commercial building located at 47-44 31st Street, Queens, New York, which it has owned since 1978. Associates is a New York general partnership. The general partners are Alvin Schwartz and Supervisory Management Corp., a wholly-owned subsidiary of Helmsley Enterprises, Inc. Defendant Helmsley-Spear, Inc. is the current managing agent of the property for Associates [eds. note: though the property was previously managed by SIG Management Company (SIG) and others].

. . . . There is no relationship, other than the lease, between Associates, the lessor, and the Limited Partnership, the lessee.

Plaintiffs John Carter, John Swing and John Veronis (artists or plaintiffs) are professional sculptors who work together and are known collectively as the "Three-J's" or "Jx3." On December 16, 1991 SIG entered into a one-year agreement with the plaintiffs "engaging and hiring the Artists . . . to design, create and install sculpture and other permanent installations" in the building, primarily the lobby. Under the agreement plaintiffs had "full authority in design, color and style," and SIG retained authority to direct the location and installation of the artwork within the building. The artists were to retain copyrights to their work and SIG was to receive 50 percent of any proceeds from its exploitation. On January 20, 1993 SIG and the artists signed an agreement extending the duration of their commission for an additional year. When Corporate Life became a general partner of the Limited Partnership, the Limited Partnership assumed the agreement with plaintiffs and in December 1993 again extended the agreement.

The artwork that is the subject of this litigation is a very large "walk-through sculpture" occupying most, but not all, of the building's lobby. The artwork consists of a variety of sculptural elements constructed from recycled materials, much of it metal, affixed to the walls and ceiling, and a vast mosaic made from pieces of recycled glass embedded in the floor and walls. Elements of the work include a giant hand fashioned from an old school bus, a face made of automobile parts, and a number of interactive components. These assorted elements make up a theme relating to environmental concerns and the significance of recycling.

The Limited Partnership's lease on the building was terminated on March 31, 1994. It filed for bankruptcy one week later. The property was surrendered to defendant Associates on April 6, 1994 and defendant Helmsley-Spear, Inc. took over management of the property. Representatives of defendants informed the artists that they could no longer continue to install artwork at the property, and instead had to vacate the building. These representatives also made statements indicating that defendants intended to remove the artwork already in place in the building's lobby.

As a result of defendants' actions, artists commenced this litigation. On April 26, 1994 the district court issued a temporary restraining order enjoining defendants from taking any action to alter, deface, modify or mutilate the artwork installed in the building. In May 1994 a hearing was held on whether a preliminary injunction should issue. The district court subsequently granted a preliminary injunction enjoining defendants from removing the artwork pending the resolution of the instant litigation. See Carter v. Helmsley-Spear, Inc., 852 F. Supp. 228 (S.D.N.Y. 1994).

A bench trial was subsequently held in June and July 1994, at the conclusion of which the trial court granted the artists the permanent injunction prohibiting defendants from distorting, mutilating, modifying, destroying and removing plaintiffs' artwork. Carter v. Helmsley-Spear, Inc., 861 F. Supp. 303, 337 (S.D.N.Y. 1994). The injunction is to remain in effect for the lifetimes of the three plaintiffs. Plaintiffs' other claims, including their cause of action for tortious interference and a request for an award of costs and attorney's fees and that they be allowed to continue to add to the artwork in the lobby, as well as defendants' counterclaim for waste, were all dismissed with prejudice. This appeal and cross-appeal followed.

Discussion

I Artists' Moral Rights

A. History of Artists' Moral Rights

Because it was under the rubric of the Visual Artists Rights Act of 1990 that plaintiffs obtained injunctive relief in the district court, we must explore, at least in part, the contours of that Act. In doing so it is necessary to review briefly the concept of artists' moral rights and the history and development of those rights in American jurisprudence, which led up to passage of the statute we must now examine.

The term "moral rights" has its origins in the civil law and is a translation of the French le droit moral, which is meant to capture those rights of a spiritual, non-economic and personal nature. The rights spring from a belief that an artist in the process of creation injects his spirit into the work and that the artist's personality, as well as the integrity of the work, should therefore be protected and preserved. See Ralph E. Lerner & Judith Bresler, Art Law 417 (1989) (Art Law). Because they are personal to the artist, moral rights exist independently of an artist's copyright in his or her work. See, e.g., 2 Nimmer on Copyright 8D-4 & n.2 (1994) (Nimmer).

While the rubric of moral rights encompasses many varieties of rights, two are protected in nearly every jurisdiction recognizing their existence: attribution and integrity. See Art Law at 420. The right of attribution generally consists of the right of an artist to be recognized by name as the author of his work or to publish anonymously or pseudonymously, the right to prevent the author's work from being attributed to someone else, and to prevent the use of the author's name on works created by others, including distorted editions of the author's original work. See, e.g., id. at 419-20; Nimmer at 8D-5. The right of integrity allows the author to prevent any deforming or mutilating changes to his work, even after title in the work has been transferred. See, e.g., Art Law at 420.

In some jurisdictions the integrity right also protects artwork from destruction. Whether or not a work of art is protected from destruction represents a fundamentally different perception of the purpose of moral rights. If integrity is meant to stress the public interest in preserving a nation's culture, destruction is prohibited; if the right is meant to emphasize the author's personality, destruction is seen as less harmful than the continued display of deformed or mutilated work that misrepresents the artist and destruction may proceed. See Art Law at 421; see also 2 William F. Patry, Copyright Law and Practice 1044 n.128 (1994) (Copyright Law) (noting the different models but suggesting that "destruction of a work shows the utmost contempt for the artist's honor or reputation").

Although moral rights are well established in the civil law, they are of recent vintage in American jurisprudence. Federal and state courts typically recognized the existence of such rights in other nations, but rejected artists' attempts to inject them into U.S. law. See, e.g., Vargas v. Esquire, Inc., 164 F.2d 522, 526 (7th Cir. 1947); Crimi v. Rutgers Presbyterian Church, 194 Misc. 570, 573-76, 89 N.Y.S.2d 813 (N.Y. Sup. Ct. 1949). Nonetheless, American courts have in varying degrees acknowledged the idea of moral rights, cloaking the concept in the guise of other legal theories, such as copyright, unfair competition, invasion of privacy, defamation, and breach of contract. See Nimmer at 8D-10; Art Law at 423.

In the landmark case of Gilliam v. American Broadcasting Companies, Inc., 538 F.2d 14 (2d Cir. 1976), we relied on copyright law and unfair competition principles to safeguard the integrity rights of the "Monty Python" group, noting that although the law "seeks to vindicate the economic, rather than the personal rights of authors . . . the economic incentive for artistic . . . creation . . . cannot be reconciled with the inability of artists to obtain relief for mutilation or misrepresentation of their work to the public on which the artists are financially dependent." Id. at 24. Because decisions protecting artists rights are often "clothed in terms of proprietary right in one's creation," we continued, "they also properly vindicate the author's personal right to prevent the presentation of his work to the public in a distorted form." Id.

Artists fared better in state legislatures than they generally had in courts. California was the first to take up the task of protecting artists with the passage in 1979 of the California Art Preservation Act, Cal. Civ. Code § 987 et seq. (West 1982 & Supp. 1995), followed in 1983 by New York's enactment of the Artist's Authorship Rights Act, N.Y. Arts & Cult. Aff. Law § 14.03 (McKinney Supp. 1995). Nine other states have also passed moral rights statutes, generally following either the California or New York models. See generally Art Law at 430-35; id. at 301-09 (Supp. 1992) (describing the different states' laws).

B. Visual Artists Rights Act of 1990

Although bills protecting artists' moral rights had first been introduced in Congress in 1979, they had drawn little support. See Copyright Law at 1018 n.1. The issue of federal protection of moral rights was a prominent hurdle in the debate over whether the United States should join the Berne Convention, the international agreement protecting literary and artistic works. Article 6bis of the Berne Convention protects attribution and integrity, stating in relevant part:

> Independently of the author's economic rights, and even after the transfer of the said rights, the author shall have the right to claim authorship of the work and to object to any distortion, mutilation or other modification of, or other derogatory action in relation to, the said work, which would be prejudicial to his honor or reputation.

Berne Convention for the Protection of Literary and Artistic Works, September 9, 1886, art. 6bis, S. Treaty Doc. No. 27, 99th Cong., 2d Sess. 41 (1986).

The Berne Convention's protection of moral rights posed a significant difficulty for U.S. adherence. See Copyright Law at 1022 ("The obligation of the United States to provide droit moral ... was the single most contentious issue surrounding Berne adherence."); Nimmer at 8D-15 ("During the debate over [the Berne Convention Implementation Act], Congress faced an avalanche of opposition to moral rights, including denunciations of moral rights by some of the bill's most vociferous advocates."); H.R. Rep. No. 514, 101st Cong., 2d Sess. 7 (1990), reprinted in 1990 U.S.C.C.A.N. 6915, 6917 ("After almost 100 years of debate, the United States joined the Berne Convention .... Consensus over United States adherence was slow to develop in large part because of debate over the requirements of Article 6bis.").

Congress passed the Berne Convention Implementation Act of 1988, Pub. L. No. 100-568, 102 Stat. 2853 (1988), and side-stepped the difficult question of protecting moral rights. It declared that the Berne Convention is not self-executing, existing law satisfied the United States' obligations in adhering to the Convention, its provisions are not enforceable through any action brought pursuant to the Convention itself, and neither adherence to the Convention nor the implementing legislation expands or reduces any rights under federal, state, or common law to claim authorship of a work or to object to any distortion, mutilation, or other modification of a work. See id. §§ 2, 3; see also S. Rep. No. 352, 100th Cong., 2d Sess. 9-10 (1988), reprinted in 1988 U.S.C.C.A.N. 3706, 3714-15.

Two years later Congress enacted the Visual Artists Rights Act of 1990 (VARA or Act), Pub. L. No. 101-650 (tit. VI), 104 Stat. 5089, 5128-33 (1990). Construing this Act constitutes the subject of the present appeal. The Act protects both the reputations of certain visual artists and the works of art they create. It provides these artists with the rights of "attribution" and "integrity." ...

> These rights are analogous to those protected by Article 6bis of the Berne Convention, which are commonly known as "moral rights." The theory of moral rights is that they result in a climate of artistic worth and honor that encourages the author in the arduous act of creation

H.R. Rep. No. 514 at 5 (internal quote omitted). The Act brings to fruition Emerson's insightful observation.

Its principal provisions afford protection only to authors of works of visual art — a narrow class of art defined to include paintings, drawings, prints, sculptures, or photographs produced for exhibition purposes, existing in a single copy or limited edition of 200 copies or fewer. 17 U.S.C. § 101 (Supp. III 1991). With numerous exceptions, VARA grants three rights: the right of attribution, the right of integrity and, in the case of works of visual art of "recognized stature," the right to prevent destruction. 17 U.S.C. § 106A (Supp. III 1991). For works created on or after June 1, 1991 — the effective date of the Act — the rights provided for endure for the life of the author or, in the case of a joint work, the life of the last surviving author. The rights cannot be transferred, but may be waived by a writing signed by the author. Copyright registration is not required to bring an action for infringement of the rights granted under VARA, or to secure statutory damages and attorney's fees. 17 U.S.C. §§ 411, 412 (1988 & Supp. III 1991). All remedies available under copyright law, other than criminal remedies, are available in an action for infringement of moral rights. 17 U.S.C. § 506 (1988 & Supp. III 1991). With this historical background in hand, we pass to the merits of the present litigation.

II Work of Visual Art

Because VARA is relatively new, a fuller explication of it is helpful. In analyzing the Act, therefore, we will follow in order the definition set forth in § 101, as did the district court when presiding over this litigation. The district court determined that the work of art installed in the lobby of Associates' building was a work of visual art as defined by VARA; that distortion, mutilation, or modification of the work would prejudice plaintiffs' honor and reputations; that the work was of recognized stature, thus protecting it from destruction (including removal that would result in destruction); and that Associates consented to or ratified the installation of the work in its building. The result was that defendants were enjoined from removing or otherwise altering the work during the lifetimes of the three artists.

A. Singleness of the Work

As a preliminary matter, we must determine whether the trial court correctly found that the work is a single piece of art, to be analyzed under VARA as a whole, rather than separate works to be considered individually. This finding was a factual one reviewed under the clearly erroneous standard. For purposes of framing the issues at trial the parties entered into a joint stipulation relating to numerous facts, including a definition of "the Work." This stipulated definition contained a long, detailed list of all the sculptural elements contained in the building's lobby. The district court found that, with a few precise exceptions determined to be separate works of art, the artwork created by plaintiffs in the lobby was a single work. See 861 F. Supp. at 314-15. This finding was based on testimony, credited by the trial judge, of the artists themselves and of their expert witnesses.

The trial court found further support for its conclusion in the method by which the artists created the work — each additional element of the sculpture was based on the element preceding it so that they would mesh together. The result was a thematically consistent, interrelated work whose elements could not be separated without losing continuity and meaning. See id. at 315. The record evidence of singleness was confirmed at the request of the parties by the district court's own inspection of the work.

Appellants' primary contention is that the finding of singleness is inconsistent with a finding that certain works of art were separate from the work that is the subject of this appeal. This assertion rests on the mistaken belief that the parties' joint stipulation to a definition of "the Work" precluded an ultimate determination by the factfinder that most but not all of the work installed in the lobby was a single artwork. In other words, according to appellants, either every component in the stipulated definition is part of a single work or every component is an individual work; there is no middle ground. Appellants' goal is to have VARA applied to each element of the sculpture individually, so that components that may not be visual art standing alone cannot be considered visual art when they are combined by the artists to create a whole that has a nature different than the mere sum of its parts.

Appellants' goal is not attainable. The parties stipulated that when they used the term "the Work" it included a list of sculptural components. The result was that during the trial there was no dispute as to the parties' meaning when referring to "the Work." The trial court was free to find that a few items of "the Work" were separate works of art, while the remainder of "the Work" was a single, interrelated, indivisible work of art. The finding of singleness was based on determinations of witness credibility as well as the district court's own inspection of the artwork. We cannot say that such a finding was clearly erroneous.

B. The Statutory Definition

A "work of visual art" is defined by the Act in terms both positive (what it is) and negative (what it is not). In relevant part VARA defines a work of visual art as "a painting, drawing, print, or sculpture, existing in a single copy" or in a limited edition of 200 copies or fewer. 17 U.S.C. § 101. Although defendants aver that elements of the work are not visual art, their contention is foreclosed by the factual finding that the work is a single, indivisible whole. Concededly, considered as a whole, the work is a sculpture and exists only in a single copy. Therefore, the work satisfies the Act's positive definition of a work of visual art. We next turn to the second part of the statutory definition — what is not a work of visual art.

The definition of visual art excludes "any poster, map, globe, chart, technical drawing, diagram, model, applied art, motion picture or other audio-visual work." 17 U.S.C. § 101. Congress meant to distinguish works of visual art from other media, such as audio-visual works and motion pictures, due to the different circumstances surrounding how works of each genre are created and disseminated. See H.R. Rep. No. 514 at 9. Although this concern led to a narrow definition of works of visual art,

> the courts should use common sense and generally accepted standards of the artistic community in determining whether a particular work falls within the scope of the definition. Artists may work in a variety of media, and use any number of materials in creating their works. Therefore, whether a particular work falls within the definition should not depend on the medium or materials used. Id. at 11.

"Applied art" describes "two- and three-dimensional ornamentation or decoration that is affixed to otherwise utilitarian objects." Carter, 861 F. Supp. at 315, citing Kieselstein-Cord v. Accessories By Pearl, Inc., 632 F.2d 989, 997 (2d Cir. 1980). Defendants' assertion that at least parts of the work are applied art appears to rest on the fact that some of the sculptural elements are affixed to the lobby's floor, walls, and ceiling — all utilitarian objects. Interpreting applied art to include such works would render meaningless VARA's protection for works of visual art installed in buildings. A court should not read one part of a statute so as to deprive another part of meaning. See, e.g., United States Nat'l Bank of Or. v. Independent Ins. Agents of America, Inc., 124 L. Ed. 2d 402, 113 S. Ct. 2173, 2182 (1993); United States v. LaPorta, 46 F.3d 152, 156 (2d Cir. 1994).

Appellants do not suggest the entire work is applied art. The district court correctly stated that even if components of the work standing alone were applied art, "nothing in VARA proscribes protection of works of visual art that incorporate elements of, rather than constitute, applied art." 861 F. Supp. at 315. VARA's legislative history leaves no doubt that "a new and independent work created from snippets of [excluded] materials, such as a collage, is of course not excluded" from the definition of a work of visual art. H.R. Rep. No. 514 at 14. The trial judge correctly ruled the work is not applied art precluded from protection under the Act.

III Work Made for Hire

Also excluded from the definition of a work of visual art is any work made for hire. 17 U.S.C. § 101(B). A "work made for hire" is defined in the Copyright Act, in relevant part, as "a work prepared by an employee within the scope of his or her employment." Id. § 101(1). Appellants maintain the work was made for hire and therefore is not a work of visual art under VARA. The district court held otherwise, finding that the plaintiffs were hired as independent contractors.

A. Reid Tests

The Copyright Act does not define the terms "employee" or "scope of employment." In Community for Creative Non-Violence v. Reid, 490 U.S. 730, 104 L. Ed. 2d 811, 109 S. Ct. 2166 (1989), the Supreme Court looked to the general common law of agency for guidance. It held that a multi-factor balancing test was required to determine if a work was produced for hire (by an employee) or was produced by an independent contractor. Reid, 490 U.S. at 751. The Court elaborated 13 specific factors:

> the hiring party's right to control the manner and means by which the product is accomplished. . . . the skill required; the source of the instrumentalities and tools; the location of the work; the duration of the relationship between the parties; whether the hiring party has the right to assign additional projects to the hired party; the extent of the hired party's discretion over when and how long to work; the method of payment; the hired party's role in hiring and paying assistants; whether the work is part of the regular business of the hiring party; whether the hiring party is in business; the provision of employee benefits; and the tax treatment of the hired party.

Reid, 490 U.S. at 751-52. While all of these factors are relevant, no single factor is determinative. Id. at 752. See also Hilton International Company v.

NLRB, 690 F.2d 318, 321 (2d Cir. 1982). Instead, the factors are weighed by referring to the facts of a given case. See Aymes v. Bonelli, 980 F.2d 857, 861 (2d Cir. 1992).

The district court determined that the sculpture was not "work for hire" and therefore not excluded from the definition of visual art. The Reid test is a list of factors not all of which may come into play in a given case. See Aymes, 980 F.2d at 861. The Reid test is therefore easily misapplied. We are usually reluctant to reverse a district court's factual findings as to the presence or absence of any of the Reid factors and do so only when the district court's findings are clearly erroneous. By contrast, the ultimate legal conclusion as to whether or not the sculpture is "work for hire" is reviewed de novo. The district court correctly stated the legal test. But some of its factual findings, we think, were clearly erroneous.

B. Factors Applied

The district court properly noted that Aymes established five factors which would be relevant in nearly all cases: the right to control the manner and means of production; requisite skill; provision of employee benefits; tax treatment of the hired party; whether the hired party may be assigned additional projects. See 980 F.2d at 861. Analysis begins with a discussion of these factors.

First, plaintiffs had complete artistic freedom with respect to every aspect of the sculpture's creation. Although the artists heeded advice or accepted suggestions from building engineers, architects, and others, such actions were not a relinquishment of their artistic freedom. The evidence strongly supports the finding that plaintiffs controlled the work's "manner and means." This fact, in turn, lent credence to their contention that they were independent contractors. See Hilton, 690 F.2d at 320. While artistic freedom remains a central factor in our inquiry, the Supreme Court has cautioned that "the extent of control the hiring party exercises over the details of the product is not dispositive." Reid, 490 U.S. at 752. Hence, resolving the question of whether plaintiffs had artistic freedom does not end the analysis.

The district court also correctly found the artists' conception and execution of the work required great skill in execution. Appellants' contention that the plaintiffs' reliance on assistants in some way mitigates the skill required for this work is meritless, particularly because each of the plaintiffs is a professional sculptor and the parties stipulated that professional sculpt-ing is a highly skilled occupation. The right to control the manner and means and the requisite skill needed for execution of this project were both properly found by the district court to weigh against "work for hire" status.

The trial court erred, however, when it ruled that the defendants could not assign the artists additional projects. First, the employment agreement between SIG Management Company and the artists clearly states that the artists agreed not only to install the sculpture but also to "render such other related services and duties as may be assigned to [them] from time to time by the Company." By the very terms of the contract the defendants and their predecessors in interest had the right to assign other related projects to the artists. The district court incorrectly decided that this language supported the artists' claim to be independent contractors. While the artists' obliga-tions were limited to related services and duties, the defendants nonetheless did have the right to assign to plaintiffs work other than the principal sculp-ture.

Further, the defendants did, in fact, assign such other projects. The district court concedes as much, explaining that "plaintiffs did create art work on the property other than that in the Lobby." Carter, 861 F. Supp. at 319. The record shows the artists performed projects on the sixth floor of the building, on the eighth floor, and in the boiler room. Thus, on at least three different occasions the plaintiffs were assigned additional projects, which they completed without further compensation. The trial court sug-gests this fact "does not undermine plaintiffs' contention that they were hired solely to install art work on the Property." Id. We disagree. If the artists were hired to perform work other than the sculpture (as both their em-ployment agreement and their actual practice suggests) then they were not hired solely to install the sculpture.

It makes no difference that all work performed by the plaintiffs was artistic in nature. The point is that the performance of other assigned work not of the artists' choosing supports a conclusion that the artists were not independent contractors but employees.

We must also consider factors the district court correctly found to favor finding the sculpture to be work for hire. Specifically, the provision of employee benefits and the tax treatment of the plaintiffs weigh strongly in favor of employee status. The defendants paid payroll and social security taxes, provided employee benefits such as life, health, and liability insurance and paid vacations, and contributed to unemployment insurance and workers' compensation funds on plaintiffs' behalf. Moreover, two of the three artists filed for unemployment benefits after their positions were terminated, listing the building's management company as their former employer. Other formal indicia of an employment relationship existed. For instance, each plaintiff was paid a weekly salary. The artists also agreed in their written contract that they would work principally for the defendants for the duration of their agreement on a 40-hour per week basis and they would only do other work to the extent that it would not "interfere with services to be provided" to the defendants. All of these facts strongly suggest the artists were employees.

Some of the other Reid factors bolster this view. The artists were provided with many (if not most) of the supplies used to create the sculpture. This factor was not, as the district court found, "inconclusive." The court also wrongly ruled that plaintiffs were hired for a "finite term of engagement." In fact, they were employed for a substantial period of time, their work continuing for over two years with no set date of termination (other than the sculpture's completion). Nor was the fact that the artists could not hire paid assistants without the defendants' approval "inconclusive" as the trial court erroneously found. Instead, this and the other just enumerated factors point towards an employer-employee relationship between the parties.

In reaching its conclusion, the district court also relied partly on the artists' copyright ownership of the sculpture, viewing such ownership as a "plus factor." We are not certain whether this element is a "plus factor," and therefore put off for another day deciding whether copyright ownership is probative of independent contractor status. Even were it to be weighed as a "plus factor," it would not change the outcome in this case.

C. Employee Status

Our review of the legal conclusion drawn from balancing the various Reid factors persuades us that the factors that weigh in favor of finding the artists were employees outweigh those factors supporting the artists' claim that they were independent contractors. One of the factors that did not persuade us was the appellants' simplistic contention that usage of the words "employ" or "employment" in the agreements between the artists and SIG or the Limited Partnership establishes that the plaintiffs were employees.

The use of these terms does not transform them into "magic words" imbued with legally controlling significance.

Again, we emphasize that despite the conclusion reached we do not intend to marginalize factors such as artistic freedom and skill, making them peripheral to the status inquiry. The fact that artists will always be retained for creative purposes cannot serve to minimalize this factor of the Reid test, even though it will usually favor VARA protection. Also, that the work was produced on the employer's premises is a necessary incident to all nonremovable art and therefore should not carry great weight. Similarly, we were not swayed by the boilerplate contract language or the accounting decision to deduct FICA taxes. To so read § 101 runs against the broad remedial purposes of VARA. As discussed earlier, the moral rights of the artist whose artistic work comes under VARA's umbrella are to be protected, not ignored, in light of Congress' pathbreaking legislation.

Moreover, because the Reid test is fact-dependent, future cases involving the work for hire question will not always fit neatly into an employee or independent contractor category. We also recognize that by counting indicia such as health insurance and paid vacations against the artists' independent contractor status, it may appear that artists regrettably are being forced to choose between the personal benefits inuring in an employment relationship and VARA's protection of the artists' work afforded only to independent contractors. Of course, when an employer today denies an artist "basic attributes of employment" like vacation time or health benefits, such denial will be wholly inconsistent with a "work for hire" defense. See Aymes, 980 F.2d at 862-63.

Consequently, while the existence of payroll formalities alone would not be controlling, see Reid, 490 U.S. at 742 n.8, in combination with other factors, it may lead to a conclusion that a given work is one made for hire. Such other factors include: plaintiffs under their contract could be and were in fact assigned projects in addition to the work in the lobby; they were paid a weekly salary for over two years for a contracted 40 hours of work per week; they were furnished many of the needed supplies necessary to create the work; and plaintiffs could not hire paid assistants without defendants' consent. These factors, properly considered and weighed with the employee benefits granted plaintiffs and the tax treatment accorded them, are more than sufficient to demonstrate that the artists were employees, and the sculpture is therefore a work made for hire as a matter of law.

IV Defendants' Counterclaim and Plaintiffs' Cross-appeal

Finally, since we have determined that the work is one made for hire and therefore outside the scope of VARA's protection, we need not discuss that Act's broad protection of visual art and the protection it affords works of art incorporated into a building. Also, as plaintiffs' sculpture was not protected from removal because the artists were employees and not independent contractors, we need not reach the defendants' Fifth Amendment takings argument.

Moreover, because the sculpture is not protected by VARA from removal resulting in its destruction or alteration, we do not address plaintiffs' contentions that VARA entitles them to complete the "unfinished" portion of the work, that they are entitled to reasonable costs and attorney's fees, and that appellants tortiously interfered with the artists' contract with SIG and the Limited Partnership. Finally, the district court dismissed defendants' counterclaim against the artists for waste, finding, inter alia, that such a cause of action under New York law may only be brought by a landlord against a tenant. See 861 F. Supp. at 334-36. Appellants have failed to persuade us that it was error to dismiss this counterclaim.

Conclusion

Accordingly, the district court's order insofar as it held the work was one not made for hire is reversed and the injunction vacated. In all other respects, the order of the district court is affirmed. Each party to bear its own costs.

Notes and Questions

1. The Court of Appeals recounts the tremendous opposition to incorporation of Article 6bis of the Berne Convention into U.S. law. The act implementing the Berne Convention into U.S. law expressly precludes direct reliance on the Convention as a source of rights.[1]

---

[1] 17 U.S.C. §104(c).

2. The "work made for hire" doctrine in U.S. law finds its counterpart in other countries and regions. The essence of the doctrine is that when a work is produced by an author or artist within the course and scope of employment by another person, that other person will hold the copyright to the work. As the court observes in the preceding case, there are a variety of factors that may go into determining whether an author or artist stands in an employee-employer relationship. The work made for hire doctrine is of paramount importance in the business context, and lawyers who represent businesses that contract for expressive works — including computer software — must pay very close attention to which party will hold the copyright at the end of the day.

Q. Computer Software

The importance of computer software to modern economic life is self-evident. Yet computer software entered the mainstream legal world only about two decades ago, as its commercial exploitation began to be commonplace. There were many questions about computer software that lawyers confronted. It is generally quite easy to copy software. In making a program available to a purchaser or test-user, how could the creator be assured that the software would not be copied and used? The commercialization of software appeared to depend upon some form of legal protection. Yet what form?

Patents are fairly cumbersome. The application process is lengthy and technical. Both novelty and inventive step are elements that would often be difficult to satisfy in the software patenting context. Moreover, commercial software is always changing. One version of a program is soon superceded by another as new features are added and bugs (programming errors) are worked out. A single concept may be embodied in several different versions of the same program written in different programming languages. Would it be possible to draft individual patent applications in a way that would encompass the evolutionary and differentiated character of software? Would a new application need to be filed each time some substantial change to a program was made? Finally, and perhaps most importantly, it was (and remains) unclear whether the basic algorithms underlying computer programs are patentable subject matter, since it has long been understood that mathematical formulas are not patentable as such (in that they are thought to represent laws of nature or discoveries).[1]

One potential alternative to the patent was *sui generis* protection that would take into account the unique characteristics of software. *Sui generis* protection might include several characteristics of the patent — such as a prohibition against independent creation and protection of the overall concept — while perhaps enjoying a moderate term of protection. The government of Japan advocated the development of a form of *sui generis* protection, and there was no shortage of proposals in Europe and the United States.

Ultimately, the practical needs of industry triumphed over the government policy-makers. Lawyers used the tools at hand to fashion protection for their clients under the copyright laws. There were (and are) decided advantages to copyright. First, copyright laws were in place throughout most of the world, so there would be no time lost in the negotiation and implementation of new norms. Second, copyright protection is automatic. Under the Berne Convention the absence of formalities is prescribed. (Though recall that in the early 1980s the United States was not party to the Berne Convention.) Thus, assuming that software would be considered copyrightable subject matter, protection would be easy to obtain. Third, copyright law is flexible. Each addition or change to a program would automatically be the subject of protection. Fourth, copyright is of long duration, and while this long duration may not always be of practical use, it was perceived as preferable to the shorter terms generally proposed for *sui generis* protection.

---

[1] Just what an *algorithm* is may not always be entirely clear. One of the authors of this book was some years ago jogging in the hills of Los Angeles with a pioneer of the personal computer industry when the author realized he needed to return to their hotel for a meeting. Not knowing how to get back to the hotel, he asked direction from the computer scientist. "Well," queried the scientist, "Do you know what an algorithm is?" The author replied, "Perhaps, but in any event why don't you tell me?" "Allow me to explain by illustration," said the scientist. "To return to the hotel, you will always run straight, except that you will turn right at every third stoplight, and left at the only stop sign between here and the hotel. In other words," he continued, "an algorithm is a set of instructions expressed as a mathematical formula." This story is true, and historical accuracy demands that the author note he became quite lost on his solo return to the hotel. He does not know whether this was due to proper execution of a flawed algorithm, or to flawed execution of a sound algorithm.

Finally, there was the perspective of the practicing lawyers who represented clients in the computer industry. The patent bar of each country is highly specialized, and qualification for the patent bar generally requires technical training. Many lawyers representing the computer industry were (and are) not patent lawyers, and these lawyers stood to lose substantial business if representation of the software industry was channeled to the patent bar. There was an incentive for the non-patent lawyer to promote copyright protection or a form of *sui generis* protection outside the specialized patent field.

The adoption of the copyright as the accepted method for protecting computer software left a myriad of questions to be answered. Though some of the most basic questions have been the subject of fairly consistent legislative and judicial rule-making, many questions remain unevenly answered (or not answered at all). Moreover, the computer software industry is dynamic — the "thing" that is covered by copyright protection continues to evolve. Legislatures and courts are continually pressed for answers to new questions.

1. The European Union

a. The Inventive Step in Germany

The German Supreme Court stimulated the approximation of computer software law in the European Union by its 1985 decision in the so-called *Inkasso* case *(Re The Protection of Computer Programs)* which follows. This decision was sharply criticized by major computer firms which invest heavily in the creation and distribution of software. The response of the European Commission took the form of the Software Directive, which we will examine after *Inkasso*. What is of great interest to observe is that the "radical" approach of the German Supreme Court may have ultimately struck a resonating chord in the U.S. federal courts. Though the terminology used by the Second Circuit Court of Appeals in the 1992 *Computer Associates v. Altai* decision reviewed *infra* may differ, as you study *Computer Associates* keep in mind the question whether the approach taken by the Second Circuit is in fact similar to that of the *Inkasso* Court.

Re The Protection of Computer Programs (I ZR 52/83)

Bundesgerichtshof (German Federal Supreme Court)
[1986] ECC 498
9 MAY 1985

Panel: The President, Prof. Dr. Frhr. von Gamm; Drs. Piper, Erdmann, Teplitzky and Scholz-Hoppe, Judges

Headnote:

Appeal from the Oberlandesgericht (Regional Court of Appeal), Karlsruhe.

*****

Facts:

The plaintiff firm is a debt-collection agency whose business is concerned with the recovery of outstanding liabilities. The first defendant is a partnership active in the sector of electronic data processing, which was established by the second and third defendants in 1979 and began trading on 1 September of that year. The second defendant is the managing director with authority to represent the firm; until 24 April 1981 the third defendant was a joint managing director. The two parties are in dispute as to whether the defendants are entitled to install a computer program for debt collection (produced for the plaintiff with the co-operation, if not more, of the second defendant), for other purposes and to market the program.

By a contract of 24 March 1976 the plaintiff commissioned the second defendant, who at the time was still active with the Company N — Computer AG as a programmer, to produce a program for debt collection. The purpose of the program was to enable the working procedures arising in connection with the process of collecting outstanding payments to be carried out using an N — Computer-Systems 8870/2 computer already acquired by the plaintiff. For producing the program, including the specification book, and for giving introductory instruction to the staff operating it, a fixed sum of 20,000 DM was agreed.

The second defendant carried out his work for the plaintiff on free evenings and at weekends almost exclusively on the plaintiff's business premises. He began by formulating the program to be developed in its basic features in a set of specifications. The final product of his work was the "S — -Inkasso-Programm" (S — - debt-collection program) submitted by the plaintiff in printed form with its pleadings as Annex A (the so-called S — version). That program, transferred to the plaintiff in the source code, has been in operation in its business since the end of 1978. The program is drawn up in the computer language COBOL. For the purposes of his work the plaintiff made information and documents available to the second defendant. Parts of the program (including the data files on postal codes, courts and debtors) were worked out in the plaintiff's place of business.

In spring 1979 the plaintiff under a licensing agreement allowed the company M — GmbH in Munich to use the S — debt-collection program in the object code in return for payment of 80,000 DM. The copyright mark of the program subject to licence referred to the plaintiff, and the second defendant was named as author. The second defendant carried out the installation work necessary to adapt the program to the business requirements of the company M — . He also developed further subsidiary programs for the company M — making use of the source program on which the plaintiff's program was based. For that additional work he received about 5,000 DM from the company M — . The plaintiff had agreed with the second defendant to pay him 10,000 DM. He regarded that payment as being in consideration of his agreement to the granting of the licence; the plaintiff sees it as remuneration for the additional programming work which he did for the company M — . The plaintiff added the debt-collection program installed for M — to its pleadings in printed form as Annex B (the so-called M — version).

In 1979 the plaintiff also entered into negotiations for a licensing agreement in favour of the firm E — -Inkasso — und Handelsauskunftei F — KG in Munich. By a letter of 24 July 1979 the firm E — -Inkasso informed the plaintiff that it was withdrawing its offer to buy. A few days earlier, on 19 July 1979, E — -Inkasso had concluded a licensing agreement with the second defendant for a data-processing program package called "integrierte Inkassoabrechnung" in the COBOL language for use on the N — -Computer-System 8870. The agreed remuneration was 45,000 DM of which the defendants according to their statements have so far received 41,000 DM. The program installed by the second defendant in the autumn of 1979 was put into operation by the firm E — -Inkasso in January 1980. The documents on which the program was based were seized by the Landeskriminalamt Baden-Wurttemberg in the course of an official search carred out as a step in investigative proceedings commenced as a result of an information laid by the plaintiff against the second defendant. The program found on the premises of E — -Inkasso was transcribed by the Landeskriminalamt on to its own disks. The program involved is the one submitted by the plaintiff with its pleadings printed out as Annex C (the so-called E — -version).

In the course of his work in the plaintiff's business, which ceased after November 1979, the second defendant made two copies of the program for himself. On 13 October 1979 he transcribed the whole of the S — debt-collection program including data files on postal codes and local courts on to disks which he had brought with him.

The plaintiff maintains that the commercialisation by the defendants of the debt-colection program produced for it is wrongful under the rules of the law on copyright, competition and contract and asks for an injunction against them, for an order requiring them to produce information, for damages and for the destruction of the data supports.

*****

The plaintiff asked the court:

1. to order the defendants to desist from, and refrain from keeping any means of, holding for sale, selling, marketing and/or advertising in the commercial sphere for the purposes of competition any computer programs and stored data with an integrated debt-collection, processing and accounting system relating to notices to debtors for the purposes of legal proceedings or otherwise and to all stages of enforcement, no matter in what sequence of programs or what programming language or computer system is used. . . .

*****

5. to order the defendants to destroy, or in the case of magnetic disks physically to erase, all data supports in their possession, and in particular magnetic disks and print-outs incorporating or containing computer programs under paragraph 1.

The defendants defended those claims. They argued that the second defendant was the sole author of the debt-collection program produced for the plaintiff; the plaintiff had merely given suggestions and acted in the capacity of an assistant. The second defendant as programmer had made the real creative contribution by building up the master file and the allocation of data. The master file included any of the debtor's personal data considered to be necessary and the allocation of data concerned the determination of the way in which the programmer's individual elements and sentences were to be treated. From that followed the arrangement of the fields and the attribution of letters, numbers and other symbols to specific places on the storage memory or the screen.

The second defendant (according to the defense) only granted the plaintiff a simple right to use the S — -debt-collection program, so that the defendants remained at liberty to market the program by the granting of licences. At the time when the contract for the production of the debt-collection program was concluded none of the parties had yet given any thought to marketing it and consequently, as was not in dispute, they had not dealt with the question of the right to use it in the written contract. The level of the remuneration paid was also evidence against the transfer to the plaintiff of an exclusive right to use the program.

The defendants also denied that they had marketed the S — -debt-collection program. They had installed a considerably improved program.

The defendants also took the view that they had a right to retain possession of the program. The application of the S — program by the plaintiff had subsequently been extended to the processing of more than 200,000 outstanding cases, which under section 36 of the Copyright Act (Urhebergesetz (UrhG)) made an adjustment of the remuneration paid to the second defendant necessary.

*****

Decision:

I.

The appellate court, disagreeing with the Landgericht, considered that the claim was well-founded mainly on the grounds of infringement of copyright (sections 97 and 98 in conjunction with sections 15(1), 16, 17, 23 and 31(3) of the Copyright Act) rather than infringement by the defendants of competition law. It held that the S — -debt-collection program was a work protected by copyright and found there was the necessary personal intellectual creativeness in the collection and arrangement of the processed material. In so doing it left undecided the question of the stage in the development towards a program ready for operation at which services were performed which were capable of protection. It also left undecided the question whether the second defendant was to be seen as the sole author or as co-author. It did not regard the matter as relevant because the second defendant had in any case granted the plaintiff the exclusive right to use the debt-collection program (section 31(3) of the Copyright Act). The defendants were therefore not entitled to market the program. According to the court, in addition to the claim for an injunction prohibiting the marketing of the program against all three of the defendants on copyright grounds, the plaintiff also had a corresponding contractual claim against the second defendant.

Since the defendants set themselves up as entitled to market the program, according to the appellate court, the plaintiff's claim for an injunction was well-founded. *****

The claims for information, compensation for damage and destruction, in so far as the defendants were in breach of the plaintiff's marketing rights to the programs. . . . The second defendant did not have any right to retain possession.

II.

*****

2. Claims in copyright

The appellate court's reasoning on the possibility of copyright protection for the S — -debt-collection program in issue in this case cannot be sustained on further consideration of the law.

The court was certainly correct in regarding computer programs as being in principle entitled to copyright protection. But the findings made by the court are not sufficient for a decision that the S — -debt-collection program is capable of being protected by copyright. The defendants' appeal must lead to the quashing of the judgment in dispute and remission of the matter to the appellate court.

(a) Computer programs fall within the area of science for the purposes of section 1 of the Copyright Act, and copyright protection is therefore in principle available to them. The relevant protection, according to whether they are represented linguistically (symbolically) or graphically, is that for a literary work (section 2(1)(1) of the Copyright Act) or that for a presentation of a scientific or technical nature (section 2(1)(7) of the Act).

(aa) The concept of a work for the purposes of section 2 of the Act entails that the work in its material form must be accessible to intellectual comprehension. That does not only apply to the completed work in the form of a computer program ready for operation. In the case of works which (as with computer programs as a rule) come about in stages the specific levels of formulation which are necessary for the availability of protection can also be achieved in the preceding stages of development. For the decision of the question of copyright there is no need for a very detailed differentiation between the individual phases of development, which in the literature on data processing are categorised in different ways (See Wittmer: Der Schutz von Computersoftware — Urheberrecht oder Sonderrecht, Bern, 1981, p 38); for it is irrelevant to the question of protecton as a literary work or as a presentation of a scientific or technical nature at what stage in the creation a sufficient level of formulation for copyright purposes becomes ascertainable. In order to understand the levels of formulation occurring in the production of a computer program a broad classification into three phases of development is sufficient.

In the first phase the general problem-solving takes place (also known as problem — or systems analysis). It is based on mathematical premises and logical proofs. (For further details see Reimar Kohler: Der urheberrechtliche Schutz der Rechenprogramme, Munich 1968, p 11 et seq, with further references). The result of the analysis phase is the proposed solution, which is described in a study (also called the specification). This description is to be regarded as a specific formulation falling under the concept of a written work (section 2(1)(1) of the Act). The fact that, in addition to the colloquial language, mathematical signs, numbers, letters and symbols are used does not prevent that conclusion (See the BGH judgment of 25 November 1958, I ZR 15/18: [1959] GRUR 251 (Standardised Travel Ticket); it is likewise irrelevant that such signs and symbols are not understandable by everyone but only by experts.

In the second phase follows the more specific formulation of the solution to the problem. In a data-flow chart (flow diagram), which is not necessary in simple programs, the proposed solution which has been devised is represented in the form of a graphic presentation of the sequence of instructions and information in the manner required for the purposes of the data-processing equipment. The sequence of events is usually presented by means of a series of blocks, switches and loops, for which there are a number of symbols available, which are written down by the person drawing the chart accordingly. The data-flow chart falls within the category of presentations of a scientific and technical nature (section 2(1)(7) of the Act) since it uses graphic representation as the means of expression. Here too the use of mathematical, technical and graphic symbols does not rule out the possibility of copyright protection. (See the BGH judgment of 3 July 1964, I b ZR 146/62: [1965] GRUR 45-6 (Town Plans)). In accordance with the data-flow chart or in some cases directly on the basis of the general solution to the problem the specific program-flow chart (block diagram) is produced. It shows the way in which the proposed solution will proceed on the actual equipment in question, that being done in the form of a symbolic program making use of (largely standardised) visual symbols, short descriptions and sequences of marks which are often derived from the language in which the program is to be drafted. The chart is mostly a mixed form of written work and presentation of a scientific or technical nature.

In the third phase follows the actual encoding of the program. There the program-flow chart is transformed into a sequence of instructions understandable by the computer. The encoding is usually done in the first instance in a programming language not taking account of the language of the actual computer to be used; the result is the so-called primary or source program which can be read by the expert. By means of mechanical translation of the source program the so-called object program comes about, which corresponds directly to the language of the machine. The definitive encoded program is contained in a data support (magnetic tape, disk etc). The complete computer program is formulated as a sequence of instructions which when recorded on a support readable by the machine makes it possible for a machine with data-processing capacities to signal, carry out or achieve a specific function or task. (See DIN standard 44 300: s 1(1) of the Model Rules for the Protection of Computer Software). In the case of the finished program copyright protection as a written work under section 2(1)(1) of the Act comes into consideration. Such protection is not ruled out by the use of symbolic language even if the program can only be read with the help of the machine. (See von Gamm, [1969] WRP 96-7).

The foregoing summary of the kinds of formulation which usually occur in the development of programs does not exclude the possibility that in the preliminary stages further results of the work (such as descriptions, documentation or sub-programs) may be produced in respect of which copyright protection is available. To complete the picture, accessory material subject to copyright may also be produced which, like computer programs and program descriptions, may also be classified under the main concept of computer software. (See s 1 of the Model Rules, in [1978] GRUR Int 290, also at [1979] GRUR 306 et seq.)

Differentiation in the assessment of the availability of copyright protection, conditioned by the production of the program in stages, does not become superfluous even if one understands modern software development as a uniform creative process of work completion having a single purpose and aimed entirely at the production of the final program, in which all the circumstances and features of the earlier stages of development which are important for the character of the computer program as a work are fused into the end product, namely the program in its form ready for operation. It is true that the real object in dispute in most cases is the computer program in its form ready for operation (in source or object code). Nevertheless differentiation does become important inter alia when infringing activities are confined to the taking over of only individual programming phases from a third party's complete program or when there is a dispute about authorship (or co-authorship) where there are several parties interested who have contributed in different ways to the work.

(bb) Computer programs and their preliminary stages can in principle also manifest the personal intellectual creativity which is necessary for copyright protection by virtue of section 2(2) of the Act.

In the individual phases of programming work of an intellectual nature is performed by systems analysts or programmers. The intellectual content of the ideas is embodied and expressed in the formation and direction of the ideas in the matter presented and/or in a special ingenuity of form or manner in the collection, application and arrangement of the material proffered. (See BGH judgment of 29 March 1984, I ZR 32/82: [1984] GRUR 659-60, [1985] ECC 562, (Documents in Support of Tender)). For the purposes of a decision on the availability of copyright for scientific or technical works a substantial level of intellectual creativity in the direction and formation of ideas in the matter presented is frequently lacking; scientific learning and the results of science are free for copyright purposes and accessible to everyone (See BGH judgment of 21 November 1980, I ZR 106/78: [1981] GRUR 325-3 (State Examination Papers), and of 27 February 1981, I ZR 29/79: [1981] GRUR 520-2 (Collection of Questions)); their presentation and formulation, in so far as they have to be in their actual form offered for scientific reasons or are in a usual form because of the application of the methods of expression usual in the technical area in question, lack the necessary original character. The rule of calculation used in the computer program, therefore, relating to a given calculator (the so-called algorithm) is just as little entitled to copyright protection as other mathematical or technical learning applied in the production of the program, which as parts of general scientific learning must be free and available to everyone.

For the purposes of copyright protection for computer programs and their preliminary stages, therefore, only the form and nature of the collection, application and arrangement of the material comes into consideration. In this area there is adequate room for individual and original solutions, and that is so in all three phases of development. This is predominantly acknowledged nowadays in the cases of problem analysis, data-flow charts and program-flow charts. (See Frankfurt OLG: [1983] GRUR 753, 755 and [1985] BB 139, 141; BAG: [1984] GRUR 429, 431; von Gamm [1969] WRP 96, 98; Kolle: [1974] GRUR 7, 9 and [1982] GRUR 443, 453; Sieber: [1981] BB 1547, 1551; Haberstumpf: [1982] GRUR 142, 147). But also in the actual encoding, at least of the source program, originality of composition cannot be excluded a priori. (See BAG: [1984] GRUR 429, 431, (aliter for the object program); E Ulmer: Der Urheberrechtsschutz wissenschaftlicher Werke unter besonderer Berucksichtigung der Programme elektronischer Rechenanlagen, Munich, 1967, pp 17 et seq; E Ulmer: Comment on BAG judgment above; Kolle: [1974] GRUR, 7, 9 and [1982] GRUR 443, 453). It is conceivable that in an individual case an insufficiently original program-flow chart may still leave sufficient room for individuality of choice and allocation in relation to the encoding.

Finally, the possibility of copyright protection for computer programs does not founder on the requirement of an intellectual-aesthetic content. An aesthetic content defined in terms of beauty is not required by section 2(2) of the Copyright Act. In so far as the concept of aesthetics is applied in the case of literary works in the traditional sense of the word as a mentally perceptible original composition produced by intellectual effort (Thus von Gamm: [1969] WRP 96, 97; cf E Ulmer/Kolle [1982] GRUR 489, 493) it coincides with the interpretation set out above.

(cc) While it must be allowed that copyright protection is in principle possible for computer programs, it remains to be considered in individual cases whether the program and its preliminary stages do achieve a sufficiently creative level of originality within the meaning of section 2(2) of the Copyright Act. The question has to be answered in accordance with the principles developed hitherto in judicial decisions. On that basis the question of the level of originality is to be assessed according to the total impression of intellectual creativity of the specific composition, and that must be done moreover through an overall comparison with pre-existing compositions. (See 27 BGH 351, 356, et seq ("Candida" Script). Such a comparison does not contain any test of novelty (which is not relevant to the question of copyright protection (See 18 BGHZ 319, 322 (Building Plan)), but answers the question whether the specific composition has individual characteristics compared with compositions already known. The starting point is known programs and the work produced in the individual stages of development with such known and usual arrangements, systems and principles of construction and treatment as they may have. Any forms of composition which remain in proximity to them do not possess a sufficiently creative level of originality; merely mechanical or technical advances on and developments of existing knowledge remain in this category. (Cf von Gamm: [1969] WRP 96, 99). If creative characteristics are established by the test of an overall comparison with what is already known, they must then be set against the products of an average programmer. What the average composer can do, the merely workmanlike mechanical or technical combination and connection of the material, cannot be subject to any protection. Only after a substantial advance does the lower level of protectability begin, and it presupposes a clear superiority of the compositional activity in the matter of the selection, collection, arrangement and treatment of the information and instructions over the current average of achievement. (Thus the decided cases, most recently BGH: [1984] GRUR 659, 661, [1985] ECC

562 (Documents in Support of Tender). Especial originality can also be achieved by the processing, reworking, and working-in of known elements and forms.

The question of the creative level of composition does not in principle depend on the quantitative scope of the program, nor on the expenditure and costs with which it was created or on whether the problem posed was new. Furthermore, it is not decisive for the question of the quality of the work that a number of programmers given the same commission would develop differing programs. (See Frankfurt OLG: [1983] GRUR 753, 755).

If it appears in a particular case that a sufficient level of creativity in composition can be established only in respect of the initial phase in the production of a program (e.g. only the general solution to the problem and the data-flow chart), but not in the later stages of the work (the program-flow chart and particularly the encoding), that does not in principle prevent the possibility of copyright protection for the completed work, that is, for the program ready for operation. In the case of an undivided production of a work the creative preliminary work enters into the final product. Where a work is created by separate stages the general problem-solving would have to be treated as an individual work, the creatively composed data-flow chart as a reworking dependent on that work (section 3 of the Act) and the program-flow chart and encoding as dependent use in the form of copying (section 16 of the Act). If several authors participate in the production of the program as a homogenous work then, unless the participants intend a contrary result, there would be a joint production of a work (section 8 of the Act) of which the computer program ready to be put into operation constitutes the final work entitled to copyright protection.

(b) The appellate court did in essence begin correctly from the principles set out above. But its acceptance that the debt-collection program in dispute constitutes a creative achievement (section 2(2) of the Act) is not supported by its findings as to fact. This point of the defendants' appeal is correct.

(aa) The appellate court set out the position on the level of creative composition as follows: creative performance in the composition of the program can be perceived in the collection and treatment of the material processed. That is apparent from the presentation of the debt-collection procedure by means of the printed-out program, from the arrangement of the necessary procedural steps and the assessment of the data and their treatment in relation to each other, all of which went beyond what was already available by reference to the existing legal and procedural provisions. A characteristic treatment of differing data sources was already apparent in the specification produced by the second defendant. The program is not confined to the sequence of individual steps in the procedure for the giving of notices for judicial and other purposes. The master file, such as the files on creditors, debtors and local courts, which taken by themselves do not give any indication of original achievement as regards their composition, have been combined with other elements, such as the analysis of cost effectiveness (analysis of the margin of cover), structural analysis of debtors and, to take a particular example, a progam with variable fees for different creditors. . . . . .To decide this issue it is not necessary (in the appellate court's opinion) to decide whether individual elements of the program in detail or the printed-out forms manifest the quality of original work or again whether the transformation of the systems analysis into the so-called source program is by itself of original quality.

(bb) However that may be, the appellate court's findings are not sufficient to establish copyright protection because the court in essence confined itself to describing the working procedures which the plaintiff's program enabled to be performed. The working procedures presented are not entitled to protection as to their contents. They cannot be monopolized by the plaintiff but must remain freely available to other producers and users of debt-collection programs, especially as they predominantly involve the self-evident features of debt-collection procedures (such as the procedures for ordinary notices, notices for the purposes of court proceedings, card indexes on the processing of cases and the data files). The appellate court was aware of this and saw the creative achievement as being in the arrangement, treatment, connection and combination of the individual features of the work. But the relevant findings of the court are of an overall nature and without detailed reasoning. It is not clear in what the individuality of the arrangement and combination consists. It has not been established that the arrangement and combination of the individual elements are not already available from the ordinary operation of the debt-collection program and constitute more than a technical or mechanical relating of each to the other; in the same way it has not been clarified how the program in dispute disginguishes itself from other available programs. In the absence of the relevant findings this Court is not in a position to ascertain whether this is a case of a creative work which is clearly above the average. . . . .

In view of the no more than general finding by the appellate court that the features of the work set out are combined with each other in an original way, there must be additional doubt as to the certainty of the injunction against marketing granted by the court. For it would not be clear to the defendants in which actual arrangement and grouping the various working stages of the debt-collection process (the contents of which are in the public domain) were subject to protection in favour of the plaintiff.

In the result therefore the question of the availability of copyright protection for the S — -debt-collection program requires further clarification by the court with jurisdiction as to fact.

*****

Notes and Questions

1. The German Supreme Court observes that there are a number of phases in the development of a computer program, and that copyright protection may be available at the various stages of development. In this Court's view, it is not necessarily — or primarily — at the level of the programming code that copyright infringement may take place.

2. In the key passages of the decision, the Court holds that copyright attaches only to program elements that reflect a substantial advance over known computer programming elements, and only if the advance embodies a skill level above that of the average programmer. "What the average composer can do, the merely workmanlike mechanical or technical combination and connection of the material, cannot be subject to any protection . . . and it presupposes a clear superiority of the compositional activity in the matter of the selection, collection, arrangement and treatment of the information and instructions over the current average of achievement."

Compare the language of the German Supreme Court in *Inkasso* to the language of the U.S. Supreme Court in *Feist, supra*. Both Courts indicate that copyright protection is predicated on a minimum level of creativity. Where do the courts differ?

3. The German Supreme Court is apparently seeking to leave the fundamental elements necessary to construct computer programs open to public

use. What other legal routes might be taken to achieve this goal? Is this a goal we should seek to achieve?

---

b. Rejection of the Inventive Step by the Union: The Software Directive

The approach of the German Supreme Court was decisively rejected by the EU in the Software Directive. In addition to eliminating any test of creativity beyond that of originality, the Software Directive addressed the important and controversial question of reverse engineering. The Software Directive gives express recognition to a right of rental that is distinct from the right of first sale.

COUNCIL DIRECTIVE of 14 May 1991 on the legal protection of computer programs (91/250/EEC)*

The Council of the European Communities, [recitals omitted]
Has Adopted this Directive:

Article 1
Object of protection

1. In accordance with the provisions of this Directive, Member States shall protect computer programs, by copyright, as literary works within the meaning of the Berne Convention for the Protection of Literary and Artistic Works. For the purposes of this Directive, the term "computer programs" shall include their preparatory design material.

2. Protection in accordance with this Directive shall apply to the expression in any form of a computer program. Ideas and principles which underlie any element of a computer program, including those which underlie its interfaces, are not protected by copyright under this Directive.

---

*91/250/EEC, 1991 OJ L 122, Document Date: May 14, 1991.

3. A computer program shall be protected if it is original in the sense that it is the author's own intellectual creation. No other criteria shall be applied to determine its eligibility for protection.

Article 2
Authorship of computer programs

1. The author of a computer program shall be the natural person or group of natural persons who has created the program or, where the legislation of the Member State permits, the legal person designated as the rightholder by that legislation. Where collective works are recognized by the legislation of a Member State, the person considered by the legislation of the Member State to have created the work shall be deemed to be its author.

2. In respect of a computer program created by a group of natural persons jointly, the exclusive rights shall be owned jointly.

3. Where a computer program is created by an employee in the execution of his duties or following the instructions given by his employer, the employer exclusively shall be entitled to exercise all economic rights in the program so created, unless otherwise provided by contract.

Article 3
Beneficiaries of protection

Protection shall be granted to all natural or legal persons eligible under national copyright legislation as applied to literary works.

Article 4
Restricted Acts

Subject to the provisions of Articles 5 and 6, the exclusive rights of the rightholder within the meaning of Article 2, shall include the right to do or to authorize:

(a) the permanent or temporary reproduction of a computer program by any means and in any form, in part or in whole. Insofar as loading, displaying, running, transmission or storage of the computer program necessitate such reproduction, such acts shall be subject to authorization by the rightholder;

(b) the translation, adaptation, arrangement and any other alteration of a computer program and the reproduction of the results thereof, without prejudice to the rights of the person who alters the program;

(c) any form of distribution to the public, including the rental, of the original computer program or of copies thereof. The first sale in the Community of a copy of a program by the rightholder or with his consent shall exhaust the distribution right within the Community of that copy, with the exception of the right to control further rental of the program or a copy thereof.

Article 5
Exceptions to the restricted acts

1. In the absence of specific contractual provisions, the acts referred to in Article 4(a) and (b) shall not require authorization by the rightholder where they are necessary for the use of the computer program by the lawful acquirer in accordance with its intended purpose, including for error correction.

2. The making of a back-up copy by a person having a right to use the computer program may not be prevented by contract insofar as it is necessary for that use.

3. The person having a right to use a copy of a computer program shall be entitled, without the authorization of the rightholder, to observe, study or test the functioning of the program in order to determine the ideas and principles which underlie any element of the program if he does so while performing any of the acts of loading, displaying, running, transmitting or storing the program which he is entitled to do.

Article 6
Decompilation

1. The authorization of the rightholder shall not be required where reproduction of the code and translation of its form within the meaning of Article 4(a) and (b) are indispensable to obtain the information necessary to

achieve the interoperability of an independently created computer program with other programs, provided that the following conditions are met: (a) these acts are performed by the licensee or by another person having a right to use a copy of a program, or on their behalf by a person authorized to to so; (b) the information necessary to achieve interoperability has not previously been readily available to the persons referred to in subparagraph (a); and (c) these acts are confined to the parts of the original program which are necessary to achieve interoperability.

2. The provisions of paragraph 1 shall not permit the information obtained through its application:

(a) to be used for goals other than to achieve the interoperability of the independently created computer program;

(b) to be given to others, except when necessary for the interoperability of the independently created computer program; or

(c) to be used for the development, production or marketing of a computer program substantially similar in its expression, or for any other act which infringes copyright.

3. In accordance with the provisions of the Berne Convention for the protection of Literary and Artistic Works, the provisions of this Article may not be interpreted in such a way as to allow its application to be used in a manner which unreasonably prejudices the right holder's legitimate interests or conflicts with a normal exploitation of the computer program.

Article 7
Special measures of protection

1. Without prejudice to the provisions of Articles 4, 5 and 6, Member States shall provide, in accordance with their national legislation, appropriate remedies against a person committing any of the acts listed in subparagraphs (a), (b) and (c) below:

(a) any act of putting into circulation a copy of a computer program knowing, or having reason to believe, that it is an infringing copy;

(b) the possession, for commercial purposes, of a copy of a computer program knowing, or having reason to believe, that it is an infringing copy;

(c) any act of putting into circulation, or the possession for commercial purposes of, any means the sole intended purpose of which is to facilitate the unauthorized removal or circumvention of any technical device which may have been applied to protect a computer program.

2. Any infringing copy of a computer program shall be liable to seizure in accordance with the legislation of the Member State concerned.

3. Member States may provide for the seizure of any means referred to in paragraph 1(c).

Article 8
Term of protection

1. Protection shall be granted for the life of the author and for fifty years after his death or after the death of the last surviving author; where the computer program is an anonymous or pseudonymous work, or where a legal person is designated as the author by national legislation in accordance with Article 2(1), the term of protection shall be fifty years from the time that the computer program is first lawfully made available to the public. The term of protection shall be deemed to begin on the first of January of the year following the abovementioned events.

2. Member States which already have a term of protection longer than that provided for in paragraph 1 are allowed to maintain their present term until such time as the term of protection for copyright works is harmonized by Community law in a more general way.

Article 9
Continued application of other legal provisions

1. The provisions of this Directive shall be without prejudice to any other legal provisions such as those concerning patent rights, trade-marks, unfair competition, trade secrets, protection of semi-conductor products or the

law of contract. Any contractual provisions contrary to Article 6 or to the exceptions provided for in Article 5(2) and (3) shall be null and void.

2. The provisions of this Directive shall apply also to programs created before 1 January 1993 without prejudice to any acts concluded and rights acquired before that date.

Article 10
Final provisions

1. Member States shall bring into force the laws, regulations and administrative provisions necessary to comply with this Directive before 1 January 1993. When Member States adopt these measures, the latter shall contain a reference to this Directive or shall be accompanied by such reference on the occasion of their official publication. The methods of making such a reference shall be laid down by the Member States.

2. Member States shall communicate to the Commission the provisions of national law which they adopt in the field governed by this Directive.

Article 11

This Directive is addressed to the Member States. Done at Brussels, 14 May 1991.

Notes and Questions

1. Article 1(3) of the Software Directive sets forth the rule against application of a qualitative standard in evaluating programs for copyright protection. What other meaningful guidance does the Directive contain regarding the tests courts might use to determine whether copyright protection should be afforded?

2. Article 2(3) of the Software Directive incorporates a work made for hire doctrine. Yet the Directive speaks only in terms of the author's "economic rights." What other rights might an author have in a computer program?

3. Consider article 4(c) of the Directive. Does an over-the-counter sale of a program to an end-user/consumer necessarily constitute a sale in accordance with the terms of the Directive? Other than the rental right which is expressly reserved, what other rights might the vendor retain?

4. Article 6 allows a person with the right to use the program to decompile it, but only for limited purposes. Consider article 6(2)(c). Is this limitation consistent with those ordinarily attaching to copyrighted material? Is the EU following the American "substantial similarity" standard for evaluating copyright infringement?

5. The life of the author plus fifty-year term of protection has been superceded by the life of the author plus seventy-year term of the Copyright Directive, *supra*.

---

c. The New European Software Environment

The changes to European copyright law brought about by the Software Directive were significant. By eliminating doubt about the copyrightability of software, the Directive enabled software developers to market their products on the assumption that they would be protected against misappropriation even in the absence of detailed contractual arrangements. At the same time, the Software Directive (and related implementing legislation) reduced the scope of restrictions that might be included in sale and license agreements. The Directive reinforced the conclusion in German law that off-the-shelf sales of computer programs may not be characterized as "licenses" by vendors for purposes such as restricting resales or transfers. The importance of these various changes is described and analyzed by Michael Lehmann.

The New Software Contract Under European and German Copyright Law — Sale and Licensing of Computer Programs

Michael Lehmann*

The recent reform of the German Copyright Act not only brings about an improvement of the protection of computer programs, but also regulates anew the contractual relations vis-à-vis program users. Consequently program suppliers would be well-advised to develop a licensing culture which takes into account adequately the minimum rights of software users as prescribed by European and German law; in this context the correct choice of one of the forms of distribution, i.e. the sale or the licensing of programs, acquires considerable legal significance.

I. As a Rule Computer Programs Are Literary Works Protected By Copyright

On June 24, 1993 the Second Law in Order to Amend the Copyright Act entered into force, the exclusive object of which is to implement EC Council Directive No. 91/250/EC of May 14, 1991 on the Legal Protection of Computer Programs. As a result of this an amendment the legal situation has changed completely, for in future it must be assumed that as a rule every slightly more complex computer program will enjoy copyright protection; the "small change" of software can also claim such protection, which applies equally to old and new programs, for Art. 9 (2) of the EC Directive 91/250/EC and the new Sec. 137d of the German Copyright Act based on this clause prescribe retroactive, positive application. This means that the economic commodity software is granted the property right character it has earned for some time; the achievements of software engineers are recognized to be, and protected as, intellectual property, whereby computer programs qualify as literary works both nationally and internationally, i.e. in particular pursuant to Art. 2 Revised Berne Convention (Paris version). Thus, the uncertainty engendered by the case law of the German Federal Supreme Court has been swept away completely. Today, every creator of a

---

*25 IIC 39 (1994).

program can normally assume that his or her computer literary works which are the result of individual "programming skills" are entitled to copyright protection. Section 69a(3) Copyright Act only requires that programs are individual works in the sense that they are the result of their author's own intellectual creation, whereby determination of their eligibility for protection cannot be made dependent upon other, in particular qualitative or other aesthetic, criteria.

This utterly new legal situation, which is tantamount to a kind of reversal of the previously valid norm/exemption relationship, acquires significance not only for copyright law itself, but also for the contract law based on copyright and regulating the sale or licensing of software. Whereas in earlier years in computer practice trade and commerce endeavored to fill the vacuum as regards protection by means of broad standard or individual contractual agreements, so to speak by wrapping a finely spun contractual cocoon around the insufficiently protected but commercially particularly vulnerable software, they can now release this butterfly into free flight into the unknown expanses of the market. The new foundation of computer program protection anchored in copyright law has now become so stable and steadfast, not least under the influence of EC law, that it does not require further contractual reinforcement.

However, this means that contractual structures for the sale of software can and must venture onto new, ultimately consumer-friendly paths. Relations to customers must no longer be secured contractually as tightly as possible, whereby in earlier years some clients were veritably bound and gagged in order to exclude to the greatest possible extent the danger of product piracy; rather, proceeding from the basis of a secure exclusive right, software suppliers can develop a new licensing culture. In the computer branch just as elsewhere, increasing competitive pressure has transformed the retailers' market into a consumers' market, with the result that the customer should now be the boss again — not least in view of marketing considerations. Software suppliers must first take note of the minimum rights granted to their customers under the EC Directive and consequently under the new Copyright Act, for there are numerous new mandatory provisions permitting customers to undertake certain acts of use in relation to the software; pursuant to Sec. 134 German Civil Code these rights cannot be contracted out of an agreement. Mark you, these rights merely constitute minimal legal equipment for users, endeavoring to protect software users adequately in their legitimate interests. The primary intention of the new provisions in the Copyright Act is indeed to provide adequate legal protection for software suppliers, but not at the expense of thus restricting the customers' utilization possibilities. Therefore, the strengthening of the software suppliers' legal status must be countered by securing the minimum rights of software users, so that a harmonious balance of interests can evolve.

II. Minimum Rights of Legitimate Software Users

Any legitimate user, no matter whether purchaser or licensee, is allowed by law to undertake certain acts of utilization, so that in future corresponding contractual "permission" will only have a clarifying function. Pursuant to Art. 9(1), second sent., of EC Directive No. 91/250/ EC and Sec. 69g(2) Copyright Act, contractual provisions which are contrary to these minimum rights of legitimate users are null and void. In detail, the following utilization rights are involved:

1. Back-Up Copy

Pursuant to Sec. 69d(2) Copyright Act and Art. 5(2) of the EC Directive a legitimate user has the right to make one back-up copy, if this is necessary to ensure future use of the program. In practice, the software supplier frequently delivers two copies of the program to the customer from the outset, one working copy and a back-up copy, or the customer is permitted to make and keep a back-up copy of the one program delivered to him. If the program is equipped with a technical anti-copy device (e.g. a dongle), then the supplier must always deliver two copies if a back-up copy is required to ensure the smooth running and use of the program, for example where the working copy might be destroyed or damaged. It is true that use of such technical devices to prevent copying is allowed by law, indeed these devices are even specifically protected by virtue of Sec. 69f(2) Copyright Act, but their use must not entail restrictions on the right of lawful acquirers to utilize programs. It is only illegal copying that may be prevented by these anti-copying mechanisms, not the right to possess a back-up copy generally required for the operation of a computer according to its intended purpose.

2. Test Run and Observation

According to Sec. 69d(3) of the Copyright Act and Art. 5(3) of the EC Directive, a user is entitled to observe the functioning of a program, to study or test that functioning, provided that these acts can be carried out by loading, displaying, running, transmitting or storing the program; reproduction and in particular decompilation are not permitted under this clause. Observation is permitted for the purpose of ascertaining the ideas and principles underlying the program as a whole, or underlying a certain element of the program; for in accordance with both the fundamental concept of German copyright law and Sec. 69a(2)(2) Copyright Act these ideas do not attract copyright protection. They can be determined freely for the purpose of independent programming, even if the programmer receives his or her stimulation from the ideas, e.g. of a competing product. The limitation in relation to acts done "by any person entitled to use" the program means that the authorization to make a test run does not encompass the making of an unauthorized copy. Restrictions on use that have been agreed contractually and which are allowed in principle are not revoked by the clause.

3. Error Correction, Not Maintenance

Pursuant to Sec. 69d(1) Copyright Act deriving from Art. 5(4) of the Directive, which is not a mandatory provision according to Sec. 69g(2) Copyright Act and Art. 9(2) EC Directive, but would nevertheless appear to contain a "mandatory nucleus," a legitimate user is entitled to correct errors; and he is permitted to decompile or reproduce the entire program for this sole purpose. Furthermore, he may splice, patch, etc., errors, without such activity being qualified as an alteration of the software that is subject to authorization under copyright law. As a rule, therefore, a person entitled to use a program will be allowed to remove all program errors, bugs, viruses, etc., in the absence of any other solution being offered by contract. The user has the right to use a program which is as free of errors as possible, so that he is either allowed to undertake the necessary corrections himself or the rightholder must promise to remedy errors or have these remedied by a third party, if he as a supplier wishes to restrict this right by contract vis-à-vis the user. In such a case, the principle of Sec. 538(2) German Civil Code should be applied analogously as regards the error correction right, because as a matter of principle any person entitled to use the program does possess an independent right to correct errors.

This must be distinguished from acts of software maintenance, in particular program improvements, or the installation of program updates or upgrades, for these possibilities touch upon the interests of the program creator in participation; the program creator should be able to share in the revenue generated by maintenance or improvement work. It was also the intention of the framers of the EC Directive that the general maintenance right remained reserved to the rightholder, i.e. the author of the work, especially since decompilation for the sole purpose of maintenance is not permitted under Sec. 69e Copyright Act and Art. 6 of the EC Directive. Obvious considerations connected to software specificities lead to the conclusion that successful and relatively inexpensive maintenance can only be carried out by the person or company which possesses or is entitled to use the source code; however, the source code is frequently one of the best kept secrets in software matters, so that pursuant to Secs. 631 et seq. Civil Code a programmer working under a contract for work is *per se* not obliged to hand over the source code to the contractor together with the finished program.

4. Decompilation Subject to Strict Conditions

By virtue of Sec. 69e Copyright Act in conjunction with Art. 6 EC Directive No. 91/250/EC a legitimate user can, subject to very strict conditions, decompile the acquired program for the purpose of achieving interoperability, i.e. can ascertain in particular information on the interfaces by means of reverse analysis from the machine code back to the source code, in order to possibly bring about the application of an independently created computer program together with one or more other programs. The functional connection and interaction of software and [respectively or hardware] is described as interoperability and defined as the ability "to exchange information and mutually to use the information which has been exchanged."

The purchaser or licensee is only permitted to carry out the reverse analyses necessary in order to achieve interoperability if the required information on interfaces had not been made "readily available" to the user by the rightholder; objectively necessary acts of reproduction or alteration in relation to the acquired software, undertaken during this process, do not infringe copyright, nor can they be forbidden contractually, by virtue of Sec. 69g in conjunction with Sec. 69e Copyright Act; pursuant to Sec. 134 Civil Code such contractual provisions are deemed null and void. Nevertheless, on the basis of the widespread effects of European and German antitrust law it can be expected that on the part of customers it will not be necessary to invoke Sec. 69e Copyright Act very often in order to gain access to the desired information on interfaces.

5. Loading and Running as Use of a Computer Program in Accordance with Its Intended Purpose

By virtue of Sec. 69d(1) Copyright Act acts of reproduction and adaptation in the sense of Sec. 69c(1) and (2) do not require the authorization of the rightholder if they are necessary for use of the program "in accordance with its intended purpose." In this connection, application of the norm/exception rule laid down in the EC Directive must be assumed, according to which the author is first granted broad exclusive rights, which he can assign as subsidiary rights to persons or entities thus entitled to use the program. Where the rightholder permits his customers or licensees to use his programs against payment, he in any case grants them a certain minimum kit of user rights, so that they can work with the software they have acquired. In this respect, the explanatory reasoning to Sec. 69d(1) Copyright Act points out a "certain mandatory nucleus," and the 18th recital of the EC Directive is even more explicit: "in the absence of specific contractual provisions, including when a copy of the program has been sold, any other act necessary for the use of the copy of a program may be performed in accordance with its intended purpose by a lawful acquirer of that copy."

The explanatory memorandum relates to Art. 5 EC Directive, which led to the new Sec. 69d(1) of the German Copyright Act, and which concern "the acts of loading and running necessary for the use of a copy of a program which has been lawfully acquired, and the act of correction of its errors;" these acts of utilization cannot be prohibited by contract. In this respect, this represents the "mandatory nucleus" of Sec. 69d(1) Copyright Act, for this interpretation is mandatory under European law. This means that every purchaser or licensee is permitted by law to load and run the program he has acquired and to remedy errors, and that these minimum rights may not be restricted contractually. This also corresponds with the general principles of the Copyright Act, for the enjoyment of a work cannot be governed by the author's exclusive rights; the participation interest of the rightholder does not encompass how often a record is heard, a book read or software employed by a lawful acquirer. Consequently, the simple running of a program cannot be rendered subject to a license or remuneration. Every legitimate program user has a right to load, run, and to remedy errors, if he has acquired the software by means of a sale or license agreement.

However, beyond these minimum rights the purpose-of-grant theory determines which concrete restrictions may be imposed on the user, in which respect the contractual provision in Sec. 69d(1) Copyright Act gains significance. First, it must be distinguished whether the software was sold or licensed.

6. Sale of a Computer Program — Exhaustion

If software, in particular a standard or off-the-shelf program, is acquired definitively by a customer by means of a transaction, for utilization, whereby such a contract might be called "one-off license," "software leasing" or any other misleading title, then the prevailing opinion in the literature and in case law in fact qualifies this contract as a contract of sale and applies Sec. 433 et seq. Civil Code and Secs. 377, 378 Commercial Code either directly or at least in analogy. Under copyright law, the sale of a copy of a work, that is of a certain copy of a program, results in exhaustion of the distribution right pursuant to Secs. 17(2), 69c(3) Copyright Act; the rightholder was rewarded for the first sale of this copy of the work (first sale doctrine), he has participated adequately in the success on the market of his intellectual property, so that he may not determine over the further sale of this copy of the program *qua* the Copyright Act. The exhaustion does not concern the reproduction right or the new rental right within the meaning of Sec. 69c Copyright Act, but relates exclusively to the distribution right with regard to the copy of a program provided in each respective individual case and the relevant back-up copy, which, however, must be resold together as joint accessories.

Consequently, the minimum rights of every acquirer of software include the right to load and run the program, to correct errors and to resell the acquired program, for the principle of exhaustion is also anchored in both German and European law as a mandatory legal principle, which cannot be contracted out. *Inter partes* prohibitions on resale which may be valid in principle, cannot become effective under copyright vis-à-vis third parties; they are not covered by the Copyright Act, do not belong to the content, to the specific subject matter of this property right, and are thus governed in all aspects by the control pursuant to Sec. 9 Law on Standard Business Conditions and Secs. 15, 18, 22, 26(2) and 37(a)(3) of the Act Against Restraints of Competition, in addition to Arts. 85 and 86 of the EEC Treaty. According to Sec. 9(2) Law on Standard Business Conditions a valid prohibition on resale cannot be agreed in standard form contracts if the object was first provided on the basis of a contract of sale; a similar interpretation can be derived from Secs. 15 and 18 Act Against Restraints of Competition (unlawful binding to conditions). This means that in standard software contracts with the character of a contract of sale, prohibitions on resale cannot be validly agreed upon. Therefore, every second-hand buyer is a legitimate user in the sense of Sec. 69d(1) Copyright Act and is thus entitled to use the program without the authorization of the rightholder, i.e. pursuant to Sec. 69c Copyright Act in particular can load and run it, correct errors and undertake alterations within the scope of its intended use.

7. License Agreements and Restrictions on Use

If, within the framework of a long-term obligation, the rightholder only grants the user a license of limited duration to use a software, exhaustion pursuant to Secs. 17 and 69c(3) Copyright Act is not applicable, because the program is not sold. In such a case a prohibition on resale is covered by copyright, for Sec. 32 Copyright Act provides that the grant of a license can be limited as to place, time or purpose. By virtue of Sec. 31 Copyright Act, the purpose-of-grant theory influences the scope of the license granted, so that in this connection the contractual fixation of the "intended purpose" of a computer program attains decisive significance.

Consequently, within the framework of a license agreement a licensor is able to impose contractual restrictions of use on his licensee, in order to ensure his economic participation interests, to a far greater extent than is possible in the case of the sale of software. The licensee must only be allowed to carry out those acts of use which are necessary for the use of the software in accordance with its intended purpose, namely the acts of reproduction and adaptation and the correction of errors. Thus, under copyright law, field-of-use restrictions, CPU clauses, floating licenses, network restrictions, etc., in short all those restrictions are permitted which in the opinion of the relevant interested circles adequately describe clear and distinctive, different possibilities of exploitation; this is permitted just as is the distinction of the hard-cover license from the paperback and book club license in a publishing contract for a literary work. However, in principle the determination in a license agreement of "use in accordance with the intended purpose" must be guided by the participation interest of the rightholder; therefore, it must not be formulated in an arbitrary manner or primarily for the purpose of restricting competition, but must be able to serve the purpose of ensuring for the rightholder adequate remuneration in different sectors of the market (e.g. private, scientific or commercial use of software, software in a work station, software in a network). Any prohibitions on passing on software must be susceptible to classification under this purpose of participation. To put it in a nutshell, this kind of restriction on use must be suitable and necessary in order to secure to the creator of the program, and to make sure he receives, the fruits of his work; an adequate possibility of participation in the market yields of every use of his intellectual property must be opened. Therefore, every contractual determination of the "use in accordance with the intended purpose" of a program in the sense of Sec. 69d Copyright Act should be classified according to and under this principle, for the possibility of a grant of a restricted license according to Sec. 31 et seq. Copyright Act in conjunction with Sec. 69d Copyright Act serves primarily to fulfill this concern as to the adequate participation of every author. The principle of the division of copyright exploitation rights in various, distinctive rights has its boundaries in the protection of the market interests of the general public and in the principle of freedom of competition. Consequently, from a copyright point of view, only remuneration-relevant use restrictions may be imposed on a licensee, e.g. prohibitions on reproduction, passing on, adaptation and maintenance, but not pure cite-clauses, obliging the user to use programs only at a certain place or even only in a certain room, or tie-in clauses. Such far-reaching restrictions on use are no longer legitimated under copyright by the possibility of determining the "use in accordance with the intended purpose" of software within the meaning of Sec. 69d Copyright Act and Art. 5(1) EC Directive; thus, individual contractual agreements of this nature are governed without restriction by the Law on Standard Business Conditions and by antitrust law. From the perspective of freedom of competition, the user should only be subject to those restrictions which are necessary in order to enforce the Copyright Act, whereby the scope of protection of this exclusive right shall also be dimensioned accordingly. This means that the fundamental freedom of contractual determination of the "use in accordance with the intended purpose" of computer programs comes up against these copyright and competition law boundaries. In this respect, every license agreement must therefore grant the user of software the following acts in the form of minimum rights: the loading and running of the acquired program, the correction of errors, the making of a back-up copy, a test run, decompilation within the above-mentioned rigid boundaries of Sec. 69e Copyright Act and all acts of adaptation and alteration which are necessary for the use of the software in accordance with its intended purpose. An issue which is still undecided and hotly disputed in this context is whether, and to which degree, this also applies to the portation of programs.

III. Summary

On the one side, the new Copyright Act improves considerably the protection afforded software, yet on the other side it prescribes the mandatory grant of certain use rights to the benefit of program users. Consequently, the buyer of software may undertake the following acts without the authorization of the rightholder: he may load the program into his computer and run it, test it, correct possible errors, make a back up copy, carry out the alterations necessary for the use of the program in accordance with its intended purpose and, subject to very strict conditions, even decompile the program. In addition, the purchaser's right to resell the acquired program cannot be prohibited validly in standard contracts. However, the latter does not apply to a licensee, who as a matter of principle can be made subject to more extensive restrictions on use than a buyer. Yet a licensee must also be granted the above-mentioned minimum rights, with the exception of the right of resale; furthermore, the contractual determination of the intended purpose of the software must be oriented to the legitimate remuneration and participation interests of the author(s) of computer programs, as protected by the Copyright Act.

Notes and Questions

1. As we noted in introducing this article by Michael Lehmann, one of the key features of the Software Directive was to clarify that an off-the-shelf sale

of computer software exhausts the vendor's control over resale of the product — regardless of whether the vendor attempts to characterize the sale as a "license." Under the Software Directive and Rental Rights Directive, the buyer of the program is nevertheless restricted from renting out the program. The result should be the same under section 109 of the U.S. Copyright Act, which grants to the owner of a particular copy of a copyrighted work the right to resell or otherwise dispose of that copy without the consent of the copyright holder, provided that the owner of a copy of the computer program may not rent, lease or lend the copy without permission of the copyright holder. Why are software developers anxious to characterize their transactions with the public as "licenses"?

2. The off-the-shelf sale of software is distinguished by Lehmann from a genuine license. In the latter case, restrictions on the use and transfer of software which reflect a legitimate purpose in allowing the copyright holder to adequately exploit an economic interest are permitted. It is a frequent practice of software developers to license their programs for use on a network, and to charge fees for the use of the program based on the number of users of the network. Does a license term which varies the fee for the program depending on the number of users strike you as the kind of restriction that legitimately reflects the copyright holder's economic interest in the program?

---

2. The United States

a. The State of the Art in U.S. Software Doctrine

In Chapter I we reviewed the *Lotus v. Borland* decision of the First Circuit Court of Appeals which discussed the distinction between non-protectable method of operation and protectable expression. In that case, the court took pains to distinguish its process of analysis from the process used by the Second Circuit Court of Appeals in *Computer Associates v. Altai.* You will recall that the court in *Lotus* distinguished the facts in that case from those in *Computer Associates* on the grounds that *Lotus* involved questions surrounding "literal infringement," whereas *Computer Associates* involved "non-literal infringement." The *Lotus* court suggested that it would be a mistake to follow the approach of the court in *Computer Associates* because, in the view of the *Lotus* court, the analytical approach in *Computer Associates* encouraged the finding of some kernel of protectable expression.

Taken together, the *Lotus v. Borland* decision and the *Computer Associates v. Altai* decision (which follows) substantially shape the "state of the art" in U.S. case law concerning software as copyrightable subject matter. Whereas the *Lotus* decision is rather straightforward — addressing what the *Lotus* court regarded as a fairly straightforward question — the *Computer Associates v. Altai* decision is rather complex. As you read *Computer Associates*, consider whether the mode of analysis the Court adopts is within the capacity of the typical court, and particularly whether it is within the capacity of a court in a country with a developing legal system.

Computer Associates International v. Altai

United States Court of Appeals for the Second Circuit
982 F.2d 693; 1992 U.S. App. LEXIS 33369
December 17, 1992, Filed

Judges: Before Altimari, Mahoney and Walker, Circuit Judges. Judge Altimari concurs in part and dissents in part in a separate opinion.

Opinion: Amended Opinion

Walker, Circuit Judge:

In recent years, the growth of computer science has spawned a number of challenging legal questions, particularly in the field of copyright law. As scientific knowledge advances, courts endeavor to keep pace, and sometimes — as in the area of computer technology — they are required to venture into less than familiar waters. This is not a new development, though. "From its beginning, the law of copyright has developed in response to significant changes in technology." Sony Corp. v. Universal City Studios, Inc., 464 U.S. 417, 430, 78 L. Ed. 2d 574, 104 S. Ct. 774 (1984).

Article I, section 8 of the Constitution authorizes Congress "to promote the Progress of Science and useful Arts, by securing for limited Times to Authors and Inventors the exclusive Right to their respective Writings and Discoveries." The Supreme Court has stated that "the economic philosophy behind the clause . . . is the conviction that encouragement of individual effort by personal gain is the best way to advance public welfare . . . ." Mazer v. Stein, 347 U.S. 201, 219, 98 L. Ed. 630, 74 S. Ct. 460 (1954). The author's benefit, however, is clearly a "secondary" consideration. See United States v. Paramount Pictures, Inc., 334 U.S. 131, 158, 92 L. Ed. 1260, 68 S. Ct. 915 (1948). "The ultimate aim is, by this incentive, to stimulate artistic creativity for the general public good." Twentieth Century Music Corp. v. Aiken, 422 U.S. 151, 156, 45 L. Ed. 2d 84, 95 S. Ct. 2040 (1975).

Thus, the copyright law seeks to establish a delicate equilibrium. On the one hand, it affords protection to authors as an incentive to create, and, on the other, it must appropriately limit the extent of that protection so as to avoid the effects of monopolistic stagnation. In applying the federal act to new types of cases, courts must always keep this symmetry in mind. Id.

Among other things, this case deals with the challenging question of whether and to what extent the "non-literal" aspects of a computer program, that is, those aspects that are not reduced to written code, are protected by copyright. While a few other courts have already grappled with this issue, this case is one of first impression in this circuit. As we shall discuss, we find the results reached by other courts to be less than satisfactory. Drawing upon long-standing doctrines of copyright law, we take an approach that we think better addresses the practical difficulties embedded in these types of cases. In so doing, we have kept in mind the necessary balance between creative incentive and industrial competition.

This appeal comes to us from the United States District Court for the Eastern District of New York, the Honorable George C. Pratt, Circuit Judge, sitting by designation. By Memorandum and Order entered August 12, 1991, Judge Pratt found that defendant Altai, Inc.'s ("Altai"), OSCAR 3.4 computer program had infringed plaintiff Computer Associates' ("CA"), copyrighted computer program entitled CA-SCHEDULER. Accordingly, the district court awarded CA $ 364,444 in actual damages and apportioned profits. Altai has abandoned its appeal from this award. With respect to CA's second claim for copyright infringement, Judge Pratt found that Altai's OSCAR 3.5 program was not substantially similar to a portion of CA-SCHEDULER called ADAPTER, and thus denied relief. Finally, the district court concluded that CA's state law trade secret misappropriation claim against Altai had been preempted by the federal copyright act. CA appealed from these findings.

Because we are in full agreement with Judge Pratt's decision and in substantial agreement with his careful reasoning regarding CA's copyright infringement claim, we affirm the district court's judgment on that issue. However, we vacate the district court's preemption ruling with respect to CA's trade secret claim, and remand the case to the district court for further proceedings.

Background

We assume familiarity with the facts set forth in the district court's comprehensive and scholarly opinion. See Computer Assocs. Int'l, Inc. v. Altai, Inc., 775 F. Supp. 544, 549-55 (E.D.N.Y. 1991). Thus, we summarize only those facts necessary to resolve this appeal.

I. Computer Program Design

Certain elementary facts concerning the nature of computer programs are vital to the following discussion. The Copyright Act defines a computer program as "a set of statements or instructions to be used directly or indirectly in a computer in order to bring about a certain result." 17 U.S.C. § 101. In writing these directions, the programmer works "from the general to the specific." Whelan Assoc., Inc. v. Jaslow Dental Lab., Inc., 797 F.2d 1222, 1229 (3d Cir. 1986), cert. denied, 479 U.S. 1031, 93 L. Ed. 2d 831, 107 S. Ct. 877 (1987). See generally Steven R. Englund, Note, Idea, Process, or Protected Expression?: Determining the Scope of Copyright Protection of the Structure of Computer Programs, 88 MICH. L. REV. 866, 867-73 (1990) (hereinafter "Englund"); Peter S. Menell, An Analysis of the Scope of Copyright Protection for Application Programs, 41 STAN. L. REV. 1045, 1051-57 (1989) (hereinafter "Menell"); Mark T. Kretschmer, Note, Copyright Protection for Software Architecture: Just Say No!, 1988 COLUM. BUS. L. REV. 823, 824-27 (1988) (hereinafter "Kretschmer"); Peter G. Spivack, Comment, Does Form Follow Function? The Idea/Expression Dichotomy in Copyright Protection of Computer Software, 35 U.C.L.A. L. REV. 723, 729-31 (1988) (hereinafter "Spivack").

The first step in this procedure is to identify a program's ultimate function or purpose. An example of such an ultimate purpose might be the creation and maintenance of a business ledger. Once this goal has been achieved, a programmer breaks down or "decomposes" the program's ultimate function into "simpler constituent problems or 'subtasks,'" Englund, at 870, which are also known as subroutines or modules. See Spivack, at 729. In the context of a business ledger program, a module or subroutine might be responsible for the task of updating a list of outstanding accounts receivable. Sometimes, depending upon the complexity of its task, a subroutine may be broken down further into sub-subroutines.

Having sufficiently decomposed the program's ultimate function into its component elements, a programmer will then arrange the subroutines or modules into what are known as organizational or flow charts. Flow charts map the interactions between modules that achieve the program's end goal. See Kretschmer, at 826.

In order to accomplish these intra-program interactions, a programmer must carefully design each module's parameter list. A parameter list, according to the expert appointed and fully credited by the district court, Dr. Randall Davis, is "the information sent to and received from a subroutine." See Report of Dr. Randall Davis, at 12. The term "parameter list" refers to the form in which information is passed between modules (e.g. for accounts receivable, the designated time frame and particular customer identifying number) and the information's actual content (e.g. 8/91-7/92; customer No. 3). Id. With respect to form, interacting modules must share similar parameter lists so that they are capable of exchanging information.

"The functions of the modules in a program together with each module's relationships to other modules constitute the 'structure' of the program." Englund, at 871. Additionally, the term structure may include the category of modules referred to as "macros." A macro is a single instruction that initiates a sequence of operations or module interactions within the program. Very often the user will accompany a macro with an instruction from the parameter list to refine the instruction (e.g. current total of accounts receivable (macro), but limited to those for 8/91 to 7/92 from customer No. 3 (parameters)).

In fashioning the structure, a programmer will normally attempt to maximize the program's speed, efficiency, as well as simplicity for user operation, while taking into consideration certain externalities such as the memory constraints of the computer upon which the program will be run. See id.; Kretschmer, at 826; Menell, at 1052. "This stage of program design often requires the most time and investment." Kretschmer, at 826.

Once each necessary module has been identified, designed, and its relationship to the other modules has been laid out conceptually, the resulting program structure must be embodied in a written language that the computer can read. This process is called "coding," and requires two steps. Whelan, 797 F.2d at 1230. First, the programmer must transpose the program's structural blue-print into a source code. This step has been described as "comparable to the novelist fleshing out the broad outline of his plot by crafting from words and sentences the paragraphs that convey the ideas." Kretschmer, at 826. The source code may be written in any one of several computer languages, such as COBAL, FORTRAN, BASIC, EDL, etc., depending upon the type of computer for which the program is intended. Whelan, 797 F.2d at 1230. Once the source code has been completed, the second step is to translate or "compile" it into object code. Object code is the binary language comprised of zeros and ones through which the computer directly receives its instructions. Id., at 1230-31; Englund, at 868 & n.13.

After the coding is finished, the programmer will run the program on the computer in order to find and correct any logical and syntactical errors. This is known as "debugging" and, once done, the program is complete. See Kretschmer, at 826-27.

II. Facts

CA is a Delaware corporation, with its principal place of business in Garden City, New York. Altai is a Texas corporation, doing business primarily in Arlington, Texas. Both companies are in the computer software industry — designing, developing and marketing various types of computer programs.

The subject of this litigation originates with one of CA's marketed programs entitled CA-SCHEDULER. CA SCHEDULER is a job scheduling program designed for IBM mainframe computers. Its primary functions are straightforward: to create a schedule specifying when the computer should run various tasks, and then to control the computer as it executes the schedule. CA-SCHEDULER contains a sub-program entitled ADAPTER, also developed by CA. ADAPTER is not an independently marketed product of CA; it is a wholly integrated component of CA-SCHEDULER and has no capacity for independent use.

Nevertheless, ADAPTER plays an extremely important role. It is an "operating system compatibility component," which means, roughly speaking, it serves as a translator. An "operating system" is itself a program that manages the resources of the computer, allocating those resources to other programs as needed. The IBM System 370 family of computers, for which

CA-SCHEDULER was created, is, depending upon the computer's size, designed to contain one of three operating systems: DOS/VSE, MVS, or CMS. As the district court noted, the general rule is that "a program written for one operating system, e.g., DOS/VSE, will not, without modification, run under another operating system such as MVS." Computer Assocs., 775 F. Supp. at 550. ADAPTER's function is to translate the language of a given program into the particular language that the computer's own operating system can understand.

The district court succinctly outlined the manner in which ADAPTER works within the context of the larger program. In order to enable CA-SCHEDULER to function on different operating systems, CA divided the CA-SCHEDULER into two components:

— a first component that contains only the task-specific portions of the program, independent of all operating system issues, and

— a second component that contains all the interconnections between the first component and the operating system.

In a program constructed in this way, whenever the first, task-specific, component needs to ask the operating system for some resource through a "system call", it calls the second component instead of calling the operating system directly.

The second component serves as an "interface" or "compatibility component" between the task-specific portion of the program and the operating system. It receives the request from the first component and translates it into the appropriate system call that will be recognized by whatever operating system is installed on the computer, e.g., DOS/VSE, MVS, or CMS. Since the first, task-specific component calls the adapter component rather than the operating system, the first component need not be customized to use any specific operating system. The second, interface, component insures that all the system calls are performed properly for the particular operating system in use. Id. at 551. ADAPTER serves as the second, "common system interface" component referred to above.

A program like ADAPTER, which allows a computer user to change or use multiple operating systems while maintaining the same software, is highly desirable. It saves the user the costs, both in time and money, that otherwise would be expended in purchasing new programs, modifying existing systems to run them, and gaining familiarity with their operation.

The benefits run both ways. The increased compatibility afforded by an ADAPTER-like component, and its resulting popularity among consumers, makes whatever software in which it is incorporated significantly more marketable.

Starting in 1982, Altai began marketing its own job scheduling program entitled ZEKE. The original version of ZEKE was designed for use in conjunction with a VSE operating system. By late 1983, in response to customer demand, Altai decided to rewrite ZEKE so that it could be run in conjunction with an MVS operating system.

At that time, James P. Williams ("Williams"), then an employee of Altai and now its President, approached Claude F. Arney, III ("Arney"), a computer programmer who worked for CA. Williams and Arney were longstanding friends, and had in fact been co-workers at CA for some time before Williams left CA to work for Altai's predecessor. Williams wanted to recruit Arney to assist Altai in designing an MVS version of ZEKE.

At the time he first spoke with Arney, Williams was aware of both the CA-SCHEDULER and ADAPTER programs. However, Williams was not involved in their development and had never seen the codes of either program. When he asked Arney to come work for Altai, Williams did not know that ADAPTER was a component of CA-SCHEDULER.

Arney, on the other hand, was intimately familiar with various aspects of ADAPTER. While working for CA, he helped improve the VSE version of ADAPTER, and was permitted to take home a copy of ADAPTER's source code. This apparently developed into an irresistible habit, for when Arney left CA to work for Altai in January, 1984, he took with him copies of the source code for both the VSE and MVS versions of ADAPTER. He did this in knowing violation of the CA employee agreements that he had signed.

Once at Altai, Arney and Williams discussed design possibilities for adapting ZEKE to run on MVS operating systems. Williams, who had created the VSE version of ZEKE, thought that approximately 30% of his original program would have to be modified in order to accommodate MVS. Arney persuaded Williams that the best way to make the needed modifications was to introduce a "common system interface" component into ZEKE. He did not tell Williams that his idea stemmed from his familiarity with ADAPTER. They decided to name this new component-program OSCAR.

Arney went to work creating OSCAR at Altai's offices using the ADAPTER source code. The district court accepted Williams' testimony that no one at Altai, with the exception of Arney, affirmatively knew that

Arney had the ADAPTER code, or that he was using it to create OSCAR/VSE. However, during this time period, Williams' office was adjacent to Arney's. Williams testified that he and Arney "conversed quite frequently" while Arney was "investigating the source code of ZEKE" and that Arney was in his office "a number of times daily, asking questions." In three months, Arney successfully completed the OSCAR/VSE project. In an additional month he developed an OSCAR/MVS version. When the dust finally settled, Arney had copied approximately 30% of OSCAR's code from CA's ADAPTER program.

The first generation of OSCAR programs was known as OSCAR 3.4. From 1985 to August 1988, Altai used OSCAR 3.4 in its ZEKE product, as well as in programs entitled ZACK and ZEBB. In late July 1988, CA first learned that Altai may have appropriated parts of ADAPTER. After confirming its suspicions, CA secured copyrights on its 2.1 and 7.0 versions of CA-SCHEDULER. CA then brought this copyright and trade secret misappropriation action against Altai.

Apparently, it was upon receipt of the summons and complaint that Altai first learned that Arney had copied much of the OSCAR code from ADAPTER. After Arney confirmed to Williams that CA's accusations of copying were true, Williams immediately set out to survey the damage. Without ever looking at the ADAPTER code himself, Williams learned from Arney exactly which sections of code Arney had taken from ADAPTER.

Upon advice of counsel, Williams initiated OSCAR's rewrite. The project's goal was to save as much of OSCAR 3.4 as legitimately could be used, and to excise those portions which had been copied from ADAPTER. Arney was entirely excluded from the process, and his copy of the ADAPTER code was locked away. Williams put eight other programmers on the project, none of whom had been involved in any way in the development of OSCAR 3.4. Williams provided the programmers with a description of the ZEKE operating system services so that they could rewrite the appropriate code. The rewrite project took about six months to complete and was finished in mid-November 1989. The resulting program was entitled OSCAR 3.5.

From that point on, Altai shipped only OSCAR 3.5 to its new customers. Altai also shipped OSCAR 3.5 as a "free upgrade" to all customers that had previously purchased OSCAR 3.4. While Altai and Williams acted responsibly to correct Arney's literal copying of the ADAPTER program, copyright infringement had occurred.

After CA originally instituted this action in the United States District Court for the District of New Jersey, the parties stipulated its transfer in March, 1989, to the Eastern District of New York where it was assigned to Judge Jacob Mishler. On October 26, 1989, Judge Mishler transferred the case to Judge Pratt who was sitting in the district court by designation. Judge Pratt conducted a six day trial from March 28 through April 6, 1990. He entered judgment on August 12, 1991, and this appeal followed.

Discussion

While both parties originally appealed from different aspects of the district court's judgment, Altai has now abandoned its appellate claims. In particular, Altai has conceded liability for the copying of ADAPTER into OSCAR 3.4 and raises no challenge to the award of $ 364,444 in damages on that score. Thus, we address only CA's appeal from the district court's rulings that: (1) Altai was not liable for copyright infringement in developing OSCAR 3.5; and (2) in developing both OSCAR 3.4 and 3.5, Altai was not liable for misappropriating CA's trade secrets.

CA makes two arguments. First, CA contends that the district court applied an erroneous method for determining whether there exists substantial similarity between computer programs, and thus, erred in determining that OSCAR 3.5 did not infringe the copyrights held on the different versions of its CA-SCHEDULER program. CA asserts that the test applied by the district court failed to account sufficiently for a computer program's non-literal elements. Second, CA maintains that the district court erroneously concluded that its state law trade secret claims had been preempted by the federal copyright act, see 17 U.S.C. § 301(a). We shall address each argument in turn.

I. Copyright Infringement

In any suit for copyright infringement, the plaintiff must establish its ownership of a valid copyright, and that the defendant copied the copyrighted work. See Novelty Textile Mills, Inc. v. Joan Fabrics Corp., 558 F.2d 1090, 1092 (2d Cir. 1977); see also 3 Melville B. Nimmer & David Nimmer, Nimmer on Copyright § 13.01, at 13-4 (1991) (hereinafter "Nimmer"). The plaintiff may prove defendant's copying either by direct evidence or, as is most often the case, by showing that (1) the defendant had access to the plaintiff's copyrighted work and (2) that defendant's work is substantially similar to the plaintiff's copyrightable material. See Walker v. Time Life Films, Inc., 784 F.2d 44, 48 (2d Cir.), cert. denied, 476 U.S. 1159, 90 L. Ed. 2d 721, 106 S. Ct. 2278 (1986).

For the purpose of analysis, the district court assumed that Altai had access to the ADAPTER code when creating OSCAR 3.5. See Computer Assocs., 775 F. Supp. at 558. Thus, in determining whether Altai had unlawfully copied protected aspects of CA's ADAPTER, the district court narrowed its focus of inquiry to ascertaining whether Altai's OSCAR 3.5 was substantially similar to ADAPTER. Because we approve Judge Pratt's conclusions regarding substantial similarity, our analysis will proceed along the same assumption.

As a general matter, and to varying degrees, copyright protection extends beyond a literary work's strictly textual form to its non-literal components. As we have said, "it is of course essential to any protection of literary property . . . that the right cannot be limited literally to the text, else a plagiarist would escape by immaterial variations." Nichols v. Universal Pictures Co., 45 F.2d 119, 121 (2d Cir. 1930) (L. Hand, J.), cert. denied, 282 U.S. 902, 75 L. Ed. 795, 51 S. Ct. 216 (1931). Thus, where "the fundamental essence or structure of one work is duplicated in another," 3 Nimmer, § 13.03[A][1], at 13-24, courts have found copyright infringement. See, e.g., Horgan v. Macmillan, 789 F.2d 157, 162 (2d Cir. 1986) (recognizing that a book of photographs might infringe ballet choreography); Twentieth Century-Fox Film Corp. v. MCA, Inc., 715 F.2d 1327, 1329 (9th Cir. 1983) (motion picture and television series); Sid & Marty Krofft Television Prods., Inc. v. McDonald's Corp., 562 F.2d 1157, 1167 (9th Cir. 1977) (television commercial and television series); Sheldon v. Metro-Goldwyn Pictures Corp., 81 F.2d 49, 55 (2d Cir.), cert. denied, 298 U.S. 669, 80 L. Ed. 1392, 56 S. Ct. 835 (1936) (play and motion picture); accord Stewart v. Abend, 495 U.S. 207, 238, 109 L. Ed. 2d 184, 110 S. Ct. 1750 (1990) (recognizing that motion picture may infringe copyright in book by using its "unique setting, characters, plot, and sequence of events"). This black letter proposition is the springboard for our discussion.

A. Copyright Protection for the Non-literal Elements of Computer Programs

It is now well settled that the literal elements of computer programs, i.e., their source and object codes, are the subject of copyright protection.

See Whelan, 797 F.2d at 1233 (source and object code); CMS Software Design Sys., Inc. v. Info Designs, Inc., 785 F.2d 1246, 1247 (5th Cir. 1986) (source code); Apple Computer, Inc. v. Franklin Computer Corp., 714 F.2d 1240, 1249 (3d Cir. 1983), cert. dismissed, 464 U.S. 1033, 104 S. Ct. 690, 79 L. Ed. 2d 158 (1984) (source and object code); Williams Electronics, Inc. v. Artic Int'l, Inc., 685 F.2d 870, 876-77 (3d Cir. 1982) (object code). Here, as noted earlier, Altai admits having copied approximately 30% of the OSCAR 3.4 program from CA's ADAPTER source code, and does not challenge the district court's related finding of infringement.

In this case, the hotly contested issues surround OSCAR 3.5. As recounted above, OSCAR 3.5 is the product of Altai's carefully orchestrated rewrite of OSCAR 3.4. After the purge, none of the ADAPTER source code remained in the 3.5 version; thus, Altai made sure that the literal elements of its revamped OSCAR program were no longer substantially similar to the literal elements of CA's ADAPTER.

According to CA, the district court erroneously concluded that Altai's OSCAR 3.5 was not substantially similar to its own ADAPTER program. CA argues that this occurred because the district court "committed legal error in analyzing [its] claims of copyright infringement by failing to find that copyright protects expression contained in the non-literal elements of computer software." We disagree.

CA argues that, despite Altai's rewrite of the OSCAR code, the resulting program remained substantially similar to the structure of its ADAPTER program. As discussed above, a program's structure includes its nonliteral components such as general flow charts as well as the more specific organization of inter-modular relationships, parameter lists, and macros. In addition to these aspects, CA contends that OSCAR 3.5 is also substantially similar to ADAPTER with respect to the list of services that both ADAPTER and OSCAR obtain from their respective operating systems. We must decide whether and to what extent these elements of computer programs are protected by copyright law.

The statutory terrain in this area has been well explored. See Lotus Dev. Corp. v. Paperback Software Int'l, 740 F. Supp. 37, 47-51 (D. Mass. 1990); see also Whelan, 797 F.2d at 1240-42; Englund, at 885-90; Spivack, at 731-37. The Copyright Act affords protection to "original works of authorship fixed in any tangible medium of expression . . . ." 17 U.S.C. § 102(a). This broad category of protected "works" includes "literary works," id. at § 102(a)(1), which are defined by the Act as works, other than audiovisual works, expressed in words, numbers, or other verbal or numerical symbols or indicia, regardless of the nature of the material objects, such as books, periodicals, manuscripts, phonorecords, film tapes, disks, or cards, in which they are embodied. 17 U.S.C. § 101. While computer programs are not specifically listed as part of the above statutory definition, the legislative history leaves no doubt that Congress intended them to be considered literary works. See H.R.Rep. No. 1476, 94th Cong., 2d Sess. 54, reprinted in 1976 U.S.C.C.A.N. 5659, 5667 (hereinafter "House Report"); Whelan, 797 F.2d at 1234; Apple Computer, 714 F.2d at 1247.

The syllogism that follows from the foregoing premises is a powerful one: if the non-literal structures of literary works are protected by copyright; and if computer programs are literary works, as we are told by the legislature; then the non-literal structures of computer programs are protected by copyright. See Whelan, 797 F.2d at 1234 ("By analogy to other literary works, it would thus appear that the copyrights of computer programs can be infringed even absent copying of the literal elements of the program."). We have no reservation in joining the company of those courts that have already ascribed to this logic. See, e.g., Johnson Controls, Inc. v. Phoenix Control Sys., Inc., 886 F.2d 1173, 1175 (9th Cir. 1989); Lotus Dev. Corp., 740 F. Supp. at 54; Digital Communications Assocs., Inc. v. Softklone Distrib. Corp., 659 F. Supp. 449, 455-56 (N.D.Ga. 1987); Q-Co Indus., Inc. v. Hoffman, 625 F. Supp. 608, 615 (S.D.N.Y. 1985); SAS Inst., Inc. v. S & H Computer Sys., Inc., 605 F. Supp. 816, 829-30 (M.D.Tenn. 1985). However, that conclusion does not end our analysis. We must determine the scope of copyright protection that extends to a computer program's non-literal structure.

As a caveat, we note that our decision here does not control infringement actions regarding categorically distinct works, such as certain types of screen displays. These items represent products of computer programs, rather than the programs themselves, and fall under the copyright rubric of audiovisual works. If a computer audiovisual display is copyrighted separately as an audiovisual work, apart from the literary work that generates it (i.e., the program), the display may be protectable regardless of the underlying program's copyright status. See Stern Elecs., Inc. v. Kaufman, 669 F.2d 852, 855 (2d Cir. 1982) (explaining that an audiovisual works copyright, rather than a copyright on the underlying program, extended greater protection to the sights and sounds generated by a computer video game because the same audiovisual display could be generated by different programs). Of course, the copyright protection that these displays enjoy extends only so far as their expression is protectable. See Data East USA, Inc.

v. Epyx, Inc., 862 F.2d 204, 209 (9th Cir. 1988). In this case, however, we are concerned not with a program's display, but the program itself, and then with only its non-literal components. In considering the copyrightability of these components, we must refer to venerable doctrines of copyright law.

1) Idea vs. Expression Dichotomy

It is a fundamental principle of copyright law that a copyright does not protect an idea, but only the expression of the idea. See Baker v. Selden, 101 U.S. 99, 25 L. Ed. 841 (1879); Mazer v. Stein, 347 U.S. 201, 217, 98 L. Ed. 630, 74 S. Ct. 460 (1954). This axiom of common law has been incorporated into the governing statute. Section 102(b) of the Act provides:

> In no case does copyright protection for an original work of authorship extend to any idea, procedure, process, system, method of operation, concept, principle, or discovery, regardless of the form in which it is described, explained, illustrated, or embodied in such work.

17 U.S.C. § 102(b). See also House Report, at 5670 ("Copyright does not preclude others from using ideas or information revealed by the author's work.").

Congress made no special exception for computer programs. To the contrary, the legislative history explicitly states that copyright protects computer programs only "to the extent that they incorporate authorship in programmer's expression of original ideas, as distinguished from the ideas themselves." Id. at 5667; see also id. at 5670 ("Section 102(b) is intended . . . to make clear that the expression adopted by the programmer is the copyrightable element in a computer program, and that the actual processes or methods embodied in the program are not within the scope of copyright law.").

Similarly, the National Commission on New Technological Uses of Copyrighted Works ("CONTU") established by Congress to survey the issues generated by the interrelationship of advancing technology and copyright law, see Pub.L. No. 93-573, § 201, 88 Stat. 1873 (1974), recommended, inter alia, that the 1976 Copyright Act "be amended . . . to make it explicit that computer programs, to the extent that they embody the author's original creation, are proper subject matter for copyright." See National Commission on New Technological Uses of Copyrighted Works, Final Report 1

(1979) (hereinafter "CONTU Report"). To that end, Congress adopted CONTU's suggestions and amended the Copyright Act by adding, among other things, a provision to 17 U.S.C. § 101 which defined the term "computer program." See Pub.L. No. 96-517, § 10(a), 94 Stat. 3028 (1980). CONTU also "concluded that the idea-expression distinction should be used to determine which aspects of computer programs are copyrightable." Lotus Dev. Corp., 740 F. Supp. at 54 (citing CONTU Report, at 44).

Drawing the line between idea and expression is a tricky business. Judge Learned Hand noted that "nobody has ever been able to fix that boundary, and nobody ever can." Nichols, 45 F.2d at 121. Thirty years later his convictions remained firm. "Obviously, no principle can be stated as to when an imitator has gone beyond copying the 'idea,' and has borrowed its 'expression,'" Judge Hand concluded. "Decisions must therefore inevitably be ad hoc." Peter Pan Fabrics, Inc. v. Martin Weiner Corp., 274 F.2d 487, 489 (2d Cir. 1960).

The essentially utilitarian nature of a computer program further complicates the task of distilling its idea from its expression. See SAS Inst., 605 F. Supp. at 829; cf. Englund, at 893. In order to describe both computational processes and abstract ideas, its content "combines creative and technical expression." See Spivack, at 755. The variations of expression found in purely creative compositions, as opposed to those contained in utilitarian works, are not directed towards practical application. For example, a narration of Humpty Dumpty's demise, which would clearly be a creative composition, does not serve the same ends as, say, a recipe for scrambled eggs — which is a more process oriented text. Thus, compared to aesthetic works, computer programs hover even more closely to the elusive boundary line described in § 102(b).

The doctrinal starting point in analyses of utilitarian works, is the seminal case of Baker v. Selden, 101 U.S. 99, 25 L. Ed. 841 (1879). In Baker, the Supreme Court faced the question of "whether the exclusive property in a system of bookkeeping can be claimed, under the law of copyright, by means of a book in which that system is explained?" Id. at 101. Selden had copyrighted a book that expounded a particular method of bookkeeping. The book contained lined pages with headings intended to illustrate the manner in which the system operated. Baker's accounting publication included ledger sheets that employed "substantially the same ruled lines and headings. . . ." Id. Selden's testator sued Baker for copyright infringement on the theory that the ledger sheets were protected by Selden's copyright.

The Supreme Court found nothing copyrightable in Selden's book-keeping system, and rejected his infringement claim regarding the ledger sheets. The Court held that:

> The fact that the art described in the book by illustrations of lines and figures which are reproduced in practice in the application of the art, makes no difference. Those illustrations are the mere language employed by the author to convey his ideas more clearly. Had he used words of description instead of diagrams (which merely stand in the place of words), there could not be the slightest doubt that others, applying the art to practical use, might lawfully draw the lines and diagrams which were in the author's mind, and which he thus described by words in his book.
>
> The copyright of a work on mathematical science cannot give to the author an exclusive right to the methods of operation which he propounds, or to the diagrams which he employs to explain them, so as to prevent an engineer from using them whenever occasion requires.

Id. at 103.

To the extent that an accounting text and a computer program are both "a set of statements or instructions . . . to bring about a certain result," 17 U.S.C. § 101, they are roughly analogous. In the former case, the processes are ultimately conducted by human agency; in the latter, by electronic means. In either case, as already stated, the processes themselves are not protectable. But the holding in Baker goes farther. The Court concluded that those aspects of a work, which "must necessarily be used as incident to" the idea, system or process that the work describes, are also not copyrightable. 101 U.S. at 104. Selden's ledger sheets, therefore, enjoyed no copyright protection because they were "necessary incidents to" the system of accounting that he described. Id. at 103. From this reasoning, we conclude that those elements of a computer program that are necessarily incidental to its function are similarly unprotectable.

While Baker v. Selden provides a sound analytical foundation, it offers scant guidance on how to separate idea or process from expression, and moreover, on how to further distinguish protectable expression from that expression which "must necessarily be used as incident to" the work's underlying concept. In the context of computer programs, the Third Circuit's noted decision in Whelan has, thus far, been the most thoughtful attempt to accomplish these ends.

The court in Whelan faced substantially the same problem as is presented by this case. There, the defendant was accused of making off with the non-literal structure of the plaintiff's copyrighted dental lab management program, and employing it to create its own competitive version. In assessing whether there had been an infringement, the court had to determine which aspects of the programs involved were ideas, and which were expression. In separating the two, the court settled upon the following conceptual approach:

> The line between idea and expression may be drawn with reference to the end sought to be achieved by the work in question. In other words, the purpose or function of a utilitarian work would be the work's idea, and everything that is not necessary to that purpose or function would be part of the expression of the idea. . . . Where there are various means of achieving the desired purpose, then the particular means chosen is not necessary to the purpose; hence, there is expression, not idea. 797 F.2d at 1236 (citations omitted).

The "idea" of the program at issue in Whelan was identified by the court as simply "the efficient management of a dental laboratory." Id. at n.28.

So far, in the courts, the Whelan rule has received a mixed reception. While some decisions have adopted its reasoning, see, e.g., Bull HN Info. Sys., Inc. v. American Express Bank, Ltd., 1990 Copyright Law Dec. (CCH) P 26,555 at 23,278 (S.D.N.Y. 1990); Dynamic Solutions, Inc. v. Planning & Control, Inc., 1987 Copyright Law Dec. (CCH) P 26,062 at 20,912 (S.D.N.Y. 1987); Broderbund Software Inc. v. Unison World, Inc., 648 F. Supp. 1127, 1133 (N.D.Cal. 1986), others have rejected it. See Plains Cotton Co-op v. Goodpasture Computer Serv, Inc., 807 F.2d 1256, 1262 (5th Cir.), cert. denied, 484 U.S. 821, 108 S. Ct. 80, 98 L. Ed. 2d 42 (1987); cf. Synercom Technology, Inc. v. University Computing Co., 462 F. Supp. 1003, 1014 (N.D.Tex. 1978) (concluding that order and sequence of data on computer input formats was idea not expression).

Whelan has fared even more poorly in the academic community, where its standard for distinguishing idea from expression has been widely criticized for being conceptually overbroad. See, e.g., Englund, at 881; Menell, at 1074, 1082; Kretschmer, at 837-39; Spivack, at 747-55; Thomas M. Gage, Note, Whelan Associates v. Jaslow Dental Laboratories: Copyright Protection for Computer Software Structure — What's the Purpose?, 1987

WIS. L. REV. 859, 860-61 (1987). The leading commentator in the field has stated that, "the crucial flaw in [Whelan's] reasoning is that it assumes that only one 'idea,' in copyright law terms, underlies any computer program, and that once a separable idea can be identified, everything else must be expression." 3 Nimmer § 13.03[F], at 13-62.34. This criticism focuses not upon the program's ultimate purpose but upon the reality of its structural design. As we have already noted, a computer program's ultimate function or purpose is the composite result of interacting subroutines. Since each subroutine is itself a program, and thus, may be said to have its own "idea," Whelan's general formulation that a program's overall purpose equates with the program's idea is descriptively inadequate.

Accordingly, we think that Judge Pratt wisely declined to follow Whelan. See Computer Assocs., 775 F. Supp. at 558-60. In addition to noting the weakness in the Whelan definition of "program-idea," mentioned above, Judge Pratt found that Whelan's synonymous use of the terms "structure, sequence, and organization," see Whelan, 797 F.2d at 1224 n.1, demonstrated a flawed understanding of a computer program's method of operation. See Computer Assocs., 775 F. Supp. at 559-60 (discussing the distinction between a program's "static structure" and "dynamic structure"). Rightly, the district court found Whelan's rationale suspect because it is so closely tied to what can now be seen — with the passage of time — as the opinion's somewhat outdated appreciation of computer science.

2) Substantial Similarity Test for Computer Program Structure: Abstraction-Filtration-Comparison

We think that Whelan's approach to separating idea from expression in computer programs relies too heavily on metaphysical distinctions and does not place enough emphasis on practical considerations. Cf. Apple Computer, 714 F.2d at 1253 (rejecting certain commercial constraints on programming as a helpful means of distinguishing idea from expression because they did "not enter into the somewhat metaphysical issue of whether particular ideas and expressions have merged"). As the cases that we shall discuss demonstrate, a satisfactory answer to this problem cannot be reached by resorting, a priori, to philosophical first principals.

As discussed herein, we think that district courts would be well-advised to undertake a three-step procedure, based on the abstractions test utilized by the district court, in order to determine whether the non-literal elements of two or more computer programs are substantially similar. This approach breaks no new ground; rather, it draws on such familiar copyright doctrines as merger, scenes a faire, and public domain. In taking this approach, however, we are cognizant that computer technology is a dynamic field which can quickly outpace judicial decisionmaking. Thus, in cases where the technology in question does not allow for a literal application of the procedure we outline below, our opinion should not be read to foreclose the district courts of our circuit from utilizing a modified version.

In ascertaining substantial similarity under this approach, a court would first break down the allegedly infringed program into its constituent structural parts. Then, by examining each of these parts for such things as incorporated ideas, expression that is necessarily incidental to those ideas, and elements that are taken from the public domain, a court would then be able to sift out all non-protectable material. Left with a kernel, or possibly kernels, of creative expression after following this process of elimination, the court's last step would be to compare this material with the structure of an allegedly infringing program. The result of this comparison will determine whether the protectable elements of the programs at issue are substantially similar so as to warrant a finding of infringement. It will be helpful to elaborate a bit further.

Step One: Abstraction

As the district court appreciated, see Computer Assocs., 775 F. Supp. at 560, the theoretic framework for analyzing substantial similarity expounded by Learned Hand in the Nichols case is helpful in the present context. In Nichols, we enunciated what has now become known as the "abstractions" test for separating idea from expression:

> Upon any work . . . a great number of patterns of increasing generality will fit equally well, as more and more of the incident is left out. The last may perhaps be no more than the most general statement of what the [work] is about, and at times might consist only of its title; but there is a point in this series of abstractions where they are no longer protected, since otherwise the [author] could prevent the use of his "ideas," to which, apart from their expression, his property is never extended.

Nichols, 45 F.2d at 121.

While the abstractions test was originally applied in relation to literary works such as novels and plays, it is adaptable to computer programs. In contrast to the Whelan approach, the abstractions test "implicitly recognizes that any given work may consist of a mixture of numerous ideas and expressions." 3 Nimmer § 13.03[F] at 13-62.34-63.

As applied to computer programs, the abstractions test will comprise the first step in the examination for substantial similarity. Initially, in a manner that resembles reverse engineering on a theoretical plane, a court should dissect the allegedly copied program's structure and isolate each level of abstraction contained within it. This process begins with the code and ends with an articulation of the program's ultimate function. Along the way, it is necessary essentially to retrace and map each of the designer's steps — in the opposite order in which they were taken during the program's creation. See Background: Computer Program Design, supra.

As an anatomical guide to this procedure, the following description is helpful:

> At the lowest level of abstraction, a computer program may be thought of in its entirety as a set of individual instructions organized into a hierarchy of modules. At a higher level of abstraction, the instructions in the lowest-level modules may be replaced conceptually by the functions of those modules. At progressively higher levels of abstraction, the functions of higher-level modules conceptually replace the implementations of those modules in terms of lower-level modules and instructions, until finally, one is left with nothing but the ultimate function of the program.... A program has structure at every level of abstraction at which it is viewed. At low levels of abstraction, a program's structure may be quite complex; at the highest level it is trivial.

Englund, at 897-98. Cf. Spivack, at 774.

Step Two: Filtration

Once the program's abstraction levels have been discovered, the substantial similarity inquiry moves from the conceptual to the concrete. Professor Nimmer suggests, and we endorse, a "successive filtering method" for separating protectable expression from non-protectable material. See generally 3 Nimmer § 13.03[F]. This process entails examining the structural components at each level of abstraction to determine whether their particular inclusion at that level was "idea" or was dictated by considerations of efficiency, so as to be necessarily incidental to that idea; required by factors external to the program itself; or taken from the public domain and hence is nonprotectable expression. See also Kretschmer, at 844-45 (arguing that program features dictated by market externalities or efficiency concerns are unprotectable). The structure of any given program may reflect some, all, or none of these considerations. Each case requires its own fact specific investigation.

Strictly speaking, this filtration serves "the purpose of defining the scope of plaintiff's copyright." Brown Bag Software v. Symantec Corp., 960 F.2d 1465, 1475 (9th Cir.) (endorsing "analytic dissection" of computer programs in order to isolate protectable expression), cert. denied, 113 S. Ct. 198, 121 L. Ed. 2d 141 (1992). By applying well developed doctrines of copyright law, it may ultimately leave behind a "core of protectable material." 3 Nimmer § 13.03[F][5], at 13-72. Further explication of this second step may be helpful.

(a) Elements Dictated by Efficiency

The portion of Baker v. Selden, discussed earlier, which denies copyright protection to expression necessarily incidental to the idea being expressed, appears to be the cornerstone for what has developed into the doctrine of merger. See Morrissey v. Procter & Gamble Co., 379 F.2d 675, 678-79 (1st Cir. 1967) (relying on Baker for the proposition that expression embodying the rules of a sweepstakes contest was inseparable from the idea of the contest itself, and therefore were not protectable by copyright); see also Digital Communications, 659 F. Supp. at 457. The doctrine's underlying principle is that "when there is essentially only one way to express an idea, the idea and its expression are inseparable and copyright is no bar to copying that expression." Concrete Machinery Co. v. Classic Lawn Ornaments, Inc., 843 F.2d 600, 606 (1st Cir. 1988). Under these circumstances, the expression is said to have "merged" with the idea itself. In order not to confer a monopoly of the idea upon the copyright owner, such expression should not be protected. See Herbert Rosenthal Jewelry Corp. v. Kalpakian, 446 F.2d 738, 742 (9th Cir. 1971).

CONTU recognized the applicability of the merger doctrine to computer programs. In its report to Congress it stated that:

Copyrighted language may be copied without infringing when there is but a limited number of ways to express a given idea. . . . In the computer context, this means that when specific instructions, even though previously copyrighted, are the only and essential means of accomplishing a given task, their later use by another will not amount to infringement.

CONTU Report at 20. While this statement directly concerns only the application of merger to program code, that is, the textual aspect of the program, it reasonably suggests that the doctrine fits comfortably within the general context of computer programs.

Furthermore, when one considers the fact that programmers generally strive to create programs "that meet the user's needs in the most efficient manner," Menell, at 1052, the applicability of the merger doctrine to computer programs becomes compelling. In the context of computer program design, the concept of efficiency is akin to deriving the most concise logical proof or formulating the most succinct mathematical computation. Thus, the more efficient a set of modules are, the more closely they approximate the idea or process embodied in that particular aspect of the program's structure.

While, hypothetically, there might be a myriad of ways in which a programmer may effectuate certain functions within a program, — i.e., express the idea embodied in a given subroutine — efficiency concerns may so narrow the practical range of choice as to make only one or two forms of expression workable options. See 3 Nimmer § 13.03[F][2], at 13-63; see also Whelan, 797 F.2d at 1243 n.43 ("It is true that for certain tasks there are only a very limited number of file structures available, and in such cases the structures might not be copyrightable . . . ."). Of course, not all program structure is informed by efficiency concerns. See Menell, at 1052 (besides efficiency, simplicity related to user accommodation has become a programming priority). It follows that in order to determine whether the merger doctrine precludes copyright protection to an aspect of a program's structure that is so oriented, a court must inquire "whether the use of this particular set of modules is necessary efficiently to implement that part of the program's process" being implemented. Englund, at 902. If the answer is yes, then the expression represented by the programmer's choice of a specific module or group of modules has merged with their underlying idea and is unprotected. Id. at 902-03.

Another justification for linking structural economy with the application of the merger doctrine stems from a program's essentially utilitarian nature and the competitive forces that exist in the software marketplace. See Kretschmer, at 842. Working in tandem, these factors give rise to a problem of proof which merger helps to eliminate.

Efficiency is an industry-wide goal. Since, as we have already noted, there may be only a limited number of efficient implementations for any given program task, it is quite possible that multiple programmers, working independently, will design the identical method employed in the allegedly infringed work. Of course, if this is the case, there is no copyright infringement. See Roth Greeting Cards v. United Card Co., 429 F.2d 1106, 1110 (9th Cir. 1970); Sheldon, 81 F.2d at 54.

Under these circumstances, the fact that two programs contain the same efficient structure may as likely lead to an inference of independent creation as it does to one of copying. See 3 Nimmer § 13.03[F][2], at 13-65; cf. Herbert Rosenthal Jewelry Corp., 446 F.2d at 741 (evidence of independent creation may stem from defendant's standing as a designer of previous similar works). Thus, since evidence of similarly efficient structure is not particularly probative of copying, it should be disregarded in the overall substantial similarity analysis. See 3 Nimmer § 13.03[F][2], at 13-65.

We find support for applying the merger doctrine in cases that have already addressed the question of substantial similarity in the context of computer program structure. Most recently, in Lotus Dev. Corp., 740 F. Supp. at 66, the district court had before it a claim of copyright infringement relating to the structure of a computer spreadsheet program. The court observed that "the basic spreadsheet screen display that resembles a rotated 'L'. . ., if not present in every expression of such a program, is present in most expressions." Id. Similarly, the court found that "an essential detail present in most if not all expressions of an electronic spreadsheet — is the designation of a particular key that, when pressed, will invoke the menu command system." Id. Applying the merger doctrine, the court denied copyright protection to both program elements.

In Manufacturers Technologies, Inc. v. Cams, Inc., 706 F. Supp. 984, 995-99 (D. Conn. 1989), the infringement claims stemmed from various alleged program similarities "as indicated in their screen displays." Id. at 990. Stressing efficiency concerns in the context of a merger analysis, the court determined that the program's method of allowing the user to navigate within the screen displays was not protectable because, in part, "the process or manner of navigating internally on any specific screen displays . . . is limited in the number of ways it may be simply achieved to facilitate user comfort." Id. at 995.

The court also found that expression contained in various screen displays (in the form of alphabetical and numerical columns), was not the proper subject of copyright protection because it was "necessarily incident to the ideas" embodied in the displays. Id. at 996-97. Cf. Digital Communi-cations, 659 F. Supp. at 460 (finding no merger and affording copyright protection to program's status screen display because "modes of expression chosen . . . are clearly not necessary to the idea of the status screen").

We agree with the approach taken in these decisions, and conclude that application of the merger doctrine in this setting is an effective way to eliminate non-protectable expression contained in computer programs.

(b) Elements Dictated By External Factors

We have stated that where "it is virtually impossible to write about a particular historical era or fictional theme without employing certain 'stock' or standard literary devices," such expression is not copyrightable. Hoehling v. Universal City Studios, Inc., 618 F.2d 972, 979 (2d Cir.), cert. denied, 449 U.S. 841, 66 L. Ed. 2d 49, 101 S. Ct. 121 (1980). For example, the Hoehling case was an infringement suit stemming from several works on the Hindenberg disaster. There we concluded that similarities in represen-tations of German beer halls, scenes depicting German greetings such as "Heil Hitler," or the singing of certain German songs would not lead to a finding of infringement because they were "'indispensable, or at least stan-dard, in the treatment of'" life in Nazi Germany. Id. (quoting Alexander v. Haley, 460 F. Supp. 40, 45 (S.D.N.Y. 1978)). This is known as the scenes a faire doctrine, and like "merger," it has its analogous application to com-puter programs. Cf. Data East USA, 862 F.2d at 208 (applying scenes a faire to a home computer video game).

Professor Nimmer points out that "in many instances it is virtually im-possible to write a program to perform particular functions in a specific computing environment without employing standard techniques." 3 Nim-mer § 13.03[F][3], at 13-65. This is a result of the fact that a programmer's freedom of design choice is often circumscribed by extrinsic considerations such as (1) the mechanical specifications of the computer on which a par-ticular program is intended to run; (2) compatibility requirements of other programs with which a program is designed to operate in conjunction; (3) computer manufacturers' design standards; (4) demands of the industry being serviced; and (5) widely accepted programming practices within the computer industry. Id. at 13-66-71.

Courts have already considered some of these factors in denying copy-right protection to various elements of computer programs. In the Plains Cotton case, the Fifth Circuit refused to reverse the district court's denial of a preliminary injunction against an alleged program infringer because, in part, "many of the similarities between the ... programs [were] dictated by the externalities of the cotton market." 807 F.2d at 1262.

In Manufacturers Technologies, the district court noted that the program's method of screen navigation "is influenced by the type of hardware that the software is designed to be used on." 706 F. Supp. at 995. Because, in part, "the functioning of the hardware package impacted and constrained the type of navigational tools used in plaintiff's screen displays," the court denied copyright protection to that aspect of the program. Cf. Data East USA, 862 F.2d at 209 (reversing a district court's finding of audiovisual work infringement because, inter alia, "the use of the Commodore computer for a karate game intended for home consumption is subject to various constraints inherent in the use of that computer").

Finally, the district court in Q-Co Industries rested its holding on what, perhaps, most closely approximates a traditional scenes a faire rationale. There, the court denied copyright protection to four program modules employed in a teleprompter program. This decision was ultimately based upon the court's finding that "the same modules would be an inherent part of any prompting program." 625 F. Supp. at 616.

Building upon this existing case law, we conclude that a court must also examine the structural content of an allegedly infringed program for elements that might have been dictated by external factors.

(c) Elements taken From the Public Domain

Closely related to the non-protectability of scenes a faire, is material found in the public domain. Such material is free for the taking and cannot be appropriated by a single author even though it is included in a copyrighted work. See E.F. Johnson Co. v. Uniden Corp. of America, 623 F. Supp. 1485, 1499 (D. Minn. 1985); see also Sheldon, 81 F.2d at 54. We see no reason to make an exception to this rule for elements of a computer program that have entered the public domain by virtue of freely accessible program exchanges and the like. See 3 Nimmer § 13.03[F][4]; see also Brown Bag Software, 960 F.2d at 1473 (affirming the district court's finding that "'plaintiffs may not claim copyright protection of an ... expression that is, if not standard, then commonplace in the computer software industry.'"). Thus, a court must also filter out this material from the allegedly infringed program before it makes the final inquiry in its substantial similarity analysis.

Step Three: Comparison

The third and final step of the test for substantial similarity that we believe appropriate for non-literal program components entails a comparison. Once a court has sifted out all elements of the allegedly infringed program which are "ideas" or are dictated by efficiency or external factors, or taken from the public domain, there may remain a core of protectable expression. In terms of a work's copyright value, this is the golden nugget. See Brown Bag Software, 960 F.2d at 1475. At this point, the court's substantial similarity inquiry focuses on whether the defendant copied any aspect of this protected expression, as well as an assessment of the copied portion's relative importance with respect to the plaintiff's overall program. See 3 Nimmer § 13.03[F][5]; Data East USA, 862 F.2d at 208 ("To determine whether similarities result from unprotectable expression, analytic dissection of similarities may be performed. If . . . all similarities in expression arise from use of common ideas, then no substantial similarity can be found.").

3) Policy Considerations

We are satisfied that the three step approach we have just outlined not only comports with, but advances the constitutional policies underlying the Copyright Act. Since any method that tries to distinguish idea from expression ultimately impacts on the scope of copyright protection afforded to a particular type of work, "the line [it draws] must be a pragmatic one, which also keeps in consideration 'the preservation of the balance between competition and protection. . . .'" Apple Computer, 714 F.2d at 1253 (citation omitted).

CA and some amici argue against the type of approach that we have set forth on the grounds that it will be a disincentive for future computer program research and development. At bottom, they claim that if programmers are not guaranteed broad copyright protection for their work, they will not invest the extensive time, energy and funds required to design and improve program structures. While they have a point, their argument cannot carry the day. The interest of the copyright law is not in simply conferring a monopoly on industrious persons, but in advancing the public welfare through rewarding artistic creativity, in a manner that permits the free use and development of non-protectable ideas and processes.

In this respect, our conclusion is informed by Justice Stewart's concise discussion of the principles that correctly govern the adaptation of the copyright law to new circumstances. In Twentieth Century Music Corp. v. Aiken, he wrote:

> The limited scope of the copyright holder's statutory monopoly, like the limited copyright duration required by the Constitution, reflects a balance of competing claims upon the public interest: Creative work is to be encouraged and rewarded, but private motivation must ultimately serve the cause of promoting broad public availability of literature, music, and the other arts.
>
> The immediate effect of our copyright law is to secure a fair return for an "author's" creative labor. But the ultimate aim is, by this incentive, to stimulate artistic creativity for the general public good. . . . When technological change has rendered its literal terms ambiguous, the Copyright Act must be construed in light of this basic purpose. 422 U.S. 151, 156, 95 S. Ct. 2040, 45 L. Ed. 2d 84 (1975) (citations and footnotes omitted).

Recently, the Supreme Court has emphatically reiterated that "the primary objective of copyright is not to reward the labor of authors. . . ." Feist Publications, Inc. v. Rural Tel. Serv. Co., 113 L. Ed. 2d 358, 111 S. Ct. 1282, 1290 (1991) (emphasis added). While the Feist decision deals primarily with the copyrightability of purely factual compilations, its underlying tenets apply to much of the work involved in computer programming. Feist put to rest the "sweat of the brow" doctrine in copyright law. Id. at 1295. The rationale of that doctrine "was that copyright was a reward for the hard work that went into compiling facts." Id. at 1291. The Court flatly rejected this justification for extending copyright protection, noting that it "eschewed the most fundamental axiom of copyright law — that no one may copyright facts or ideas." Id.

Feist teaches that substantial effort alone cannot confer copyright status on an otherwise uncopyrightable work. As we have discussed, despite the fact that significant labor and expense often goes into computer program flow-charting and debugging, that process does not always result in inherently protectable expression. Thus, Feist implicitly undercuts the Whelan rationale, "which allowed copyright protection beyond the literal computer code . . . [in order to] provide the proper incentive for programmers by protecting their most valuable efforts. . . ." Whelan, 797 F.2d at 1237 (footnote omitted). We note that Whelan was decided prior to Feist when the "sweat of the brow" doctrine still had vitality. In view of the Supreme Court's recent holding, however, we must reject the legal basis of CA's disincentive argument.

Furthermore, we are unpersuaded that the test we approve today will lead to the dire consequences for the computer program industry that plaintiff and some amici predict. To the contrary, serious students of the industry have been highly critical of the sweeping scope of copyright protection engendered by the Whelan rule, in that it "enables first comers to 'lock up' basic programming techniques as implemented in programs to perform particular tasks." Menell, at 1087; see also Spivack, at 765 (Whelan "results in an inhibition of creation by virtue of the copyright owner's quasi-monopoly power").

To be frank, the exact contours of copyright protection for non-literal program structure are not completely clear. We trust that as future cases are decided, those limits will become better defined. Indeed, it may well be that the Copyright Act serves as a relatively weak barrier against public access to the theoretical interstices behind a program's source and object codes. This results from the hybrid nature of a computer program, which, while it is literary expression, is also a highly functional, utilitarian component in the larger process of computing.

Generally, we think that copyright registration — with its indiscriminating availability — is not ideally suited to deal with the highly dynamic technology of computer science. Thus far, many of the decisions in this area reflect the courts' attempt to fit the proverbial square peg in a round hole. The district court, see Computer Assocs., 775 F. Supp. at 560, and at least one commentator have suggested that patent registration, with its exacting up-front novelty and non-obviousness requirements, might be the more appropriate rubric of protection for intellectual property of this kind. See Randell M. Whitmeyer, Comment, A Plea for Due Processes: Defining the Proper Scope of Patent Protection for Computer Software, 85 NW. U. L. REV. 1103, 1123-25 (1991); see also Lotus Dev. Corp. v. Borland Int'l, Inc., 788 F. Supp. 78, 91 (D. Mass. 1992) (discussing the potentially supplemental relationship between patent and copyright protection in the context of computer programs). In any event, now that more than 12 years have passed since CONTU issued its final report, the resolution of this specific issue could benefit from further legislative investigation — perhaps a CONTU II.

In the meantime, Congress has made clear that computer programs are literary works entitled to copyright protection. Of course, we shall abide by these instructions, but in so doing we must not impair the overall integrity of copyright law. While incentive based arguments in favor of broad copyright protection are perhaps attractive from a pure policy perspective, see Lotus Dev. Corp., 740 F. Supp. at 58, ultimately, they have a corrosive effect on certain fundamental tenets of copyright doctrine. If the test we have outlined results in narrowing the scope of protection, as we expect it will, that result flows from applying, in accordance with Congressional intent, long-standing principles of copyright law to computer programs. Of course, our decision is also informed by our concern that these fundamental principles remain undistorted.

B. The District Court Decision

We turn now to our review of the district court's decision in this particular case. At the outset, we must address CA's claim that the district court erred by relying too heavily on the court appointed expert's "personal opinions on the factual and legal issues before the court."

1) Use of Expert Evidence in Determining Substantial Similarity Between Computer Programs

Pursuant to Fed.R.Evid. 706, and with the consent of both Altai and CA, Judge Pratt appointed and relied upon Dr. Randall Davis of the Massachusetts Institute of Technology as the court's own expert witness on the issue of substantial similarity. Dr. Davis submitted a comprehensive written report that analyzed the various aspects of the computer programs at issue and evaluated the parties' expert evidence. At trial, Dr. Davis was extensively cross-examined by both CA and Altai.

The well-established general rule in this circuit has been to limit the use of expert opinion in determining whether works at issue are substantially similar. As a threshold matter, expert testimony may be used to assist the fact finder in ascertaining whether the defendant had copied any part of the plaintiff's work. See Arnstein v. Porter, 154 F.2d 464, 468 (2d Cir. 1946). To this end, "the two works are to be compared in their entirety ... [and] in making such comparison resort may properly be made to expert analysis. . . ." 3 Nimmer § 13.03[E][2], at 13-62.16.

However, once some amount of copying has been established, it remains solely for the trier of fact to determine whether the copying was "illicit," that is to say, whether the "defendant took from plaintiff's works so much of what is pleasing to [lay observers] who comprise the audience for whom such [works are] composed, that defendant wrongfully appropriated something which belongs to the plaintiff." Arnstein, 154 F.2d at 473. Since the test for illicit copying is based upon the response of ordinary lay observers, expert testimony is thus "irrelevant" and not permitted. Id. at 468, 473. We have subsequently described this method of inquiry as "merely an alternative way of formulating the issue of substantial similarity." Ideal Toy Corp. v. Fab-Lu Ltd. (Inc.), 360 F.2d 1021, 1023 n.2 (2d Cir. 1966).

Historically, Arnstein's ordinary observer standard had its roots in "an attempt to apply the 'reasonable person' doctrine as found in other areas of the law to copyright." 3 Nimmer § 13.03[E][2], at 13-62.10-11. That approach may well have served its purpose when the material under scrutiny was limited to art forms readily comprehensible and generally familiar to the average lay person. However, in considering the extension of the rule to the present case, we are reminded of Holmes' admonition that, "the life of the law has not been logic: it has been experience." O. W. Holmes, Jr., THE COMMON LAW 1 (1881).

Thus, in deciding the limits to which expert opinion may be employed in ascertaining the substantial similarity of computer programs, we cannot disregard the highly complicated and technical subject matter at the heart of these claims. Rather, we recognize the reality that computer programs are likely to be somewhat impenetrable by lay observers — whether they be judges or juries — and, thus, seem to fall outside the category of works contemplated by those who engineered the Arnstein test. Cf. Dawson v. Hinshaw Music Inc., 905 F.2d 731, 737 (4th Cir.) ("departure from the lay characterization is warranted only where the intended audience possesses 'specialized expertise'"), cert. denied, 112 L. Ed. 2d 523, 111 S. Ct. 511 (1990). As Judge Pratt correctly observed:

> In the context of computer programs, many of the familiar tests of similarity prove to be inadequate, for they were developed historically in the context of artistic and literary, rather than utilitarian, works.

Computer Assocs., 775 F. Supp. at 558.

In making its finding on substantial similarity with respect to computer programs, we believe that the trier of fact need not be limited by the strictures of its own lay perspective. See Dawson, 905 F.2d at 735; Whelan, 797 F.2d at 1233; Broderbund, 648 F. Supp. at 1136 (stating in dictum: "an integrated test involving expert testimony and analytic dissection may well be the wave of the future in this area. . . ."); Brown Bag Software, 960 F.2d at 1478-79 (Sneed, J., concurring); see also 3 Nimmer § 13.03[E][4]; but see Brown Bag Software, 960 F.2d at 1475 (applying the "ordinary reasonable person" standard in substantial similarity test for computer programs). Rather, we leave it to the discretion of the district court to decide to what extent, if any, expert opinion, regarding the highly technical nature of computer programs, is warranted in a given case.

In so holding, we do not intend to disturb the traditional role of lay observers in judging substantial similarity in copyright cases that involve the aesthetic arts, such as music, visual works or literature.

In this case, Dr. Davis' opinion was instrumental in dismantling the intricacies of computer science so that the court could formulate and apply an appropriate rule of law. While Dr. Davis' report and testimony undoubtedly shed valuable light on the subject matter of the litigation, Judge Pratt remained, in the final analysis, the trier of fact. The district court's use of the expert's assistance, in the context of this case, was entirely appropriate.

2) Evidentiary Analysis

The district court had to determine whether Altai's OSCAR 3.5 program was substantially similar to CA's ADAPTER. We note that Judge Pratt's method of analysis effectively served as a road map for our own, with one exception Judge Pratt filtered out the non-copyrightable aspects of OSCAR 3.5 rather than those found in ADAPTER, the allegedly infringed program. We think that our approach — i.e., filtering out the unprotected aspects of an allegedly infringed program and then comparing the end product to the structure of the suspect program — is preferable, and therefore believe that district courts should proceed in this manner in future cases

We opt for this strategy because, in some cases, the defendant's program structure might contain protectable expression and/or other elements that are not found in the plaintiff's program. Since it is extraneous to the allegedly copied work, this material would have no bearing on any potential substantial similarity between the two programs. Thus, its filtration would be wasteful and unnecessarily time consuming. Furthermore, by focusing the analysis on the infringing rather than on the infringed material, a court may mistakenly place too little emphasis on a quantitatively small misappropriation which is, in reality, a qualitatively vital aspect of the plaintiff's protectable expression.

The fact that the district court's analysis proceeded in the reverse order, however, had no material impact on the outcome of this case. Since Judge Pratt determined that OSCAR effectively contained no protectable expression whatsoever, the most serious charge that can be leveled against him is that he was overly thorough in his examination.

The district court took the first step in the analysis set forth in this opinion when it separated the program by levels of abstraction. The district court stated:

> As applied to computer software programs, this abstractions test would progress in order of "increasing generality" from object code, to source code, to parameter lists, to services required, to general outline. In discussing the particular similarities, therefore, we shall focus on these levels. Computer Assocs., 775 F. Supp. at 560. While the facts of a different case might require that a district court draw a more particularized blueprint of a program's overall structure, this description is a workable one for the case at hand.

Moving to the district court's evaluation of OSCAR 3.5's structural components, we agree with Judge Pratt's systematic exclusion of non-protectable expression. With respect to code, the district court observed that after the rewrite of OSCAR 3.4 to OSCAR 3.5, "there remained virtually no lines of code that were identical to ADAPTER." Id. at 561. Accordingly, the court found that the code "presented no similarity at all." Id. at 562.

Next, Judge Pratt addressed the issue of similarity between the two programs' parameter lists and macros. He concluded that, viewing the conflicting evidence most favorably to CA, it demonstrated that "only a few of the lists and macros were similar to protected elements in ADAPTER; the others were either in the public domain or dictated by the functional demands of the program." Id. As discussed above, functional elements and elements taken from the public domain do not qualify for copyright protection. With respect to the few remaining parameter lists and macros, the district court could reasonably conclude that they did not warrant a finding of infringement given their relative contribution to the overall program. See Warner Bros., Inc. v. American Broadcasting Cos., Inc., 720 F.2d 231, 242 (2d Cir. 1983) (discussing de minimis exception which allows for literal copying of a small and usually insignificant portion of the plaintiff's work); 3 Nimmer § 13.03[F][5], at 13-74. In any event, the district court reasonably found that, for lack of persuasive evidence, CA failed to meet its burden of proof on whether the macros and parameter lists at issue were substantially similar. See Computer Assocs., 775 F. Supp. at 562.

The district court also found that the overlap exhibited between the list of services required for both ADAPTER and OSCAR 3.5 was "determined by the demands of the operating system and of the applications program to which it [was] to be linked through ADAPTER or OSCAR. . . ." Id. In other words, this aspect of the program's structure was dictated by the nature of other programs with which it was designed to interact and, thus, is not protected by copyright.

Finally, in his infringement analysis, Judge Pratt accorded no weight to the similarities between the two programs' organizational charts, "because [the charts were] so simple and obvious to anyone exposed to the operation of the programs." Id. CA argues that the district court's action in this regard "is not consistent with copyright law" — that "obvious" expression is protected, and that the district court erroneously failed to realize this. However, to say that elements of a work are "obvious," in the manner in which the district court used the word, is to say that they "follow naturally from the work's theme rather than from the author's creativity." 3 Nimmer § 13.03[F][3], at 13-65. This is but one formulation of the scenes a faire doctrine, which we have already endorsed as a means of weeding out unprotectable expression.

CA argues, at some length, that many of the district court's factual conclusions regarding the creative nature of its program's components are simply wrong. Of course, we are limited in our review of factual findings to setting aside only those that we determine are clearly erroneous. See Fed. R. Civ. P. 52. Upon a thorough review of the voluminous record in this case, which is comprised of conflicting testimony and other highly technical evidence, we discern no error on the part of Judge Pratt, let alone clear error.

Since we accept Judge Pratt's factual conclusions and the results of his legal analysis, we affirm his dismissal of CA's copyright infringement claim based upon OSCAR 3.5. We emphasize that, like all copyright infringement cases, those that involve computer programs are highly fact specific. The amount of protection due structural elements, in any given case, will vary according to the protectable expression found to exist within the program at issue.

II. Trade Secret Preemption

In its complaint, CA alleged that Altai misappropriated the trade secrets contained in the ADAPTER program. Prior to trial, while the proceedings were still before Judge Mishler, Altai moved to dismiss and for summary judgment on CA's trade secret misappropriation claim. Altai argued that section 301 of the Copyright Act preempted CA's state law cause of action. Judge Mishler denied Altai's motion, reasoning that "'the elements of the tort of appropriation of trade secrets through the breach of contract or confidence by an employee are not the same as the elements of a claim of copyright infringement.'" Computer Assocs., 775 F. Supp. at 563.

The parties addressed the preemption issue again, both in pre-and post-trial briefs. Judge Pratt then reconsidered and reversed Judge Mishler's earlier ruling. The district court concluded that CA's trade secret claims were preempted because "CA — which is the master of its own case — has pleaded and proven facts which establish that one act constituted both copyright infringement and misappropriation of trade secrets [namely, the] copying of ADAPTER into OSCAR 3.4 . . . ." Computer Assocs., 775 F. Supp. at 565.

In our original opinion, Computer Assocs. Int'l, Inc. v. Altai, Inc., 1992 U.S. App. LEXIS 14305 (2d Cir. 1992), we affirmed Judge Pratt's decision. CA petitioned for rehearing on this issue. In its petition for rehearing, CA brought to our attention portions of the record below that were not included in the appendix on appeal. CA argued that these documents, along with Judge Mishler's disposition of Altai's motion to dismiss and for summary judgment, established that CA advanced non-preempted trade secret misappropriation claims before both Judge Mishler and Judge Pratt. CA further contended that Judge Pratt failed to consider its theory that Altai was liable for wrongful acquisition of CA's trade secrets through Arney. Upon reconsideration, we have granted the petition for rehearing, withdrawn our initial opinion, and conclude in this amended opinion that the district court's preemption ruling on CA's trade secret claims should be vacated. We accordingly vacate the judgment of the district court on this point and remand CA's trade secret claims for a determination on the merits.

A. General Law of Copyright Preemption Regarding Trade Secrets and Computer Programs

Congress carefully designed the statutory framework of federal copyright preemption. In order to insure that the enforcement of these rights remains solely within the federal domain, section 301(a) of the Copyright Act expressly preempts all legal or equitable rights that are equivalent to any of the exclusive rights within the general scope of copyright as specified by section 106 in works of authorship that are fixed in a tangible medium of expression and come within the subject matter of copyright as specified by sections 102 and 103 .... 17 U.S.C. § 301(a). This sweeping displacement of state law is, however, limited by section 301(b), which provides, in relevant part, that nothing in this title annuls or limits any rights or remedies under the common law or statutes of any State with respect to ... activities violating legal or equitable rights that are not equivalent to any of the exclusive rights within the general scope of copyright as specified by section 106. ... 17 U.S.C. § 301(b)(3). Section 106, in turn, affords a copyright owner the exclusive right to: (1) reproduce the copyrighted work; (2) prepare derivative works; (3) distribute copies of the work by sale or otherwise; and, with respect to certain artistic works, (4) perform the work publicly; and (5) display the work publicly. See 17 U.S.C. § 106(1)-(5).

Section 301 thus preempts only those state law rights that "may be abridged by an act which, in and of itself, would infringe one of the exclusive rights" provided by federal copyright law. See Harper & Row, Publishers, Inc. v. Nation Enters., 723 F.2d 195, 200 (2d Cir. 1983), rev'd on other grounds, 471 U.S. 539, 85 L. Ed. 2d 588, 105 S. Ct. 2218 (1985). But if an "extra element" is "required instead of or in addition to the acts of reproduction, performance, distribution or display, in order to constitute a state-created cause of action, then the right does not lie 'within the general scope of copyright,' and there is no preemption." 1 Nimmer § 1.01[B], at 1-14-15; see also Harper & Row, Publishers, Inc., 723 F.2d at 200 (where state law right "is predicated upon an act incorporating elements beyond mere reproduction or the like, the [federal and state] rights are not equivalent" and there is no preemption).

A state law claim is not preempted if the "extra element" changes the "nature of the action so that it is qualitatively different from a copyright infringement claim." Mayer v. Josiah Wedgwood & Sons, Ltd., 601 F. Supp. 1523, 1535 (S.D.N.Y. 1985); see Harper & Row, Publishers, Inc., 723 F.2d at 201. To determine whether a claim meets this standard, we must determine "what plaintiff seeks to protect, the theories in which the matter is thought to be protected and the rights sought to be enforced." 1 Roger M. Milgrim, Milgrim on Trade Secrets § 2.06A[3], at 2-150 (1992) (hereinafter "Milgrim"). An action will not be saved from preemption by elements such as awareness or intent, which alter "the action's scope but not its nature . . . ." Mayer, 601 F. Supp. at 1535.

Following this "extra element" test, we have held that unfair competition and misappropriation claims grounded solely in the copying of a plaintiff's protected expression are preempted by section 301. See, e.g., Walker v. Time Life Films, Inc., 784 F.2d 44, 53 (2d Cir.), cert. denied, 476 U.S. 1159, 90 L. Ed. 2d 721, 106 S. Ct. 2278 (1986); Warner Bros. Inc. v. American Broadcasting Cos., 720 F.2d 231, 247 (2d Cir. 1983); Durham Indus., Inc. v. Tomy Corp., 630 F.2d 905, 919 & n. 15 (2d Cir. 1980). We also have held to be preempted a tortious interference with contract claim grounded in the impairment of a plaintiff's right under the Copyright Act to publish derivative works. See Harper & Row, Publishers, Inc., 723 F.2d at 201.

However, many state law rights that can arise in connection with instances of copyright infringement satisfy the extra element test, and thus are not preempted by section 301. These include unfair competition claims based upon breach of confidential relationship, breach of fiduciary duty and trade secrets. Balboa Ins. Co. v. Trans Global Equities, 218 Cal. App. 3d 1327, 1339-53, 267 Cal. Rptr. 787, 793-803 (Ct. App. 3rd Dist.), cert. denied, 111 S. Ct. 347, 112 L. Ed. 2d 311 (1990).

Trade secret protection, the branch of unfair competition law at issue in this case, remains a "uniquely valuable" weapon in the defensive arsenal of computer programmers. See 1 Milgrim § 2.06A[5][c], at 2-172.4. Precisely because trade secret doctrine protects the discovery of ideas, processes, and systems which are explicitly precluded from coverage under copyright law, courts and commentators alike consider it a necessary and integral part of the intellectual property protection extended to computer programs. See id.; Integrated Cash Management Servs., Inc. v. Digital Transactions, Inc., 920 F.2d 171, 173 (2d Cir. 1990) (while plaintiff withdrew copyright infringement claim for misappropriation of computer program, relief for theft of trade secret sustained); Healthcare Affiliated Servs., Inc. v. Lippany, 701 F. Supp. 1142, 1152-55 (W.D.Pa. 1988) (finding likelihood of success on trade secret claim, but not copyright claim); Q-Co Indus., Inc., 625 F. Supp. at 616-18 (finding likelihood of success on trade secret claim, but no merit to copyright claim); Kretschmer, at 847-49.

The legislative history of section 301 states that "the evolving common law rights of . . . trade secrets . . . would remain unaffected as long as the causes of action contain elements, such as . . . a breach of trust or confidentiality, that are different in kind from copyright infringement." House Report, at 5748. Congress did not consider the term "misappropriation" to be "necessarily synonymous with copyright infringement," or to serve as the talisman of preemption. Id.

Trade secret claims often are grounded upon a defendant's breach of a duty of trust or confidence to the plaintiff through improper disclosure of confidential material. See, e.g., Mercer v. C.A. Roberts Co., 570 F.2d 1232, 1238 (5th Cir. 1978); Brignoli v. Balch Hardy and Scheinman, Inc., 645 F. Supp. 1201, 1205 (S.D.N.Y. 1986). The defendant's breach of duty is the gravamen of such trade secret claims, and supplies the "extra element" that qualitatively distinguishes such trade secret causes of action from claims for copyright infringement that are based solely upon copying. See, e.g., Warrington Assoc., Inc. v. Real-Time Eng'g Sys., Inc., 522 F. Supp. 367, 369 (N.D. Ill. 1981); Brignoli, 645 F. Supp. at 1205; see also generally Balboa Ins. Co., 218 Cal. App. 3d at 1346-50, 267 Cal. Rptr. at 798-802 (reviewing cases).

B. Preemption in this Case

The district court stated that:

> Were CA's [trade secret] allegations premised on a theory of illegal acquisition of a trade secret, a charge that might have been alleged against Arney, who is not a defendant in this case, the preemption analysis might be different, for there seems to be no corresponding right guaranteed to copyright owners by § 106 of the copyright act.

Computer Assocs., 775 F. Supp. at 565. However, the court concluded that CA's trade secret claims were not grounded in a theory that Altai violated a duty of confidentiality to CA. Rather, Judge Pratt stated that CA proceeded against Altai solely "on a theory that the misappropriation took place by Altai's use of ADAPTER — the same theory as the copyright infringement count." Id. The district court reasoned that "the right to be free from trade secret misappropriation through 'use', and the right to exclusive reproduction and distribution of a copyrighted work are not distinguishable." Id. Because he concluded that there was no qualitative difference between the elements of CA's state law trade secret claims and a claim for federal copyright infringement, Judge Pratt ruled that CA's trade secret claims were preempted by section 301.

We agree with CA that the district court failed to address fully the factual and theoretical bases of CA's trade secret claims. The district court relied upon the fact that Arney — not Altai — allegedly breached a duty to CA of confidentiality by stealing secrets from CA and incorporating those secrets into OSCAR 3.4. However, under a wrongful acquisition theory based on Restatement (First) of Torts § 757 (1939), Williams and Altai may be liable for violating CA's right of confidentiality. Section 757 states in relevant part:

> One who discloses or uses another's trade secret, without a privilege to do so, is liable to another if . . . . (c) he learned the secret from a third person with notice of the fact that it was a secret and that the third person discovered it by improper means or that the third person's disclosure of it was otherwise a breach of his duty to the other . . . .

Actual notice is not required for such a third party acquisition claim; constructive notice is sufficient. A defendant is on constructive notice when, "from the information which he has, a reasonable man would infer [a breach of confidence], or if, under the circumstances, a reasonable man would be put on inquiry and an inquiry pursued with reasonable intelligence and diligence would disclose the [breach]." Id., comment 1; Metallurgical Indus., Inc. v. Fourtek, Inc., 790 F.2d 1195, 1204 (5th Cir. 1986); Vantage Point, Inc. v. Parker Bros., Inc., 529 F. Supp. 1204, 1210 n.2 (E.D.N.Y. 1981), aff'd, 697 F.2d 301 (2d Cir. 1982); see also Rohm and Haas Co. v. Adco Chem. Co., 689 F.2d 424, 431 (3rd Cir. 1982) ("Defendants never asked where the 'Harvey process' had come from. Defendants therefore were charged 'with whatever knowledge such inquiry would have led to.'") (citation omitted); Colgate-Palmolive Co. v. Carter Prods., Inc., 230 F.2d 855, 864 (4th Cir.) (per curiam) (defendant "'must have known by the exercise of fair business principles'" that its employee's work was covered by an agreement not to disclose) (citation omitted), cert. denied, 352 U.S. 843, 1 L. Ed. 2d 59, 77 S. Ct. 43 (1956); 1 Milgrim § 5.04[2][c].

We agree with the district court that New Jersey's governing governmental interest choice of law analysis directs the application of Texas law to CA's trade secret misappropriation claim. See Computer Assocs., 775 F. Supp. at 566. Texas law recognizes trade secret misappropriation claims grounded in the reasoning of Restatement section 757(c), see, e.g., Fourtek, 790 F.2d at 1204, and the facts alleged by CA may well support such a claim.

It is undisputed that, when Arney stole the ADAPTER code and incorporated it into his design of OSCAR 3.4, he breached his confidentiality agreement with CA. The district court noted that while such action might constitute a valid claim against Arney, CA is the named defendant in this lawsuit. Additionally, the district court found, as a matter of fact, that "no one at Altai, other than Arney, knew that Arney had the ADAPTER code . . . ." Computer Assocs., 775 F. Supp. at 554. However, the district court did not consider fully Altai's potential liability for improper trade secret acquisition. It did not consider the question of Altai's trade secret liability in connection with OSCAR 3.4 under a constructive notice theory, or Altai's potential liability under an actual notice theory in connection with OSCAR 3.5.

The district court found that, prior to CA's bringing suit, Altai was not on actual notice of Arney's theft of trade secrets, and incorporation of those secrets into OSCAR 3.4. However, by virtue of Williams' close relationship with Arney, Williams' general familiarity with CA's programs (having once been employed by CA himself), and the fact that Arney used the ADAPTER program in an office at Altai adjacent to Williams during a period in which he had frequent contact with Williams regarding the OSCAR/VSE project, Williams (and through him Altai) may well have been on constructive notice of Arney's breach of his duty of confidentiality toward CA. The district court did not address whether Altai was on constructive notice, thereby placing it under a duty of inquiry; rather the court's finding that only Arney affirmatively knew of the theft of CA's trade secrets and incorporation of those secrets into OSCAR 3.4 simply disposed of the issue of actual notice in connection with the creation of OSCAR 3.4. CA's claim of liability based on constructive notice, never considered in the district court's opinion, must be determined on remand.

With respect to actual notice, it is undisputed that CA's first complaint, filed in August 1988, informed Altai of Arney's trade secret violations in connection with the creation of OSCAR 3.4. The first complaint alleged that Arney assisted in the development of ADAPTER, thereby obtaining knowledge of CA's related trade secrets. It also alleged that Altai misappropriated CA's trade secrets by incorporating them into ZEKE.

In response to CA's complaint, Altai rewrote OSCAR 3.4, creating OSCAR 3.5. While we agree with the district court that OSCAR 3.5 did not contain any expression protected by copyright, it may nevertheless still have embodied many of CA's trade secrets that Arney brought with him to Altai. Since Altai's rewrite was conducted with full knowledge of Arney's prior misappropriation, in breach of his duty of confidentiality, it follows that OSCAR 3.5 was created with actual knowledge of trade secret violations. Thus, with regard to OSCAR 3.5, CA has a viable trade secret claim against Altai that must be considered by the district court on remand. This claim is grounded in Altai's alleged use of CA's trade secrets in the creation of OSCAR 3.5, while on actual notice of Arney's theft of trade secrets and incorporation of those secrets into OSCAR 3.4. The district court correctly stated that a state law claim based solely upon Altai's "use", by copying, of ADAPTER's non-literal elements could not satisfy the governing "extra element" test, and would be preempted by section 301. However, where the use of copyrighted expression is simultaneously the violation of a duty of confidentiality established by state law, that extra element renders the state right qualitatively distinct from the federal right, thereby foreclosing preemption under section 301.

We are also convinced that CA adequately pled a wrongful acquisition claim before Judge Mishler and Judge Pratt. In ruling that CA failed to properly plead a non-preempted claim, Judge Pratt relied heavily upon two allegations in CA's amended complaint. Id. at 563-64. They read as follows:

P 57. By reason of the facts stated in paragraph 39 and by copying from CA-SCHEDULER into ZEKE, ZACK and ZEBB the various elements stated in paragraphs 39-51, 54 and 55, defendant Altai has infringed [CA's] copyright in CA-SCHEDULER.

* * *

P 73. Defendant's incorporation into its ZEKE, ZACK and ZEBB programs of the various elements contained in the ADAPTER component of [CA's] CA-SCHEDULER program as set out in paragraphs 39-51, 54 and 55 constitutes the willful misappropriation of the proprietary property and trade secrets of plaintiff [CA].

From these pleadings, Judge Pratt concluded that the very same act, i.e., Altai's copying of various elements of CA's program, was the basis for both CA's copyright infringement and trade secret claims. See id. at 564. We agree with Judge Pratt that CA's allegations are somewhat inartfully stated. However, when taken together, the terms "incorporation" and "misappropriation" in paragraph 73 above suggest to us an act of a qualitatively different nature than the infringement pled in paragraph 57. House Report, at 5748 ("'misappropriation' is not necessarily synonymous with copyright infringement").

In support of our reading, we note that paragraphs 65-75 of CA's amended complaint alleged facts that reasonably comprise the elements of a wrongful acquisition of trade secrets claim. CA averred that, while he was employed at CA, Arney learned CA's trade secrets regarding the ADAPTER program. CA further alleged that after Arney went to work for Altai, Altai misappropriated those trade secrets by incorporating CA's ADAPTER program into its own product. Finally, CA claimed that the trade secret misappropriation was carried out "in a willful, wanton and reckless manner in disregard of [CA's] rights." In other words, Altai could have reasonably inferred from CA's allegations that CA's claim, in part, rested on Williams' "wanton and reckless" behavior in the face of constructive notice.

In addition, while responding to Altai's preemption argument in its motion to dismiss and for summary judgment, CA specifically argued in its brief to Judge Mishler that "it can easily be inferred that Mr. Arney was hired by Altai to misappropriate [CA's] confidential source code for Altai's benefit." At oral argument, CA further contended that:

The circumstances of Mr. Arney's hiring suggested that Mr. Williams wanted more than Mr. Arney's ability and in fact got exactly what he wanted. And that is Computer Associates' confidential Adapter technology.

* * *

[Arney testified that he] surreptitiously took that code home from Computer Associates after giving notice he was going to go to work for Altai, and after being hired by Mr. Williams to come to Altai and reconstruct Zeke, to work on the MVS operating system.

In the aftermath of Judge Mishler's ruling in its favor on Altai's motion to dismiss and for summary judgment, CA reasonably believed that it had sufficiently alleged a non-preempted claim. And, in light of CA's arguments and Judge Mishler's ruling, Altai clearly was on notice that the amended complaint placed non-preempted trade secret claims in play. See 5 Charles A. Wright & Arthur R. Miller, Federal Practice and Procedure § 1215, at 136-38 (2d ed. 1990) (federal pleading standards require plaintiff to provide defendant with fair notice of claim and grounds it rests on).

Accordingly, we vacate the judgment of the district court and remand for reconsideration of those aspects of CA's trade secret claims related to Altai's alleged constructive notice of Arney's theft of CA's trade secrets and incorporation of those secrets into OSCAR 3.4. We note, however, that CA may be unable to recover damages for its trade secrets which are embodied in OSCAR 3.4 since Altai has conceded copyright liability and damages for its incorporation of ADAPTER into OSCAR 3.4. CA may not obtain a double recovery where the damages for copyright infringement and trade secret misappropriation are coextensive.

However, additional trade secret damages may well flow from CA's creation of OSCAR 3.5. Judge Pratt correctly acknowledged that "if CA's claim of misappropriation of trade secrets did not fail on preemption grounds, it would be necessary to examine in some detail the conflicting claims and evidence relating to the process by which Altai rewrote OSCAR and ultimately produced version 3.5." Computer Assocs., 775 F. Supp. at 554-55; see also 1 Milgrim § 5.04[2][d], at 5-148 ("after notice, the [innocent] second user should cease the use, and if he does not he can be enjoined and held liable for damages arising from such use subsequent to notice"). Since we hold that CA's trade secret claims are not preempted, and that, in writing OSCAR 3.5, Altai had actual notice of Arney's earlier trade secret violations, we vacate and remand for such further inquiry anticipated by the district court. If the district court finds that CA was injured by Altai's unlawful use of CA's trade secrets in creating OSCAR 3.5, CA is entitled to an award of damages for trade secret misappropriation, as well as consideration by the district court of CA's request for injunctive relief on its trade secret claim.

Conclusion

In adopting the above three step analysis for substantial similarity between the non-literal elements of computer programs, we seek to insure two things: (1) that programmers may receive appropriate copyright protection for innovative utilitarian works containing expression; and (2) that non-protectable technical expression remains in the public domain for others to use freely as building blocks in their own work. At first blush, it may seem counter-intuitive that someone who has benefited to some degree from illicitly obtained material can emerge from an infringement suit relatively unscathed. However, so long as the appropriated material consists of non-protectable expression, "this result is neither unfair nor unfortunate. It is the means by which copyright advances the progress of science and art." Feist, 111 S. Ct. at 1290.

Furthermore, we underscore that so long as trade secret law is employed in a manner that does not encroach upon the exclusive domain of the Copyright Act, it is an appropriate means by which to secure compensation for software espionage.

Accordingly, we affirm the judgment of the district court in part; vacate in part; and remand for further proceedings. The parties shall bear their own costs of appeal, including the petition for rehearing.

Dissent: Altimari, Circuit Judge, Concurring in part and Dissenting in part:

Because I believe that our original opinion, see Computer Assoc. Int'l v. Altai, 1992 U.S. App. LEXIS 14305, 1992 WL 139364 (2d Cir. 1992), is a reasoned analysis of the issues presented, I adhere to the original determination and therefore concur in Part 1 and respectfully dissent from Part 2 of the amended opinion.

Notes and Questions

1. The second step in the court's analytical process is "filtration." The court observes that the expression in computer programs is often dictated by

functional concerns — e.g., the microprocessor requests that data be transmitted from the disk drive — and that there are a limited number of relatively efficient ways to frame such requests. The court does not want expression that is dictated by such functional concerns to be protected by copyright. Moreover, the Court notes that some types of program instruction are commonplace — analogizing to *scenes a faire* doctrine which precludes the copyrighting of commonplace descriptions and events (e.g., "under a clear blue sky"). Recall the German Supreme Court's much-criticized decision in *Inkasso*. What was the German Court trying to accomplish with its qualitative test of the skill level of the programmer? Was it trying to exclude functional and commonplace elements from copyright protection, or did it have some other objective in view?

2. In the notes following the *Lotus v. Borland* case, we suggested that many Courts may find it difficult to apply the tests articulated in *Computer Associates*. We asked whether you might propose a different kind of test for infringement in the computer software context. We also indicated that some experts believe the kind of non-literal infringement addressed in *Computer Associates* would be unlikely to take place in the developing countries. They suggest it will be more likely to find simple copying or counterfeiting in these countries. We ask you to revisit these issues. Is the *Computer Associates* analysis practical in the global context? Should we assume that developing country entrepreneurs will limit their misappropriation to copying program CDs without altering the programs?

3. In the second part of its opinion, the Second Circuit considers the relationship between state trade secret law and federal copyright law. The court holds that state trade secret law is not preempted by federal copyright law to the extent that there is an additional substantive element to a state trade secret law cause of action. What is the additional element in Computer Associate's trade secret law claim that was not encompassed within its copyright claim?

---

b. Copyright Versus Patent Revisited

In connection with our study of the patent policy of the European Union/EPO, we noted that so far there has been an aversion to the use of patents to protect computer software. We also noted that the U.S. PTO and U.S. courts have exhibited a more receptive attitude toward the patenting of software over the past several years. In the following excerpt from an article by Pamela Samuelson and others, the U.S. trend toward allowing the patenting of software is described. In the view of the authors of the article, patent protection as a mechanism for protecting computer software remains beset by difficulties.

A Manifesto Concerning the Legal Protection of Computer Programs*

Pamela Samuelson, Randall Davis, Mitchell D. Kapor, & J.H. Reichman

*****

2.2.2 Why Patent Law Is Ill-Suited to Protecting Software Innovation

The dual character of computer programs — which are both writings and machines at the same time — has presented some difficulties for those wanting to use patent law as a means of legal protection for software innovations. Patent law has traditionally excluded texts ("printed matter"), as well as methods embodied in texts, from its domain.[121] Under this doctrine, program code is unpatentable even though, once in machine readable form, it is unquestionably a technological process.[122]

Under the "printed matter" rule and the kindred "mental process"

---

*94 Colum. L. Rev. 2308 (1994).

[121]See, e.g., In re Rice, 132 F.2d 140, 141 (C.C.P.A. 1942) (holding that a pictorial method of writing music was not patentable subject matter under the "printed matter" rule); In re Russell, 48 F.2d 668, 669 (C.C.P.A. 1931) (holding method of arranging directories in phonetic order unpatentable). See generally Note, The Patentability of Printed Matter: Critique and Proposal, 18 Geo. Wash. L. Rev. 475 (1950) (exploring case law development of "printed matter" doctrine). The Patent and Trademark Office currently relies on the "printed matter" rule as its basis for excluding programs from the subject matter of patent law. See, e.g., United States Patent and Trademark Office & United States Copyright Office, Patent-Copyright Laws Overlap Study 46 (1991) [hereinafter Overlap Study].

[122]It is because programs in machine-readable form are utilitarian processes that Professor Chisum has argued that program instructions should be regarded as patentable subject matter. See 1 Donald S. Chisum, Patents 1.02[4] (1994).

doctrine,[123] more abstract elements of programs should also be unpatentable.[124] Perhaps out of deference to their traditionally separate domains, patent law has generally left innovations in the representation, ordering, and presentation of information to copyright.[125] The Patent and Trademark Office and the courts have historically explained that such innovations lacked an industrial character.[126]

In reliance on these doctrines, the Patent Office for nearly two decades, refused patent applications for software innovations on subject matter grounds.[127] The U.S. Supreme Court seemed to concur in this legal

---

[123]A number of appellate courts have ruled that information processes are unpatentable. See, e.g., In re Abrams, 188 F.2d 165, 168 (C.C.P.A. 1951) (holding that method involving "calculating," "measuring," "observing," and "comparing" of data elements was unpatentable). The Patent Office has regarded information processes to be unpatentable even if an applicant claims more than a mental implementation of them (e.g., use of some technology, such as pen or calculator, to carry them out). See Samuelson, Benson Revisited, supra note 5 [Pamela Samuelson, Benson Revisited: The Case Against Patent Protection for Algorithms and Other Computer Program-Related Inventions, 39 Emory L.J. 1025(1990) [hereinafter Samuelson, Benson Revisited]], at 1043-44. The United States Supreme Court has stated that "mental processes" are unpatentable subject matter. See Gottschalk v. Benson, 409 U.S. 63, 67 (1972); see also In re Meyer, 688 F.2d 789, 79596 (C.C.P.A. 1982) (rejecting claims for programmable medical diagnosis system as merely simulating thought processes of doctors). The name generally given to the doctrine established in this line of cases is the "mental step" or "mental process" doctrine. See 1 Chisum, supra note 122, 1.03[6].

[124]Mathematical principles, like laws of nature and other scientific principles, have also been regarded as unpatentable in character. See, e.g., Gottschalk, 409 U.S. at 71-72 (program algorithm held unpatentable mathematical principle).

[125]See generally Ginsburg, supra note 74 [Jane C. Ginsburg, Creation and Commercial Value: Copyright Protection of Works of Information, 90 Colum. L. Rev. 1865, 1893 (1990)] (tracing development of copyright protection for selection, arrangement, and manner of presentation of information).

[126]Both relied on Cochrane v. Deener, 94 U.S. 780 (1877), as having established that patentable "processes" were those that involved the transformation of matter from one physical state to another. See Gottschalk, 409 U.S. at 69-70; see also Samuelson, Benson Revisited, supra, at 1033-40, 1056-57 (discussing cases and reasons for this interpretation of process). For a discussion of some processes that have long been thought to be ineligible for patent protection, see 1 Chisum, supra note 122, 1.03. But see Chisum, Algorithms, supra note 1 [Donald S. Chisum, The Patentability of Algorithms, 47 U. Pitt. L. Rev. 959 (1986)], at 1020 (arguing that program algorithms should be patented).

[127]The Court of Customs and Patent Appeals overturned some of these subject matter rulings. See Samuelson, Benson Revisited, supra, at 1041-48.

position, and its decisions influenced the patent policies of other nations.[128] Since the mid-1980s,[129] however, patent protection has become available for a wide range of software innovations, seemingly because of the perceived need for more legal protection of programs than copyright alone could provide.[130]

Apart from subject matter concerns, one reason that patents have limited application in the protection of behavior is that patents typically issue for particular methods of achieving results, rather than for results themselves.[131] It is quite possible to produce functionally indistinguishable program behaviors through use of more than one method.[132] This means that holding a patent on one method of generating certain results could not prevent the use of another method, even if those results were the program's principal source of value.[133] Hence, patents on methods would not protect behavior and therefore would not protect the primary entity of value in software. Yet if the Patent and Trademark Office were willing to issue a

---

[128]See Diamond v. Diehr, 450 U.S. 175, 185-87 (1981) (holding rubber curing process that included computer program patentable, but reaffirming Benson and Flook on unpatentability of algorithms); Parker v. Flook, 437 U.S. 584 (1978) (holding algorithm unpatentable, even though industrial application specified); Gottschalk, 409 U.S. at 63 (holding algorithm unpatentable). For international influences, see Henri Hanneman, The Patentability of Computer Software 243 (1985) (discussing impact on European patent policy for software innovations); see also Samuelson, Benson Revisited, supra note 5, at 1132-33 & n.426 (discussing standards for patenting software-related innovations in Europe).

[129]See Samuelson, Benson Revisited, supra, at 1093-94.

[130]See Barton, supra note 6 [John H. Barton, Adapting the Intellectual Property System to New Technologies, in Global Dimensions of Intellectual Property Rights in Science and Technology 256, 266 (Mitchel B. Wallerstein et al. eds., 1993)], at 265 (suggesting this rationale for the revised patent policy).

[131]See, e.g., U.S. Patent No. 4,821,211 to Torres, issued Apr. 11, 1989 (Method of Navigating Among Program Menus Using a Graphical Menu Tree); U.S. Patent No. 4,796,220 to Wolfe, issued Jan. 3, 1989 (Method of Controlling the Copying of Software).

[132]See, e.g., 3 Knuth, supra note 64 [Donald E. Knuth, Sorting and Searching (4th ed. 1975)] (volume describing various ways to accomplish sorting and searching).

[133]Some holders of software-related patents have, however, tried to claim all means of achieving particular results. See, e.g., Brian Kahin, The Software Patent Crisis, Tech. Rev., Apr. 1990, at 53, 58 (giving examples of overbroad patents for performing certain functions by computer).

patent with claims for any means of achieving a particular set of results, such a patent would issue at a high level of generality and would inhibit competition in development of useful program behaviors out of proportion to the innovation actually contributed by the claimant.[134]

However, the more profound problem with using patent law to protect functional program behavior, user interfaces, and the industrial design of programs that produce behavior is that these innovations are typically of an incremental sort. Classical intellectual property regimes do not protect this kind of innovation.[136] Patent law requires an inventive advance over the prior art before it grants protection.[137] Protecting incremental innovations in program behavior through patent law would thwart the economic goals of the patent system: to grant exclusive rights only when an innovator has made a substantial contribution to the art and advanced competition to a new level.[138]

---

[134]See, e.g., U.S. Patent No. 5,317,757 to Medicke & Posharow, issued May 31, 1994 (System and Method for Finite State Machine Processing Using Action Vectors); U.S. Patent No. 5,105,184 to Pirani & Ekedal, issued Apr. 14, 1992 (Methods for Displaying and Integrating Commercial Advertisements with Computer Software).

Other factors thought by some to impede the utility of patents in the software industry include the high costs and long delays required to obtain such protection for program innovations. See, e.g., Garfinkel et al., supra note 5 [Simson L. Garfinkel et al., Why Patents Are Bad for Software, Issues in Sci. & Tech., Fall 1991, at 50.], at 52; Kahin, supra note 133, at 55. As a practical matter, these barriers might make patent protection unavailable to small software developers with limited resources. Software developers generally need legal protection most in the first few years after they introduce an innovation to the market, a need which patents cannot meet. United States patent law provides no protection to an invention (except if it can be kept as a trade secret) until the patent actually issues. This rule makes many software innovations vulnerable to appropriation in the first years after they are introduced into the market. If and when a patent finally issues, it may also come after the useful commercial life of the product embodying the innovation, because of the fast pace of innovation in the industry. A form of legal protection for the first years of a technical innovation in software would, accordingly, be better tailored to the needs of software entrepreneurs. See infra text accompanying notes 411, 414.

[136]Trade secrecy law protects incremental innovations that can be kept a secret. See Reichman, Legal Hybrids, supra note 100 (concerning legal hybrid regimes, created to protect some publicly disclosed incremental innovations).

[137]See 35 U.S.C. 101 (1988).

[138]See U.S. Const. art. I, 8, cl. 8; Michael Lehmann, The Theory of Property Rights and the Protection of Intellectual and Industrial Property, 16 I.I.C. (1985)

In this respect, software resembles semiconductor chips whose industrial designs are rarely inventive. Congress recognized that the chip industry's products were both patentable and vulnerable to rapid imitative copying that undermined innovators' ability to recoup research and development costs; this undermined incentives to make the substantial investments necessary to develop new chip designs.[139] To provide proper incentives for semiconductor designs, Congress passed the Semiconductor Chip Protection Act of 1984 (SCPA).[140] It may eventually need to do the same for computer software, where the typically incremental nature of innovation also impedes the utility of patent protection.

In addition, the application of both copyright and patent law to software innovations may impair the effectiveness of both forms of protection. It has also created considerable uncertainty about the scope of protection available from each.[141] No one knows just where the boundary line between these domains does or should lie.[142] The economic goals of both regimes can be thwarted when both are applied to a dual-character subject matter such as computer programs.[143] This is especially true if copyright law, with its long duration of protection, its low creativity threshold, and its automatic protection, is construed so broadly that it encompasses technical innovations that should be regulated by patent law.[144]

---

[139]See H.R. Rep. No. 781, 98th Cong., 2d Sess. 140, (1984), reprinted in U.S.C.C.A.N. 5750, 575060.

[140]17 U.S.C. 901914 (1988).

[141]See Pamela Samuelson, Survey on the Patent/Copyright Interface for Computer Programs, 17 AIPLA Q.J. 256, 25961 (1989) (showing differences of opinion among computer lawyers).

[142]Is a program's data structure copyrightable, patentable, both, or neither? For discussion of this issue under each law without regard to the other, see Whelan Assocs. v. Jaslow Dental Lab., Inc., 797 F.2d 1222 (3d Cir. 1986) (seeming to regard data structures as copyrightable), cert. denied, 479 U.S. 1031 (1987); In re Bradley, 600 F.2d 807 (C.C.P.A. 1979) (data structure for microcode function held patentable), aff'd sub nom. Diamond v. Bradley, 450 U.S. 381 (1981) (equally divided court); see also In re Lowry, 32 F.3d 1579 (Fed. Cir. 1994) (holding data structure patentable subject matter); In re Warmerdam, 3 U.S.P.Q.2d (BNA) 1754 (Fed. Cir. 1994) (holding data structure unpatentable, although claim for machine implementation of data structure was patentable).

[143] See Reichman, Legal Hybrids, supra note 100 [J.H. Reichman, Legal Hybrids Between the Patent and Copyright Paradigms, 94 Colum. L. Rev. 2432], at 2451-52 (discussing the economic goals of the classical intellectual property regimes).

[144]See OTA Report, supra note 6 [Office of Technology Assessment, United States Con-

Notes and Questions

1. In an earlier part of the same article, the authors describe the drawbacks to "traditional" copyright protection for computer software. They make a proposal for "anti-cloning" legislation as a *sui generis* form of software protection. They do not suggest a particular piece of legislation, but rather lay out a number of the features which they believe such legislation might usefully include. The authors do not make a specific proposal regarding the term of protection, yet it seems clear that for at least an initial strong stage of protection, the term would be more limited than that of traditional copyright.

The authors do not purport that their anti-cloning proposal would put an end to the difficulties that surround determining which elements of a program should be protected. What they do suggest is that it may be easier to base such a determination (in non-literal infringement cases) on factors like the overall design and functioning of a program, rather than on expression in the source code.

Do you think some form of anti-cloning protection might provide a more practical basis on which courts could evaluate claims of non-literal infringement?

2. In July, 1998 the U.S. Court of Appeals for the Federal Circuit decided *State Street Bank & Trust Co. v. Signature Financial Group.*[1] The court upheld a decision of the U.S. PTO to grant a patent for a data processing system operating on a personal computer. The computer program at the heart of this system essentially calculated on a daily basis the value of various mu-

---

gress, Intellectual Property Rights in an Age of Electronics and Information (1986)], at 83. This problem is especially serious in light of the interchangeability of software and hardware. At the moment it is generally not feasible to transform hardware into software embodiments. If the technology develops to make this transition trivial, however, the inventor of any piece of digital electronics could acquire 75 years of protection without having to prove nonobviousness or to pass an examination of the prior art. It would be odd if the choice between two interchangeable media in which a given innovation could be embodied, rather than the innovation itself, determined the form of legal protection available for it.

[1] 1998 U.S. App Lexis 16869 (decided July 23, 1998).

tual funds tied together in a partnership arrangement, and allowed the preparation of various complex financial reports. The CAFC said:

> Today, we hold that the transformation of data, representing discrete dollar amounts, by a machine through a series of mathematical calculations into a final share price, constitutes a practical application of a mathematical algorithm, formula, or calculation, because it produces a "useful, concrete and tangible result" — a final share price momentarily fixed for recording and reporting purposes and even accepted and relied upon by regulatory authorities and in subsequent trades.[2]

3. In spite of all the issues surrounding copyright and other forms of protection for computer software, the software industry has on the whole been dynamic and economically successful. Is it possible that the programming industry is not heavily dependent on IPRs protection? What distinguishes successful software producers from unsuccessful producers? Are factors such as rate of innovation and lead time in the marketplace more critical to success than legal protection? Is the fairly low cost of standard end-user software (e.g., word processing and spreadsheet software) a factor which might minimize the importance of legal protection?

R. Satellites Signals and Cable Transmission

1. The Brussels Convention of 1974

The transmission of broadcast signals by satellite has become a commonplace mode of distributing copyrighted works. The signal transmitted from a satellite to the earth creates a "footprint" or "zone of illumination" which is often larger than a single country, and it may often exceed a particular geographical area for which rights to broadcast, retransmit, etc. have been secured from the copyright holder. We now turn to the question of what copyright law is applicable in the case of satellite signals.

The Brussels Convention of 1974 establishes a few basic principles regulating satellite transmissions, such as the principle obligating contracting states to take steps to prevent the misappropriation of signals within their

---

[2]*Id.* at 14-15.

territory. However, the rules of the Brussels Convention are limited. They do not seek to establish what country's rules should govern the interests of copyright holders. As of April 1, 1999, only twenty-three countries are party to the Brussels Convention. The text of Articles 1 through 8 of the Brussels Convention follows.

Convention Relating to the Distribution of Programme-Carrying Signals Transmitted by Satellite

Done at Brussels on May 21, 1974

The Contracting States,

Aware that the use of satellites for the distribution of programme-carrying signals is rapidly growing both in volume and geographical coverage;

Concerned that there is no world wide system to prevent distributors from distributing programme-carrying signals transmitted by satellite which were not intended for those distributors, and that this lack is likely to hamper the use of satellite communications;

Recognizing, in this respect, the importance of the interests of authors, performers, producers of phonograms and broadcasting organizations;

Convinced that an international system should be established under which measures would be provided to prevent distributors from distributing programme-carrying signals transmitted by satellite which were not intended for those distributors;

Conscious of the need not to impair in any way international agreements already in force, including the International Telecommunication Convention and the Radio Regulations annexed to that Convention, and in particular in no way to prejudice wider acceptance of the Rome Convention of October 26, 1961, which affords protection to performers, producers of phonograms and broadcasting organizations,

Have agreed as follows:

Article 1

For the purposes of this Convention:

(i) "signal" is an electronically-generated carrier capable of transmitting programmes;

(ii) "programme" is a body of live or recorded material consisting of images, sounds or both, embodied in signals emitted for the purpose of ultimate distribution;

(iii) "satellite" is any device in extraterrestrial space capable of transmitting signals;

(iv) "emitted signal" or "signal emitted" is any programme-carrying signal that goes to or passes through a satellite;

(v) "derived signal" is a signal obtained by modifying the technical characteristics of the emitted signal, whether or not there have been one or more intervening fixations;

(vi) "originating organization" is the person or legal entity that decides what programme the emitted signals will carry;

(vii) "distributor" is the person or legal entity that decides that the transmission of the derived signals to the general public or any section thereof should take place;

(viii) "distribution" is the operation by which a distributor transmits derived signals to the general public or any section thereof.

Article 2

(1) Each Contracting State undertakes to take adequate measures to prevent the distribution on or from its territory of any programme-carrying signal by any distributor for whom the signal emitted to or passing through the satellite is not intended. This obligation shall apply where the originating organization is a national of another Contracting State and where the signal distributed is a derived signal.

(2) In any Contracting State in which the application of the measures referred to in paragraph (1) is limited in time, the duration thereof shall be fixed by its domestic law. The Secretary-General of the United Nations shall be notified in writing of such duration at the time of ratification, acceptance or accession, or if the domestic law comes into force or is changed thereafter, within six months of the coming into force of that law or of its modification.

(3) The obligation provided for in paragraph (1) shall not apply to the distribution of derived signals taken from signals which have already been distributed by a distributor for whom the emitted signals were intended.

Article 3

This Convention shall not apply where the signals emitted by or on behalf of the originating organization are intended for direct reception from the satellite by the general public.

Article 4

No Contracting State shall be required to apply the measures referred to in Article 2(1) where the signal distributed on its territory by a distributor for whom the emitted signal is not intended

(i) carries short excerpts of the programme carried by the emitted signal, consisting of reports of current events, but only to the extent justified by the informatory purpose of such excerpts, or

(ii) carries, as quotations, short excerpts of the programme carried by the emitted signal, provided that such quotations are compatible with fair practice and are justified by the informatory purpose of such quotations, or

(iii) carries, where the said territory is that of a Contracting State regarded as a developing country in conformity with the established practice of the General Assembly of the United Nations, a programme carried by the emitted signal, provided that the distribution is solely for the purpose of teaching, including teaching in the framework of adult education, or scientific research.

Article 5

No Contracting State shall be required to apply this Convention with respect to any signal emitted before this Convention entered into force for that State.

Article 6

This Convention shall in no way be interpreted to limit or prejudice the protection secured to authors, performers, producers of phonograms, or broadcasting organizations, under any domestic law or international agreement.

Article 7

This Convention shall in no way be interpreted as limiting the right of any Contracting State to apply its domestic law in order to prevent abuses of monopoly.

Article 8

(1) Subject to paragraph (2) and paragraph (3), no reservation to this Convention shall be permitted.

(2) Any Contracting State whose domestic law, on May 21, 1974, so provides may, by a written notification deposited with the Secretary-General of the United Nations, declare that, for its purposes, the words "where the originating organization is a national of another Contracting State" appearing in Article 2(1) shall be considered as if they were replaced by the words "where the signal is emitted from the territory of another Contracting State."

(3)

    (a) Any Contracting State which, on May 21, 1974, limits or denies protection with respect to the distribution of programme-carrying signals by means of wires, cable or other similar communications channels to subscribing members of the public may, by a written notification deposited with the Secretary-General of the United Nations, declare that, to the extent that and as long as its domestic law limits or denies protection, it will not apply this Convention to such distributions.

(b) Any State that has deposited a notification referred to in Article 9(1), as well as the accordance with subparagraph (a) shall notify the Secretary-General of the United Nations in writing, within six months of their coming into force, of any changes in its domestic law whereby the reservation under that subparagraph becomes inapplicable or more limited in scope.

*****

Note

1. The Brussels Convention establishes obligations only with respect to satellite signals intended for retransmission to the public. It does not apply to signals that are intended for direct reception by the public.

2. Satellite Signals in the European Union

In 1992, the Austrian Supreme Court considered the choice of copyright law in the context of signals transmitted by satellite. This decision preceded both the adoption by the EU of the Satellite Broadcast Directive (SBD), and Austria's joining of the EU. The decision illustrates some of the difficulties countries confront in respect to satellite signals. It is followed by the text of the Satellite Broadcast Directive, which takes an approach different from that of the Austrian Court. As you read the text of the Satellite Broadcast Directive, consider how closely the EU solution to the choice of law problem is tied to the approximation or harmonization of national copyright and broadcast laws. Austria is now, of course, a member state of the EU.

Re Satellite Television Broadcasting (Case 4 Ob 44/92)

Oberster Gerichtshof (Austrian Supreme Court)
[1994] ECC 526

16 June 1992

Panel: The President, Dr. Friedl; Drs. Gamerith, Kodek, Niederreiter and Redl, Judges

Headnote:

Appeal from the Oberlandesgericht (Regional Court of Appeal), Wien (Vienna).

Decision:

In its appeal the plaintiff is essentially attacking the so-called "Bogsch theory". It says that the travaux prepartoires on the Austrian Copyright Act and the writings of the reputable authors concentrate on the place where the broadcaster is situated. For the purposes of broadcasting rights, there-fore, the decisive factor is the process of transmission; the actual form of re-ception is not decisive. It says that the rules on cable broadcasting in section 17(2) of the Copyright Act cannot provide any support for the legality of a television broadcast by direct satellite. Furthermore the "Bogsch theory" re-quires intricate application in all respects as regards satellite operators be-cause its effect is that the broadcasting rights have to be obtained for every country within the satellite's "footprint".

The parties' dispute is not about the territorial limits of the exclusive broadcasting right granted by the plaintiff under the contract of 16 August 1951; they do not dispute that the plaintiff (among others) was granted the exclusive broadcasting right for the area of the Federal Republic of Ger-many. But that does not involve the interpretation of the contract (which under section 43(1), first sentence, of the Private International Law Act would have to take place in accordance with German law); it concerns the decision of the question whether the broadcasting right granted to the plaintiff for the territory of Germany is sufficient to authorise a direct satel-lite broadcast transmitted from Germany which can intentionally be re-ceived not only there but also in Austria (among other countries). Under section 34(1) of the Act the creation, content and extinction of rights in in-tangible property are to be assessed in accordance with the law of the state in which an act of exploitation or infringement takes place. In an action for infringement the decisive issue is whether the infringing conduct is to be regarded as a breach of national intellectual-property rights under the law of the state for whose sovereign territory protection is claimed. The court that has to decide on an infringement claim must decide the question of whether an infringement has taken place according to the law of the state whose protection is claimed. (The so-called "protection-country theory", RV 784 BlgNR 14 GP 49.) Exploitation rights under copyright law also fall within that rule of allocation. (See Schwimann, in Rummel, ABGB, n 1 on s 34 IPRG.)

The plaintiff is claiming for itself, on the basis of the broadcasting right granted to it (solely) for the territory of Germany, the right to transmit direct-satellite broadcasts from Germany to the territory of Austria as well and to issue broadcasting licences for that purpose; it regards the defendant's actions in issue as an infringement of the exclusive broadcasting right granted to it by the defendant. According to the protection-country principle, therefore, the question whether there is an infringement must be decided according to Austrian law. (That was also the conclusion of the decision at [1991] Obl 181, [1992] ECC 456, referred to in what follows.)

The Supreme Court, in its judgment at [1991] Obl 181, has already dealt in detail with the treatment of trans-border television broadcasts for copyright purposes. Adopting the view of Dillenz, M Walter, Katzenberger and Schricker (Dillenz, Urheberrechtliche Probleme der Direktsatelliten in FS-50 Jahre UrhG, 43; M Walter, Grundlagen und Ziele der osterreichischen UrhRReform, op cit at 236; Katzenberger, in Schricker, Komm Z UrhG, preliminary n 89 to s 120 et seq dUrhG, and Elektronische Textkommunikation, [1983] GRUR Int 916: Schricker, Grenzuberschreitende Fernseh-und Horfunksendungen im Gemeinsamen Markt, [1984] GRUR Int at 594) and rejecting the contrary view of Ungern-Sternberg (Grenzuberschreitende Rundfunk-und Drahtfunksendungen, pp 113 et seq), the Court concluded that the acquisition of a licence to broadcast in the country of transmission is not sufficient by itself if the broadcasting organisation deliberately transmits the protected works to other countries in radio or television broadcasts. In such cases the exploitation rights must also be obtained for the countries of reception in order to protect the exploitation rights of the copyright-holders in those countries. At the same time it expressly refused to apply to the case of a broadcast deliberately transmitted to a specific country the considerations stated in the travaux preparatoires on the section 17(1) of the Copyright Act to the effect that the broadcasting organisation could not be expected to acquire the rights for all conceivable countries for which the broadcast was not intended but in which it could be heard simply because of the circumstances of reception conditions there; the position is, rather, that in such a case it is entirely reasonable to expect the broadcasting organisation to acquire the rights for those countries of reception as well. Finally, the Supreme Court also stated in that judgment that a transmission intentionally aimed at Austria from abroad is not (merely) a "foreign broadcast" within the meaning of section 59a of the Copyright Act but is also an "internal" one, so that, as in the case of a broadcast transmitted from this country, the copyright-holder's consent is required (for internal purposes).

There is no reason to depart from this judgment, which follows the so-called "Bogsch theory". Although its principles were stated in relation to the specific case of a deliberate cross-border terrestrial transmission, they are also fully applicable to the intentional transmission to one or more foreign areas of reception that is typical of direct-satellite broadcasting. The reference in the appeal to the fact that such broadcasts take place with the help of Hertzian waves, so that under section 17(1) of the Copyright Act one must refer here too to the location of the transmitter and the location of the country of reception, is without significance for copyright purposes, and therefore cannot lead to any other conclusion. But it is not disputed that Austria is also within the "footprint" of the satellites which are relevant here and that the broadcasting organisation is deliberately beaming the musico-dramatic works in issue to Austria (among other countries).

According to a proposal of the Council of the European Communities on the co-ordination of copyright and neighbouring rights relating to satellite broadcasting and cable retransmission the Member States are to introduce rules under which the place of transmission which is relevant for copyright-law purposes is that at which the broadcasting organisation takes the single decision on the content and transmission of the programme-bearing signals, for which purposes account can also be taken of the public in the country of reception in assessing the remuneration. This directive, which is still being worked on and is only binding on the Member States of the European Community, presupposes the transmission of direct-satellite signals from one Member State of the Community to another, and therefore can have no influence on the decision of the present case, which has been reached on the basis of the current Austrian Copyright Act. (The Directive (93/83) was adopted on 27 September 1993: [1993] OJ L248/15 — Ed.)

It must therefore be held that there has been no breach by the defendant of the plaintiff's German broadcasting right as alleged by the latter, and the appeal must therefore fail.

*****

1210

Appeal dismissed.

Council Directive 93/83/EEC of 27 September 1993 on the coordination of certain rules concerning copyright and rights related to copyright applicable to satellite broadcasting and cable retransmission*

The Council of the European Communities, [recitals omitted]
Has Adopted this Directive:

Chapter I Definitions

Article 1
Definitions

1. For the purpose of this Directive, "satellite" means any satellite operating on frequency bands which, under telecommunications law, are reserved for the broadcast of signals for reception by the public or which are reserved for closed, point-to-point communication. In the latter case, however, the circumstances in which individual reception of the signals takes place must be comparable to those which apply in the first case.

2. (a) For the purpose of this Directive, "communication to the public by satellite" means the act of introducing, under the control and responsibility of the broadcasting organization, the programme-carrying signals intended for reception by the public into an uninterrupted chain of communication leading to the satellite and down towards the earth.

(b) The act of communication to the public by satellite occurs solely in the Member State where, under the control and responsibility of the broadcasting organization, the programme-carrying signals are introduced into an uninterrupted chain of communication leading to the satellite and down towards the earth.

(c) If the programme-carrying signals are encrypted, then there is communication to the public by satellite on condition that the means for de-

---

*1993 OJ L 248, Doc. Date, Sept. 27, 1993.

crypting the broadcast are provided to the public by the broadcasting organization or with its consent.

(d) Where an act of communication to the public by satellite occurs in a non-Community State which does not provide the level of protection provided for under Chapter II,

(i) if the programme-carrying signals are transmitted to the satellite from an uplink situation situated in a Member State, that act of communication to the public by satellite shall be deemed to have occurred in that Member State and the rights provided for under Chapter II shall be exercisable against the person operating the uplink station; or

(ii) if there is no use of an uplink station situated in a Member State but a broadcasting organization established in a Member State has commissioned the act of communication to the public by satellite, that act shall be deemed to have occurred in the Member State in which the broadcasting organization has its principal establishment in the Community and the rights provided for under Chapter II shall be exercisable against the broadcasting organization.

3. For the purposes of this Directive, "cable retransmission" means the simultaneous, unaltered and unabridged retransmission by a cable or microwave system for reception by the public of an initial transmission from another Member State, by wire or over the air, including that by satellite, of television or radio programmes intended for reception by the public.

4. For the purposes of this Directive "collecting society" means any organization which manages or administers copyright or rights related to copyright as its sole purpose or as one of its main purposes.

5. For the purposes of this Directive, the principal director of a cinematographic or audiovisual work shall be considered as its author or one of its authors. Member States may provide for others to be considered as its co-authors.

Chapter II Broadcasting of Programmes by Satellite

Article 2
Broadcasting right

Member States shall provide an exclusive right for the author to authorize the communication to the public by satellite of copyright works, subject to the provisions set out in this chapter.

Article 3
Acquisition of broadcasting rights

1. Member States shall ensure that the authorization referred to in Article 2 may be acquired only by agreement.
2. A Member State may provide that a collective agreement between a collecting society and a broadcasting organization concerning a given category of works may be extended to rightholders of the same category who are not represented by the collecting society, provided that:
— the communication to the public by satellite simulcasts a terrestrial broadcast by the same broadcaster, and
— the unrepresented rightholder shall, at any time, have the possibility of excluding the extension of the collective agreement to his works and of exercising his rights either individually or collectively.
3. Paragraph 2 shall not apply to cinematographic works, including works created by a process analogous to cinematography.
4. Where the law of a Member State provides for the extension of a collective agreement in accordance with the provisions of paragraph 2, that Member States shall inform the Commission which broadcasting organizations are entitled to avail themselves of that law. The Commission shall publish this information in the Official Journal of the European Communities (C series).

Article 4
Rights of performers, phonogram producers and broadcasting organizations

1. For the purposes of communication to the public by satellite, the rights of performers, phonogram producers and broadcasting organizations shall

be protected in accordance with the provisions of Articles 6, 7, 8 and 10 of Directive 92/100/EEC.

2. For the purposes of paragraph 1, "broadcasting by wireless means" in Directive 92/100/EEC shall be understood as including communication to the public by satellite.

3. With regard to the exercise of the rights referred to in paragraph 1, Articles 2 (7) and 12 of Directive 92/100/EEC shall apply.

Article 5
Relation between copyright and related rights

Protection of copyright-related rights under this Directive shall leave intact and shall in no way affect the protection of copyright.

Article 6
Minimum protection

1. Member States may provide for more far-reaching protection for holders of rights related to copyright than that required by Article 8 of Directive 92/100/EEC.

2. In applying paragraph 1 Member States shall observe the definitions contained in Article 1 (1) and (2).

Article 7
Transitional provisions

1. With regard to the application in time of the rights referred to in Article 4 (1) of this Directive, Article 13(1), (2), (6) and (7) of Directive 92/100/EEC shall apply. Article 13(4) and (5) of Directive 92/100/EEC shall apply mutatis mutandis.

2. Agreements concerning the exploitation of works and other protected subject matter which are in force on the date mentioned in Article 14(1) shall be subject to the provisions of Articles 1(2), 2 and 3 as from 1 January 2000 if they expire after that date.

3. When an international co-production agreement concluded before the date mentioned in Article 14(1) between a co-producer from a Member State and one or more co-producers from other Member States or third countries expressly provides for a system of division of exploitation rights

between the co-producers by geographical areas for all means of communication to the public, without distinguishing the arrangement applicable to communication to the public by satellite from the provisions applicable to the other means of communication, and where communication to the public by satellite of the co-production would prejudice the exclusivity, in particular the language exclusivity, of one of the co-producers or his assignees in a given territory, the authorization by one of the co-producers or his assignees for a communication to the public by satellite shall require the prior consent of the holder of that exclusivity, whether co-producer or assignee.

Chapter III Cable Retransmission

Article 8
Cable retransmission right

1. Member States shall ensure that when programmes from other Member States are retransmitted by cable in their territory the applicable copyright and related rights are observed and that such retransmission takes place on the basis of individual or collective contractual agreements between copyright owners, holders of related rights and cable operators.
2. Notwithstanding paragraph 1, Member States may retain until 31 December 1997 such statutory licence systems which are in operation or expressly provided for by national law on 31 July 1991.

Article 9
Exercise of the cable retransmission right

1. Member States shall ensure that the right of copyright owners and holders of related rights to grant or refuse authorization to a cable operator for a cable retransmission may be exercised only through a collecting society.
2. Where a rightholder has not transferred the management of his rights to a collecting society, the collecting society which manages rights of the same category shall be deemed to be mandated to manage his rights. Where more than one collecting society manages rights of that category, the rightholder shall be free to choose which of those collecting societies is deemed to be mandated to manage his rights. A rightholder referred to in this paragraph

shall have the same rights and obligations resulting from the agreement between the cable operator and the collecting society which is deemed to be mandated to manage his rights as the rightholders who have mandated that collecting society and he shall be able to claim those rights within a period, to be fixed by the Member State concerned, which shall not be shorter than three years from the date of the cable retransmission which includes his work or other protected subject matter.

3. A Member State may provide that, when a rightholder authorizes the initial transmission within its territory of a work or other protected subject matter, he shall be deemed to have agreed not to exercise his cable retransmission rights on an individual basis but to exercise them in accordance with the provisions of this Directive.

Article 10
Exercise of the cable retransmission right by broadcasting organizations

Member States shall ensure that Article 9 does not apply to the rights exercised by a broadcasting organization in respect of its own transmission, irrespective of whether the rights concerned are its own or have been transferred to it by other copyright owners and/or holders of related rights.

Article 11
Mediators

1. Where no agreement is concluded regarding authorization of the cable retransmission of a broadcast. Member States shall ensure that either party may call upon the assistance of one or more mediators.

2. The task of the mediators shall be to provide assistance with negotiation. They may also submit proposals to the parties.

3. It shall be assumed that all the parties accept a proposal as referred to in paragraph 2 if none of them expresses its opposition within a period of three months. Notice of the proposal and of any opposition thereto shall be served on the parties concerned in accordance with the applicable rules concerning the service of legal documents.

4. The mediators shall be so selected that their independence and impartiality are beyond reasonable doubt.

Article 12
Prevention of the abuse of negotiating positions

1. Member States shall ensure by means of civil or administrative law, as appropriate, that the parties enter and conduct negotiations regarding authorization for cable retransmission in good faith and do not prevent or hinder negotiation without valid justification.
2. A Member State which, on the date mentioned in Article 14(1), has a body with jurisdiction in its territory over cases where the right to retransmit a programme by cable to the public in that Member State has been unreasonably refused or offered on unreasonable terms by a broadcasting organization may retain that body.
3. Paragraph 2 shall apply for a transitional period of eight years from the date mentioned in Article 14(1).

Chapter IV General Provisions

Article 13
Collective administration of rights

This Directive shall be without prejudice to the regulation of the activities of collecting societies by the Member States.

Article 14
Final provisions

1. Member States shall bring into force the laws, regulations and administrative provisions necessary to comply with this Directive before 1 January 1995. They shall immediately inform the Commission thereof. When Member States adopt these measures, the latter shall contain a reference to this Directive or shall be accompanied by such reference at the time of their official publication. The methods of making such a reference shall be laid down by the Member States.
2. Member States shall communicate to the Commission the provisions of national law which they adopt in the field covered by this Directive.
3. Not later than 1 January 2000, the Commission shall submit to the European Parliament, the Council and the Economic and Social Committee a

report on the application of this Directive and, if necessary, make further proposals to adapt it to developments in the audio and audiovisual sector.

Article 15

This Directive is addressed to the Member States.

Notes and Questions

1. The SBD establishes that the rights of copyright holders will be exclusively determined by the law of the EU member state from which a signal is transmitted up to a satellite (art. 1(2)(b)). Why does the EU consider it important that the law of a single member state be applied in this context?

2. The SBD provides that the author's right to authorize satellite broadcast to the public may be acquired only "by agreement" (art. 3(1)). What other mode of acquiring the right to broadcast might otherwise be available in the member states?

3. The SBD provides that in respect of cable retransmission rights, a copyright owner may only exercise his or her rights through a collecting society. The SBD is protecting certain interests of cable operators. What are those interests?

4. According to the SBD, what member state's copyright law applies in the case in which a satellite transmission originates in a non-EU member?

5. We suggested earlier that the approach taken by the SBD might be dependent on a certain level of approximation or harmonization of copyright law among the member states of the EU. Do you think this is the case?

INDEX

A

Administrative dispute resolution, 1921–1924, *see also* Domain name management
African Intellectual Property Organization, 478–480
African Regional Industrial Property Organization, 476–478
Agreement on Trade-Related Aspects of Intellectual Property Rights. *See* TRIPS Agreement
American Intellectual Property Law Association, 483
ANCOM. *See* Andean Pact
Andean Pact
  development strategy, 384
  institutions, 301, 391
  patent norms, 825–837
  technology transfer provisions, 818–825
APEC. *See* Asia-Pacific Economic Cooperation forum
Appellation of origin. *See* Geographical indication of origin
Arbitration, 1732–1739, 2024–2025
Asia-Pacific Economic Cooperation forum
  institutional arrangement, 384, 390–394
  IPRs regime 455–461

B

Berne Convention
  criticisms of, 328–329
  direction application, 896–906
  dispute settlement, 1569
  enforcement, 630, 722–729, 731–732, 1569
  historical, 2–3, 303, 328, 860–870
  intellectual step requirement, 615
  International Court of Justice, 896
  moral rights, 81, 895, 1084, 1106–1110
  most favored nation treatment, 597–601
  national law, 896–906
  national treatment, 590–596
  patent-copyright demarcation, 285–291
  priority, right of unknown, 609
  registration of copyrights, 1427
  retroactive application, 896
  terms, 870–895
  TRIPS Agreement, incorporation by reference, 722–723, 984–991
Bilateral agreements, 481–483, 488
Biotechnology
  genetic resources and, 1819–1850
  patent practices, 837–844
  traditional intellectual property rights and, 1819–1850

Breeder's right, 66–67
Broadcast rights. *See also* Satellite
  signals, WIPO Performances
  and Phonograms Treaty
  Berne Convention and, 873
  European Union, 1040–1046
  neighboring rights of copyright,
  23
  TRIPS Agreement and, 985–991
Brussels Convention, 1202–1207

C

China
  copyright law, 1066–1083
  history, comparison with Japan,
    854–859
  patent system, 844–854
  United States, agreements on
    IPRs protection, 1592–1608
Color as trademark, 131–146,
  1248–1249
Community Patent Convention,
  465–468, 776, 779, 781–796
Community Plant Variety Rights
  Office, 474–475
Community Trade Mark Regulation, *see also* Office for Harmonisation in the Internal
  Market
  historical, 1269–1272
  provisions of, 1299–1337,
    1535–1567
  registration process, 1535–1543
Competition
  antitrust law, 1742
  cartels, 1756, 1758–1761
  conflicting rights and interests,
    1741–1743, 1754–1756

dominant position, 1744–1745,
  1767–1779
global technological integration,
  1743–1750
international trade law, 1742
market power, 1749
market share, 1741
Microsoft, 1743, 1745
monopoly, 1745, 1749
parallel imports, 1758–1760,
  1762–1766, 1789–1790
regulations, 1743, 1762–1766
safe-harbors, 1743
TRIPS Agreement, 1746,
  1750–1761
Compulsory licensing, 262, 264,
  640–641, 709–718, 837, 1855
Computers. *See also* Database protection; Internet
  intellectual property rights, ef-
    fects on, 269–271
  software. *See* Software protection
Consistent interpretation doctrine,
  558–572
Convention on Biological Diversity,
  see Biotechnology, traditional
  intellectual property rights
  and
Copyright
  Berne Convention, 328–329,
    860–906
  broadcasts, 1040–1046
  China, 1066–1083, *see also* China
  competition 1767–1779
  database protection, 82,
    1012–1030, *see also* Database
    protection
  design and, 111–115
  dissemination, 618

duration, 22, 81, 611–612
enforcement, 1569, 1651
EU Directive, 1006–1012
expression vs. idea, 83–84
fair use rights, 81, 895, 922–927,
    1861–1863
films, 1040–1046
freedom of information and,
    1861–1863
free movement of copyrighted
    works, 1040–1062
human rights and, 506–507
imports, 1046–1062
infringement, 85–92, *see also* en-
    forcement
integrated circuits and, 164
intellectual step, 615
international trade and,
    1046–1062
moral rights. *See* Moral rights
most favored nation treatment,
    597–601
NAFTA, 1062–1066
national treatment, 589–596
nature of right, 81–110
Online Copyright Infringement
    Liability Limitation Act,
    1863–1875
neighboring rights, 23, 860
price discrimination, 1791
priority, right of, 609
registration, 1427–1428, 1673
rental rights, 346, 941–950,
    986–1006, 1151–1152
satellite transmission, 1202–1218
software. *See* Software protection
subject matter of, 81–84
telephone directories, 82,
    1012–1030

territoriality, 602–604
translations, 894
TRIPS Agreement, 346, 860,
    984–991
WIPO Copyright Treaty,
    906–949
Counterfeit goods
    criminal penalties, 1728–1732
    imports. *See* Infringing imports
Courts. *See* European Court of Jus-
    tice; International Court of
    Justice; Judicial systems
Criminal penalties, 1728–1732

D

Database protection
    copyright protection, 82,
        1012–1030
    Database Directive, 1012–1013,
        1030–1040
    U.S. digital agenda, 931–935
Designs, *see* Industrial designs
Direct effect doctrine, 403–404,
    421, 572–586
Dispute settlement
    arbitration, 1732–1739,
        2024–2025
    Berne Convention, 328, 1569
    GATT, 328–332, 353–354
    NAFTA, 387–388, 442–443
    Paris Convention, 328, 1569
    TRIPS Agreement, 357, 363–364,
        510–572, 628–632, 718–733,
        1569–1575, 1995–1997,
        2001–2002, 2006
    WIPO, 359, 364–366, 371,
        1732–1739, 2024–2025, *see also*
        Domain name management

Dispute settlement (*cont.*)
  WTO, 325, 353–359, 363–366,
    371–372, 435–438, 510–572,
    718–733, 1569–1575,
    1995–1997, 2001–2002, 2006
Dissemination principle, 618–625
Domain name management
  Internet Corporation for As-
    signed Names and Numbers,
    1879–1880, 1967–1986
  WIPO Internet Domain Name
    Process, 1878–1967
    Administrative dispute
      resolution, 1921–1924
Droit moral. *See* Moral rights

E

ECJ. *See* European Court of Justice
Economic development, *see* Intel-
  lectual property, economic
  foundations of
EPC. *See* European Patent Conven-
  tion
EPO. *See* European Patent Office
Equity, 494–501
Equivalents, doctrine of, 250–254
EU. *See* European Union
European Coal and Steel Commu-
  nity, 386, 400
European Commission, 388, 401,
  422–423, 1608–1609,
  1622–1628, 1763–1766
European Community and Euro-
  pean Communities, *see* Euro-
  pean Union
European Council
  composition, 422

decisions, 422
directives, 422, *see also* specific
  directives, *e.g.,* Database Directive
legislative power, 388, 418–421
regulations, 422, *see also* specific
  regulations, *e.g.,* Community
  Trade Mark Regulation
European Court of Justice, case decisions referenced by subject
  matter in table of contents
  doctrines of, 400–421
  jurisdiction and review, 409–
    416
  role of, 388, 400–423
European Economic Area, 384,
  1364–1372
European Free Trade Area, 384,
  481, 1364–1372
European Parliament, 388, 423
European Patent Convention, *see*
  also European Patent Office
  application process, 734–739,
    1468–1491, *see also* Commis-
    sion Green Paper
  Commission Green Paper analy-
    sis and proposals, 777–808
  dissemination principle and, 620
  historical, 461–469, *see also*
    Commission Green Paper
  implemented, national law,
    48–49
  member states, 44, 468, 779
  norms, 733–739
  provisions of, 740–749,
    1470–1491
European Patent Office, *see also* European Patent Convention

appeals, 732
biotechnology patent practices, 837–844
divisions, 749–750
grant procedures, 734–739, 1468–1491
historical, 461–469
location, 1468–1470
Technical Boards, *see* decisions referenced by subject matter in table of contents, decisions, 749–776, decisions and national courts, 62–63
trilateral cooperation, 837–838
European Union, *see also* European Council, European Court of Justice, European Parliament
Anticounterfeiting Regulation, 1650–1662
broadcast rights and free movement, 1041–1046
Community Trade Mark Regulation, *see* Community Trade Mark Regulation,
Copyright Directive, 1006–1012
First Trade Marks Directive, 1265–1286, *see also* exhaustion of rights doctrine
exhaustion of rights doctrine, 146–162, 605–608, 1342–1363, 1763–1766
external relations power, 422–438
goals and history, 386–390, 399–421
Industrial Design Directive, 113–114

New Instrument, *see* Trade Barriers Regulation
OHIM, 469–474
plant variety registration, 474–475
Rental Rights Directive, 998–1006
Satellite Broadcast Directive, 1211–1218
Software Directive, 1135–1152
structure, 386–390, 399–421
Trade Barriers Regulation, 1608–1628
trade mark registration, *see* Community Trade Marks Regulation, First Trade Mark Directive and Madrid Agreement and Protocol
Exhaustion of rights, *see also* Competition, European Union, exhaustion of rights doctrine, International Exhaustion of Rights
international. *See* International exhaustion of rights
national, regional and international, compared, 605–608
TRIPS Agreement, 604, 1779–1819, 1856–1857

F

Fair use rights, 81, 895, 922–927, 1861–1863
Farmer's privilege, 66, 68–81, 1860
Food and Agriculture Organization, 301, 374–375, 1845

Free Trade Area of the Americas,
389–394
FTAA. *See* Trade Area of the Americas

G

GATT, *see generally* World Trade
Organization
dispute settlement, 331–332,
353–354, 1629–1649
intellectual property, mandate,
332–333
intellectual property, historical
treatment, 5–9
reciprocity, 337–338
General Agreement on Trade and
Tariffs. *See* GATT
Genetic engineering, 29–64,
837–844, 1819–1850
Geographical indication of origin
definition, 185
functions of, 185–196
indication of source distinguished, 185
registration, 186–187
TRIPS Agreement, 347–348,
1999–2000

H

Hague Agreement Concerning the
International Deposit of Industrial designs, 114, 304,
306
Human rights
doctrine, 501–504
instruments and IPRs, 504–
507

I

Implied powers doctrine, EU,
430–433
Import right
NAFTA, 1062–1063
parallel. *See* Parallel imports
TRIPS Agreement, patent and,
709, 1805–1806, 1816–
1817
Indication of source, 185
Industrial designs
EU Directive, 113–114
Hague Agreement, 114, 304,
306
intellectual step, 616
protection of, 110–128
TRIPS Agreement and, 114–115,
348
Infringing imports
Anticounterfeiting Regulation,
1650–1662
civil litigation, 561–572, 1662,
1694–1727
European Union, 561–572,
1650–1662
Section 337, U.S., 1629–1649,
1662–1675
TRIPS Agreement, 349–350,
561–572, 1662
United States, 1662–1732
Integrated circuit layout-design
protection
duration of, 329
holder, rights of, 163
intellectual step, 616
mask work, 162–163
nature of, 162–165
origin of, 162–164, 329

reverse engineering, 164–165,
174–182
substantial similarity, 164–165,
171–173
TRIPS Agreement, 162, 329,
349
Intellectual capital, 13–16
Intellectual property, *see* specific
subject matter headings, *e.g.,*
Copyright
definition, 21–25, 1887–
1888
economic foundations of,
222–300, 1851–1861,
2008–2017
Intellectual step, 613, 618
International Court of Justice, 328,
485–496, 661–662, 896
International exhaustion of rights,
see also Exhaustion of Rights,
Parallel Imports
cartels and, 1758–1760
competition law and, 1762–
1766
copyright and, 992–998,
1040–1062
defined, 604–608
parallel importation and,
1736–1760
patent and, 674–678, 1752
trademark rights and,
1342–1426, 1675–1693
TRIPS Agreement and,
1779–1819
International Federation of Pharmaceuticals Manufacturers
Associations, 483
International Intellectual Property
Alliance, 483

International law
customary, 488–491, 517–519,
542–543
doctrine, 491–496
equity, 494–501
general principles, 496–501
sources of, 485–508
precedents, 485–496
trade law, 1698
treaty law, 487–488, 517–519,
542–543
International Telecommunications
Union, 301, 374–375
International Trade Law Committee, 320–326, 1762–1766,
1779–1796
International Trademark Association, 483
Internet, *see also* Database protection
defined, 1883–1885
domain names. See Domain
name management
economic impact of, 269–271
global electronic commerce,
1986–1989, 2002–2003
Online Copyright Infringement
Liability Limitation Act,
1861–1875
patent information systems,
618
regulation of, 1877–1878, *see also*
Domain name management

J

Japan Patent Office
biotechnology patent practices,
838–844
trilateral cooperation, 837–838

Judicial systems
European Community and European Union. *See* European Court of Justice
Switzerland, 84
United Kingdom, 42
United States, 28–29

L

Legitimate expectations doctrine, 518–519, 526–533, 537–548, 557
Life forms, artificially created, 28–42

M

Madrid Agreement and Protocol
application process, 1493–1494
geographical coverage, 304–306, 310–311
guide to, 1502–1513
provisions of, 1513–1535
relationship between, 1494, 1506–1507, 1534
statistics, 310
United States adherence, 310–311, 1453, 1454
Mercosur, 4, 301, 387–391, 394–398, 443–455
Moral rights
Berne Convention, 81, 873, 895
China and, 1074–1077
continental Europe, 81, 1083–1087
differences between legal systems, 81, 1083–1084
mandatory application, 1085–1087

Switzerland and, 89–90, 956
TRIPS Agreement and, 895
United States and, 81, 1087–1119
Visual Artists Rights Act, 1102–1119
Most favored nation treatment, 596–601

N

NAFTA
copyright provisions, 1062–1066
dispute settlement, 387–388
goals, 386–390
IPRs regime, 438–443, 601
patent norms, 808–818
trademark provisions, 1337–1340
National treatment principle, *see also* Berne Convention, Paris Convention, TRIPS Agreement, 587–596, 1622–1649
Neighboring Rights, *see also* Broadcast rights, Satellite signals, WIPO Performances and Phonograms Treaty, 23, 950–984
New Instrument, *see* Trade Barriers Directive
Nice Agreement, 1492, 1499–1501
Norms, *see* specific subject matter, *e.g.,* Copyright

O

Office for Harmonisation in the Internal Market, 469–474, 1266, 1297–1337, 1535–1567

Organisation for Economic Cooperation and Development, 6,
301, 376–383, 1986,
1988–1989
Origin. *See* Geographical indication
of origin

P

Parallel imports, *see also* Exhaustion of Rights, International
Exhaustion of Rights
cartels and, 1758–1760
competition law and, 1762–1766
copyright and, 992–998,
1040–1062
GATT, 1715, 1754–1757
patented products, 674–678,
1752
Trademark rights and,
1342–1426, 1675–1693
TRIPS Agreement and,
1779–1819
Paris Convention
compulsory licensing, 640–641,
649, 661, 710
criticisms of, 327–328
dispute settlement, 328, 661–662,
1569
economic background of,
254–265
enforcement, 629, 1569
generally, 633–686
historical, 2–3, 633–646
independence, principle of,
662–676
most favored nation treatment,
597

national treatment principle,
588–590, 594–595, 648, 692
negotiations, 633–646
paradigm, 286
party states, 647
patent provisions, 652–662
principles, 587–590, 594–597,
602–604, 608, 610, 629
priority, right of, 608–610, 648,
676–685
revisions, 633, 625–635, 645, 648
terms of, 647–662
trademarks and, 1219–1247
trade secret protection, 196
TRIPS Agreement and, 344–345,
700, 722–732
WIPO and, 303–304
Patent Cooperation Treaty
application process, 310,
1430–1441
dissemination principle and,
619–620
generally, 1430–1467
historical, 1430
provisions of, 1441–1464
statistics, 310, 1438–1441
timeline, 1464–1467
WIPO, administration of, 310,
371–372
Patents, *see also* Competition, European Patent Convention, Paris
Convention
Andean Pact provisions, 818–
837
biotechnology patent practices,
837–844
China, 844–854, 859, *see also*
China

Patents (*cont.*)
  compulsory licensing, 262–264,
    640–641, 649–650, 710–718
  compulsory working, 262–264,
    640–641, 649–650, 708–709
  criteria for granting, 26–28,
    42–64
  design patent, 112–113, 115–124
  development and, *see* economics
    of
      administration in develop-
        ing countries, 2009–2011
  discovery and invention distin-
    guished, 25
  duration, 612, 701
  economics of, 222–300
  enabling disclosure, 42–64,
    761–776, *see also* TRIPS
    Agreement
  equivalents, doctrine of, 250–254
  European Patent Convention.
    See European Patent Conven-
    tion
  European Patent Office. *See* Eu-
    ropean Patent Office
  first-to-file and first-to-invent,
    701, 1428–1429
  genetic engineering, 29–64,
    837–844, 1819–1850
  independence of, 662–676
  intellectual step, 613–618
  international applications. *See*
    Patent Cooperation Treaty
  international system, economics
    of, 254–284
  inventive step, 26, 42–64, *see also*
    intellectual step and TRIPS
    Agreement

life forms, artificially created,
  28–42
monopoly, 237–238, 1741–1750
NAFTA provisions, 808–818
nature of, 25–28
new, *see* novelty
non-obviousness, 26–27, 42–64,
  see also TRIPS Agreement
novelty, 26, 42–64, *see also* TRIPS
  Agreement
parallel importation of patented
  products, 674–678, 1752
Paris Convention. *See* Paris Convention
Patent Law Treaty, draft, 624
plants. *See* Plant variety protection
procedures for securing,
  1427–1430, *see* European
  Patent Convention, Patent Cooperation Treaty and specific
  national and regional headings
subject matter of, 25–42, *see also*
  TRIPS Agreement
trade secret and patent law, relationship between, 198–218
TRIPS Agreement, 348, 685–710,
  1806–1809
United States patenting procedures, 1428–1429
utility, 26
PCT. *See* Patent Cooperation Treaty
Pirated goods. *See* Infringing imports
Plant variety protection, *see also*
  Biotechnology, Genetic engineering
  breeder's right, 66–67
  criteria for granting, 65–67

European Union, 475
farmer's privilege, 65–81
generally, 23, 34–37, 65–81
historical, 34–37, 65–66
TRIPS Agreement and, 67, 2001, 2012
Priority, right of, 608–610, 648, 676–685, 1220, 1233

R

R & D. *See* Research and development
Reciprocity, national treatment and, 587–596, 1039–1040
Rental rights, 346, 941–950, 986–1006, 1151–1152
Research and development
generally, 13–21
increases in, 13
inter-firm alliances, 15
protection standards and, 243–244, 251–254, 266–268
spending patterns, 16–18
TRIPS Agreement, impact of, 279–280
Reverse engineering, 164–165, 174–182, 1141, 1146–1147
Rome Convention
most favored nation treatment, 597–599
national treatment, 589–596
provisions of, 960–961, 974–984
Switzerland and, 950
TRIPS Agreement and, 987–988

S

Satellite signals
Brussels Convention, 1202–1207
European Union, 1207–1218
Satellite Broadcast Directive, 1211–1218
SEA. *See* Single European Act
Section 301 and Special 301
China, actions under, 1592–1608
critique of, 330–332, 1576–1588
democratisation function, 1577
generally, 1575–1608
priority countries, 1578–1579, 1591–1592
provisions of, 1580–1591
Trade Barriers Regulation compared, 1608
trade sanctions, 1576–1580, 1592
U.S. Trade Representative, authority of, 1591–1592, 1576–1579
Section 337
discrimination complaint, 1622–1628
GATT panel report, 1629–1649
generally, 1662–1675
Presidential discretion under, 1664–1667
provisions of, 1667–1675
Semiconductor devices, 162, *see* Integrated circuit layout-design protection
Service marks, 128–129, 1229–1230, 1253, *see also* Domain name management
Single European Act, 416–420

Software
  copyright protection, 24, 94–110,
    346
  European Union, 1135–1152
  generally, 93–110, 1119–1202
  Germany, 1121–1135, 1142–1152
  historical, 81–82, 293–94,
    1119–1121
  inventive step, 1121–1135
  licensing of programs,
    1142–1152
  method of operation, 94–110
  network externalities, 270
  patenting, 93–94, 1119–1121,
    1196–1202
  rental rights, 346, 985,
    1151–1152
  sale of programs, 1148–1151
  Software Directive, provisions of,
    1135–1141
  TRIPS Agreement and, 346, 985,
    987
  United States, 93–110,
    1152–1202
  user rights, 1144–1152
  WIPO Copyright Treaty and,
    941–942, 949
Supremacy doctrine, 404–405
Sustainable development, 507–508,
    see also Biotechnology, tradi-
    tional intellectual property
    rights

                    T

Telephone directories, 82,
    1012–1030
Territoriality, 602–604, see also International exhaustion of
    rights
Trade Barriers Regulation,
    1608–1628
Trademarks
  color as trademark, 131–145
  Community Trade Mark Regula-
    tion. See Community Trade
    Mark Regulation
  duration, 610, 612
  European, 469–474, see Commu-
    nity Trade Mark Regulation,
    First Trade Marks Directive
  First Trade Marks Directive,
    1265–1286
  historical, 1219–1220
  intellectual step, 617
  international exhaustion of
    rights, 1342–1426, 1675–
    1693, see also European
    Union, exhaustion of rights
    doctrine
  Madrid Agreement. See Madrid
    Agreement and Protocol
  marketing tools, 1219
  NAFTA, 1337–1340
  nature and function, 128–131
  Nice Agreement, 1492,
    1499–1501
  Paris Convention, 1219–1247
  registration, 4, 129, 469–474,
    1502–1567
  renewal, 129, 1256
  risk of confusion, 1287–1297
  service marks, 128–129,
    1229–1230, 1253, see also Do-
    main name management
  signs, 128–130

Trademark Law Treaty,
1492–1498
TRIPS Agreement, 346–347,
1247–1265
Trade Secrets
criteria for, 196–197
disclosure, 198, 217
duration, 22, 217, 610–611
employees and, 217–218
generally, 196–222
governmental proceedings and,
218–222
intellectual step, 617
Paris Convention, 196
patent and trade secret law, relationship between, 198–218
subject matter, 196–197
TRIPS agreement, 197–198,
349
Transparency, 625–627
TRIPS Agreement, see also specific
IPRs subject matter
amendment procedures,
361–363
anti-competitive practices, control of, 349, see Competition,
TRIPS Agreement
Berne Convention provisions,
986–988, see Berne Conven
tion, TRIPS Agreement
competence to conclude,
422–435
competition, 1746, 1750–1761
copyright and, 346, 860, 984–991
counterfeit goods, 349–350,
561–572, 1662
dispute settlement, 357, 363–364,
510–572, 628–632, 718–733,

1569–1575, 1995–1997,
2001–2002, 2006
duration norms, 611–613
effective date of, 2, 341, 358
enforcement, 2, 349–350,
628–632, 1569–1575
exhaustion of rights, see International exhaustion of rights,
TRIPS Agreement and
future development, 1991–2006
geographical indications of origin protection, 347–348,
1999–2000
implementation, 1991–2006,
2015–2016
industrial design protection,
114–115, 348
infringing imports, 349–350,
561–572, 1662
integrated circuit layout-design
protection, 162, 329, 349
intellectual step requirements,
615–618
mailbox provision, 510–558
most favored nation treatment,
596–601
national treatment principle,
587–596
negotiations, 5–12, 302, 341–343,
686–696, 985–988
objectives, 2, 343, 359, 686–691
overview of, 340–353
patents and, 348, 685–710,
1806–1809
plant variety protection, 67,
2001, 2012, see also Biotechnology, traditional intellectual
property rights

TRIPS Agreement (*cont.*)
  rent transfers, 277–278
  research and development, impact on, 279–280
  sanctions, 2, 1569–1592
  trade mark protection, 346–347, 1247–1265
  trade secret protection, 197–198, 349
  transition arrangements, 336–337, 352, 358–359, 1992–1997
  transparency provision, 625–627

U

Ubiquity, 22, 604–608
Undisclosed information. *See* Trade secrets
United Nations Conference on Trade and Development, 301, 374–376
United Nations Development Program, 301, 375–376
United Nations Environment Program, 301, 375–376
United States
  China, agreements on IPRs protection, 1592–1608
  copyright registration, 1427–1428, 1673
  database protection, 1012–1030
  digital agenda, 908–940
  infringing imports, 1662–1732
  judicial system, 28–29
  Madrid Agreement and Protocol, 310–311, 1493, 1534

moral rights protection, 81, 1087–1119
  patenting procedures, 1428–1429
  software protection, 93–110, 1152–1202
United States Customs Service, 1673–1676, 1692–1693
United States Patent and Trademark Office
  biotechnology patent practices, 837–844
  trilateral cooperation, 837–838, 844
United States Trade Representative
  See Section 301 and Special 301

V

Vienna Convention, *see* International law, treaty law
Visual Artists Rights Act, 1102–1119

W

WIPO
  arbitration, 1732–1739, 2024–2025,
  budget, 308
  Copyright Treaty, 906–949, 2005
  developmental assistance, 307, 360, 366, 371
  dispute settlement, 359, 364–366, 371, 1732–1739, 2024–2025, *see also* Domain name management
  governing bodies, 303–304, 372

history, 303
International Bureau, 303
Internet domain name process,
    1878–1967
membership, 304
objectives, 301–308, 354,
    359–360, 362–364, 369
Performances and Phonograms
    Treaty, 950–984
rights, mechanisms for securing,
    308–312
rule-making, 361–363, 370
United Nations, agency of, 303,
    313
WTO, relationship between
    WIPO and, 312–314, 358–374,
    1998
World Bank, 301, 374–375,
    2014–2017
World Health Organization,
    375–376

World Intellectual Property Orga-
    nization. *See* WIPO
World Trade Organization. *See*
    WTO
WTO
    agreements, 320–327, *see also*
        Dispute settlement, WTO,
        TRIPS Agreement
    dispute settlement, *see* Dispute
        settlement, WTO
    framework, 320–326, 358–359
    functions, 312–326
    global electronic commerce dec-
        laration, 1986–1987,
        2002–2003
    objectives, 315, 368–369
    principles, 315–320
    rule-making, 361–363
    WIPO, relationship between
        WTO and, 312–314, 358–374,
        1998